Lecture Notes in Artificial Intelligence 13457

Subseries of Lecture Notes in Computer Science

Series Editors

Randy Goebel
University of Alberta, Edmonton, Canada

Wolfgang Wahlster
DFKI Berlin, Germany

Zhi-Hua Zhou
Nanjing University, Nanjing, China

Founding Editor

Jörg Siekmann
DFKI and Saarland University, Saarbrücken, Germany

More information about this subseries at https://link.springer.com/bookseries/1244

Honghai Liu · Zhouping Yin · Lianqing Liu ·
Li Jiang · Guoying Gu · Xinyu Wu ·
Weihong Ren (Eds.)

Intelligent Robotics and Applications

15th International Conference, ICIRA 2022
Harbin, China, August 1–3, 2022
Proceedings, Part III

Editors
Honghai Liu
Harbin Institute of Technology
Shenzhen, China

Lianqing Liu
Shenyang Institute of Automation
Shenyang, Liaoning, China

Guoying Gu
Shanghai Jiao Tong University
Shanghai, China

Weihong Ren
Harbin Institute of Technology
Shenzhen, China

Zhouping Yin
Huazhong University of Science
and Technology
Wuhan, China

Li Jiang
Harbin Institute of Technology
Harbin, China

Xinyu Wu
Shenzhen Institute of Advanced Technology
Shenzhen, China

ISSN 0302-9743   ISSN 1611-3349 (electronic)
Lecture Notes in Artificial Intelligence
ISBN 978-3-031-13834-8   ISBN 978-3-031-13835-5 (eBook)
https://doi.org/10.1007/978-3-031-13835-5

LNCS Sublibrary: SL7 – Artificial Intelligence

This Springer imprint is published by the registered company Springer Nature Switzerland AG
The registered company address is: Gewerbestrasse 11, 6330 Cham, Switzerland

Preface

With the theme "Smart Robotics for Society", the 15th International Conference on Intelligent Robotics and Applications (ICIRA 2022) was held in Harbin, China, August 1–3, 2022, and designed to encourage advancement in the field of robotics, automation, mechatronics, and applications. It aims to promote top-level research and globalize the quality research in general, making discussions, presentations more internationally competitive and focusing on the latest outstanding achievements, future trends, and demands.

ICIRA 2022 was organized by Harbin Institute of Technology, co-organized by Huazhong University of Science and Technology, Shanghai Jiao Tong University, and Shenyang Institute of Automation, Chinese Academy of Sciences, undertaken by State Key Laboratory of Robotics and Systems, State Key Laboratory of Digital Manufacturing Equipment and Technology, State Key Laboratory of Mechanical Systems and Vibration, and State Key Laboratory of Robotics. Also, ICIRA 2022 was technically co-sponsored by Springer. On this occasion, ICIRA 2022 was a successful event this year in spite of the COVID-19 pandemic. It attracted more than 440 submissions, and the Program Committee undertook a rigorous review process for selecting the most deserving research for publication. The advisory Committee gave advice for the conference program. Also, they help to organize special sections for ICIRA 2022. Finally, a total of 284 papers were selected for publication in 4 volumes of Springer's Lecture Note in Artificial Intelligence. For the review process, single-blind peer review was used. Each review took around 2–3 weeks, and each submission received at least 2 reviews and 1 meta-review.

In ICIRA 2022, 3 distinguished plenary speakers and 9 keynote speakers had delivered their outstanding research works in various fields of robotics. Participants gave a total of 171 oral presentations and 113 poster presentations, enjoying this excellent opportunity to share their latest research findings. Here, we would like to express our sincere appreciation to all the authors, participants, and distinguished plenary and keynote speakers. Special thanks are also extended to all members of the Organizing Committee, all reviewers for peer-review, all staffs of the conference affairs group, and all volunteers for their diligent work.

August 2022

Honghai Liu
Zhouping Yin
Lianqing Liu
Li Jiang
Guoying Gu
Xinyu Wu
Weihong Ren

Organization

Honorary Chair

Youlun Xiong — Huazhong University of Science and Technology, China

General Chairs

Honghai Liu — Harbin Institute of Technology, China
Zhouping Yin — Huazhong University of Science and Technology, China
Lianqing Liu — Shenyang Institute of Automation, Chinese Academy of Sciences, China

Program Chairs

Li Jiang — Harbin Institute of Technology, China
Guoying Gu — Shanghai Jiao Tong University, China
Xinyu Wu — Shenzhen Institute of Advanced Technology, Chinese Academy of Sciences, China

Publication Chair

Weihong Ren — Harbin Institute of Technology, China

Award Committee Chair

Limin Zhu — Shanghai Jiao Tong University, China

Regional Chairs

Zhiyong Chen — The University of Newcastle, Australia
Naoyuki Kubota — Tokyo Metropolitan University, Japan
Zhaojie Ju — The University of Portsmouth, UK
Eric Perreault — Northwestern University, USA
Peter Xu — The University of Auckland, New Zealand
Simon Yang — University of Guelph, Canada
Houxiang Zhang — Norwegian University of Science and Technology, Norway

Advisory Committee

Jorge Angeles	McGill University, Canada
Tamio Arai	University of Tokyo, Japan
Hegao Cai	Harbin Institute of Technology, China
Tianyou Chai	Northeastern University, China
Jie Chen	Tongji University, China
Jiansheng Dai	King's College London, UK
Zongquan Deng	Harbin Institute of Technology, China
Han Ding	Huazhong University of Science and Technology, China
Xilun Ding	Beihang University, China
Baoyan Duan	Xidian University, China
Xisheng Feng	Shenyang Institute of Automation, Chinese Academy of Sciences, China
Toshio Fukuda	Nagoya University, Japan
Jianda Han	Shenyang Institute of Automation, Chinese Academy of Sciences, China
Qiang Huang	Beijing Institute of Technology, China
Oussama Khatib	Stanford University, USA
Yinan Lai	National Natural Science Foundation of China, China
Jangmyung Lee	Pusan National University, South Korea
Zhongqin Lin	Shanghai Jiao Tong University, China
Hong Liu	Harbin Institute of Technology, China
Honghai Liu	The University of Portsmouth, UK
Shugen Ma	Ritsumeikan University, Japan
Daokui Qu	SIASUN, China
Min Tan	Institute of Automation, Chinese Academy of Sciences, China
Kevin Warwick	Coventry University, UK
Guobiao Wang	National Natural Science Foundation of China, China
Tianmiao Wang	Beihang University, China
Tianran Wang	Shenyang Institute of Automation, Chinese Academy of Sciences, China
Yuechao Wang	Shenyang Institute of Automation, Chinese Academy of Sciences, China
Bogdan M. Wilamowski	Auburn University, USA
Ming Xie	Nanyang Technological University, Singapore
Yangsheng Xu	The Chinese University of Hong Kong, SAR China
Huayong Yang	Zhejiang University, China

Jie Zhao   Harbin Institute of Technology, China
Nanning Zheng   Xi'an Jiaotong University, China
Xiangyang Zhu   Shanghai Jiao Tong University, China

Contents – Part III

Wearable Sensing and Robot Control

Wearable Ultrasound Interface for Prosthetic Hand Manipulation 3
  Zongtian Yin, Hanwei Chen, Xingchen Yang, Yifan Liu, Ning Zhang,
  Jianjun Meng, and Honghai Liu

3D Printed Soft Robotic Hand Combining Post-Stroke Rehabilitation
and Stiffness Evaluation 13
  Chang Qiu Zhou, Xiang Qian Shi, Zheng Li, and Kai Yu Tong

Wearable Sensing Based Virtual Reality Rehabilitation Scheme for Upper
Limb Training 24
  Jialiang Zhang, Yaojie Liu, and Juan Liu

Gait Analysis and Phase Recognition Based on Array Fiber Optic Sensing
Insole 37
  Nian Peng, Wei Meng, Quan Liu, and Shengquan Xie

Gait Phase Detection Based on Time Sequence Adapting to Various
Walking Posture and Frequency 49
  Siyu Liu, Zhiyong Zhou, Linjun Lu, Xiaohui Xiao, and Zhao Guo

In Situ Calibration of a Six-Axis FBG Force/Moment Sensor for Surgical
Robot 59
  Tianliang Li, Fayin Chen, and Yifei Su

**Wearable Robotics to Characterize, Retrain, and Restore Human
Movements**

Effects of Brain-Computer Interface and Classical Motor Imagery
for Upper Limb Impairment After Stroke: A Case Report 71
  Yi-Qian Hu, Rong-Rong Lu, Tian-Hao Gao, Jie Zhuang, and Yu-Long Bai

A Synchronous Acquisition System of Ultrasound, sEMG and IMU
for Human Motion Prediction 79
  Yifan Liu, Zongtian Yin, Hongyu Yang, Xingchen Yang, and Honghai Liu

Gait Time Parameter Analysis-Based Rehabilitation Evaluation System
of Lower Limb Motion Function 90
  Yue-Peng Zhang, Guang-Zhong Cao, Jiang-Cheng Chen, Ye Yuan,
  Ling-Long Li, Dong-Po Tan, and Zi-Qin Ling

A Portable Fully Coupled Parallel Continuum Manipulator for Nursing
Robot: Mechanical Design and Modeling 103
  Chuanxin Ning and Ting Zhang

A Perturbation Platform and Exoskeleton Simulator for Studying Balance
Control of Hip Exoskeleton: Design and Preliminary Validation 113
  Kaixiang Feng and Ting Zhang

Disturbance Observer Compensation Based on Sliding-Mode Approach
for Solving Compliant Actuator Tracking Control Problems 127
  Changxian Xu, Jian Gu, Yongbai Liu, Liming Zhao, and Zhongbo Sun

Impedance Control of Upper Limb Rehabilitation Robot Based on Series
Elastic Actuator 138
  Jian Gu, Changxian Xu, Keping Liu, Liming Zhao, Tianyu He,
  and Zhongbo Sun

Flexible Lightweight Graphene-Based Electrodes and Angle Sensor
for Human Motion Detection 150
  Wenbin Sun, Quan Liu, Qiang Luo, Qingsong Ai, and Wei Meng

The Study of Ankle Assisted Exoskeleton 162
  Yali Han, Jiachen Chang, Zhuangzhuang Jin, Shunyu Liu, and Lei Zhou

Motor Learning-Based Real-Time Control for Dexterous Manipulation
of Prosthetic Hands 174
  Kemal Balandiz, Lei Ren, and Guowu Wei

Robotic Environment Perception

A Method for Object Recognition and Robot Grasping Detection
in Multi-object Scenes 189
  Jiajun Zheng, Yuanyuan Zou, Jie Xu, and Lingshen Fang

Reinforcement Learning for Mobile Robot Obstacle Avoidance with Deep
Deterministic Policy Gradient 197
  Miao Chen, Wenna Li, Shihan Fei, Yufei Wei, Mingyang Tu,
  and Jiangbo Li

An Improved Beetle Antennae Search Optimization Based Particle
Filtering Algorithm for SLAM 205
  Wei-Dian Ni and Guang-Zhong Cao

Simulation Study of Wireless Coverage in Straight Long Corridors
on Container Ship Deck 216
  Yu Zhu and Bing Han

Research on Path Planning Based on the Fusion Algorithm of Adaptive
Ant Colony Optimization and Artificial Potential Field Method 229
  Ran Wang, Qingxin Zhang, Tong Cui, and Xinggang Wu

A State-of-the-Art Review on SLAM 240
  Xuewei Zhou and Ruining Huang

Swarm Robotic Technology and System in Space and Underwater

Synthesis of One DOF Single-Loop Mechanisms with Prismatic Pairs
Based on the Atlas Method 255
  Yang Zhang, Changqing Gao, Hailin Huang, and Bing Li

Research on the Hydrodynamic Calculation of Variable Structure
Underwater Vehicle Based on CFD 268
  Xiaomeng Liu, Qifeng Zhang, Qiyan Tian, Yaxing Wang, Xuejiao Yang,
  Dehao Li, and Xiaohui Wang

SOINS: A Real-Time Underwater Sonar-Inertial System for Pipeline 3D
Reconstruction 279
  Wenzhi Gong, Li Xiao, Tian Zeng, Yuchong Li, Zhigang Sun,
  and Zhuo Wang

Subsea Pipeline Inspection Based on Contrast Enhancement Module 289
  Ming Zhao, Lin Hong, Zhen-Long Xiao, and Xin Wang

Numerical Investigation on Turbulence Models and the Hydrodynamics
of a UVMS 299
  Hang Xu, Lin Hong, Xin Wang, and Ming Zhao

Design of Enveloping Underwater Soft Gripper Based on the Bionic
Structure 311
  Jiansong Dou, Daohui Zhang, Yanxu Sun, Xin Fu, and Xingang Zhao

Research on Formation Obstacle Avoidance Algorithm of Multiple AUVs
Based on Interfered Fluid Dynamical System 323
  Wen Pang, Daqi Zhu, and Linling Wang

Research on Thermage Robot System Based on Constant Force Control 335
  Fengyi Liu and Chengtao Yue

An Active Obstacle Avoidance Method 345
  Wei Zhu, Yuanzhe Cui, Pengjie Xu, Yichao Shen, and Qirong Tang

Medical Robot

Design of Wireless Force Sensing Module of Vascular Interventional Robot 357
  Zhuang Fu, Jianfeng Yao, Zeyu Fu, Chenxin Sui, and Jian Fei

Deep Motion Flow Estimation for Monocular Endoscope 367
  Min Tan, Lijuan Feng, Zeyang Xia, and Jing Xiong

Constant Force Control Method of Grinding Device 378
  Jia Wen duo, Jiang Zi feng, and Dai Yu

Shape Reconstruction Method for Continuum Robot Using FBG Sensors 388
  Licheng Hou, Sikyuen Tam, Xingwei Zhao, and Bo Tao

Safety Motion Control and End Force Estimation Based on Angle
Information in Robotic Flexible Endoscopy 396
  *Bo Guan, Xingchi Liu, Zhikang Ma, Jianchang Zhao, Yuelin Zou,
  and Jianmin Li*

Design and Modeling of a Lightweight Concentric Tube Robot
for Nasopharyngeal Surgery 409
  *Gang Zhang, Hangxing Wei, Peng Qi, Honghui Wang, Hao Cheng,
  and Fuxin Du*

Research on Puncture Status Perception of Venipuncture Robot Based
on Electrical Impedance 420
  Tianbao He, Chuangqiang Guo, Hansong Liu, and Li Jiang

An IMU and EMG-Based Simultaneous and Proportional Control Strategy
of 3-DOF Wrist and Hand Movements 430
  Zihao Li, Jianmin Li, and Lizhi Pan

Application of Feedforward-Cascade Control in an External Pulling Robot
for Nerve Restoration 440
  Hongrui Fu, Gang Zhang, Han Zeng, Fuxin Du, and Rui Song

**Intelligent Co-operation in Mobile Robots for Learning, Optimization,
Planning, and Control**

Crawling Trajectory Generation of Humanoid Robot Based on CPG
and Control 453
  Weilong Zuo, Gunyao Gao, Jingwei Cao, Tian Mu, and Yuanzhen Bi

A System Integration Method of Product Data Management Based
on UG/NX Secondary Development 466
  Kai Wang, Pengfei Zeng, Chunjing Shi, Weiping Shao, and Yongping Hao

Research on Feature Matching Based on Improved RANSAC Algorithm 477
  Xianfeng Wang, Baitong Wang, Zilin Ding, and Tong Zhao

Global Optimal Trajectory Planning of Mobile Robot Grinding
for High-Speed Railway Body 485
  Xiaohu Xu, Songtao Ye, Zeyuan Yang, Sijie Yan, and Han Ding

Design of Control Software for a Reconfigurable Industrial Robot Training
Platform 497
  Dianyong Yu, Sui Yingnun Bian, and Ye Duan

Observer-Based H_∞-Consensus Control of Multi-agent Systems Under
WTOD Protocol 509
  Jinbo Song, Yafei Jiao, Fan Yang, and Chao Xu

Applications of Kalman Filtering in Time Series Prediction 520
  Xuegui Li, Shuo Feng, Nan Hou, Hanyang Li, Shuai Zhang, Zhen Jian,
  and Qianlong Zi

Non-fragile Consensus Control for MASs with Dynamical Bias 532
  Jinnan Zhang, Dongyan Dai, Xuerong Li, and Pengyu Wen

ResNet-BiGRU-Attention Based Facial Expression Analysis Model
for a Humanoid Robot 541
  Yang Lu, Xiaoxiao Wu, Pengfei Liu, Wanting Liu, Xinmeng Zhang,
  and Yixuan Hou

Overtaking Trajectory Planning Based on Model Predictive Control 553
  Zihan Yuan and Jun Xu

H_∞ Switching Adaptive Tracking Control for Manipulator with Average
Dwell Time 564
  Hongmei Zhang and Junpeng Shang

An Inspection Planning Method for Steam Generators
with Triangular-Distributed Tubes 573
  Biying Xu, Xuehe Zhang, Yue Ou, Kuan Zhang, Zhenming Xing,
  Hegao Cai, Jie Zhao, and Jizhuang Fan

Memory-Based STOMP for Local Path Planning 585
  Wenjie Li, Tao Cao, Yunfan Wang, and Xian Guo

Research and Verification of Robot Master-Slave Control Algorithm
for Nuclear Power Maintenance Scenarios 595
  Feng Yang, Haihua Huang, Yanzheng Chen, Weiming Li, Quanbin Lai,
  Rui Ma, Binxuan Sun, and Xingguang Duan

Research on Force Perception of Robot End-Effector Based on Dynamics
Model 604
  Zhongshuai Yao, Ming Hu, Yufeng Guo, Jianguo Wu, and Jing Yang

Tactile Robotics

Perceptual Properties of Fingertips Under Electrotactile Stimulation 617
  Ziliang Zhou, Yicheng Yang, Jia Zeng, Xiaoxin Wang, Jinbiao Liu,
  and Honghai Liu

A Brief Review Focused on Tactile Sensing for Stable Robot Grasping
Manipulation 628
  Zhenning Zhou, Zhuangzhuang Zhang, Kaiyi Xie, Xiaoxiao Zhu,
  and Qixin Cao

A Soft Neuromorphic Approach for Contact Spatial Shape Sensing Based
on Vision-Based Tactile Sensor 640
  Xiaoxin Wang, Yicheng Yang, Ziliang Zhou, Guiyao Xiang,
  and Honghai Liu

Contact Information Prediction Based on Multi-force Training for Tactile
Sensor Array with Elastomer Cover 652
  Qiang Diao, Wenrui Chen, Yaonan Wang, Qihui Jiang, and Zhiyong Li

Hand Rehabilitation Modes Combining Exoskeleton-Assisted Training
with Tactile Feedback for Hemiplegia Patients: A Preliminary Study 661
  Bo He, Min Li, and Guoying He

Co-manipulation System with Enhanced Human-Machine Perception

Behavior Tree Based Dynamic Task Planning Method for Robotic
Live-Line Maintenance 673
  Feng Jiabo, Shi Lirong, Liu Lei, and Zhang Weijun

Design of Multi-unit Passive Exoskeleton for Running 686
  Nianfeng Wang, Fan Yue, Jiegang Huang, and Xianmin Zhang

Force Tracking Impedance Control Based on Contour Following Algorithm 698
  Nianfeng Wang, Jianbin Zhou, Kaifan Zhong, Xianmin Zhang,
  and Wei Chen

Guidance Method for UAV to Occupy Attack Position at Close Range 710
    Xu Bingbing, Meng Guanglei, Wang Yingnan, and Zhao Runnan

The Variation Characteristic of EMG Signal Under Varying Active Torque:
A Preliminary Study 722
    Boxuan Zheng, Xiaorong Guan, Zhong Li, Shuaijie Zhao, Zheng Wang,
    and Hengfei Li

A VPRNN Model with Fixed-Time Convergence for Time-Varying
Nonlinear Equation 731
    Miaomiao Zhang and Edmond Q. Wu

Surface Electromyography-Based Assessment of Muscle Contribution
in Squatting Movements 742
    Zheng Wang, Xiaorong Guan, Zhong Li, Boxuan Zheng, Hengfei Li,
    and Yu Bai

Energy Gradient Descent Method for Actuation of a Direct-Drive
Spherical Robotic Wrist 753
    Mengke Li, Yaqing Deng, and Kun Bai

Compliant Mechanisms and Robotic Applications

Design and Modeling of a Novel Compliant Ankle Mechanism
with Flexible Slider-Crank Limbs 767
    Shujie Tang, Genliang Chen, Wei Yan, and Hao Wang

Adaptive Compliance Control of Flexible Link Manipulator in Unknown
Environment 779
    Cianyi Yannick, Xiaocong Zhu, and Jian Cao

A Novel Discrete Variable Stiffness Gripper Based on the Fin Ray Effect 791
    Jiaming Fu, Han Lin, I. V. S. Prathyush, Xiaotong Huang, Lianxi Zheng,
    and Dongming Gan

Author Index 803

Wearable Sensing and Robot Control

Wearable Ultrasound Interface for Prosthetic Hand Manipulation

Zongtian Yin[1] , Hanwei Chen[1] , Xingchen Yang[2] , Yifan Liu[3] ,
Ning Zhang[4] , Jianjun Meng[1(✉)] , and Honghai Liu[3,5(✉)]

[1] Shanghai Jiao Tong University, Shanghai, China
mengjianjunxs008@sjtu.edu.cn
[2] Swiss Federal Institute of Technology Lausanne (EPFL), Lausanne, Switzerland
[3] Harbin Institute of Technology, Shenzhen, China
[4] National Research Center for Rehabilitation Technical Aids, Beijing, China
honghai.liu@icloud.com
[5] The University of Portsmouth, Portsmouth PO1 3HF, UK

Abstract. Ultrasound can non-invasively detect muscle deformations, which has great potential applications in prosthetic hand control. This research developed a miniaturized ultrasound device that could be integrated into a prosthetic hand socket. This compact system included four A-mode ultrasound transducers, a signal processing module, and a prosthetic hand control module. The size of the ultrasound system was $65 * 75 * 25$ mm, weighing only 85 g. For the first time, we integrated the ultrasound system into a prosthetic hand socket to evaluate its performance in practical prosthetic hand control. We designed an experiment to perform six commonly used gestures, and the classification accuracy was $95.33\% \pm 7.26\%$ for a participant. These experimental results demonstrated the efficacy of the designed prosthetic system based on the miniaturized A-mode ultrasound device, paving the way for an effective HMI system that could be widely used in prosthetic hand control.

Keywords: A-mode ultrasound · Miniaturized HMI system · Prosthetic hand control

1 Introduction

With the development of human-machine interface (HMI) technology, the application of intelligent prosthetics has become widespread. Subjects' movement intention needs to be detected to control the prosthetic movement naturally. For prosthetic hand control, decoding human bio-signals provides an intuitive and natural way to control the artificial hand.

This work was supported by the China National Key R&D Program (Grant No. 2020YFC207800), Shanghai Pujiang Program (Grant No. 20PJ1408000), the National Natrual Science Foundation of China (Grant No. 52175023), and the Guangdong Science and Technology Research Council (Grant 2020B1515120064).

H. Liu et al. (Eds.): ICIRA 2022, LNAI 13457, pp. 3–12, 2022.
https://doi.org/10.1007/978-3-031-13835-5_1

4 Z. Yin et al.

The miniaturized ultrasonic devices [1] was expected to be an alternative of sEMG sensing [2,3]. There are three common modes of ultrasound techniques: A-mode, B-mode, and M-mode. Some early HMI studies used B-mode ultrasound to acquire images of muscle tissues. They were applied to the classification of hand gestures [4,5], and the estimation of continuous finger joint angles [6,7]. Huang et al. demonstrated that ultrasound images could perform better than sEMG on gesture classification [8]. Although miniaturized B-mode ultrasound devices (such as VSCAN, General Electric, USA) are portable, transducer probes are too bulky to be wearable for amputees. Studies related to B-mode ultrasound images have shown the possibility of applying ultrasound technology in the field of HMI.

Some research teams started using smaller-sized A-mode ultrasound sensors. Compared to ultrasound images, the signal of A-mode ultrasound is one-dimensional, containing less information about human tissue movements. Yang et al. carried out virtual hand control experiments, showing the great potential of A-mode ultrasound for HMI. The A-mode ultrasound devices used in many studies were still not portable. Until now, there is no research that could be able to integrate ultrasound devices into prostheses for online control.

This research aims to develop a miniaturized ultrasound system that could be integrated into a prosthetic hand socket for practical control. Firstly, a miniaturized ultrasound device with four-channel probes was developed. Four probes of A-mode ultrasound were worn around the forearm to obtain information of muscle morphological deformations. The wearable A-mode ultrasound system has demonstrated favorable performance in online gesture control. Section 2 provides an overview of the integrated prosthetic hand system. Section 3 evaluates the system's performance in the application of hand gesture recognition and conclusion are presented in Sect. 4.

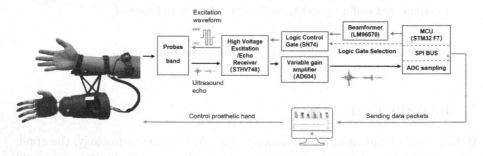

Fig. 1. Block diagram of the prosthetic hand control system based on the miniaturized A-mode ultrasound device.

2   Overview of Integrated Ultrasound System

Figure 1 presents the integrated prosthetic hand control system based on a minia-turized A-mode ultrasound device. The micro-controller unit (MCU, STM32F7, STMicroelectronics Inc., Switzerland) was responsible for waveform genera-tion/excitation and signal sampling/transmission. The A-mode ultrasound probe was excited with high voltage to generate ultrasound waves. Echo signals of dif-ferent tissue groups were captured using positive piezoelectric effects [9]. The data was eventually transferred to a Laptop via the high-speed Wi-Fi module. A customized software integrating pattern recognition algorithms on the PC delivered commands to control prosthetic hand movements. Details about the integrated prosthetic hand system are presented below.

2.1   Ultrasound Transducers Module

The schematic diagram of the A-mode ultrasound signal acquisition was shown in Fig. 2. In particular, Fig. 2(a) showed the structure of a single A-mode trans-ducer, including a matching layer, a piezoelectric layer, and a backing layer [10]. The piezoelectric layer was 1–3 composite materials with an acoustic impedance

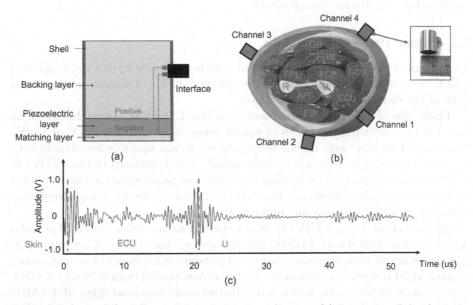

Fig. 2. Diagram of A-mode ultrasound signal acquisition: (a) Structure of the A-mode transducer probe. (b) Cross-section view of the forearm and the distribution of the probes. R = radius; U = ulna; BR = brachioradialis; FCR = flexor carpi radialis; FCU = flexor carpi ulnaris; ECU = extensor carpi ulnaris; ED: extensor digitorum; ECR = extensor carpi radialis; FPL = flexor pollicis longus; FDP = flexor digitorum profundus; FDS = flexor digitorum superficialis; APL = abductor pollicis longus. (c) Demonstrated positions estimated from the ultrasound echo signal of channel 1.

of about 10 MRayls (Z_a). It is close to the human soft tissues' acoustic impedance $(Z_t,$ 1 MRayls). The transmission coefficient of sound pressure (t_p) is:

$$t_p = \frac{2Z_t}{Z_t + Z_a} \tag{1}$$

Considering that the maximum sampling frequency of MCU was 2.5 MHz, the center frequency of the designed probes was set to 1MHz to obey the Nyquist-Shannon sampling theorem. The size of the designed probes was approximately Φ12 mm × 16 mm.

The arrangement of four probes around the forearm was shown in Fig. 2(b). This cross-section of muscle tissues (Complete Anatomy, Elsevier, Netherlands) was 5 cm away from the elbow joint in the forearm. The one-dimensional ultrasound echo signals obtained from channel 1 was shown in Fig. 2(c). The horizontal axes were the propagation time of the ultrasound echo signals, and the vertical axes were the amplitude of the echo signals. Several large amplitudes were marked as dashed red lines in the ultrasound echo signal. For example, the two dashed lines of channel 1 indicated the physiological quantities from left to right: the interface between surface skin and Extensor Carpi Ulnaris (ECU) muscle, ECU and Ulna (U). Hand movements caused contraction of the forearm muscle groups, and A-mode ultrasound signals reflected muscle deformations through the amplitudes' changements.

2.2   Signal Processing Module

The designed electrical system generated a high-frequency square wave signal of ±50 V to excite the transducers. The two pictures in Fig. 3 showed the front and back of the electrical board, respectively.

First, the MCU issued a instruction to the LM96570 (Texas Instruments Inc., USA), generating two cycles of square wave signal within 0–3.3 V at 1 MHz frequency. Two logic gate circuit were used to obtain square wave signals with negative voltage. Then, the low-voltage signals were transfered to the STHV748 (STMicroelectronics Inc., Switzerland), which was responsible for the waveform excitation and echo reception. The STHV748 can generate a high-frequency square wave signal of ±50 V in the excitation mode.

After a short time, STHV748 was switched to reception mode. The echo signals were amplified with AD604 (Analog Devices, Inc., USA). A low-pass filter module removed high-frequency noise components entrained in the ultrasound signals. Valid frequency components of the probes ranged from 0.75 to 1.3 MHz. After several experiments, a 6th order Butterworth low-pass filter of 1.7 MHz was designed. High-frequency noise components (e.g., 3.2, 5.5, and 6.5 MHz) were clearly suppressed significantly.

Finally, the filtered ultrasound echo signal was stored in the MCU temporarily. The data were transferred to the PC for further feature extraction and classification through Ethernet or high-speed Wi-Fi modules (ESP8266, Espressif, China). The size of miniaturized A-mode ultrasound device was 65 * 75 * 25 mm, weighing only 85 g.

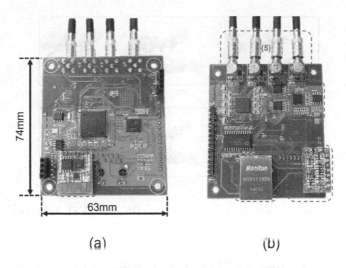

(a)   (b)

Fig. 3. The Electric system design: (a) Front: (1) MCU, (2) Wi-Fi module. (b) Back: (3) Beamformer and logic control gate module, (4) Waveform excitation/Echo receiver and amplifier module, (5) Probes connection module, (6) Low-pass filter module, (7) Ethernet module.

2.3 Prosthetic Hand Module

A command was issued to control a prosthetic hand (eCon-Limb, SHANGHAI IDEA-INTERACTION Inc., China) via a Bluetooth module. The time for collecting and processing data to get one control command was about 70 ms. In this study, the majority vote strategy [11] were used, and the past three outcomes determined the final output. Therefore, the time from data acquisition to the start of prosthetic hand movement was about 210 ms (<300 ms), which was less than the threshold of an acceptable time delay for amputee patients [12].

3 Experiment Evaluation

3.1 Experimental Protocol

The experiment protocol was approved by the SJTU's Institutional Review Board (E2021103). An armband containing four A-mode ultrasound probes was placed about 5 cm away from the elbow joint. In each echo channel, data points within block of a 55 μs duration were recorded at a sampling frequency of 2.5 MHz. The propagation speed of ultrasound in human soft tissues is approximately 1540 m/s [13]. The maximal inspecting depth can reach 8.47 cm theoretically, which satisfied the requirements of detecting. The overall weight of the integration prosthetic hand system was 1120 g.

This research investigated six gestures commonly used in the daily lives of amputees, as shown in Fig. 4, including resting state (RS) gesture, fist (FS)

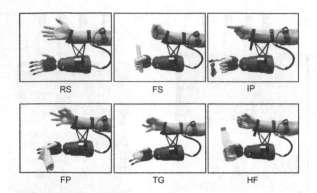

Fig. 4. The involved six hand gestures: rest state (RS), fist (FS), index point (IP), fine pinch (FP), tripod grasp (TG), and half fist (HF).

gesture, index point (IP) gesture, fine pinch (FP) gesture, tripod grasp (TG) gesture, half fist (HF) gesture.

This study consisted of two sessions for each participanta. First, an offline session including four trials was carried out. Each gesture was held for 5 s, and each trial consisted of six gestures, taking 30 s in total. Considering the subjects' reaction time, data in the first and last 1 s (data in transient state) were removed during the front-end processing, and the 3 s data (data in steady state) in the middle were kept for offline analysis. The entire duration of the procedure was two minutes. Second, in the online prediction session, subjects were instructed to perform the same gesture displayed on the screen.

3.2 Data Processing Procedures

A common machine learning strategy was adopted to decode the multiple gesture motions using ultrasound signals, as shown in Fig. 5. In the training phase, the front-end processing and feature extraction was designed. Then, linear discriminant analysis (LDA) classifier was trained based on the data of training trials [14].

Front-end processing and feature extraction were performed for each frame of data. First, the envelope for each frame of ultrasound signals was obtained according to the discrete Hilbert transform. Then, the sliding window method was applied to the envelope waveforms, and the window length was set to 15 points. The mean and root mean square error (RMSE) values were extracted based on each window's data points [15].

3.3 Feature Classification and Validation

To assess the performance of the proposed system, a cross-validation method within trials was used. In detail, three of the trials were used for training, the remaining one trial was used for testing. Each gesture had 75 non-overlapping

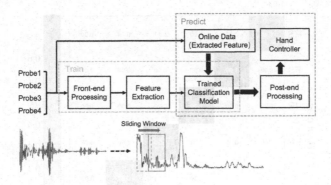

Fig. 5. Schematic diagram of the typical data processing steps of pattern-recognition-based classifiers.

frames of data (40 ms) in a single trial. The classification accuracy was the average of 4 times cross-validation calculated with formula 2.

$$CA = \frac{Number\ of\ correctly\ recognized\ motions}{Total\ number\ of\ testing\ motions} \times 100\% \qquad (2)$$

In this study, the PC's configuration was AMD Ryzen9 3900 CPU, 3.1 GHz clock speed, and 16 G RAM. Offline data analysis was done in the MATLAB R2021a platform, and the online test was completed in the customized software developed by C++.

4   Data Analysis

The parameters of window length and dimensions after PCA, were specified. After a lot of experimental comparisons, the range of window length was set to 15 points. To avoid the curse of dimensionality, principal component analysis (PCA) was used to reduce the dimension of feature to 30 (> 90% explained variance) [16].

One subject participated in the experiment and the offline data was analyzed. Calculating the classification accuracy with formula 2, the confusion matrix result for subject 1 was shown in Fig. 6. The mean and standard error values were 95.33% and 7.26%, respectively.

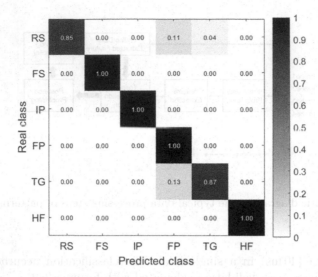

Fig. 6. Confusion matrix of 6 different finger motions based on LDA classifier.

5   Discussion and Conclusion

5.1   Discussion

Many studies have begun to explore the advantages of ultrasound on the HMI field. He et al. showed that A-mode ultrasound was superior to sEMG on discrete gestures, but the resting state was worse [17]. Zeng et al. experimentally proved that ultrasound was more tolerant to muscle fatigue than sEMG [18].

A miniaturized ultrasound system with one channel was manufactured by David et al. [19]. Vasilios et al. designed a wearable ultrasound system consisting of two small devices, weighing 298 g totally [20]. Yang et al. developed an eight-channel ultrasound device for HMI applications [21]. However, these studies for ultrasound applications have not miniaturized the hardware systems sufficiently to allow its integration into the prosthetic hand socket.

In this study, small size and wearable A-mode ultrasound probes were developed. The size of the signal acquisition and processing device was only 65 mm width, 75 mm length, 25 mm height, and 85 g weight. Precise recognition of six commonly used gestures was achieved. Compared to the three miniaturized devices mentioned above, the device designed in this research reduced the size and weight substantially.

There are still many aspects for further improvement. The main challenge for the integrated A-mode ultrasound system was movement robustness. It was inevitable that transducers had relative movements with the skin surface. This problem affected the repeatability of the echo signal and caused a degradation of the classification accuracy. Deep learning methods for feature representation may provide a solution for this problem [22].

5.2 Conclusion

This research developed a miniaturized A-mode ultrasound devices, which can be integrated into a prosthetic hand socket. This research described the customized probe's design and functional modules of the circuit device. Offline data analysis was performed for six classes of gestures (RS, FS, IP, FP, TG, and HF). The LDA algorithm was finally selected for the classification. The classification accuracy for one participant was $95.33\% \pm 7.26\%$. This research demonstrated that the designed miniaturized A-mode ultrasound system is reliable in the prosthetic hand control application.

References

1. Smith, S.: MO-F-220-02: imaging educational course - ultrasound miniaturization. Med. Phys. **38**(6), 3732–3732 (2011)
2. Loram, I.D., Maganaris, C.N., Lakie, M.: Use of ultrasound to make noninvasive in vivo measurement of continuous changes in human muscle contractile length. J. Appl. Physiol. **100**(4), 1311–1323 (2006)
3. Botter, A., Vieira, T.M.M., Loram, I.D., Merletti, R., Hodson-Tole, E.F.: A novel system of electrodes transparent to ultrasound for simultaneous detection of myoelectric activity and B-mode ultrasound images of skeletal muscles. J. Appl. Physiol. **115**(8), 1203–1214 (2013)
4. Shi, J., Guo, J.Y., Hu, S.X., Zheng, Y.P.: Recognition of finger flexion motion from ultrasound image: a feasibility study. Ultrasound Med. Biol. **38**(10), 1695–704 (2012)
5. Akhlaghi, N., et al.: Real-time classification of hand motions using ultrasound imaging of forearm muscles. IEEE Trans. Biomed. Eng. **63**(8), 1687–98 (2016)
6. Castellini, C., Passig, G., Zarka, E.: Using ultrasound images of the forearm to predict finger positions. IEEE Trans. Neural Syst. Rehabil. Eng. **20**(6), 788–797 (2012)
7. Bimbraw, K., Nycz, C.J., Schueler, M., Zhang, Z., Zhang, H.K.: Prediction of Metacarpophalangeal joint angles and Classification of Hand configurations based on Ultrasound Imaging of the Forearm. arXiv:2109.11093 [cs] (2021)
8. Huang, Y., Yang, X., Li, Y., Zhou, D., He, K., Liu, H.: Ultrasound-based sensing models for finger motion classification. IEEE J. Biomed. Health Inform. **22**(5), 1395–1405 (2018)
9. Manbachi, A., Cobbold, R.S.C.: Development and application of piezoelectric materials for ultrasound generation and detection. Ultrasound **19**(4), 187–196 (2011)
10. Mason, W.P.: Piezoelectricity, its history and applications. J. Acoust. Soc. Am. **70**(6), 1561–1566 (1980)
11. Huang, Y., Englehart, K.B., Hudgins, B., Chan, A.D.: A Gaussian mixture model based classification scheme for myoelectric control of powered upper limb prostheses. IEEE Trans. Biomed. Eng. **52**(11), 1801–1811 (2005)
12. Kevin Englehart, K.B., Englehart, K., Englehart, B.H., Hudgins, B.: A robust, real-time control scheme for multifunction myoelectric control. IEEE Trans. Biomed. Eng. **50**(7), 848–854 (2003)
13. Aldrich, J.E.: Basic physics of ultrasound imaging. Critical Care Med. **35**(Suppl), S131–S137 (2007)

14. Waris, A., Niazi, I.K., Jamil, M., Englehart, K., Jensen, W., Kamavuako, E.N.: Multiday evaluation of techniques for EMG-based classification of hand motions. IEEE J. Biomed. Health Inform. **23**(4), 1526–1534 (2019)
15. Narayan, Y., Mathew, L., Chatterji, S.: SEMG signal classification with novel feature extraction using different machine learning approaches. J. Intell. Fuzzy Syst. **35**, 1–11 (2018)
16. Parker, P., Englehart, K., Hudgins, B.: Myoelectric signal processing for control of powered limb prostheses. J. Electromyogr. Kinesiol. **16**(6), 541–548 (2006)
17. He, J., Luo, H., Jia, J., Yeow, J.T.W., Jiang, N.: Wrist and finger gesture recognition with single-element ultrasound signals: a comparison with single-channel surface electromyogram. IEEE Trans. Biomed. Eng. **66**(5), 1277–1284 (2019)
18. Zeng, J., Zhou, Y., Yang, Y., Yan, J., Liu, H.: Fatigue-sensitivity comparison of sEMG and a-mode ultrasound based hand gesture recognition. IEEE J. Biomed. Health Inform. **26**, 1–8 (2021)
19. Piech, D.K., Kay, J.E., Boser, B.E., Maharbiz, M.M.: Rodent wearable ultrasound system for wireless neural recording. In: 2017 39th Annual International Conference of the IEEE Engineering in Medicine and Biology Society (EMBC), pp. 221–225 (2017)
20. Protopappas, V., Baga, D., Fotiadis, D., Likas, A., Papachristos, A., Malizos, K.: An ultrasound wearable system for the monitoring and acceleration of fracture healing in long bones. IEEE Trans. Biomed. Eng. **52**(9), 1597–1608 (2005)
21. Yang, X., Chen, Z., Hettiarachchi, N., Yan, J., Liu, H.: A wearable ultrasound system for sensing muscular morphological deformations. IEEE Trans. Syst. Man Cybern. Syst. **51**, 1–10 (2019)
22. Shi, J., Zhou, S., Liu, X., Zhang, Q., Lu, M., Wang, T.: Stacked deep polynomial network based representation learning for tumor classification with small ultrasound image dataset. Neurocomputing **194**, 87–94 (2016)

3D Printed Soft Robotic Hand Combining Post-Stroke Rehabilitation and Stiffness Evaluation

Chang Qiu Zhou[1], Xiang Qian Shi[1] (ID), Zheng Li[2] (ID), and Kai Yu Tong[1]([envelope]) (ID)

[1] Department of Biomedical Engineering,
The Chinese University of Hong Kong, Hong Kong, SAR, China
xqshi@link.cuhk.edu.hk, kytong@cuhk.edu.hk
[2] Department of Surgery, The Chinese University of Hong Kong,
Hong Kong, SAR, China
lizheng@cuhk.edu.hk

Abstract. Soft rehabilitation devices have been invented and applied for hand function recovery. In this paper, we propose a new Ring-reinforced 3D printed soft robotic hand, which combines hand rehabilitation and joint stiffness evaluation. The elastomer body of Ring-reinforced Soft-Elastic Composite Actuator (R-SECA) is 3D printed directly for fitting different sizes of fingers and the Iterative learning model predictive control (ILMPC) algorithm is used for controlling. Torque compensating layer inside R-SECA enables finger flexion and extension despite finger spasticity. Plastic rings are used to refrain radial expansion and reinforce the actuator. Bending angle and output tip force at different air pressure inputs are explored with four different R-SECA (120 mm, 112 mm, 96 mm, 72 mm length). Four-stroke survivors are recruited to evaluate the effectiveness of the soft robotic hand, and hand function improvement can be observed from the clinical evaluation data and stiffness evaluation outcomes.

Keywords: Ring-reinforced soft-elastic composite actuator (R-SECA) · Stroke rehabilitation · Spasticity · Stiffness evaluation · Soft robotic hand

1 Introduction

Among all causes of death, considered separately from other Cardiovascular Diseases (CVDs), stroke ranks No.5, following heart, cancer, chronic lower respiratory disease, and unintentional injuries/accidents [1]. Disability is often observed in stroke survivors, including hand disability, which upsets them in the activities of daily life (ADL) and lowers the level of quality of life (QOL) [2]. Especially,

Supported by the Guangdong Science and Technology Research Council (Grant No. 2020B1515120064) and the Hong Kong Innovation and Technology Fund (ITS/065/18FP).

H. Liu et al. (Eds.): ICIRA 2022, LNAI 13457, pp. 13–23, 2022.
https://doi.org/10.1007/978-3-031-13835-5_2

hand disability affects them largely in daily activities such as grabbing a bottle, writing, and other independent tasks. Thus, hand rehabilitation training for hand function recovery has been an important and urgent affair for stroke survivors. However, the loss of motor function and the inability of controlling muscles precisely [3] impede the rehabilitation process goes smoothly. To facilitate hand rehabilitation training for motor function recovery, In [4], the effectiveness of repetitive movement on impaired hand has been demonstrated. However, this process can be very labour-consuming and costly if the rehabilitation training is conducted by physical therapist (PT) or occupational therapist (OT) [5].

To solve this problem, lots of hand rehabilitation robotic devices, which can bring out accurate and repetitive movement, have been invented and applied in the stroke community for hand function recovery, including some commercial products, such as Hand of Hope and HandCARE [6,7]. However, the rigid components like linear motors, rigid linkages and metal frame of these products have resulted in the heavy body weight and large size, which cannot make stroke survivors feel comfortable during hand rehabilitation training and also make it incapable of assisting daily activities. Thus, there is an apparent need for designing smaller, lighter and more comfortable hand rehabilitation devices. Several researchers have proposed some novel design of soft robotic hand [5,8,9]. Elastomeric-based soft actuators of the device developed by H. K. Yap et al. [10] can be actuated to bend on pressurization, while the extension is passively driven by the elastomer elasticity when depressurization, which is very limited. This can affect the hand rehabilitation effects. So, in our previous work [11], we proposed a solution to solve this problem by inserting an torque-compensating layer into the actuator, which can provide enough extension force although spasticity exists. And the former design of the actuator consists of a 3D printed elastomer body, fibre wrapping and a strain-limiting layer (torque-compensating layer) [11]. But some problems occur when experimenting with the formerly designed actuator: the fibre wrapping process is very time-consuming and the actuator can be very vulnerable when the fibre is broken. In view of this, we propose a new 3D printed soft robotic hand with Ring-reinforced Soft-Elastic Composite Actuator (R-SECA) (See Fig. 1). The reinforced ring is made of polypropylene by casting method, and polypropylene is a kind of plastic with strong mechanical properties. On the other hand, it is easy to assemble R-SECA if using reinforced ring rather than fibre wrapping. Based on the former 3D printed soft robotic hand, we proposed a preliminary method and platform to evaluate finger joint stiffness

Fig. 1. Demo design of the new 3D printed soft robotic hand

[12] as there is no objective method for finger stiffness evaluation when doing hand rehabilitation training. However, we just did preliminary test for evaluating finger joint stiffness, without post evaluation to compare. Further verification should be conducted to evaluate its effectiveness. Thus, for the purpose, we propose a 3D printed Soft robotic hand that combines post-stroke rehabilitation and joint stiffness evaluation.

In this paper, we design and 3D print four different lengths of R-SECA and then explore the relationship between the bending angle and output tip force at different input air pressure. Integrating with the pressurizing source and control system, the 3D printed soft robotic hand system can generate enough bending angle and flexion and extension torque for finger movement. Four recruited stroke survivors participate in the hand rehabilitation training and the improvement of hand function can be observed from the clinical evaluation data. The finger joint stiffness evaluation method and device are also presented and the evaluation results (pre and post) have been compared.

The rest of the paper is organised as follows. In Sect. 2, we introduce the design, performance of the 3D printed actuator and the stiffness estimation method and platform. In Sect. 3, we introduce the whole 3D printed soft robotic hand system, including the hardware components and control logic. In Sect. 4, four post-stroke patients are recruited to evaluate the clinical effectiveness of the 3D printed soft robotic hand system. In Sect. 5, we make a summary of our project progress and the future objectives.

2 Ring-reinforced Soft-Elastic Composite Actuator (R-SECA)

2.1 Actuator Design for the Soft Robotic Hand

Elastomeric chamber, fibre reinforcement and strain-limiting layer are key elements of the existing soft fibre-reinforced actuators [5]. In view of this, we have proposed the concept of SECA for soft robotic hand already in our previous work [11], in which the detailed design as well as its modeling has been clearly illustrated.

In this paper, we adopt 3D printing method for elastomeric-based actuator body as the traditional molding method can be usually time-consuming and multiple steps are needed to produce one actuator. Furthermore, the size of soft actuator is normally fixed since more different molds are needed to cast soft actuators in different sizes. The elastomeric-based actuator body is 3D printed directly by ACEO® - WACKER Chemie AG, which can not only produce high quality of R-SECA quickly, but also easy to adjust the size of soft actuator by altering the model. The material of ACEO Silicone GP Shore A 30 offered by ACEO® - WACKER Chemie AG is selected as printing material of elastomeric actuator body, which can offer sufficient elongation (450%) and tensile strength (6 MPa) [13].

As for the fibre wrapping method we introduced in [11], we replace it by polypropylene plastic ring to refrain radial expansion and reinforce the actuator. The polypropylene is a thermoplastic polymer that can be used in a wide variety of applications because of its strong mechanical properties. And the torque compensating layer is a thin stainless steel plate with 0.25 mm thickness, which is placed beneath the actuator. The R-SECA is separated into two segments, PIP segment and MCP segment, to allow it to be compatible with the human fingers (See Fig. 2). In previous study [14], authors have demonstrated that human index and ring fingers are about the same length, so we design the R-SECA with the length of 120 mm, 112 mm, 96 mm, 72 mm for fitting middle, index/ring, little and thumb fingers, separately. In the next section, we experiment to test the performance of R-SECA, including free space bending angle and output tip force under different input air pressure.

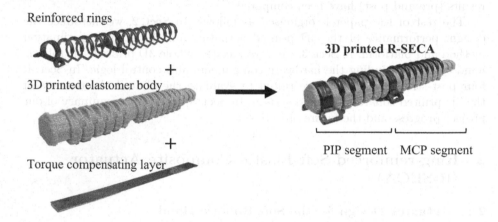

Fig. 2. Composition of the new 3D Printed R-SECA

2.2   Performance of the Ring-reinforced Soft-Elastic Composite Actuator

Free Space Bending Angle Measurement. To learn more about the relationship between the bending angle and input air pressure, We conduct experiments by inputting different air pressure (take 60KPa as the step) and record the bending angle. The measurement method of the bending angle is shown in Fig. 3B, which is the same as the method in [13]. In this section, the R-SECAs' free bending angles with different lengths (120 mm, 112 mm, 96 mm, 72 mm) are compared at different air pressure inputs (See Fig. 3C).

It is clear that the bending angle of R-SECA increases with air pressure and the longer R-SECA bends larger than other shorter R-SECAs at the same air pressure. At the maximal air pressure inputs 300KPa, the bending angle of 120 mm length R-SECA can reach 187°.

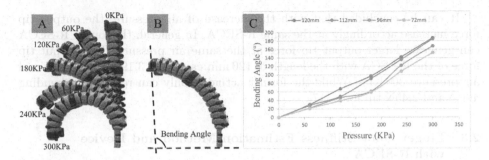

Fig. 3. (A) Free bending of the double-segmented R-SECA (120 mm) under different pressure inputs. (B) Illustration of the bending angle measurement. (C) Relationship between the air pressure inputs and bending angle with different length (120 mm, 112 mm, 96 mm, 72 mm)

Tip Force Measurement. In this paper, we propose a personalized output tip force measuring platform (See Fig. 4A), which is similar to the measurement setup in [5,15,16]. Our tip force measurement platform consists of a mounting platform, constraining platform, a clamp and a load cell (accuracy: 0.05%, TDA-02A, AUTODA Automation Equipment Co., Ltd.), with the proximal end of the actuator mounted on the clamp and distal end of the actuator contacted with the load cell. A constraining platform was placed on the top of the actuator, which was being used to constrain the curvature of the actuator. The air source was input into the actuator via an air tube, which was connected to the proximal end of the actuator. The relationship between the output tip force and the air pressure inputs is illustrated (see Fig. 4B).

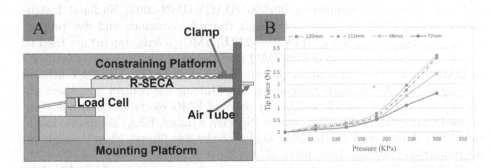

Fig. 4. (A) Schematic of the tip force measurement platform. (B) The relationship between tip force and pressure with different length (120 mm, 112 mm, 96 mm, 72 mm) of R-SECA

It can be concluded that with the increase of air pressure, the output tip force increase accordingly at the same R-SECA. In general, the longer R-SECA can generate larger output tip force at the same air pressure. The output tip force of the R-SECA with the length of 120 mm can reach 3.19N at the maximal air pressure 300 KPa. While the former actuator only can reach 137° bending angle and 2.45N tip force [17].

2.3 Finger Joint Stiffness Estimation Method and Device with R-SECA

In our previous work [12], we built a standard MCP joint stiffness measurement device, which mainly consists of two load cells (Model 1021, Range 0–100 N, Arizon Inc., China), DC servomotor (RDS5160, Torque 60 kg.cm, DSservo Inc., China) and an index finger splint. The testing and measurement platform has been illustrated. Inspired by [18,19], we have rebuilt Ground-Truth stiffness evaluation with standard mechatronic devices to evaluate its effectiveness. We experimented to evaluate MCP stiffness of index fingers on recruited subjects (Four chronic stroke survivors and four subjects with no neurological deficit) with the two different stiffness evaluation devices. The experiment results show that there is no evident difference in the stiffness evaluation by these two different devices. Based on this finding and research, we build again the joint stiffness measurement device with R-SECA and conduct the experiment to evaluate joint stiffness in the recruited subjects.

3   3D Printed Soft Robotic Hand System

The 3D printed soft robotic hand system is shown in Fig. 5A. Inside the control box, three data acquisition devices (DAQ) (USB-6009, National Instruments, Corp., USA) are used to transmit control commands and five proportional solenoids valves (PSV) (ITV1030-212 L, SMC, Tokyo, Japan) are used to receive the control commands from DAQ and also send the pressure values back to DAQ. Each PSV regulated air pressure for each R-SECA. One 24 V lithium battery is also placed inside the control box. Outside the control box, there are one 3D printed soft robotic hand, four pairs of EMG electrodes and one compressed CO_2 cylinder. Five flex sensors (Spectra Symbol, USA) are placed inside the R-SECA to record the bending angles of the five fingers when doing hand rehabilitation training. Four pairs of Ag/AgCl EMG electrodes (SE-00-S/50, Ambu® Blue Sensor, Denmark) are attached to the skin surface of FD, ED, BIC and TRI muscles. The reference electrode is attached to the skin surface of olecranon, and EMG values from EMG electrodes are read by DAQ directly [20]. The compressed CO_2 cylinder serves as pressurizing source. Figure 5B illustrate the task-oriented training by the 3D printed soft robotic hand system. For the control strategy, we adopt the iterative learning model predictive control (ILMPC) as we introduced in [21]. This method has the ability to improve model accuracy gradually and its good tracking performance has also been demonstrated.

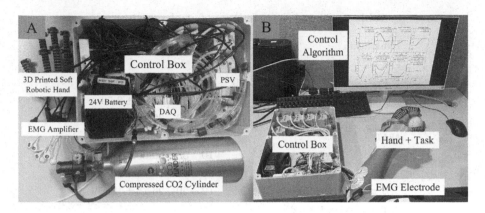

Fig. 5. (A) The 3D printed soft robotic hand and pneumatic control setup (B) Task-oriented hand rehabilitation training with the 3D printed soft robotic hand system

4   Pilot Test on Stroke Survivors

Considering the advantages of the soft robotic hand in assisting ADL tasks, a task-oriented intention-driven training model is adopted to improve stroke survivors' hand functions. In [22], the authors have shown that spherical grasp (all five fingers), tripod pinch (thumb, index and middle fingers) and tip pinch (thumb and index fingers) were frequently used during ADL tasks. Thus, in this study, we adopt the training mode as same as our previous study in [20], in which the experimental procedure has also been illustrated.

In this pilot study, four stroke survivors were recruited to evaluate the effect of rehabilitation training with the 3D printed R-SECA, together with the finger joint stiffness assessment before and after the training. The demographic information of the stroke survivors is listed in (Table 1). 20 sessions (3 sessions per week) of hand function rehabilitation training were given to each subject. Each session lasted for 45 min, while 5 min break time was given in each session to prevent muscle fatigue.

Table 1. Demographics of the recruited stroke survivors.

Subject	Age	Gender	Impaired side	Stroke type	Stroke onset (years)
S1	65	Male	Hemorrhagic	Left	9.2
S2	61	Male	Ischemic	Right	5.6
S3	55	Female	Ischemic	Left	6.4
S4	72	Female	Ischemic	Left	6.5

Table 2. Clinical characteristics of stroke survivors.

Evaluation	S1	S2	S3	S4	Mean ± S.D
FMA-UE					
Pre	27	29	15	36	26.75 ± 8.73
Post	32	38	22	42	33.50 ± 8.70
3 months follow up	36	31	19	43	32.25 ± 10.11
ARAT					
Pre	25	7	10	38	20.00 ± 14.35
Post	32	16	20	51	29.75 ± 15.71
3 months follow up	34	11	12	50	26.75 ± 18.79
BBT (Impaired hand)					
Pre	2	0	0	5	1.75 ± 2.36
Post	7	2	0	13	5.50 ± 5.80
3 months follow up	12	1	0	14	6.75 ± 7.27
Grip force (Kg)					
Pre	2.3	8.7	1.4	6.8	4.80 ± 3.51
Post	8.7	20	3.8	9.9	10.60 ± 6.80
3 months follow up	7.2	12.2	1.6	8.9	7.48 ± 4.43

The assessment of wrist and hand scale of the Fugl-Meyer Assessment for upper extremity (FMA-UE), Action Research Arm Test (ARAT), Box-and-Block (BBT), and grip force (Jamar® Dynamometers, JLW Instruments, U.S.A) have been given to stroke survivors before and after 20 sessions (See Table 2) and the stiffness evaluation of MCP and PIP joint is also conducted with the personalized stiffness evaluation device (See Table 3). FMA-UE is one of the most widely accepted measurement for upper extremity motor impairment post-stroke to evaluate the voluntary motor function [23]. ARAT evaluates full upper-limb capacity [24]. BBT measures unilateral gross manual dexterity [25]. MAS (motor assessment scale) is used to assess the muscle tone of fingers [26], a higher MAS grade reflects larger stiffness.

From the results, it is observed that improvement of the hand function can be found in all of the four subjects after the hand rehabilitation training with the above-mentioned 3D printed soft robotic hand system. This is consistent with our previous research findings [27]. For the subjects S1, S2 and S4, a stable improvement can be observed in FMA-UE, ARAT, BBT and Grip force, comparing the pre, post and 3 months follow-up assessment scores. For subject S3, an increase of the score of FMA-UE, ARAT and Grip force is observed, except BBT. Subject S3 cannot move any block from one compartment of the box to another side in one minute after finishing 20 sessions of rehabilitation training.

The decreased resting angle of MCP and PIP joint for all of the four subjects can be observed in (Table 3). Subjects S1 and S3 get a lower MAS-Finger grade after 20 sessions of training, which reflects both of them improved their muscle

Table 3. Clinical tone and stiffness evaluation of MCP and PIP joint.

	S1	S2	S3	S4
MAS-Finger				
Pre	1+	2	3	1+
Post	1	2	2	1+
MCP resting angle (°)				
Pre	54	71	90	60
Post	50	69	78	59
PIP resting angle (°)				
Pre	47	56	61	43
Post	46	53	51	44
Stiffness (MCP)				
Pre	0.0809 (±0.0025)	0.5011 (±0.0408)	0.6255 (±0.0231)	0.0857 (±0.0106)
Post	0.0610 (± 0.0083)	0.5237 (± 0.0186)	0.4760 (± 0.0342)	0.0733 (± 0.0037)
Stiffness (PIP)				
Pre	0.0910 (± 0.0017)	0.5683 (± 0.0283)	0.7123 (± 0.0601)	0.0483 (± 0.0041)
Post	0.0831 (± 0.0101)	0.5446 (± 0.0295)	0.4947 (± 0.0681)	0.0554 (± 0.0068)

tone of fingers. For subjects S2 and S4, there is no change of the MAS-Finger grade, compared to the pre and post-assessment.

5 Conclusion

In this work, we present a new 3D printed soft robotic hand system and conduct post-stroke rehabilitation training and finger stiffness evaluation with it. The Ring-reinforced Soft-Elastic Composite Actuator (R-SECA) can facilitate the finger flexion and extension effectively, while the key advantage is the different finger size can be achieved easily by 3D printing technology. Iterative learning model predictive control (ILMPC) is used to control the motion of the R-SECA, facilitating stroke survivors to complete the task-training tasks. The relationship between bending angle and the output tip force and input air pressure of R-SECA with different length is also explored. Improvement is also observed on the four recruited subjects after completing 20 sessions rehabilitation training with the 3D printed soft robotic hand system. In summary, the new 3D printed soft robotic hand system has preliminary demonstrated its effectiveness on hand rehabilitation training and more subjects will be recruited to compare the clinical efficacy in our future work.

References

1. Benjamin, E.J., et al.: Heart disease and stroke statistics-2017 update: a report from the American heart association. Circulation **135**(10), e146–e603 (2017)
2. Takahashi, C.D., Der-Yeghiaian, L., Le, V., Motiwala, R.R., Cramer, S.C.: Robot-based hand motor therapy after stroke. Brain **131**(2), 425–437 (2008)

3. Gerloff, C., Corwell, B., Chen, R., Hallett, M., Cohen, L.G.: The role of the human motor cortex in the control of complex and simple finger movement sequences. Brain J. Neurol. **121**(9), 1695–1709 (1998)
4. Bütefisch, C., Hummelsheim, H., Denzler, P., Mauritz, K.-H.: Repetitive training of isolated movements improves the outcome of motor rehabilitation of the centrally paretic hand. J. Neurol. Sci. **130**(1), 59–68 (1995)
5. Polygerinos, P., Wang, Z., Galloway, K.C., Wood, R.J., Walsh, C.J.: Soft robotic glove for combined assistance and at-home rehabilitation. Robot. Autonom. Syst. **73**, 135–143 (2015)
6. Ho, N.S.K., et al.: An EMG-driven exoskeleton hand robotic training device on chronic stroke subjects: task training system for stroke rehabilitation. In: 2011 IEEE International Conference On Rehabilitation Robotics, pp. 1–5. IEEE (2011)
7. Dovat, L., et al.: Handcare: a cable-actuated rehabilitation system to train hand function after stroke. IEEE Trans. Neural Syst. Rehabil. Eng. **16**(6), 582–591 (2008)
8. Feng, N., Shi, Q., Wang, H., Gong, J., Liu, C., Zhiguo, L.: A soft robotic hand: design, analysis, sEMG control, and experiment. Int. J. Adv. Manuf. Technol. **97**(1), 319–333 (2018)
9. Zhou, J., et al.: A soft-robotic approach to anthropomorphic robotic hand dexterity. IEEE Access **7**, 101483–101495 (2019)
10. Yap, H.K., Lim, J.H., Nasrallah, F., Goh, J.C.H., Yeow, C.-H.: Characterisation and evaluation of soft elastomeric actuators for hand assistive and rehabilitation applications. J. Med. Eng. Technol. **40**(4), 199–209 (2016)
11. Heung, K.H.L., Tong, R.K.Y., Lau, A.T.H., Li, Z.: Robotic glove with soft-elastic composite actuators for assisting activities of daily living. Soft Robot. **6**(2), 289–304 (2019)
12. Shi, X.Q., Heung, H.L., Tang, Z.Q., Tong, K.Y., Li, Z.: Verification of finger joint stiffness estimation method with soft robotic actuator. Front. Bioeng. Biotechnol. **8**, 1479 (2020)
13. Heung, H.L., Tang, Z.Q., Shi, X.Q., Tong, K.Y., Li, Z.: Soft rehabilitation actuator with integrated post-stroke finger spasticity evaluation. Front. Bioeng. Biotechnol. **8**, 111 (2020)
14. Peters, M., Mackenzie, K., Bryden, P.: Finger length and distal finger extent patterns in humans. Am. J. Phys. Anthropol. Official Publ. Am. Assoc. Phys. Anthropol. **117**(3), 209–217 (2002)
15. Polygerinos, P., et al.: Modeling of soft fiber-reinforced bending actuators. IEEE Trans. Robot. **31**(3), 778–789 (2015)
16. Yap, H.K., Sebastian, F., Wiedeman, C., Yeow, C.-H.: Design and characterization of low-cost fabric-based flat pneumatic actuators for soft assistive glove application. In: 2017 International Conference on Rehabilitation Robotics (ICORR), pp. 1465–1470. IEEE (2017)
17. Heung, K.H.L., Tang, Z.Q., Ho, L., Tung, M., Li, Z., Tong, R.K.Y.: Design of a 3d printed soft robotic hand for stroke rehabilitation and daily activities assistance. In: 2019 IEEE 16th International Conference on Rehabilitation Robotics (ICORR), pp. 65–70. IEEE (2019)
18. Esteki, A., Mansour, J.M.: An experimentally based nonlinear viscoelastic model of joint passive moment. J. Biomech. **29**(4), 443–450 (1996)
19. Kuo, P.-H., Deshpande, A.D.: Muscle-tendon units provide limited contributions to the passive stiffness of the index finger metacarpophalangeal joint. J. Biomech. **45**(15), 2531–2538 (2012)

20. Tang, Z.Q., Heung, H.L., Shi, X.Q., Tong, R.K., Li, Z.: Probabilistic model-based learning control of a soft pneumatic glove for hand rehabilitation. IEEE Trans. Biomed. Eng. **69**, 1016–1028 (2021)
21. Tang, Z.Q., Heung, H.L., Tong, K.Y., Li, Z.: A novel iterative learning model predictive control method for soft bending actuators. In: 2019 International Conference on Robotics and Automation (ICRA), pp. 4004–4010. IEEE (2019)
22. Bullock, I.M., Zheng, J.Z., De La Rosa, S., Guertler, C., Dollar, A.M.: Grasp frequency and usage in daily household and machine shop tasks. IEEE Trans. Haptics. **6**(3), 296–308 (2013)
23. Camilla Biering Lundquist and Thomas Maribo: The Fugl-Meyer assessment of the upper extremity: reliability, responsiveness and validity of the Danish version. Disabil. Rehabil. **39**(9), 934–939 (2017)
24. Hoonhorst, M.H., et al.: How do Fugl-Meyer arm motor scores relate to dexterity according to the action research arm test at 6 months poststroke? Arch. Phys. Med. Rehabil. **96**(10), 1845–1849 (2015)
25. Hsiao, C.-P., Zhao, C., Do, E.Y.-L.: The digital box and block test automating traditional post-stroke rehabilitation assessment. In: 2013 IEEE International Conference on Pervasive Computing and Communications Workshops (PERCOM workshops), pp. 360–363. IEEE (2013)
26. Carr, J.H., Shepherd, R.B., Nordholm, L., Lynne, D.: Investigation of a new motor assessment scale for stroke patients. Phys. Ther. **65**(2), 175–180 (1985)
27. Shi, X.Q., Heung, H.L., Tang, Z.Q., Li, Z., Tong, K.Y.: Effects of a soft robotic hand for hand rehabilitation in chronic stroke survivors. J. Stroke Cerebrovasc. Dis. **30**(7), 105812 (2021)

Wearable Sensing Based Virtual Reality Rehabilitation Scheme for Upper Limb Training

Jialiang Zhang, Yaojie Liu, and Juan Liu[✉]

School of Information Engineering, Wuhan University of Technology, Wuhan 430070, China
juanliu@whut.edu.cn

Abstract. Upper limb rehabilitation training is an important method for stroke patients with hemiplegia to restore their upper limb motor ability. The combination of virtual reality (VR) technology and rehabilitation training can increase the effectiveness and interest of the training process. In the process of virtual reality rehabilitation training, dynamic uncertainty factors will affect the effectiveness of rehabilitation training, so it is necessary to adjust the decision of rehabilitation training in real time according to the status of patients. In this paper, a virtual reality upper limb rehabilitation training game with controllable difficulty parameters is designed to collect the electromyographic (EMG) signals and motion signal of patients in the process of movement. Through the fuzzy neural network rehabilitation training decision-making method optimized based on the cuckoo algorithm, the control parameters of virtual reality rehabilitation training scene are adjusted to make the difficulty of rehabilitation training task match the upper limb movement ability of patients adaptively. We recruited 23 stroke patients with different stages of Brunnstrom rehabilitation participated in this experiment. The accuracy of the rehabilitation training decision-making method has an accuracy rate of 96.23%. It can accurately make rehabilitation training decisions, adjust the difficulty of training tasks to a challenging but feasible level, and improve the rehabilitation training effect.

Keywords: Wearable sensing · Virtual reality · Cuckoo algorithm · Upper limb rehabilitation training

1 Introduction

Studies have shown that there are 11 million patients with acute ischemic stroke and intracranial hemorrhage in China [1], and the number of new cases is increasing by 2.4 million every year. Since 2010, stroke has become the disease with the highest rate of death and disability in China, and the number of patients with dyskinesia caused by stroke and other reasons is also growing rapidly [2, 3]. The disability of the upper limb will seriously affect the daily life of the patients. It is necessary to recover the movement ability of the limbs through rehabilitation training. However, the existing rehabilitation medical resources in China are very scarce. When the clinical rehabilitation carries out limb rehabilitation training, the rehabilitation doctors usually carry out one-to-one

H. Liu et al. (Eds.): ICIRA 2022, LNAI 13457, pp. 24–36, 2022.
https://doi.org/10.1007/978-3-031-13835-5_3

passive training on the rehabilitation treatment parts of the patients with bare hands or with the aid of equipment, and guide the patients' limb movement repeatedly until they can return to the normal movement. After training for a period of time, the evaluation is carried out to adjust the training program [4–6]. This traditional rehabilitation training mode has many problems, such as high manpower consumption, long rehabilitation cycle, low rehabilitation enthusiasm of patients, boring rehabilitation training process and low efficiency [7].

The application of virtual reality (VR) technology in the field of medical rehabilitation makes up for the shortcomings of traditional rehabilitation training methods. It enables rehabilitation doctors and patients free from the repetitive and boring rehabilitation training tasks [8, 9]. Rehabilitation doctors can focus more on the improvement of the treatment scheme, and patients can be more independent and active in rehabilitation training, so as to promote the development of centralized rehabilitation medicine and family rehabilitation medicine exhibition [10, 11]. Winso et al [12] developed an adaptive interactive learning system based on 3D video games named "The Number Race" to improve learning efficiency. John et al. [13] developed physiological adaptive fitness games for the elderly to control the human body's exercise load in the current affordable state, avoid excessive exercise and maintain a good level of entertainment. Shabnam et al. [14] developed an integrated system named "ReHabGame", which uses fuzzy logic guidance to adjust rehabilitation robot and virtual reality scene. Karime et al. [15] designed a set of adaptive family wrist rehabilitation training framework, which uses fuzzy logic to control the position and attitude of quilt and plate in virtual environment to realize adaptive wrist rehabilitation training. Buttussi et al. [16] proposed a situational awareness and user adaptive fitness game system. One-way ANOVA was used to analyze the adaptive algorithm to predict the real-time participation of players, so that the game environment could automatically adapt to the degree of people seeking to experience perceived challenges when playing games, and guide and motivate players to continue to exercise. Borghese et al. [17] developed a set of family serious game rehabilitation system using fuzzy logic continuous monitoring, and updated game parameters through Bayesian framework to provide games of different levels of difficulty, so as to continuously adapt to the current state of patients and avoid patients doing wrong or harmful exercises to recovery. From the perspective of rehabilitation, self-adaptive rehabilitation training can not only scientifically guide patients to complete personalized rehabilitation training, improve the effectiveness of rehabilitation training, but also avoid secondary injuries caused by improper exercise [18, 19].

However, at present, the scene parameters controlled by the rehabilitation training decision-making method are single, which can't meet the needs of rehabilitation training; the patients' movement can't be fed back to the virtual reality rehabilitation training scene; the rehabilitation training decision-making and rehabilitation training process need manual intervention, which costs manpower and time. Therefore, this paper designs the upper limb rehabilitation training game based on virtual reality to enhance the interest of rehabilitation training. The rehabilitation status and motor ability of patients can be assessed by collecting the motor signals and physiological signals. We also use an algorithm to make the rehabilitation training intelligent.

2   Design of VR-Based Rehabilitation System

This paper designs an upper limb rehabilitation training system based on virtual reality, which is composed of wearable sensing data acquisition hardware equipment and human-computer interaction software. The wearable sensing data acquisition device consists of myoelectric signal acquisition equipment and 3D motion capture system. The system software is mainly composed: (a) Virtual reality rehabilitation training module, (b) Adaptive decision-making module, and (c) Data communication module.

2.1   Wearable Sensing Device

In this paper, a three-dimensional motion acquisition and analysis system (Qualisys, Sweden), a wireless surface electromyography acquisition device (Delsys Trigno, USA), a signal synchronous trigger and computer are used as the signal acquisition platform to synchronously collect the angle signals of the elbow joint and the two major upper limb joints of the wrist joint. During the upper limb flexion and extension movement, the surface electromyogram signals of the two head muscles of the humorous, the triceps, the extensor carpi radialis and the flexor carpi radialis four muscles are wearable monitored. The wearable sensing data acquisition system is shown in Fig. 1. The Qualisys 3D motion analysis system consists of eight infrared high-speed motion capture cameras, one video camera, a set of calibration equipment, several marker balls and Qualisys Track Manager analysis software. Trigno™ wireless surface EMG signal acquisition system mainly includes wireless EMG patch electrode, signal receiving base station and signal acquisition and analysis software. The signal synchronous trigger enables the motion capture system and the surface EMG acquisition instrument to be triggered synchronically to complete the collection of motion signals and surface EMG signals during movement.

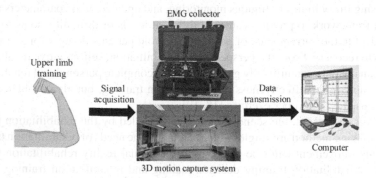

Fig. 1. Wearable sensing hardware device

2.2   Rehabilitation Games Design

The main purpose of rehabilitation training is to guide the patients to carry out rehabilitation sports training [20]. The Bruunstrom rehabilitation assessment stage of the trained patients is at least stage III. In this paper, we design a game called "catching small experts". In the game, a virtual food will be randomly generated within a certain range. The patient will control the virtual arm movement through their own motion. The game interface is shown in Fig. 2(a).

The game sets two initial difficulties: static mode and dynamic mode. In the static mode, set the existence time of each virtual food as 15 s, and the virtual food will not move. After the random position is generated, the virtual food will stay still. The patient controls the virtual arm to grasp the virtual food and get points, and the next virtual food goal will appear. If the patient cannot move the arm to the corresponding position to capture the virtual food within 15 s, the virtual food will disappear, and the task fails without score. The next target object appears. In the dynamic mode, after the virtual food is generated at a certain time interval, it falls at a certain speed, and disappears when it touches the virtual seabed rock. The patient is required to control the virtual arm to capture the virtual food before it falls into the seabed, and score after capture. Because the location and falling speed of the virtual food are different, the patient needs to consider which object to capture first, which greatly exercises hand-eye coordination of patients. The game flow is shown in Fig. 2(b).

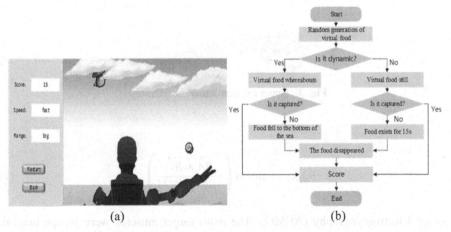

(a)   (b)

Fig. 2. (a) Rehabilitation game interface for upper limb (b) Game flow chart

The system software is based on the Unity 3D game engine and uses C# language programming to build the human-computer interaction platform. For rehabilitation training games, the communication connection between the upper computer software QTM of the Qualisys motion capture system and the Unity 3D platform is required. In this paper, UDP communication protocol is adopted to realize data transmission between two applications. The motion data of the subjects were transmitted to the virtual scene by QTM, the upper computer software of the Qualisys 3D motion capture system with an integrated server port. The client is then built in Unity 3D for real-time data transmission with QTM.

3 Decision-Making for Rehabilitation Training

3.1 Selection of Upper Limb Motion Feedback Parameters

In the process of rehabilitation training, the parameters of patients' movement can reflect the patients' movement ability and rehabilitation state. Range of motion is the most direct indicator of motor function in stroke patients with dyskinesia. ROM is the range of motion of the patients. EMG signals occur during the human body muscle activity in the process of human body muscle contraction in tiny electrical signals, studies [21–23] have shown that EMG signal amplitude related to muscle size, velocity and acceleration, the RMS of EMG reflects the number of motor unit to activate muscle activity, and integral values of EMG reflect the neuromuscular activity in a certain time range of motor unit discharge total amount.

ROM: The range of motion can be calculated from the coordinates of the markers in the motion capture system. 4 markers are selected, the positions of which are shown in the Fig. 3. Equation (1) can be used to calculate the range of motion of the elbow joint. The difference between the average values of the maximum 1000 angles and the minimum 1000 angles will be the ROM.

Fig. 3. Upper extremity marker location

$$\theta_{elbow} = \arccos\left(\frac{\overrightarrow{BA} * \overrightarrow{BC}}{\left|\overrightarrow{BA}\right| * \left|\overrightarrow{BC}\right|} \right) \tag{1}$$

Average Electromyography (AEMG): The main target muscles were biceps brachii, triceps brachii, extensor carpi radialis and flexor carpi radialis. Firstly, preprocessing is carried out to reduce the influence of artifact noise and baseline drift, so as to make the EMG signal more accurate. The initial EMG signal is filtered by a 5-order Baxter high pass filter with a cut-off frequency of 20 Hz. The calculation method of AEMG is shown in formula (2), Where x_m is the m-th EMG signal value.

$$AEMG = \frac{1}{m}\sum\nolimits_{m=1}^{m} x_m \tag{2}$$

3.2 Cuckoo Search-Fuzzy Based Decision-Making Scheme

In the decision-making of virtual reality rehabilitation training, it is necessary to effectively and accurately establish the relationship between the patients' movement state and the parameters in the virtual training scene, namely, to establish a non-linear mapping relationship between the input and output data, to control the parameters of virtual reality training scene through the mapping relationship, establish a rehabilitation training system with real-time regulation of exercise load, so as to make the patients with personalized, adaptability of rehabilitation training [24].

Fuzzy neural network has good learning and adaptive ability [25, 26]. But in the fuzzy neural network, the gradient descent method is usually used to train and adjust the weights. In the process of training, the prediction result of the neural network may be inaccurate because it converges to the local optimal solution. Therefore, this paper uses the cuckoo algorithm to find the optimal weights of the neural network and optimize the rehabilitation training decision-making method of the fuzzy neural network. The decision-making process of rehabilitation training is shown in Fig. 4.

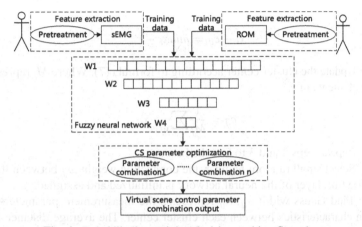

Fig. 4. Rehabilitation training decision-making flow chart

Input: The ROM values of the two joints are formed into a feature matrix A_j of the range of motion. The AEMG composition of four channels (biceps brachii, triceps brachii, extensor carpi radialis and flexor carpi radialis) constitute A_m. By A_j and A_m constitutes the characteristic matrix X of rehabilitation training state as (3).

$$X = [A_j, A_m] \tag{3}$$

Output: There are two control parameters of virtual reality scene, which are the speed and range of motion required for rehabilitation training. The control parameter set Y is (4). V_i is the scene action speed control coefficient, i range is [1, 2], the larger i is, the faster the scene action control speed is. R_j is the control coefficient of scene action range, j range is [1, 2], the larger the j is, the larger the scene action range is.

$$Y = [V_i, R_j](i = 1, 2, j = 1, 2,) \tag{4}$$

$\delta(t)$ is the movement status indicators during rehabilitation training, including the objective function of rehabilitation training decision-making method constructed by angular acceleration and variation of joint range of motion, as shown in (5).

$$\delta(t) = min(\mu \cdot \Delta A_j + \lambda \cdot \Delta A_m) \qquad (5)$$

ΔA_j represents the change of ROM, ΔA_m represents the mean change of RMS. μ and λ represent the weight coefficients of the cost function for two input eigenvalues. X and Y are substituted into the fuzzy neural network as input and output respectively, the training steps of fuzzy neural network are as follows:

Step 1: Initialize the cluster center, and the cluster center is c_{ij}, where i = 1,2..., m, j = 1, 2,..., m.

Step 2: All input variables x_i are grouped according to the nearest clustering center principle, as long as (6) is satisfied. x_i is divided into sets θ_j, which is the same group. θ_j represents the set of training patterns clustered around c_{ij} in the cluster center.

$$x_i - c_{ij} = \min_{j \in N_m} x_i - c_{ij} \qquad (6)$$

Step 3: Update the cluster center according to formula (7). Where M_j represents the number of elements in θ_i.

$$c_{ij} = \frac{1}{M_j} \sum_{x_i \in \theta_i} x_i \qquad (7)$$

Step 4: Repeat steps 2 and 3 to find the best c_{ij}.

Step 5: Select small random number, the connection weight ω_{ij} between the fourth layer and the fifth layer of the neural network is initialized and assigned.

Step 6: Find Gauss width σ_{ij}. σ_{ij} represents the measurement parameters of data distribution characteristics between each cluster center. The average distance between training mode and cluster center is calculated by (8).

$$\sigma_{ij} = \sqrt{\frac{1}{M_j} \sum_{x_i \in \theta_i} (x_i - c_{ij})^T (x_i - c_{ij})} \qquad (8)$$

Step 7: By determining the width and center of Gauss membership degree, we can start to update the weight, usually using gradient descent method. In this paper, cuckoo algorithm is used to replace gradient descent method.

Step 8: Finally, the Mean-Square Error (MSE) value is calculated by (9). When MSE $< 10^{-4}$, the training output is finished. Otherwise, step 6 is returned.

$$MSE = \frac{1}{N} \sum_{i=1}^{N} (y_{ki} - y_i)^2 \qquad (9)$$

In Step 7, cuckoo is used to calculate the update weight. Cuckoo algorithm uses Levi flight to update the nest position [27, 28], as shown in (10).

$$X_{g+1,i} = X_{g,i} + \alpha \otimes Levy(\beta)(i = 1, 2, ...n) \qquad (10)$$

$X_{g+1,i}$ is the nest position of the i-th nest in the g-th generation. α is the step size scaling factor, $Levy(\beta)$ is the levy random path. Generally, $\alpha = 1$.

4   Experiments and Results Discussion

A total of 23 stroke patients with hemiplegia were tested in the rehabilitation department of XX Hospital, including 19 males and 4 females, aged between 25 and 63. The 23 patients were in stage I–VI of Bruunstrom's rehabilitation stage. The trials were approved by Human Participants Ethics Committees from Wuhan University of Technology, and written informed consent was obtained from each participant.

4.1   Inclusion and Exclusion Criteria

All patients meet the following requirements: (1) Informed of the purpose of the experiment and participate voluntarily; (2) Have the ability of cognition and communication, can follow the guidance; (3) There are no other injuries affecting the motor ability in the affected upper limb, and other factors influencing the rehabilitation assessment of stroke are excluded; (4) No strenuous exercise within 24 h, excluding the influence of muscle fatigue; (5) There is no damage to the upper limb muscle epidermis, which is not easy to be allergic to skin. It is convenient to paste marker ball and electromyographic patch electrode; (6) It is not easy to produce spasm, the muscle tension is small, and the influencing factors of sEMG signal are reduced; (7) During the experiment, there is a professional rehabilitation physician.

4.2   Experimental Protocol

Step 1: The subjects participate in the rehabilitation training when the brain and limbs are not excessively tired. At the same time of completing the task, repeat the four training actions of elbow extension, flexion, wrist dorsiflexion and palm flexion, record the subjects movement characteristic values, normalize for $\tilde{A}_j$ and $\tilde{A}_m$.

Step 2: Adjust training scenarios parameters, make subjects to complete $C = [V_i, R_j](i = 1, 2j = 1, 2)$ combination of four different training difficult task cycle, record the task completion is the most close to 60% of control parameters combination, the motion characteristics of the subjects to complete the training task to remember is $[\tilde{A}_{j0}, \tilde{A}_{m0}]$, just as a set of Cuckoo Search- Fuzzy Neural Network(CS-FNN) rehabilitation training decision model of the training sample $[\tilde{A}_j, \tilde{A}_m, V_i, R_j]$.

Step 3: Repeat the above steps several times to obtain a total of 200 sets of data from subjects as a sample database.

Step 4: The training sample base is substituted into the CS-FNN rehabilitation training decision model. The probability of host abandonment of cuckoo's eggs P_a is set as 0.25, the step-size scaling factor α is 1.0, the step-size scaling factor is 1.0, the Levi flight parameter β is 1.5, the weight factors and in the objective function are both 0.5, and the number of iterations is 100.

Step 5: Online experiment. When patients complete a cycle task, the exercise data enters into the CS-FNN rehabilitation training decision model completed by training, and the combination of scene control parameters is output.

4.3   Results Discussion

Based on the Brunnstrom rehabilitation assessment scale, the rehabilitation status and motor ability of patients in different stages are different. Two joint angle data changes as shown in Fig. 5. Patients with stage III's motion are much smaller than the VI period patients. Patients with stage III can't completely make joint separate separatist movement, each body in the process of movement control is poor, joint angular motion curves have obvious shaking; In stage VI, the motion angle curve is smooth and the motion of the two joints has obvious sequence, which is separation motion.

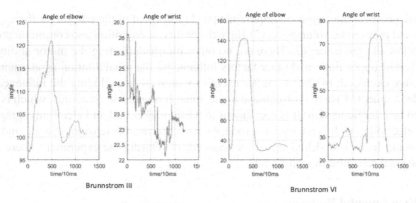

Fig. 5. ROM of brunnstrom III and VI

The EMG signals before and after the filtering of the upper limb muscle groups of the two patients are shown in Fig. 6. It can be seen from the figure that the EMG amplitude of stage III patients is less than that of stage VI patients, and the period of flexor movement of stage III patients is not obvious.

In the absence of CS algorithm optimization, 80% of the data is randomly divided into test sets. The decision-making results of FNN and CS-FNN rehabilitation training are shown in Fig. 7. The two scene parameters in the figure are combined and divided into four situations: 1 represents [small range, slow speed], 2 represents [large range, slow speed], 3 represents [small range, fast], and 4 represents [large range, fast].

Other algorithms are used as rehabilitation training decision making methods. The accuracy of the improved fuzzy-neural network rehabilitation training decision making method based on cuckoo in this paper is similar to that shown in Table 1.

After the optimization based on the cuckoo algorithm, the prediction results of fuzzy neural network are significantly improved. The decision-making method of rehabilitation training based on the cuckoo optimization is helpful for the more accurate adaptive adjustment of the parameters of the virtual reality rehabilitation training scene, and helps the patients to carry out the rehabilitation training with high efficiency and scientific difficulty to adapt to their own sports ability.

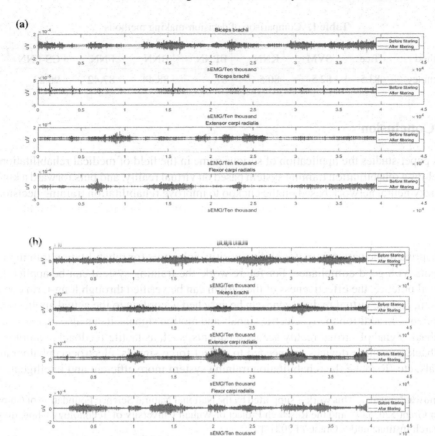

Fig. 6. (a) Brunnstrom stage III (b) Brunnstrom stage VI

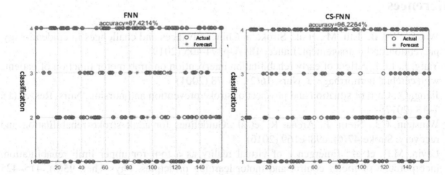

Fig. 7. Results of rehabilitation training decision

Table 1. Comparison of decision-making methods

Method	Tree	SVM	KNN	BPNN	BNN	FNN	CS-FNN
Accuracy	83.5	82.5	80.5	87	88.44	87.42	96.23

5 Conclusion

This paper studies the application of serious game in the field of medical rehabilitation, develops a rehabilitation training system based on virtual reality, and puts forward a kind of fuzzy neural network based on the cuckoo to improve rehabilitation training decision methods. Build rehabilitation training in patients with movement to the rehabilitation training task difficulty mapping model, the motion state of the patients with feedback to the rehabilitation training scenario, the control of rehabilitation training task difficulty is adaptive to the patient's motor ability, positive incentive for rehabilitation training in patients with good compliance. For future work, the training system can be applied to clinical practice, the effectiveness of the system can be verified through long-term comparison, and the virtual reality scene can be enriched according to the actual application of patients. In addition to myoelectric signals and motion signals, it can also increase the feedback signal of virtual reality scene to patients, such as tactile feedback, emotional feedback, etc. more devices are needed to collect force signals, electroencephalogram signals, etc. To make the rehabilitation training system more efficient and intelligent.

Acknowledgments. This work is supported by the National Natural Science Foundation of China under Grant 52075398 and the Research Project of Wuhan University of Technology Chongqing Research Institute under Grant YF2021-17.

References

1. Wu, S., Wu, B., Liu, M., et al.: Stroke in China: advances and challenges in epidemiology, prevention, and management. Lancet **18**(4), p394-405 (2019)
2. Yang, J., Li, J.: Effect of early rehabilitation intervention on limb motor function of patients with cerebral hemorrhage. J. Nurs. **16**(2), 76–78 (2001)
3. Jiang, Q.: Current situation and prospect of stroke prevention and nursing. Nurs. Res. **31**(1), 7–13 (2017)
4. Winstein, C.J., Stein, J., Arena, R., et al.: Guidelines for adult stroke rehabilitation and recovery. Stroke **47**(6), e98–e169 (2016)
5. Levin, M.F., et al.: Emergence of virtual reality as a tool for upper limb rehabilitation: incorporation of motor control and motor learning principles. Phys Ther. **95**(3), 415–425 (2015)
6. Fang, D., Zhu, Y.: Neurorehabilitation. Chin. J. Neuropsychol. **28**(4), 23–238 (1995)
7. Gu, J., Huang, H., Yu, R., et al.: Progress in rehabilitation evaluation and treatment of traumatic brain injury. Chongqing Med. **38**(8), 909–911 (2009)
8. Wiley, E., Khattab, S., Tang, A., et al.: Examining the effect of virtual reality therapy on cognition post-stroke: a systematic review and meta-analysis. Disability and rehabilitation. Assistive Technol. 1–11 (2020)

9. Liu, T., Liu, Z., Pang, Q., et al.: Research on virtual reality system design for body and psychological rehabilitation. J. China Univ. Posts Telecommun. **26**(6), 73–82 (2019)
10. Yang, X., Wang, D., Zhang, Y., et al.: An adaptive strategy for an immersive visuo-haptic attention training game. In: Proceedings of the International Conference On Human Haptic Sensing and Touch Enabled Computer Applications, Part I (2016)
11. Chen, Y., Abel, K.T., Janecek, J.T., et al.: Home-based technologies for stroke rehabilitation: a systematic review. Int. J. Med. Inform. **123**, 11–22 (2019)
12. Wilson, A.J., Dehaene, S., Pinel, P., et al.: Principles underlying the design of "The Number Race", an adaptive computer game for remediation of dyscalculia. Behav. Brain Funct. **2**(1), 19 (2006)
13. Munoz, J.E., Cameirao, M., Bermudez, I., Badia, S., et al.: Closing the loop in exergaming - health benefits of biocybernetic adaptation in senior adults. In: Proceedings of the 5th ACM SIGCHI Annual Symposium on Computer-Human Interaction in Play, CHI PLAY, pp. 329–339, Association for Computing Machinery, Inc. (2018)
14. Esfahlani, S.S., Cirstea, S, Sanaei, A., et al.: An adaptive self-organizing fuzzy logic controller in a serious game for motor impairment rehabilitation. In: Proceedings of the IEEE International Symposium on Industrial Electronics (2017)
15. Karime, A., Eid, M., Alja'am, J.M., et al.: A fuzzy-based adaptive rehabilitation framework for home-based wrist training. IEEE Trans. Instrum. Measur. **63**(1), 135–144 (2013)
16. Buttussi, F., Chittaro, L., Ranon, R., Verona, A.: Adaptation of graphics and gameplay in fitness games by exploiting motion and physiological sensors. In: Butz, A., Fisher, B., Krüger, A., Olivier, P., Owada, S. (eds.) SG 2007. LNCS, vol. 4569, pp. 85–96. Springer, Heidelberg (2007). https://doi.org/10.1007/978-3-540-73214-3_8
17. Borghese, N.A., Mainetti, R., Pirovano, M., et al.: An intelligent game engine for the at-home rehabilitation of stroke patients. In: Proceedings of the IEEE International Conference on Serious Games & Applications for Health (2013)
18. Dhiman, A., Solanki, D., Bhasin, A., et al.: An intelligent, adaptive, performance-sensitive, and virtual reality-based gaming platform for the upper limb. Comput. Anim. Virt. Worlds **29**(2), e1800 (2018)
19. Dash, A., Lahiri, U., et al.: Design of virtual reality-enabled surface electromyogram-triggered grip exercise platform. Des. Virt. Real. Enabled Surf. Electro. Triggered Grip Exerc. Platform **28**(2), 444–452 (2020)
20. Bonnechère, B.: Serious games in physical rehabilitation. Serious Games in Rehabilitation (Chapter 4), pp. 41–109 (2018). https://doi.org/10.1007/978-3-319-66122-3
21. Wang, B., Zhang, X.: Research progress of upper limb rehabilitation assessment methods based on artificial intelligence and clinical diagnosis. Beijing Biomed. Eng. **37**(1), 103–108 (2018)
22. Sy, A.C., Bugtai, N.T., Domingo, A.D., et al.: Effects of movement velocity, acceleration and initial degree of muscle flexion on bicep EMG signal amplitude (2016)
23. Saad, I., Bais, N.H., Bun, S.C., et al.: Electromyogram (EMG) signal processing analysis for clinical rehabilitation application. In: Proceedings of the 2015 3rd International Conference on Artificial Intelligence, Modelling & Simulation (AIMS) (2015)
24. Wang, D., Zheng, Y., Teng, L.I., et al.: Multi-modal human-machine interaction for human intelligence augmentation. Scientia Sinica (Informationis) **48**(4), 95–111 (2018)
25. Jia, L., Xiao, L., Dai, J., et al.: Design and application of an adaptive fuzzy control strategy to zeroing neural network for solving time-variant QP problem. IEEE Trans. Fuzzy Syst. **99**, 1–1 (2020)
26. Dian, S., Hu, Y., Zhao, T., Han, J.: Adaptive backstepping control for flexible-joint manipulator using interval type-2 fuzzy neural network approximator. Nonlinear Dyn. **97**(2), 1567–1580 (2019). https://doi.org/10.1007/s11071-019-05073-8

27. Walton, S., Hassan, O., Morgan, K., et al.: Modified cuckoo search: a new gradient free optimization algorithm. Chaos Solit. Fract. **44**(9), 710–718 (2011)
28. Yang, X.S., Deb, S.: Cuckoo search via levy flights. Mathematics, pp. 210–214 (2010)

Gait Analysis and Phase Recognition Based on Array Fiber Optic Sensing Insole

Nian Peng[1], Wei Meng[1(✉)], Quan Liu[1], and Shengquan Xie[2]

[1] School of Information Engineering, Wuhan University of Technology, Wuhan 430070, China
weimeng@whut.edu.cn
[2] School of Electronic and Electrical Engineering, University of Leeds, Leeds LS2 9JT, UK

Abstract. In order to realize gait assessment and robot-assisted control in lower extremity rehabilitation scenarios, prevention and diagnosis of lower extremity diseases, a sensitivity-enhanced array fiber optic sensing insole for plantar pressure monitoring was designed by taking advantage of the characteristics of fiber optic sensor, such as lightness, anti-electromagnetic interference, strong multiplexing capability, and sensitivity to stress and strain. The gait parameters were effectively analyzed by collecting the plantar pressure data under natural walking. A gait recognition method based on plantar pressure at different walking speeds was proposed to solve the problems of the complexity and poor accuracy of gait recognition. The support vector machine was used to classify four gait periods: the initial double-limb support phase, the single-limb stance phase, the second double-limb support phase and the swing phase. The overall gait phase recognition rate of the classifier was 90.37%. The experiment verifies the validity of the fiber optic pressure insole to measure gait parameters and the accuracy of gait recognition.

Keywords: Fiber bragg grating · Plantar pressure · Gait analysis · Gait phase recognition

1 Introduction

According to the data of the seventh census of the National Bureau of Statistics in 2021, the population of China aged 60 and above is 264 million, accounting for 18.7% of the total population. This is an increase of 5.44% points compared with the data of the sixth census, and the aging situation is becoming increasingly severe [1]. The aging population's physiology declines, causing health problems such as diabetes, stroke, cerebral palsy, spinal cord injury, and Parkinson's disease, which greatly affect their daily movement. Exercise capacity is one of the key parameters for human health assessment, especially gait analysis is an important metric of a person's health status. As part of gait analysis, plantar pressure

H. Liu et al. (Eds.): ICIRA 2022, LNAI 13457, pp. 37–48, 2022.
https://doi.org/10.1007/978-3-031-13835-5_4

can assess the development and evolution of foot ulcers in diabetic patients [2]; in the process of rehabilitation training for patients with limb movement disorders, plantar pressure monitoring can assist rehabilitation therapists in evaluating the patient's walking function before and after training; moreover, by collecting the patient's plantar pressure data, the precise division of the gait phase can provide accurate control for the wearable device [3]. Therefore, the analysis of plantar pressure data and the accurate identification of gait phase are of great significance in the prevention and diagnosis of diseases and the rehabilitation treatment of patients.

The current gait information collection systems include: (1) the gait recognition systems based on machine vision, including video capture systems, human color and depth images collected by Kinect cameras, etc. However, the system based on visual collection of information has high requirements on computer software and hardware, high-performance cameras are relatively expensive, and the shooting effect is easily affected by the location of the camera and the surrounding environment. (2) the force measuring plate, which embeds the arrayed electronic pressure sensing elements into a rigid plate. Although it does not need to be worn, the measurement is limited to a fixed area and it is not portable. (3) the wearable sensing devices, including EMG sensors, electronic plantar pressure sensors [4], acceleration sensors, gyroscopes, etc. The EMG sensor can collect biological signals on the surface of the subject's muscles, which can be used to identify the subject's movement intention and solve the synchronization problem with the control system. However, the requirements for the installation location of the EMG sensor are relatively high, and it must be close to the skin, and the patch is easy to fall off during walking, which is inconvenient for signal acquisition, and the EMG signal is easily affected by the environment, so it is not suitable for use in complex environments. Although other electronic sensors are more stable and reliable than EMG sensors, these electronic sensors are susceptible to electromagnetic interference, are sensitive to humidity, lack safety, and are not suitable for human body installation and long-term monitoring [5]. In contrast, the fiber optic sensor has the advantages of light weight, anti-electromagnetic interference, strong multiplexing ability, and sensitivity to stress and strain. It can be made into a wearable pressure insole, making the monitoring process safe, comfortable and unconstrained.

Gait recognition has wide applications in clinical medicine, rehabilitation training, posture recognition, and other fields [6]. In the field of rehabilitation, gait phase recognition can assist exoskeleton robot to formulate reasonable control strategies. The representative BLEEX lower limb exoskeleton robot [7] measures the inclination angle of the human body's center of gravity, plantar pressure, inclination angle of the limbs, and the force of each joint by using gyroscope, plantar pressure sensor, inclination sensor, and force sensor, respectively. It integrates multi-source signals to divide and identify gait. Deng Qinglong's team from the University of Electronic Science and Technology of China has designed a lower-limb exoskeleton robot that can recognize gait. By installing pressure sensors on the soles of the feet, encoders on the knee joints, and gyroscopes on the lower limbs, the gait characteristic data such as the joint angle of the human body and the plantar pressure were collected, and phase recognition and gait prediction for different groups of people were realized [8]. Meng et al. proposed a practical gait feedback method that can provide sufficient feedback without precise alignment of the inertial measurement unit (IMU), which enables simultaneous detection of gait stance and swing phase and measurement of ankle joint angle [9]. Ledoux et al. proposed a method to detect walking gait events using a single IMU mounted on the lower leg. It provides a robust, simple and inexpensive method for gait event detection [10]. Based on the content of gait acquisition and gait recognition of human body or exoskeleton robots at home and abroad, most of them use one or more types of sensors such as electronic pressure sensors, encoders, gyroscopes, IMU or EMG sensors to collect gait data and divide gait features.

In this paper, combined with the advantages of fiber optic sensing such as light weight, anti-electromagnetic interference, strong multiplexing ability, and stress-strain sensitivity, an array-type fiber optic sensing insole was designed and fabricated for plantar pressure signal acquisition. The support vector machine (SVM) classification method was used to identify the four phases of the initial double-limb support, the single-limb stance, the second double-limb support and the swing phase at different walking speeds, and the effectiveness of the sensing insole in gait analysis and phase identification was verified. It is of great significance to realize gait assessment and robot-assisted control in lower extremity rehabilitation scenarios, prevention and diagnosis of lower extremity diseases. Section 2 presents the design, printing and packaging of the fiber optic sensor insole, as well as sensor performance testing and pressure calibration; Sect. 3 presents the results and analysis of gait testing experiments; and the last part is the conclusion of this work.

2 Array Fiber Optic Sensing Insole

2.1 Fiber Bragg Grating Sensing

The sensing principle of the fiber Bragg grating is shown in Fig. 1. When a beam of light with a broad spectrum is incident on the grating, the light with the center wavelength λ_B is reflected. The grating is equivalent to a narrowband filter, filtering out the light of wavelength λ_B from the broad light source. The reflected wavelength can be expressed as:

$$\lambda_B = 2n_{eff}\Lambda. \tag{1}$$

where n_{eff} is the effective refractive index of the fiber core, and Λ is the grating period. According to the different center wavelengths reflected by different grating parameters, multiple FBGs are connected in series to realize the multiplexing function of the array fiber Bragg grating. Under the action of external strain or temperature, both n_{eff} and Λ will change, which will lead to the change of the reflected wavelength [11], it can be expressed as:

$$\frac{\Delta\lambda_B}{\lambda_B} = (\alpha + \xi)\Delta T + (1 - P_e)\Delta\varepsilon. \tag{2}$$

where $\Delta\lambda_B$ is the change in the center wavelength of the grating, ΔT and $\Delta\varepsilon$ are the changes in strain and temperature, respectively. α, ξ, and P_e are the thermal expansion coefficient, thermo-optic coefficient, and photoelastic constant of the fiber optic, respectively, which are determined by the mechanical properties of the grating itself. The wavelength change of the reflection spectrum of the fiber grating can be detected by the fiber grating interrogator, and the strain or temperature acting on the fiber grating can be calculated by calibrating the corresponding relationship between the wavelength change and the actual strain or temperature change.

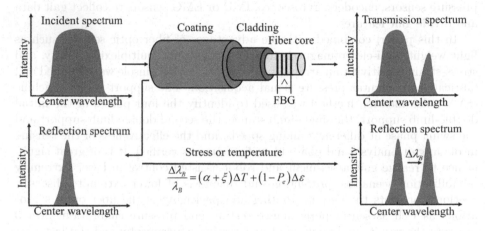

Fig. 1. Sensing principle of fiber Bragg grating.

2.2   Insole Design and Fabrication

The foot area can be divided into heel, midfoot, metatarsal, and toe areas [12,13], and we selected the 5 most relevant points in natural walking as the sensitive points of the pressure insole. First, we used SOLIDWORKS to design the insole, and planned the position and connection lines of the sensitive points. Since the fiber optic at the fusion point of the two FBG sensors is easy to break, it needs to be fixed with a heat-shrinkable tube. Therefore, the placement of the heat-shrinkable tube needs to be considered when planning the path. Then, the thermoplastic polyurethane(TPU) material was selected for 3D printing of the insole. This material has the advantages of flexibility, wear resistance, high waterproofness, and antibacterial properties. It is the best choice for the insole material. The thickness of the insole is 5 mm, the depth of the groove of the insole is 2.5 mm and the width is 2 mm, the FBG was encapsulated in a cylinder with a depth of 5 mm and a diameter of 20 mm, and which was then glued to the corresponding groove of the insole with superglue. For the encapsulation materials of sensitive points, related researches mostly use epoxy resin [14], PDMS

[15], and other materials. In this paper, in order to increase the sensitivity of the sensor, a flexible silicone material (Dragon Skin® 10 Very Fast) was selected to encapsulate the FBG. The mechanical analysis of the silica gel cannot rely on the elastic modulus and Poisson's ratio like a linearly elastic body, but needs to collect the stress-strain data of the material through tensile/compression tests, and obtain the material constitutive model coefficients by fitting the data. The hyperelastic material model relies on the definition of the strain energy function [16,17].

After the packaging material was determined, the A and B liquids of the silicone were mixed and injected into the sensing element mold. It was then put into a vacuum box for defoaming and cured at room temperature, and finally the silicone substrate was peeled off from the mold and attached to the insole. When a force is applied to the sensitive element, the silicone structure is primarily subjected to axial strain, which transmits this strain to the embedded FBG, resulting in a corresponding shift in the wavelength of the FBG. Figure 2 shows a schematic diagram of the sensor design, printing, and packaging.

It should be noted here that in the process of splicing and packaging the fiber optic sensing array, the strength and precision of the manual operation will have a great impact on the finished product. After many experiments and considering cost-effectiveness, each sensing element on the insole was finally connected by a single fiber optic. However, entrusting a third-party organization to realize the recording of the fiber grating array instead of pure manual fusion can better realize the multiplexing function of the fiber optic sensing array.

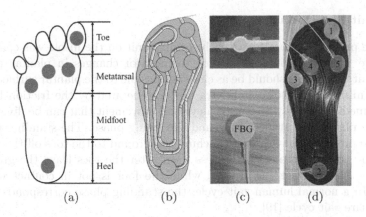

Fig. 2. Design, printing and packaging of insole (a) Foot area; (b) Insole design; (c) Sensing element packaging; (d) Insole packaging.

2.3 Sensor Pressure Calibration

To achieve plantar pressure monitoring, the insole was connected to a fiber Bragg interrogator (Wuhan O-Optics Technology Co., Ltd.), which operates at a maximum sampling rate of 8 KHz and a wavelength resolution of 0.1 pm for collecting the shift of the fiber Bragg wavelength. Figure 3(a) shows a monitoring system for plantar pressure. Figure 3(b) shows the reflectance spectra of the 5 FBGs after flexible encapsulation. We used QLW-5E microcomputer type electronic tensile testing machine (Xiamen Group Lung Instrument Co., Ltd.) to perform pressure calibration on 5 sensitive points respectively. The force calibration range is from 0 to $100N$, and the step size is $10N$. The wavelength offset of the sensor was obtained by the interrogator, and the relationship between the wavelength offset and the pressure change was established. We found that the force-wavelength curve of the sensing element encapsulated by the flexible material was nonlinear (which was caused by the mechanical properties of the encapsulating material), as shown in Fig. 3(c). In order to effectively characterize the relationship between fore and wavelength, an exponential function was used to fit it, and the fitting formula is

$$f(x) = a \cdot exp(b \cdot x) + c \cdot exp(d \cdot x). \tag{3}$$

where a, b, c, and d are fitting coefficients.

3 Experiments

3.1 Gait Monitoring

After the pressure calibration of each sensing unit on the insole was completed, the insole was placed inside the shoe to monitor changes in plantar pressure during gait. The insole should be as close as possible to the plantar surface, which helps to mitigate the noise and extra power generated by the friction between the intermediate layers [18]. Gait is a cyclical movement that can be divided into two main phases: the stance phase and the swing phase. The standing phase is the entire process from the heels touching the ground to the toes off the ground. The swing phase is the entire process from after the toes leave the ground to before the heel touches the ground, while the foot is not in contact with the ground. In a normal human gait cycle, the standing phase corresponds to 62% of the entire gait cycle [19].

A subject (weight about 55 kg) was asked to put on the insole, walk on the treadmill at various speeds ranging from 0.5 km/h to 3 km/h for about 30 s each, and recorded the wavelength offset with the fiber optic interrogator. According to the force-wavelength curve calibrated in Sect. 2.3, the corresponding plantar pressure curve was obtained. We intercepted the response data in a gait cycle and detected the sequence in which the sensors were activated by the maximum amplitude recorded [19]. FBG2 was first activated at the beginning of the stance phase of the gait cycle, when the heel began to make contact with the floor.

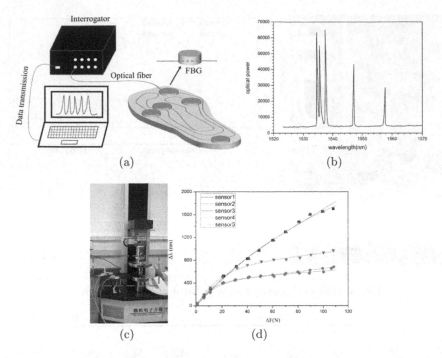

Fig. 3. (a) Plantar pressure monitoring system; (b) Reflectance spectrum; (c) Sensor pressure calibration.

As the cycle progressed, FBG3 to FBG5 (located at the metatarsals) were activated to enter the single-limb stance phase, and the increased rate of amplitude of FBG3 was more pronounced than that of FBG4 and FBG5, reflecting that the patient had a certain degree of foot varus. With gait motion, FBG3 and FBG5 had stronger responses at forefoot contact during the second double-limb support. Finally, the amplitude change of FBG1 at the toe-off moment marked the end of the stance phase and the beginning of the swing phase of the gait cycle. The plantar pressure curve is shown in Fig. 4, according to the pressure characteristics during gait walking, the stance phase is divided into three phases: the initial double-limb support phase, the single-limb stance phase, and the second double-limb support phase using dotted lines. This curve shows that the insole using fiber optic sensing can accurately display the gait progression.

3.2   Gait Phase Recognition

Perry [13] divided the gait events and gait phases in detail after statistical analysis of experimental data, the four phases of the initial double-limb support, the single-limb support, the second double-limb support, and the swing period accounted for 12%, 38%, 12% and 38% of the gait cycle, respectively, as shown in Fig. 5.

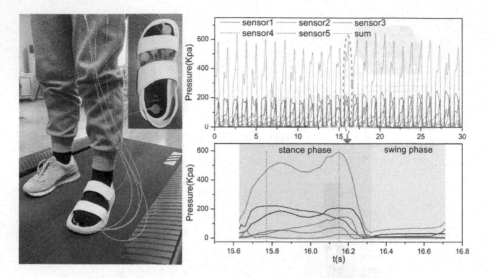

Fig. 4. Gait cycle curve during natural walking (3 km/h).

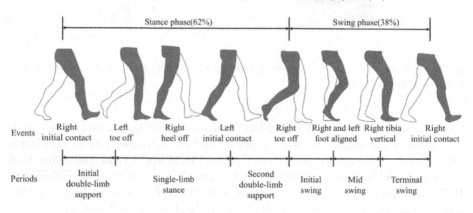

Fig. 5. Gait phase division.

In a complete gait cycle, the rational division of gait phases is very critical, which lays the foundation for gait recognition and subsequent control strategy formulation. If the number of divided phases is too small, the available effective information will be insufficient, which is not conducive to the formulation of the system control scheme, and will also affect the final control effect; on the contrary, the available information is more detailed and can better reflect the laws of human motion. However, as the switching frequency between gait phases becomes faster, the control strategy becomes more difficult. In this paper, a four-phase method was used to divide a gait cycle. We subdivided the standing phase into three phases, and considered that the duration of the swing phase was short, too many phases would cause the control system to switch frequently, so the swing phase was not subdivided. Finally, the gait cycle was divided into an initial double-limb support phase, a single-limb stance phase, a second double-limb support phase, and a swing phase.

We employed support vector machines (SVM) for phase identification. The main idea of SVM is to map the low-dimensional vectors to the high-dimensional spaces, and find the mapping relationship between the input and output in the high-dimensional spaces. The optimal weight vector ω^* and optimal bias b^* of SVM are defined as

$$\omega^* = \sum_{i=1}^{M} \alpha_i^* y_i x_i. \tag{4}$$

$$b^* = y_i - \sum_{i=1}^{M} \alpha_i^* (x_i^T x_i). \tag{5}$$

where x_i is the feature vector of the ith sample point, y_i is the category label of x_i; α_i^* is the ith element in the support vector. The kernel function of SVM selects the Gaussian kernel function, which is expressed as

$$K(x,z) = exp[-\frac{\|x - z\|^2}{2\sigma^2}]. \tag{6}$$

The recognition function is defined as

$$f(x) = sgn((\sum_{i=1}^{M} a_i^* y_i K(x, x_i)) + b^*). \tag{7}$$

where x is the unknown input vector. The gait phase identification steps are described in detail as follows:

1. The participant walked on a treadmill at a speed of 1.5 km/h, 2 km/h, and 3 km/h for about 30 s, respectively, while the plantar pressure data were collected.
2. The plantar pressure data of the five sensitive points at different speeds were used as feature data, and we divided the plantar pressure data into the initial double-limb support phase, the single-limb stance phase, the second double-limb support phase, and the swing phase (see Fig. 4) as label data. The first 70% of the participant's walking data at different speeds were used as the training set, and the remaining data were used as the test set.
3. The training data was input to the SVM classifier for training the gait phase classification model.
4. The test samples were input into the trained SVM classifier for gait phase recognition. The recognition results are shown in Fig. 6.

In order to verify the effectiveness of the algorithm in this paper, the gait phase recognition rate *accuracy*, class precision *precision_k* and class recall *recall_k* are defined as follows

$$accuracy = \frac{\sum x_{correct}}{\sum x} * 100\%. \tag{8}$$

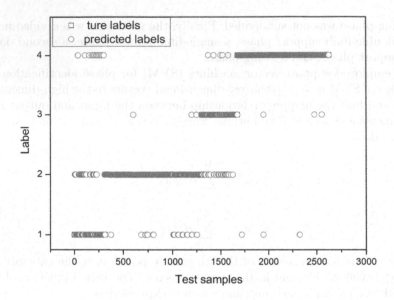

Fig. 6. The result graph of gait phase recognition

$$precision_k = \frac{\sum x_{correct\_k}}{\sum x_{predict\_k}} * 100\%. \tag{9}$$

$$recall_k = \frac{\sum x_{correct\_k}}{\sum x_k} * 100\%. \tag{10}$$

where $\sum x_{correct}$ is the number of correctly classified samples, $\sum x$ is the total number of samples, $\sum x_{correct\_k}$ is the number of correctly classified samples in the kth class, $\sum x_{predict\_k}$ is the number of samples of the kth class predicted by SVM classifier, and $\sum x_k$ is the number of samples of the kth class. The gait phase identification evaluation indicators of the test samples are shown in Table 1. The gait recognition results show that the multi-class SVM model constructed in this paper can realize the gait phase recognition at different walking speeds based on the plantar pressure feature, and the total recognition accuracy is 90.37%.

Table 1. Phase recognition evaluation indicators of the test samples.

Evaluation indicators	Initial double-limb support	Single-limb stance	Second double-limb support	Swing phase
Predict	78.46	86.11	95.54	96.53
Recall	64.76	93.62	80.65	99.26

4   Conclusion

In this paper, a plantar pressure insole based on sensitized encapsulated fiber optic array was designed and fabricated. By collecting the gait data in natural walking, the pressure changes of the sensors under different gait phases were analyzed, and the SVM classification method was used to accurately identify the four gait stages: the initial double-limb support phase, the single-limb stance phase, the second double-limb support phase, and the swing phase. The plantar pressure-based sensing system realized the functions of gait monitoring, feature analysis, and gait recognition in natural walking at different speeds. Since the pressure insole is a consumable and needs to be customized, incorrect packaging and use will lead to fiber damage. Therefore, this study only conducts experiments on a single plantar pressure insole, which has certain shortcomings and limitations.

Acknowledgements. This project is supported by National Natural Science Foundation of China (Grant 52075398), Application Foundation Frontier Project of Wuhan Science and Technology Program (Grant 2020020601012220), and Research Project of Wuhan University of Technology Chongqing Research Institute (Grant YF2021-17).

References

1. National Bureau of Statistics of China: Communiqué of the seventh national population census of the People's Republic of China (No. 5) - Age composition of the population (2021). https://www.stats.gov.cn
2. Morag, E., Cavanagh, P.R.: Structural and functional predictors of regional peak pressures under the foot during walking. J. Biomech. **32**(4), 359–370 (1999)
3. Villa-Parra, A.C., Delisle-Rodriguez, D., Souza Lima, J., Frizera-Neto, A., Bastos, T.: Knee impedance modulation to control an active orthosis using insole sensors. Sensors **17**(12), 2751 (2017)
4. Amralizadeh, A., Marjani, T., Masouleh, M.T., Kalhor, A.: Design and fabrication of a flexible pressure-sensitive insole based on barometric tactile sensors. In: 2020 28th Iranian Conference on Electrical Engineering (ICEE), pp. 1–5 (2020). https://doi.org/10.1109/ICEE50131.2020.9260811
5. Li, C.: Research on gait recognition method based on sensor information fusion. Master's thesis, Shc. Automation, WHUT, Wuhan, China (2019)
6. Li, W., et al.: Wearable gait recognition systems based on MEMS pressure and inertial sensors: a review. IEEE Sens. J. **22**(2), 1092–1104 (2022). https://doi.org/10.1109/JSEN.2021.3131582
7. Zoss, A.B., Kazerooni, H., Chu, A.: Biomechanical design of the Berkeley lower extremity exoskeleton (BLEEX). IEEE/ASME Trans. Mechatron. **11**(2), 128–138 (2006)
8. Deng, Q.: Design and application of smart sensor system on lower-limb exoskeleton. Master's thesis, Shc. ME, UEST, Chengdu, China (2017)
9. Meng, L., Martinez-Hernandez, U., Childs, C., Dehghani-Sanij, A.A., Buis, A.: A practical gait feedback method based on wearable inertial sensors for a drop foot assistance device. IEEE Sens. J. **19**(24), 12235–12243 (2019)

10. Ledoux, E.D.: Inertial sensing for gait event detection and transfemoral prosthesis control strategy. IEEE Trans. Biomed. Eng. **65**(12), 2704–2712 (2018)
11. Hill, K.O., Meltz, G.: Fiber Bragg grating technology fundamentals and overview. J. Lightwave Technol. **15**(8), 1263–1276 (1997)
12. Abdul Razak, A.H., Zayegh, A., Begg, R.K., Wahab, Y.: Foot plantar pressure measurement system: a review. Sensors **12**(7), 9884–9912 (2012)
13. Tao, W., Liu, T., Zheng, R., Feng, H.: Gait analysis using wearable sensors. Sensors **12**(2), 2255–2283 (2012)
14. Tavares, C., et al.: Optically instrumented insole for gait plantar and shear force monitoring. IEEE Access **9**, 132480–132490 (2021)
15. Song, J.: The perception mechanism and experiment research on robot fiber-optic array skin. Master's thesis, Shc. CSE, Shandong University, Jinan, China (2016)
16. Martins, P., Natal Jorge, R., Ferreira, A.: A comparative study of several material models for prediction of hyperelastic properties: application to siliconerubber and soft tissues. Strain **42**(3), 135–147 (2006)
17. Marechal, L., Balland, P., Lindenroth, L., Petrou, F., Kontovounisios, C., Bello, F.: Toward a common framework and database of materials for soft robotics. Soft Robot. **8**(3), 284–297 (2021)
18. Wang, L., Jones, D., Chapman, G.J., Siddle, H.J., Russell, D.A., Alazmani, A., Culmer, P.: A review of wearable sensor systems to monitor plantar loading in the assessment of diabetic foot ulcers. IEEE Trans. Biomed. Eng. **67**(7), 1989–2004 (2019)
19. Domingues, M.F., et al.: Insole optical fiber Bragg grating sensors network for dynamic vertical force monitoring. J. Biomed. Optics **22**(9), 091507 (2017)

Gait Phase Detection Based on Time Sequence Adapting to Various Walking Posture and Frequency

Siyu Liu, Zhiyong Zhou, Linjun Lu, Xiaohui Xiao, and Zhao Guo[✉]

School of Power and Mechanical Engineering, Wuhan University, Wuhan, China
guozhao@whu.edu.cn

Abstract. This study designs a deep neural network to detect gait phases, including heel-strike (HS), foot-flat (FF), heel off (HO) and swing (SW). Proposed the concept of "gait image" to be the input and "phase image" to be the output of the model. The model (CFCT) adopts Convolution layers to extract gait-image's feature, Fully-Connected layers to vary the feature non-linearly and Convolution-Transpose layers to upgrade feature's dimension to output the phase-image. The CFCT model is capable to predict multi-dimensional gait phases in 1.5 s time sequence and adapt to various walking posture and walking frequency of different people, indicating the model's robustness. The maximum accuracy of current moment's gait phase prediction is 98.37%. Results of predicted phases are analyzed according to the time sequence in past 1 s, current moment and future 0.5 s, remaining high and stable accuracy. The maximum accuracy is 96.80% at the time step of future 0.35 s, verifying the effectiveness and stability of the CFCT model.

Keywords: Gait phase detection · Time sequence · Gait image · Phase image · Neural network

1 Introduction

We can often distinguish different people according to their walking posture. People may have various gait even with the same height, weight and body proportion. The gait will show a strong periodicity, such as the rotation angle, angular velocity, axes acceleration of the thighs and shanks, and the interactive force between the foot and the ground in the process of walking. Ashutosh Kharb [1] divides a gait cycle into two periods, stance and swing. Stance is subdivided into initial contact, opposite toe off, heel rise, opposite initial contact. Swing is subdivided into toe off, feet adjacent, tibia vertical. Human gait characteristics can be analyzed through the division of these gait phases. Gait phases detection has great applications in many fields, such as the assessment of rehabilitation training, the control of lower limb exoskeleton robot, assistance control, etc.

A variety of sensors are used in gait data acquisition, such as inertial measurement unit (IMU), ground contact force measurement, Vicon, etc. Ioannis Papavasileiou [2] uses infinite Gaussian mixture model based on the value of ground contact measurement

H. Liu et al. (Eds.): ICIRA 2022, LNAI 13457, pp. 49–58, 2022.
https://doi.org/10.1007/978-3-031-13835-5_5

to classify gait phases. Xianta Jiang [3] uses force myography (FMG) to do the automatic gait phases detection and investigate the feasibility. Yi Chiew Han [4] uses a single IMU which is attached to the shank to detect normal and abnormal gait phase. Tao Zhen [5] presents a gait phase detection system contains three acceleration sensors, based on four detection algorithms. Lingyun Yan [6] designs a low-cost multisensor integrated system for online gait phase detection. The system contains manual switches, foot switches, shank inclinations, force-sensitive resistors, goniometers, gyroscopes, accelerometers, and electromyography (EMG) sensors. Julià Camps [7] uses a waist-worn measurement to detect Parkinson's disease patients' gait.

In the past years, with the advanced intelligent algorithm proposed, more and more algorithms are applied to the detection of gait phases. Huong Thi [8] makes a review of gait phases detection for lower limb prostheses, listing number of sensor-based and method-based publications from 2010 to 2020. Tze-Shen Chen [9] uses k-nearest neighbors algorithm to estimate gait phases. Long Liu [10] detects gait phases using the method of Hidden Markov Model and parameter adaptive model with 15-dimensional temporal characteristic feature. Tao Zhen [11] proposes a spatiotemporal network, considering the inherent correlation in high-dimensional spaces to detect gait phase. David Kreuzer [12] combines deep 2D-convolutional and LSTM networks to divide five different gait phase and proposed some methods to optimize the model. Keehong Seo [13] replaces foot sensors with inertial measurement unit to estimate gait phase in 10ms with recurrent neural networks. Jing Tang [14] proposes a self-tuning triple threshold to adjust human walking to detect gait phase, making up for the poor adaptability of the fixed threshold method in the past. Dongfang Xu [15] uses an adaptive oscillator to conduct the gait phase estimation and recruited three transtibial amputees to evaluate this method.

Considering the excellent performance of neural network in classification and regression, we select it to do the classification work of gait phases. Input the shank's and thigh's posture data in time sequence and output four categories of gait phases in time sequence, which are heel-strike (HS), flat-foot (FF), heel-off (HO), swing (SW). The outputs do not only contain current moment's gait phase, also contain past 1 s's and future 0.5 s's gait phases sequence. The accuracy rates of the model in different time sequences are analyzed. Compared with other gait phases detection algorithms, we can provide more dimensional information, which plays a great role in gait evaluation and prediction in a certain period of time.

2   Experiment

2.1   Volunteer Setup

We recruited Ten volunteers to participate in the experiment, including 3 female and 7 male. The more volunteers, the richer the datasets. The information of volunteers is shown in the Table 1 below. Volunteers walk in a normal walking posture on a flat in the process of walking, the walking frequency and speed should be changed appropriately to enrich the diversity of data.

Table 1. Volunteer Information

No	Height (cm)	Weight (kg)	Gender
1	163	51	Female
2	157	50	Female
3	158	48	Female
4	176	68	Male
5	166	68	Male
6	183	65	Male
7	174	75	Male
8	176	80	Male
9	170	58	Male
10	162	50	Male

2.2 Wearable System

In this experiment, we designed a wearable system, including two Bluetooth inertial measurement units(IMUs), a force sensitive resistors(FSR) and a Raspberry Pi 4b. Both of these two sensors use wireless communication with Raspberry Pi, intending to reduce the discomfort of too many wired connections to volunteers when collecting data.

We use elastic bandage to fixed IMUs and thighs together, as well as shanks. The convenience of putting on and taking off makes switching volunteers between experiments flexibly. Each IMU is able to measure and transfer multi-dimensional data, such as acceleration, angular velocity and angle of three axes at the frequency of 25 Hz. The installation direction and shaft orientation of IMU are shown in the Fig. 1 below. Thighs and shanks rotate mainly around the Y-axis of IMU.

As shown below, the detectors of FSR are pasted on the bottom of slippers from toe to heel, the data acquisition and transmission module of FSR is pasted on the top of the shoe.

The layout of ours wearable system is shown below.

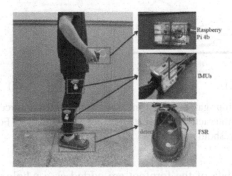

Fig. 1. The layout of wearable system for data acquisition.

2.3 Data Acquisition

Volunteers are not required to bind IMUs strictly horizontally and vertically but within a proper range. The purpose is to enrich the datasets and enhance the robustness of CFCT model. Because in practical application, it is reluctantly to ensure that everyone binds the IMU in the same accurate position every time. The trained model can pay more attention to the intrinsic law of data when the initial position of binding is different, avoiding model errors caused by tiny installation difference. For convenience and walking comfortably, we fixed FSR on slippers.

The maximum acquisition and transmission rate of each IMU is 25 Hz and that of FSR is 30 Hz. The data recording frequency is 20 Hz, which should be lower than sensors acquisition frequency (Fig. 2).

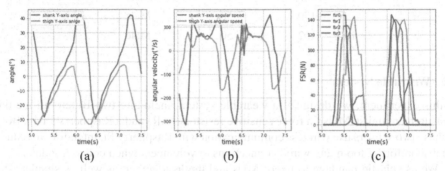

(a)   (b)   (c)

Fig. 2. Recorded data of experiments. (a) Shank's and thigh's Y-axis angle. (b) Shank's and thigh's angular velocity. (c) FSR's 4 channel interaction data.

2.4 Data Labeling

Angular velocity and angle of each IMU's Y-axis and four channels of FSR's pressure information are recorded. The unit of angle is degrees, angular velocity is deg/s and FSR is N (Fig. 3).

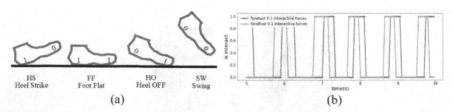

(a)   (b)

Fig. 3. (a) Schematic of four gait phases. 1 indicates the interactive forces between the foot and the ground. 0 indicates no interactive forces between foot and ground. (b) Forefoot's and hindfoot's interactive forces after threshold process.

The two pressure data of the forefoot are added as a whole, as well as hindfoot. When the pressure sum is greater than the threshold, it is set to 1, which means there is an interactive force between foot and ground. When the pressure sum is less than the threshold, it is set to 0, representing no interactive force between foot and ground. According to the division standard of gait phase, we can use these 0–1 pressure data to label the data. Gait phases are classified into four categories, heel strike (HS), foot flat (FF), heel off (HO) and swing (SW).

These four categories of gait phase are independent from each other. It is equivalent to telling the model which category has a greater weight if there is a comparison relationship between categories, which is critically negative for model training. Therefore, encoding these four labels by methods of one-hot encoder [16] is essential. Each gait phase is transformed into a four-dimensional tensor. The four dimensions here are determined according to the total number of gait phases. Each value of this four-dimensional tensor is 1 only on the index of the corresponding gait phase, and the other values are 0. The model training problem caused by the comparison relationship between labels can be avoided.

The rule of labeling gait phases are as follows (Table 2).

Table 2. The rule of labeling gait phases

	Heel Strike	Foot Flat	Heel Off	Swing
Forefoot's interactive force	0	1	1	0
Hindfoot's interactive force	1	1	0	0
Label	0	1	2	3
One-hot label	[1, 0, 0, 0]	[0, 1, 0, 0]	[0, 0, 1, 0]	[0, 0, 0, 1]

3 CFCT Model Structure

Gait phases can be accurately depicted in the time sequence and be predicted for a certain length of time sequence in the future according to the historical walking posture, considering its strong regularity and periodicity. Therefore, we use the data of IMU in a time sequence as the input of the model to output a time sequence of gait phases. We don't use FSR as the input of the model due to its inconvenience to wear in the process of gait phase prediction in the. FSR here is only used for labeling data.

3.1 Construct Inputs and Outputs

We set a time window containing 30 columns and 4 rows of historical data as input. Taking a consideration of the data recording frequency is 20 Hz, it means 1.5 s data of IMU being used as the input. Each column of data contains 4 dimensions data of IMU, shank Y-axis angle, shank Y-axis angular speed, thigh Y-axis angle and thigh Y-axis angular speed. Reshape these data into a two-dimensional "gait image" in the time sequence, and its dimension is (4 * 30).

Set a time window containing 30 columns and 4 rows of gait phases data as output. 20 columns of the output are earlier than current moment and 10 of it are later than current moment. Each column of the output is a one-hot tensor of a gait phase. Considering the data recording frequency, the CFCT model will predict 1 s of historical gait phase and 0.5 s of future gait phases. The output gait phases are also transformed into a two-dimensional "phase image", similar to "gait image". Therefore, the output dimension of "phase image" is also (4 * 30) (Figs. 4 and 5).

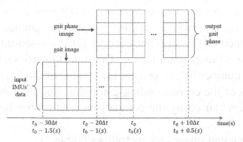

Fig. 4. Input and output of CFCT model. t_0 represents the current time. Δt represents sampling interval.

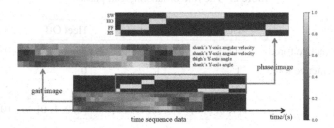

Fig. 5. Demonstration of "gait image" and "phase image".

3.2 Model Layers

Convolution Layers. Convolution is widely used in traditional image processing, such as image filtering, edge detection, image sharpening, etc. Further more, convolution operation promotes the extraction of image features by neural network [17]. The first half of CFCT model also adopts convolution network to extract the features of gait image due to its capability.

$$Out = \sigma(W * X + b) \tag{1}$$

where Out is the output tensor of a layer. σ is an activation function. W is the value of convolution kernel. X is the input tensor. $*$ is convolution operation. b is the bias tensor.

Fully-Connected Layers. Then the featured two-dimensional tensor is flatten into one-dimensional tensor, and be input into the fully-connected network to do the nonlinear transformation using the activate function of relu[18]. At the end of fully-connected network, the output tensor will be reshaped into the two-dimensional tensor, which size is same to the featured tensor.

$$Out = relu(XW + b) \tag{2}$$

$$relu(x) = max(x, 0) \tag{3}$$

where Out is the output tensor of a layer. Function relu is an nonlinear activation operation, shown as formula (3). W is the weights between neurons. X is the input tensor. b is the bias tensor between neurons.

Convolution Transpose Layers. When the extracted two-dimensional featured tensor is obtained, the third part convolution-transpose [19] network is adopted to restore it into the dimension of phase image, which is (4 * 30). The calculation of convolution transpose is equivalent to the reverse operation of convolution.

Softmax Layers. At last of the model, use softmax layer to turn all output results into probability values between 0–1, and the sum of probability values is 1. The largest value's index in the tensor is selected as the gait phase.

$$softmax(x) = \frac{e^{x_i}}{\sum_i e^{x_i}} \tag{4}$$

The structure of CFCT model is shown as follows (Fig. 6).

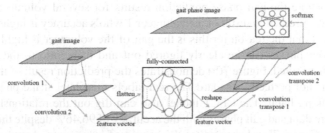

Fig. 6. CFCT model's structure, including two convolution layers, a fully-connected layer, two convolution transpose layers and a softmax layer.

3.3 Model Training

Paddpaddle deep learning framework is selected for CFCT model training. Cross entropy function is used to calculate the loss value for the multi classification. In the parameter training stage of neural network back propagation, the Adam optimizer was selected for loss reduction with the learning rate of 0.001.

4 Result

The CFCT model can predict the gait phase in a certain time sequence, including the historical 1 s, the current moment and the future 0.5 s. Accuracy rates of the CFCT model prediction in these time sequence are analyzed after training the model in training datasets.

4.1 Current Moment's Gait Phase Prediction

Current moment's prediction is very capital for gait phase detection, which reflects the real-time effectiveness and plays a guiding role in perception and decision-making.

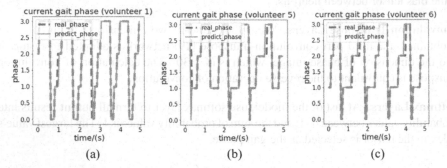

Fig. 7. (a) Result of current moment's phase prediction on volunteer 1. (b) Result of current moment's phase prediction on volunteer 5. (c) Result of current moment's phase prediction on volunteer 6.

We demonstrate the gait phase prediction results for several volunteers as above. Figure 7(a) is the prediction result of the volunteer 1 who's accuracy is highest, 98.37%. It's no surprised that the reason for this is the gait of the volunteer is highly regulated. Each of the four phases can be clearly figured out and their ratio to the overall gait cycle is well distributed. Figure 7(b) demonstrates the prediction result of the volunteer 5 whose gait is not perfectly standard.The real labels miss heel strike phase probably due to his walking habit. The CFCT model also can dig out the relationship between walking posture data and gait phases with the accuracy of 96.46% despite this, revealing its robustness. Figure 7(c) demonstrates the source of inaccuracy. As we can see, the reason why the actual curve and the predicted curve do not fit perfectly is not that there is a mistaken value with the predicted phase, but that there is some over-or-lag in the phase between the two. The accuracy is 94.97% (Table 3).

Table 3. Results of current moment's gait phase detection

No	Accuracy rate	No	Accuracy rate
1	98.37%	6	94.97%
2	97.84%	7	93.67%
3	96.43%	8	92.34%
4	96.70%	9	95.33%
5	96.46%	10	97.65%
Average	95.95%		

4.2 Historical and Future Phase Prediction

Figure 8 show the accuracy and its trend in the sequence of 1.5 s. Maximum accuracy rate is 96.80%. From the current time to 0.35 s in the future, the accuracy rate remains stable and high.

Future time sequence's gait phases prediction depends on the past historical state. If there is a latency in the gait detection system, such as exoskeleton control combined with gait detection, the predicted gait phase at a certain time step in the future can be used as the current phase to alleviate the latency.

We predicted 20 gait phases in history, which is 1 s of historical phases. A complete gait cycle of normal walking is often less than 1 s, from another perspective, these 20 points can cover more than one gait cycle. The model has the ability to accurately classify the gait phases according to these data. These phases information of historical sequence can be used to estimate the gait feature, such as gait assessment for rehabilitation training.

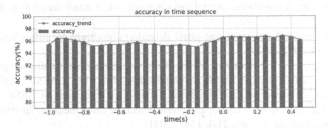

Fig. 8. Accuracy and its trend in the sequence of 1.5 s, including past 1.0 s and future 0.5 s.

5 Conclusion

The study constructs a deep neural network to detect gait phases with high accuracy in the condition of ten different people with various walking frequency. Proposed the concept of gait image and phase image, reshaping the 1.5 s historical gait data and phases' one-hot tensor of 1.5 s time sequence into two-dimensional image. The accuracy of overall sequence's gait detection is high, especially for prediction of current moments and future time.

For future work, we will collect multi-modal data, including flat roads, slopes, walking up and down stairs, standing up and sitting down to enrich our datasets, for both normal people and patients with hemiplegia of lower limbs. Then We will elaborate our model to output multi-dimensional data, such as walking patterns, trajectories, torque, etc. Aimed at merging the model and algorithm with the lower limb exoskeleton to assist people's walking and patient's rehabilitation.

Acknowledgments. Research supported by the Research Project of China Disabled Persons' Federation-on assistive technology (Grant No. 2021CDPFAT-27), the National Natural Science Foundation of China (Grant No. 51605339), and the Key Research and Development Program of Hubei Province (Grant NO. 2020BAB133).

References

1. Ashutosh, K., et al.: A review of gait cycle and its parameters. IJCEM Int. J. Comput. Eng. Manage. **13**, 78–83 (2011)
2. Papavasileiou, I., Zhang, W., Han, S.: Real-time data-driven gait phase detection using ground contact force measurements: algorithms, platform design and performance. Smart Health **1**, 34–49 (2017)
3. Xianta, J., et al.: A wearable gait phase detection system based on force myography techniques. Sensors **18**.4, 1279 (2018)
4. Chiew, H.Y., Wong, K.I., Murray, I.: Gait phase detection for normal and abnormal gaits using IMU. IEEE Sensors J. **19**.9, 3439–3448 (2019)
5. Zhen, T., Yan, L., Yuan, P.: Walking gait phase detection based on acceleration signals using LSTM-DNN algorithm. Algorithms **12**(12), 253 (2019)
6. Lingyun, Y., et al.: Low-cost multisensor integrated system for online walking gait detection. J. Sensors **2021** (2021)
7. Julia, C., et al.: Deep learning for freezing of gait detection in Parkinson's disease patients in their homes using a waist-worn inertial measurement unit. Knowl. Based Syst. **139**, 119–131 (2018)
8. Thu, V.H.T., et al.: A review of gait phase detection algorithms for lower limb prostheses. Sensors **20**.14, 3972 (2020)
9. Tze-Shen, C., Lin, T.Y., Peter Hong, Y.-W.: Gait phase segmentation using weighted dynamic time warping and k-nearest neighbors graph embedding. In: ICASSP 2020–2020 IEEE International Conference on Acoustics, Speech and Signal Processing (ICASSP). IEEE (2020)
10. Long, L., et al.: Ambulatory human gait phase detection using wearable inertial sensors and hidden markov model. Sensors **21**.4, 1347 (2021)
11. Zhen, T., Yan, L., Kong, J.-L.: An acceleration based fusion of multiple spatiotemporal networks for gait phase detection. Int. J. Environ. Res. Public Health **17**(16), 5633 (2020)
12. Kreuzer, D., Munz, M.: Deep convolutional and lstm networks on multi-channel time series data for gait phase recognition. Sensors **21**(3), 789 (2021)
13. Keehong, S., et al.: RNN-based on-line continuous gait phase estimation from shank-mounted IMUs to control ankle exoskeletons. In: 2019 IEEE 16th International Conference on Rehabilitation Robotics (ICORR). IEEE (2019)
14. Jing, T., et al.: Self-tuning threshold method for real-time gait phase detection based on ground contact forces using FSRs. Sensors **18**.2, 481 (2018)
15. Xu, D., et al. "Online estimation of continuous gait phase for robotic transtibial prostheses based on adaptive oscillators. In: 2020 IEEE/ASME International Conference on Advanced Intelligent Mechatronics (AIM). IEEE (2020)
16. Potdar, K., Pardawala, T.S., Pai, C.D.: A comparative study of categorical variable encoding techniques for neural network classifiers. Int. J. Comput. Appl. **175**(4), 7–9 (2017)
17. Saad, A., Mohammed, T.A., Al-Zawi, S.: Understanding of a convolutional neural network. In: 2017 International Conference on Engineering and Technology (ICET). IEEE (2017)
18. Li, Y., Yuan, Y.: Convergence analysis of two-layer neural networks with relu activation. Adv. Neural Inf. Process. Syst. **30** (2017)
19. Vincent, D., Visin, F.: A guide to convolution arithmetic for deep learning. arXiv preprint arXiv:1603.07285 (2016)

In Situ Calibration of a Six-Axis FBG Force/Moment Sensor for Surgical Robot

Tianliang Li[✉], Fayin Chen, and Yifei Su

Wuhan University of Technology, Wuhan 430070, China
tianliangli@whut.edu.cn

Abstract. This paper developed a layered six-axis FBG force/moment sensor to measure the force/moment during robot-assisted bone drilling. The design that eight unique C-shaped beams form a layered elastic structure and eight FBGs are mounted on the structure to sense six-axis force/moment, leads to low chirping risk and low fabrication cost. An in situ calibration method done with a robot and standard weight has been proposed to calibrate the designed sensor and overcome the performance degradation caused by installing and removing sensors. The calibration results that the sensor has excellent measurement accuracy with a relative error of 6.92%. A robot-assisted bone drilling test has been implemented to further prove the potential application of the proposed sensor and the in situ calibration method for high-precision Force/Moment measurement in surgical robots.

Keywords: In situ calibration · Fiber Bragg grating · Six-Axis force/moment sensor · Surgical robot

1 Introduction

In the past few years, robotic-assisted surgery has proven to be a safe and viable alternative to traditional open approaches due to its inherent advantages of high positioning accuracy, excellent stability, and fatigue resistance [1]. Typical such as the da Vinci surgical robot [2] could improve the accuracy and stability of operations with its four arms and three-dimensional video system, which is used in urinary surgery, cardio-thoracic surgery, and abdominal surgery. However, some downsides limit the further development of modern surgical robotics, including steep learning curves and high risk of tissue damage [3]. Force feedback is one of the most basic safety requirements for robot-assisted surgery [4], which could help surgical robotics overcome the shortcomings mentioned above. Consequently, precise force sensing is vital for reducing the risk and achieving better surgical outcomes in robotic-assisted surgery [5].

Traditional electrical sensors are vulnerable to electromagnetic interference. In recent years, fiber Bragg grating (FBG)-based force sensors, which have the advantages of high sensitivity, small in size, anti-electromagnetic interference, biocompatibility, and MRI-compatible, are widely used in the field of medical robots [6–8]. To meet the force reflection requirements of surgical tools, Hyundo et al. proposed a FBG-based three-axis force sensor with an annular deformation structure [9], the sensor has a high sensitivity of

H. Liu et al. (Eds.): ICIRA 2022, LNAI 13457, pp. 59–68, 2022.
https://doi.org/10.1007/978-3-031-13835-5_6

0.06 N, but lacks torque measurement. A six-axis FBG force/moment sensor was consisting of a four-layered elastic structure and 12 FBGs [10], which achieved the measurement of six-axis force/moment information and low coupling error of 2.3%. However, there is a risk of chirping due to the pasted installation method, and the aluminum alloy used in the sensor is not compatible with MRI.

The vast majority of FBG-based sensor is assembled by gluing the FBG to the deformed structure. There is a decrease in performance that arise from the mounting of the sensor and long-time use of the sensor [11]. Thus, in-situ calibration methods are widely explored to improve the accuracy of FBG six-axis force sensors output signals. Sun et al. [12] proposed an online calibration and decoupling method based on the shape from motion combined with a complex algorithm. This method reduces the calibration time greatly, and the error is below 2.1%. By using accelerometer measurements, Silvio et al. proposed an in situ calibration technique that requires neither the knowledge of the inertial parameters nor the orientation of the rigid body but depends on accurate acceleration data [13]. Francisco et al. [14] presented a new in situ calibration technique for six-axis F/T sensors which assumes that the inertial parameters of robot links are known. But the calibration error is more than 14%, and the inertial parameters of robots are hard to get. Moreover, other in situ calibration methods can be found in [15, 16], which relied on reference force/moment sensors yet.

Herein, a six-axis FBG force/moment sensor and its in-situ calibration method have been developed for surgical robots. The proposed sensor is designed as 8 unique C-shaped beams form a layered elastic structure and 8 FBGs are tensely suspended on the beam. The layered elastic structure is processed by 3D printing technology with the material of Acrylonitrile Butadiene Styrene (ABS). Such a configuration enables the sensor to overcome the chirping risk, and also leads to the advantages of lightweight, biocompatibility, and MRI compatibility. Meanwhile, an in situ calibration done with a robot and standard weight has been presented and realized high precision of in situ calibration for six-axis force/moment sensors, which could avoid the decrease in performance that arise from mounting and removing the sensors during offline calibration.

The rest of the paper is organized as follows. Section 2 introduces the sensor design, sensing principle, and sensor assembly. In situ calibration method and experiments are shown in Sect. 3. Section 4 carries out the robot-assisted bone drilling experiment to validate the performance of the sensor further and the feasibility of situ calibration. Section 5 features conclusion.

2   Design and Fabrication of the Sensor

2.1   Structure Design

The designed six-axis force/moment sensor is composed of a layered elastomer structure and eight suspended optical fibers. The elastic body is designed as a layered structure, as shown in Fig. 1(a). Layer I consists of a fixing loop, connecting loop, and four horizontal C-shaped beams (HCSBs) (Fig. 1(b)). The connecting loop, four diagonal C-shaped beams (DCSBs), and loading loop form layer II, as depicted in Fig. 1(c). Four FBGs (noted FBG 1-4) are arranged on the concave side of HCSBs, as shown in Fig. 1(b). Another four FBGs (noted FBG 5-8) are arranged on the concave side of DCSBs to form another sensing layer (Fig. 1(c)). Thus, the max diameter of the designed sensor is 134 mm and the height is 29 mm. Moreover, there are four uniformly distributed holes on the fixing loop to connect the sensor to the end of the robot, and another four on the connecting loop to fix with the surgery tool. Different from beam-based structures, such a layered structure enables the sensor to have high sensitivity and low chirping risk.

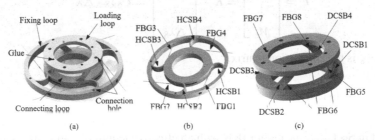

Fig. 1. Structural design of the sensor. (a) Three-dimensional diagram of the designed sensor. The sensor consists of two layers, which are layer I (b), and layer II (c).

2.2 Sensing Principle

FBG can serve as a wavelength-specific reflector. This characteristic achieved by a periodic variation in the refractive index of the fiber core is utilized to perceive force. Shifts in the central wavelength are related to the changes in strain, as follows:

$$\Delta\lambda = \lambda_0(1 - P_e)\varepsilon \tag{1}$$

where $\Delta\lambda$ and λ_0 are the central wavelength shift of FBG and its initial value, respectively, P_e is the elastic-optic coefficient and the corresponding value is 0.22, ε is the strain that occurs in FBG.

When a single-dimensional external load is applied to the sensor, all the DCSBs and HCSBs will undergo elastic deformation, which causes the corresponding strains of eight FBGs and then causes the shift of central wavelength. The relationship between the shift of central wavelength and force can be described as:

$$\Delta\lambda_{ij} = \lambda_0(1 - P_e)\varepsilon_{ij} = K_{ij}F_j \tag{2}$$

where $\Delta\lambda_{ij}$ is the central wavelength shift of FBG i, λ_0 is the initial central wavelength of the eight FBGs, ε_{ij} is the strain of FBG i when the load F_j is applied on the sensor, K_{ij} is strain response factor.

When the six-axis F/M is applied to the designed sensor, the correlation between load and central wavelength shift of FBGs can be indicated as:

$$\Delta\lambda = \begin{bmatrix} \Delta\lambda_1 \\ \Delta\lambda_2 \\ \vdots \\ \Delta\lambda_8 \end{bmatrix} = \begin{bmatrix} K_{11} & K_{12} & \cdots & K_{16} \\ K_{21} & K_{22} & \cdots & K_{26} \\ \vdots & \vdots & \ddots & \vdots \\ K_{81} & K_{82} & \cdots & K_{86} \end{bmatrix} \begin{bmatrix} F_x \\ F_y \\ \vdots \\ M_z \end{bmatrix} = KF \tag{3}$$

where $\Delta\lambda$ is the wavelength variation vector which represents the central wavelength shift of FBG 1 to FBG 8 and consists of $\Delta\lambda_1$ to $\Delta\lambda_8$. Based on the above analysis, the six-axis force from the designed sensor can be determined as:

$$F = \begin{bmatrix} F_x \\ F_y \\ \vdots \\ M_z \end{bmatrix} = K^{-1} \begin{bmatrix} \Delta\lambda_1 \\ \Delta\lambda_2 \\ \vdots \\ \Delta\lambda_8 \end{bmatrix} = C_{6\times8} \cdot \Delta\lambda \tag{4}$$

where $C_{6\times8}$ is the calibration matrix.

2.3 Sensor Fabrication

The 3-D printer and ABS plastic have been used to manufacture the elastic body. As discussed in Sect. 2.1, the eight FBGs with an effective length of 5 mm are used in this sensor.

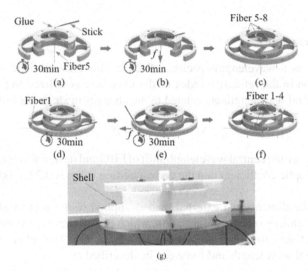

Fig. 2. The assembly process (a–f) and photograph (g) of the designed sensor.

The detailed fabrication process flow of the designed sensor is shown in Fig. 2(a–f). Firstly, the distal end of fiber 5 is pulled through the hole in connecting loop into a hole in the loading loop, and a stick is used to fill the hole with glue to fix the fiber. It takes about 30 min to wait for the glue to set completely, as shown in Fig. 2(a). Secondly, a preliminary load is applied in fiber, and the hole in the connecting loop is filled with glue (Fig. 2(b)). Then, fibers 6-8 is been installed in the same way in Fig. 2(c). As shown in Fig. 2(d–f), Fiber 1's distal end is pulled through the hole in the fixing loop into a hole in the connecting loop, and then it is fixed in the same way as fiber 5. Fibers 2-4 are installed in the same way afterward. A 3-D printed shell is used to protect the fibers, as illustrated by a real photograph in Fig. 2(g).

3   In Situ Calibration and Result

3.1   Setup and Principle

The calibration experimental setup has been established, as shown in Fig. 3(a). It mainly consists of a robot arm (UR5), a loading frame, a 500-g weight, an FBG interrogator, and a PC. The loading frame like an L shape acts as a force arm with a length of 50 mm in the horizontal and vertical directions (Fig. 3(b)). The designed sensor is fixed on the end of UR5 and will not be removed after calibration, and the loading frame is fixed on the loading loop. The weight is suspended from the top of the loading frame by a wire. Thus, the gravity of the weight will exert an eccentric load on the sensor when the sensor is in different postures driven by the UR5.

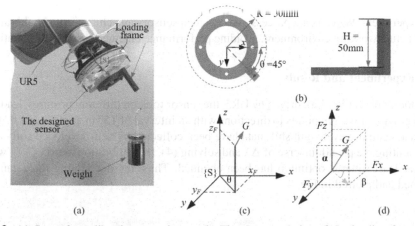

Fig. 3. (a) Setup for calibration experiment. (b) The shape and size of the loading frame. (c) Coordinate diagram of the loading point. (d) The diagram of the decompositions of weight gravity in the sensor coordinate system.

From Fig. 3(c), the coordinate of the loading point can be obtained as follows.

$$\begin{cases} x_F = \cos(\theta)R \\ y_F = \sin(\theta)R \\ z_F = H \end{cases} \tag{5}$$

From Fig. 3(d), the decompositions of weight gravity in the sensor coordinate system can be obtained as follows.

$$\begin{cases} F_x = \sin(\alpha)\cos(\beta)G \\ F_y = \sin(\alpha)\sin(\beta)G \\ F_z = \cos(\alpha)G \end{cases} \tag{6}$$

where G is the gravity of weight. Thus, the six-axis load applied to the sensor can be calculated as:

$$F = \begin{bmatrix} 1 & 0 & 0 \\ 0 & 1 & 0 \\ 0 & 0 & 1 \\ 0 & z_F & -y_F \\ -z_F & 0 & x_F \\ y_F & -x_F & 0 \end{bmatrix} \cdot \begin{bmatrix} F_x \\ F_y \\ F_z \end{bmatrix} \tag{7}$$

With the driving of UR5, the pose of the designed sensor will change, leading to the change of angle α and β, thus the six-axis load generated by the gravity of weight will be applied to the designed sensor as reference force. The calibration matrix C could be obtained by solving (4) using the central wavelength shift and force/moment data during this experiment. With such a process, the designed sensor can achieve in situ calibration in the actual working environment, avoiding performance change caused by installation.

3.2 Experiment and Result

With the setup in Fig. 3(a), driven by UR5, the sensor took on different postures, leading to the gravity of weight points to directions with an interval of 15° in angle α and β. The load and central wavelength shift data have been collected by self-developed software. Via counting the pseudoinverse of $\Delta\lambda$ and solving (4), the calibration matrix $C_{6\times8}$ with a linear least-squares optimum has been obtained. Thus, the decoupling force can be obtained and plotted in Fig. 4.

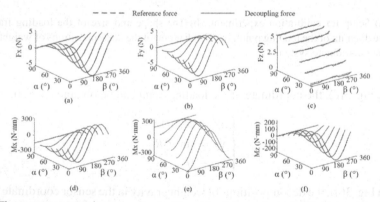

Fig. 4. The contrast curve between decoupling and reference force in the dimension of (a) Fx, (b) Fy, (c) Fz, (d) Mx, (e) My, (f) Mz.

From Fig. 4, the decoupling force is in agree with the reference force. Figure 5 shows the error cloud charts, it can be seen that most areas of the figure are blue, indicating that the designed sensor has a high decoupling accuracy. According to the range of load, the scale ranges are set as $[-5, 5]$ N for force components and $[-200, 200]$ N·mm for moment components. After such an in situ calibration, the static performance of the designed sensor can be obtained and displayed in Table 1. Moreover, distribution maps of absolute errors are obtained to analyze the absolute error confidence intervals as shown in Fig. 6. Under the confidence of 0.95, the absolute error confidence intervals of six-axis F/M detection are $[-0.130, 0.143]$ N, $[-0.093, 0.119]$ N, $[-0.249, 0.259]$ N, $[-6.021, 8.439]$ N·mm, $[-5.782, 6.156]$ N·mm, $[-3.279, 3.810]$ N·mm, respectively. These narrow confidence intervals explain the excellent static characteristic of the sensor and the feasibility of in situ calibration method.

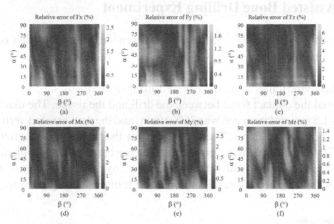

Fig. 5. Cloud charts of decoupling error. (a) Fx. (b) Fy. (c) Fz. (d) Mx. (e) My. (f) Mz. (Color figure online)

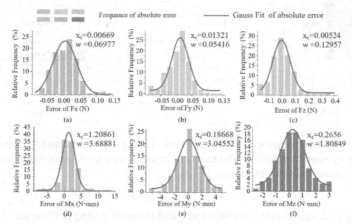

Fig. 6. Decoupling error distribution maps and their fitted normal distribution curves. (a) Fx. (b) Fy. (c) Fz. (d) Mx. (e) My. (f) Mz.

Table 1. Static performance of the designed sensor

Component	Fx	Fy	Fz	Mx	My	Mz
Max error (%)	2.63	1.95	6.92	4.60	2.90	1.49
Sensitivity (pm/N or pm/N·mm)	133.17	327.12	284.97	4.84	3.43	8.02
R-square		0.9998	0.9998	0.9975	0.9998	0.9999	0.9999

4 Robot-Assisted Bone Drilling Experiment

To further validate the reliability of the designed sensor in bone drilling operation, a surgery robot system has been built, which retains the configuration shown in Fig. 3(a) and only replace the loading frame with a motor, as illustrated in Fig. 7(a). The robot was used to drill the bovine femur to simulate bone drilling operation in surgery. The designed sensor monitored the contact force between the drill and the tissue. The diameter of the twist drill was 1.5 mm, rotate speed was 7500 r/min, and the drill was fed vertically down with the feed speed of 0.1 mm/s. The photograph of the bone segment after drilling is shown in Fig. 7(b). The central wavelength shift data has been collected with the sampling rate of 2000 Hz, and converted into force/moment data by calibration matrix. Figure 7(c) and (d) display the variations of resultant force and moment during drilling.

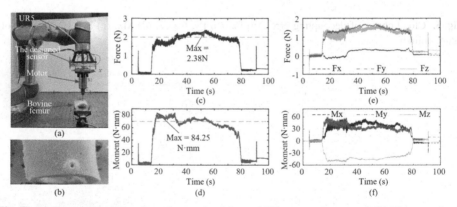

Fig. 7. (a) Experiment setup for robot-assisted bone drilling experiment and (b) Photograph of bovine femur segment after drilling. The resultant (c) and components (e) of force, and resultant (d) and components (f) of moment during drilling.

From Fig. 7(c, d), the max variation force and moment during drilling are 2.38 N and 84.25 N·mm. It can be seen that variation of force appears a peak at 4.7 s due to start of the motor. At 15 s, the force rose to about 1.8 N, indicating that the cutting begins. From 15 s, the force was staying around 2 N, until 79 s when the drill pierced the bone. The peak at 91 s illustrated that the motor stopped. In Fig. 7(e), the peaks at 4.7 s and 91 s are in the opposite direction, because the inertia is opposite when the motor starts and stops. A similar analysis can be performed on the axial moment variation in Fig. 7(d), and the same conclusion can also be obtained. Such results prove the reliability of the designed sensor and the feasibility of in situ calibration method proposed in this paper.

5 Conclusion

In this paper, a layered six-axis FBG force/moment sensor has been proposed and used to detect the force/moment information during robot-assisted orthopedic surgery. The sensor is a unique designed that eight unique C-shaped beams form a two-layer sensor structure manufactured by 3D printing, and eight FBGs are mounted tightly on the concave side of C-shaped beams to sense six-axis force/moment. Compared with the existing sensor design, this configuration gives the sensor the advantage of low chirping risk, high sensitivity, and MRI compatibility, it also leads to a lower cost than commercial sensors such as ATI. To overcome the performance degradation caused by installing and removing sensors, in situ calibration method has been proposed and employed to calibrate the designed sensor. Such a calibration leads to the excellent measurement accuracy of the designed sensor, with the max relative error of 6.92% which is lower than the FBG six-axis force sensor in [17] (18.65%). The normal distribution analysis of absolute error shows that the measurement error of the sensor has a narrow confidence interval in the range of 5.18%. Furthermore, during the robot-assisted bone drilling, the proposed sensor could detect the force/moment information between drill and tissue in real-time. The peak force and moment detected are much less than the mean value investigated in study [18], due to the high rotate speed and small diameter of the drill. Moreover, the various stages of the drilling process can be reflected by the force variation and consistent with the actual situation. In conclusion, the proposed in situ calibration can be used to improve the performance of the designed FBG force/ moment sensor with good feasibility and features huge application potential for high-precision Force/Moment measurement at the tip of a surgical robot.

References

1. Staub, B.N., Sadrameli, S.S.: The use of robotics in minimally invasive spine surgery. J. Spine Surg. 5(Suppl 1), S31 (2019)
2. Lippross, S., et al.: Robot assisted spinal surgery-A technical report on the use of DaVinci in orthopaedics. J. Orthop. 19, 50–53 (2020)
3. Niesche, A., Müller, M., Ehreiser, F., Teichmann, D., Leonhardt, S., Radermacher, K.: Smart bioimpedance-controlled craniotomy: concept and first experiments. Proc. Inst. Mech. Eng. 231(7), 673–680 (2017)
4. Al-Abdullah, K.I., Lim, C.P., Najdovski, Z., Yassin, W.: A model-based bone milling state identification method via force sensing for a robotic surgical system. Int. J. Med. Robot. Comput. Assist. Surg. 15(3), e1989 (2019)
5. Doulgeris, J.J., Gonzalez-Blohm, S.A., Filis, A.K., Shea, T.M., Aghayev, K., Vrionis, F.D.: Robotics in neurosurgery: evolution, current challenges, and compromises. Cancer Control 22(3), 352–359 (2015)
6. Akinyemi, T.O., et al.: Fiber Bragg grating-based force sensing in robot-assisted cardiac interventions: a review. IEEE Sens. J. 21, 10317–10331 (2021)

7. Lai, W., et al.: Force sensing with 1 mm fiber bragg gratings for flexible endoscopic surgical robots. IEEE/ASME Trans. Mechatron. **25**(1), 371–382 (2019)

8. Li, T., King, N.K.K., Ren, H.: Disposable FBG-based tridirectional force/torque sensor for aspiration instruments in neurosurgery. IEEE Trans. Industr. Electron. **67**(4), 3236–3247 (2019)

9. Choi, H., Lim, Y., Kim, J.: Three-axis force sensor with fiber Bragg grating. In: 2017 39th Annual International Conference of the IEEE Engineering in Medicine and Biology Society (EMBC), pp. 3940–3943. IEEE (2017)

10. Xiong, L., Guo, Y., Jiang, G., Zhou, X., Jiang, L., Liu, H.: Six-dimensional force/torque sensor based on fiber Bragg gratings with low coupling. IEEE Trans. Industr. Electron. **68**(5), 4079–4089 (2020)

11. Andrade Chavez, F.J., Traversaro, S., Pucci, D.: Six-axis force torque sensor model-based in situ calibration method and its impact in floating-based robot dynamic performance. Sensors **19**(24), 5521 (2019)

12. Sun, Y., Li, Y., Liu, Y., Liu, H.: An online calibration method for six-dimensional force/torque sensor based on shape from motion combined with complex algorithm. In: 2014 IEEE International Conference on Robotics and Biomimetics (ROBIO 2014), pp. 2631–2636. IEEE (2014)

13. Traversaro, S., Pucci, D., Nori, F.: In situ calibration of six-axis force-torque sensors using accelerometer measurements. In: 2015 IEEE International Conference on Robotics and Automation (ICRA), pp. 2111–2116 IEEE (2015)

14. Chavez, F.J.A., Traversaro, S., Pucci, D., Nori, F.: Model based in situ calibration of six axis force torque sensors. In: 2016 IEEE-RAS 16th International Conference on Humanoid Robots (Humanoids), pp. 422–427. IEEE (2016)

15. Cursi, F., Malzahn, J., Tsagarakis, N., Caldwell, D.: An online interactive method for guided calibration of multi-dimensional force/torque transducers. In: 2017 IEEE-RAS 17th International Conference on Humanoid Robotics (Humanoids), pp. 398–405. IEEE (2017)

16. Roozbahani, H., Fakhrizadeh, A., Haario, H., Handroos, H.: Novel online re-calibration method for multi-axis force/torque sensor of ITER welding/machining robot. IEEE Sens. J. **13**(11), 4432–4443 (2013)

17. Haslinger, R., Leyendecker, P., Seibold, U.: A fiberoptic force-torque-sensor for minimally invasive robotic surgery. In: 2013 IEEE International Conference on Robotics and Automation, pp. 4390–4395. IEEE (2013)

18. Golahmadi, A.K., Khan, D.Z., Mylonas, G.P., Marcus, H.J.: Tool-tissue forces in surgery: a systematic review. Ann. Med. Surg. **2**, 102268 (2021)

Wearable Robotics to Characterize, Retrain, and Restore Human Movements

Effects of Brain-Computer Interface and Classical Motor Imagery for Upper Limb Impairment After Stroke: A Case Report

Yi-Qian Hu[1], Rong-Rong Lu[1], Tian-Hao Gao[1], Jie Zhuang[2], and Yu-Long Bai[1(✉)]

[1] Department of Rehabilitation, Huashan Hospital, Fudan University, No. 12 Middle Wulumuqi Road, Shanghai 200040, China
dr_baiyl@fudan.edu.cn

[2] School of Psychology, Shanghai University of Sport, Shanghai 200438, China

Abstract. Background. There still exists limitations in the recovery of severe upper limb impairment after stroke, and brain computer interface maybe a hopeful therapy. **Methods.** A 76-year-old male hemiplegic patient with severe paretic upper limb was admitted. In the first four weeks, 20 sessions classic motor imagery was added in addition to routine treatments. Then, 20 sessions brain-computer interface training was added over the next four weeks. Behavioral characteristics, neuroelectrophysiology and neuroimaging were assessed at multiple time, such as the FuglMeyer Assessment Upper Extremity, the Motor Status Scale (MSS), the Action Research Arm Test (ARAT), Active range of motion of the paretic wrist and Modified Barthel Index (MBI). Functional magnetic resonance imaging (fMRI) was used to investigate the effect of the above interventions on the recovery of brain and its structural plasticity. **Results.** The patient's upper limb motor function improved after two different therapy interventions, however, the efficacy of BCI training was more obvious: after classic motor imagery, the paretic wrist could actively flex, but extension is still irrealizable. However, after BCI training, the paretic wrist was able to extend proactively. The fMRI findings revealed positive and dynamic changes on brain structure and function. **Conclusion.** BCI training could effectively promote the movement recovery after stroke than traditional motor imagery even if they showed apparent initial paralysis. An association between functional improvement and brain structure remodeling was observed. These findings serve as a conceptual investigations to encourage further relevant research.

Keywords: Brain-computer interface · Motor imagery · Chronic stroke · Brain plasticity

1 Introduction

Globally, stroke is still the third leading cause of disability [1]. Stroke patients mostly left different functional disorders, such as motor dysfunction, cognitive impairment, speech disorder, dysphagia, etc., among which motor dysfunction is the most common [2].

Y.-Q. Hu, R.-R. Lu and T.-H. Gao—Contributed equally to this work.

H. Liu et al. (Eds.): ICIRA 2022, LNAI 13457, pp. 71–78, 2022.
https://doi.org/10.1007/978-3-031-13835-5_7

Although a proportion of patients can obtain a certain degree of functional recovery through rehabilitation training, such as constrained induced movement therapy [3], task-oriented training [4]. However, existing rehabilitation interventions have shown very little efficacy for those chronic stroke patients with severe motor impairment [5], which cause great economic and mental burden on the families of stroke patients and society [6]. Therefore, it is urgent to find more effective treaments. Previous studies have proved that classical motor imagery could promote the motor recovery, which has a lower requirements for patients' actual retained motor function [7, 8]. Intensive training could be avoided which might cause abnormal movement patterns and compensatory movements, meanwhile, there was an internal stimulation to their brain which could increase the familiarity of movement [9]. However, classical motor imagery also have some limitations. During training, patients are required to have inact cognitive function to match with motor imagery activities, and maintain attention simultaneously. This is difficult in practical training. Therefore, the researches about it were heterogeneous and had different clinical efficacy [10–12]. Brain-computer interface (BCI) is a new rehabilitation technology, which can directly convert the signals generated by brain activities into computer commands to interact with the surrounding environment without the participation of peripheral nerves and muscles [13]. This stimulation process may have an impact on brain plasticity, thus promoting the motor function recovery for stroke patients [14]. This is a good supplement to the current clinical treatment. The purpose of this study was to compare the clinical efficacy of classical motor imagery and brain-computer interface on severe upper limb impairment in stroke patients. Functional Magnetic Resonance Imaging (fMRI) was applied to observe brain functional and structural plasticity to explore the potential mechanism of brain-computer interface to promote functional recovery.

2 Methodology

2.1 Patients

A 76-year-old man with left hemiplegia caused by cerebral infarction in the right lateral paraventricular and basal ganglia was recruited. He had severe left hemiplegia—there was no active movement on his wrist, his left finger could only co-flex within a range of 1.5 cm and the initiation of flexion was slow. He has significantly limitations for activities of daily living. He depended on assistance for his personal hygiene and dressing and he walked slowly with the aid of a cane. Moreover, the paretic hand prevented him from lifting his arm. The absence of speech and cognitive impairments allowed him to perform motor imagery and BCI training accurately under guidance. The patient had hypertension in the past, which was controlled by oral drugs and was stable. He received regular rehabilitation immediately after stroke, but there was no substantial improvement in the left wrist and hand more than 4 months later (P1). Before entering the study, we had fully communicated with the patient and signed the informed consent form, which was approved by the Ethics Committee of Huashan Hospital affiliated to Fudan University.

2.2 Intervention

Classical Motor Imagery. In the first four weeks, the patient underwent classical motor imagery (P2) [15]. The treatment was carried out in a relatively quiet and comfortable environment. Firstly, the patient was told to keep in a comfortable sitting position, then closed his eyes and imagined that he was in a familiar environment under the guidance of the therapist. Secondly, the therapist helped him to relax the body, and start instructing him to imagine the relevant movements. The content of the imagery task was adjusted by the therapist which could be combined with occupational therapy. For example, "extending slowly the paretic arm to touch the red apple placed in front of him, and then withdrawing it slowly", "imaging the active flexion and extension of the paretic wrist and fingers" or "stretching out the affected side arm, picking up the water cup on the table to drink water" and so on. Each imagery task could be repeated several times. After the imagery task, patient was asked to lift both hands for 10 times. Each training consisted of 3–4 sessions, and there was 2 min to break between each session. The whole last approximately 30 min, 5 times a week last for 4 weeks. In the process of training, the therapist should pay attention to keep the patient focused and avoid interference. After each session, the patient underwent routine rehabilitation therapy, including physical therapy, occupational therapy, etc.

BCI Training. Over the next four weeks, the patient underwent brain-computer interface (P3). In this study, a new brain-computer interface technology based on motor imagery was applied, combined with light touch stimulation and visual feedback from VR which we call it "multimodal perceptual feedback training". Before the treatment, the patient was given an EEG cap and connected to the electrode with a conductive ointment. After the training, the patient first received light touch input from both hands (completed by a brush), at the same time, the patient wore a pair of VR glasses which could see the movement of the virtual hands. After the sensory stimulation stopped, the patient conducted an imagery task about extension of the left or right wrist according to the prompt in the screen, meanwhile, the screen would give a feedback on the degree of imagery task completion through the action of the virtual hands, during which the patient continuously received visual stimulation and feedback. Each training session was 30 min with four cycles, each containing 20 random left or right hand imagery tasks lasting approximately 6 min with a 2-min rest between cycles. Five times a week, for a total of 20 training sessions. Similarly, the patient would undergo the same routine treatment after BCI training.

The brief procedure is listed in Fig. 1.

2.3 Functional Magnetic Resonance Imaging

fMRI scans were performed before and after BCI training. The task was designed as the motor imagery of both hands, consisting of three types of tasks which were named left hand grip, right hand grip and rest respectively. A, B, and C were used to represent the three tasks, each performed for 20 s with no interval between task. In sequence of ABC, BCA, CAB and repeated three times.

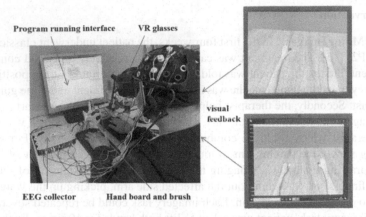

Fig. 1. A brief illustration of the BCI training process.

Echo planer imaging (EPI) was used to acquire functional MR images data: TR (repetition Time) = 2000 ms, TE(Echo Time) = 30 ms, FOV(Field of view) = 192 mm × 192 mm, flip angle = 90, voxel size = 3 mm × 3 mm × 3mm, matrix size = 64 × 64. slice thickness = 3 mm, and slice gap = 0 mm. Forty-two slices of axial planer images were acquired, including the whole cerebral cortex and the cerebellum.

Preprocessing of fMRI data was performed using the SPM12 software, the main steps included: ① Time difference correction between all scan layers was performed. ② The interlayers of the rigid body were rearranged for head movement correction. ③ The structural images of T1 are divided into different components such as gray matter and white matter and matched into the functional images, which the structural and functional images are converted into the Montreal Neurological Institute (MNI) standard space. ④ Finally, spatial smoothing was performed to form a spatial smoothing of a half-height full-width 6 mm Gaussian smoothing core. Statistical significance was considered at $p < 0.001$ (after FWE correction) to observe the changes in the activated brain regions.

3 Results

All assessments were conducted by the same physician who did not participate the study before and after treatment.

Fugl-Meyer Assessment Upper Extremity (FMA-UE), Motor Status Scale (MSS), Action Research Arm Test (ARAT) and the active motion range of paretic wrist were observed during P1, P2 and P3 to assess the arm and hand motor function. Modified Barthel index (MBI) was used to assess the daily living ability. Functional magnetic resonance imaging (fMRI) was applied to assess the brain change of structure and function.

3.1 Clinical Outcome

The parameters were improved in both different treatment options (Table 1). After classic motor imagery, the motor range and strength of the left shoulder was increased. Moreover, the patient was able to actively flex his wrist (flexion angle was about 10°), the active range co-flexion of the fingers increased from 1.5 cm to about 2.5 cm, and the muscle strength increased in the flexion of fingers, but he still could not extend his paretic wrist or finger. However, after BCI training, the patient could actively extend his paretic wrist (extension angle was about 15–20°) and the flexion angle of wrist also increased to about 60°. He could pinch a piece of A4 paper by his thumb and index finger and maintain a certain strength. The sEMG results also improved, with synergistic contraction rates (extensor/extensor + flexor * 100%) calculated for both treatments.

Table 1. Test Parameters of clinical assessment in P1, P2, P3

Period	The active flexion and extension angle of the paretic wrist (°)	FMA-UE	MSS	ARAT	MBI
P1 (baseline)	0/0	12	13.8/0.8	0	75
P2	10/0	16	17.8/1.8	3	75
Number change from baseline	**10/0**	**4**	**4.0/1.0**	**3**	**0**
P3	60/15	22	20.4/3.4	7	75
Number change from P2	**50/15**	**6**	**2.6/1.6**	**4**	**0**

Note: FMA-UE = Fugl-Meyer assessment-upper extremity; ARAT = action research arm test; MSS = motor status scale; MBI = Modified Barthel Index; Change values are shown in font-bold

3.2 fMRI

No significant brain region activation was observed during the motor imagery task of the paretic hand before the BCI training. While, after 20 sessions of BCI training, extensive regional activation occurred in both cerebral hemispheres, including bilateral motor cortex, superior frontal gyrus, middle frontal gyrus and posterior-temporal lobe among which the strongest activation was the bilateral motor cortex.

Combined with the results of the clinical evaluation in the previous chapter (Table 1), the patient showed a more pronounced improvement in upper limb motor function after BCI training. The positive result suggested that the activation of bilateral motor cortex may play a meaningful role in functional recovery, which might achieve functional remodeling after injury.

In the motor imagery of the unaffected hand, the differences all appeared in the motor cortex of the left hemisphere both before and after intervention, but there were significant differences in the specific brain regions of activation.

Prior to the intervention, standard left motor cortex activation was performed during the right-hand motor imagery task, while the activation area changed after the intervention and began to move downward (although it was still in the motor cortex, but closer to the facial muscles area). The change seemed to suggest a functional remodeling occurred in the left motor cortex after intervention, in which a part of the left motor cortex was "seconded" to dominate the motor function of the paretic hand to promote the functional recovery (Fig. 2).

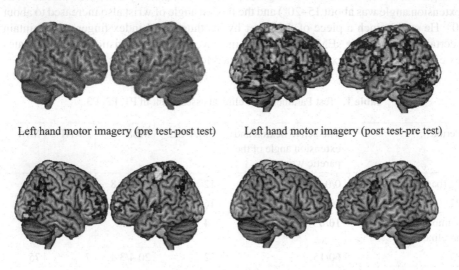

Left hand motor imagery (pre test-post test)   Left hand motor imagery (post test-pre test)

Right hand motor imagery (pre test-post test)   Right hand motor imagery (post test-pre test)

Fig. 2. The significant activated brain regions in the left or right hand during the motor imagery tasks before and after BCI training (p < 0.001, after the FWE correction).

4 Discussion

According to our study, after 20 sessions intervention, brain-computer interface based on motor imagery showed a better rehabilitation superiority than classical motor imagery that change value of each evaluation index showed more obvious improvement (Table 1), especially functional recovery in wrist and hand. Those previous stroke patients with severe hemiplegia rarely or even cannot obtain the functional recovery of wrist and hand, which also strikes the patients' enthusiasm and confidence in recovery. Therefore, we believe that this finding is a great encouragement and has great significance for the existing clinical rehabilitation. As we know, stroke patients with severe paretic upper limb rarely or even unable to recover their wrist and hand functions, which greatly struck the patients' enthusiasm and confidence in recovery. Therefore, we believed that what we found in this study had a massive inspiration and important significance to the current clinical rehabilitation. Pichiorri had demonstrated that the rehabilitation effects of motor imagery could be enhanced in BCI system using a randomized controlled trial [16], which also indicated the clinical feasibility and effectiveness of this study from the side. Recently, our research group has also carried out relevant clinical trials, and the results showed that compared with classical motor imagery, the BCI system based on motor imagery had a better trend of promoting the recovery of upper limb motor function [17].

Of course, we needed to recognize that this was just a case report and may be with some contingency. Refining and expanding studies need be done in future, preferably to conduct randomized controlled trials to obtain more reliable conclusions. The results of this study still indicate huge promise for patients with severe paretic upper limb.

From the fMRI results, corresponding structural changes occurred in both bilateral brains after BCI training. Motor cortex of the ipsilateral hemisphere showed obviously enhanced activity which suggested that BCI training might help to enhanced the activity in motion regions of the ipsilateral hemisphere to achieve functional recovery. Meanwhile, It should also be noted that the motor cortex of the contralateral hemisphere also showed corresponding changes. The brain area activated during the task of right-hand motor imagery was shifted downward from the standard M1 region to the facial muscle group region. The dynamic change might suggest that the contralateral hemisphere might "second" some part of motor region to assist the ipsilateral hemisphere to complete the control to motion function. This was different from the previous theory of contralateral compensation or ipsilateral compensation [18, 19]. This might suggest that function recovery after stroke do not depend on a simple brain structural change, but might be related to the lesion location and severity, thus showing changeable structural restructuring and functional improvement. These above still need to be verified by more rigorous randomized controlled trials.

In addition, the ability of daily life did not show visible changes, considering that might be related to the choice of assessment scale, and we also should realize that the improvement of motor function did not directly represent the improvement of life ability because of the transformation from motor function to life ability still need many aspects to cooperate which also suggested that we need to consider more in the future research.

5 Conclusion

As an exploratory case-report, this study has a suggestive and encouraging effect that BCI training may be effective in promoting functional recovery in chronic stroke patients with severe hemiplegic upper limb, especially in those with severely paretic wrist. The fMRI results also suggest that BCI training may facilitate brain structural remodeling.

Acknowledgements. This work was supported by Natural Science Foundation of China (NSFC) [grant number 81902280].

References

1. GBD 2019 Stroke Collaborators: Global, regional, and national burden of stroke and its risk factors, 1990–2019: a systematic analysis for the Global Burden of Disease Study 2019. Lancet Neurol. **20**(10), 795–820 (2021). https://doi.org/10.1016/S1474-4422(21)00252-0
2. Feigin, V.L.: Stroke: practical management. JAMA **300**(19), 2311–2312 (2008). https://doi.org/10.1001/jama.2008.633
3. Wolf, S.L., Winstei, C.J., Mille, J.P., et al.: Effect of constraint-induced movement therapy on upper extremity function 3 to 9 months after stroke: the EXCITE randomized clinical trial. JAMA **296**(17), 2095–2104 (2006). https://doi.org/10.1001/jama.296.17.2095

4. Winstein, C.J., Wolf, S.L., Dromerick, A.W., et al.: Effect of a task-oriented rehabilitation program on upper extremity recovery following motor stroke: the ICARE randomized clinical trial. JAMA 315(6), 571–581 (2016). https://doi.org/10.1001/jama.2016.0276

5. Caria, A., Weber, C., Brötz, D., et al.: Chronic stroke recovery after combined BCI training and physiotherapy: a case report. Psychophysiology 48(4), 578–582 (2011). https://doi.org/10.1111/j.1469-8986.2010.01117.x

6. Pandian, J.D., Sebastian, I.A.: Integrated approach to stroke burden: are we doing enough? Lancet Neurol. 20(10), 774–775 (2021). https://doi.org/10.1016/S1474-4422(21)00287-8

7. Page, S.J., Levine, P., Leonard, A.: Mental practice in chronic stroke: results of a randomized, placebo-controlled trial. Stroke 38(4), 1293–1297 (2007). https://doi.org/10.1161/01.STR.0000260205.67348.2b

8. Wang, H., Xu, G., Wang, X., et al.: The Reorganization of resting-state brain networks associated with motor imagery training in chronic stroke patients. IEEE Trans. Neural Syst. Rehabil. Eng. 27(10), 2237–2245 (2019). https://doi.org/10.1109/TNSRE.2019.2940980

9. Hétu, S., Grégoire, M., Saimpont, A., et al.: The neural network of motor imagery: an ALE meta-analysis. Neurosci. Biobehav. Rev. 37(5), 930–949 (2013). https://doi.org/10.1016/j.neubiorev.2013.03.017

10. Liu, H., Song, L.P., Zhang, T.: Mental practice combined with physical practice to enhance hand recovery in stroke patients. Behav. Neurol. 2014, 876416 (2014). https://doi.org/10.1155/2014/876416

11. Rayegani, S.M., Raeissadat, S.A., Sedighipour, L., et al.: Effect of neurofeedback and electromyographic-biofeedback therapy on improving hand function in stroke patients. Top Stroke Rehabil. 21(2), 137 (2014). https://doi.org/10.1310/tsr2102-137

12. Schuster, C., Butler, J., Andrews, B., et al.: Comparison of embedded and added motor imagery training in patients after stroke: results of a randomised controlled pilot trial. Trials 13, 11 (2012). https://doi.org/10.1186/1745-6215-13-11.PMID: 22269834

13. Nicolas-Alonso, L.F., Gomez-Gil, J.: Brain computer interfaces, a review. Sensors (Basel) 12(2), 1211–1279 (2012). https://doi.org/10.3390/s120201211

14. Daly, J.J., Cheng, R., Rogers, J., et al.: Feasibility of a new application of noninvasive Brain Computer Interface (BCI): a case study of training for recovery of volitional motor control after stroke. J. Neurol. Phys. Ther. 33(4), 203–211 (2009). https://doi.org/10.1097/NPT.0b013e3181c1fc0b

15. Page, S.J., Levine, P., Sisto, S.A., Johnston, M.V.: Mental practice combined with physical practice for upper-limb motor deficit in subacute stroke. Phys. Ther. 81(8), 1455–1462 (2001). https://doi.org/10.1093/ptj/81.8.1455

16. Pichiorri, F., Morone, G., Petti, M., et al.: Brain-computer interface boosts motor imagery practice during stroke recovery. Ann. Neurol. 77(5), 851–865 (2015). https://doi.org/10.1002/ana.24390

17. Hu, Y.Q., Gao, T.H., Li, J., et al.: Motor imagery-based brain-computer interface combined with multimodal feedback to promote upper limb motor function after stroke: a preliminary study. Evid Based Complement Alternat. Med. 2021, 1116126 (2021). https://doi.org/10.1155/2021/1116126

18. Johansen-Berg, H., Rushworth, M.F., Bogdanovic, M.D., et al.: The role of ipsilateral premotor cortex in hand movement after stroke. Proc. Natl. Acad. Sci. USA 99(22), 14518–14523 (2002). https://doi.org/10.1073/pnas.222536799

19. Schaechter, J.D., Perdue, K.L.: Enhanced cortical activation in the contralesional hemisphere of chronic stroke patients in response to motor skill challenge. Cereb Cortex. 18(3), 638–647 (2008). https://doi.org/10.1093/cercor/bhm096

A Synchronous Acquisition System of Ultrasound, sEMG and IMU for Human Motion Prediction

Yifan Liu[1], Zongtian Yin[2], Hongyu Yang[1], Xingchen Yang[2],
and Honghai Liu[1(✉)]

[1] State Key Laboratory of Robotics and System, Harbin Institute of Technology,
Shenzhen, China
honghai.liu@icloud.com
[2] State Key Laboratory of Mechanical System and Vibration,
Shanghai Jiao Tong University, Shanghai, China

Abstract. At present, due to the limited information, the single man-machine interface control has some defects in human motion prediction, such as low accuracy and poor robustness. In this work, a multi-modal real-time acquisition system that combines surface electromyography (sEMG), inertial measurement (IMU) and A-mode ultrasound (AUS) information is used to upper limb motion prediction. The device we developed can simultaneously collect three kinds of signals, eliminating the operation of manual alignment. sEMG can reflect the electrical activity of muscle contraction, AUS can detect the deformation of deep muscles, and IMU can obtain information such as the speed and acceleration of the limbs. One healthy subjects participated in the experiment. The results show that the motion prediction accuracy of three modal information fusion is higher than that of any one or two information fusion, which is expected to provide a better control method in exoskeleton or prosthesis.

Keywords: A-mode ultrasound · sEMG · IMU · Motion prediction

1 Introduction

In recent years, human motion perception has attracted more and more attention, which is an important research link in the control of prosthetic hand and exoskeleton. The methods of obtaining human motion information can be divided into the following: computer vision, IMU, sEMG, encoder and so on.

sEMG is the electrical manifestation of neuromuscular activation detected from the surface skin [1], and it obtains rich electrophysiological information related to movement intention non-invasively, so it has been verified as an effective interface for gesture recognition. EMG-based technology has been widely used in context awareness, motor control analysis, rehabilitation training, and

H. Liu et al. (Eds.): ICIRA 2022, LNAI 13457, pp. 79–89, 2022.
https://doi.org/10.1007/978-3-031-13835-5_8

motion pattern recognition and interaction [2,3]. The application of electromyography (EMG) has already been shown to perform well when classifying hand and wrist function as part of an automated sensor system. However, the application the EMG in such sensor systems is limited in practice by factors including requirements for careful skin preparation and electrode placement, and a signal which is dependent on humidity and skin impedance.

Ultrasonic human-machine interface technology is being widely used. Ultrasound can not only provide static images of anatomical structures, but also pro vide real-time dynamic images of internal tissue movements related to physical and physiological activities. It can detect the deformation state of subcutaneous muscles in a more intuitive way, and its energy compared to semg Deep muscles are detected [4], and more and more researches are oriented to ultrasound. Shi et at. utilized ultrasound images of different finger flexion to recognize motions in distinct pat terns and achieved an overall accuracy of 94 and promising performance of ultrasound-based finger motion decoding [5]. Akhlaghi et al. set up fifteen classes of hand gestures for off-line recognition and four classes real-time de- coding. Their experiment results presented a higher robustness of ultrasound, in comparison with other muscle-based HMIs [6].

The inertial measurement unit (IMU) is a device that combines the acceleration readings in the accelerometer and the angular rotation speed detection of the gyroscope. There have been some studies using imu to measure movement after stroke [7]. Patel et al. [8] selected 8 tasks from the evaluation scale, and provided estimated scores for each task through pattern recognition and analysis of accelerometer data. Anne et al. [9] used multiple IMUs to evaluate spatial movement indicators to assess the movement ability of reach-to-grasp and displacement movements in the upper limbs. imu can have a good estimate of wrist rotation, but when it needs to sense finger movement, imu needs to deploy a large number of sensors in each finger segment.

Recently, multi-source information fusion technology has become the focus of research in the field of human motion analysis. The common ones are imu and sEMG. Li [10] combined IMU and EMG data yielded superior performance over the IMU data alone and the EMG data alone, in terms of decreased normal data variation rate (NDVR) and improved determination coefficient (DC) from a regression analysis between the derived indicator and routine clinical assessment score. There are also IMU and MMG. The system is composed of wearable inertial sensing and MMG sensors. The output of the system combines classified FMA-UE scores with a series of fine-grained supplementary features which have been formulated as a means of complementing the low resolution clinical rating scores.

In this paper, a portable hybrid sEMG/AUS/IMU system is designed, which can simultaneously acquire the three modal information of myoelectricity, ultrasound, and IMU from the same part, eliminate the time difference between different acquisition information, and verified that multi-source information fusion is better than single information through the experiment of upper limb motion recognition.

2 Three Mode Information Synchronous Acquisition System

As shown in Fig. 1, the overall system framework consists of 8 parts, including ultrasonic acquisition module, sEMG acquisition module, IMU acquisition module, main control processor, data communication module, power module, upper computer graphical user interface and sensor wearing module. The three signals are filtered, amplified and collected by each module, then transmitted to the main control chip, and then transmitted to the upper computer by the communication module through WiFi for subsequent acceptance, display and storage.

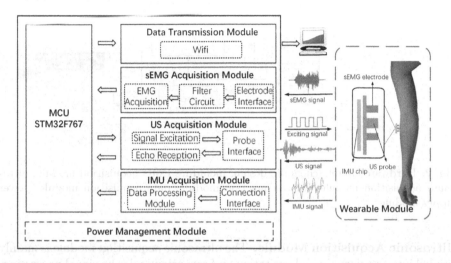

Fig. 1. The overall structure frame. The arm band including ultrasonic probe, EMG electrode and IMU sensor is worn on the arm. The signal is collected and processed by the hardware system and uploaded to the upper computer for subsequent processing.

2.1 Acquisition Function Module

sEMG Acquisition Module. The system hardware design is shown in Fig. 2. In order to obtain high-quality and stable EMG signals, a high-precision and low-noise ADC acquisition chip ads1299 (Texas Instrument) is selected. It has up to 8 low-noise programmable gain amplifiers (PGAs) and 8 high-resolution synchronous sampling analog-to-digital converters (ADCs). The signals are differentially amplified to improve the common mode rejection ratio and signal-to-noise ratio. RC capacitor placed behind the electrode is used to filter high-frequency interference. The original EMG signal is input into ads1299 after RC filtering. It is amplified, sampled and low-pass filtered inside 1299. The obtained digital signal is transmitted to the main control chip through SPI, and the main control interrupt is triggered by pulling down the drdy pin, so as to read the data transmitted by 1299. Digital filtering will be carried out in the main chip, and 50 Hz comb filter is set to reduce the interference 50 Hz common frequency signal. There is also a high pass filter with a cut-off frequency 20 Hz to reduce motion artifact noise.

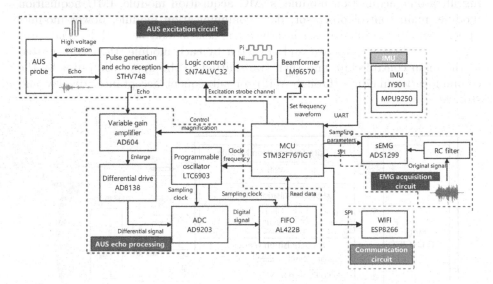

Fig. 2. Hardware circuit schematic design, including EMG acquisition module, ultrasound acquisition module, IMU acquisition module, data acquisition module, power supply module

Ultrasonic Acquisition Module. The ultrasonic acquisition module is mainly divided into two parts: signal excitation and reception and echo signal processing.

The main controller stm32f767 realizes data transmission and communication with each functional chip through the general I/O pin or the peripheral function pin on the chip, so as to configure the registers of each functional chip to set the excitation frequency, excitation waveform, magnification, sampling frequency and other relevant parameters.

The ultrasonic signal excitation and receiving module includes beamformer circuit, logic control circuit, high voltage excitation and echo receiving circuit. The beamformer circuit lm96570 chip first generates multiple pairs of low-voltage square wave control signals PI and Ni, and is gated by the logic control circuit sn74alvc32 to control the sthv748 high-speed high-voltage pulse generator chip. After excitation, it switches to the echo receiving state and transmits the ultrasonic echo signal to the ultrasonic echo processing module. In this paper, the parameters of low-voltage square wave control signal are set as follows: frequency 5 MHz, square wave duty cycle 50%, two square wave periods, and the phase difference of PI and Ni is 180°. The positive and negative peak value ± HV of high-voltage square wave excitation signal is ±50 V, with two square wave cycles and a duty cycle of 50%.

The ultrasonic echo processing module includes variable gain amplifier circuit, differential driving circuit and sampling clock setting circuit, analog-to-digital conversion circuit, first in first out buffer circuit. The ultrasonic echo signal first passes through the RC filter circuit and then successively enters the above circuits for amplification, differential and sampling processing. The sampled echo data is cached in the first in first out cache circuit. The dual output low-noise variable gain amplifier chip ad604 is used as the core of the amplification circuit, and the analog voltage is generated by the digital to analog converter on the main controller to set the amplification factor of ad604. The ad8138 differential chip processes the amplified echo signal and converts it into differential signal to reduce common mode noise, and is used to drive the analog-to-digital conversion circuit ad9203. In order to prevent the main controller from having time to read and process the sampling data, a first in first out buffer circuit based on al422b chip is set up to avoid this problem.

IMU Acquisition Module. Using the jy901 electronic device module, the internal integration of high-precision gyroscope, accelerometer and geomagnetic field sensor, high-performance microprocessor and advanced dynamic solution and Kalman dynamic filter algorithm can quickly solve the current real-time motion attitude of the module. Each module is connected to the main chip through the serial port, with a maximum support of 921600bps. The sampling frequency of the module 100 Hz, and the collected three-axis acceleration, angular velocity and angle are transmitted to the main chip.

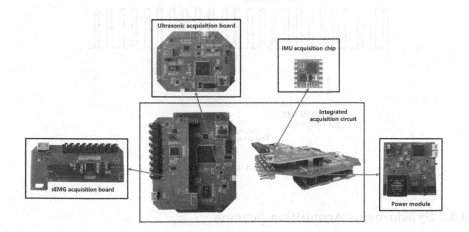

Fig. 3. Hardware circuit board

Data Communication Module. The whole synchronous information can be transmitted to the upper computer through WiFi. The high-speed WiFi module ALK8266WIFI based on ESP8266EX chip, which can support the standard wireless communication protocol. It provides a high-speed SPI slave interface with a maximum clock frequency of 25 MHz, which is suitable for high-speed acquisition and other applications.

Physical Design of Hardware. As shown in Fig. 3, the whole system is divided into three layers. The lowest layer is the power module, which is powered by 12V battery. The middle layer is the ultrasonic acquisition module and the main control chip, and the top layer is the EMG acquisition module and IMU acquisition circuit. The real object is small and easy to carry.

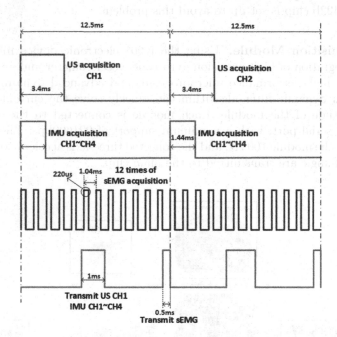

Fig. 4. System timing diagram

2.2 Synchronous Acquisition Scheme

As shown in Fig. 4, In order to synchronize various information, some information needs to be downsampled. One cycle of each acquisition and transmission is 12.5 ms. The time from excitation to acquisition of each ultrasonic frame is 3.4 ms, the sampling frequency of IMU 80 Hz, and the data is read through interruption. Because the amount of data is small, the use time can be ignored. The sampling frequency of EMG is 960 Hz, and 220 us is required for each interruption of acquisition. The existing EMG data are accessed every 1.04 ms, and 12 acquisitions are carried out in 12.5 ms. After the acquisition of ultrasound and IMU, it takes 3–4 ms to transmit the ultrasound and IMU through the communication module, and the last EMG data needs to be sent within 0.8 ms.

2.3   Host Computer Acquisition System

The GUI of the upper computer receives data according to the communication protocol and packet structure of the data packet sent by the lower computer, analyzes three kinds of information respectively through the packet header, and displays the graphic pictures of the three kinds of information. As shown in Fig. 5, you can view 4-channel ultrasonic data, 8-Channel EMG data and 4-channel IMU data. At the same time, it can save data and design experimental paradigm on the host computer.

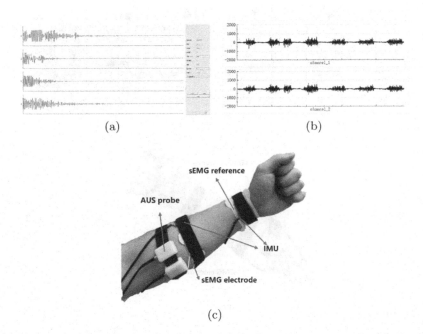

(a)   (b)

(c)

Fig. 5. (a) US Waveform drawing (b) sEMG Waveform drawing (c) IMU Waveform drawing

3   Upper Limb Movement Experiment

3.1   Experimental Protocols

To assess the effect of unimodal and multimodal recognition in upper limb movements, 1 able-bodied male subject (25 years old, without any history of neuromuscular or joint disease) was pre-experimented. The subject was familiarized with 12 upper limb movements, as shown in Fig. 6, which included 4 finger movements, 4 wrist movements, and 4 wrist combined with elbow movements that balanced the dominance of each modality. To perform the first 8 movements, the subject placed the elbow on the table with the small arm vertically upward; for the last 4 movements, the elbow joint was straightened and the small arm and large arm were in a 180° horizontal line. The subjects repeated the experiment four times, with each movement lasting 5 s and a 30 s rest between each experiment.

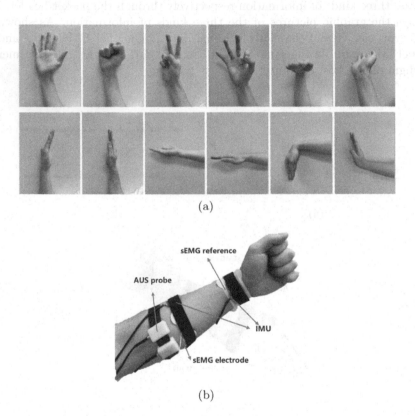

(a)

(b)

Fig. 6. (a) The 20 pre-set motions for hand recognition experiment: fingers abduction (FA), fist (FS), index and middle finger point (IMP), thumb and index finger flexion (TIF), wrist flexion (WF), wrist extension (WE), wrist supination (WS), wrist pronation (WP), wrist supination with elbow straight (WSES), wrist pronation with elbow straight (WPES), wrist flexion with elbow straight (WFES), wrist extension with elbow straight (WEES). (b) Sensor placement position

3.2   Feature Extraction and Feature Fusion

Feature extraction is needed for the three modal information to reduce the dimensionality to obtain useful information. Here seven features are compared, ultrasound features, EMG features, IMU features, a mixture of each two features and a mixture of three features. The ultrasound features are one-dimensional spatial signals, and their features are obtained by segmental linear fitting of ultrasound data after time gain compensation, Gaussian filtering, Hilbert transform and logarithmic compression [4]. Both the EMG and IMU signals are temporal signals, and TD-AR6 [11] was chosen as their features. When performing data fusion, the time window of the EMG signal is set to 250 and the step size is set to 48 in order to ensure the data dimensional alignment, and the time window of IMU is set to 20 and the step size is set to 4. In order to avoid the modal failure of one signal due to excessive difference in values, the normalization operation is performed on the respective signals, and the feature spliced data are later subjected to PCA dimensionality reduction to obtain the final features.

3.3   Classification

The LDA classifier is used here, which is constructed based on Gaussian assumptions with Bayesian decision criterion and is one of the most widely used classifiers in the field of discrete gesture recognition based on physiological signals [12]. The LDA classifier does not need to set hyperparameters, and the classifier parameters are all calculated based on the data in the training set.

4   Results

As shown in the figure, the classification accuracy is 81.25% for ultrasound features in unimodal, 62.33% for surface EMG signals, 43.96% for IMU features, 83.83% for ultrasound + EMG features in bimodal, 82% for ultrasound + IMU, 65.08% for IMU + EMG, and 85% for trimodal features (Fig. 7).

The experiments show that feature fusion of different types of information possesses better performance in upper limb gesture motion decoding. The EMG signal is mainly able to capture the surface neuroelectric signal, IMU mainly uses the Euler angle to obtain the gesture of the limb, while ultrasound is able to obtain the subcutaneous muscle morphology information, ultrasound can detect deeper muscle information and has good stability, so ultrasound unimodal is superior to the other two modalities in motion classification. Ultrasound features are better than EMG signals in finger motion classification, precisely because finger motion is associated with deeper muscles in the small arm, whereas EMG can only obtain surface information. And the four gestures performed by EMG in the two cases of elbow flexion and elbow extension, respectively, are prone to misclassification because the angular change of the elbow joint does not involve the muscle information of the small arm, so the EMG signals acquired from the small arm are not necessarily classified accurately. The reason for the low recognition rate of IMU unimodality is that the information acquired by IMU is almost always the same when performing finger movements, and only when it involves elbow joint rotation, the information from the IMU becomes useful. The recognition rate improved from both bimodal and trimodal features. It can be

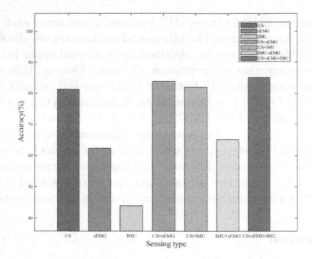

Fig. 7. Classification accuracy of various modes

analyzed as the ultrasound information provides the main role after PCA down-scaling, while EMG and IMU can provide more information from physiological electrical signals and axial joint perspective. The pre-experiment in this paper is to verify that multimodal information fusion is superior to unimodal information, and subsequent experiments are needed to increase the number of subjects and increase the number of classifications to validate multi-subject action prediction experiments in a more complex upper limb motion environment. In terms of mul-timodal fusion algorithm, the feature fusion approach may instead bring some negative effects, such as the information provided by IMU in finger classification is redundant information, which may pull down the accuracy. Subsequently, a multi-level classification approach can be considered to first determine the over-all upper limb pose using IMU, and then continue to subdivide the finger gesture or wrist angle in each pose.

5 Conclusion

Finally, this paper proposes a synchronous acquisition system of Ultrasound, sEMG and IMU. A PCB hardware design scheme and a synchronous acquisition timing scheme are proposed. The system can simultaneously acquire 4 channels 20 Hz A-type ultrasound signals, 8 channels 960 Hz EMG signals, and 4 channels 80 Hz IMU signals. Meanwhile, a pre-experimental analysis of upper limb motion recognition based on this system was conducted to verify that the combination of sEMG, AUS and IMU can improve the decoding accuracy of complex motions. In addition to the application in upper limb gesture motion, this device and the multimodal information approach are expected to provide better help in finger-elbow joint angle estimation, force judgment, fatigue judgment, and lower limb gait recognition.

References

1. De Luca, C.J.: Physiology and mathematics of myoelectric signals. IEEE Trans. Biomed. Eng. **6**, 313–325 (1979)
2. Lee, K.H., Min, J.Y., Byun, S.: Electromyogram-based classification of hand and finger gestures using artificial neural networks. Sensors **22**(1), 225 (2021)
3. McDonald, C.G., Sullivan, J.L., Dennis, T.A., O'Malley, M.K.: A myoelectric control interface for upper-limb robotic rehabilitation following spinal cord injury. IEEE Trans. Neural Syst. Rehabil. Eng. **28**(4), 978–987 (2020)
4. Yang, X., Sun, X., Zhou, D., Li, Y., Liu, H.: Towards wearable a-mode ultrasound sensing for real-time finger motion recognition. IEEE Trans. Neural Syst. Rehabil. Eng. **26**(6), 1199–1208 (2018)
5. Shi, J., Hu, S.-X., Liu, Z., Guo, J.-Y., Zhou, Y.-J., Zheng, Y.-P.: Recognition of finger flexion from ultrasound image with optical flow. a preliminary study. In: 2010 International Conference on Biomedical Engineering and Computer Science, pp. 1–4. IEEE (2010)
6. Akhlaghi, N., et al.: Real-time classification of hand motions using ultrasound imaging of forearm muscles. IEEE Trans. Biomed. Eng. **63**(8), 1687–1698 (2015)
7. Lou, Y., Wang, R., Mai, J., Wang, N., Wang, Q.: IMU-based gait phase recognition for stroke survivors. Robotica **37**(12), 2195–2208 (2019)
8. Patel, S., et al.: A novel approach to monitor rehabilitation outcomes in stroke survivors using wearable technology. Proc. IEEE **98**(3), 450–461 (2010)
9. Schwarz, A., Bhagubai, M., Wolterink, G., Held, J.P., Luft, A.R., Veltink, P.H.: Assessment of upper limb movement impairments after stroke using wearable inertial sensing. Sensors **20**(17), 4770 (2020)
10. Li, Y., Zhang, X., Gong, Y., Cheng, Y., Gao, X., Chen, X.: Motor function evaluation of hemiplegic upper-extremities using data fusion from wearable inertial and surface EMG sensors. Sensors **17**(3), 582 (2017)
11. Hargrove, L., Englehart, K., Hudgins, B.: The effect of electrode displacements on pattern recognition based myoelectric control. In: International Conference of the IEEE Engineering in Medicine and Biology Society, pp. 2203–2206. IEEE (2006)
12. Englehart, K., Hudgins, B.: A robust, real-time control scheme for multifunction myoelectric control. IEEE Trans. Biomed. Eng. **50**(7), 848–854 (2003)

Gait Time Parameter Analysis-Based Rehabilitation Evaluation System of Lower Limb Motion Function

Yue-Peng Zhang [ID], Guang-Zhong Cao[✉] [ID], Jiang-Cheng Chen, Ye Yuan,
Ling-Long Li, Dong-Po Tan, and Zi-Qin Ling

Guangdong Key Laboratory of Electromagnetic Control and Intelligent Robots, College of
Mechatronics and Control Engineering, Shenzhen University, Shenzhen 518060, China
gzcao@szu.edu.cn

Abstract. Aiming at the problems of low accuracy and high time cost of existing
motion function rehabilitation evaluation methods, this paper proposes a rehabilitation evaluation method and system of lower limb motion function based on
gait parameter analysis. Firstly, according to the calculation method of gait information related parameters, compare the differences of age and gender in healthy
people and the differences of gait information between healthy and disabled group,
and preliminarily determine the characteristic parameters of lower limb motion
function evaluation. Then, the evaluation indexes are determined through multicollinearity and significance analysis, and the multiple linear regression model
of Fugl-Meyer assessment (FMA) score is established. The goodness-of-fit test
method is used to prove that the proposed evaluation method can replace the lower
limb score of FMA as the evaluation method of lower limb motor function in stroke
patients. Finally, the lower limb motor function evaluation system is built in the
upper computer, so that the model can be used concretely.

Keywords: Gait parameter · Gait analysis · Rehabilitation evaluation

1 Introduction

Rehabilitation refers to the ability of patients to resume exercise, including rehabilitation training and rehabilitation evaluation. Rehabilitation training is paid more and
more attention in the rehabilitation process of stroke patients. Many rehabilitation training researches have made positive progress, such as lower limb rehabilitation exercise
assisted exoskeleton robot developed by colleges and research institutions, which is one
of its main research directions. However, the existing rehabilitation evaluation research
pays much less attention than rehabilitation training. Scientific and effective evaluation
methods can play a role of feedback and guidance for rehabilitation training.

Scholars and institutions have conducted research on rehabilitation evaluation. Makihara et al. [1] evaluated the safety and effectiveness of HAL exoskeleton robot, and its
main evaluation index is human bioelectrical signal. Pérez-Nombela et al. [2] evaluated the rehabilitation effect by comparing the physiological parameters of patients in

H. Liu et al. (Eds.): ICIRA 2022, LNAI 13457, pp. 90–102, 2022.
https://doi.org/10.1007/978-3-031-13835-5_9

trajectory mode, compliance mode and without exoskeleton. Rodgers et al. [3] studied robot assisted training and improving limb motor function of stroke patients through randomized controlled trial. The rehabilitation effect is scored with action research arm test (ARAT), Barthel scale and FMA scale, and the assisted training scheme of rehabilitation robot is determined according to the results. Nam et al. [4] proposed an image assisted human-computer interactive exoskeleton robot rehabilitation system, which scores the subjects according to the questionnaire and judges the effectiveness of the robot through the subjective feedback of the subjects. Wu et al. [5] arranged two patients to wear the developed exoskeleton rehabilitation robot for 8 weeks of rehabilitation training. The study conducted a walking ability test before and after each training to assess people's exercise ability, speed, and endurance.

Objective evaluation parameter comparison is an effective rehabilitation evaluation method, which conduct rehabilitation evaluation based on kinematic parameters and physiological parameters [6]. The Medical Research Council (MRC) scale is graded according to limb resistance to gravity and muscle contraction [7]. Brunnstrom scale is a qualitative grading evaluation scale, which makes judgments according to the state of coordinated movement, separated movement and completion of specific actions during movement [8]. Rivermead Mobility Index (RMI) [9], modified Ashworth scale [10], Fugl-Meyer motor function score [11] and Berg Balance Scale [12] are quantitative evaluation methods refined based on the above-mentioned grading scale, with medical theoretical basis, and evaluation results are accurate. However, the above evaluation scale needs to comprehensively evaluate multiple items, and the time cost is high.

Gait analysis is the study of human movement based on gait parameters, including the measurement, description, and evaluation of human movement characteristics [13]. The gait cycle can be divided into a series of gait events [14], and analyze the motor function of patients according to the time and proportion of gait events, objectively and quantitatively display the effect of rehabilitation treatment.

This paper researches and develops a set of lower limb motion function rehabilitation evaluation method and system based on gait parameter analysis. The system combines the advantages of gait analysis and scale method, obtains the gait characteristic parameters of healthy people and stroke patients through gait information data acquisition experiment, and analyzes the characteristic differences of the two parameters. Based on this characteristic difference, the rehabilitation evaluation regression model of FMA lower limb motor function score is established and applied to the rehabilitation evaluation software system. In addition, the system can also be used for the rehabilitation evaluation of people with lower limb motor dysfunction after the rehabilitation training of lower limb rehabilitation exoskeleton robot.

2 Design of Multi-index Rehabilitation Evaluation Model

Compare the sample characteristic parameters, explore the key information that can reflect the motion ability of stroke patients is weaker than that of healthy people, and use it as the information source for the rehabilitation evaluation index.

Multiple linear regression analysis on FMA score is performed for characteristic parameters. The multiple linear regression model is shown in (1)

$$Y = \beta_0 + \beta_1 X_1 + \beta_2 X_2 + \ldots + \beta_n X_n + \varepsilon \tag{1}$$

where Y is the explained variable, which is an n-dimensional vector, representing n samples, independent variable X_i is the $n \times p$ matrix, β_0 is the constant term coefficient, β_i is the regression coefficient ($i = 1, 2, \ldots, n$), and ε is the random error vector.

The regression coefficient is obtained by the least square regression method. Calculate the partial derivative of the sum of squares of residuals (SSE) with respect to their respective variables, and the result should be 0 to obtain (2) and solve it to obtain the estimated value of regression coefficient.

$$\frac{\partial SSE}{\partial \beta_i} = -2 \sum \left(Y - \widehat{Y} \right) X_i = 0 \tag{2}$$

To avoid the correlation of characteristic parameters affecting the accuracy of regression model, it is necessary to check the multicollinearity between characteristic parameters. When collinearity occurs, the accuracy of the model can be ensured by gradually excluding independent variables with strong correlation.

The degree of collinearity of the model is measured by the Variance Inflation Factor (VIF), that is, the ratio of the variance of the regression coefficient estimator to the variance that the assumed independent variables are not linearly correlated, as shown in (3).

$$VIF_i = \frac{1}{1 - R_i^2} \tag{3}$$

where, R_i is the multiple correlation variable of the independent variable X_i for the regression analysis to other independent variables. The larger the VIF, the stronger the collinearity. When $0 < VIF < 10$, there is no multicollinearity. When $10 \leq VIF < 100$, the variable has multicollinearity. When $VIF \geq 100$, multicollinearity is very serious.

After the collinearity test of each parameter, the significance test of each regression coefficient is also required to determine the influence of each variable on the dependent variable. First, propose hypotheses $H_0 : \beta_i = 0$, $H_1 : \beta_i \neq 0$, and then calculate the test statistic t, as shown in (4)

$$t_i = \frac{\widehat{\beta_i}}{S_i} \, t(n - k - 1) \tag{4}$$

where, S_i represents the standard deviation of the sampling distribution corresponding to the regression coefficient $\widehat{\beta_i}$.

When t_i is greater than the critical value, accept H_1, and the regression coefficient has a significant impact on the value of the dependent variable; otherwise, accept H_0, and the regression coefficient has no significant impact on the value of the dependent variable.

3 Gait Data Acquisition and Characteristic Parameter Calculation

3.1 Gait Data Selection

Collect the gait data of healthy people and stroke patients, extract the data characteristics, and analyze the differences of characteristic parameters, and establish the evaluation system of lower limb motion function of stroke patients according to the characteristics.

(1) Inclusion criteria of lower limb motor dysfunction group:

- Conform the diagnostic criteria of stroke
- Unilateral lower limb motor dysfunction
- Can walk independently for more than 60m without assistance
- Cognitive function Mini-mental State Examination score > 16

(2) Exclusion Criteria:

- Nerve injury or bone and joint disease, lower limb soft tissue injury
- Patients with severe heart, lung, liver, and kidney function diseases
- Visual conditions such as cataracts, hemianopia, and severe refractive errors

(3) Falling off and removal standard:

- The deviation from the straight line along with walk is too large
- Withdrawal from gait experiment

3.2 Gait Information Collection

The structure of gait measurement system shown in Fig. 1. In the experiment, the 9-axis inertial sensor is fixed on the human foot, and the kinematics information of the subject's foot can be measured in real time. The data is transmitted to the gait information management software of the upper computer through Bluetooth communication and saved for subsequent data analysis. The subjects move from one end to the other at a constant speed along the test site with a linear distance of 10 m, then stop for 3S, turn around, stand still, and repeat the process for 6 times. The rehabilitation training physician gave FMA scores to the subjects in the dysfunction group, and the researchers recorded the scores.

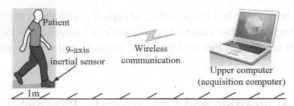

Fig. 1. Gait measurement system and data collector

3.3 Calculation of Gait Characteristic Parameters

Gait time parameter refers to the time when the left and right lower limbs of the subject are at rest and moving in a gait cycle. It is obtained by measuring the triaxial acceleration data of the subject's foot movement through the gait measurement system. Take the modulus value of the acceleration values of the three axes to obtain the sum acceleration of foot movement. Figure 2(a) and (b) show the sensor installation method and gait sequence respectively. Figure 3 shows the triaxial acceleration curve of the subject during normal walking, in which ax, ay, Az and sum represent the x-axis, y-axis, z-axis and sum acceleration respectively. Ay and Az fluctuate around 0, while ax mainly fluctuates around 1, which means that they are always affected by the gravity component.

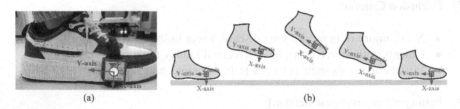

(a)   (b)

Fig. 2. Sensor installation method and gait sequence

Conduct zero position test on the sum acceleration, compare the sum acceleration with the upper and lower threshold range of zero position and determine the motion state of the foot. This paper set the threshold to 0.1. Detect the sum acceleration waveform and filter out the mutation points with too small time interval, and get the results as shown in Fig. 4. In Fig. 4, the red curve is the sum acceleration curve, the blue is the motion state detection result curve, the value of 0 represents rest and the value of 1 represents motion. It can be observed that the motion state of the foot can be well distinguished.

• Gait time proportion parameter

The time proportion parameter can reflect the difference in walking mode between healthy people and stroke patients. Formulas (5) and (6) are the calculation methods of

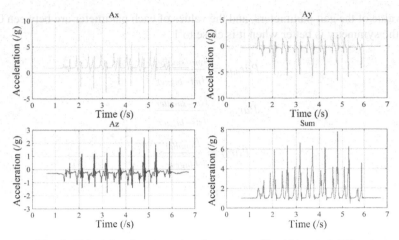

Fig. 3. Triaxial and sum acceleration curves of healthy people's feet

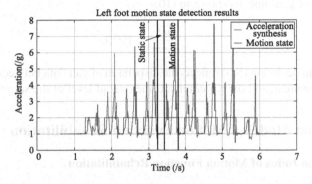

Fig. 4. Motion state detection

gait time proportion parameters. Where Par_{mt} is the motion time proportion parameter and Par_{st} is the static time proportion parameter.

$$Par_{mt} = \frac{t_{nor-mt}}{T} \tag{5}$$

$$Par_{st} = \frac{t_{nor-st}}{T} \tag{6}$$

where t_{mt} is motion time, t_{st} is static time, and T is gait cycle.

- Gait time symmetry parameters

The lower limb motion of stroke patients showed asymmetry in motion time and rest time compared with healthy people. Formulas (7)–(9) represent the motion time symmetry parameters, static time symmetry parameters and gait cycle symmetry parameters of both lower limbs. The denominators of the three gait cycle parameters are set to the larger value of the gait parameters, and the values of each parameter are between 0 and 1, and the symmetry is better when it is close to 1.

$$Par_{mts} = \frac{t_{mt-smaller}}{t_{mt-bigger}} \tag{7}$$

$$Par_{sts} = \frac{t_{sts-smaller}}{t_{sts-bigger}} \tag{8}$$

$$Par_{Ts} = \frac{T_{smaller}}{T_{bigger}} \tag{9}$$

- Gait time variability parameters (GTVP)

Confirmed that gait variability can reflect motion ability. Due to the comparison of the degree of variability of parameters in different dimensions, to facilitate the determination of rehabilitation evaluation model, the ratio of SD and mean is used as the coefficient of variation (CV) of gait time, as shown in (10).

$$CV = \frac{SD}{mean} \times 100\% \tag{10}$$

The standard deviation (SD) reflects the dispersion of gait data between steps during lower limb movement, and the mean reflects the overall level of the sample.

4 Evaluation Model of Motion Function Rehabilitation

4.1 Evaluation Index of Motion Function Rehabilitation

The selection of evaluation indexes of lower limb motor function should consider the influence of age, gender, and disease of motion ability. After analysis, the parameters of healthy people are not related to gender but related to age. The characteristic parameters of healthy people and dyskinesia are analyzed and compared, and the following conclusions are drawn:

(1) The parameters are selected as the evaluation index of motor function in the age group of 20–50-years-old: a) the static time and gait cycle of the affected side and unaffected side. b) the affected and unaffected side motion time proportional parameter and the static time proportional parameter. c) the motion and static time symmetry parameters. d) the CV of motion time of the affected side and the unaffected side, and the CV of the cycle.
(2) The parameters are selected as the evaluation index of motor function in the age group of 51–80-year-old: a) the motion time symmetry parameters and static time symmetry parameters of the affected and unaffected sides. b) the CV of the motion time of the affected side and the unaffected side, and the CV of the cycle.

4.2 Multi-index-Based Evaluation Model of Motion Function Rehabilitation

- Characteristic parameter preprocessing

Before using each indicator to determine the evaluation model, dimensionless and reverse indicator forward processing is performed on the selected features. Since the characteristic parameters of the 20–50 age group include the characteristic parameters of the 51–80 age group, the two processing methods are the same.

The evaluation indexes of motor function are selected for the age group of 20–50 years old: a) the static time and gait cycle of the affected side and unaffected side; b) the affected and unaffected side motion time proportional parameter and the static time proportional parameter; c) the motion and static time symmetry parameters; d) the CV of motion time of the affected side and the unaffected side and the CV of the cycle. The parameters in a) and b) are absolute values of time, which need to be transformed into relative values reflecting the motor function of the lower limbs, the processing method as shown in (11).

$$P = \frac{Comp_{max} - Comp}{Comp_{max} - Comp_{min}} \tag{11}$$

where $Comp_{max}$ is the maximum modulus of the difference between the mean values of the characteristic parameters of the samples in the disabled group and the healthy group, and $Comp_{min}$ is the minimum modulus value, which is generally 0. From (11) that the gait time parameters and gait time proportional parameters of the affected are transformed into values between 0–1, and the closer to 1, the motor function is better.

The gait time symmetry parameter reflects the ability of people to control the motion of the lower limbs. Too large parameter will lead to unstable walking, which is a reverse index. Carry out the reverse index forward processing, and the processing method is the same as (11), in which $Comp_{max}$ takes the empirical value of 30%, $Comp_{min} = 0$.

- Rehabilitation evaluation model

The characteristic parameters of the 20–50-year-old age group are analyzed for collinearity diagnosis, and the proportion of motion time on the affected side among the characteristic parameters with the highest variance inflation factor is repeatedly excluded until the VIF value of all characteristic parameters is less than 10, and the results in Table 1 are obtained. The independent variables of the model are the proportion of motion time of unaffected side, the proportion of static time of affected side and the symmetry parameters of motion time. To avoid the reduction of accuracy, the independent variables of the model are in a fixed range, and the 95% confidence interval lists the variation range of the parameters.

The model for the age group of 20–50 is as (12)

$$Score_1 = Ra_{hm} * 15.463 + Ra_{as} * 8.384 + Sym_m * 10.06 \tag{12}$$

where, Ra_{hm} is the proportion of motion time of unaffected side, Ra_{as} is the proportion of static time of affected side, and Sym_m is the motion time symmetry parameter.

Table 1. Multiple linear regression results of 20–50 years old

Par	RC	SD	Sta	95% CI	Sig	VIF
Proportional of unaffected motion time	15.46301	2.303	5.310	[0.599, 1]	0.001	4.847
Proportional of unaffected static time	8.383562	2.006	3.169	[0.142, 0.979]	0.016	3.984
Motion time symmetry parameter	10.06027	1.324	2.656	[0.265, 1]	0.033	8.207
Static time symmetry parameter	1.33516	7.368	0.557	~	0.595	3.297
CV of motion time on affected	−1.24201	8.025	-0.397	~	0.703	5.709

* Par = Parameter, RC = regression coefficient, Sta = Statistic, CI = confidence interval, Sig = Significant

The same operation is performed for the age group of 51–80, and the results in Table 2 are obtained. The model is as (13).

$$Score_2 = Sym_m * 11.976 + CV_{hm} * 7.337 + CV_{ap} * 15.911 \tag{13}$$

where Sym_m is the symmetry parameter of motion time, CV_{hm} is the CV of motion time of unaffected side, and CV_{ap} is the CV of cycle on the affected side.

Table 2. Multiple linear regression results of 51–80 years old

Par	RC	SD	Sta	95% CI	Sig	VIF
Motion time symmetry parameter	11.976	1.854	6.459	[0.67,1]	< 0.001	3.961
CV of motion time on unaffected	7.337	2.386	3.075	[0.14,1]	0.018	6.810
CV of affected side cycle	15.911	3.136	5.073	[0.749,1]	0.001	9.385

- Goodness of fit test of rehabilitation evaluation model

In statistics, R^2 is used to determine the fitting degree of multiple linear regression, and its definition is shown in (14).

$$R^2 = 1 - \frac{SSE}{SST} = 1 - \frac{\sum \left(Y_i - \hat{Y}_i \right)^2}{\sum \left(Y_i - \overline{Y} \right)^2} \tag{14}$$

where SSE is the sum of squares of residuals and SST is the sum of squares of total deviations.

From (14) that $0 \leq R^2 \leq 1$, when R^2 is closer to 1, the fitting degree of the regression model is higher. Since R^2 is affected by the number of independent variables, the influence needs to be eliminated. By dividing the residual sum of squares and the sum of squares of the total deviation by their respective degrees of freedom, it becomes the ratio of the mean square error, the adjusted R^2 is shown in (15).

$$\bar{R}^2 = 1 - \frac{SSE/(n - k - 1)}{SST/(n - 1)} \tag{15}$$

The $\bar{R}^2$ of the regression model for the 20–50 age group is 0.978, and the model has a good fitting effect. The samples of the healthy group and the disabled group are respectively brought into the model, the score of the disabled group is 16.81 ± 3.16, and the score of the healthy group is 30.75 ± 3.62, and the scores of the two groups are significantly different.

The $\bar{R}^2$ of the regression model for the 51–80 age group is 0.982, and the model has a good fitting effect. The two groups of samples were brought into the model, and the score of the disabled group is 21.75 ± 2.9, and the score of the healthy group is 30.63 ± 1.433, and the scores of the two groups were significantly different. Formula (14), (15) can well distinguish between healthy and motion dysfunction patients aged 20–50 and 51–80.

All samples of the patient group are divided into 0–10 group, 11–20 group and 21–34 group according to the score. After being brought into the model, the score of 0–10 group is 6.23 ± 1.542, that of 11–20 group is 17.12 ± 2.03, and that of 21–34 group is 29.03 ± 1.424. There are significant differences in the scores of the three groups. The evaluation model can well distinguish the degree of illness of patients.

Compared with other studies [15], this paper comprehensively considers various characteristic parameters that affect gait movement quality, and establishes a rehabilitation evaluation model, which can more accurately and truly reflect the movement and rehabilitation degree of different populations.

5 Development of Rehabilitation Evaluation System

5.1 Rehabilitation Evaluation System Architecture

The architecture of rehabilitation evaluation system is shown in Fig. 5. The data collected by the sensor interacts with the rehabilitation evaluation software system through Bluetooth wireless communication. The video monitoring device transmits the picture taken by the camera to the upper computer. The upper computer receives and processes the data, and realizes the functions of storage, analysis, and display through the rehabilitation evaluation software system.

Fig. 5. The architecture of rehabilitation evaluation system

5.2 Software Development

The software system is windows10, the compilation environment is QT 5.14.1, and the development language is C++. The video equipment is raspberry pie V3b+, and the camera is Raspberry PI Camera. The composition of each module of the system is shown in Fig. 6, which is divided into four parts: communication module, real-time data display module, historical data analysis module and database interface module.

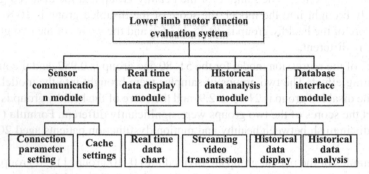

Fig. 6. The composition of each functional module of motion function evaluation system

5.3 System Function Verification

Login system: the first login requires user registration, including name, age, gender, contact information, date of birth, location of affected party, login password. The login interface is shown in Fig. 7(a). And then, establish a connection with the sensor by setting the wireless communication format and enter the main interface, as shown in Fig. 7(b). The left part of Fig. 7(b) is to view by accessing the IP address of the webcam. The right part of Fig. 7(b) is the data collected by the sensor.

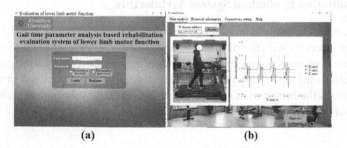

(a)   (b)

Fig. 7. Scoring system interface

Enter the score evaluation interface to observe the user's historical gait scores, as shown in Fig. 8(a). The interface filters data through time in the background and uses the model to analyze the data. Figure 8(b) is the historical data information display interface, from which the user's lower limb motion ability has been significantly improved.

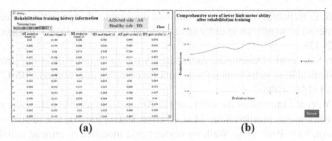

(a)   (b)

Fig. 8. Historical gait of a user

6 Conclusion

This paper proposes a rehabilitation evaluation method and system of lower limb motor function based on gait parameter analysis. The methods based on the calculation of gait information-related parameters, the age and gender differences of healthy people, and the gait information differences between health and lower limb motion disorders were compared to determine the characteristic parameters of motion function evaluation. Multicollinearity and significance analysis were used to determine the rehabilitation evaluation indexes, and a multiple linear regression model of Fugl-Meyer motor function evaluation score is established to replace the lower limb score of FMA as the evaluation method of lower limb motor function of stroke patients. The goodness of fit test method is used to prove the excellence of the proposed evaluation method, and a lower limb motor function evaluation system is established for the rehabilitation evaluation of lower limb motor function in stroke patients.

Acknowledgment. This work was supported in part by the National Natural Science Foundation of China under Grant NSFC U1813212, in part by the Science and Technology Planning Project of Guangdong Province, China under Grant 2020B121201012.

References

1. Makihara, T., et al.: Shoulder motion assistance using a single-joint Hybrid Assistive limb® robot: evaluation of its safety and validity in healthy adults. J. Orthop. Surg. **25**(3), 1–6 (2017)
2. Pérez-nombela, S., et al.: Physiological Evaluation of Different Control Modes of Lower Limb Robotic Exoskeleton H2 in Patients with Incomplete Spinal Cord Injury, vol. 15, pp. 343–348 (2017)
3. Rodgers, H., et al.: Robot assisted training for the upper limb after stroke (RATULS): a multicentre randomised controlled trial. Lancet **394**(10192), 51–62 (2019)
4. Nam, H.S., Hong, N., Cho, M., Lee, C., Seo, H.G., Kim, S.: Vision-assisted interactive human-in-the-loop distal upper limb rehabilitation robot and its clinical usability test. Appl. Sci. **9**(15), 1–12 (2019)
5. Wu, C.H., Mao, H.F., Hu, J.S., Wang, T.Y., Tsai, Y.J., Hsu, W.L.: The effects of gait training using powered lower limb exoskeleton robot on individuals with complete spinal cord injury. J. Neuroeng. Rehabil. **15**(1), 1–10 (2018)

6. Blackwood, J.: Reliability, validity and minimal detectable change in the Timed Up and Go and five times sit to stand tests in older adults with early cognitive loss. J. Physiother. Rehabil **5**, 58–65 (2017)
7. Olafsdottir, S.A., et al.: Developing ActivABLES for community-dwelling stroke survivors using the Medical Research Council framework for complex interventions. BMC Health Serv. Res. **20**(1), 1–14 (2020)
8. Huang, C.Y., et al.: Improving the utility of the Brunnstrom recovery stages in patients with stroke: validation and quantification. Med. (United States) **95**(31), 1–8 (2016)
9. Lim, J.Y., An, S.H., Park, D.S.: Walking velocity and modified rivermead mobility index as discriminatory measures for functional ambulation classification of chronic stroke patients. Hong Kong Physiother. J. **39**(2), 125–132 (2019)
10. Freire, B., Bochehin do Valle, M., Lanferdini, F.J., Foschi, C.V.S., Abou, L., Pietta-Dias, C.: Cut-off score of the modified Ashworth scale corresponding to walking ability and functional mobility in individuals with chronic stroke. Disabil. Rehabil. 1–5 (2022)
11. Rech, K.D., Salazar, A.P., Marchese, R.R., Schifino, G., Cimolin, V., Pagnussat, A.S.: Fugl-Meyer assessment scores are related with kinematic measures in people with chronic hemiparesis after stroke. J. Stroke Cerebrovasc. Dis. **29**(1), 1–8 (2020)
12. Liao, W.L., Chang, C.W., Sung, P.Y., Hsu, W.N., Lai, M.W., Tsai, S.W.: The berg balance scale at admission can predict community ambulation at discharge in patients with stroke. Med. **57**(6), 1–8 (2021)
13. Liu, X., et al.: Wearable devices for gait analysis in intelligent healthcare. Front. Comput. Sci. **3**(May), 1–8 (2021)
14. Wu, J., et al.: An intelligent in-shoe system for gait monitoring and analysis with optimized sampling and real-time visualization capabilities. Sensors **21**(8), 1–19 (2021)
15. Serrao, M., et al.: Prediction of responsiveness of gait variables to rehabilitation training in Parkinson's disease. Front. Neurol. **10**(JUL), 1–12 (2019)

A Portable Fully Coupled Parallel Continuum Manipulator for Nursing Robot: Mechanical Design and Modeling

Chuanxin Ning and Ting Zhang[✉]

Robotics and Microsystems Center, College of Mechanical and Electrical Engineering,
Soochow University, Suzhou, China
tzhang@suda.edu.cn

Abstract. Robot nurses have become well-known for their contributions to the healthcare industry. Compared with traditional manipulators, cable-driven continuum manipulators have many advantages, such as small manipulator rotational inertia, high dexterity, and large workspace. It is especially suitable for working environment with complex structure and narrow space. In this paper, a portable fully coupled parallel continuum manipulator is designed. The manipulator adopts a spherical parallel mechanism as the basic drive unit. Multiple identical spherical parallel mechanisms are connected in series to form a continuum manipulator. The continuum manipulator installs the motor on the base of the manipulator. To drive the operating platform through the cable, the moment of inertia of the manipulator is reduced, the forward kinematics and inverse kinematics modeling of the basic drive unit are carried out, and the statics modeling of the mechanism is carried out. It solves the problem that the existing traditional manipulator cannot work in a space with a complex structure and a high degree of narrowness, and improves the problems that the existing continuum manipulator has a weak carrying capacity and a small movement space.

Keywords: Parallel continuum robot · Statics analysis · Kinematics

1 Introduction

The development of nursing robots presents a major step forward in the fields of robotics in healthcare. Many older adults have been isolated at home due to COVID-19 pandemic. Nursing robots can assist with food and medication delivery, and patient movement and transfer. Traditional rigid robots have been widely used in various industries such as military, industry, agriculture, and service industries. However, most of these rigid robots have six or less degrees of freedom, so they are not suitable for work environments with complex structures and confined spaces [1, 2], for example, space docking, rescue and disaster relief, bending pipes, inside collapsed buildings search and rescue work. Therefore, there is an increasing need to develop robotic structures with redundancy that can work in spaces with complex shapes. Currently, continuum robots are an important solution to this problem.

© The Author(s), under exclusive license to Springer Nature Switzerland AG 2022
H. Liu et al. (Eds.): ICIRA 2022, LNAI 13457, pp. 103–112, 2022.
https://doi.org/10.1007/978-3-031-13835-5_10

In nature, fish, snakes, and other vertebrates rely on the dense arrangement of vertebral joints to achieve continuous deformation; invertebrates such as octopuses and earthworms can achieve continuous deformation by relying on their own skeletal muscles or muscles. Similar to the body structure of animals, current continuum robots can also be divided into two categories: hyper-redundant robots with a spine structure [3–6] and a spineless continuum robot structure [6–10]. Hyper-redundant robots have high load-carrying capacity due to the use of joints with rigid components, but poor flexibility. Invertebrate continuum robots use flexible components that increase the robot's flexibility but reduce the robot's load capacity.

Different from the traditional robot, the cable-driven robot is a special kind of robot, the motor is installed at the bottom of the drive joint, and the operating platform is driven by the cable. Compared with traditional direct-drive methods, cable-drive technology offers a new approach to the design of robotic systems and a new solution to overcome existing problems. Because the cable-driven robot can design the layout of the drive module more flexibly, it has the advantages of light weight, easy modification, simple structural design, fast response, and low inertia. Cable-driven robots have been widely used in production and life, and scholars from all over the world have also conducted a lot of research on cable-driven robots [11, 12].

Combining the cable drive with the continuum manipulator, heavy-duty motors and other drives can be placed on the base, which further reduces the size of the continuum manipulator and improves its flexibility, enabling it to adapt to complex working conditions. However, during the operation, the operation accuracy of the robotic arm will be affected by factors such as the object's own weight and load, and the carrying capacity is weak. Therefore, this paper proposes a new type of continuum manipulator with a parallel mechanism as the motion unit, and conducts kinematic modeling and static modeling for the motion unit of the manipulator, which lays the foundation for the subsequent research on the manipulator.

2 Structural Design of Continuum Manipulator

In the current design and application of cable-driven continuum robots [13, 14], influenced by factors such as continuum structure, elastic bending characteristics and driving mode, the continuum robot has shortcomings such as low carrying capacity and poor stiffness performance. It is greatly limited when it is used in practical working conditions, in order to solve the shortcomings of traditional rigid continuum manipulators such as complex structure, small movement space, high cost and low bearing capacity, and improve the load capacity and position accuracy of the continuum robot. In this paper, a parallel continuum manipulator is designed, and its structure is shown in Fig. 1.

The parallel continuum manipulator adopts multiple spherical parallel mechanisms in series to form the manipulator, the use of spherical parallel mechanism can not only increase the overall rigidity of the manipulator, but also bend the manipulator to a larger angle to meet the needs of any working condition, the outside of the robotic arm is wrapped with soft silicone to protect the robotic arm. Each spherical parallel mechanism is connected together by connecting rods in turn, the spherical parallel mechanism is composed of a moving platform, a static platform and a link mechanism, in which the

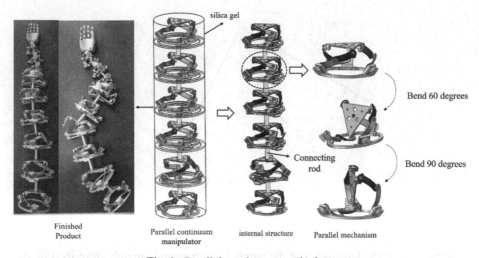

Fig. 1. Parallel continuum manipulator

link mechanism consists of three active parts and three driven parts. The moving platform is fixed on the static platform through three symmetrically distributed link mechanisms. In each linkage, the two ends of the driving piece are respectively connected with the static platform and the driven piece through the rotating pair, and the other end of the driven piece is connected with the moving platform through the spherical pair. Its specific structure is shown in the parallel mechanism in Fig. 1.

3   The Kinematics of Parallel Mechanism

Figure 1 shows the kinematic model of the parallel mechanism. It is composed of the static platform, the moving platform and the link mechanism. The link mechanism has three identical limbs structure, Each ink mechanism consists of two kinematic branches.

In each link mechanism, there are two revolute pairs R and one spherical pair S. The point O represents the spherical center of the parallel mechanism. The point D represents the center of the moving platform. The point E represents the center of the static platform. $A_i, B_i, C_i(i = 1, 2, 3)$ represent the kinematic centers of the corresponding branch chains, respectively (Fig. 2).

The static coordinate system O–XYZ is established on the static platform, O–X, O–Y and O–Z pass through A_1, A_2 and A_3 on the static platform, respectively. The moving coordinate system O–xyz is established on the moving platform, O–x, O–y and O–z pass through C_1, C_2 and C_3 on the moving platform, respectively. The radius of the two kinematic branches are r_1 and r_2 respectively. The angle between the two ends of the branch chain is δ_1 and δ_2.

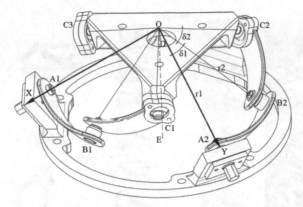

Fig. 2. The parallel mechanism

In this paper, the kinematics of the parallel mechanism is mainly described by the Euler angle method in the form of Z–Y–X [15, 16].

$$R = \begin{bmatrix} \cos\alpha\cos\beta & \cos\alpha\sin\beta\sin\gamma - sin\alpha cos\gamma & \sin\alpha\sin\gamma + \cos\alpha\sin\beta\cos\gamma \\ \sin\alpha\cos\beta & \cos\alpha\cos\gamma + \sin\alpha\sin\beta\sin\gamma & \sin\alpha\sin\beta cos\gamma - \cos\alpha\sin\gamma \\ -\sin\beta & \cos\beta\sin\gamma & \cos\beta\cos\gamma \end{bmatrix}$$

(1)

3.1 The Forward Kinematic Analysis of Parallel Mechanism

The forward kinematic analysis of the parallel mechanism is the process of solving the position of the moving platform by knowing the three driving angles θ_1, θ_2 and θ_3 of the static platform of the parallel mechanism.

When the parallel mechanism is in the initial position, as shown in Fig. 1. The moving platform and the static platform are parallel to each other, and the crank and connecting rod of each branch chain are parallel to each other. It can be seen from the graph analysis.

The coordinates A_i of the static platform in the $O - XYZ$ system are obtained as follows:

$$\begin{bmatrix} A_1 \\ A_2 \\ A_3 \end{bmatrix} = \begin{bmatrix} r_1 & 0 & 0 \\ 0 & r_1 & 0 \\ 0 & 0 & r_1 \end{bmatrix}$$

(2)

The coordinates B_i of the static platform in the $O - XYZ$ system are obtained as follows:

$$B_i = \begin{bmatrix} B_1 \\ B_2 \\ B_3 \end{bmatrix} = \begin{bmatrix} cos\delta_1 & sin\delta_1 sin\theta_1 & sin\delta_1 cos\theta_1 \\ sin\delta_1 cos\theta_2 & cos\delta_1 & sin\delta_1 sin\theta_2 \\ sin\delta_1 sin\theta_3 & sin\delta_1 cos\theta_3 & cos\delta_1 \end{bmatrix} \times r_1$$

(3)

The coordinates C_i of the static platform in the $O - XYZ$ system are obtained as follows:

$$C_i = \begin{bmatrix} C_1 \\ C_2 \\ C_3 \end{bmatrix} = \begin{bmatrix} \cos(\delta_1 + \delta_2) & \sin(\delta_1 + \delta_2)\sin\theta_1 & \sin(\delta_1 + \delta_2)\cos\theta_1 \\ \sin(\delta_1 + \delta_2)\cos\theta_2 & \cos(\delta_1 + \delta_2) & \sin(\delta_1 + \delta_2)\sin\theta_2 \\ \sin(\delta_1 + \delta_2)\sin\theta_3 & \sin(\delta_1 + \delta_2)\cos\theta_3 & \cos(\delta_1 + \delta_2) \end{bmatrix} \times r_2 \quad (4)$$

Assume that the centers C_i of the three spherical pairs connecting each connecting rod to the moving platform are all located on the unit sphere, When the rotation angle of the crank is $\theta_i(i = 1, 2, 3)$, the coordinates C_i of the static platform in the $O - XYZ$ system, based on the Rodriguez and index formula, can be expressed as

$$C_i(\theta_i) = e^{\hat{a}_i\theta_i} e^{\hat{b}_i\eta_i} c_i \quad (5)$$

where a_i, b_i, and c_i are the unit vectors of A_i, B_i, and C_i, respectively, η_i is the angle between the crank and the connecting rod called passive angle.

In the parallel mechanism, The following equation can be obtained

$$\left\| \overline{C_iC_j} \right\|^2 = (C_i - C_j)^T (C_i - C_j) \quad (6)$$

In Eq. 6, $i = 1, 2, 3, j = 1, 2, 3; i \neq j$.
The derivative of both sides of Eq. 6 can be obtained:

$$dl_{ij} = \frac{(C_i - C_j)^T}{\left\| \overline{C_iC_j} \right\|} (dC_i - dC_j) \quad (7)$$

From Eq. 7, the following expression can be obtained

$$d\eta_i = J^{-1}dl \quad (8)$$

where

$$J = \begin{bmatrix} \frac{(C_2-C_1)^T}{\|\overline{C_1C_2}\|}\dot{C}_1 & \frac{(C_2-C_1)^T}{\|\overline{C_1C_2}\|}\dot{C}_2 & 0 \\ 0 & -\frac{(C_3-C_2)^T}{\|\overline{C_3C_2}\|}\dot{C}_2 & \frac{(C_3-C_1)^T}{\|\overline{C_1C_3}\|}\dot{C}_3 \\ -\frac{(C_3-C_1)^T}{\|\overline{C_1C_3}\|}\dot{C}_1 & 0 & \frac{(C_3-C_1)^T}{\|\overline{C_1C_3}\|}\dot{C}_3 \end{bmatrix}$$

$$\dot{C}_i = e^{\hat{a}_i\theta_i} e^{\hat{b}_i\eta_i} \hat{b}_i c_i$$

$$dl = \begin{bmatrix} dl_{12} & dl_{23} & dl_{13} \end{bmatrix}^T$$

From Eq. 8, The iterative formula can be obtained

$$\eta^{k+1} = \eta^k + (J^{-1}dl)^k \quad (9)$$

Using the above-formula iterative formula and Rodriguez and index volume formulas can calculate the position of the moving platform of the parallel mechanism relative to the position of the static platform, the coordinates of any point in the moving coordinate system can be obtained by using formula (10).

$$O_0 = RO \quad (10)$$

where O_0 is the coordinate of the static coordinate system, O is the coordinate of the moving coordinate system.

3.2 The Inverse Kinematic Analysis of Parallel Mechanism

The inverse kinematic analysis of the parallel mechanism is to solve the three driving angles $\theta 1$, $\theta 2$ and $\theta 3$ for a given orientation (α, β, γ) of the moving platform.

the coordinates C_i of the moving platform in the $O - xyz$ system are obtained as follows:

$$C_0 = \begin{bmatrix} C_1 \\ C_2 \\ C_3 \end{bmatrix} = \begin{bmatrix} r_2 & 0 & 0 \\ 0 & r_2 & 0 \\ 0 & 0 & r_2 \end{bmatrix} \tag{11}$$

When the moving platform moves, the coordinates C_i of the static platform in the $O - XYZ$ system are obtained as follows:

$$C_i = R \times C_0$$

$$= \begin{bmatrix} cos\alpha cos\beta & cos\alpha sin\beta sin\gamma - sin\alpha cos\gamma & sin\alpha sin\gamma + cos\alpha sin\beta cos\gamma \\ sin\alpha cos\beta & cos\alpha cos\gamma + sin\alpha sin\beta sin\gamma & sin\alpha sin\beta cos\gamma - cos\alpha sin\gamma \\ -sin\beta & cos\beta sin\gamma & cos\beta cos\gamma \end{bmatrix} \times r_2 \tag{12}$$

When the three angles α, β and γ of the moving platform are known, the rotating pair B_i in the middle of each branch is connected to the spherical pair C_i on the moving platform by a connecting rod, and the dimensional angle of link B_iC_i is δ_2. The relationship that can be established is as follows: the constraint equation is

$$\begin{cases} cos\delta_1 \cos\alpha\cos\beta + sin\delta_1 sin\theta_1 \sin\alpha\cos\beta - \sin\beta \, sin\delta_1 cos\theta_1 = cos\delta_2 \\ sin\delta_1 cos\theta_2 (\cos\alpha\sin\beta\sin\gamma - sin\alpha cos\gamma) + cos\delta_1(\cos\alpha\cos\gamma + \sin\alpha\sin\beta\sin\gamma) \\ \qquad + sin\delta_1 sin\theta_2 \cos\beta\sin\gamma = cos\delta_2 \\ sin\delta_1 sin\theta_3 (\sin\alpha\sin\gamma + \cos\alpha\sin\beta\cos\gamma) + sin\delta_1 cos\theta_3 (\sin\alpha\sin\beta cos\gamma - \cos\alpha\sin\gamma) \\ \qquad + cos\delta_1 \cos\beta\cos\gamma = cos\delta_2 \end{cases} \tag{13}$$

Therefore, arranged from Eq. 13, the inverse kinematic analysis of the parallel mechanism is obtained as follows

$$\theta_i = 2arctan\frac{F_i \pm \sqrt{F_i{}^2 + G_i{}^2 - H_i{}^2}}{H_i + G_i} \tag{14}$$

where

$$\begin{cases} F_1 = sin\delta_1 \sin\alpha cos\beta \\ G_1 = -\sin\beta \, sin\delta_1 \\ H_1 = cos\delta_2 - cos\delta_1 \cos\alpha\cos\beta \end{cases} \tag{15}$$

$$\begin{cases} F_2 = sin\delta_1 \cos\beta\sin\gamma \\ G_2 = sin\delta_1(\cos\alpha\sin\beta\sin\gamma - sin\alpha cos\gamma) \\ H_2 = cos\delta_2 - cos\delta_1(\cos\alpha\cos\gamma + \sin\alpha\sin\beta\sin\gamma) \end{cases} \tag{16}$$

$$\begin{cases} F_3 = sin\delta_1(\sin\alpha\sin\gamma + \cos\alpha\sin\beta\cos\gamma) \\ G_3 = sin\delta_1(\sin\alpha\sin\beta cos\gamma - \cos\alpha\sin\gamma) \\ H_3 = cos\delta_2 - cos\delta_1 \cos\beta\cos\gamma \end{cases} \tag{17}$$

4   Static Analysis of the Continuum Robotic Arm

Because the actual force analysis of the parallel mechanism is relatively complex, it is necessary to ignore the weight of the platform and the friction at each connection when performing static analysis.

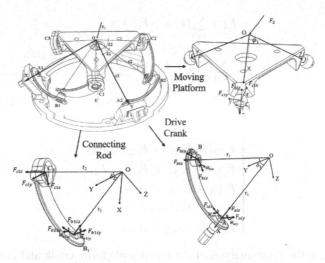

Fig. 3. Parallel mechanism is subjected to external load

Because the parallel mechanism is subjected to the action of the external load F_2 passing through the center O of the sphere. Thus, as illustrate in Fig. 3, the force analysis of the parallel mechanism needs to consider the static analysis of the force F_2 on the moving platform. When the parallel mechanism is in equilibrium, the force analysis of each connecting rod of the parallel mechanism is carried out separately.

Since the crank mechanism and the connecting rod mechanism of the parallel mechanism are not completely coincident at points B and B_1, OB_1 and OB are on the same straight line, when the angle between them is φ, the relationship between the two coordinates can be obtained from the rotation matrix in the homogeneous transformation matrix as follows [17],

$$R = \begin{bmatrix} \cos\varphi & -\sin\varphi & 0 \\ \sin\varphi & \cos\varphi & 0 \\ 0 & 0 & 1 \end{bmatrix} \tag{18}$$

So the force of B_1 at point B can be expressed as $R \bullet F_{b1ix}$, then according to the action and reaction forces, we can get:

$$F_{bix} = F_{b1ix}\cos\varphi \tag{19}$$

$$F_{biy} = F_{b1ix}\sin\varphi \tag{20}$$

$$F_{biz} = F_{b1iz} \tag{21}$$

According to the force analysis of the moving platform, crank and connecting rod mechanism, simplify the moving platform to get the new force condition of the moving platform,

$$F_2 + \sum_{i=1}^{3}(F_{cix} + F_{ciz}) = 0 \tag{22}$$

$$\sum_{i=1}^{3}(F_{cix} + F_{ciy})R_1 = 0 \tag{23}$$

Simplify F_2, F_{cix}, F_{ciz} to O–XYZ, the following expression can be obtained:

$$\begin{cases} F_{c1xx} + F_{c1xy} + F_{c1z} = F_{2z} \\ F_{c2xy} + F_{c2xz} + F_{c2z} = F_{2x} \\ F_{c3xx} + F_{c3xz} + F_{c3z} = F_{2y} \\ F_{c1xy} + F_{c2xx} = 0 \\ F_{c1xz} + F_{c3xy} = 0 \\ F_{c2xy} + F_{c3xx} = 0 \end{cases} \tag{24}$$

According to the force analysis of the moving platform, crank and connecting rod mechanism, get the new stress state of the crank,

$$\begin{cases} F_{biz} \cos \delta_1 - F_{bix} \sin \delta_1 = F_{aiz} \\ F_{biz} \sin \delta_1 - F_{bix} \cos \delta_1 = F_{aix} \\ F_{aiy} = F_{b1ix} \sin \varphi \\ M_{bix} \sin \delta_1 + F_{bix} \cdot \sqrt{2r_1^2(1 - \cos \delta_1)} = 0 \\ F_{bix} = F_{b1ix} \cos \varphi \\ F_{biy} = F_{b1ix} \sin \varphi \end{cases} \tag{25}$$

According to the force analysis of the moving platform, crank and connecting rod mechanism, the connecting rod is simplified according to the above formula:

$$\begin{cases} F_{b1iz} \cos \delta_2 - F_{b1ix} \sin \delta_2 = F_{ciz} \\ F_{b1iz} \sin \delta_2 + F_{b1ix} \cos \delta_2 = F_{cix} \\ F_{ciy} = 0 \\ F_{b1iy} = 0 \end{cases} \tag{26}$$

5 Conclusion

This paper presents a portable fully coupled parallel continuum manipulator. The manipulator is mainly composed of a parallel mechanism as the basic driving unit. Multiple parallel mechanisms are connected in series to form a continuum manipulator. The kinematics and statics modeling of the basic motion unit of the manipulator is carried out. It solves the problem that the traditional rigid manipulator cannot work in a complex and highly narrow space, and improves the problem that the existing continuum manipulator has weak carrying capacity and small movement space.

Acknowledgement. This work was supported in part by the National Key R&D Program of China (2020YFC2007804), the Natural Science Foundation of the Jiangsu Higher Education Institutions of China (19KJA180009), the Natural Science Foundation of Jiangsu Province (BK20191424), the Jiangsu Frontier Leading Technology Fundamental Research Project (BK20192004D), and the Distinguished Professor of Jiangsu province.

References

1. Wolf, A., et al.: A mobile hyper redundant mechanism for search and rescue tasks. In: IEEE/RSJ International Conference on Intelligent Robots and Systems, vol. 3, pp. 2889–2895 (2003)
2. Lane, D.M., et al.: The AMADEUS dextrous subsea hand: design, modeling, and sensor processing. IEEE J. Oceanic Eng. **24**(1), 96–111 (1999)
3. Hannan, M.W., Walker, I.D.: Analysis and initial experiments for a novel elephant's trunk robot, Proceedings. In: IEEE/RSJ International Conference on Intelligent Robots and Systems, vol. 1, pp. 330–337 (2000)
4. Walker, I.D., Hannan, M.W.: A novel 'elephant's trunk' robot. In: IEEE/ASME International Conference on Advanced Intelligent Mechatronics, pp. 410–415 (1999)
5. Brown, H.B., Schwerin, M., Shammas, E., Choset, H.: Design and control of a second-generation hyper-redundant mechanism. In: IEEE/RSJ International Conference on Intelligent Robots and Systems, pp. 2603–2608 (2007)
6. Zhang, Q., Zhou, L., Wang, Z.: Design and implementation of wormlike creeping mobile robot for EAST remote maintenance system. Fusion Eng. Des. **118**, 81–97 (2017)
7. McMahan, W., et al.: Field trials and testing of the OctArm continuum manipulator. In: IEEE International Conference on Robotics and Automation, pp. 2336–2341 (2006)
8. Buckingham, R.: Snake arm robots for flexible delivery. Insight **44**, 150–151 (2002)
9. Rolf, M., Steil, J.J.: Constant curvature continuum kinematics as fast approximate model for the Bionic Handling Assistant. In: IEEE/RSJ International Conference on Intelligent Robots and Systems, pp. 3440–3446 (2012)
10. Barrientos-Diez, J., Dong, X., Axinte, D., Kell, J.: Real-time kinematics of continuum robots: modelling and validation. Robot. Comput. Integ. Manuf. **67**, 102019 (2021)
11. Kawamura, S., Kino, H., Won, C.: High-speed manipulation by using parallel wire-driven robots. Robotica **18**(1), 13–21 (2000)
12. Pott, A., et al.: Cable-driven parallel robots for industrial applications: the IPAnema system family. In: IEEE ISR, pp. 1–6 (2013)
13. Dong, X., et al.: Development of a slender continuum robotic system for on-wing inspection/repair of gas turbine engines. Robot. Comput. Integ. Manuf. **44**, 218–229 (2017)
14. Yang, Z., Zhao, B., Bo, L., Zhu, X., Xu, K.: CurviPicker: a continuum robot for pick-and-place tasks. Assem. Autom. **39**(3), 410–421 (2019)
15. Bai, S., Hansen, M.R., Angeles, J.: A robust forward-displacement analysis of spherical parallel robots. Mech. Mach. Theory **44**(12), 2204–2216 (2009)

16. Bai, S.: Optimum design of spherical parallel manipulators for a prescribed workspace. Mech. Mach. Theory **45**(2), 200–211 (2010)
17. Xiangzhou, Z., Yougao, L.; Zhiyong, D., Hongzan, B.: Statics of rotational 3-UPU parallel mechanisms based on principle of virtual work. In: IEEE International Conference on Robotics and Biomimetics, pp. 1954–1959 (2007)

A Perturbation Platform and Exoskeleton Simulator for Studying Balance Control of Hip Exoskeleton: Design and Preliminary Validation

Kaixiang Feng and Ting Zhang(✉)

College of Mechanical and Electrical Engineering, Soochow University, Suzhou 215000, China
tzhang@suda.edu.cn

Abstract. In order to deal with the problem of imbalance of the elderly in the process of walking on level ground, this paper proposes a hip exoskeleton with series elastic actuator (SEA) to assist the wearer to adjust the step width, step length and step frequency in real time during walking to maintain balance walking. Through the built multi-sensor fusion gait perturbation and perception integrated platform, the experimenter's autonomous recovery of balance experiment and exoskeleton-assisted human body's recovery of balance experiment under external wrench state were carried out respectively. The perturbations were applied in four directions to the experimenter while walking, which verified the validity of the balance evaluation model and the assisting effect of the exoskeleton in restoring the balance of human walking. Firstly, according to the established kinematics model, the displacement and velocity of the experimenter's center of mass during walking are calculated, and the system is simplified to a linear inverted pendulum model (LIPM) to evaluate the motion state. Secondly, a balance state evaluation model is established based on the instantaneous capture point (ICP) theory, and the balance state evaluation of the human body is realized by judging the positional relationship between the instantaneous capture point and the support range of the feet. Finally, according to the step strategy in the human body balance strategy, the magnitude of the auxiliary torque when the experimenter is out of balance is calculated through the relative position of the center of mass and the instantaneous capture point. Therefore, it can be shown that the balance evaluation model and exoskeleton control strategy we established can provide the balance restoring torque for the experimenter to swing the leg when the system is about to become unbalanced, which can effectively slow down the unbalanced trend.

Keywords: Hip exoskeleton · Perturbation platform · Series elastic actuator · Balance recovery

1 Introduction

Aging is reflected by reduced physical capabilities due to physiological changes. The reduced physical performance due to muscle deterioration, loss of motor units, and reduced neuromuscular activation may lead to gait disorders in senior adults [1, 2].

© The Author(s), under exclusive license to Springer Nature Switzerland AG 2022
H. Liu et al. (Eds.): ICIRA 2022, LNAI 13457, pp. 113–126, 2022.
https://doi.org/10.1007/978-3-031-13835-5_11

The major concerns for senior citizens are handicap for falling during walking. The hip exoskeleton [3, 4], a rising research topic in recent years due to the small inertia added to the leg and the device's ability to reduce the wearer's ankle and hip joints' activation with only hip assistance [5].

When it is difficult to maintain balance during walking, the human body will use different strategies to restore balance autonomously according to the current state. By studying the perturbation in different directions and magnitude of the human body, and giving a short-term control strategy to realize the hip exoskeleton-assisted balance movement, this is the key issues that need to be addressed [6, 7]. In order to study the relationship between the balance state of the human body and perturbation, external wrench is applied to the wearer during walking on the treadmill to analyze the balance mechanism of the human body through the wearer's kinematic and dynamic parameters. The wrench applied can be of any magnitude and direction [8], so as to achieve the purpose of losing the balance. Relevant studies have shown that the joint output torque of the elderly during walking is 18% to 20% lower than that of the young [5]. Therefore, when designing a hip exoskeleton, it is necessary to select an appropriate output power. At the same time, by adjusting the hip flexion/extension and abduction/adduction of the human hip joint in the coronal and sagittal planes, the walking step width, step length and step frequency is adjusted in real time to maintain a balanced walk.

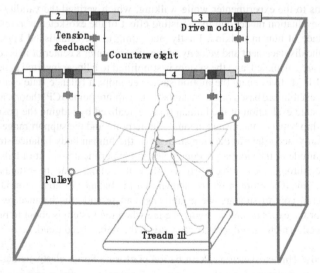

Fig. 1. The overall system of the perturbation platform

As a product of the combination of robotics and medical technology, the hip exoskeleton robot came into being. Its purpose is to provide assistance to the aging population to improve normal motor function [9]. Compared with the existing exoskeleton robots, there are problems such as large volume and weight, poor interaction comfort and low safety. Therefore, for the elderly with mobility problems who still have exercise ability, the hip exoskeleton robot has shown great practical application value due to its advantages of comfort and high interaction. The hip exoskeleton can avoid the decrease in comfort caused by increasing the inertia of the end limb, and further improve the comfort of human-machine interaction by reducing the non-alignment problem [10] between the joints of the coupling system caused by the multi-link design.

For the perturbation platform, in order to meet the requirement of transparency, it should have two working modes: perturbation mode and transparent mode. The perturbation platform with transparent mode is a key factor for studying the relationship between external wrench and equilibrium state when the human body is walking, so the system needs to simulate the external perturbation to the greatest extent, and will not interfere with the human walking gait during walking. In order to meet the transparency of the perturbation platform, the driving module adopts a clutch structure to reduce the interaction force of normal walking. When external wrench is required, the drive module provides pulling force to the cable fixed to the pelvic girdle after the clutch is closed. When no pulling force is required, the clutch is disconnected, and at this time, the tension exerted on the cable is generated by the counterweight on the other side.

This paper offers the following two major contributions:

1) The design of a perturbation platform with clutch structure is used to study the relationship between perturbation and balance state during the human motion, so as to simulate the external wrench to the greatest extent, and to minimize the interaction force of the human body during normal walking when the disturbance is not needed.
2) The design of a hip exoskeleton simulator with SEA and clutch to drive both hip abduction/adduction (HAA) and hip flexion/extension (HFE), which makes the hip exoskeleton compliant and transparent.

The paper is structured as follows. The hardware design is described in Sect. 2. Section 3 presents the bench-top testing, which show the performance of the exoskeleton in isolation. Experiments with human subject walking on level ground after perturbation, as well as assistance by exoskeleton are shown in this section. The conclusion is described in Sect. 4.

2 Methods

This paper is designing a perturbation platform to study how human's effort when she/he lost balance, and generalize the balance policy. This policy will be help to design wearable hip exoskeleton's balance strategy. And this paper also presents a hip exoskeleton simulator to study the wearer's reaction when hip exoskeleton offers the balance assistance to real-time adjusting the step length, step width, and step frequency.

Based on the motivation described above, we develop a novel perturbation platform and a hip exoskeleton simulator to study balance assistance during walking and running. Figure 1 shows the overall system of the proposed system. Perturbation platform consists of four actuation modules with clutch structure, pelvic belt driven by cables, and five gyroscopes for each leg and trunk. Components of the hip exoskeleton simulator are updated from those reported earlier [11], including torso module, HFE and HAA joint, thigh linear guide.

2.1 Perturbation Platform Design

The goal of the perturbation platform is to provide perturbation at the hip joint position to study the relationship between the human's motion recovery mechanism and external perturbation. In order to interfere with the walking process of the human body when needed, horizontal pulling is applied to the pelvis. Falling during walking may be in any direction, thus four cables were used during the human experiment. In addition, as a wearable device, the interaction force of the system should be transparent to avoid affecting the gait during normal walking when perturbation is not required. A maximum target tension of 150 N can be applied to each cable. When pulling force is not required, the clutch is disengaged and the pulley rotates in the reverse direction, at this time, the tension of the cable (approximately 4 N) is generated by the counterweight fixed on the other side of the pulley.

In order to meet the requirements of transparency when the subject is walking, the perturbation platform is configured in two working modes: perturbation mode and transparent mode, as shown in Fig. 2. The end of the first cable is fixed on the pelvic belt and the other end is wound clockwise on the first step of the reel. The end of the second cable is fixed with a counterweight and the other end is wound on the second step of the wheel counterclockwise. In the perturbation mode, the clutch of one or more drive modules is closed. At this time, the motor output torque T is far greater than the tension force G provided by the counterweight. Therefore, the drive module rotates clockwise to provide tension on the pelvis. The equation for the tension F_p during perturbation mode is given by

$$F_p = \frac{T}{r_1} - \frac{G}{r_2}, \quad T \gg G, \tag{1}$$

where T is the torque provided by the drive module, r_1 and r_2 are the diameters of the two steps of the reel, which are designed to be 60 and 90 mm respectively, and G is the tension force generated by the counterweight under the action of gravity. In the

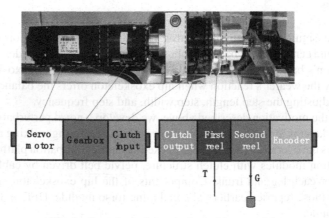

Fig. 2. Overview of the platform driver module

transparent mode, the clutches of all drive modules are disengaged and there is no output torque. At this time, only the tension provided by the counterweight makes the reel rotate counterclockwise. The equation for the tension F_t during transparent mode is given by

$$F_t = \frac{G}{r_2}, \ T = 0. \tag{2}$$

2.2 Hip Exoskeleton Simulator Design

Figure 3 shows the mechanical design and implementation of the hip exoskeleton joint driven by series elastic actuator. The exoskeleton prototype for balance walking for the elderly is designed and proposed, It has four degrees of freedom of HFE and HAA. Modules with series elastic actuator are used as driving joints, which makes the exoskeleton have excellent performance to improve coronal and sagittal balance assistance during walking. The brushless DC motor acts as a drive module to output continuous torque, which is amplified by the harmonic gearbox, and finally assists the wearer through the drive binding mechanism. According to the characteristic parameters of the DC brushless motor and the harmonic gearbox, the continuous torque that the lower limb exoskeleton joint can output is 18 NM, and the output speed is 390°/s.

In order to meet the requirements of the output torque and speed of the drive joint, a brushless DC motor with a rated power of 200 W was selected as the drive motor of the exoskeleton joint (EC 60 flat, Maxon Motor, Sachseln, Switzerland), and its rated torque and velocity were 0.536 Nm and 3240 rpm, respectively. A harmonic gearbox (CSD-17-50-2A-GR-BB, Harmonic Drive, Limburg, Germany) with small size, high positioning accuracy and high load capacity is selected as the reduction mechanism, and its transmission ratio is 50:1. In order to achieve the transparency of the exoskeleton, the joint module has a clutch function. When the wearer needs an auxiliary torque from the exoskeleton device, the clutch will be turned on to work; in the normal walking gait of the wearer, the clutch will be disconnected to ensure that the interaction force between the exoskeleton and the human body is zero.

During walking, the motor drive system has high servo stiffness, which can cause discomfort to the wearer. Therefore, combining the motor with the SEA can improve the structural compliance of the joint drive system. After the structural design is completed, the strength and stiffness of the SEA need to be analyzed [12] to meet the usage requirements. The torque of the SEA was measured indirectly by measuring the deflection of the torsion spring with a high-resolution magnetic encoder (Avago AEDA-3300 series, Broadcom Inc., South Carolina). The performance of the torque sensor depends on the stiffness of the elastic element and the resolution of the encoder [13]. The SEA is fixed on the platform and the motor is locked when the torque output side is connected to the load, results show that the actual stiffness of the spring is 392.743 Nm/rad.

2.3 Control Scheme

The goal of the low-level controller of the exoskeleton is to output a torque signal according to the command, and provide torque to the wearer through the servo driver,

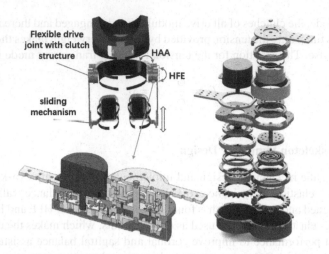

Flexible drive
joint with clutch
structure

HAA

HFE

sliding
mechanism

Fig. 3. The hip exoskeleton with series elastic actuator

so that the drive joint can output enough torque to drive the exoskeleton to achieve coordinated movement during the unbalanced process. Each drive joint is equipped with a commercial brushless motor driver to drive the motor and provide feedback from hall and motor current data to the advanced control system, the driver is configured in torque output mode. Each joint is also equipped with an absolute magnetic encoder (RMB08, RLS, Komenda, Slovenia) to acquire data and monitor the deflection of the SEA to measure the interaction force. The engagement and disengagement of the clutch is controlled by the transistor amplifier circuit which controls the power connection of the clutch via the relay (3.3 V). The torque input signal of the joint driver communicates with the visual studio C# system running on the laptop through the NI controller (USB-6343, National Instruments, State of Texas).

The high-level controller performs balance evaluation when detecting the imbalance of the human body, and calculates the output torque of the hip exoskeleton in combination with the human body posture model. The exoskeleton system needs to integrate multiple position sensors to provide motion and other information for the coupled control system. In order to accurately perceive and calculate the motion state of the limbs, the degrees of freedom of HFE and HAA are all arranged with an inertial measurement unit (IMU). Real-time perception of the wearer's posture is achieved by fixing the IMU on the surface of each limb, and the wearer's motion state in the world coordinate system is calculated by combining the kinematics and dynamics models.

In the control of the humanoid biped robot, the robot model can be simplified to a Linear Inverted Pendulum Model (LIPM) composed of the human body's center of mass and a weightless lightweight rod. When moving on flat ground, we assume that the center of mass of the pendulum moves in the horizontal direction, and the motion state in the vertical direction is ignored. The limbs are simplified as a LIPM model, and the movement posture of each limb of the human body is normalized to the position of the centroid for analysis. As shown in Fig. 4, when the human body is simplified as LIPM, the model includes a point foot located at the r_{ankle} position, a point mass m located at the

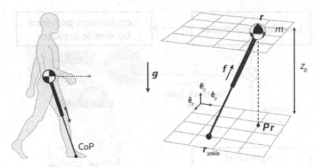

Fig. 4. Diagram of instantaneous capture point based on LIPM model

r position, and a massless telescopic leg with a linear driving force exerts a magnitude f on the point mass r, keeps the point mass at a constant height z_0. The projection matrix P projects the point mass positions to the P_r positions on the x-y plane. The angle between the massless rod and the vertical direction is θ, the mass of the mass point is m, the gravitational acceleration vector is g, and the position supporting the ankle joint is r_{ankle}. In order for the LIPM model to move continuously and stably, a method is needed to characterize and evaluate the motion state of the inverted pendulum, and use this as a reference to dynamically calculate the next foothold. In this case, the point where the LIPM model contacts the ground has only one fulcrum. At this time, the center of mass of the linear inverted pendulum is kept approximately on the horizontal line, that is, a constant center of mass height z0 is maintained.

Based on the state where the target orbital energy is zero, Jerry Pratt et al. proposed the theory of dynamic capture point X_{ICP} [8], which enables the human body to obtain a new dynamic balance control process after being subjected to external interference. The horizontal motion equation of a linear inverted pendulum can be obtained:

$$X_{ICP} = x \mp \frac{z_0}{g}\dot{x} \qquad (3)$$

Analogy to the balance strategy of the human body, when the external system exerts a disturbance force on the human body, then the human body is bound to take a step to maintain the balance posture again. As shown in Fig. 5, the specific balancing strategy is:

1) The ICP is inside the supporting polygon, that is, inside the Stability Zone: it is in a state of equilibrium at this time, and no balance assistance is needed.
2) ICP is outside the Stability Zone: triggers the "stepping strategy". In order to maximize the stability after the step action, the position of the new ICP should be in the center of the supporting polygon.

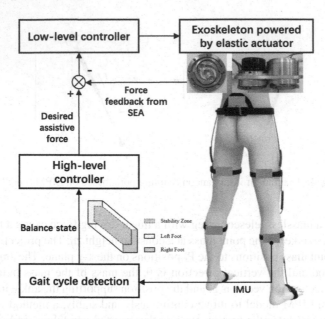

Fig. 5. Flowchart of the control system

According to the balance assistance strategy, it is necessary to calculate the assistance force of the external driving torque to the human body when the human body is out of balance according to the relative positions of the COM and the ICP. The moment acting on the center of mass required to maintain a balanced walking can be obtained as

$$W_{corr,\mathrm{COM}} = \begin{bmatrix} mg/z_0(X_{GCOM} - X_{COP}) \\ 0 \end{bmatrix} \tag{4}$$

Among them, m is the quality of the system, X_{GCOM} represent the position and acceleration of the center of mass of the system, X_{COP} represents the cartesian coordinate system position of the plantar pressure center point COP. According to above calculation, it can be obtained that the moment acting on the center of mass of the system to maintain balance is

$$W_{act,\mathrm{COM}} = W_{corr,\mathrm{COM}} - W_{dyn,\mathrm{COM}} \tag{5}$$

Among them, $W_{dyn,\mathrm{COM}}$ are the biological joint moments acting on the system center of mass by the human leg joints, $W_{corr,\mathrm{COM}}$ represent the required corrective torque acting on the system center of mass, after obtaining the corrective torque $W_{corr,\mathrm{COM}}$. The balance state calculates the auxiliary moments of the left and right legs of the exoskeleton.

3 Experimental Characterization

3.1 Transparency Characterization

In order to verify the transparency of the perturbation platform, that is, the influence of the system on the human gait under the state of "zero force mode", the interaction force information between the wearer and the perturbation platform is collected through the tension sensor, and the analog voltage output by the tension sensor is read. According to the interaction force of the wearer in one walking cycle, it can be concluded that the maximum interaction force of the human body in the static state is 3.25 N, and the maximum interaction force of the human body in the walking state is 6.9 N.

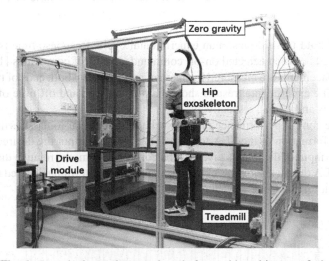

Fig. 6. Perturbation and perception platform with multi-sensor fusion

The platform and exoskeleton should not interfere with the normal movement of the wearer. In order to further verify the transparency of the wearer when walking on the platform, as shown in Fig. 6, the gait analysis experiment of walking outside the platform without wearing the exoskeleton and walking on the platform with the exoskeleton was carried out. The data was collected by a motion capture system (Perception Neuron 2.0, Noitom Technology Ltd.), the changes of the hip joint angle under two different conditions were compared and the impact on the wearer's normal gait was comprehensively analyzed.

From a gait perspective, the data of the two groups of experimental results are very similar. Only in the first 50% of the gait cycle, the hip joint angle when wearing the exoskeleton is slightly smaller than that when walking normally. While for the hip flexion angle, the flexion angle in the case of wearing the exoskeleton ($25.41 \pm 4.59°$) is slightly larger than that in the normal walking state ($24.09 \pm 2.18°$), which may be caused by the increased inertia of the end structure of the exoskeleton. Therefore, the designed hip exoskeleton and platform have little impact on the wearer's normal gait, and the interaction moment during walking is negligible, which can be regarded as transparent to the wearer.

3.2 Actuator Performance During Walking

Aiming at the experimental verification of the hip exoskeleton for the elderly, based on the design idea of the rigid-flexible hybrid mechanism, the pre-designed hip exoskeleton robot with the clutch function of the series elastic driver drive joint was tested, including the clutch on-off test, torque control performance experiments and bandwidth tests to generate the required torque.

In order to verify the influence of the clutch structure of the modular joint on the response time of the system, an experimental study on the delay time of the clutch on and off was carried out. The modular joint was fixed on the experimental bench, and the clutch signal was provided by a 24 V switching power supply. It was commanded to engage and hold for 1000 ms in an experimental cycle. Response time is defined as the time elapsed between detected on-off commands or on-off commands [14], and the resulting displacements are measured by magnetic encoders on both ends of the modular joint clutch. The experimental results show that the on time and off time of the clutch are about 24 ms and 12 ms, respectively.

The torque control performance of the exoskeleton modular joint is verified by controlling the deformation of the SEA to control the joint to output the desired torque. A desired torque input of the joint is given by the control system, the relative displacement curve of the SEA output terminal is obtained, and the output terminal is fixed to calculate the joint output torque.

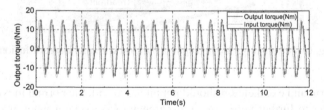

Fig. 7. The joint torque response curve of the hip exoskeleton

Figure 7 shows the joint torque response curve when the expected input torque varies from −15 Nm to 15 Nm with a period of 500 ms. From the above torque response curves, it can be calculated that the torque output error (peak-to-peak) of the joint with series elastic actuators under normal gait is less than 6.89%. Specifically, it is realized by measuring the linear voltage value of the magnetic encoder arranged at the input end and output end of the SEA.

The joint bandwidth is measured by the step method, and the rise time of the system is defined as the range of the joint output torque reaching 10%–90% of the input torque. When the input torque is 8 N · m, the calculated frequency of the system is 13.46 Hz; When the torque is 16 N · m, the calculated frequency is 11.29 Hz. It can be found that with the gradual increase of the output torque, the joint output torque bandwidth gradually decreases, which proves the correctness of the above theoretical analysis, and the system bandwidth is much larger than the 2 Hz bandwidth when the human body is walking, which can meet the assistance requirements of the hip exoskeleton.

3.3 Perturbation Tests

The walking experiments are carried out on a balanced perturbation and perception experimental platform based on multi-sensor fusion. The platform adopts the developed drive unit with clutch function to drive the winding wheel to drive the rope to pull the waist of the human body in four directions. At the same time, the motion capture system records the movement trajectory of the human body, and the four tension sensors of the perturbation platform record the perturbation force information. By observing and recording the balance recovery mechanism of the experimenter under the perturbation force, the accuracy of the balance evaluation model is judged.

The experimenter completed the walking motion on the treadmill. When the speed of the treadmill is 1 m/s, the perturbation in the front, back, left and right directions were applied to the pelvis of the experimenter through the platform, and the balance was restored by the body's autonomy. The applicability of the model was evaluated by the strategy research balance, where the perturbation force magnitude and duration were 50 N and 150 ms, respectively.

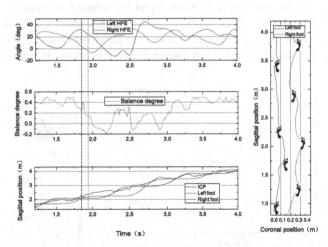

Fig. 8. Autonomous recovery diagram with forward perturbation at 1 m/s

The state recovery diagram of forward disturbance during low-speed walking is shown in Fig. 8. Hip flexion/extension is defined as the hip joint rotation angle in the sagittal plane, ICP is defined as the position scalar of the dynamic capture point relative to the initial position, and the black vertical line is the time when the disturbance is applied, the red vertical line is the time when the imbalance is detected, and the balance degree [11] μ is defined as

$$\mu = \frac{r_s - |(x_l + x_r)/2 - x_{ICP}|}{\varphi_s} \tag{6}$$

where r_s is the radius of the stable support area, x_l and x_r are the left and right foot positions in the sagittal plane, x_{ICP} is the component of the dynamic capture point position scalar in the sagittal plane, and φ_s is the walking step length. It can be seen from the balance degree diagram that when the disturbance is applied for 170 ms, the balance degree rapidly drops to a negative value, and is determined to be an unbalanced state by the balance evaluation model. Then through the joint torque output of the human limb, the system autonomously returns to the equilibrium state after 500 ms.

3.4   Balance Assistance Tests

By wearing the hip exoskeleton robot, the experimenter conducted perturbation experiments when walking on the experimental platform, and then compared the balance recovery of the exoskeleton participating in balance recovery and not participating in balance recovery when walking during an unbalanced state. By comparing and analyzing the step width, step length, stride frequency, and the phase relationship between the center of mass and the legs, the walking balance assistance effect of the hip walking exoskeleton on the wearer's imbalance is verified.

As shown in Fig. 9, comparing the two situations of the process of self-restoring balance during walking and the process of restoring balance with exoskeleton assistance, it can be found that by assisting the swinging leg to obtain a larger support range, the time it takes for the wearer to restore balance can be reduced, compared with 400 ms when there is no assistance. After returning to the balance state, the balance recovery time when assisted by the exoskeleton is reduced to about 300 ms, and it can be found from the figure that the degree of balance when assisted is relatively improved.

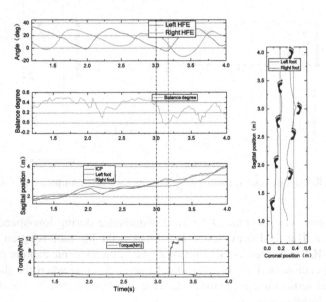

Fig. 9. Exoskeleton-assisted recovery diagram with forward perturbation at 1 m/s

To evaluate the biomechanical and physiological effects of exoskeleton-assisted motion in the recovery model, the wearer was disturbed in four directions, and then the balance restoration effect of wearing the exoskeleton and not wearing the exoskeleton was compared, and the joint angle and kinematic parameters of the wearer were recorded by the motion capture device. Table 1 shows the biological results of the subject under the four perturbation conditions, including the degree of balance and the time required to restore balance at different walking speeds.

Table 1. Walking recovery at 1 m/s on treadmill

		Assist off	Assist on
Forward	Balance degree	−0.2	−0.01
	Recovery time (ms)	503	316
Backward	Balance degree	−0.13	−0.09
	Recovery time (ms)	232	189
Left	Balance degree	−0.05	0.04
	Recovery time (ms)	263	216
Right	Balance degree	−0.27	−0.17
	Recovery time (ms)	406	220

4 Conclusion

Therefore, it can be shown that the balance evaluation model and exoskeleton control strategy we established can provide the balance restoring torque for the experimenter to swing the leg when the system is about to become unbalanced, which can effectively slow down the tendency of the human body to reduce the degree of balance and fall, and provide a good foundation for the subsequent multiple balanced walking within the gait cycle.

Acknowledgement. This work was supported in part by the National Key R&D Program of China (2020YFC2007804), the Natural Science Foundation of the Jiangsu Higher Education Institutions of China (19KJA180009), the Natural Science Foundation of Jiangsu Province (BK20191424), the Jiangsu Frontier Leading Technology Fundamental Research Project (BK20192004D), and the Distinguished Professor of Jiangsu province.

References

1. Population Division of the Department of Economic and Social Affairs of the United Nations Secretariat. 2019 Revision of World Population Prospects (2019). https://population.un.org/wpp/

2. Zhou, M.G., Wang, H.D., Zeng, X.Y., et al.: Mortality, morbidity, and risk factors in China and its provinces, 1990–2017: a systematic analysis for the Global Burden of Disease Study 2017. Lancet **394**(10204), 1145–1158 (2019)
3. Yasuhara, K., Shimada, K., Koyama, T., Ido, T., Kikuchi, K., Endo, Y.: Walking assist device with stride management system. Honda R&d Tech. Rev. **21**, 54–62 (2009)
4. Monaco, V., et al.: An ecologically-controlled exoskeleton can improve balance recovery after slippage. Sci. Rep. **7**, 46721 (2017)
5. Sanchez-Villamañan, M.D.C., Gonzalez-Vargas, J., Torricelli, D., et al.: Compliant lower limb exoskeletons: a comprehensive review on mechanical design principles. J. NeuroEng. Rehab. **16**(1) (2019)
6. Winter, D.A.: Human balance and posture control during standing and walking. Gait Posture **3**(4), 193–214 (1995)
7. Horak Fay, B., Nashner, L.M.: Central programming of postural movements: adaptation to altered support-surface configurations. J. Neurophysiol. **55**(6), 1369–1381 (1986)
8. Pratt, J., Carff, J., Drakunov, S., et al.: Capture point: a step toward humanoid push recovery. In: 6th IEEE-RAS International Conference on Humanoid Robots (2007)
9. Young, A., Ferris, D.: State-of-the-art and future directions for robotic lower limb exoskeletons. IEEE Trans. Neural Syst. Rehab. Eng. 1 (2016)
10. Schiele, A.: Ergonomics of exoskeletons: objective performance metrics. In: 3rd Joint Euro-Haptics Conference and Symposium on Haptic Interfaces for Virtual Environment and Teleoperator Systems, pp. 103–108 (2009)
11. Zhang, T., Tran, M., Huang, H.: Design and experimental verification of hip exoskeleton with balance capacities for walking assistance. IEEE/ASME Trans. Mechatron. **23**(1), 274–285 (2018)
12. Arno, H.A.S., Hekman, E.E.G., et al.: Design of a rotational hydroelastic actuator for a powered exoskeleton for upper limb rehabilitation. IEEE Trans. Biomed. Eng. **57**, 728–735 (2010)
13. Kashiri, N., Malzahn, J., Tsagarakis, N.G.: On the sensor design of torque controlled actuators: a comparison study of strain gauge and encoder based principles. IEEE Robot. Autom. Lett. **2**, 1 (2017)
14. Tucker, M.R., Shirota, C., Lambercy, O., et al.: Design and characterization of an exoskeleton for perturbing the knee during gait. IEEE Trans. Biomed. Eng. **64**(10), 2331–2343 (2017)

Disturbance Observer Compensation Based on Sliding-Mode Approach for Solving Compliant Actuator Tracking Control Problems

Changxian Xu, Jian Gu, Yongbai Liu, Liming Zhao, and Zhongbo Sun[(✉)]

Department of Control Engineering, Changchun University of Technology, Changchun 130012,
People's Republic of China
zhongbosun2012@163.com

Abstract. The rehabilitation robot needs directly physical interaction in the process of rehabilitation training for patients. Considering the safety of patients, the actuator of the rehabilitation robot should have the advantages of flexibility. Based on the requires of rehabilitation robots, an accurate dynamics model is considered the interaction force between the parts of the compliant actuator, which is established, and the control scheme of the compliant actuator end trajectory tracking is designed. The disturbance observer is designed to estimate the disturbance value and actively eliminate the influence of some disturbances on the compliant actuator. A nonlinear sliding mode controller is designed to reduce the tracking error and shaking the compliant actuator. Through the simulation experiments, compared with the traditional proportional-integral-derivative (PID) controller, it is obvious that the tracking effect of sliding mode control is more efficient on the basis of using the disturbance observer to dispose the disturbance.

Keywords: Compliant actuator · Disturbance observer · Nonlinear sliding mode

1 Introduction

At present, due to the serious aging at home and abroad, stroke is become one of the main causes of adult disability. These stroke patients can't stand, walk and squat like normal people, which will bring them additional diseases, such as muscle atrophy, muscle weakness, obesity and other diseases. Therefore, in families and hospitals, there is a growing demand for rehabilitation robots [1–3] and walking robots [4] to help patients with rehabilitation training and assisted walking, so as to improve their quality of life.

With the increasing needs of rehabilitation robot, as the core component of rehabilitation robot, driver can determine the output torque and speed of robot, so as to determine the performance of rehabilitation robot. In traditional engineering applications, most of the actuators are also rigid and non back-drivable [5]. These actuators can provide excellent accuracy, speed and repeatability to robot system. However,

The work is supported in part by the National Natural Science Foundation of China under grants 61873304, 62173048 and in part by the China Postdoctoral Science Foundation Funded Project under grants 2018M641784 and 2019T120240, and also in part by the Changchun Science and Technology Project under grant 21ZY41.

H. Liu et al. (Eds.): ICIRA 2022, LNAI 13457, pp. 127–137, 2022.
https://doi.org/10.1007/978-3-031-13835-5_12

for rehabilitation robot system using rigid actuators, the system will be unsafe and unfriendly to patients. In [6], based on the theory of human anatomy, a limb rehabilitation robot under AutoLEE-II with 12 degrees of freedom composed of series parallel hybrid mechanism is developed. The limb rehabilitation robot under AutoLEE-II lacks flexibility when cooperating with patients, which reduces the safety of patients. Considering the safety of patients is the crucial factor in the human-robot interaction, this paper proposes a new type of compliant actuator [7–9]. The compliant actuator is mainly to add a device with elastic and damping characteristics between the driving device and the end effector of the rehabilitation robot. The compliant actuator has the advantages of passive compliance, low impedance, impact resistance and friendly interaction with patients.

Generally speaking, the main purpose of using disturbance observer is to infer external unknown or uncertain disturbance torque without using additional sensors [8, 10, 11]. In [12], a general system method is used to solve the problem of disturbance observer design of robot, which is not limited by degrees of freedom, joint type or manipulator configuration. PID controller is widely used in the field of compliant actuator control [13]. In [14, 15], proportional-derivative (PD) feedback plus feedforward controller is used to control the position of serial variable stiffness actuator (SVSA). The simulation results show that the controller has the advantages of fast response and high precision. In [16], based on the linear quadratic regulator method, PD controller is used to control the series elastic actuator, so that the series elastic actuator has good control performance in both low force range and high force range. PID controller has the advantage of not relying on the dynamics model of compliant actuator, but the large starting torque of PID control leads to the damage of compliant actuator and the destitute motion quality of rehabilitation robot. In addition, the robust controller is also to be used as compliant actuators [18–20]. The robustness of the system is the key to the survival of the system in emergencies. Due to its special flexible structure and motion characteristics, the compliant actuator system is prone to various uncertainties and disturbances, and the robust controller can just compensate the system uncertainty. Therefore, the robust controller has been widely used in the compliant actuator.

The rest of this paper is organized as follows, In Sect. 2, the accurate dynamics model of the novel compliant actuator is established. In Sect. 3, a sliding mode controller based on disturbance observer compensation are designed to reduce the tracking error of the compliant actuator. The rationality of the design of disturbance observer and sliding mode controller is proved. In Sect. 4, the simulation results are obtained through Simulink. Section 5 gives a brief conclusion.

2   Dynamics Modeling and Control Scheme

2.1   Compliant Actuator Dynamics Model

General compliant actuator system model is composed of control system, driving system, elastic element, sensing system and end load. Because the actuator of the rehabilitation robot should have the advantages of flexibility, lightweight and modularization, it is improved on the basis of the general compliant actuator system model to obtain the compliant actuator system model diagram suitable for the rehabilitation robot as shown in Fig. 1.

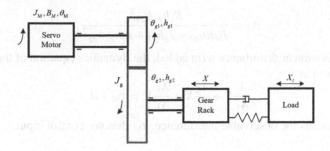

Fig. 1. Dynamics model diagram of compliant actuator

Figure 1 is the compliant actuator system model suitable for the rehabilitation robot, which is comprised of motor, a pair of spur gear devices, gear rack devices, spring devices and output devices. The use of rack and pinion device can improve the load bearing capacity of compliant actuator. Working principle of compliant actuator is that the servo motor drives the rack and pinion through a pair of spur gears with large reduction ratio. The use of spur gears with large reduction ratio has the advantages of improving the output torque of compliant actuator and improving the compactness of compliant actuator mechanism structure. The rotary motion is transformed into linear motion through the gear rack device, and the rack realizes the linear motion of the load by pushing the spring.

Based on the working principle and mechanical structure of compliant actuator, the dynamics model of compliant actuator is established by Newton Euler method.

$$J_M \ddot{\theta}_M = \tau_M - h_{g1} F_{g1} - B_M \dot{\theta}_M \tag{1}$$

$$J_g \ddot{\theta}_{g2} = h_{g2} F_{g1} - h_{g3} F_{g2} \tag{2}$$

$$m\ddot{X} = F_{g2} - K_s(X - X_l) - B_s(\dot{X} - \dot{X}_l) \tag{3}$$

where $X_l = 0$, $\theta_M = R\theta_{g1}$. In addition, R represents the transmission ratio between gears, J_M denotes the moment of inertia of the motor, J_g denotes the moment of inertia of the gear, F_{g1} expresses the interaction force between the driving and driven gears, F_{g2} expresses the interaction force between the gear and rack, h_{g1} represents the rotation radius of the driving gear, h_{g2} represents the radius of rotation of the driven gear, h_{g3} represents the radius of the spur gear engaged with the rack and K_s connotes the stiffness coefficient of the spring. After sorting out the above formulae (1–3), the dynamics model equation of compliant actuator is defined as

$$\ddot{X} = A_1 \tau_M - A_2 \dot{X} - A_3 X \tag{4}$$

where

$$A_1 = \frac{h_{g2} h_{g3}}{J_M R h_{g2} + J_g h_{g1} + m h_{g1} h_{g3}^2}$$

$$A_2 = \frac{B_M R h_{g2} + B_s h_{g1} h_{g3}^2}{J_M R h_{g2} + J_g h_{g1} + m h_{g1} h_{g3}^2}$$

$$A_3 = \frac{K_s h_{g1} h_{g3}{}^2}{J_M R h_{g2} + J_g h_{g1} + m h_{g1} h_{g3}{}^2}$$

With the nonlinear disturbance term added, the dynamics equation of the compliant actuator is given as

$$\frac{1}{A_1}\ddot{X} + \frac{A_2}{A_1}\dot{X} + \frac{A_3}{A_1}X = \tau_M + d \tag{5}$$

where d represents the observable interference, τ_M denotes control input.

2.2 Compliant Actuator Control Scheme

The tracking error of compliant actuator comes from the design tolerance, assembly error and the influence of external interference of compliant actuator. The above disturbance or error could be divided into observable part and unobservable part. For the observable part disturbance, the disturbance observer is designed to estimate the disturbance size and compensate in the controller. For the unobservable part, the sliding mode variable structure control is used to improve the control accuracy. The control scheme of the compliant actuator designed in this paper is shown in Fig. 2.

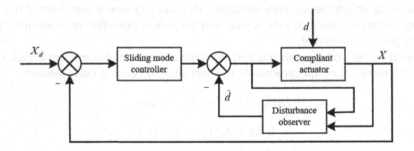

Fig. 2. Control scheme of compliant actuator system.

As shown in Fig. 2, X_d is the desired displacement of the compliant actuator, X is the actual displacement of the compliant actuator, $\hat{d}$ is the observed value of disturbance.

3 Sliding Mode Control Based on Disturbance Observer

3.1 Design and Prove the Stability of Disturbance Observer

The design principle of disturbance observer is to input the pre disturbance state and post disturbance state into the observer for comparison, and take the difference as the estimated value of disturbance momentum. The basic idea of realizing the disturbance controller is to use the error between the actual disturbance value and the observed value to adjust the observed value, so as to reduce the error. Based on above principle, the nonlinear disturbance observer of compliant actuator is designed as

$$\dot{z} = H\left(\frac{A_2}{A_1}\dot{X} + \frac{A_3}{A_1}X - u\right) - H\hat{d} \tag{6}$$

$$\hat{d} = z + q$$

The gain matrix of disturbance observer is designed as

$$H = Y^{-1}\left(\frac{1}{A_1}\right)^{-1} \tag{7}$$

of which Y is a scalar to be determined in this paper. The auxiliary vector of the disturbance observer is given by

$$q - Y^{-1}\dot{Y} \tag{8}$$

Theorem 1. *Consider the compliant actuator subject to disturbances described by (5). The disturbance observer is given in (6) with the disturbance observer gain matrix H defined in (7) and the disturbance observer auxiliary vector q defined in (8). The disturbance tracking error $\tilde{d}$ converges exponentially to zero.*

Proof. Consider the following Lyapunov function candidate as:

$$V_o = \tilde{d}^\top Y^\top \frac{1}{A_1} Y \tilde{d} \tag{9}$$

According to the disturbance observer (6), the formula can be obtained as:

$$\begin{aligned}
\dot{\tilde{d}} &= \dot{d} - \dot{z} - \dot{q} \\
&= \dot{d} - H\left(\frac{A_2}{A_1}\dot{X} + \frac{A_3}{A_1}X - \tau_M\right) + H\hat{d} - H\frac{1}{A_1}\ddot{X} \\
&= \dot{d} + H\hat{d} - H\left(\frac{1}{A_1}\ddot{X} + \frac{A_2}{A_1}\dot{X} + \frac{A_3}{A_1}X - \tau_M\right) \\
&= \dot{d} + H\hat{d} - Hd \\
&= \dot{d} - H\tilde{d}
\end{aligned} \tag{10}$$

therefore, the observation error can be obtained from (10)

$$\dot{\tilde{d}} + H\tilde{d} = 0 \tag{11}$$

Substituting Eq. (7) into Eq. (11) yields the following equations

$$\dot{\tilde{d}} = -Y^{-1}\left(\frac{1}{A_1}\right)^{-1}\tilde{d} \tag{12}$$

$$\dot{\tilde{d}}^\top = -\tilde{d}^\top\left(\frac{1}{A_1}\right)^{-\top}Y^{-\top}$$

The time-derivative of V_0 could be computed as

$$
\begin{aligned}
\dot{V}_o &= \mathring{\tilde{d}}^{\top} Y^{\top} \frac{1}{A_1} Y \tilde{d} + \tilde{d}^{\top} Y^{\top} \frac{1}{A_1} Y \mathring{\tilde{d}} \\
&= -\tilde{d}^{\top} \left(\frac{1}{A_1}\right)^{-\top} Y^{-\top} Y^{\top} \frac{1}{A_1} Y \tilde{d} - \tilde{d}^{T} Y^{\top} \frac{1}{A_1} Y Y^{-1} \left(\frac{1}{A_1}\right)^{-1} \tilde{d} \\
&= -\tilde{d}^{\top} Y \tilde{d} - \tilde{d}^{\top} Y^{\top} \tilde{d} \\
&= -\tilde{d}^{\top} \left(Y + Y^{\top}\right) \tilde{d}
\end{aligned}
\tag{13}
$$

The following inequality is constructed:

$$
Y + Y^{\top} \geq \Gamma
\tag{14}
$$

where $\Gamma > 0$ is a symmetric positive definite matrix, so Eq. (13) could be computed as:

$$
\dot{V}_o \leq -\tilde{d}^{T} \Gamma \tilde{d}
\tag{15}
$$

It can be seen that the disturbance observer converges exponentially to zero, and the convergence accuracy depends on the parameter Γ value. With the growth of Γ value, the convergence speed and accuracy are faster.

3.2   Design Sliding Mode Controller and Proof System Stability

The compliant actuator designs an external disturbance observer to observe and compensate the disturbance in the sliding mode control, which can effectively reduce the switching gain and chattering. For unobservable disturbances and other uncertain factors, the sliding mode controller can weaken the influence on the compliant actuator, so that the system still has excellent position tracking performance and robustness in the case of external disturbances.

Based on the dynamics model of the compliant actuator described in Sect. 2, the sliding mode controller can be reasonably designed. The control objective of the sliding mode controller is to make the actual trajectory X of the compliant actuator as close to the given trajectory X_d as possible.

The sliding mode function is defined as

$$
s = \dot{e} + \lambda e
\tag{16}
$$

where $e = X - X_d$. The derivative of Eq. (16) can be obtained as follows:

$$
\begin{aligned}
\dot{s} &= \ddot{e} + \lambda \dot{e} \\
&= \ddot{X} - \ddot{X}_d + \lambda \dot{e} \\
&= A_1 \left(\tau_M - \frac{A_2}{A_1} \dot{X} - \frac{A_3}{A_1} X + d \right) - \ddot{X}_d + \lambda \dot{e}
\end{aligned}
\tag{17}
$$

Based on the dynamics model (5) and sliding mode function (16) of the compliant actuator, the controller of the compliant actuator is designed as

$$\tau_M = \frac{1}{A_1}\omega + \frac{A_2}{A_1}\dot{X} + \frac{A_3}{A_1}X - \hat{d} - \eta\,\mathrm{sgn}(s) - \frac{A_2}{A_1}s \tag{18}$$

where, $\eta > |\tilde{d}(0)| + \eta_0, \eta_0 > 0$.

It can be obtained by formula (17)

$$\frac{1}{A_1}\dot{s} = \frac{1}{A_1}\omega - \eta\,\mathrm{sgn}(s) - \hat{d} + d - \frac{A_2}{A_1}s + \frac{1}{A_1}\left(\lambda\dot{e} - \ddot{X}_d\right)$$

$$= \frac{1}{A_1}\left(\omega + \lambda\dot{e} - \ddot{X}_d\right) - \eta\,\mathrm{sgn}(s) + \tilde{d} - \frac{A_2}{A_1}s \tag{19}$$

Taking $\omega = \ddot{X}_d - \lambda\dot{e}$ and simplifying formula (19), which generates the following formula can be achieved as:

$$\frac{1}{A_1}\dot{s} = -\eta\,\mathrm{sgn}(s) + \tilde{d} - \frac{A_2}{A_1}s \tag{20}$$

Theorem 2. *Consider the system of the compliant actuator (5), the disturbance of compliant actuator system (5) is observed by disturbance observer (6). When $t \to \infty$, the system is asymptotically stable.*

Proof. Consider a Lyapunov function.

$$V = \frac{1}{2}s^{\top}\frac{1}{A_1}s + V_o \tag{21}$$

Since the disturbance observer is exponentially convergent, $\|\tilde{d}\| \le \|\tilde{d}(t_0)\|$. If $\|\eta\| > \|\tilde{d}(t_0)\|$, the time-derivative of V could be computed as

$$\dot{V} = s^{\top}\frac{1}{A_1}\dot{s} + \dot{V}_o$$

$$= s^{\top}\left(-\frac{A_2}{A_1}s - \eta\,\mathrm{sgn}(s) + \tilde{d}\right) + \dot{V}_o$$

$$= -\eta\,\|s\| - s^{\top}\tilde{d} + \dot{V}_o$$

$$\le -\eta_0\,\|s\| - \tilde{d}^T\Gamma\tilde{d} \tag{22}$$

When $\dot{V} \equiv 0$, $s \equiv 0$, $\tilde{d} = 0$ is obtained. According to LaSalle invariance principle, the closed-loop system is asymptotically stable.

4 Numerical Results

To further illustrate the design idea as well as the above analysis, computational simulations are performed using simulink program. The specific parameters required in the dynamics model of the compliant actuator are shown in Table 1. The target trajectory selected in this paper is $X_d = 0.1\sin(t)$. The disturbance observer is designed as a friction observer. In other words, the disturbance observer is used to estimate the friction

Table 1. Research on parameters of compliant actuator prototype.

Variable	Parameter
J_M	$8.6 \times 10^{-6}\ kg \cdot m^2$
J_g	$5.5 \times 10^{-6}\ kg \cdot m^2$
h_{g1}	9 mm
h_{g2}	18 mm
h_{g3}	20 mm
Motor power	70 W
Spring stiffness	36 N/mm

for compliant actuator. The friction considered is viscous friction, given by $d = v * \dot{X}$. The design parameter v is chosen as 2.

In this paper, two groups of comparative simulation experiments are designed: (1) The traditional PID controller is used to track the end trajectory of the compliant actuator without adding the disturbance observer; (2) The disturbance observer is operated to observe the disturbance, and the sliding mode control algorithm is applied to control the compliant actuator to track the target trajectory. Through the comparison of two groups of simulation experiments, it can be well reflected that the tracking effect of sliding mode controller compensated by disturbance observer is better than that of traditional PID controller without disturbance observer compensation.

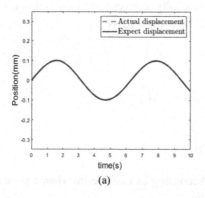
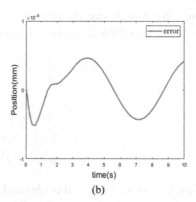

(a)   (b)

Fig. 3. (a) The trajectory tracking of compliant actuator based on PID control, (b) The tracking error of compliant actuator based on PID control.

The trajectory tracking effect of using traditional PID controller for compliant actuator without adding disturbance observer is presented in Fig. 3. By using the traditional PID algorithm to control the compliant actuator, the path of the actual position variable X and the reference variable X_d is shown in Fig. 3(a). The corresponding tracking error is shown in Fig. 3(b), which is less than $\pm 10^{-4}$ mm. The tracking effect of sliding mode

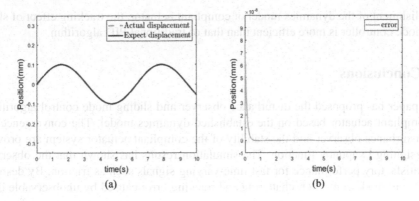

Fig. 4. (a) The trajectory tracking of compliant actuator based on sliding mode control and observer compensation, (b) The tracking error of compliant actuator based on sliding mode control and observer compensation.

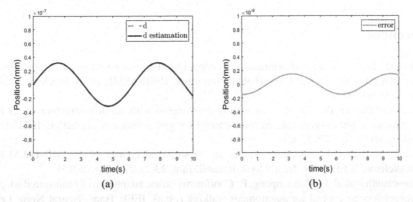

Fig. 5. (a) The trajectory tracking of disturbance observer, (b) The tracking error of disturbance observer.

control for compliant actuator with disturbance observer is presented in Fig. 4. The path of the actual position variable X and the reference variable X_d is shown in Fig. 4(a). The corresponding tracking error is shown in Fig. 4(b), which is less than $\pm 10^{-8}$ mm. The tracking effect of the viscous friction of the compliant actuator through the disturbance observer is shown in Fig. 5(a). The corresponding tracking error is shown in Fig. 5(b), which is less than $\pm 10^{-9}$ mm. Through experimental comparison, it can be seen that the tracking error of the sliding mode controller with disturbance observer to the compliant actuator is better than that of the traditional PID controller.

In conclusion, it can be seen from the simulation results that the difference of tracking effect fully proves the effectiveness of disturbance observer in trajectory tracking. This is because observing the disturbance and then compensating the control torque is an active measure to eliminate the influence of disturbance, which can effectively suppress the trajectory tracking error caused by disturbance. Based on the accurate establishment of the dynamics model of compliant actuator, the tracking effect of sliding mode controller is more efficient than that of traditional PID algorithm.

5 Conclusions

This paper has proposed the disturbance observer and sliding mode control algorithm of compliant actuator based on the established dynamics model. The convergence of the disturbance observer and the stability of the compliant actuator system are proved by designing Lyapunov function. The simulation results has shown that the observer has satisfactory performance for fast time-varying signals such as friction. By designing sliding mode controller, chattering and tracking error caused by unobservable disturbance are reduced. Eventually, high tracking accuracy and good tracking effect are achieved through simulation experiments. In the next stage of our research, we will design the compliant actuator according to the dynamics model of the compliant actuator, design the control algorithm into the controller and complete trajectory tracking.

References

1. Zhou, J., Li, Z., Li, X., et al.: Human-robot cooperation control based on trajectory deformation algorithm for a lower limb rehabilitation robot. IEEE/ASME Trans. Mechatron. **26**(6), 3128–3138 (2021)
2. Aguirre-Ollinger, G., Yu, H.: Lower-limb exoskeleton with variable-structure series elastic actuators: phase-synchronized force control for gait asymmetry correction. IEEE Trans. Robot. **37**(3), 763–779 (2021)
3. Wang, S., Wang, L., Meijneke, C., et al.: Design and control of the MINDWALKER exoskeleton. IEEE Trans. Neural Syst. Rehabil. Eng. **23**(2), 277–286 (2015)
4. Homchanthanakul, J., Manoonpong, P.: Continuous online adaptation of bioinspired adaptive neuroendocrine control for autonomous walking robots. IEEE Trans. Neural Netw. Learn. Syst. **33**(5), 1833–1845 (2022)
5. Martínez, A., Lawson, B., Durrough, C., et al.: A velocity-field-based controller for assisting leg movement during walking with a bilateral hip and knee lower limb exoskeleton. IEEE Trans. Robot. **35**(2), 307–316 (2019)
6. Liu, J.S., He, Y., Yang, J.T., et al.: Design and analysis of a novel 12-DOF self-balancing lower extremity exoskeleton for walking assistance. Mech. Mach. Theory **167**, 104519 (2022)
7. Sariyildiz, E., Chen, G., Yu, H.: A unified robust motion controller design for series elastic actuators. Trans. Mechatron. **22**(5), 2229–2240 (2017)
8. Sariyildiz, E., Chen, G., Yu, H.: An acceleration-based robust motion controller design for a novel series elastic actuator. IEEE Trans. Ind. Electron. **63**(3), 1900–1910 (2016)
9. Li, X., Pan, Y., Chen, G., et al.: Adaptive human-robot interaction control for robots driven by series elastic actuators. IEEE Trans. Robot. **33**(1), 169–182 (2017)
10. Guo, Z., Sun, J., Ling, J., et al.: Robust control of a serial variable stiffness actuator based on nonlinear disturbance observer (NDOB). In: International Conference on Advanced Robotics and Mechatronics (ICARM), pp. 171–176 (2018)
11. Han, S., Wang, H., Yu, H.: Nonlinear disturbance observer-based robust motion control for multi-joint series elastic actuator-driven robots. In: International Conference on Robotics and Automation (ICRA), pp. 10469–10475 (2021)

12. Mohammadi, A., Tavakoli, M., Marquez, H.J., et al.: Nonlinear disturbance observer design for robotic manipulators. Control. Eng. Pract. **21**(3), 253–267 (2013)
13. Zhang, J., Cong, M., Liu, D., Du, Y., Ma, H.: Design of an active and passive control system for a knee exoskeleton with variable stiffness based on a shape memory alloy. J. Intell. Robot. Syst. **101**(3), 1–15 (2021). https://doi.org/10.1007/s10846-021-01319-z
14. Sun, J., Guo, Z., Sun, D., et al.: Design, modeling and control of a novel compact, energy-efficient, and rotational serial variable stiffness actuator (SVSA-II). Mech. Mach. Theory **130**, 123–136 (2018)
15. Sun, J., Guo, Z., Zhang, Y., et al.: A novel design of serial variable stiffness actuator based on an archimedean spiral relocation mechanism. IEEE/ASME Trans. Mechatron. **23**(5), 2121–2131 (2018)
16. Yu, H., Huang, S., Chen, G., et al.: Control design of a novel compliant actuator for rehabilitation robots. Mechatronics **23**, 1072–1083 (2013)
17. Kong, K., Bae, J., Tomizuka, M.: Mechatronic considerations for actuation of human assistive wearable robotics: robust control of a series elastic actuator. In: Mohammed, S., Moreno, J.C., Kong, K., Amirat, Y. (eds.) Intelligent Assistive Robots. STAR, vol. 106, pp. 401–429. Springer, Cham (2015). https://doi.org/10.1007/978-3-319-12922-8_16
18. Oh, S., Kong, K.: High-precision robust force control of a series elastic actuator. IEEE/ASME Trans. Mechatron. **22**(1), 71–80 (2017)
19. Calanca, A., Fiorini, P.: A rationale for acceleration feedback in force control of series elastic actuators. IEEE Trans. Robot. **34**(1), 48–61 (2018)
20. Kim, D.H., Oh, J.H.: Hysteresis modeling for torque control of an elastomer series elastic actuator. IEEE/ASME Trans. Mechatron. **24**(3), 1316–1324 (2019)

Impedance Control of Upper Limb Rehabilitation Robot Based on Series Elastic Actuator

Jian Gu[1], Changxian Xu[1], Keping Liu[1,2(✉)], Liming Zhao[1], Tianyu He[1], and Zhongbo Sun[1]

[1] Department of Control Engineering, Changchun University of Technology, Changchun 130012, People's Republic of China
liukeping@ccut.edu.cn
[2] School of Electrical and Information Engineering, Jilin Engineering Normal University, Changchun 130052, China

Abstract. In this paper, to address motor dysfunction caused by factors such as stroke or traffic accidents, a kind of upper limb rehabilitation robot is designed for rehabilitation training. The rehabilitation robot is driven by series elastic actuator (SEA) to make the upper limb rehabilitation robot have flexible output. Flexible output can improve the compliance and safety between the patient and the rehabilitation robot, but impedance control method is needed to ensure the compliance of human–robot interaction. In order to solve the human–robot interaction problem of SEA–based upper limb rehabilitation robot, the dynamic model and an impedance control are established for the SEA–based upper limb rehabilitation robot. The impedance control method of upper limb rehabilitation robot based on terminal position is designed in detail. Aiming at the designed impedance control method, a numerical simulation model is established for the upper limb rehabilitation robot, and the accuracy of the model is verified by the simulation of the upper limb rehabilitation robot. The numerical results show that the impedance controller can meet the needs of the rehabilitation training of the upper limb rehabilitation robot, which improves the coordination of human–robot interaction in the rehabilitation process.

Keywords: Upper limb rehabilitation robot · Impedance control · Series elastic driver

1 Introduction

In recent years, social problems such as the aging of the population and the younger age of stroke have led to a sharp increase in the number of patients with

The work is supported in part by the National Natural Science Foundation of China under grants 62173048, 61873304 and in part by the China Postdoctoral Science Foundation Funded Project under grants 2018M641784 and 2019T120240, and also in part by the Changchun Science and Technology Project under grant 21ZY41.

H. Liu et al. (Eds.): ICIRA 2022, LNAI 13457, pp. 138–149, 2022.
https://doi.org/10.1007/978-3-031-13835-5_13

motor dysfunction. Survivors of stroke suffer varying degrees of central nervous system damage [1–3]. However, the traditional simple medical equipment and the hands–free treatment by physicians have some outstanding problems, such as low rehabilitation efficiency, high labor intensity of physicians, which are difficult to satisfy the huge demand for rehabilitation medical equipment and artificial rehabilitation resources [4–6]. Therefore, the robot technology is introduced into the field of rehabilitation medicine to assist patients to carry out more scientific and effective rehabilitation training [7–9].

Rehabilitation robot is a combination of mechanical engineering, rehabilitation engineering, artificial intelligence and other interdisciplinary research results [10–13]. Most of the traditional upper limb rehabilitation robots are of the rigid output type. The rehabilitation robot with rigid output has the advantages of high precision of terminal trajectory tracking, simple mechanical structure, easy to control and establish its dynamic model [14,15]. MIT developed the first upper limb rehabilitation robot [16]. Professor Hogan proposed an impedance control algorithm to improve the compliance of human–robot interaction during rehabilitation training. As the inventor of the upper limb rehabilitation robot, it serves as an excellent guide for scholars conducting rehabilitation robot research at a later stage, particularly in terms of structural form, control algorithm, sensing, and monitoring. The upper limb rehabilitation robot in the form of rigid output structure limits the complexity of rehabilitation training tasks, which is difficult to achieve complex movement training. So it is necessary to study the flexibility of the upper limb rehabilitation robot [17,18].

In the rehabilitation training process, the reliability and comfort of the upper limb rehabilitation robot are the primary performance indicators. Compliance is a prerequisite for the safety of human–robot interaction. Improving the compliance of the upper limb rehabilitation robot, which can effectively reduce the mechanical impedance of the human body during rehabilitation training, thus ensuring that rehabilitation training can be carried out in a safe and comfortable interactive environment. Alex used the moment sensor to provide real-time feedback and carried out research on the force position control method, which realized the normalization of patients' gait [19]. In [19], the rehabilitation robots improved patients' gait patterns and increased their walking speed on the treadmill. Hu used impedance control system to achieve the state of interaction force and human position balance of rehabilitation machine [20]. Appropriate training strategies and impedance parameters were selected according to different patients, which realized the auxiliary training and training process of safety and flexibility. Rienrd proposed a control strategy based on the combination of impedance method and adaptive control [21]. Because biofeedback control is difficult to be combined with impedance or adaptive control strategy, impedance and adaptive controller can be combined into an impedance amplitude adaptive controller in [21]. The controller includes the advantages of both control strategies so that patients can adapt to a more personalized, more appropriate and more convenient gait pattern. Although some upper limb rehabilitation robots have been developed, comfort and flexibility remain the main challenges for upper limb rehabilitation robots.

In this paper, impedance control integrates the robot into the same system as the surrounding environment, establishes the expected relationship of target impedance, and carries out real–time position control and force control of the robot. Impedance control method is utilized to dynamically follow the upper limb of the rehabilitation robot. The design simulation and experimental study of the terminal position impedance controller of the rehabilitation robot are emphasized.

This paper is organized as follows: In Sect. 2, introduces the modeling process of the upper limb rehabilitation robot. In Sect. 3, the impedance controller of the upper limb rehabilitation robot is set. The accuracy of the dynamic model of the upper limb rehabilitation robot is verified by the end trajectory tracking experiment in Sect. 4. The Sect. 5 is the conclusion and the prospect of future work.

2   Dynamic and Kinematic Modeling of an Upper Limb Rehabilitation Robot

2.1   Kinematics Analysis

In this section, kinematics analysis is carried out for the schematic diagram of the mechanism in Fig. 1. In Fig. 1, the upper limb rehabilitation robot consists of two SEAs and two links. Among them, there is resistance constraint at the end of the upper limb rehabilitation robot. When the end of the robot touches the obstacle, it slides down parallel to x_2 and continues to track the desired trajectory x_d.

In the Cartesian coordinate system, according to the position of the end points of the upper limb rehabilitation robot in the work space, joint angles q_1 and q_2 are calculated. According to Fig. 1, the position of the terminal workspace as follows:

$$\begin{cases} x_1 = l_1 \cos q_1 + l_2 \cos(q_1 + q_2) \\ x_2 = l_1 \sin q_1 + l_2 \sin(q_1 + q_2) \end{cases}, \tag{1}$$

where q_1 and q_2 are the rotation angles of rods l_1 and q_2, respectively. x_1 and x_2 are the terminal coordinates of the upper limb rehabilitation robot, which are calculated by trigonometric function. According to the law of cosines, the angles q_1 and q_2 are described as:

$$q_1 = \begin{cases} \beta - \gamma & q_2 > 0 \\ \beta + \gamma & q_2 \leq 0 \end{cases}, \tag{2}$$

$$q_2 = \cos^{-1}\left(\frac{x_1^2 + x_2^2 - l_1^2 - l_2^2}{2 l_1 l_2}\right), \tag{3}$$

where β and γ can be represented by trig functions as:

$$\beta = \arccos \frac{x_1^2 + x_2^2 - l_1^2 - l_2^2}{2 l_1 \sqrt{x_1^2 + x_2^2}}, \tag{4}$$

$$\gamma = \begin{cases} \arctan\frac{x_2}{x_1} & \text{if } x_1 \geq 0 \\ \pi + \arctan\frac{x_2}{x_1} & \text{if } x_1 < 0 \end{cases}, \tag{5}$$

Jacobian matrix is defined to express the relationship between the terminal velocity and joint angular velocity of the upper limb rehabilitation robot. Jacobian matrix $\mathbf{J}(\mathbf{q})$ is defined as:

$$\mathbf{J}(\mathbf{q}) = \begin{bmatrix} -l_1\sin(q_1) - l_2\sin(q_1 + q_2) & -l_2\sin(q_1 + q_2) \\ l_1\cos(q_1) + l_2\cos(q_1 + q_2) & l_2\cos(q_1 + q_2) \end{bmatrix}, \tag{6}$$

it can be seen from Jacobian matrix $\mathbf{J}(\mathbf{q})$, which $\mathbf{J}(\mathbf{q})$ is determined by the structure of the upper limb rehabilitation robot. It is assumed to be nonsingular in the bounded workspace Ω.

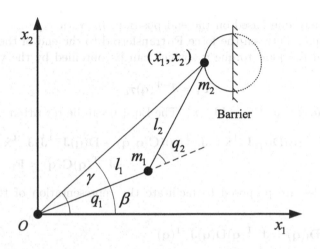

Fig. 1. Mechanism diagram of upper limb rehabilitation robot.

2.2 Dynamic Analysis

In this paper, the upper limb rehabilitation robot is driven by SEA, and the flexible output of SEA realizes the protection of joint drive of the rehabilitation robot. The coupling of the output of the SEA joint to the patient's upper limb needs to be considered during dynamic modeling. Assuming that the spring is linear, the torque generated by the spring can be expressed as:

$$\tau_c = \mathbf{k_m}(\theta - q), \tag{7}$$

where θ is the angle of motor, $\mathbf{k_m}$ is the spring's elastic coefficient. The input torque formula of the motor can be defined as follows:

$$\tau_m = \mathbf{J}\ddot{\theta} + \mathbf{b_m}\dot{\theta} + \tau_c, \tag{8}$$

where b_m is the damping coefficient of the motor. According to Lagrange dynamics theory, the dynamic equation of the upper limb rehabilitation robot can be expressed as:

$$\mathbf{D}(\mathbf{q})\ddot{\mathbf{q}} + \mathbf{C}(\mathbf{q},\dot{\mathbf{q}})\dot{\mathbf{q}} + \mathbf{G}(\mathbf{q}) = \tau_c, \tag{9}$$

where $\mathbf{q} \in \mathbf{R}^n$ is a vector of joint variable, $\tau_c \in \mathbf{R}^n$ is the joint torque vector applied by SEA, $\mathbf{D}(\mathbf{q}) \in \mathbf{R}^{n \times n}$ is a symmetric positive definite inertia matrix, $\mathbf{C}(\mathbf{q},\dot{\mathbf{q}}) \in \mathbf{R}^{n \times n}$ is the vector of Coriolis force and centrifugal force, $\mathbf{G}(\mathbf{q}) \in \mathbf{R}^n$ is the gravity vector. In order to describe the constraint relationship between the motor position and the connecting rod position of the connecting rod end dynamic model, it can be written in the following form:

$$\mathbf{D}(\mathbf{q})\ddot{\mathbf{q}} + \mathbf{C}(\mathbf{q},\dot{\mathbf{q}})\dot{\mathbf{q}} + \mathbf{G}(\mathbf{q}) + \mathbf{k}_m\mathbf{q} = \mathbf{k}_m\theta, \tag{10}$$

in order to control the end position, the dynamic equation of joint angle is transformed into one based on the end position. In static equilibrium, there is a linear mapping between the force $\mathbf{F}_i$ transferred to the end of the rehabilitation robotand the joint torque τ_c, which can be obtained by the virtual work principle as:

$$\mathbf{F}_i = \mathbf{J}^{-T}(\mathbf{q})\tau_c, \tag{11}$$

where $\dot{\mathbf{x}} = \mathbf{J}\dot{\mathbf{q}}$, $\ddot{\mathbf{x}} = \mathbf{J}^{-1}(\ddot{\mathbf{x}} - \dot{\mathbf{J}}\mathbf{J}^{-1}\dot{\mathbf{x}})$. The Eq. (9) can be rewritten as:

$$\mathbf{J}^{-T}(\mathbf{q})\mathbf{D}(\mathbf{q})\mathbf{J}^{-1}\ddot{\mathbf{x}} + \mathbf{J}^{-T}(\mathbf{q})(\mathbf{C}(\mathbf{q},\dot{\mathbf{q}}) - \mathbf{D}(\mathbf{q})\mathbf{J}^{-1}\dot{\mathbf{J}})\mathbf{J}^{-1}\dot{\mathbf{x}}$$
$$+\mathbf{J}^{-T}(\mathbf{q})\mathbf{G}(\mathbf{q}) = \mathbf{F}_i. \tag{12}$$

Three variables are proposed to facilitate the representation of the dynamic model as:

$$\mathbf{D}_i(\mathbf{q}) = \mathbf{J}^{-T}(\mathbf{q})\mathbf{D}(\mathbf{q})\mathbf{J}^{-1}(\mathbf{q})$$
$$\mathbf{C}_i(\mathbf{q},\dot{\mathbf{q}}) = \mathbf{J}^{-T}(\mathbf{q})(\mathbf{C}(\mathbf{q},\dot{\mathbf{q}}) - \mathbf{D}(\mathbf{q})\mathbf{J}^{-1}(\mathbf{q})\dot{\mathbf{J}}(\mathbf{q}))\mathbf{J}^{-1}(\mathbf{q}) \tag{13}$$
$$\mathbf{G}_i(\mathbf{q}) = \mathbf{J}^{-T}(\mathbf{q})\mathbf{G}(\mathbf{q}),$$

Considering the uncertainty of the dynamic model of the upper limb rehabilitation robot, the compensation terms are designed, the following dynamic model is obtained as:

$$\mathbf{D}_i(\mathbf{q})\ddot{\mathbf{x}} + \mathbf{C}_i(\mathbf{q},\dot{\mathbf{q}})\dot{\mathbf{x}} + \mathbf{G}_i(\mathbf{q}) + \varpi(\mathbf{q},\mathbf{q},\dot{\mathbf{q}}) = \mathbf{F}_i, \tag{14}$$

the inertia matrix $\mathbf{D}_i(\mathbf{q})$ in the dynamic equation designed in this section is symmetric and positive definite, and $\|\varpi(\mathbf{q},\mathbf{q},\dot{\mathbf{q}})\| \leq \eta$. According to the proposed dynamic model, the impedance model of the upper limb rehabilitation robot is established as follows:

$$\mathbf{M}_m(\ddot{\mathbf{x}}_r - \ddot{\mathbf{x}}) + \mathbf{B}_m(\dot{\mathbf{x}}_r - \dot{\mathbf{x}}) + \mathbf{K}_m(\mathbf{x}_r - \mathbf{x}) = \mathbf{F}_r, \tag{15}$$

where $\mathbf{M}_m$, $\mathbf{B}_m$, and $\mathbf{K}_m$ are mass, damping, and stiffness coefficients, respectively. The contact force at the end of the upper limb rehabilitation robot is $\mathbf{F}_r$,

$\mathbf{x_r}$ is the instruction locus of the contact position. In order to realize the track tracking of $\mathbf{x_r}$ at the ideal contact position in the Cartesian coordinate system, according to Eq. (14) and Eq. (15), the following model is obtained as:

$$\mathbf{D_i(q)\ddot{x}} + \mathbf{C_i(q,\dot{q})\dot{x}} + \mathbf{G_i(q)} + \mathbf{F_r} + \varpi(\mathbf{q,q,\dot{q}}) = \mathbf{F_i}, \qquad (16)$$

in the impedance model, the impedance control objective is $\mathbf{x}$ tracking the ideal impedance track $\mathbf{x_d}$, which can be obtained from the following model as:

$$\mathbf{M_m\ddot{x}_d} + \mathbf{B_m\dot{x}_d} + \mathbf{K_m x_d} = -\mathbf{F_r} + \mathbf{M_m\ddot{x}_r} + \mathbf{B_m\dot{x}_r} + \mathbf{K_m x_r}, \qquad (17)$$

here, $\mathbf{x_d}(0) = \mathbf{x_r}(0)$, $\dot{\mathbf{x}}_d(0) = \dot{\mathbf{x}}_r(0)$. Next, according to the proposed dynamic model, the control law $\mathbf{F_i}$ is designed, the actual joint torque τ_c is obtained by the relation between $\mathbf{F_i}$ and τ_c.

3   Design of Impedance Controller

The principle of impedance control is to replace the actual contact force to be controlled with equivalent impedance. When there is a deviation between the rehabilitation robot and the human body, impedance compensation force will be generated at the contact point to realize the dynamic interaction between position and force. In this paper, the contact force to be applied is obtained through the position deviation, and the position based impedance control is obtained by calculating the contact force deviation between the rehabilitation robot and the patients. In Fig. 2, the desired position is calculated, which translates the compensation of the force into the compensation of the position. In the position control model, the end motion of the robot is regarded as the expected motion. Define $\mathbf{x_d}$ as the ideal trajectory in workspace, $\dot{\mathbf{x}}_d$ and $\ddot{\mathbf{x}}_d$ are ideal velocities and accelerations, respectively. According to the control block diagram in Fig. 2, the sliding variable $\mathbf{s(t)}$ is proposed as:

$$\begin{cases} \mathbf{e(t)} = \mathbf{x_d(t)} - \mathbf{x(t)} \\ \dot{\mathbf{x}}_c(t) = \dot{\mathbf{x}}_d(t) + \Lambda\mathbf{e(t)} \\ \mathbf{s(t)} = \dot{\mathbf{x}}_c(t) - \dot{\mathbf{x}}(t) = \dot{\mathbf{e}}(t) + \Lambda\mathbf{e(t)} \end{cases}, \qquad (18)$$

where $\mathbf{e(t)}$ is the end displacement error of the upper limb rehabilitation robot, the matrix Λ is a positive definite matrix. According to the dynamic model and impedance model, the controller is designed as:

$$\mathbf{F_i} = \mathbf{D_i(q)\ddot{x}_c} + \mathbf{C_i(q,\dot{q})\dot{x}_c} + \mathbf{G_i(q)} + \mathbf{F_r} + \mathbf{K}s + \eta\tan\frac{s}{\varepsilon}, \qquad (19)$$

where $\mathbf{K} > 0$, $\varepsilon > 0$. The dynamic model described by Eq. (19) and Eq. (14) can be written as:

$$\mathbf{D_i(q)\ddot{x}} + \mathbf{C_i(q,\dot{q})\dot{x}} + \mathbf{G_i(q)} + \varpi(\mathbf{q,q,\dot{q}}) = \mathbf{D_i(q)\ddot{x}_c} +$$
$$\mathbf{C_i(q,\dot{q})\dot{x}_c} + \mathbf{G_i(q)} + \mathbf{F_r} + \mathbf{K}s + \eta\tan\frac{s}{\varepsilon}, \qquad (20)$$

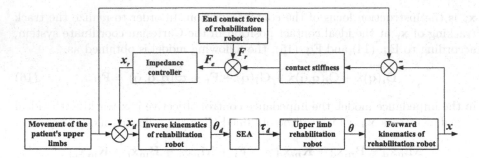

Fig. 2. Block diagram of impedance control of upper limb rehabilitation robot.

defining $\dot{x}(t) = \dot{x}_c(t) - s(t)$ and $\ddot{x}(t) = \ddot{x}_c(t) - \dot{s}(t)$, then

$$D_i(q)\dot{s} + C_i(q,\dot{q})s + G_i(q) + Ks + \eta \tan\frac{s}{\varepsilon} - \varpi(q,\dot{q},\ddot{q}). \tag{21}$$

In Fig. 2, when the actual joint position of the upper limb rehabilitation robot deviates from the operator's position, the actual contact force is calculated by the action of the position deviation and contact stiffness. Impedance controller is a second–order system, and impedance parameters are related to system performance. The damping coefficient B_m will affect the stability process of the step response of the system, so the damping parameter should be set as the critical damping state or over–damping state to complete the tracking of the joint relative to the human upper limb. Stiffness parameter K is the key of impedance control for compliant following, and affects response speed at the same time. Selecting lower stiffness may produce slow following image. The inertia parameter M_m is determined by the actual inertia matrix, and the K value is optimized through simulation test. Then inertia parameter M_m and stiffness parameter K were set to select damping coefficient B_m. Finally, the inertial parameter M_m is selected. Appropriate parameters are selected for simulation experiments to verify the accuracy of the designed model.

4   Simulation Results

In this section, the accuracy and stability of the proposed model and algorithm are proved by the end trajectory tracking control of the upper limb rehabilitation robot.

4.1   Trajectory Tracking of an Upper Limb Rehabilitation Robot

In this subsection, impedance control method is used to realize the end tracking motion of the upper limb rehabilitation robot. Since the cartesian position of the joint of the upper limb rehabilitation robot is corresponding to the joint position, the joint position is utilized to comparative analysis of the following effect. The simulation environment is adopted as Matlab software. In order to better realize the end track tracking of the upper limb rehabilitation robot, it is necessary to analyze the end track tracking of x_1 and x_2 and set reasonable parameters.

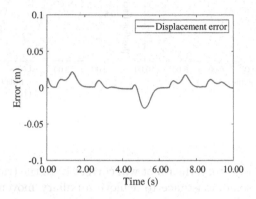

Fig. 3. The results of x_2 tracking trajectory.

In parameter selection, the inertia parameter $M_m = 0.9$ is similar to the inertia of the system, and the damping parameter $B_m = 10$. Different stiffness parameters K_m are used for simulation tests. When $K_m = 50$, the position trajectory tracking of joint nodes of the upper limb rehabilitation robot is obtained as shown in the Fig. 4. In the simulation process, it finds that with the increase of the stiffness parameters, the response time of the actual position relative to the expected position shortens, the stability time decreases, but there will be overshoot. The overshoot increases with the increase of the contact torque. As there is resistance at the end of the upper limb rehabilitation robot, when $x_1 \leq 0.6$, the end of the rehabilitation robot does not contact the obstacle, namely $\mathbf{F_r} \begin{bmatrix} 0 & 0 \end{bmatrix}$, when $x_1 \geq 0.6$, the end point of the rehabilitation robot contacts the obstacle $x_1 = 0.6$. Therefore, in Fig. 4(a), there is an error between the actual trajectory of peak value and the expected trajectory.

It can be seen from Fig. 4(b) that the model established in this paper can track the x_2 track stably through impedance control, and the error curve is shown in Fig. 3. The error mainly occurs at the peak of the desired trajectory, and the error is less than 0.03 rad as shown in Fig. 4(b). Based on the accurate track tracking effect of the x_1 and x_2 coordinate axes of the upper limb rehabilitation robot in Fig. 4, the $\mathbf{x_r}$ trajectory tracking by the end of the upper limb rehabilitation robot is realized.

The end trajectory tracking of the upper limb rehabilitation robot is shown in Fig. 5. The desired trajectory x_1 is defined as $x_1 = 0.6 - 0.3\cos(\pi t)$, and the x_2 is defined as $x_2 = 0.6 - 0.3\sin(\pi t)$. The purpose of using the upper limb rehabilitation robot to track the terminal trajectory is to let the patient control the affected limb to move along the given reference trajectory. When the movement

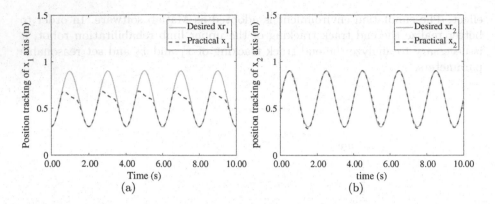

Fig. 4. Position tracking of joint nodes of rehabilitation robot.

deviates from this trajectory, the robot will correct it. In the training process, the robot can provide some assistance to achieve auxiliary movement and provide some resistance to achieve resistance movement.

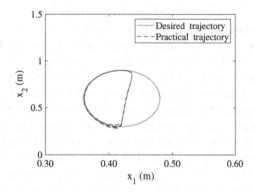

Fig. 5. The tracking terminal trajectory of rehabilitation robot.

4.2   Contact Force and Joint Torque of Upper Limb Rehabilitation Robot

The contact force simulation test can ensure the contact safety between the joint and the patient. Equation (15) is exploited to calculate the contact force F_r at the end of the upper limb rehabilitation robot. From Fig. 6, the contact force F_r corresponding to each moment when the upper limb rehabilitation robot completes the trajectory tracking task. Figure 6 shows the contact forces generated during the simulated experiment, which ensures that the human–robot

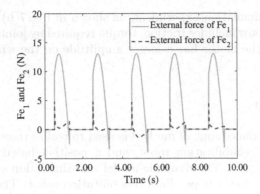

Fig. 6. External forces on the end joint.

interaction force of the affected limb is maintained in a safe range in the rehabilitation process. To prevent secondary damage to the affected limb, a safety
threshold can be set. When the contact force is greater than the set threshold,
the rehabilitation robot stops moving.

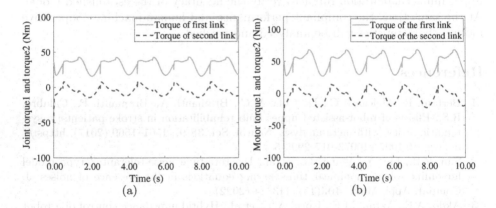

Fig. 7. The actual input torque of the joint.

The impedance control result equates the force between human and joint as
a spring–damping system. The joint based on the impedance control method can
achieve real-time interaction of motion and force with the human body to complete the obedient following. Figure 7(a) show the magnitude τ_c of the torque
required to follow the motion of the arm from the end joint. The value τ_c of the
control torque fluctuates slightly at the peak of the desired trajectory, but soon
returns to normal, and the overall curve is smooth without large fluctuation and
changes periodically. Equation (9) is used to calculate τ_c in the simulation experiment, which provides reference for the design of SEA in the prototype experiment. Equation (7) and Eq. (8) are utilized to obtain the torque τ_m required by

the motor in the simulation experiment, as shown in Fig. 7(b). The torque τ_m provided by the motor includes friction, torque required by joints, etc. Therefore, the torque τ_m of the motor has a larger amplitude on the whole and its peak torque is 68 Nm.

5   Conclusion

In this paper, impedance control method is used to realize the compliant control of the upper limb rehabilitation robot, and a position–based impedance control method is designed. The dynamic model and simulation system are established for the SEA–based upper limb rehabilitation robot. The position–based impedance control method can achieve more accurate and stable interaction between the rehabilitation robot and the patient. Impedance control is utilized to track the end displacement of an upper limb rehabilitation robot. The results show that the impedance control can enable the upper limb rehabilitation robot to accurately complete the end trajectory tracking task. The proposed impedance control method can solve the interaction between motion and force of SEA-based upper limb rehabilitation robot during rehabilitation. In the future, a prototype will be built, and impedance control tests will be carried out on the designed upper limb rehabilitation robot to verify the accuracy of the established model. At the same time, the compliant performance and human-machine cooperative motion characteristics will be analyzed and verified.

References

1. Bertani, R., Melegari, C., De Cola, M.C., Bramanti, A., Bramanti, P., Calabrò, R.S.: Effects of robot-assisted upper limb rehabilitation in stroke patients: a systematic review with meta-analysis. Neurol. Sci. **38**(9), 1561–1569 (2017). https://doi.org/10.1007/s10072-017-2995-5
2. Sun, Z.B., Liu, Y., Wang, G., et al.: Discrete-time noise-tolerant Z-type model for online solving nonlinear time-varying equations in the presence of noises. J. Comput. Appl. Math. **403**(15), 113824 (2022)
3. Akdo, A.E., Aktan, M.E., Koru, A.T., et al.: Hybrid impedance control of a robot manipulator for wrist and forearm rehabilitation: performance analysis and clinical results. Mechatronics **49**, 77–91 (2017)
4. Brahmi, B., Driscoll, M., El Bojairami, I.K., Saad, M., Brahmi, A.: Novel adaptive impedance control for exoskeleton robot for rehabilitation using a nonlinear time-delay disturbance observer. ISA Trans. **108**, 381–392 (2020)
5. Wu, Q., Wang, X., Bai, C., et al.: Development of an RBFN-based neural-fuzzy adaptive control strategy for an upper limb rehabilitation exoskeleton. Mechatronics **53**, 85–94 (2018)
6. Jalaeian, F.M., Fateh, M.M., Rahimiyan, M.: Optimal predictive impedance control in the presence of uncertainty for a lower limb rehabilitation robot. J. Syst. Sci. Complexity **33**, 310–1329 (2020)
7. Mancisidor, A., Zubizarretaa, A., Cabanes, I., et al.: Kinematical and dynamical modeling of a multipurpose upper limbs rehabilitation robot. Robot. Comput. Integr. Manuf. **49**(7), 374–387 (2018)

8. Yang, T., Gao, X., Dai, F.: New hybrid AD methodology for minimizing the total amount of information content: a case study of rehabilitation robot design. Chin. J. Mech. Eng. **33**(1), 51–60 (2020)

9. Sun, Z., Zhao, L., Liu, K., Jin, L., Yu, J., Li, C.: An advanced form-finding of tensegrity structures aided with noise-tolerant zeroing neural network. Neural Comput. Appl. **34**(8), 6053–6066 (2021). https://doi.org/10.1007/s00521-021-06745-6

10. Sun, Z.B., Wang, G., Jin, L., et al.: Noise-suppressing zeroing neural network for online solving time-varying matrix square roots problems: a control-theoretic approach. Expert Syst. Appl. **192**(15), 116272 (2022)

11. Ji, L.: Quantitative assessment of motor function by an end-effector upper limb rehabilitation robot based on admittance control. Appl. Sci. **11**, 112–132 (2021)

12. Meng, Q., Jiao, Z., Yu, H., et al.: Design and evaluation of a novel upper limb rehabilitation robot with space training based on an end effector. Mech. Sci. **1**, 639–648 (2021)

13. Madani, M., Moallem, M.: Hybrid position/force control of a flexible parallel manipulator. J. Franklin Inst. **348**(6), 999–1012 (2011)

14. Wang, J., Liu, J., Zhang, G., et al.: Periodic event-triggered sliding mode control for lower limb exoskeleton based on human-robot cooperation. ISA Trans. **123**, 87–97 (2022)

15. Chai, Y.Y., Liu, K.P., Li, C.X., et al.: A novel method based on long short term memory network and discrete-time zeroing neural algorithm for upper-limb continuous estimation using sEMG signals. Biomed. Signal Process. Control **67**, 1746–8094 (2021)

16. Krebs, H.I., Volpe, B.T., Aisen, M.L., et al.: Increasing productivity and quality of care: robot-aided neuro-rehabilitation. J. Rehabil. Res. Dev. **37**(6), 639–652 (2000)

17. Zhang, Q., Sun, D., Qian, W., et al.: Modeling and control of a cable-driven rotary series elastic actuator for an upper limb rehabilitation robot. Front. Neurorobot. **14**, 13 (2020)

18. Chen, T., Casas, R., Lum, P.S.: An elbow exoskeleton for upper limb rehabilitation with series elastic actuator and cable-driven differential. IEEE Trans. Robot. **35**(6), 1464–1474 (2019)

19. Banala, S.K., Kim, S.H., Agrawal, S.K., et al.: Robot assisted gait training with active leg exoskeleton (ALEX). IEEE Trans. Neural Syst. Rehabil. Eng. **17**(1), 2–8 (2009)

20. Hu, J., Hou, Z., Zhang, F., et al.: Training strategies for a lower limb rehabilitation robot based on impedance control. In: 2012 Annual International Conference of the IEEE Engineering in Medicine and Biology Society, pp. 6032–6035 (2012)

21. Riener, R., Lunenburger, L., Jezernik, S., et al.: Patient-cooperative strategies for robot-aided treadmill training: first experimental results. IEEE Trans. Neural Syst. Rehabil. Eng. **13**(3), 380–394 (2055)

Flexible Lightweight Graphene-Based Electrodes and Angle Sensor for Human Motion Detection

Wenbin Sun, Quan Liu, Qiang Luo, Qingsong Ai, and Wei Meng[✉]

School of Information Engineering, Wuhan University of Technology, Wuhan 430070, China
weimeng@whut.edu.cn

Abstract. Flexible wearable sensors can assist patients with physical injuries or disabilities in auxiliary treatment and rehabilitation, which are of great importance to the development of the future medical field. Most flexible wearable sensors convert physiological signal changes or the changes of body states caused by motion into electrical signals to realize human motion information sensing. Two typical examples are EMG sensors and angle sensors. However, the existing EMG electrodes have many disadvantages such as high manufacturing cost and inferior contact with skin, which makes it impossible to guarantee a stable signal acquisition when the body is in kinetic state. Moreover, angle sensors need to develop in the direction of high sensitivity, ease of use and low cost. Graphene has thus entered the field of vision of researchers. In this work, we tested and analyzed two flexible sensors based on graphene. Firstly, we prepared graphene flexible electrodes and performed human sEMG sensing tests. Meanwhile, we proposed a graphene-based strain gauge with grid structure and performed angle sensing tests. The experimental results show that the graphene electrodes can effectively monitor human movement information such as blink and arm movement with high sensitivity. The graphene grid strain gauge is able to detect flexion angle of joints with high linearity from 20° to 90°. As a flexible sensing material, graphene has the characteristics of high sensitivity, repeatability and ease of use, and can be widely used in different types of sensing, which means that graphene may become one of the prime materials for future wearable sensors.

Keywords: Flexible wearable sensor · Graphene · Surface EMG sensing · Angle sensing

1 Introduction

Smart wearable technology is one of the cores of the future development of medical rehabilitation field, which can realize a variety of functions such as telemedicine, rehabilitation training assistance and real-time monitoring [1]. Flexible wearable sensor is the functional core of intelligent wearable devices and also the main research object in the field of flexible wearable. The preparation of flexible wearable sensor needs to measure a

H. Liu et al. (Eds.): ICIRA 2022, LNAI 13457, pp. 150–161, 2022.
https://doi.org/10.1007/978-3-031-13835-5_14

variety of indicators such as flexibility, sensitivity and sensing range, repeatability, hysteresis effect and time response, which means that an excellent flexible wearable device needs to strike a balance among all indicators and have a good sensing performance.

The choice of sensing materials is crucial for flexible wearable devices. Among many flexible materials, low-dimensional carbon materials (graphene, carbon nanotubes and fullerene) have gradually become a research focus. Graphene has become one of the sensing materials for flexible wearable sensors due to its excellent mechanical and electrical properties [2–7]. Research on flexible sensors based on graphene is diverse, as it can be widely applied on different parts of the body, depending on different preparation methods and sensing mechanisms. For example, by integrating flexible graphene-based rosette strain gauge into gloves, the sensor can detect multidirectional strain with a strain detection range of up to 7.1% [8]. Researchers also use graphene electrode for electro-oculogram (EOG) detection, which is simple in structure and can detect eye movements such as blink and saccade due to its high sensitivity [9]. In some studies, graphene is mixed with other sensing materials to obtain better sensing properties [10–12]. For instance, SWCNT is mixed with graphene to obtain stable temperature compensation properties [12]. A large number of studies have shown that graphene does have the development potential as a sensing material for flexible wearable devices. Therefore, the use of graphene to prepare flexible wearable sensing systems with lower cost, easier operation and better sensing performance is the focus of current research.

There are still some problems in today's flexible wearable devices, such as poor skin suppleness, easy damage and poor repeatability, especially in traditional sEMG sensing electrodes and flexible strain sensors. In this study, graphene electrodes and graphene grids were prepared to test the sEMG sensing characteristics and bending angle sensing characteristics, respectively. The experimental results verify the feasibility and excellent sensing performance of graphene electrodes for sEMG sensing and graphene grids for angle sensing, and also show that graphene has excellent versatility as a sensing material, i.e., depending on the preparation method, sensing mechanism and sensing system construction, it can be used to detect human body information under different needs, which reflects the application prospects of graphene in the field of wearable sensing.

2 Methods

2.1 Flexible Graphene Electrode for sEMG Sensing

The electrodes used in conventional sEMG sensors are generally Ag/AgCl electrodes, which are not inherently flexible. Since graphene has excellent electrical conductivity and skin fit, we prepared circular graphene sheets to replace Ag/AgCl electrodes, and also prepared copper and aluminum electrodes of the same size for control experiments, as shown in Fig. 1.

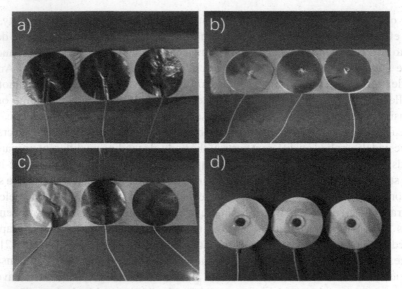

Fig. 1. Four sEMG sensing electrodes: a) Graphene electrode; b) Aluminum electrode; c) Copper electrode; d) Ag/AgCl electrode.

An impedance model is established based on the electrodes shown in Fig. 1, as shown in Fig. 2a, where R_G represents the impedance of a single graphene electrode, and R_1–R_3 represent the equivalent human body impedance.

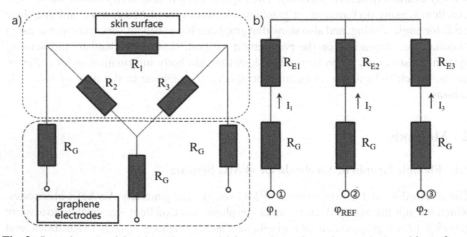

Fig. 2. Impedance model: a) impedance model for graphene electrodes attached on skin surface; b) impedance model transformation.

Transform the delta connected impedance network composed of R_1, R_2 and R_3 into a star connected network, and the result is shown in Fig. 2b. It can be seen from Fig. 2 that R_{E1}, R_{E2} and R_{E3} have a specific relationship with R_1, R_2 and R_3, as shown in Eq. 1.

$$\begin{cases} R_{E1} = \dfrac{R_1 R_2}{R_1 + R_2 + R_3} \\ R_{E2} = \dfrac{R_2 R_3}{R_1 + R_2 + R_3} \\ R_{E3} = \dfrac{R_1 R_3}{R_1 + R_2 + R_3} \end{cases} \tag{1}$$

Now specify the potential difference between electrode 1 and electrode 2 is U_1; the potential difference between electrode 2 and electrode 3 is U_2; and the potential difference between electrode 1 and electrode 3 is U_3, then Eq. 2 is established.

$$\begin{cases} U_1 = \varphi_{REF} - \varphi_1 = I_2(R_{E2} + R_G) - I_1(R_{E1} + R_G) \\ U_2 = \varphi_3 - \varphi_{REF} = I_3(R_{E3} + R_G) - I_2(R_{E2} + R_G) \\ U_3 = \varphi_3 - \varphi_1 = I_3(R_{E3} + R_G) - I_1(R_{E1} + R_G) \\ I_1 + I_2 + I_3 = 0 \end{cases} \tag{2}$$

Take electrode 2 as reference electrode, corresponding to the electrode in the middle in Fig. 1a. When the sensing system is attached to the forehead to detect blinks, the value of sEMG signals measured by the electrodes (U_{sEMG}) satisfies Eq. 3.

$$U_{sEMG} = U_3 = \varphi_3 - \varphi_1 = I_3(R_{E3} + R_G) - I_1(R_{E1} + R_G)$$
$$= (I_3 - I_1)R_G + I_3 R_{E3} - I_1 R_{E1} \tag{3}$$

It can be seen from Eq. 3 that the change of the conductivity of the sensing material will have an impact on the measurement of sEMG signal. The resistance stability of graphene is better than that of Ag/AgCl electrodes, and thus the sEMG signal measured by graphene electrodes will be more accurate.

2.2 Flexible Graphene Grid for Angle Sensing

The working principle of resistance strain gauges is based on strain effect, that is, when a conductor or semiconductor material is mechanically deformed under the action of external force, its resistance value changes correspondingly. Graphene also has strain effect, and in order to make this effect more obvious, our group prepared a graphene grid strain gauge, as shown in Fig. 3a. After processing and sealing, it is shown in Fig. 3b. The graphene grid is more sensitive to bending than an uncarved graphene sheet.

The grid structure of graphene strain gauge is shown in Fig. 4. If the resistivity of graphene is ρ and the strain gauge thickness is h, the initial resistance of the graphene strain gauge is shown in Eq. 4. The resistance of the graphene strain gauge during bending is shown in Eq. 5.

$$R = \rho \frac{n(L + d)}{dh} \tag{4}$$

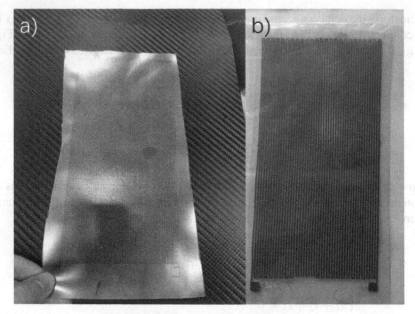

Fig. 3. Flexible graphene grid strain gauge.

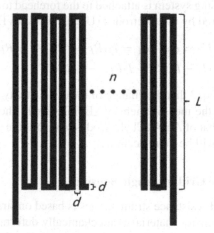

Fig. 4. Structure of the graphene grid strain gauge.

$$R' = \rho \frac{n(L + \Delta L + d - \Delta d)}{(d - \Delta d)(h - \Delta h)} \tag{5}$$

ΔL is the longitudinal length change of each grid caused by strain gauge bending, ΔD and Δh are the length changes of grid width and thickness caused by strain gauge bending, respectively. The change in resistance value caused by bending is shown in Eq. 6.

$$\Delta R = R' - R = \rho n(\frac{\Delta L}{dh - h\Delta d - d\Delta h + \Delta d\Delta h} + \frac{L}{dh - h\Delta d - d\Delta h + \Delta d\Delta h} + \frac{1}{h - \Delta h} - \frac{L}{dh} - \frac{1}{h}) \tag{6}$$

Since d >> Δd, and h >> Δh, Eq. 3 can be reduced to:

$$\Delta R = R' - R = \rho n(\frac{\Delta L}{dh} + \frac{L}{dh} + \frac{1}{h} - \frac{L}{dh} - \frac{1}{h}) = \rho n\frac{\Delta L}{dh} = \rho n\frac{L}{dh}\frac{\Delta L}{L} = k\varepsilon \tag{7}$$

In Eq. 7, k is a constant and ε is the strain resulting from bending. Therefore, the resistance of the graphene strain gauge theoretically varies linearly with the bending strain. It also can be seen from Eq. 7 that the graphene strain gauge will not be interfered by the transverse strain caused by sticking the strain gauge to the skin, so the device is very suitable for measuring the angle of human joints.

3 Experiments

3.1 Flexible Graphene Electrode for sEMG Sensing

The sEMG sensing system was built using electrodes, a sEMG sensor (Muscle Sensor V3), a signal processing unit (Arduino), and a terminal (PC), as shown in Fig. 5a–b. The sensor is powered by a ±9 V power supply (6F22ND). We first applied graphene electrodes to the arm and conducted sEMG sensing test by bending the arm to verify the usability of graphene electrodes, as shown in Fig. 5c. Thereafter, electrodes of different materials were applied to the forehead to detect blink information and the results were compared, as shown in Fig. 6.

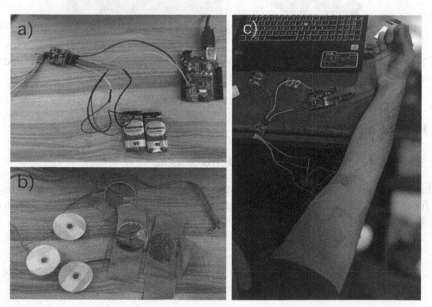

Fig. 5. The whole sEMG sensing system: a) sEMG sensor, power supply and signal processing unit; b) graphene electrodes; c) sEMG sensing test for arm movement.

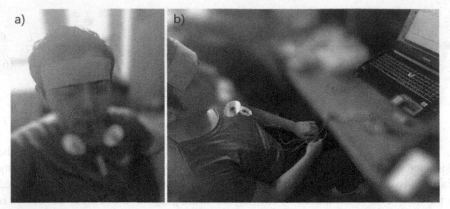

Fig. 6. Eye movement detection: a) graphene electrodes placed on the forehead; b) blink and observe the sensing output on PC.

3.2   Flexible Graphene Grid for Angle Sensing

The bending angle sensing system is composed of a strain gauge sensor (RunesKee), a graphene grid strain gauge and a signal processing unit (Arduino), as shown in Fig. 7.

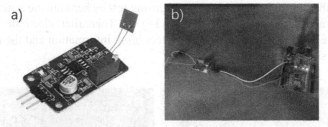

Fig. 7. Bending angle sensing test: a) strain gauge sensor; b) angle sensing system; c) and d) graphene grid strain gauge attached on elbow for angle sensing.

4   Results and Discussion

4.1   Flexible Graphene Electrode for sEMG Sensing

In this study, four electrodes of the same material were applied to different positions of the forehead in parallel to detect blink signals. The experimental results are shown in Fig. 8.

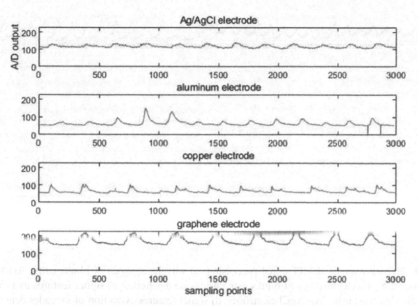

Fig. 8. Blink detection by different flexible electrodes.

As can be seen from Fig. 8, the Ag/AgCl electrode has relatively high repeatability, but its amplitude range is the smallest among the four electrodes, which indicates that its sensitivity is low. The repeatability of the aluminum electrode for human blink sensing is poor and the output is accompanied by glitch, which may be due to the fact that the fit of the aluminum piece to the skin is not good enough and its output amplitude is too small compared with the other three flexible electrodes, which shows that the aluminum electrode is not suitable enough for detecting small physiological activities such as human blink and pulse, and as a metal electrode, its suppleness to the skin is relatively poor. As for the copper electrode, although its output amplitude is larger than that of the aluminum electrode, reflecting a more excellent sensing sensitivity, the results show that it still has problems such as unstable output results and poor repeatability. It is worth noting that the copper electrode is also a metal electrode. Although it can be prepared as a flexible electrode for wearable devices, it still has problems of poor skin suppleness and low sensing sensitivity. The graphene electrode has a significant improvement over the previous three electrodes. The output amplitude of the graphene electrode is the largest among the four electrodes, which means that it has better sensing sensitivity than the other three electrodes. In addition, the graphene-based sEMG sensor has stability and repeatability for the same blink motion.

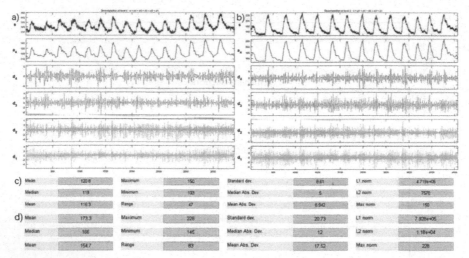

Fig. 9. Eye movements sEMG signal processing: a) wavelet analysis of blinks using Ag/AgCl electrodes; b) wavelet analysis of blinks using graphene electrodes; c) signal features extraction of blinks detection using Ag/AgCl electrodes; d) signal features extraction of saccades detection using graphene electrodes.

After wavelet analysis of sEMG signals, the differences between the traditional Ag/AgCl electrode and the flexible graphene electrode can be seen more intuitively, as shown in Fig. 9. In the figure, a_4 in Fig. 9a–b represents the low-frequency component after filtering. Obviously, the graphene electrode has better repeatability. According to the comparison in Fig. 9c–d, the output amplitude of graphene electrode is $228 - 145 = 83$, which is larger than the output amplitude of Ag/AgCl electrode with value of $150 - 103 = 47$. The results of wavelet analysis show that the sensitivity and repeatability of graphene electrode are better than that of traditional Ag/AgCl electrode.

The graphene electrode is capable of detecting not only small physiological activities such as blink and saccade, but also physical activities such as arm movements, as shown in Fig. 10. The subject first straightens the arm and then gradually bends it to perform this process in a cycle. The experimental results show that the graphene-based sEMG sensor has excellent sensing sensitivity and repeatability, and the sensing range is large, ranging from small physiological activities to limb movements. If the collected sEMG signals be processed by wavelet analysis and feature extraction, then the sensor can be applied to various rehabilitation medical scenarios such as artificial limb control and gait recognition and analysis.

4.2 Flexible Graphene Grid for Angle Sensing

The bending angle - resistance relationship test was performed on the prepared graphene grid strain gauge, and the results are shown in Fig. 11. With the increase of bending Angle, the resistance of strain gauge gradually increases, which shows that the sensing mechanism is consistent with the theory.

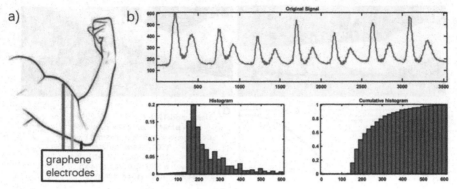

Fig. 10. Arm movement detection: a) position of the graphene electrodes; b) detection results of arm movement sensing.

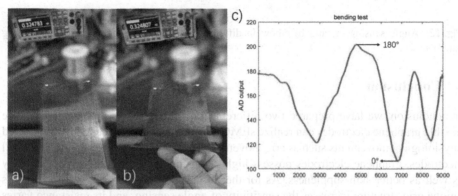

Fig. 11. Qualitative measurement of the angle sensing characteristics: a) and b) graphene grid strain gauge bent to different degrees; c) sensing result of bending the strain gauge.

From Fig. 11c, it can be seen that the maximum bending-induced sensor output voltage change is about $(202 - 107)/4096 \times 5\ V = 116\ mV$. Thus, this graphene strain gauge has a good sensitivity for bending angle sensing.

After conducting the above qualitative tests, we attached graphene strain gauges to the elbow joint for bending sensing test to verify the usability of graphene strain gauges, as shown in Fig. 12a–b. Curve fitting has been performed based on the experiment data, and the fitting results are shown in Fig. 12c–d. It can be seen that the voltage change caused by the bending angle is not strictly linear, which is because the relationship between the bending angle and the strain generated by bending is not linear, thus leading to the nonlinear results of the bending angle sensing curve.

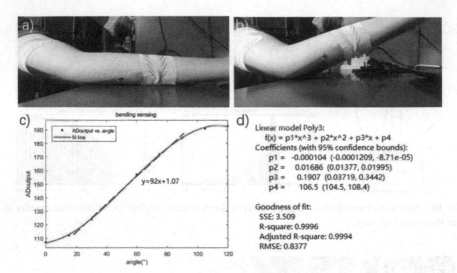

Fig. 12. Angle sensing: a) and b) elbow in different angle; c) fitting curve; d) curve-fitting parameters.

5 Conclusion

In conclusion, we have prepared two different graphene-based wearable sensors. The flexible graphene electrodes can realize sEMG sensing and have successfully monitored physiological movements such as arm movements and blinks. Compared with Ag/AgCl electrodes, graphene electrodes possess higher sensing sensitivity, better repeatability as well as better skin suppleness. As for the proposed graphene grid strain gauge, its unique grid structure increases the sensitivity of angle sensing, and its resistance varies linearly with the bending strain. Experiments show that the strain gauge is effective in bending angle sensing and has a high linearity between 20° and 90°. The two graphene-based sensing systems proposed in this paper outperform most conventional flexible wearable devices due to their excellent skin suppleness, sensing performance and wide applicability, which demonstrate broad application prospects in wearable sensing.

Acknowledgments. This work is supported by the Wuhan Application Frontier Project under Grant 20200206601012220 and the National Natural Science Foundation of China under Grant 52075398.

References

1. Shyamal, P.: A review of wearable sensors and systems with application in rehabilitation. J. Neuroeng. Rehabil. **9**(1), 1–17 (2012)
2. Du, D.: Graphene coated nonwoven fabrics as wearable sensors. J. Mater. Chem. C **4**(15), 3224–3230 (2016)
3. Xuan, X.: A wearable electrochemical glucose sensor based on simple and low-cost fabrication supported micro-patterned reduced graphene oxide nanocomposite electrode on flexible substrate. Biosens. Bioelectron. **109**, 75–82 (2018)

4. Yu, L., et al.: All VN-graphene architecture derived self-powered wearable sensors for ultra-sensitive health monitoring. Nano Res. **12**(2), 331–338 (2018). https://doi.org/10.1007/s12 274-018-2219-1

5. Wei, Y.: Graphene-based multifunctional textile for sensing and actuating. ACS Nano **15**(11), 17738–17747 (2021)

6. Zhang, H.: Graphene-enabled wearable sensors for healthcare monitoring. Biosens. Bioelectron. **197**, 113777 (2022)

7. Yu, T.: Graphene foam pressure sensor based on fractal electrode with high sensitivity and wide linear range. Carbon **182**, 497–505 (2021)

8. Bae, S.: Graphene-based transparent strain sensor. Carbon **51**, 236–242 (2013)

9. Golparvar, A.J.: Graphene smart textile-based wearable eye movement sensor for electro-ocular control and interaction with objects. J. Electrochem. Soc. **166**(9), B3184–B3193 (2019)

10. Lü, X.: Wide-range and high-stability flexible conductive graphene/thermoplastic polyurethane foam for piezoresistive sensor applications. Adv. Mater. Technol. **6**(10), 2100248 (2021)

11. Zou, X.: Ultrahigh sensitive wearable pressure sensors based on reduced graphene oxide/polypyrrole foam for sign language translation. Adv. Mater. Technol. **6**(7), 2001188 (2021)

12. Guo, X.: Highly stretchable strain sensor based on SWCNTs/CB synergistic conductive network for wearable human-activity monitoring and recognition. Smart Mater. Struct. **26**(9), 095017 (2017)

The Study of Ankle Assisted Exoskeleton

Yali Han[(✉)], Jiachen Chang, Zhuangzhuang Jin, Shunyu Liu, and Lei Zhou

Nanjing Institute of Technology, Nanjing 211167, Jiangsu, China
S966237@163.com

Abstract. This article proposes a design of a multidegree-of-freedom ankle assisted exoskeleton based on the gait phase and motion mechanism of human ankle joint. Firstly, the model of the exoskeleton mechanism is designed, and the size parameters of each part are determined through structural analysis. Then, the control strategy of the exoskeleton is analyzed, the gait is obtained by identifying the foot pressure signal through the finite state machine, and the ankle exoskeleton is controlled by matching the corresponding PID parameters according to different gaits. At last, a prototype experiment is carried out. The results show that the ankle exoskeleton can reduce the EMG signal of the calf by 28.91% on average, and has a good effect of rehabilitation.

Keywords: Ankle assisted exoskeleton · Gait recognition · Finite state machine · Exoskeleton wear experiment

1 Introduction

Ankle assisted exoskeleton is a wearable device. It generally has the functions of assisting the human body to walk, and is a kind of strength and rehabilitation equipment. At present, a variety of exoskeletons have been designed to assist ankle motion, which are divided into passive and active ankle assisted exoskeletons.

The passive ankle assisted exoskeleton designed by Collins team of Carnegie Mellon University [1, 2] uses springs to collect energy during human walking, and releases it when lifting the foot to help the human ankle. Various active ankle assist systems developed by Wyss Laboratory of Harvard University [3–8] all use a motor-driven Bowden wire rotating joint, which can reduce the wearer's metabolic consumption by 6.4% and 10% respectively. ReWalk Robotics Israel and Wyss Lab at Harvard University jointly developed the flexible ankle assisted exoskeleton restore Exo-Suit [9]. It is composed of two motors at the back waist and Bowden line. The motor transmits the force to the flexible fabric of heel and foot surface through Bowden line, so that the ankle joint is assisted by dorsiflexion and plantar flexion. The team of Charles Khazoom from the University of Sherbrooke in Canada used a magnetorheological clutch as a driver to design a high-power, low-mass ankle-assisted exoskeleton [10]. By adjusting the current in the magnetorheological clutch, the pressure of the hydraulic cylinder was controlled, thereby helping ankle plantar flexion. Minhyung Lee developed a compact ankle exoskeleton with a multi-axis parallel mechanism [11, 12], which can generate dorsiflexion and plantar flexion movements by applying torque to the ankle joint. The mechanism accommodates up to 12 N·m of torque within a thickness constraint of 40 mm, and can recognize gait phases through the data from foot pressure sensors.

This paper aims to conduct a comprehensive study of the ankle exoskeleton, and design an ankle assisted exoskeleton with two degrees of freedom of plantar flexion/dorsiflexion and adduction/abduction. The ankle exoskeleton consists of a linkage mechanism, which is driven by a motor. The designed exoskeleton can reduce the electromyographic signal of the main muscles of the calf when the human body is walking, indicating that it has a sufficient rehabilitation effect on the human body.

2   Ankle Assisted Exoskeleton Design

2.1   Structural Design of Ankle Assisted Exoskeleton

The designed ankle-assisted exoskeleton system and motion schematic are shown in Fig. 1. Including drive motor, gear box, encoder, fixed plate, pulley, synchronous belt, lead screw support seat, ball screw, lead screw nut, sleeve, connecting pin, movable cross bar, curved connecting rod, fisheye bearing, foot plate, foot connector, ear connector, movable link, connecting rod structure fixed side and active side of connecting rod structure. The synchronous belt drive is used to place the motor and the ball screw in parallel, which is conducive to saving space and making the overall structure more compact. The ball screw can convert the rotary motion of the motor into the linear motion of the sleeve, and can amplify the torque output by the motor. Ear connectors provide passive degrees of freedom for ankle adduction or ankle abduction. The spatial linkage structure can transform the linear motion of the sleeve into the rotational motion of the ankle joint.

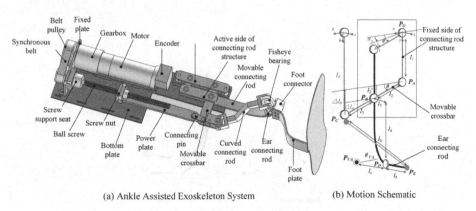

(a) Ankle Assisted Exoskeleton System   (b) Motion Schematic

Fig. 1.   Ankle assisted exoskeleton system and motion schematic

P_O and P_A are the fixed side of the connecting rod structure, P_B is the intersection of the movable side of the connecting rod structure and the movable cross bar. θ_0 is the initial offset angle of the connecting rod machine. l_0 is the initial length of the end of the ball screw power plate from the starting position. P_C is the position where the end of the power plate is connected to the movable crossbar. P_D is the connection point between the foot connector and the previous structure. P_E is the connection point between the curved link and the fisheye pair. The P_{VA} is a virtual ankle joint whose center of rotation coincides with the actual ankle joint position.

2.2 Structural Analysis of Ankle Assisted Exoskeleton

The ankle joint exoskeleton rotation schematic diagram is shown in Fig. 2.

Analyze the structural diagram of ankle exoskeleton, define a set of design variables $L = [\theta_0, l_2, l_3, l_4, l_5, l_6, l_7, l_s]$. The change of the linkage's rotation angle θ_1 will drive the position P_{VA} of the virtual ankle joint point to change. The coordinates of point P_{VA} can be obtained by solving the coordinates of the rotation point on the ankle exoskeleton. In xyz coordinate system, the coordinate vector expression of each rotation point is as follows:

$$P_B = l_2 \cos \theta\, x + (l_1 + l_2 \sin \theta)y \tag{1-1}$$

$$P_C = (l_2 + l_3) \cos \theta\, x + (l_1 + (l_2 + l_3) \sin \theta)y \tag{1-2}$$

$$P_D = l_2 \cos \theta\, x + (l_1 + l_2 \sin \theta + l_4)y + l_7 z \tag{1-3}$$

The total length of the motor is 103.7 mm, according to the size of ankle exoskeleton determined by the size of adult human body, the specific size of each part is: $l_1 = 40$ mm, $l_2 + l_3 = 60$ mm, $l_4 = 103$ mm, $l_5 = 29$ mm, $l_6 = 108$ mm, $l_7 = 29$ mm.

The principle of ankle rotation driven by the linkage mechanism is shown in Fig. 2(b).

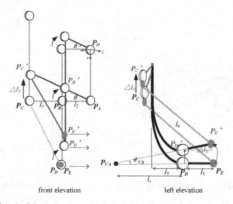

front elevation   left elevation

Fig. 2. Ankle joint exoskeleton rotation schematic diagram

P_C is the end of the sleeve, which is driven by the lead screw to produce a displacement of Δl_0, and P_B displacement is: $l'_2 = (l_2/(l_2 + l_3))\Delta l_0$. This displacement difference is transmitted to P_D and P_E to make the end rotate. The points marked after rotation are $P_{D'}$ and $P_{E'}$, the intersection of the connecting line between $P_{E'}$ and $P_{D'}$ and the connecting line between P_D and P_E is the virtual ankle point P_{VA}. The included angle θ_{VA} between them is the angle of ankle rotation, and the expression is:

$$\tan \theta_{VA} = \Delta l_0'/l_5 \tag{1-4}$$

It can be obtained by substituting into Eq. 1-4:

$$\theta_{VA} = \arctan[(l_3/(l_2 + l_3)l_5)\Delta l_0] \tag{1-5}$$

According to Eq. 1-5, by substituting different l_2 and l_3 ratios, the relationship image between the rotation angle θ_{VA} of the ankle exoskeleton and the linear displacement Δl_0 of the ball screw sleeve can be obtained, as shown in Fig. 3. Referring to the straight line $y = x$, it can be seen that when $l_2:l_3 = 1:1$, the relationship between θ_{VA} and Δl_0 is also the closest to 1:1. This means that for every 1 mm movement of the sleeve, the ball screw rotates for half a cycle and the ankle exoskeleton rotates by 1°, and the linearity is the best when the ankle angle changes little. Therefore, $l_2:l_3 = 1:1$, that is, $l_2 = l_3 = 30\,\text{mm}$ is selected as the design size.

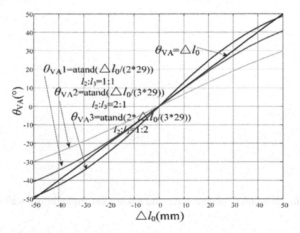

Fig. 3. The relationship between θ_{VA} and Δl_0 under different ratios of l_2 and l_3

3 Study on Control Strategy of Ankle Assisted Exoskeleton

3.1 Design of Gait Recognition System

Whether the plantar force can be accurately identified has a great impact on the ankle joint control system. Gait recognition is carried out to facilitate the design of ankle control system. The membrane pressure sensor combined with flexible bending sensor is selected as the sensing module element. Multiple pressure sensors are used to measure the pressure at different positions of the sole, and the flexible bending sensor is used to measure the angle of the ankle.

Signals of the plantar force and the angle of the ankle are collected. Three pressure sensors are placed at the bottom of the insole, respectively on the toe, heel and forefoot of the sole, the specific location is shown in Figs. 4 and Figs. 5. The toe is set to signal A, the heel is set to signal B, and the forefoot is set to signal C.

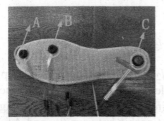
Fig. 4. Pressure sensor location diagram

Fig. 5. Bend sensor location diagram

The plantar force and ankle joint angle at different walking speeds is shown in Fig. 6.

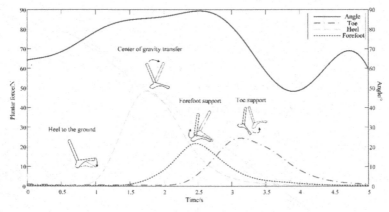
Fig. 6. Diagram of plantar force and ankle joint angle during walking

It can be seen from Fig. 6 that when the heel touches the ground as the beginning of a gait cycle, the plantar force at three positions (Toe, Heel and Forefoot) is 0 N and the ankle angle is about 64°. As the heel touches the ground, its pressure and ankle angle begin to increase.

When the body's center of gravity is fully shifted to the support side, the pressure on the heel is at its maximum, and the pressure on the forefoot and the angle of the ankle also increases. When the center of gravity of the human body continues to move forward, the heel pressure decreases rapidly and transmits to the front end of the foot. At this time, the forefoot pressure is about to reach the maximum value, and the angle of the ankle joint almost reaches the peak value of 90°. When the heel is lifted, the plantar pressure is all transferred to the toe. At this point, the pressure between the heel and forefoot is almost zero, and the ankle angle begins to drop rapidly to about 30° with the lifting of the heel. When the toe is off the ground, the plantar pressure is all zero, and the ankle angle begins to adjust with the lower leg swinging in the air until it enters the next gait cycle.

3.2 Research on Control Strategy

The PID angle control strategy and the layered control block diagram of the ankle joint exoskeleton are shown in Fig. 7.

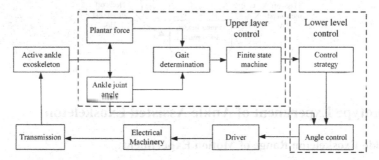

Fig. 7. A block diagram of the hierarchical control strategy of the ankle exoskeleton

Set the signal activation state when the pressure ratio of the toe, mid-foot and heel is greater than 40%, the activation signal is set to 1. The finite state transition rules of ankle joint can be obtained, as shown in Table 1.

Table 1. Ankle exoskeleton finite state transition table

Phase	Signal status		
	A	B	C
ZC	0	1	0
BC	0	0	1
ZD	1	0	0
WC	1	1	0

When the ankle exoskeleton is in a certain phase and the plantar force signals A, B and C reach the corresponding state in the above table, the ankle exoskeleton will transfer the state to the next phase. The state transfer process is shown in Fig. 8.

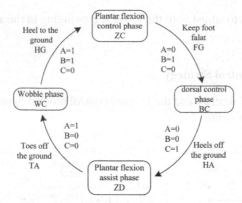

Fig. 8. Ankle joint exoskeleton state transition process diagram

4 Prototype Experiment of Ankle Assisted Exoskeleton

4.1 Ankle Exoskeleton Range of Motion Experiment

The range experiments of ankle adduction/abduction and plantar flexion/dorsiflexion is performed, the results are shown in Figs. 9 and Figs. 10.

It can be seen from Fig. 9 and Fig. 10 that the ankle exoskeleton can provide a range of motion of 35° in the adduction direction and 15° in the abduction direction. The rotation angle of the ankle exoskeleton can reach 20° in the dorsal flexion direction and 30° in the plantar flexion direction.

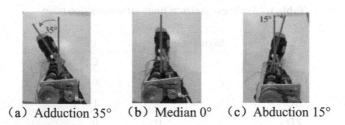

(a) Adduction 35°   (b) Median 0°   (c) Abduction 15°

Fig. 9. Movement angle range diagram of prototype in adduction/abduction direction

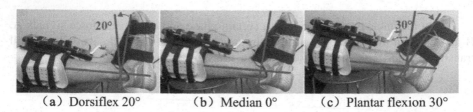

(a) Dorsiflex 20°   (b) Median 0°   (c) Plantar flexion 30°

Fig. 10. Range of motion angle in plantar flexion/dorsiflexion direction of prototype

4.2 Angle Following Experiment of Ankle Exoskeleton

The angle following control experiment of ankle exoskeleton is carried out, and the PID control method is used to help the ankle during walking. The plantar force and ankle angle of the wearer during normal walking are collected. The plantar force data are processed by the finite state machine according to the proportion of each pressure to obtain the phase of the gait.

The finite state machine divided the phases into plantar flexion control phase (ZC), dorsiflexion control phase (BC), plantar flexion assist phase, swing control phase (WC). Each phase outputs different parameters as selection conditions for PID parameters.

The plantar force and the output of the state machine are shown in Fig. 11.

It can be seen from Fig. 11 that the output of the state machine accurately reflects different phase periods. The experimental process of wearing and walking of ankle exoskeleton is shown in Fig. 12, and the angle following curve is shown in Fig. 13.

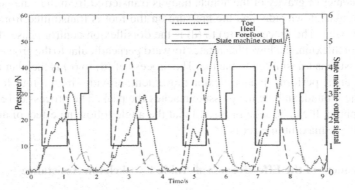

Fig. 11. Plantar force and state machine output results

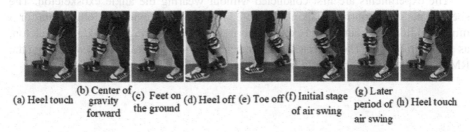

(a) Heel touch (b) Center of gravity forward (c) Feet on the ground (d) Heel off (e) Toe off (f) Initial stage of air swing (g) Later period of air swing (h) Heel touch

Fig. 12. Angle following process diagram of ankle exoskeleton

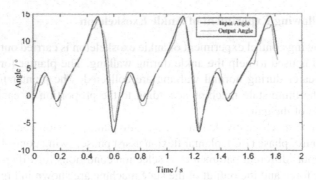

Fig. 13. Angle following curve of ankle exoskeleton

As can be seen from Fig. 12, the process of (a) to (c) is the plantar flexion control phase, the center of gravity of the human body is transferred from the other side of the body to the touchdown side, and the pressure on the foot is transmitted from the heel to the front palm. The process of (c) to (d) is the dorsiflexion control phase. The ankle performs dorsiflexion, the lower leg rotates forward perpendicular to the ground, and the plantar pressure is transmitted to the toe. The process of (d) to (e) is the plantar flexion phase. The ankle performs plantar flexion movement, provides high torque to push the ankle off the ground, and the toe pressure reaches the peak. The process of (e) to (h) is the swing phase. It can be seen in Fig. 13 that the angle following effect of ankle joint is good, and the maximum error is 2°.

4.3 Assessment of the Effectiveness of Ankle Exoskeleton Assistance

As shown in Fig. 14, an experiment for evaluating the effect of the ankle joint-assisted exoskeleton is performed.

The experiments are first conducted without wearing the ankle exoskeleton. The speed is set as the normal walking speed: 2 km/h, and continuously collect data for 3 min. In addition, the same set of experiments is done with wearing the ankle exoskeleton, as shown in Fig. 15. The collected electromechanical signals are processed by using the RMS, and the results are shown in Fig. 16 and Fig. 17.

There are two groups of curves in each of the graphs from Fig. 16 and Fig. 17. The upper part is the original surface EMG signal, and the lower part is the root mean square algorithm (RMS) processing of the original signal. It can be seen from the figure that the EMG signal data of gastrocnemius and soleus muscles after wearing ankle assisted exoskeleton are significantly smaller than those during normal walking, Among them, the electrical signal of gastrocnemius decreased by about 61.67%, and soleus decreased by about 10.31%. Therefore, it can be concluded that the assistance effect of ankle exoskeleton is better.

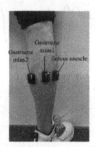

Fig. 14. Location diagram of EMG signal sensor

Fig. 15. Experimental diagram of exoskeleton wearing and walking

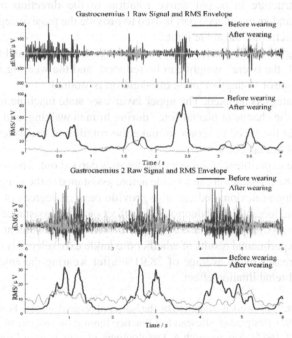

Fig. 16. Electromyography of gastrocnemius muscle 1&2

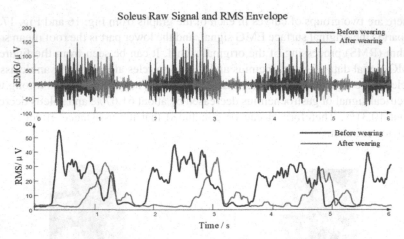

Fig. 17. Electromyography of soleus muscle

5 Conclusion

An ankle assisted exoskeleton is designed in this study, the conclusions are as follows:

For the mechanism design of the ankle joint exoskeleton, a motor is used to drive the link structure to output active rotation in the direction of plantar flexion/dorsiflexion, and an ear-shaped part is used to provide the passive degree of freedom of adduction/abduction of the ankle joint.

The total weight of the current prototype is 1.5 kg, the structure and material can be further optimized, the overall weight can be reduced, and the wearing comfort can be improved. The control strategy of ankle exoskeleton is studied.

A layered strategy is adopted. The upper layer uses state machine to recognize the gait according to the change of plantar force during human walking, and the lower layer uses PID to adjust the speed of motor to make the rotation of exoskeleton conform to the current gait of human body.

The prototype experiment of ankle exoskeleton is carried out. The results of experiments show that the exoskeleton can provide active assistance in the range of 30° plantar flexion and 20° dorsal flexion, and can also provide passive degrees of freedom in the range of 35° adduction and 15° abduction. The effect of ankle assistance was evaluated, and the EMG signals of the main muscle groups of lower limb movement were collected. Comparing the experimental results of whether the ankle exoskeleton is worn or not, the EMG signal decreases by an average of 28.91% after wearing the ankle exoskeleton, which has a good rehabilitation effect.

Acknowledgement. This work is supported by the National Natural Science Foundation of China (Grant No. 51205182), Postgraduate Research & Practice Innovation Program of Jiangsu Province (Grant No. SJCX21_0915), Key research & Development plan of Jiangsu Province (Grant No. BE2019724).

References

1. Collins, S.H., Wiggin, M.B., Sawicki, G.S.: Reducing the energy cost of human walking using an unpowered exoskeleton. Nature **522**(7555), 212 (2015)
2. Sawicki, G.S., Beck, O.N., Kang, I., et al.: The exoskeleton expansion: improving walking and running economy. J. Neuroeng. Rehabil. **17**(1), 1–9 (2020)
3. Asbeck, A.T., Rossi, S.M.M.D., Galiana, I., et al.: Stronger, smarter, softer: next-generation wearable robots. IEEE Robot. Autom. Mag. **21**(4), 22–33 (2014)
4. Asbeck, A.T., de Rossi, S.M.M., Holt, K.G., et al.: A biologically inspired soft exosuit for walking assistance. Int. J. Robot. Res. **34**(6), 744–762 (2015)
5. Lee, S., Crea, S., Malcolm, P., et al.: Controlling negative and positive power at the ankle with a soft exosuit. In: IEEE International Conference on Robotics and Automation. Piscataway, pp. 3509–3515. IEEE, USA (2016)
6. Quinlivan, B.T., Lee, S., Malcolm, P., et al.: Assistance magnitude versus metabolic cost reductions for a tethered multiarticular soft exosuit. Sci. Robot. **2**(2) (2017)
7. Bae, J., Siviy, C., Rouleau, M., et al.: A lightweight and efficient portable soft exosuit for paretic ankle assistance in walking after stroke. In: IEEE International Conference on Robotics and Automation. Piscataway, pp. 2820–2827. IEEE (2018)
8. Awad, L.N., Bae, J., O'Donnell, K., et al.: A soft robotic exosuit improves walking in patients after stroke. Sci. Transl. Med. **9**(400) (2017)
9. Plaza, A., Hernandez, M., Puyuelo, G., et al.: Lower-limb medical and rehabilitation exoskeletons: A review of the current designs. IEEE Rev. Biomed. Eng. (2021)
10. Khazoom, C., Veronneau, C., Bigue, J., et al.: Desigh and control of a multifunctional ankle exoskeleton powered by magnetorheological actuators to assist walking, jumping and landing. IEE Robot. Autom. Lett. **4**(3), 3083–3090 (2019)
11. Lee, M., et al.: A compact ankle exoskeleton with a multiaxis parallel linkage mechanism. IEEE/ASME Trans. Mechatron. **26**(1), 191–202 (2021)
12. Choi, H., Park, Y., Seo, K., Lee, J., Lee, S., Shim, Y.: A multifunctional ankle exoskeleton for mobility enhancement of gait-impaired individuals and seniors. IEEE Robot. Autom. Lett. **3**(1), 411–418 (2018)

Motor Learning-Based Real-Time Control for Dexterous Manipulation of Prosthetic Hands

Kemal Balandiz[1](✉), Lei Ren[1], and Guowu Wei[2]

[1] The University of Manchester, Sackville Street, Manchester M13 9PL, UK
kemal.balandiz@manchester.ac.uk
[2] Salford University, Newton Building, Salford M5 4WT, UK

Abstract. Recent studies on myoelectric-based prosthetic control have shown that surface electromyography (sEMG) can enhance prosthetic intuitiveness by improving motion detection algorithms and continuous data processing. This study aims to use a combination of feature extraction techniques and machine learning approaches to map sEMG signals to 10 upper-limb motions for real-time control. The study implements four machine learning methods (i.e., k-nearest neighbours (k-NN), artificial neural networks (ANN), support vector machines (SVM), linear discriminant analysis (LDA)) as classifiers and six time-domain features (i.e., root mean square (RMS), integrated absolute value (IAV), mean absolute value (MAV), simple square integration (SSI), waveform length (WL), average amplitude change (AAC)) to extract sEMG features to differentiate six individual fingers and four-hand griping patterns. Five subjects volunteered in the research and training datasets were recorded using seven sEMG electrodes for three static and three dynamic arm positions. The modalities were assessed with offline classification performance from the collected datasets and real-time evaluation metrics such as motion completion rate, motion detection accuracies and reach and grasp experiments. Based on the above, the control methodology differentiates independent finger motions with high accuracy, 94% completion rates with 0.23 s data processing and prediction time.

Keywords: Dexterous manipulation · EMG-based control · Pattern recognition · Prosthetic hand

1 Introduction

With a complicated kinematic structure, tactile sensory system, and bidirectional communication with the brain, limb autonomy is a significant factor influencing individuals' life. The upper limb possesses exceptional dexterity, allowing it to investigate and manipulate various items by transferring sensory information and fine motor control of about thirty different muscles.

Amputation of the upper limb significantly reduces human autonomy, and severe amputation can cause a variety of psychological and physical problems in amputees. According to studies, around 30% of amputees suffer from despair or anxiety and are socially isolated [1]. According to a survey, nearly two million amputees live in the

© The Author(s), under exclusive license to Springer Nature Switzerland AG 2022
H. Liu et al. (Eds.): ICIRA 2022, LNAI 13457, pp. 174–186, 2022.
https://doi.org/10.1007/978-3-031-13835-5_16

United States of America (USA), which is estimated to be doubled by 2050 [2]. Although some advanced prosthetics hands have been developed, the cost of these devices ranges from $25,000 to $75,000 [3]. Some statistics show that the rejection rate of commercially available prostheses is between 40% to 50% due to issues related to cosmetic appearance, lack of functionality, high cost and poor intuitiveness [4].

Numerous studies have been carried out in order to develop myoelectric-based prostheses by combining muscle group synergies with machine learning algorithms. This method allows control of the wrist and individual fingers by monitoring EMG signals generated as a series of muscle group contractions stating intended tasks. Non-invasive (sEMG) interfaces have primarily been used to control prostheses with multiple degrees of freedom (DoF). The traditional prosthetics viewpoint uses pattern recognition from two input EMGs to control the limited DoF (moving from one state to another). On the other hand, these devices lack robustness and dexterous object manipulation. As an alternative to the simple EMG classifier, a new control approach with multiclass classifications has been developed [5]. Various machine learning methods have been used to identify hand manipulation patterns. This approach has influenced pattern recognition to progress beyond basic movements and has evolved into a new trend of sensing muscle movements to control individual fingers.

In the initial investigations, sEMG signals were obtained from the individuals' arms as they performed a variety of activities and produced force patterns. Digital filters were utilized to pre-process dynamic and kinematic data before it was used to train supervised ML models. This study investigates the applicability and efficiency of ML methods in sEMG-based pattern recognition. It analyses the key approaches in developing prosthetic hands, including signals processing, feature extraction techniques, different types of classifiers, socket design, sensory modality, and performance evaluation methods. The study presents improvements to address some of the major issues raised by myoelectric control of prosthetic hands, such as reduced functionality, limited controllability, the accuracy of movement selection and response time delay.

1.1 Background and Related Work

Several adaptive mechanisms have been developed and implemented in prosthetic hands. By imitating the kinematics of the human hand, it has been possible to achieve high dexterity to perform multiple tasks, such as detecting a sliding object between fingers and increasing compensating force to reconstruct accurate movements. While many concepts and attempts have been made to develop prosthetics, only a few procedures and technologies have been widely accepted and introduced from laboratories to everyday clinical use [6]. In order to connect the prosthesis to the remaining muscles, alternative invasive methods such as targeted muscle reinvention (TMR) and Peripheral Nervous System (PNS) have been used since it is challenging to measure sEMG corresponding to all possible motions [7]. However, these procedures are limited and more applicable for laboratory investigations due to surgical problems and contamination from numerous noises in the surrounding environment.

Even though contemporary hybrid approaches have enhanced prosthetic performance with sensory feedback to execute the autonomous movement, they have also introduced new drawbacks, such as higher costs, design problems, and increased user training load. Furthermore, the stiff form and propagation of anchoring pressures can harm nerves and may cause significant damage. Therefore, the correlation of the pattern recognition approach in laboratory results to the actual world is unsatisfactory. It has been claimed that the completion rate of real-time control in pattern recognition by transradial amputees was 55%, while the offline classification accuracy was 85% [8].

This paper constructs a systematic framework to achieve continuous real-time control by identifying independent finger motions driven by muscle groups and employing diverse sensory locations to improve grab grip accuracy. Lastly, a compact combination of all compartments that enables permanent and continuous connection with users was proposed to reduce the problem's complexity and give a dependable solution to instability. Using a new sensory modality and embedded data processing: (1) the study monitored muscle activity simultaneously, (2) investigated the impact of using fewer electrodes, different windowing sizes, and variation in dynamic and static arm postures with designed bypass socket, and (3) the performance of continuous motion detection was evaluated on a real-time robotic hand while taking into account amputees' real-life conditions.

2   Materials and Methods

2.1   EMG Data Acquisition

The muscle activities of participants were recorded as part of the EMG data acquisition employing seven high-performance Delsys™ Trigno Wireless System® with recently released Quattro sensors. The experiment was divided into two halves, each being conducted at a different time. The surface electrodes were targeted to specific muscles during the first half of the research, as presented in Fig. 1(a). In contrast, seven electrodes were equally distributed over the right forearm muscles (approximately 5 cm from the elbow joint) in the second half, as illustrated in Fig. 1(b).

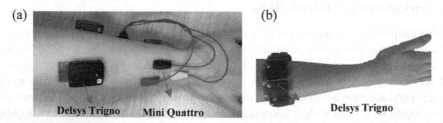

(a)   (b)

Delsys Trigno   Mini Quattro   Delsys Trigno

Fig. 1. EMG electrode placement on the right forearm for the targeted (TR) muscle (a). Equally distributed EMG electrodes for untargeted (UT) muscle in the circumference of the right arm (b). The electrode pairs are placed onto the extensor and flexor muscles.

In targeted muscles, four Quattro electrodes were mainly placed around the forearm to obtain the dense sampling of the muscles at the forearm's proximal part. The remaining three Trigno electrodes were placed on the main activity spots of the flexor digitorum superficialis and flexor digitorum profundus. The precise locations of muscles were chosen based on their significance for motor control of finger and hand motions. After finding the optimal locations of muscles, which were identified by palpation while the participants were continually contracting muscles, the data collection procedure for the targeted muscle session was meticulously repeated concerning the forearm's muscular physiology.

In the second phase of the studies, seven electrodes were placed throughout the forearm circumference without targeting muscles to detect flexion/extension and abduction/adduction of fingers and thumb separately for the untargeted (UT) muscle condition (see Fig. 1(b)). Because conventional targeted electrode placement ignores the participant's stump with the short remaining arm, the primary objective of this electrode placement is to record as many different muscles as feasible. Differences in sensory locations create considerable classification degradation in each trial. Thus, a bypass socket (see Fig. 2) resists elbow rotation, decreases electrode shifting, and standardizes electrode localization was designed to improve classification performance.

Fig. 2. Different views of the custom-made socket for electrode placement in the circumference of the user's arm.

2.2 Experimental Protocol

The first stage of the experiment involves collecting data sets and examining individual participants' influence on classification performance with five able-bodied males ranging in age from 24 to 28 years old. The individuals have no musculoskeletal or motor control diseases that could impact the speed of activities or natural manipulation. The experimenter recorded trials when the subjects had rested their arm and were ready to begin. The individuals were instructed to perform finger motions and manipulate all hand joint axes in accordance with induction displayed on a PC screen. The movements were defined as six basic finger motions and four object grasping gestures, including individual finger flexion and extension of five fingers, as well as thumb abduction/adduction. Within every manipulation, the participants completed the desired motions for 10 s. The tests were conducted on different days to collect information from five distinct sessions. The experiments were carried out using static and dynamic arm orientations to examine dynamic limb postures' implications.

In the second and third phases, the subjects were asked to hold their arm horizontal, upright and downside for the same finger movements as seen in Fig. 3. Each finger manipulation duration was 10 s with at least 3 s maintain fingers in the flexion position. Participants were introduced to reaching and grasping objects from three different distances and returning to the initial arm position in the final part of data collection (see

Fig. 3). Objects were located at three different lengths and heights (i.e., 10 cm, 20 cm, and 30 cm) from the initial arm position. Subjects followed and imitated the same trajectories displayed on a computer screen to eliminate the impact of various motion speeds.

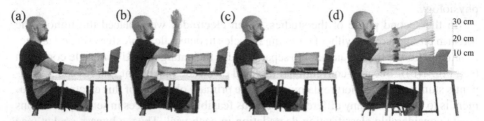

Fig. 3. Experiment setup displaying arm postures and electrode allocation for six fingers and three dynamic arm motions. (a) The arm is horizontal, (b) the arm is upright, and (c) the arm is up-down (vertical) (d) the object is gripping in three different positions. The identifiable person gave permission for the use of his image and resubmitted it.

2.3   Data Pre-processing and Feature Extraction

EMG signals were collected at 2 kHz before being band-pass filtered (20 Hz to 450 Hz) and normalized concerning the target muscle contraction level. A 4th order Butterworth filter with a cut-off frequency of 5 Hz was employed to remove interference and motion artefacts. Signals were segmented at the 125 ms window length with a 65 ms overlap. In order to analyze windowing size effects, a larger windowing size of 300 ms with 150 ms overlap was implemented. Six features of raw signal in the time domain were computed for each window: Root Mean Square (RMS), Mean Absolute Value (MAV), Integrated Absolute Value (IAV), Waveform Length (WL), Simple Square Integration (SSI), and Average Amplitude Change (AAC).

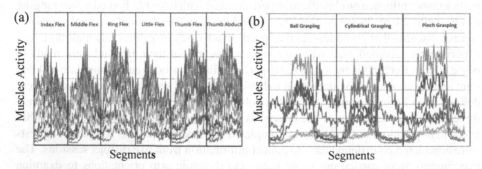

Fig. 4. Illustration of seven sEMG signals for RMS features. Samples are collected from the subject while performing six finger motions (a) and three grabbing types (b) for targeted muscle analysis. Seven channels are plotted for six-finger motions.

In this study, six features mentioned above extraction methods were used following the sEMG signal processing procedure presented in [9]. Figure 4(a) and 4(b) shows pre-processed EMG signals acquired from a human counterpart while the user performs a sequence of defined motion patterns for individual finger manipulation and object grabbing, respectively. In addition to feature extraction and data acquisition techniques, machine learning also plays a significant role in the performance of EMG-based control. To improve the efficiency of classifiers for a group of fingers or individual finger movements, researchers have investigated and compared a variety of machine learning approaches, from the linear discriminant model (LDA) to nearest-neighbours (k-NN) support vector machine (SVM) to artificial neural network (ANN) [10] with several kernels.

The research demonstrates the effectiveness of classifier performances and extracted features with high accuracy and low computational costs. The performance of each class was measured using the value of the F1 score, and average accuracy metrics measured the performance of each feature. The low classification performance suggests that it is challenging to identify motions due to postural muscles. Training data points were normalized to obtain mean zero and standard deviation in each dimension or electrode. The data sets for each user were split into 70% training and 30% for testing sets. Consequently, feature representation is the value of each EMG signal (i.e., seven channels for each motion) from each channel.

3 Results

3.1 Offline Learning

Classification, regression, and control algorithms have been developed to understand the intended movement of users. The motion detection results proposed in the literature vary by a large margin to 80–95% accuracy. However, this accuracy is affected by various factors, including amputation degree, the number of classes, experiment settings, and observed muscles. During the training phase, a three hidden dropout multilayer feed-forward neural network was adopted for classification. The model contains 128 units (nodes) at the hidden layers, and the output layer has units. The network was trained using the "ReLU" activation function in hidden layers, and the linear function was used for the output layer. All other network parameters such as weights and biases were randomly selected in the initial stages, and the optimization algorithms minimized the cost function for adaptive learning. In order to optimize weights, a back-propagation algorithm with an adaptive "Adam" optimizer was employed. The performance of sEMG features was assessed by the k-NN, SVM and LDA to compare the performance of the first classifier, ANN, considering both performance and computational cost.

The performance of machine learning models and feature extraction techniques for individual finger movements are summarized in Fig. 5(a). The average recognition rate of RMS for ANN was (93.4%), higher than SVM (90.4%), k-NN (87.8%), and LDA (82.8%) through the statistical analysis. RMS's highest average recognition rate was found for flexion of the ring (94 ± 1.53) %, and the lowest recognition rate was observed for thumb abduction with average (90 ± 4.53)% accuracy. The same models were used for the untargeted (UT) muscle condition. The average accuracy for seven electrodes placed around the arm for six-movement classes was observed as the highest average recognition rate for flexion of the ring finger with $(93 \pm 3.059)\%$, and the lowest performance was thumb abduction with $(80 \pm 7.22)\%$. The classification results suggest that there is no significant difference between the three main features ($p = 0.93$) but a significant difference between trials ($p = 0.0026$). Although targeting muscle improves classification accuracies considerably for some machine learning algorithms such as ANN (88.8%) and SVM (89.4), the fact that the targeting surface does not offer an advantage in LDA (87%) and k-NN (88.8%) methods as shown in Fig. 5(b).

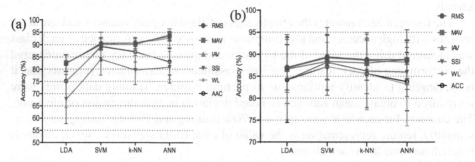

Fig. 5. Average classification accuracy for targeted (TR) (a) and untargeted (UT) muscles (b) using varied learning techniques in 125 ms windowing size.

The results show that all proposed feature sets' classification performance degraded significantly when dropping windowing size from 300 ms to 125 ms except for ANN (as seen in Fig. 6(a)). This study also showed that when comparing 6–7 sensor deployments for targeted and untargeted muscles, the motion detection performance for all features decreased considerably ($p < 0.001$) by reducing the number of sensors (shown in Fig. 6(b)).

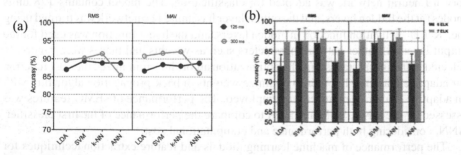

Fig. 6. The effect of windowing size (a) and the number of electrodes (b) on classification performance.

For individual finger detection (see Fig. 7(a)), there is no significant accuracy difference between three different arm positions ($p = 0.7879$), with the best performance while the arm is in an upright position. For object grasping (see Fig. 7(b)), there is a significant difference between the three different arm positions ($p = 0.0059$), and the best performance was recorded while the arm is in the horizontal position for SVM 92.8 ± 3.8%. According to the findings, training datasets with dynamic arm postures may have a significant effect on the robustness of the myoelectrical-based control system. Figure 8 shows the average classification performance for grasping during dynamic limb orientation. It performed a more reliable method than static arm positions, improving the average classification for ANN from 89% to 91.6%. On average, 92% classification performance was achieved for the ANN for all grasping types. The analysis of the presented ML techniques and pre-processing approach were comparable to those obtained in previous sEMG acquisition and data processing in the literature [11].

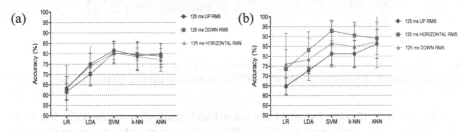

Fig. 7. Classification accuracy for individual finger (a) and object grabbing (b) motion detection in various static arm postures. The blue line represents the arm in an upright position, the red line in a horizontal position, and the green line in a downward position.

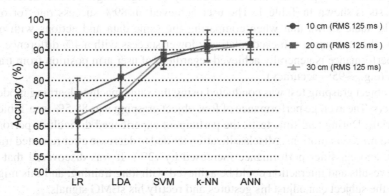

Fig. 8. Classification accuracy rate in different distances. Respectively, the blue line corresponds to 10 cm, the red line 20 cm distances, and the green line 30 cm distances.

3.2 Real-Time Control Performance

The potential of non-invasive EMG-based real-time control has been extensively investigated in the literature with task-related measures [12]. One of the standardized setups for evaluating myoelectrical hand performance is the box and block test (B&B) [13]. It is the most straightforward and commonly used test, implemented explicitly for grasping and object manipulation functioning tests. It consists of transferring an object from one location to another in a fixed time (usually in one minute). In order to evaluate the performance of the proposed pattern recognition system in real-time applications, an anthropomorphic robotic hand that can implement independent finger motion, flexion/extension of five fingers and thumb abduction was chosen.

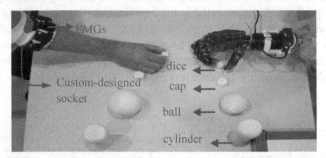

Fig. 9. Object grasping of the right hand is illustrated using four objects. The prosthesis was connected to the PC during training through TCP/IP protocol to capture EMG signals.

Four objects reflecting the most common hand manipulations in daily life were placed on the table, as illustrated in Fig. 9. The weights of the objects are neglected in the testing because they were designed and preferred in light materials. The subject was instructed to pick up the objects one at a time and hold them for three seconds each. Two performance metrics were determined for each of the four grasping types: completion rate and average completion time. The accuracy of single-finger motion detection for online tests is shown in Table 1. The user achieved an 89% success rate for overall tasks. The table shows that when comparing the same data and actions with offline accuracy, the participant achieved relatively lower success with a 4% difference. High offline performance is generally achieved regardless of user arm position from training sessions (e.g., >95% accuracy).

The object grasping test was conducted using the same machine learning model and parameters. The average performance of four object grasping was 88.5% (see Table 1) in online trials. During real-time tests, the participant experienced difficulties performing pinch and precision motions. Misclassification tended to decrease after repeated training sessions, and classifier performance increased by (2%). It was discovered that more accurate results and interaction could be achieved with long training, and this might be because the subject can adjust his gestures and rectify his sEMG signals.

Under this combined control method, the prosthetic hand can rapidly grasp objects with 0.23 s. It was found that the failure possibility, which was presented as the number of failure times divided by the total transporting times, was considerably reduced compared to early studies [14]. According to the findings, objects of similar sizes and shapes cannot be distinguished with high accuracy. Nonetheless, dropping possibility is reduced by a long-time training period. In the bottle/ block transfer test the subject successfully transferred 92% object for 30 cm, 88% for 50 cm, and 76% for 80 cm. The number of bottles/blocks dropped during bottle transfer is similar per round for each distance. The time to transfer the object was 7 ± 2 s for 30 cm, 8 ± 1 s for 50 cm, and 10 ± 3 s for 80 cm distances, respectively. The main benefits of this control scheme in terms of the three key concerns mentioned earlier are its intuitiveness, robustness, and quick response to user intention, which were achieved through the use of independent fingers, continuous operation regardless of arm position, and embedded system.

Table 1. Real-time control performance for individual finders.

Type of motion	Number of electrodes	Motion detection rate (%)
Rest	7	92
Thumb Flexion	7	90
Index Flexion	7	88
Middle Flexion	7	86
Ring Flexion	7	90
Little Flexion	7	88
Cylinder grasping	7	94
Ball grasping	7	92
Pinch grasping	7	86
Precision grasping	7	82

4   Discussion

This study carried out a detailed analysis with particular emphasis on prosthesis rejection and developing a combined embedded data collecting and motion execution challenges. This study aims to provide a factual basis for stressing the disparities in datasets and ML performance for offline and real-time control. A series of datasets (TR, UT) was developed to compare feature sets' impact. Two different windowing lengths with static and dynamic arm positions were utilized to assess the performance of a prosthetic hand in real-time.

The findings indicated that features derived from RMS and MAV might lead to the maximum classification rate in 300 ms windowing length, with RMS performing better for real-time implementation with a 3% higher overall recognition performance than MAV. Although ANN outperforms SVM in offline learning for 125 ms windowing size, SVM appears more accurate at 300 ms windowing size. However, a windowing size of about 65–125 ms in feature extraction using ANN was employed for real-time control to enhance practical implementation and decrease real-time delays.

The data show that classification performance dropped significantly (by 7%) when classifiers were trained on one arm and tested on another for the same user. Despite variations in approach, the results found for sEMG while studying the impact of arm position were comparable to those published in [13, 14], where similarity is focused on certain specific arm positions (arm down position). Although the classification performance is comparable to earlier research, it differs for two primary reasons. Previous studies looked at classification performance with various hand and wrist movements. This

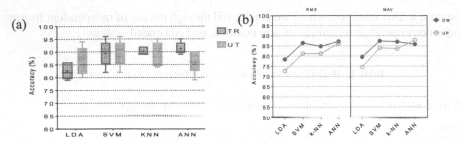

Fig. 10. The classification performance for RMS features in 125 ms windowing size. (TR) denotes targeted muscular conditions, whereas (UT) denotes untargeted muscle conditions (a). Performance of four classifiers with two arm postures for object grasping (b). (DW) symbolizes the arm vertically, whereas (UP) represents the arm upright.

study concentrated on individual finger manipulations to investigate the performance of a non-amputee individual from the standpoint of real prosthesis users. The results revealed that the UT state was slightly less accurate than the TR muscle condition. However, the UT scenario is more realistic because most amputees lack the necessary muscles, and it is challenging to identify a precise muscle placement [9]. Aside from classification accuracy (see Fig. 10(a)), the UT approach's practicality and possible application in daily activities for amputees is a significant benefit.

The overall assessment (see Fig. 10(b)) reveals that the offline classification performance for RMS with SVM was 86.4% when the subject's arm was vertical down and 81.2% upright. The average classification in the ANN performance evaluation using RMS was 87.2% when the subject's arm was vertical down and 86.2% when the subject's arm was upright. These findings show that, whereas arm position substantially alters muscle arrangement and EMG amplitude value, it has no significant effect on specific classifiers' performance in various arm positions ($p = 0.3692$). The results outperformed those of other studies that employed comparable techniques in the literature (i.e., [15, 16]).

The findings of real-time object grasping show that motion detection performance and motion completion time for four object grabbing and individual finger manipulations are competent and similar to the development of prosthetic devices [17]. The control architecture may enable robust data acquisition in 0.23 s with 88.5% for object grabbing and 89% accuracy for individual finger manipulation. The real-time object grasping test was performed to determine the best control settings and provide insight on clinically implementing sEMG-based continuous control for upper prostheses. The experimental results demonstrate that a high DoF robotic hand paired with dynamic feature extraction provides an ~84% success in real-time control. The findings suggest that applying this combined method could address the research problem of robustness and capability to continue operating despite various interferences, electrode shifting, force variations, and limb position.

Although data collected from healthy individuals is critical for assessing prostheses, more participation of amputees would reveal even more clearly what is lacking in order to develop a more intuitive prosthesis. Furthermore, a potential next step would be including a strategy for sensory feedback, either invasive or non-invasive, that employs vibrotactile afferent feedback to strengthen the robustness of prostheses and the execution of motions.

5   Conclusions

This study investigated six time-domain feature extraction approaches and four machine learning methods to differentiate six individual fingers and four gripping motions using sEMG signals as inputs. The study describes a novel control approach for real-time control of a prosthetic hand that continuously and independently monitors and predicts user forearm muscle activities. The experimental results demonstrate that features derived from dynamic arm motion with new sensory modality and embedded control architecture can lead to robust motion recognition in real-time control. A five-finger tendon-driven robotic hand was used to examine and test the proposed real-time control approach. The proposed control unit demonstrated system robustness and reliability for real-time myoelectrical pattern recognition with high accuracy in object grasping and block transfer tests.

References

1. Darnall, B.D., et al.: Depressive symptoms and mental health service utilization among persons with limb loss: results of a national survey. Arch. Phys. Med. Rehabil. **86**(4), 650–658 (2005)
2. Ziegler-Graham, K., MacKenzie, E.J., Ephraim, P.L., Travison, T.G., Brookmeyer, R.: Estimating the prevalence of limb loss in the United States: 2005 to 2050. Arch. Phys. Med. Rehabil. **89**(3), 422–429 (2008)
3. Resnik, L., et al.: Advanced upper limb prosthetic devices: implications for upper limb prosthetic rehabilitation. Arch. Phys. Med. Rehabil. **93**(4), 710–717 (2012)
4. Furui, A., et al.: A myoelectric prosthetic hand with muscle synergy–based motion determination and impedance model–based biomimetic control. Sci. Robot. **4**(31), eaaw6339 (2019)
5. Farrell, T.R., ff Weir, R.F.: A comparison of the effects of electrode implantation and targeting on pattern classification accuracy for prosthesis control. IEEE Trans. Biomed. Eng. **55**(9), 2198–2211 (2008)
6. Roche, A.D., Rehbaum, H., Farina, D., Aszmann, O.C., Aszmann, O.C.: Prosthetic myoelectric control strategies: a clinical perspective. Curr. Surg. Reports **2**(3) (2014)
7. Raspopovic, S., et al.: Restoring natural sensory feedback in real-time bidirectional hand prostheses: supplemental material. Sci. Transl. Med. **6**(222), 222ra19 (2014)
8. Jarque-Bou, N.J., Sancho-Bru, J.L., Vergara, M.: A systematic review of EMG applications for the characterization of forearm and hand muscle activity during activities of daily living: results, challenges, and open issues. Sensors **21**(9) (2021)
9. De Luca, C.J., Donald Gilmore, L., Kuznetsov, M., Roy, S.H.: Filtering the surface EMG signal: movement artifact and baseline noise contamination. J. Biomech. **43**(8), 1573–1579 (2010)
10. Tenore, F.V.G., Ramos, A., Fahmy, A., Acharya, S., Etienne-Cummings, R., Thakor, N.V.: Decoding of individuated finger movements using surface electromyography. IEEE Trans. Biomed. Eng. **56**(5), 1427–1434 (2009)

11. Benatti, S., Milosevic, B., Farella, E., Gruppioni, E., Benini, L.: A prosthetic hand body area controller based on efficient pattern recognition control strategies. Sensors (Switzerland) **17**(4), 869 (2017)
12. Vujaklija, I., et al.: Translating research on myoelectric control into clinics-are the performance assessment methods adequate? Front. Neurorobot. **11**, 1–7 (2017)
13. Patel, G.K., Castellini, C., Hahne, J.M., Farina, D., Dosen, S.: A classification method for myoelectric control of hand prostheses inspired by muscle coordination. IEEE Trans. Neural Syst. Rehabil. Eng. **26**(9), 1745–1755 (2018)
14. Jochumsen, M., Waris, A., Kamavuako, E.N.: The effect of arm position on classification of hand gestures with intramuscular EMG. Biomed. Signal Process. Control **43**, 1–8 (2018)
15. Atzori, M., et al.: Electromyography data for non-invasive naturally-controlled robotic hand prostheses. Sci. Data **1**, 1–13 (2014)
16. Palermo, F., Cognolato, M., Gijsberts, A., Müller, H., Caputo, B., Atzori, M.: Repeatability of grasp recognition for robotic hand prosthesis control based on sEMG data. In: IEEE International Conference on Rehabilitation Robotics, pp. 1154–1159 (2017)
17. Yang, D., Gu, Y., Jiang, L., Osborn, L., Liu, H.: Dynamic training protocol improves the robustness of PR-based myoelectric control. Biomed. Signal Process. Control **31**, 249–256 (2017)

Robotic Environment Perception

A Method for Object Recognition and Robot Grasping Detection in Multi-object Scenes

Jiajun Zheng[1,2], Yuanyuan Zou[1,2(✉)], Jie Xu[1,2], and Lingshen Fang[3]

[1] School of Mechanical Engineering, Shenyang Jianzhu University, No. 25, Hunnan Middle Road, Shenyang 110168, China
yyzou@sjzu.edu.cn

[2] National-Local Joint Engineering Laboratory of NC Machining Equipment and Technology of High-Grade Stone, Shenyang 110168, China

[3] Kunshan Intelligent Equipment Research Institute, Shenyang Institute of Automation, Chinese Academy of Sciences, Shenyang 110016, China

Abstract. Due to robot grasping has always been an open challenge and a difficult problem, it has attracted many researches. With the wide application of deep learning methods in robot grasping, the grasping performance of robots has been greatly improved. Traditionally, many robot grasp detection approaches focus on how to find the best grasp. However, it is very important for robots to have an object recognition function during the grasping process to meet more industrial requirements, such as industrial assembly tasks and sorting tasks. In addition, the problem of missed detection has always existed in the current multi-object grasping detection. To solve the above problems, this paper proposes a two-stage robot grasping method to recognize objects and detect the most likely grasp for every object in multi-object scenes. Our approach achieved a detection accuracy of 65.7% on the VMRD dataset and outperformed the benchmark algorithm by 11.2%. The simulation experimental results showed that our approach achieved a recognition success rate of 96.7% and a grasp success rate of 85% for robotic grasp detection in multi-object scenes.

Keywords: Robot grasping · Object detection · Grasping detection · Deep learning

1 Introduction

In order to enable robots to assist people to better complete tasks in more complex unstructured environments [1], robots are expected to have more efficient and reliable, sensitive perception, autonomous response and autonomous decision-making capabilities. Grasping and placing are common execution operation in industrial production and daily life. The ability of traditional industrial robots to grasp known object in fixed scenes has propelled the development and production of industry in the past. But this ability also limits the application of traditional industrial robots in the present and the future. Robots in unstructured environments will face practical challenges under various non-ideal conditions such as uncertain operating environments, uncertain scene illumination,

H. Liu et al. (Eds.): ICIRA 2022, LNAI 13457, pp. 189–196, 2022.
https://doi.org/10.1007/978-3-031-13835-5_17

unknown operation instances, and diverse placement poses when performing grasping operations. In a complex environment, there are still problems such as object recognition errors and insufficient grasping positioning accuracy when the robot performs grasping operations. In response to the above problems, more and more scholars are also conducting in-depth research on improving the grasping ability of robots in unstructured environments. With the development of deep convolutional neural networks, computer vision technology has also made breakthroughs, and the filling of visual perception systems can make the robot more intelligent.

The successful application of deep learning in the field of computer vision has also attracted people's attention to grasp detection technology, and grasp detection methods based on deep learning have been proposed one after another. According to the different forms of output results, robot grasping detection methods can be divided into methods based on grasping robust functions and methods based on structured grasping expressions. However, most of the above-mentioned grasping detection methods can only detect single-object scenes, and grasping detection for multi-object complex environments can meet the current needs of people. In this paper, a method for robot grasp detection in multi-object scenes is proposed. In a nutshell, the contributions of this paper are:

- In this method, the object recognition function is added to the method based on grasp detection, which further meets the needs of the industry for sorting and grasp tasks.
- Aiming at the missing detection of multi-object scenes and the problem of grasping unknown objects, the method proposed in this paper can effectively solve the above problems.

In this paper, Sect. 2 describes the details of the related works. We describe the proposed method in Sect. 3. The experimental results can be found in Sect. 4. The conclusions are summarized in Sect. 5.

2 Related Works

In recent years, object recognition technology based on deep learning has become more and more popular. Various network frameworks have been continuously proposed and used, and the target detection performance has been significantly improved. Current object detection algorithms can be divided into two-stage detection frameworks that require candidate regions and single-stage detection frameworks that do not require candidate regions according to the network structure. Compared with single-stage detection methods, two-stage detection methods generally have higher detection accuracy and can also achieve good detection of small objects. Representative methods include R-CNN [2], Faster R-CNN [3], and R-FCN [4]. However, since the two-stage detection method introduces candidate regions, its detection speed is not as fast as that of the single-stage detection method. With the continuous improvement of single-stage detection methods such as YOLO [5–8] and SSD [9], the detection accuracy has also been greatly improved. In industrial applications, the single-stage detection method has been widely used because of its simplified network structure and fast running speed.

Different from other grasp detection methods based on deep learning, the GR-ConvNet model [10] has shorter network structure and better detection accuracy. The model can realize fast grasp detection of n-channel input images. Compared with other advanced algorithms, it performs best on Cornell grasp dataset [11] and Jacquard grasp datasets [12]. The trained GR-ConvNet model can also performs grasp detection on unknown objects, and has the ability to generalize to any type of object. However, when grasping in a multi-object scenes, the model has missed detection. Therefore, the model can not grasp multiple objects through an input picture information, and can not realize the task of selection and sorting. The method proposed in this paper can effectively solve the above problems by segmenting multiple objects and the simultaneous strategy of recognition and grasping algorithm.

3   Proposed Method

In this paper, a method for robot grasp detection in multi-object scenes is proposed. Figure 1 shows an overview of the proposed grasp detection network. The task is divided into two stages. The detection of the object recognition stage belongs to the category of general object detection, and the YOLOX object detection framework is used to complete the corresponding detection task. The detection of grasp positions uses the GR-ConvNet object grasp detection network.

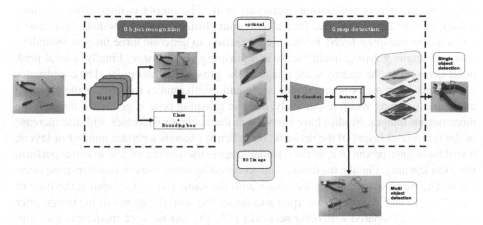

Fig. 1. Overview of the proposed grasp detection network

3.1   Object Recognition

In the first stage, a single-stage object recognition algorithm is used for detection, and the multi-object scene is segmented by the detection results, and the target bounding box containing a single object is used as the target ROI as the input of the second stage. As shown in Table 1, by comparing the four algorithms of Faster R-CNN, SSD, YOLO V3 [6] and YOLOX [8], the YOLOX algorithm was selected for object recognition at this stage.

Table 1. Results on VOC 2007 test set. All methods were trained on union of VOC 2007 trainval and VOC 2012 trainval.

Method	mAP (%)	FPS
SSD [9]	78.5	15
YOLOV3 [6]	82.6	27
YOLOX-s [8]	**85.7**	**43**
Faster R-CNN [3]	81.4	5

3.2 Grasp Detection

In the second stage, the input target ROI image is detected by the grasping detection algorithm, and a five-dimensional grasping rectangular frame is output to complete the picking and grasping of the target object. At this stage, the grasp detection is optimized based on the GR-ConvNet model. Different from the grasp detection task of single-object scenes, grasping detection of multi-object scenes need to locate the position of the object and detect the graspable position of the object.

The GR-ConvNet model first pre-processes the input ROI image and performs cropping, resizing and normalization operations in it. The output is three-channel image information of 224 * 224 size. Then after 3 convolution layers, 5 residuals layer and 3 convolution transpose layers for feature extraction to generate three images, including grasping angle, grasping quality score and grasping width image. Finally, a local peak point is found on the quality score image as the grasping center point. The coordinates of the peak point are brought into the angle and width images to generate the grasping angle and grasping width respectively, and the grasping pose is generated through the three output images. Studies have shown that the accuracy increases with the increase of the number of layers of the network, but when it exceeds a certain number of layers, it will be counterproductive, so the residual layer is used in the middle to better perform function learning. Finally, the image is up-sampled by using convolution transpose operation. The purpose is to obtain the image with the same size as the input at the time of output, and make it easier to interpret and retain the spatial features of the image after convolution. Compared with other networks [13, 14], our network model has a shorter structure and contains 1,900,900 parameters, so the calculation is more streamlined and the running speed is faster.

The loss function is:

$$L(G_i, \widehat{G}_i) = \frac{1}{n} \sum^{k} Z_k \tag{1}$$

where Z_k is represented as:

$$Z_k = \begin{cases} 0.5 \left(G_{i_k} - \widehat{G}_{i_k} \right)^2, & if \left| G_{i_k} - \widehat{G}_{i_k} \right| < 1 \\ \left| G_{i_k} - \widehat{G}_{i_k} \right| - 0.5, & \text{otherwise} \end{cases} \tag{2}$$

Among them, G_i is the grasp predicted by the network, and $\widehat{G}_i$ is the ground truth grasp.

4 Experiments

In experiments, the proposed method is verified through three experiments, including object recognition stage, grasp detection stage and simulation stage.

4.1 Object Recognition Experiments

In the above, by comparing several object recognition algorithms, the feasibility of YOLOX-s on the dataset is verified, and the specific performance of YOLOX on the standard dataset can be learned from the literature. This paper studies the method for robot grasping, but the above two datasets are not for graspable objects, so here we use the Visual Manipulation Relationship Dataset (VMRD) multi-object grasping dataset [15] provided by Xi'an Jiaotong University to train in the object recognition stage. The VMRD grasp dataset contains 4,233 training images and 450 testing images, each containing 2 to 5 stacked objects. There are a total of 31 object categories in the dataset with over 100,000 grasp detection labels. Divide the data set into train set and test set classification with a ratio of 9:1, and the trained model uses the mean average precision (mAP) as the evaluation metric to analyze its performance, including the mean precision (AP) thresholds are set to 0.5 and 0.75 (AP_{50}, AP_{75}). The results are shown in Fig. 2, and the detection accuracy on the test set of VMRD $AP_{50} = 98.4\%$, $AP_{75} = 92.3\%$.

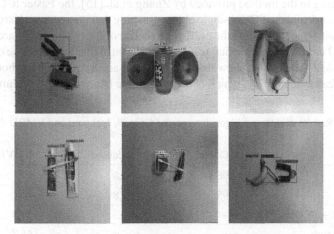

Fig. 2. Examples of detection results on VMRD

4.2 Grasp Detection Experiments

In this stage, the performance of the model is evaluated on the Cornell and Jacquard datasets, and the evaluation metric use the rectangle criterion [11] to evaluate the grasp detection results. If a predicted grasp rectangle satisfies both of the following conditions, the predicted grasp rectangle is considered to be an accurate grasp rectangle:

(1) The difference between the rotation angle of the predicted detection rectangle and the ground-truth detection rectangle is within 30°;
(2) The Jaccard index between the predicted detection rectangle and the ground-truth detection rectangle is more than 0.25.

The Jaccard index is defined as follows:

$$J(G_p, G_r) = \frac{G_p \cap G_r}{G_p \cup G_r} \qquad (3)$$

where, G_p is the area of the predicted detection rectangle; G_r is the area of the ground-truth detection rectangle; $G_p \cap G_r$ is the intersection of the two detection rectangle; $G_p \cup G_r$ is the union of the two detection rectangle.

The method proposed in this paper is only for RGB images as input information. When training the model, the Adam optimizer [16] and the SGD optimizer (momentum = 0.9) [17] are used to train the model, and the Adam optimizer is finally selected. The learning rate is set to 0.001, using a mini-batch size of 8, and training epochs set to 600000, the model is trained using three random seeds, and the average of the three seeds is reported.

In this section, an advanced grasping detection method FCGN [14] is selected as the comparison benchmark. First, the evaluation indicators on the two datasets are compared. FCGN algorithm slightly outperforms GR-ConvNet model on two standard datasets. Finally, referring to the method provided by Zhang et al. [15], the Faster R-CNN object detection network and the FCGN single object grasping detection network are combined as a comparison benchmark, and the evaluation metric of the two methods are compared on the VMRD dataset. Experimental results of different algorithms on three datasets are shown in Table 2. The results show that the detection accuracy of the method proposed in this paper can reach 65.7%, which is better than the benchmark algorithm.

Table 2. Results of different algorithms on the Cornell, Jacquard and VMRD datasets.

Algorithm	Cornell	Jacquard	RMVD
FCGN	96.1	91.8	–
GR-ConvNet	95.5	91.8	–
Fsater-RCNN + FCGN	–	–	54.5
Proposed Method	–	–	65.7

4.3 Simulation Experiments

V-REP (Virtual Robot Experiment Platform) is one of the most commonly used robot simulation modeling tools [18]. It is often used to build a robot operation simulation environment. It can use embedded scripts, plug-ins, nodes, custom solutions and other methods to achieve distributed control, and is suitable for Common programming languages such as C/C++, Python, Matlab, etc. The simulation experiment environment of this section is set up as shown in Fig. 3. In this paper, the combined model of the robotic arm UR3 and the gripper RG2 is imported into V-REP to build a simulation environment for grasping experiments. The feasibility of the method proposed in this paper is verified by training the collaborative strategy model based on Pytorch. The results are shown as Table 3.

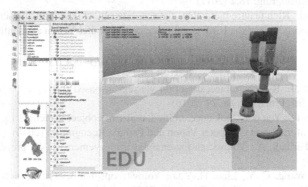

Fig. 3. Construction of simulation experiment environment.

Table 3. Simulation results of the proposed method

Object	Prediction success rate	Grasping success rate
Banana	10/10	7/10
Box	10/10	10/10
Knife	9/10	9/10
Cup	10/10	8/10
Toothpaste	9/10	9/10
Pliers	10/10	8/10
Accuracy	**96.7%**	**85%**

5 Conclusions

In this paper, an object grasp detection method based on deep learning is proposed for multi-object scenes. A two-stage grasp detection method is realized by combining object recognition algorithm and grasp detection algorithm. Compared with the original grasp detection methods, the method proposed in this paper can effectively solve the problem of missing detection in multi-object scenes, and can recognize the types of objects to realize the task of sorting and selection. Finally, experiments show the effectiveness of the proposed algorithm by comparing the existing advanced detection algorithms. And the practicability of the algorithm is proved by simulation experiments.

References

1. Zheng, N., et al.: Hybrid-augmented intelligence: collaboration and cognition. Front. Inf. Technol. Electron. Eng. **18**.2 (2017)
2. Ross, G., et al.: Rich feature hierarchies for accurate object detection and semantic segmentation. In: Proceedings of the IEEE Conference on Computer Vision and Pattern Recognition (2014)
3. Shaoqing, R., et al.: Faster R-CNN: Towards real-time object detection with region proposal networks. Adv. Neural Inf. Process. Syst. **28** (2015)
4. Jifeng, D., et al.: R-FCN: Object detection via region-based fully convolutional networks. Adv. Neural Inf. Process. Syst. **29** (2016)
5. Joseph, R., et al.: You only look once: unified, real-time object detection. In: Proceedings of the IEEE Conference on Computer Vision and Pattern Recognition (2016)
6. Joseph, R., Farhadi, A.: Yolov3: an incremental improvement. arXiv preprint arXiv:1804.02767 (2018)
7. Alexey, B., Wang, C.-Y., Liao, H.-Y.M.: Yolov4: optimal speed and accuracy of object detection. arXiv preprint arXiv:2004.10934 (2020)
8. Zheng, G., et al.: Yolox: exceeding yolo series in 2021. arXiv preprint arXiv:2107.08430(2021).
9. Wei, L., et al.: SSD: single shot multibox detector. European Conference on Computer Vision. Springer, Cham (2016)
10. Sulabh, K., Joshi, S., Sahin, F.: Antipodal robotic grasping using generative residual convolutional neural network. In: 2020 IEEE/RSJ International Conference on Intelligent Robots and Systems (IROS). IEEE (2020)
11. Yun, J., Moseson, S., Saxena, A.: Efficient grasping from RGBD images: learning using a new rectangle representation. In: 2011 IEEE International Conference on Robotics and Automation. IEEE (2011)
12. Amaury, D., Dellandréa, E., Chen, L.: Jacquard: a large scale dataset for robotic grasp detection. In: 2018 IEEE/RSJ International Conference on Intelligent Robots and Systems (IROS). IEEE (2018)
13. Sulabh, K., Kanan, C.: Robotic grasp detection using deep convolutional neural networks. In: 2017 IEEE/RSJ International Conference on Intelligent Robots and Systems (IROS). IEEE (2017)
14. Xinwen, Z., et al.: Fully convolutional grasp detection network with oriented anchor box. In: 2018 IEEE/RSJ International Conference on Intelligent Robots and Systems (IROS). IEEE (2018)
15. Hanbo, Z., et al.: Roi-based robotic grasp detection for object overlapping scenes. In: 2019 IEEE/RSJ International Conference on Intelligent Robots and Systems (IROS). IEEE (2019)
16. Diederik, P.K., Ba, J.: Adam: A Method for Stochastic Optimization. arXiv e-prints (2014)
17. Atsushi, N.: Stochastic proximal gradient descent with acceleration techniques. Adv. Neural Inf. Process. Syst. **27** (2014)
18. Eric, R., Singh, S.P.N., Freese, M.: V-REP: a versatile and scalable robot simulation framework. In: 2013 IEEE/RSJ International Conference on Intelligent Robots and Systems. IEEE (2013)

Reinforcement Learning for Mobile Robot Obstacle Avoidance with Deep Deterministic Policy Gradient

Miao Chen, Wenna Li[(✉)], Shihan Fei, Yufei Wei, Mingyang Tu, and Jiangbo Li

Liaoning Petrochemical University, Fushun 113001, China
liwenna0810224@126.com

Abstract. This paper proposed an improved reinforcement learning (RL) algorithm to develop a strategy for a mobile robot to avoid obstacles with deep deterministic policy gradient (DDPG) in order to solve the problem that the robot spends invalid time exploring obstacles in the initial exploration and speed up the stability and speed of the robot learning. An environment map is used to generate range sensor readings, detect obstacles, and check collisions that the robot may make. The range sensor readings are the observations for the DDPG agent, and the linear and angular velocity controls are the action. The experiment scenario trains a mobile robot to avoid obstacles given range sensor readings that detect obstacles in the map. The objective of the reinforcement learning algorithm is to learn what controls including linear and angular velocity, the robot should use to avoid colliding into obstacles. Simulations results show that the feasibility and certain application value of the method and the algorithm can effectively solve the rewards problem in the process of robot moving, and the execution efficiency of the algorithm is significantly improved. Therefore there are some value of reference and application for development of mobile robot obstacle avoidance system owing to the work of this paper.

Keywords: Reinforcement learning · Avoiding obstacles · Deep deterministic policy gradient

1 Introduction

Reinforcement learning has some important applications in controlling mobile robots [1, 2] and has a powerful ability to solving the various control problems, such as robot soccer [3], unmanned aerial vehicle [4] and humanoid robot [5]. Reinforcement learning is a goal-oriented interactive learning approach which seeks the optimal strategy which makes agent get the maximum cumulative reward in time series. TP et al. proposed a Deep Deterministic Policy Gradient (DDPG) method [6], which has the advantage of handling high dimensional continuous state. Bin Zhang et al. proposed reinforcement Learning Energy Management for Hybrid Electric Tracked Vehicle with Deep Deterministic Policy Gradient [7].

H. Liu et al. (Eds.): ICIRA 2022, LNAI 13457, pp. 197–204, 2022.
https://doi.org/10.1007/978-3-031-13835-5_18

Recently, mobile robot system has become one of the hottest topics in robotics. A key point in the research of mobile robot system is collision avoidance in the field of machine learning. At present, there are many achievements about avoiding obstacles for mobile robots based on static environment. It is difficult for the mobile robots to make a correct and reasonable prediction of behavior in the training process because of the complexity and change of dynamic environment [8]. Therefore, the movement of obstacles in a dynamic environment makes it more difficult for the mobile robots to choose the optimal strategy. Chun-Ta Chen [9] presented a collision avoidance system based on theresearch of cockroach avoiding to be caught. He solved the problems by recognizing moving-obstacle and selecting collision avoidance behavior, but the system failed to solve the problem of avoiding multi-obstacles [10].

2   Relevance Theory

2.1   Reinforcement Learning

Reinforcement learning is another machine learning method different from supervised learning and unsupervised learning. It can optimize the decision of behavior via estimating feedback signals got from interactive process with environment, so it is more valuable in solving complex optimization control problem [10]. A computer learns to perform a task by interacting with an unknown dynamic environment by reinforcement learning which is regarded a goal-directed computational approach. Without human intervention and explicit programming, this learning method enables the computer to make a series of decisions which maximize the cumulative reward of the task. The following diagram shows a general representation of a reinforcement learning scenario as shown in Fig. 1.

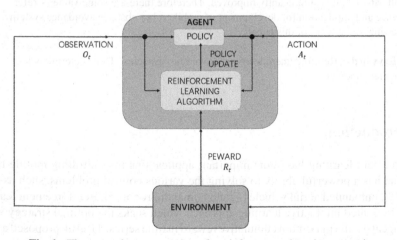

Fig. 1. The general representation of a reinforcement learning scenario

The goal of reinforcement learning is to train an agent to complete a task within an uncertain environment. At each time interval, the agent receives observations and a reward from the environment and sends an action to the environment. The reward is a measure of how successful the previous action which taken from the previous state was with respect to completing the task goal. The agent contains a policy and a learning algorithm. The policy is a mapping that selects actions based on the observations from the environment. Typically, the policy is a function approximator with tunable parameters, such as a deep neural network. The learning algorithm continuously updates the policy parameters based on the actions, observations, and rewards. Depending on the learning algorithm, an agent maintains one or more parameterized function approximators for training the policy. Approximators can be used in two ways including critics and actors. The critic can return the predicted discounted value of the cumulative long-term reward for given observation and action. The actor can return as output the action that often maximizes the predicted discounted cumulative long-term reward for a given observation. Agents that use only critics to select their actions rely on an indirect policy representation. These agents are also referred to as value-based, and they use an approximator to represent a value function. In general, these agents work better with discrete action spaces but can become computationally expensive for continuous action spaces. Agents that use only actors to select their actions rely on a direct policy representation. These agents are also referred to as policy-based. The policy can be either deterministic or stochastic. In general, these agents are simpler and can handle continuous action spaces, though the training algorithm can be sensitive to noisy measurement and can converge on local minima. Agents that use both an actor and a critic are referred to as actor-critic agents. In these agents, during training, the actor learns the best action to take using feedback from the critic. At the same time, the critic learns the value function from the rewards so that it can properly criticize the actor. In general, these agents can handle both discrete and continuous action spaces.

2.2 Deep Deterministic Policy Gradient Agents

The deep deterministic policy gradient (DDPG) algorithm is a model-free, online, off-policy reinforcement learning method. A DDPG agent is an actor-critic reinforcement learning agent that searches for an optimal policy that maximizes the expected cumulative long-term reward.

A DDPG agent with default actor and critics based on the observation and action specifications from the created environment. There are five steps to do this task. Step 1 is to create observation specifications for the environment. Step 2 is to create action specifications for your environment. Step 3 is to specify the number of neurons in each learnable layer or whether to use an LSTM layer if needed. To do so, create an agent initialization option object. Step 4 is to specify agent options if needed. Step 5 is to create the agent.

A DDPG agent can update the actor and critic properties at each time step during training. The experiences using a circular experience buffer is stored. The agent can update the actor and critic using a mini-batch of experiences randomly sampled from the buffer. The action chosen by the policy using a stochastic noise model at each training step is perturbed.

3 Improved Reinforcement Learning Based on DDPG

DDPG is a combination of actor-critic and DQN algorithm. In the basic RL structure, the agent chooses an action at each time step according to an internal policy, which maps an action to each observable state s_t. For every chosen action the environment feedbacks an instant reward r_t and a new state s_{t+1}. The object of the RL agent is to maximize the accumulative return r_t at any time step by adjusting the policy and r_t is defined as the weighted sum of the instant rewards. DDPG calculates the deterministic strategy gradient by different strategy method. The heterogeneous strategy approach is that an agent uses exploratory strategies to generate data from which gradients are calculated, β represents a behavioral policy. The deterministic strategy gradient is:

$$\nabla_\theta J_\beta(\mu_\theta) = \nabla_\theta E_{s-\rho^\beta}[Q(s,a)] = E_{s-\rho^\beta}[\nabla_\theta \mu_\theta \cdot \nabla_a Q(s,a)|a = \mu_\theta] \tag{1}$$

The behavior value function is a function of state and action, which can be approximated by neural network. $Q(s,a) = w_{out} \cdot relu(w_a A + w_s S) + b_{out}$.

Actor network input status is s, The loss function is:

$$loss = -Q(s, u_\theta(s)) \tag{2}$$

Critic network input status is s, sampling action is a, the network output is a behavior-value function. The loss function is:

$$loss = (r + \gamma Q(s', a; w) - Q(s, a; w))^2 \tag{3}$$

The trainable parameter is w.

The updating formula of parameters can be obtained form the formula (1)-(3),

$$\delta_t = r_t + \gamma Q^w(s_{t+1}, \mu_\theta(s_{t+1})) - Q^w(s_t, a_t)$$
$$w_{t+1} = w_t + a_w \delta_t \nabla_w Q^w(s_t, a_t) \tag{4}$$
$$\theta_{t+1} = \theta_t + a_\theta \nabla_\theta \mu_\theta(s_t) \cdot \nabla_a Q^w(s_t, a_t)|_{a=\mu_\theta(s)}$$

The TD goal is $\delta_t = r_t + \gamma Q^w(s_{t+1}, \mu_\theta(s_{t+1}))$ here. Independent target network means that parameters in TD target use independent network parameters w and θ. They can be set to w^- and θ^-. The independent target network parameters are updated as follows:

$$\delta_t = r_t + \gamma Q^{w^-}(s_{t+1}, \mu_\theta(s_{t+1})) - Q^w(s_t, a_t)$$
$$w_{t+1} = w_t + a_w \delta_t \nabla_w Q^w(s_t, a_t)$$
$$\theta_{t+1} = \theta_t + a_\theta \nabla_\theta \mu_\theta(s_t) \cdot \nabla_a Q^w(s_t, a_t)|_{a=\mu_\theta(s)} \tag{5}$$
$$\theta^- = \tau\theta + (1-\tau)\theta^-$$
$$w^- = \tau w + (1-\tau)w^-$$

Simulate the model in Simulink after the trained agent can be saved.

4 Experimental Result

In this section, simulation is carried out to verify the proposed algorithm the proposed approach is implemented by one actor network, one critic network and a replay buffer. The simulations are carried out using MATLAB/Simulink software. As shown in Fig. 2, simulation model diagram of the obstacle avoidance system for mobile robots is implemented.

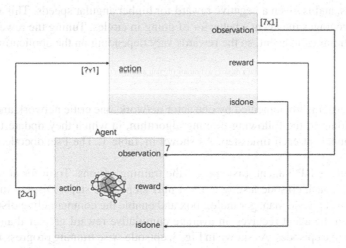

Fig. 2. Simulation model diagram of the obstacle avoidance system

4.1 Experimental Environment

Simulated physical environments of varying levels of difficulty is constructed to test the proposed algorithm. Load a map matrix and then set up a range Sensor object which simulates a noisy range sensor. The range sensor readings are considered observations by the agent. Define the angular positions of the range readings, the max range, and the noise parameters. Environment Interface can create an environment model that takes the action, and gives the observation and reward signals. Specify the provided example model name, the simulation time parameters, and the agent block name. There is a model for simulating the robot and sensor data inside the environment subsystem block. The subsystem takes in the action, generates the observation signal based on the range sensor readings, and calculates the reward based on the distance from obstacles, and the effort of the action commands. Build the environment interface object and Specify the model, agent block name, observation parameters, and action parameters. Set the reset function for the simulation. This function restarts the simulation by placing the robot in a new random location to begin avoiding obstacles.

A DDPG agent approximates the long-term reward given observations and actions using a critic value function representation. To create the critic, first create a deep neural network with two inputs, the observation and action, and one output. Next, specify options for the critic optimizer. Finally, create the critic representation using the specified deep neural network and options. Specify the action and observation specifications for the critic obtained from the environment interface. A DDPG agent decides which action to take given observations using an actor representation. To create the actor, first create a deep neural network with one input, the observation, and one output, the action. Finally, construct the actor in a similar manner as the critic. Create DDPG agent object and specify the agent options. The agent is rewarded to avoid the nearest obstacle, which minimizes the worst-case scenario. Additionally, the agent is given a positive reward for higher linear speeds, and is given a negative reward for higher angular speeds. This rewarding strategy discourages the agent's behavior of going in circles. Tuning the rewards is key to properly training an agent, so the rewards vary depending on the application.

4.2 Train Agent

The DDPG agent is implemented by one actor network, one critic network and a replay buffer according to the following training algorithm, in which they update their actor and critic models at each time step. As shown in Table 1. The Pseudocode of DDPG algorithm.

To train the DDPG agent, first specify the training options. Train for at most 1000 episodes, with each episode lasting at most max steps time steps. Display the training progress in the episode manager dialog box and enable the command line display. Stop training when the agent receives an average cumulative reward greater than 400 over fifty consecutive episodes. As shown in Fig. 3, episode-wise training progress is tracked.

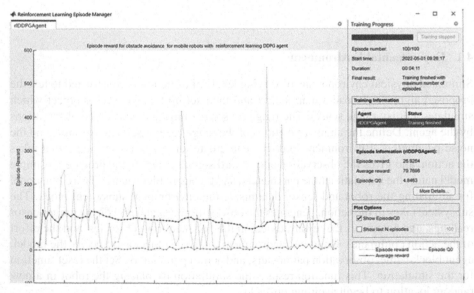

Fig. 3. Training progress of the episode reward for obstacle avoidance for mobile robots

Table 1. The pseudocode of DDPG algorithm

Algorithm	DDPG algorithm

Randomly initialize critic network $Q(s, a|\theta^Q)$ and actor $\mu(s|\theta^\mu)$ with weights θ^Q and θ^μ

Initialize target network Q' and μ' with weights $\theta^{Q'} \leftarrow \theta^Q$, $\theta^{\mu'} \leftarrow \theta^\mu$

Initialize replay buffer R

for episode = 1, M do

for

Initialize a random process N for action exploration

Receive initial observation state s_1

for t = 1, T do

Select action $a_t - \mu(s_t|\theta^\mu) + N_t$ according to the current policy and exploration noise

Execute action a_t and observe reward r_t and observe new state s_{t+1}

Store transition $(s_t, a_t, r_t, s_{t+1},)$ in R

Sample a random minibatch of N transitions (s_i, a_i, r_i, s_{i+1}) from R

Set $y_i = r_i + \gamma Q'(s_{i+1}, \mu'(s_{i+1}|\theta^{\mu'})|\theta^{Q'})$

Update critic by minimizing the loss: $L = \frac{1}{N}\Sigma_i(y_i - Q(s_i, a_i|\theta^Q))^2$

Update the actor policy using the sampled policy gradient:

$$\nabla_{\theta_\mu}J \approx \frac{1}{N}\Sigma_i \nabla_a Q(s, a|\theta^Q)|s = s_i, a = \mu(s_i)\nabla_{\theta_\mu}\mu(s|\theta^\mu)|s_i$$

Update the target networks:

$$\theta^{Q'} \leftarrow \tau\theta^Q + (1-\tau)\theta^{Q'}$$
$$\theta^{\mu'} \leftarrow \tau\theta^\mu + (1-\tau)\theta^{\mu'}$$

end for

end for

After the DDPG agent training is finished, the trained agent is used to simulate the robot driving in the map and avoiding obstacles.

5 Conclusion

The paper has given a reinforcement learning for mobile robot obstacle avoidance system with deep deterministic policy gradient based on the results of collision avoidance system's research. The simulation experiment indicated that this algorithm is feasible and valid and the system could solve the problem of collision avoidance of motion obstacles in a complex environment.

Support
Liaoning Province 2022 Provincial Innovation Project for College Students Project Number: D202204171351579117.

References

1. Levine, S., Pastor, P., Krizhevsky, A., et al.: Learning hand-eye coordination for robotic grasping with deep learning and large-scale data collection. Int. J. Robot. Res. **37**, 421–436 (2017)
2. Tang, L., Liu, Y.-J., Tong, S.: Adaptive neural control using reinforcement learning for a class of robot manipulator. Neural Comput. Appl. **25**(1), 135–141 (2013). https://doi.org/10.1007/s00521-013-1455-2
3. Yu, H., Gao, H., Deng, Z.: Toward a unified approximate analytical representation for spatially running spring-loaded inverted pendulum model. IEEE Trans. Rob. **99**, 1–8 (2020)
4. Xu, Y., Ding, S.X., Luo, H., et al.: A real-time performance recovery framework for vision-based control systems. IEEE Trans. Industr. Electron. **99**, 1 (2020)
5. Riedmiller, M., Gabel, T., Hafner, R., et al.: Reinforcement learning for robot soccer. Auton. Robot. **27**(1), 55–73 (2009)
6. Lillicrap, T.P., Hunt, J.J., Pritzel, A ., et al.: Continuous control with deep reinforcement learning. In: Computer Science (2015)
7. Zhang, B.W., Jinlong, Z., et al.: Reinforcement Learning Energy Management for Hybrid Electric Tracked Vehicle with Deep Deterministic Policy Gradient, 2020 China Society of Automotive Engineering Annual Conference and Exhibition (2020)
8. Cai, K., et al.: mobile robot path planningin dynamic environments: a survey. Instrumentation **6**(02), 92–102(2019)
9. Chen, CT., Quinn, R.D., Ritzmann, R.E.: A crash avoidance system based upon the cockroach escape response circuit. In: IEEE International Conference on Robotics & Automation, Pp. 2007–2012. IEEE (2002)
10. Fan, J., Wu, G., Ma, F., Liu, J.: Reinforcement learning and ART2 neural network based collision avoidance system of mobile robot. In: Yin, F.-L., Wang, J., Guo, C. (eds.) ISNN 2004. LNCS, vol. 3174, pp. 35–41. Springer, Heidelberg (2004). https://doi.org/10.1007/978-3-540-28648-6_6

An Improved Beetle Antennae Search Optimization Based Particle Filtering Algorithm for SLAM

Wei-Dian Ni and Guang-Zhong Cao$^{(\boxtimes)}$

Guangdong Key Laboratory of Electromagnetic Control and Intelligent Robots, College of
Mechatronics and Control Engineering, Shenzhen University, Shenzhen 518060, China
gzcao@szu.edu.cn

Abstract. Particle filter localization technology is the key technology of mobile
robot Simultaneous Localization and Mapping (SLAM). To solve the problem of
particle degradation in the process of particle pose estimation, an improved optimization strategy of swarm intelligence Beetle Antennae Search (BAS) algorithm
is proposed. The key novelty of the proposed particle optimization strategy is that
it considers both the randomness and the depth of the particle, improves the global
optimization ability of the particle and reduces the RMSE of the particle estimation. The feasibility and effectiveness of the optimization strategy are verified by
theoretical comparison and application simulation.

Keywords: SLAM · Beetle antennae search · Particle filter · ROS

1 Introduction

For mobile robots capable of autonomously performing predetermined tasks, whether
the robot can locate autonomously in the environment is crucial [1]. Lidar Simultaneous Localization and Mapping (SLAM) technology is still a key technology [2] for
autonomous mobile robots to locate and map because it does not require site installation
and is not affected by ambient light. At the same time, when mobile robots use lidar sensors for positioning and mapping functions, Particle filter-based positioning algorithms
are the most widely used [3]. Because of its nonlinear system filtering and multimodal
distribution characteristics, the particle filter algorithm is suitable for solving global
positioning and pose tracking problems for mobile robots.

The basic idea of Particle Filter (PF) is to generate a set of random samples in the
state space according to the empirical distribution of the state vector of the system,
and then adjust the weight and position of the particles according to the error with
the measurement system, and modify the particle information to the initial empirical
conditional distribution. Although the particle filter algorithm is an effective nonlinear
filtering technology, it will face the problem of particle degradation. The reason of
particle degradation is that the unreasonable resampling process leads to the reduction
of particle diversity. For this reason, many scholars have done many in-depth studies

on solving the problem of particle degradation caused by resampling. Zhou N [4] has proposed a resampling process method based on genetic optimization particles; Xu C [5] has proposed a particle filter algorithm based on error ellipse resampling. These algorithms improve the filtering performance to a certain extent, but in essence, they do not completely eliminate the problem of particle degradation, and even discard some effective particles, reducing particle diversity.

Swarm intelligence optimization theory [6] provides a new direction for improving the performance of particle filter. Classical intelligent algorithms have the advantages of high robustness and strong search. Many intelligent optimization theory has been successfully applied to particle filter, such as whale swarm algorithm [7], firefly algorithm [8] and so on. In order to further enrich the particle filter optimization theory, based on the above research results, and absorbing the advantages of single Beetle Antennae Search (BAS) algorithm and particle filter, a particle filter algorithm based on improved BAS optimization is proposed. The BAS algorithm is a new intelligent optimization algorithm [9]. Because of its simple structure and strong convergence, it has been widely used in fault diagnosis [10], pipeline leak detection [11], COVID-19 case prediction [12], etc. At the same time, its theoretical convergence analysis has been proved [13]. So far, there is no application of the BAS algorithm for SLAM. The improved particle filter algorithm proposed in this paper optimizes the weight assignment of particles, makes the distribution of particles closer to the true posterior probability density, solves the problem of particle degradation fundamentally and improves the accuracy of particle filter. The innovations of this paper are as follows:

- Aiming at the problem that the original monomer BAS algorithm is easily trapped into local optimum, the idea of swarm intelligence is introduced into BAS algorithm, and an improved optimization algorithm of BAS is proposed;
- In order to solve the problem of particle degradation in importance sampling, a heuristic method based on BAS algorithm was proposed to optimize the process of particle distribution and improve the state estimation accuracy of particle filter;
- The idea of BAS-PF is applied into Gmapping-SLAM algorithm to optimize the position estimation accuracy of particles in scanning matching, so as to improve the quality of the mapping.

The rest of this chapter is organized as follows: In the second part, the principle of BAS algorithm is analyzed and the shortcoming of the algorithm is optimized and improved. The improved BAS algorithm is applied into particle filter state estimation. In the third part, the improved particle filter algorithm is applied into the Gmapping-SLAM of mobile robot. The fourth part uses MATLAB and ROS-Gazebo simulation platform to simulate improved BAS-PF algorithm and improved Gmapping algorithm, and the results are analyzed and discussed.

2 BAS-PF Strategy

2.1 Principle and Improvement of BAS Algorithm

The BAS algorithm is a new bio-inspired intelligent optimization algorithm, which inspired by the phenomenon of BAS foraging. The beetle search principle of the algorithm is: one beetle forages for food by recognizing the intensity of a food odor. The individual foraging behavior of beetle is shown in Fig. 1.

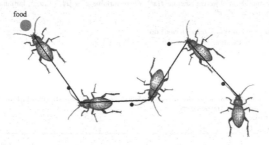

Fig. 1. The individual foraging behavior of beetle

At first, the beetle doesn't know the location of the food, but the two tentacles above the head are used to detect the intensity of the food odor. If the intensity of the food odor received by the left whisker is greater than that of the food odor received by the right whisker, the beetle will move a distance to the left and do the next feeding. The cycle goes on until the calf finds the most concentrated food gas to complete the foraging work. The mathematical model of the bionic search algorithm of beetle is as follows:

Assuming that the beetle foraged in an n-dimensional space, the center of mass is set to x, the left whisker of the beetle is x_{wl}, the right whisker is x_{wr}, the distance between the two whiskers is d, and the coefficient between the distance between the two whiskers and the first step *step* of the beetle is δ.

Because the head orientation of beetle is random every time, if beetle's head orientation is $\vec{b}$ by Eq. 1.

$$\vec{b} = \frac{\text{rand}(n, 1)}{\|\text{rand}(n, 1)\|} \tag{1}$$

where rand $(n, 1)$ denotes the randomly generated n-dimensional vector. According to the above-established head orientation of the Albatross, the coordinates of left and right whiskers of the Albatross can be expressed as Eq. 2.

$$x_{wl} = x^t - d\vec{b}, \; x_{wr} = x^t + d\vec{b} \tag{2}$$

where x^t is the location of the center of mass corresponding to the time t when foraging. The fitness values $f(x_{wl})$ and $f(x_{wr})$ are obtained by the coordinates of the left and right whiskers of the ascend, and the position of the centroid of the next ascend is affected by the difference between the two values, namely Eq. 3.

$$x^t = x^{t-1} + step^t\vec{b}\text{sign} \left(f(x_{wl}) - f(x_{wr}) \right) \tag{3}$$

where $step^t$ is the t foraging step, and its value is related to the distance between the two whiskers, namely Eq. 4.

$$step^t = step^{t-1} \delta d \tag{4}$$

The pseudo-code of the BAS is as **Algorithm 1**:

Algorithm 1 BAS algorithm

Input: Estabilsh an objective function $f(x^t)$, where variable $x^t = [x_1, \cdots, x_i]^T$, initialize the parameters x^0, d^0, δ^0.
Output: x_{bst}, f_{bst}.
1: **while** $(t > times)$ or $(stop\ criterion)$ **do**
2:    Generate the direction vector unit $\vec{b}$ according to (1).
3:    Search in variable space with two kinds of antennae according to (2).
4:    Update the state variable x^t according to (3).
5:    **if** $f(x^t) > f_{bst}$ **then**
6:        $f_{bst} = f(x^t)$, $x_{bst} = x^t$.
7:    **end if**
8:    Update step size $step^t$ with decreasing functions (4) and respectively, which could be further studied by the designers.
9: **end while**
return x_{bst}, f_{bst}.

A detailed performance analysis is carried out for the BAS algorithm [13]. From this, it can be concluded that the original beetle search algorithm is a method for finding the optimal value of a single individual. Although the system assigns the initial values of the distance between the two tentacles and the step size of the beetle individual, but there is still the problem of beetle individuals falling into local optima. In response to this problem, fully consider the individual foraging behavior and cluster mate-seeking behavior of beetles, introduce the idea of cluster intelligence, form beetles into groups, and combine elite individual information in the process of population renewal to survive the fittest, so as to avoid individuals falling into local optima and improve their global optimization ability. The pseudo-code of the improved BAS algorithm is as **Algorithm 2**:

Algorithm 2 improved BAS algorithm

Input: Estabilsh an objective function $f(x(n_{bst}, t))$, where variable $x(n_{bst}, t) = [x_{bst}^1, \cdots, x_{bst}^i]^T$, n_{bst} is the best individual in the colony of beetle at time i, N_{Bee} is the number of beetles, initialize the parameters $x(n_0, 0)$, d^0, δ^0, N_{Bee}.
Output: $x(n_{bst}, :)$, f_{bst}.
1: **while** $(t > times)$ or $(stop\ criterion)$ **do**
2:    Suppose there is a beetle as a local optimum x_{locBst}.
3:    Generate the direction vector unit $\vec{b_0}$ according to (1).
4:    That beetle search in variable space with two kinds of antennae according to (2).
5:    Update the state variable x_{locBst} according to (3).
6:    $x(n_{bst}, t) = x_{locBst}$, $f_{locBst} = f(x_{locBst})$, $f_{bst} = f_{locBst}$.
7:    **while** $(n < N_{Bee})$ **do**
8:        Generate the direction vector unit $\vec{b_n}$ according to (1).
9:        Every beetle search in variable space with two kinds of antennae according to (2).
10:       Update the state variable x_n according to (3) by x_{locBst}.
11:       **if** $f(x_n) > f_{locBst}$ **then**
12:           $f_{locBst} = f(x_n)$, $x_{locBst} = x_n$
13:       **end if**
14:   **end while**
15:   **if** $f_{locBst} > f_{bst}$ **then**
16:       $f_{bst} = f_{locBst}$, $x(n_{bst}, t) = x_{locBst}$.
17:   **end if**
18:   Update step size $step^t$ with decreasing functions (4) and respectively, which could be further studied by the designers.
19: **end while**
return $x(n_{bst}, :)$, f_{bst}.

2.2 Optimization Strategy Design of Particle Filter

The improved particle filter algorithm of BAS optimization is the idea of the swarm BAS algorithm is introduced into the standard particle filter. Because the swarm BAS algorithm is a random search optimization, and the particle filter algorithm mainly has the problem that the probability function of the importance density is difficult to converge quickly, so the random search optimization algorithm is adopted to solve the problem of particle degradation. The basic idea is to introduce the foraging behavior and the cluster seeking behavior of the population beetles in the process of calculating the importance weight of particles, so that the majority of prior particles move to the high likelihood region, thereby improving the estimation accuracy of particles and improving the performance of particle filter algorithm. The flow of BAS-PF algorithm is as shown in Fig. 2.

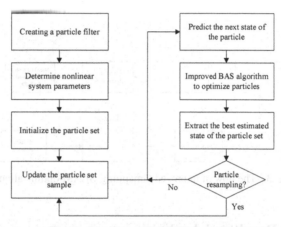

Fig. 2. The flow of BAS-PF algorithm

3 Application of BAS-PF in Gmapping-SLAM

Gmapping-SLAM uses Rao-Blackwellized particle filter [14] as the algorithm core of mobile robot localization and mapping. In the process of constructing particle filter's proposal distribution, the lidar's environment ranging information and odometer's moving distance information are fused into particle's proposal distribution, and an adaptive resampling mechanism is introduced, which reduces the number of particle sets to some extent, improves the calculation efficiency and satisfies most real-time application scenarios.

In the process of studying and analyzing the source code of Gmapping-SLAM algorithm, the idea of applying particle filter is in the scanning and matching link, among them, the hill-climbing search algorithm is used, the algorithm also adopts the heuristic search strategy, but has the following shortcomings [15]:

• This algorithm is not a comprehensive blanket search, and the search results may be only local optimal solution rather than global optimal solution;

- When the search reaches the flat area of the highland, the best search direction can not be determined, which will reduce the search efficiency.

Aiming at the above shortcomings, the idea of improved BAS algorithm was introduced into the scanning and matching link, and the single foraging characteristic and the group seeking characteristic of beetle group were fully utilized. The next head orientation of the single reflected the randomness of the search, the size of the single determined the length of the search step and the size difference between the single reflected the competition behavior of the survival of the fittest. The particles in the high-likelihood region are further optimized to the regional optimal particles by the improved BAS algorithm, while the particles in the low-likelihood region are optimized to the low-likelihood region optimal particles, which avoids all particles approaching to the same optimal value and maintains the particle diversity to some extent. The flow of improved Gmapping-SLAM optimization is as shown in Fig. 3.

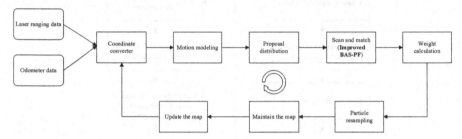

Fig. 3. The flow of improved Gmapping-SLAM optimization

4   Simulation Result and Analysis

4.1   Simulation of Improved BAS-PF

In order to verify the effectiveness of the proposed algorithm, Univariate Nonstationary Growth Model (UNGM) is selected as the evaluation object. The improved BAS-PF and the standard PF are used to compare the system state estimation. The simulation results of Fig. 4 and Fig. 5 are all done on the parameter settings of Table 1.

Table 1.   The parameters of UNGM filter

Parameters	Value	Parameters	Value
Process noise variance(Q)	10	Measuring noise variance(R)	1
Number of particles(N_p)	100	Initial state of particle(x_0)	0.1
Step size(*step*)	0.2	Step attenuation coefficient (δ)	0.8
Maximum iterations	5	Number of beetles(N_b)	5

Figure 4 is the simulation experiment of nonlinear system state estimation of PF and improved BAS_PF filter. From Fig. 4(a), we can see that the improved BAS_PF method proposed in this paper has a higher degree of coincidence with the state truth value at each moment than the traditional PF method in the state estimation trajectory tracking, which can also draw the same conclusion on the comparison of the maximum posteriori estimation error curves of the two filters in Fig. 4(b).

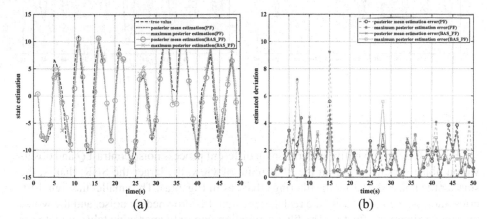

Fig. 4. Filter status comparison between PF and improved BAS_PF. (a) State trajectory. (b) Error estimation.

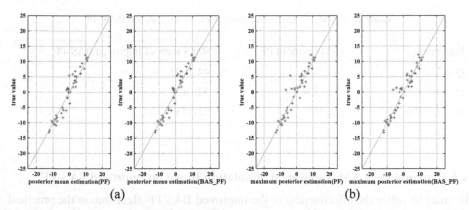

Fig. 5. Comparison of state truth values with distributions of estimated states of PF and improved BAS_PF filters. (a) Posterior state. (b) Maximum posterior state.

The results of Fig. 5 show that the improved BAS_PF method has better performance than PF method in estimating the state of the system along the straight line.

212   W.-D. Ni and G.-Z. Cao

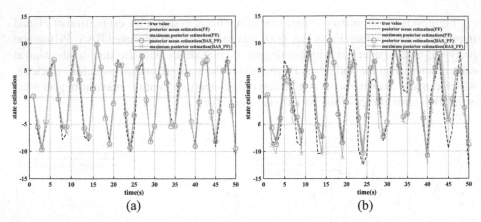

Fig. 6. State trajectory comparison between PF and improved BAS_PF. (a) $Q = 1, R = 1$. (b) $Q = 10, R = 10$.

Figure 6 is a comparative experiment in different process noise contrast Q and observation noise variance R. From the SNR point of view, the larger the SNR, that is, the smaller the noise, the easier the filtering effect, as in Fig. 6(a); The smaller the signal-to-noise ratio is, the more easily the real system signal is drowned by noise, and the worse the state estimation effect is. The filter estimation can only approximately simulate the changing trend of the system, as shown in Fig. 6(b). But from the comparison of the RMS error of the two filters in Table 2, the RMS error of the improved BAS_PF method is slightly smaller than that of the PF method, and the state estimation effect is better.

Table 2. RMSE comparison between PF and improved BAS_PF

Parameters	RMS error of PF	RMS error of improved BAS-PF
$Q = 1, R = 1$	44.2039	44.1895
$Q = 10, R = 1$	52.6230	52.6125
$Q = 10, R = 10$	52.5801	52.5730

4.2 Gmapping-SLAM Application Simulation Based on Improved BAS-PF

In order to verify the effectiveness of the improved BAS-PF algorithm in the practical application scenario of mobile robot mapping, according to the actual size of a factory's production site, the factory's production environment is built by 1:1 scale reduction on the ROS's Gazebo physical simulation platform, and the mechanical model of the self-developed AGV prototype is built into a 1:1 scale URDF model to move into the simulation environment for simulation experiments. Then, a AGV forward segment is recorded by the ROS's bag recording tool, and the original Gmapping-SLAM mapping function package and the improved Gmapping-SLAM are used to optimize the graph. A factory-based Gazebo simulation environment is shown in the Fig. 7.

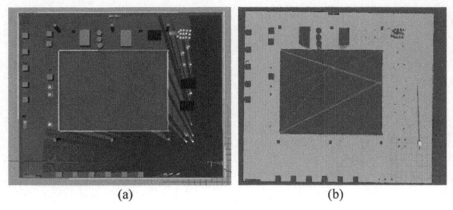

Fig. 7. Factory-based Gazebo simulation environment. (a) Gazebo environment setup. (b) Gmapping-SLAM mapping effect optimized based on improved BAS-PF.

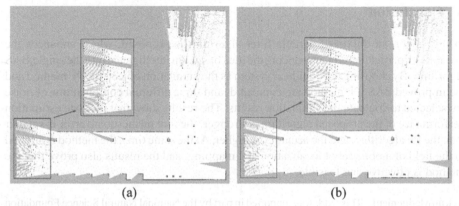

Fig. 8. Mapping with 1 particle number. (a) The original Gmapping-SLAM method. (b) The proposed method.

Figure 8 is the original Gmapping-SLAM method and the improved method proposed in this paper on the particle number 1 positioning mapping, can be more obvious from the red box to see the wall edge of the method is clearer; Fig. 9 is in the particle number of 20 on the positioning mapping, you can see from the red and blue box comparison of the map of the environment in this method updates faster, pose estimation efficiency is higher.

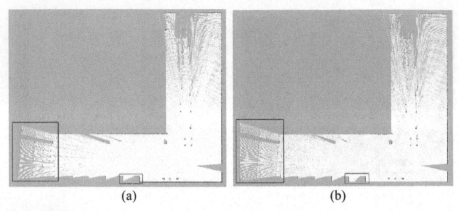

(a)   (b)

Fig. 9. Mapping with 20 particles number. (a) The original Gmapping-SLAM method. (b) The proposed method.

5 Conclusion

In this paper, an improved particle filter algorithm is proposed, which enhances the diversity of particle sets by introducing the idea of swarm intelligence into the single BAS algorithm. By choosing the nonlinear system as the simulation object, the PF method and the improved BAS_PF method are compared, and three different combinations of noise are selected to compare the simulation results. The results show that the state estimation performance of the proposed algorithm is stronger, the root mean square error is smaller than the PF algorithm, and the accuracy is higher. At the same time, the method is applied to the field of mobile robot localization and mapping, and the results also prove that the method is effective and feasible.

Acknowledgement. This work was supported in part by the National Natural Science Foundation of China under Grant NSFC U1813212, in part by the Science and Technology Planning Project of Guangdong Province, China under Grant 2020B121201012.

References

1. Reis, W.P., Couto, G.E., Junior, O.M.: Automated guided vehicles position control: a systematic literature review. J. Intell. Manuf. 1–63 (2021).https://doi.org/10.1007/s10845-021-018 93-x
2. Zou, Q., Sun, Q., Chen, L., Nie, B., Li, Q.: A comparative analysis of LiDAR SLAM-based indoor navigation for autonomous vehicles. IEEE Trans. Intell. Transp. 1–15 (2021)
3. Zhu, D., Wang, M., Su, M., Liu, S., Guo, P.: SLAM of mobile robot for wireless communication based on improved particle filter. Wirel. Commun. Mob. Com. **2021**, 1–14 (2021)
4. Zhou, N., et al.: A genetic optimization resampling based particle filtering algorithm for indoor target tracking. Rem. Sens. **13**(1), 132 (2021)
5. Xu, C., Wang, X.X., Duan, X.X., Wan, J.W.: Particle filter tracking algorithm based on error ellipse resampling. Chinese J. Sci. Instrum. **41**(12), 76–84 (2020)

6. Osamy, Walid, Ahmed, A., El, S., Ahmed, S.: CSOCA: Chicken swarm optimization based clustering algorithm for wireless sensor networks. IEEE Access. **8**, 60676–60688 (2020)
7. Wu, F.B., Liu, Y., Zhu, D.X., Wang, M.B.: Research on particle filter algorithm for whale swarm optimization. J. Appl. Optics. **42**(05), 859–866 (2021)
8. Zhu, D., et al.: Mobile robot SLAM algorithm based on improved firefly particle filter. In. 2019 International Conference on Robots and Intelligent System (ICRIS), pp. 35–38. IEEE (2019)
9. Wang, T., Yang, L., Liu, Q.: Beetle swarm optimization algorithm: theory and application. Filomat. **34**(15), 5121–5137 (2020)
10. Cao, Z., Du, X.: An intelligent optimization-based particle filter for fault diagnosis. IEEE Access. **9**, 87839–87848 (2021)
11. He, N., et al.: An improved pipeline leak detection and localization method based on compressed sensing and event-triggered particle filter. J. Franklin Inst. **358**(15), 8085–8108 (2021)
12. Zivkovic, M., et al.: COVID-19 cases prediction by using hybrid machine learning and beetle antennae search approach. Sustain. Cities Soc. **66**, 102669 (2021)
13. Zhang, Y., Li, S., Xu, B.: Convergence analysis of beetle antennae search algorithm and its applications. Soft. Comput. **25**(16), 10595–10608 (2021). https://doi.org/10.1007/s00500-021-05991-z
14. Grisetti, G., Stachniss, C., Burgard, W.: Improved techniques for grid mapping with rao-blackwellized particle filters. IEEE Trans. Robot. **23**(1), 34–46 (2007)
15. Wang, X.Y., Wang, X.L.: Improvement and implementation of heuristic search strategy (mountain climbing method). J. Shaanxi Normal Univ. (Nat. Sci. Edn.). **01**, 63–65+70 (1999)

Simulation Study of Wireless Coverage in Straight Long Corridors on Container Ship Deck

Yu Zhu[1,3] and Bing Han[1,2,3](✉)

[1] Shanghai Ship and Shipping Research Institute Co. Ltd., Shanghai 200135, China
han.bing@coscoshipping.com
[2] College of Physics and Electronic Information Engineering, Minjiang University,
Fuzhou 350108, China
[3] National Engineering Research Center for Ship Transportation Control System,
Shanghai 200135, China

Abstract. A wireless coverage simulation based on the ray tracing method is constructed to realize the wireless coverage prediction of the straight long corridor on the container ship deck. The ray reflection model based on the reverse algorithm of the ray tracing method is established to realize the simulation calculation of the point-to-point propagation path. Referring to the recommendations given by the International Telecommunication Union, the Fresnel loss of the straight long corridors and the first Fresnel loss point are calculated, and the ray reflection model is effectively corrected. The least square method is used to fit the double slope of the simulation curve, and the loss formula of the straight long corridors on the deck is obtained. Through experimental simulation, the path loss factors of the fully enclosed corridor are 1.248 and 3.245, and the path loss factors of the semi-closed corridor are 1.251 and 3.444. The simulation results agree with the general conclusions of the ITU recommendation. The simulation can provide the prediction of wireless coverage effect in the design of container ships and provide guidance for the layout design and optimization of base stations of the straight long corridor on container ship deck with different scales.

Keywords: Ray tracing · Ship · Path loss · Fresnel loss · Multipath propagation

1 Introduction

Various technologies are becoming more and more mature with the continuous deepening of the application of ICT (Information and Communications Technology) technologies such as wireless network, IOT (the Internet of Things), artificial intelligence in all walks of life. The shipbuilding industry is also developing in the direction of informatization and intelligence, and more and more informatization and intelligent equipment are deployed on ships. The installation and layout of intelligent information equipment on board is constrained because the wired deployment of ships depends on the cable holes reserved during shipbuilding. Therefore, ship-wide wireless coverage has become a realistic requirement. Similarly, it is difficult to lay the wireless base station due to the limitation of cable holes. It is impossible to lay wireless base stations in the field directly based on past experience, like the traditional indoor wireless layout: if there is a lack of coverage, it will be supplemented. Consequently, it is necessary to carry out wireless coverage simulation to improve the accuracy and effectiveness of ship wireless coverage planning and design.

The straight long channel on the deck of container ship, as a typical scene of ship wireless coverage, not only has the steel environment, but also has the characteristics of tunnel. The existing traditional wireless signal propagation model and distance loss formulas are difficult to be directly applied to ship platform [1, 2]. In the steel tunnel environment, in addition to direct radiation, electromagnetic waves will also be reflected by the surrounding bulkheads multiple times. There-fore, the electromagnetic signal received by the receiver is a synthetic wave that pass-es through multiple paths and propagates from multiple directions and has obvious multipath effect [3]. Based on Recommendation ITU-R P.1238, such a long straight channel scenario will also generate Fresnel loss and have a great impact on electro-magnetic wave propagation.

At present, there is little research on the straight long channel of ships all over the world. But there are many researches on the similar scene of tunnel and mine. References [4, 5] verified the simulation feasibility of ray tracing method for tunnels and corridors. References [6, 7] realized the channel modeling and simulation for the subway tunnel environment. References [8, 9] realizes the modeling and simulation of visual channel for closed environment. In the Reference [10], the frequency model is modified based on the ray tracking of narrow-band channel for ultra-wideband mine channel.

In this study, the large-scale path loss model of LTE (Long Term Evolution) channel is simulated for straight long corridors of container ship deck. Firstly, the reflection model of narrow-band channel is simulated. According to the ITU-R series of recommendations and the characteristics of tunnel environment, the loss correction of the propagation model is carried out. The simulation model is established for the loss prediction of wireless network path of the straight long corridors on the container ship deck.

2 Ray Reflection Model

Ray tracing is an effective method widely used in wireless coverage simulation [11, 12], which is used to approximate the propagation of high frequency electromagnetic field. In the case of high frequency, the transmission characteristics of electromagnetic wave and other relevant parameters change slowly, so its propagation can be simulated by light according to the principle of GO (Geometric Optics) [13].

Ray tracing method is mainly divided into two types: forward propagation and back propagation. The forward algorithm tracks each ray emitted by the transmitter. The forward propagation algorithm can directly obtain the wireless coverage of the whole area after completing one calculation, but the accuracy is limited, and the amount of rays tracked is large. The overall calculation complexity is large. The reverse algorithm starts from the receiver and tracks the propagation path between all transmitters and receivers in reverse. It is more difficult to calculate than the forward algorithm, but it can complete the point-to-point propagation path and achieve more accurate calculations and obtain the corresponding phase, delay and other propagation information [14].

In this study, the reverse algorithm is selected as the core algorithm of the simulation, and the propagation path is calculated by the mirror image method. The principle of the mirror image method is showed as Fig. 1. The position information of the transmitter, reflector and receiver is known. The mirror image position of the transmitter and the physical position of the transmitter are symmetrical with respect to the reflector. The transmission path from the transmitter to the reflecting surface and then to the receiver can be directly equivalent to the mirror position of the transmitter directly radiating to the receiver. The overall first-order mirror radiation field can be obtained from the radiation characteristics of the transmitter and the electromagnetic characteristics of the reflecting surface. In the actual propagation, the ray will be reflected more than once. So in order to simulate the actual electromagnetic wave propagation process, it is necessary to calculate the high-order reflection. Similar to the first-order reflection, the mirror point of the transmitter is used as a virtual transmitter, then the mirror point of the virtual transmitter relative to other reflection surfaces is calculated, and the reflection point of the second reflection is calculated to obtain the propagation path of the secondary reflection. By analogy, the calculation of higher-order reflection is completed.

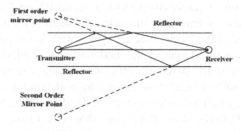

Fig. 1. Principle of mirror image method

After calculating the effective propagation path between the transmitter and receiver by the mirror image method, the receiving power can be calculated by Eq. (1)

$$P_r = P_t \left\{ \frac{\lambda}{4\pi} \right\}^2 \times \left\{ \left| \frac{1}{r} + \sum_{i=1}^{N-1} \frac{\rho_s R_i \exp(j\varphi_i)}{r_i} \right|^2 \right\} \tag{1}$$

where P_r is the receiving power of the receiver; PT is the transmitting power of the transmitter; λ is the wavelength of electromagnetic wave; N is the total number of propagation paths to the receiver; R_i is the reflection coefficient of the i-th ray that reaches the receiver through the reflection surface; r_i is the path length of the i-th ray; r is the length of the direct ray path; ρ_s is the scattering loss factor of the rough reflection surface; φ_i is the phase difference of the signal transmitted at the receiver between the i-th ray path and the direct path, wherein

$$\rho_s = \exp\left[-8\left(\frac{\pi \sigma_h \cos(\theta_i)}{\lambda} \right)^2 \right] \tag{2}$$

$$\varphi_i = \frac{2\pi \Delta l_i}{\lambda} \tag{3}$$

In Eq. (2) and (3), σ_h is the variance of the reflection surface roughness; θ_i is the incident angle of the i-th ray; Δl_i is the difference between the path length of the i-th ray and the line-of-sight path.

The electromagnetic wave will be lost in the process of reflection because there is no ideal conductor in the actual propagation. In general, the reflection loss can be expressed by Fresnel reflection coefficient.

$$R = \frac{E_r}{E_i} \tag{4}$$

where E_r is the intensity of reflected electric field and E_i is the intensity of the incident electric field.

For the incident wave of electromagnetic wave, two polarization modes are adopted, vertical and parallel.

$$E_h = E_{hm} \cos(\omega t - \phi_h) \tag{5}$$

$$E_v = E_{vm} \cos(\omega t - \phi_v) \tag{6}$$

where E_h is the energy of parallel polarization wave and E_v is the energy of vertical polarization wave; w is the angular frequency; ϕ is the initial phase. In linear polarization, the initial phase ϕ_h and ϕ_v are 0.

$$E = \sqrt{E_{hm}^2 + E_{vm}^2}\cos\omega t$$
$$= \sqrt{E_h^2 + E_v^2} \tag{7}$$

On the reflecting surface, the electromagnetic waves will be incident and reflected at different angles depending on the propagation path. For parallel and vertical polarization waves, the reflection coefficients R_h and R_v are showed as Eq. (8) and Eq. (9).

$$R_h = \frac{\cos(\theta)-\sqrt{(\varepsilon-\sin^2(\theta))}}{\cos(\theta)+\sqrt{(\varepsilon-\sin^2(\theta))}} \tag{8}$$

$$R_v = \frac{\varepsilon\cos(\theta)-\sqrt{(\varepsilon-\sin^2(\theta))}}{\varepsilon\cos(\theta)+\sqrt{(\varepsilon-\sin^2(\theta))}} \tag{9}$$

where θ is the incidence angle of electromagnetic wave; ε is the relative permittivity of the reflecting surface.

By introducing Eq. (8) and (9) into Eq. (7) and (4) respectively, the equivalent reflection coefficient of the i-th electromagnetic wave for the reflecting surface under the condition of this incident angle can be obtained.

$$R_i = \sqrt{\frac{(E_h R_h)^2+(E_v R_v)^2}{E_h^2+E_v^2}} \tag{10}$$

3 Model Correction

According to the Recommendation ITU-R P.1238 given by ITU (International Telecommunication Union), Fresnel loss may begin to occur at a certain point away from the transmitter for a long unobstructed path with corridor path characteristics. It means that the turning point of the first Fresnel zone may occur.

The Fresnel zone is between the transmitter and the receiver and is formed by the effective reflection point where the difference between the direct path and the refracted path of the electromagnetic wave is $\frac{n\lambda}{2}$. Its geometric composition is an ellipse with the position of the transceiver as the focus and the direct path as the axis. Among them, the first Fresnel zone is the Fresnel zone with $n = 1$, which has the greatest impact on signal propagation. The concentric radius of Fresnel zone can be expressed by the following equation.

$$r_n = \sqrt{\frac{n\lambda d_1 d_2}{d_1 + d_2}} \tag{11}$$

where n is the number of ellipses, d_1 is the distance between the Fresnel zone and the transmitter, d_2 is the distance between the Fresnel zone and the receiver, λ is the wavelength of the electromagnetic wave.

From Eq. (11), the first Fresnel zone between the transmitter and the receiver has the largest radius when the electromagnetic wavelength is determined. The Fresnel radius decreases when the electromagnetic wave frequency increases, if the receiving and transmitting position is determined and the electromagnetic wavelength decreases.

According to Recommendation ITU-R P.526, the Fresnel loss of a long straight channel can be approximately fitted by the composite rectangular aperture diffraction model. The Fresnel-Kirchhoff diffraction parameters of the first Fresnel zone are:

$$v = H \sqrt{\frac{2}{\lambda \left(\frac{1}{d_1} + \frac{1}{d_2} \right)}} \tag{12}$$

where d_1 is the distance between the Fresnel zone and the transmitter, d_2 is the distance between the Fresnel zone and the receiver, λ is the wavelength of electromagnetic wave and H is the length of the line connecting the top of the obstacle to the transmitter and receiver.

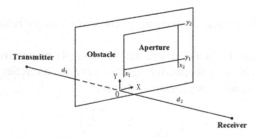

Fig. 2. Diffraction model of rectangular aperture

The positions of the aperture edges are showed as Fig. 2. The origin is the intersection of the connecting line between transmitter and receiver and the shielding surface, and the propagation of electromagnetic wave is parallel to the Z-axis. The distance between the transmitter and the receiver from the shield is d_1 and d_2 respectively. The field strength at the receiver is given by Eq. (13)

$$\frac{e_a(x_1, x_2, y_1, y_2)}{= 0.5(C_x C_y - S_x S_y) + j0.5(C_x S_y + S_x C_y)} \tag{13}$$

where:

$$C_x = C(v_{x2}) - C(v_{x1}) \tag{14}$$

$$C_y = C(v_{y2}) - C(v_{y1}) \tag{15}$$

$$S_x = S(v_{x2}) - S(v_{x1}) \tag{16}$$

$$S_y = S(v_{y2}) - S(v_{y1}) \tag{17}$$

$$F_c(v) = C(v) + jS(v) = \int_0^v \exp\left(j\frac{\pi s^2}{2}\right) ds \tag{18}$$

$C(v)$ and $S(v)$ are derived from the complex Fresnel integral $F_c(v)$.

In Eq. (12), replace H with x_1, x_2, y_1 and y_2, respectively, to obtain 4 v values. The diffraction loss La of a single rectangular aperture can be obtained from Eq. (19):

$$L_a = -20\log(e_a) \tag{19}$$

In the propagation path of the composite rectangular aperture propagation model, the single rectangular aperture with the maximum v value is the main obstacle, which is the main component of the overall diffraction loss and is recorded as position a.

The diffraction loss at the maximum v value for a single rectangular aperture also needs to be calculated twice for calculating the approximation of the composite model loss.

1. v_b and L_b are obtained from the transmitter to point a
2. v_c and L_c are obtained from point a to the receiver

The diffraction loss of the composite rectangular aperture model is obtained by the following equation.

$$L = L_a + T[L(v_b) + L(v_c) + C] \tag{20}$$

where:

$$C = 10.0 + 0.04D \tag{21}$$

$$T = 1.0 - \exp\left[-\frac{L(v)}{6.0}\right] \tag{22}$$

where C is the empirical correction, D is the total path length (km), and T is the loss caused by two sub rectangular aperture obstacles.

4 Modeling and Simulation Analysis

4.1 Container Ship Straight Long Corridor Modeling

According to the layout drawing of 21000TEU (Twenty-feet Equivalent Unit) container ship, there are two main arrangements for the straight long corridor of the container ship.

The first is a fully enclosed corridor, which is located at the lower deck inside the container ship. The overall feature is fully enclosed and the bulkhead is made of all-metal. The fully enclosed corridor is about 380 m long and the width height is about 2.5 m of a standard TEU.

The second is semi-closed corridor which is located on the edge of the container ship. The overall feature is embodied as semi-closed, as shown in Fig. 3. The top, the area associated with the container, are effective reflection walls; There is no effective reflection wall in the side and the area associated with the container. Other parts are effective metal bulkheads. As a whole, it is a semi-closed corridor, about 380 m long, the same width and height as a standard TEU, about 2.5 m.

Fig. 3. Schematic diagram of the semi-closed corridor of a container ship

According to the characteristics and layout drawings of the container captain's straight channel, the fully closed channel and the semi closed channel are modeled by ZW3D modeling software, and the modeling accuracy reaches 0.1M, as shown in Fig. 4. At the same time, in order to reduce the complexity and calculation of the overall model simulation, the irregular reflection and scattering characteristics caused by the gap of the metal bulkhead in the straight long corridor and all kinds of small sundries that may appear in the straight long corridor are not considered.

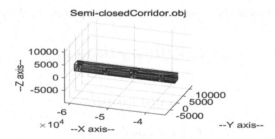

Fig. 4. 3D model of the semi-closed corridor of a container ship

4.2 Simulation Conditions

The nodes are arranged at the center of the transverse section in the corridor because the energy of electromagnetic waves in the straight long corridor of the container ship is concentrated in the center of the corridor. The corridor is with width and height of 2.4 m. The transmitter position is fixed and the receiving node is on the midline. The simulation is carried out every meter. Both the transmitter and the receiver adopt omnidirectional antennas. Due to the limitation of the frequency band of ship-borne LTE private network, the frequency of the electromagnetic wave in this simulation is 1.8 GHz. Considering the reflection loss of the bulkhead to the ray, the electromagnetic wave reflected more than three times has little impact on the receiver [15]. In the simulation, the maximum reflection times is taken as 3. The specific simulation parameters are shown in Table 1.

Table 1. Parameters of the simulation.

Simulation parameters	Numerical value
Signal frequency f/GHz	1.8
Vacuum permittivity ε_0/(F/m)	8.854×10^{-12}
Relative permittivity of long straight channel ε_r	12.5
Long straight channel conductivity σ/(s/m)	710
Bandwidth B/MHz	20
Effective reflection times	3

4.3 Model Correction

In the ray reflection model, the blocking of the first Fresnel zone is not considered in the simulation of wireless coverage. According to the Recommendation ITU-R P.526, it can be considered that there is no Fresnel loss in the propagation of electromagnetic waves when the blocked area of the first Fresnel zone is less than 45%. When the effective blocking area is more than 45%, the Fresnel diffraction loss needs to be calculated and the ray reflection model needs to be corrected. According to Eq. (11), the position in the middle of the transmitter and the receiver has the largest radius of the first Fresnel zone when the wavelength of the electromagnetic wave is determined. The calculation of Fresnel diffraction loss will be carried out based on this radius. Under the condition of fixed width and height of the straight long corridor, the first Fresnel loss point and the overall Fresnel diffraction loss at different frequencies are simulated. The simulation results show that the first Fresnel loss point is about 107 m at 1.8 GHz.

The frequency of electromagnetic wave is set to 1.8 GHz by combining the ray re-flection model and the correction quantity. The relationship curve between distance variation and distance loss is obtained by simulation. And the simulation results show that the first Fresnel loss point is about 107 m at 1.8 GHz.

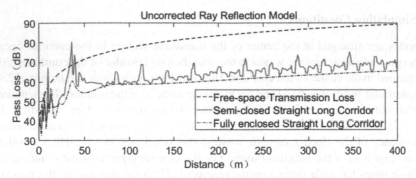

Fig. 5. Uncorrected ray reflection model

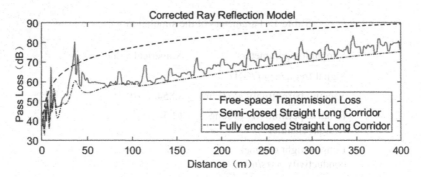

Fig. 6. Corrected ray reflection model

The simulation results of the uncorrected ray reflection model and the corrected ray reflection model are showed as the Fig. 5 and Fig. 6. It shows that the overall trend of change is similar to that of the uncorrected model. Before the first Fresnel loss point, the loss curve shows the characteristics of fast fading as a whole, which is greatly affected by multipath fading. Because the phase between multipath signals changes dramatically, the received signal amplitude changes dramatically. After the first Fresnel loss point, the phase change period between multipath signals tends to be stable. The change of signal loss curve is related to the actual reflection conditions of the propagation scene. In the fully enclosed scene, the reflection condition is stable and the loss curve rises gently; In the semi-closed scene, the loss curve also shows regular fluctuations due to the regular changes of the top and side effective reflection walls. In the fully enclosed straight long corridor, the maximum pass loss is 75.34 dB; In the semi-closed straight long corridor, the maximum path loss is 83.57 dB, which will increase the Fresnel loss by 5–10 dB compared with the uncorrected model.

4.4 Fitting and Analysis of Simulation Results

The path loss can be fitted and predicted by logarithmic distance model, and its expression is

$$PL = PL_0 + 10n\lg d \tag{23}$$

where PL_0 is the path loss of the reference distance, which is generally related to the electromagnetic wave frequency and the reference distance, and the reference distance is generally 1 m; n is the distance loss factor; d is the distance between the transmitter and the receiver.

By the least square method, the single-slope and double-slope logarithmic fittings are carried out for the fully enclosed corridor and the semi-closed corridor respectively. The fitting effect is evaluated by RMSE (Root Mean Square Error), and its expression is

$$RMSE = \sqrt{\frac{1}{N} \sum_{i=1}^{N} (L(i) - PL(i))^2} \tag{24}$$

Fully Enclosed Corridor Fitting. The path loss Eq. (25) and the RMSE (26) of the fully enclosed straight long corridor are obtained by single-slope fitting:

$$PL_{quan} = 25.71 + 17.59\lg d \tag{25}$$

$$RMSE_{quan\_dan} = 2.8661 \tag{26}$$

The double-slope model takes the first Fresnel loss point as the turning point, and the fitted path loss Eq. (27) and the RMSE (28) of the fully enclosed straight long corridor (Fig. 7):

$$\begin{cases} PL_{quan1} = 34.16 + 12.48\lg d & d \le 107 \\ PL_{quan2} = -9.72 + 32.45\lg d & d > 107 \end{cases} \tag{27}$$

$$RMSE_{quan\_shuang} = 1.7374 \tag{28}$$

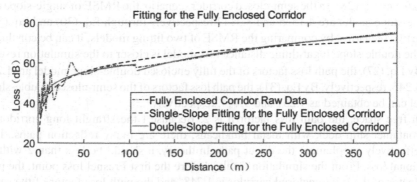

Fig. 7. Fitting for the fully enclosed corridor

Semi-closed Corridor Fitting. The path loss Eq. (29) and the RMSE (30) of semi-closed straight long corridor are obtained by single-slope fitting:

$$PL_{ban} = 28.41 + 18.02 \lg d \tag{29}$$

$$RMSE_{ban\_dan} = 4.1535 \tag{30}$$

The path loss Eq. (31) and the RSME (32) of semi-closed straight long corridor are obtained by double-slope fitting (Fig. 8):

$$\begin{cases} PL_{ban1} = 37.58 + 12.51 \lg d & d \le 107 \\ PL_{ban2} = -10.73 + 34.44 \lg d & d > 107 \end{cases} \tag{31}$$

$$RMSE_{ban\_shuang} = 3.3117 \tag{32}$$

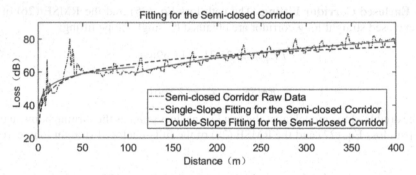

Fig. 8. Fitting for the semi-closed corridor

Simulation Fitting Data Analysis. In the fully enclosed corridor scenario, the RMSE of single-slope and double-slope model are 2.8661 and 1.7374 respectively through Eq. (26) and Eq. (28); In the semi-closed corridor scenario, the RMSE of single-slope and double-slope model are 4.1535 and 3.3117 respectively through Eq. (30) and Eq. (32). In the two scenarios, by comparing the RMSE of two fitting models, it can be concluded that the double-slope logarithmic distance loss model is closer to the simulation results.

By Eq. (27), the path loss factors of the fully enclosed double-slope model are 1.248 and 3.245, respectively. By Eq. (31), the path loss factors of the semi-closed double-slope model can be obtained as 1.251 and 3.444, respectively.

In free space, the path loss factor n is 2. Because t the straight long corridor of the container ship deck with metal bulkheads, there are many reflection paths. This can effectively supplement the direct path. In theory, n should be less than 2 without additional loss. From the simulation results, before the first Fresnel loss point, the path loss factor of the fully enclosed corridor is 1.248, and the path loss factor of the semi-closed corridor is 1.251, which are both less than 2, which conforms to the general conclusion given in ITU Recommendation. Moreover, the loss factor of the fully enclosed corridor is only 0.003 smaller than that of semi-closed corridor, which indicates that the influence of the propagation scene is small when the reflection component is sufficient before the first Fresnel loss point. After the first Fresnel loss point, due to the large Fresnel loss, the path loss factor of the fully enclosed corridor is 3.245, and the path loss factor of the semi-closed corridor is 3.444, which are greater than 2, which conforms to the general conclusion given in ITU Recommendation. Compared with semi-closed corridor, the path loss factor of the fully closed corridor is 0.199 smaller, which reflects the difference of two propagation scenarios.

The simulation results show that the modified double-slope logarithmic distance loss model can obtain more accurate prediction results.

5   Conclusion

In this paper, the wireless coverage simulation of the straight long corridor of the container deck is realized based on the ray tracing method. The electromagnetic wave propagation path is calculated by the mirror image method. Through the calculation of direct and reflected propagation, the point-to-point distance loss model is obtained in this specific scene. Fresnel loss is calculated to complete the correction of the ray reflection model in this scene. At the frequency of 1.8 GHz electromagnetic wave, the fully enclosed corridor and semi-closed corridor are simulated and analyzed, and the distance loss factor meets the theoretical expectation. In the scenario of straight long corridor on container deck, it can be determined that the maximum distance loss of fully closed channel is 75.34 dB and that of semi closed channel is 83.57 dB based on the simulation model. The model can effectively predict the signal coverage in this scenario and provide guidance for the layout and optimization of wireless base stations in the long straight channel of different scales container ships.

In the future, the calculation of repeated paths and invalid paths can be reduced and the overall calculation efficiency can be improved by optimizing the intersection test phase of ray visibility. Thus, more scene details can be covered in the modeling stage to further improve the simulation accuracy.

Acknowledgment. This manuscript is supported by National Key Research and Development Program (2019YFB1600600).

This manuscript is supported by the Natural Science Foundation of Fujian Province of China (2022J01131710).

References

1. Athanasiadou, G.E., Nix, A.R., McGeehan, J.P.: A ray tracing algorithm for microcellular and indoor propagation modeling. Antennas Propag. **2**, 231–235 (1995)
2. Rizki, K., WagenJ, F., Gardiol, F.: Two-dimensional ray-tracing modeling for propagation prediction in microcellular environments. IEEE Trans. Veh. Technol. **46**(2), 508–518 (1997)
3. Rao, T.R., Balachander, D., Tiwari, N.: Short-range near floor path gain measurements in indoor corridors at UHF for wireless sensor communications. In: IEEE International Conference on Communication Systems. IEEE (2013)

4. Sun, R., Song, K., Tao, C., et al.: Research of radio channel characteristics under tunnel scenario. J. China Railw. Soc. **39**(2), 58–66 (2017)
5. Zhang, S.: Study of the law of radio ray transmission in tunnel. Chin. J. Radio Sci. **17**(2), 114–118 (2002)
6. Jiang, Y., Zheng, G., Yin, X., et al.: Performance study of millimeter-wave MIMO channel in subway tunnel using directional antennas. IET Microwaves Antennas Propag. **12**(5), 833–839 (2017)
7. Song, K.: Simulation and analysis of radio channel characteristic in tunnel. Beijing Jiaotong University (2017)
8. El Khaled, M., Fortier, P., Ammari, M.L.: A performance study of line-of-sight millimeter-wave underground mine channel. IEEE Antennas Wirel. Propag. Lett. **13**, 1148–1151 (2014)
9. Batalha, I.S., Lopes, A.V.R., Jasmine, J., et al.: Indoor corridor and office propagation measurements and channel models at 8, 9, 10 and 11 GHz. IEEE Access **7**, 55005–55021 (2019)
10. Wang, Y., Chen, Y., Sun, Y.: Construction and simulation of the path loss model for mine UWB. J. Taiyuan Univ. Technol. (2012)
11. Remley, K.A., Anderson, H.R., Weisshar, A.: Improving the accuracy of ray-tracing techniques for indoor propagation modeling. IEEE Trans. Veh. Technol. **49**(6), 2350–2358 (2000)
12. Chen, S.-H.: An SBR/image approach for radiowave propagation in indoor environments with metallic furniture. IEEE Trans. Antennas Propag. **45**(1), 98–106 (1997)
13. Ying, W., Zhang, Z.W.: Study on the propagation characteristic of the electromagnetic waves in limited space. Shanxi Electron. Technol. (2011)
14. Cheng, T., You, M., Tan, Z., et al.: Radio channel character in tunnels based on theray-tracing method. J. Beijing Jiaotong Univ. (2016)
15. Yan, C., Ge, L.-H., Fan, X.P., et al.: Simulation and analysis of radio wave propagation characteristics in ship Cabin. J. Shanxi Datong Univ. (Nat. Sci. Ed.) **34**(6), 17–20 (2018)

Research on Path Planning Based on the Fusion Algorithm of Adaptive Ant Colony Optimization and Artificial Potential Field Method

Ran Wang, Qingxin Zhang(✉), Tong Cui, and Xinggang Wu

College of Artificial Intelligence, Shenyang Aerospace University, Shenyang 110136, China
Zhy9712@sau.edu.cn

Abstract. It is a hot topic in the field of road landscape planning technology that a mobile robot can quickly and safely find an optimal path in a multi obstacle environment. In path planning, in light of the problems of poor cooperation and slow convergence of ant colony algorithm in a known environment, the existing potential field method in the local path environment focuses on avoiding dynamic obstacles but cannot guarantee an optimal path. This study provides a new fusion algorithm for path planning optimization in both static and dynamic environments. Firstly, to prevent slipping into a local optimum, create a pheromone diffusion model and adaptively tweak the population information entropy factor to speed up the convergence speed of the Adaptive Ant Colony Optimization (AACO) algorithm. Secondly, on the basis of the globally planned path, by designing the local stability detection and escape functions, the Improved Artificial Potential Field (IAPF) method is utilized to solve the problem of unreachable destination. Finally, we conduct simulation experiments through MATLAB to compare the indicators for evaluating paths, it verifies that the fusion algorithm proposed in this research has obvious advantages in path planning in both static and dynamic environments.

Keywords: Path planning · Adaptive ant colony optimization · Population information entropy · Improved artificial potential field

1 Introduction

Path navigation technology has been extensively studied and is now widely employed in the domains of robot dynamic obstacle avoidance that need more accuracy and flexibility. The path planning of the mobile robot is critical in robot navigation technology, its mission is to find an optimal path in a working environment.

The ant colony optimization algorithm is implemented for global path planning, local path obstacle avoidance often uses the artificial potential field method. With the advancement of path navigation research, the dominant position of fusion algorithms

---

Foundation Item: Liaoning Education Department General Project (LJKZ0231); Huaian Natural Science Research Plan Project (HAB202083).

H. Liu et al. (Eds.): ICIRA 2022, LNAI 13457, pp. 229–239, 2022.
https://doi.org/10.1007/978-3-031-13835-5_21

is prominent. In this work, the contributions of the improved fusion algorithm to robot path planning are as follows. 1) The pheromone diffusion mechanism was established to enhance the cooperative ability of the population and the efficiency of searching for the · optimal path. 2) The population information entropy adaptively adjusts the probability of searching for the next node and dynamically changes the pheromone concentration to prevent local optimal solutions from occurring. 3) The rules of gravitational and repulsive potential fields were improved to safely avoid the unknown and moving obstacles. 4) The problems of unreachable destinations are eliminated by implementing local stability detection and escape mechanisms.

2 Related Works

2.1 Ant Colony Optimization

The Ant Colony Optimization (ACO) is a random heuristic search algorithm. Initially, the ants would hunt aimlessly and emit pheromone as a bridge to sharing information about the course they have traveled. The ants will wish to explore along the path with the highest accumulated pheromone concentration during the search process, eventually finding an optimal path after so many iterations.

State transition and pheromone updating are the two most prominent processes. The ACO adopts whether nodes are randomly chosen or deterministically according to the parameter $q_0 \in [0, 1]$, as given in formula (1).

$$S = \begin{cases} \arg\max[\tau_{ij}^{\alpha}(t)][\eta_{ij}^{\beta}(t)] & if \ q \leq q_0 \\ s & otherwise \end{cases} \tag{1}$$

The ACO is more likely to construct candidate solutions in the deterministic model as q_0 rises; otherwise, candidate solutions are constructed randomly. Where τ_{ij} is the pheromone concentration of nodes i to j, α is the pheromone heuristic factor, which indicates how pheromone concentration affects transition probabilities. η_{ij} is heuristic information, β is the expected heuristic factor, which evaluates whether to fall into local optimum.

The pheromone must be updated after the candidate solution is generated. The ACO only modifies the pheromone on the global optimal solution to ensure that the algorithm always uses the optimal solution. The updating rule is shown in formula (2).

$$\tau_{ij}(t+1) = (1 - \rho) \cdot \tau_{ij}(t) + \rho \cdot \Delta\tau_{ij}^{gb}(t) \tag{2}$$

where $\rho \in [0, 1]$ is the volatilization coefficient of the pheromone, $\Delta\tau_{ij}^{gb}$ represents the pheromone increment produced on the globally optimal path segment.

A local pheromone update is required in addition to a global pheromone update to promote exploration of unexplored areas and avoid slipping into local optimum. The local information update rule is as formula (3).

$$\tau_{ij}(t+1) = (1 - \xi) \cdot \tau_{ij}(t) + \xi \cdot \tau_0 \tag{3}$$

where ξ is the local pheromone volatilization coefficient, and τ_0 is the initial value of the pheromone.

2.2 Artificial Potential Field

The Artificial Potential Field (APF) method simulates the moving surroundings of a mobile robot as a force field. The repulsive potential field drives it to move away from obstacles, while the gravitational potential field provides attraction that propels it towards the destination. The resultant determines the robot's movement direction and speed. Figure 1 shows a schematic diagram of force analysis using the APF method.

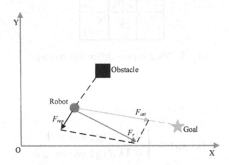

Fig. 1. The schematic diagram of a mobile robot force in APF.

The field strength shown below formulas.

$$F_{att}(X_p) = -k_{att} \cdot \rho(X_p, X_{goal}) \tag{4}$$

$$F_{rep}(X_p) = \begin{cases} k_{rep} \cdot (\frac{1}{\rho(X_p, X_{obs})} - \frac{1}{d_0}) \cdot \frac{1}{\rho^2(X_p, X_{obs})} & if \ \rho(X_p, X_{obs}) \le d_0 \\ 0 & otherwise \end{cases} \tag{5}$$

where X_p is the current position of the mobile robot, is the position coordinates of the obstacle, $\rho(X_p, X_{goal})$ is the relative distance between the mobile robot and the destination, $\rho(X_p, X_{obs})$ is the relative distance between the mobile robot and the obstacle.

From Eq. (5), (6), the attraction is proportional to the distance between the mobile robot and the destination, while the repulsion is inversely related to the distance between the robot and the obstacle. The resultant enables the mobile robot to avoid obstacles to the destination. The resultant calculation is shown in formula (6).

$$F_{total}(X_p) = F_{att}(X) + \sum_{i=1}^{n} F_{repi}(X) \tag{6}$$

3 Algorithm Improvement

3.1 ACCO

Although the ACO has optimization capability in mobile robots global path planning, there still exist problems such as slow convergence speed, local optimization, and weak cooperation between ants. Therefore, the AACO is proposed by introducing population information entropy. The following are concrete improvement strategies:

Pheromone Diffusion Mechanism. The pheromone only diffuses to the surrounding 8 grids. The corresponding pheromone diffusion model is shown in Fig. 2, assuming that the current grid's pheromone concentration is 1.

Fig. 2. Pheromone diffusion model.

The grid at each position around the current grid sets variable pheromone diffusion values. The calculation is shown in formula (7).

$$f(g, g_0) = \begin{cases} 0.5 & d(g, g_0) = 1 \\ 0.33 & d(g, g_0) = \sqrt{2} \end{cases} \tag{7}$$

Parameter Adaptive Adjustment Based on Population Information Entropy. The proportion of various states in a system is represented by information entropy. A probabilistic optimization algorithm is the ant colony algorithm. The length of the candidate solution's path and its proportion is random in each iteration. The proportion of the candidate solution might well be treated as the state of the colony, allowing information entropy to be used to characterize the diversity characteristics of the ant colony algorithm's evolution process [10].

The value of the parameter q_0 is automatically adjusted during the optimization process based on changes in population information entropy, and the proportion of random candidate solutions is adaptively altered in the next iteration. It effectively alleviates the local optimal problem caused by a rapid decrease of algorithmic diversity, not only accelerating convergence speed but also strengthening searchability. The adaptive adjustment rule of parameter q_0 is shown in formula (8).

$$q_0 = q_{0\min} + (q_{0\max} - q_{0\min}) \cdot HR_{pop}^{0.5}(t) \tag{8}$$

where $HR_{pop}(t) \in [0, 1]$ represents relative information entropy of the AACO in the t-th iteration. To ensure the optimization quality of the algorithm, the value of q_0 should be reduced to increase the proportion of candidate solutions in random mode, which will boost the exploration capacity of the algorithm. For accelerating the convergence speed of the algorithm, the value of q_0 should be increased to make use of the optimal solution.

Global Pheromone Update Rule Based on Population Information Entropy. The ACO only updates the pheromone of the global optimal solution, without considering high quality information contained in an iterative optimal solution [11]. Therefore, a new global pheromone update rule with population information entropy is designed to optimize the algorithm. The update method is shown as formula (9).

$$\tau_{ij}(t + 1) = (1 - \rho) \cdot \tau_{ij}(t) + \rho \cdot \Delta\tau_{ij}^{gb}(t) + (1 - HR_{pop}(t)) \cdot \Delta\tau_{ij}^{ib}(t) \tag{9}$$

where $\Delta \tau_{ij}^{ib}$ represennts the pheromone increment produced on local optimal path segment. According to population information entropy, pheromone release intensity is dynamically regulated to make full use of the iterative optimal solution.

3.2 IAPF

When a mobile robot moves along the path that the AACO has planned in a global static environment, unknown or moving obstacles should be avoided with the APF. By analyzing the force model of the APF which exists deficiencies in local path planning. Therefore, a rolling programming window that includes global optimal path information all along is designed on the mobile robot. If the sensor detects dynamic obstacles, the current programming window invokes the IAPF to avoid obstacles in a local dynamic environment. Then, analyzing deficiencies of the APF model and proposing improvement strategies.

Reduce the Risk of Collision. When a mobile robot detects obstacles far away from the destination, since the attraction of the destination is considerably larger than the repulsion of the obstacles, the mobile robot quickly moves towards the destination, resulting in the inability to avoid obstacles in time, which increases the risk of collision with obstacles.

Learned from the experience of repulsive potential field, the influence range of destination is set to improve the timeliness of gravitational potential field. The gravitational field strength shown in formula (10).

$$F_{att}(X_p) = \begin{cases} -k_{att} \cdot \rho(X_p, X_{goal}) \ if \ \rho(X_p, X_{goal}) \leq d_g \\ -d_g \cdot k_{att} \qquad\qquad\quad otherwise \end{cases} \tag{10}$$

where d_g is influence scope of the destination, if a mobile robot exceeds the scope, the attraction is a fixed value. Thus, solving the risk of collision when the mobile robot approaches obstacles.

The Solution to an Unreachable Destination. When there exists obstacles near the destination, a mobile robot enters the scope of the obstacles and destination. The obstacles exert too strong repulsion on the mobile robot, yet the attraction is weak preventing the mobile robot from reaching the destination. Figure 3 shows the situation of the unreachable destination.

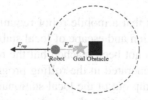

Fig. 3. The schematic diagram of unreachable destination.

A mobile robot cannot arrive at the destination without considering the effect of the destination on the repulsive potential field. Drawing on the design notion of the gravitational potential field function, the distance information between the mobile robot's current position and the destination is designed to repulsive potential field function, reducing repulsion near the destination.

The improved repulsive potential field function is shown in below formulas, where represents distance gain coefficient.

$$F_{rep}(X_p) = \begin{cases} F_{rep1}(X_p) + F_{rep2}(X_p) & if \ \rho(X_p, \ X_{obs}) \le d_0 \\ 0 & otherwise \end{cases} \qquad (11)$$

$$F_{rep1}(X_p) = k_{rep} \cdot (\frac{1}{\rho(X_p, \ X_{obs})} - \frac{1}{d_0}) \cdot \frac{\rho^n(X_p, \ X_{goal})}{\rho^2(X_p, \ X_{obs})} \qquad (12)$$

$$F_{rep2}(X_p) = -\frac{n}{2} \cdot k_{rep} \cdot (\frac{1}{\rho(X_p, \ X_{obs})} - \frac{1}{d_0}) \cdot \rho^{n-1}(X_p, \ X_{goal}) \qquad (13)$$

where $F_{rep1}(X_p)$ is the direction of obstacles pointing to the mobile robot, $F_{rep2}(X_p)$ is similar to the direction of attraction generated by the destination on the mobile robot. The improved repulsive potential field decreases the repulsion near the destination while also increasing the attraction, allowing the mobile robot to reach the destination.

The Solution to Stuck in Local Stability. Assuming that before a mobile robot reaches its destination, repulsion is equal to attraction but in opposite direction, so the resultant is zero [12]. Resulting in the mobile robot traps in local stability and is unable to continue moving to the destination, as shown in Fig. 4.

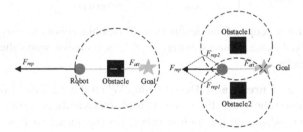

Fig. 4. The schematic diagram of local stability.

Given the above situations that a mobile robot remains in its current position. So designing functions that detection and escape of local stability. When the mobile robot detects that the destination has not been reached but the resultant is zero, a temporary point near the destination is generated in the rolling programming window. The point enables the mobile robot to jump out of the local stationary position. After the mobile robot escapes from its stationary position, the window removes the temporary point and restores the original destination. Then the mobile robot continues to move forward to the destination under the resultant. The effect of the temporary point is shown in Fig. 5.

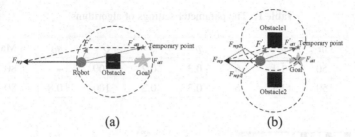

(a)   (b)

Fig. 5. The schematic diagram of escaping local stability.

3.3 Fusion Algorithm

This study proposes a two-stage path planning that integrates global and local information. In the offline operation phase, the initial optimal path of a mobile robot is planned with the AACO based on known static environment information, it is also a reference path for the online operation phase. During the online operation phase, the rolling programming window includes path information. Based on local information collected from sensors, the mobile robot decides whether to invoke the IAPF. The structure of the hierarchical fusion algorithm in a dynamic environment is shown in Fig. 6.

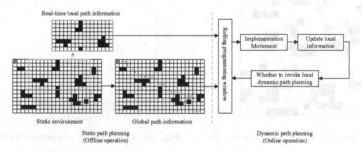

Fig. 6. The schematic diagram of hierarchical path planning.

4   Simulation Experiment and Analysis

4.1   The AACO Algorithm Simulation Experiment

We conduct two sets of comparative experiments with the ACO in 2D grid maps. The same parameters are set in two algorithms, the specific parameters value are shown in Table 1. The average value of 30 independent runs was used as the experimental result. And the comparison results of the simulation experiments are shown in Fig. 7 and Fig. 8, Fig. 9 and Fig. 10.

The performance comparison for two grid maps shows clearly that the path planned by the AACO is shorter and has fewer inflection points than the ACO. The superiority indexes are shown in Table 2.The AACO shows advantages, especially the larger optimal fitness ratio reflects the efficiency of the AACO.

Table 1. The parameter settings of algorithms

Algorithm	m	α	β	ρ	ξ	Q	q_0	MaxIter
ACO	50	1.1	6	0.3	0.2	100	–	80
AACO	50	1.1	6	0.3	0.2	100	0.8	80

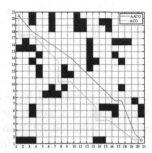

Fig. 7. Comparison of simulation results.

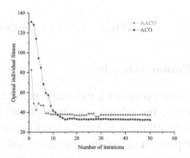

Fig. 8. Comparison of convergence curve.

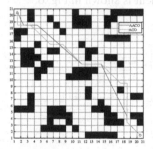

Fig. 9. Comparison of simulation results.

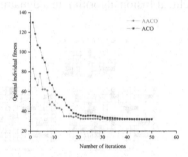

Fig. 10. Comparison of convergence curve.

Table 2. Comparison of evaluation indexes under two grid maps

Environment	Algorithm	Optimal fitness	Average fitness	FirstIter	Optimal fitness ratio
Map one	ACO	**32.3**	43.1	41	75.0%
	AACO	37.2	**39.3**	**31**	**94.7%**
Map two	ACO	32.0	47.6	40	67.2%
	AACO	**31.8**	**39.2**	**29**	**81.1%**

4.2 The IAPF Fusion Algorithm Simulation Experiment

There are two main changes in the fusion algorithm: One is to randomly place unknown static obstacles near-global path in the generated 2D grid environment, and the other is to add a dynamic obstacle with low speed. The whole dynamic obstacle avoidance process of the mobile robot in the complex working environment is shown in follow figures.

In the Fig. 11, the blue dotted line represents the global path planned by the AACO algorithm, the gray grid represents unknown static obstacles, and the red line represents the moving path of a dynamic obstacle.

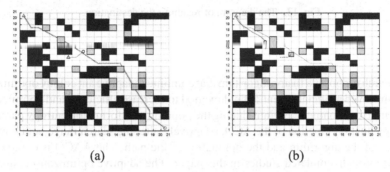

| (a) | (b) |

Fig. 11. The diagram of avoiding unknown obstacles

In the Fig. 12, due to an unknown obstacle on the global path, the mobile robot can avoid it accurately. In addition, the mobile robot can make timely judgments after sensing surrounding environment information and refind a feasible path.

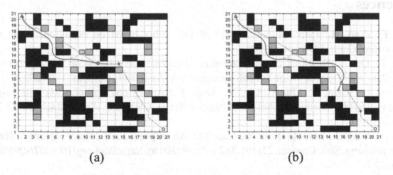

| (a) | (b) |

Fig. 12. The diagram of the re-planning path.

In the Fig. 13, in the case of the mobile robot passing through a narrow path segment, the trajectory of the mobile robot is affected by unknown obstacles which increases the chaos of potential fields. However, the mobile robot still follows the global path direction and does not collide with surrounding obstacles. Finally, the mobile robot avoids obstacles accurately and reaches the destination.

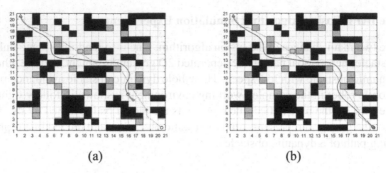

(a)   (b)

Fig. 13. The diagram of reaching the destination.

5 Conclusion

This research proposes a fusion algorithm that combines adaptive ant colony optimization and an improved artificial potential field method to increase efficiency and optimize path in a dynamic environment. By introducing the population information entropy parameter into the evaluation function of the ACO, adaptively alter the search range, and boost the efficiency of the algorithm and the optimality of the path. The AACO is compared to the ACO through simulated studies in this paper. The adaptive optimization algorithm shows clear advantages in terms of path length and optimal fitness ratio, according to the results of the experiments. In the dynamic simulation experiment, the key points of the AACO are extracted as temporary points of the IAPF. The fusion algorithm can guide the mobile robot to avoid unknown and dynamic obstacles to reach the destination, which verifies the obstacle avoidance flexibility of the algorithm in the dynamic environment.

References

1. Li, T., Zhao, H.: Path optimization for mobile robot based on evolutionary ant colony algorithm. Control Decis.1–9 (2022)
2. Ma, F., Qu, Z.: Research on path planning of mobile robot based on heterogeneous dual population and global vision ant colony algorithm. Appl. Res. Comput. 1–6 (2022)
3. Zhang, Q., Chen, B., Liu, X., Liu, X., Yang, H.: Ant colony optimization with improved potential field heuristic for robot path planning. Trans. Chin. Soc. Agric. Mach. **50**(5), 23–32, 42 (2019)
4. Liu, J., Yang, J., Liu, H., Tian, X., Gao, M.: An improved ant colony algorithm for robot path planning. Soft. Comput. **21**(19), 5829–5839 (2016). https://doi.org/10.1007/s00500-016-2161-7
5. Chne, Y., Li, T., Yu, S., Shen, Z.: Global path planning of robots based on potential field ant colony algorithm. J. Dalian Univ. Technol. **59**(3), 316–322 (2019)
6. Jin, Q., Tang, C., Cai, W.: Research on dynamic path planning based on the fusion algorithm of improved ant colony optimization and rolling window method. IEEE Access **10**, 28322–28332 (2021)
7. Skackauskas, J., Kalganova, T., Dear, I., et al.: Dynamic impact for ant colony optimization algorithm. Swarm Evol. Comput. **69**, 100993 (2022)
8. Peng, H., Ying, C., Tan, S., et al.: An improved feature selection algorithm based on ant colony optimization. IEEE Access **6**, 69203–69209 (2018)

9. Ning, J., Zhang, Q., Zhang, C., et al.: A best-path-updating information-guided ant colony optimization algorithm. Inf. Sci. **433**, 142–162 (2018)
10. Hwang, J., Lee, J., Park, C.: Collision avoidance control for formation flying of multiple spacecraft using artificial potential field. Adv. Space Res. **69**(5), 2197–2209 (2022)
11. Chen, G., Liu, J.: Mobile robot path planning using ant colony algorithm and improved potential field method. Comput. Intell. Neurosci. (2019)
12. Liu, L., Yao, J., He, D., et al.: Global dynamic path planning fusion algorithm combining jump-A* algorithm and dynamic window approach. IEEE Access **9**, 19632–19638 (2021)

A State-of-the-Art Review on SLAM

Xuewei Zhou and Ruining Huang[✉]

School of Mechanical Engineering and Automation, Harbin Institute of Technology,
Shenzhen 518055, China
hrn@hit.edu.cn

Abstract. SLAM (Simultaneous Localization and Mapping), also
known as CML (Concurrent Mapping and Localization), refers to real-
time positioning and map building, or concurrent mapping and positioning. After nearly 30 years of research on SLAM, there have been quite a
few breakthroughs in the SLAM community. This paper aims to provide
an insightful review of information background, recent development, feature, implementation, and recent issue in SLAM. This paper includes the
following parts: First of all, it gives an overview of the basic development
of SLAM from its introduction to the present. Then, and most impor-
tantly, it summarizes the mainstream SLAM technology and theoretical
basis. In addition, some cutting-edge and novel SLAM research results
are discussed respectively. Finally, this paper summarizes and introduces
some practical applications of SLAM technology.

Keywords: Simultaneous localization and mapping · Perception ·
Robots · Sensing

1 Introduction

SLAM is the abbreviation of simultaneous positioning and mapping. It contains
two main tasks: positioning and mapping. This is an important open problem
in mobile robots: to move accurately, mobile robots must have an accurate environmental map. However, to build an accurate map, the mobile robot must
accurately perceive the position [30].

In 1990, Randall Smith [43] first proposed to use EKF to incrementally estimate the posterior distribution of the robot's posture and the position of the
landmark.

In 2006, Durrant-Whyte and Bailey proposed the term SLAM for the first
time and determined a detailed probabilistic theoretical analysis framework for
SLAM problems. Computational efficiency, data association, convergence, and
consistency of SLAM are discussed [12]. SLAM has entered the era of systematic
research.

With the rapid development of SLAM, in terms of sensors, SLAM, which
has emerged in recent years, is equipped with LiDAR, camera, IMU, and other
sensors [11]; in terms of the method of state estimation, SLAM's initial system
based on filters (KF, EKF, PF) has gradually developed into a system based on

© The Author(s), under exclusive license to Springer Nature Switzerland AG 2022
H. Liu et al. (Eds.): ICIRA 2022, LNAI 13457, pp. 240–251, 2022.
https://doi.org/10.1007/978-3-031-13835-5_22

graph optimization [8,29]; in terms of the perspective of algorithm architecture, the single thread has been replaced by multi-thread [28]; with the integration of multi-sensors, SLAM technology has changed from the earliest military proto- type to the necessary application technology of robots today.

Many scholars have reviewed the evolution of SLAM, but most of them focus on a specific topic. Generally, researchers summarized the development process of SLAM so far into three main stages [7].

Classic Age (1986–2004). In the early stage, the definition of SLAM problem, modeling and solving method based on probability framework.

Algorithm-Analysis Age (2004–2015). In-depth study of some properties of SLAM problems, such as sparsity, convergence, consistency, and more diverse and efficient algorithms have been proposed one after another.

Robust-Perception Age (2015–). Start to consider the robustness, scalabil- ity, efficient algorithm under resource constraints, high-level semantic cognitive task orientation.

This paper gives a broad overview of the current state of SLAM research and offers the perspective of part of the community on the open problems and future directions for the SLAM study. Our main focus is on multi-sensor fusion, dynamic environment, and semantic SLAM, which are the hot spots that most scholars have studied and paid attention to in SLAM research. Then, some other potential research directions are summarized. Finally, we discuss the application scenarios of SLAM technology in real life.

2   Implementation of SLAM System

SLAM system mainly includes front-end and back-end. The front-end is respon- sible for extracting features and data association from sensor data, while the back-end is responsible for maximum posterior estimation, filtering, and closed- loop detection.

2.1   The Structure of SLAM System

The specific SLAM system can be regarded as the combination of sensor, map structure, and solution method, and different combination methods can produce different technical frameworks. Here are some commonly used sensors, map struc- tures, and solutions in SLAM.

Sensors. Angle measuring sensors such as LiDAR, millimeter-wave radar, and sonar. Various cameras, such as RGB-D cameras, Stereo cameras, and Event cameras. Other sensors such as wheeled odometer, IMU, and GPS.

Map Structure. The structure is closely related to the sensor. When sensors measure distance and angle or extract feature points from vision, maps are usually based on landmarks. Grid map and points cloud map are also used in LiDAR SLAM. Besides, there are other types of maps such as geometric maps which are based on edge or surface, octree maps [23], and so on.

Solution Method. Bayesian-framework-based recursive filtering, such as EKF, PF, and IF. Optimization-based method, one is the Bundle Adjustment [34]; The other is graph optimization [29].

2.2 LiDAR SLAM System

In the early stage of SLAM development, the complete SLAM was basically based on LiDAR. The data acquired by the laser is the depth value with angle, which can also be regarded as a points cloud. The rigid body motion of laser radar at two adjacent moments can be obtained by inter-frame matching of the point clouds scanned by laser radar. The most important and classic algorithm is the ICP [4], which is not limited to laser SLAM but is widely used in SLAM problems.

It is worth noting that it takes time for LiDAR to acquire complete data, which will cause each laser spot to be generated at a different reference pose in the process of robot movement. When the scanning frequency of LiDAR is relatively low, the error caused by robot motion can't be ignored. engineers can use the pure state estimation method, such as the variant of the ICP: VICP [22], to remove the motion distortion, or use sensor-assisted methods, such as odometer and IMU.

Early LiDAR SLAM algorithms did not include loop closing detection. Later, Scan Context [26] was used for fast inter-frame matching to achieve closed-loop detection. Recently, the paper [9] has proposed a state-of-the-art closed-loop detection method, which uses Deep Learning to search the loop closing based on different clues from LiDAR data. This method is more effective and demonstrates the great potential of deep learning.

SLAM based on LiDAR is the most mature and commonly used solution in business. Classical LiDAR SLAM systems include Gmaping [19], Catigrapher [21], and LOAM-SLAM [25], etc. LiDAR SLAM in indoor environment has a very good practical effect.

2.3 Visual SLAM System

Different from LiDAR, a vision sensor has a lot of information, which can provide us with a large amount of data. The cameras used in visual SLAM can be divided into three categories according to their working modes: monocular camera, stereo camera, and depth camera (RGB-D). Among them, the monocular vSLAM has scale uncertainty in theory, because the distance of the object is lost in the projection process of the monocular camera [36].

The practice shows that VO has the most significant influence on SLAM [40]. According to the map structure, VO can be divided into dense and sparse; according to the form of error, VO can be divided into two categories: indirect method, also known as feature-base method, and direct method.

Indirect method means that by detecting the feature points of an image, calculating the descriptors, and then matching the feature points of two adjacent images, the corresponding relationship between the feature points of two images can be obtained. When there are enough corresponding feature points, we can use geometric constraints [20] to solve the relative pose of two adjacent frames and get the 3D coordinates of feature points. RANSAC is used [13] to remove the unreliable matching point pairs.

The direct method is directly evolved from the Optical Flow method [3], and has the same assumption. The method directly estimates the motion of the camera according to the brightness information of the pixels in two adjacent frames of the camera. Image Pyramid [1] is introduced to improve the convergence of the algorithm.

As result, Map points are more parameterized by inverse depth [10], and vSLAM is more inclined to be used in conjunction with IMU [42]. Bag of words model [17] is often used in closed-loop detection and feature matching.

3   Current Mainstream SLAM

The state-of-the-art SLAM is divided into three main research directions, including multi-sensor fusion, using semantic information, and ensuring the robustness of the SLAM system in a dynamic environment. These three directions also overlap each other.

3.1   Multi-sensor Fusion

In multi-sensor fusion, it is inevitable to calibrate the external parameters of sensors, and the fusion algorithms can basically be classified into two categories: filter and graph optimization. This section will introduce VIO and LVIO, and the research status of multi-sensor fusion.

Visual Inertial Odometry. IMU has a high sampling frequency, is not affected by the external environment, and can estimate the absolute scale. At the same time, it can use the information of visual positioning to estimate the bias of IMU, which is complementary to the visual positioning scheme. Therefore, there are quite a few achievements in recent years [24]. How to integrate vision with IMU can be divided into two schemes: loose coupling and tight coupling.

Loose coupling refers to the direct fusion of IMU positioning and vision /GNSS pose. The fusion process does not influence the initial systems, and it is output as a post-processing mode. A typical example is the Kalman filter. The tightly coupled fusion process will affect the parameters of vision and IMU. The current open-source packages are basically based on tight coupling because tight coupling can model all the motion and measurement information at once, and it is easier to get the best estimation.

IMU's pre-integration was first put forward by Lupton in 2012 [35], and further extended to Lie algebra by Forster in 2015 [14,15]. This set of pre-integration theories has been widely used in VIO based on the BA optimization framework, which can greatly reduce the calculation amount of the algorithm and ensure the real-time performance of the algorithm.

Optimization-Based Example: VINS-Mono [48] is a well-known monocular VIO algorithm that was opened in 2018 by the Flying Robot Laboratory of Hong Kong University of Science and Technology. While ensuring the high-precision odometer effect, it can also estimate the sensor external parameters, IMU bias, and sensor time delay at the same time. It is a very classic and excellent VIO framework.

Filter-Based Example: MSCKF [38] stands for Multi-State Constraint Kalman Filter, which is a VIO algorithm based on filtering. It was first proposed by Mourikis in 2007. MSCKF fuses IMU and visual information under the framework of EKF. MSCKF is widely used in robots, UAVs, and AR/VR. For example, Google Project Tango uses MSCKF for pose estimation.

Lidar-Visual-Inertial Odometry. There are three ways to fusion LiDAR and vision. Use visual information to improve the accuracy of LiDAR, use LiDAR information to improve the accuracy of vision, and use both LiDAR and visual information [11].

3.2   Using Semantic Information

The research work of the traditional SLAM algorithm is faced with relatively simple geometric features such as points, lines, and surfaces, and almost no object-level features are involved. Secondly, the map constructed by the traditional SLAM algorithm cannot be "reused" in practice and lacks the visual map that can be directly used in actual production.

The original purpose of using Semantic information in SLAM is to match object-level features and build a map with semantic information. It has made great progress under the impetus of deep learning and has become a relatively independent branch. There are two main aspects of the combination of SLAM and semantics.

One is semantics help SLAM. Information about objects can help to get maps with object labels, which are easier to be understood by human thinking. In addition, the tag information of the object can bring more constraints for loop detection and BA optimization.

The other one is SLAM help semantics. In SLAM, engineers can collect data on objects from different perspectives and estimate their pose, automatically generate high-quality sample data for semantic recognition, avoid manual calibration of data, and speed up the training process of classifiers.

The concept of semantic SLAM is vague. At present, the so-called semantic segmentation based on neural networks, object detection, instance segmentation, and other technologies are used in SLAM, mostly for feature point selection and camera pose estimation. More broadly, the methods that use neural networks such as end-to-end image pose, marking point cloud from segmentation results, scene recognition, feature extraction, and loop detection can be called Semantic SLAM.

Semantic SLAM-related work involves a wide range of aspects, mainly including feature selection [18,31], dynamic scene [6,49,51], monocular scale restoration [16,45], long-term positioning [44] and improving algorithm accuracy [5,32].

3.3 Dynamic Environment

The main problem in dynamic SLAM is handling dynamic data associations. By choosing whether to cull dynamic correspondences or use them to track objects, the dynamic SLAM problem can be considered a robustness problem or an extension of standard SLAM [39]. To understand the dynamic environment SLAM problem, developers must first understand what disadvantages the dynamic environment has brought to SLAM so that researchers need to solve it.

The first is the SLAM registration level. No matter which point cloud registration method, it is based on static assumption. In theory, dynamic points will definitely affect the registration accuracy. At this level, dynamic points can only be identified and killed in real-time before or during registration. As for how to identify? Traditional methods, such as eliminating points that are too far away in the process of registration iteration, the more popular method at present is to directly identify and kill dynamic objects based on deep learning.

Secondly, the level of map building. It is assumed that the interference of dynamic objects to the registration is limited, which does not affect the trajectory accuracy, but it is still unbearable that the final generated map is full of ghosts of a large number of dynamic objects, which will have an adverse impact on map-based positioning or map-based feasible area planning.

Target Classification. At present, the main solution is to divide all objects in the environment into four categories according to their dynamic degree:

  a) High dynamic objects;
  b) Low-dynamic objects;
  c) Semi-static objects;
  d) Static objects.

Except for static objects, the other three types of objects all have dynamic attributes to different degrees, and their coping strategies are different. For high dynamic objects: online real-time filtering; For low dynamic objects: after a SLAM process, post-processing filtering; For semi-static objects: life-long mapping (or long-term mapping). The above three ways are upward compatible. No matter which one of these three coping ways, more papers have been published, and the selective excerpts are as follows.

Online Real-Time Filtering. Dynamic filtering must require reference frames to compare dynamic points. To achieve real-time, there will not be too many reference frames.

Dynamic Filtering in Post-processing Mode. As the post-processing method does not need to worry about real-time, all frames in the whole SLAM period can be used as reference information to identify dynamic points. Compared with the real-time method, the post-processing method pursues the accuracy and sufficiency of dynamic point cloud filtering. On the premise of post-processing, common dynamic object filtering methods can be divided into three typical categories: segmentation-based, ray-casting-based [41], and visibility-based [27].

Life-Long Mapping. In fact, the core problem of life-long mapping is far more than dynamic/semi-static object filtering. Dynamic/semi-static object filtering is only a part of map fusion among different sessions in the process of life-long, and map fusion is only a part of life-long mapping [50].

4   The Future of SLAM

The front part is just an overview of several main research directions of current SLAM, and there are many other aspects with the same research potential. In some classical SLAM theories, there are also outstanding works like ICE-BA [33].

4.1   Implicit Map Representation

Using a neural network to implicitly store the information of a 3D space, instead of using vectors or sets to explicitly store feature points or mesh as in the traditional SLAM, is a new technical route to solve old problems, which has a promising research prospect and has become a research hotspot since 2020. It is equivalent to putting cartography into the network, so there is no need for dense point clouds to save the map, and only small network parameters are needed to restore the scene.

iMAP. Drawing on the idea of NeRF [37], iMAP [46] in Andrew Davison's lab first proposed to use MLP (Multilayer Perceptron, a feedforward artificial neural network model) to represent the scene map in the SLAM process. This implicit map representation method can not only solve the problem of map storage but also control the details of scene reconstruction, such as the reconstruction of objects that cannot be observed by the camera.

NICE-SLAM. In this paper [52], the author puts forward NICE-SLAM, which is an intensive SLAM system, which combines multi-level local information by introducing hierarchical scene representation. By optimizing this representation with pre-trained geometric prior, details can be reconstructed on large indoor scenes. Compared with the recent neural implicit SLAM system, this method is more scalable, efficient, and robust.

4.2 Event Camera

The event camera is a new type of sensor, which outputs the change of pixel brightness. The amount of data in the event stream is much smaller than the data transmitted by the traditional camera, and the event stream has no minimum time unit, so it has low delay characteristics, unlike the traditional camera which outputs data regularly. The overall method framework of the camera is basically the same as that of the traditional camera field, that is, data association, observation model, residual calculation, and problem-solving. To sum up, the following three issues need to be considered in designing the event camera SLAM.

1) How to design a method directly based on event camera data, and meet the requirement of low computation.
2) How to find some kind of information, which is used to establish the data association of events.
3) Whether to use a monocular event camera or a binocular event camera.

4.3 Active SLAM

Active SLAM is different from the general SLAM method in that: the general SLAM method is to give the input data, and get the location and map by analyzing and calculating the input data; Active SLAM combines SLAM with path planning to explore the environment by planning the path of mobile robots, which makes SLAM algorithm get high-precision maps faster and better. The problem of controlling robot motion to minimize the uncertainty of its map representation and positioning is usually called active SLAM. This definition is derived from the well-known Bajcsy's active perception [2] and Thrun's robot exploration [47].

Active SLAM is a decision problem, and several general decision frameworks can be used as the backbone of exploration-development decisions.

A complete framework for active SLAM can be divided into three main steps [7]:

1) The robot identifies possible locations to explore or exploit in its current estimation of the map, i.e. vantage points.
2) The robot calculates the effect of visiting each vantage point and selects the action with the highest effect.

3) The robot performs the selected action and decides whether to continue or terminate the task.

For active SLAM to have an impact in practical applications, there are still many problems to be solved, including fast and accurate prediction of future states and convergence of mathematical optimal solutions.

5 The Application of SLAM

At present, SLAM technology is mainly used in UAVs, unmanned driving, robot, AR, smart home, and other fields, starting from various application scenarios to promote consumption upgrades.

5.1 Autonomous Vehicles

Unmanned driving is one of the hot topics in recent years, Google, Uber, Baidu, and other enterprises are accelerating the research and development of driverless technology, to seize the initiative. With the improvement of the Internet of things and intelligent systems in cities, driverless driving is bound to be the general trend. Unmanned vehicles use LiDAR sensors (Velodyne, IBEO, etc.) as tools to obtain map data and construct maps to avoid obstacles and achieve path planning. Similar to the application of SLAM technology in the field of robotics, but compared with the application of SLAM in robotics, unmanned radar requirements and costs are significantly higher than robots.

5.2 UAV

UAVs need to know where there are obstacles, how to avoid them, and how to re-plan their route during flight. Obviously, this is the application of SLAM technology. However, the UAV flight range is large, so the accuracy of the requirements are not high, some other optical flow, and ultrasonic sensors on the market can be used as auxiliary.

5.3 AR

AR applies virtual information to the real world through computer technology, and the real environment and virtual objects are superimposed into the same picture or space in real-time. The realization of this picture is inseparable from the real-time positioning of SLAM technology. Although there are many alternative technologies in the AR industry, SLAM is the most ideal positioning and navigation technology. Compared with the application of LAM in robotics, unmanned driving and other fields, the application of LAM in the AR industry has many differences.

6 Conclusion

Multi-sensor fusion, optimization of data association and loopback detection, integration with front-end heterogeneous processor, enhancement of robustness, and repositioning accuracy are the next development directions of SLAM technology, but these will be gradually solved with the development of consumption stimulation and industrial chain. Just like in mobile phones, SLAM technology will enter People's Daily life in the near future and change people's lives.

Acknowledgment. This work was funded by the National Natural Science Foundation of China (No. 51975155), the Natural Science Foundation of Guangdong Province (No. 2021A1515011823) and the Shenzhen Basic Research Program (No. JCYJ202008-24082533001).

References

1. Adelson, E.H., Anderson, C.H., Bergen, J.R., Burt, P.J., Ogden, J.M.: Pyramid methods in image processing. RCA Eng. **29**(6), 33–41 (1983)
2. Bajcsy, R.: Active perception. Proc. IEEE **76**(8), 966–1005 (1988)
3. Baker, S., Matthews, I.: Lucas-Kanade 20 years on: a unifying framework. Int. J. Comput. Vision **56**(3), 221–255 (2004)
4. Besl, P.J., Mckay, H.D.: A method for registration of 3-D shapes. IEEE Trans. Pattern Anal. Mach. Intell. **14**(2), 239–256 (1992)
5. Bowman, S.L., Atanasov, N., Daniilidis, K., Pappas, G.J.: Probabilistic data association for semantic slam. In: 2017 IEEE International Conference on Robotics and Automation (ICRA) (2017)
6. Brasch, N., Bozic, A., Lallemand, J., Tombari, F.: Semantic monocular slam for highly dynamic environments. In: 2018 IEEE/RSJ International Conference on Intelligent Robots and Systems (IROS) (2018)
7. Cadena, C., et al.: Past, present, and future of simultaneous localization and mapping: toward the robust-perception age. IEEE Trans. Rob. **32**(6), 1309–1332 (2016)
8. Castellanos, J.A., Neira, J., Tardos, J.D.: Limits to the consistency of EKF-based slam. In: Symposium on Intelligent Autonomous Vehicles (2004)
9. Chen, X., Läbe, T., Milioto, A., Röhling, T., Behley, J., Stachniss, C.: OverlapNet: a siamese network for computing LiDAR scan similarity with applications to loop closing and localization. Auton. Robots **46**, 61–81 (2021). https://doi.org/10.1007/s10514-021-09999-0
10. Civera, J., Davison, A.J., Montiel, J.: Inverse depth parametrization for monocular SLAM. IEEE Trans. Rob. **24**(5), 932–945 (2008)
11. Debeunne, C., Vivet, D.: A review of visual-lidar fusion based simultaneous localization and mapping. Sensors **20**(7), 2068 (2020)
12. Durrant-Whyte, H., Bailey, T.: Simultaneous localisation and mapping (SLAM): part 2. IEEE Robot. Autom. Mag. **13**(3), 108–117 (2006)
13. Fischler, M.A., Bolles, R.C.: Random sample consensus: a paradigm for model fitting with applications to image analysis and automated cartography. In: Readings in Computer Vision, pp. 726–740 (1987)
14. Forster, C., Carlone, L., Dellaert, F., Scaramuzza, D.: IMU preintegration on manifold for efficient visual-inertial maximum-a-posteriori estimation (supplementary material). Georgia Institute of Technology (2015)

15. Forster, C., Carlone, L., Dellaert, F., Scaramuzza, D.: On-manifold preintegration theory for fast and accurate visual-inertial navigation. Comput. Sci. (2015)
16. Frost, D., Prisacariu, V., Murray, D.: Recovering stable scale in monocular slam using object-supplemented bundle adjustment. IEEE Trans. Rob. **34**, 736–747 (2018)
17. Galvez-Lpez, D., Tardos, J.D.: Bags of binary words for fast place recognition in image sequences. IEEE Trans. Rob. **28**(5), 1188–1197 (2012)
18. Ganti, P., Waslander, S.L.: Visual slam with network uncertainty informed feature selection (2018)
19. Grisetti, G., Stachniss, C., Burgard, W.: Improved techniques for grid mapping with rao-blackwellized particle filters. IEEE Trans. Rob. **23**(1), 34–46 (2007)
20. Hartley, R.I., Zisserman, A.: Multi-view geometry in computer vision. Kybernetes **30**(9/10), 1865–1872 (2019)
21. Hess, W., Kohler, D., Rapp, H., Andor, D.: Real-time loop closure in 2D LIDAR SLAM. In: 2016 IEEE International Conference on Robotics and Automation (ICRA) (2016)
22. Hong, S., Ko, H., Kim, J.: VICP: velocity updating iterative closest point algorithm. In: IEEE International Conference on Robotics and Automation (2012)
23. Hornung, A., Wurm, K.M., Bennewitz, M., Stachniss, C., Burgard, W.: OctoMap: an efficient probabilistic 3D mapping framework based on octrees. Auton. Robot. **34**(3), 189–206 (2013)
24. Huang, G.: Visual-inertial navigation: a concise review. In: 2019 International Conference on Robotics and Automation (ICRA) (2019)
25. Zhang, J., Singh, S.: Low-drift and real-time lidar odometry and mapping. Auton. Robot. **41**(2), 401–416 (2016). https://doi.org/10.1007/s10514-016-9548-2
26. Kim, G., Kim, A.: Scan context: egocentric spatial descriptor for place recognition within 3D point cloud map. In: 2018 IEEE/RSJ International Conference on Intelligent Robots and Systems (IROS) (2018)
27. Kim, G., Kim, A.: Remove, then revert: static point cloud map construction using multiresolution range images. In: 2020 IEEE/RSJ International Conference on Intelligent Robots and Systems (IROS) (2020)
28. Klein, G., Murray, D.: Parallel tracking and mapping for small AR workspaces. In: IEEE and ACM International Symposium on Mixed and Augmented Reality (2008)
29. Kummerle, R., Grisetti, G., Strasdat, H., Konolige, K., Burgard, W.: G2o: a general framework for graph optimization. In: IEEE International Conference on Robotics and Automation (2011)
30. Leonard, J.J., Durrant-Whyte, H.F.: Simultaneous map building and localization for an autonomous mobile robot. In: Proceedings IROS 1991. IEEE/RSJ International Workshop on Intelligent Robots and Systems 1991. Intelligence for Mechanical Systems (1991)
31. Liang, H.J., Sanket, N.J., Fermüller, C., Aloimonos, Y.: SalientDSO: bringing attention to direct sparse odometry. IEEE Trans. Autom. Sci. Eng. **16**(4), 1619–1626 (2018)
32. Lianos, K.N., Schnberger, J.L., Pollefeys, M., Sattler, T.: VSO: visual semantic odometry. In: European Conference on Computer Vision (ECCV) (2018)
33. Liu, H., Chen, M., Zhang, G., Bao, H., Bao, Y.: ICE-BA: incremental, consistent and efficient bundle adjustment for visual-inertial slam. In: 2018 IEEE/CVF Conference on Computer Vision and Pattern Recognition (CVPR) (2018)
34. Lourakis, M.: SBA: a software package for generic sparse bundle adjustment. ACM Trans. Math. Softw. **36**(1), 2 (2009)

35. Lupton, T., Sukkarieh, S.: Visual-inertial-aided navigation for high-dynamic motion in built environments without initial conditions. IEEE Press (2012)
36. Martinezmontiel, J.: Scale drift-aware large scale monocular SLAM. In: Robotics: Science and Systems VI, Universidad de Zaragoza, Zaragoza, Spain, 27–30 June 2010 (2010)
37. Mildenhall, B., Srinivasan, P.P., Tancik, M., Barron, J.T., Ren, N.: NeRF: representing scenes as neural radiance fields for view synthesis. Commun. ACM **65**(1), 99–106 (2022)
38. Mourikis, A.I., Roumeliotis, S.I.: A multi-state constraint Kalman filter for vision-aided inertial navigation. In: 2007 IEEE International Conference on Robotics and Automation (2007)
39. Saputra, M.R.U., Markham, A., Trigoni, N.: Visual slam and structure from motion in dynamic environments: a survey. ACM Comput. Surv. (CSUR) **51**(2), 1–36 (2018)
40. Scaramuzza, D., Fraundorfer, F.: Visual odometry [tutorial]. IEEE Robot. Autom. Mag. **18**(4), 80–92 (2011)
41. Schauer, J., Nuechter, A.: The peopleremover-removing dynamic objects from 3-D point cloud data by traversing a voxel occupancy grid. IEEE Robot. Autom. Lett. **3**(3), 1679–1686 (2018)
42. Serviéres, M., Renaudin, V., Dupuis, A., Antigny, N.: Visual and visual-inertial slam: state of the art, classification, and experimental benchmarking. J. Sens. **2021**(1), 1–26 (2021)
43. Smith, R., Self, M., Cheeseman, P.: Estimating uncertain spatial relationships in robotics, pp. 435–461 (1988)
44. Stenborg, E., Toft, C., Hammarstrand, L.: Long-term visual localization using semantically segmented images, pp. 6484–6490 (2018)
45. Sucar, E., Hayet, J.B.: Bayesian scale estimation for monocular slam based on generic object detection for correcting scale drift (2017)
46. Sucar, E., Liu, S., Ortiz, J., Davison, A.J.: iMAP: implicit mapping and positioning in real-time (2021)
47. Thrun, S.: Probabilistic robotics. Commun. ACM **45**(3), 52–57 (2005)
48. Qin, T., Li, P., Shen, S.: VINS-mono: a robust and versatile monocular visual-inertial state estimator. IEEE Trans. Robot. **34**(4), 1004–1020 (2018)
49. Yu, C., et al.: DS-SLAM: a semantic visual slam towards dynamic environments. In: 2018 IEEE/RSJ International Conference on Intelligent Robots and Systems (IROS) (2018)
50. Zhao, M., et al.: A general framework for lifelong localization and mapping in changing environment. arXiv e-prints (2021)
51. Zhong, F., Sheng, W., Zhang, Z., Chen, C., Wang, Y.: Detect-slam: making object detection and slam mutually beneficial. In: 2018 IEEE Winter Conference on Applications of Computer Vision (WACV) (2018)
52. Zhu, Z., et al.: NICE-SLAM: neural implicit scalable encoding for slam (2021)

Swarm Robotic Technology and System in Space and Underwater

Synthesis of One DOF Single-Loop Mechanisms with Prismatic Pairs Based on the Atlas Method

Yang Zhang[1] , Changqing Gao[1] , Hailin Huang[1] , and Bing Li[1,2](✉)

[1] School of Mechanical Engineering and Automation, Harbin Institute of Technology,
Shenzhen 518055, China
libing.sgs@hit.edu.cn

[2] State Key Laboratory of Robotics and System, School of Mechanical Engineering and
Automation, Harbin Institute of Technology, Harbin 150001, China

Abstract. This paper proposes a new method to synthesize one DOF single-loop mechanisms (SLMs) with prismatic pairs based on the atlas method. Compared with the traditional synthesis method of SLMs, this method is simple, intuitive, and has a definite physical meaning. Besides, it is a method that is used to synthesize the SLMs with prismatic pairs. It fills the gap in the synthesis of SLM considering prismatic pairs. All constraint types (including overconstraints and non-overconstraints) of SLMs are analyzed comprehensively. The cases containing the lazy pairs are also discussed. The idea of this method is to give a prismatic pair first, and then synthesize other kinematic pairs based on the condition that the motion of this prismatic pair is not constrained. In this paper, a variety of new models are proposed using this method, which verifies the feasibility of this method.

Keywords: Synthesis · Single-loop mechanism · The atlas method

1 Introduction

The single-loop mechanism (SLM) has attracted the interest of many researchers because of its short kinematic chain, low manufacturing cost, low weight, low transmission error, high transmission efficiency, high stiffness, and large workspace [1]. It is widely used in origami mechanism [2] aviation deployment mechanism [3], olyhedral grasping mechanism [4] mobile robot [5], metamorphic mechanism of the bionic robot leg [6], nd generalized kinematic pair [7] and reconfigurable moving platform of parallel mechanism [8], etc.

The existing synthesis methods of one DOF SLMs are as follows: construction methods [9], geometric methods [10], algebraic methods [11], numerical methods [12], screw theory [13], the improved atlas methods [14], etc. The core idea of construction methods [9] is to assemble some classical SLMs to obtain some new mechanisms. This method does not use synthesis theory for the systematic synthesis of SLMs. Because the existing classical SLMs are limited, so the acquired SLMs are rare. Besides, all obtained mechanisms do not include prismatic pairs. Deng et al. [10] used symmetrical branch

© The Author(s), under exclusive license to Springer Nature Switzerland AG 2022
H. Liu et al. (Eds.): ICIRA 2022, LNAI 13457, pp. 255–267, 2022.
https://doi.org/10.1007/978-3-031-13835-5_23

chains composed only of revolute pairs to synthesize a class of deployable/foldable SLMs using motion symmetry. The core idea of the geometric methods is to find the intersection of the motion of sub-chains based on intuitive geometric symmetry. Some SLMs are obtained by using this principle to assemble kinematic branch chains. This method is only suitable for synthesizing some special mechanisms with symmetry. The algebraic method is to analyze and synthesize overconstrained 6R mechanisms using the inverse kinematics algorithm [11]. However, it is impossible that use arbitrary design parameters to algebraically solve the resulting system of nonlinear equations. So this approach only can synthesize mobile 6R chains without offsets. For numerical methods, Gan [12] proposed a systematic study of the kinematics of closed-loop structures, and presented a numerical scheme for simulating their deployment. Based on screw theory, Fang et al. [13] synthesized one-DOF overconstrained SLMs. Their basic ideas are the same. Firstly, the synthesis requirements of SLMs were obtained based on the virtual work principle. Then, the corresponding relations of the constituent elements of SLMs were obtained using the DOF formula. Finally, they constructed the structure that meets the conditions based on this relation and the synthesis conditions. However, the schemes of some non-overconstraints are not considered, and some kinds of overconstraints are not discussed. For example, the synthesis of 1F1C, 1F2C, 1F3C, and 3C (F represents force constraint and C represents couple constraint) is not considered [13]. As a result, there are still some corresponding overconstrained mechanisms that have not been synthesized. Their synthesis results have not been well classified, and we can not see the specific geometric relationship of the mechanism. We can't see what kind of geometric relationship redundant constraints have. Reference [14] used the improved atlas method to synthesize SLMs. This method uses the screw theory and the atlas method. This method synthesizes the mechanism on the basis of giving two revolute pairs with a special relationship. Using this method, only a few special SLMs contain prismatic pairs. The constraints of prismatic pairs are not specially considered, and the synthesized mechanism has no lazy pairs, which is good for the assembly of the prototype. (Lazy pair means that it does not affect the movement of the mechanism and will not move during the movement of the mechanism). This paper further perfects the work of reference [14]. Moreover, this paper mainly analyzes the types with prismatic pairs and discusses some cases of lazy pairs. This paper does not use the screw theory, only uses the atlas method [15, 16], and classifies the constraints based on the dual constraint equivalent graphs of prismatic pairs. Therefore, this paper can more clearly see the geometric relationship of constraints in the equivalent graphs, which is more conducive to the induction and classification of constraints. It fills the gap in the synthesis of SLM considering prismatic pairs.

This paper is laid out as follows. The one DOF SLM with prismatic pairs and the atlas method are introduced in Sect. 2. The method of synthesizing one DOF SLMs with prismatic pairs is presented in Sect. 3. In Sect. 4, we analyze the constraints provided by branch chain 1 using the atlas method. We further determine and classify the constraints provided by branch chain 2 based on the constraint graph of branch chain 1. Non-overconstrained SLMs with prismatic pairs are synthesized in Sect. 5. Overconstrained SLMs with prismatic pairs are synthesized in Sect. 6. We draw some conclusions in Sect. 7

2   Introduction of the One DOF SLM with Prismatic Pairs and the Atlas Method

The idea of this paper is to give a prismatic pair first, and then synthesize other kinematic pairs based on the condition that the motion of this prismatic pair is not constrained, so the SLM is split into two branch chains, as shown in Fig. 1. Branch chain 1 is a prismatic pair. Other residual bars and kinematic pairs constitute branch chain 2. Therefore, the mechanism needs to meet the requirements: branch chain 2 cannot limit the movement of branch chain 1.

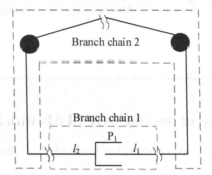

Fig. 1. The conceptual diagram of SLMs with a prismatic pair.

In this paper, the atlas method [14–16] is used to synthesis SLMs. Table 1 shows the atlas elements, where the red straight line denotes the rotation axis of the rotational DOF of a mechanism or the rotation axis of a revolute pair in a branch chain structure. A black straight line denotes the force constraint provided by a mechanism. The red double arrow line denotes the direction of movement of translational DOF of a mechanism or the moving direction of a prismatic pair of a branch structure. The black double arrow line denotes the couple direction provided by a mechanism. The orange double arrow lines indicate the moving direction of ^yP.

The duality criteria that we use in this paper are as follows [14–16].

(1)   When a graph has n non-redundant lines, its dual graph should have $(6 - n)$ lines. (If the dimension of a graph is n, then the dimension of its dual graph is $(6 - n)$).

(2)   Each line vector in one graph is intersecting or parallel with each one of the line vectors in its dual graph.

(3)   Each line in one graph is perpendicular to each one of the couple vectors in its dual graph.

(4)   Each couple vector in one graph does not affect all couple vectors in its dual graph.

Table 1. Elemental representation of the atlas

Atlas elements	Physical significance	Helical vector type
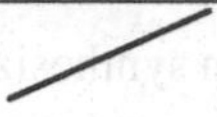	Force constraints	Line vector
	Couple constraint	Couple vector
	Revolute DOF	Line vector
	Moving DOF	Couple vector
	Moving DOF of ^yP	Couple vector

3 Synthesis Method of the One DOF SLMs with Prismatic Pairs

The main steps of the synthesis of SLMs can be divided as follows:

(1) SLM is divided into two branch chains. We analyze the constraints provided by branch chain 1 using the atlas method.
(2) We determine and classify the constraints provided by branch chain 2 based on the constraint graph of branch chain 1.
(3) Based on step (2), we determine the synthesis requirements and further design the synthesis schemes. Then, according to these synthesis schemes, we construct and arrange the kinematic pairs of the SLMs with prismatic pairs.
(4) We eliminate instantaneity SLMs and further obtain SLMs that meet the synthesis requirements.

4 Analysis and Classification of the Constraints

To facilitate the subsequent discussion, we establish a coordinate system shown in Fig. 2. The Y-axis is along the moving direction of this prismatic pair, the Z-axis is perpendicular to the moving direction of this prismatic pair, and the X-axis is obtained by the right-hand rule. The constraint graph shown in Fig. 2(a) is obtained according to the graph method. Their equivalent constraint graph with redundancy is shown in Fig. 2(b). We can see from Fig. 2(b) that branch chain 2 has at most five constraints. To avoid the incomplete synthesis schemes, the constraints that branch chain 2 may provide can be divided into overconstraints and non-overconstraints to discuss. Among them, the overconstraints is divided into 17 cases: 1F, 1C, 1F1C, 2F, 2C, 1F2C, 2F1C, 3C, 3F, 1F3C, 2F2C, 3F1C, 4F, 2F3C, 3F2C, 4F1C, and 5F (F means force and C means couple). The couple constraints can be arranged arbitrarily, and the force constraints must be located in the planes parallel to the XOZ plane. Based on this classification, we synthesize the one DOF SLMs with prismatic pairs. We do not discuss the case of screw constraints in this paper.

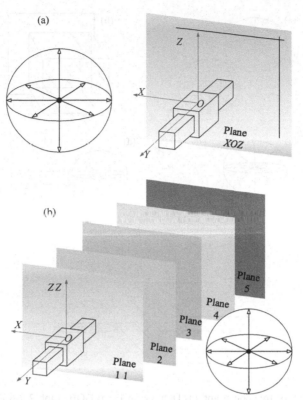

Fig. 2. The constraints graph and equivalent constraint graph of prismatic pair. (a) Constraint graph of prismatic pair, (b) Equivalent constraint graph with the redundancy of prismatic pair

5 Synthesis of Non-overconstrained SLMs with Prismatic Pairs

In this mechanism, branch chain 2 does not provide any constraints. Figure 3 shows the 6-DOF graphs of branch chain 2. Branch chain 2 is constructed according to Fig. 3, and the result is shown in Table 2. The specific structure of branch chain 2 in Table 2 and branch chain 1 are assembled to obtain some SLMs with prismatic pairs, whose typical CAD model is shown in Fig. 4.

Instantaneity Analysis: We use SolidWorks to model the three-dimensional (3D) shape of mechanisms, and then watch the variation of the geometric relationships between constituent elements of the branch chain in finite displacement. **According to the duality criteria, we can know whether the constraints have changed.** On this basis, we can see the constraint satisfaction of the mechanisms, so as to judge whether the mechanism is instantaneous. We found that when branch chain 2 contains three linearly independent prismatic pairs, there are four prismatic pairs in the whole SLM, so there is a redundant prismatic pair. Although it does not affect the DOF of the whole SLM, the other revolute pairs of this kind of branch chain 2 will become lazy pairs. The constraint line graphs of all SLMs do not change in the finite displacement, so all SLMs are not instantaneous.

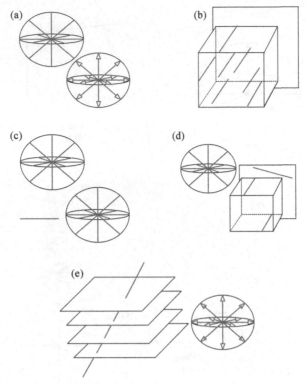

Fig. 3. DOF graph of free constraint. (a) DOF graph 1, (b) DOF graph 2, (c) DOF graph 3, (d) DOF graph 4, (e) DOF graph 5.

Table 2. Synthesis of non-overconstrained branch chain 2

Types	Enumeration
No prismatic pairs	$(^iR^jR^kR)_NR(^iR^jR^kR)_N$, $R(^iR^jR)_N(^iR^jR^kR)_N$, $R_cR_cR(^iR^jR^kR)_N$, $(^iR^jR)_NR_cR_c(^kR^iR)_N$, $RR_cR_cR_c(^iR^jR)_N$, $^iR_c^iR_c^jR_c^jR_c(^jR^kR)_N$, $^zR_c^zR_c^xR_c^xR_c^yR_c^yR_c$, $(^iR^jR^kR)_N{}^{d1}R^{d2}R^{d3}R$, $R_cR_c{}^{d1}R^{d2}R(^iR^kR)_N$, $^iR_c^iR_c{}^{d1}R^{d2}R^jR_c^jR_c$, $^iR_c^iR_c^jR_c^jR_c^jR_cR$, $R_cR_cR_c{}^{d1}R^{d2}R^{d3}R$
One prismatic pair	$(^iR^jR^kR)_NP(^iR^jR^kR)_N$, $P(^iR^jR)_N(^iR^jR^kR)_N$, $R_cR_cP(^iR^jR^kR)_N$, $RPR_cR_c(^iR^jR)_N$, $(^iR^jR)_NRP(^kR^lR)_N$, $P^{d1}R^{d2}R(^iR^jR^kR)_N$, $(^iR^jR)_NRP(^kR^lR)_N$, $RR_cR_cP(^iR^jR)_N$, $PR^iR_c^iR_c^jR_c^jR_c$, $RP^{d1}R^{d2}R(^jR^kR)_N$, $PR^{d1}R^{d2}R^jR_c^jR_c$, $^iR_c^iR_c^iR_c^jR_c^jR_cP$, $PR_cR_c{}^{d1}R^{d2}R^{d3}R$
Two prismatic pairs	$RPP(^iR^jR^kR)_N$, $RPPR_c(^iR^jR)_N$, $PPR(^iR^jR^kR)_N$, $RRPP(^iR^jR)_N$, $PR^iR_c^iR_cRP$, $PR^{d1}R^{d2}RRP$, $P^iR_c^iR_c^jR_c^jR_cP$, $PPR^{d1}R^{d2}R^{d3}R$
Three prismatic pairs	$^iR^uP^jR^vP^kR^wP$, $(^iR^jR^kR)_N{}^uP^vP^wP$

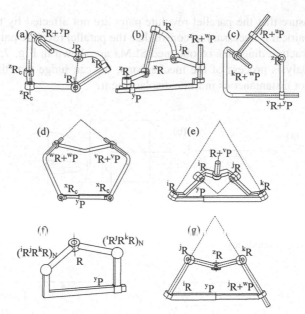

Fig. 4. Typical CAD model of non-overconstrained SLMs. (a) $^zR_c{}^zR_c{}^xR(^iR^jR^kR)_N\text{-}^yP$, (b) $^zR_c{}^xR(^iR^jR)_N{}^zR_c{}^wP\text{-}^yP$, (c) $^zR^uP^yR^wP(^jR^kR)_N\text{-}^yP$, (d) $^wR^wP^xR_c{}^xR_c{}^vR^vP\text{-}^yP$, (e) $(^kR^iR)_N{}^vPR(^iR^jR)_N\text{-}^yP$, (f) $(^iR^jR^kR)_NR(^iR^jR^kR)_N\text{-}^yP$, (g) $^zR^wP(^iR^jR)_N(^jR^kR)_N\text{-}^yP$.

6 Synthesis of Overconstrained SLMs with Prismatic Pairs

6.1 Synthesis of 1F Overconstrained SLMs with Prismatic Pairs

When branch chain 2 provides 1F, the direction of this force constraint should be perpendicular to the moving direction of ^yP. According to the duality criterion, branch chain 2 has five kinematic pairs. Therefore, the synthesis of SLMs becomes how to design the five kinematic pairs in branch chain 2.

First, we analyze and discuss the geometric properties of this kind of branch chain that provide a force constraint. Figure 5 shows 1F constraint graph and its dual DOF graph. Its equivalent constraint graph refer to reference [14, 15]. We can see from the graph the geometric characteristics between the kinematic pairs. As shown in Fig. 5(b), we can use a combination of the parallel revolute pairs and the spherical sub-chain to ensure that the direction of the force constraint is perpendicular to the moving direction of this prismatic pair of branch chain 1.

According to the duality criterion, this force constraint provided by this kind of branch chain passes through the center of the spherical branch chain and is parallel to the rotation axis of the parallel revolute pairs. Therefore, as long as the rotation axes of the parallel revolute pairs are perpendicular to the direction of ^yP, the requirements can be ensured. Because some parallel revolute pairs can produce equivalent movement, so the prismatic pairs can also be used. The specific synthesis schemes are shown in Fig. 6. According to the synthesis schemes in Fig. 6, branch chain 2 is constructed, then assembled with branch chain 1 to obtain the one DOF SLM with prismatic pairs. During assembly, to ensure that the parallel revolute pairs are not affected by the rotation of other revolute pairs, it is necessary to consolidate the parallel revolute pairs with branch chain 1. The structure diagrams of obtained SLMs are shown in Fig. 7. As the above instantaneity analysis process of the mechanisms, we can judge that the synthesized mechanism is not instantaneous in finite displacement.

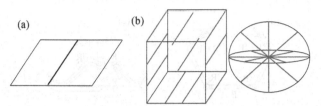

Fig. 5. Constraint and dual DOF graphs of 1F constraint. (a) 1F constraint graph, (b) the dual DOF graph including redundancy.

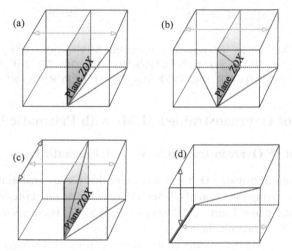

Fig. 6. Synthesis schemes of 1F SLMs with prismatic pairs. (a) Scheme 1, (b) Scheme 2, (c) Scheme 3, (d) Scheme 4.

6.2 Synthesis of Other Constraint Type Overconstrained SLMs with Prismatic Pairs

Similarly, we can get SLMs of other constraint types using this method, as shown in Table 3, and some representative mechanisms are shown in Fig. 8. For 2F constraint, it is not guaranteed that the two forces are always in the plane perpendicular to the moving direction of ^yP in the finite displacement. This kind of constraint can not be used to synthesize one DOF SLM with prismatic pairs. Like the branch chain of 2F1C constraints, the branch chain of 2F2C, 2F3C, 3F, 3F1C, 3F2C, 4F, 4F1C, and 5F reduces the kinematic pairs and increases the constraints based on the branch chain of 2F constraints. Therefore, this kind of branch chain can not guarantee that the force constraints are perpendicular to the direction of ^{y}P in the finite displacement. These constraints can not synthesize the satisfaction SLMs.

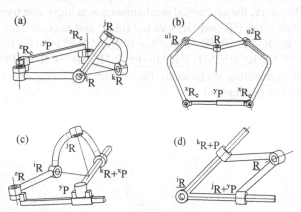

Fig. 7. Typical CAD model of 1F overconstrained SLMs. (a) $^zR_c(^iR^jR^kR)_N{}^zR_c$-^{y}P, (b) $^{u1}\underline{R}^xR_cR^xR_c{}^{u2}\underline{R}$-^{y}P, (c) $^zR(^iR^jR^kR)_N{}^xP$-^{y}P, (d) $(^i\underline{R}^jR^kR)_N\underline{R}P$-^{y}P.

Table 3. SLMs of other constraint types

Constraint types	Enumeration
1C	$^zR_c{}^zR_c{}^xR_c{}^xR_c{}^xR_c$-^{y}P, $^zR_c{}^zR_c{}^zP^xR_c{}^xR_c$-^{y}P, $^zR^wP^uP^xR_c{}^xR_c$-^{y}P, $^zR_c{}^zR_c{}^{u1}P^{u2}P^xR$-^{y}P, $^zR^vP^wP^uP^xR$-^{y}P
1F1C	$(^iR^jR)_N{}^xR_c{}^xR_c$-^{y}P, $^zR^xR_c{}^xR_c{}^xR_c$-^{y}P, $^zR^xR_c{}^xR_c{}^uP$-^{y}P, $^zR^xR^{u1}P^{u2}P$-^{y}P, $^{i1}\underline{R_c}^{i2}R_c{}^{j1}\underline{R_c}^{j2}R_c$-^{y}P, $^{u1}\underline{R}^{u1}P^{u2}\underline{R}^{u2}P$-^{y}P
2F	None
2C	$^xR_c{}^xR_c{}^{v1}P^{v2}P$-^{y}P, $^yR_c{}^yR_c$ $^yR_c{}^vP$-^{y}P
1F2C	^{u1}P ^{u2}P R-^{y}P, $^xR_c{}^xR_c{}^xR_c$-^{y}P, $^xR_c{}^xR_c{}^uP$-^{y}P, $^xR^{u1}P^{u2}P$-^{y}P, $^yR_c{}^yR_cP$-^{y}P, PPR-^{y}P
2F1C	None
3C	$^uP^vP^wP$-^{y}P
1F3C	^{u1}P ^{u2}P-^{y}P
2F2C, 2F3C, 3F, 3F1C, 3F2C, 4F, 4F1C, 5F	None

As the above instantaneity analysis process of the mechanisms, we can judge that all mechanisms not instantaneous but $(^iR^jR)_N{}^xR_c{}^xR_c$-^{y}P, $^yR_c{}^yR_cP$-^{y}P is instantaneous in finite displacement. However, there are lazy pairs in some SLMs. For example, the

1C branch chain needs at least two revolute pairs in the same direction to ensure such revolute pairs rotate. Otherwise, the mechanism will produce lazy pair. The couple constraint provided by branch chain 2 of $^zR^vP^wP^uP^xR$-^yP mechanism in Fig. 8(4) is always perpendicular to the rotational axes of the two revolute pairs (^zR and ^xR). It does not provide the possibility of rotation for such revolute pairs because of branch chain 1 is a prismatic pair. Therefore, the assembled mechanism can achieve one translational DOF, but the two revolute pairs (^zR and ^xR) will not rotate and become lazy pairs. In addition, $^zR_c{}^zR_c{}^yR_c{}^yR_c{}^yR_c$-$^yP$, $^zR_c{}^zR_c{}^vP^yR_c{}^yR_c$-$^yP$, and $^zR^vP^wP^uP^xR$-^yP, $^zR^xR_c{}^xR_c{}^xR_c$-^yP, $^zR^xR_c{}^xR_c{}^uP$-^yP, $^zR^xR^{u1}P^{u2}P$-^yP, $\underline{^{u1}R}^{u1}P^{u2}\underline{R}^{u2}P$-$^yP$, ^{u1}P ^{u2}P R-^yP, PPR-^yP also contain lazy pairs. In engineering applications, the existence of lazy pairs can be beneficial to the assembly of the mechanism.

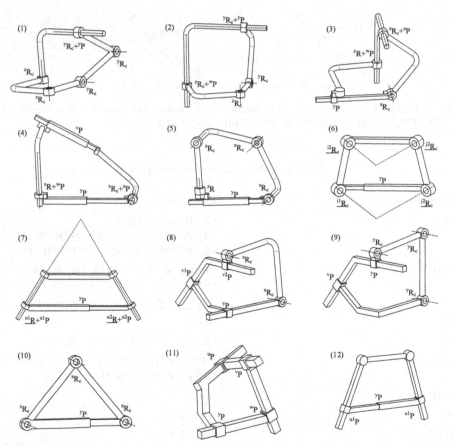

Fig. 8. Typical CAD model of overconstrained SLMs. (1) $^zR_c{}^zR_c{}^yR_c{}^yR_c{}^yR_c$-$^yP$, (2) $^zR_c{}^zR_c{}^vP^yR_c{}^yR_c$-$^yP$, (3) $^zR^wP^uP^xR_c{}^xR_c$-^yP, (4) $^zR^wP^vP^uP^xR$-^yP, (5) $^zR^xR_c{}^xR_c{}^xR_c$-^yP, (6) $^{i1}\underline{R_c}{}^{i2}\underline{R_c}{}^{j1}\underline{R_c}{}^{j2}\underline{R_c}$-$^yP$, (7) $\underline{^{u1}R}^{u1}P^{u2}\underline{R}^{u2}P$-$^yP$. (8) $^xR_c{}^xR_c{}^{v1}P^{v2}P$-$^yP$, (9) $^yR_c{}^yR_c$ $^yR_c{}^vP$- ^yP. (10) $^xR_c{}^xR_c{}^xR_c$-^yP, (11) $^uP^vP^wP$-^yP, (12) ^{u1}P ^{u2}P-^yP.

7   Conclusion

In this paper, a synthesis method of one DOF SLM with prismatic pairs based on the graph method is presented. The idea of this method is to give a prismatic pair first, and then synthesize other kinematic pairs based on the condition that the motion of this prismatic pair is not constrained. So we split the SLM into two branch chains, one of which contains only one prismatic pair. Based on such a prismatic pair, the synthesis of the SLM is changed into the synthesis of the branch chain 2 structure. Using this method, 35 non-overconstrained novel SLMs with prismatic pairs and 23 overconstrained novel SLMs with prismatic pairs are proposed, which verify the feasibility of this method. The constraints of $1FnC$, nC ($n = 0, 1, 2, 3$) can synthesize the SLMs that satisfy the conditions, while the constraint of 2F, 2F1C, 2F2C, 2F3C, 3F, 3F1C, 3F2C, 4F, 4F1C, and 5F can not synthesize the SLMs because multiple force constraints cannot be in a plane parallel to the XOZ plane in the motion of the SLMs. Among them, we also discuss the cases of lazy pairs, non-overconstraints, and overconstraints.

Acknowledgment. This   work   is   supported   by   Shenzhen   Peacock   Team Project (20210810140836002), and the Shenzhen Research and Development Program of China (Grant No. JCYJ20200109112818703).

Nomenclature

DOF	Degree of freedom
R	Revolute pair or rotational DOF
P	Prismatic pair or translational DOF
SLM	Single-loop mechanism
$(^iR^jR)_N$	2 revolute pairs with their rotational axes are intersecting
$(^iR^jR^kR)_N$	3 revolute pairs with their rotational axes are intersecting at point N
$R_c, R_c,$	Revolute pairs with their rotational axes are parallel
$^{d1}R, ^{d2}R$	Two revolute pairs whose axes are not intersecting or parallel in space
$^{d1}R, ^{d2}R, ^{d3}R$	Three revolute pairs whose axes are not intersecting or parallel in space
^yP	Prismatic pair with its translational direction parallel to the Y-axis
^uP	Prismatic pair with its translational direction parallel to the YOZ plane
^vP	Prismatic pair with its translational direction parallel to the XOZ plane
^wP	Prismatic pair with its translational direction parallel to the XOY plane

(continued)

(*continued*)

DOF	Degree of freedom
^{i1}R, ^{j1}R or ^{i2}R, ^{j2}R	Two revolute pairs with their axes parallel to the YOZ plane and intersecting at a point
^{x}R	Revolute pair with its axis parallel to the X-axis
^{y}R	Revolute pair with its axis parallel to the Y-axis
^{z}R	Revolute pair with its axis parallel to the Z-axis

References

1. Wang, N., Fang, Y., Zhang, D.: A spatial single loop kinematotropic mechanism used for biped/wheeled switchable robots. Int. J. Mech. Mater. Des. **11**(3), 287–299 (2014). https://doi.org/10.1007/s10999-014-9274-x

2. Chen, Y., Peng, R., You, Z.: Origami of thick panels. Science **349**(6246), 396–400 (2015). https://doi.org/10.1126/science.aab2870

3. Huang, H., Li, B., Zhang, T., Zhang, Z., Qi, X., Hu, Y.: Design of large single-mobility surface-deployable mechanism using irregularly shaped triangular prismoid modules. Trans. ASME J. Mech. Des. **141**(1), 012301 (2019). https://doi.org/10.1115/1.4041178

4. Teoh, Z.E., Phillips, B.T., Becker, K.P., et al.: Rotary-actuated folding polyhedrons for mid-water investigation of delicate marine organisms. Sci. Robot. **3**(20), eaat5276 (2018). https://doi.org/10.1126/scirobotics.aat5276

5. Liu, C., Chao, X.D., Yao, Y.A.: Ground mobile bricard mechanism. Trans. ASME J. Mech. Robot. **12**(4), 041010 (2020). https://doi.org/10.1115/1.4046028

6. Li, L.Q., et al.: Synthesis of a class of novel 3-DOF single loop parallel leg mechanisms for walking robots. Mech. Mach. Theory **145**, 103695 (2020). https://doi.org/10.1016/j.mechmachtheory.2019.103695

7. Tian, C., Fang, Y., Guo, S., Qu, H.: A class of reconfigurable parallel mechanisms with five-bar metamorphic linkage. Proc. Inst. Mech. Eng. Part C J. Mech. Eng. Sci. **231**(11), 2089–2099 (2017). https://doi.org/10.1177/0954406216628558

8. Xu, Y., Liang, Z., Liu, J.: A new metamorphic parallel leg mechanism with reconfigurable moving platform. Math. Probl. Eng. **2020**, 3234969 (2020). https://doi.org/10.1155/2020/3234969

9. Guo, H.W., et al.: Synthesis of deployable single loop overconstrained linkages based on Bennett linkages. Mech. Mach. Theory **120**, 1–29 (2018). https://doi.org/10.1016/j.mechmachtheory.2017.09.013

10. Deng, Z., Huang, H., Li, B., Liu, R.: Synthesis of deployable/foldable SLMs with revolute joints. J. Mech. Robot. **3**(3), 31006 (2011). https://doi.org/10.1115/1.4004029

11. Li, Z., Schicho, J.: A technique for deriving equational conditions on the Denavit-Hartenberg parameters of 6R linkages that are necessary for movability. Mech. Mach. Theory **94**, 1–8 (2015). https://doi.org/10.1016/j.mechmachtheory.2015.07.010

12. Gan, W.W., Pellegrino, S.: Numerical approach to the kinematic analysis of deployable structures forming a closed loop. Proc. Inst. Mech. Eng. Part C J. Mech. Eng. Sci. **220**(7), 1045–1056 (2006). https://doi.org/10.1243/09544062JMES245

13. Fang, Y., Tsai, L.W.: Enumeration of a class of overconstrained mechanisms using the theory of reciprocal screws. Mech. Mach. Theory **39**(11), 1175–1187 (2004). https://doi.org/10.1016/j.mechmachtheory.2004.06.003

14. Zhang, Y., Huang, H.L., Mei, T., Li, B.: Type synthesis of single loop deployable mechanisms based on improved graph method for single-DOF grasping manipulators. Mech. Mach. Theory **169**, 104656 (2022). https://doi.org/10.1016/j.mechmachtheory.2021.104656

15. Xie, F.G., Liu, X.J., Zheng, Y., Wang, J.S.: Synthesis of 2T1R-type parallel kinematic mechanisms and the application in manufacturing. Robot. Comput.-Integr. Manuf. **30**(1), 1–10 (2014). https://doi.org/10.1016/j.rcim.2013.07.002

16. Hopkins, B.J., Culpepper, M.L.: Synthesis of multi-degree of freedom, parallel flexure system concepts via freedom and constraint topology (FACT) part II: practice. Precis. Eng. **34**(2), 271–278 (2010). https://doi.org/10.1016/j.precisioneng.2009.06.007

Research on the Hydrodynamic Calculation of Variable Structure Underwater Vehicle Based on CFD

Xiaomeng Liu[1,2,4,5], Qifeng Zhang[1,2,3,4](✉), Qiyan Tian[1,2,4], Yaxing Wang[1,2,4], Xuejiao Yang[1,2,4,5], Dehao Li[1,2,4,5], and Xiaohui Wang[1,2,4]

[1] State Key Laboratory of Robotics, Shenyang Institute of Automation, Chinese Academy of Sciences, Shenyang 110016, China
zqf@sia.cn

[2] Institutes for Robotics and Intelligent Manufacturing, Chinese Academy of Sciences, Shenyang 110169, China

[3] Southern Marine Science and Engineering Guangdong Laboratory (Guangzhou), Guangzhou 511458, China

[4] Key Laboratory of Marine Robotics, Shenyang 110169, Liaoning, China

[5] University of Chinese Academy of Sciences, Beijing 100049, China

Abstract. In order to speed up the construction of ocean intelligence, improving the intelligent operation level of Underwater Vehicles is one of the current research directions. This paper takes the Variable Structure Underwater Vehicle (VS-UV) as the research object. Through statics analysis and direct navigation simulation analysis, it is verified that the VS-UV has the ability of large-range low resistance navigation and short-range stable operation. CFD simulation method was used to simulate the 6-DOF motion of the vehicle in the two states before and after the deformation for hydrodynamic calculation. The least square method was used to fit the data to obtain the hydrodynamic coefficient and establish the dynamics model. The comparison between simulation results and real navigation results proves that the method can be used to obtain a reliable model for the VS-UV.

Keywords: Underwater vehicle · CFD · Hydrodynamic modelling · Multi-mode operations

1 Introduction

With the development of technology, the demand for intelligent operation in the marine field has increased, and autonomy and intelligence have become the development trend in the field of underwater vehicles. Underwater vehicles are divided into manned and unmanned ones, and in the field of unmanned underwater vehicles, they mainly include Autonomous Underwater Vehicles (AUV) and Remotely Operated Vehicles (ROV). The underwater operation mode is mostly a collaborative mode of AUVs for wide-range observation and ROV for close-range operation [1]. In recent years, the research on Underwater Vehicle Manipulator System (UVMS) consisting of AUV and vehicleic

© The Author(s), under exclusive license to Springer Nature Switzerland AG 2022
H. Liu et al. (Eds.): ICIRA 2022, LNAI 13457, pp. 268–278, 2022.
https://doi.org/10.1007/978-3-031-13835-5_24

arm has become one of the hot spots to achieve free capability [2]. However, UVMS is constrained by the limited stable center height, and it is difficult to perform fine collaborative operations in hovering state. Synthesizing the characteristics of various types of current underwater vehicles, researchers proposed an underwater vehicle based on variable structure for the integration of detection operations.

In order to ensure that the Variable Structure Underwater Vehicle (VS-UV) can have good stability and maneuverability in navigation mode and accurate attitude control ability in operation mode, considering the particularity of underwater environment, it is very important to obtain a reliable hydrodynamic coefficient and establish accurate dynamic model. Currently, the commonly used methods for obtaining hydrodynamic coefficients are divided into Empirical formula method [3], Constraint Mode Test (CMT) [4, 5], Computational Fluid Dynamics (CFD) [6, 7] and System Identification Method (SI) [8, 9]

In recent years, the shapes of underwater vehicles are not only torpedo-shaped but also more complex shapes. To improve the autonomous ability of underwater vehicles, more and more attention has been paid to establishing the dynamic model with complex shapes. Xu took DOE HD2 + 2 ROV as the research object, combined CFD and WAMIT methods to obtain hydrodynamic coefficients, simulated translational oscillatory motion by sinusoidal velocity, and simulated translational and rotational occasional motion by changing the radius of rotating flow field [10]. Juan performed steady-state motion calculations for the Visor 3 ROV using CFD, without considering other coupled motions under the joint action of movement and rotation [11]. Liu made a 1:1.6 scale model of Haima ROV, and obtained hydrodynamic coefficients by using planar mechanism motion method, this paper focuses on the underwater vehicle rotation in situ and large drift angle [12]. Xu investigated the effect of geometric asymmetry on hydrodynamic coefficients of open-frame ROVs using the planar mechanism method [13]. Sven compared the open-frame ROV droop motion model using CMT and SI to analyze the error sources [14]. Liu used CFD to analyze the hydrodynamic performance of the streamlined vertical flat ARV and proposed a simplified method of hydrodynamic coefficients [15]. Yu Simulation of finned underwater vehicle motion by CFD method and analysis of wake effect of bionic finned thruster by fluid-solid coupling method [16]. Ji calculated the linear and nonlinear terms in the spherical AUV hydrodynamic coefficients by setting up static [17]. Liu proposed to calculate the additional mass coefficient by simulating the 6-DOF free harmonic damping oscillations for SILVER SHARK ROV [18].

In this paper, the hydrodynamic analysis of the VS-UV is performed and its hydrodynamic coefficients are calculated. The paper is organized as follows: in Sect. 2, the basic characteristics of the VS-UV are introduced, and the kinematics and dynamics models are established. In Sect. 3, CFD simulations of spatially constraint motion are used to calculate the hydrodynamic coefficients in both modes. In Sect. 4, the CFD simulation results are analyzed. Section 5 summarizes and outlooks on the article content.

2   Hydrodynamic Modeling for the VS-UV

2.1   Overview of the VS-UV

As shown in Fig. 1, the VS-UV is externally wrapped with two buoyancy materials, which provide a streamline shape and buoyancy in water. The VS-UV can work in two ways: Before deformation, it is in navigation mode, which has a streamline shape and can be used for long distance low resistance and agile navigation; after deformation, the vehicle is in operation mode. The upper and lower parts of the vehicle can be expanded to increase the metacenter and attitude stability during hovering operation. Eight vector thrusters are used to provide redundant degrees of freedom and ensure the flexibility of the VS-UV.

Fig. 1. (a) navigation mode (b) operation mode

The main parameters of VS-UV are shown in Table 1 below (the origin is the position of the center of gravity in the navigation mode). When the robot switches to the operation mode, the metacentric height will increase, which provides a larger righting moment to improve the operation stability of the VS-UV.

Table 1. Main parameters of VS-UV

Parameters		Values	Parameters		Values
Mass in air (M)		97 kg	Buoyancy (B)		97 kg
Mass in water		0	Length (l)		1772 mm
Width (b)		1256 mm	Height (h)		[1118–1518] mm
Navigation mode	Centre of gravity	(0,0,0) mm	Operation mode	Centre of gravity	(0,0,45) mm
	Center of buoyancy	(51,−15,49) mm		Center of buoyancy	(51,−15,156) mm
	Metacentric height	(51,−15,49) mm		Metacentric height	(51,−15,156) mm

2.2 Kinematics Modeling

In order to express the position and attitude of the vehicle, the fixed coordinate system and the body coordinate system are introduced as shown in Fig. 2, the coordinate origin Oe of the fixed coordinate system $E - \xi\eta\zeta$ is located at a point in the sea. $E\xi$ pointing to the underwater vehicle main heading is positive, $E\zeta$ pointing to the center of the earth is positive, represents the position of the vehicle in the flow field; The origin O of the body coordinate system $O - xyz$ is taken at the center of gravity of the underwater vehicle. The Ox, Oy, Oz three axes are the intersecting lines of waterplane, transverse section and longitudinal middle section passing through the origin respectively. The Ox-axis pointing to the bow is positive, the Oy-axis pointing to the starboard is positive, and the Oz-axis pointing to the bottom of the underwater vehicle is positive, which are used to represent the attitude of the vehicle. Both coordinate systems meet the rule of the right hand coordinate system.

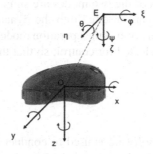

Fig. 2. Definition of coordinate systems

Through coordinate transformation, the kinematics equation of the vehicle can be obtained as follows:

$$\dot{\eta} = \mathbf{J}(\eta)\mathbf{v} \tag{1}$$

$$\mathbf{J}(\eta) = \begin{bmatrix} \mathbf{J}_1(\eta_2) & 0 \\ 0 & \mathbf{J}_2(\eta_2) \end{bmatrix} \tag{2}$$

$$\mathbf{J}_1(\eta_2) = \begin{bmatrix} \cos\psi\cos\theta & -\sin\psi\cos\varphi + \cos\psi\sin\theta\sin\varphi & \sin\psi\sin\varphi + \cos\psi\cos\varphi\sin\theta \\ \sin\psi\cos\theta & \cos\psi\cos\varphi + \sin\varphi\sin\theta\sin\psi & -\cos\psi\sin\varphi + \sin\theta\sin\psi\cos\varphi \\ -\sin\theta & \cos\theta\sin\varphi & \cos\theta\cos\varphi \end{bmatrix} \tag{3}$$

$$\mathbf{J}_2(\eta_2) = \begin{bmatrix} 1 & \sin\varphi\tan\theta & \cos\varphi\tan\theta \\ 0 & \cos\varphi & -\sin\varphi \\ 0 & \sin\varphi/\cos\theta & \cos\varphi/\cos\theta \end{bmatrix} \tag{4}$$

Which η represents the position and attitude vector of the vehicle, $\mathbf{v}$ represents the velocity vector of the vehicle in the following coordinate system. φ, θ, ψ represent the vehicle's roll angle, pitch angle and heading angle.

2.3 Dynamic Modeling

Referring to the standard motion equation of submarine and combined with the main motion forms of vehicle in two modes, the overall dynamic equation is established as follows [19]:

$$M_{RB}\dot{V} + C_{RB}(V)V = F_I(\dot{V}) + F_D(V) + F_R + F_{Thr} \tag{5}$$

where M_{RB} is the the rigid-body system inertia matrix and obtained by statics, $C_{RB}(V)$ is the coriolis-centripetal matrix, $F_I(\dot{V})$ and $F_D(V)$ are the inertia term and viscosity term of hydrodynamic force, which are obtained by CFD simulation, F_R is static force, F_{Thr} is the thrust of the propellers.

This paper only focuses on the long-distance navigation and the short distance movement of the VS-UV in the navigation mode and the operation mode, so the influence of the manipulator is not taken into account temporarily. In the following paragraphs, the hydrodynamic coefficients of the two modes are simulated and calculated, and the coefficients of the two modes are inserted into the dynamic equation respectively to obtain the two dynamics models. When the operation mode is switched, the corresponding dynamics model can be selected for control, so that the vehicle can achieve better control performance.

3 Simulation

In this paper, STARCCM + software is used to conduct CFD simulation of vehicles in two modes. Firstly, pre-processing is carried out to simplify the model. As shown in Fig. 3, the vehicle has a smooth and complete shape in long-distance navigation mode. In the operation mode, due to the deformation of the mechanism, the upper and lower buoyancy materials are separated, and the internal equipment is exposed in the flow field, the model is complicated, so the model is greatly simplified to ensure the basic appearance while ignoring details.

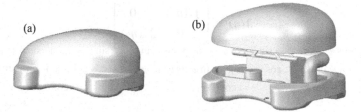

Fig. 3. Simplified model: (a) navigation mode (b) operation mode

Considering the operation mode of our vehicle, although the direct flight motion is the main one, the motion of other degrees of freedom cannot be neglected. Therefore, in this paper, we first simulate the direct flight motion of the vehicle in two modes, analyze the characteristics of direct flight hydrodynamic resistance, and then calculate the complete hydrodynamic coefficients using the spatial constrained motion simulation method proposed in the literature [20]. In this method, different 6-DOF velocities and angular velocities were set in each time step. During the simulation process, the forces and torques of the vehicle at each time step were recorded by CFD. Finally, data fitting was carried out by the least square method to obtain the hydrodynamic coefficient. The advantages of this method are that the input and output of the simulation are processed at one time, which is simple and efficient, and the multi-velocity coupling is considered, so the model established is more reliable in the real uncertain marine environment.

In this paper, according to the design requirements of the vehicle, the velocities/angular velocities simulation interval are set, and the random method is used to generate the 6-DOF random velocity as the input item. In view of the characteristics of the simulation input, this paper set up the cube outflow field with a size of $14l * 14l * 14l$, set the sphere field with a radius of $2l$ with the center of gravity of the vehicle as the origin (as shown in Fig. 4), carry out grid encryption(as shown in Fig. 5), and calculate the additional mass matrix.

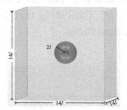 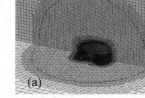 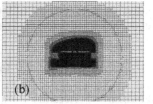

Fig. 4. Calculation model of the flow fiel

Fig. 5. Volumetric Meshing (a) navigation mode (b) operation mode

Through comparison of grid performance, the cut body grid model is finally selected. In the navigation mode, the number of nodes is 5.22 million, the number of cells is 5.01 million, and the average cell quality is 0.9914; in the operation mode, the number of nodes is 5.72 million, the number of cells is 5.45 million, and the average cell quality is 0.9937.

4 Comparison of Results

4.1 Comparison of Hydrodynamic Resistance in Forward Motion

The VS-UV performs the comb scanning observation mission in the navigation mode with a straight motion and an expected speed of 2 to 3 knots. And when entering the operation mode, the VS-UV moves at a slower speed toward the close target with a speed of 0.5 to 1 knot in general. As shown in Fig. 6: (a) shows the pressure diagram of VS-UV moving forward at 1.5 m/s during navigation mode; (b) shows the pressure diagram of VS-UV moving forward at 0.5 m/s during operation mode; (c) shows the relationship between the speed and straight heading water resistance of VS-UV in both modes. Based on the simulation results, it can be observed that the vehicle water resistance is lower than operation mode, which indicates that VS-UV does have the characteristics of low resistance navigation.

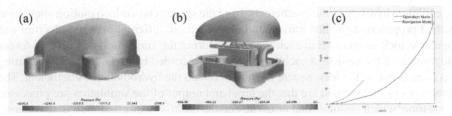

Fig. 6. Forward pressure diagram: (a) navigation mode (1.5 m/s) (b) operation mode (0.5 m/s) (c) Diagram of velocity versus resistance for forward motion

4.2 Simulation Results Analysis of Navigation Mode

The least square method is used to fit the simulation data of the 6-DOF equations. The accuracy of the simulation results is shown in the Table 2. The fitted plots are shown in Fig. 7 The hydrodynamic coefficients of the complete navigation model were obtained. Table 3 shows part of the navigation mode hydrodynamic coefficients. The accuracy of the fitted regressions of the 6-DOF equations are all above 0.95, indicating that the model has small errors and can meet the needs of subsequent calculations.

Table 2. Fitted regression accuracy

Equation	Accuracy	Equation	Accuracy	Equation	Accuracy
Fx	0.869904	Fy	0.8577352	Fz	0.987667
Mx	0.974303	My	0.9574258	Mz	0.877874

Table 3. Part of the hydrodynamic coefficient of the navigation mode

Item	Value	Item	Value	Item	Value	Item	Value
X'_{qq}	−0.002432	X'_{ww}	0.010896	Y'_{wp}	0.428249	Y'_{vw}	−0.262823
X'_{rr}	−0.246231	$Y'_{\dot{r}}$	0.033681	Y'_{wr}	0.212812	$Z'_{\dot{q}}$	−0.07663
X'_{rp}	−0.081337	$Y'_{\dot{p}}$	−0.078947	Y'_*	0.065661	Z'_{pp}	−0.02371
$X'_{\dot{u}}$	−0.01198	$Y'_{p|p|}$	−0.207251	Y'_{uv}	−0.197632	Z'_{rp}	0.276189
X'_{vr}	0.786715	Y'_{pq}	0.064058	Y'_{up}	0.941828	Z'_{rr}	−0.19811
X'_{wq}	−0.20315	Y'_{qr}	0.272707	Y'_{ur}	0.836368	$Z'_{\dot{w}}$	−0.68384
X'_{uu}	0.18711	$Y'_{\dot{v}}$	−0.13911	$Y'_{v|r|}$	−0.115178	Z'_{up}	−0.5124
X'_{vv}	−0.35254	Y'_{vq}	0.16918	$Y'_{v|v|}$	−0.317730	......	

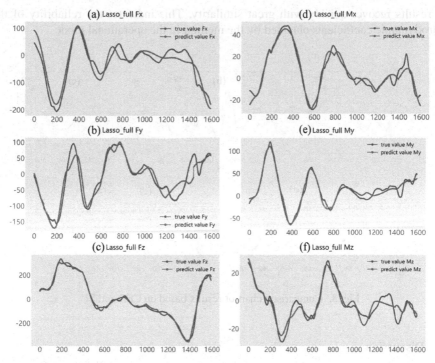

Fig. 7. Comparison chart of fitting results: (a) Fx, (b) Fy, (c) Fz, (d) Mx, (e) Mx, (f) Mx

4.3 Comparison of Operation Mode Simulation Results

The simulation results of the VS-UV 6-DOF motion in the operating mode were fitted using the least squares method to obtain the complete hydrodynamic coefficients. The regression accuracy of the simulation results is shown in the following Table 4.

Table 4. Fitted regression accuracy

Equation	Accuracy		Equation	Accuracy		Equation	Accuracy	
	CFD	SI		CFD	SI		CFD	SI
Fx	0.985	0.776	Fy	0.969	0.632	Fz	0.988	0.736
Mx	0.984	-	My	0.979	0.667	Mz	0.976	0.685

The simulation results were compared with the identification results of the actual navigation of the vehicle, and the intercepted 80-180s comparison graph is shown in Fig. 8. The roll motion comparison is ignored because of its value was small in the real flight. Figure 8 shows the surge, sway, heave, pitch and yaw motions in order from (a) to (e). The two curves have the same trend, and although there are occasional errors, the results recover quickly with great similarity. This indicates the reliability of the hydrodynamic coefficients obtained by the method in the operational mode.

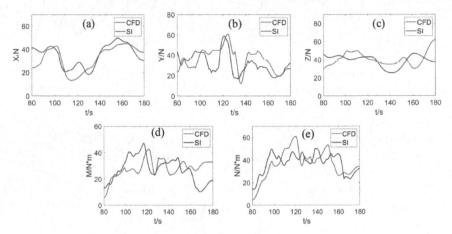

Fig. 8. Comparison chart of results based on CFD and SI

4.4 Discussion

Although the simulation result curves are closer to the real flight fitting curves in operation modes, they are not exactly the same, and the analysis of early errors may be due to the following reasons: (1) From the simulation point of view, the input data are randomly generated, which may be limited by the number of samples, and the samples are not complete enough to represent all velocity intervals. The calculation errors caused by the grid division is still not detailed enough. Maybe for some time steps when calculating The stability is still not reached when the stopping condition is reached, resulting in some data affecting the overall fitting effect. For the operation mode, the internal structure of the vehicle is complex, and the simplification of the model may weaken the effect on the flow field. (2) Analyzed from the perspective of real navigation, the uncertainty of the actual natural underwater environment brings unpredictable disturbances to the vehicle, adding an unknown disturbance term to the dynamics model, and the system may have a delay in processing the disturbance, resulting in a period of time afterwards always maintaining a similar error value and returning to normal after a period of time, which also reflects that it is very important to improve the real-time performance of the system.

5   Conclusions

In this paper, the VS-UV is taken as the research object. Through statics calculation, it is verified that the vehicle has a large metacentric height after deformation to provide the righting moment, which can improve the attitude control stability of hovering operation. Through CFD simulation of direct navigation movement of the vehicle in two working modes, analysis of hydrodynamic resistance changes, verify that the vehicle has the ability of low resistance navigation before deformation, so as to prove that the vehicle has the characteristics of integration of large range navigation observation and short-range stability operation, and meet the design expectations. At the same time, CFD simulation was carried out to calculate the hydrodynamic coefficient of the vehicle under the two states, and the two dynamics models were established. The comparison between the two dynamics models was carried out through the real flight test, which proves that the VS-UV can obtain accurate and reliable results by using the simulation method.

This paper only analyzes the 6-DOF motion before and after deformation, without involving the action of manipulator. However, in the operation mode, the influence of the manipulator cannot be ignored. Then, the influence of the manipulator action on the dynamics model should be studied, and the control method should be studied based on the established dynamics model.

Acknowledgment. This work was supported by the National Key Research and Development Program of China (2021YFF0306200).

References

1. Vu, M.T., Choi, H.S., Kang, J., et al.: A study on hovering motion of the underwater vehicle with umbilical cable. Ocean Eng. **135**, 137–157 (2017)
2. Antonelli, G.: Underwater vehicles. In: Encyclopedia of Systems and Control, pp. 2384–2388. Springer, Cham (2021)
3. Rehman, F.U., Huang, L., Anderlini, E., et al.: Hydrodynamic modelling for a transportation system of two unmanned underwater vehicles: semi-empirical, numerical and experimental analyses. J. Mar. Sci. Eng. **9**(5), 500 (2021)
4. Aage, C., Smitt, L.W.: Hydrodynamic manoeuvrability data of a flatfish type AUV. In: Proceedings of OCEANS 1994, vol. 3, pp. III–425. IEEE (1994)
5. Koh, T.H., Lau, M.W., et al.: Preliminary studies of the modelling and control of a twin-barrel underactuated underwater robotic vehicle. In: 7th International Conference on Control, Automation, Robotics and Vision, ICARCV 2002, vol. 2, pp. 1042–1047. IEEE, December 2002
6. Stern, F., Yang, J., Wang, Z., et al.: Computational ship hydrodynamics: Nowadays and way forward. Int. Shipbuild. Prog. **60**(1–4), 3–105 (2013)
7. Stern, F., et al.: Recent progress in CFD for naval architecture and ocean engineering. J. Hydrodyn. **27**(1), 1–23 (2015). https://doi.org/10.1016/S1001-6058(15)60452-8
8. Alessandri, A., Bono, R., Caccia, M., et al.: Experiences on the modelling and identification of the heave motion of an open-frame UUV. In: IEEE Oceanic Engineering Society. OCEANS 1998. Conference Proceedings (Cat. No. 98CH36259, vol. 2, pp. 1049–1053. IEEE (1998)
9. Chen, H.H.: Vision-based tracking with projective mapping for parameter identification of remotely operated vehicles. Ocean Eng. **35**(10), 983–994 (2008)
10. Xu, M.M., Feng, Z.P., Bi, A.Y., et al.: Dynamical modeling of complex shape submersible. Naval Sci. Technol. **39**(9), 23–28 (2017)
11. Ramírez-Macías, J.A., Brongers, P., Rúa, S., et al.: Hydrodynamic modelling for the remotely operated vehicle Visor3 using CFD. IFAC-PapersOnLine **49**(23), 187–192 (2016)
12. Liu, C.H.: Research on distributed coordination and fault-tolerant control strategy for deep-sea operational ROVs (2016)
13. Xu, S.J.: Study on hydrodynamic characteristics and motion simulation of open-frame ROV (2018)

14. Lack, S., Rentzow, E., Jeinsch, T.: Experimental parameter identification for an open-frame ROV: comparison of towing tank tests and open water self-propelled tests. IFAC-PapersOnLine **52**(21), 271–276 (2019)
15. Liu, J.F., Wang, Y.X., Tang, Y.G., et al.: Dynamical modeling and simplification study of full-sea-depth ARV. J. Mar. Technol. **38**(2), 21–29 (2019)
16. Wang, Y., Bai, X., Cheng, L., et al.: Data-driven hydrodynamic modeling for a flippers-driven underwater vehicle-manipulator system. In: 2020 IEEE 9th Data Driven Control and Learning Systems Conference (DDCLS), pp. 342–349. IEEE (2020)
17. Ji, D., Wang, R., Zhai, Y., et al.: Dynamic modeling of quadrotor AUV using a novel CFD simulation. Ocean Eng. **237**, 109651 (2021)
18. Hammoud, A., Sahili, J., Madi, M., et al.: Design and dynamic modeling of ROVs: estimating the damping and added mass parameters. Ocean Eng. **239**, 109818 (2021)
19. Fossen, T.I.: Handbook of Marine Craft Hydrodynamics and Motion Control. Wiley, Hoboken (2011)
20. Gao, T., Wang, Y., Pang, Y., et al.: A time-efficient CFD approach for hydrodynamic coefficient determination and model simplification of submarine. Ocean Eng. **154**, 16–26 (2018)

SOINS: A Real-Time Underwater Sonar-Inertial System for Pipeline 3D Reconstruction

Wenzhi Gong, Li Xiao[✉], Tian Zeng, Yuchong Li, Zhigang Sun, and Zhuo Wang

Huazhong University of Science and Technology, Wuhan 430074, China
wh_xl@hust.edu.cn

Abstract. In this paper, we propose a real time underwater sonar-inertial system for pipeline reconstruction. In our approach, the sonar data is preprocessed by the likelihood method, from which we calculate the optimal estimation of obstacles position. The cluster center, feature vector and the feature point of sonar point cloud are computed by our cluster-based method, the feature information are utilized to state estimate and 3D reconstruction. During the state estimation step, an IEKF (iterative extended Kalman filter) are used to fuse IMU and sonar data, which are suitable for real-time calculation on the embedded platforms. The proposed method is validated in underwater experiment, the result shows our method have great performance in real-time and accuracy, in which process time can achieve 53 ms and relative translation error can be reduced to 2.5%. The 3D point cloud reconstructed in our method is shown at the end of article.

Keywords: Sonar-inertial system · State estimation · Simultaneous localization and mapping · 3D reconstruction

1 Introduction

Simultaneous localization and mapping (SLAM) has been intensive researched on the terrestrial area. As in underwater environment, the state estimation of robot remains a challenge for researcher due to the complex environment underwater, especially in closed, sewage filled pipeline in-wall. Optimization-based method can perform its strength in its accuracy, [1] combine IMU pre-integration constrains and plane constrains [2] from LiDAR feature points by tight-coupled graph optimization. Ye *et al.* [3] propose a module named LIOM similar graph optimization based on edge and plane features. While in mini robot, filter-based methods have advantages in its rapidity and real-time, [4] fuse IMU data with planar sonar utilizing Gaussian Partial Filter. With the rapid growth of computation complexity of particle filter, Kalman filters and its variants which including EKF [5], UKF [6] and IEKF [7] are widely used in practical. However, traditional on land sensor can hardly adopt to underwater robot. In this case, Global Navigation Satellite System can't work because of the electromagnetic shielding effectiveness of water, LiDAR and camera can rarely perform their full properties as well. Therefore, we adopt omnidirectional sonar to acquire the environmental information, sonar has excellent advantage in wide-covering, deep-measurement range and visibility in turbid water. In this paper, we propose a tight-coupled Sonar-inertial system to estimate the state of the underwater robot equipped with sonar and low-cost IMU.

© The Author(s), under exclusive license to Springer Nature Switzerland AG 2022
H. Liu et al. (Eds.): ICIRA 2022, LNAI 13457, pp. 279–288, 2022.
https://doi.org/10.1007/978-3-031-13835-5_25

The Visualization of point cloud underwater can help human and machines recognize and classify the object, Song Y E *et al.* in [8] adopt the 2-dimention multi-beam imaging sonar to gather high resolution image underwater; Kwon S *et al.* in [9] generate the 3-dimention point cloud by detect box, cylinder with multi-beam sonar.

The paper organized as follows:

- The second section will illustrate our data pre-process method, including sonar likelihood estimation and clustering-based omnidirectional sonar process.
- In third section, we adopt iterative extended Kalman filter constrained with the cluster feature acquired at the first step.
- In the fourth section, we compare our method with extended Kalman filter and normal extended Kalman filter using our clustering-based features

The structure of proposed sonar-inertial state estimator is shown in Fig. 1. The process begins at processing measurement data, including omnidirectional sonar feature-tracking, buoy-odometer counter and IMU measurement pre-integrating. Influenced by the unpredicted diffuse reflection underwater, the sonar data contains all obstacles reflection information as well as plenty of noise underwater. Thus, we are supposed to derive the interested feature in series of sonar data frame, we adopt a sonar measurement likelihood estimation method. After that, we propose a cluster-based method to assist the state estimation, which makes full use of the sparse sonar point, and can achieve beneficial result, this method is detailed description in Sect. 2. The sonar-inertial odometer algorithm adopts iterated extended Kalman filter, this algorithm will be specifically illustrated in Sect. 3.

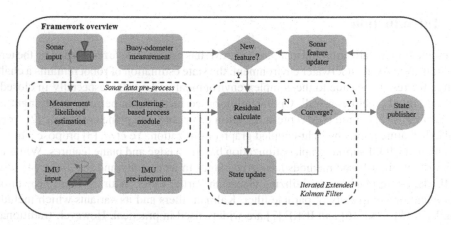

Fig. 1. The full pipeline of proposed sonar-inertial system.

2   Omnidirectional Sonar Data Preprocess

The omnidirectional sonar spin while emitting ultrasound signal, omnidirectional sonar has tinier size than normal sonar inside pipeline. However, the imprecise obstacle position cause by low power emitter remain a pendent problem, as well as the plenty of noise underwater. We adopt a method to optimally estimate the position of obstacles underwater, along with cluster-based method in order to eliminate the outlier and optimally estimate the state in unknown environment.

2.1 Sonar Measurement Likelihood Estimate

In this section, we adopt the model introduced in [10] in our system to eliminate the error produced in obstacle detection. The sonar can detect the environment and offer the likelihood the scalar distance series $d \in R$ between the robot body and the suspected obstacles.

In our system, the wave signal is rarely focused in boundary area while its intensity is low as well. Therefore, we model the phenomenon by calculating the probability distribution of triggering a measurement in a time interval, we denote I as the wave intensity, θ as the zenith angle, θ as the distant of obstacle, Ω as the corresponds to the dihedral angle, $A(d)$ as the attenuation coefficient in the water, we can calculate the incident power of the obstacle:

$$P(d, \theta, \Omega) = I(\theta)A(d)\Omega \tag{1}$$

The proportion of reflected signal power can be approximated by a Gaussian distribution:

$$p(P_R(d)|\mathbf{x}) \approx \mathcal{N}(P_R(d); \alpha P_{max}(r, \mathbf{x}), \alpha(1-\alpha)P_R(r, \mathbf{x})) \tag{2}$$

where P_{max} denote the maximum power that the ultrasound signal reflected by obstacles toward the receiver, from (2) we can notice that P_{max} decide the mean and variance of sonar value probability distribution, Fig. 2 is an example of our sonar maximum power and its corresponding likelihood estimation.

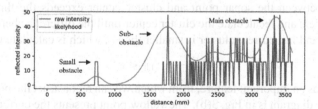

Fig. 2. Sonar maximum power correcting.

From this method, we can eliminate the sonar data error and get correct position p^b of the main obstacles in body frame. From the optimal estimation of $\mathbf{R}$ and $\mathbf{p}$ in Sect. 3, the position in world frame p^w can be calculate by (3).

$$p^w = p^b \mathbf{R} + \mathbf{p} \tag{3}$$

2.2 Clustering-Based Process Module

After transferring original sonar data to likelihood estimate, there are still a mass of noise cloud point, shown in the Fig. 3. Because the diameter of the sonar transmitter is in the same order of magnitude as its wavelength and the diffuse reflection in the water, the noise points distribute mostly in the out-wall of the pipeline, to solve this problem, we propose a clustering-based method to filter the outliers as well as recording feature points for state estimation.

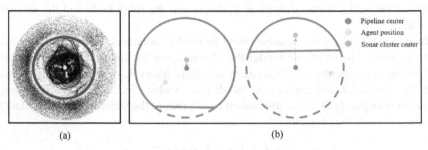

(a)   (b)

Fig. 3. (a) The profile map of the raw sonar data, we use cluster method to classify the data and select the feature points. (b) The diagram of pipeline center, agent position and the sonar cluster center.

We can notice in Fig. 3(a) that the truth sonar value and the noise can be divided by a circle, so we propose a method to separate this point cloud. We initial the cluster center **c** as the current position estimate of the robot, we calculate the cluster center by:

$$\mathbf{c}_t = \left[\frac{1}{m} \sum_{i=1}^{m} x_i \; \frac{1}{m} \sum_{i=1}^{m} y_i \; \frac{1}{m} \sum_{i=1}^{m} z_i \right]^T \tag{4}$$

where x, y, z denote the position of sonar point, m denote the number of point, when the distance between the sonar point and cluster center exceeds the threshold d_{thre}^t, removing outliers and recalculate the cluster center until the difference between current cluster center and last current cluster is smaller than ε, which is calculate in (5).

$$\|c_k - c_{k-1}\| < \varepsilon \tag{5}$$

We use c_k as an important feature, from which we can reconstruct the pipeline shape. The schematic diagram is in Fig. 3(b). The yellow point presents the current position of robot, orange point presents the sonar cluster center c_k, blue point presents the pipeline center, the arrow points to sonar cluster from pipeline center present the vector ρ_k. And the sonar feature points are recoded as $\mathbf{G}_k$, which will be utilized in state estimation. If a frame of sonar data is an ellipse, we transform the frame of data to circle instead.

3   Real-Time State Estimator

3.1   Sonar-Inertial System Description

In this section, we list the notations we will use following. $\mathbf{R} \in SO(3)$ is the rotation matrix, $\mathbf{p} \in \mathbb{R}^3$ is the position in space, $\mathbf{v} \in \mathbb{R}^3$ is the velocity, $\mathbf{b}_\omega$ and $\mathbf{b}_a$ is the gyroscope and the accelerometer bias, i is the ith IMU frame and k is the kth Sonar frame. The state of robot $\mathbf{x}$ can be modeled as:

$$\mathbf{x} = \left[\mathbf{R}^T, \mathbf{p}^T, \mathbf{v}^T, \mathbf{b}_\omega^T, \mathbf{b}_a^T \right]^T \tag{6}$$

We calibrate the gyroscope and accelerometer noise $\mathbf{n}_\omega$, $\mathbf{n}_a$. As well as bias noise $\mathbf{n}_{b\omega}$, $\mathbf{n}_{ba}$, the noise matrix is defined below:

$$\mathbf{w} = \left[\mathbf{n}_\omega^T, \mathbf{n}_a^T, \mathbf{n}_{b\omega}^T, \mathbf{n}_{ba}^T \right]^T \tag{7}$$

We adopt iterative extended Kalman filter as our estimator. Assuming that the optimal state estimation of the last sonar feature set at t_{k-1} is $\bar{\mathbf{x}}_k$ while the covariance matrix is $\overline{\mathbf{P}}_{k-1}$ which represent the covariance of random error state vector between the truth state $\mathbf{x}_\lambda$ and the optimal state estimation $\bar{\mathbf{x}}_\lambda$. The states got small variation in movement, the state differential $\dot{\mathbf{x}}$ linearization is:

$$\dot{\mathbf{x}} = \begin{bmatrix} \omega - \mathbf{b}_\omega - \mathbf{n}_\omega \\ \mathbf{v} \\ \mathbf{R}(a - \mathbf{b}_a - \mathbf{n}_a) + \mathbf{g} \\ \mathbf{n}_{b\omega} \\ \mathbf{n}_{ba} \end{bmatrix} \tag{8}$$

$[a]^\times$ denote the skew symmetric matrix of vector a, the propagation state $\hat{\mathbf{x}}_{i+1}$ is:

$$\hat{\mathbf{x}}_i = \hat{\mathbf{x}}_{i-1} + \dot{\mathbf{x}}_i \Delta t \hat{\mathbf{x}}_0 = \bar{\mathbf{x}}_k \tag{9}$$

To propagate the covariance, the matrix $\mathbf{F}_{\tilde{\mathbf{x}}}$, $\mathbf{F}_{\tilde{\mathbf{w}}}$ can be shown as:

$$\mathbf{F}_{\tilde{\mathbf{x}}} = \begin{bmatrix} \mathrm{Exp}(-[\omega_i]^\times \Delta t) & \mathbf{p} & -\mathbf{A}(\omega_i \Delta t)^T \Delta t & 0 & 0 \\ 0 & 1 & 0 & 0 & 0 \\ -\mathbf{R}_i[a_i]^\times \Delta t & 0 & I_{3\times3} & -\mathbf{R}_i \Delta t\, I_{3\times3} \Delta t \\ 0 & 0 & 0 & I_{3\times3} & 0 \\ 0 & 0 & 0 & 0 & I_{3\times3} \end{bmatrix} \tag{10}$$

$$\mathbf{F}_{\mathbf{w}} = \begin{bmatrix} -\mathbf{A}(\omega_i \Delta t)^T \Delta t & 0 & 0 & 0 \\ 0 & -\mathbf{R}_i \Delta t & 0 & 0 \\ 0 & 0 & I_{3\times3} \Delta t & 0 \\ 0 & 0 & 0 & I_{3\times3} \Delta t \end{bmatrix} \tag{11}$$

$$\mathrm{Exp}_{SO(3)}(\mathbf{R}) = I + sin\|\mathbf{R}\| \frac{\mathbf{R}}{\|\mathbf{R}\|} + (1 - cos\|\mathbf{R}\|) \frac{\mathbf{R}^2}{\|\mathbf{R}\|^2} \tag{12}$$

$$A_{SO(3)}(\mathbf{R}) = I + \frac{1 - cos(\mathbf{R})}{\|\mathbf{R}\|} \frac{\mathbf{R}}{\|\mathbf{R}\|} + \left(1 - \frac{sin(\|\mathbf{R}\|)}{\|\mathbf{R}\|} \right) \frac{\mathbf{R}^2}{\|\mathbf{R}\|^2} \tag{13}$$

where Δt denote the time interval between 2 IMU samples i and $i + 1$. The matrix $\mathrm{Exp}(\cdot)$ and $\mathrm{A}(\cdot)$ is computed in (11), (12). Thus the state error can be modeled as following

$$\tilde{\mathbf{x}}_{i+1} = \mathbf{x}_{i+1} - \hat{\mathbf{x}}_{i+1} \simeq \mathbf{F}_{\tilde{\mathbf{x}}} \tilde{\mathbf{x}}_i + \mathbf{F}_{\mathbf{w}} \mathbf{w}_k \tag{14}$$

3.2 System State Estimator

We denote the covariance matrix $\mathbf{Q}$ of white noise $\mathbf{w}$. Denoting the predictive covariance matrix $\hat{\mathbf{P}}_i$, which is initialized as $\hat{\mathbf{P}}_0 = \overline{\mathbf{P}}_{k-1}$ and is updated as following:

$$\hat{\mathbf{P}}_{i+1} = \mathbf{F}_{\bar{x}}\hat{\mathbf{P}}_i\mathbf{F}_{\bar{x}}^T + \mathbf{F}_{\mathbf{w}}\mathbf{Q}\mathbf{F}_{\mathbf{w}}^T \tag{15}$$

The prediction propagates until receiving next frame of sonar feature c_k, ρ_k and $\mathbf{G}_k$, The observation matrix is:

$$\mathbf{z}_k = \begin{bmatrix} c_k & \rho_k & \mathbf{G}_k & d_k \end{bmatrix}^T \tag{16}$$

While c_k denote the cluster center of the sonar point, ρ_k denote the vector from the pipeline center to cluster center, $\mathbf{G}_k$ is the set of sonar feature adopt from ICP (Iterative Center Point), d_k present the buoy-odometer measurement, the specific sonar feature derive method is shown in Sect. 2.2. The IEKF begins at initiating the iteration times, when the optimal estimate available, computing the Jacob matrix $\mathbf{H}_k^I$, Kalman gain$\mathbf{K}_k^I$. the process of IEKF is shown below

$$\mathbf{H}_k^I = \frac{\partial \mathbf{h}_k(\mathbf{x})}{\partial \mathbf{x}}\bigg|_{x=\hat{\mathbf{x}}_k^I} \tag{17}$$

$$\mathbf{S}_k^I = \mathbf{H}_k^I\mathbf{P}_k\mathbf{H}_k^T + \mathbf{R} \tag{18}$$

$$\mathbf{K}_k^I = \mathbf{P}_k\mathbf{H}_k^T\mathbf{S}_k^{-1} \tag{19}$$

Then we calculate the next iteration of state estimation $\hat{\mathbf{x}}_k^{I+1}$, the I denote the Ith iteration, the process continue until the change $\Delta\hat{\mathbf{x}}$ between two consecutive iterations is negligible or the iteration times reach threshold, the iteration process is shown followed:

$$\hat{\mathbf{x}}_k^{I+1} = \hat{\mathbf{x}}_{k-1} + \mathbf{K}_k^I\left(\mathbf{z}_k - \mathbf{h}_k\left(\hat{\mathbf{x}}_k^I\right) - \mathbf{H}_k^I\left(\hat{\mathbf{x}}_{k-1} - \hat{\mathbf{x}}_k^I\right)\right) \tag{20}$$

$$\Delta\hat{\mathbf{x}} = \left\|\hat{\mathbf{x}}_k^{I+1} - \hat{\mathbf{x}}_k^I\right\| \le \epsilon \tag{21}$$

After convergence the optimal state estimation, the optimal state and covariance estimation is:

$$\overline{\mathbf{x}}_k = \hat{\mathbf{x}}_k^{I+1} \tag{22}$$

$$\overline{\mathbf{P}}_{\mathbf{k}} = (\mathbf{I} - \mathbf{K}_k\mathbf{H}_k)\mathbf{P}_k \tag{23}$$

The sonar feature points will be constructed as point cloud for underwater pipeline 3D reconstruction, when the new sonar feature points are available, the state estimator begin fusing IMU state propagation and sonar feature, if the residual calculation converge, the sonar feature points cloud will get updated and the state estimation will be published to odometer and other node of the robot system.

4 Experiment

In city area, the underground pipelines are difficult to clean for scrubber, to solve the problem, we mount a tiny robot (340 mm * 270 mm * 130 mm) with the sensors and our algorithm, the robot gathers IMU and sonar measurement, and process them instantly. We conduct our experiment in real pipeline underwater. We present our results and compare our method with other Kalman filter variants.

(a)   (b)

Fig. 4. Experiment environment underwater. (a) Experiment robot. (b) Underwater pipeline. (Provided by Guoqing Wu)

4.1 Experiment Underwater

This experiment environment is shown in Fig. 4. The robot equipped with embedded platform NVIDIA Jetson TX2, IMU, omnidirectional sonar and buoy-odometer, in this

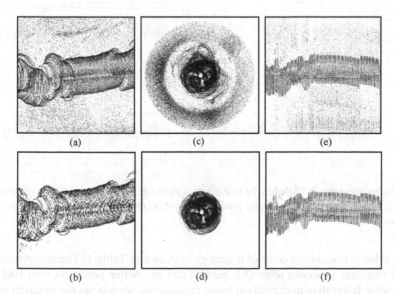

(a)   (c)   (e)

(b)   (d)   (f)

Fig. 5. (a), (c), (e) is before our preprocess, (b), (d), (f) is after our preprocess.

experiment, we gather raw measurement of sonar, buoy-odometer and IMU, then pre-process them using our proposed method. Our method can get good result in underwater situation, compared with sonar point cloud, our preprocess can remove outlier and reconstruction rapidly, which is shown in Fig. 5 and Table 1.

4.2 Evaluation

We compared our method with EKF, but the experiment in EKF is also using our pre-process sonar method. The experiment results are shown in Fig. 6. Including trajectory and linear velocity prediction using different method, angular velocity and acceleration are raw data from IMU. We can notice that our method can predict the trajectory and linear velocity rate accurately in underwater environment.

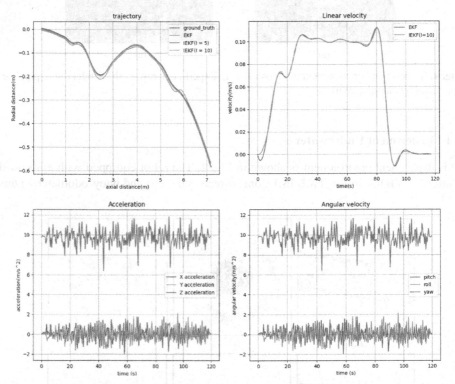

Fig. 6. Experiment result diagram. The first diagram show the trajectory prediction of robot. The second picture show the linear velocity prediction of robot, the third and the fouth pictrue show the raw data of IMU.

The relative translation error of trajectory is shown in Table 1. The computing time on TX2 platform is shown also. Our method can get better precision than EKF, and can calculate faster than optimization based method and we can set the iteration time to balance the accuracy and computing time during state estimate.

Table 1. The algorithm process time and precision

Method	Process time	Relative translation error
EKF	40 ms	12.5%
Our method (I = 5)	45 ms	4.8%
Our method (I = 10)	53 ms	2.3%
Optimization based method	120 ms	1.9%

5 Conclusion and Future Work

In this paper, we propose a method to solve the hard work in state estimation underwater for pipeline. To process the raw sonar data, we propose a cluster-based method to calculate the measurement likelihood estimate and compute the sonar data center, then we match the sonar feature for next estimation. We adopt iterative extended Kalman filter as our state estimator, our experiment is performed underwater in pipeline, from the result we can conclude that our method can achieve great score in practice. In the future, we will couple the sonar data and IMU data tightly, in order to enhancement of accuracy.

References

1. Geneva, P., Eckenhoff, K., Yang, Y., Huang, G.: LIPS: LiDAR-inertial 3D plane slam. In: 2018 IEEE/RSJ International Conference on Intelligent Robots and Systems (IROS), pp. 123–130. IEEE (2018). https://doi.org/10.1109/IROS.2018.8594463
2. Hsiao, M., Westman, E., Kaess, M.: Dense planar-inertial slam with structural constraints. In: 2018 IEEE International Conference on Robotics and Automation (ICRA), pp. 6521–6528. IEEE (2018).https://doi.org/10.1109/ICRA.2018.8461094
3. Ye, H., Chen, Y., Liu, M.: Tightly coupled 3D lidar inertial odometry and mapping. In: 2019 International Conference on Robotics and Automation (ICRA), pp. 3144–3150. IEEE (2019). https://doi.org/10.1109/ICRA.2019.8793511
4. Bry, A., Bachrach, A., Roy, N.: State estimation for aggressive flight in GPS-denied environments using onboard sensing. In: 2012 IEEE International Conference on Robotics and Automation, pp. 1–8. IEEE (2012). https://doi.org/10.1109/ICRA.2012.6225295
5. Hesch, J.A., Mirzaei, F.M., Mariottini, G.L., Roumeliotis, S.I.: A laser-aided inertial navigation system (l-ins) for human localization in unknown indoor environments. In: 2010 IEEE International Conference on Robotics and Automation, pp. 5376–5382. IEEE (2010). https://doi.org/10.1109/ROBOT.2010.5509693
6. Cheng, Z., et al.: Practical phase unwrapping of interferometric fringes based on unscented kalman filter technique. Opt. Express **23**(25), 32337–32349 (2015). https://doi.org/10.1364/OE.23.032337
7. Qin, C., Ye, H., Pranata, C.E., Han, J., Zhang, S., Liu, M.: LINS: a lidar-inertial state estimator for robust and efficient navigation. In: 2020 IEEE International Conference on Robotics and Automation (ICRA), pp. 8899–8906. IEEE (2020). https://doi.org/10.1109/ICRA40945.2020.9197567
8. Song, Y.E., Choi, S.J.: Underwater 3D reconstruction for underwater construction robot based on 2D multibeam imaging sonar. South Korean Soc. Oceanogr. **30**(3), 227–233 (2016). https://doi.org/10.5574/KSOE.2016.30.3.227

9. Kwon, S., Park, J., Kim, J.: IEEE 2017 IEEE Underwater Technology (UT) - Busan, South Korea (2017.2.21–2017.2.24)] 2017 IEEE Underwater Technology (UT) - 3D reconstruction of underwater objects using a wide-beam imaging sonar, pp. 1–4 (2017). 10.1109/UT.2017.7890306
10. Müller, J., Rottmann, A., Burgard, W.: A probabilistic sonar sensor model for robust localization of a small-size blimp in indoor environments using a particle filter. In: Proceedings of the IEEE International Conference on Robotics and Automation (ICRA), pp. 3589–3594 (2009). https://doi.org/10.1109/ROBOT.2009.5152283

Subsea Pipeline Inspection Based on Contrast Enhancement Module

Ming Zhao, Lin Hong, Zhen-Long Xiao, and Xin Wang[✉]

The School of Mechanical Engineering and Automation,
Harbin Institute of Technology, Shenzhen, Guangdong 518055, China
wangxinsz@hit.edu.cn

Abstract. Due to the high turbidity of the water and lack of lighting in deep sea, the image of subsea pipeline are blurred and lack of brightness. In the paper an algorithm is proposed to extract centerline of underwater pipeline using image enhancement and pipeline edge detection. The enhancement module based on the color space transformation is given to improve image contrast. Also the threshold segmentation algorithm is put forward to calculate the parameters of Canny operator for edge detection. The centerline of the pipeline is extracted based on the probabilistic Hough transform. Experimental results show that the proposed algorithm is effective and robust.

Keywords: Underwater pipeline inspection · Edge detection · Probability hough transform

1 Introduction

With the development of underwater fields exploitation, more and more people use subsea pipelines to transport natural gas, oil and other energy, and communication between continents is also dependent on subsea cables. Because the change of geological structure, sea water corrosion and other problems will lead to pipeline defects. Therefore, it is great important for maintenance and safety to have regular inspection of subsea pipelines.

Underwater vehicles are divided into ROVs and AUVs, ROVs (Remotely Operated Underwater Vehicles) employ sensors and cameras and are controlled through radio or cable connections, but data needs to be checked manually, It wastes human resources. AUVs(Autonomous Underwater Vehicles) can work in underwater without supervision compared to ROVs. Therefore, most of the current pipeline inspection is still using AUVs, which is by far the most cost-effective method. However, the high turbidity of the subsea, lack of lighting and artificial light attenuation present significant challenges for the camera, which can greatly degrade image quality. Vision-based methods often work well in indoor pool but tend to be fragile in real-world subsea scenarios [1].

For AUV underwater pipeline detection, there are two methods: traditional method and deep learning method. The traditional method can be divided into two types: (a) the method of pipeline segmentation is used to generate an over-all mask; (b) The method of edge detection and Hough transform is used to obtain the pipe boundary. The paper [2] use segmentation based on clustering of 2d image histogram; Shi et al. designed a robot can move along the pipeline by extracting the contour of the pipeline using Hough transform [3]; Zhang et al. uses improved OTSU threshold processing and Kalman filter to detect the pipeline [4]. The deep learning method performs well in complex scenes, but requires a large number of data sets for training. The paper [5] is based on the method of deep learning, using U-NET network for training and using the contour point cloud map obtained by sonar for supervision. Grau et al. proposed a cable detection algorithm based on machine learning, which is also suitable for subsea pipelines [6]. But even with all kinds of methods, the detection of blurred scenes is always unsatisfactory.

In this paper, we propose a vision-based underwater pipeline centerline detection algorithm. Firstly, we analyze the underwater pipeline image characteristics and propose a contrast enhancement module, which consists of contrast limited adaptive histogram equalization(CLAHE) and filtering algorithms. Then we use Canny operator and probability Hough transform to obtain the edge of the pipeline, and use a selection method to improve the detection accuracy. Finally, we obtain the centerline of the pipeline based on the above results, and evaluated each step of the algorithm through ablation experiments to prove the effectiveness of the proposed model, the results can provide specific implementation of underwater AUV with corresponding reference.

2   Methodology

This section introduces the image processing methods that constitute the underwater pipeline detection algorithm. Our algorithm include image enhancement and line detection. The algorithm process is shown in Fig. 1.

2.1   Image Enhancement

The subsea light source mainly came from artificial auxiliary light sources, due to the selective absorption of light by water body, the contrast of underwater image is low and the image is blue-green [7]. According to the above characteristics, in order to ensure the real-time performance of pipeline detection, we use the color space transform method to enhance the subsea image. Converting an RGB image into a color space with chromaticity components such as HSV, YUV and Lab for the algorithm resistant to light changes and enhances the contrast between pipeline and background.

We converted the underwater images to HSV, Lab and YUV color space for comparison, we select five lines evenly distributed in the image to calculate the average deviation, and take the average of the selected five rows deviation as the image average deviation. We can see through the Table 1 the average difference of Y-channel is larger than other channels for blurred or normal underwater

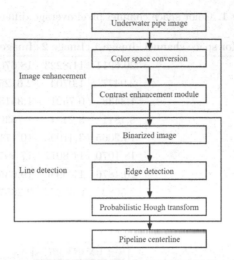

Fig. 1. Subsea pipeline detection algorithm.

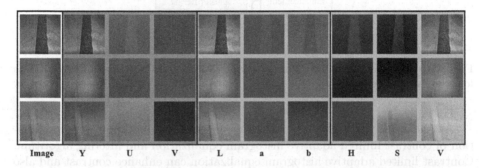

Fig. 2. White background is RGB image. Blue background is the image of each channel in the YUV color space. Yellow background is the image of each channel in the Lab color space. Green background is the image of each channel in the HSV color space. (Color figure online)

image, this represents the Y-channel of the image have a greater contrast, and contains more useful image information. It can also be seen from Fig. 2 that other channels will generate a lot of noise, It is not helpful for subsequent image gradient processing, so we chose Y channel for enhancement.

Because the pixel distribution of the subsea image is not uniform, we use histogram equalization to process the image. However, when processing images with very similar pixel values, the histogram transformation function will map pixels in a very narrow range to the whole pixel range, which makes a amount of noise in some flat areas over-magnify after histogram equalization processing. Our subsea pipeline images are also images with very similar pixel values, therefore, we propose a contrast enhancement module to better improve the contrast of our images.

Table 1. Color space channel pixel average difference

Color space channel	Image 1	Image 2	Image 3
Y	20.6911	11.8223	18.6702
U	2.9477	1.0704	2.6125
V	1.3438	0.7621	1.3518
H	8.4811	3.2494	7.7630
S	10.2065	3.4199	10.1713
V	18.1070	11.8077	17.5970
L	20.4876	11.5986	19.6359
a	2.5682	0.6737	2.2657
b	3.9672	1.2177	3.5731

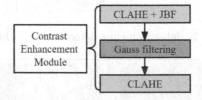

Fig. 3. (a) CLAHE is contrast limited adaptive histogram equalization. (b) JBF is joint bilateral filtering.

As shown in the Fig. 3, our contrast enhancement module use a combination of contrast limited adaptive histogram equalization and filtering algorithm. Contrast limited adaptive histogram equalization can enhance contrast and also magnify part of noise, and filtering algorithm can solve this problem well. This paper chooses joint bilateral filtering [8], which can suppress the noise and keep the image edge information. Then eliminate the original noise of the image by Gaussian filtering, and contrast limited adaptive histogram equalization is used again to improve the edge condition. The final result can not only improve the contrast, but also keep the edge information of the pipeline and eliminate some image noise.

2.2 Pipeline Division

Due to the obvious grayscale difference between the subsea pipeline and the background, in order to better identify the subsea pipeline and obtain the relevant parameters of edge extraction, it is necessary to carry out binarization processing on the image, generally speaking, we need to specify a threshold value, which divides the image into two types higher than this threshold value and lower than this threshold value, so that objects with different pixel values in the image can be effectively segmented. In the present, there are many researches on threshold segmentation. Considering the characteristics of subsea pipelines, we choose

Otsu threshold segmentation method [9]. Otsu algorithm is often used for clustering problems based on image segmentation. The algorithm assumes that the image is composed of foreground and background, so that the optimal threshold value can be calculated to separate foreground and background elements.

If n_i is the number of pixels in the image whose gray scale is i, the number of image pixels with a grayscale value of i is n_i, the probability is:

$$p_i = \frac{n_i}{n_0 + n_1 + \ldots + n_{255}} \tag{1}$$

We suppose a threshold k divides the pixels in the image into two categories: A(greater than k) and B(less than k). Then the value range of k is $[0, 255]$. In the case of the assumed threshold k, $p_A(k)$ or $p_B(k)$ is the probability that the pixel is assigned to category A or B. calculated as the accumulation of p_i in the category A or B. The average gray value of the pixels assigned to A and B is:

$$m_A(k) = \frac{\sum_{i=0}^{k} i p_i}{p_A(k)} \tag{2}$$

$$m_B(k) = \frac{\sum_{i=k+1}^{255} i p_i}{p_B(k)} \tag{3}$$

The mean value of the whole image is:

$$p_A(k) * m_A(k) + p_B(k) * m_B(k) = m_G \tag{4}$$

$$\sigma^2 = p_A(k) \left(m_A(k) - m_G\right)^2 + p_B(k) \left(m_B(k) - m_G\right)^2 \tag{5}$$

When σ^2 is the maximum value, the corresponding k value is the optimal threshold. The result obtained by Ostu is not only a binary image that has been segmentation, but also a threshold value k, which is very important for the following work of edge detection.

The edge detection of pipeline image is to identify the boundary of pipeline by using the rapidly changing area in the image. In this paper, Canny operator is used for edge detection. Canny edge detection is a method of edge detection using multi-stage edge detection algorithm [10], As shown in the Fig. 4, which is mainly divided into the following steps:

(1) **Image denoising.** Because the image edges are susceptible to noise interference, so in order to avoid misidentifying detected edge information, we need to use filter algorithm to remove noise, the purpose is to smooth some texture detail features, weak edge information and preserve strong edge information. In this paper, we adopt Gaussian filtering with a kernel size of 5 * 5 and sigma of 1.
(2) **Computing gradient.** The gradient of gray-level image can be approximated using the first-order difference, the difference formula is:

$$G = \sqrt{G_x^2 + G_y^2} \tag{6}$$

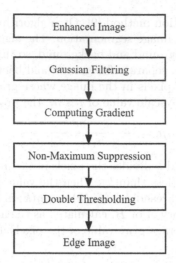

Fig. 4. Canny operator calculation process.

$$\theta = \arctan\left(\frac{G_y}{G_x}\right) \tag{7}$$

G_x and G_y represent a pair of convolution arrays in Sobel operator, and the corresponding gradient amplitude G and gradient angle θ can be obtained after the convolution calculation of the convolution check image.

(3) **Non-maximum suppression(NMS)**. In order to refine the edge features and eliminate the noise of non-edge, we use NMS to process the images, NMS can suppress those pixels whose gradient is not large enough and only retain the largest gradient within the range.

The algorithm compares two gradient amplitude along the gradient direction of the current point, if it is a local maximum in the positive or negative gradient direction, we preserves the point, if not, let the gradient amplitude at that point be zero.

(4) **Double thresholding**. After the above operation, the strong edges are already inside the edge image, However, there are still some weak edges which enhance the image noise and must be filtered out. Therefore, the algorithm sets two corresponding thresholds, one as Maxval and the other as Minval, as shown in the Fig. 5. The selection of double threshold parameters is subjective, so how to determine the double threshold of Canny algorithm is a difficult thing. For our subsea image, we use the threshold extracted by Otsu in the previous step to determine it the threshold. According to the test results, 1/4 of the threshold value as Maxval and 1/8 as Minval are the optimal results. The advantage of this method is to reduce the number of parameters requiring subjective judgment, automatically select the corresponding threshold based on the selection of different images.

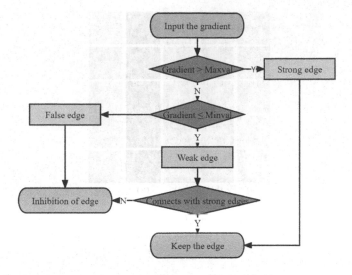

Fig. 5. Non-maximum suppression calculation process.

Because Canny operator will treat the noise in the image with a high gradient as an edge, we must use a method to detect the real pipe edge. The subsea pipeline has obvious linear characteristics, so Hough transform is the most commonly used method for line detection at present, which is used for image line detection based on slope and intercept parameterization. Hough transform is mainly used to deal with the line detection of binary images. Hough transform uses the transformation between two coordinate Spaces to map curves or lines with the same shape in one space to a point in another coordinate space to form a peak value, thus transforming the problem of detecting arbitrary shapes into a statistical peak value problem.

However, it is inherently limited by high computing costs due to the large memory space required to store cumulative votes. In order to improve the computational efficiency of line detection, Kiryati et al. (1991) proposed the probabilistic Hough transform [11], which uses random sampling to select a number of edge points to be stored in voting. They found that using probabilistic Hough transform for line detection can significantly reduce calculation. In order to improve the speed, we use probabilistic Hough transform for edge fitting in this paper.

Probabilistic Hough transform results in many pairs of point sets, which are mainly distributed at the edge of the pipeline and a few points at the image noise points. In order to reduce the influence of the wrong point set on the following work, we first calculated the inclination Angle of each pair of points and counted the inclination Angle, eliminated the inclination Angle with large deviation from most of the current inclination Angle, and calculated the average value of the remaining inclination Angle. Then, by taking the method of moment, the centroid of the pipeline is calculated according to the set of points after screening

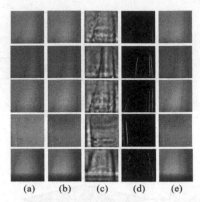

(a)   (b)   (c)   (d)   (e)

Fig. 6. (a) RGB subsea pipeline image (b) Y color space subsea pipeline image. (c) Enhanced subsea pipeline image. (d) Subsea pipeline edge image. (e) Our final results

in the previous step, and finally the coordinates and orientation inclination of the centroid of the pipeline are obtained and draw the corresponding line.

3   Experiments and Analysis

Our results are shown Fig. 6. It can be seen that our algorithm has good performance in blur and non-blur subsea image, and can accurately predict the extension direction and position of the pipeline, which is conducive to our subsequent control.

We conducted an ablation study on the algorithm, and extract five types of images from about 100 number of images, the experimental results are shown in Fig. 7. The first row to the last row is clear subsea pipeline image, multinoise subsea pipeline image, blurred subsea pipeline image, incomplete subsea pipeline image and strongly shadowed subsea pipeline image. We delete the contrast enhancement module, CLAHE and joint bilateral filtering, compared them with the complete algorithm in this paper. We found that the result was unsatisfactory of subsea images after removing these modules.

As mentioned above, the function of module is to improve image contrast and suppress excessive amplification of noise. Column (c) represents the deletion of contrast enhancement module. Although there is no significant difference in image performance and pipelines have been successfully identified, but the overall error detection rate has increased a lot. The reason is that a large number of false edges will be generated in the process of edge detection for low contrast images. Column (d) represents the deletion of CLAHE algorithm, which is mainly used to balance image histograms to improve contrast and improve weak boundary gradient. Experiments and images show that after CLAHE algorithm is deleted, the algorithm can only detect strong edges, but not weak edges. Apart from a clear image, it is almost impossible to inspect our subsea pipeline properly. The reason is that without enhancing weak edges, weak edges of blurred images

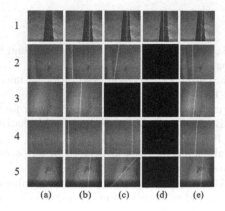

Fig. 7. (a) RGB image. (b) Our algorithm result. (c) Remove contrast enhancement module. (d) Remove contrast limited adaptive histogram equalization. (e) Remove joint bilateral filtering.

cannot be recognized as boundaries by Canny operators. Column (e) represents the deletion of joint bilateral filtering algorithm, which is mainly used to suppress the noise caused by histogram equalization in coordination with CLAHE as described above. The result was consistent with our prediction. After deleting this part, pipelines could still be detected in the image, but all the high-noise images were incorrectly detected. In this way, we verify the original intention of the design and prove that the noise points will be amplified after CLAHE algorithm. If Joint is not used, the recognition of high-noise images will indeed be affected.

4   Conclusion

This paper propose an efficient and robust algorithm for subsea pipeline detection in AUV navigation. The algorithm is divide into two stages: image enhancement and pipeline detection. In the first stage of the algorithm, we transformer underwater pipeline image into brightness space in YUV color space. Then we propose a module to enhance the contrast of subsea images and suppress image noise. We also use Otsu threshold segmentation method to get a value. it split the image pixels into two parts and is used as the threshold for Canny operator. The probabilistic Hough transform is adopted to detect lines in the edge map, the centerline of pipeline is obtained. Experiment results verify the feasibility of our algorithm. Further more, we evaluate the process parameters which need for each part of the algorithm and determine the optimal parameters for each section. We performer ablation studies and successfully verify the effectiveness of the contrast enhancement module.

Acknowledgments. This work was supported in part by the Joint Funds of the National Natural Science Foundation of China (No. U1913206) and Shenzhen Science and Technology Program (No. JSGG20211029095205007).

References

1. Paull, L., Saeedi, S., Seto, M., Li, H.: AUV navigation and localization: a review. IEEE J. Ocean. Eng. **39**(1), 131–149 (2013)
2. Ortiz, A., Simó, M., Oliver, G.: A vision system for an underwater cable tracker. Mach. Vision App. **13**(3), 129–140 (2002)
3. Shi, L., et al.: An underwater pipeline tracking system for amphibious spherical robots. In: 2017 IEEE International Conference on Mechatronics and Automation (ICMA), pp. 1390–1395. IEEE (2017)
4. Zhang, H., et al.: Subsea pipeline leak inspection by autonomous underwater vehicle. Appl. Ocean Res. **107**, 102321 (2021)
5. Bharti, V., Lane, D., Wang, S.: Learning to detect subsea pipelines with deep segmentation network and self-supervision. In: Global Oceans: Singapore-US Gulf Coast, pp. 1–7. IEEE 2020 (2020)
6. Grau, A., Climent, J., Aranda, J.: Real-time architecture for cable tracking using texture descriptors. In: IEEE Oceanic Engineering Society. OCEANS 1998. Conference Proceedings (Cat. No. 98CH36259), vol. 3, pp. 1496–1500. IEEE (1998)
7. Hong, L., Wang, X., Xiao, Z., Zhang, G., Liu, J.: WSUIE: weakly supervised underwater image enhancement for improved visual perception. IEEE Robot. Autom. Lett. **6**(4), 8237–8244 (2021)
8. Tomasi, C., Manduchi, R.: Bilateral filtering for gray and color images. In: Sixth International Conference on Computer Vision (IEEE Cat. No. 98CH36271), pp. 839–846. IEEE (1998)
9. Otsu, N.: A threshold selection method from gray-level histograms. IEEE Trans. Syst. Man Cybern. **9**(1), 62–66 (1979)
10. Canny, J.: A computational approach to edge detection. IEEE Trans. Pattern Anal. Mach. Intell. **6**, 679–698 (1986)
11. Kiryati, N., Eldar, Y., Bruckstein, A.M.: A probabilistic Hough transform. Pattern Recogn. **24**(4), 303–316 (1991)

Numerical Investigation on Turbulence Models and the Hydrodynamics of a UVMS

Hang Xu, Lin Hong, Xin Wang[✉], and Ming Zhao

School of Mechanical Engineering and Automation,
Harbin Institute of Technology, Shenzhen 518055, Guangdong, China
wangxinsz@hit.edu.cn

Abstract. Underwater vehicle-manipulator systems (UVMS) have been widely used in many underwater tasks. In this paper, a numerical investigation of the hydrodynamic performances of a small-size UVMS is carried out by using the computational fluid dynamics (CFD) method. Firstly, based on the standard DARPA SUBOFF model, the performance of several common turbulence models is compared, and the SST k-ω turbulence model is adopted in our numerical simulations. Then, the three-dimensional model of the UVMS with a complex mechanical structure is simplified to improve the mesh quality and reduce the calculation cost on the premise of ensuring the accuracy of the results. Finally, based on the CFD method, towing test simulations are carried out to obtain the essential hydrodynamic coefficients of the UVMS.

Keywords: Underwater vehicle-manipulator system · Computational fluid dynamics (CFD) · Turbulence model · Hydrodynamic coefficients

1 Introduction

Autonomous underwater vehicles (AUVs) have been increasingly popular in recent years as the importance of marine resources and the workload of underwater operations have grown. The focus and difficulty in its research process is AUV control. As a result, an accurate dynamic model which includes sophisticated hydrodynamic models must be constructed [1]. The values of the coefficients in the hydrodynamic model which represent forces and moments are critical for the AUV's autonomous maneuverability.

The hydrodynamic coefficient can be determined by three kinds of methods: analytical and semi-empirical (ASE) methods, experimental evaluation methods, and numerical investigation methods [2]. The ASE method relies on empirical findings and analytic expressions. Cardenas et al. [3] proposed a method for calculating an AUV's hydrodynamic coefficient based solely on its geometry. However, because the ASE method relies on empirical conclusions based on conventional geometries, estimating the hydrodynamic coefficients of AUVs

H. Liu et al. (Eds.): ICIRA 2022, LNAI 13457, pp. 299–310, 2022.
https://doi.org/10.1007/978-3-031-13835-5_27

with complicated body geometry is almost impossible. Experimental evaluation methods typically use the planar motion mechanism (PMM) for towing tank experiments. Nouri et al. [4] devised a method for measuring the forces and moments caused by the AUV's velocity and acceleration, as well as estimating the hydrodynamic coefficients in the dynamic model, based on planar experiments in a water tunnel. With the advancement of computer performance and turbulence models, the CFD method has been widely used in the work of solving hydrodynamic coefficients. Zhandong Li et al. [5] developed a complex-shaped AUV with devices that can weld nuclear reactors in emergency situations and perform routine inspections. The numerical simulation of the hydrodynamic coefficient calculation of the AUV was carried out based on CFD. By simulating the steady-state motion simulation test and unsteady motion simulation test in CFD, the inertial hydrodynamic coefficients and viscous hydrodynamic coefficients are solved respectively. Huang Hai et al. [6] developed a novel small streamlined 1-AUV for autonomous cruise and handling. To study the hydrodynamic performance of the 1-AUV during manipulation, PMM experiments and CFD analysis were carried out for the 1-AUV under various manipulation postures. The CFD method still needs verification at the physical experimental level, but it greatly improves the convenience of hydrodynamic research.

Existing AUVs can be divided into open-frame and torpedo-shaped [7]. AUVs began to perform operational functions other than marine exploration and inspection as they evolved. Because the structure of a torpedo-shaped AUV is constrained, the design and implementation of AUVs with complicated shapes are becoming more popular, increasing the complexity of determining the hydrodynamic coefficient. The UVMS used in this study has an underwater operable manipulator that can execute tasks in difficult underwater conditions. UVMS is typically found on big Remote Operated Vehicles (ROVs) because of its complex structure, and its downsizing trend emerges later. The force and moment communicated by the manipulator to the body cannot be ignored in a portable UVMS, which puts increased demands on the correctness of the UVMS model coefficients.

The remainder of this document is structured as follows: Sect. 2 covers the basic principles of CFD, evaluates several turbulence models using the SUBOFF-5563 [8] model and its experimental data, and determines the properties and applicability of these models. Section 3 builds UVMS' equation of motion, optimizes and validates UVMS' three-dimensional model, simulates the optimized model's steady motion, and estimates the appropriate hydrodynamic coefficients. The conclusion is presented in Sect. 4.

2   Computational Fluid Dynamics

2.1   FVM and Turbulence Models

The finite volume method (FVM) is one of the pervasive numerical solution methods used in CFD to solve the differential equations (DEs). This method is based on conservation equations that describe every individual control volume defined by the meshes. Divergence-containing terms in volumetric integration

are transformed into surface integration using the divergence formula [9]. FVM
has two significant advantages, one is that it shows excellent adaptability to
the meshes, and can yield correct results in both structured and non-structured
solution networks, the other is that it can be perfectly integrated with the finite
element method when conducting fluid-structure interaction analysis.

As Eq. 1 shows, the continuity equation expresses the mass conservation of
every control volume in a flow, where ρ is the density of fluid, u, v and w are
fluid velocities in x, y and z directions. The amount of flux arriving at a volume
is equivalent to the flux leaving its adjacent volume.

$$\frac{\delta\rho}{\delta t} + \frac{\partial(\rho u)}{\partial x} + \frac{\partial(\rho v)}{\partial y} + \frac{\partial(\rho w)}{\partial z} = 0 \tag{1}$$

Usually, laminar flow problems can be easily solved using CFD, but it is almost
impossible to solve a flow problem numerically in practice if the motion of the
fluid is turbulent. The features of the flow are ordinarily characterized by the
dimensionless R_e which is defined by the fluid's velocity, density, dynamic viscosity, and characteristic length. The Navier-Stokes equations are converted into
time-averaged Navier-Stokes equations when the flow is turbulent, therefore the
stochastic flow properties and their parameters can be obtained by statistical
methods using normal and joint normal probabilistic distributions. Various turbulence models have been used to solve these time-averaged equations. The
widely used turbulence models include the Standard k-ϵ model, Renormalisation-
group (RNG) k-ϵ model, and Shear-stress-transport (SST) k-ω model.

2.2   Comparison of Turbulence Models

There is no turbulence model which is suitable for all types of flow problems. The
accuracy of turbulence models is limited by the geometry of the flow, R_e and the
limitations of experimental data and empirical formulas. Therefore, it is necessary to verify the numerical analysis results with experimental data before solving the hydrodynamic simulation to ensure the correctness of the CFD method
and meshing. This paper uses several turbulence models including the Standard
k-ϵ model, RNG k-ϵ model, and SST k-ω model to calculate the forces on the
SUBOFF-5563 model, separately. We noticed that the growth rate, face sizing,
and the number of layers of the inflation mesh can cause the transition shape
of the meshes to behave very differently (see Fig. 1), and therefore also analyzed the effect of the transition mesh with the SST k-ω model. The simulation
results of the SUBOFF-5563 model are shown in Table 1, and the line charts of
these data are shown in Fig. 2. The experimental drag of SUBOFF-5563 should
be artificially increased by 20%, because the fairing installed in the experiment
allows the SUBOFF-5563 to avoid an additional drag which is created by tip
losses and vortices [8]. Figure 2 shows that the line graphs of the Standard k-ϵ
model and RNG k-ϵ model have similar trends, their numerical results are more
than 50% higher compared with the experimental data when the speed exceeds
0.5 m/s. The numerical results of the SST k-ω model without considering the

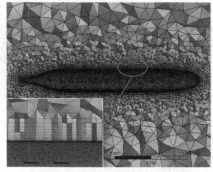 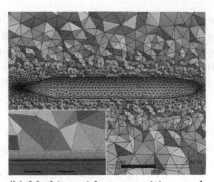

(a) Meshing with transition mesh   (b) Meshing without transition mesh

Fig. 1. Meshing results after improving mesh quality by adjusting the growth rate, face sizing, and the number of layers of the inflation mesh

mesh transition coherence are smaller than the experimental data, which may be due to the loss of information when the calculation proceeds to the faces where the mesh shape suddenly changes. The more accurate results are obtained when mesh transitions are improved.

Table 1. Towing tank and simulation results of SUBOFF-5563

Force(N)　　　　　Velocity(m/s)　Item	0.1	0.2	0.6	0.7	0.9	1.05
Experimental data of SUBOFF-5563	0.0409	0.0617	0.3188	0.4226	0.7904	0.9181
Standard k-ϵ model	0.0195	0.0693	0.4830	0.6353	1.0955	1.3092
RNG k-ϵ model	0.0193	0.0666	0.4711	0.6199	1.0696	1.2791
SST k-ω model(without transition mesh)	0.0153	0.0449	0.2278	0.3081	0.5604	0.6676
SST k-ω model(with transition mesh)	0.0177	0.0591	0.4020	0.5372	0.9526	1.1479

3   Hydrodynamic Performance Investigation of the UVMS

The UVMS studied in this work consists of a 5 degrees-of-freedom (DOF) robot body with two cabins and a 2 DOF manipulator with two robotic arms and a 1 DOF gripping mechanism. As shown in Fig. 3, the manipulator is installed in the front of the subcompartment of the robot body, the gripping mechanism is mounted on the end of the manipulator. The design parameters of the UVMS are shown in Table 2. The center of gravity of the UVMS coincides with the center of buoyancy by adjusting the weight and position of the counterweight.

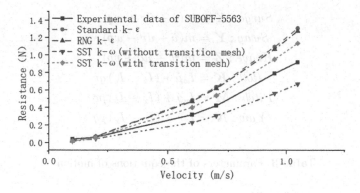

Fig. 2. Towing tank and simulation results of SUBOFF-5563

Table 2. The Design parameters of the UVMS

Parameter	Value
Boundary dimension (mm × mm × mm)	712 × 400 × 380
Weight (kg)	15.5
Sailing speed (knot)	1 to 2
Degrees of freedom	5 (without pitch)

3.1 Equations of Motion

As Fig. 3 shows, earth-fixed frame $(E - \xi\eta\zeta)$ and body-fixed frame $(O - xyz)$ are introduced to describe the motion of the UVMS. The origin of the body-fixed frame is set at the center of gravity of the UVMS, the positive Ox is the forward-cruising direction of the UVMS. The equation of motion of the UVMS in the body-fixed frame is shown in Eq. 2, Parameters of the equations are given in Table 3.

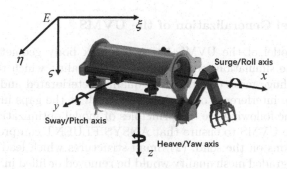

Fig. 3. System overview and coordinate systems of the UVMS

$$Surge : \boldsymbol{X} = m(\dot{u} - vr + wq)$$
$$Sway : \boldsymbol{Y} = m(\dot{v} + ur - wp)$$
$$Heave : \boldsymbol{Z} = m(\dot{w} - uq + vp)$$
$$Roll : \boldsymbol{K} = I_x \dot{p} + (I_z - I_y)\, qr \tag{2}$$
$$Pitch : \boldsymbol{M} = I_y \dot{q} + (I_x - I_z)\, pr$$
$$Yaw : \boldsymbol{N} = I_z \dot{r} + (I_y - I_x)\, pq$$

Table 3. Parameters of the equations of motion

Parameter	Description
$\boldsymbol{X}, \boldsymbol{Y}$ and $\boldsymbol{Z}$	Resultant forces respect to x, y and z axes
$\boldsymbol{K}, \boldsymbol{M}$ and $\boldsymbol{N}$	Moments respect to x, y and z axes
u, v and w	Velocity of surge, sway, and heave motion
p, q and r	Angular velocity of roll, pitch, and yaw motion
I_x, I_y and I_z	Inertia momentum of the UVMS about the axes Ox, Oy and Oz

The underwater working environment of the UVMS is regarded as an infinite domain of water. Only the UVMS' shape and motion factors dictate its hydrodynamic performance. For this low-speed UVMS, just velocity and its first-order derivative are taken into account. The hydrodynamic force τ_x along the x-axis can be expressed as

$$\tau_x = f_x(u, v, w, p, q, r, \dot{u}, \dot{v}, \dot{w}, \dot{p}, \dot{q}, \dot{r}) \tag{3}$$

Using Taylor series expansion on Eq. 3, and dimensionless hydrodynamic coefficients of velocity and acceleration with $1/2\rho U^2 L^2$ and $1/2\rho U^2 L^3$ respectively, then the equations of motion of the UVMS with unknown hydrodynamic coefficients are obtained [2].

3.2   3D Model Generalization of the UVMS

The original model of the UVMS has a complex body geometry with many appendages. The simulation requires good mesh quality, which results in small mesh sizes and huge mesh counts. Mesh quality deteriorated and even meshing failed due to the interference of the inflation mesh at the gaps in the model, as Fig. 4 shows. The following are the principles of model optimization: (1) Fill the cavity inside the UVMS to ensure that ANSYS FLUENT can properly perform boolean operations on the solid. (2) Small structures which lead to large mesh numbers and degraded mesh quality would be removed or filled in to improve the time occupancy and convergence of the simulation. (3) The main feature shape and projected shape of the UVMS cannot be changed to prevent simplification from making the simulation inaccurate in other directions. (4) Simulations should be utilized to test the optimized model's forces and flow field, and errors within 5% are considered to be acceptable. The models before and after optimization and the numerical results of their simulations are shown in Fig. 4.

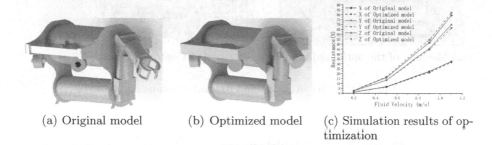

(a) Original model   (b) Optimized model   (c) Simulation results of optimization

Fig. 4. The 3D model and the numerical simulation results along the x, y, and z axes before and after optimization

3.3 Towing Test Simulation of the UVMS

The optimized model is used for meshing and numerical solutions. The size of the computational domain is $7L \times 10H \times 10W (L = 712$ mm, $W = 400$ mm, $H = 380$ mm) to avoid the blocking effects. Water will have a large R_e and a non-negligible boundary layer on the surface of the UVMS at the same time when it is at the sailing speed of this UVMS. The SST k-ω model is selected according to the previous simulation of the SUBOFF model. The y^+ is controlled to be around 1, and the equation for calculating the mesh thickness of the first layer at each speed can be expressed as

$$y = \frac{y^+\mu}{\sqrt{0.029 \left(\frac{\rho u L}{\mu}\right)^{-0.2} \rho^2 U_m^2}} \tag{4}$$

where μ is the dynamic viscosity of water(1.01×10^{-3} Pa · s), ρ is the density of water (998.2 kg/m^2), L is the equivalent length of the UVMS, u and U_∞ are the local and steady-state velocities, respectively. y^+y is preset to 1 and the local velocity u is assumed to be equal to the steady-state velocity U_∞. Meshing based on this thickness and using these meshes for simulation (see Fig. 5). A more accurate local velocity u is obtained after completing the simulation, using Eq. 4 to calculate the true y^+, the range of y^+ value is 0 to 1.5, as shown in Fig. 5. Other initial parameters of CFD simulation are given in Table 4. The mesh independence of the UVMS has been verified using these settings.

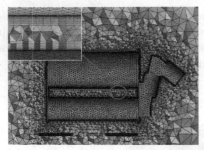

(a) Meshing of the optimized model   (b) Contour of local y^+

Fig. 5. Meshing situation and its evaluation using y^+

Table 4. Setting of some initial parameters of CFD

Parameter	Initial setting
Time	Steady state
Turbulence model	SST k-ω model
Discrete format	Second-order upwind discrete scheme
Solving algorithm	SIMPLE
Fluid type	Water (liquid)

Straight-Line Motion Along x-axis. The stationary motion simulation is to measure the drag of the UVMS at different speeds, obtain the speed-resistance curve and then determine the corresponding hydrodynamic coefficient. The hydrodynamic coefficient X_{uu} is equal to the quadratic term coefficient of the fitted curve according to the main equation of straight-line motion along the x-axis, as shown in Eq. 5. Set the incoming flow velocity in both directions since the UVMS is not completely symmetrical about the yOz plane, and then use the correction coefficient to unify the expression of X_{uu} as

$$X = X_{u|u|}u|u| + X_{uu}uu$$
$$X_{u|u|} = \frac{1}{2}\left(X_{u|u|}^{(+)} + X_{u|u|}^{(-)}\right) \tag{5}$$
$$X_{uu} = \frac{1}{2}\left(X_{u|u|}^{(+)} - X_{u|u|}^{(-)}\right)$$

where $X_{u|u|}^{(+)}$ and $X_{u|u|}^{(-)}$ are the hydrodynamic parameters along the positive and negative directions of the 0x axis respectively, $X_{u|u|}$ is the hydrodynamic coefficient, X_{uu} is the correction coefficient. In straight-line motion simulation, the drags at speeds between 0.2 m/s to 1.1 m/s are solved, as Table 5 shows. Figure 6 shows the curve fitted by the least squares method using these drags, where $X_{u|u|}^{(+)} = 26.25$ and $X_{u|u|}^{(-)} = 26.61$. Dimensionless $X_{u|u|} = 26.43$ and $X_{uu} = -0.18$ to get $X'_{u|u|} = 0.0907$ and $X'_{uu} = -0.00062$.

Table 5. Numerical results of straight-line motion along x-axis

Velocity (m/s)	0.2	0.3	0.4	0.5	0.6	0.7	0.8	0.9	1.0	1.1
X^+ (N)	1.084	2.384	4.240	6.500	9.522	12.94	16.89	21.44	26.47	31.80
X^- (N)	1.132	2.528	4.534	6.980	9.868	13.77	17.48	21.95	26.98	33.08

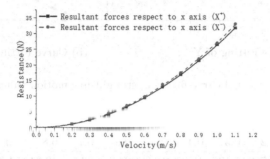

Fig. 6. Polynomial curve fitting of straight-line motion along x-axis

Straight-Line Motion Along y-axis. Only the positive velocities are considered when simulating the straight-line motion along the y-axis since the UVMS is symmetrical about the xOz plane. Set different fluid velocities to simulate the drags of the UVMS with straight-line motion along the y-axis at different speeds in the water (see Table 6). Use the least-squares method to fit the speed-drag curve and speed-yaw moment curve, as shown in Fig. 7. According to the quadratic coefficients of the polynomials obtained by fitting, $Y_{vv} = 56.55$ and $N_{vv} = 4.635$. These two hydrodynamic coefficients are dimensionless, where $Y'_{vv} = 0.1954$ and $N'_{vv} = 0.02103$.

Table 6. Numerical results of straight-line motion along y-axis

Velocity (m/s)	0.2	0.3	0.4	0.5	0.6	0.7	0.8	0.9	1.0	1.1
Y (N)	2.198	4.968	8.743	13.41	19.91	25.76	36.45	44.78	56.36	66.76
N (N·m)	0.188	0.447	0.780	1.217	1.642	2.298	2.723	3.763	4.797	5.559

Straight-Line Motion Along z-axis. The UVMS is asymmetric about the xOy plane, so the simulation work is required to get the drag due to movement along both positive and negative directions of z-axis. Use correction values to represent the relevant hydrodynamic coefficients. The numerical results of the simulation and their fitted curves are shown in Table 7 and Fig. 8, respectively. The relevant dimensionless hydrodynamic coefficients are: $Z'_{w|w|} = 0.2195$, $Z'_{ww} = 0.01348$, $M'_{w|w|} = 0.00622$ and $M'_{ww} = -0.00163$.

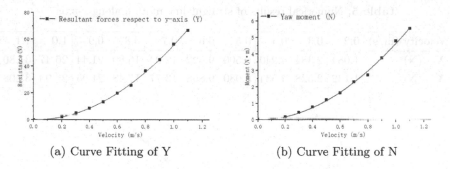

(a) Curve Fitting of Y   (b) Curve Fitting of N

Fig. 7. Polynomial curve fitting of straight-line motion along y-axis

Table 7. Numerical results of straight-line motion along z-axis

Velocity (m/s)	0.2	0.3	0.4	0.5	0.6	0.7	0.8	0.9	1.0	1.1
Z^+ (N)	2.759	6.106	10.95	16.89	24.61	33.15	43.34	54.67	67.07	82.25
Z^+ (N)	2.468	5.555	9.997	15.82	22.52	30.75	40.37	49.67	61.12	74.03
M^+ (N·m)	0.043	0.108	0.175	0.306	0.437	0.561	0.683	0.832	1.057	1.335
M^+ (N·m)	0.079	0.169	0.316	0.495	0.734	0.996	1.241	1.510	1.848	2.259

Oblique Motion in xOy Plane. When the UVMS turns while moving forward, the velocity vector presents an angle (the drift angle) with the x-axis due to its inertia. Therefore, it is necessary to simulate the oblique motion of UVMS in the horizontal plane (xOy plane) [10]. The fluid velocity is kept constant at 1m/s and the angle between the UVMS and the incoming flow direction is changed between 0° to 20°. The numerical results are shown in Table 8. These numerical results are linearly fitted with the intercept set to 0 (see Fig. 9). By processing the slope of the fitted straight line, the hydrodynamic coefficients which are important for the turning motion are obtained, where $Y_v' = 0.23153$ and $N_v' = 0.02617$.

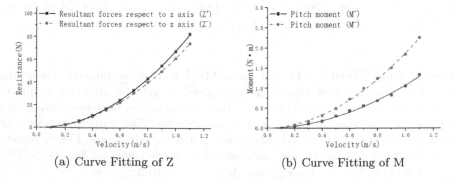

(a) Curve Fitting of Z   (b) Curve Fitting of M

Fig. 8. Polynomial curve fitting of straight-line motion along z-axis

Table 8. Numerical results of oblique motion in xOy plane

Drift angle (°)	Lateral velocity (m/s)	Y (N)	N (N·m)
5	0.08716	3.4116	1.8804
10	0.17364	11.699	1.5496
15	0.25882	17.334	0.9739
20	0.34202	23.214	0.3559

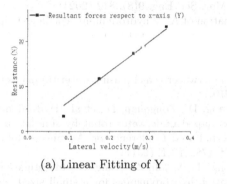

(a) Linear Fitting of Y

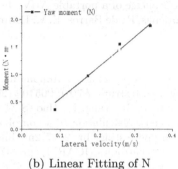

(b) Linear Fitting of N

Fig. 9. Linear fitting of oblique motion in xOy plane

4   Conclusions

In this study, experimental data of the SUBOFF-5563 model were used to validate and compare three commonly used turbulence models, including the Standard k-ε model, RNG k-ε model, and SST k-ω model. The SST k-ω model was proved to be more suitable than the Standard k-ε model and RNG k-ε model for the simulation of low-speed and portable AUVs with R_e between 100,000 and 1.5 million. Furthermore, it was found that the smoothness of the transition between the inflation layer mesh and the outer mesh has a great impact on the accuracy of the simulation results when the correct turbulence model has already been used. After confirming to use SST k-ω model to analyze the self-built UVMS, the initial model was optimized, and several principles and techniques for model optimization were summarized. As a consequence, the number of meshes and computation time were decreased to less than half of what they were before, mesh quality was considerably improved, while the simulation results only altered by no more than 5%. The simulation for the optimized model of straight-line motion along the three coordinate axes and oblique Motion in the xOy plane are carried out. Some hydrodynamic coefficients in the equations of motion are estimated. In the future, the UVMS' unsteady motion and capabilities in other spatial degrees of freedom will be investigated. Additionally, a controller will be designed based on the estimated hydrodynamic coefficients to enhance the ability of the UVMS to track to the specified location accurately.

Acknowledgments. This work was supported in part by the Joint Funds of the National Natural Science Foundation of China (No. U1913206) and Shenzhen Science and Technology Program (No. JSGG20211029095205007).

References

1. Yan, H., et al.: Design approach and hydrodynamic characteristics of a novel bionic airfoil. Ocean Eng. **216**, 108076 (2020)
2. Hong, L., Fang, R., Cai, X., Wang, X.: Numerical investigation on hydrodynamic performance of a portable AUV. J. Mar. Sci. Eng. **9**(8), 812 (2021)
3. Cardenas, P., de Barros, E.A.: Estimation of AUV hydrodynamic coefficients using analytical and system identification approaches. IEEE J. Oceanic Eng. **45**(4), 1157–1176 (2019)
4. Nouri, N.M., Mostafapour, K., Bahadori, R.: An apparatus to estimate the hydrodynamic coefficients of autonomous underwater vehicles using water tunnel testing. Rev. Sci. Instrum. **87**(6), 065106 (2016)
5. Zhandong, L., Yang, L., Hao, S., Liang, D., Zongquan, D., et al.: Hydrodynamic coefficients calculation of a complex-shaped underwater robot by simulation and prototype testing. In: 2017 2nd International Conference on Advanced Robotics and Mechatronics (ICARM), pp. 474–478. IEEE (2017)
6. Hai, H., Zexing, Z., Jiyong, L., Qirong, T., Wanli, Z., Wang, G.: Investigation on the mechanical design and manipulation hydrodynamics for a small sized, single body and streamlined I-AUV. Ocean Eng. **186**, 106106 (2019)
7. Sahoo, A., Dwivedy, S.K., Robi, P.S.: Advancements in the field of autonomous underwater vehicle. Ocean Eng. **181**, 145–160 (2019)
8. Hait, M.W.: A hydrodynamic analysis and conceptual design study for an external storage enclosure system for unmanned underwater vehicles. Ph.D. thesis, Massachusetts Institute of Technology (2021)
9. Yilmaz, S., Yılmaz, G.A.: Identification of particular hydrodynamic parameters for a modular type 4 DOF underwater vehicle by means of CFD method. Ind. Robot Int. J. Robot. Res. Appl. (2022)
10. Mitra, A., Panda, J.P., Warrior, H.V.: Experimental and numerical investigation of the hydrodynamic characteristics of autonomous underwater vehicles over sea-beds with complex topography. Ocean Eng. **198**, 106978 (2020)

Design of Enveloping Underwater Soft Gripper Based on the Bionic Structure

Jiansong Dou[1,2(✉)], Daohui Zhang[2], Yanxu Sun[3], Xin Fu[2], and Xingang Zhao[2]

[1] Shenyang University of Technology, Shenyang 110870, China
1140837474@qq.com
[2] Shenyang Institute of Automation, Chinese Academy of Sciences, Shenyang 110016, China
{zhangdaohui,zhaoxingang}@sia.cn
[3] Northeastern University, Shenyang 110870, China

Abstract. The ocean has been an important research site for scientists in recent years. Many marine creatures with soft bodies such as sea cucumbers are fragile and easily deformed, so it is difficult when grasping these kinds of targets. In this regard, this study developed an underwater soft robot gripper based on a bionic structure. By imitating the envelope structure of the Venus flytrap, the soft robot gripper was designed with a soft finger envelope plate, and the structure was designed by imitating human finger fingerprints. The large and small pressure chambers of soft fingers were designed with the characteristics of different lengths of the segments. By adopting these bionic elements, the grasping ability of the gripper has been greatly improved. The structural parameter optimization design of soft fingers, based on finite element simulation, has been described detailed in the paper. The declination between the simulation results and the actual results is very small, which proves that the accuracy of the optimization method is high. In the simulated underwater environment, some models and living sea cucumbers were grasped for tests. Finally, the experimental results proved that the soft robot gripper can achieve the goal of stable grasping for different objects.

Keywords: Soft robot · Underwater soft robot gripper · Bionics

1 Introduction

The ocean occupies 71% of the earth's surface area, contains many treasures that we have never discovered, and is one of the important areas we want to explore [1]. However, the deep-sea environment is harsh, so it is difficult for humans to conduct scientific research and explorations in the deep sea without the aid of tools [2]. By 2022, the deepest human diving record is 105 m, which is far from supporting human research and exploration in the deep-sea environment. Therefore, underwater robots have become important work equipment for scholars to conduct deep-sea sampling, antique salvage, and biological collection [3]. Most underwater robots need to be equipped with the end effector of the underwater manipulator, and the operation efficiency of the underwater manipulator will directly affect the performance of the underwater robots [4, 5]. Most of the traditional underwater manipulators are made of rigid materials, although they can achieve better

H. Liu et al. (Eds.): ICIRA 2022, LNAI 13457, pp. 311–322, 2022.
https://doi.org/10.1007/978-3-031-13835-5_28

force and position control. The greater rigidity of them is easy to damage the objects. The underwater soft robot gripper provides a new option for underwater operations due to its good flexibility and safety [2, 6].

The design of the soft gripper is inspired by the creatures in nature, such as octopus, starfish, jellyfish, etc. [7]. Relying on its great deformation and infinite DOF, when grasping objects, it can pass through according to the shape of the object. The resulting deformation is firmly attached to the surface of the object to achieve stable grasping action [8].

At present, scholars have created many kinds of soft robot grippers. Galloway et al. [9, 10] succeeded in a non-destructive sampling of benthic animals in the ocean by using a soft gripper with a rigid robotic arm. In the follow-up research [4, 11], the bellows-type soft gripper combined with the soft arm was mounted on the ROV to realize the sampling of marine organisms. However, this soft gripper has no envelope structure, and the grasped object is easy to escape when grasping. Luo Zhaojun et al. [12] proposed a bending actuator with independent control of three joints according to the motion law of human fingers and designed a bionic hand on this basis. Due to its softness, this soft manipulator can adapt to the shape and size of objects in unstructured and complex environments to achieve the purpose of grasping and manipulating objects [13–15]. The ultra-soft robotic actuator developed by Sinatra, Nina R et al. [16] of Harvard University is capable of grasping gelatinous marine organisms. However, the driver captures jellyfish and other creatures by winding, and the capture is limited, and the captured object is easy to escape after being caught. Jiangnan University Dong Hu et al. [17] designed a soft gripper based on a one-way pneumatic actuator. The fingers of the soft gripper can be bent and deformed, and the unidirectional actuator at the base of the finger can achieve swing deformation. The finite element simulation study of the soft gripper is carried out, and also the correctness of the theoretical model is verified. However, it has not carried out the finger deformability experiment and has not carried out physical verification, so it cannot further verify its accuracy. Shanghai Jiao Tong University Liu Wenhai et al. [18] designed a complete grasping configuration for the four-finger soft gripper and verified the effectiveness of the proposed grasping model through open-source databases and self-built databases. However, it can only be used in the air and cannot be used underwater. Wu Zhaoping from Nanjing University of Science and Technology [19] proposed a new design idea for a new type of articulated endoskeleton pneumatic soft manipulator with the decomposition of drive and load-bearing functions and completed the specific structural design of the soft hand. However, it does not have an effective envelope structure, and its system envelope still needs to be improved.

In summary, the underwater soft robot grippers are of great value for application in deep-sea non-destructive grasping. However, existing underwater soft grippers have defects such as unsatisfactory grasping effect and low grasping success rate, which have a certain impact on underwater operations. The main reason for these defects is that the existing underwater soft grippers do not have an effective enveloping structure and cannot withstand huge underwater pressure. Therefore, around these problems, this paper designs an underwater soft robot gripper with a bionic enveloping structure, conducted structural optimization through finite element analysis, and finally built a relevant test platform to test its underwater operation capability.

2 Structural Design and Finite Element Method

2.1 Structural Design

Finger Structure Design. When refering to bionic structures, most soft fingers are often designed as human hands [20]. Human fingers are relatively flexible, and the fingerprint structure on the finger can increase the friction between the finger and the object being grasped, which can improve the success rate of grasping. However, there is no connection between two human fingers, so it is easy to "slip through the net" when grasping some slippery and soft objects.

The reason for the high success rate of catching Venus flytrap is mainly due to its thorn-like envelope structure, as shown in Fig. 1(a), which can prevent the grasped object from slipping out between the fingers during the grasping process. So an envelope plate is designed on the side of the fingers, imitating the envelope structure of the thorns of the Venus flytrap. When a soft gripper grasps an object, the bending angles of each section of the finger are different, which can better fit the surface of the grasped object. In this study, the matching structure of the large and small pressure chambers is shown in Fig. 1(b). In this structure, the large pressure chamber is distributed near the base of the finger, and the small pressure chamber is distributed near the fingertip, which can realize a large bending of the finger near the fingertip and a small bending near the base of the finger under the condition of a single pressure input, which greatly reduces the complexity of the structure on the premise of satisfying the function. To improve the success rate of grasping, by imitating the structure of human fingerprints, a fingerprint structure is designed at the bottom of the fingernail to increase the friction force.

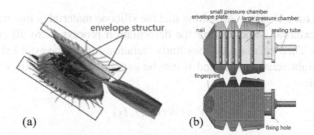

Fig. 1. Bionic design (a) The capture mechanism of the Venus flytrap (b) The structure of fingers.

Gripper Structure Design. Based on the finger structure designed in Fig. 1(c), a three-finger soft robot gripper as shown in Fig. 2 was designed. Including a three-finger handle, clamping part A, clamping part B, pagoda joint, and soft fingers. The three soft fingers are centrally and symmetrically distributed on the three-finger handle. Clamping part A fixes the finger on the three-finger handle through-bolt connection, one end of the pagoda joint is inserted into the soft finger sealing tube, and the pagoda joint is clamped and sealed with the finger through the bolt connection of clamping part B, and another end of the pagoda joint is connected by a hose connect pressure source. The upper part of the three-finger handle can be connected to a robotic arm or an underwater ROV for testing.

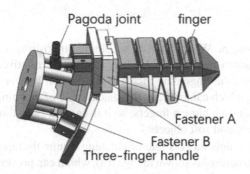

Fig. 2. Assembly drawing of three-finger soft robot hand.

2.2 Finite Element Method

The shape and thickness of the back wall in front of the finger are important parameters that affect the performance of the finger. So the finite element simulation optimization of the finger will be carried out based on these properties. Based on previous studies, silicone material LR3003 was used in this study with a shore hardness of 40A from Wacker, Germany. In this analysis, the Yeoh [21] model under ABAQUS software is used to analyze the constitutive model of the soft gripper. The parameters of the Yeoh model can be measured by uniaxial tensile experiments.

Gripper Structure Design. Assuming that the silicone material is incompressible and isotropic, the external works during the deformation process were all converted into internal energy. Then the material constitutive relationship can be established according to the stress-strain relationship, and it can be expressed as the strain energy density function (W) as:

$$W = W(I_1, I_2, I_3) \tag{1}$$

For incompressible materials, the strain energy density function of the Yeoh model binomial parameter form is:

$$W = C_{10}(I_1 - 3) + C_{20}(I_1 - 3)^2 \tag{2}$$

Which can be transformed into:

$$\frac{\sigma 1}{2\left(\lambda_1 - \frac{1}{\lambda_1^2}\right)} = C_{20}\left[2\left(\lambda_1^2 + \frac{2}{\lambda_1}\right) - 6\right] + C_{10} \tag{3}$$

The test points corresponding to different principal stretching ratios λ_1 and principal stress $\sigma 1$ are obtained through uniaxial tensile experiments, and then the abscissa is $x = 2\left(\lambda_1^2 + \frac{2}{\lambda_1}\right) - 6$, the ordinate is $y = \dfrac{\sigma 1}{2\left(\lambda_1 - \frac{1}{\lambda_1^2}\right)}$, fits the experimental data points to a straight line by using MATLAB software, it can be known that the intercept of the fitted straight line and the slope is C_{10} and C_{20} from formula 3, so we can find two material parameters of the obtained Yeoh model.

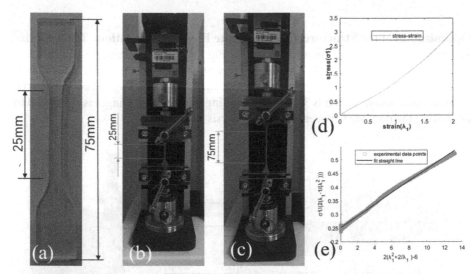

Fig. 3. Tensile test (a) Tensile specimen (b) Initial state (c) End state (d) Stress-strain curve (e) Yeoh model fitting curve

The tensile test of the material was carried out by the national standard "GBT 528-2009 Determination of Tensile Stress-Strain Properties of Vulcanized Rubber or Thermoplastic Rubber". As shown in Fig. 3(a), a type 2 dumbbell-shaped standard style was selected as the silicone sample.

To reduce the random errors, three identical experimental samples were used to conduct the test at the same time in this experiment, and finally, the measured results were averaged. This article only shows the experimental process of the No. 1 sample.

The tensile process of the dumbbell-shaped specimen is shown in Fig. 3(b, c). Figure 3(b) is the initial state of the sample when the elongation is zero, and Fig. 3(c) is the end state of the experiment when the elongation is 50 mm. As shown in Fig. 3(d), the stress-strain curve was fitted according to the experimental data. As shown in Fig. 3(e), the stress-strain data is plotted according to Eq. 3 and regressed to a straight line, the slope of the fitted straight line is C_{20}, and the intercept is C_{10}. According to the data in Table 1, the material constants can be calculated: $C_{10} = 0.2467$, $C_{10} = 0.0212$.

Table 1. Parameter calculation results for three test samples.

	C_{10}	C_{20}
Sample 1	0.2513	0.0215
Sample 2	0.2317	0.0215
Sample 3	0.2571	0.0207
Average value	0.2467	0.0212

Optimization of the Structure Through Finite Element Simulation. The optimized structure diagram of one finger is shown in Fig. 4(a), the parameter p and whether there is an arc structure on the front and rear walls of the finger are the indicators to be optimized. Three analysis points are set on the side of the finger, and the interval between each analysis point is 38 mm, the bending angle φ of the finger is calculated by measuring the distance between the three analysis points.

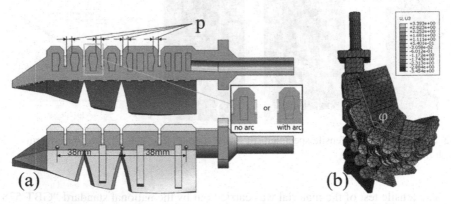

Fig. 4. Finger optimization (a) Finger structure (b) Finite element analysis diagram.

In the process of finger design, the thickness of the front and rear walls of the finger is an important factor affecting the bending angle and mechanical properties of the finger. According to the design requirements, the pressure in the pressure bladder is set successively from 0 Mpa–0.2 Mpa with an interval of 0.02 Mpa. As shown in Fig. 4(b), the finite element simulation analysis is carried out for different wall thicknesses, and by observing the relationship between the pressure and the angle, the optimal wall thickness value required for the design was obtained.

The relationship between the angle φ and the pressure changes when the wall thickness p = 2 mm, p = 3 mm, and p = 4 mm has a circular arc which was analyzed respectively. The analysis results are shown in Fig. 5(a). According to the analysis results, the bending angle of the finger increases with the thickness of the anterior and posterior walls of the pressure capsule. When the wall thickness is 2 mm, the change of the finger angle with the pressure is too large, and when the wall thickness is 4 mm, the change of the finger angle with the pressure is too small. When the wall thickness p = 3 mm, the finger angle changes moderately with the pressure.

According to the analysis results, it can be seen that the increasing speed of the finger angle with the pressure in the case of an arc is greater than that without an arc. Adding an arc structure can effectively reduce the stress concentration and expand the balloon effect of the front and rear walls.

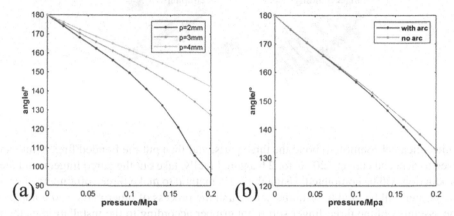

Fig. 5. Simulation results (a) Finite element simulation of the relationship between different wall thickness angles and pressure (b) Influence of arc structure on fingers.

Through the finite element analysis results, it is finally determined that the front and rear wall thickness of the finger pressure chamber is p = 3 mm, and with a circular arc structure.

3 Soft Finger Production and OptiTrack Calibration Experiment

3.1 Soft Finger Production

The soft fingers in this study were made of silicone material LR3003 with a Shore hardness of 40A from Wacker, Germany. According to the material properties, this study was carried out using injection molding. The soft finger is divided into a sealing tube, the upper part of the finger, and the lower part of the finger for injection molding, and then the three parts are bonded. The specific steps are shown in Fig. 6.

First, put components A and B of the silica gel into a vacuum mixer, according to the ratio of 1:1, for full stirring. The vacuum mixer can ensure that there are no bubbles in the mixed silica gel while fully stirring, which can greatly improve the success rate of the finger makes. Then, the stirred silica gel is injected into the finger mold through a glue injector. The finger abrasive tool adopts an aluminum mold processed by a CNC machine tool. The aluminum mold has good thermal conductivity and is not easily deformed by heat, which can ensure the injection molding accuracy and accelerate curing time. After that, the aluminum mold filled with silica gel will be placed in an oven, then heated and cured at 120 °C for 2 h. Then take out the three parts of the cured fingers, using the

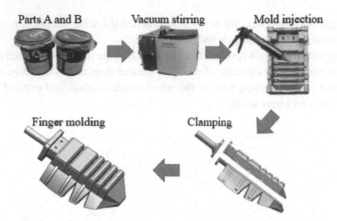

Fig. 6. Preparation process of the soft finger

same silica gel solution to bond the three parts, and then put the bonded fingers into an oven to heat and cure at 120 °C for 2 h again. Finally, take out the cured fingers, and the production will be completed. Using the same method to make three soft fingers, then a 3D printer will be used to print the handle and the process of other parts, and complete the assembly of the three-finger soft robot gripper according to the installation method shown in Fig. 2.

3.2 OptiTrack Calibration Experiment

The OptiTrack motion capture system can accurately capture the motion trajectory of objects through reflective markers, which has great advantages over traditional manual measurement. In this experiment, the measurement of the angle of the soft finger will be completed by the OptiTrack motion capture system as shown in Fig. 7(a).

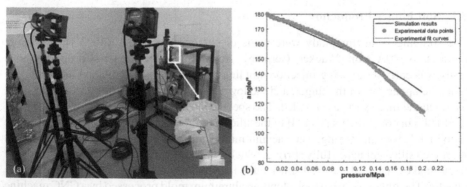

Fig. 7. Finger specification (a) OptiTrack motion capture system (b) Experiment-simulation comparison curve of the finger bending. (Color figure online)

To make the angle measured in the experiment the same as the bending information of the finger represented by the finite element simulation angle, the reflective markers are pasted on the same position of the finite element analysis model corresponding to the actual finger, and the distance was set as 38 mm, and the quantity is three. The bending angle of the finger is calculated from the arc cosine of the coordinates of the three points.

The experimental test results are shown in Fig. 7(b), the blue points are data points obtained from the experiment, and the quadratic fitting curve obtained by MATLAB software fitting is $y = -1232x^2 - 81.54x + 178.5$. The yellow curve is the finite element analysis result curve. Through calculation, the error between the simulation results and the experimental results is very small and within a reasonable range.

The experimental test results show that the finite element simulation can effectively simulate the actual performance of the finger, which can play an important role in predicting the finger structure design process.

4 Grabbing Experiment

The grasping ability of the soft gripper is an important performance. To test the grasping ability of the soft robot gripper, this study carried out the grasping test of the soft robot gripper by simulating an underwater gripping environment. The safety and grasping stability of the soft robot gripper were verified by grasping the marine life models and live sea cucumbers in the simulated experiment environment. The grasping environment and grasping objects are shown in Fig. 8(a).

In the grasping environment shown in Fig. 8(a), the grasped object was picked up from the bottom and hold for 10 s. The pufferfish, octopus, hermit crab, starfish, crab, and live sea cucumber were grasped 20 times respectively. Figure 8(b–m) shows the grasping effects. The grasping results show that the success rate of pufferfish and hermit crab is 100%, octopus, starfish, and crab is 80%, and sea cucumber is 90%. Overall, the high success rate of the grasping shows that the grabbing effect is ideal. Octopus, starfish, and crab failed to grasp four times, the reason for failures was that the shape of the grasping object was relatively flat, and the grasping contact point was too close to the fingertip, which lead to unstable force and slippage. The rest of grasping objects can achieve stable and safe grasping effects in different placement positions. The sea cucumber was inspected after the experiment, and it was found that the sea cucumber was alive and had not been damaged at all, which fully proved the safety of the soft robot gripper.

Fig. 8. Grab experiment.

5 Conclusion

In this paper, a bionic soft robot gripper imitating the Venus flytrap and human fingers was designed, which is suitable for grasping underwater creatures and objects. The soft robot gripper was made of flexible silicone material, which can fit the surface of the grasped object of different shapes without causing damage to it. The soft robot gripper can firmly wrap the grasped object through its enveloping structure, greatly improving the success rate of grasping. Through the coordinated design of large and small pressure chambers, it realized the large bending of the finger near the fingertip under the condition of single pressure input, which produced a small curvature near the base of the finger. The shape and thickness of the front and rear walls of the soft finger are optimized through finite element simulation analysis of Abaqus software. And through the experiment, it is concluded that the average error between the simulation value angle and the experimental angle is very small, which verified the accuracy of the simulation results. The grasping ability and safety of the soft robot gripper were verified by grasping experiments on underwater creature models and living sea cucumbers.

Taking into account the design of the soft robot gripper in this study, it is easy to find that it has a high grasping success rate and safety, which can meet the needs of underwater grasping. In the follow-up research, the finger structure will be further optimized, the soft robot gripper will be assembled, and connected with the underwater robot to realize the field grasping of the ocean.

References

1. Teoh, Z.E., Phillips, B.T., Becker, K.P., et al.: Rotary-actuated folding polyhedrons for mid-water investigation of delicate marine organisms. Sci. Robot. **3**(20) (2018). https://doi.org/10.1126/scirobotics.aat5276
2. Xie, Z.X., Domel, A.G., An, N., et al.: Octopus arm-inspired tapered soft actuators with suckers for improved grasping. Soft Robot. **7**(5), 639–648 (2020)
3. Vogt, D.M., Becker, K.P., Phillips, B.T., et al.: Shipboard design and fabrication of custom 3D-printed soft robotic manipulators for the investigation of delicate deep-sea organisms. PLoS One **13**(8) (2018). https://doi.org/10.1371/journal.pone.0200386
4. Phillips, B.T., Becker, K.P., Kurumaya, S., et al.: A dexterous, glove-based teleoperable low-power soft robotic arm for delicate deep-sea biological exploration. Sci. Rep. **8**(1) (2018). https://doi.org/10.1038/s41598-018-33138-y
5. Aguzzi, J., Costa, C., Calisti, M., et al.: Research trends and future perspectives in marine biomimicking robotics. Sensors **21**(11) (2021). https://doi.org/10.3390/s21113778
6. Chen, Y.Z., Zhang, Q.F., Tian, Q.Y., et al.: Research status of underwater multi-fingered hands. Robot **42**(6), 749–768 (2020)
7. Marvi, H., Gong, C.H., Gravish, N., et al.: Sidewinding with minimal slip: snake and robot ascent of sandy slopes. Science **346**(6206), 224–229 (2014)
8. Zhang, Z., Ni, X.Q., Gao, W.L., et al.: Pneumatically controlled reconfigurable bistable bionic flower for robotic gripper. Soft Robot. (2021). https://doi.org/10.1089/soro.2020.0200
9. Galloway, K.C., Becker, K.P., Phillips, B., et al.: Soft robotic grippers for biological sampling on deep reefs. Soft Robot. **3**(1), 23–33 (2016)
10. Mosadegh, B., Polygerinos, P., Keplinger, C., et al.: Pneumatic networks for soft robotics that actuate rapidly. Adv. Funct. Mater. **24**(15), 2163–2170 (2014)
11. Kurumaya, S., Phillips, B.T., Becker, K.P., et al.: A modular soft robotic wrist for underwater manipulation. Soft Robot. **5**(4), 399–409 (2018)
12. Luo, S.J., Wang, S., Cheng, G.G., et al.: Designing, manufacturing and controlling of the elastic materials based bionic hand. J. Mech. Eng. **55**(11), 69–75 (2019)
13. Terryn, S., Brancart, J., Lefeber, D., et al.: Self-healing soft pneumatic robots. Sci. Robot. **2**(9) (2017). https://doi.org/10.1126/scirobotics.aan4268
14. Nasab, A.M., Sabzehzar, A., Tatari, M., et al.: A soft gripper with rigidity tunable elastomer strips as ligaments. Soft Robot. **4**(4), 411–420 (2017)
15. Feng, N., Shi, Q., Wang, H., et al.: A soft robotic hand: design, analysis, sEMG, control, and experiment. Int. J. Adv. Manuf. Technol. **97**(1–4), 319–333 (2018). https://doi.org/10.1007/s00170-018-1949-2
16. Sinatra, N.R., Teeple, C.B., Vogt, D.M., et al.: Ultragentle manipulation of delicate structures using a soft robotic gripper. Sci. Robot. **4**(33) (2019). https://doi.org/10.1126/scirobotics.aax5425
17. Dong, H., Wang, B.X., Li, W., et al.: The deformation mechanism of soft hand based on one-way pneumatic actuator. J. Donghua Univ. **46**(2), 288–296 (2020)
18. Liu, W.H., Hu, J., Wang, W.M.: Soft gripper grasping based on complete grasp configuration and multi-stage network. J. Shanghai Jiaotong Univ. **54**(5), 507–514 (2020). https://doi.org/10.16183/j.cnki.jsjtu.2020.05.008
19. Wu, Z.P., Li, X.N.: Grasping strategy of a soft gripper with endoskeleton structure. Chin. Hydraul. Pneumatics **45**(4), 61–68 (2021)

20. Subramaniam, V., Jain, S., Agarwal, J., et al.: Design and characterization of a hybrid soft gripper with active palm pose control. Int. J. Robot. Res. **39**(14), 1668–1685 (2020)
21. Huang, J.L., Xie, G.J., Liu, Z.W.: FEA of hyperelastic rubber material based on Mooney-Rivlin model and Yeoh model. China Rubber Ind. **55**(8), 467–471 (2008)

Research on Formation Obstacle Avoidance Algorithm of Multiple AUVs Based on Interfered Fluid Dynamical System

Wen Pang[1], Daqi Zhu[2(✉)], and Linling Wang[1]

[1] Logistics Engineering College, Shanghai Maritime University,
Shanghai 201306, China
[2] School of Mechanical Engineering, University of Shanghai for Science
and Technology, Shanghai 200093, China
zdq367@aliyun.com

Abstract. This paper focuses on planning a two-dimensional (2-D) obstacle avoidance path for the formation of autonomous underwater vehicles (AUVs) in an ocean environment with complicated static obstacles. Inspired by the natural phenomenon of a flowing stream avoiding obstacles, a novel strategy based on an interfered fluid dynamical system (IFDS) is designed. In view of the particular features of the ocean environment, the obstacles are modeled first. Then, by imitating the phenomenon of fluid flow, the IFDS method is used to quickly plan a smooth and safe path for formation AUVs, which conforms to the general characteristic of the phenomenon that running water can avoid rock and arrive at its destination. Finally, formation control is achieved using rigid graph theory. The planned route serves as a known virtual AUV to the leader AUV. The simulation results show that this method has the characteristics of curve continuity and smoothness, enhances obstacle avoidance effects, and has good performance in obstacle avoidance in 2-D path planning.

Keywords: Multi-AUV systems · Formation control · Obstacle avoidance · Interfered fluid dynamical system (IFDS)

1 Introduction

The developments in the technology of autonomous underwater vehicles (AUVs) make AUVs play a more and more important role in the exploration of marine resources. An AUV can complete a variety of subsea tasks in civil and military fields, such as ocean pollutant monitoring, mine hunting, marine biology exploration, pipeline following and inspection, and anti-submarine warfare, etc.

This work was supported by the Shanghai Science and Technology Innovation Funds under Grant 20510712300 and Grant 21DZ2293500.

H. Liu et al. (Eds.): ICIRA 2022, LNAI 13457, pp. 323–334, 2022.
https://doi.org/10.1007/978-3-031-13835-5_29

[1–4]. When carrying out large and complicated missions, compared with a single AUV, a multi-AUV system has received widespread attention from academia and industry due to its good reliability, efficiency, flexibility, scalability, and fault tolerance. One of the main concerns in the discussion of multi-AUV systems is formation control. Research on AUV formation control is attracting more and more researchers attention [5]. While navigating in formation, the AUVs may encounter hazards that endanger their safety, such as undulating terrain, currents, enemy torpedoes, and so on, and it is necessary to avoid these hazards. So, how to make multi-AUV maintain good formation and avoid obstacles simultaneously is still under exploration [6].

A variety of research has been conducted in the past few decades, concentrating on the path planning framework. According to the path-planning problem of obstacle avoidance, the current methods can be summarized into the following seven kinds: (1) Graphical based method [7], e.g. Voronoi Map, vector field histogram; (2) sampling based methods [8], e.g. Rapidly Random-Trees (RRT), Probabilistic RoadMap (PRM); (3) heuristic search based method [9], e.g. A* method or Dijkstra method; (4) optimization based method [10], e.g. mixed integer linear programming (MILP), intelligent algorithms (e.g. Particle Swarm Optimization (PSO), genetic algorithm (GA) and gravitational search algorithm (GSA), etc.); (5) reinforcement learning; (6) model predictive control (MPC) methods; (7) potential field based method [11], e.g. Virtual Force (VF), stream function and Artificial Potential Field (APF). These methods can be applied to 2-dimensional (2D) path planning as well. Most of the abovementioned obstacle avoidance algorithms basically have some kind of shortcomings. They only consider the obstacle avoidance mechanism and do not plan the obstacle avoidance path effectively. In contrast, due to their simple structure, APF methods have good real-time performance and are widely used in practice. Nevertheless, this type of method still has the following non-negligible drawbacks: When an agent is located in a narrow gallery or in a position near an obstacle, the planned path of the agent can easily cause oscillation, resulting in an unsmooth path. Moreover, the problems of the trap area and the local minimum caused by APF methods are also incompatible with obstacle avoidance.

To overcome the drawbacks of the abovementioned obstacle avoidance methodologies, in recent years, inspired by the phenomenon that water in rivers avoids rocks smoothly and ultimately reaches its destination, a series of novel fluid-based methodologies for real-time path planning and obstacle avoidance have been proposed in complex obstacle environments. Wang et al. [12] proposed a path planning algorithm based on an interfered fluid dynamical system (IFDS), which is applied to unmanned aerial vehicle (UAV) path planning. Stream-function based obstacle avoidance algorithms have been introduced in the field of path planning. Compared with the traditional APF, IFDS has a small amount of calculation, and at the same time, it can avoid the problem that the controlled object is easy to fall into a local minimum.

In this paper, a new obstacle avoidance method based on IFDS is designed, which provides a safe and flyable route matching the formation width for the swarm in the area with obstacles, and the planned route as a virtual AUV is taken as the known information to the leader AUV to realize the overall obstacle avoidance. Overall, the main contributions can be divided into several parts as follows: 1) The AUV kinematic constraints and model are introduced to the traditional IFDS on the basis of the formation control strategy, which can generate feasible paths and control inputs for AUVs. Our scenario is that the movement of the leader AUV is tracking the planed path, and the follower AUVs are following the position of the leader AUV to achieve formation and obstacle avoidance. 2) For the obstacle avoidance aspect, the characteristics of the fluid methodology are considered and a novel formation obstacle avoidance strategy is proposed to achieve AUV formation obstacle avoidance as a hole framework for the first time. The proposed fluid-based framework can balance obstacle avoidance and formation maintenance. The results showed that multi AUVs can maintain the desired formation around ground vehicles and avoid obstacles at the same time in a complex environment.

2   Preliminaries

2.1   Modeling the AUVs Dynamics

In this paper, the formation obstacle avoidance for a fleet of AUVs is considered. For the motion description of the AUV, we define an earth-fixed inertial frame $\{E\} := \{X_E, Y_E, Z_E\}$ and a body-fixed frame $\{B\} := \{X_B, Y_B, Z_B\}$ as shown in Fig. 1. The moving frame $\{B\}$ is attached to the ith AUV and the X_i-axis aligned with its heading direction, the angle φ_i describes the orientation of the AUV. Assume that the AUV's center of mass c_i is coincident with its center of rotation. Neglecting the motions in heave, roll, and pitch, a three degree-of-freedom (DOF) dynamic model for the ith AUV in horizontal plane is described in [13], and consists of kinematic and dynamic:

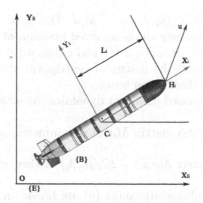

Fig. 1. Schematic model of AUV.

$$\begin{cases} \dot{x}_{ci} = v_i cos\varphi_i \\ \dot{y}_{ci} = v_i sin\varphi_i \\ \dot{\varphi}_i = w_i \end{cases} \tag{1a}$$

$$\bar{M}_i \dot{\eta}_i + \bar{D}_i \eta_i = \bar{\tau}_i \tag{1b}$$

where, $p_{ci} = (x_{ci}, y_{ci}) \in R^2$ denotes the position, and φ_i represents the heading angle of the ith AUV in the $\{E\}$ frame. $\eta_i = (v_i, w_i) \in R^2$ is the velocities of the AUV (surge velocity: v_i, and yaw velocity: w_i). $\bar{M}_i = diag(m_i, I_i)$, m_i denotes AUV mass and I_i represents the moment of inertia about the vertical axis. $\bar{D}_i \in R^{2\times2}$ indicates the constant damping matrix, $\bar{\tau}_i = (F_i, T_i) \in R^2$ denotes the control signal (surge force: F_i, and yaw moment: T_i).

Motivated by the ideas developed in [14], by considering the nonholonomic constraint $\dot{x}_{ci} sin\varphi_i - \dot{y}_{ci} cos\varphi_i = 0$ the head point H_i position $p_i = (x_i, y_i)$ can be utilized instead of the center point $p_{ci} = (x_{ci}, y_{ci})$. Consequently, it follows that:

$$p_i = [x_i \ y_i]^T = [x_{ci} + L_i cos\varphi_i \ y_{ci} + L_i sin\varphi_i] \tag{2}$$

where L_i denotes the distance between the head position and the AUV center. Furthermore, one has:

$$\dot{p}_i = [\dot{x}_i \ \dot{y}_i]^T = [u_{xi} \ u_{yi}] \tag{3}$$

with

$$\eta_i = \begin{bmatrix} v_i \\ w_i \end{bmatrix} = \begin{bmatrix} cos\varphi_i & sin\varphi_i \\ -(sin\varphi_i)/L_i & (cos\varphi_i)/L_i \end{bmatrix} \begin{bmatrix} u_{xi} \\ u_{yi} \end{bmatrix} = J(\varphi_i)p_i \tag{4}$$

Taking the time derivative of (4) and premultiplying the equation using the matrix $\bar{M}_i$, using (1b), we obtain:

$$\bar{\tau}_i - \bar{D}_i J(\varphi_i)\dot{p}_i = \bar{M}_i \dot{J}(\varphi_i)\dot{p}_i + \bar{M}_i J(\varphi_i)\ddot{p}_i \tag{5}$$

Then premultiplying (5) by $J^T(\varphi_i)$, we have equation:

$$M_i(p_i)\ddot{p}_i + C_i(p_i, \dot{p}_i)\dot{p}_i + D_i(p_i)\dot{p}_i = \tau_i \tag{6}$$

where $M_i(p_i) = J^T \bar{M}_i J$, $C_i(p_i, \dot{p}_i) = J^T \bar{M}_i \dot{J}$, $D_i(p_i) = J^T \bar{D}_i J$, $\tau_i = J^T \bar{\tau}_i$. In this model, $P_i \in R^2$ represents the generalized position of the ith AUV, $\tau_i \in R^2$ denotes the control force. $M_i(p_i) \in R^{2\times2}$ and $C_i(p_i, \dot{p}_i) \in R^{2\times2}$ are the positive-definite inertia matrix and the matrix of centripetal and Coriolis torque, and $D_i(p_i) \in R^{2\times2}$ involves the friction terms.

Note that the transformed nonlinear dynamics (6) satisfy the following properties [15].

Property 1: The inertia matrix $M_i(p_i)$ is symmetric and uniformly positive definite.

Property 2: The matrix $\dot{M}_i(p_i) - 2C_i(p_i, \dot{p}_i)$ is skew symmetric and for any μ.

Property 3: The nonlinear dynamics (6) are linear on a dynamic parameter vector α_i:

$$M_i(p_i)\dot{\mu}_i + C_i(p_i, \dot{p}_i)\mu + D_i(p_i)\dot{p}_i = Y_i(p_i, \dot{p}_i, \mu, \dot{\mu})\alpha_i \tag{7}$$

$\forall \mu \in R^2$ where μ is the derivative of p from (6), $Y_i \in R^{2\times 6}$ is a known regression matrix, and is a proper parameter vector, describe the manipulators mass property, and can be defined as:

$$\alpha_i = (m_i, I_i/L_i^2, [D_i]_{11}, [D_i]_{12}/L_i^2, [D_i]_{21}/L_i, [D_i]_{22}/L_i^2) \qquad (8)$$

where $[\cdot]_{ij}$ denotes the ijth component of the matrix.

2.2 Algebraic Graph Theory

A formation of n AUVs can be represented by an undirected graph $G = (V, E)$, where $V = \{1, 2, ..., n\}$ is the node set that represents the AUVs and $E \subseteq V \times V$ is the edge set that represents the communication links between the AUVs. If node i can send information to node j, the edge (i, j) is said to exist, i.e., $(i, j) \in E$, then i and j are called to be adjacent. The topology of an inter AUV network can be modeled with an adjacency matrix $A = [a_{ij}]$, where a_{ij} represents a direct connection between a pair of AUVs. The element $a_{ij} = 1$, if there exists an edge between vertices (AUVs) i and j; otherwise $a_{ij} = 0$. The neighbours of a node are those nodes it can receive information from, the set of neighbours of a node is denoted by $N_i = \{j \in V : (i, j) \in E\}$. The number of edges l is given by $l = \{1, 2, ..., n(n-1)/2\}$, respectively [16]. Given an arbitrary ordering of the edges of G, an edge function $f_G : R^{2n} \in R^l$ associated with (G, p) is given by:

$$f_G(p) = (..., \|p_i - p_j\|^2, ...), (i, j) \in E \qquad (9)$$

where $\|\cdot\|$ denotes the Euclidean norm. The rigidity matrix $R(p) : R^{2n} \to R^{l \times 2n}$ of (G, p) is defined as:

$$R(p) = \frac{1}{2}\frac{\partial f_G(p)}{\partial p} \qquad (10)$$

3 Obstacle Avoidance Design

3.1 Environment Modeling

In this article, the formation AUV navigates at a constant depth, so we can build a 2-D obstacle environment. The positions of the virtual leader AUV can be denoted as $p_v = (x_v, y_v)$. In practical tasks, the obstacles encountered during navigation are irregular. In order to reduce the complexity of the obstacle environment, the obstacles can be enveloped by standard convex polygons. Suppose there are K obstacles in the planning plane. After pretreatment, any obstacle is described as a standard convex polygon, such as a circle or a rectangle [17]. It is shown as follows:

$$\Gamma(p_v) = (\frac{x_v - x_{obs}}{a})^{2q} + (\frac{y_v - y_{obs}}{a})^{2r} \qquad (11)$$

where a, b and q, r are the size and shape parameters respectively, among them, a, b are constants greater than 0, q, r are constants greater than or equal to 1. $p_{obs} = (x_{obs}, y_{obs})$ is the center of obstacle. $\Gamma(p_v) > 1$ refers to the space outside the obstacle; $\Gamma(p_v) = 1$ means that is on the surface of obstacle; $\Gamma(p_v) < 1$ refers to the space in the internal of obstacle.

3.2 Obstacle Avoidance Based on IFDS

When no obstacle exists in the navigation environment, the AUV should navigate in a straight line from the current position to the goal. Suppose that $p_g = (x_g, y_g)$ is the goal position and the cruising speed of the AUV is a constant, the distance between the virtual leader AUV and the goal is $d(p_v, p_g) = \sqrt{(x_v - x_g)^2 + (y_v - y_g)^2}$, then the original expected fluid velocity in 2-D inertial frame can be described as:

$$V(p_v) = -\left(\frac{C(x_v - x_g)}{d(p_v, p_g)} \quad \frac{C(y_v - y_g)}{d(p_v, p_g)} \right) \tag{12}$$

When there are obstacles in the navigation environment. The effect of the obstacles on the original fluid speed can be described by the total interfered modulation matrix M:

$$\bar{M}(p_v) = \sum_{k=1}^{K} \omega_k(p_v) M_k(p_v) \tag{13}$$

where $\omega_k(p_v)$ indicates the weight coefficient of the kth obstacle, and the value mainly depends on the distance between the virtual leader AUV and the surface of the obstacle. Generally, the larger the distance is, the smaller the weight coefficient is, i.e., the smaller the disturbance of the obstacle on the initial vector field is. $\omega_k(p_v)$ is expressed as follows:

$$\omega_k(p_v) = \begin{cases} 1, & \text{if } K = 1 \\ \prod_{i=1, i \neq k}^{K} \frac{(\Gamma_i - 1)}{(\Gamma_i - 1) + (\Gamma_k - 1)}, & \text{if } K \neq 1 \end{cases} \tag{14}$$

where Γ_i, Γ_k is the obstacle equation, see the formula (13). Because of $\omega_{sum} = \sum_{k=1}^{K} \omega_k < 1$, it need to be normalized as $\omega_k = \omega_k / \omega_{sum}$. M_k is the interfered modulation matrix of the kth obstacle, and M_k is defined as follows:

$$M_k(p_v) = I - \frac{n_k n_k^T}{\Gamma_k^{1/\rho_k} n_k^T n_k} \tag{15}$$

where I is a second-order unit matrix. ρ_k is the reaction coefficient related to the perturbation matrix closely. n_k is the radial normal vector, which is the partial derivative vector of the obstacle function and perpendicular to the surface of the obstacle. It can be expressed as follows:

$$n_k = \left[\frac{\partial \Gamma_k}{\partial x} \quad \frac{\partial \Gamma_k}{\partial y} \right]^T \tag{16}$$

Then the initial flow field $V(p_v)$ can be calculated by the perturbation matrix to obtain the disturbance flow field:

$$\bar{V}(p_v) = \bar{M}(p_v) V(p_v) \tag{17}$$

Figure 2(a) illustrates the original flow from a series of start points to the only goal point $(0,0)$. In Fig. 2(b), four circle obstacles is constructed, and the effect on original flow is illustrated. It can be seen that the modified streamlines will avoid the obstacles smoothly, follow the shape of obstacles effectively and reach the destination eventually. Finally, waypoint along time can be computed by integrating $\bar{V}(p_v)$ recursively:

$$\{p_v\}_{t+1} = \{p_v\}_t + \bar{V}(p_v)\Delta t \tag{18}$$

where Δt is the iteration time step. The cycle of the above steps, can get all the way points in turn, the smaller the calculation step size, the smoother the route. Eventually we can obtain all the planned waypoints, forming the modified streamline i.e. the planned route, as show in Fig ?(c)

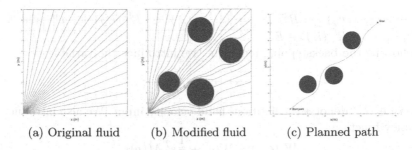

(a) Original fluid   (b) Modified fluid   (c) Planned path

Fig. 2. Modification of flow.

4   Obstacle Avoidance Design

We begin by rewriting (6) as:

$$\dot{p} = v_i \tag{19a}$$

$$M_i(p_i)\dot{v}_i = \tau_i - C_i(p_i, v_i)v_i - D_i(p_i)v_i \tag{19b}$$

where $v_i \in R^2$ represents the AUV's hand velocity relative to the {E} frame. Define the relative position of two AUVs in the formation as:

$$\tilde{p}_{ij} = p_i - p_j, \ (i,j) \in E^* \tag{20}$$

The distance error for the group of n AUVs and the corresponding distance error dynamics are given by:

$$e_{ij} = \|\tilde{p}_{ij}\| - d_{ij}(t), (i,j) \in E^* \tag{21}$$

$$\dot{e}_{ij} = (\tilde{p}_{ij}^T \tilde{p}_{ij})^{-\frac{1}{2}} \tilde{p}_{ij}^T (v_i - v_j) - \dot{d}_{ij} = \frac{\tilde{p}_{ij}^T(v_i - v_j)}{e_{ij} + d_{ij}} - \dot{d}_{ij} \tag{22}$$

Define a term $z_{ij} = \|\tilde{p}_{ij}\|^2 - d_{ij}^2 = e_{ij}(\|\tilde{p}_{ij}\|^2 + d_{ij}) = e_{ij}(e_{ij} + 2d_{ij}), (i,j) \in E^*$, with which the Lyapunov function for the first iteration of backstepping is defined as:

$$W_{ij} = \frac{1}{4}z_{ij}^2 \tag{23}$$

We now define the following Lyapunov function for all the edges:

$$W_{(e)} = \sum_{(i,j) \in E^*} W_{ij}(e_{ij}) \tag{24}$$

where $W_{(e)} = \sum_{(i,j) \in E^*} W_{ij}(e_{ij})$. The time derivative of (24) is given by:

$$\dot{W} = \sum_{(i,j) \in E^*} e_{ij}(e_{ij} + 2d_{ij})[\tilde{p}_{ij}^T(v_i - v_j) - d_{ij}\dot{d}_{ij}] = z^T(R(p)v - d_v) \tag{25}$$

$v = (v_1, v_2, ..., v_n) \in R^{2n}$, $z = (..., z_{ij}, ...) \in R^l, (i,j) \in E^*$ and $d_v = (..., d_{ij}\dot{d}_{ij}, ...) \in R^l, (i,j) \in E^*$.

Following the backstepping technique, we introduce the variable:

$$s = v - v_d \tag{26}$$

where $v_d \in R^{2n}$ denotes the fictitious hand velocity input. We also introduce the Lyapunov function:

$$W_v(e, s) = W(e) + \frac{1}{2}s^T M(p)s \tag{27}$$

where $M(p) = diag(M_1(p_1), M_2(p_2), ..., M_n(p_n))$. After taking the time derivative of (27), we obtain:

$$\dot{W}_v = z^T(R(p)v - d_v) + \frac{1}{2}s^T \dot{M}(p)s + s^T M(p)\dot{s} = z^T(R(p)v_d - d_v) \\ + s^T[\tau - Y(p, \dot{p}, v_d, \dot{v}_d)\alpha + R^T(p)z] \tag{28}$$

where $Y(p, \dot{p}, v_d, \dot{v}_d) = diag(Y_1(p_1, \dot{p}_1, v_{d1}, \dot{v}_{d1}), Y_2(p_2, \dot{p}_2, v_{d2}, \dot{v}_{d2}), ..., Y_n(p_n, \dot{p}_n, v_{dn}, \dot{v}_{dn}))$, to form the estimation control law using adaptive backstepping, the Lyapunov function is modified as:

$$W_\alpha(e, s, \tilde{\alpha}) = W_v(e, s) + \frac{1}{2}\tilde{\alpha}^T \Gamma^{-1}\tilde{\alpha} \tag{29}$$

where $\Gamma \in R^{6n \times 6n}$ is a diagonal, constant, and positive definite matrix. Assuming $\dot{\alpha} = 0$, the time derivative of W_α is:

$$\dot{W}_\alpha = \dot{W}_v + \tilde{\alpha}^T \Gamma^{-1}\dot{\tilde{\alpha}} = z^T(R(p)v_d - d_v) + s^T[\tau - Y(p, \dot{p}, v_d, \dot{v}_d)(\hat{\alpha} - \tilde{\alpha}) \\ + R^T(p)z] + \tilde{\alpha}^T \Gamma^{-1}\dot{\hat{\alpha}} \\ = z^T(R(p)v_d - d_v) + s^T[\tau - Y(p, \dot{p}, v_d, \dot{v}_d)\hat{\alpha} + R^T(p)z] \\ + \tilde{\alpha}^T \Gamma^{-1}(\dot{\hat{\alpha}} + \Gamma Y^T s) \tag{30}$$

The proposed control law for making $\dot{W}_\alpha$ negative definite is:

$$\tau = -k_a s + Y(p, \dot{p}, v_d, \dot{v}_d)\hat{\alpha} - R^T(p)z \tag{31a}$$

$$v_d = R^+(p)(-k_v z + d_v) + (1_n \otimes \bar{V}(p)) \tag{31b}$$

$$\dot{\hat{\alpha}} = -\Gamma Y^T(p, \dot{p}, v_d, \dot{v}_d)s \tag{31c}$$

where k_a and k_v are positive constants and $R^+(p) = R^T(p)[R(p)R(p)^T]^{-1}$ is the Moore-Penrose Pseudo inverse of $R(p)$.

5 Simulation Results Analysis

A numerical simulation example for identifying the effectiveness of the proposed formation obstacle avoidance control approach is given. The AUV parameters are choose as in [18], and $L_i = 0.5m$ for $i = 1, 2, ..., 7$. The simulation consisted of applying control law (13) to (33) using the fact that $\bar{\tau}_i = J_i^{-1}\tau_i$. The desired formation is the regular convex hexagon. The initial position of the ith AUV $p_i(0)$ is randomly chosen as a perturbation about p_i^*, while its initial orientation $\varphi_i(0)$ is randomly set to a value between 0 and 2π. The initial position of each AUV's mass center (x_{ci}, y_{ci}) is then obtained from (2). The initial translational and angular speed of each AUV is set to $v_i(0) = [0, -0.15, 0.45, -0.35, 0.35, 0.5, -0.25]$ m/s and $\dot{\varphi}_i(0) = [0.1, -0.1, -0.3, 0.4, 0.05, -0.05, 0.2]$ rad/s, respectively. The initial conditions for the parameter estimates are $\hat{\alpha}(0) = 0$. The control and adaptation gains are set to $k_v = 1$, $k_a = 2$.

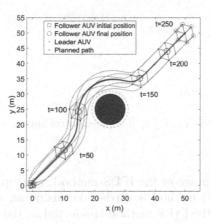

Fig. 3. Obstacle avoidance trajectories of formation AUVs in single obstacle environment.

There are seven AUVs move on the 2-D plane which have three obstacles, the initial positions of obstacle are $p_{obs1} = (16, 26)$, $p_{obs2} = (28, 12)$, $p_{obs3} = (35, 40)$

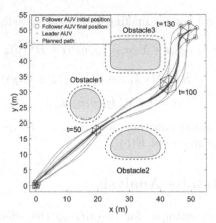

Fig. 4. Obstacle avoidance trajectories of formation AUVs in multiple obstacles environment.

and the goal point set as $p_g = (50, 50)$. The final simulation status of the formation AUVs is shown in Figs. 3, 4, 5 and 6. Figure 3 shows the formation obstacle trajectories of the AUVs when maneuvering in single obstacle environment, while Fig. 4 shows the trajectories in multiple obstacles environment. Under multiple obstacles environment, from Fig. 5(a) one can find that the distance errors $e_{ij}, i, j \in V^*$ between any two of AUVs approaching zero or a constant. The control inputs of each AUV are shown in Fig. 5(b).

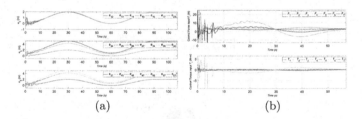

(a)   (b)

Fig. 5. (a) Distance errors $e_{ij}, i, j \in V^*$, (b) Control inputs forces $F_i(t)$ and torques $T_i(t)$.

To verify the advantage of the IFDS method, a comparative item with the improved APF (IAPF) method is carried out using an AUV with one obstacle. The reasons why the IAPF method is selected as the comparative item are illustrated as follows. First, both of the proposed fluid-based method and the IAPF method belong to the potential-based path planning methodology. There are many similar concepts in these two methods, such as the attractive fields and repulsive fields. Therefore, these two methods have the comparability. Second, the IAPF method is one of the most widely used path planning methods. The comparative results can be more persuasive if it is selected as the comparative item. The paths by two methods are shown in Fig. 6. Intuitively, there is a poly-line in the path by IAPF, which AUV formation cannot track. Comparatively speaking, the path of IFDS method is smoother. On the other hand, in terms of path length, the length of improved IAPF is also longer, $L_{IFDS} = 76.2737$, $L_{IAPF} = 84.4336$.

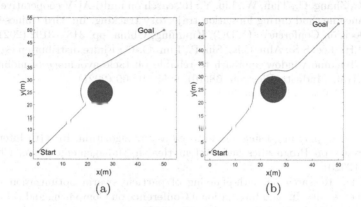

(a)   (b)

Fig. 6. Comparison of obstacle avoidance paths of IFDS and IAPF with single obstacle. (a) IFDS, (b) IAPF

6   Conclusion

This paper focuses on the obstacle avoidance of formation AUVs in a 2-D static complex environment based on interfered fluid and graph rigidity. And this proposed hybrid method has the advantage of being simple in principle, high computational efficiency, and strong practicality. The method can plan a smooth obstacle avoidance path in the case of single and multiple obstacles, which not only satisfies the maneuverability constraints of AUVs, but also has the natural characteristics of flow around obstacles. The relevant simulations have demonstrated that the planned route can guide the AUVs to maintain the formation and avoid obstacles at the same time. In this paper, obstacles are static and well known. Future work will take into account the formation obstacle avoidance problem under uncertain terrain or threat and extend it to 3-D space.

References

1. Wei, H., Shen, C., Shi, Y.: Distributed Lyapunov-based model predictive formation tracking control for autonomous underwater vehicles subject to disturbances. IEEE Trans. Syst. Man Cybern. Syst. **51**(8), 5198–5208 (2021)
2. Li, X.: An adaptive SOM neural network method for distributed formation control of a group of AUVs. IEEE Trans. Ind. Electron. **65**(10), 8260–8270 (2018)
3. Yuan, C.: Formation learning control of multiple autonomous underwater vehicles with heterogeneous nonlinear uncertain dynamics. IEEE Trans. Cybern. **48**(10), 2920–2934 (2018)

4. Suryendu, C., Subudhi, B.: Formation control of multiple autonomous underwater vehicles under communication delays. IEEE Trans. Circuits Syst. II Express Br. **67**(12), 3182–3186 (2020)
5. Yang, Y.: A survey of autonomous underwater vehicle formation: performance, formation control, and communication capability. IEEE Commun. Surv. Tutor. **23**(2), 815–841 (2021)
6. Yan, Z., Zhang, C., Tian, W., Liu, Y.: Research on multi-AUV cooperative obstacle avoidance method during formation trajectory tracking. In: 33rd Chinese Control and Decision Conference (CCDC), Kunming, China, pp. 3187–3192 (2021)
7. Lee, D.H., Lee, S.S., Ahn, C.K., Shi, P., Lim, C.-C.: Finite distribution estimation-based dynamic window approach to reliable obstacle avoidance of mobile robot. IEEE Trans. Industr. Electron. **68**(10), 9998–10006 (2021)
8. Chen, L.: A fast and efficient double-tree RRT?-Like sampling-based planner applying on mobile robotic systems. IEEE/ASME Trans. Mechatron. **23**(6), 2568–2578 (2018)
9. Ju, C.: Path planning using an improved a-star algorithm. In: 11th International Conference on Prognostics and System Health Management, Jinan, China, pp. 23–26 (2020)
10. Yuan, D.: Research on path-planning of particle swarm optimization based on distance penalty. In: 2nd International Conference on Computing and Data Science (CDS), Stanford, CA, USA, pp. 149–153 (2021)
11. Wang, Y.: Formation control of multi-UAV with collision avoidance using artificial potential field. In: 11th International Conference on Intelligent Human-Machine Systems and Cybernetics (IHMSC), Hangzhou, China, pp. 296–300 (2019)
12. Wang, H.: Three-dimensional path planning for unmanned aerial vehicle based on interfered fluid dynamical system. Chin. J. Aeronaut. **28**(1), 229–239 (2015)
13. Wang, J.: Neuroadaptive sliding mode formation control of autonomous underwater vehicles with uncertain dynamics. IEEE Syst. J. **14**(3), 3325–3333 (2020)
14. Paliotta, C.: Trajectory tracking of under-actuated marine vehicles. In: 55th Conference on Decision and Control (CDC), Las Vegas, NV, USA, pp. 5660–5667 (2016)
15. Cai, X.: Adaptive rigidity-based formation control for multirobotic vehicles with dynamics. IEEE Trans. Control Syst. Technol. **23**(1), 389–396 (2015)
16. Asimow, L.: The rigidity of graphs, II. J. Math. Anal. Appl. **68**(1), 171–190 (1979)
17. Wei, X.: Comprehensive optimization of energy storage and standoff tracking for solar-powered UAV. IEEE Syst. J. **14**(4), 5133–5143 (2020)
18. Gao, Z.: Adaptive formation control of autonomous underwater vehicles with model uncertainties. Int. J. Adapt. Control Signal Process. **32**(7), 1067–1080 (2018)

Research on Thermage Robot System Based on Constant Force Control

Fengyi Liu(✉) and Chengtao Yue

Shanghai Robot Industrial Technology Research Institute, Shanghai 200063, China
liufy@seari.com.cn

Abstract. Nowadays more and more people pay attention to the medical cosmetology industry. This paper presents a study of thermage robot system. In the first, a thermage robot system via hardware design and software design was built. Then, hand-eye calibration, visual recognition and localization, constant force control algorithm were applied to the system. Finally, the experiments based on facial model and human face were carried out, and the feasibility of the proposed thermage robot system was validated effectively.

Keywords: Thermage robot system · Hand-eye calibration · Visual recognition and localization · Constant force control

1 Introduction

Thermage is a technology that transforms electric energy into heat energy through electromagnetic waves in order to tighten and improve skin tissue [1–7]. Skin and subcutaneous tissue will produce resistance when the radiofrequency current acts on the human body, making the water molecules in the tissue vibrate to produce heat, and the heat generated can destroy cells and shrink the skin after acting on the target tissue. Due to the impedance principle, radiofrequency can reach deeper skin tissues than laser, namely the dermis and superficial fascia layers. Specifically, in radiofrequency, tridimensional heating combined with impedance properties of different tissues allows selective targeting of collagen-rich skin tissue, resulting in immediate shrinkage and denaturation of collagen fibers. At the same time, fibroblasts are activated to produce new collagen fibers and elastic fibers, and the reconstruction of collagen fiber bundles and production of new collagen will continue for several months. On the basis of the above principle, radiofrequency improves skin elasticity of face and neck, and even has a slight fat-melting effect. A course of radiofrequency treatment can usually maintain rejuvenation of the face for more than a year. Many people prefer radiofrequency treatment to surgery on account of no recovery period, no scars and fewer side effects.

In this study, an overall conceptual design with hardware and software design was proposed firstly. In the second, a constant force control algorithm was presented. To verify the validity of the proposed algorithm, we have carried out the experiments based on thermage robot system. And the effectiveness of the proposed method was validated.

H. Liu et al. (Eds.): ICIRA 2022, LNAI 13457, pp. 335–344, 2022.
https://doi.org/10.1007/978-3-031-13835-5_30

2 Overall Conceptual Design

Thermage requires professional physicians to operate personally. In the process of operation, physicians need to repeat the operation of dotting in the grid with high precision, which will cause fatigue during lengthy operation, resulting in the problems of positioning accuracy and strength deviation. Therefore, a thermage robot is indispensable to the 3D modeling of customer's face, grid positioning, path planning and correction. At the same time, it is required that it can track to the desired position accurately, and the precision control is mainly reflected in the position accuracy and track accuracy of the robot. Finally, it is required to ensure the safety of the thermage robot system during operation to avoid medical accidents.

2.1 Technical Proposal

3D modeling technology is adopted to automatic facial modeling in the robot design. The recognition and location of grids to be dotted are carried out by positioning technology of profiled surface. Adaptive path planning technology is used for dotting path planning of the robot. Visual inspection technology is applied for dot detection. The expert decision system is used to deal with common operation failures of robot system. The above technologies are integrated to realize the automatic dotting function of the thermage robot.

The thermage robot system is composed of manipulator (including gripper), 3D camera, screen monitoring camera, all-in-one system of operation, system software, monitoring unit of posture and face temperature, etc. Figure 1 shows a system architecture diagram.

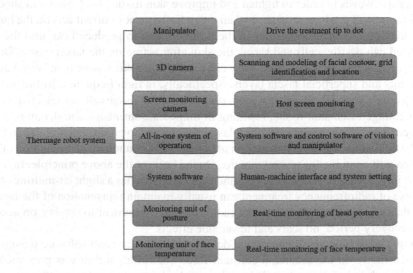

Fig. 1. System architecture of the researched thermage robot system

2.2 Hardware Design

Structure of Basis. The manipulator frame is used for the positioning of the manipulator, control cabinet and visual components. It has the following requirements:

(a) Easy to move and position fixed, casters with brakes or horizontal adjustment;
(b) Ensure relative fixation between manipulator and visual components, and can resist the inertial load when manipulator moves.

Manipulator. The manipulator is used to drive the treatment tip to complete the operation, and shall not be placed directly above the customer's face. An elastic displacement of about 10 mm in the axial direction exists in treatment tip.

(a) The payload capacity of the manipulator is no less than 2 kg;
(b) The motion range of the treatment tip should not be less than $250 \times 250 \times 300$ mm in 3D area;
(c) The repeat position error of treatment tip should be less than ± 0.25 mm, attach and detach time of treatment tip should be less than 15 s.

3D Camera. 3D camera is applied for scanning and modeling of customer's face based on 3D modeling technology. Grid is recognized and located based on profiled surface positioning technology.

(a) Time of scanning and modeling of whole face should be less than 5 s, and the time of scanning and modeling of single dot area should be less than 3 s;
(b) The number of recognition points in the forehead area is not less than 2×6, and the number of recognition points in the unilateral cheek area is not less than 5×5.

2.3 Software Design

System Software. It is used to provide human-machine operation interface and system setting with the following functions

(a) Dot area selection (forehead, left cheek or right cheek);
(b) Starting point selection;
(c) Provide start, pause and emergency stop button;
(d) Provide status display of each functional unit;
(e) Provide alarm display of customer's head movement;
(f) Provide function of one-button calibration, which is used for the calibration of the disassembly and assembly of the manipulator and camera or position change.

Monitoring Unit of Posture. It is used for the real-time monitoring of the customer's head posture changes. The fluctuation caused by breathing, speaking or temporary change of facial expression should be eliminated, otherwise the alarm will be triggered frequently. When the grid position changes more than ± 1.5 mm relative to the previous recognition due to the change of head posture, the alarm will be triggered. Area scanning will be restarted automatically after the reset of manipulator. The remaining work shall be finished in accordance with the order of the previous operated grids.

3 System Algorithm

During the actual operation, the nurse manually transfers grid paper onto the customer's face (around the forehead and cheek), marks and assigns dot points and areas. The 3D camera scans the customer's dot area and models automictically. Grid position is converted to robot coordinate system for dotting with constant force. The system process is shown as follows (Fig. 2).

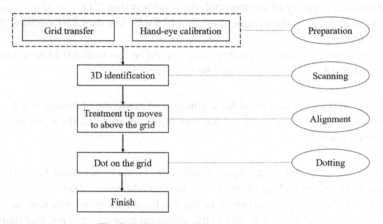

Fig. 2. Thermage robot system process

3.1 Hand-Eye Calibration

Calibration must be carried out first in order to realize the conversion between pixel coordinate and actual coordinate in robot vision system, which includes not only camera calibration but also hand-eye calibration of the robot system. In fact, robot hand-eye calibration is the calibration of the transformation relationship between robot coordinate system and camera coordinate system.

Hand-eye calibration usually adopts checkerboard calibration method to calibrate the camera [8–12]. A 12 × 9 checkerboard is applied in the calibration test. The relation between checkerboard and base is kept unchanged during calibration. The camera is mounted at the end of the manipulator. The hand-eye matrix with minimum error is calculated via transforming the end position of the manipulator. Finally, the error can be measured by calculating the checkerboard position (Fig. 3).

Fig. 3. Checkerboard during calculation

The position of the checkerboard in the camera coordinate system during calibration process is calculated by hand-eye matrix as shown in Fig. 4. Result shows that the error is within 2 mm, which meets system requirement.

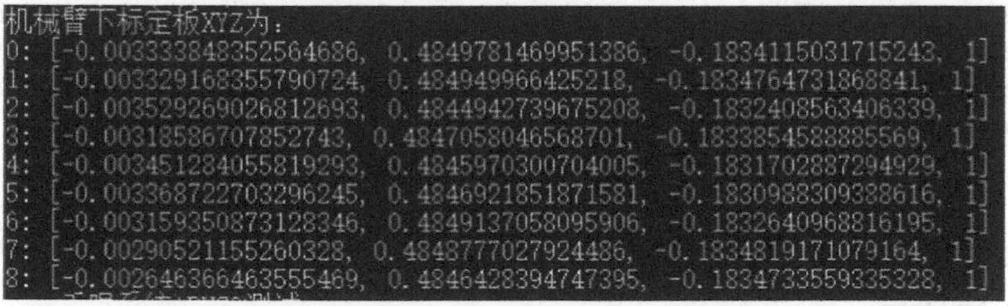

```
机械臂下标定板XYZ为：
0: [-0.0033338483352564686, 0.4849781469951386, -0.1834115031715243, 1]
1: [-0.003329168355790724, 0.484949966425218, -0.1834764731868841, 1]
2: [-0.003529269026812693, 0.4844942739675208, -0.1832408563406339, 1]
3: [-0.00318586707852743, 0.4847058046568701, -0.1833854588885569, 1]
4: [-0.003451284055819293, 0.4845970300704005, -0.1831702887294929, 1]
5: [-0.003368722703296245, 0.4846921851871581, -0.1830988309388616, 1]
6: [-0.003159350873128346, 0.4849137058095906, -0.1832640968816195, 1]
7: [-0.00290521155260328, 0.4848777027924486, -0.1834819171079164, 1]
8: [-0.002646366463555469, 0.4846428394747395, -0.1834733559335328, 1]
```

Fig. 4. Verification of hand-eye calibration result

3.2 Visual Recognition and Localization

Target detection of grid intersections is realized by using YOLO neural network algorithm [13, 14]. YOLO transforms the target detection problem into a regression problem when performing target detection at intersection points. Given the input image, the bounding box of the target and its classification category can be regressed directly in multiple positions of the image. At the same time, it can predict multiple frames for location and category at one time, so as to achieve end-to-end target detection and recognition.

3.3 Constant Force Control Algorithm

To achieve constant force control, a six-dimensional force sensor is installed at the end of manipulator to obtain external contact force. Since the constant force direction is the normal direction of the end, it is necessary to calibrate and decouple the force sensor [15–17]. When manipulator moves along the normal direction, the normal force is obtained in real time. Admittance control is adopted to control the speed and position of the manipulator, so as to achieve the purpose of maintaining constant force.

The control system adopts inner loop strategy based on position control and outer loop strategy based on force control. The contact force between the robot system and the outside world can be detected by six-dimensional force sensor, and an additional position is generated through a second-order admittance model. The additional position is then corrected to the preset position trajectory, and finally sent into the inner loop of position control to complete the final position control.

The admittance model of the manipulator is

$$M\,\ddot{x}_e + B\,\dot{x}_e + Kx_e = F_e \tag{1}$$

where F_e is the difference between the environmental force collected by the sensor in the tool coordinate system and the required constant force, x_e is the deviation between the actual position and the expected position of the manipulator, $\ddot{x}_e$ and $\dot{x}_e$ are the first derivative and the second derivative respectively.

Rewrite Eq. (1),

$$\ddot{x}_e = M^{-1}(F_e - B\dot{x}_e^t - K) \tag{2}$$

And then,

$$\dot{x}_e^{t+1} = \dot{x}_e^t + \ddot{x}_e\,\Delta t \tag{3}$$

$$x_e^{t+1} = x_e^t + \dot{x}_e^{t+1}\,\Delta t \tag{4}$$

The desired position can be obtained.

4 Experiments

Set the constant force at −6.5 N, the above algorithm is used to control the constant force of the manipulator. Firstly, a facial model is used for simulation test. The spatial surface of 3D face modeling and the calculated normal vector are shown in Fig. 5, where the normal line is marked as the normal direction of the treatment tip. The dotting test of facial model is shown in Fig. 6, and the tip is in good fitting condition.

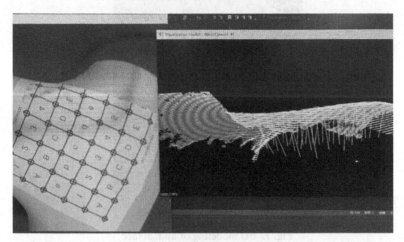

Fig. 5. 3D modeling of facial model

Fig. 6. Dotting test of facial model

Secondly, a human face test is carried out. The 3D modeling space surface and the calculated normal vector are shown in Fig. 7. The dotting test of human face is shown in Fig. 8. The test result shows that the maximum force is −6.82 N, and the error is 4.92%, as shown in Fig. 9, which meets the system requirements.

Fig. 7. 3D modeling of human face

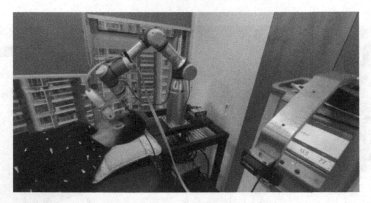

Fig. 8. Dotting test of human face

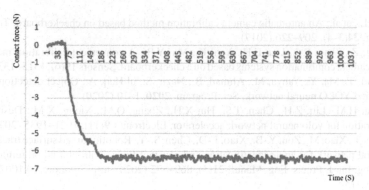

Fig. 9. Constant force control of dotting test

5 Conclusion

Thermage robot system is designed to assist physicians to perform face dotting operation automatically in the process of thermage treatment, which will improve standardized operation execution and reduce the labor intensity of physicians. Thermage treatment should be adjusted according to state of skin aging, pain tolerance and individual requirements of different consumers. Repetitive operation requirements are put forward for physicians, which is quite a challenge for physicians' operation ability. The research of thermage robot system will hopefully solve the pain points of medical cosmetology industry and alleviate the shortage of professional physicians to a certain extent.

References

1. Jesitus, J.: Thermage FLX: single-session standout. Dermatol. Times 76–77 (2018)
2. Polder, K.D., Bruce, S.: Radiofrequency: thermage. Facial Plast. Surg. Clin. North Am. **19**(2), 347–359 (2011)
3. Jones, J.K.: Nonsurgical skin tightening with three heat-producing devices. Plast. Surg. Nurs. **33**(3), 137–139 (2013)
4. Ingrid, M.: Thermage bolsters aesthetic skin treatment offerings via reliant purchase. The Gray Sheet (2008)
5. Ault, A.: Thermage's new look. Skin Allergy News (2009)
6. Hodgkinson, D.J.: Clinical applications of radiofrequency: nonsurgical skin tightening (thermage). Clin. Plast. Surg. **36**(2), 261–268 (2009)
7. Sukal, S.A., Geronemus, R.G.: Thermage: the nonablative radiofrequency for rejuvenation. Clin. Dermatol. **26**(6), 602–607 (2008)
8. Lin, W.W., Liang, P.D., Luo, G.T., Zhao, Z.Y., Zhang, C.T.: Research of online hand-eye calibration method based on ChArUco board. Sensors **22**(10), 3805 (2022)
9. Su, S.H., Gao, S., Zhang, D.Y., Wang, W.Q.: Research on the hand-eye calibration method of variable height and analysis of experimental results based on rigid transformation. Appl. Sci. **12**(9), 4415 (2022)
10. Fu, J.S., Ding, Y.B., Huang, T., Liu, H.T., Liu, X.P.: Hand–eye calibration method based on three-dimensional visual measurement in robot-ic high-precision machining. Int. J. Adv. Manuf. Technol. **119**, 3845–3856 (2022). https://doi.org/10.1007/s00170-021-08591-1

11. Bi, Q.L., et al.: An automatic camera calibration method based on checkerboard. Traitement du Sig. **34**(3–4), 209–226 (2017)
12. Zhang, Z., Zhao, R.J., Liu, E.H., Yan, K., Ma, Y.B.: A convenient calibration method for LRF-camera combination systems based on a checkerboard. Sensors **19**(6), 1315–1334 (2019)
13. Ahmad, T., Ma, Y., Yahya, M., Ahmad, B., Nazir, S., ul Haq, A.: Object detection through modified YOLO neural network. Sci. Program. **2020**, 1–10 (2020)
14. Huang, H.M., Liu, Z.H., Chen, T.S., Hu, X.H., Zhang, Q.M., Xiong, X.M.: Design space exploration for yolo neural network accelerator. Electronics **9**(11), 1921–1935 (2020)
15. Zhang, T., Xiao, M., Zou, Y.-B., Xiao, J.-D., Chen, S.-Y.: Robotic curved surface tracking with a neural network for angle identification and constant force control based on reinforcement learning. Int. J. Precis. Eng. Manuf. **21**(5), 869–882 (2020). https://doi.org/10.1007/s12541-020-00315-x
16. Zhang, X.Z., Xu, Q.S.: Design and testing of a novel 2-DOF compound constant-force parallel gripper. Precis. Eng. **56**, 53–61 (2019)
17. Ding, B.X., Zhao, J.Y., Li, Y.M.: Design of a spatial constant-force end-effector for polishing/debur-ring operations. Int. J. Adv. Manuf. Technol. **116**(11), 3507–3515 (2021). https://doi.org/10.1007/s00170-021-07579-1

An Active Obstacle Avoidance Method

Wei Zhu, Yuanzhe Cui, Pengjie Xu, Yichao Shen, and Qirong Tang[✉]

Laboratory of Robotics and Multibody System, School of Mechanical Engineering,
Tongji University, Shanghai, China
qirong.tang@outlook.com

Abstract. Swarm robots often encounter dynamic obstacles when performing tasks, such as moving objects in the scene or other individuals in the robot group. The traditional passive obstacle avoidance method makes the robots take emergency avoidance behaviour when it is about to encounter obstacles. Hoverer this may destroy the group cooperation behaviour, thereby affecting the efficiency of the system. Active obstacle avoidance perceives a dynamic target and predicts the movement of the target and takes the initiative to avoid obstacles, minimizes the impact of obstacle avoidance on the system's cooperative behaviour. Considering that the defects in the structural design of swarm robots and the avoidance strategy of swarm robots, it is necessary to focus on active obstacle avoidance of swarm robots that is based on the prediction of dynamic targets. An improved obstacle avoidance method is therefore proposed, which enables robots to avoid both static and dynamic obstacles.

Keywords: Dynamic target prediction · Swarm robots · Active obstacle avoidance

1 Introduction

Due to swarm robots' abilities of robustness, flexibility and scalability, more and more scholars pay attention to swarm robots. When performing the tasks, swarm robots usually encounter dynamic obstacles, such as moving objects or other individuals in the robot group. Therefore, in order to complete the tasks successfully, it is necessary for the swarm robots to avoid obstacles.

There are several common obstacle avoidance methods for robots, such as Artificial Potential Field, VFH, Reciprocal Velocity Obstacle, etc.

This work is supported by the projects of National Natural Science Foundation of China (No. 61873192), the Quick Support Project (No. 61403110321), the Innovative Projects (No. 20-163-00-TS-009-125-01; 21-163-00-TS-011-011-01; 2021-JCJQ-LB-010-11), and the Key Pre-Research Project of the 14th-Five-Year-Plan on Common Technology (No. 50912030501). Meanwhile, this work is also partially supported by the Fundamental Research Funds for the Central Universities, as well as the project of Shanghai Key Laboratory of Spacecraft Mechanism (18DZ2272200). All these supports are highly appreciated.

H. Liu et al. (Eds.): ICIRA 2022, LNAI 13457, pp. 345–353, 2022.
https://doi.org/10.1007/978-3-031-13835-5_31

Khabit proposed the concept of Artificial Potential Field [1]. Its disadvantage is that the gravitational force is very large when robot is far away from the target point, thus the relatively small repulsive force can't be completely offset, which leads to collision.

Fiorini and Shiller proposed the concept of Velocity Obstacle (VO) at 1998 [2]. This method is applied for dynamic obstacle. Under the premise of observing dynamic obstacles, the robot calculates the set of velocities that will eventually cause a collision. The robot is supposed to adapt a new velocity that isn't belong to the set. Dynamics isn't considered in VO.

Borenstein et al. proposed the Vector Field Histogram (VFH), VFH permits the detection of unknown obstacles and avoids collisions while simultaneously steering the mobile robot towards the target [3]. However, VFH doesn't take the size and dynamics of robot into consideration and regards robot as a point. Iwan et al. proposed a method based on VFH and it is called VFH+, which takes size, trajectory and dynamics of robots in to consideration [4]. It doesn't take movable obstacle into consideration, which may lead to collision.

Fox et al. divided obstacle avoidance methods into two categories, global planning and local planning [5]. The former applies for static obstacle while the latter applies for dynamic obstacle. In addition, Fox also proposed Dynamic Window Approach (DWA), which considered the kinematics of the robot, leading to selection of velocity more reasonable. However, it may lead to collision because it focuses on the obstacles on the trajectory of the robots, while the obstacles near the trajectory may lead to collision.

Piyapat et al. proposed a method based on Dynamic Window Approach which is called Field Dynamic Window Approach (F-DWA). It solves the problem that obstacles near the trajectory of robots may lead to collision. However, F-DWA focus single robot, it doesn't consider collision avoidance of multiple robots [6].

Zhang Zhiwen et al. proposed a method that combines improved A* algorithm with Dynamic Window [7]. It achieves real-time dynamic obstacle avoidance and performs well in path planning. However, the method applies for collision avoidance and path planning of single robot, while there exists multiple robots that need to avoid collision, it fails.

Jur Van den Berg et al. proposed Reciprocal Velocity Obstacle that is based on the Velocity Obstacle [8]. This method calculates the set of velocities that make the robot avoid collision with others by linear programming, then the robot selects the optimal velocity in the set. It is simple and fast but it doesn't consider dynamics.

Some of the above method focus on single robot's collision avoidance such as method proposed by Zhang Zhiwen and Piyapat. Others ignore dynamics such as the method proposed by Michele. Those method used in swarm robots will lead to collision or destruction of swarm robots' formation. Therefore a method is proposed in this article, which aims to avoid collision. In this method, both static obstacles and dynamic ones are considered.

2 Proposed Method Based on ORCA

Based on Reciprocal Velocity Obstacle, Van den berg and so on proposed Optimal Reciprocal Collision Avoidance (ORCA) [9], which works better than Reciprocal Velocity Obstacle.

The core of ORCA is to establish a velocity set. Each velocity in the set makes sure that robots would be free from collision with other robots and static obstacles. The set is an area of the two-dimensional velocity plane and the area is defined by equations caused by other robots and static obstacles. A robot is supposed to select a velocity in the area as its new velocity in the next iteration.

However, there also exists limitation in ORCA. Dynamic obstacles in ORCA only refers to robots that are adherence to ORCA. Therefore, ORCA doesn't work well if there exist robots that aren't adherence to ORCA.

It's necessary to take robots that aren't adherence to ORCA into consideration and it is what the proposed method achieves in this article.

2.1 Establishing the Velocity Set

Taking the case of two robots as an example. Robot A and Robot B is described by the equation as follows, see Fig. 1(a):

$$D(\mathbf{p}, r) = \{\mathbf{q}|\ ||\mathbf{q} - \mathbf{p}|| < r\}. \tag{1}$$

To establish the velocity set, the first step is to establish the velocity obstacle. For robot A and robot B, velocity obstacle $VO_{A|B}^{\tau}$ is defined by the equation as follows, see Fig. 1(b):

$$VO_{A|B}^{\tau} = \{\mathbf{v}|\ \exists t \in [0, \tau] :: t\mathbf{v} \in D(\mathbf{p}_B - \mathbf{p}_A, r_A + r_B)\}. \tag{2}$$

The next step is to establish the velocity set. If in the next time of τ, robot A and B will not collide at their maximum velocity, both robot A and B don't have to choose a velocity through ORCA. If robot A and B will collide in the

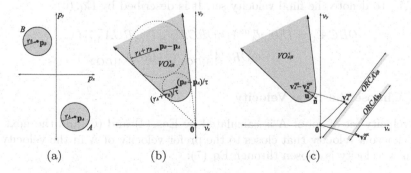

$$(a) \qquad\qquad (b) \qquad\qquad (c)$$

Fig. 1. Configuration, velocity obstacle and ORCA of robots.

next time of τ, vector $\mathbf{u}$ exists and vector $\mathbf{u}$ is used to establish the velocity set. Vector $\mathbf{u}$ is defined as follows, geometric interpretation is displayed in Fig. 1(c):

$$\mathbf{u} = \left(\underset{\mathbf{v} \in \partial VO^{\tau}_{A|B}}{\arg\min} \left\| \mathbf{v} - \left(\mathbf{v}^{\mathrm{opt}}_A - \mathbf{v}^{\mathrm{opt}}_B \right) \right\| \right) - \left(\mathbf{v}^{\mathrm{opt}}_A - \mathbf{v}^{\mathrm{opt}}_B \right). \tag{3}$$

Vector $\mathbf{n}$ is an outer normal vector at the boundary point $v^{opt}_A - v^{opt}_B + \mathbf{u}$ of $VO^{\tau}_{A|B}$. Vector $\mathbf{u}$ is the smallest change of velocity for robot A and B to be away from collision in next time τ. As robot A and B have the same status, each of robot A and B take half the responsibility to change their velocity. Therefore, velocity of robot A is supposed to add $0.5\mathbf{u}$ and velocity of robot B is supposed to add $-0.5\mathbf{u}$. Finally, the velocity set of robot A is calculated by Eq. (4), see Fig. 1(c):

$$ORCA^{\tau}_{A|B} = \left\{ \mathbf{v} \mid \left(\mathbf{v} - \left(\mathbf{v}^{\mathrm{opt}}_A + \frac{1}{2}\mathbf{u} \right) \right) \cdot \mathbf{n} \geq 0 \right\}. \tag{4}$$

In the proposed method, a dynamic obstacle which is adherence to ORCA is considered, the velocity set using $ORCA^{\tau}_{A|DO}$ to denote, and it is calculated by Eq. (5).

$$ORCA^{\tau}_{A|DO} = \left\{ \mathbf{v} \mid \left(\mathbf{v} - \left(\mathbf{v}^{\mathrm{opt}}_A + \mathbf{u} \right) \right) \cdot \mathbf{n} \geq 0 \right\}. \tag{5}$$

The difference between Eq. (4) and Eq. (5) is the coefficient of $\mathbf{u}$. In ORCA, it ignores the dynamic obstacles that aren't adherence to ORCA. The dynamic obstacle towards a certain robot in ORCA means other robots, therefore each robot takes half responsibility to avoid collision. While in the proposed method, the dynamic obstacles includes other robots that aren't adherence to ORCA. Therefore robot in the proposed method is supposed to take full responsibility to avoid collision when facing dynamic obstacle that aren't adherence to ORCA.

As for robot B, the velocity set $ORCA^{\tau}_{B|A}$ is defined symmetrically, geometric interpretation is shown in Fig. 1(c).

The final velocity set is the intersection of velocity set caused by other robots, dynamic obstacles and its maximum velocity if there exists a lot of robots, such as robot A, B, C, etc. and dynamic obstacle 1, dynamic obstacle 2 etc. Using $ORCA^{\tau}_A$ to denote the final velocity set. It is described by Eq. (6):

$$\begin{aligned} ORCA^{\tau}_A = D(\mathbf{0}, v^{max}_A) &\cap ORCA^{\tau}_{A|B} \cap ORCA^{\tau}_{A|C} \cap \dots \\ &\cap ORCA^{\tau}_{A|DO1} \cap ORCA^{\tau}_{A|DO2} \cap \dots. \end{aligned} \tag{6}$$

2.2   Choose the New Velocity

The velocity set of robot A is calculated by Eqs. (4) and (6) and the next step is to choose a velocity that closes to the prefer velocity of A in the velocity set. The new velocity is chosen through Eq. (7):

$$\mathbf{v}^{\mathrm{new}}_A = \underset{\mathbf{v} \in ORCA^{\tau}_A}{\arg\min} \left\| \mathbf{v} - \mathbf{v}^{\mathrm{pref}}_A \right\|, \tag{7}$$

where $\mathbf{v}_A^{\text{pref}}$ is the velocity robot A prefers to select. To simplify, $\mathbf{v}_A^{\text{pref}}$ and $\mathbf{v}_A^{\text{opt}}$ are set as $\mathbf{v}_A$. Finally robot A selects a new velocity that guarantees it be away from collision.

2.3   Combined with Kalman Filter

In ORCA, the most important information is the position of robots. By using Kalman filter, more accurate position information of robots can be obtained. Kalman filter mainly processes position information of robots, the processed information is converted to ORCA to calculate the new velocity set. Considering that position information matters in ORCA, Kalman filter [10] can be simplified in the proposed method. And the simplified Kalman filter is used to improve the accuracy of robots' position information and it is described by Eq. (8).

$$\hat{x}_n = \hat{x}_{n-1} + K_n\left(y_n - \hat{x}_{n-1}\right),$$
$$p_n = (1 - K_n)\,p_{n-1},$$
$$K_n = \frac{p_{n-1}}{p_{n-1} + \sigma^2},$$

(8)

where $\hat{x}_n$ is the current estimate, $\hat{x}_{n-1}+K_n$ is the former estimate, K_n is Kalman gain, y_n is the measurement value of sensor, p_{n-1} is based on the state of the previous moment to find the variance of the current state, p_n is the updated variance, σ^2 is the variance of the sensor measurement.

3   Simulations Between ORCA and Proposed Method

The simulation is conducted in the Virtual Robot Experiment Platform (VREP). And there are three scenes conducted in VREP.

3.1   Setup

All the parameters of the robots in the scenes in VREP are the same as the physical robots. The mass of each wheel is 0.2 kg and principal moment of inertia is 9×10^{-5} kg·m^2. The maximum torque is 10 N·m. The mass of the whole robot is 1.1 kg. The maximum velocity of the robot is 0.94 m/s. The friction coefficient is set as default. Both x-coordinate and y-coordinate of robots are disturbed by Gaussian noise with variance of 1 cm^2 and mean value of 0 cm.

3.2   Scenes

There are several scenes to show the effect of method to achieve collision avoidance. All of the scenes are created in VREP.

Scene 1 aims to show the collision avoidance among robots. Twelve robots are distributed on a circle with the radius of 2 m, which is centred on the coordinate origin. In this scene, the task of the robots is to approach the origin and rotate around the origin for a certain period time when the distance between the origin and the robot is less than 1.1 m. Then each robot is supposed to move back to the initial position, see Fig. 2(a). Scene 2 aims to show robots using the proposed method to go through a narrow aisle to arrive target position, see Fig. 2(b).

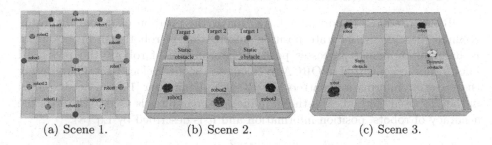

(a) Scene 1.   (b) Scene 2.   (c) Scene 3.

Fig. 2. Scenes of simulations.

Scene 3 aims to show the collision avoidance among robots, static obstacles and dynamic ones. The task of the robots is the same as it in scene 1, though some parameters differ, such as the initial position and the center of the rotation, see Fig. 2(c).

3.3 Effectiveness

The proposed method is both applied in the three scenes and ORCA is applied in scene 3.

In the scene 1, as envisaged, the proposed method successfully makes robots approach the target and rotate around it without collision. It shows the proposed method performs well in collision avoidance among robots that are adherence to ORCA, see Fig. 3(a).

In the scene 2, it shows that the proposed method enables robots to avoid collision with static obstacles, see Fig. 3(b). In the scene 3, it shows that the proposed method successfully makes each robot in the scene complete task without collision with other robots and dynamic object, see Fig. 4(a). In this scene, the dynamic object aren't adherence to ORCA, which means they are highly possible to collision with robots. Therefore, they don't take responsibility of collision avoidance. In ORCA, each robot is responded for half responsibility to avoid collision. When facing the dynamic obstacles, it is very likely to happen collision between robots and dynamic obstacles if robots take only half responsibility to avoid collision, see Fig. 4(b).

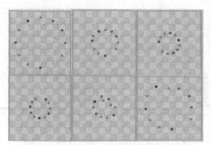 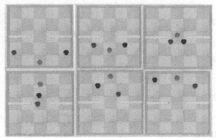

(a) Simulation for scene 1(using pro- posed method and ORCA). Both make the robots achieve task.

(b) Simulation for scene 2(using proposed method and ORCA). Both make robots achieve task.

Fig. 3. Scene 1 and scene 2 of simulations

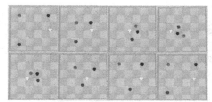 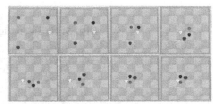

(a) Simulation for scene 3(using proposed method). No collision happens.

(b) Simulation for scene 3(using ORCA). Collision happens between robot(the red object) and the dynamic obstacle(the white object).

Fig. 4. Scene 3 of simulations. (Color figure online)

In simulation, the proposed method is able to solve the scenes like scene 3 with some limits that the velocitie of dynamic obstacles is supposed to have the same maximum velocity as robots. If dynamic obstacles' maximum velocity is faster than robots', there will be collision between them. Collision happens in scene 3 with ORCA beacause Gaussian noise disturb position information of robots and there are robots in scene 3, which aren't adherence to ORCA. All trajectories of scenes 1, 2 and 3 are displayed in Fig. 5 and Fig. 6.

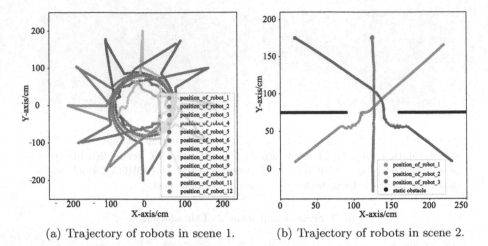

(a) Trajectory of robots in scene 1.   (b) Trajectory of robots in scene 2.

Fig. 5. Trajectories of scene 1, 2.

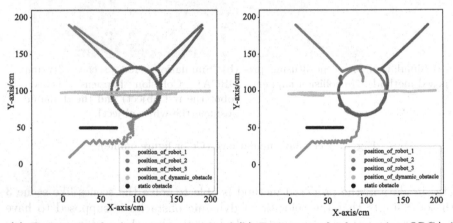

(a) Trajectory of robots using proposed method in scene 3.   (b) Trajectory of robots using ORCA in scene 3(Collision happens).

Fig. 6. Trajectories of scene 3.

4   Conclusion

A collision avoidance method based on ORCA is proposed in this article. The Kalman filter used in the method is supposed to make ORCA better to be applied in simulation and is able to play a role in experiment. The proposed method Combines it with the improved ORCA, which is able to predict the position of dynamic obstacle and therefore helps the robots to avoid collision with dynamic obstacles that aren't adherence to ORCA. In a word, this study makes contribution of collision avoidance of multi-robot navigation especially in the environment with dynamic obstacles. Future works can focus on the point that how to make robots avoid collision with dynamic obstacles whose velocity is higher than the maximum velocity of the robot and strengthen robot's ability of robustness towards larger disturbance of position.

References

1. Huang, Y., Hu, H., Liu, X.: Obstacles avoidance of artificial potential field method with memory function in complex environment. In: 8th World Congress on Intelligent Control and Automation, Jinan, pp. 6414–6418. IEEE (2010)
2. Paolo, F., Zvi, S.: Motion planning in dynamic environments using velocity obstacles. Int. J. Robot. Res. **17**(7), 760–772 (1998)
3. Borenstein, J., Koren, Y.: The vector field histogram-fast obstacle avoidance for mobile robots. IEEE Trans. Robot. Autom. **7**(3), 278–288 (1991)
4. Ulrich, I., Borenstein, J.: VFH+: reliable obstacle avoidance for fast mobile robots. In: IEEE International Conference on Robotics and Automation, Leuven, pp. 1572–1577. IEEE (1998)
5. Dieter, F., Wolfram, B., Sebastian, T.: The dynamic window approach to collision avoidance. IEEE Robot. Autom. Mag. **4**(1), 23–33 (1997)
6. Saranrittichai, P., Niparnan, N., Sudsang, A.: Robust local obstacle avoidance for mobile robot based on dynamic window approach. In: 10th IEEE International Conference on Electrical Engineering/Electronics, Computer, Telecommunications and Information Technology, Krabi, pp. 1–4. IEEE (2013)
7. Zhang, Z., Zhang, P., Mao, H., Li, X., Sun, Q.: Global dynamic path planning combining improved A* algorithm and dynamic window method. Electron. Opt. Control 1–6 (2021)
8. Van den Berg, J., Lin, M., Manocha, D.: Reciprocal velocity obstacles for real-time multi-agent navigation. In: IEEE International Conference on Robotics and Automation, Pasadena, pp. 1928–1935. IEEE (2008)
9. Van den Berg, J., Guy, S.J., Lin, M., Manocha, D.: Reciprocal n-body collision avoidance. In: Pradalier, C., Siegwart, R., Hirzinger, G. (eds.) Robotics Research. STAR, vol. 70, pp. 3–19. Springer, Heidelberg (2011). https://doi.org/10.1007/978-3-642-19457-3_1
10. Rudof, K.: A new approach to linear filtering and prediction problems. J. Basic Eng. Trans. **82**(1), 35–45 (1960)

that how to make robots avoid collision with dynamic obstacles whose velocity is higher than the maximum velocity of the robot and strengthen robot's ability of robustness towards large disturbance of position.

References

Medical Robot

Design of Wireless Force Sensing Module of Vascular Interventional Robot

Zhuang Fu[1]([✉]), Jianfeng Yao[1], Zeyu Fu[1], Chenxin Sui[1], and Jian Fei[2]

[1] State Key Lab of Mechanical System and Vibration, Shanghai Jiao Tong University,
Shanghai 200240, China
zhfu@sjtu.edu.cn

[2] Ruijin Hospital Affiliated to Shanghai Jiao Tong University, Shanghai 200025, China

Abstract. Force information is an indispensable and essential factor in vascular interventional surgery, which significantly affects the accuracy and safety of the procedure. This paper designs a new force sensing module for the vascular interventional robot, which measures the propulsion resistance and twisting torque during catheter and guidewire actuation. The FEA simulation is used to analyze the stress of the elastic body, and to establish the appropriate structure statically. The voltage signal is amplified, filtered and then transmitted wirelessly via Bluetooth. Finally, the force sensing module is subjected to a static calibration experiment, and the acquired signal is filtered using the Kalman filter algorithm. The experimental results have shown that the force sensing module exhibits good linearity and accuracy.

Keywords: Vascular interventional robot · Force sensing · Kalman filter

1 Introduction

According to WHO data, cardiovascular disease has been the largest cause of mortality globally in recent years [1, 2]. In 2016, over 9 million people died from coronary artery disease [3]. Despite the effectiveness of prevention and therapy, the prevalence of the disease continues to climb. The vascular interventional procedure is becoming more popular in the treatment of cardiovascular disease due to its advantages of small incisions, quick healing, and minimal complications. By introducing a surgical robot, the surgeon can remotely manipulate the robot to drive the catheter guidewire to the lesion and complete the surgery, minimizing the exposure to the extended X-ray radiation and resolving some of the procedure's perceptual and operational issues [4]. Furthermore, force sensory information has a substantial impact on the precision, efficiency, and safety of the surgical procedure.

Many companies and colleges in China and overseas have recently carried out extensive studies in this area. Interventional surgery robots are developing rapidly, yet there are still some problems. The substitution of force sensory information with visual and other information is often impossible for an accurate procedure assessment and can easily result in vascular damage to the patient [5–7]. Due to the size and mounting technique

H. Liu et al. (Eds.): ICIRA 2022, LNAI 13457, pp. 357–366, 2022.
https://doi.org/10.1007/978-3-031-13835-5_32

constraints of the force sensor, the overall dimension of the module is normally enormous [8, 9]. Furthermore, the surgical robot's stroke is limited, necessitating various operational adjustments due to how the surgical robot is driven and how the signal wires are entangled. Special surgical equipment with force sensing can obtain the force on the guidewire's head, yet they are less adaptable and more costly [10].

In this paper, a force sensing module is designed for vascular interventional robots based on catheter guidewire movement and force circumstances, with remote force feedback on the surgical instruments via Bluetooth communication.

2   Force Sensing Module's Structural Design

During vascular interventional surgery, doctors push and twist surgical instruments like catheters and guidewires into vascular lesions to achieve therapy approaches such as balloon dilation or stent implantation. According to the degrees of freedom analysis, the driving system must be capable of both linear propulsion and circular rotation. The forces are derived from two primary sources when the catheter guidewire movement comes into touch or collides with the vasculature. (1) Axial resistance during propulsion. (2) Rotational torque during rotation. The driving friction wheel is subjected to forces operating on the catheter guidewire when the friction wheel is utilized as the driving portion, as shown in Fig. 1. The propulsion resistance and the rotational torque correspond to the axial force and the circular torque of the friction wheel, respectively. Therefore, the force sensing module has to analyze and calculate the drive shaft's rotational torque and axial force.

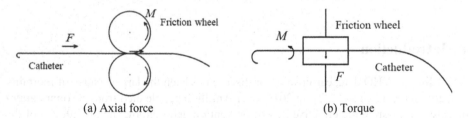

(a) Axial force   (b) Torque

Fig. 1. Catheter guide wire force diagram

2.1   Force Sensing Module's Structural Arrangement

The force sensing module consists of a driving gear shaft with integrated sensitive elements, a friction wheel, a miniature slip ring, a bearing, a signal acquisition circuit and a battery. This subsection will be detailed in conjunction with a partial cross-sectional picture of the drive unit for the convenience of functional description. The friction wheel drives the guidewires' movement by clamping them tightly, as indicated in Fig. 2. Gear shaft 1 is the drive gear shaft with integrated sensitive parts, whereas gear shaft 2 is the active shaft for incoming power. Strain gauges are fastened to the center section of the elastomeric part of gear shaft 1, which are coupled to the signal collection circuit at the bottom via a small slip ring and transmitted wirelessly through Bluetooth. The rotation of gear shaft 1 produces the axial force on the catheter guidewire. Moreover, the torque on the catheter guidewire is generated by rotating the housing.

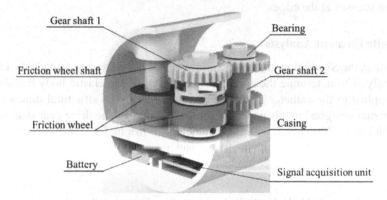

Fig. 2. Sectional view of force sensing module

2.2 Elastic Body Structural Design

In order to reduce the overall size of the vascular intervention robot's driving unit, the size of the drive shaft should be minimized. Considering factors such as the positioning of strain gauges, the forces on the surgical instruments, and the strain on the elastic body, in Fig. 3, the elastic body adopts a thin-walled cylindrical structure and is integrated in the middle region of the transmission gear shaft. The inner bore of the shaft enables the alignment of strain gauges. And they are attached to a micro slip ring to keep signal wires from tangling. The elastomer is arranged in a two-layer configuration, with the upper strain gauge measuring the rotational torque and oriented at 45° to the axis to balance the axial force (Fig. 4).

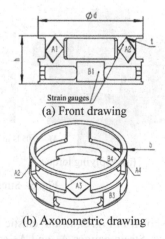

(a) Front drawing

(b) Axonometric drawing

Fig. 3. Model of gear shaft   **Fig. 4.** Structure of elastic body

---

While the lower strain gauge, which is applied in the direction of the axis, measures the axial force. The elastic body is composed of thin-walled, uniformly perforated cylinders to increase the strain on the acting surface, with rounded corners around the holes to relieve stresses at the edges.

2.3 Finite Element Analysis

In this paper, the Simulation module in Solidworks was used to carry out a finite element static analysis to determine the appropriate structure of the elastic body based on the forces applied to the catheter guidewire during surgery. The structural dimensions of the elastomer designed in this paper are shown in Table 1. The drive gear shaft was 3D printed in Future 7000 nylon with the parameters shown in Table 2. A new Simulation case is created in Solidwork with the fixture and mesh set. Moreover, the corresponding rotational torque and axial force are loaded for finite element analysis.

Table 1. Elastic body construction dimensions (*mm*)

Diameter (d)	Height (H)	Thickness (b)	Slot depth (t)
24	11	1.2	≤0.4

Table 2. 7000-nylon material parameters

Tensile modulus	Constrained modulus	Yield strength	Density
1600 MPa	1300 MPa	46 MPa	1200 g/mm^3

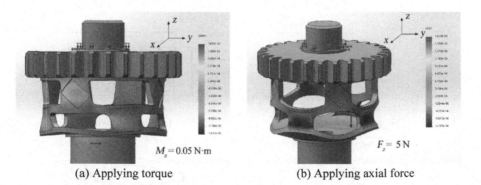

(a) Applying torque   (b) Applying axial force

Fig. 5. Stress contours with Ansys

As shown in Fig. 5(a), the elastic body is subjected to shear stress when a torque is applied. Strain gauges A_1 and A_3 are subjected to isotropic stresses, A_2 and A_4 are subjected to the opposite stresses, the maximum strain at the strain gauge attachment position is 8.417×10^{-4} and the RMS is 6.048×10^{-4}. As the lower strain gauges are mounted in the axial direction, the stress's direction is different from the direction of the sensitive grid. It has less influence on the measurement of the lower layer.

As shown in Fig. 5(b), when an axial force $F_z = 5\,\mathrm{N}$ is applied, the elastomer is subjected to positive stress. Strain gauges B_1 and B_3 are subjected to isotropic stresses, B_2 and B_4 are subjected to the opposite and smaller stresses, the maximum strain at the strain gauge attachment position is 8.938×10^{-4}, and the RMS is 6.048×10^{-4}. As the higher strain gauges are oriented at 45° to the axis to balance the axial force, the axial strain is smaller. Based on the forces applied to the catheter guidewire during surgery, the force sensing module is configured to a complete range of 5 N for axial force and 0.05 N · m for torque. The maximum stress on the gear shaft was 2.091 MPa and 3.175 MPa when full scale torque and axial load were applied respectively, which were less than the material yield strength of 40 MPa, corresponding to a safety factor of 22.0 and 14.5. The gear shaft was verified to be safe.

3 Hardware Circuit Design

The measurement and signal acquisition units are the major components of the force sensing module's hardware circuit. The sensitive element of the measuring unit is strain gauges, which convert the elastomeric strain into voltage in the presence of an auxiliary power supply. An amplifier filter module, an A/D acquisition module, and a Bluetooth communication module make up the signal acquisition circuit. The system block diagram is shown in Fig. 6.

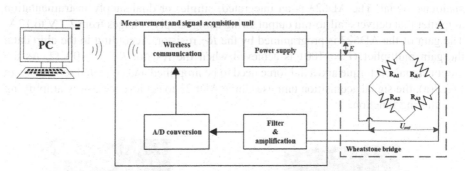

Fig. 6. System block diagram of force sensing module

3.1 Measurement Unit

The force detection module uses resistance strain gauges for the measurement of torque and axial force. Measurements are made via two Wheatstone bridge circuits with a total of 8 strain gauges. Taking Wheatstone bridge A as an example, the output voltage of the circuit can be expressed as

$$U_{out} = \left(\frac{R_{A3}}{R_{A3} + R_{A4}} - \frac{R_{A2}}{R_{A1} + R_{A2}} \right) E \tag{1}$$

It can be assumed that strain gauge A_1 is under tensile stress and A_2 is under compressive stress based on the finite element analysis results. According to the piezoresistive effect of the resistance strain gauge, the resistance change satisfies the following formula

$$\frac{\Delta R}{R} = K \times \varepsilon \tag{2}$$

where K is the sensitivity coefficient of the strain gauge, ε is the strain, and ΔR is the change in resistance caused by the deformation of the strain gauge. Define ΔR_{A1}, ΔR_{A2}, ΔR_{A3}, ΔR_{A4} as the resistance changes of the strain gauges. To estimate the magnitude of the output voltage, define the bridge A strain gauges' resistance equals R. Combining Eqs. (1) and (2), the output voltage of the circuit can be expressed as

$$U_{out} = \frac{\Delta R}{R}E = K \times \varepsilon \times E \tag{3}$$

According to the finite element simulation results, when the applied torque is 0.05 N · m, the shear strain $\gamma = 6.048 \times 10^{-4}$ and the strain generated in the sensitive direction is 4.277×10^{-4}. Furthermore, when the input voltage is 3.7 V and the strain gauge sensitivity factor K = 2, the output voltage $U_{out} = 3.165$ mV. The above calculation shows that the axial force output voltage is in the order of mV and the subsequent circuit needs to meet this voltage signal acquisition requirements.

3.2 Signal Acquisition Unit

Depending on the order of output voltage, operational amplifiers are used to amplify small analogue signal. The AD623 is an integrated, single- or dual-supply instrumentation amplifier that delivers rail-to-rail output swing using supply voltages from 2.7 V to 12 V. The gain of the AD623 is programmed by the R_G resistor. According to the chip data, the gain multiplier $G = 1001$ is achieved when the resistor $R_G = 100$ Ω. As the output signals of torque and axial force need to be amplified and collected separately, in Fig. 7(a), the signal acquisition unit uses three AD623 to achieve the 3-way amplifying and filtering function.

(a) Amplifying and filtering unit   (b) CurieNano

Fig. 7. Signal acquisition unit

The A/D acquisition and Bluetooth communication are mainly implemented using the CurieNano control board, as shown in Fig. 7(b). CurieNano is a compact development tool based on Intel Curie, integrating Bluetooth 4.0, 10-bit A/D conversion module and other features. The integrated Bluetooth 4.0 module features conventional Bluetooth technology, high speed technology and low-energy technology (BLE). The amplifying filter module and CurieNano are connected through pin headers to form a signal acquisition module, which has the characteristics of modularity, small size, and low power consumption.

4 Calibration and Experiments

4.1 Calibration Experimental Platform

In order to reflect the force of the catheter guidewire more accurately during calibration, the constraint condition should be restored as much as possible. The static calibration device is shown in Fig. 8 and Fig. 9.

Fig. 8. Force sensing module prototype

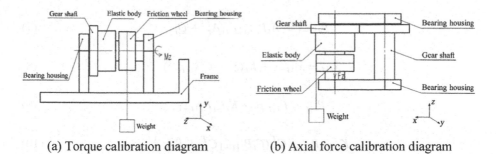

(a) Torque calibration diagram   (b) Axial force calibration diagram

Fig. 9. Calibration experimental platform

4.2 Data Acquisition and Analysis

When loaded, the output signals from bridges A and B are transmitted via Bluetooth to the remote upper computer after amplification and A/D conversion. The upper computer uses Qt as the development platform for Bluetooth data acquisition and storage. Because of the adhesive's disturbance, the working circuit's thermal noise, and the external environmental noise, the output signal is frequently unstable. This paper applies Kalman filter to process the collected voltage signal. Kalman filter is an algorithm permitting exact inference in a linear dynamical system. The great success of the Kalman filter is due to its small computational requirement, elegant recursive properties, and its status as the optimal estimator for one-dimensional linear systems with Gaussian error statistics. The Kalman filter model assumes that the state of a system at a time t evolved from the prior state at time t − 1 according to the equation

$$x_t = A_t x_{t-1} + B_t u_t + w_t \tag{4}$$

where x_t is the output voltage of the bridge circuit at time t, A_t is the state transition matrix, u_t is the applied force, B_t is the control input matrix, w_t is the vector containing the process noise terms for each parameter in the state vector. Measurements of the system can also be performed, according to the model

$$z_t = C_t x_t + v_t \tag{5}$$

where z_t is the vector of measurements, C_t is the transformation matrix, v_t is the vector containing the measurement noise terms for each observation in the measurement vector. The process and the measurement noise are assumed to be zero mean Gaussian white noise with covariance Rt. The elastic body, strain bridge circuit and signal conditioning circuit are equivalent to first-order inertial element, and the A/D conversion is simplified to zero-order holder. The Kalman filter algorithm involves two stages: prediction and measurement update. The information from the predictions and measurements are combined to provide the best possible estimation. The standard Kalman filter equations for the prediction stage and the measurement update stage are

$$\hat{x}_{t|t-1} = A_t \hat{x}_{t-1|t-1} + B_t u_t \tag{6}$$

$$P_{t|t-1} = A_t P_{t-1|t-1} A_t^T + Q_t \tag{7}$$

$$\hat{x}_{t|t} = \hat{x}_{t|t-1} + K_t(z_t - C_t \hat{x}_{t|t-1}) \tag{8}$$

$$P_{t|t} = P_{t|t-1} - K_t C_t P_{t|t-1} \tag{9}$$

$$K_t = P_{t|t-1} C_t^T (C_t P_{t|t-1} C_t^T + R_t)^{-1} \tag{10}$$

where $\hat{x}_{t-1|t-1}$ is the estimated state vector at time $t - 1$, $\hat{x}_{t|t-1}$ is the predicted state vector at time t, $\hat{x}_{t|t}$ is the estimated state vector after update at time t, Q_t is the process noise covariance matrix associated with noisy control inputs.

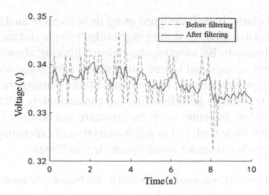

Fig. 10. Filtering effect under Kalman method algorithm

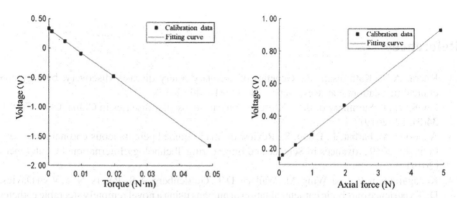

Fig. 11. Torque M_z fitting results   **Fig. 12.** Axial forces F_z fitting results

The acquired voltage signal is processed with the Kalman filter algorithm and then analyzed. Figure 10 shows the voltage signal before and after Kalman filtering when the load is 0, which effectively suppresses the signal noise. The calibration experiment uses weights with masses of 10 g, 50 g, 100 g, 200 g, and 500 g. Through the method of step-by-step loading and unloading, three groups of experiments of torque and axial force are respectively calibrated. The voltage-load data are fitted with least squares method to obtain curves as shown in Fig. 11 and Fig. 12. The fitting curve between voltage and torque is $y = -40.4625x + 0.3138$, with the coefficient of determination $R^2 = 0.9997$. Furthermore, the fitting curve between voltage and axial force is $y = 0.1612x + 0.1402$, with the coefficient of determination $R^2 = 0.9993$. The negative voltage in Fig. 11 is obtained by calculating the difference between the observed and the reference voltage of the AD623 chip. The positive and negative of the graph line represent the direction of the loading.

5   Conclusions

In this paper, a two-dimensional wireless force detection module is designed based on the force conditions of catheter guidewire during vascular interventional procedures.

The structure of the elastic body is designed using finite element analysis, and a sensing module is constructed to collect the strain gauge bridge voltage and transmit it wirelessly via a low-power Bluetooth. By adopting the Kalman filtering algorithm, the mapping relationships between voltage and torque, voltage and axial force are finally obtained through the calibration experiment. The presented force sensing module is simple in construction, small in size, has good linearity, and can accurately reflect the load condition of the friction wheel. In future work, the structure and design of the force sensing module will be further improved, and in-depth analysis and experiments will be carried out on the catheter guidewire under actual operating conditions.

Acknowledgment. This work was greatly supported by the National Natural Science Foundation of China (Grant No. 61973210) and the Medical-engineering Cross Projects of SJTU (Grant Nos. YG2019ZDA17, ZH2018QNB23).

References

1. Khera, A.V., Kathiresan, S.: Genetics of coronary artery disease: discovery, biology and clinical translation. Nat. Rev. Genet. **18**(6), 331–344 (2017)
2. Hu, S., et al.: Summary of the 2018 report on cardiovascular diseases in China. Chin. Circ. J. **34**(3), 12 (2019)
3. Alatoom, A., Farhat, J., Dhou, S.: Review of image-guided percutaneous coronary interventions. In: 2019 Advances in Science and Engineering Technology International Conferences (2019)
4. Kanagaratnam, P., Koa-Wing, M., Wallace, D.T., Goldenberg, A.S., Peters, N.S., Wyn Davies, D.: Experience of robotic catheter ablation in humans using a novel remotely steerable catheter sheath. J. Intervent. Card. Electrophysiol. **21**(1), 19–26 (2008). https://doi.org/10.1007/s10 840-007-9184-z
5. Swaminathan, R.V., Rao, S.V.: Robotic-assisted transradial diagnostic coronary angiography. Cathet. Cardiovas. Interv. **92**(1), 54–57 (2018)
6. Khan, E.M., et al.: First experience with a novel robotic remote catheter system: Amigo™ mapping trial. J. Interv. Card. Electrophysiol. **37**(2), 121–129 (2013). https://doi.org/10.1007/ s10840-013-9791-9
7. Payne, C.J., Rafii-Tari, H., Yang, G.Z.: A force feedback system for endovascular catheterisation. In: IEEE/RSJ International Conference on Intelligent Robots & Systems. IEEE (2012)
8. Guo, S., et al.: Study on real-time force feedback for a master–slave interventional surgical robotic system. Biomed. Microdev. **20**(2) (2018). Article number: 37. https://doi.org/10.1007/ s10544-018-0278-4
9. Guo, J., et al.: A vascular interventional surgical robotic system based on force-visual feedback. IEEE Sens. J. **19**(23), 11081–11089 (2019)
10. Noh, Y., et al.: Image-based optical miniaturized three-axis force sensor for cardiac catheterization. IEEE Sens. J. **16**(22), 7924–7932 (2016)

Deep Motion Flow Estimation
for Monocular Endoscope

Min Tan[1,2], Lijuan Feng[3], Zeyang Xia[1,2], and Jing Xiong[1,2(✉)]

[1] Shenzhen Institute of Advanced Technology, Chinese Academy of Sciences,
Shenzhen 518055, China
jing.xiong@siat.ac.cn
[2] University of Chinese Academy of Sciences, Beijing 101400, China
[3] Department of Gastroenterology and Hepatology,
Shenzhen University General Hospital, Shenzhen 518055, China

Abstract. For monocular endoscope motion estimation, traditional algorithms often suffer from poor robustness when encountering uninformative or dark frames since they only use prominent image features. In contrast, deep learning methods based on an end-to-end framework have achieved promising performance by estimating the 6-DOF pose directly. However, the existing techniques overly depend on the mass high-precision labelled 6-DOF pose data, which is difficult to obtain in practical scenarios. In this work, we propose a fast yet robust method for monocular endoscope motion estimation named Deep Motion Flow Estimation (DMFE). Specifically, we propose an innovative Key Points Encoder (KPE) supervised by Speeded-up Robust Features (SURF) flow to extract the salient features of endoscopic images. Aiming to ensure real-time capability, we propose a novel 3D motion transfer algorithm to reduce the computational complexity of the essential matrix. Extensive experiments on clinical and virtual colon datasets demonstrate the superiority of our method against the traditional methods, which can provide visual navigation assistance for doctors or robotic endoscopes in real-world scenarios.

Keywords: Colonoscopy · Motion pattern · SURF · Swin transformer

1 Introduction

Endoscopes with a tip monocular camera can help doctors visualize the location of lesions. Colonoscopy is one of the endoscopes for detecting polyps and lesions in the colon, and these inflammations can be developed into the highest prevalence rate of digestive cancer [5]. The motion estimation is vital for robotic

Supported by National Natural Science Foundation of China (62073309), Guangdong Basic and Applied Basic Research Foundation (2022B1515020042) and Shenzhen Science and Technology Program (JCYJ20210324115606018).

H. Liu et al. (Eds.): ICIRA 2022, LNAI 13457, pp. 367–377, 2022.
https://doi.org/10.1007/978-3-031-13835-5_33

endoscopy, especially for colonoscopy [4,19], since we can provide automated navigation or position tracking of the colonoscopy.

Many algorithms have been developed for visual navigation and motion estimation in the endoscope environment, broadly divided into traditional and learning-based approaches. Traditional algorithms use the dark area or the colon contour for recognition clues [16,21]. Zhao *et al.* [21] set the Region of Interest (ROI) to limit the search coverage around the last navigation point. Stap *et al.* [16] proposed a navigation algorithm that is based on image classification followed by dark region segmentation. However, these methods lack robustness and generalization when encountering uninformative frames since dark areas and clear outlines are not always visible during colon surgery.

Deep learning methods have more powerful feature extracting and the adaptive ability for uninformative frames, thus having better performance in endoscope motion estimation [3,17]. Armin *et al.* [1] proposed a convolutional neural network (CNN)-based framework to predict the camera pose. Turan *et al.* proposed a Long Short Term Memory (LSTM) [17] network framework to map the RGB image and camera pose. However, external high-precision labelled 6-DOF magnetic location pose data is required for these supervised end-to-end frameworks, which is difficult to obtain in practical scenarios. The synthetic [13] or phantom data [1] were used for training in the above methods, but it is challenging to narrow the gap between fake data and the clinical colonoscopic image. Conversely, some unsupervised frameworks that do without pose ground truth have been proposed [14,18]. Nevertheless, the performance requires improvement since the colon environment contains low texture and tortuous paths. In other methods [9,20], the optical flow technique has been integrated into the deep learning framework to estimate monocular endoscope motion. However, the dense optical flow is brightness sensitive and only can handle tiny movements with redundant information [15]. By contrast, the traditional Speeded-up Robust Features (SURF) [2] flow with a more robust feature points descriptor can substitute the optical flow as the supervised signal to train the deep network.

Motivated by the above observation, we propose a fast yet robust method for monocular endoscope motion estimation named Deep Motion Flow Estimation (DMFE). Specifically, we propose an innovative Key Points Encoder (KPE) to extract the salient features from endoscopic images, which leverages a Swin Transformer as the backbone supervised by SURF flow. We craft the SURF flow by the traditional SURF algorithm and employ the coordinate, length, and angle of SURF flows as the supervised motion parameters. In addition, we propose a novel 3D motion transfer algorithm via geometric operation to reduce the computational complexity of the essential matrix [8,20]. Extensive experiments on clinical and virtual colon datasets demonstrate the superiority of our method. Moreover, the experiment on real clinical colonic videos shows that our method is fast yet robust, especially for insufficient brightness images, which can provide visual navigation assistance for doctors or robotic endoscopes in real-world scenarios.

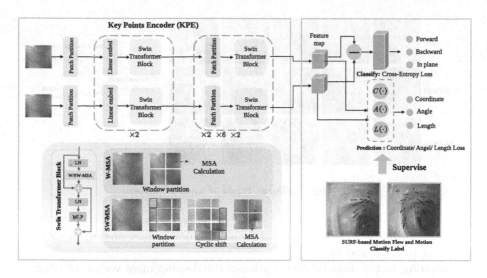

Fig. 1. The framework of the Deep Motion Flow Estimation method.

2 Method

The framework of our Deep Motion Flow Estimation (DMFE) method showed in Fig. 1. Two consecutive colon frames were input into the Key Points Encoder (KPE), which is employed by the Swin Transformer network for feature points extraction. A classifying loss and three prediction loss functions, calculated by the feature map and external SURF flow labels, were implemented to optimize the weights of the deep network.

2.1 Supervised SURF Flow Label

For the supervised signals, we used the SURF algorithm to generate the motion pattern label and the feature points information. The 64-dimensional feature vectors can be obtained after the SURF [2] feature point detecting algorithm. The Fast Library for Approximate Nearest Neighbors (FLANN) [11] method matches the feature points of two consecutive images. The matching result will be a list of correspondences between the train feature and query sets. The FLANN library will train a matcher, and an index tree of the feature set will be built to find the best match of the query set with the train matcher. In the process of filtering outliers, we primarily perform the coarse filtering operation, which calculates the minimum distances $dist_{min}$ between these pair of key points. Then, the point pairs whose distance is greater than $3 \times dist_{min}$ would be filtered out. The fine filtering operation with Random Sample Consensus (RANSAC) [6] algorithm has been carried out to estimate the parameters of the mathematical model from a set of observed outliers sets. Finally, the $t-1$ frame and the t frame are made 50% transparent to make a fusion image with SURF flow. Finally, we

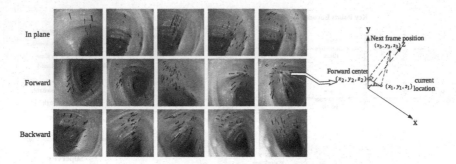

Fig. 2. Three different types of motion pattern

save the coordinate of the select m feature points coordinates, angles, and lengths according to Eq. 5 and Eq. 7.

According to the different distribution of the displacement vector, the motion posture of the lens can be judged, as shown in Fig. 2. Based on the length and angle of the displacement vector, motion patterns can be divided into three following types: **(1) Forward:** The displacement vector presents a divergent shape with a large difference between the length and the angle when forwarding. Moreover, the reverse connection of the displacement vector can be gathered into a forward center. **(2) Backward:** The backward pattern is the opposite of the forward when the lens is retracted. The direction of the displacement vector arrow can be gathered into a backward center. **(3) In-plane:** The posture of the motion in the image plane includes rotation and translation. In this situation, the length and angle of the displacement vector are not much different, and the vector connection cannot be gathered into the center. According to the distribution pattern of the displacement vector, the motion posture of the lens can be roughly determined, and the forward center coordinates also can be calculated (as shown in Fig. 2). When the current position $p_1 = (x_1, y_1, z_1)$ is known, the forward center $p_2 = (x_2, y_2, z_2)$ can be calculated by our 3D Motion Transfer Algorithm (detail in Fig. 3). The forward distance l takes the average length of the displacement vector. The calculation formula of the next frame position coordinate p_3 is as follows:

$$p_3 = \left(x_2, y_2, \sqrt{l^2 - (x_2 - x_1)^2 - (y_2 - y_1)^2} \right), l = \frac{1}{m} \sum^m \text{distance}\,(p_1, p_2) \quad (1)$$

where the m is the number of SURF flow pairs and the *distance* is the Euclidean distance, and x_3 and y_3 of p_3 are equal to x_2 and y_2, respectively.

2.2   Key Points Encoder

The KPE module is employed by the Swin Transformer network [10]. The hierarchical structure and shifted windows of the Swin Transformer bring high efficiency to extract multi-level spatial features. Thus, its performance surpasses the previous state-of-the-art methods in image classification and other tasks. As shown on the left of Fig. 1, each stage of the Swin Transformer will reduce the resolution of the input feature map and expand the receptive field layer by layer. The Patch Embedding cuts the image into smaller windows and patches at the beginning of the input, then transforms them into the linear embedding and Swin Transformer Block layers, as shown in the left bottom of Fig. 1. The most important two parts of the Swin Transformer block are window multi-head self-attention (W-MSA) and shifted window multi-head self-attention (SW-MSA). **(1) W-MSA:** The image will split into $n \times n$ windows and calculate the multi-head self-attention in each window to reduce the time complexity. There are m patches for each window, and the calculation process of MSA is presented in Eq. 2:

$$\text{Attention}\,(Q, K, V) = \text{SoftMax}\left(QK^T \sqrt{d} + B\right) V \tag{2}$$

where Q, K and $V \in \mathbb{R}^{M^2 \times d}$ are three matrices Q_i (query), K_i (key), and V_i (value), respectively, which are obtained by applying three different linear transformations for each input window. The M^2 represents the number of patches in one window, and the B is the relative position bias for every patch. The d is the encoding dimension in Patch Embedding. **(2) SW-MSA:** The partition operation of the W-MSA layer makes Windows independent of each other, thus losing global attention information. Therefore, SW-MSA is proposed to combine more information in different image windows, as show in Fig. 1. The window partition operation is different from W-MSA, which splits into more pieces and changes the position of different blocks. After the cyclic shift, the image will be combined into image blocks with the same number of W-MSA Windows. Finally, the MSA calculation is made to obtain attention feature maps.

2.3 Loss Function

Motion Pattern Classify. The traditional SURF method has been used to label the image data into three categories and obtain motion parameters. As shown in Fig. 1 right, we first do the minus operation to imitate the SURF flow features, and then the cross-entropy loss is calculated with Eq. 3:

$$\text{loss}(x, c) = -\log\left(\frac{\exp(x_c)}{\sum_j \exp(x_j)}\right) = -x_c + \log\left(\sum_j \exp(x_j)\right) \tag{3}$$

where x with the size of categories numbers C denotes the input one-hot encoding vector, and the $c \in [0, C]$ denotes the index of categories.

Motion Parameters Prediction. Every output feature map with the size of $m \times 2$ represents m feature points with x and y 2-dimension coordinate values in one single image. Then, the three parameters loss calculation of coordinate, angle, and length are based on the position of m points.

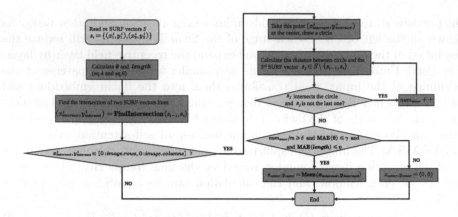

Fig. 3. The process of the 3D motion transfer algorithm

(1) Coordinate Loss: The coordinate loss is directly calculated by the euclidean distance between ground truth and output position of m points. The process can be formulated as follows:

$$C(\boldsymbol{x}, \boldsymbol{y}) = \lambda_{\text{coord}} \sum_i^m \sum_j^n \left(\sqrt{(x_{ij} - \hat{x}_{ij})^2 + (y_{ij} - \hat{y}_{ij})^2} \right) \tag{4}$$

where the $\boldsymbol{x}$ and $\boldsymbol{y}$ are the coordinate vectors of m points in 2-dimension, respectively, and the λ_{coord} is the normalization factor.

(2) Angle Loss: We use the arctangent function (measured in radians) to calculate the angle θ using the m points. After that, we need to normalize the angle to a positive integer in the range of $[0, 1]$ to ensure better convergence in training propagation. The same normalizing operation has been utilized in the output features of the KPE module. Then we can calculate angle loss with Wasserstein distance [7], which can be formulated as:

$$\theta = \arctan(\boldsymbol{y}/\boldsymbol{x}), \mathrm{A}(\boldsymbol{\theta}, \hat{\boldsymbol{\theta}}) = \lambda_{\text{angle}} \sum_i^m W\left(\theta_i^{\text{truth}}, \hat{\theta}_i \right) \tag{5}$$

where the function of $W(\cdot)$ is Wasserstein distance used to measure the similarity of two $\boldsymbol{\theta}$ distributions. Wasserstein distance can still reflect the distance even if the two distributions do not overlap or overlap very little, which can be formulated as:

$$W(P_1, P_2) = \inf_{\gamma \sim \prod(P_1, P_2)} \mathrm{E}_{(x,y) \sim \gamma}[\|x - y\|] \tag{6}$$

(3) Length Loss: We calculate the euclidean distance between two coordinates in two consecutive images, which can be formulated as:

$$length^i = \sqrt{(x_{t+1}^i - x_t^i)^2 + (y_{t+1}^i - y_t^i)^2} \tag{7}$$

Table 1. Key points extracting results

Data sequence/model	Test-1	Test-2	Test-3	Test-4	Test-5	Mean
Type (clinical/virtual)	C	V	V	C	C	–
Frames	200	50	150	100	50	–
Traditional SURF [2]	3120	2361	10095	2078	2104	3951
DMFE (ours)	5154	4936	15015	2649	3146	**6180**

where $i \in [1, m]$, and the subscript t and $t+1$ denote the first and second image, respectively. We use the same Wasserstein distance to measure the two distributions of $Length$.

$$L(\boldsymbol{\theta}, \hat{\boldsymbol{\theta}}) = \lambda_{\text{length}} \sum_i^m W\left(length_i^{\text{truth}}, \hat{length}_i\right) \qquad (8)$$

2.4 3D Motion Transfer Algorithm

The forward or backward center is computed based on motion flow vectors, and the procedure of our transfer algorithm is shown in Fig. 3. We read m SURF/motion flows from one fusion image, and calculate the θ and $length$. After that, we need to find the intersection center (forward or backward) according to the distribution of motion flows. Firstly, we take the intersection point $(x_{intersect}^i, y_{intersect}^i)$ of first two motion vector lines. If this point is in the image plane, we draw a circle with this intersection as the center. After that, we substitute other motion flows into the circle equation. If other motion flow lines intersect this circle, the counter num_{inner} will plus one. We iteratively conducted this process. Eventually, according to the counter num_{inner} and the MAE values to judge, we acquired the mean value of forwarding or backward centre (x_{center}, y_{center}).

3 Experiments and Results

3.1 Dataset and Implementation Details

1726 frames from 38 clinical colonic video streams were acquired in accordance with approval from Shenzhen University General Hospital as our training data. Furthermore, we used 2000 virtual colon images (with pose ground truth) from the Endoslam [12] dataset. In testing, we used 3 video sequences of clinical colonic images and 2 virtual colon images to evaluate the performance of our method.

We implement our DMFE method to predict the motion pattern and parameters. In the KPE module, we utilize a 32-dimensional embedding layer for the input embedding, four headers for the multi-head attention, seven for the window size, the MLP with 2048, and 64 hidden units for the feed-forward layer.

For loss design, we set λ_{coord}, λ_{angle}, and λ_{length} to 0.2, 0.4, and 0.4 according to experimental results. In the 3D transfer algorithm (Fig. 3), we set the threshold parameters δ, γ, η to 0.2, 0.5, and 50, respectively. Our approach is implemented with Pytorch 1.5.0 and trained for 100 epochs by the Adam optimizer. For all datasets, the batch size is set to 16, and the learning rate is set to 0.1e−2 for training. All experiments in this paper are trained on NVIDIA RTX 2080 GPU with 8 G memory and Intel Xeon E5 CPU with 2.30 GHz.

3.2 Feature Extracting Results

The feature extracting results are shown in Table 1 and Fig. 4. According to Table 1, the mean number of feature flows extracted by DMFE is 6180, which significantly outperforms the traditional SURF feature method (the mean value is 3951) in all test sequences. The mean classification accuracy of DMFE is 67.06% in clinical test data and 70.89% in virtual test data. From Fig. 4, we can observe that our KPE module can extract more prominent feature points even in low light conditions. Due to virtual images being clear, without too many reflections and motion blur, the classification accuracy and motion flow extracting performance in virtual images are better than in clinical images.

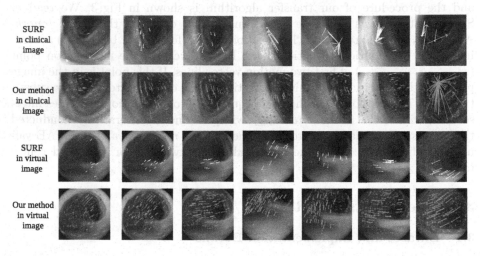

Fig. 4. The feature extracting comparison between the traditional SURF method (white arrow) and our DMFE module (green arrow) in clinical and visual testing data. (Color figure online)

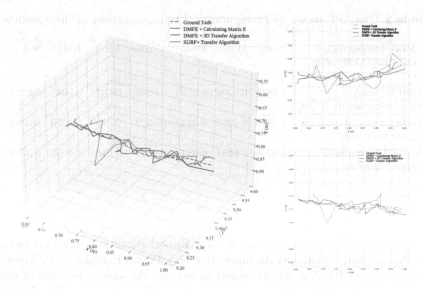

Fig. 5. Three-dimensional trajectory comparison of different models in Test-2. (Color figure online)

3.3 Motion Trajectory Generating Results

We calculated the coordinates of the forward or backward center point according to our transfer algorithm (Fig. 3), and used the average of the vector lengths for the forward distance. Figure 5 vividly shows that the trajectory error obtained by the traditional method (green line) is substantial. In contrast, the trajectory predicted using the DMFE (red line and blue line) is smoother and closer to the ground truth. We calculate the absolute trajectory error (APE) metric of three models to measure the fitting trajectory degree. According to Table 2, our DMFE and transfer algorithm outperform the traditional method (mean APE error is 0.0243 m, the RMSE is 0.0076 m and the std is 0.0362 m). On the other hand, since our transfer algorithm simplified the iteration process and obtained a coarse spatial position estimation, it is not as good as the calculating essential matrix method. Nevertheless, The computational time of our transfer algorithm (3.6896 ms) is faster than the essential matrix calculation method [20] (8.3858 ms) in mean computing time according to Table 2.

Table 2. The APE metric and computational time comparison of three models

Model/computational time (ms)/APE value (m)	Time	Max	Mean	Median	Min	RMSE	Std
DMFE (ours) + calculating matrix E [20]	8.3858	0.0208	0.0194	0.0206	0.0074	0.0049	0.0221
DMFE (ours) + transfer algorithm (ours)	3.6896	0.0266	0.0243	0.0222	0.0108	0.0076	0.0362
SURF [2] + transfer algorithm (ours)	3.4705	0.0384	0.0345	0.0317	0.0169	0.0098	0.0754

4   Conclusion

In this work, we proposed a Deep Motion Flow Estimation (DMFE) method for the monocular endoscope. An innovative Key Points Encoder (KPE) module supervised by SURF flow was proposed to extract the salient features of endoscopic images. In addition, we proposed a novel 3D motion transfer algorithm to reduce the computational complexity of the essential matrix aiming to ensure real-time capability. Experimental results show that our method can obtain a faster and more robust performance in feature extraction and movement estimation. We will implement our method in colon phantom and compare more deep-learning methods to improve our approach further. The real-time clinical trials will further consider providing visual navigation assistance for doctors or robotic endoscopy in the future.

References

1. Armin, M.A., Barnes, N., Alvarez, J., Li, H., Grimpen, F., Salvado, O.: Learning camera pose from optical colonoscopy frames through deep convolutional neural network (CNN). In: Cardoso, M.J., et al. (eds.) CARE/CLIP -2017. LNCS, vol. 10550, pp. 50–59. Springer, Cham (2017). https://doi.org/10.1007/978-3-319-67543-5_5
2. Bay, H., Tuytelaars, T., Van Gool, L.: SURF: speeded up robust features. In: Leonardis, A., Bischof, H., Pinz, A. (eds.) ECCV 2006. LNCS, vol. 3951, pp. 404–417. Springer, Heidelberg (2006). https://doi.org/10.1007/11744023_32
3. Bell, C.S., Obstein, K.L., Valdastri, P.: Image partitioning and illumination in image-based pose detection for teleoperated flexible endoscopes. Artif. Intell. Med. **59**(3), 185–196 (2013)
4. Chen, G., Pham, M.T., Redarce, T.: Sensor-based guidance control of a continuum robot for a semi-autonomous colonoscopy. Robot. Auton. Syst. **57**(6–7), 712–722 (2009)
5. Chen, H., et al.: Participation and yield of a population-based colorectal cancer screening programme in China. Gut **68**(8), 1450–1457 (2019). https://doi.org/10.1136/gutjnl-2018-317124
6. Fischler, M.A., Bolles, R.C.: Random sample consensus: a paradigm for model fitting with applications to image analysis and automated cartography. Commun. ACM **24**(6), 381–395 (1981)

7. Givens, C.R., Shortt, R.M.: A class of Wasserstein metrics for probability distributions. Mich. Math. J. **31**(2), 231–240 (1984)
8. Hartley, R., Zisserman, A.: Multiple View Geometry in Computer Vision. Cambridge University Press, Cambridge (2003)
9. Jiang, W., Zhou, Y., Wang, C., Peng, L., Yang, Y., Liu, H.: Navigation strategy for robotic soft endoscope intervention. Int. J. Med. Robot. Comput. Assist. Surg. **16**(2), e2056 (2020)
10. Liu, Z., et al.: Swin transformer: hierarchical vision transformer using shifted windows. In: Proceedings of the IEEE/CVF International Conference on Computer Vision, pp. 10012–10022 (2021)
11. Muja, M., Lowe, D.G.: Scalable nearest neighbor algorithms for high dimensional data. IEEE Trans. Pattern Anal. Mach. Intell. **36**(11), 2227–2240 (2014)
12. Ozyoruk, K.B., et al.: EndoSLAM dataset and an unsupervised monocular visual odometry and depth estimation approach for endoscopic videos. Med. Image Anal. **71**, 102058 (2021)
13. Puerto-Souza, G.A., Staranowicz, A.N., Bell, C.S., Valdastri, P., Mariottini, G.-L.: A comparative study of ego-motion estimation algorithms for teleoperated robotic endoscopes. In: Luo, X., Reichl, T., Mirota, D., Soper, T. (eds.) CARE 2014. LNCS, vol. 8899, pp. 64–76. Springer, Cham (2014). https://doi.org/10.1007/978-3-319-13410-9_7
14. Recasens, D., Lamarca, J., Fácil, J.M., Montiel, J., Civera, J.: Endo-depth-and-motion: reconstruction and tracking in endoscopic videos using depth networks and photometric constraints. IEEE Robot. Autom. Lett. **6**(4), 7225–7232 (2021)
15. Sevilla-Lara, L., Sun, D., Learned-Miller, E.G., Black, M.J.: Optical flow estimation with channel constancy. In: Fleet, D., Pajdla, T., Schiele, B., Tuytelaars, T. (eds.) ECCV 2014. LNCS, vol. 8689, pp. 423–438. Springer, Cham (2014). https://doi.org/10.1007/978-3-319-10590-1_28
16. van der Stap, N., Slump, C.H., Broeders, I.A.M.J., van der Heijden, F.: Image-based navigation for a robotized flexible endoscope. In: Luo, X., Reichl, T., Mirota, D., Soper, T. (eds.) CARE 2014. LNCS, vol. 8899, pp. 77–87. Springer, Cham (2014). https://doi.org/10.1007/978-3-319-13410-9_8
17. Turan, M., Almalioglu, Y., Araujo, H., Konukoglu, E., Sitti, M.: Deep EndoVO: a recurrent convolutional neural network (RCNN) based visual odometry approach for endoscopic capsule robots. Neurocomputing **275**, 1861–1870 (2018)
18. Turan, M., et al.: Unsupervised odometry and depth learning for endoscopic capsule robots. In: 2018 IEEE/RSJ International Conference on Intelligent Robots and Systems (IROS), pp. 1801–1807. IEEE (2018)
19. Wang, K., Wang, Z., Zhou, Y., Yan, G.: Squirm robot with full bellow skin for colonoscopy. In: 2010 IEEE International Conference on Robotics and Biomimetics, pp. 53–57. IEEE (2010)
20. Xu, Y., Feng, L., Xia, Z., Xiong, J.: Camera pose estimation based on feature extraction and description for robotic gastrointestinal endoscopy. In: Liu, X.-J., Nie, Z., Yu, J., Xie, F., Song, R. (eds.) ICIRA 2021. LNCS (LNAI), vol. 13015, pp. 113–122. Springer, Cham (2021). https://doi.org/10.1007/978-3-030-89134-3_11
21. Zhao, Y., Lou, Y.: Vision guided navigation based on dark regions and template matching for capsule endoscopies. In: 2013 IEEE International Conference on Information and Automation (ICIA), pp. 533–538. IEEE (2013)

Constant Force Control Method of Grinding Device

Jia Wen duo, Jiang Zi feng, and Dai Yu(✉)

College of Artificial Intelligence, Nankai University, Tianjin, China
daiyu@nankai.edu.cn

Abstract. At present, the traditional robot grinding has some shortcomings in output constant force control. As a result, the output force on the grinding object is frequently instable. Improper force can damage the object during grinding and lead huge economic loss. Therefore, how to improve the accuracy of the output force of robot grinding, has become an urgent problem to be solved. In this paper, aim to improve the grinding force control accuracy, a new control framework which is suitable for cylinder driven grinding device is proposed. The control framework is applied to control the cylinder output force of the grinding device, thereby improving the control ability of the high-precision grinding process robot. In the framework, a PID controller with nonlinear differential gain parameters is used, and parameters are optimized by using the Particle Swarm Optimization Algorithm (PSO). The proposed control method, based on the model of the actual cylinder driven grinding device, is verified in MATLAB. The results show that it controls the actual force of the grinding object near the ideal force accurately. The overshoot of the output force on the grinding object is zero and the system stability is very good.

Keywords: Grinding device · Nonlinear differential gain PID controller · Particle Swarm Optimization Algorithm

1 Introduction

1.1 A Subsection Sample

Grinding is a finishing process. It is widely used in high-precision design, such as fan blades [1], aerospace, automobiles [2], medical supplies [3], gear wheel [4], bone-cutting operation [5–7] and other high-tech and sophisticated fields [8]. Robot grinding is mainly used for workpiece surface grinding, sharp corners deburring, weld grinding, holes of internal cavity deburring and other scenarios [9]. So, if the robot's cutting force is not properly controlled in the grinding process, it may cause irreversible damage to the grinding object. And it will give rise to unimaginable terrible consequences when a large error robot grinding is used in the high precision requirements fields. In recent years, with the increasing demand for efficient and economical flexible precision machining equipment,

Funded by National Natural Science Foundation of China(62173190, U1913207).

it is urgent to realize robot high-precision grinding. So, the research of high-precision robot grinding technology is of great value to achieve technological breakthroughs in industrial automation and even other fields [10].

Automated grinding requires not only precise position control, but also flexible force mixing control [11]. At present, the research on the flexible control of robot grinding mainly focuses on the following two aspects. One is the active compliance, achieved by force/position hybrid control and impedance control of the robot control algorithm [12]. The other is the passive compliance whose buffering is realized by using compliance mechanisms such as abrasive bands and so on [13]. It is noteworthy that, although good robustness is eventually obtained, the active compliance control of the mechanical arm generally has problems such as complex control algorithms and complicated realizing processes [14]. The passive compliance avoids the rigid contact between the grinding device and the grinding object. It is natural obedience. Not only due to low accuracy requirements of the robot, but also the force control and position control are decentralized, passive compliance has a wider application prospect in the industrial field. However, passive compliance control method has low accuracy and long response time for the output force, so it is not suitable for high precision grinding [15].

Therefore, focusing on the basic problems of passive compliance robot high-precision grinding control, we carried out research on improving the control accuracy of grinding device output force. In this paper, based on the model of an actual cylinder driven grinding device, a new controller with nonlinear differential gain is designed. Parameters optimization is made by introducing The Particle Swarm Optimization Algorithm (PSO) to obtain a more accurate output force of the grinding device. The new controller is expected to significantly improve the grinding accuracy and effectively reduces the probability of damage to the grinding objects.

The other components of this paper are as follows. Section 2 describes the mechanism model of the cylinder driven grinding device through the grinding tool dynamic model and the cylinder model respectively. Section 3 discusses the establishment of a nonlinear PID controller for the force output of the cylinder driven grinding device, and how to obtain the optimal PID controller parameters by introducing the Particle Swarm Optimization Algorithm. Section 4 simulates and verifies the control effect, and compares it with the original controller. And Sect. 5 summarizes the work and prospects finally (Table 1).

Table 1. Variables used in this paper and their meanings

Name	Meaning	Unit
M_0	Total mass of the grinding device active end	kg
α	Angle between the axial and gravity directions of the grinding device	rad
F_n	Contact force between the grinding tool and the surface of the grinding object	N
g	Acceleration of gravity	m/s^2
$x, X(s)$	Displacement of the piston in the cylinder	mm

(*continued*)

Table 1. (*continued*)

Name	Meaning	Unit
F_d	Output force of the grinding device	N
f	Cylinder friction and rail friction	N
A_d	Effective force area of the piston	mm^2
$P_d, P_d(s)$	Air pressure of the cylinder	kPa
F_{n0}	Expected force on the grinded object	N
$F_{d0}(s)$	Expected output force of grinding device	N
$U, U(s)$	Voltage signal output by the controller to the regulator	V
$F_d(s)$	Actual output force of the grinding device	N
k, B	Constants	–
k_p	Proportional element parameter of PID controller	–
k_i	Integral element parameter of PID controller	–
k_d	Differential element parameter of PID controller	–
$e(t)$	Adjustment error	–
$K(e(t))$	Nonlinear differential gain	–
a_d, b_d, c_d, d_d	Parameters of nonlinear differential gain	–
n	Number of initial populations	–
S	Spatial dimensions	–
N	Maximum number of iterations	–
w	Inertia weights	–
T_1	Self-learning factor	–
T_2	Group learning factor	–

2 Mechanism Model of the Grinding Device

2.1 Grinding Tool Dynamics Model

The research object is a two-part grinding device, one is a cylinder and the other is a grinding tool. The device is equipped with force sensor and inclination sensor. Force sensor is used to obtain the force on the tool. Inclination sensor measures angle between gravity and the direction perpendicular to the contact surface in real time. A pressure regulating valve is selected as the pressure difference regulating actuator of the system.

When the force or inclination changes, the pressure regulating valve will change its output voltage. Then, the air pressure on both sides of the cylinder piston will be adjusted, and the pressure difference will make the piston displaced. Since the expand and contract of the tool relates to the piston displacement, the air pressure difference can indirectly control the output force of the device. The appropriate output force control can maintain the grinding force constantly. The force analysis of the grinding tool during operation is shown in Fig. 1.

According to Newton's Second Law, we can obtain the kinetic equation of the grinding device as follows:

$$M_0\ddot{x} + M_0g\cos\alpha = F_d + F_n + f \tag{1}$$

where M_0 can be obtained by weighing, f can be obtained by identifying friction forces at different speeds, and F_d is calculated as follows:

$$P_dA_d - f = F_d \tag{2}$$

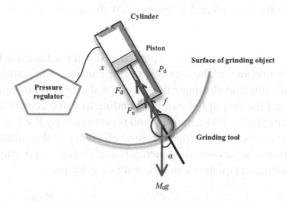

Fig. 1. Force analysis of the grinding device

2.2 Cylinder Model

The research object is a two-part grinding device, one is a cylinder and the other is a grinding tool. The device is equipped with force sensor and inclination sensor. Force sensor is used to obtain the force on the tool. Inclination sensor measures angle between gravity and the direction perpendicular to the contact surface in real time. A pressure regulating valve is selected as the pressure difference regulating actuator of the system.

Cylinders have obvious nonlinear properties, and it is difficult to model a nonlinear system directly. Therefore, by taking the pressure regulating valve and the cylinder as a whole, the model form U to P_d is established. This model greatly reduces the difficulty and error of modeling.

By comparing the fitting results of different order transfer equations, the second-order model of the optimal fitting system is finally obtained as follows:

$$G(s) = \frac{a}{s^2 + bs + c} \tag{3}$$

where the parameters are as follows: $a = 0.008$, $b = 0.048$, $c = 1.601$ [15].

In summary, the grinding device system model used in this paper is as follows:

$$\begin{cases} G(s) = \frac{a}{s^2 + bs + c} \\ M_0\ddot{x} + M_0g\cos\alpha = F_d + F_n + f \end{cases} \tag{4}$$

3   Control of the Output Force of the Grinding Device

3.1   Control Framework Based on a Nonlinear Differential Gain PID Controllers

The input F_{n0} is set value of constant grinding force on the grinding object in the actual operation process. $F_{d0}(s)$ is calculated by the model shown in Sect. 2. $P_d(s)$ is measured value of the air pressure. We want to get a grinding device that can realize the function of constant force grinding. This means that the device can restore the expected value F_{n0} in a short time after the force on the grinding object fluctuates. In order to meet this condition, we must ensure that $F_d(s)$ follows $F_{d0}(s)$ efficiently in the simulation experiment.

The PID controller is used and it ensures that the actual value of the output force follows the ideal value quickly and stably. At the same time, PID controller can reduce the possibility of overshoot damage to the grinded object. When the controller receives the ideal value and actual values of the output force, it will use the error between the two to calculate a correction value. The correction value can make the actual value gradually approach the ideal value and eliminate the error in a short period of time.

In order to adjust the output force of the grinding tool, the controller is designed as a nonlinear differential gain PID controller and is optimized by PSO. It can increase the damping ratio and improve the dynamic response efficiency of the output force under the condition of ensuring that the natural frequency is unchanged. According to the principle of PID control system, an equation can be construct as follows:

$$u(t) = k_p e(t) + k_i \int_0^t e(t)dt + k_d K(e(t)) \frac{de(t)}{dt} \tag{5}$$

where e(t) is calculated as follows:

$$e(t) = F_{d0} - F_d \tag{6}$$

The nonlinear part K is a function of $e(t)$, so Eq. (5) can be seen as adding a nonlinear sector to the general PID. The structural diagram of the nonlinear differential gain PID control system is shown in Fig. 3.

Since the response of the grinding device is basically without overshoot, it is only necessary to slowly increase the parameters of the differential sector to suppress overshoot. Therefore, the differential gain equation is constructed as follows:

$$K(e(t)) = a_d + \frac{b_d}{1 + c_d \exp(-d_d e(t))} \tag{7}$$

where the parameters a_d, b_d, c_d, d_d are all positive real numbers. The adjustment error $e(t)$ is positively correlated with the differential gain and the output control amount. So, it can effectively make the system quickly tend to the target value (Fig. 2).

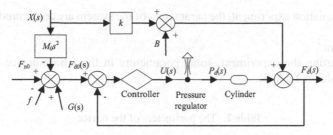

Fig. 2. Schematic diagram of the control framework

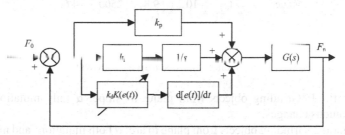

Fig. 3. Nonlinear differential gain PID control system structure diagram

3.2 Controller Parameter Selection Based on the Particle Swarm Optimization Algorithm

The parameters of the differential gain are expected to adjust to an optimal state, in which the controller will have the best output force following effect. There are seven parameters in the designed nonlinear differential gain PID controller altogether. What's more, the interaction between each parameter is completely complex. The results obtained by using the general optimization algorithm are instable. Therefore, we choose to use the Particle Swarm Optimization Algorithm. The PSO has high stability, and can accurately identify the optimal regions that can meet the needs of the particle swarm in complex particle interactions. Moreover, the PSO is efficient and has relatively simple implementation.

Therefore, the whole controller is used as the optimized object in this paper. Thus, the optimal parameter can be founded through continuous evolutionary iteration of the algorithm.

4 Simulation Experiments

4.1 Simulation Configuration and Methods

In this paper, Simulink is used for simulation experiments. Generally grinding work is usually slow and smooth and the acceleration of the grinding tool is small. So, the effect of acceleration on the calculation of the ideal output force is ignored in the simulation experiment.

In the simulation experiment, the parameters of the system are configured as follows:

- Assignment
  Before starting the experiment, some parameters in the whole device were given specific values (Table 2):

Table 2. The parameters of the device

Parameter	M_0	F_{n0}	g	A_d	F
Value	1	10	9.8	2500	4.66

- Classification
  In this paper, three grinding scenarios are set up as follows:

  a) Scenario 1: Grinding objects from plane to slope: α only mutations and no continuous changes.
  b) Scenario 2: Grinding objects from plane to arc: α both mutations and monotonous continuous changes.
  c) Scenario 3: Grinding objects have only an arc surface: α no mutations and only nonmonotonic continuous changes.

- Particle Swarm Optimization Algorithm:
  The parameters of the controller before optimization [15] are shown as follows (Table 3):

Table 3. The parameters of the original controller

Parameter	k_p	k_i	k_d	a_d	b_d	c_d	d_d
Value	12	3	1	3.5	2.8	5	3

The relevant parameter settings for using the Particle Swarm Optimization Algorithm are showed as follows (Table 4):

Table 4. The parameter setting of PSO

Parameter	n	S	N	w	T_1	T_2
Value	10	6	50	0.1	1.495	1.495

To prevent overshoots from appearing, we set a penalty for overshooting that is greater than a penalty for not overshooting. After the program runs, the changes of objective function are shown in Fig. 4(a).

After optimizing the parameters of the controller using the Particle Swarm Optimization Algorithm, we get the results as follows (Table 5):

Table 5. The parameters of the new controller

Parameter*	Value	Parameter**	Value
k_p	14.5859	a_d	1.0453
k_i	1.1674	b_d	2.7797
k_d	2.3436	c_d	1.2435
–	–	d_d	1.4542

* Three parameters of the PID controller
**Four parameters of the nonlinear differential gain.

As the iteration increases, the variation curves of each parameter are shown in the Fig. 4 and Fig. 5.

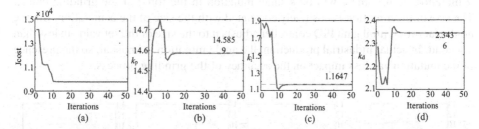

Fig. 4. The change of the parameter: (a) changes in the objective function of the PSO; (b) variation curve of parameter k_p; (c) variation curve of parameter k_i; (d) variation curve of parameter k_d.

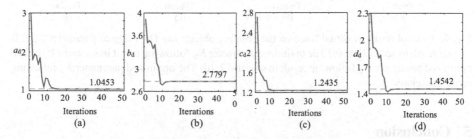

Fig. 5. The change of the parameter: (a) variation curve of parameter a_d; (b) variation curve of parameter b_d; (c) variation curve of parameter c_d; (d) variation curve of parameter d_d.

To test its control performance in different grinding states, we conduct a virtual simulation experiment on the model according to the three scenarios proposed in the previous section. We use scenario 1 to compare the effect before the controller parameter optimization and the effect after.

a) Scenario 1: Fig. 6(a) is the following result of F_n before parameter optimization, and Fig. 6(b) is the following result of F_n after parameter optimization.

From the comparison of Fig. 6(a) and Fig. 6(b), it can be seen that after optimizing the parameters, the performance of PID controller has been proved. When the α suddenly changes, not only the response time becomes faster, but also the accuracy of following the set point becomes higher. The control effect of the constant force is significantly higher than that of the PID controller Using the original parameters. Therefore, the optimization, Using the PSO, can indeed significantly improve the following effect of the actual output force of the grinding device on the ideal output force.

b) Scenario 2: In Scenario 2, the effect of the actual value following the ideal value is shown in Fig. 6(c).

c) Scenario 3: In Scenario 3, the effect of the actual value following the ideal value is shown in Fig. 6(d).

From the following results of the above three scenarios, when the α is unchanged or continuously changed, the control method designed in this paper can accurately control the force received by the grinding object around the set constant force. When the angle α mutation occurs, there will be a small mutation in the force of the grinding object. The size of the mutation is positively correlated with the size of the α mutation. But the nonlinear differential gain PID controller adjusts it to the size of the set value in less than a second. In actual industrial production, the angle mutation is unusual, so the presence of the mutation has less impact on the accuracy of the grinding process.

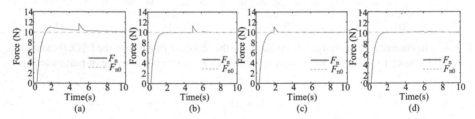

Fig. 6. Control result of actual force on the grinding object: (a) The original parameter F_n following result in scenario 1; (b) The optimized parameter F_n following result in scenario 1; (c) The optimized parameter F_n following result in scenario 2; (d) The optimized parameter F_n following result in scenario 3.

5   Conclusion

This paper studies how to more effectively realize the constant force grinding based on cylinder control. Firstly, the entire system's two parts, the grinding tool and the cylinder, are respectively modeled. Then a framework based on the nonlinear differential gain PID controller is build. The parameters are optimized using the Particle Swarm Optimization Algorithm. Finally, the optimized controller's advantage, can get a more accurate control and faster response to the constant force following effect, is verified through simulation experiments. However, there is shortcoming in this paper. The operating environment of the simulation experiment is very ideal. In actual operation process, there will be other uncontrollable factors that affect the system. Therefore, the following effect of the controller in real work needs to be verified by further practical experiments.

References

1. Chong, Z., Xie, F., Liu, X.J., et al.: Design of the parallel mechanism for a hybrid mobile robot in wind turbine blades polishing. Robot. Comput.-Integr. Manuf. **61**, 101857-1–101857-9 (2020)
2. Pereira, B., Griffiths, C.A., Birch, B., Rees, A.: Optimization of an autonomous robotic drilling system for the machining of aluminum aerospace alloys. Int. J. Adv. Manuf. Technol. **119**, 2429–2444 (2021). https://doi.org/10.1007/S00170-021-08483-4
3. Preciado, D., Wilson, E., Fooladi, H., Sang, H., Cleary, K., Monfaredi, R.: A new surgical drill instrument with force sensing and force feedback for robotically assisted otologic surgery. J. Med. Dev. **11**(3), 031009 (2017). https://doi.org/10.1115/1.4036490
4. Klingelnberg GmbH: Apparatus for grinding machining of gear wheel workpieces. Patent Application Approval Process (USPTO 20190329339). Politics & Government Week (2019)
5. Xia, G., Zhang, L., Dai, Y., Xue, Y., Zhang, J.: Vertebral lamina state estimation in robotic bone milling process via vibration signals fusion. IEEE Trans. Instrum. Measur. **71**(1), 1–10 (2022). https://doi.org/10.1109/TIM.2022.3161704
6. Xia, G., Jiang, Z., Zhang, J., Wang, R., Dai, Y.: Sound pressure signal based bone cutting depth control in robotic vertebral lamina milling. IEEE Sens. J. **22**(11), 10708–10718 (2022). https://doi.org/10.1109/JSEN.2022.3167664
7. Xia, G., Dai, Y., Zhang, J., Jia, B.: A method of bone cutting depth control for surgical robot based on acoustic signals. Robot **43**(1), 101–111 (2021). https://doi.org/10.13973/j.cnki.robot.200035
8. Wu, X., Huang, Z., Wan, Y., et al.: A novel force-controlled spherical polishing tool combined with self-rotation and co-rotation motion. IEEE Access **8**, 108191–108200 (2020)
9. Guo, W., Zhu, Y., He, X.: A robotic grinding motion planning methodology for a novel automatic seam bead grinding robot manipulator. IEEE Access **8**, 75288–75302 (2020)
10. Zhu, D., Feng, X., Xu, X., et al.: Robotic grinding of complex components: a step towards efficient and intelligent machining–challenges, solutions, and applications. Robot. Comput.-Integr. Manuf. **65**, 101908-1–101908-15 (2020)
11. Luo, Z., Li, J., Bai, J., Wang, Y., Liu, L.: Adaptive hybrid impedance control algorithm based on subsystem dynamics model for robot polishing. In: Yu, H., Liu, J., Liu, L., Ju, Z., Liu, Y., Zhou, D. (eds.) ICIRA 2019. LNCS, pp. 163–176. Springer, Cham (2019). https://doi.org/10.1007/978-3-030-27529-7_15
12. Zhang, Y.D.: Research on robot control method based on six-dimensional force sensor. Master's degree, Huazhong University of Science & Technology (2019)
13. Li, J., Guan, Y., Chen, H., et al.: A high-bandwidth end-effector with active force control for robotic polishing. IEEE Access **8**, 169122–169135 (2020)
14. Xu, X., Chen, W., Zhu, D., et al.: Hybrid active/passive force control strategy for grinding marks suppression and profile accuracy enhancement in robotic belt grinding of turbine blade. Robot. Comput.-Integr. Manuf. **67**, 102047-1 (2021)
15. Li, P.W.: Research on constant force control method of compliance device for high precision grinding operation. Master's degree, Naikai University (2021)

Shape Reconstruction Method for Continuum Robot Using FBG Sensors

Licheng Hou, Sikyuen Tam, Xingwei Zhao$^{(\boxtimes)}$, and Bo Tao

School of Mechanical Science and Engineering, Huazhong University of Science
and Technology, Wuhan 430074, China
zhaoxingwei@hust.edu.cn

Abstract. In this paper, we propose an improved shape reconstruction method based on FBG sensors. Two optical fibers with five uniformly distributed FBG sensors are bonded on a rod, and the curvature of each measuring point can be measured. The relationship between curvature and the rod arc length is obtained by cubic spline interpolation and partial linear interpolation. The rod is differentiated into sufficiently small constant curvature arcs, then the shape of the rod is reconstructed by means of integration. A fourth-order Bezier curve is used as a virtual bending rod to verify the proposed method. Experiments are conducted to reconstruct the shape of actual bending rod. Simulation and experiment results show that the proposed method has higher shape reconstruction accuracy in most cases.

Keywords: Fiber Bragg Grating (FBG) · Shape reconstruction · Spline interpolation methods

1 Introduction

Continuum robots have a completely different structure compared with the traditional industrial robots composed of multiple rigid joints. This kind of design offers them the characteristics of ease of miniaturization, high dexterity and inherent structural compliance, giving them congenital advantages in minimally invasive surgery (MIS) [1]. In recent years, continuum robots have attracted extensive attention in the field of medical robotics [2–5]. However, these characteristics make the continuum robots vulnerable to the influence of external complex environment and significantly reduce their control accuracy.

In order to improve the control accuracy of the continuum robots, various modalities and techniques have been employed to obtain their shape and terminal position, such as ultrasound (US) images [6], computed tomography (CT) images, magnetic resonance imaging (MRI), stereo vision [3] and electromagnetic (EM) tracking [7]. However, some drawbacks are discovered within these approaches in practice. The US image-guided approach has good real-time performance, but its low signal-to-noise ratio as well as image artifacts caused by metal instruments result in low accuracy. The resolution of MRI images is high enough, but it is difficult to achieve real-time performance, while

H. Liu et al. (Eds.): ICIRA 2022, LNAI 13457, pp. 388–395, 2022.
https://doi.org/10.1007/978-3-031-13835-5_35

the material requirements for surgical instruments are strict. There exists a high dose of radiation in CT, the human body cannot be exposed to the radiation environment for a long time. Stereo vision's targets are easily polluted by blood while EM tracking is susceptible to electromagnetic interference. In the last few years, fiber Bragg grating (FBG), a kind of sensor which can measure strain and temperature, has been favored by researchers. Current technology allows FBG interrogator to sample the reflected light signal at a very high speed (up to 1 kHz), which is fast enough for real-time applications. FBG sensors are small in size and light in weight, therefore, they can be integrated into surgical instruments. Moreover, FBG sensors are immune to electromagnetic, which allows them to be used with surgical devices without causing electromagnetic interference. Utilizing the FBG characteristics, we can calculate the strain and temperature at the sensor position [8].

Obviously, a shape sensor can be designed to convert the strain measured by FBGs into curvature. And multiple sets of FBGs obtain a group of discrete curvatures. To solve the problem of reconstructing the sensor shape with discrete curvature, Hoffman et al. [9] proposed a constant curvature reconstruction method. They assumed that the curvature of a distance around each measurement point was constant, then they reconstructed the shape of the curved rod. Farvardin et al. [10] used linear interpolation and partial constant curvature method to obtain the relationship between curvature and sensor arc length, and reconstructed the shape of the continuum robot.

Based on the structure of shape sensing rod and the characteristics of FBG, the calculation formula of local curvature is derived in this paper. In order to obtain higher shape reconstruction accuracy, a cubic spline interpolation method is proposed. To verify the superiority of this method, a fourth-order Bezier curve is used as a virtual bending rod to reconstruct its shape, and then the shape of the actual bending rod is reconstructed based on images. Simulation and experiment results show that the proposed method has higher reconstruction accuracy in most cases than the other two methods mentioned above.

2 Shape Sensing Methods

In this section, the principle of FBG sensors is reviewed. Temperature decoupling and calculation of local curvature are introduced. Based on the obtained local curvature, the relationship between curvature and shape sensing rod's arc length is acquired. Assuming the differential arc segment's curvature is constant, the shape can be reconstructed by integration.

2.1 Strain Measurement and Curvature Computations

When broadband light from FBG interrogator propagates along an optical fiber, each FBG connected in series to the fiber reflects a specific portion of the light, and the light with different wavelength is transmitted. The wavelength which is reflected by FBG is called the Bragg wavelength (λ_B). It satisfies:

$$\lambda_B = 2n_{eff}\Lambda \tag{1}$$

where n_{eff} is the effective refractive index of optical fiber, Λ is the grating period. The change of external strain and temperature will cause the change of n_{eff} and Λ, as well as the Bragg wavelength λ_B, the relationship can be expressed as:

$$\frac{\Delta\lambda_B}{\lambda_B} = (1 - P_e)\varepsilon + (\alpha + \zeta)\Delta T \qquad (2)$$

where, $\Lambda\lambda_B$ is the Bragg wavelength shifts, P_e is the elastic-optic coefficient, ε is the axial strain in the gate region, α is the thermal-optic coefficient, ζ is the thermal expansion coefficient, ΔT is the change in temperature.

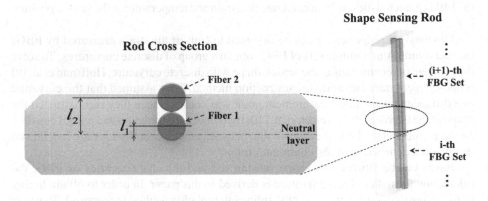

Fig. 1. Schematic of the shape sensor, where 2 optical fibers are glued in groove along the entire rod. There are 5 FBGs which are evenly distributed in the shape sensor in each fiber. The purpose of placing 2 optical fibers is to perform temperature decoupling. The width of the shape sensor is 1.8 mm and the thickness is 0.5 mm. The length can be varied as required.

The principle of calculating local curvature by strain is based on the pure bending model. For the shape sensor shown in Fig. 1, when plane bending occurs along the neutral layer, the relationship between strain and curvature of fiber 1 and fiber 2 satisfies:

$$\varepsilon_1 = \frac{l_1}{\rho} + \varepsilon_0 = l_1\kappa + \varepsilon_0$$
$$\varepsilon_2 = \frac{l_2}{\rho} + \varepsilon_0 = l_2\kappa + \varepsilon_0 \qquad (3)$$

where ρ is the radius of curvature, κ is the curvature, ε_0 is the common strain caused by the axial stress of the rod. Limited by the maximum strain of the fiber and the rod, the minimum radius of curvature of the shape sensor can be bent is 50 mm. Assuming that the temperature changes (ΔT) of the fiber in the same FBG set are equal, combining (2) and (3), the formula of local curvature can be obtained as follows:

$$\kappa = \frac{(\frac{\Delta\lambda_1}{\lambda_1} - \frac{\Delta\lambda_2}{\lambda_2})}{(1 - P_e)(l_1 - l_2)} \qquad (4)$$

2.2 Shape Reconstruction Model

The Bragg wavelength reflected from each Bragg grating can be captured in real time from the FBG interrogator. The local curvature ($\kappa_1 \sim \kappa_5$) corresponding to the arc length ($s_1 \sim s_5$) shown in Fig. 2(a) can be obtained using Eq. (4). In order to reconstruct the shape of the rod and acquire the terminal position, the relationship between the curvature and arc length along the whole rod needs to be predicted firstly using discrete local curvature, as follows:

$$\kappa = f(s) \tag{5}$$

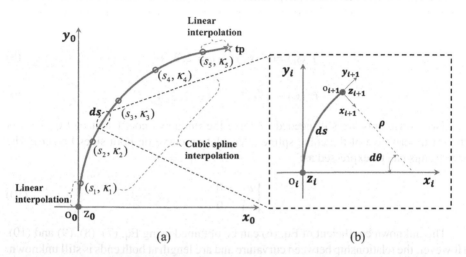

Fig. 2. (a) Diagram of bent rod. Red circles represent locations where the local curvature is known. "tp" stands for terminal position. (b) Diagram of constant curvature differential arc segment. (Color figure online)

Combining with the calculated local discrete curvature information, we propose cubic spline interpolation between measuring points and linear interpolation at both ends, to speculate the relationship between curvature (κ) and rod's arc length (s). The cubic spline interpolation part of the equation ($f(s)$) is as follows:

$$f(s) = \begin{cases} a_1 s^3 + b_1 s^2 + c_1 s + d_1, & s_1 \le s < s_2, \\ a_2 s^3 + b_2 s^2 + c_2 s + d_2, & s_2 \le s < s_3, \\ a_3 s^3 + b_3 s^2 + c_3 s + d_3, & s_3 \le s < s_4, \\ a_4 s^3 + b_4 s^2 + c_4 s + d_4, & s_4 \le s < s_5, \end{cases} \tag{6}$$

There are 16 unknown coefficients ($a_1 \sim a_4$, $b_1 \sim b_4$, $c_1 \sim c_4$, $d_1 \sim d_4$) in Eq. (6), which need 16 constraints to solve. Since each interpolation segment passes through two endpoints, the following equation gives eight constraints:

$$\begin{cases} f(s_1) = \kappa_1 \\ f(s_2^-) = \kappa_2 \\ \quad \vdots \\ f(s_4) = \kappa_4 \\ f(s_5^-) = \kappa_5 \end{cases} \tag{7}$$

In addition, in cubic spline interpolation, the first and second derivatives are continuous at the common points of every two interpolation segments, resulting in the following six constraints:

$$f'(s_i) = f'(s_i^+) \quad i = 2, 3, 4 \tag{8}$$

$$f''(s_i) = f''(s_i^+) \quad i = 2, 3, 4 \tag{9}$$

Two constraints are still needed to solve the unknown coefficient of Eq. (6). Let the third derivative of the cubic spline interpolation curve on both sides be zero. The constraints can be expressed as:

$$\begin{cases} a_1 = 0 \\ a_4 = 0 \end{cases} \tag{10}$$

The unknown coefficient of Eq. (6) can be obtained using Eq. (7), (8), (9) and (10). However, the relationship between curvature and arc length at both ends is still unknown. Linear interpolation is used to derive this relationship, shown as follows:

$$f(s) = \begin{cases} f'(s_1)(s - s_1) + \kappa_1, \ 0 \le s < s_1 \\ f'(s_5^-)(s - s_5) + \kappa_5, \ s_5 \le s < s_t \end{cases} \tag{11}$$

where s_t is the total length of the shape sensing rod.

The arc length direction of the shape sensing rod is evenly divided into n sufficiently small constant curvature arcs, as shown in Fig. 2(b), with the following geometric relationship:

$$\kappa = \frac{d\theta}{ds} \quad \Rightarrow \quad d\theta = \kappa ds = \frac{ds}{\rho} \tag{12}$$

where ds is the arc length of the arc segment, $d\theta$ is the central angle corresponding to arc length, ρ is the radius of curvature. Utilizing the frames established in Fig. 2, the homogeneous transformation matrix ($_{i+1}^{i}\mathbf{T}$) of the frame $\{i + 1\}$ relative to the frame $\{i\}$ can be acquired.

$$_{i+1}^{i}\mathbf{T} = Trans((1-\cos d\theta)/\kappa \quad \sin d\theta/\kappa \quad 0)Rot(z, -d\theta)$$

$$= \begin{bmatrix} \cos d\theta & \sin d\theta & 0 & (1-\cos d\theta)/\kappa \\ -\sin d\theta & \cos d\theta & 0 & \sin d\theta/\kappa \\ 0 & 0 & 1 & 0 \\ 0 & 0 & 0 & 1 \end{bmatrix} \tag{13}$$

The homogeneous transformation matrix $(_n^0\mathbf{T})$ of the sensor's terminal frame $\{n\}$ with respect to the base frame $\{0\}$ can be obtained by multiplication.

$$_n^0\mathbf{T} = {_1^0\mathbf{T}}\,{_2^1\mathbf{T}}\cdots{_{i+1}^{i}\mathbf{T}}\cdots{_n^{n-1}\mathbf{T}} \tag{14}$$

Hence, the terminal position was obtained, and the intermediate data was used to reconstruct the shape of the rod.

3   Simulation Study

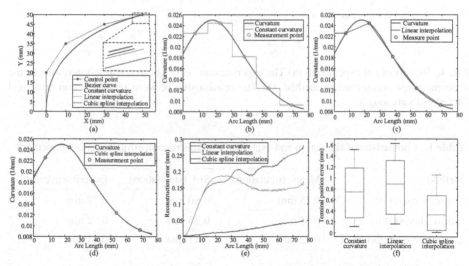

Fig. 3. Results of the simulation. (a) Bezier curve and the results of the different shape reconstruction method. (b), (c), and (d) correspond to constant curvature, linear interpolation, and cubic spline interpolation approximation methods, respectively. (e) The relationship between reconstruction error and shape sensing rod's arc length. (f) Terminal position error comparison of the different methods.

To simulate the shape reconstruction method, a fourth-order Bezier curve is used as the virtual bending rod. The curvature of Bezier curve corresponding to the FBG set's position in shape sensing rod is calculated. Then the shape of the curve is reconstructed using the shape reconstruction method proposed in the previous section. Reconstructed results are compared with the constant curvature shape reconstruction method in literature [9] and linear interpolation shape reconstruction method in literature [10]. And the result of comparison is shown in Fig. 3.

According to Fig. 3(b), (c) and (d), the relationship between curvature and arc length obtained by cubic spline interpolation is obviously more accurate than the other two methods, and the reconstruction error is also lower, as shown in Fig. 3(e). In order to verify the generality of the method, shape reconstruction was carried out for multiple Bezier curves, and the reconstruction errors of their terminal positions were shown in Fig. 3(f).

4   Experiment

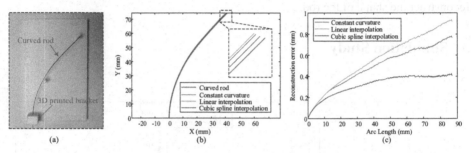

(a)   (b)   (c)

Fig. 4. Results of the experiment. (a) The experimental setup. (b) Reconstruction results of the different shape reconstruction method. (c) The relationship between reconstruction error and curved rod's arc length.

Table 1. Comparison of simulation and experiment reconstruction errors of different methods.

Method	Mean (simulation)	Std. (simulation)	Experiment error
Constant curvature	0.75 mm	0.50 mm	0.77 mm
Linear interpolation	0.84 mm	0.55 mm	0.92 mm
Cubic spline interpolation	0.42 mm	0.41 mm	0.41 mm

Experiment is conducted in this section to verify the shape reconstruction method. The experimental setup is shown in Fig. 4(a). Instead of fabricating a shape sensing rod and using FBG interrogator to capture data, then reconstruct the rod shape. An easier image analysis method was used in this experiment. The camera attitude was adjusted to face the bending rod and the image was taken. Threshold segmentation was performed on the image to extract the pixels corresponding to the bending rod, and a set of discrete points were obtained. Smooth filtering was performed on these points to get a smooth curve. Then the discrete curvature was calculated. The shape reconstruction method proposed in this paper, the constant curvature shape reconstruction method in literature

[9] and the linear interpolation shape reconstruction method in literature [10] were used to reconstruct the shape of the bending rod. The reconstruction results are shown in Fig. 4(b) and (c). Experimental results shown in Table 1 confirm that the proposed method has higher reconstruction accuracy.

5 Conclusion

Aiming at the shape reconstruction problem of the shape sensing rod with two optical fibers, an improved shape reconstruction method is proposed. The cubic spline interpolation and partial linear interpolation is used to acquire the relationship between the curvature and the arc length of the rod. Afterward, the shape of the rod can be reconstructed. The fourth-order Bezier curve is used to verify the proposed shape reconstruction method. Simulation results show that the proposed method can improve the reconstruction accuracy of the shape sensing rod compared with the other two construction methods in [9, 10]. The average terminal error is more than 40% lower than that of the other two methods. In the experiment, the reconstruction method proposed in this paper also has smaller shape reconstruction error compared to the other two methods.

References

1. Burgner-Kahrs, J., Rucker, D.C., Choset, H.: Continuum robots for medical applications: a survey. IEEE Trans. Rob. **31**(6), 1261–1280 (2015)
2. Yan, J., et al.: A continuum robotic cannula with tip following capability and distal dexterity for intracerebral hemorrhage evacuation. IEEE Trans. Biomed. Eng. (2022). https://doi.org/10.1109/TBME.2022.3158539
3. Wu, B.B., et al.: Closed-loop pose control and automated suturing of continuum surgical manipulators with customized wrist markers under stereo vision. IEEE Robot. Autom. Lett. **6**(4), 7137–7144 (2021)
4. Sefati, S., et al.: A dexterous robotic system for autonomous debridement of osteolytic bone lesions in confined spaces: human cadaver studies. IEEE Trans. Robot. **38**, 1–17 (2021)
5. Goldman, R.E., et al.: Design and performance evaluation of a minimally invasive telerobotic platform for transurethral surveillance and intervention. IEEE Trans. Biomed. Eng. **60**(4), 918–925 (2013)
6. Boctor, E.M., et al.: Three-dimensional ultrasound-guided robotic needle placement: an experimental evacuation. Int. J. Med. Robot. Comput. Assist. Surg. **4**(2), 180–191 (2008)
7. Franz, A.M., et al.: Electromagnetic tracking in medicine-a review of technology, validation, and applications. IEEE Trans. Med. Imaging **33**(8), 1702–1725 (2014)
8. Oh, S.T., et al.: Discrimination of temperature and strain with a single FBG based on the birefringence effect. Opt. Express **12**(4), 724–729 (2004)
9. Hoffman, J., et al.: Shape sensing of polymer core composite electrical transmission lines using FBG sensors. IEEE Trans. Instrum. Meas. **69**(1), 249–257 (2020)
10. Farvardin, A., et al.: Towards real-time shape sensing of continuum manipulators utilizing fiber Bragg grating sensors. In: 2016 6th IEEE International Conference on Biomedical Robotics and Biomechatronics (BioRob) (2016)

Safety Motion Control and End Force Estimation Based on Angle Information in Robotic Flexible Endoscopy

Bo Guan, Xingchi Liu, Zhikang Ma, Jianchang Zhao, Yuelin Zou, and Jianmin Li[✉]

Tianjin University, Tianjin 300072, China
mjli@tju.edu.cn

Abstract. Precise motion control and clear contact force information play an important role in robot-assisted endoscopy. It allows the surgeon to estimate soft tissue stiffness, understand the anatomy, and enables the robot to perform the surgeon's movement intentions more accurately. However, the ability of surgeon to perceive contact force information and motion status through the flexible endoscope is severely impaired. In this work, we proposed a rotational joint with torque estimation functions based on angle information to achieve the motion control and end force estimation of the flexible endoscope during the robot-assisted endoscopy. Furthermore, the joint consists of two wheels, which are connected with cables and springs. And then, two encoders have been utilized to check the joint positions. In the meantime, a feedforward PID control strategy has been proposed to realize an accurate position control for the designed joint. According to the force estimation study, the perception performance of the proposed joint was characterized with an excellent linearity error (0.53%), a high resolution (7.778×10^{-3} N · mm) and a wide measurement range (-500 N · mm to $+500$ N · mm), while the tracking performance demonstrates high sensitivity of the control strategy. The proposed joint has the capability to observe the external interference by estimating the change of the torque. Thus, the proposed method has important application potential in force detection, force feedback and control strategy with enhanced safety during Natural Orifice Transluminal Endoscopic Surgery (NOTES).

Keywords: Torque sensing · Flexible endoscopy · NOTES

1 Introduction

Flexible endoscopy techniques have been rapidly developed and widely applied in natural orifice transluminal endoscopic surgery (NOTES) [1–3]. During NOTES, a flexible endoscope is inserted into human body along specific natural orifice, such as, respiratory tract, digestive tract, and urinary tract, with minimal trauma, blood loss and complications. Surgeons perform flexible endoscopies guided by endoscopic image, and the above operations require the necessary training practice on phantoms and animals. To get rid of the dependence of endoscopy on operator experience, robot-assisted technology is

H. Liu et al. (Eds.): ICIRA 2022, LNAI 13457, pp. 396–408, 2022.
https://doi.org/10.1007/978-3-031-13835-5_36

increasingly employed in flexible endoscopy due to its high flexibility, comfort, and stability [4–9]. Meantime, surgeons cannot perceive tactile information due to the lack of contact force information, which may affect the safety and efficiency of robot-assisted surgery. Moreover, the endoscope is often contacted with different organs and most of these interactions are happened out of the view of endoscope. Therefore, it is necessary to implement force sensing and precise motion control on the flexible endoscope for enhanced safety [10].

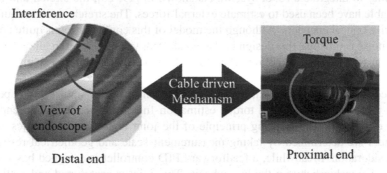

Fig. 1. Distal bending of a flexible endoscope and the schematic diagram of the unobserved interference between the endoscope and the organs

To achieve accurate contact force perception, many researches have been performed. Puangmali et al. summarized the force sensing techniques that utilized in minimally invasive surgery [11]. Several methods have been applied into this domain, including displacement-based, current-based, pressure-based, resistive-based, optical-based and piezoelectric-based sensing. The current of the actuators have been used to estimate tool-tissue forces and this method performs short time delay and it is compatible with existing sterilization methods [12, 13]. However, there are some inherent disturbances that influence estimation accuracy, such as motor effort. The cable tension has been applied to sense external force sensing of minimally invasive surgical manipulators [14]. Force sensors have been utilized to test the tension on cables. The whole system is complicated and hard to integrate on medical robots. As shown in [15], a capacitive-based sensor has been fabricated to check pressure based on stretchable composite electrodes and dielectric elastomer with microstructures. This sensor behaves a high sensitivity and an outstanding linearity, and its flexibility is an advantage to realize integration on flexible endoscope. Fiber Bragg grating (FBG) sensors are also utilized to perform force or torque sensing based on the strain of the fiber [16–18]. A miniature FBG-based force sensor has been designed for tissue palpation. A force-sensitive flexure has been designed and FBG sensor is glued on it to realize a single-axis force sensing. The main advantage of FBG sensor is higher sensitivity [18]. However, the transformation between the wavelength changes and force depends on several devices.

For the motion control of the endoscope, the main control is distal bending. Figure 1 shows the main components of an endoscope. A lever mechanism is designed to maneuver the distal bending movement with stainless wires that pass through the endoscope.

Once the unexpected interaction appeared at the distal end, the torque that applied on the lever mechanism will be different from that of without interaction. If this torque can be acquired and applied into control strategy, the safety of robots for endoscopy will be promoted. Conventional 6-axis sensors can be directly mounted on relative joints to check this torque. This method is relatively available compared to the sensor integration on the distal tip, which is even not compatible with some sterilization methods. However, they are expensive instruments with lots of additional elements, such as, data acquisition device, amplifiers, power supply and even host computer, which increase the complexity to integrate a robot system. As shown in [19, 20], the stretch and tension of the cable have been used to estimate external forces. The stretch can be acquired by the precise optical encoders. Although the model of this configuration is quite complex and the noise is obvious, this design is also an alternative approach to realize the torque estimation with compact structure. Therefore, the work in this paper is inspired by this research.

Based on the above requirements and the current research status, this paper proposes a joint with model-based torque estimation functions for the distal bending of flexible endoscope. The working principle of the joint is analyzed by statics and the parameters are determined by taking measurement scale and geometrical restrictions into consideration. Meanwhile, a feedforward PID controller is designed based on the motion relationship between the two wheels. This joint is prototyped and realized by integrating a servo motor and an encoder. Calibration experiment has been performed to demonstrated the higher linearity and sensitivity of the torque estimation function. Further trajectory response performance experiments and application research experiments have validated the perfect following error and effectiveness of this design.

2 Methods

2.1 Working Principle of the Proposed Joint with End Force Estimation

As illustrated in Fig. 2, the basic structures of the proposed joint include two wheels, two extension springs and cables that connect them to form a rotational transmission mechanism. The left wheel is defined as the driven wheel with a radius R_1. The right wheel is regarded as the driving wheel with a radius R_2. Two springs with initial length L_{10} and L_{20} have different spring constant K_1 and K_2. respectively. The whole mechanism is pre-tensioned with a tension force T_0 on each cable. After the pre-tension process, the elongations of the springs are Δ_1 and Δ_2. Meanwhile, the lengths of for cables at two side are denoted as L_1, L_2, L_3 and L_4 respectively.

A constant torque M_1 is applied on the driven wheel to rotate the endoscope, and the rotation angle is θ_1. This motion is driven by the driving wheel and its rotation angle is θ_2, and the corresponding torque supported by the motor is M_2. At this status, the elongations of the two springs are Δ_{11} and Δ_{21}, respectively. The tension force on the cables at two sides are T_1 and T_2.

According to the above description, the relationship between the elongation and tension on cables can be expressed as:

$$T_0 = K_1\Delta_1 = K_2\Delta_2$$
$$T_1 = K_1\Delta_{11} \tag{1}$$
$$T_2 = K_2\Delta_{21}$$

Meanwhile, the torque M_1 and M_2 can be calculated based on the tension as:

$$M_1 = (T_2 - T_1)R_1$$
$$M_2 = (T_2 - T_1)R_2 \tag{2}$$

As for the length change of the cables, considering two sides are always tensioned during the movement, the total length of the lengths for two cables and one spring at each side is a constant. All the elongations of cables are neglected since they are too small compared to the elongation of springs. Furthermore, the total lengths at two sides are same. This relationship can be written as:

$$L_1 + L_{10} + \Delta_1 + L_2 = L_3 + L_{20} + \Delta_2 + L_4$$
$$L_1 + L_{10} + \Delta_1 + L_2 = L_1 - R_1\theta_1 + L_{10} + \Delta_{11} + L_2 + R_2\theta_2 \tag{3}$$
$$L_3 + L_{20} + \Delta_2 + L_4 = L_3 + R_1\theta_1 + L_{20} + \Delta_{21} + L_4 - R_2\theta_2$$

Meanwhile, the torque M_1 and M_2 can be calculated based on the tension as:

$$M_1 = (K_1 + K_2)(R_2\theta_2 - R_1\theta_1)R_1$$
$$M_2 = (K_1 + K_2)(R_2\theta_2 - R_1\theta_1)R_2 \tag{4}$$

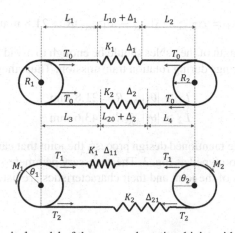

Fig. 2. Mechanical model of the proposed rotational joint with force sensing

2.2 Parameters Determination and System Integration

To prototype the above model and apply it for the endoscope control, the parameters should be determined according to the requirements analysis. To simplify the design, some parameters are selected as the same values:

$$R_1 = R_2 = R = 25 \text{ mm}$$
$$K_1 = K_2 = K$$
$$L_1 = L_3$$
$$L_2 = L_4$$

(5)

Therefore, the torque can be described as:

$$M = 2K(\theta_2 - \theta_1)R^2$$

(6)

The requirements mainly include the rotation range and the maximum torque that the joint can provide. The rotation angle is from $[-45°, 45°]$, where the $0°$ is defined as the joint position at which the distal end is released. Therefore, the motion range for θ_1 is designed as $[-50°, 50°]$. According to direction of the desired torque, the motion range for θ_2 should be larger than θ_1. In this design, it is determined as $[-100°, 100°]$. Generally, the maximum torque is less than 350 N·mm, and the maximum torque appears at the limited joint position. Our design determined the maximum torque $M_{max} = 400$ N·mm. Therefore, the spring constant can be determined as

$$K \geq \frac{M_{max}}{2(|\theta_2|_{max} - |\theta_1|_{max})R^2} = 0.366 \text{ N/mm}$$

(7)

In addition, to ensure the tension exists over the whole range movement, the elongation during pretension is determined as

$$\Delta_1 = \Delta_2 \geq (|\theta_2|_{max} - |\theta_1|_{max})R = 21.8 \text{ mm}$$

(8)

Meanwhile, the length of the cables should be enough to avoid interference between the wheels and the springs during rotation transmission. Thus, they are restricted as:

$$L_1 \geq |\theta_1|_{max}R = 21.8 \text{ mm}$$
$$L_2 \geq |\theta_2|_{max}R = 43.6 \text{ mm}$$

(9)

According to above mentioned design process, the joint that can realize torque sensing is designed and prototyped as Fig. 3. The necessary parameters are listed in Table 1. The main components of the joint and their characteristics are listed in Table 2.

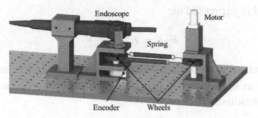

Fig. 3. Integration of the proposed rotational joint

Table 1. Parameters of the designed joint.

Parameters	Values
R	25 mm
θ_1	$[-50°, 50°]$
θ_2	$[-100°, 100°]$
L_1	25 mm
L_2	50 mm
Δ_1	25 mm
Δ_2	25 mm
M_{max}	400 N · mm

Table 2. Components of the designed joint

Components	Specifications
Motor	Maxon DCmax-16 s, 100:1 harmonic reducer, encoder with 4096 counts per circle
Encoder	HEDL5540, 2000 counts per circle
Extension spring	Wire diameter: 1.2 mm Out diameter: 12 mm Free length: 70 mm Length range: 70–139.7 mm Spring constant: 0.399 N/mm after calibrated

2.3 Control Strategy of the Proposed Mechanism

To realize an accurate position control, a PID controller has been designed to achieve higher accuracy in trajectory tracking. Meanwhile, A feedforward unit has been established to speed up the convergence and enhance the stability based on the geometrical relationship between the two wheels.

The feedforward is expressed as:

$$\theta_{2,k} = K_{E1}^{E2} \cdot \theta_{1,k} \tag{10}$$

where k represents an arbitrary time in the control process. In the meanwhile, the error at time k is denoted as e_k, which can be calculated according the actual joint positions and desired joint positions as:

$$e_k = \theta_{1,k} - \tilde{\theta}_{1,k} \tag{11}$$

where k represents an arbitrary time in the control process. In the meanwhile, the error

$$\Delta_k = K_P(e_k - e_{k-1}) + K_I e_k + K_D(e_k - 2e_{k-1} + e_{k-2}) \tag{12}$$

Therefore, the desired joint positions of the driver wheel at time $k + 1$ is

$$\theta_{2,k+1} = \tilde{\theta}_{2,k} + K_{E1}^{E2} \cdot \Delta_k \tag{13}$$

Based on the above-mentioned procedure, the structure of the control strategy can be illustrated as Fig. 4.

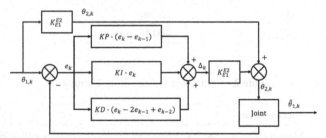

Fig. 4. Structure of parallel proportional-integral-derivatives (PID) position controller with feedforward

3   Experiments and Results

The experimental setup mainly consists of a PMAC controller (CK3M, Omron, Japan), an amplifier (ESCON Module 24/2, Maxon, Switzerland), a six-axis force/torque sensor (Nano17 SI-12-0.12, ATI Industrial Automation, Apex, NC, USA) and an NI data acquisition (DAQ) card, as illustrated in Fig. 5. The CK3M is connected with the PC through Ethernet to monitor and control the joint positions of two wheels. It has also been utilized to collect the joint positions with a sampling rate of 280 Hz. The ATI sensor has been installed on a 3D-printed support to check force. It is connected to the DAQ to provide force information with a resolution of 1/320N and a sampling rate of 50 Hz via USB.

3.1 Static Torque Calibration Experiments

The calibration experiment was performed at first. Due to the torque measuring range of the sensor at z axis is quite limited, a beam was fabricated by 3D-print to transform the torque to a force. The length direction of the beam is orthogonal to the z axis of the sensor. it is fixed with the left wheel at one side and the other side is fixed with the sensor. The length of beam is $L = 75$ mm. Therefore, the relationship between the required torque M_{measured} and the measured force N is:

$$M_{\text{measured}} = LN \tag{14}$$

The left wheel is set at 0 position and the angle difference is changed within the range of $-50°$–$50°$ with an interval of $5°$. The force applied on the sensor was also recorded. Three repeated procedures have been finished with both increasing and decreasing stages. The average values captured at each step are used to determine the *Torque-Difference of angle* relationship, as illustrated in Fig. 6. The measured results have been fitted based on least square method. The results calculated based on the model and the error between the model-based and the measure-based torque have also been listed in Fig. 6. Some quantitative parameters are listed in Table 3.

The maximum error 8 N · mm appears when the difference of angle is $-40°$, which determines the excellent linearity 0.53%. The R^2 is 0.9999 and it reflects the fitting degree between the two variables. The sensitivity is 7.778×10^{-3} N · mm and it is determined by the resolutions of the encoder on the servo motor, which reflects the sensitive performance of the joint.

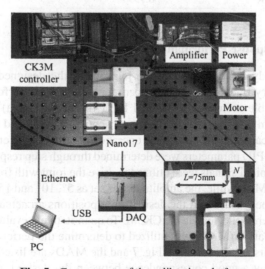

Fig. 5. Components of the calibration platform

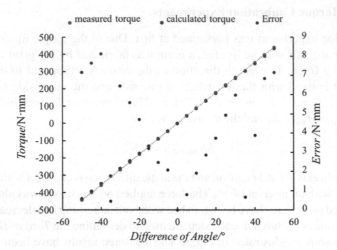

Fig. 6. Calibration results of the designed joint

Table 3. Mechanical property of the designed joint

Sensitivity	7.778×10^{-3} N · mm
Fitted equation	$M = 8.85 \times (\theta_1 - \theta_2) - 0.4952$
Linearity error (%)	0.53
R^2	0.9999

3.2 Tracking Response Performance Investigation

To investigate the dynamic features of the joint under the designed control strategy, a group of trajectory tracking response experiments have been performed. Before the experiment, a flexible ureteroscope (Model DPG II, Hawk, China) was fixed on the experiment platform and the lever of the ureteroscope was mounted on the left wheel. This configuration can simulate the robotic operation of commercial endoscopes. Before the experiment, the PID parameters were determined through step response (2°, 500 ms). The typically sinusoidal signals were utilized to drive the joint with frequency at 0.2 Hz, 0.5 Hz and 0.8 Hz. Meanwhile, the amplitude was set as 5°, 10° and 15°. Therefore, nine experiments were performed and the desired joint positions an actual joint position of the driven wheel were collected via the CK3M. To quantitatively evaluate the results, the mean absolute deviation (MAD) was utilized to determine the performance of tracking response. The results are illustrated in Fig. 7 and the MADs are listed in Table 4.

The results show a good correspondence between the desired joint positions and the actual joint positions, and the MADs are small, which reflects the efficiency of the control strategy.

Table 4. Mechanical property of the designed joint

Sensitivity	5°	10°	15°
0.2 Hz	0.222°	0.269°	0.342°
0.5 Hz	0.375°	0.552°	0.777°
0.8 Hz	0.423°	0.602°	0.876°

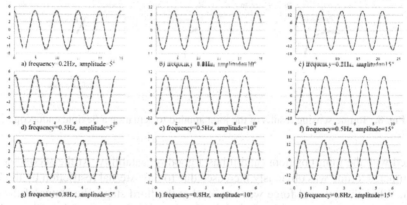

a) frequency 0.2Hz, amplitude 5°   b) frequency 0.2Hz, amplitude 10°   c) frequency=0.2Hz, amplitude=15°

d) frequency=0.5Hz, amplitude=5°   e) frequency=0.5Hz, amplitude=10°   f) frequency=0.5Hz, amplitude=15°

g) frequency=0.8Hz, amplitude=5°   h) frequency=0.8Hz, amplitude=10°   i) frequency=0.8Hz, amplitude=15°

Fig. 7. Tracking response performances of the proposed joint under sinusoidal excitation with different frequencies and amplitudes

3.3 Application Research of the Joint on the Bending Movement for the Endoscope

The application research was achieved by controlling the endoscope's bending and checking the applied torques on the endoscope to estimate whether there is unobservable interaction on the distal end. The previous endoscope was mounted on the proposed joint once again. A ureteral access sheath (UAS) (12-14F, COOK, USA) was used to restrict the distal end to simulate the un observable interaction. The joint was stimulated by a sinusoidal signal with a frequency of 0.2 Hz and an amplitude of 15°. The whole experiment was divided into 3 stages. At the beginning of the experiment, the distal end is out of the sheath to be set free. Then the UAS was moved along the endoscope to cover the most of the distal end. At last, the UAS was moved to the original position to expose the whole distal end. During the experiment, the desired joint positions and the actual joint positions of the driven wheel was recorded. In the meanwhile, the estimated torque was calculated by the CK3M in real time. It was also collected and analyzed. The results are illustrated in Fig. 8.

The three pictures at the bottom of the Fig. 8 shows the three stages of the experiment. The top diagram describes the tracking response of the proposed joint during the experiment. The results show a good performance on tracking no matter if there is interaction and external force on the distal end, which indicates the stability of the control strategy. The middle diagram reflects the variation of the estimated torque with the joint position and the external restriction. At the first stage, the estimated torque is

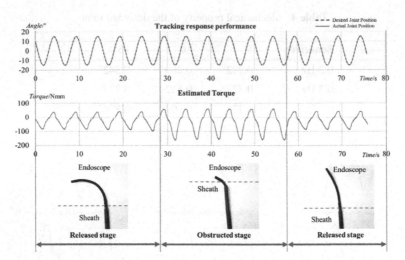

Fig. 8. Torque sensing results of the joint applied to actuating a flexible endoscope

changed with the joint positions, and it has a good repeatability. At the second stages, the estimated torque was obviously increased due to the external restriction by the UAS sheath. When the external force was removed at the third stage, the status of the estimated torque was the same as the first stage. However, the fluctuate of the estimated was not symmetrical about 0 Nmm, which was not conform to the normal conditions. Some reasons might lead to this circumstance, including: 1) the 0 position of the driven wheel is not a position that can make the distal end free; 2) the internal design of the endoscope is not symmetrical.

4 Conclusion

In summary, this paper proposes a joint with torque estimation function for distal bending of flexible endoscope. It provides a higher linearity and accuracy for torque estimation and a better tracking response performance for joint position control. The proposed joint has been applied to check the torque change of a flexible endoscope in the experiment to simulate unobserved interference and the results have demonstrated the effectiveness. This research only uses the joint positions to realize torque estimation without any force/torque or elongation measurement equipment. It is a quite exploration towards practical application. This design can provide a low-cost way to realize force/torque measurement. Furthermore, the whole procedure is accomplished by the CK3M controller, avoiding any software interfaces, and lessening the latency, which is a very dangerous factors for medical robots. The future work may mainly be focused on the integration on the multi-DOF endoscopic robotic system. Therefore, more research can be developed, such as force feedback and control strategy with more safe considerations.

Acknowledgments. This research is supported by National Natural Science Fund of China under grants 52122501, 51875394, and Science and Technology Program of Tianjin under grant

20JCZDJC00790. These funders had no role in study design, data collection, data analysis, decision to publish, or preparation of the manuscript.

References

1. Yip, H.C., Chiu, P.W.: Recent advances in natural orifice transluminal endoscopic surgery dagger. Eur. J. Cardiothorac. Surg. **49**(1), 25–30 (2016)
2. Min, Y.W., Min, B.H., Lee, J.H., Kim, J.J.: Endoscopic treatment for early gastric cancer. World J. Gastroenterol. **20**(16), 4566–4573 (2014)
3. Balmadrid, B., Hwang, J.H.: Endoscopic resection of gastric and esophageal cancer. Gastroenterol. Rep. **3**(4), 330–338 (2015)
4. Saglam, R., et al.: A new robot for flexible ureteroscopy: development and early clinical results. Eur. Urol. **66**(6), 1092–1100 (2014)
5. Iwasa, T., et al.: A new robotic-assisted flexible endoscope with single-hand control: endoscopic submucosal dissection in the ex vivo porcine stomach. Surg. Endosc. **32**(7), 3386–3392 (2018). https://doi.org/10.1007/s00464-018-6188-y
6. Zorn, L., et al.: A novel telemanipulated robotic assistant for surgical endoscopy: preclinical application to ESD. IEEE Trans. Biomed. Eng. **65**(4), 797–808 (2018)
7. Jiang, W., Zhou, Y., Wang, C., Peng, L., Yang, Y., Liu, H.: Navigation strategy for robotic soft endoscope intervention. Int. J. Med. Robot. Comput. Assist. Surg. **16**(2), 2056 (2019)
8. Ma, X., Song, C., Chiu, P.W., Li, Z.: Autonomous flexible endoscope for minimally invasive surgery with enhanced safety. IEEE Robot. Autom. Lett. **4**(3), 2607–2613 (2019)
9. Hwang, M., Kwon, D.S.: K-FLEX: a flexible robotic platform for scar-free endoscopic surgery. Int. J. Med. Robot. **16**(1), 2078 (2020)
10. Wagner, C.R., Stylopoulos, N., Howe, R.D.: The role of force feedback in surgery: analysis of blunt dissection. In: 10th Symposium on Haptic Interfaces for Virtual Environment and Teleoperator Systems, Proceedings, Orlando, FL, pp. 73–79. IEEE Computer (2002)
11. Puangmali, P., Althoefer, K., Seneviratne, L.D., Murphy, D., Dasgupta, P.: State-of-the-art in force and tactile sensing for minimally invasive surgery. IEEE Sens. J. **8**(4), 371–381 (2008)
12. Zhao, B.L., Nelson, C.A.: Sensorless force sensing for minimally invasive surgery. J. Med. Devices **9**(4), 14 (2015)
13. Tholey, G., Pillarisetti, A., Green, W., Desai, J.P.: Design, development, and testing of an automated laparoscopic grasper with 3-D force measurement capability. In: Cotin, S., Metaxas, D. (eds.) ISMS 2004. LNCS, vol. 3078, pp. 38–48. Springer, Heidelberg (2004). https://doi.org/10.1007/978-3-540-25968-8_5
14. Yu, L., Wang, W., Zhang, F.: External force sensing based on cable tension changes in minimally invasive surgical micromanipulators. IEEE Access **6**(1), 5362–5373 (2018)
15. Hao, W., Guo, J., Wang, C., Wang, S., Shi, C.: A novel capacitive-based flexible pressure sensor based on stretchable composite electrodes and a dielectric elastomer with microstructures. IEEE Access **8**, 142810–142818 (2020)
16. Lo Presti, D., et al.: Fiber bragg gratings for medical applications and future challenges: a review. IEEE Access **8**, 156863–156888 (2020)
17. Shi, C., Li, M., Lv, C., Li, J., Wang, S.: A high-sensitivity fiber bragg grating-based distal force sensor for laparoscopic surgery. IEEE Sens. J. **20**(5), 2467–2475 (2020)
18. Lv, C., Wang, S., Shi, C.: A high-precision and miniature fiber bragg grating-based force sensor for tissue palpation during minimally invasive surgery. Ann. Biomed. Eng. **48**(2), 669–681 (2020)

19. Kosari, S.N., Ramadurai, S., Chizeck, H.J., Hannaford, B.: Robotic compression of soft tissue. In: 2012 IEEE International Conference on Robotics and Automation (ICRA), pp. 4654–4659. IEEE (2012)

20. Haghighipanah, M., Miyasaka, M., Hannaford, B.: Utilizing elasticity of cable-driven surgical robot to estimate cable tension and external force. IEEE Robot. Autom. Lett. 2(3), 1593–1600 (2017)

Design and Modeling of a Lightweight Concentric Tube Robot for Nasopharyngeal Surgery

Gang Zhang[1,2] , Hangxing Wei[1] , Peng Qi[3] , Honghui Wang[1] , Hao Cheng[1] , and Fuxin Du[1,2(✉)]

[1] School of Mechanical Engineering, Shandong University, Jinan, China
dufuxin@sdu.edu.cn
[2] Key Laboratory of High Efficiency and Clean Mechanical Manufacture of Ministry of Education, Shandong University, Jinan 250061, Shandong, China
[3] Tongji University, Shanghai, China

Abstract. The millimeter diameter of the concentric tube robot enables it to pass through the human nasal cavity for surgery. However, plenty of concentric tube robots adopt a bulky design scheme, forcing the limited space in the operating room to be occupied. In this paper, a lightweight concentric tube robot for nasopharyngeal surgery is proposed. The robot can be mounted on a 6-DOF robot. The length of the concentric tube robot can be adjusted in real-time to perform surgery in different positions. Then, the curvature of the tubes is determined by analyzing the coupling between the tubes. The effect of the stiffness on the curvature of the tubes is analyzed. The forward kinematics model considering the coupling of the concentric tube robot is established. The simulation showed that the stiffness ratio between the tubes is contrary to the changing trend of coupling levels. Finally, the inverse kinematics model of the concentric tube robot is established using the LM algorithm. A simulation is proposed to prove the feasibility of this algorithm. This paper has implications for the motion control of the concentric tube robot.

Keywords: Concentric tube robot · Design · Decouple · Nasopharyngeal surgery

1 Introduction

The excellent dexterity makes continuum robots widely concerned in the medical field [1–3]. Single-segment continuum robots have been commonly used in commercial surgical robots, such as the dexterous wrist of the Da Vinci surgical robot [4]. However, with the development of medical technology, the treatment difficulty is concentrated on the operation of the deeper human body [5, 6]. It is difficult for a single-segment continuum robot to bypass vital organs for surgery. There is an increasing demand for surgical instruments capable of bypassing vital organs in surgical applications, such as transnasal surgery [7]. Existing nasopharyngeal surgical instruments are mostly rigid straight rods with operable forceps or other surgical tools. The instruments are difficult to reach deeper into the nose and do extra damage to surrounding tissue during surgery.

H. Liu et al. (Eds.): ICIRA 2022, LNAI 13457, pp. 409–419, 2022.
https://doi.org/10.1007/978-3-031-13835-5_37

Further developments in continuum robots have possible to address this problem. Multi-segment continuum robots can bypass organs easily and penetrate deep into the human body. The structure of the continuum robot is bionic from the vertebrae and muscles of snakes [8]. In recent years, cables-driven continuum robots with various structures have been proposed [9–11]. These structures have their unique characteristics and application scenarios. But cable-driven designs limit their size, and there is a clear trade-off between the central channel for surgical instruments and the size [12]. The emergence of concentric tube robots has brought new opportunities to develop minimally invasive surgical instruments.

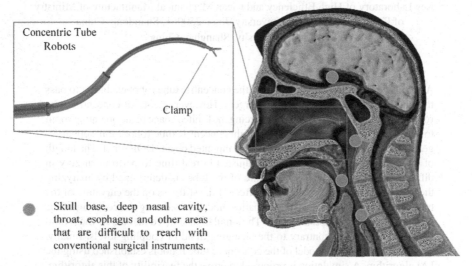

Fig. 1. Schematic diagram of the concentric tube robot for nasal surgery.

The concentric tube robot is a special kind of continuum robot. As shown in Fig. 1, the small diameter and dexterous performance allow the robot to perform complex operations through the natural orifice of human [13–16]. At present, the concentric tube robot has been widely used in the cardiac intervention [17], skull base tumor resection [18], lung puncture [19], and so on. However, the development has not brought innovation to the drive form of concentric tube robots. Most robots need to occupy a vast operating room space. Robots are challenging to dispatch between operating rooms [20]. Lightweight designs of concentric tube robots have been proposed in recent years. The design of the new drive unit still needs to be further explored [21, 22]. In addition, the anisotropy of the tube is often ignored in the establishment of the kinematic model of the concentric tube robot. But the anisotropy will affect the coupling between the tubes, thereby reducing the kinematic accuracy. Recent studies have found that increasing the anisotropy between the tubes can improve the robot's performance [23, 24].

This paper proposed a lightweight concentric tube robot for nasopharyngeal surgery. The contributions of this paper are as follows:

- A lightweight concentric tube robot for nasopharyngeal surgery is proposed. The robot has 6 degrees of freedom, and modules can be added to expand the degrees of freedom.
- A static model of the concentric tube robot is established to analyze the coupling of the robot. Simulations show the effect of coupling on the robot's end trajectory.
- An inverse kinematics algorithm for the coupled concentric tube robot is proposed based on the LM method. Simulations demonstrate the feasibility of the algorithm.

The rest of the paper is as follows. Section 2 presents the structure of the concentric tube robot. Section 3 analyzes the coupling effect of the concentric tube robot, and a kinematic model considering the coupling is established. Section 4 simulates end motion curves at different stiffness ratios. Simulation of inverse kinematics is presented. Section 5 summarizes the whole paper.

2 Structure of the Lightweight Concentric Tube Robot

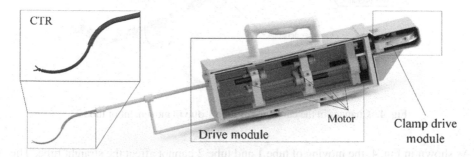

Fig. 2. The structure of the concentric tube robot.

The structure of the concentric tube robot is shown in Fig. 2. The robot has 6 degrees of freedom, including the feeding and opening of the gripper. Concentric tube parts include one straight tube and two pre-bent NITI alloy tubes. The rotation and feeding of the concentric tube parts are carried out by four motors located in the drive module. The control of the clamp is realized through the clamp drive module.

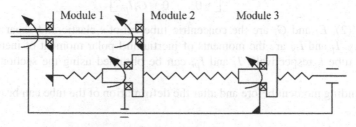

Fig. 3. Schematic diagram of the concentric tube robot.

The motion diagram of the concentric tube robot is shown in Fig. 3. Module 3 lets modules 2 and 1 move by rotating the guide screw. The motor in Modules 1 and 2 turn the connected pre-bent tubes. The swivel below module 2 enables module 2 to move on the lead screw. This design makes the machine more compact. And by adding more modules, the degree of freedom of the robot can be expanded easily.

3   Kinematics Model Considering Coupling

3.1   Decoupling of Concentric Tube Robot

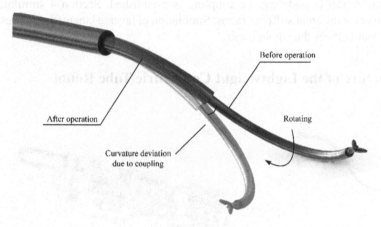

Fig. 4. Changes in the curvature of tube 1 due to movement of tube 2.

As shown in Fig. 4, the moving of tube 1 and tube 2 cannot affect the straight tube. The interaction between tube 1 and tube 2 will affect the curvature of tube 1.

The tubes' curvature can be expressed by Eq. (1), ignoring the torsional deformation.

$$\mathbf{u}_i = [u_{ix}, u_{iy}, 0]^T \tag{1}$$

where i represents the i-th tube, and u_{ix} and u_{iy} are the components of the curvature of tube i in the X and Y directions, respectively. Suppose the stiffness of the tube is K.

$$\mathbf{K_i} = \begin{bmatrix} E_{xi}I_{xi} & 0 & 0 \\ 0 & E_{yi}I_{yi} & 0 \\ 0 & 0 & G_iI_{pi} \end{bmatrix} \tag{2}$$

In Eq. (2), E_i and G_i are the concentric tube robot's elastic and shear modulus, respectively. I_i and I_{pi} are the moments of inertia and polar moment of inertia of the section of tube i, respectively. I_i and I_{pi} can be obtained using the section distance equation.

The bending moment before and after the deformation of the tube can be expressed by Eq. (3).

$$M_i = \mathbf{K_i}(\mathbf{u}_i^e - \mathbf{u}_i^0) \tag{3}$$

In the equation, $\mathbf{u}_i^e$ is the curvature of tube i after deformation, and $\mathbf{u}_i^0$ is the curvature of tube i before deformation. The curvature change due to the coupling can be solved by Eq. (4).

$$\sum_1^i M_i = \sum_1^i \mathbf{K}_i(\mathbf{u}_i^e - \mathbf{u}_i^0) = 0 \tag{4}$$

Take the analysis of two tubes as an example. This method can be easily extended to analyze the coupling between multiple tubes. The relationship between the stiffness of tube 2 and tube 1 can be expressed by Eq. (5).

$$f_K = \frac{\mathbf{K}_2}{\mathbf{K}_1} = \mathbf{c} \tag{5}$$

In Eq. (5), $\mathbf{c}$ is the ratio of the moment of inertia of an area.

The initial stat curvature of tube 1 is only in the x-direction, the curvature vector of tube 1 can be expressed by Eq. (6).

$$\mathbf{u}_i^0 = [u_{1x}^0, 0, 0]^T \tag{6}$$

Assuming that the deflection angle between the two tubes is φ_1, the curvature of tube 2 can be expressed by Eq. (7).

$$\mathbf{u}_2^0 = [u_{2x}^0 \cos \varphi_1, u_{2x}^0 \sin \varphi_1, 0]^T \tag{7}$$

According to Eqs. (5) to (7), the tube's curvature after coupling can be calculated.

$$\sum_{i=1}^2 M_i = \mathbf{K}_1(\mathbf{u}_1^e - \mathbf{u}_1^0) + \mathbf{K}_2(\mathbf{u}_1^e - \mathbf{u}_2^0) = 0 \tag{8}$$

$$\mathbf{u}_1^e = \frac{\mathbf{u}_1^0 + c\mathbf{u}_2^0}{1 + c} \tag{9}$$

When the material used is anisotropic:

$$\mathbf{u}_1^e = \frac{\mathbf{K}_1 \mathbf{u}_1^0 + \mathbf{K}_2 \mathbf{u}_2^0}{\mathbf{K}_1 + \mathbf{K}_2} \tag{10}$$

For the convenience of calculation, it is assumed that

$$\mathbf{c} = \begin{vmatrix} c_1 & & \\ & c_2 & \\ & & c_3 \end{vmatrix} \tag{11}$$

When the structure and material are determined, c can be quickly determined from Eq. (5). Then the curvature of the coupling is considered as:

$$u_x^e = \frac{u_{1x}^0 + c_1 u_{2x}^0 \cos \varphi_1}{1 + c_1} \tag{12}$$

$$u_y^e = \frac{c_2 u_{2x}^0 \sin \varphi_1}{1 + c_2} \tag{13}$$

3.2 Kinematics Model

Establish the coordinate system shown in Fig. 5. P_o is the initial coordinate system, and the end of tube 1 is set as P_M. The end of tube 2 is set as P_E. The concentric tube robot has 4 degrees of freedom. The feed of tube 1 is set as S_1, and the parameter of the rotational motion is set as φ_1. S_2 and φ_2 are the parameters of the feeding motion and rotation of tube 2, respectively.

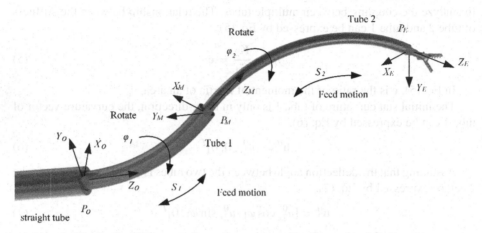

Fig. 5. Establishment of coordinate system for concentric tube robot.

According to the conclusion of the previous section, the motion of tube 2 will have a coupling effect on tube 1. When the relative angle between the two tubes is $\Delta\varphi$, the curvature of tube 1 after changing can be obtained by Eq. (14).

$$
k_1 = \sqrt{\left(\frac{c_2 u_{2x}^0}{1+c_2}\sin\Delta\varphi\right)^2 + \left(\frac{c_1 u_{2x}^0}{1+c_1}\cos\Delta\varphi\right)^2 + \left(\frac{c_1 u_{1x}^0}{1+c_1}\right)^2 + \frac{2c_1 u_{1x}^0 u_{2x}^0 \cos\Delta\varphi}{(1+c_1)^2}}
$$

$$(14)$$

In addition to changing the curvature of tube 1, the coupling of tube 1 and tube 2 also causes a rotational coupling motion of tube 1. The rotation angle can be solved by Eqs. (12) and (13).

$$
\Delta\varphi_1 = a\tan(\frac{u_y^e}{u_x^e})
$$

$$(15)$$

The motion of tube 1 has no coupling effect on the curvature of tube 2. The curvature of tube 2 is:

$$
k_2 = \left|\mathbf{u}_2^0\right|
$$

$$(16)$$

The DH method was used to establish the forward kinematics of the concentric tube robot. The DH parameters are shown in Table 1.

Table 1. DH parameters

DH parameters	φ	a	θ	d
Segment 1	$\varphi_1 + \Delta\varphi$	$\sin k_1 S_1 / k_1$	$k_1 S_1$	$(1-\cos k_1 S_1)/ k_1$
Segment 2	$\pi/2$	0	φ_2	0
	$-\pi/2$	$\sin k_2 S_2 / k_2$	$k S_2$	$(1-\cos k_2 S_2)/ k_2$

According to the DH method, the pose of the end of the concentric tube robot is:

$$T_{end} = T_1 T_2 T_3 \tag{17}$$

In Eq. (17):

$$T_i = \begin{vmatrix} c\theta i & -s\theta i c\alpha i & s\theta i s\alpha i & ai c\theta i \\ s\theta i & c\theta i c\alpha i & -c\theta i s\alpha i & ai s\theta i \\ 0 & s\alpha i & c\alpha i & di \\ 0 & 0 & 0 & 1 \end{vmatrix} \tag{18}$$

In Eq. (18), $c\theta i = \cos\theta i$, $s\theta i = \sin\theta i$, $c\alpha i = \cos\alpha i$, $s\alpha i = \sin\alpha i$.
According to Eq. (18), the position of the robot end is:

$$\begin{cases} x_E = Tend(1,4) \\ y_E = Tend(2,4) \\ z_E = Tend(3,4) \end{cases} \tag{19}$$

The inverse kinematics of concentric tube robot is when given partial information, solving Eq. (19) or Eq. (17).

The LM algorithm [25] is introduced to solve Eq. (19), given only positional information. All inverse kinematic solutions of the robot are obtained.

$$q_{n+1} = q_n + H_n^{-1} g_n \tag{20}$$

$$H_k = J_k^T W_E J_k + W_N \tag{21}$$

4 Simulation and Experiments

4.1 The Relationships Between Stiffness and Coupling

The material of the tubes is nylon. The numerical values that define the physical parameters of the concentric tube robot are shown in Table 2.

Fix the concentric tube robot and make tube 2 rotate. During the rotation, the curvature of tube 1 will change due to the coupling. As shown in Fig. 6, the trajectory of the robot end (red curve) is a standard circle when the coupling effect is not considered. The curve of the robot end in the front stiffness configuration is the blue curve in Fig. 6.

Table 2. Physical parameters of the concentric tube robot

Parameters	u_{1x}^{0}	u_{2x}^{0}	$Max(S_1)$	$Max(S_1)$	c_1	c_2
Value	$\pi/120$	$\pi/120$	60	60	6.85	7.37

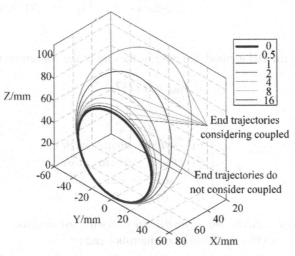

Fig. 6. End trajectories at different stiffness ratios. (Color figure online)

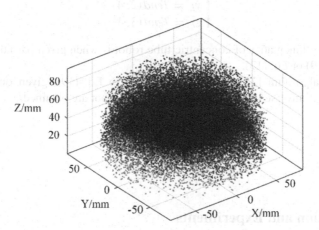

Fig. 7. End trajectories at different stiffness ratios. (Color figure online)

The end trajectory curves corresponding to different stiffness ratios are drawn to make the relationship clearer. As the stiffness ratio increases, the end curve is closer to the situation without considering the coupling. The magnification ratio can be found in the legend.

As shown in Fig. 7, the red dots enclose the workspace of the concentric tube robot, considering the coupling. The blue dots enclose the workspace of the concentric tube robot without considering the coupling. The robot's workspace considering the coupling and the robot's workspace not considering the coupling are primarily coincident. However, considering the coupling, the value on the Z-axis of the robot's workspace is larger than before. It is caused by the reduction of the curvature of tube 1 due to the coupling between the tubes.

4.2 Simulation of Inverse Kinematics

Verify the inverse kinematics solution method in MATLAB. All solutions are solved by a set point P_E ($\pi/4$, $\pi/4$, 30, 30), as shown in Fig. 8. Each colored curve in the figure represents the robot skeleton curve corresponding to one of its solutions. The red point P_M is the end of tube 1. It should be noted that the continuum robot has a high degree of symmetry, and its inverse kinematics solution is symmetric about plane A. Using this property, another inverse kinematics solution of the continuum robot can be easily obtained.

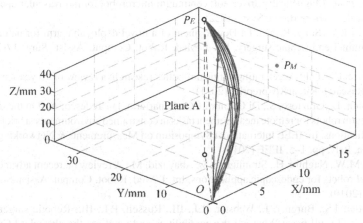

Fig. 8. Inverse kinematics solution for the concentric tube robot. All solutions have a corresponding solution that is symmetrical to plane A.

5 Conclusion and Discussion

This paper proposed a lightweight concentric tube robot to address the problem that traditional rigid instruments are difficult to reach the deeper human body. The robot has 6 degrees of freedom, and the degree of freedom can be expanded by adding the driving module. The coupling of the concentric tube robot was analyzed. The anisotropy of the tube was considered. Then, a forward kinematic model considering the coupling was established. The simulation showed that the stiffness ratio of the outer and inner tubes of the robot is inversely proportional to the coupling level. Finally, an inverse kinematics model considering the coupling was established based on the LM algorithm. Simulations show that this method can obtain all inverse kinematics solutions for a given position. This paper has reference significance for developing micro-surgical instruments, especially the instruments through the nasal approach.

In the future, the vibration problem caused by the mutual movement of the concentric tube robots will be solved.

Acknowledgments. This work was supported by the China Postdoctoral Science Foundation funded project (Grant No. 2019M662346), Shandong Provincial Postdoctoral Innovative Talents Funded Scheme (Grant No. 238226), the Focus on Research and Development Plan in Shandong province (Grant No. 2022CXGC010503), the Intelligent Robots and Systems High-precision Innovation Center Open Fund (Grant No. 2019IRS06), the Fundamental Research Funds for the Central Universities and Young Scholars Program of Shandong University.

References

1. Dupont, P., Simaan, N., Choset, H., Rucker, C.: Continuum robots for medical interventions. Proc. IEEE 1–24 (2022)
2. Liu, D., et al.: Magnetically driven soft continuum microrobot for intravascular operations in microscale. Cyborg Bionic Syst. (2022)
3. Lei, Y., Li, Y., Song, R., Du, F.: Development of a novel deployable arm for natural orifice transluminal endoscopic surgery. Int. J. Med. Robot. Comput. Assist. Surg. 17(3), e2232 (2021)
4. D'Ettorre, C., et al.: Accelerating surgical robotics research: a review of 10 years with the da Vinci Research Kit. arXiv preprint (2021)
5. Angrisani, L., Grazioso, S., Di Gironimo, G., Panariello, D., Tedesco, A.: On the use of soft continuum robots for remote measurement tasks in constrained environments: a brief overview of applications. In: IEEE International Symposium on Measurements & Networking (M&N), Catania, Italy, pp. 1–5. IEEE (2019)
6. Gifari, M.W., Naghibi, H., Stramigioli, S., Abayazid, M.: A review on recent advances in soft surgical robots for endoscopic applications. Int. J. Med. Robot. Comput. Assist. Surg. 15(5), e2010 (2019)
7. Schneider, J.S., Burgner, J., Webster, R.J., III., Russell, P.T., III.: Robotic surgery for the sinuses and skull base: What are the possibilities and what are the obstacles? Curr. Opin. Otolaryngol. Head Neck Surg. 21(1), 11–16 (2013)
8. Li, Z., Du, R., Lei, M.C., Yuan, S.M.: Design and analysis of a biomimetic wire-driven robot arm. In: Proceedings of the ASME 2011 International Mechanical Engineering Congress and Exposition, Denver, Colorado, vol. 7, pp. 191–198. ASME, USA (2011).
9. Chirikjian, G.S.: Conformational modeling of continuum structures in robotics and structural biology: a review. Adv. Robot. 29(13), 817–829 (2015)
10. Janabi-Sharifi, F., Jalali, A., Walker, I.D.: Cosserat rod-based dynamic modeling of tendon-driven continuum robots: a tutorial. IEEE Access 9, 68703–68719 (2021)
11. Fonseca, L.M., Rodrigues, G.V., Savi, M.A.: An overview of the mechanical description of origami-inspired systems and structures. Int. J. Mech. Sci. 233, 107316 (2022)
12. Zhang, G., et al.: Design and modeling of a bio-inspired compound continuum robot for minimally invasive surgery. Machines 10, 468 (2022)
13. Webster, R.J., III., Jones, B.A.: Design and kinematic modeling of constant curvature continuum robots: a review. Int. J. Robot. Res. 29(13), 1661–1683 (2010)

14. Wang, J., Yang, X., Li, P., Song, S., Liu, L., Meng, M.-H.: Design of a multi-arm concentric-tube robot system for transnasal surgery. Med. Biol. Eng. Comput. **58**(3), 497–508 (2020). https://doi.org/10.1007/s11517-019-02093-9
15. Madoglio, A., et al.: Robotics in endoscopic transnasal skull base surgery: literature review and personal experience. Control Syst. Des. Bio-Robot. Bio-mechatron. Adv. Appl. 221–244 (2020)
16. Mahoney, A.W., Gilbert, H.B., Webster III, R.J.: A review of concentric tube robots: modeling, control, design, planning, and sensing. The Encyclopedia of MEDICAL ROBOTICS: Volume 1 Minimally Invasive Surgical Robotics, pp. 181–202 (2019)
17. Bergeles, C., Gosline, A.H., Vasilyev, N.V., Codd, P.J., Nido, P.J., Dupont, P.E.: Concentric tube robot design and optimization based on task and anatomical constraints. IEEE Trans. Rob. **31**(1), 67–84 (2015)
18. Swaney, P.J., Gilbert, H.B., Webster, R.J., III., Russell, P.T., III., Weaver, K.D.: Endonasal skull base tumor removal using concentric tube continuum robots: a phantom study. J. Neurol. Surg. Part B: Skull Base 76(02) 145–149 (2015)
19. Swaney, P.J., et al.: Tendons, concentric tubes, and a bevel tip: three steerable robots in one transoral lung access system. In: 2015 IEEE International Conference on Robotics and Automation (ICRA), Seattle, WA, USA, pp. 5378–5383. IEEE (2015)
20. Gilbert, H.B., Rucker, D.C., Webster III, R.J.: Concentric tube robots: the state of the art and future directions. In: Inaba, M., Corke, P. (eds.) Robotics Research. STAR, vol. 114, pp. 253–269. Springer, Cham (2016). https://doi.org/10.1007/978-3-319-28872-7_15
21. Florea, A.N., Ropella, D.S., Amanov, E., Herrell III, S.D., Webster III, R.J.: Design of a modular, multi-arm concentric tube robot featuring roller gears. In: Medical Imaging 2022: Image-Guided Procedures, Robotic Interventions, and Modeling, vol. 12034, pp. 37–42 (2022)
22. Bodani, V., Azimian, H., Looi, T., Drake, J.: Design and evaluation of a concentric tube robot for minimally-invasive endoscopic paediatric neurosurgery. In: The Hamlyn Symposium on Medical Robotics, vol. 1, no. 1, pp. 25–26 (2014)
23. Rucker, C., Childs, J., Molaei, P., Gilbert, H.B.: Transverse anisotropy stabilizes concentric tube robots. IEEE Robot. Autom. Lett. **7**(2), 2407–2414 (2022)
24. Girerd, C., Schlinquer, T., Andreff, N., Renaud, P., Rabenorosoa, K.: Designof concentric tube robots using tube patterning for follow-the-leader deployment. J. Mech. Robot. **13**(1) (2021)
25. Sugihara, T.: Solvability-unconcerned inverse kinematics by the Levenberg–Marquardt method. IEEE Trans. Rob. **27**(5), 984–991 (2011)

Research on Puncture Status Perception of Venipuncture Robot Based on Electrical Impedance

Tianbao He, Chuangqiang Guo, Hansong Liu, and Li Jiang(✉)

State Key Laboratory of Robotics and System, Harbin Institute of Technology, Harbin 150001, China
jiangli01@hit.edu.cn

Abstract. With the development of robotics and bioengineering technologies, venipuncture robots are expected to replace manual venipuncture under the supervision of medical staff and free up scarce medical resources. However, current venipuncture robots are still unable to be applied in medical procedures because they still lack in vivo puncture state sensing. A robotic venipuncture decision method based on bio-tissue electrical impedance is proposed in this paper to solve this problem. In this study, the electrical impedance properties of biological tissues are first analyzed, and a robotic venipuncture decision method is proposed based on this property. Then an improved puncture needle that can measure electrical impedance is introduced. Experiments are conducted on a pork model using a self-developed six-degree-of-freedom venipuncture robot. The experimental results show that successful venipuncture has more than a 35% reduction of electrical impedance, and the venipuncture robot based on this method can successfully enter the venous vessels.

Keywords: Electrical impedance · Venipuncture · Medical robot

1 Introduction

Venipuncture is a standard medical tool widely used in health screening, disease treatment, and other medical procedures. According to statistics, up to 3.5 million venipunctures are performed worldwide every day [1], and all of these tasks are performed manually by medical professionals. The success rate of venipuncture depends not only on the competence and experience of the medical staff. However, it is also influenced by the patient's physical characteristics, resulting in a still high failure rate of venipuncture. The failure rate of first venipuncture in the general adult population is 20–33% [2, 3], rising to 47–70% for specific patients (e.g., high body fat percentage, dark skin tone, and dense hair) [2, 4–6], with an average of 2.18 attempts required to perform a successful venipuncture in a single patient [7].

To improve the success rate of venipuncture, there have been several studies related to venipuncture robots [8–10]. These robots use a near-infrared imaging approach for vein identification, which allows for high accuracy. At the same time, these robots have multiple degrees of freedom, which enables the localization of the vessels suitable for venipuncture. However, these venipuncture robots are still not applicable in medical procedures due to their lack of state perception during venipuncture to determine the position of the puncture needle, which has a high risk.

Ultrasound has been widely used in the medical field due to its flexibility. In some robots, ultrasound has been used for the real-time detection of needles in venipuncture [11–14], but there are still some limitations. When imaging, ultrasound devices produce image speckles and artifacts, making it difficult to judge and identify needles and vessels (Fig. 1) [13, 15]. For example, in obese patients, the sound signal is severely backscattered or attenuated due to the high amount of fat in the subcutaneous tissue [16]. Moreover, for venipuncture purposes, ultrasound imaging has a long learning time and complex image processing [17]. Also, in order to determine the needle position, it is necessary to always keep the puncture needle within the imaging range of the ultrasound device, increasing the structural complexity and control difficulty of the robot.

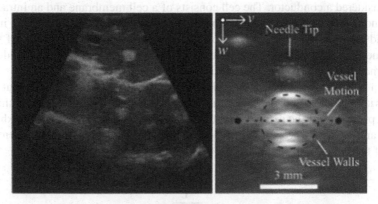

Fig. 1. Ultrasound is performed on veins and puncture needles.

This paper presents a bioelectrical impedance-based method to determine the puncture state of the robot in venipuncture. This method is based on the fact that the electrical impedance of different biological tissues varies greatly. The electrical impedance changes significantly when the needle enters biological tissues from the air and then into veins. There have been some studies to determine the type of tissue based on the difference in electrical impedance of biological tissues, such as skin, fat, and muscle [18]. Different types of tissues, somatic and cellular tissues, have significant differences in their electrical impedance. Kalvoy et al. measured the impedance spectrum of living pig tissues and demonstrated that subcutaneous tissues such as muscle and fat could be distinguished by impedance [19]. In a study by Cheng et al., the electrical impedance of adipose tissue was approximately three times that of skin and more than ten times that of blood [20]. Satio et al. performed animal studies in rabbit ear veins, using a syringe needle with conductive electrodes for a venous puncture, and used the conductivity of blood to detect changes in electrical impedance [21].

Inspired by these studies, we determined whether the puncture needle successfully entered the venous vessels by detecting the change of electrical impedance during venipuncture. In this paper, an impedance needle for a venipuncture robot is designed and experimented with in a venipuncture model of pork. The puncture needle can be installed in a self-developed six-degree-of-freedom venipuncture robot to detect the change of electrical impedance during puncture in real-time.

The structure of this paper is as follows. The second part presents the electrical impedance-based venipuncture decision method and the experimental system. In the third part, we present the experiments, show the experimental results, and discuss the experimental results. Finally, the paper is summarized.

2   Materials and Method

2.1   Bioelectrical Impedance Analysis

Biological tissue structure consists of chemical substances such as cells and other extracellular fluids. Extracellular fluid fills between cells and contains many conductive ions to be considered a conductor. The cell consists of a cell membrane and an intracellular fluid. Among them, the main components of the cytoplasm and nucleus of the intracellular fluid are proteins, salts, and aqueous solutions. The main components of the cell membrane are the phospholipid and proteins, which have very low electrical conductivity and are therefore generally regarded as insulators [22].

When an alternating current is applied to biological tissues, the biological tissues characterize complex impedance information. At low frequencies, it will exhibit the resistive properties of the extracellular fluid, and at high frequencies, it will exhibit the resistive and capacitive properties of the cell membrane. Therefore, the equivalent model circuit of the bioimpedance model is shown in Fig. 2 [23].

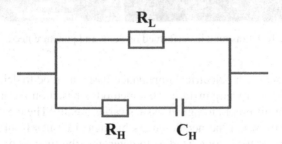

Fig. 2. Bioimpedance equivalent model.

The electrical impedance of the equivalent model of biological tissue is

$$Z = \frac{R_L(1 + j\omega C_H R_H)}{1 + j\omega C_H(R_L + R_H)}$$
$$= \frac{R_L + \omega^2 C_H R_L R_H(R_L + R_H)}{1 + (R_L + R_H)^2 \omega^2 C_H^2} - j\frac{\omega C_H R_L^2}{1 + (R_L + R_H)^2 \omega^2 C_H^2} \quad (1)$$

where R_L is the resistance value at low frequency, R_H and C_H are the resistance and capacitance values at high frequency, respectively.

Bioelectrical impedance measurements are limited to the frequency range of 1 to 1000 kHz due to surface electrodes [24]. Therefore, the capacitive characteristics of bioimpedance are not prominent. The main components of skin and fat are cells and extracellular fluid, while the main component of blood contains water, electrolytes, and other inorganic substances and 40–50% of cells. Consequently, it will exhibit a much lower bioelectrical impedance.

Therefore, the venipuncture robot can determine the position of the needle in venipuncture based on the electrical impedance characteristics of biological tissues, solving the problem that the venipuncture robot cannot sense the puncture state.

The puncture needle enters the skin, fat, and blood sequentially from the air during venipuncture. Due to the different compositions of different biological tissues, their electrical impedance also has a considerable variation, with blood having a minor electrical impedance [20]. Therefore, a significant decrease in electrical impedance occurs when the puncture needle enters the blood. The workflow is shown in Fig. 3. The venipuncture robot detects the electrical impedance in real-time and sends the data to the host computer for processing and analysis. When the host computer judges that the puncture needle has successfully entered the blood vessel based on the electrical impedance change, it controls the robot to stop the movement.

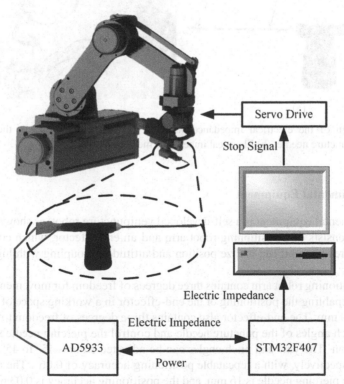

Fig. 3. Electrical impedance-based workflow for venipuncture robot puncture state perception.

2.2 Design of Electrical Impedance Needle

The puncture needle used to measure electrical impedance is based on a modified design of the universal disposable venipuncture needle (model 24G, $\Phi 0.55$ mm $\times$ 19 mm). One electrode, a copper wire with an insulating coating, is placed inside the needle. The outer wall of the needle is used as the other electrode. The modified puncture needle is shown in Fig. 4a.

The AD5933 negative impedance test module was used with an AC signal frequency of 30–50 kHz to achieve high precision impedance measurement. Meanwhile, the stm32F407 microcontroller was used to communicate between the electrical impedance measurement module and the robot host computer and supply power to the electrical impedance measurement module. The electrical impedance measurement module is shown in Fig. 4b.

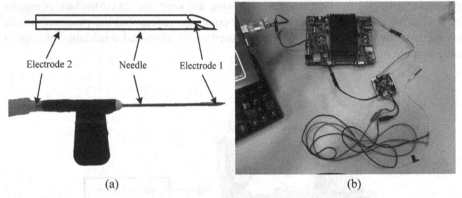

(a)　　　　　　　　　　　　　　　　　　　(b)

Fig. 4. Design of the electrical impedance puncture needle. (a) Structure of the electrical impedance puncture needle. (b) Electrical impedance measurement module.

2.3 Experimental Equipment

The experimental equipment is a self-developed venipuncture robot, as shown in Fig. 5. The robot consists of a positioning robot arm and an end-effector, which contains six degrees of freedom and can realize position and attitude decoupling with high motion accuracy.

The positioning robot arm contains three degrees of freedom for movement in Cartesian space, enabling the positioning of the end-effector in a working space of 70 mm $\times$ 80 mm $\times$ 40 mm. The end-effector also contains three degrees of freedom to adjust the yaw and pitch angles of the puncture needle and control the piercing needle's insertion and extraction. The yaw and pitch angles can be adjusted from $-45°$ to $45°$ and from 0 to $30°$, respectively, with a repeatable positioning accuracy of $0.06°$. The movement stroke of the piercing needle is 16 mm, and the positioning accuracy is 0.03 mm, which can realize high precision movement in a small range.

Fig. 5. Six-degree-of-freedom venipuncture robot.

2.4 Experimental Phantom

The experimental model is based on the anatomical model of the human body. The human forearm blood vessels are located in the fat layer with the skin above. Therefore, pork adipose tissue with pigskin was used to simulate human tissues, and rubber tubes with inner and outer diameters of 3 mm and 4 mm, respectively, were embedded in the adipose layer to simulate blood vessels. Also, the simulated blood vessels were filled with simulated blood, as shown in Fig. 6.

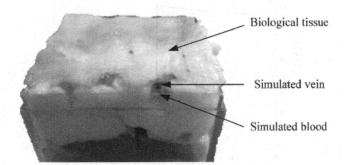

Biological tissue

Simulated vein

Simulated blood

Fig. 6. Pork model for venipuncture.

3 Experiments

3.1 The Process of the Experiments

The center axis of the yaw angle of the robot's positioning robot arm control end-effector is located directly above the venous vessels of the pork model, and the yaw angle is adjusted to 0°, the pitch angle to 30°, and the needle feed speed to 5 mm/s. At the same time, the pork model is placed at a certain height to ensure that the simulated vessels are within the travel range of the puncture needle.

426 T. He et al.

Since in air, the impedance is more significant than in biological tissue. Therefore, to reduce the interference of the external environment with venipuncture, the electrical impedance measurement is started only when the needle tip touches the skin. This process is detected by the force sensor at the end of the robot. When the needle tip touches the skin, the force sensor will have data changes, and then start to measure the electrical impedance. This avoids the disturbance to the system caused by a sudden drop in electrical impedance when the puncture needle enters the biological tissue from the air. When the electrical impedance drops, the robot stops moving. The experiment has repeated a total of ten times.

3.2 Results and Discussion

Table 1 shows the mean electrical impedance values in adipose tissue and after entering the bloodstream for ten puncture experiments. Also, the degree of decrease in electrical impedance is shown in the table. In these ten experiments, when the puncture needle enters the adipose tissue, the electrical impedance remains stable at 9.96 ± 0.25 kΩ. When the needle enters the bloodstream, the electrical impedance drops by more than 35% and remains at 6.15 ± 0.24 kΩ. Figure 7 shows the results of two of these experiments.

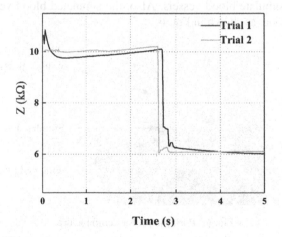

Fig. 7. Changes in electrical impedance during puncture.

The experimental results show that the venipuncture robot effectively relies on the difference in electrical impedance of different tissues for puncture state feedback. After the puncture needle enters the blood from the adipose tissue, a sudden drop of more than 3 kΩ is generated. The change is significant and can be easily detected by the robot.

The method has the merit of simple signal processing, low noise, and reliable accuracy compared to ultrasound imaging. At the same time, it has low structural requirements for the robot; only the puncture needle needs to be mounted on the end of the robot, and no complex motion and control mechanism needs to be designed.

Table 1. The average value and degree of change of electrical impedance during puncture.

Trials	Z_{fat}(kΩ)	Z_{blood}(kΩ)	ΔZ(kΩ)	$\Delta Z/Z_{fat}$(%)
T1	9.928	6.174	3.754	37.8
T2	10.068	6.107	3.961	39.3
T3	9.911	6.122	3.789	38.2
T4	9.906	6.359	3.547	35.8
T5	10.066	6.030	4.036	40.1
T6	9.954	6.392	3.562	35.8
T7	9.751	5.956	3.795	38.9
T8	10.213	6.311	3.902	38.2
T9	9.706	6.269	3.437	35.4
T10	9.873	5.902	3.971	40.2

The electrical puncture needle is a practical and straightforward modification of the universal venipuncture needle. Satio et al. used the puncture needle as one electrode and the other electrode fixed to the skin when detecting the electrical impedance of the blood [21]. When the tip of the needle enters the vessel, blood flows into the needle, and the electrodes on the skin's surface and inside the needle are conducted through the blood. Compared with this method, the puncture needle designed in this paper is more convenient in use and does not require additional manipulation.

The puncture needle passes through the skin and tissue in sequence before entering the vessel in venipuncture. In the study by Cheng et al., the skin's electrical impedance was less than the fat [20]. Therefore, the electrical impedance during puncture should rise and then produce a sudden drop. However, there was no significant rising trend of electrical impedance in the experiment. This phenomenon may be related to the size of the puncture needle and the speed of needle entry. Since the thickness of the skin is about 0.07 mm–1.2 mm, the tip length of a standard general-purpose venipuncture needle (about 4 mm) is too small in comparison. Moreover, the puncture speed is 5 mm/s, so the needle tip has already entered the adipose tissue when the electrical impedance produces a change.

4 Conclusion

The electrical impedance-based decision method for robotic venipuncture enables the robot to detect the electrical impedance change in real-time by the puncture needle with electrodes during venipuncture to determine the puncture status. In this paper, firstly, the electrical impedance-based venipuncture decision method is proposed by analyzing the bioelectrical impedance. Then an improved electrical impedance puncture needle based on a universal venipuncture needle is introduced, which is simple to make and easy to use. In venipuncture experiments with the pork model, there was a decrease in electrical impedance of more than 35%. These results show that using electrical impedance for venipuncture robot puncture state sensing is effective. The method has the advantages of low cost, low noise, and simple signal processing.

Acknowledgment. This work was supported by the National Natural Science Foundation of China (U1813209), Self-Planned Task (No. SKLRS202112B) of State Key Laboratory of Robotics and System (HIT).

References

1. De Boer, T., Steinbuch, M., Neerken, S., Kharin, A.: Laboratory study on needle-tissue interaction: towards the development of an instrument for automatic venipuncture. J. Mech. Med. Biol. **07**, 325–335 (2007). https://doi.org/10.1142/S0219519407002297
2. Jacobson, A.F., Winslow, E.H.: Variables influencing intravenous catheter insertion difficulty and failure: an analysis of 339 intravenous catheter insertions. Heart Lung **34**, 345–359 (2005). https://doi.org/10.1016/j.hrtlng.2005.04.002
3. Rauch, D., Dowd, D., Eldridge, D., Mace, S., Schears, G., Yen, K.: Peripheral difficult venous access in children. Clin. Pediatr. **48**, 895–901 (2009). https://doi.org/10.1177/000992280933 5737
4. Carr, P.J., et al.: Development of a clinical prediction rule to improve peripheral intravenous cannulae first attempt success in the emergency department and reduce post insertion failure rates: the Vascular Access Decisions in the Emergency Room (VADER) study protocol. BMJ Open **6**, 7 (2016)
5. Black, K.J.L., Pusic, M.V., Harmidy, D.: Pediatric intravenous insertion in the emergency department. Pediatr. Emerg. Care **21**, 5 (2005). https://doi.org/10.1097/01.pec.0000186422. 77140.1f
6. Lininger, R.A.: Pediatric peripheral IV insertion success rates. Pediatr. Nurs. **29**, 351–354 (2003)
7. Lillis, K.A., Jaffe, D.M.: Prehospital intravenous access in children. Ann. Emerg. Med. **21**, 1430–1434 (1992). https://doi.org/10.1016/S0196-0644(05)80054-X
8. Qiao, Z., Li, Y., Wu, Z., Kou, J.: Automatic puncture system based on NIR image and ultrasonic image. In: MATEC Web Conference, vol. 108, p. 15002 (2017). https://doi.org/10.1051/mat ecconf/201710815002
9. Cheng, Z., Davies, B.L., Caldwell, D.G., Barresi, G., Xu, Q., Mattos, L.S.: A hand-held robotic device for peripheral intravenous catheterization. Proc. Inst. Mech. Eng. H. **231**, 1165–1177 (2017). https://doi.org/10.1177/0954411917737328
10. Leipheimer, J.M.: First-in-human evaluation of a hand-held automated venipuncture device for rapid venous blood draws. Technology **7**, 98–107 (2019)
11. Chen, A., Nikitczuk, K., Nikitczuk, J., Maguire, T., Yarmush, M.: Portable robot for autonomous venipuncture using 3D near infrared image guidance. Technology **01**, 72–87 (2013). https://doi.org/10.1142/S2339547813500064
12. Balter, M.L., Chen, A.I., Maguire, T.J., Yarmush, M.L.: The system design and evaluation of a 7-DOF image-guided venipuncture robot. IEEE Trans. Robot. **31**, 1044–1053 (2015). https://doi.org/10.1109/TRO.2015.2452776
13. Balter, M.L., Chen, A.I., Maguire, T.J., Yarmush, M.L.: Adaptive kinematic control of a robotic venipuncture device based on stereo vision, ultrasound, and force guidance. IEEE Trans. Ind. Electron. **64**, 1626–1635 (2017). https://doi.org/10.1109/TIE.2016.2557306

14. Chen, A.I., Balter, M.L., Maguire, T.J., Yarmush, M.L.: Real-time needle steering in response to rolling vein deformation by a 9-DOF image-guided autonomous venipuncture robot. In: 2015 IEEE/RSJ International Conference on Intelligent Robots and Systems (IROS), Hamburg, Germany, pp. 2633–2638. IEEE (2015)
15. Freschi, C., Troia, E., Ferrari, V., Megali, G., Pietrabissa, A., Mosca, F.: Ultrasound guided robotic biopsy using augmented reality and human-robot cooperative control. In: 2009 Annual International Conference of the IEEE Engineering in Medicine and Biology Society, pp. 5110–5113 (2009)
16. Maecken, T., Grau, T.: Ultrasound imaging in vascular access. Critical Care Med. **35**, S178–S185 (2007). https://doi.org/10.1097/01.CCM.0000260629.86351.A5
17. Perry, T.: Profile: veebot [Resources_Start-ups]. IEEE Spectr. **50**, 23 (2013). https://doi.org/10.1109/MSPEC.2013.6565554
18. Kalvøy, H.: Needle Guidance in Clinical Applications based on Electrical Impedance (2010)
19. Kalvøy, H., Frich, L., Grimnes, S., Martinsen, Ø.G., Hol, P.K., Stubhaug, A.: Impedance-based tissue discrimination for needle guidance. Physiol. Meas. **30**, 129–140 (2009). https://doi.org/10.1088/0967-3334/30/2/002
20. Cheng, Z., Davies, B.L., Caldwell, D.G., Mattos, L.S.: A new venous entry detection method based on electrical bio-impedance sensing. Ann. Biomed. Eng. **46**(10), 1558–1567 (2018). https://doi.org/10.1007/s10439-018-2025-7
21. Saito, H., Mitsubayashi, K., Togawa, T.: Detection of needle puncture to blood vessel by using electric conductivity of blood for automatic blood sampling. Sens. Actuators A **125**, 446–450 (2006). https://doi.org/10.1016/j.sna.2005.06.012
22. Wang, P.: Study on Human Body Composition Analysis Method Based on Bioelectrical Impedance Technique (2021). https://kns.cnki.net/kcms/detail/detail.aspx?dbcode=CMFD&dbname=CMFD202201&filename=1021704205.nh&uniplatform=NZKPT&v=Fn8RAn55gYIfaCf3DXj6oXr0fycgDo4HmFRsi-7AVscLOXY6oHsZ6V9H5-cLR0se
23. Zhang, H.: The Research on the Method of Water Injection Meat Testing Based on Bioelectric Impedance Spectrum (2017). https://kns.cnki.net/kcms/detail/detail.aspx?dbcode=CMFD&dbname=CMFD201802&filename=1018039514.nh&uniplatform=NZKPT&v=ssOnWZf_YRCRwpyXFGTQuA_xH5V8Zixr8o_64md0rYHOlmmcBCkQ8zOXjtGQOnYk
24. Jaffrin, M.Y., Morel, H.: Body fluid volumes measurements by impedance: a review of bioimpedance spectroscopy (BIS) and bioimpedance analysis (BIA) methods. Med. Eng. Phys. **30**, 1257–1269 (2008). https://doi.org/10.1016/j.medengphy.2008.06.009

An IMU and EMG-Based Simultaneous and Proportional Control Strategy of 3-DOF Wrist and Hand Movements

Zihao Li, Jianmin Li, and Lizhi Pan[✉]

Key Laboratory of Mechanism Theory and Equipment Design
of Ministry of Education, School of Mechanical Engineering,
Tianjin University, Tianjin 300350, China
melzpan@tju.edu.cn

Abstract. Multiple degrees-of-freedom (DOFs) simultaneous and proportional control (SPC) is the trend of the electromyography (EMG)-driven human-machine interfaces. Recent studies demonstrated the capability of the musculoskeletal model in SPC. However, the supinator was a deep muscle and the signal-to-noise ratio (SNR) of the supinator surface EMG signal was relatively low. The musculoskeletal model had poor performance when decoding the joint angles of wrist rotation. This study proposed a control strategy intended to address this issue. The proposed decoder utilized an inertial measurement unit (IMU) to record the residual limb movements. The recorded residual limb movements were used to substitute EMG signals from a pair of agonist-antagonist muscles to control the wrist pronation/supination. Meanwhile, the decoder employed EMG signals for control of MCP flexion/extension and wrist flexion/extension. The EMG signals, IMU data and kinematic data were collected simultaneously from an able-bodied subject. To quantify the performance of the decoder, the Pearson's correction coefficient (r) and the normalized root mean square error (NRMSE) between estimated and measured angles were computed. The results demonstrated that the decoder provided accurate estimations of wrist rotation while the performance of the decoder was not affected by the simultaneous movements with the MCP and wrist flexion/extension.

Keywords: Inertial measurement unit · Electromyography · Residual limb movements · Human-machine interface

1 Introduction

Electromyography (EMG) is the electrical manifestation of muscle contractions [1]. Since the EMG signals carry rich information from the human physiological system, they are widely used as the input signals of the human-machine interface (HMI) [2-4]. The current commercial prosthetics are still dominated by traditional control methods, which require non-intuitive switching commands

[5]. With the development of pattern recognition algorithms, the classification accuracy of healthy people by pattern recognition is over 95% [6–9]. However, the algorithms of pattern recognition only classify EMG signals into several discrete joint angles, which is inconsistent with the natural movements of human limbs. Consequently, the commercial prosthesis based on pattern recognition algorithms has a limited clinical application in upper limb amputation [1].

To realize intuitive prosthetic control, the EMG-based simultaneous and proportional control (SPC) algorithms have been widely studied [10]. Artificial neural network (ANN), linear regression (LR), non-negative matrix factorization (NMF) and other advanced data-driven algorithms were used to establish models for SPC [11–14]. However, the above algorithms for SPC belonged to model-free approaches. They depended on the black-box method that used numerical mapping between input and output signals. There were several limitations in the black-box method, such as the need for a large amount of data to train the model and the possible inability to accurately predict new movements that not appeared in training data [15]. To reveal the relationships between muscle activation and corresponding movements, the prior knowledge of the human body's physiological structure was applied to the musculoskeletal model [16–18]. A recent study demonstrated that the musculoskeletal model could predict the trend and magnitude better than ANN and LR [19].

Wrist flexion/extension, MCP flexion/extension and wrist pronation/supination were the main DOFs of hand movements. However, the supinator associated with supination movements was in the deep of the forearm. The surface EMG signal of the supinator had a relatively low signal-to-noise ratio (SNR). To address this issue, Pan et al. substituted supinator with biceps. The controller performed well when the elbow flexed to 90° [20]. Since the biceps contributed to both elbow flexion and wrist supination, the controller had a poor performance during weightlifting. In addition, the approach based on movements synergistic between shoulder and wrist joints has also been applied to control wrist rotation [21,22].

In this study, we proposed an IMU and EMG-based SPC strategy of 3-DOF wrist and hand movements. In this decoder, four-channel EMG signals were used to control the movements of MCP and wrist flexion/extension. Given the difficulty of prosthesis control by solely using EMG, we used IMU to sense residual limb movements and used the recorded residual limb movements to control wrist pronation/supination. To evaluate the performance of the decoder, an able-body subject was recruited to conduct different types of tasks. The EMG signals, IMU data and kinematic data were collected simultaneously.

2 Method

2.1 Subject

One able-bodied subject (male, age 23, right hand dominant) was recruited and tested in this study. The subject had no known neurological disorders. The experimental protocol was approved by the Ethics Committee of Tianjin University

(Approval: TJUE-2021-114, Approval date: 06/10/2021) and in accordance with the Declaration of Helsinki.

2.2 Experimental Paradigm

The subject was asked to sit on the chair while the torso was straight and elbow flexed to 90°. The forearm and hand were fully relaxed and the fingers bent to the palm naturally. There were seven different types of tasks in this experiment, including rhythm and random movements: (1) rhythm MCP flexion/extension only; (2) rhythm wrist flexion/extension only; (3) rhythm wrist pronation/supination only; (4) random MCP flexion/extension only; (5) random wrist flexion/extension only; (6) random wrist pronation/supination only; (7) random simultaneous MCP flexion/extension, wrist flexion/extension and wrist pronation/supination.

During the rhythm trials, the subject performed the movements at a fixed frequency (1/4 Hz). During the random trials, the subject performed movements randomly. Each type of task was conducted for 20 s in each trial and four repetitive trials were performed for each task. The subjects performed a total of 28 trials. To avoid muscle fatigue, a 30-s break was taken between two consecutive trials.

2.3 Data Collection

In each trial, the EMG signals, IMU data and kinematic data were collected simultaneously (Fig. 1).

For EMG signals collection, DTS sensors (Noraxon U.S.A. Inc., USA) were used to record the EMG signals with a sampling frequency of 3000 Hz. The skin surface was rubbed with alcohol to reduce the contact impedance before placing the electrode. Four DTS sensors were attached to the four muscles: extensor carpi radials longus (ECRL), extensor digitorum (ED), flexor carpi radialis (FCR) and flexor digitorum (FD).

The kinematic data of the wrist and MCP were collected by the M-hand data glove (Guangzhou Virdyn Network Technology Co., Ltd, China) 120 Hz.

As for the IMU data, the IMU (Dongguan Wheeltec Technology Co., China) was mounted on the middle part of the lateral forearm using adhesive tape. There were six data streams (3 accelerometers, 3 gyroscopes) collected by IMU with a sampling frequency 200 Hz.

2.4 Data Processing

The raw EMG signals were band-pass filtered at cut-off frequencies 10 Hz and 1000 Hz. Then, the signals were full-wave rectified and low-pass filtered by a 4th-order Butterworth filter 5 Hz. To match the frequency of kinematic data collected by the data glove, a moving root mean square filtering (window length: 600 sample points, increment: 25 sample points) was used to down-sample the

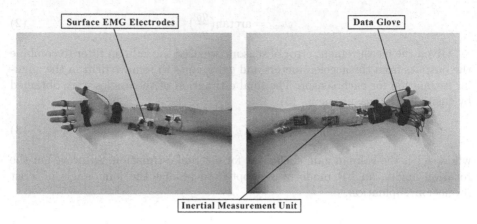

Fig. 1. Experimental setup. The positions of the surface EMG electrodes, IMU and data glove.

EMG signals 120 Hz. Finally, the processed EMG signals were normalized to the interval of 0 to 1.

For IMU data, three-axis gyroscope data and three-axis accelerometer data were up-sampled 600 Hz and down-sampled 120 Hz by moving average filtering (window length: 10 sample points, increment: 5 sample points).

2.5   Data Analysis

The joint angles of the wrist and MCP flexion/extension were predicted by the 2-DOF musculoskeletal model. Half of the experimental data were used to optimize the parameters of the model, while the rest of the experimental data were used to evaluate the performance of the model. In the 2-DOF musculoskeletal model, each muscle was represented as a Hill-type actuator with a contractile unit and a parallel elastic unit [16,17]. Furthermore, each muscle possessed six parameters (optimal muscle length, maximum isometric force, moment arms at the MCP flexion/extension and wrist flexion/extension joints, parallel elastic element stiffness and muscle length at neutral position). Every parameter was constrained to approximate ranges of physiologic values [18]. To minimize the weighted sum of squared difference between measured and predicted joint angles, the Matlab's GlobalSearch function was used to optimize the muscle's parameters. Since the ECRL and FCR did not cross the MCP joint anatomically, the moment arms at the MCP joint were set to zero.

For wrist pronation/supination angles decoding, the rotation angles of forearm residual limb were used as the control signal. The rotation angles can be measured using (1) and (2), where g_y and g_z are the values measured by y-axis and z-axis accelerometers, respectively, ω_x is the value measured by x-axis gyroscope and Δt is set at 1/120 s.

$$\psi_{gyro}(k) = \psi_{gyro}(k-1) + \omega_x \times \Delta t \tag{1}$$

$$\psi_{acc} = \arctan(\frac{g_y}{g_z}) \tag{2}$$

Given the measurement error of sensors, we used the kalman filter to combine the outputs from the accelerometers and gyroscopes to remove drift in the angular estimation for each sensor. The final estimation of the angles were obtained by fusing both measurements (3):

$$\psi_{roll} - \psi_{gyro} \mid K_k \times (\psi_{acc} - \psi_{gyro}) \tag{3}$$

where K_k is the kalman gain coefficient for optimal estimation. After we got the rotation angles, an LR model was adopted to predict the joint angle of wrist pronation/supination.

$$\theta_{pronation/supination} = K \times \psi_{roll} + b \tag{4}$$

where K and b are the coefficients of linear regression. Half of the experiments data were used to train the LR model.

2.6   Evaluation Metrics and Methods

To quantify the performance of the controller, the Pearson's correction coefficient (r) and the normalized root mean square error (NRMSE) between estimated and measured angles were computed. It should be noted that the r values of single DOF movements were computed at the corresponding joint being moved only.

$$r = \frac{\sum_{i=1}^{n} (x_i - \bar{x})(y_i - \bar{y})}{\sqrt{\sum_{i=1}^{n} (x_i - \bar{x})^2 (y_i - \bar{y})^2}} \tag{5}$$

$$NRMSE = \frac{\sqrt{\frac{1}{n} \sum_{i=1}^{n} (x_i - y_i)^2}}{x_{\max} - x_{\min}} \tag{6}$$

where x is the measured joint angles, y is the predicted joint angles, $\bar{x}$ is the mean value of the measured joint angles, $\bar{y}$ is the mean value of the predicted joint angles, $x_{\max}$ is the maximum value of the measured joint angles, $x_{\min}$ is the minimum value of the measured joint angles, n is the length of the data.

3   Result

For single joint rhythm movements, the mean r values between measured and predicted joints were 0.85, 0.91 and 0.95 at the MCP extension/flexion, wrist extension/flexion and wrist pronation/supination trials, respectively (Fig. 2(a)). The mean r values during MCP extension/flexion only, wrist extension/flexion only and wrist pronation/supination only random trials were 0.84, 0.84 and 0.95, respectively. In the simultaneous 3-DOF random movements trials, the mean r values for MCP extension/flexion, wrist extension/flexion and wrist pronation/supination were 0.71, 0.78 and 0.94, respectively.

Figure 2(b) shows the NRMSE values between measured and predicted joint angles during different kinds of movements. The mean NRMSE values during MCP extension/flexion, wrist extension/flexion and wrist pronation/supination rhythm trials were 0.17, 0.15 and 0.10, respectively. The mean NRMSE values during MCP extension/flexion, wrist extension/flexion and wrist pronation/supination random trials were 0.19, 0.20 and 0.09, respectively. The mean NRMSE values for MCP extension/flexion, wrist extension/flexion and wrist pronation/supination during simultaneous 3-DOF random movements trials were 0.20, 0.22 and 0.12, respectively.

Figure 3 presents the measured and predicted joint angles during single DOF random movements and simultaneous 3-DOF random movements. The results of the trials denote that the proposed model could feasibly estimate the movements of the wrist and hand in single DOF movements and simultaneous 3-DOF movements.

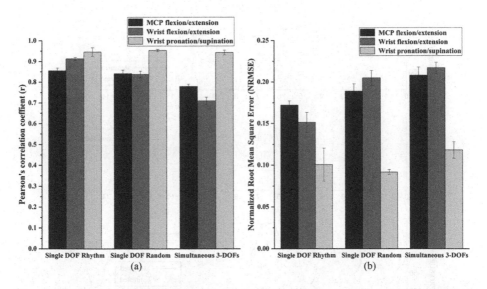

Fig. 2. The performance of the proposed controller. (a) Pearson's correlation coefficient (r) between measured and predicted joint angles during different kind of movement. (b) Normalize root mean square error (NRMSE) between measured and predicted joint angles during different kind of movement.

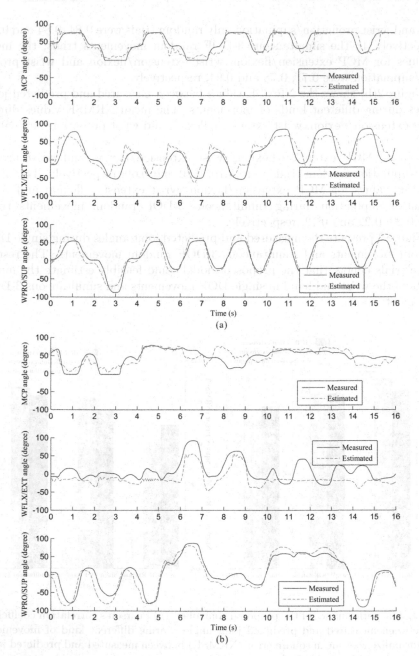

Fig. 3. Measured and estimated joint angles during different kinds of movements. (a) single DOF random movements of MCP flexion/extension, wrist flexion/extension and wrist pronation/supination, respectively. In the shown trials, the r values are 0.86, 0.85 and 0.95 respectively. The NRMSE values are 0.18, 0.19 and 0.09 respectively. (b) simultaneous 3-DOF random. In this trial, the r values for MCP extension/flexion, wrist extension/flexion and wrist pronation/supination were 0.70, 0.80 and 0.95, respectively. The NRMSE values are 0.21, 0.22 and 0.12 respectively.

4   Discussion

Our study proposed an SPC strategy of 3-DOF wrist and hand movements. The controller essentially used residual limb movements to substitute EMG signals from a pair of agonist-antagonist muscles to control wrist pronation/supination. Meanwhile, the decoder employed EMG signals for control of the MCP and wrist flexion/extension. The results demonstrated that the proposed model could reliably estimate the movements of the wrist and hand in single DOF and simultaneous 3-DOF movements.

As shown in Fig. 2, the mean r value and NRMSE value of wrist pronation/supination decoding was 0.95 and 0.10 respectively, which meant that the proposed decoder could accurately estimate the joint angle of wrist pronation/supination. Since the sEMG signal of the supinator had relatively low SNR, the sEMG-driven HMI had poor performance when decoding the movements of wrist rotation. The proposed decoder provided a feasible control strategy for HMI. Different from the motion of the other two DOFs, the movements of wrist pronation/supination could be partially reflected on the amputee's residual forearm. That was the main reason why we only applied this method to estimate the joint angles of wrist pronation/supination. Meanwhile, given the source of the input signals, the subject using the proposed decoder should reserve at least part of the forearm.

The 2-DOF musculoskeletal model was employed to decode the joint angles of MCP flexion/extension and wrist flexion/extension. For the decoding of MCP flexion/extension movement, the r values in single DOF rhythm, single DOF random and simultaneous 3-DOF random movements were 0.91, 0.84 and 0.71, respectively. For the decoding of wrist flexion/extension movement, the r values in single DOF rhythm, single DOF random and simultaneous 3-DOF random movements were 0.85, 0.84 and 0.78, respectively. This result indicated that the performance of the model was affected by the types of the tasks. The estimation performance of wrist was better than that of MCP in the simultaneous 3-DOF movements trials. We attribute the above results to the following two reasons: (1) Due to the limited independent sites at the residual limb, the forearm surface EMG signals were subject to crosstalk while the hand and wrist were moving simultaneously. (2) there is a greater cross-talk from wrist-related EMG signals in simultaneous 3-DOF movements trials.

The result indicated the feasibility of using the information of residual limb movements as the control inputs of the decoder. However, there existed several limitations in the current study. We only attempted to use the rotation angles of the forearm to predict the joint angles of the wrist by LR. In the future, different data streams and models will be applied to predict joint angles. The proposed decoder will be compared with the state-of-the-art methods. On the other hand, there is a limited number of able-bodies subjects. More subjects will be recruited to test the performance of the decoder in future studies.

5   Conclusion

In this study, we proposed an IMU and EMG-based SPC strategy of 3-DOF wrist and hand movements. The proposed controller used EMG signals to control the movements of the MCP and wrist flexion/extension. Meanwhile, we used IMU to sense residual limb movements and used the recorded residual limb movements to control wrist pronation/supination. The off-line results demonstrated that the proposed control strategy could estimate the movements of wrist and hand in single DOF movements and simultaneous 3-DOF movements. Note that the rotation of the limbs measured by IMU could always provide an accurate estimation of wrist pronation/supination movements (mean r value is 0.95, mean NRMSE value is 0.10).

Acknowledgments. The authors thank all participants who took part in the study. This work was supported in part by National Natural Science Foundation of China (Grant No. 52005364, 52122501). This work was also supported by the Key Laboratory of Mechanism Theory and Equipment Design of Ministry of Education (Tianjin University).

References

1. Jiang, N., Dosen, S., Muller, K.R., Farina, D.: Myoelectric control of artificial limbs-is there a need to change focus? [in the spotlight]. IEEE Sig. Process. Mag. **29**(5), 150–152 (2012)
2. Huang, H., Jiang, L., Liu, Y., Hou, L., Cai, H., Liu, H.: The mechanical design and experiments of HIT/DLR prosthetic hand. In: 2006 IEEE International Conference on Robotics and Biomimetics, pp. 896–901. IEEE (2006)
3. Bi, L., Guan, C., et al.: A review on EMG-based motor intention prediction of continuous human upper limb motion for human-robot collaboration. Biomed. Sig. Process. Control **51**, 113–127 (2019)
4. Li, K., Zhang, J., Wang, L., Zhang, M., Li, J., Bao, S.: A review of the key technologies for sEMG-based human-robot interaction systems. Biomed. Sig. Process. Control **62**, 102074 (2020)
5. Davidson, J.: A survey of the satisfaction of upper limb amputees with their prostheses, their lifestyles, and their abilities. J. Hand Ther. **15**(1), 62–70 (2002)
6. Englehart, K., Hudgins, B.: A robust, real-time control scheme for multifunction myoelectric control. IEEE Trans. Biomed. Eng. **50**(7), 848–854 (2003)
7. Huang, H., Zhou, P., Li, G., Kuiken, T.: Spatial filtering improves EMG classification accuracy following targeted muscle reinnervation. Ann. Biomed. Eng. **37**(9), 1849–1857 (2009). https://doi.org/10.1007/s10439-009-9737-7
8. Chen, X., Zhang, D., Zhu, X.: Application of a self-enhancing classification method to electromyography pattern recognition for multifunctional prosthesis control. J. Neuroeng. Rehabil. **10**(1), 1–13 (2013)
9. Ortiz-Catalan, M., Håkansson, B., Brånemark, R.: Real-time and simultaneous control of artificial limbs based on pattern recognition algorithms. IEEE Trans. Neural Syst. Rehabil. Eng. **22**(4), 756–764 (2014)
10. Jiang, N., Englehart, K.B., Parker, P.A.: Extracting simultaneous and proportional neural control information for multiple-DOF prostheses from the surface electromyographic signal. IEEE Trans. Biomed. Eng. **56**(4), 1070–1080 (2008)

11. Ameri, A., Akhaee, M.A., Scheme, E., Englehart, K.: Real-time, simultaneous myoelectric control using a convolutional neural network. PLoS ONE **13**(9), e0203835 (2018)
12. Hahne, J.M., et al.: Linear and nonlinear regression techniques for simultaneous and proportional myoelectric control. IEEE Trans. Neural Syst. Rehabil. Eng. **22**(2), 269–279 (2014)
13. Hahne, J.M., Graimann, B., Muller, K.R.: Spatial filtering for robust myoelectric control. IEEE Trans. Biomed. Eng. **59**(5), 1436–1443 (2012)
14. Jiang, N., Rehbaum, H., Vujaklija, I., Graimann, B., Farina, D.: Intuitive, online, simultaneous, and proportional myoelectric control over two degrees-of-freedom in upper limb amputees. IEEE Trans. Neural Syst. Rehabil. Eng. **22**(3), 501–510 (2013)
15. Sartori, M., Lloyd, D.G., Farina, D.: Corrections to "neural data-driven musculoskeletal modeling for personalized neurorehabilitation technologies" [May 16 879–893]. IEEE Trans. Biomed. Eng. **63**(6), 1341–1341 (2016)
16. Crouch, D.L., Huang, H.: Musculoskeletal model predicts multi-joint wrist and hand movement from limited EMG control signals. In: 2015 37th Annual International Conference of the IEEE Engineering in Medicine and Biology Society (EMBC), pp. 1132–1135. IEEE (2015)
17. Pan, L., Crouch, D.L., Huang, H.: Comparing EMG-based human-machine interfaces for estimating continuous, coordinated movements. IEEE Trans. Neural Syst. Rehabil. Eng. **27**(10), 2145–2154 (2019)
18. Crouch, D.L., Huang, H.: Lumped-parameter electromyogram-driven musculoskeletal hand model: a potential platform for real-time prosthesis control. J. Biomech. **49**(16), 3901–3907 (2016)
19. Crouch, D.L., Pan, L., Filer, W., Stallings, J.W., Huang, H.: Comparing surface and intramuscular electromyography for simultaneous and proportional control based on a musculoskeletal model: a pilot study. IEEE Trans. Neural Syst. Rehabil. Eng. **26**(9), 1735–1744 (2018)
20. Pan, L., Crouch, D., Huang, H.: Musculoskeletal model for simultaneous and proportional control of 3-DOF hand and wrist movements from EMG signals. In: 2017 8th International IEEE/EMBS Conference on Neural Engineering (NER), pp. 325–328. IEEE (2017)
21. Montagnani, F., Controzzi, M., Cipriani, C.: Exploiting arm posture synergies in activities of daily living to control the wrist rotation in upper limb prostheses: a feasibility study. In: 2015 37th Annual International Conference of the IEEE Engineering in Medicine and Biology Society (EMBC), pp. 2462–2465. IEEE (2015)
22. Bennett, D.A., Goldfarb, M.: IMU-based wrist rotation control of a transradial myoelectric prosthesis. IEEE Trans. Neural Syst. Rehabil. Eng. **26**(2), 419–427 (2017)

Application of Feedforward-Cascade Control in an External Pulling Robot for Nerve Restoration

Hongrui Fu[1,2] (iD), Gang Zhang[3] (iD), Han Zeng[3] (iD), Fuxin Du[3(✉)] (iD), and Rui Song[1,2(✉)] (iD)

[1] School of Control Science and Engineering, Shandong University, Jinan, China
rsong@sdu.edu.cn
[2] Engineering Research Center of Intelligent Unmanned System of Ministry of Education, Jinan, China
[3] School of Mechanical Engineering, Shandong University, Jinan, China
dufuxin@sdu.edu.cn

Abstract. The regeneration process of severed nerves is extremely slow, and the distance and direction of growth are affected by many factors, making it difficult for doctors to determine the time of suture surgery. Existing treatments, which require doctors to manually pull on an external cord to pull the nerve, are highly uncertain. In this paper, we propose an external pulling robot, which connects the fractured nerve to an implanted tendon sheath system (TSS) and automatically pulls the nerve by an external drive module that can be fixed on the body surface. The external driver module is 16 cm by 8 cm by 6 cm. In this paper, a feedforward link is designed to compensate for friction hysteresis in the transmission process of the tendon sheath system. The traction force, speed, and displacement are precisely controlled by the cascade control strategy. The experimental results show that the control system can effectively reduce the errors in the traction process. This paper is of great significance for reducing the cost of nerve restoration and improving the reliability of nerve traction.

Keywords: External pulling robot · Design · Tendon sheath system · Nerve traction

1 Introduction

In recent years, medical robot technology has made significant progress in numerous application fields [1, 2], including laparoscopic surgery, exoskeleton and orthopedic navigation [3, 4]. Implantable robots should give the human body environmental awareness and the ability to act to properly integrate with the human body and regulate biological and metabolic processes similar to natural organs [5]. Research on implantable robots has reported some preliminary results in recent years, such as urination [6], drug delivery [7], and tissue regeneration [8], and these methods inspire restoring the function of the injured site.

© The Author(s), under exclusive license to Springer Nature Switzerland AG 2022
H. Liu et al. (Eds.): ICIRA 2022, LNAI 13457, pp. 440–449, 2022.
https://doi.org/10.1007/978-3-031-13835-5_40

The restoration of peripheral nerve defects is a difficult problem in clinical surgery, which can lead to sensory and motor dysfunction in innervated areas [9]. Small nerve defects can be directly sutured by dissociation and other means [10], but the restoration of large nerve defects needs to be combined with the natural growth of the nerve and regular pulling [11, 12]. The traditional procedure for repairing a broken nerve involves inserting a Kirschner wire into the patient's bone and periodically manually rotating the externally fixed nut to pull the drive wire stitched onto the nerve. This type of traction is extremely dependent on the surgeon's surgical experience, and the amount of traction provided varies greatly each time. Key parameters of the actual nerve growth process, such as traction force and traction distance, cannot be accurately controlled. In addition, the device is bulky and puts most of the force of gravity on a patient's bones which will cause unpredictable bone damage, especially in patients with osteoporosis.

The tendon sheath system plays an indispensable role in reducing surgical wounds and improving the degree of freedom and flexibility of surgical robots, which has been widely used in the field of laparoscopic surgical robots [13]. However, friction hysteresis exists in the long-distance bending transmission process, which greatly affects the transmission effect of the displacement and the driving force [14–16]. Due to the narrow working environment in the body, it is difficult for existing methods to integrate sensors into the end of surgical instruments, which causes an obstacle to the precision control of surgical robots.

To solve the practical problems in the treatment process mentioned above, the following research contents are completed in this paper:

- An external pulling robot is proposed to assist the directional growth of fractured nerves. The robot can be fixed on the surface of the body and automatically achieve regular traction according to the law of nerve growth.
- The friction hysteresis characteristic of the tendon sheath system is analyzed. A cascade control system with feedforward compensation of tendon sheath in a low-speed state is proposed. Experiments show the corresponding relationship between traction force and traction distance.

The rest of the paper is as follows. Section 2 presents the working principle of the external pulling robot. Section 3 analyzes the friction hysteresis model of the tendon sheath system, and a feedforward compensation is proposed to improve the accuracy of actual output displacement. Section 4 describes an experimental method and gives experimental results that are consistent with the analysis process. Finally, the limitations of this paper and the methods to reduce the error are discussed.

2 Structure of the External Pulling Robot

The structure of the external pulling robot is shown in Fig. 1. The robot can only achieve single-direction nerve traction, which ensures the reliability of the actual growth length of the nerve. The wire in the traction tube is connected with the nerve or sutured line, and the traction part pulls the nerve according to the set force.

The motion diagram of the external pulling robot is shown in Fig. 2. The motor drives the pulley to rotate through the coupling, and then drives the lead screw to achieve the traction wire. The overall movement relationship is as follows: servo motor - coupling - belt - lead screw - lead screw nut - connecting block - tension sensor - traction wire. The tension sensor is used to sense and adjust the traction force of the nerve. Belt drive ensures that the traction will not fluctuate greatly.

Fig. 1. The structure of the external pulling robot.

This design makes the overall size of the robot more compact. It is friendly for patients to carry around, opening up the possibility of adding other power modules.

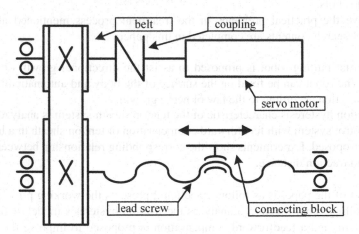

Fig. 2. Schematic diagram of the external pulling robot.

3 Mathematical Model

In this section, the control system of the external pulling robot is analyzed. The traction force, velocity, and displacement are controlled by a cascade control strategy. The friction model of the tendon sheath system is calculated by using the data collected by the force sensor, which is used as a feedforward link to compensate for the output displacement of the end.

3.1 Cascade Control of Drive System

To quantitatively analyze the dynamic performance of the external pulling robot, the dynamic mathematical model of the driving system must be established first. When the armature current is constant, we have:

$$E_b = K_1 \frac{d\theta_m}{dt}, T_m = K_2 I_a \qquad (1)$$

where E_b is the inverse electromotive force of the motor, K_1 is the inverse emf coefficient, θ_m is the rotation angle of the rotor shaft, T_m is the electromagnetic torque, K_2 and I_a are torque coefficient and armature current respectively.

The differential equation of armature current is derived by Kirchhoff's voltage law:

$$L_a \frac{dI_a}{dt} + R_a I_a + E_b = E_a \qquad (2)$$

where L_a and E_a are armature inductance and armature voltage respectively.

Considering the rotor dynamics equation, we have:

$$2\pi J_m \frac{d\omega}{dt} = T_m - M_L \qquad (3)$$

Set E_a as the control input and load torque M_l as the disturbance input, then the armature time constant T_a, armature gain K_a, and mechanical time constant T_b are shown below respectively.

$$T_a = \frac{L_a}{R_a}, K_a = \frac{1}{R_a}, T_b = \frac{1}{2\pi J} \qquad (4)$$

Taking the Laplace transform of this linear system, we have:

$$I_a(s) = \frac{K_a T_b s}{T_a T_b s^2 + T_b s + K_1 K_2 K_a} U_a(s) + \frac{K_a K_1}{T_a T_b s^2 + T_b s + K_1 K_2 K_a} M_L(s) \qquad (5)$$

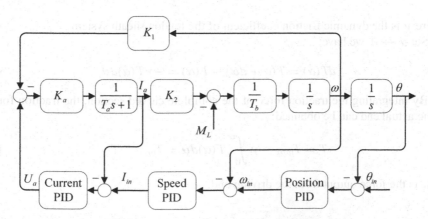

Fig. 3. Drive system structure block diagram.

The motion control of an external traction robot needs to consider three States simultaneously: traction force, traction speed, and traction distance. The current, speed, and angle of the servo motor are mutually coupled, so a multi-loop cascade PID control strategy can be designed to realize the cooperative control of the three states. The control flow of this method is shown in Fig. 3.

3.2 Feedforward Compensation of Tendon Sheath System

As is shown in Fig. 4, assuming that the sheath is bent with a constant radius of curvature, a section of the flexural segment of the tendon sheath system is analyzed.

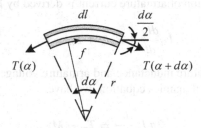

Fig. 4. Stress analysis of single-segment tendon sheath system.

$$T(\alpha)\cos(\frac{d\alpha}{2}) - T(\alpha + d\alpha)\cos(\frac{d\alpha}{2}) = f \tag{6}$$

where $d\alpha$ is the bending angle of the section, $T(\alpha)$ is the system tension near the driving end, and f is the total friction force.

Considering that the process of neural traction runs entirely at lower velocities, the effect of velocity on friction is negligible in the viscous model, we obtain:

$$f = 2\gamma T(\alpha)\sin(\frac{d\alpha}{2}) \tag{7}$$

where γ is the dynamic friction coefficient of the tendon sheath system.

Set $\alpha \to 0$, we have:

$$dT(\alpha) = T(\alpha + d\alpha) - T(\alpha) = -\gamma T(\alpha)d\alpha \tag{8}$$

By integrating the traction force of the complete curved section, the traction force of the actual end can be obtained:

$$T = T_{prox} - \gamma \int_0^\alpha T(\alpha)d\alpha = T_{prox}e^{-\gamma\alpha} \tag{9}$$

T_{prox} is the force output from the driving end.

It is assumed that the tendon system works within the elastic range of Hooke's law, the tension of each section will lead to the change of elongation:

$$\frac{T}{A} = E\frac{d\delta}{dl} = \frac{E}{r}\frac{d\delta}{d\alpha} \tag{10}$$

where A is the cross-sectional area, E and $d\delta$ are young's modulus of tendon sheath material and elongation of the segment.

Integral over the complete curved section, we obtain:

$$\delta = \frac{T_{prox}}{EA}\int_0^\alpha r(\alpha)e^{-\gamma\alpha}d\alpha - \frac{T_0L}{EA} \tag{11}$$

It is assumed that the bending radius R of the tendon sheath system in the working state is unchanged, we can obtain the analytical solution of δ as follows:

$$\delta = \frac{T_{prox}R}{EA\gamma}(1 - e^{-\gamma\alpha}) - \frac{T_0L}{EA} \tag{12}$$

The elongation obtained from the friction model is compensated to the control system as a feedforward link:

$$X_a = X_d + \delta(\alpha, L, R, T_{prox}) \tag{13}$$

where X_a is the adjusted displacement, X_d is the expected displacement, and $\delta(\alpha, L, R, T_{prox})$ is the elongation compensated by the tendon sheath system.

The system block diagram obtained is shown in Fig. 5.

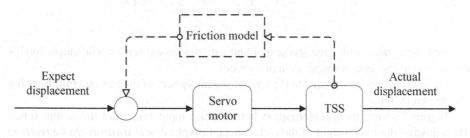

Fig. 5. Block diagram of the external pulling robot system.

4 Simulation and Experimental Verification

The complete experimental rig is shown in Fig. 6. The input terminal is composed of the external pulling robot, circuit board (main control chip is RT1064), battery, and displacement sensor. In addition to the servo control function, the circuit board also has power detection, and voltage compensation. The displacement sensor is fixed with the connecting block to eliminate the displacement deviation caused by the violent movement of the connecting block. The driving wire is made of Nitinol alloy. The

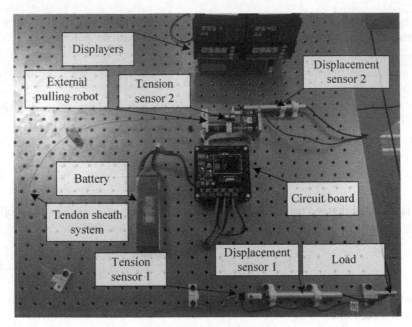

Fig. 6. Experimental device.

Table 1. Physical parameters of the tendon sheath system

Parameters	γ	r	L	A	E
Value	0.31	16.2	90	0.126	199

output is integrated with a tension sensor and a displacement sensor. The output load is connected to the tendon sheath system by wool.

Physical parameters related to the tendon sheath system of the external pulling robot are shown in Table 1.

Figure 7 shows the transformation between the input force and the output force. By adjusting the load weight of the end, constant displacement traction can be realized within a limited speed range. The traction force of the input end is linear with the output force after passing through the tendon sheath system. The friction in the transmission process also increases linearly with the increase of the input and output tension.

When the bending angle of the tendon sheath system is constant, the displacement relationship between the output end and the input end of the robot under directional traction is shown in Fig. 8. Under the condition of 50g heavy load at the end, the pulling speed is 1mm/s, and the calculated elongation of the driving wire is 0.07mm, which is very similar to the experimental results. The elongation is almost constant under a fixed load.

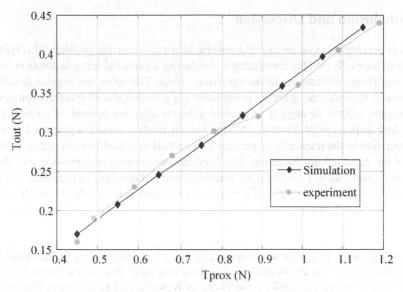

Fig. 7. Input-output force relationship.

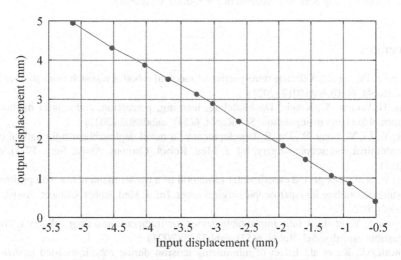

Fig. 8. The elongation of the driving wire at diffident displacements.

5   Conclusion and Discussion

In this paper, we propose an external pulling robot to solve the problem of relying on doctors to manually pull the connecting wires during traditional nerve restoration, resulting in significant differences in each traction effect. The robot has regular directional traction and is connected to nerves in the body via a tendon sheath transmission system. The cascade control strategy is utilized to achieve effective control of traction force, speed, and displacement. Finally, a tendon sheath friction model is proposed in which the elongation in the transmission process is regarded as a feedforward step to compensate for the expected displacement. The friction force during transmission can also be calculated quantitatively to obtain the traction force at the output in real-time.

In future work, the problem of a large circuit board will be solved, and the overall size of the external pulling robot will be further reduced. New control strategies will be proposed to improve the flexibility and accuracy of the control system.

Acknowledgments. This work was supported by the China Postdoctoral Science Foundation funded project (Grant No. 2019M662346), Shandong Provincial Postdoctoral Innovative Talents Funded Scheme (Grant No. 238226), the Focus on Research and Development Plan in Shandong province (Grant No. 2022CXGC010503), the Fundamental Research Funds for the Central Universities and Young Scholars Program of Shan-dong University.

References

1. Dupont, PE., et al.: A decade retrospective of medical robotics research from 2010 to 2020. Sci. Robot. **6**(60), eabi8017 (2021)
2. Yin, H.,Varava, A., Kragic, D.: Modeling, learning, perception, and control methods for deformable object manipulation. Sci. Robot. **6**(54), eabd8803 (2021)
3. Lei, Y., Li, Y., Song, R., Du, F.: Development of a novel deployable arm for natural orifice transluminal endoscopic surgery. Int. J. Med. Robot. Comput. Assist. Surg. **17**(3), e2232 (2021)
4. Lei, Y., et al.: Design and experimental validation of a master manipulator with position and posture decoupling for laparoscopic surgical robot. Int. J. Med. Robot. Comput. Assist. Surg. e2398 (2022)
5. Iacovacci, V., et al.: A fully implantable device for intraperitoneal drug delivery refilled by ingestible capsules. Sci. Robot. **6**(57), eabh3328 (2021)
6. Kowalczyk, K., et al.: Effect of minimizing tension during robotic-assisted laparoscopic radical prostatectomy on urinary function recovery. World J. Urol. **31**(3), 515–521 (2013)
7. Zhi, C., et al.: Fabrication and characterization of micro electromagnetic linear actuators. J. Micromech. Microeng. **30**(12), 125011 (2020)
8. Damian, DD., et al.: In vivo tissue regeneration with robotic implants. Sci. Robot. **3**(14), eaaq0018 (2018)
9. Faroni, A., Mobasseri, S., Kingham, P., Reid, A.J.: Peripheral nerve regeneration: experimental strategies and future perspectives. Adv. Drug Deliv. Rev. **82**, 160–167 (2015)
10. Bhadra, N., Peckham, P.H.: Peripheral nerve stimulation for restoration of motor function. J. Clin. Neurophysiol. **14**(5), 378–393 (1997)
11. Li, X., et al.: In vivo DTI longitudinal measurements of acute sciatic nerve traction injury and the association with pathological and functional changes. Eur. J. Radiol. **82**(11), e707–e714 (2010)

12. Plastaras, C., Chhatre, A., Kotcharian, A.: Perioperative upper extremity peripheral nerve traction injuries. Orthop. Clin. **45**(1), 47–53 (2014)
13. Phee, S., Low, S., Huynh, V., Kencana, A., Sun, Z., Yang, K.: Master and slave transluminal endoscopic robot (MASTER) for natural orifice transluminal endoscopic surgery (NOTES). In: Annual International Conference of the IEEE Engineering in Medicine and Biology Society, Minneapolis, MN, pp. 1992–1995. IEEE (2009)
14. Zhang, T., Liu, M., Lei, Y., Du, F., Song, R., Li, Y.: Analysis of dynamic friction and elongation characteristics of the tendon sheath system. In: Liu, X.-J., Nie, Z., Yu, J., Xie, F., Song, R. (eds.) ICIRA 2021. LNCS (LNAI), vol. 13015, pp. 145–154. Springer, Cham (2021). https://doi.org/10.1007/978-3-030-89134-3_14
15. Phee, S., Low, S., Dario, P., Menciassi, A.: Tendon sheath analysis for estimation of distal end force and elongation for sensorless distal end. Robotica **28**(7), 1073–1082 (2010)
16. Xu, W., Poon, C.C.Y., Yam, Y., Chiu, P.W.Y.: Motion compensated controller for a tendon-sheath-driven flexible endoscopic robot. Int. J. Med. Robot. Comput. Assist. Surg. **13**(1), e1747 (2017)

Intelligent Co-operation in Mobile Robots for Learning, Optimization, Planning, and Control

Crawling Trajectory Generation of Humanoid Robot Based on CPG and Control

Weilong Zuo[1,2], Gunyao Gao[1,2(✉)], Jingwei Cao[1,2], Tian Mu[1,2], and Yuanzhen Bi[1,2]

[1] School of Mechanical Engineering, Beijing Institute of Technology, Beijing, China
gaojunyao@bit.edu.cn

[2] Beijing Advanced Innovation Center for Intelligent Robots and Systems, Beijing, China

Abstract. There were various gait generation and motion control methods implemented on humanoid robot, while research on humanoid robot crawling and control seems to be litter. In this paper, we establish the CPG model based on Hopf oscillator and get the trajectory of each joint when the robot crawls. Compared with the traditional CPG method, we use the layered and coupled method to establish the CPG expression of robot joint, which reduces the whole amount of computation. In order to correct the problem of the robot's climbing deviation, we simplified the robot above the waist joint into an inverted pendulum model, and established a position controller to make the robot crawl forward after being disturbed. To increase the robot's ability to adapt to different environment, we established a compliance control model for the robot's arm and estimated the force generated when the robot's arm collided with the ground. Finally, we performed crawling experiments outdoors, the results show that the robot can pass through an environment with a fluctuation height of 3 cm.

Keywords: Crawl · CPG · Inverted pendulum · VMC · Controller

1 Introduction

Compared with traditional wheeled robot and crawler robot, legged robot have attracted widespread attention because of their strong environmental adaptability. Legged robot include biped, quadruped, hexapod etc. [1]. Among all legged robot, bipedal robot have received extensive attention due to their strong coupling and nonlinearity. The main research direction focuses on walking, running, jumping and other movement [2]. In order to work in a variety of challenging environment, it's important for the robot complete various movement, thus we consider the crawling gait, because crawling can reduce the impact on the robot and reduce the risk of injury when the robot fallen. In this work, we present a new method to generate crawling gait based on Central Pattern Generators (CPG) and adopt posture control for the rotational degrees of freedom of the waist joint, compliance control for the arm joint, which constitutes a closed loop.

Biologist have found that some movement patterns of vertebrates, such as walking, running and jumping, are simple rhythmic movements, which are mainly controlled by CPG [3–6]. The main function of CPG is to generate rhythm signals, control effectors

H. Liu et al. (Eds.): ICIRA 2022, LNAI 13457, pp. 453–465, 2022.
https://doi.org/10.1007/978-3-031-13835-5_41

to realize movement, and they can smoothly adjust the shape of oscillation with simple control signals for different disturbances [7]. In the past time, Many scholars have devoted themselves to using CPG to generate rhythmic movement patterns. In [8], the author made use of four non-linear oscillators to generate ellipse-shaped trajectories and filters the output of the oscillators. In [9] and [10], Hopf oscillators were proposed, and incorporated inertial feedback into the CPG framework for the control of body posture during legged locomotion on uneven terrain. Ludovic Righetti presents a way of designing CPG with coupled oscillators in which he can independently control the ascending and descending phases of the oscillations, and the feedback system method was adopted to make the controller strongly coupled with the mechanical system [11]. Endo successfully cope with unknown 3mm bump with Matsuoka neural oscillators, which use the extensor response and vestibulo-spinal Reflex as the feedbacks [12]. In order to overcome the problem that there is no direct relationship between model parameters and workspace in CPG, [13] adopts Workspace-Based Central Pattern Generators (WCPG) establish the relationship. Chengju Liu used CPG generate toe trajectories online in workspace for a robot rather than to generate joint control signals in joint space, which were validated using a quadruped robot [14]. Li adopted the general CPG modeling method to conduct crawling experiments on NAO and iCub robots, which proved the adaptability of the CPG structure and the degree of ability to transfer it to different robot morphologies [15], but his equation requires a lot of calculation. Huang based on CPG generated the robot's crawling trajectory, and solved the problem of difficult to plan crawling motion of robot with rigid-flexible mechanism [16], but her approach didn't constitute a closed loop. From the above summary, many CPG methods have been applied to robot fish swimming, quadruped or biped walking, however most of them need larger calculation or didn't form a closed-loop control.

Considering the limitation of the work mentioned above, a framework based on Central Pattern Generators and control feedback were proposed in this paper to achieve robust crawling (see Fig. 1). The main contributions of this paper are as follows:

(1) We divide nine Hopf oscillators into two stages and construct a hierarchical CPG network. In the first stage, a fully symmetrical network topology is adopted, and in the second stage, a unidirectional coupling method is adopted to establish the relationship between the knee and hip joints of the robot. In the actual experiment, in order to prevent the robot from backsliding, we used the roll freedom of lumbar joint, whose direction was synchronized with the pitch joint of the left hip leg.

(2) In order to correct the problem of the robot crawling deviation, we simplified the above of the robot waist joint into an inverted pendulum model, constructed the relationship between the gain coefficient and the damping and oscillation frequency.

(3) In order to adapt to different ground environments, we simplify the arm into a viscoelastic model, and use the LQR method to construct the relationship between the arm variation, the force on the arm and the position of the arm. And a method similar to PD was used to estimate the force of the robot arm when it collides with the ground.

(4) The proposed method is verified on an actual robot, and the experimental results show that the robot can successfully pass through obstacles with a ground height of 3 cm in an outdoor environment.

The remainder of the paper is organized as follows. Section 2 presents the structure of humanoid robot, including the parameters of each connecting link. Section 3 provides background on the CPG framework and describes our CPG model. Section 4 describes the control methods we use, including posture controller and VMC controller. In Sect. 5, we use CPG and controllers do some experiments, both with simulation and real robot. And the results show that our method have a good effect. Section 6 summarizes our work and offers suggestions for future work.

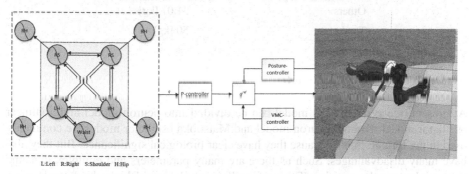

Fig. 1. Overviews of the CPG and control framework. Where q^{ref} is the joint reference.

2 Humanoid Robot Model

Figure 2 shows a humanoid robot structure which was depend on the height of adult men. The total weight of the robot is 50 kg and 20 degrees of freedom in all. In order to prevent the deformation of the robot after violent impact, we install the matching pads on the waist, chest, back, left arm and right arm of the robot. To control the whole body motion, the robot body is equipped with a CPU board, an inner measurement unit (IMU) was installed on the upper body of the robot, and two six-dimensional force sensors are attached on the two ankles respectively. Table 1 shows the overall mass of the robot and the length values of each link.

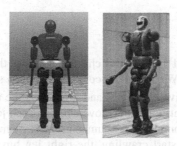

Fig. 2. Snapots of humanoid robot

Table 1. The parameters of our robot.

Parameters	size	Mass
Thigh	361 [mm]	7.36 [kg]
Shank	330 [mm]	5.12 [kg]
Boom	350 [mm]	4.15 [kg]
Jib	360 [mm]	2.30 [kg]
Others	–	31.07 [kg]
Total mass	–	50 [kg]

3 Design of CPG Network

At present, the general CPG model can be divided into neuron model and nonlinear oscillator model. Kimura neuron model and Matsuoka oscillator model are commonly used in the former, that's because they have clear biological significance. But they also have many disadvantages. Such as there are many parameters and complex dynamic characteristics in the equation. The hopf oscillator model is widely used in latter because of its simple parameters and easy to control the frequency and amplitude of the oscillator. The traditional method is to build an oscillator model for each joint, and then send the solved joint value to each joint. This method needs to establish a large number of equations, and occupy a lot of computer memory in the process of calculation.

Compared with quadruped walking, the crawling action of humanoid robot has many similarities. Therefore, we refer to the literature [17] and the form of quadruped robot motion, and design a layered CPG network. The control network is mainly divided into two layers, the first layer mainly includes left and right arm shoulder joint, left and right leg hip joint; the second layer mainly includes left and right arm elbow joint, left and right arm joint knee joint. The first layer adopts omnidirectional coupling connection mode; the second layer adopts one-way coupling connection mode. The mathematical expression of traditional Hopf oscillator were Eq. 1 and Eq. 2.

$$\dot{x} = \alpha(\mu - r^2)x - \omega y \tag{1}$$

$$\dot{y} = \alpha(\mu - r^2)y + wx \tag{2}$$

In order to better control the coupling characteristics of the oscillator, and make the output become adjustable. We added the coupling term, as shown in the right term of Eq. 3, where θ_i^j is the relative phase of i and j, $R(\theta_i^j)$ is the rotation matrix. Literature [18] and [19] respectively introduce the movements of each joint of human body during crawling, considering the complexity of human muscle, we made a simplification, that's when the humanoid robot start crawling, the right leg hip joint and knee joint start swing, the left shoulder joint start swing, the elbow joint start contracting, at the same time the left leg hip joint and knee joint start contracting, the right shoulder joint start contracting, the elbow joint start swing, from above gait pattern, we can get θ_i^j. Then the final equation expression were shown in Eq. (3)–Eq. (8), where α and μ represent the convergence speed and amplitude of the oscillator respectively, β represents the duty cycle. Considering the convenience, here we use the output of y_i as the input value of each joint of the robot.

$$\begin{bmatrix} \dot{x}_i \\ \dot{y}_i \end{bmatrix} = \begin{bmatrix} \alpha(\mu - r_i^2) & -w_i \\ w_i & \alpha(\mu - r_i^2) \end{bmatrix} \begin{bmatrix} x_i \\ y_i \end{bmatrix} + \sum_{j=1}^{i} R(\theta_j^i) \begin{bmatrix} x_i \\ y_i \end{bmatrix}, i = 1, 2, 3, 4 \qquad (3)$$

$$r_i^2 = x_i^2 + y_i^2 \qquad (4)$$

$$w_i = \frac{w_{st}}{e^{-ay_i} + 1} + \frac{w_{sw}}{e^{ay_i} + 1} \qquad (5)$$

$$w_{st} = \frac{1 - \beta}{\beta} w_{sw} \qquad (6)$$

$$\theta_{ji} = 2\pi(\varphi_i - \varphi_j) \qquad (7)$$

$$R(\theta_i^j) = \begin{bmatrix} \cos\theta_{ji} & -\sin\theta_{ji} \\ \sin\theta_{ji} & \cos\theta_{ji} \end{bmatrix} \qquad (8)$$

During the experiment, we found that only relying on the above joints, the robot will fall back in the process of crawling. To avoid this problem, we added a roll degree of freedom of the lumbar joint, whose direction was consistent with that of the thigh pitch joint, but have different amplitude. Because the trajectories generated by CPG were dimensionless, considering the actual size of our robot, we add a P control parameter here, $P = [k_1, k_2, k_3, k_4, k_5, k_6, k_7, k_8, k_9]$, like Eq. (9).

$$\theta_i^{ref} = k_i y_i (i = 1, 2, 3, 4, 5, 6, 7, 8, 9) \qquad (9)$$

4   Crawling Control

4.1   Crawling Posture Control

When the robot crawls forward, its torso remains upright, but when it encounters interference, the robot may deviate. Therefore, in view of the problem that the robot's trunk cannot remain vertical after being disturbed, this paper proposes a trunk vertical controller based on an inverted pendulum model, which simplifies the waist joint and above into an inverted pendulum model, and constructs a waist joint PD controller. Through the measured deviation angle between the trunk and the forward direction, the compensation angle of the rotation direction of the waist joint is calculated, and its expressions are shown in Eq. 10 and Eq. 11. Where θ_{waist}^{ref} represents the angle reference value of the rotation direction of the lumbar joint, $\triangle \theta_{wasit}^{control}$ represents the compensation value. φ represents the deviation angle of the torso from the forward direction, which obtained from the IMU, and the IMU was placed at the position of the robot head. k_p and k_d are the coefficients of the PD controller.

$$\theta_{waist}^{mod\,fied} = \theta_{waist}^{ref} + \Delta\theta_{wasit}^{control} \tag{10}$$

$$\Delta\dot{\theta}_{waist}^{control} = k_p * \varphi + k_d * \dot{\varphi} \tag{11}$$

Assuming that the mass of the robot's waist joint and above is evenly distributed, the waist joint can be simplified as an inverted pendulum, as shown in Fig. 3. The rod length is 1/2 of the length from the waist joint to the head, which is recorded as l_0. Assuming that the mass of the robot is concentrated at one point, which is recorded as m_0, we can carry out dynamic analysis of the waist joint and get:

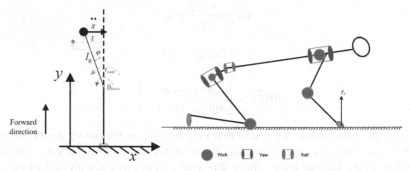

Fig. 3. Robot crawling diagram. The left represents the top view of robot crawling, and the right represents the left view of robot crawling.

$$m_0gx + m_0\ddot{x}\,l_0\cos\varphi - F_N(L+x) = \tau_{waist} \tag{12}$$

$$\tau_{waist} = I(\ddot{\theta}_{waist}^{ref} + \Delta\ddot{\theta}_{wasit}^{control}) \tag{13}$$

where x is the deviation distance between the trunk and the horizontal direction, φ is the deviation angle between the trunk and the forward direction, which can be measured by IMU, τ_{waist} is the moment of the waist joint, I is the moment of inertia of the inverted pendulum, and F_N is the force acting on the arm when the arm collides with the ground, here we adopted the reference value, L is the distance between the arm contact point and the y-axis in the x direction. Because the roll deviation between the torso and the forward direction is less than $\pm 5°$, so we can get the Eq. (14).

$$x = l_0\sin\varphi \approx l_0\varphi$$
$$\cos\varphi \approx 1 \tag{14}$$

From Eq. (12), Eq. (13) and Eq. (14), we can obtain

$$(m_0g - F_N)l_0\varphi + m_0l_0^2\ddot{\varphi} = I(\ddot{\theta}_{waist}^{ref} + \Delta\ddot{\theta}_{wasit}^{control}) + F_NL \tag{15}$$

Take the derivative of Eq. (11)

$$\Delta \ddot{\theta}_{waist}^{control} = k_p * \dot{\varphi} + k_d * \ddot{\varphi} \tag{16}$$

From Eq. (15) and Eq. (16), we can obtain

$$\ddot{\varphi} + \frac{-Ik_p}{m_0 l_0^2 - Ik_d} \dot{\varphi} + \frac{(m_0 g - F_N) l_0}{m_0 l_0^2 - Ik_d} \varphi = \frac{I}{m_0 l_0^2 - Ik_d} \ddot{\theta}_{waist}^{ref} + \frac{F_N L}{m_0 l_0^2 - Ik_d} \tag{17}$$

It can be seen that Eq. 17 is a second-order system. According to the principle of the second-order system,

$$\frac{-Ik_p}{m_0 l_0^2 - Ik_d} = 2\xi w_n$$
$$\frac{(m_0 g - F_N) l_0}{m_0 l_0^2 - Ik_d} = w_n^2 \tag{18}$$

Through the given damping ratio and oscillation frequency, we can calculate the values of k_p and k_d. Then bring k_p and k_d into Eq. 11, we can obtain $\Delta \dot{\theta}_{waist}^{control}$, integrate it, obtain $\Delta \theta_{waist}^{control}$. This is the compensation value obtained by our solution.

4.2 Compliance Control

When the human body is crawling, the muscles of the arm can absorb and restrain the impact between the hand and the ground, and have a certain viscoelasticity. Therefore, by simulating the muscles of the human arm, a virtual viscoelastic model is constructed in the form of multiple spring damping in parallel. According to the estimated force generated by the arm in the process of collision with the ground, the height to be adjusted in the vertical direction is calculated, the adjusted height is brought into the inverse kinematics of the arm, and the changes of each joint angle of the arm are solved, so that the supporting arm can be closely combined with the ground, The swinging arm can land more smoothly, so as to reduce the impact on the ground.

The virtual model established in this paper is shown in Fig. 4. Here, a spring and a damping block are used on the left and a spring and a telescopic unit are used on the right. The coefficient of the left spring is k_1, the coefficient of the right spring is k_2, and the coefficients of the damping block and the expansion unit are b and e respectively. Assume the first group of spring variable on the left is ε_1 and the group of spring variable on the right is ε_2, the total spring variable is ε, then we can get the Eq. 19 and Eq. 20.

$$\varepsilon = \varepsilon_1 + \varepsilon_2 \tag{19}$$

$$f = k_1 \varepsilon_1 + b \dot{\varepsilon}_1 = k_2 \varepsilon_2 + e \tag{20}$$

Laplace transform Eq. (20), we can obtain

$$\varepsilon_1 = \frac{\sigma}{k_1 + bs}$$
$$\varepsilon_2 = \frac{\sigma - e}{k_2} \tag{21}$$

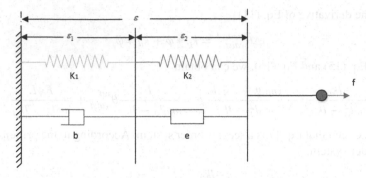

Fig. 4. Viscoelastic Model, the meaning of the specific parameters has been introduced above.

Substituting Eq. 21 into 19 and performing the inverse Laplace transform, we get

$$k_1 k_2 \varepsilon + k_2 b \varepsilon s = (k_1 + k_2)\sigma + b \varepsilon s - k_1 e - b e s$$
$$k_1 k_2 \varepsilon + k_2 b \dot{\varepsilon} = (k_1 + k_2)\sigma + b \dot{\varepsilon} - k_1 e - b \dot{e} \tag{22}$$

When the arm collides with the ground, the force of the ground on the arm is $-f_z$, and the whole variation was h_z, substituting it into Eq. 22, we can obtain:

$$\dot{f}_z = -(\frac{k_1 + k_2}{b})f_z - \frac{k_1 k_2}{b}h_z - k_2 \dot{h}_z - \frac{k_1}{b}e - \dot{e} \tag{23}$$

$$\ddot{f}_z = -(\frac{k_1 + k_2}{b})\dot{f}_z - \frac{k_1 k_2}{b}\dot{h}_z - k_2 \ddot{h}_z - \frac{k_1}{b}\dot{e} - \ddot{e} \tag{24}$$

Rewrite Eqs. 23 and 24 as equations of state, where $x = [f_z \dot{f}_z \, h_z \, \dot{h}_z]^T$, $u = [e \, \dot{e} \, \ddot{e} \, \dot{h}_z]^T$

$$\dot{x} = Ax + Bu \tag{25}$$

$$\frac{d}{dt}\begin{bmatrix} f_z \\ \dot{f}_z \\ h_z \\ \dot{h}_z \end{bmatrix} = \begin{bmatrix} -\frac{k_1+k_2}{b} & 0 & -\frac{k_1 k_2}{b} & -k_2 \\ 0 & -\frac{k_1+k_2}{b} & 0 & -\frac{k_1 k_2}{b} \\ 0 & 0 & 0 & 1 \\ 0 & 0 & 0 & 0 \end{bmatrix}\begin{bmatrix} f_z \\ \dot{f}_z \\ h_z \\ \dot{h}_z \end{bmatrix} + \begin{bmatrix} -\frac{k_1}{b} & -1 & 0 & 0 \\ 0 & \frac{-k_1}{b} & -1 & 0 \\ 0 & 0 & 0 & 0 \\ 0 & 0 & 0 & -k_2 \end{bmatrix}\begin{bmatrix} e \\ \dot{e} \\ \ddot{e} \\ \dot{h}_z \end{bmatrix} \tag{26}$$

Similarly, a relationship similar to Eq. 25 can be established between the desired force on the arm and the desired joint height

$$\dot{x}^d = Ax^d + Bu^d \tag{27}$$

Equation 25 minus Eq. 27 obtain

$$\dot{\Delta}x = A\Delta x + B\Delta u \tag{28}$$

Let $\Delta u = -K\Delta x$, and we use the LQR method to solve the coefficient matrix K. Define the objective function as,

$$J = \frac{1}{2}\int_0^\infty \Delta x^T Q \Delta x + \Delta u^T R \Delta u dt$$
$$= \frac{1}{2}\int_0^\infty \Delta x^T (Q + K^T RK)\Delta x dt \tag{29}$$

where Q and R are the weight matrices of the state variables x and u, respectively, and let P be a constant matrix, solve the following Riccati equation, and get P. Then we can calculate the gain coefficient matrix K.

$$A^T P + PA + Q - PBR^{-1}B^T P = 0 \tag{30}$$

$$K = R^{-1}B^T P \tag{31}$$

When we solve the gain coefficient, we plug it into Eq. 32 can obtain the $\ddot{\Delta h_z}$, then integrate twice get Δh_z. After get it, we put it into arm inverse kinematics, solve the angle of each joint of the arm.

$$\ddot{\Delta h_z} = -k_{41}(f - f_d) - k_{42}(\dot{f} - \dot{f_d}) - k_{43}(h_z - h_z^d) - k_{44}(\dot{h_z} - \dot{h_z^d}) \tag{32}$$

In the actual robot, we do not have force sensors on the robot arm. Therefore, we need to estimate the magnitude of the collision force of the robot. Assuming the initial value of the robot arm was p_0, When the robot crawling forward, the arm begin to extend forward, set the value at this time was p_{hand}, and the acceleration at this time was $\dot{p}_{hand}$. By refer to the literature of 21, we can imitate the ground force on the arm at this time, specifically as Eq. 33. Where K_p, D_p, V are the scaling coefficients and variable respectively.

$$F_p = -K_p(p_{hand} - p_0) - D_p\dot{p}_{hand} + V \tag{33}$$

5   Simulation and Experiment

In order to verify the effectiveness of our proposed trajectory generation and motion control, we put the robot model in Vrep, Select bullet 2.78 physical simulator, set the simulation dt = 5 ms, set the crawling time of the robot to 10s and the number of crawling steps to 10 steps, about the model's detailed parameters and weight of the whole robot have been introduced in Chapter 2 before. The main parameters of the controller are listed in Table 2.

Through the CPG method proposed above, we generate the joint crawling trajectory of the robot. Here we set the crawl time was 10 s, using the ode45 solver, and set the initial value to[0.01;0;0;0;0;0;0], we got the curves of the robot leg hip and knee joint, arm hip and forearm joint, and waist joint respectively, which were shown on Fig. 5. In each line, the title tells the cures belong who. Since the curve generated by CPG is dimensionless, it needs to be deformed to meet the actual needs. Figure 6 shows the actual intention of the centroid position in the XY plane after the robot adopt PD control. We define the forward direction of the robot as the Y-axis and the right direction as the X-axis. The blue curve indicates that the robot is not controlled by PD, and the red curve indicates that it is controlled by PD. It can be seen that the left and right deflection angle of the robot is improved after PD control.

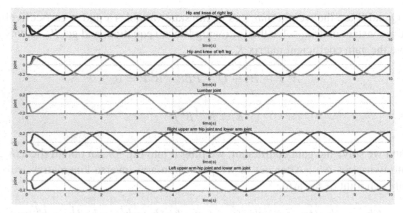

Fig. 5. Joint curve trajectory. The abscissa represents time from 0 to 10 s and the ordinate represents each joint angle, unit is radian.

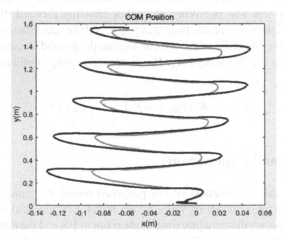

Fig. 6. The position of the COM in the XY direction, we define the robot forward as y and right as x.

Finally, Fig. 7 shows the simulation effect of the overall crawling experiment of the robot after adopting PD control and compliance control. The yellow object represents the uneven terrain. It can be seen that the robot can easily pass through the creeping ground with an obstacle of 3 cm.

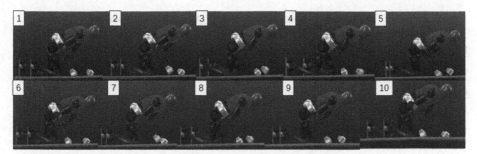

Fig. 7. Crawling simulation experiment

Fig. 8. Crawling snapshots of humanoid robot using CPG, position control and compliance control.

Figure 8 shows a crawling experiment done by an actual robot. At the beginning of the picture, the robot's arms and knees are on the ground. The robot's right leg steps forward, while the left arm begins to move forward, then the left leg and right hand step forward, the left hand begins to move backward, and the body moves forward. In order to verify the feasibility of robot compliance, we completed it in outdoor environment. There are many wooden floors, which were uneven. We can see that the robot can crawl smoothly, which proves the effectiveness of our proposed trajectory generation method and the rationality of control.

6   Conclusion and Future Work

In this paper, we propose a method of generating crawling trajectory based on CPG, and establish the robot joint coupling equation, which reduces the calculation parameters and makes the equation more concise. In view of the phenomenon that the robot is easy to deviate when crawling, we simplified the robot above the waist joint into an inverted pendulum model, and established a position controller. In view of the phenomenon that the robot arm is easy to be damaged under different environmental conditions, we estimated the force on the robot arm, and used the established compliance control model to control the robot arm to adapt to different ground environments. And we use experiments to prove the correctness of the proposed method. Because this paper only considers the state of the robot when crawling, but does not consider the switching state of the robot from bipedal to quadruped, it will be studied later.

Table 2. Mechanical parameters of the simulation model

Description	Value	Description	Value
α	100	k_1	500
β	0.5	k_2	2500
μ	0.4	b	100
w	π	Q	$\begin{bmatrix} 0.1 & 0.001 & 1 & 1 \end{bmatrix}$
a	100	K_{4x4}	$\begin{matrix} 0.0020 & -0.0003 & -0.0596 & -0.0005 \\ 0.0001 & 0.0000 & 0.1343 & -0.0001 \\ -0.0001 & 0.0000 & 0.0292 & -0.0000 \\ -0.2747 & -0.0118 & 17.2883 & 1.2966 \end{matrix}$
$[k_1, k_2, k_3, k_4, k_5, k_6, k_7, k_8, k_9]$	$\begin{matrix} \frac{1}{3} & \frac{1}{3} & \frac{1}{3} & \frac{1}{3} & \frac{1}{3} & - \\ \frac{1}{3} & \frac{1}{3} & -\frac{1}{3} & \frac{1}{3} \end{matrix}$	K_p	800
ξ	2.86	D_p	1
ω_n	$\frac{4\pi}{3}$	V	$\begin{bmatrix} 100 & 100 & 100 \end{bmatrix}$

Acknowledgement. This work was supported in part by the National Natural Science Foundation of China under Grant 91748202, Grant 61973039, the Beijing Municipal Science and Technology Project under Grant Z191100008019003. The author is very grateful to the teachers and researchers for their help.

References

1. Raibert, M.H., Tello, E.R.: Legged robots that balance. IEEE Expert **1**(4), 89 (1986)
2. Holmes, P., Full, R.J., Koditschek, D.E., et al.: The dynamics of legged locomotion: models, analyses, and challenges. SIAM Rev. **48**(2), 207–304 (2006)
3. Brown, T.G.: The intrinsic factors in the act of progression in the mammal. Proc. R. Soc. Lond. **84**(572), 308–319 (1911)
4. Brown, T.G.: The factors in rhythmic activity of the nervous system. Proc. R. Soc. Lond. **85**(579), 278–289 (1912)
5. Shik, M.: Organization of locomotion synergism. Biophysics **13**, 127–135 (1966)
6. Bussel, B, et al.: Evidence for a spinal stepping generator in man. Electrophysiological Study **56**(1) 465–468(1996)
7. Ijspeert, A.J.: Central pattern generator for locomotion control in animals and robots: a review. Neural Netw. **21**, 642–653 (2008)
8. Barasuol, V., Buchli, J., Semini, C., et al.: A reactive controller framework for quadrupedal locomotion on challenging terrain. In: IEEE International Conference on Robotics and Automation, pp. 2554–2561 (2013)
9. Sartoretti, G.: Central pattern generator with inertial feedback for stable locomotion and climbing in unstructured terrain. In: IEEE International Conference on Robotics and Automation (2018)

10. Ajallooeian, M., et al.: Central pattern generators augmented with virtual model control for quadruped rough terrain locomotion. In: IEEE International Conference on Robotics and Automation (2013)
11. Righetti, L., Ijspeert, A.J.: Pattern generators with sensory feedback for the control of quadruped locomotion. In: IEEE International Conference on Robotics and Automation (2008)
12. Endo, G.,et al.: Experimental studies of a neural oscillator for biped locomotion with QRIO. In: IEEE International Conference on Robotics and Automation (2006)
13. Barasuol, V., et al.: WCPG: a central pattern generator for legged robots based on workspace intentions. In: ASME Dynamic Systems and Control Conference and Bath/ASME Symposium on Fluid Power and Motion Control (2011)
14. Liu, C., Chen, Q., Wang, D.: CPG-inspired workspace trajectory generation and adaptive locomotion control for quadruped robots. IEEE Trans. Syst. Man Cybern. **41**(3), 867–880 (2011)
15. Cai, L., et al.: Humanoids that crawl: comparing gait performance of iCub and NAO using a CPG architecture. In: IEEE International Conference on Computer Science and Automation Engineering (2011)
16. Huang, Z., et al.: Design of crawling motion for a biped walking humanoid with 3-DoF rigid-flexible waist. In: 2018 IEEE-RAS 18th International Conference on Humanoid Robots (2018)
17. Qing, L., Xiao, L.: Bionic Quadruped Robot Technology. Beijing Institute of Technology Press (2016)
18. Maclellan, M.J., et al.: Features of hand-foot crawling behavior in human adults. J. Neurophysiol. **107**(1), 114–125 (2012)
19. Patrick, S.K., Noah, J.A., Yang, J.F.: Developmental constraints of quadrupedal coordination across crawling styles in human infants. J. Neurophysiol. **107**(11), 3050–3061 (2012)
20. Li, Q., et al.: A compliance control method based on viscoelastic model for position-controlled humanoid robots. In: IEEE/RSJ International Conference on Intelligent Robots and Systems (2020)

A System Integration Method of Product Data Management Based on UG/NX Secondary Development

Kai Wang[1,2], Pengfei Zeng[1,2(✉)], Chunjing Shi[1,2], Weiping Shao[1,2], and Yongping Hao[2]

[1] School of Mechanical Engineering, Shenyang Ligong University, Shenyang 110159, China
pfzeng@163.com
[2] Key Laboratory of Advanced Manufacturing Technology and Equipment of Liaoning Province, Shenyang Ligong University, Shenyang 110159, China

Abstract. An integrated development methodology of UG/NX and product data management (PDM) system is carried out based on the UG/NX secondary development technology, aiming at the needs of the PDM system to manage the product design information exported by CAD software tools and multi-user collaborative operation in the product design link, in order to unify the information and file format in the system and simplify user operation. The integrated system based on the Client/Server (C/S) architecture is designed and implemented to manage various product design documents and information. The basic model, software architecture, function flow and realization method of the integrated system are established and analyzed, and some key interfaces of the integrated system are completed. In addition, the architecture and functions of the integrated system are analyzed and evaluated, and the future development work is presented. This development methodology has certain reference application value in the CAD software secondary development, integrated system architecture establishment, functional flow construction as well as related system implementation.

Keywords: UG/NX secondary development · PDM system integration · C/S architecture system

1 Introductions

In modern industrial production, with the gradual popularization of CAD technology and PDM system, enterprise productivity and production quality are greatly improved [1]. Meanwhile, effective management means are provided for the data generated in the whole life cycle of product design and manufacturing [2, 3]. However, there are various CAD tools at present, and the types and formats of the output design information are also different, which may lead to the disunity of the types and formats of design information, and the PDM system cannot directly manage the information or files output by CAD tools, thus forming information islands [4, 5]. At the same time, due to poor information transmission in design and management within the product life cycle [6], the

H. Liu et al. (Eds.): ICIRA 2022, LNAI 13457, pp. 466–476, 2022.
https://doi.org/10.1007/978-3-031-13835-5_42

data management advantage of PDM system will be affected. Therefore, the industry generally seeks a development idea or system architecture to closely integrate CAD software with PDM system and unify the types and formats of files and information in the system, so as to reduce the appearance of information islands to the greatest extent and improve the work efficiency of PDM system [7].

The integrated development of CAD tools and PDM system is to use the secondary development technology of CAD tools to directly call the PDM system Application Programming Interface (API) to implement data interaction in its process, or use middleware to call the secondary development API of CAD tools to implement product design information output, upload and download in a specified format. This development method simplifies complex information format conversion steps, which is conducive to optimizing product design process and shortening product design link [8, 9].

In this paper, the integrated system has realized data or file transfer between local and server, management of design files and output of design information and files from UG/NX three kinds of management functions. The overall architecture of the system is designed as C/S type, which is mainly composed of server and client computer. The server can exchange information with several client computers to realize cooperative operation.

2 Key Development Techniques

2.1 System Integration Process

The basic model of the integrated system in this study is shown in Fig. 1. The basic components of the server include application layer, service layer and database. UG/NX and middleware should be installed on each client, and appropriate disk storage space should be used as local workspace.

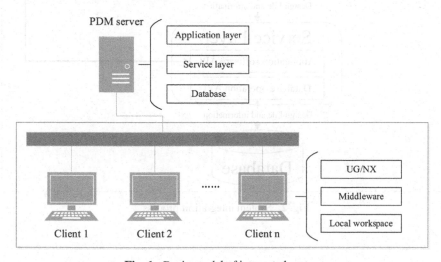

Fig. 1. Basic model of integrated system

Based on the basic model of integrated system, the integration process of the system is analyzed. The system integration process designed is shown in Fig. 2.

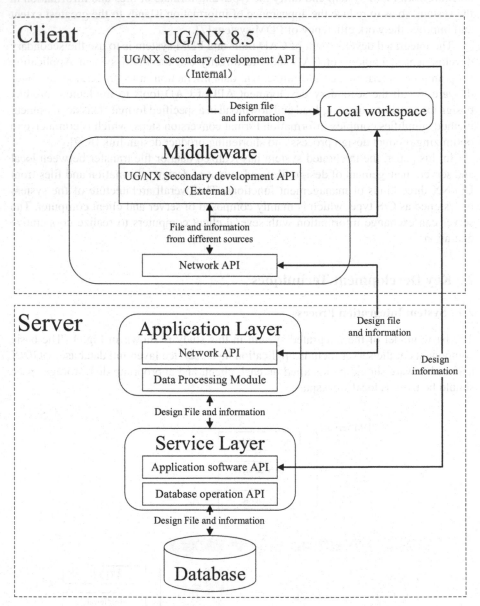

Fig. 2. System integration process

Service Layer. The service layer is mainly responsible for completing three tasks: connecting and operating the database, providing files or information from the database for the application layer and providing API for UG/NX to call, so that users can operate the database directly in UG.

Application Layer. The application layer mainly has two modules: network communication API and data processing module. The network communication API is used to receive requests, information and files sent to the server by the user through interaction with the middleware. The data processing module is used to judge the correctness of user request, encode and decode the sent and received information and process the sent and received files.

Middleware. It is essentially an application. Middleware is mainly composed of user interface, UG/NX secondary development API and network communication API. Middleware is the key to connecting users, user machines and system servers.

2.2 UG/NX Secondary Development Technology

UG/NX secondary development technology is commonly used to expand the UG/NX native function means, the purpose is to let users according to their own business needs to customize CAD tools. At present, the mainstream secondary development methods of UG/NX include Graphics Interactive Programming (GRIP), Knowledge Fusion (KF), NXOpen C, NXOpen C++, NXOpen Java, etc. Theoretically, NXOpen C and NXOpen C++ have the most comprehensive API [10]. Therefore, this research is developed in the form of combining the two methods.

This study uses UG/NX 8.5 as CAD tool and Microsoft Visual Studio 2010 as development tool for UG/NX secondary development. For the consideration of the functional flexibility and user operation convenience of the integrated system, two UG/NX secondary development modes are used simultaneously, namely internal mode and external mode. The compiler file generated by the former code is a dynamic link library (DLL), and its functional API must be loaded and called in UG/NX environment, so it is used to implement the functions that need to be used in UG/NX. The compiler file generated by the latter code is an executable file, which can run independently from UG/NX environment. During the development of middleware, functions implemented in external mode of UG/NX secondary development can be directly integrated into the middleware for users to call. In addition, the MenuScript technology and Block UI Styler Modules provided by UG/NX are used to design and create custom function menu and some interfaces when developing system functions [11].

2.3 Middleware Development

In the integrated system, the primary task of middleware is to make the format of design information consistent between the clients and the server of the system, and establish network communication channels between the clients and the server to send or receive information and files [12]. Secondly, the middleware also needs to have a user interface for users to interact with. In this study, the middleware also integrates some NXOpen API in external mode of UG/NX secondary development, which makes the middleware extend its functions on the basis of basic functions.

This study uses Microsoft Visual Studio 2010 as a development tool for the development of middleware. Based on the characteristics of C/S system architecture, the Microsoft Foundation Class (MFC) library is used to develop the main framework of middleware, the basic functions and user interface of middleware are implemented by the classes defined by MFC. In addition, on the basis of middleware framework, Microsoft WinHTTP API is invoked to implement network communication, NXOpen API is invoked to implement the integration of middleware and UG/NX secondary development function.

It should be mentioned that this study is mainly aimed at the development of client side. The PDM server in the system is provided by other partners and provides data services and relevant API.

2.4 Information Specification of Integrated System

In order to ensure the unification of file and information formats in the integrated system and reduce the transmission difficulty of product design information in the integrated system [13], the files or information that need to be managed in the integrated system are mainly defined as product model files and product design information documents. Product model files include product original design model (.prt) and lightweight files under JT, STEP, STL and IGES standards that are widely used at present [14]. Product design file refers to a document that contains the product type, specification, attribute, version, batch [15] and other information extracted from the product model by using secondary development technology and formatted in XML format [16]. NXOpen C/C++ API is used to output model files in specific format, and tinyxml2 function library is used to output formatted design information.

3 Key Management Process Design and Function Implementation Method

3.1 File Management

A workspace is a directory or folder where product design files are stored. After logging in to the integrated system, users can create, delete, open, and synchronize files in the workspace. The flow of the above functions is shown in Fig. 3.

The functions of file deletion and opening are implemented by the member functions of CFile class defined by MFC and shell function, and the creation of prt file is implemented by the function of uf_part header file defined by NXOpen C. During file synchronization, the middleware requests the server to query the file version. If the latest version file exists on the server, the server sends the query result and the latest version file to the middleware. The middleware receives the file and overwrites the local old version file.

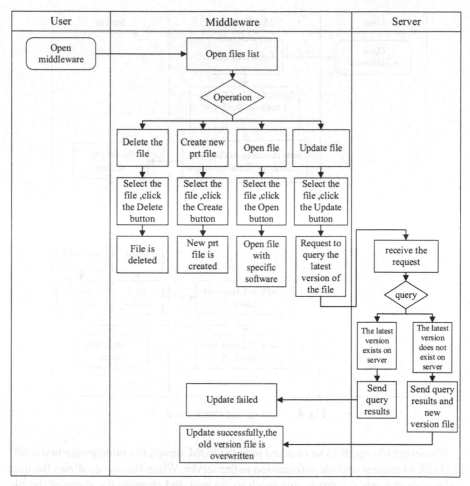

Fig. 3. File management flow

3.2 Check-In and Check-Out of Files

Check-in and check-out are the key process for PDM system to manage files and realize multi-user cooperative operation. After the design file is checked into the PDM system, the file and its information will be uploaded to the PDM server and become the managed object of the PDM system. When a file is checked out from the PDM system, it will be downloaded from server to the client computer that sent the check-out request, and the user can then edit the file. At this time, other users cannot check out the file again until the design file is checked in to the server and passes the signature link. The check-in and check-out process can effectively avoid the confusion caused by multiple users designing at the same time in the product design process. The flow of check-in and check-out functions is shown in Fig. 4.

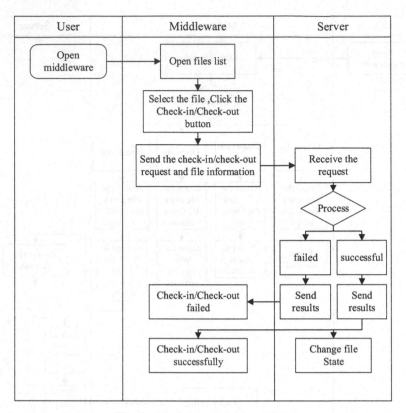

Fig. 4. Check-in and check-out flow

If a design file needs to be checked in to the PDM server, the middleware first sends the check-in request and file information to the server. When the server allows the user to check-in, it sends the processing result to the user and changes the status of the file on the server to "check-in". The implementation of the check-out function requires the middleware to send the check-out request and file information to the server, and the server will query the status of the file on the server after receiving the request. If the file can be checked out, a successful check out message is sent to the middleware along with the file, and the status of the file on the server changes to "check-out".

3.3 Extraction and Export of Information

Block UI Styler module of UG/NX is used to design information export function interfaces. At the same time, corresponding buttons are added in UG/NX custom function menu. Users can open the functional interface in UG/NX by clicking the menu button.

By calling the functions of uf_attr, uf_assem, uf_drf header files defined by the NXOpen C or the JtCreator, the Drawings_DrawingSheetCollection, the Drawings_DraftingViewCollection and other header files defined by the NXOpen C++, the function of exporting model attribute information, model assembly structure, engineering drawing information, lightweight model and other information and files can be implemented. At the same time, the research uses external mode and internal mode of UG secondary development, so that users can use UG/NX function module or middleware to export design information. The flow of the above functions is shown in Fig. 5 and Fig. 6.

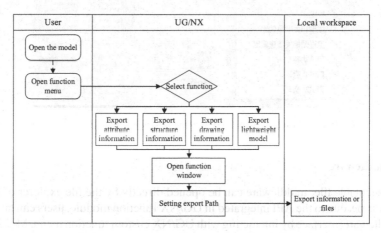

Fig. 5. Using UG/NX to export information

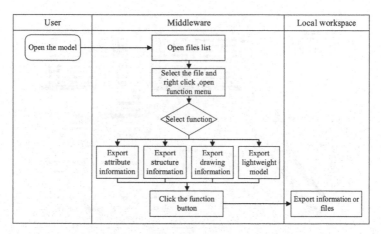

Fig. 6. Using middleware to export information

4 Main Function Modules of System

4.1 UG/NX Function Module

UG/NX functional module is realized by using internal mode of UG/NX secondary development. Users can open the corresponding function interface by interacting with the custom function menu in UG/NX. The functions of the module include user login and logout, model check-in and check-out, opening middleware, exporting model related information, exporting drawing information, etc. (Fig. 7).

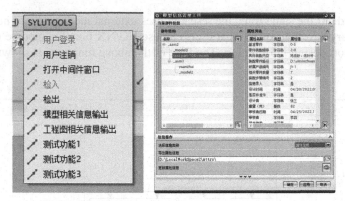

Fig. 7. Customize function menu and interface to export model related information

4.2 Middleware

As an executable file, middleware can be opened directly by the file explorer of PC. At the same time, due to the API integrated in UG/NX function module, users can also open the middleware interface by interacting with UG/NX custom function menu. Middleware interface in Windows 10 system is shown in Fig. 8.

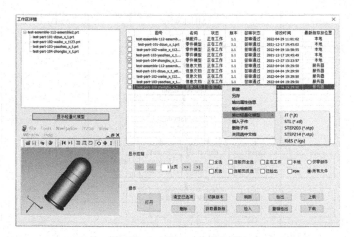

Fig. 8. Middleware files list

In the middleware workspace files list interface, users can manage files in the workspace. The user interface uses the Tree control to express the structure of the model assembly. At the same time, the JT2Go browser window is embedded, so the lightweight model in JT format can be viewed in the interface.

In this interface, users can open, delete, synchronize, check-in and check-out any file in the workspace. In addition, the interface also integrates create new.prt file, export attribute information, export lightweight model, insert parts model and other UG/NX secondary development functions for users (Fig. 9).

Fig. 9. Batch export attribute information and attribute information in XML format

5 Conclusions

Based on the secondary development technology of UG/NX, this study developed the integrated system of UG/NX 8.5 and PDM, standardized the format of files and information in the integrated system, and optimized the management of design files and information exported by UG/NX. However, in the process of system development, there are still some problems to be analyzed and improved.

The C/S architecture system has high requirements on user equipment performance and high system maintenance costs, and according to the analysis of actual business needs, some production links or enterprise departments do not need staff to modify the product design model, such as product signature, resource management, product after-sales and other work. Based on the above considerations, the overall architecture of the system can be designed as C/S and B/S hybrid architecture in the later development. In this case, the product design department can use UG/NX and middleware to achieve product design and management, other departments can use the browser to complete the work.

Since UG/NX is used as integration software in this study, the design and development of middleware are based on the characteristics of UG/NX. In order to better meet the production needs of different enterprises, we can use the secondary development technology of different CAD tools to integrate the integrated system with more mainstream CAD tools.

Acknowledgements. This work was supported by the State Administration of Science, Technology and Industry for National Defense under Grant No. JSZL2020208A001, and the project is sponsored by "Liaoning BaiQianWan Talents Program" and Applied Basic Reserach Program of Liaoning Province.

References

1. Pfouga, A., Stjepandić, J.: Leveraging 3D geometric knowledge in the product lifecycle based on industrial standards. J. Comput. Des. Eng. **5**, 54–67 (2018)
2. Zhu, Y., Liu, C., Ge, W., Duan, S., Guo, H.: Practice of improving efficiency of space product technical document archiving based on PDM system. Xinxi Jilu Cailiao. **23**(5), 104–107 (2022)

3. Lanza, R., Haenisch, J., Bengtsson, K., Rølvåg, T.: Relating structural test and FEA data with STEP AP209. Adv. Eng. Softw. **127**, 96–105 (2019)
4. Zhang, M., Ma, Q., Zhang, W., Wang, J.: Research on CAD/CAM/CAPP/ERP integration technology under PDM framework. Mod. Manuf. Eng. **7**, 27–29 (2009)
5. Kutin, A., Dolgov, V., Sedykh, M., Ivashin, S.: Integration of different computer-aided systems in product designing and process planning on digital manufacturing. Procedia CIRP **67**, 476–481 (2018)
6. Camba, J.D., Contero, M., Company, P., Pérez, D.: On the integration of model-based feature information in product lifecycle management systems. Int. J. Inf. Manag. **37**(6), 611–621 (2017)
7. Wang, B., Wen, W.: Research and implementation of CAD/CAPP/ERP integration scheme based on PDM. Mech. Eng. Autom. **4**, 213–214 (2015)
8. Gong, J.: CATIA and PDM integrated interface design and development. Electron. Technol. Softw. Eng. **14**, 41–42 (2015)
9. Prashanth, B.N., Venkataram, R.: Development of modular integration framework between PLM and ERP systems. Mater. Today Proc. **4**(2), 2269–2278 (2017)
10. Tang, K.: Siemens NX Secondary Development. Publishing House of Electronics Industry, Beijing (2021)
11. Hou, Y., Ding, X.: UG/Open Secondary Development and Examples of Fine Solution. Chemical Industry Press, Beijing (2007)
12. Ji, M., Leng, S.: Research on MES and BOM Information integration based on middleware. Mach. Des. Manuf. Eng. **39**(01), 1–4 (2010)
13. Xiang, G.: Optimization integration of monitoring data of ship communication network based on XML. Ship Sci. Technol. **43**(12), 136–138 (2021)
14. Wu, Z., Chen, H.: Application of MBD digital model to lightweight engineering of complex shell. Technol. Innov. Appl. **16**, 37–38 (2017)
15. Zhang, Z.: Design and manufacturing integration technology for discrete manufacturing enterprises based on PDM. Plant Maint. Eng. **2**, 28–29 (2022)
16. Mandolini, M., Marconi, M., Rossi, M., Favi, C., Germani, M.: A standard data model for life cycle analysis of industrial products: a support for eco-design initiatives. Comput. Ind. **109**, 31–44 (2019)

Research on Feature Matching Based on Improved RANSAC Algorithm

Xianfeng Wang, Baitong Wang, Zilin Ding$^{(\boxtimes)}$, and Tong Zhao

Northeast Petroleum University, Daqing 163000, China
740857185@qq.com

Abstract. Aiming at the problems that the current RANSAC (Random Sample Consensus) algorithm has too large randomness and is susceptible to external point interference, which leads to the reduction of matching accuracy, an improved RANSAC algorithm combining feature matching confidence and grid clustering is proposed. Firstly, rough matching is carried out by the FLANN algorithm, and confidence analysis is carried out on the coarse matching point pairs, then expanding grid clustering around the high confidence point pairs. Multiple local optimal interior points are screened to optimize the global interior points and improve the matching accuracy of feature points. The experimental results show that the improved RANSAC in this paper increases the existence probability of interior points, avoids too many wrong feature matching affecting the model effect of the homography matrix, and improves the accuracy of feature matching.

Keywords: RANSAC algorithm · Grid clustering · Confidence analysis

1 Introduction

Image feature matching refers to finding the same feature points between adjacent frames and matching them one by one, which plays an important role in map construction, target detection, and navigation and positioning [1]. The current mainstream feature matching process generally first performs feature detection on images, then generates descriptors for image feature points, and finally performs matching based on the similarity of descriptors between different images. However, this kind of rough matching is generally due to the fact that the feature points in different poses will be distorted due to lighting transformation, perspective transformation and other factors, and the texture of the image with too high a degree of similarity leads to different feature points at different positions. Therefore, the RANSAC algorithm is usually used after rough matching to eliminate the false matching. However, this algorithm is sensitive to noise, and the operation time will increase and the model accuracy will decrease due to obvious error points. Therefore, some improvements are proposed. Algorithms, such as the GraphSAC algorithm proposed by Barath et al. [2], separates interior and exterior points through local optimization, thereby eliminating false matches, but this method must first ensure that there is a priori knowledge that can be used for classification, and there is To ensure the validity and real-time performance of the classification algorithm. The Lo-RANSAC

© The Author(s), under exclusive license to Springer Nature Switzerland AG 2022
H. Liu et al. (Eds.): ICIRA 2022, LNAI 13457, pp. 477–484, 2022.
https://doi.org/10.1007/978-3-031-13835-5_43

algorithm proposed by Chum et al. [3], a method is to sample the calculation model
from the in-class points of the returned result, set a fixed number of iterations, and then
select the optimal local result as the improved result, However, this algorithm is also too
random and susceptible to external interference.

The traditional RANSAC algorithm is too random and needs to assume that the
matching results are correct, without considering the confidence difference between
different feature matching points, and if there are a large number of wrong points in
the data points selected during random sampling, it will affect the model. In view of the
shortcomings of the above algorithms, this paper proposes an improved feature matching
algorithm based on the RANSAC algorithm.

2 RANSAC Algorithm

RANSAC algorithm: This algorithm randomly selects several pairs of feature points
from the feature points of the two images, solves the homography matrix through the
spatial variation relationship between the feature points, and regards the feature matching
points that conform to the homography matrix as interior points. The homography matrix
with the most interior points is selected as the final matrix by multiple iterations, and
the feature points that conform to the matrix model are regarded as the correct matching
feature points. This chapter will improve the algorithm, so the principle of the algorithm
is described below elaborate.

The selection of the number of iterations should not only ensure the real-time performance of the algorithm, but also ensure that the iterative model contains enough
interior points. The assumption means that after the next iteration, at least one randomly
selected feature point is the probability that all the interior points are interior points. The
occupancy rate of interior points should satisfy:

$$k > \frac{log(1-z)}{log(1-\omega^n)} \tag{1}$$

For a pair of matched feature point pairs $p_1(x_1, y_1)$, $p_2(x_2, y_2)$, they are all projections of points P in space under different camera poses, and spatial affine is realized
through a homography matrix M, which M is a 3×3 matrix:

$$p_2 = Mp_1 \Leftrightarrow \begin{bmatrix} x_2 \\ y_2 \\ 1 \end{bmatrix} = \begin{bmatrix} M_{11} & M_{12} & M_{13} \\ M_{21} & M_{22} & M_{23} \\ M_{31} & M_{32} & M_{33} \end{bmatrix} \begin{bmatrix} x_1 \\ y_1 \\ 1 \end{bmatrix} \tag{2}$$

Since a homography matrix M is a homogeneous matrix, so M_{33} will be normalized
to:

$$x_2 = \frac{M_{11}x_1 + M_{12}y_1 + M_{13}}{M_{31}x_1 + M_{32}y_1 + 1} y_2 = \frac{M_{21}x_1 + M_{22}y_1 + M_{23}}{M_{31}x_1 + M_{32}y_1 + 1} \tag{3}$$

The above matrix contains 8 unknowns, and a pair of matching feature points can
provide two constraints, so at least 4 sets of matching feature points are needed to solve
the homography matrix. In turn, the homography matrix is used, the feature points are

substituted into the matrix and the number of feature points conforming to the model is counted, and the optimal solution is selected by the projection errors generated by different models in the iterative process. The projection error function is as follows:

$$e = \sum_{i=1}^{n=4} \left[\left(\frac{M_{11}x_i+M_{12}y_i+M_{13}}{M_{31}x_i+M_{32}y_i+1} x_i\right)^2 + \left(\frac{M_{21}x_i+M_{22}y_i+M_{23}}{M_{31}x_i+M_{32}y_i+1} y_i\right)^2 \right] \tag{4}$$

After many iterations, the model with the smallest projection error is considered the best model.

3   Improved RANSAC Algorithm

This paper conducts confidence analysis on feature matching points. Matching points with higher confidence are more likely to be interior points [4, 5], and feature point groupings that are consistent in space may contain more interior points, that is, when the feature When the point set can be divided into clusters, it means that these feature points have similar features in the spatial domain or texture details. When the feature points in the cluster can be correctly matched, they belong to the same cluster and have similar characteristics. The remaining feature points of spatial features or texture features have higher inlier ratios than discrete feature points [6, 7]. Therefore, the improved algorithm in this paper sorts the samples according to their confidence, and preferentially selects the feature matching points with high confidence as the initial interior points; The dense density quickly divides the clusters, performs local RANSAC analysis on all the feature points included in the cluster, and obtains the local optimal interior points in the cluster, and repeats the above steps in the remaining feature points to obtain multiple sets of local optimal interior points. Using the homography matrix obtained from all the local optimal interior point sets to calculate the interior point set for the global feature points to achieve the effect of eliminating false matching. The specific steps are as follows:

Step1: Rough matching is carried out through the fast nearest neighbor algorithm, and the quality of matching points is estimated, and the confidence function is defined $q = \frac{D_1}{D_2}$, Among them, it represents the Euclidean distance of the ORB feature point descriptor q, D_1 and D_2 represent the minimum and sub-minimum values of the Euclidean distance, respectively. The smaller the value of q, the better the matching quality. Select the four pairs of matching feature points with the highest confidence as the initial interior points;

Step2: Divide the data space of two adjacent frames into a grid according to the pixel length of L, and map the image features to the grid space; take the selected initial interior point as the center, calculate the data density of adjacent grid cells, the data density is the ratio of the number of feature points in the current grid to the total number of pixels in the grid, and judges whether each grid cell is a high-density cell according to a preset threshold, merges adjacent high-density cells and sets them as the same cluster class, set the feature point set in the cluster as the point set S_n to be matched;

Step3: Judging by the S_n matching distance of the Hamming distance pair, for the feature matching point whose Hamming distance is twice the minimum Hamming distance, it is considered as a wrong match, and the point pair is directly eliminated;

Step4: Carry out the local RANSAC algorithm, use the selected initial interior points to calculate the homography matrix, and calculate the interior points existing in S_n according to the projection error, and then recalculate the homography matrix and new interior points from the updated interior points., until the local optimal interior point set within the current cluster is selected;

Step5: Remove the feature point set S_n in the cluster from the total feature point set, and repeat the above steps for the remaining feature points. Until all feature points are scanned. After multiple iterations, multiple sets of local optimal interior points are obtained, and the local optimal interior point sets of all clusters are extracted for the global RANSAC algorithm, and all feature matching point pairs are purified after obtaining the global homography matrix.

The improved RANSAC algorithm in this paper selects feature matching point pairs with high confidence on the initial interior points, and selects other feature point pairs with spatial consistency and texture consistency through clustering to increase the existence probability of interior points and avoid too many The erroneous feature matching affects the model effect of the homography matrix, thereby improving the accuracy of feature matching.

4 Experiment and Result Analysis

In order to verify the effect of the improved RANSAC algorithm, the matching effect of the original RANSAC algorithm is compared after the image data is rotated, scaled and illuminated. The test images of rotation, scaling and illumination changes are shown in Fig. 1, Fig. 2, and Fig. 3. The experimental results are shown in Fig. 4, Fig. 5, Fig. 6, Fig. 7, and Fig. 8, respectively. The detailed experimental results are shown in Table 1 shown:

(a) Original image   (b) rotated 45°   (c) rotated90°

Fig. 1. Original image and rotated 45°, 90° images

(a) Original image   (b) partial image enlarged   (c)image reduced by 50%
                            by 50%

Fig. 2. Original image, partial image enlarged by 50%, and image reduced by 50%

(a) light brightness+50%   (b) light brightness-50%

Fig. 3. Illuminated test image

(a) original RANSAC matching results   (b) improved RANSAC matching results

Fig. 4. Matching results of original RANSAC and improved RANSAC rotated by 45°

(a) original RANSAC matching results   (b) improved RANSAC matching results

Fig. 5. Matching results of original RANSAC and improved RANSAC rotated by 90

(a) original RANSAC matching results   (b) improved RANSAC matching results

Fig. 6. Matching results of original RANSAC and improved RANSAC by 50% reduction

(a) original RANSAC matching results   (b) improved RANSAC matching results

Fig. 7. Matching results of the original RANSAC and the improved RANSAC by 50% enlarge

(a) original RANSAC matching results   (b) improved RANSAC matching results

Fig. 8. Matching results between the original RANSAC and the improved RANSAC by ±50%

It can be seen from the experimental results that although the improved RANSAC algorithm in this paper increases the division of grid clustering and multiple local optimal interior point analysis, the average matching time is only increased by 2.26 ms, and because the improved algorithm in this paper can pass the internal clustering The homography matrix model can quickly converge to the local optimal solution, and the wrong matching with too large Hamming distance can be quickly eliminated, so the matching accuracy of each data set has been improved, and the average matching accuracy has increased by 2.34%, which verifies that the algorithm in this paper can improve the feature matching performance of images in different situations.

Table 1. Experimental comparison results of the original RANSAC algorithm and the improved algorithm

Match result	Algorithm	Number of matches after filtering	Number of correct matches	Accuracy	Time
Figure 4	Original RANSAC	436	407	93.3%	46.3 ms
	Improved RANSAC	397	377	94.9%	47.6 ms
Figure 5	Original RANSAC	611	578	94.5%	48.3 ms
	Improved RANSAC	466	448	96.1%	51.1 ms
Figure 6	Original RANSAC	823	751	91.2%	51.2 ms
	Improved RANSAC	710	667	93.9%	54.4 ms
Figure 7	Original RANSAC	682	667	97.8%	51.7 ms
	Improved RANSAC	638	627	98.2%	53.8 ms
Figure 8	Original RANSAC	287	264	91.9%	31.7 ms
	Improved RANSAC	226	220	97.%3	33.6 ms

5 Conclusion

The traditional RANSAC algorithm is susceptible to the error of outliers, which leads to the reduction of model accuracy, and does not consider the difference of different feature matching points. This paper improves the algorithm through confidence analysis, and expands the clustering with high-confidence feature matching points as the center, finds feature points with spatial and feature consistency, improves the probability of interior points, and uses multiple local optimal interior points to screen the global optimal inside point. The experimental results show that the improved algorithm in this paper can effectively avoid the influence of incorrect matching points, and effectively improve the feature matching accuracy in different situations.

References

1. Ma, J., Jiang, X., Fan, A., et al.: Image matching from handcrafted to deep features: a survey. Int. J. Comput. Vision **129**(1), 23–79 (2021)

2. Ni, K., Jin, H., Dellaert, F.: GroupSAC: efficient consensus in the presence of groupings. In: Proceedings of 12th IEEE International Conference on Computer Vision, October 2009
3. Chum, O., Matas, J.: Optimal randomized RANSAC. IEEE Trans. Pattern Anal. Mach. Intell. **30**(8), 1472–1482 (2008)
4. Chum, O., Matas, J.: Matching with PROSAC - progressive sample consensus. In: IEEE Computer Society Conference on Computer Vision and Pattern Recognition, CVPR 2005. IEEE (2005)
5. Ni, K., Jin, H., Dellaert, F.: GroupSAC: efficient consensus in the presence of groupings. In: 2009 IEEE 12th International Conference on Computer Vision, 2009, pp. 2193–2200 (2009). https://doi.org/10.1109/ICCV.2009.5459241
6. Barath, D., Ivashechkin, M., Matas, J.: Progressive NAPSAC: sampling from gradually growing neighborhoods. CoRR 2019 abs/1906.02295 (2019)
7. Matuszewski, D.J., Hast, A., Wählby, C., Sintorn, I.M.: A short feature vector for image matching: the log-polar magnitude feature descriptor. PLoS ONE **12**(11), e0188496 (2017). https://doi.org/10.1371/journal.pone.0188496. PMID: 29190737; PMCID: PMC5708636

Global Optimal Trajectory Planning of Mobile Robot Grinding for High-Speed Railway Body

Xiaohu Xu[1](✉), Songtao Ye[2], Zeyuan Yang[2,3], Sijie Yan[2], and Han Ding[2]

[1] The Institute of Technological Sciences, Wuhan University, Wuhan 430072, China
xuxiaohu@whu.edu.cn
[2] State Key Laboratory of Digital Manufacturing Equipment and Technology,
Huazhong University of Science and Technology, Wuhan 430074, China
[3] Department of Electrical and Computer Engineering, National University
of Singapore, Singapore 117576, Singapore

Abstract. Reasonable machining trajectory planning could increase the robotic maneuverability and productivity, which is a research hotspot in the field of robotic grinding, especially for large complicated components. To overcome the machining area planning challenges, an optimal robotic machining trajectory planning approach is presented by creating the robot joint configuration model. To begin, a global trajectory planning approach based on the strong surface consistency of a high-speed railway body is proposed to ensure the continuity of robot motion and the optimal configuration. The high-speed railway body is then divided into different areas to ensure robotic accessibility. Finally, the simulation experiment is employed to obtain the appropriate robotic machining trajectory and working attitude, which effectively enhance robotic accessibility and vastly increase processing efficiency and surface quality in the actual robotic grinding of high-speed railway body.

Keywords: Trajectory planning · Robot grinding · High-speed railway

1 Introduction

Large complex components such as high-speed railway, aircraft, and wind blades, etc. possess the characteristics of large size, complicated structure, and non-uniform stiffness, which have become one of most challenging manufacturing tasks [1]. The traditional machining mode represented by the multi-axis CNC machine and gantry machine is obviously insufficient in reconfigurability, flexibility, and economy, especially in the face of increasingly product diversification and high-quality requirements. The industrial robots have recently achieved remarkable advancements in performance and adaption, receiving extensive concerns in the manufacturing field [2,3]. However, the robotic workspace is not large enough

Supported by the National Key R&D Program of China (No. 2019YFA0706703), the National Nature Science Foundation of China (Nos. 52105514, 52075204).

to the size of large complex components. Naturally, adding extra rail carriages, automatic guided vehicle, or elevator machine is becoming mainstream solutions to strengthen the robotic operating range and flexibility. This raises new issues about the trajectory planning and optimization of the robotic machining process [4,5], which has attracted extensive attention.

Existing trajectory planning methods rely mostly on commercial CAD/CAM software, which ignores workpiece constraints, obstacles, and postures, etc., resulting in poor flexibility and machining accuracy [1]. Diao et al. [6] proposed an optimal trajectory planning with collision avoidance for robotic grinding by taking the length of the collision avoidance path, the weighted sum of the strokes of joints, and the duration of the collision avoidance trajectory into account. Lv et al. [7] developed an adaptive trajectory planning algorithm based on the material removal profile for robotic blade grinding that effectively enhances machining quality by combining the machining dynamics and chord-height error model. Grzegorz [8] used the extended Jacobian approach to design a revolutionary online trajectory planning method for mobile manipulators that minimized robot vibrations on the mobile manipulator. Trajectory planning methods, however, are often addressed by means of path planning algorithms, which compute a suitable path between the machining points without considering the velocity, accelerations, and singularity [9], which would cause the best route points to be sacrificed to raise the computational complexity.

Most strategies provide different indicators and target certain tasks from the preceding literature reviews, however, the accessibility and the continuity of machining paths are given less concern, especially for large complex components. Therefore, a more systematic and universal trajectory planning method is proposed to greatly improve robotic processing efficiency and surface quality for high-speed railway. The rest of this paper is organized as follows: Sect. 2.1 introduces the adjustment of robot joint configuration. Section 2.2 presents the trajectory planning of robotic machining process. Section 2.3 proposes the robotic trajectory planning for high-speed railway body. Section 3 evaluates the trajectory planning results. The conclusions are finally presented in Sect. 4.

2   Trajectory Planning of Robotic Machining System

2.1   Adjustment of Robot Joint Configuration

The D-H parameter approach [10] is developed to build the kinematics model of an industrial robot with fewer expression parameters than other methods. Therefore, the kinematics model of a serial robot is:

$$
\begin{aligned}
{}_6^0\mathbf{T} &= {}_1^0\mathbf{T}(\theta_1) \cdot {}_2^1\mathbf{T}(\theta_2) \cdot {}_3^2\mathbf{T}(\theta_3) \cdot {}_4^3\mathbf{T}(\theta_4) \cdot {}_5^4\mathbf{T}(\theta_5) \cdot {}_6^5\mathbf{T}(\theta_6) \\
&= \begin{bmatrix} n_x & o_x & a_x & p_x \\ n_y & o_y & a_y & p_y \\ n_z & o_z & a_z & p_z \\ 0 & 0 & 0 & 1 \end{bmatrix}
\end{aligned}
\tag{1}
$$

Because of multiple solutions, singularity, and other issues, the inverse kinematics of open chain robot is more complicated than the forward kinematics, which has algebraic and numerical methods. The former is more difficult to obtain the calculation formula than the numerical method, but it is faster, and numerical method has a computational speed of ms, while algebraic method is us [11]. Thus, the latter method [12] is used to determine the inverse kinematics:

$$\begin{cases} \theta_1 = atan2(p_y, p_x) - atan2(0, \pm\sqrt{p_x^2 + p_y^2}) \\ \theta_1 = atan2(s_{23}, c_{23}) - \theta_3 \\ \theta_3 = atan2(a_3, d_4) - atan2(K, \pm\sqrt{a_3^2 + d_4^2 - K^2}) \\ \theta_4 = atan2(-a_x s_1 + a_y s_1, -a_x c_1 s_{23} - a_y s_1 s_{23} - a_z c_{23}) \\ \theta_5 = atan2(s_5, c_5) \\ \theta_6 = atan2(s_6, c_6) \end{cases} \quad (2)$$

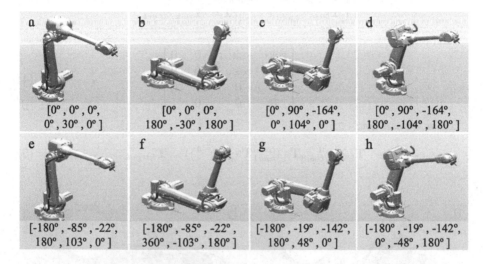

Fig. 1. The corresponding configuration of robot under zero position.

The pose of robotic end-effector operation point is calculated to obtain each group of corresponding inverse solutions, which is a vector formed of each joint angles of robot, as illustrated in Fig. 1. The joint configuration is therefore defined as the intersection of the rigid body posture in space with the vector [13]. According to off-line programming, robot configuration must be altered to minimize collisions, unreachable, and unique configurations. Under robotic machining, the normal vector of TCP would be limited to overlap with the normal of the target point, and its tangential vector can vary at any time that is redundant. To achieve the efficient functioning, a comparatively ideal arrangement of the robot end-effector may be determined [14]. The joint configuration corresponding to the discrete target points should be kept continuous without mutation due to the high precision requirement of robotic machining, and the optimal joint configuration of the robot cannot be determined by optimizing the attitude of each target point. Therefore, a configuration optimization approach is presented to adjust the TCP's joint configuration, defined as *tool0*, to all places on the machining path at the same time.

In the robotic machining process of large components, the Z-axis of the target trajectory point must coincide with the normal vector of the surface, and the attitude can only be modified by adjusting the local Z-axis angle. Since changing the attitude of a single target point during the grinding process will not ensure the continuity of the joint space, the joint configuration corresponding to all points on the machining path reached by the robot can be adjusted by changing the angle of the tool coordinate system which is defined as $tool1$, around its local Z-axis. Then the transfer matrix $tool0$ to $tool1$ is $^{tool0}_{tool1}\mathbf{T}$, the adjusted angle of the target point is $\alpha \in [-\pi, \pi]$, and its pose before and after adjusting is $\mathbf{T}_{target}$, $\mathbf{T}_{newtarget}$, respectively. Thus, it can be:

$$\begin{cases} \mathbf{T}_{target} \cdot \mathbf{T}_z = \mathbf{T}_{newtarget} \\ \mathbf{T}_{base} \cdot {}^0_{tool0}\mathbf{T} \cdot {}^{tool0}_{tool1}\mathbf{T} = \mathbf{T}_{newtarget} \end{cases} \tag{3}$$

Among,

$$\mathbf{T}_z = \begin{bmatrix} \cos a & -\sin a & 0 & 0 \\ \sin a & \cos a & 0 & 0 \\ 0 & 0 & 1 & 0 \\ 0 & 0 & 0 & 1 \end{bmatrix} \tag{4}$$

Then we can get:

$$\mathbf{T}_{base} \cdot {}^0_{tool0}\mathbf{T} \cdot ({}^{tool0}_{tool1}\mathbf{T} \cdot (\mathbf{T}_z^{-1})) = \mathbf{T}_{target} \tag{5}$$

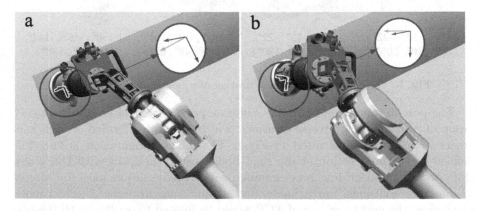

Fig. 2. Equivalence of adjusting target point and tool coordinate system: (a) the rotation of local Z-axis of target points by angle of α; (b) the rotation of local Z-axis of tool coordinate system by angle of -α.

According to the properties of the rotation matrix, the inverse of $\mathbf{T}_z$ is $\mathbf{T}_z$ when α = -α. In combination with Eq. 5, the rotation of the target point attitude around the local Z-axis by an angle of α is equivalent to the rotation of the tool coordinate system around its local Z-axis by an angle of -α, and the inverse solution is the same. The goal of adjusting the tool coordinate system is to change the robot operating configuration to correspond to all current target points without changing a single target point, which is ideal for continuous machining trajectory operations. Therefore, the robot configuration corresponding to the TCP tracking target point, as shown in Fig. 2, can be altered by modifying the angle of the tool coordinate system around the Z-axis.

2.2   Trajectory Planning of Robotic Grinding Process

The trajectory planning, which generates discrete trajectory points on the machined surface, is essential for robot machining configuration optimization. The inverse solution algorithm, which ensures motion continuity in robot joint space, should be used to transfer the machining trajectory planning to the relevant joint space. The step length and row spacing, among the path planning parameters, have a direct impact on the trajectory accuracy based on NURBS curve interpolation [15]. The cutting residual height between contiguous machining paths is determined by row spacing, while the chord height error between adjacent target points on the same trajectory is determined by step length.

Calculation of Step Length. In the theoretical machining trajectory curve, the chord height error of end tool from target points p_i to p_{i+1} is defined as δ_i and its distance is cutting step length. The lower the step length, the less the chord height error and the more precise the machining trajectory becomes, but machining efficiency diminishes. Therefore, the cutting step length between neighboring target points should be suitably estimated to realize robotic grinding of large components with higher machining accuracy and efficiency. Then the equal height error δ_i is:

$$\delta_i \approx \left| P(\frac{u_i + u_{i+1}}{2}) - \frac{P(u_i) + P(u_{i+1})}{2} \right| \tag{6}$$

Isoparametric, isometric, and equal chord height error methods are the most common approaches for calculating chord height error [16]. The isoparametric method calculates quickly and is simple to use, especially for curves with small curvature changes. However, it was unable to assure that all chord height errors met the processing criteria, and chord height errors shift dramatically when the curvature varies, reducing machining accuracy [17]. The computation of isometric approach is inefficient and unstable, making it unsuitable for machining route planning of large component [18]. The equal chord height error method uses the chord height between adjacent target points to calculate the corresponding parameters of the next processing target point on the path curve from the current target point, ensuring that the bow height error values of all processing target points on a single path are approximately equal to the allowable value.

Since the distance between neighboring interpolation points on a NURBS curve is so short, interval curves can be regarded roughly as arcs, as shown in Fig. 3. R_i is roughly equal to the curvature radius at the parameter u_i:

$$\delta_i = R_i - \sqrt{R_i^2 - \frac{L_i^2}{4}} \tag{7}$$

Then the cutting step length Δu can be calculated:

$$\Delta u = \frac{2\sqrt{2R \cdot \delta - \delta^2}}{\sqrt{(x_i')^2 + (y_i')^2 + (z_i')^2}} \tag{8}$$

The equal chord height error method could enhance machining efficiency and precision based on the permitted mistakes for surface machining. The approach also has a high level of stability, making it suited for curves with a wide range of curvature. When machined surface is close to a plane, the curvature radius of the target point on the surface is ∞, therefore, the isoparametric technique could be used when calculating machining trajectory.

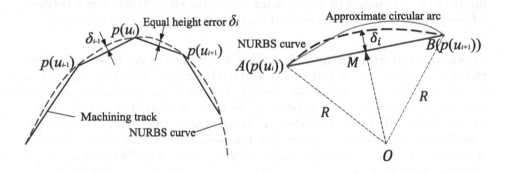

Fig. 3. Schematic of equal height error method and NURBS curve interpolation.

Calculation of Row Spacing. Cutting row spacing is an important parameter in machining path planning, and if the row spacing is too large, the trajectory distribution will be too sparse, resulting in uneven residual height between adjacent tracks and poor machining precision. Isoparametric line, isometric intercept plane, Hilbert filling curve and equal residual height method [19], illustrated in the Fig. 4, are the primary calculating methods for row spacing, respectively.

Isoparametric line method is straightforward and practicable, its track spacing is uniform and the accuracy is high with uncomplicated surface. When the machining contour is complex and the local features are inconsistent, the distance between the discrete points on the curve is not uniform to result in over-grinding or under-grinding, which could compromise machining accuracy and efficiency [20]. The isometric intercept plane approach possesses simple programming, high machining efficiency, and uniform distribution of the generated trajectory, which is especially suitable for the complex workpiece. However, when the curvature of machining surface changes too much, the machining scallop height becomes highly unpredictable, and it would even result in self-cutting. While the velocity and acceleration of the trajectory point of the Hilbert filling curve approach are abrupt, which can easily lead to intense vibration of the robot end-effector and each axis, lowing the service life and machining accuracy of the equipment [21]. The row spacing between the tracks of the equal residual height method is adjusted with the surface curvature, considerably improving processing efficiency and accuracy, however, it would must meet matching requirements [22].

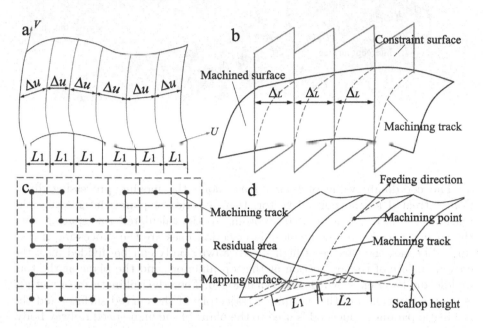

Fig. 4. Calculation methods of cutting row spacing: (a) isoparametric line method; (b) isometric intercept plane method; (c) Hilbert filling curve method; (d) equal residual height method.

In conclusion, the equal residual height approach has the best computational efficiency and accuracy when compared to other methods, while the isopararic line and isometric section method are ideal for modest changes in the local curvature. Therefore, the equal residual height method is used to compute row spacing for non-planar machining surfaces, whereas the corresponding row spacing for planar machining surfaces should be calculated according to the process and the machining track obtained using the isometric intercept plane method.

2.3   Robotic Trajectory Planning for High-Speed Railway Body

Because of the strong consistency of the high-speed railway body and the large machined area, the processing surface can be segmented based on the bounding box, which includes three directions, as shown in Fig. 5, moving machining direction, machining path direction, and main normal direction. The model's boundary information is derived from the bounding box object, which contains the bounding box's greatest vertex *corner_max* and smallest vertex *corner_min*.

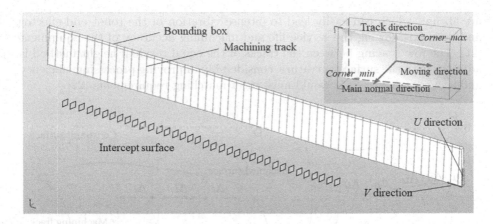

Fig. 5. The bounding box of the machined surface.

The coordinate value of *corner_max* along the moving processing direction is treated as the normal vector, then a series of planes intersecting the machined surfaces are generated according to the calculated row spacing until the *corner_max* is obtained, whose intersection lines are the processing trajectory. Whereas, the surface of high-speed railway body can be divided into: the curved surface of the arc section at the top junction, and the plane at the top, middle and lower ends, which is shown in Fig. 6. Then the isokinetic error method is adopted to generate the machining trajectory of the curved surface, and the isokinetic parameter method is used to the plane of the high-speed railway body.

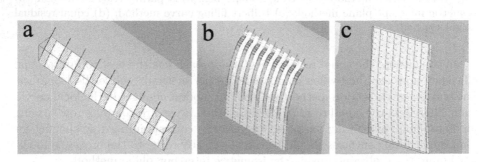

Fig. 6. The machining trajectory of the top (a), curved surface (b) and the middle and lower ends (c) of the high-speed railway body.

3 Experimental Setup and Verification

The body is the most essential huge and complicated component of the entire high-speed railway, which is characterized by its large size (22.5–26 m in length), complex structure shape, and local structural variation/weak rigidity.

Because of the limited workpiece size and operation space, the robotic grinding system of high-speed railway body requires additional guide rails and higher platforms, as well as the unique grinding tools. Therefore, an ABB 6-axis robot and a 24 × 3.9 m high-speed railway body were employed in the experiment, depicted in Fig. 7a, to validate the proposed approaches.

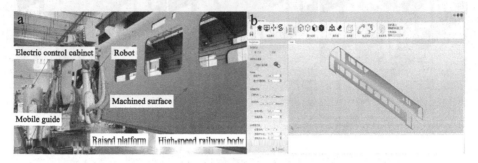

Fig. 7. Experimental setup of mobile robot grinding system (a) and the developed trajectory planning software for high-speed railway body.

According to the surface features of the high-speed railway body, the machined surface can be separated into three regions: Zoom 1, Zoom 2, and Zoom 3. And then the machining trajectory is planned using CAD/CAM technology in the configuration optimization algorithm of a mobile robot grinding system, and the indexes of collision constraints are needed to obtain the robot connecting rod and the bounding box of the detection model, therefore, the associated software is built to match the machining requirements using the OCC geometry engine and the Qt interface development framework, as shown in Fig. 7b. Whereas, the appropriate elevated platform should be selected to plan the machining trajectory and make the matching robot base height of Zoom 1 and Zoom 3 mutual decoupling, which is illustrated in Fig. 8, to improve the redundancy of the robotic grinding system for high-speed railway body.

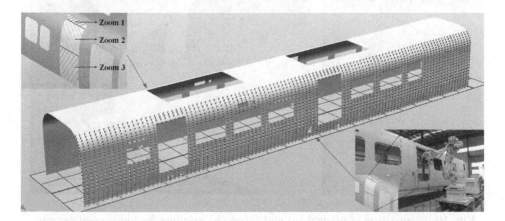

Fig. 8. Robotic machining trajectory of high-speed railway body.

The optimization effect of robot machining is simulated and evaluated using the robotic machining trajectory of high-speed railway body, as shown in Fig. 9. The robot operating space expands the robotic accessible range, reducing the risk of robotic singularity and collision, to fulfill the machining requirements.

Fig. 9. The optimal robotic machining attitude in Zoom 1 (a), Zoom 2 (b) and Zoom 3 (c) for high-speed railway body.

The practical robotic machining of high-speed railways body is shown in Fig. 10. The developed trajectory planning software could deal with poor offline programming adaptability and random defects on workpiece surfaces, reducing reliance on programming technicians and increasing trajectory planning efficiency, with the average time spent on single manual programming reduced from 3h to 0.5 h. It has been demonstrated that the surface smoothness of high-speed railways can be improved from the best 0.6 mm/m for manual repeated machining to better than 0.5 mm/m for single robotic machining, and the surface roughness can be improved from Ra3.0 to Ra2.0, which not only reduces pollution but also improves processing efficiency and surface quality.

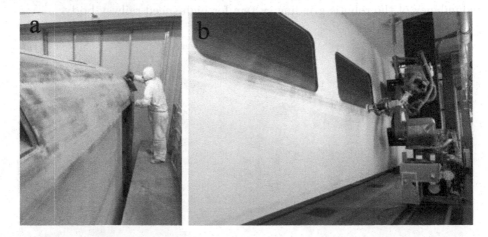

Fig. 10. Comparison of manual (a) and robot (b) grinding for high-speed railway.

4   Conclusion

The model of robot joint configuration is built to obtain the optimal robotic machining attitude, and then the robotic machining trajectory planning method is proposed to realize robotic grinding of high-speed railway body with high performance. The following findings were reached:

(1) Machined surface area divisions of Zoom 1, Zoom 2, and Zoom 3 could largely improve the smoothness of trajectory planning and robotic grinding efficiency for high-speed railway body.
(2) The optimal trajectory in the operation space is employed to actual robotic machining of high-speed railway body, which could largely improve processing efficiency and surface quality.
(3) The proposed method could significantly reduce machining configuration adjustment time, which is applicable for robot milling, robot grinding, and robot drilling of large components. Future study will concentrate on feature trajectory extraction and algorithm enhancement, which will help to increase its convergence speed even further.

References

1. Zhu, D., et al.: Robotic grinding of complex components: a step towards efficient and intelligent machining - challenges, solutions, and applications. Robot Cim-Int. Manuf. **65**, 101908 (2020)
2. Zhao, X., Tao, B., Qian, L., Yang, Y., Ding, H.: Asymmetrical nonlinear impedance control for dual robotic machining of thin-walled workpieces. Robot Cim-Int. Manuf. **63**, 101889 (2020)
3. Xu, X., Chen, W., Zhu, D., Yan, S., Ding, H.: Hybrid active/passive force control strategy for grinding marks suppression and profile accuracy enhancement in robotic belt grinding of turbine blade. Robot Cim-Int. Manuf. **67**, 102047 (2021)
4. Ren, S., Yang, X., Xu, J., Wang, G., Xie, Y., Chen, K.: Determination of the base position and working area for mobile manipulators. Assem. Autom. **36**, 80–88 (2016)
5. Tao, B., Zhao, X.W., Ding, H.: Mobile-robotic machining for large complex components: A review study. Sci. China Technol. Sci. **62**(8), 1388–1400 (2019). https://doi.org/10.1007/s11431-019-9510-1
6. Diao, S., Chen, X., Wu, L., Yang, M., Liu, J.: The optimal collision avoidance trajectory planning of redundant manipulators in the process of grinding ceramic billet surface. Math Probl. Eng **2017**, 1–12 (2017)
7. Lv, Y., Peng, Z., Qu, C., Zhu, D.: An adaptive trajectory planning algorithm for robotic belt grinding of blade leading and trailing edges based on material removal profile model. Robot Cim-Int. Manuf. **66**, 101987 (2020)
8. Pajak, G.: Trajectory planning for mobile manipulators with vibration reduction. J. Vibroeng. **23**, 877–890 (2021)
9. Beschi, M., et al.: Optimal robot motion planning of redundant robots in machining and additive manufacturing applications. Electronics **8**, 1473–1491 (2019)
10. Rocha, C., Tonetto, C.P., Dias, A.: A comparison between the Denavit-Hartenberg and the screw-based methods used in kinematic modeling of robot manipulators. Robot Cim-Int. Manuf. **27**(4), 723–728 (2011)

496 X. Xu et al.

11. Diankov, R., Rybski, P.: Automated construction of robotic manipulation programs. Carnegie Mellon University (2010)
12. Atef, A.A.: Optimal trajectory planning of manipulators: a review. J. Eng. Sci. Technol. **2**(1), 32–54 (2007)
13. Lynch, K.M., Park, F.C.: Modern robotics: mechanics, planning, and control. IEEE Control Syst. Mag. **39**, 100–102 (2017)
14. Zargarbashi, S.H.H., Khan, W., Angeles, J.: Posture optimization in robot-assisted machining operations. Mech. Mach. Theory **51**, 74–86 (2012)
15. Constantinescu, D., Croft, E.: Smooth and time-optimal trajectory planning for industrial manipulators along specified paths. J. Robot Syst. **17**(5), 233–249 (2020)
16. Dong, J., Yu, T., Chen, H., Li, B.: An improved calculation method for cutting contact point and tool orientation analysis according to the CC points. Precis. Eng. **61**, 1–13 (2019)
17. Liu, M.: Research on NURBS interpolation for NC machining. Huazhong University of Science and Technology (2015)
18. Sun, H.: Research on real-time algorithms of NURBS tool-paths interpolation. National University of Defense Technology (2008)
19. Giri, V., Bezbaruah, D., Bubna, P., Choudhury, A.R.: Selection of master cutter paths in sculptured surface machining by employing curvature principle. Int. J. Mach. Tool Manuf. **10**, 1202–1209 (2005)
20. He, W., Lei, M., Bin, H.: Isoparametric CNC tool path optimization based on adaptive grid generation. Int. J. Adv. Manuf. Tech. **41**, 538–548 (2009)
21. Griffiths, J.G.: Tool path based on Hilbert's curve. Comput. Aid. Des. **26**(11), 839–844 (1994)
22. Han, Z., Yang, D., Chuang, J.: Isophote based ruled surface approximation of freeform surfaces and its application in NC machining. Int. J. Prod. Res. **9**, 1911–1930 (2001)

Design of Control Software for a Reconfigurable Industrial Robot Training Platform

Dianyong Yu[1], Sai Yingnan Bian[1(✉)], and Ye Duan[2]

[1] State Key Laboratory of Robotics and System, Harbin Institute of Technology, Harbin 150001, China
392894475@qq.com

[2] School of Engineering and Applied Science, University of Pennsylvania, Philadelphia 19104, USA

Abstract. For this reconfigurable robot training platform, the platform is divided into 6 modules using fuzzy clustering theory. We use the STM32F407 equipped with the uCOS II system for programming and divide the system into a communication module, a motor module, and a patrol module. The lower computer accepts the instructions of the upper computer, completes the operation of each servo motor through task scheduling, and feeds back the real-time status. Based on QT, the software is built. The upper computer is divided into task module, communication module, and status module. The json class is used to set the configuration file to set the newly created task. The communication task is carried out with other subsystems through the serial port and Ethernet. Use the FUNAUC robot and Eft robot to communicate with the upper computer, accept and analyze the instructions of the upper computer, complete the corresponding training tasks according to the task number and action number, and give feedback on the completion of the robot arm and the task. The above systems cooperate with each other to complete the function of robot training.

Keywords: Training platform · Fuzzy clustering · STM32 · UCOS · QT

1 Introduction

Most of the robot training platforms on the market today have many problems such as single tasks, limited functions, and inability to secondary development. Facing the increasingly diverse task requirements in actual production, the number of corresponding training platforms is also increasing, which has pushed up the construction cost of training platforms and raised the threshold of capital access for robotics training and teaching in higher vocational colleges. It is not conducive to the popularization of industrial robot training and teaching in higher vocational and technical colleges. Therefore, in the face of this problem, a reconfigurable multi-task industrial robot training platform should be developed to meet the needs of high-frequency switching of teaching tasks, reducing the cost of training platforms, thus improving the teaching efficiency of higher vocational and technical colleges.

This paper is based on the national key research and development project (2019YFB1312602).

2 Theoretical Background

2.1 Overview

The multi-task training industrial robot platform is designed for multi-task training purposes. A sound module classification procedure can lay a solid foundation for the subsequent function allocation in the following practical engineering design of the platform. The module classification process comprises the following procedures (Fig. 1):

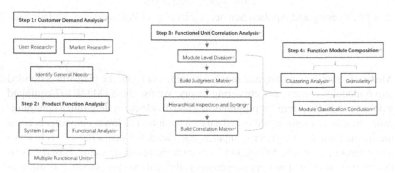

Fig. 1. Module Classification Procedure

2.2 Description of Each Step

The customer demand analysis is one of the powerful tools; using relevant user research and marketing research approaches, the subjective needs of customers can be determined into objective information of module classification [1]. The overall requirements of the platform are initially divided into modules as execution module, drive module, communication module, control module, storage module, and human-computer-interaction module. Then, the product function analysis plays a vital role in the platform's design. Based on the execution, drive, communication, control, storage, and human-computer-interaction modules summed up by the customer demand analysis, from the system level, the product function analysis method is further used to decompose the above modules to logical functional unit, physical functional unit, and mathematical functional unit [2]. Most functional units belong to non-independent functional modules, so it is necessary to analyze the correlation between non-independent functional units [3]. In our case, the functional unit correlation analysis comprises module-level division, judgment matrix built, hierarchical inspection & sorting, and the correlation matrix construction. The formula for calculating the correlation between two functional units is:

$$C_{mn} = \sum_{j=1}^{n} \omega_j r_{mn}^j \tag{1}$$

where r_{mn}^j is the degree of correlation between the mth functional unit and the nth functional unit under the jth correlation. And the corresponding correlation matrix is as follows:

$$C = \begin{bmatrix} 1 & R_{12} & R_{13} & R_{14} & R_{15} & \cdots & R_{1i} \\ & 1 & R_{23} & R_{24} & R_{25} & & R_{2i} \\ & & 1 & R_{34} & R_{35} & \cdots & R_{3i} \\ & & & 1 & R_{45} & \cdots & R_{4i} \\ & & & & 1 & \cdots & R_{5i} \\ & & & & & 1 & \cdots \\ & & & & & & 1 \end{bmatrix} \tag{2}$$

where i is the number of functional units. The final module classification of the platform needs to go through the fuzzy clustering, to be more specific, the granularity process. The correlation strength is further used in the fuzzy clustering analysis to classify the object of interest by analyzing the corresponding fuzzy relationships. Cohesion and coupling are also introduced to provide an evaluation basis for the module selection. Cohesion defines the degree to which the elements belong to each other. While coupling means the degree of interdependence between modules and it is measured by the number of relations between the modules [4, 5].

2.3 Conclusion from Theoretical Analysis

After implementing customer demand analysis, product function analysis, functional unit correlation analysis, and function module composition process, we want the one with the lowest coupling and highest cohesion. The final optimal module classification result is (Table 1):

Table 1. Conclusion from theoretical analysis

Module name	Module composition
Upper computer module	PC with QT software
Lower computer module	STM32,Transmission,Turntable,Linear
Robotic arm module	Robotic arm
Vision module	Industrial camera
Power source module	Air supply system, power(electricity) supply system
Manufacturing storage module	Raw material storage, finished product storage, fixture storage

3 The Overall Design of the Training Platform

The training platform comprises two six-axis robotic arm modules, a linear module, two turntable modules, a fixture library module, a transmission module, a vision module, an upper computer, and a control electrical module cabinet for placing the lower computer. The composition of the training platform is shown in the following Fig. 2:

Fig. 2. Industrial robot training platform

This training system adopts the classic upper and lower computer control mode. The control system of this training platform is initially divided into four main parts: the upper computer control subsystem, the lower computer control subsystem, the robotic arm control subsystem, and the visual inspection subsystem. Based on the TCP/IP protocol, the upper computer is connected to the robotic arm and the industrial camera through Ethernet, based on the TCP/IP protocol. The connection between the upper and lower computer adopts the communication method of the RS485 serial port. At the same time, the lower computer and the turntable, linear module, transmission, and other peripherals are connected through the RS485 serial port based on the Modbus protocol, as shown in the following Figs. 3 and 4:

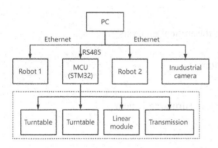

Fig. 3. System network topology

Fig. 4. The modules of the robot training platform

We choose a PC equipped with a Windows system as the upper computer and choose QT as the host computer development software. We choose STM32F407ZET6 as the lower computer. Linear modules use Delta's ASDB3 servo motor system. The six-axis robot is mounted on it. The turntable uses an ASDA3 servo motor system. It can provide different processing positions for the two manipulators. The transmission line is controlled by a Mitsubishi FR inverter. The visual inspection subsystem uses the Hikvision MV-CE050-30GM camera as an industrial camera. The robotic arm subsystem uses the FUNAUC robot and Eft robot.

The sequence of system execution process design is as follows:

1. The developer writes the technological process on the host computer;
2. The upper computer sends commands to the lower computer, robotic arm, and industrial camera;
3. The industrial robot executes the command of the upper computer, executes the corresponding action, and feeds back the status of the industrial robot in real-time;
4. The lower computer collects the status of each motor driver, and feeds it back to the upper computer regularly, executes the command of the upper computer, sends the setting command to the driver, executes actions, etc.;
5. The industrial camera executes the command of the host computer, feeds back the result of the visual judgment to the host computer, and feeds back the status of the industrial camera in real-time;
6. The upper computer analyzes the feedback and status of the robot, the lower computer, and the industrial camera and runs the process steps step by step. Each step must meet the corresponding conditions before the next process can be executed.

4   Design of Control Software for Subsystem of Lower Computer

This lower computer adopts the STM32F407ZET6 development board. The HAL library is used for development, and the development environment is Keil uVision5MDK. For this task, we use the uCOS ii operating systems.

4.1   Main Program Structure Design

The main program flow is shown in the following Fig. 5:

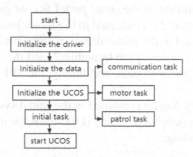

Fig. 5. Main program flow chart

After booting, STM32 first initializes the peripherals on the board, initializes the required data structures and uCOS system, and creates various subtasks.

The tasks required by the lower computer control software and their priorities are shown in the following Table 2:

Table 2. The priority of each task

Name	Priority	Function
start_task	5	Creating other tasks
pc_task	6	Communicate with the host computer
moto_task	7	Control motor
period_task	8	Patrol the flags

The start task must have the highest priority, and the division of task priority requires high real-time performance. Therefore, the priority of the pc_task with the upper computer is ranked after the start task, motor_task is the second, and patrol_task is the last (Fig. 6).

Fig. 6. Driver initialization flow chart

The Driver initialization first configures the RCC clock to 168 MHz, then sets the system timer, sets the interrupt time to 1ms, and configures the interrupt priority. To prevent interrupted nesting, except the system clock is set to high priority, the rest is set to the same low priority. Initialize the CRC peripheral to perform a CRC check on the Modbus communication, initialize the PVD peripheral for low-voltage detection, and the system voltage is lower than 3v to generate an interrupt to reset the development board. The serial port is initialized, the serial port 1 is configured as the serial port for communication, the serial port 2 is connected to the motor inverter of the conveyor line, the serial port 3 is connected to the motor driver of the turntable 1, and the serial port 4 is connected to the motor driver of the turntable 2, and the serial port 6 is connected to the motor driver of the linear module, and finally, the SPI and external FLASH are initialized.

Data initialization is the flag bit contained in the initial sys structure. This structure contains the status of each peripheral, which is the basis for us to provide the basis for subsequent running scheduling.

4.2 Communication Task Design

The communication task is mainly to realize the communication function between the upper and lower computers. The flow chart is as follows (Fig. 7):

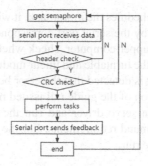

Fig. 7. Communication task flow chart

When the communication serial port receives data and generates an interruption, use the OSSemPost function to release the semaphore, read the message received in the serial port read buffer, first perform verification, extract its header, compare it with the protocol header, and calculate its data bit length and compare with the extracted length check digit data. If the verification passes, extract its command code and sub-command code to determine the action executed through the switch function. If it is an acquisition command, the serial port sends a DI command to the motor with Modbus protocol to update its flag bit. If it is a set command, it is necessary to further extract its parameters. First, by changing the flag bit of the motor part in the sys structure, wait for the motor running state to be changed when switching to the motor control task, configure the command message, and use the serial port to each motor to set specific operation information. Finally, edit the feedback message and send it to the host computer through the serial port.

4.3 Motor Task Design

The motor task is mainly to perform the task of changing the running state of each motor. The flow chart is as follows (Fig. 8):

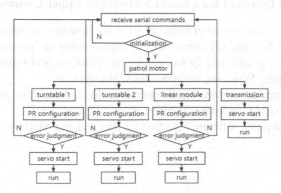

Fig. 8. Motor task flow chart

When the task scheduler schedules the motor task, it will patrol each motor, analyze the Modbus package received by the serial port corresponding to the motor, obtain the control command sent by the upper computer, check whether each motor is initialized and start the servo in turn. For the turntable and linear modules, we first set the PR mode and set the command. When it is detected that the error between the set position of the guide rail and the actual position of the guide rail issued by the host computer exceeds a certain value, start the Delta servo driver and run the motor to the corresponding position according to the command requirements. For the transmission line, according to the speed set by the message run.

4.4 Patrol Task Design

The upper computer needs to know the feedback status of the lower computer in real-time. This subsystem writes the status of each part of the system into the SYS structure. After setting the time through the system, the timer divides the flag bits in the sys into multiple groups of flag bits that are refreshed at different times. The group, at different times, is updated and written to the flash of the STM32 development board so that the upper computer can read the status of the lower computer in real-time (Fig. 9).

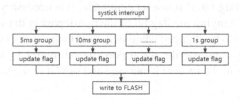

Fig. 9. Patrol task flow chart

5   Design of Control Software for Subsystem of Upper Computer

5.1   The Overall Design of the Control Software of Upper Computer

The upper computer development software used for human-computer interaction uses QT programming. Because QT comes with a large number of functional modules and interfaces, it is easy to call, and Qt has good cross-platform performance and supports compiling code under Windows, macOS, and Linux systems.

This upper computer subsystem software can be divided into three parts: task module, communication module, and status module.

The upper computer software interface of this training platform is shown in the Fig. 10:

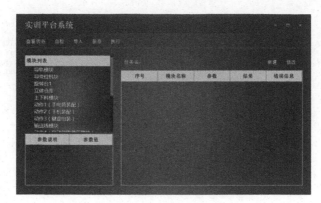

Fig. 10. PC software interface

The module list on the left represents different modules of the training platform. Click the tree control below to indicate the relevant parameters of the module at this time. The table control on the right reflects the information of each module in the ongoing task. The "View Self-Check Status" option on the toolbar can view the status of each part of the robot training platform in real-time, the "Import" option can view the local task json file and read and load it, and the "Execute" option can parse the json file. The task is then converted into a communication protocol code and sent out through the communication module for corresponding training operations (Fig. 11).

5.2 Task Module Design

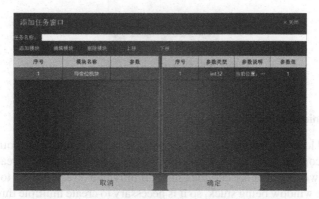

Fig. 11. Task add interface

Click "New" on the main interface to enter the window for adding tasks. This software uses the QJson library to implement the configuration file. The task structure, module structure, and parameter structure are shown in the Fig. 12:

```
struct Task                                      struct Module                    struct Paras
{                                                {                                {
    QString name;                                    ModularType type;                int paraId = 0;
    QList<Module> moduleInfos;                       QList<Paras> paras;              QString paraType;
    void Clear()                                     QString condition;//以逗          QString paraValue;
    {                                                bool isRun = false;              QString paraDesc;
        for(int i =0;i<moduleInfos.size();i++)       void Clear()                 };
        {                                            {
            moduleInfos[i].Clear();                      paras.clear();
        }                                                type = maxModule;
        moduleInfos.clear();                             isRun = false;
        name = "";                                   }
    }                                            }
};                                               };
```

Fig. 12. Task, module, parameter structure

After selecting the module and setting the parameters in the add task window, the task setting function will generate a json file in the data folder of the root directory of the upper computer software, which stores a jsondocument data structure to represent all the information of the task set this time, including the task name, the modules participating in the task, the parameters to be executed by each module, and so on.

Click the "Import" button on the main interface to view the json files of different tasks in the local data folder. After clicking "Execute," read through the read function, parse through the parsing function, and finally send it through the communication module to execute training tasks (Fig. 13).

Fig. 13. Task import interface

5.3 Communication Module Design

The upper and lower computers use serial communication, while the robotic arm adopts TCP network communication. The communication module uses multi-threading because when dealing with some more complex logic, if only one thread is used to process it, it will lead to the window being stuck, so it is necessary to create multiple threads to avoid such phenomena. In this project, we use the QThread class to create multiple threads to handle the tasks of serial communication and TCP network communication at the same time and call the moveToThread function to place the processing tasks in the thread.

For TCP communication, it mainly exists between the host computer and the manipulator. This communication adopts the CS architecture, the host computer acts as the server, the manipulator acts as the client, and the manipulator driver has a network communication module on the body and a general-purpose register for storing characters., use the socket on the host computer to establish a connection.

For serial communication, it mainly exists between the upper computer and the lower computer and is realized by the object established by QserialPort.

For sending and receiving data, we use QMap to write the corresponding command code and corresponding processing function into Map. When receiving data, the command code obtained after decoding by the corresponding decoding function can find the corresponding processing function.

5.4 Self-checking Module Design

The self-checking module of the lower computer changes the icon in front of the corresponding module according to the obtained relevant information when the upper computer sends to obtain the status of the lower computer or receives the feedback from the lower computer so that the operator can know the operation status of different modules in time (Fig. 14).

Fig. 14. Self-check module interface

6   Design of Control Software for Subsystem of Robotic Arm

The robotic arm communicates with the upper computer through TCP network communication, and the upper computer links with the robotic arm by modifying and reading its variable values.

Among them, variables 1 to 4 are responsible for placing the commands sent by the host computer to the robotic arm. While variables 33 to 39 are the feedback of the robotic arm to the upper computer.

Use the Eft robotic arm teach pendant for programming; the main function flow chart is as follows (Figs. 15 and 16):

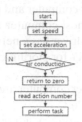

Fig. 15. Robotic arm main function flow chart

Fig. 16. Function in the pendant

In the main function, first set the speed of the robotic arm, adjust the acceleration and deceleration of the robot, set the task number feedback and action number feedback to zero, connect the air circuit, and check whether the air circuit is connected, and return the robot to the zero position, check whether the task has started, and place the task number and action number in the task and action feedback bits, and check and execute the tasks in turn.

For the task class function, it is to cyclically poll the data bits that store the action number and call the relevant action function. For the task1, there are 9 actions. When the action is completed, change the action number feedback bit so that the upper computer can obtain parameters and send new action commands. The execution of a set of training tasks can be completed through the above three steps.

7 Conclusion

In this paper, a reconfigurable robot training platform is designed. By programming the lower computer STM32, using QT to design the upper computer software to edit the training tasks, and at the same time programming the robotic arm to encapsulate its basic actions through the above. The platform modules can cooperate with each other to complete the execution of desired training tasks indicated by the user.

References

1. Li, F., Li, X., Xie, H.: Modular design research of computer numerical control machine tools oriented to customer requirements. Adv. Mech. Eng. **12**, 1–18 (2020)
2. Bonvoisin, J., Halstenberg, F., Buchert, T., Stark, R.: A systematic literature review on modular product design. J. Eng. Des. **27**(7), 488–514 (2016)
3. Kreng, V.B., Lee, T.-P.: Modular product design with grouping genetic algorithm—a case study. Comput. Ind. Eng. **46**(3), 443–460 (2004)
4. Yang, M.-S.: A survey of fuzzy clustering. Math. Comput. Model. **18**(11), 1–16 (1993)
5. Zadeh, L.A.: Fuzzy Sets and Information Granularity. Memorandum No. UCB/ERL M79/45 (1979)

Observer-Based H_∞-Consensus Control of Multi-agent Systems Under WTOD Protocol

Jinbo Song[1,2], Yafei Jiao[1,3,4], Fan Yang[1,3,4(✉)], and Chao Xu[1,3,4]

[1] Artificial Intelligence Energy Research Institute, Northeast Petroleum University, Daqing 163318, Heilongjiang, China
yangfan001luck@163.com
[2] College of Electrical Engineering and Information, Northeast Petroleum University, Daqing 163318, Heilongjiang, China
[3] Heilongjiang Provincial Key Laboratory of Networking and Intelligent Control, Northeast Petroleum University, Daqing 163318, Heilongjiang, China
[4] Sanya Offshore Oil and Gas Research Institute, Northeast Petroleum University, Sanya 572025, Hainan, China

Abstract. In this paper, the observer-based H_∞-consensus control problem is studied for multi-agent systems (MASs) under the weighted try-once-discard (WTOD) communication protocol. The WTOD protocol is implemented in the channel from observer to controller to schedule the data transmissions among the agents. Under such a protocol, for one agent, only one neighboring agent's information is received at each time instant. First, the state observers are designed based on the measurement outputs to estimate the states of the agents. Then, consensus controllers are designed based on the estimates from the observers. The sufficient condition is obtained such that the H_∞-consensus performance index is guaranteed. The parameters of the observers and the controllers are then calculated from certain matrix inequalities. Finally, a numerical example is provided to verify the effectiveness and feasibility of the method proposed in this paper.

Keywords: MASs · WTOD protocol · State observer · Consensus control · H_∞ performance

1 Introduction

Since the late 1980s, the multi-agent systems (MASs) have entered the study field of distributed control and become a hot research area. In the MASs, the agents are able to achieve cooperation through perceiving the surrounding information and sharing of the information with other agents through the communication network. Nowadays, the MASs have been widely applied in areas such as the computer network [1], the UAV formation [2] and the in-wheel-motor electric vehicles [3] by virtue of the advantages such as strong scalability, high reliability and easy maintenance.

© The Author(s), under exclusive license to Springer Nature Switzerland AG 2022
H. Liu et al. (Eds.): ICIRA 2022, LNAI 13457, pp. 509–519, 2022.
https://doi.org/10.1007/978-3-031-13835-5_46

To date, the consensus control problem of the MASs has achieved fruitful results since it is the basis for engineering application, see references [4] and [5]. In the consensus control of the MASs, each agent needs to communicate with the neighboring agents. Unfortunately, because of the limitations in the network bandwidth and energy, the simultaneous transmissions of the information of all neighboring agents will lead to network-induced problem such as packet dropouts and transmission delays. To solve such problems, the communication protocols have been used to adjust the transmission orders of the neighboring agents [6–11]. At present, the commonly used communication protocols include the weighted try-once-discard (WTOD) protocol, the stochastic communication (SC) protocol and the round-robin (RR) protocol. The references [7] and [8] have studied the application of the RR protocol in set-membership filtering and MASs consensus control, respectively. The reference [10] has investigated the H_∞-consensus control of MASs with SC protocol in finite-horizon. The reference [11] has concerned the effect of the WTOD protocol on the filtering of complex networks in finite-horizon.

On the other hand, it is known that the state-feedback control strategy can obtain better system performance than the output-feedback control strategy. Nevertheless, in most cases, the state of the system is unable to directly obtain. As an alternative solution, the observer-based control strategy has been developed and has received extensive research attentions. The references [12]-[16] have all studied the observer-based consensus control problem of MASs where the leader-following fractional-order heterogeneous nonlinear MASs has been studied in [12], the multi-rate MASs has been considered in [16], and the conventional linear/nonlinear discrete-time MASs has been investigated in [13–15].

Stimulated by the above discussions, in this study, the H_∞-consensus control problem has been investigated for discrete-time MASs under WTOD protocol. *The contributions of this study are outlined as follows: 1) the WTOD protocol is implemented in the channel from the observer to the controller to lighten the communication burden and alleviate network congestions among agents; 2) an observed-based controller is proposed that maintains a satisfactory consensus performance in case of the external disturbances; and 3) sufficient condition is acquired that ensures the H_∞-consensus performance of the controlled output dynamics.*

Notation. The symbols used in this thesis is normal. A block-diagonal matrix can be represented by the notation diag$\{A_1, A_2, \ldots, A_n\}$. $*$ denotes the symmetric vector in a symmetric matrix. A binary function $\delta(z)$ is defined with function value is 1 for $z = 0$ and 0 for $z \neq 0$. The Hadamard product operation is represented by symbol $\circ$.

2 Problem Formulation

In this thesis, the MASs considered has L agents which are arranged in the space in terms of a specific communication topology described by a directed graph $\mathcal{G}$. Let $\mathcal{G} = (\mathcal{N}, \mathcal{F}, \mathcal{H})$ be a graph of order L where the set of agents is represented by $\mathcal{N} = \{1, 2, \ldots, L\}$, the set of edges is represented by $\mathcal{F} = \mathcal{N} \times \mathcal{N}$, and the weighted adjacency matrix is represented by $\mathcal{H} = [h_{ij}]$. $h_{ij} > 0 \iff (i, j) \in \mathcal{F}$ indicates that agent j is a neighbor of agent i and agent i can receive information from agent j. Obviously, $h_{ij} = 0 \iff (i, j) \notin \mathcal{F}$ indicates that agent i cannot receive information from agent j. In this paper, self-edges (i, i) are not permitted, i.e. $h_{ii} = 0$ for any $i \in \mathcal{N}$. Define a set $\mathcal{L}_i \triangleq \{j \in \mathcal{N} : (i, j) \in \mathcal{F}\}$ to represent the neighbouring agents set of agent i with L_i being the number of neighbors of agent i.

2.1 System Model

It is assumed that all agents in the MAS have identical dynamic characteristics and the dynamics of the ith agent at time instant s is depicted by the following discrete system:

$$\begin{cases} x_{i,s+1} = Ax_{i,s} + Bu_{i,s} + D\omega_{i,s} \\ \quad y_{i,s} = Cx_{i,s} + E\nu_{i,s} \\ \quad z_{i,s} = Mx_{i,s} \end{cases} \tag{1}$$

where $x_{i,s} \in \mathbb{R}^{n_x}$, $u_{i,s} \in \mathbb{R}^{n_u}$, $y_{i,s} \in \mathbb{R}^{n_y}$ and $z_{i,s} \in \mathbb{R}^{n_z}$ represent the state vector, the control input vector, the measurement output vector, and the controlled output vector of agent i, respectively. $\omega_{i,s} \in l_2([0, \infty); \mathbb{R}^{n_\omega})$ and $\nu_{i,s} \in l_2([0, \infty); \mathbb{R}^{n_\nu})$ are the system and measurement disturbances, respectively. Matrices A, B, C, D, E, M are known of proper dimensions and matrix B is full column rank.

2.2 Controller Design

The state observer of agent i is designed as follows:

$$\hat{x}_{i,s+1} = A\hat{x}_{i,s} + Bu_{i,s} + K_o(y_{i,s} - C\hat{x}_{i,s}) \tag{2}$$

where $\hat{x}_{i,s}$ represents the estimate of $x_{i,s}$ and K_o is the observer parameter to be determined.

In the traditional consensus control problems, the consensus controller on the agent i is designed based on the state estimates from itself and the neighboring agents. Nevertheless, due to the introduction of the WTOD protocol, not all the neighboring agents can transmit the estimate to agent i at a certain time. Let $\mu_{i,s} \in \mathcal{L}_i$ indicates the chosen neighboring agent that transmits message to agent i at time s. From the scheduling rule of the WTOD protocol, $\mu_{i,s}$ denotes as

$$\mu_{i,s} = \arg\max_{j \in \mathcal{L}_i}(\hat{x}_{j,s} - \bar{x}_{j,s})^T R_j(\hat{x}_{j,s} - \bar{x}_{j,s}) \tag{3}$$

where R_j is a given positive-definite weighting matrix and $\bar{x}_{j,s}$ is the last trans-mitted estimate.

Under the schedule of the WTOD protocol, the consensus controller on agent i is designed as

$$
\begin{aligned}
u_{i,s} &= K_u \sum_{j \in \mathcal{N}} h_{i,j} \gamma_{j,s}^i (\hat{x}_{j,s} - \hat{x}_{i,s}) \\
&= K_u h_{i,\mu_{i,s}}(\hat{x}_{\mu_{i,s},s} - \hat{x}_{i,s})
\end{aligned}
\tag{4}
$$

where $\gamma_{j,s}^i \triangleq \delta(j - \mu_{i,s})$ and K_u is the controller parameter to be determined.

In order to facilitate further processing, the following lemmas are introduced.

Lemma 1 [17]. *For given matrices M, N, Q and P with suitable dimensions, the features of Kronecker product $\otimes$ are depicted as follows:*

1) $(M + N) \otimes P = M \otimes P + N \otimes P$,
2) $(M \otimes N)(P \otimes Q) = (MP) \otimes (NQ)$,
3) $(M \otimes N)^T = M^T \otimes N^T$.

Lemma 2 [18]. *If matrix $B \in \mathbb{R}^{n_x \times n_u}$ ($n_x > n_u$) is full column rank, then it can be decomposed into the following form with two orthogonal matrices $V \in \mathbb{R}^{n_x \times n_x}$ and $N \in \mathbb{R}^{n_u \times n_u}$ satisfying*

$$B = V \begin{bmatrix} \Lambda \\ 0 \end{bmatrix} N = [V_1\ V_2] \begin{bmatrix} \Lambda \\ 0 \end{bmatrix} N \tag{5}$$

where $V_1 \in \mathbb{R}^{n_x \times n_u}$, $V_2 \in \mathbb{R}^{n_x \times (n_x - n_u)}$, $\Lambda = \mathrm{diag}\{\varpi_1, \cdots, \varpi_{n_u}\}$ and $\varpi_j (j = 1, 2, \cdots, n_u)$ are non-zero singular values of matrix B. Thus, if matrix P has the following structure:

$$
\begin{aligned}
P &= [V_1\ V_2]\ \mathrm{diag}\{P_1, P_2\} [V_1\ V_2]^T \\
&= V_1 P_1 V_1^T + V_2 P_2 V_2^T
\end{aligned}
\tag{6}
$$

where $P_1 \in \mathbb{R}^{n_u \times n_u} > 0$, $P_2 \in \mathbb{R}^{(n_x - n_u) \times (n_x - n_u)} > 0$, then there exists a nonsin-gular matrix $\widetilde{P} \in \mathbb{R}^{n_u \times n_u}$ such that $B\widetilde{P} = PB$. Moreover, $\widetilde{P} = N^T \Lambda^{-1} P_1 \Lambda N$.

For simplification, defining

$$u_s \triangleq [u_{1,s}^T\ u_{2,s}^T\ \cdots\ u_{L,s}^T]^T, \quad \hat{x}_s \triangleq [\hat{x}_{1,s}^T\ \hat{x}_{2,s}^T\ \cdots\ \hat{x}_{L,s}^T]^T,$$

it can be deduced from (4) that

$$u_s = (I_L \otimes K_u)(\mathcal{H}_{\mu,s} \otimes I_{nx})\hat{x}_s \tag{7}$$

where

$$\mathcal{H}_{\mu,s} \triangleq \mathcal{H} \circ \Upsilon - d_s, \quad \Upsilon \triangleq [\gamma^i_{j,s}]_{L \times L}, \quad d_s \triangleq \text{diag}\{d_{1,s}, d_{2,s}, \ldots, d_{L,s}\},$$

$$d_{i,s} = \sum_{j \in \mathcal{L}_i} h_{i,j} \gamma^i_{j,s}, \quad i = 1, 2, \cdots, L.$$

Clear, matrix $\mathcal{H}_{\mu,s}$ is related to the sequence $\mu_{i,s}, i \in \{1, 2, \cdots, L\}$ which indicates the scheduling of the WTOD protocol.

Define the observation error as $\delta_{i,s} \triangleq x_{i,s} - \hat{x}_{i,s}$ and introduce the following symbols:

$$x_s \triangleq [x^T_{1,s} \ x^T_{2,s} \ \cdots \ x^T_{L,s}]^T, \quad z_s \triangleq [z^T_{1,s} \ z^T_{2,s} \ \cdots \ z^T_{L,s}]^T,$$

$$\omega_s \triangleq [\omega^T_{1,s} \ \omega^T_{2,s} \ \cdots \ \omega^T_{L,s}]^T, \quad \nu_s \triangleq [\nu^T_{1,s} \ \nu^T_{2,s} \ \cdots \ \nu^T_{L,s}]^T,$$

$$\delta_s \triangleq [\delta^T_{1,s} \ \delta^T_{2,s} \ \cdots \ \delta^T_{L,s}]^T.$$

According to Lemma 1, the augmented system of the closed-loop system is expressed as:

$$x_{s+1} = (I_L \otimes A + \mathcal{H}_{\mu,s} \otimes BK_u)x_s - (\mathcal{H}_{\mu,s} \otimes BK_u)\delta_s + (I_L \otimes D)\omega_s,$$

$$\delta_{s+1} = (I_L \otimes A - I_L \otimes K_o C)\delta_s + (I_L \otimes D)\omega_s - (I_L \otimes K_o E)\nu_s.$$

Define the consensus output error of agent i as:

$$\bar{z}_{i,s} = z_{i,s} - (1/L) \sum_{j=1}^{L} z_{j,s}.$$

Let $\bar{z}_s \triangleq [\bar{z}^T_{1,s} \ \bar{z}^T_{2,s} \ \cdots \ \bar{z}^T_{L,s}]^T$, it is obtained that $\bar{z}_s = (\mathcal{F} \otimes I_{n_z})z_s$, where $\mathcal{F} \triangleq I_L - 1/L\mathbf{1}_{L \times L}$. Set $\xi_s \triangleq [x^T_s \ \delta^T_s]^T, \bar{\omega}_s \triangleq [\omega_s \ \nu_s]^T$, the augmented dynamic equation of the MAS is obtained:

$$\begin{cases} \xi_{s+1} = \bar{A}\xi_s + \bar{D}\bar{\omega}_s \\ \bar{z}_s = \bar{M}\xi_s \end{cases} \tag{8}$$

where

$$\bar{A} \triangleq \begin{bmatrix} I_L \otimes A + \mathcal{H}_{\mu,s} \otimes BK_u & -\mathcal{H}_{\mu,s} \otimes BK_u \\ 0 & I_L \otimes A - I_L \otimes K_o C \end{bmatrix},$$

$$\bar{D} \triangleq \begin{bmatrix} I_L \otimes D & 0 \\ I_L \otimes D & -I_L \otimes K_o E \end{bmatrix},$$

$$\bar{M} \triangleq [\mathcal{F} \otimes M \ \ 0].$$

Definition 1. *For a given disturbance attenuation level $\gamma > 0$, the MAS (8) is said to satisfy the H_∞-consensus control performance if the following inequality holds:*

$$\sum_{s=0}^{\infty} \|\bar{z}_s\|^2 \leq \gamma^2 \sum_{s=0}^{\infty} \|\bar{\omega}_s\|^2. \tag{9}$$

The objective of this paper is to design observer-based consensus controllers (4) for MAS (1) such that:

1. the closed-loop system (8) is asymptotically stable when $\bar{\omega}_s = 0$;
2. under the zero initial condition, for the given disturbance attenuation level $\gamma > 0$, the controlled output $\bar{z}_s$ meets the H_∞ performance index (9).

3 Main Results

In this section, based on the Lyapunov stability theory, a sufficient condition is presented under which the expected H_∞-consensus performance are achieved. Moreover, the corresponding observer and controller gains are obtained by the solutions of certain matrix inequality.

Theorem 1. *Let the disturbance attenuation level $\gamma > 0$, the observer gain matrix K_o and the controller gain matrix K_u be known. Under the zero initial condition, the MAS (8) is asymptotically stable when $\bar{\omega}_s = 0$ and satisfies the H_∞-consensus control performance (9) for all $\bar{\omega}_s \neq 0$ if there exists positive definite matrix $\bar{P}$ satisfying*

$$\Phi = \begin{bmatrix} \bar{A}^T \bar{P} \bar{A} + \bar{M}^T \bar{M} - \bar{P} & * \\ \bar{D}^T \bar{P} \bar{A} & \bar{D}^T \bar{P} \bar{D} - \gamma^2 I \end{bmatrix} < 0. \tag{10}$$

Proof. The Lyapunov functional is defined as follows:

$$V_s = \xi_s^T \bar{P} \xi_s.$$

When $\bar{\omega}_s = 0$, the difference is obtained as follows:

$$\Delta V_s = \xi_{s+1}^T \bar{P} \xi_{s+1} - \xi_s^T \bar{P} \xi_s = \xi_s^T \bar{A}^T \bar{P} \bar{A} \xi_s - \xi_s^T \bar{P} \xi_s.$$

According to Schur complement lemma, if $\Phi < 0$, then $\bar{A}^T \bar{P} \bar{A} - \bar{P} < 0$. Then, the system (8) is asymptotically stable when $\bar{\omega}_s = 0$.

When $\bar{\omega}_s \neq 0$, the difference is obtained as

$$\begin{aligned} \Delta V_s &= \xi_{s+1}^T \bar{P} \xi_{s+1} - \xi_s^T \bar{P} \xi_s \\ &= \xi_s^T \bar{A}^T \bar{P} \bar{A} \xi_s + \xi_s^T \bar{A}^T \bar{P} \bar{D} \bar{\omega}_s + \bar{\omega}_s^T \bar{D}^T \bar{P} \bar{A} \xi_s + \bar{\omega}_s^T \bar{D}^T \bar{P} \bar{D} \bar{\omega}_s - \xi_s^T \bar{P} \xi_s \\ &= \eta_s^T \bar{\Phi} \eta_s \end{aligned} \tag{11}$$

where

$$\eta_s^T \triangleq \begin{bmatrix} \xi_s^T & \bar{\omega}_s^T \end{bmatrix}^T,$$

$$\bar{\Phi} \triangleq \begin{bmatrix} \bar{A}^T \bar{P} \bar{A} - \bar{P} & * \\ \bar{D}^T \bar{P} \bar{A} & \bar{D}^T \bar{P} \bar{D} \end{bmatrix}.$$

Adding the zero term $\bar{z}_s^T \bar{z}_s - \gamma^2 \bar{\omega}_s^T \bar{\omega}_s - \bar{z}_s^T \bar{z}_s + \gamma^2 \bar{\omega}_s^T \bar{\omega}_s$ to both sides of (11), it is converted to

$$
\begin{aligned}
\Delta V_s &= \eta_s^T \bar{\Phi} \eta_s + \bar{z}_s^T \bar{z}_s - \gamma^2 \bar{\omega}_s^T \bar{\omega}_s - \bar{z}_s^T \bar{z}_s + \gamma^2 \bar{\omega}_s^T \bar{\omega}_s \\
&= \eta_s^T \Phi \eta_s - \bar{z}_s^T \bar{z}_s + \gamma^2 \bar{\omega}_s^T \bar{\omega}_s.
\end{aligned}
\tag{12}
$$

Then, adding up both sides of (12) in the case of s from 0 to ∞, it is obtained

$$
\begin{aligned}
\sum_{s=0}^{\infty} \Delta V_s &= \eta_\infty^T \bar{P} \eta_\infty - \eta_0^T \bar{P} \eta_0 \\
&= \sum_{s=0}^{\infty} \eta_s^T \Phi \eta_s - \sum_{s=0}^{\infty} \bar{z}_s^T \bar{z}_s + \gamma^2 \sum_{s=0}^{\infty} \bar{\omega}_s^T \bar{\omega}_s.
\end{aligned}
$$

It follows from (10) that $\eta_s^T \Phi \eta_s < 0$. As a result

$$
\begin{aligned}
&\eta_\infty^T \bar{P} \eta_\infty - \eta_0^T \bar{P} \eta_0 + \sum_{s=0}^{\infty} \bar{z}_s^T \bar{z}_s - \gamma^2 \sum_{s=0}^{\infty} \bar{\omega}_s^T \bar{\omega}_s \\
&= \sum_{s=0}^{\infty} \eta_s^T \Phi \eta_s \leq 0.
\end{aligned}
$$

Noting that $\bar{P} > 0$, and the initial condition $\eta_0^T \bar{P} \eta_0 = 0$, it is derived

$$
\sum_{s=0}^{\infty} \bar{z}_s^T \bar{z}_s < \gamma^2 \sum_{s=0}^{\infty} \bar{\omega}_s^T \bar{\omega}_s.
$$

According to Definition 1, the proof is completed.

Next, the observer and controller gains are obtained by solving a certain matrix inequality.

Theorem 2. *Given the disturbance attenuation level $\gamma > 0$, the closed-loop MAS (8) meets the H_∞ performance constraint (9) if there exist matrices $\tilde{K}_u$, $\tilde{K}_o$ and positive definite matrices P_1, P_2 satisfying*

$$
\begin{bmatrix}
\Psi_{11} & * & * & * & * & * \\
0 & -I_L \otimes P & * & * & * & * \\
0 & 0 & -\gamma^2 I & * & * & * \\
0 & 0 & 0 & -\gamma^2 I & * & * \\
\Psi_{51} & \Psi_{52} & I_L \otimes PD & 0 & -I_L \otimes P & * \\
0 & \Psi_{62} & I_L \otimes PD & \Psi_{64} & 0 & -I_L \otimes P
\end{bmatrix} < 0
\tag{13}
$$

where

$$
\Psi_{11} \triangleq -I_L \otimes P + \mathcal{F}^T \mathcal{F} \otimes M^T M, \quad \Psi_{51} \triangleq I_L \otimes PA + \mathcal{H}_{\mu,s} \otimes B\tilde{K}_u,
$$

$$
\Psi_{52} \triangleq -\mathcal{H}_{\mu,s} \otimes B\tilde{K}_u, \quad \Psi_{62} \triangleq I_L \otimes PA - I_L \otimes \tilde{K}_o C,
$$

$$
\Psi_{64} \triangleq -I_L \otimes \tilde{K}_o E, \quad P = V_1 P_1 V_1^T + V_2 P_2 V_2^T.
$$

In addition, if the above inequality is practicable, the observer and controller gain matrices K_o and K_u can be deduced by

$$K_o = P^{-1}\tilde{K}_o,$$
$$K_u = N\Lambda^{-1}P_1^{-1}\Lambda N^T \tilde{K}_u \tag{14}$$

where matrices N, V_1 and V_2 can be obtained by Lemma 2.

Proof. By using Schur complement lemma, the inequality (10) is transformed to

$$\begin{bmatrix} \bar{P} + \bar{M}^T\bar{M} - \bar{P} & * & * \\ 0 & -\gamma^2 I & * \\ \bar{A} & \bar{D} & -\bar{P}^{-1} \end{bmatrix} < 0. \tag{15}$$

In order to convert inequality (15) to a linear matrix inequality, we perform the congruent transformation to (15) by diag$\{I, I, \bar{P}\}$. Then, from Lemma 2, matrix (13) is obtained.

4   An Illustrative Example

In this section, the effectiveness and validation of the controller designed is verified by an illustrative example.

Consider a MAS with 3 agents and the communication topology of the agents is described by a directed graph $\mathcal{G} = (\mathcal{N}, \mathcal{F}, \mathcal{H})$ with the set of agents $\mathcal{N} = \{1, 2, 3\}$ and the corresponding adjacency matrix $\mathcal{H}$ is given as follows:

$$\mathcal{H} = \begin{bmatrix} 0 & 1 & 1 \\ 1 & 0 & 1 \\ 1 & 1 & 0 \end{bmatrix}.$$

The system parameters of MAS (1) are set as follows:

$$A = \begin{bmatrix} 0.95 & 0 \\ -0.12 & 0.3 \end{bmatrix}, \quad B = \begin{bmatrix} 1 \\ 0.5 \end{bmatrix}, \quad C = \begin{bmatrix} 1 & 0 \\ 0 & 1 \end{bmatrix}, \quad M = \begin{bmatrix} 1 & 0 \\ 0 & 1 \end{bmatrix},$$
$$D = \begin{bmatrix} 0.01 & 0 \\ 0 & 0.01 \end{bmatrix}, \quad E = \begin{bmatrix} 0.01 & 0 \\ 0 & 0.01 \end{bmatrix}.$$

The initial conditions of the states are selected as $x_{1,0} = \begin{bmatrix} 1 & -1 \end{bmatrix}^T$, $x_{2,0} = \begin{bmatrix} 2 & -2 \end{bmatrix}^T$, $x_{3,0} = \begin{bmatrix} 1.5 & -1.5 \end{bmatrix}^T$. The external disturbances are chosen as $\omega_s = 0.1\sin(s)$, $\nu_s = 0.1\cos(s)$, and the H_∞ consensus control performance index is set as $\gamma = 0.6$. The simulation results are presented in Figs. 1, 2 and 3, where Fig. 1 plots the state curves of the three agents, Fig. 2 plots the consensus errors of the controlled output of three agents, and Fig. 3 plots the observation errors of three agents. Clearly, from these figures, it can be seen that the observed states are almost consistent with the actual states and the MAS (1) have good consensus behavior. Therefore, the control algorithm proposed in this paper is indeed effective.

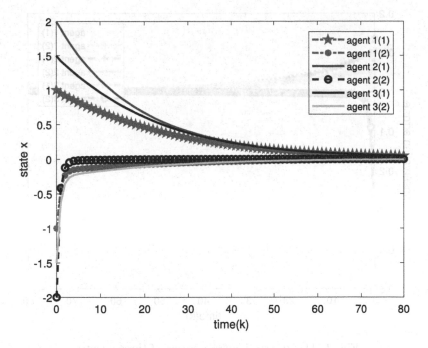

Fig. 1. The state curves of three agents

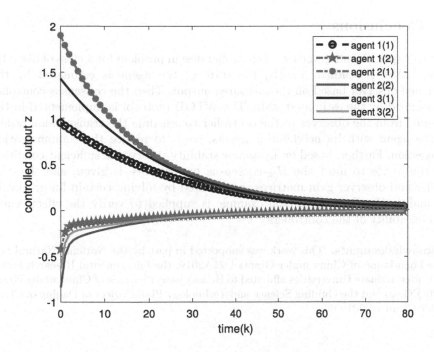

Fig. 2. The controlled output curves of three agents

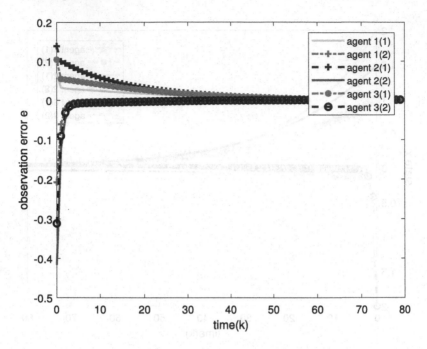

Fig. 3. The observation error curves of three agents.

5   Conclusions

In this paper, the observer-based controller design problem for a class of discrete-time MASs is studied. Firstly, the state of the agent is estimated by the designed observer based on the measured output. Then the consensus controller is designed by the estimated state. The WTOD protocol is implemented in the channel from the observer to the controller to schedule the transmission orders of the agent with its neighboring agents, so as to reduce the communication congestion. Further, based on Lyapunov stability theory, the sufficient condition for the MASs to meet the H_∞-consensus performance is given, and the controller and observer gain matrices are acquired by solving certain linear matrix inequality. Finally, a numerical example is supplied to verify the effectiveness and feasibility of the controllers.

Acknowledgements. This work was supported in part by the National Natural Science Foundation of China under Grants U21A2019, the Fundamental Research Funds for Undergraduate Universities affiliated to Heilongjiang Province of China under Grant 2020QNL-04 and the Guiding Science and Technology Plan Project of Daqing of China under Grant zd-2019-06.

References

1. Shi, T.F., et al.: Sequence to sequence multi-agent reinforcement learning algorithm. Pattern Recognit. Artif. Intell. **34**(3), 206–213 (2021)
2. Ho, F., et al.: Decentralized multi-agent path finding for UAV traffic management. IEEE Trans. Intell. Transp. Syst. **2**(23), 1–12 (2020)
3. Nguyen, B.M., et al.: Longitudinal modelling and control of in-wheel-motor electric vehicles as multi-agent systems. Energies **13**(20), 5437–5464 (2020)
4. Gao, C., et al.: Consensus control of linear multiagent systems under actuator imperfection: when saturation meets fault. IEEE Trans. Syst. Man Cybern. Syst. **52**(4), 2651–2663 (2021). https://doi.org/10.1109/TSMC.2021.3050370
5. Xu, W.Y., et al.: Finite horizon consensus for multi-agent systems with redundant channels via an observer-type event-triggered scheme. IEEE Trans. Cybern. **48**(5), 1567–1576 (2018)
6. Zou, L., et al.: Communication-protocol-based analysis and synthesis of networked systems: progress, prospects and challenges. Int. J. Syst. Sci. **52**(14), 3013–3034 (2021)
7. Li, X.R., et al.: Set-membership filtering for piecewise linear systems with censored measurements under Round-Robin protocol. Int. J. Syst. Sci. **51**(9), 1571588 (2020)
8. Song, J.B., et al.: Finite-horizon distributed H_∞-consensus control of time-varying multi-agent systems with Round-Robin protocol. Neurocomputing **364**, 219–226 (2019)
9. Zhu, K., et al.: On ℓ_2-ℓ_∞ output-feedback control scheduled by stochastic communication protocol for two-dimensional switched systems. Int. J. Syst. Sci. **52**(14), 2961–2976 (2021)
10. Zou, L., et al.: Finite-horizon H_∞-consensus control of time-varying multi-agent systems with stochastic communication protocol. IEEE Trans. Cybern. **47**(8), 1830–1840 (2017)
11. Wang, D., et al.: Finite-horizon filtering for complex networks with state saturations: the weighted try-once-discard protocol. Int. J. Robust Nonlinear Control **29**(7), 2096–2111 (2019)
12. Wen, G.G., et al.: Observer-based output consensus of leader-following fractional-order heterogeneous nonlinear multi-agent systems. Int. J. Control **10**(93), 2516–2524 (2019)
13. Xie, X.X., et al.: Observer-based consensus control of nonlinear multi-agent systems under semi-Markovian switching topologies and cyber attacks. Int. J. Robust Nonlinear Control **30**, 5510–5528 (2020)
14. Zhang, J.N., et al.: Observer-based non-fragile H_∞-consensus control for multi-agent systems under deception attacks. Int. J. Syst. Sci. **52**(6), 1223–1236 (2021)
15. Xiong, T.Y., et al.: Observer-based adaptive fixed-time formation control for multi-agent systems with unknow ncertainties. Neurocomputing **432**, 506–517 (2021)
16. Han, F., et al.: Outlier-resistant observer-based H_∞-consensus control for multi-rate multi-agent systems. J. Franklin Inst. **358**(17), 8914–8928 (2021)
17. Horn, R.A., Johnson, C.R.: Topics in Matrix Analysis. Cambridge University Press, Cambridge (1994)
18. Han, F., et al.: Finite-horizon H_∞-consensus control for multi-agent systems with random parameters: the local condition case. J. Franklin Inst. **354**(14), 6078–6097 (2017)

Applications of Kalman Filtering in Time Series Prediction

Xuegui Li[1,2,3,4], Shuo Feng[1,2,3(✉)], Nan Hou[1,2,3,4], Hanyang Li[1,2,3],
Shuai Zhang[1,2,3], Zhen Jian[2], and Qianlong Zi[2]

[1] Artificial Intelligence Energy Research Institute,
Northeast Petroleum University, Daqing, China
fengshuo12169@163.com
[2] School of Computer and Information Technology,
Northeast Petroleum University, Daqing, China
[3] Heilongjiang Provincial Key Laboratory of Networking and Intelligent Control,
Northeast Petroleum University, Daqing, China
[4] Sanya Offshore Oil and Gas Research Institute,
Northeast Petroleum University, Sanya, China

Abstract. With the development of big data techniques, various data
are accumulated and used for time series prediction. As an optimal estimation algorithm, Kalman filtering (KF) is a useful method in realizing
time series prediction for linear systems. In this paper, the characteristics
of KF and its derivative algorithms (KFDAs) are analyzed and summarized. The existing application results about KFDAs are reviewed respectively in carrying on time series prediction of wind speed and finance.
The available comparison results of KFDAs and neural network models
are surveyed and discussed on conducting time series prediction, and it
is revealed that KFDAs usually outperform neural network.

Keywords: Time series prediction · Kalman filter · Extend Kalman
filter · Unscented Kalman filter · Cubature Kalman filter · Neural
network

1 Introduction

Time series, which is a set of observations made over a period of time, offers a
basis for a significant number of applications for life [22,29]. With the development of the Internet and big data, a large amount of data has been accumulated
in various fields such as finance, industry, production and living. Time series prediction has become a recurring topic of research initiating a multitude of studies
and developments, which is a method to predict the future with known past
data and has a board range of applications. There are many methods for time
series prediction [41], such as Box-Jenkins [9,48], mean regression, autoregressive
[23], ARIMA and exponential smoothing prediction (Holt-Winters). Traditional
methods for time series prediction estimate the parameters of the time series
model to predict [42,43] and have some restrictions.

H. Liu et al. (Eds.): ICIRA 2022, LNAI 13457, pp. 520–531, 2022.
https://doi.org/10.1007/978-3-031-13835-5_47

Kalman filtering (KF) is one of the numerous novel methods frequently used for time series prediction [52]. Proposed in [40], KF has been first used by the Apollo spacecraft of the United States. KF, which is based on state space equation [59–61], used to be employed for state estimation including target tracking [30,50], noise reduction [16], location [11] and so on. Since the pioneering work in [45], a significant number of researchers have poured effort into time series prediction with KF [20,52], which would be summarized and analyzed in this paper.

Neural network (NN) is an effective method for time series prediction [2,6,31, 39,44,54,58]. The model of MLP neuron has been presented in [51]. However, due to the backwardness of computer hardware and other reasons, the development of NN has almost stagnated. The artificial program AlphaGo invented by Google has beaten the world champion of the game of Go. The success of AlphaGo has inspired scholars to pull more attention to study and develop NNs. In recent years, remarkable success has been seen on NN in a multitude of applications [3,18,28]. With the development of NN, a quantity of NN models have been put forward for time series prediction [6,35,57]. NN prediction methods, which not only have strong abilities of processing uncertainty and generalization but also have anti-interference ability, can handle uncertainty factors. It is found that NN and KF have been adopted for time series prediction by various scholars. Besides, they have also been set as control experiments in a large number of research results. However, there are few researches on the comparison of NN and KF for time series prediction. Therefore, the comparison of these two methods is searched to fill the gaps in related fields. *The contributions of this survey are summarized as follows: 1) the principle and the characteristic of KF and its derivative algorithms (KFDAs) are introduced in detail, which can help other researchers acquire relevant knowledge quickly; 2) the applications of KFDAs are summarized and analyzed for time series prediction; and 3) the KFDAs and NN are compared for time series prediction, and the research gaps and potential research directions are discussed.*

The rest of the paper is organized as follows. In Sect. 2, KFDAs are portrayed at length. Results about the utilization of KFDAs are presented in Sect. 3. The comparisons of NN and KF are summarized and analyzed in Sect. 4. Finally, conclusions are given in Sect. 5.

2   Detailed Description of KFDAs

KF, a vital tool for state estimation, has been expanding rapidly. It has been applied to a large number of fields. In this section, KFDAs will be introduced in detail.

2.1   Principle of Kalman Filtering

KF, which is calibrated by external observation, is a method of estimating objective probability based on subjective probability. In essence, KF is a method which obtains the posteriori optimal estimation according to the priori estimation and experimental observation results. KF takes the result estimated at the previous moment as the current priori estimation. Prediction step and correction step are two steps in KF. KF calculates recursively along the time chain. In fact, KF is an optimal recursive algorithm for data processing based on Markov chain. The covariance matrix $P_{k|k}$ not only estimates the uncertainty factors of the calculation process but also realizes the linkage relationships between variables. The history information of estimated variable is hidden in the covariance matrix. Consequently, KF needs a small amount of data storage to process and can update data in real time.

KF, which uses both the state equation and the observation data of the system to iterate continuously, provides a solution for prediction problem. The posterior, which is corrected by the current measurement, is obtained by the prior. KF gives an efficient recursive means of estimating the states of a process by minimizing the mean of the squared error [15, 19]. KF is not only the optimal filter among a subset of all linear filters, but also the best filter among all filters when the noise processes are Gaussian [5]. However, KF has strict application conditions. KF, which optimizes auto regressive data, is a linear-quadratic estimator. It can only be applied in linear and Gaussian systems, assuming that the process noise and the measurement noise of the system are both white Gaussian noise. Therefore, the process noise and the measurement noise obey normal distribution in the whole prediction process. Random variables with normal distribution will no longer be normally distributed after passing the nonlinear system. Thus, KF is only applicable to linear systems. However, most problems are nonlinear ones in real life. KF needs to be improved before being applied to real-world problems. Consequently, by the linearization of the nonlinear function or by other methods, the derivative algorithms of KF, such as Extended Kalman Filter (EKF), Unscented Kalman filter (UKF), Cubature Kalman filter (CKF) and so on, are designed to extend KF to nonlinear systems.

2.2 Explanation on Extended Kalman Filter

In EKF, the state mean and covariance are updated by linearization [15]. Function fitting is a mathematical transformation method for nonlinear functions to be linearized [27]. In EKF, the states of the nonlinear system are estimated by function fitting. By linearizing the nonlinear system with a linear function, the conditions of using KF are satisfied. For EKF, Taylor expansion method is adopted to linearize the nonlinear state transition function. EKF and KF have the same algorithm structure and assumption. At each time step of EKF, nonlinear system is transformed into linear time-varying system by first-order Taylor expansion to forecast and update parameters. When using Taylor expansion approximation, the high-order terms are directly ignored by EKF, which inevitably introduces linear errors. Thus, the prediction of EKF accuracy is reduced. In addition, the state transition matrix and the observation matrix of EKF, which need to be used in calculating the covariance matrix, are both obtained by Jacobi matrix of the nonlinear functions. The process of calculating Jacobian matrix is complex and requires huge computing resources, in which errors may occur. Although the use conditions of KF are met by using Taylor expansion, both the prediction error and the amount of calculation increase a lot.

EKF approximates the nonlinear function of system through Taylor expansion, which has the advantages of concise algorithm structure and easy implementation by computer. However, due to the negligence of high-order term of Taylor expansion, EKF is only suitable for systems with weak nonlinearity. Otherwise, the error will rise sharply and the filtering accuracy will be reduced heavily.

2.3   Statement of Unscented Kalman Filter

Because of its limitations, EKF can only be applied to weak nonlinear systems. To solve high dimensional nonlinear filtering problems and obtain better filtering effect, UKF has been proposed based on Unscented Transformation (UT) [46]. To update and forecast the state variable, in EKF, the nonlinear function is approximated into a linear function in the way of Taylor expansion. For UKF, the probability density function is approximated to realize the approximation of nonlinear function. The basic idea of UKF is to approximate a Gaussian distribution by calculating the statistics of a set of random variable which undergoes a nonlinear transformation [46]. The priori knowledge of the system is hidden in the mean and the covariance of sigma points which are chosen according to a specific and deterministic algorithm called UT. The mean and the covariance of the sigma points are equal to those of the state samples. Each point of sigma points set is substituted into the nonlinear function to obtain the new points set. The new points set has the same mean and covariance with the state variables after nonlinear state transition. Therefore, the expansion of sigma points set and nonlinear mapping are carried out through UT to forecast the state variable of next time step. For filtering applications, UT, which avoids the error of linearization process, is preferable than Taylor expansion method. Meanwhile, UKF does not require calculate Jacobian matrix, which can enhance operation speed.

UKF employs UT and uses the probability density function of the sigma points to approximate the probability density function of state variables. Through transferring nonlinear measurement functions, the new points set is obtained and the state variable is updated. Compared with EKF, UKF not only has excellent estimation accuracy, but also implements conveniently and fast. UKF can predict the mean and the covariance with second order accuracy [12]. If the dimension of nonlinear system is higher than third order, then UKF will become unstable and diverge. Consequently, UKF is also not applicable to high-order nonlinear systems.

2.4   Analysis on Cubature Kalman Filter

In order to solve the problem that UKF and EKF are not applicable in high-dimensional nonlinear systems, CKF has been proposed which is based on a third-degree spherical-radial cubature rule [26]. Cubature transform is adopted in CKF to generate cubature points. A good set of points, entailing $2n$ cubature points for the n-dimensional state vector, always has two properties. All the points not only have the positive weights, but also lie inside the region of integration [26]. CKF approximates the statistical characteristics of Z with $2n$ cubature points, and the posterior probability density function is calculated through the set of cubature points. The core concept of CKF is to parameterize the mean and the variance of the probability distribution. A standard update process is completed by the time update, the measurement update and the corresponding update of error covariance. The nonlinear transformation is applied to each point of the cubature points set. Thus, $2n$ functional evaluations are required to compute at each time step.

KF is only applicable to linear systems, while EKF, UKF and CKF all can handle nonlinear factors. EKF ignores the high-order term of Taylor expansion, which can only be used in first-order nonlinear system. UKF can deal with various problems in second-order nonlinear systems with ease. CKF not only can handle third-order nonlinear factors, but also has superior stability. EKF uses Taylor expansion to linearize the nonlinear function and calculate the derivative and Jacobi matrix. While UKF and CKF generate point sets through rules to approximate Gaussian probability density, which has no derivative and do not require calculation of Jacobi matrix. Thus, UKF and CKF can be written into computer programs in advance. Both UKF and CKF generate points sets and calculate the approximate Gaussian distribution after nonlinear transformation according to the transformed points sets. There are some differences between UKF and CKF due to the different generating rules of points. UKF has strong dependence on parameters, while CKF does not require any free parameter.

3   KFDAs for Wind Speed and Finance Series Prediction

In recent years, KFDAs have been investigated widely for time series prediction. In this paper, researches about KFDAs have been reviewed, which are applied in wind series prediction and finance series prediction to analyse the characteristic.

Wind energy plays a significant role in renewable energy. The accurate information of wind speed is required to be obtained, which can improve and optimize generation of wind resources. In [21], three two-year-long sets of wind speed data have been used to predict the wind speed at the wind farm site of Varese Ligure in Northern Italy. The data of the three data sets are derived from NWP simulating data, two anemometric masts measurement data and wind farm data. The first two data sets are used for KF prediction, and the last data set is used to verify the accuracy of KF prediction. The state space equations, which are rich and vary according to different problems, are obtained from previous research. With the state space equations and experiment data sets, KF implements without a hitch. The experimental results indicate that the method of KF can improve the accuracy of prediction and reduce the systematic errors. A novel hybrid method combing support vector regression (SVR) and UKF has been introduced in [7] for short-term wind speed prediction. The wind speed sequences for experiment are collected from three sites in United States every 10 min at the same position. SVR is employed to get the state space equations for UKF, and the wind sequence is estimated by UKF recursively. It is shown that the hybrid scheme can enhance the accuracy of prediction, reliability and robustness.

Financial sequences prediction is a significant branch of time series prediction which contains stock prices, market indexes, and so on. Financial time series has the characteristic of randomness, weak stationarity and aggregation, and is influenced by a large amount of factors including social policies, market changes and company operations. Many teams investigate financial time series for preferably investment strategy. We are to analyze some applications of KFDAs in financial sequences prediction to get further study of KFDAs. In [49], the method has been put forward of predicting the stock prices time sequences with KF. The state space equations of KF are established by the corresponding mathematical difference equations according to the relationship between stock prices. The presented scheme is applied to a data set of original stock price of Sichuan Changhong. It is shown that KF can calculate fast with high estimation accuracy. The UKF algorithm has been investigated in [1] for noisy multivariate financial time-series data prediction. The experiments are taken on the eleven-year-long data sets of KLCI stock indices, and the state space equations are got from previous research. The experimental simulations indicate that the estimations of UKF are smoothed with less noisy interference. In [8], KF has been adopted to obtain the relationship between contemporaneous logarithm volatility changes and logarithm stock index, and the state space equations are established on the regression model of previous research. Through working on a seven-year-long data set of daily data of OVX and oil prices, the negative relationship is found by KF method between negative crude oil spot returns and OVX changes.

By reviewing the prediction of KFDAs in wind speed and financial sequences, it can be concluded that KFDAs have the strength of fast calculation speed, easy implementation and being packaged in the program. Besides, KFDAs are capable of estimating the sequences with high accuracy by combining the priori knowledge with observation information. However, there are some limitations of KFDAs for time series prediction. The state space equations are required to be established before the estimation. The state transition function is hard to acquire which is established by various methods such as mathematical method and regression model. It is found that the number of studies is growing examining the use of NN to determine the function, which may be another research topic.

4   Comparison of KFDAs and NN in Time Series Prediction

NN is a favorable tool for prediction. To get further study of KFDAs for time series prediction, we do a survey on existing comparison results between KF and NN for prediction.

A rich body of literature has been available on comparison between KF and NN. For example, a structured neural network (SNN) algorithm has been proposed in [14] based on knowledge. SNN and EKF which is a well-established method are compared in estimating the state of health determination of lithium-ion batteries. Through experiments, it is found that SNN requires some time to train the given functions, while EKF does not. Moreover, SNN has a lower computational complexity and consumes less time than EKF which needs to calculate Kalman gain and a covariance matrix of $n \times n$ at every sample step. In [4], a wavelet neural network (WNN) model has been proposed which is established and optimized by Levenberg-Marquardt algorithm to estimate the state of charge of lithium-ion batteries. Comparing with EKF and BP, WNN has better performance not only on accuracy but also on robustness. In [13], 119 works have been reviewed on the estimation of vehicle sideslip angle in total which can not be measured directly. The approach based on KF has high robustness against input and measurement noise. The NN-based approach is more suitable for real-time environment, but has poor capability to deal with any environmental and vehicle-physical changes.

To estimate Soil Moisture Deficit, four data fusion techniques have been studied including Linear Weighted Algorithm, Multiple Linear Regression, KF and ANN [37]. The result shows that KF and ANN involve more expertise, need more time for computation, and have a higher capability for data fusion than the other two methods. Meanwhile, ANN outperforms all the other data fusion techniques. In [55], a hierarchical ANN model has been proposed to predict real-time arrival time of bus. The proposed model can be superior to the KF model in accuracy. In [38], an efficient Dempster Shafer NN algorithm has been proposed, which is more suitable for non-linear systems than EKF. The proposed method can acquire good performance by a large amount of training data. In [24], the relevance vector machine algorithm has been used for predicting bus headway. The proposed model confirms higher precision and stronger robustness than KF, SVM, KNN, GA-SVM and ANN, although it requires a large amount of computational resources. In [32], RNN and KF have been employed for sequence classification of the limit order book. RNN can capture the non-linear relationship between the near-term price-flips and a spatio-temporal representation of the limit order book. Comparing with KF, RNN is more suitable for predicting and sequence classification. BP and UKF are adopted to estimate human multi-joint angles from surface electromyography. The results show that the predictions of UKF have less large deviations from the real values than those of BP. Furthermore, the predicted results of UKF are smooth.

In [56], an ANN scheme has been portrayed for speed estimation and EKF has been set as the control experiment. The results of the experiment of calculating the speed of the mathematical model show that ANN outperforms EKF with reasonable accuracy. In [10], an adaptive network architecture has been investigated, which utilizes both fuzzy model and artificial neural network (ANN) for state-of-available-power prediction for a lithium-ion battery pack. Compared with robust extended Kalman Filter, the novel NN shows better results with the capability of real-time operation. Switching Kalman filter (SKF) has been applied in [36] for multimodal degradation prognostics. SKF ensembles display better robustness against noise and prognostic accuracy over traditional methods. In [25], NARX model and ANN have been adopted for identification of nonlinear dynamic system, which not only exhibit robust characteristics and fast convergence properties but also are computed faster. ANN based on a polynomial least-squares approximation has been presented for trajectory prediction of cyclists in [47]. The accuracy of the new method is higher than that of KF.

In [34], both BP, KF and Luenberger observer have been employed to estimate system states, disturbances and clutch torques of modular multi-speed transmission system for electric vehicles. The simulation results show that the Kalman filter has better performance than the other two methods. Short Term Memory (STM) NN has been used for simultaneous localization and consistent mapping in [53]. Compared with EKF, the creative new method has Lyapunov stability without the lag of convergence. In addition, STM enhances the performance not only in static environments but also in dynamic environments. An ANN algorithm has been brought forward in [33] for trajectory forecast of pedestrian, and 150 pedestrian trajectories have been used for testing. The results indicate that the ANN has excellent performance in position. On the other hand, in [17], a hybrid WNN model has been proposed for state of charge estimation. Compared with EKF, the proposed method has been proved to be more effective with robustness evaluation results.

KF transfers the historical information to the estimated variable by error covariance. By combing error covariance and measured value, the variable can be estimated in real time. While NN establishes model parameters according to the training and fitting of historical data and other data. Through the above literature review, it is found that in most cases, NN behaves better than KFDAs on the prediction accuracy, and KFDAs has faster calculation speed. In addition, NN can handle the nonlinear factors of nonlinear system better. Although some KFDAs, like EKF and UKF, are nonlinear transformed or fitted, the error of those methods cannot be ignored in the progress of predicting. The measure noise and the process noise of KFDAs cannot follow the change of system. By comparing some appearing results, some common features have been found of the cases that KFDAs have better performance than NN. Multi-parameters have been predicted in these literatures. So, it may be able to come to the conclusion that the effect of NN in multi-parameters prediction needs to be further improved. In general, KFDAs show preferable performance in most cases. However, the ability of KFDAs to manage the nonlinear factors is required to be further improved. Moreover, KF has excellent performance in multi-objective simultaneous prediction, and the results of KFDAs for multi-objective prediction are superior.

5 Conclusions

In this paper, a detailed discussion has been made of KF, EKF, UKF and CKF. Results have been reviewed about KFDAs prediction in wind speed and financial sequences estimation. Also, achievements have been surveyed on the comparison of KFDAs and NN in prediction. The regular pattern and the characteristics have been found out for KFDAs usage in time series prediction. KFDAs with established state space equation have been indicated to be suitable for time series prediction, which own merits including low computation cost, simple storage structure and high accuracy. It should be pointed that the state space equation is hard to be obtained according to the specific problems. A trend has been revealed of building the functions by NN through literature review, and establishing the state equation by NN has been regarded as the future work to be studied further.

Acknowledgements. This work was supported in part by the National Natural Science Foundation of China under Grants U21A2019, 61873058, 62073070, 62103096 and 11902072, the Heilongjiang Postdoctoral Foundation under Grant LBH-Z18045, the Hainan Province Science and Technology Special Fund of China under Grant ZDYF2022SHFZ105, the Fundamental Research Funds for Provincial Undergraduate Universities of Heilongjiang Province of China under Grant 2018QNL-56, the Technology Plan Project of Daqing City of China under Grants zd-2019-17 and zd-2020-26, and the Alexander von Humboldt Foundation of Germany.

References

1. Jadid Abdulkadir, S., Yong, S.-P.: Unscented Kalman filter for noisy multivariate financial time-series data. In: Ramanna, S., Lingras, P., Sombattheera, C., Krishna, A. (eds.) MIWAI 2013. LNCS (LNAI), vol. 8271, pp. 87–96. Springer, Heidelberg (2013). https://doi.org/10.1007/978-3-642-44949-9_9
2. Waibel, A.: Modular construction of time-delay neural networks for speech recognition. Neural Comput. **1**(1), 39–46 (1989)
3. Öztürk, A.E., Erçelebi, E.: Real UAV-bird image classification using CNN with a synthetic dataset. Appl. Sci. **11**(9), 3863:1–3863:17 (2021)
4. Xia, B., et al.: State of charge estimation of lithium-ion batteries using optimized Levenberg-Marquardt wavelet neural network. Energy **153**, 694–705 (2018)
5. Anderson, B.D.O., Moore, J.B., Eslami, M.: Optimal filtering. IEEE Trans. Syst. Man Cybern. **12**(2), 235–236 (1982)
6. Lim, B., Zohren, S.: Time-series forecasting with deep learning: a survey. Phil. Trans. Roy. Soc. A **379**(2194), 20200209 (2021)
7. Zuluaga, C.D., Álvarez, M.A., Giraldo, E.: Short-term wind speed prediction based on robust Kalman filtering: an experimental comparison. Appl. Energy **156**, 321–330 (2015)
8. Chen, Y., Zou, Y.: Examination on the relationship between OVX and crude oil price with Kalman filter. Procedia Comput. Sci. **55**, 1359–1365 (2015)
9. Chiu, C.-C., Su, C.-T.: A novel neural network model using Box-Jenkins technique and response surface methodology to predict unemployment rate. In: Proceedings Tenth IEEE International Conference on Tools with Artificial Intelligence (Cat. No. 98CH36294), pp. 74–80 (1998)
10. Fleischer, C., Waag, W., Bai, Z., Sauer, D.U.: Adaptive on-line state-of-available-power prediction of lithium-ion batteries. J. Power Electron. **13**(4), 516–527 (2013)
11. Hide, C., Moore, T., Smith, M.: Adaptive Kalman filtering for low-cost INS/GPS. J. Navig. **56**(1), 143–152 (2003)
12. Dini, D.H., Mandic, D.P., Julier, S.J.: A widely linear complex unscented Kalman filter. IEEE Sig. Process. Lett. **18**(11), 623–626 (2011)
13. Daniel, C., Basilio, L., Marco, G.: On the vehicle sideslip angle estimation: a literature review of methods, models, and innovations. Appl. Sci. **8**(3), 355 (2018)

14. Andre, D., Nuhic, A., Soczka-Guth, T., Sauer, D.U.: Comparative study of a structured neural network and an extended Kalman filter for state of health determination of lithium-ion batteries in hybrid electricvehicles. Eng. Appl. Artif. Intell. **26**(3), 951–961 (2013)

15. Simon, D.: Optimal State Estimation: Kalman, H_∞ and Nonlinear Approaches. Wiley, Hoboken (2006)

16. Walker, D.M., Mees, A.I.: Noise reduction of chaotic systems by Kalman filtering and by shadowing. Int. J. Bifurcat. Chaos **7**(03), 769–779 (1997)

17. Cui, D., et al.: A novel intelligent method for the state of charge estimation of lithium-ion batteries using a discrete wavelet transform-based wavelet neural network. Energies **11**(4), 995:1–995:18 (2018)

18. Luvizon, D.C., Picard, D., Tabia, H.: Multi-task deep learning for real-time 3D human pose estimation and action recognition. IEEE Trans. Pattern Anal. Mach. Intell. **43**(8), 2752–2764 (2021)

19. Lerro, D., Bar-Shalom, Y.: Tracking with debiased consistent converted measurements versus EKF. IEEE Trans. Aerosp. Electron. Syst. **29**(3), 1015–1022 (1993)

20. Xu, D., Wang, Y., Jia, L., Qin, Y., Dong, H.: Real-time road traffic state prediction based on ARIMA and Kalman filter. Front. Inf. Technol. Electron. Eng. **18**(2), 287–302 (2017). https://doi.org/10.1631/FITEE.1500381

21. Cassola, F., Burlando, M.: Wind speed and wind energy forecast through Kalman filtering of Numerical Weather Prediction model output. Appl. Energy **99**, 154–166 (2012)

22. Janacek, G.: Time series analysis forecasting and control. J. Time **31**(4), 303 (2010)

23. Box, G.E.P., Jenkins, G.M., Reinsel, G.C., Ljung, G.M.: Time Series Analysis: Forecasting and Control, 5th edn. Wiley, Hoboken (2015)

24. Yu, H., Wu, Z., Chen, D., Ma, X.: Probabilistic prediction of bus headway using relevance vector machine regression. IEEE Trans. Intell. Transp. Syst. **18**(7), 1772–1781 (2016)

25. Sahoo, H.K., Dash, P.K., Rath, N.P.: NARX model based nonlinear dynamic system identification using low complexity neural networks and robust H_∞ filter. Appl. Soft Comput. **13**(7), 3324–3334 (2013)

26. Arasaratnam, I., Haykin, S.: Cubature Kalman filters. IEEE Trans. Autom. Control **54**(6), 1254–1269 (2009)

27. Wang, J., Li, X., Zhang, H., Ma, H.: Survey of nonlinear filters in the framework of recursive Bayesian estimation. Comput. Sci. **37**(8), 21–25 (2010)

28. Liu, J.-E., An, F.-P.: Image classification algorithm based on deep learning-kernel function. Sci. Program. **2020**, 7607612:1–7607612:14 (2020)

29. Brockwell, P.J., Davis, R.A.: Introduction to Time Series and Forecasting, 2nd edn. Springer, New York (2003). https://doi.org/10.1007/b97391

30. Li, Y., Li, J.: Robust adaptive Kalman filtering for target tracking with unknown observation noise. In: 2012 24th Chinese Control and Decision Conference (CCDC), pp. 2075–2080 (2012)

31. Garnelo, M., et al.: Conditional neural processes. In: International Conference on Machine Learning, pp. 1704–1713 (2018)

32. Dixon, M.F.: Sequence classification of the limit order book using recurrent neural networks. J. Comput. Sci. **24**, 277–286 (2018)

33. Goldhammer, M., Doll, K., Brunsmann, U., Gensler, A., Sick, B.: Pedestrian's trajectory forecast in public traffic with artificial neural networks. In: 2014 22nd International Conference on Pattern Recognition, pp. 4110–4115 (2014)

34. Roozegar, M., Setiawan, Y.D., Angeles, J.: Design, modelling and estimation of a novel modular multi-speed transmission system for electric vehicles. Mechatronics **45**, 119–129 (2017)
35. Lara-Benítez, P., Carranza-García, M., Riquelme, J.C.: An experimental review on deep learning architectures for time series forecasting. Int. J. Neural Syst. **31**(03), 2130001 (2021)
36. Lim, P., Goh, C.K., Tan, K.C., Dutta, P.: Multimodal degradation prognostics based on switching Kalman filter ensemble. IEEE Trans. Neural Netw. Learn. Syst. **28**(1), 136–148 (2015)
37. Srivastava, P.K., Han, D., Rico-Ramirez, M.A., Al-Shrafany, D., Islam, T.: Data fusion techniques for improving soil moisture deficit using SMOS satellite and WRF-NOAH land surface model. Water Resour. Manag. **27**(15), 5069–5087 (2013). https://doi.org/10.1007/s11269-013-0452-7
38. Aggarwal, P., Bhatt, D., Devabhaktuni, V., Bhattacharya, P.: Dempster Shafer neural network algorithm for land vehicle navigation application. Inf. Sci. **253**, 26–33 (2013)
39. Qu, L., Lyu, J., Li, W., Ma, D., Fan, H.: Features injected recurrent neural networks for short-term traffic speed prediction. Neurocomputing **451**, 290–304 (2021)
40. Kalman, R.E.: A new approach to linear filtering and prediction problems. J. Basic Eng. **82**(1), 35–45 (1960)
41. Sharda, R., Patil, R.B.: Connectionist approach to time series prediction: an empirical test. J. Intell. Manuf. **3**(5), 317–323 (1992). https://doi.org/10.1007/BF01577272
42. Snyder, R.D., Ord, J.K., Koehler, A.B., McLaren, K.R., Beaumont, A.N.: Forecasting compositional time series: a state space approach. Int. J. Forecast. **33**(2), 502–512 (2017)
43. Dahlhaus, R., Wefelmeyer, W.: Asymptotically optimal estimation in misspecified time series models. Ann. Stat. **24**(3), 952–974 (1996)
44. Sharma, S., Elvira, V., Chouzenoux, E., Majumdar, A.: Recurrent dictionary learning for state-space models with an application in stock forecasting. Neurocomputing **450**, 1–13 (2021)
45. Sarkka, S., Vehtari, A., Lampinen, J.: Time series prediction by Kalman smoother with cross-validated noise density. In: 2004 IEEE International Joint Conference on Neural Networks (IEEE Cat. No. 04CH37541), pp. 1653–1657 (2004)
46. Julier, S.J., Uhlmann, J.K.: New extension of the Kalman filter to nonlinear systems. In: Signal Processing, Sensor Fusion, and Target Recognition VI, vol. 3068, pp. 182–193 (1997)
47. Zernetsch, S., Kohnen, S., Goldhammer, M., Doll, K., Sick, B.: Trajectory prediction of cyclists using a physical model and an artificial neural network. In: 2016 IEEE Intelligent Vehicles Symposium (IV), pp. 833–838 (2016)
48. Abidin, S.Z., Jalal, T.M.T., Razali, F.A., Hassim, N.H., Haron, N.F.: Comparison on estimating Malaysia gold price via nonlinear prediction method and Box-Jenkins model. In: AIP Conference Proceedings, vol. 1974, no. 1, p. 020057 (2018)
49. Tang, C., Peng, J., Deng, Y.: Application of a real-time tracking model based on Kalman filter in the prediction of stock price. Comput. Simul. **22**(9), 218–221 (2005)
50. Kirubarajan, T., Bar-Shalom, Y.: Kalman filter versus IMM estimator: when do we need the latter. IEEE Trans. Aerosp. Electron. Syst. **39**(4), 1452–1457 (2003)
51. McCulloch, W.S., Pitts, W.: A logical calculus of the ideas immanent in nervous activity. Bull. Math. Biophys. **5**(4), 115–133 (1943). https://doi.org/10.1007/BF02478259

52. Wu, X., Wang, Y.: Extended and unscented Kalman filtering based feedforward neural networks for time series prediction. Appl. Math. Model. **36**(3), 1123–1131 (2012)
53. Li, Y., Li, S., Ge, Y.: A biologically inspired solution to simultaneous localization and consistent mapping in dynamic environments. Neurocomputing **104**, 170–179 (2013)
54. Wang, Y., Smola, A., Maddix, D.C., Gasthaus, J., Januschowski, T.: Deep factors for forecasting. In: Proceedings of the International Conference on Machine Learning (ICML), pp. 9–15 (2019)
55. Lin, Y., Yang, X., Zou, N., Jia, L.: Real-time bus arrival time prediction: case study for Jinan, China. J. Transp. Eng. **139**(11), 1133–1140 (2013)
56. Aydogmus, Z., Aydogmus, O.: A comparison of artificial neural network and extended Kalman filter based sensorless speed estimation. Measurement **63**, 152–158 (2015)
57. Shen, Z., Zhang, Y., Lu, J., Xu, J., Xiao, G.: A novel time series forecasting model with deep learning. Neurocomputing **396**, 302–313 (2020)
58. Zhang, X., He, K., Bao, Y.: Error-feedback stochastic modeling strategy for time series forecasting with convolutional neural networks. Neurocomputing **459**, 234–248 (2021)
59. Tan, H., Shen, B., Peng, K., Liu, H.: Robust recursive filtering for uncertain stochastic systems with amplify-and-forward relays. Int. J. Syst. Sci. **51**(7), 1188–1199 (2020)
60. Shen, Y., Wang, Z., Shen, B., Dong, H.: Outlier-resistant recursive filtering for multi-sensor multi-rate networked systems under weighted try-once-discard protocol. IEEE Trans. Cybern. **51**(10), 4897–4908 (2021)
61. Mao, J., Sun, Y., Yi, X., Liu, H., Ding, D.: Recursive filtering of networked nonlinear systems: a survey. Int. J. Syst. Sci. **52**(6), 1110–1128 (2021)

Non-fragile Consensus Control for MASs with Dynamical Bias

Jinnan Zhang[1,3,4], Dongyan Dai[1,2,3,4(✉)], Xuerong Li[1,3,4], and Pengyu Wen[1,3,4]

[1] Artificial Intelligence Energy Research Institute, Northeast Petroleum University,
Daqing Heilongjiang 163318, China
crystal_ddy@126.com
[2] School of Science, Heilongjiang Bayi Agriculture University,
Daqing Heilongjiang 163319, China
[3] Heilongjiang Provincial Key Laboratory of Networking and Intelligent Control,
Northeast Petroleum University, Daqing Heilongjiang 163318, China
[4] Sanya Offshore Oil & Gas Research Institute, Northeast Petroleum University,
Sanya Hainan 572024, China

Abstract. This paper is concerned with the consensus control problem for a class of multi-agent systems with dynamical bias. In system analysis, dynamical bias is taken into account and an augmented state approach is used to deal with the dynamical bias. At the same time, considering the inaccuracy of the controller implementation caused by the complex and changeable environment, a non-fragile controller is proposed to suppress the resulted influence. The main task of this paper is to design an observer-based controller such that the system can achieve the bounded consensus under the influence of the dynamical bias and the controller perturbation. Furthermore, the observer and controller parameters are solved via inequality technique. In the end, a numerical example is given to check on the effectiveness of the proposed control scheme.

Keywords: Multi-agent systems · Non-fragile controller · Dynamical bias

1 Introduction

In recent years, the consensus problem of multi-agent systems(MASs) has become a current mainstream research topic due to its wide applications in many fields (such as UAV control, unmanned aerial vehicle, robot team) [1–8]. Consensus control refers to the design of a specific consensus algorithm according to the local neighboring information such that a group of autonomous agents reach a certain agreement. Consequently, the consensus control issue has been gaining particular attention [9–11].

When designing the controller strategy, the corresponding control strategy can be designed according to different problems. For example, considering the computational costs and communication resources, a consensus control strategy based on event-triggered mechanism is designed in literatures [12]. In the context of controller design, the controller parameter perturbation is one of the inevitable factors that may affect the control performance [13–16]. As such, designing a non-fragile controller that can suppress the effects of parameter perturbation on the controller performance is the first motivation of this paper.

In practical engineering, the ideal systems are almost impossible to obtain. Among them, system noise is one of the important factors that cannot be ignored in the analysis process, including white noise and other strongly correlated noise, and the latter one is called dynamical bias [17–19]. Dynamical bias is often described by a dynamic equation, which is attached to the state of the system [20, 21]. It is worth mentioning that there is still a gap in the consensus analysis of MASs with the consideration of the dynamical bias, which is another motivation of this paper.

Motivated by the above discussions, the main contributions of this paper are highlighted as follows: *1) considering the influence of the dynamical bias in the MASs, the system description is more comprehensive; 2) a non-fragile consensus controller is designed to suppress the influence from the parameter perturbation; and 3) sufficient conditions are given for the MASs to be ultimately bounded consensus in the mean square (UBCMS).*

2   Problem Formulation

For the MASs considered in this paper, the information interaction between all agents is shown by a directed graph $\mathcal{G} = (\mathcal{O}, \mathcal{T}, \mathcal{H})$, where $\mathcal{T} = \{1, 2, \cdots, N\}$, $\mathcal{T} \in \mathcal{O} \times \mathcal{O}$, $\mathcal{H} = [h_{ij}]$. Each edge of $\mathcal{T}$ is denoted by (i, j), and its adjacency element is $h_{ij} > 0$, which means agent j can send information to agent i. The Laplacian matrix is $L = \mathcal{Q} - \mathcal{H}$, where $\mathcal{Q}$ represents the set of the neighbor agents of agent i.

Considering a class of MASs composed of N agents, the dynamic structure of the ith agent is presented as follows:

$$\begin{cases} x_{i,\kappa+1} = \tilde{\mathcal{A}} x_{i,\kappa} + \tilde{\mathcal{B}} u_{i,\kappa} + \tilde{\mathcal{F}} \varphi_{i,\kappa} + \tilde{\mathcal{D}} w_{i,\kappa}, \\ y_{i,\kappa} = \tilde{\mathcal{C}} x_{i,\kappa} + \mathcal{N} v_{i,\kappa} \end{cases} \tag{1}$$

where $x_{i,\kappa} \in \mathbb{R}^{n_x}$, $y_{i,\kappa} \in \mathbb{R}^{n_y}$, $u_{i,\kappa} \in \mathbb{R}^{n_u}$ are the state vector, measurement output and control input of agent i, respectively. $w_{i,\kappa} \in \mathbb{R}$ and $v_{i,\kappa} \in \mathbb{R}$ represent the process noise and measurement noise, and their expectations and variances are $\mathbb{E}\{w_{i,\kappa}\} = 0$, $\mathbb{E}\{v_{i,\kappa}\} = 0$, $\mathbb{V}\{w_{i,\kappa}\} = w_0^2$ and $\mathbb{V}\{v_{i,\kappa}\} = v_0^2$ with w_0 and v_0 being known constants. $\tilde{\mathcal{A}}$, $\tilde{\mathcal{B}}$, $\tilde{\mathcal{C}}$, $\tilde{\mathcal{D}}$, $\tilde{\mathcal{F}}$ and $\mathcal{N}$ are known matrices of appropriate dimensions.

The dynamical bias is characterized by

$$\varphi_{i,\kappa+1} = \widetilde{\mathcal{M}} \varphi_{i,\kappa} + \varsigma_{i,\kappa}$$

where $\varphi_{i,\kappa} \in \mathbb{R}$ stands for the bias with unknown magnitude. $\varsigma_{i,\kappa}$ expresses the white noise whose expectation and variance are $\mathbb{E}\{\varsigma_{i,\kappa}\} = 0$, $\mathbb{V}\{\varsigma_{i,\kappa}\} = \varsigma_0^2$ with ς_0 being a scalar, $\widetilde{\mathcal{M}}$ is a given matrix.

Denoting $\tilde{x}_{i,\kappa} \triangleq [x_{i,\kappa}^T \ \varphi_{i,\kappa}^T]^T$ and $\theta_{i,\kappa} \triangleq [w_{i,\kappa}^T \ \varsigma_{i,\kappa}^T]^T$, one further has

$$\begin{cases} \tilde{x}_{i,\kappa+1} = \mathcal{A}\tilde{x}_{i,\kappa} + \mathcal{B}u_{i,\kappa} + \mathcal{D}\theta_{i,\kappa}, \\ y_{i,\kappa} = \mathcal{C}\tilde{x}_{i,\kappa} + \mathcal{N}v_{i,\kappa} \end{cases} \tag{2}$$

where

$$\mathcal{A} \triangleq \begin{bmatrix} \tilde{\mathcal{A}} & \tilde{\mathcal{F}} \\ 0 & \tilde{\mathcal{M}} \end{bmatrix}, \ \mathcal{B} \triangleq \begin{bmatrix} \tilde{\mathcal{B}} \\ 0 \end{bmatrix}, \ \mathcal{D} \triangleq \begin{bmatrix} \tilde{\mathcal{D}} & 0 \\ 0 & I \end{bmatrix}, \ \mathcal{C} \triangleq \begin{bmatrix} \tilde{\mathcal{C}} & 0 \end{bmatrix}.$$

The following control algorithm is proposed for agent i:

$$\begin{cases} \hat{x}_{i,\kappa+1} = \mathcal{A}\hat{x}_{i,\kappa} + \mathcal{B}u_{i,\kappa} + G(y_{i,\kappa} - \mathcal{C}\hat{x}_{i,\kappa}), \\ u_{i,\kappa} = (\mathcal{K} + \Delta\mathcal{K}) \sum_{j \in \mathcal{N}_i} h_{ij}(\hat{x}_{i,\kappa} - \hat{x}_{j,\kappa}) \end{cases} \tag{3}$$

where $\hat{x}_{i,\kappa} \in \mathbb{R}^{n_x}$ is the observer state of the ith agent, G and $\mathcal{K}$ are appropriately dimensioned gains to be designed later, and the gain fluctuation $\Delta\mathcal{K}$ satisfies

$$\Delta\mathcal{K} = \mathcal{K}\mathcal{S}_1\tilde{\mathcal{K}}\mathcal{S}_2, \ \tilde{\mathcal{K}}^T\tilde{\mathcal{K}} \leq I$$

where $\mathcal{S}_1$ and $\mathcal{S}_2$ are given matrices with suitable dimensions.

Denoting $e_{i,\kappa} \triangleq \tilde{x}_{i,\kappa} - \hat{x}_{i,\kappa}$, $e_\kappa \triangleq \text{col}_N[e_{i,\kappa}]$, $\tilde{x}_\kappa \triangleq \text{col}_N[\tilde{x}_{i,\kappa}]$, $\hat{x}_\kappa \triangleq \text{col}_N[\hat{x}_{i,\kappa}]$, $u_\kappa \triangleq \text{col}_N[u_{i,\kappa}]$, $v_\kappa \triangleq \text{col}_N[v_{i,\kappa}]$ and $\theta_\kappa \triangleq \text{col}_N[\theta_{i,\kappa}]$, the compact form of the system is written as

$$\begin{cases} \tilde{x}_{\kappa+1} = (I_N \otimes \mathcal{A} + L \otimes \mathcal{B}(\mathcal{K} + \Delta\mathcal{K}))\tilde{x}_\kappa \\ \qquad - L \otimes \mathcal{B}(\mathcal{K} + \Delta\mathcal{K})e_\kappa + (I_N \otimes \mathcal{D})\theta_\kappa, \\ e_{\kappa+1} = (I_N \otimes \mathcal{A} - I_N \otimes G\mathcal{C})e_\kappa + (I_N \otimes \mathcal{D})\theta_\kappa - (I_N \otimes G\mathcal{N})v_\kappa. \end{cases} \tag{4}$$

Letting $\bar{x}_\kappa \triangleq \text{col}_N[\bar{x}_{i,\kappa}]$ with $\bar{x}_{i,\kappa} = \tilde{x}_{i,\kappa} - (1/N)\sum_{j=1}^N \tilde{x}_{j,\kappa}$, we further have $\bar{x}_\kappa = (\mathfrak{L} \otimes I_{n_x})\tilde{x}_\kappa$ with $\mathfrak{L} \triangleq I_N - 1/N1_{N \times N}$.

Therefore, the following equation can be derived:

$$\begin{cases} \bar{x}_{\kappa+1} = (I_N \otimes \mathcal{A} + L \otimes \mathcal{B}(\mathcal{K} + \Delta\mathcal{K}))\bar{x}_\kappa \\ \qquad - \mathfrak{L}L \otimes \mathcal{B}(\mathcal{K} + \Delta\mathcal{K})e_\kappa + (\mathfrak{L}I_N \otimes \mathcal{D})\theta_\kappa, \\ e_{\kappa+1} = (I_N \otimes \mathcal{A} - I_N \otimes G\mathcal{C})e_\kappa + (I_N \otimes \mathcal{D})\theta_\kappa - (I_N \otimes G\mathcal{N})v_\kappa. \end{cases} \tag{5}$$

Defining $\xi_\kappa \triangleq [\bar{x}_\kappa^T \ e_\kappa^T]^T$ and $\eta_\kappa \triangleq [\theta_\kappa^T \ v_\kappa^T]^T$, the augmented system is obtained as

$$\xi_{\kappa+1} = A\xi_\kappa + B\eta_\kappa \tag{6}$$

where

$$A \triangleq \begin{bmatrix} I_N \otimes \mathcal{A} + L \otimes \mathcal{B}(\mathcal{K} + \Delta\mathcal{K}) & -\mathfrak{L}L \otimes \mathcal{B}(\mathcal{K} + \Delta\mathcal{K}) \\ 0 & I_N \otimes \mathcal{A} - I_N \otimes G\mathcal{C} \end{bmatrix},$$

$$B \triangleq \begin{bmatrix} \mathfrak{L}I_N \otimes \mathcal{D} & 0 \\ I_N \otimes \mathcal{D} & -I_N \otimes G\mathcal{N} \end{bmatrix}.$$

Definition 1. *Let M be a positive scalar. The considered MASs (1) is said to be UBCMS if the following condition is met*

$$\mathbb{E}\left\{\|\tilde{x}_{i,\kappa} - \tilde{x}_{j,\kappa}\|^2\right\} \le M. \tag{7}$$

3 Main Results

In this section, the bounded consensus of the considered system will be analyzed.

Theorem 1. *Consider the system affected by the dynamical bias and the gain perturbation. For the given parameters $\mathcal{K}$, ΔK and $0 < \mu < 1$, suppose there exists a positive definite matrix P such that*

$$A^T P A + (\mu - 1)P < 0 \tag{8}$$

holds, then the MASs (1) is UBCMS.

Proof. Choosing the Lyapunov function $V(\kappa, \xi_\kappa) \triangleq \xi_\kappa^T P \xi_\kappa$, the difference of $V(\xi_\kappa)$ in the statistical sense is calculated as follows:

$$
\begin{aligned}
\mathbb{E}\{\Delta V(\kappa, \xi_\kappa)\} &= \mathbb{E}\{\xi_{\kappa+1}^T P \xi_{\kappa+1} - \xi_\kappa^T P \xi_\kappa\} \\
&= \mathbb{E}\{\xi_\kappa^T (A^T P A - P)\xi_\kappa + \operatorname{tr}\{\Gamma\} + \mu V(\kappa, \xi_\kappa) - \mu V(\kappa, \xi_\kappa)\} \\
&= \mathbb{E}\{\xi_\kappa^T (A^T P A - P + \mu P)\xi_\kappa\} + \operatorname{tr}\{\Gamma\} - \mu \mathbb{E}\{V(\kappa, \xi(\kappa))
\end{aligned}
$$

where $\Gamma \triangleq B^T P B W_0$ with $W_0 \triangleq \operatorname{diag}\{w_0^2 I, \varsigma_0^2 I, v_0^2 I\}$. Furthermore, one has

$$\mathbb{E}\{V(\kappa + 1, \xi_{\kappa+1})\} - \mathbb{E}\{V(\kappa, \xi_\kappa)\} < \operatorname{tr}\{\Gamma\} - \mu \mathbb{E}\{V(\kappa, \xi_\kappa)\}.$$

For any scalar $\alpha > 0$ and $\varrho \triangleq \alpha - \alpha\mu - 1$, we easily have

$$
\begin{aligned}
&\alpha^{\kappa+1} \mathbb{E}\{V(\kappa + 1, \xi_{\kappa+1})\} - \alpha^\kappa \mathbb{E}\{V(\kappa, \xi_\kappa)\} \\
&< \alpha^{\kappa+1}\left(\operatorname{tr}\{\Gamma\} - \mu \mathbb{E}\{V(\kappa, \xi_\kappa)\}\right) + \alpha^\kappa(\alpha - 1)\mathbb{E}\{V(\kappa, \xi_\kappa)\} \\
&= \alpha^\kappa \varrho \mathbb{E}\{V(\kappa, \xi_\kappa)\} + \alpha^{\kappa+1}\operatorname{tr}\{\Gamma\}.
\end{aligned}
$$

Letting $\alpha = \frac{1}{1-\mu}$ and summing the both sides of κ from 0 to $\vartheta - 1$, we obtain

$$\alpha^\vartheta \mathbb{E}\{V(\vartheta, \xi_\vartheta)\} - \mathbb{E}\{V(0, \xi_0)\} < \frac{\alpha(1 - \alpha^\vartheta)}{1 - \alpha}\operatorname{tr}\{\Gamma\},$$

which indicates that

$$
\begin{aligned}
\mathbb{E}\{V(\vartheta, \xi_\vartheta)\} &< \alpha^{-\vartheta}\left(\mathbb{E}\{V(0, \xi_0)\} + \frac{\alpha}{1 - \alpha}\operatorname{tr}\{\Gamma\}\right) + \frac{\alpha}{\alpha - 1}\operatorname{tr}\{\Gamma\} \\
&= (1 - \mu)^\vartheta\left(\mathbb{E}\{V(0, \xi_0)\} - \frac{\operatorname{tr}\{\Gamma\}}{\mu}\right) + \frac{\operatorname{tr}\{\Gamma\}}{\mu}.
\end{aligned}
$$

It is worth noting that $\mathbb{E}\{V(\vartheta,\xi_\vartheta)\} \geq \lambda_{\min}(P)\mathbb{E}\{\|\xi_\vartheta\|^2\}$, and thus we acquire

$$\mathbb{E}\{\|\xi_\vartheta\|^2\} \leq \frac{\mathbb{E}\{V(\vartheta,\xi_\vartheta)\}}{\lambda_{\min}(P)}$$

$$\leq \frac{(1-\mu)^\vartheta \mathbb{E}\{V(0,\xi_0)\} + \frac{\mathrm{tr}\{\Gamma\}}{\mu}}{\lambda_{\min}(P)} \triangleq M.$$

It is obvious from the definition of ξ_κ that the system (1) is UBCMS, and the upper bound is M, which ends the proof.

On the basis of the above analysis, the observer and controller gains are designed.

Theorem 2. *Given a positive scalar $0 < \mu < 1$, the system (1) is UBCMS if there exists a symmetric positive definite matrix P, matrices Ξ_1, Ξ_2, Ξ_3, $\bar{K}$, $\bar{G}$, and a positive scalar ε satisfying the following condition:*

$$\Omega = \begin{bmatrix} (\mu-1)P & * & * & * \\ \Omega_{21} & \Omega_{22} & * & * \\ 0 & \Omega_{32}^T & -\varepsilon I & * \\ \varepsilon\Theta_2 & 0 & 0 & -\varepsilon I \end{bmatrix} < 0 \tag{9}$$

where

$$\Omega_{21} \triangleq \begin{bmatrix} I_N \otimes \Xi\Upsilon\mathcal{A} + L \otimes K & -\mathcal{L}L \otimes K \\ 0 & I_N \otimes \Xi\Upsilon\mathcal{A} - I_N \otimes \bar{G}C \end{bmatrix},$$

$$\Omega_{22} \triangleq I \otimes (P - \Xi\Upsilon - \Upsilon^T\Xi^T), \quad K \triangleq [\bar{K}^T \quad 0]^T,$$

$$\Omega_{32} \triangleq \begin{bmatrix} L \otimes KS_1 & -\mathcal{L}L \otimes KS_1 \\ 0 & 0 \end{bmatrix}, \quad \Xi \triangleq \begin{bmatrix} \Xi_1 & \Xi_2 \\ 0 & \Xi_3 \end{bmatrix},$$

$$\Theta_2 \triangleq \begin{bmatrix} I_N \otimes S_2 & 0 \\ 0 & I_N \otimes S_2 \end{bmatrix}, \quad \Upsilon \triangleq [\mathcal{B}((\mathcal{B}^T\mathcal{B})^{-1})^T \quad \mathcal{B}^\perp]^T.$$

Furthermore, if (9) is solvable, the gain matrices can be calculated as

$$K = \Xi_1^{-1}\bar{K}, \quad G = (\Xi\Upsilon)^{-1}\bar{G}. \tag{10}$$

Proof. The proof can be obtained based on Theorem 1. By using S-procedure lemma, the parameter uncertainty ΔK can be addressed, and further we have

$$\begin{bmatrix} (\mu-1)P & * & * & * \\ \bar{\mathcal{A}} & -I \otimes P^{-1} & * & * \\ 0 & \Theta_1^T & -\varepsilon I & * \\ \varepsilon\Theta_2 & 0 & 0 & -\varepsilon I \end{bmatrix} < 0 \tag{11}$$

where

$$\bar{\mathcal{A}} \triangleq \begin{bmatrix} I_N \otimes \mathcal{A} + L \otimes B\mathcal{K} & -\mathcal{L}L \otimes B\mathcal{K} \\ 0 & I_N \otimes \mathcal{A} - I_N \otimes GC \end{bmatrix},$$

$$\Theta_1 \triangleq \begin{bmatrix} L \otimes B\mathcal{K}S_1 & -\mathcal{L}L \otimes B\mathcal{K}S_1 \\ 0 & 0 \end{bmatrix}.$$

Making congruent transformation with diag$\{I, I \otimes (\Xi \Upsilon), I, I\}$ to (11) and defining $K \triangleq [\bar{K}^T \ 0]^T = \Xi \Upsilon \mathcal{B} \mathcal{K}$ and $\bar{G} \triangleq \Xi \Upsilon G$, we arrive at (9). Meanwhile, the observer and controller parameters can be solved by (10). The proof is complete.

4   Numerical Example

This section provides a numerical example to test the validity of the proposed control scheme. An MAS with three agents is considered, and the corresponding adjacency matrix is $\mathcal{H} = [0 \ 1 \ 1; 1 \ 0 \ 1; 1 \ 1 \ 0]$.

Consider that system (1) has the following parameters:

$$\tilde{\mathcal{A}} = \begin{bmatrix} 0.18 & 0.01 \\ 0.34 & -0.26 \end{bmatrix}, \quad \tilde{\mathcal{B}} = \begin{bmatrix} -0.25 \\ -0.32 \end{bmatrix}, \quad \tilde{\mathcal{F}} = \begin{bmatrix} -0.12 \\ -0.25 \end{bmatrix}^T, \quad \tilde{\mathcal{D}} = \begin{bmatrix} -0.2 \\ -0.1 \end{bmatrix},$$

$$\tilde{\mathcal{C}} = \begin{bmatrix} 2.1 & -0.1 \end{bmatrix}, \quad \mathcal{N} = -0.43, \quad \widetilde{\mathcal{M}} = -0.26.$$

The parameters of the uncertain gain matrix are as follows:

$$S1 = \begin{bmatrix} 1 & 1 & 1 \end{bmatrix}, \quad S2 = \begin{bmatrix} 0.15 & 0.23 & 0.16 \\ 0.19 & 0.27 & 0.12 \\ 0.11 & 0.21 & 0.22 \end{bmatrix}.$$

The variances of the noises are chosen as $w_0^2 = 0.18$, $v_0^2 = 0.09$, $\varsigma_0^2 = 0.11$ and the parameter μ is defined as $\mu = 0.45$.

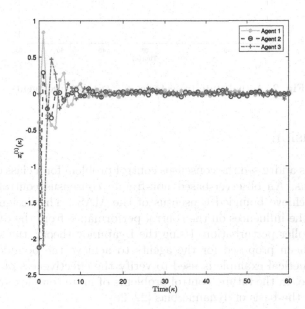

Fig. 1. Actual state trajectories $x_i^{(1)}(\kappa)$ of three agents.

By solving inequality (9), the gain matrices are calculated as

$$\mathcal{K} = \begin{bmatrix} 0.1585 & 0.0148 & -0.0446 \end{bmatrix}, \quad G = \begin{bmatrix} 0.0661 & 0.3209 & 0 \end{bmatrix}^T.$$

The state trajectories of each agent are exhibited in Figs. 1 and 2, where $x_i^{(a)}(\kappa)$ denotes the a-th element of $x_i^{(a)}(\kappa)$ $(a = 1, 2)$. It can be seen from the simulation results that after a period of time, the state of the system can eventually be consensus. Therefore, the observer-based consensus control scheme proposed in this paper can achieve a good consensus performance.

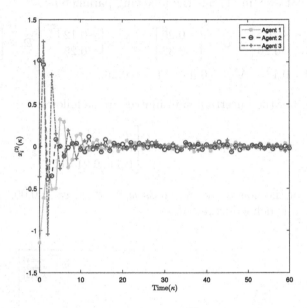

Fig. 2. Actual state trajectories $x_i^{(2)}(\kappa)$ of three agents.

5   Conclusion

This paper has addressed the consensus control problem for a class of MASs with dynamical bias. An observer-based non-fragile consensus controller has been designed to achieve bounded consensus of the MASs. The designed controller can alleviate the influences on the control performance from the dynamical bias and the controller perturbation. Using the Lyapunov theory, the sufficient conditions have been proposed for the agents to achieve the bounded consensus. Finally, a numerical example is used to verify the effectiveness of the proposed control scheme. In the future, control problems of more complex systems can be considered on the basis of dynamic bias [22–28].

Acknowledgements. This work was supported in part by the National Natural Science Foundation of China under Grants U21A2019, 61873058 and 61933007, the "Three Vertical" Scientific Research Support Project of Heilongjiang Bayi Agriculture University under Grant ZRCPY202115, the Hainan Province Science and Technology Special Fund under Grant ZDYF2022SHFZ105, and the Heilongjiang Province Postdoctoral Science Foundation of China under Grant LBH-Z21123.

References

1. Ke, J., Huang, W.C., Wang, J.Y., Zeng, J.P.: Fixed-time consensus control for multi-agent systems with prescribed performance under matched and mismatched disturbances. ISA. T. **119**, 135–151 (2021)
2. Chen, W., Wang, Z.D., Ding, D.R., Dong, H.L.: Consensusability of discrete-time multi-agent systems under binary encoding with bit errors. Automatica **133**, 109867 (2021)
3. Du, H.B., et al.: Distributed fixed-time consensus for nonlinear heterogeneous multi-agent systems. Automatica **113**, 108797 (2020)
4. Gao, C., Wang, Z.D., Dong, H.L.: Encryption-decryption-based consensus control for multi-agent systems: handling actuator faults. Automatica **134**, 1039908 (2021)
5. Xu, W.Y., Yang, S.F., Cao, J.D.: Fully distributed self-triggered control for second-order consensus of multiagent systems. IEEE. Trans. Syst. Man. Cybern. **51**(6), 3541–3551 (2021)
6. Cui, Y., Liu, Y.R., Wang, W.B., Alsaadi, F.E.: Sampled-based consensus for nonlinear multiagent systems with deception attacks: the decoupled method. IEEE. Trans. Syst. Man. Cybern. **51**(1), 561–573 (2021)
7. Liu, Z.T., et al.: Approximation-free robust synchronization control for dual-linear-motors-driven systems with uncertainties and disturbances. IEEE. Trans. Ind. Electron. **69**(10), 10500–10509 (2022)
8. Shi, P.W., et al.: Master-slave synchronous control of dual drive gantry stage with cogging force compensation. IEEE. Trans. Syst. Man. Cybern. https://doi.org/10.1109/TSMC.2022.3176952
9. Ma, T.D., et al.: Adaptive odd impulsive consensus of multi-agent systems via comparison system method. Nonlinear. Anal-Hybri. **35**, 100824 (2020)
10. Zhang, N., Zhu, J.D.: Sliding mode control for robust consensus of general linear uncertain multi-agent systems. Int. J. Control. Autom. **18**(8), 2170–2175 (2020)
11. Liu, K.X., Gu, H.B., Wang, W., Lu, J.H.: Semiglobal consensus of a class of heterogeneous multi-agent systems with saturation. IEEE. Trans. Neural Netw. Learn. **31**(11), 4946–4955 (2020)
12. Li, W., Niu, Y.G., Cao, Z.R.: Event-triggered sliding mode control for multi-agent systems subject to channel fading. Int. J. Syst. Sci. **53**(6), 1233–1244 (2022)
13. Liu, L., Ma, L.F., Zhang, J., Bo, Y.M.: Distributed non-fragile set-membership filtering for nonlinear systems under fading channels and bias injection attacks. Int. J. Syst. Sci. **52**(6), 1192–1205 (2021)
14. Zhu, K.Q., et al.: On ℓ_2-ℓ_∞ output-feedback control scheduled by stochastic communication protocol for two-dimensional switched systems. Int. J. Syst. Sci. **52**(14), 2961–2976 (2021)
15. Tian, E.G., Wang, Z.D., Zou, L., Yue, D.: Chance-constrained H_∞ control for a class of time-varying systems with stochastic nonlinearities: the finite-horizon case. Automatica **107**, 296–305 (2019)

16. Li, J.H., Dong, H.L., Liu, H.J., Han, F.: Sampled-data non-fragile state estimation for delayed genetic regulatory networks under stochastically switching sampling periods. Neurocomputing **463**, 168–176 (2021)
17. Harms, A.A., Laratta, F.: Dynamic-bias in radiation interrogation of 2-phase flow. Int. J. Heat. Mass. Transf. **16**(7), 1459–1465 (1973)
18. Qi, Y.Q., Jing, Z.L., Hu, S.Q., Zhanf, H.T.: New method for dynamic bias estimation: Gaussian mean shift registration. Opt. Eng. **47**(2), 122–122 (2008)
19. Shen, Y.X., Wang, Z.D., Dong, H.L.: Minimum-variance state and fault estimation for multi-rate systems with dynamical bias. IEEE. Trans. Circuits-II. **69**(4), 2361–2365 (2022)
20. Ching, J., Beck, J.L., Porter, K.A.: Bayesian state and parameter estimation of uncertain dynamical systems. Probabil. Eng. Mech. **21**(1), 81–96 (2006)
21. Moradkhani, H., et al.: Dual state-parameter estimation of hydrological models using ensemble Kalman filter. Adv. Water Resour. **28**(2), 135–147 (2005)
22. Li, J.H., Dong, H.L., Wang, Z.D., Bu, X.Y.: Partial-neurons-based passivity-guaranteed state estimation for neural networks with randomly occurring time-delays. IEEE. Trans. Neural Netw. Learn. **31**(9), 3747–3753 (2020)
23. Hou, N., Wang, Z.D., Ho, D.W.C., Dong, H.L.: Robust partial-nodes-based state estimation for complex networks under deception attacks. IEEE. Trans. Cybern. **50**(6), 2793–2802 (2020)
24. Li, J.H., Wang, Z.D., Dong, H.L., Yi, X.J.: Outlier-resistant observer-based control for a class of networked systems under coding-decoding mechanism. IEEE. Syst. J. **16**(1), 922–935 (2022)
25. Wen, P.Y., Dong, H.L., Huo, F.C., Li, J.H., Lu, X.Q.: Observer-based PID control for actuator-saturated systems under binary encoding scheme. Neurocomputing **499**, 54–62 (2022)
26. Bu, X.Y., Song, J.B., Huo, F.C., Yang, F.: Dynamic event-triggered resilient state estimation for time-varying complex networks with Markovian switching topologies. ISA. Trans. https://doi.org/10.1016/j.isatra.2022.05.012(2022)
27. Jiang, B., Dong, H.L., Shen, Y.X., Mu, S.J.: Encoding-decoding-based recursive filtering for fractional-order systems. IEEE-CAA. J. Autom. **9**(6), 1103–1106 (2022)
28. Song, W.H., et al.: Distributed auxiliary particle filtering with diffusion strategy for target tracking: a dynamic event-triggered approach. IEEE Trans. Signal Process. **69**, 328–340 (2021)

ResNet-BiGRU-Attention Based Facial Expression Analysis Model for a Humanoid Robot

Yang Lu[1,2]([envelope]), Xiaoxiao Wu[1], Pengfei Liu[1], Wanting Liu[1], Xinmeng Zhang[1], and Yixuan Hou[3,4]

[1] College of Information and Electrical Engineering, Heilongjiang Bayi Agricultural University, Daqing 163319, Heilongjiang, China
luyanga@sina.com
[2] Artificial Intelligence Energy Research Institute, Northeast Petroleum University, Daqing 163318, Heilongjiang, China
[3] Heilongjiang Provincial Key Laboratory of Networking and Intelligent Control, Northeast Petroleum University, Daqing 163318, Heilongjiang, China
[4] Sanya Offshore Oil and Gas Research Institute, Northeast Petroleum University, Sanya 572025, Hainan, China

Abstract. In recent years, the robot industry has developed rapidly. With the advance of technology, robots have played an important role on human life in the world. In order to achieve more and more natural and intelligent human-machine interaction, the facial expression recognition model based on ResNet-BiGRU-Attention is proposed in this paper. Firstly, RNN was introduced on the basis of ResNet, the model learns shallow features through ResNet, and learns deep features through RNN. The authors use BiGRU, an enhanced version of RNN, to learn the features of data from two aspects: forward and backward. Secondly, the authors also use the attention mechanism to enhance the weight of the key features in the facial expression. The RAF-DB facial emotion dataset samples were used to train the proposed model. At last, the bipedal humanoid robot NAO was used as an experimental platform. The simulation experiment shows that the model can identify the 7 basic expressions, including happy, angry, nausea, fear, sadness, surprise, and nature. It achieves 86.02% recognition accuracy rate. The proposed model provides a reliable solution for the facial expression recognition in humanoid robot vision.

Keywords: Facial expression · ResNet-BiGRU-Attention · Humanoid robotics · CNN · Deep learning

1 Introduction

Humanoid robots have broad application prospects in business, medical treatment, entertainment, psychology, fatigue driving and other related industries. With the development of industry, research work is increasingly focused on applications such as home service robot, medical care robot and manufacturing robot.

H. Liu et al. (Eds.): ICIRA 2022, LNAI 13457, pp. 541–552, 2022.
https://doi.org/10.1007/978-3-031-13835-5_49

At the same time, human-machine interaction system has become a hot research topic. At present, most human-machine interaction methods still use the traditional control modes such as mouse and keyboard. It is an urgent need to improve the experience of human-machine interaction.

Emotions play an important role in human interaction because they enable people express themselves without words. Without emotions, people cannot live in harmony. Therefore, emotion recognition will certainly improve the experience of human-machine interaction. The construction of human-machine interaction system for emotion recognition was inseparable from mature facial expression recognition technology. Facial expression recognition was a particularly important part of these systems.

Deep learning has been proved to be a sustainable research hotspot in the field of humanoid robot research. In the process of deep learning, the network used each layer structure to extract different levels of features of the original data. The network structure of CNN was very close to the actual biological neural network, and had unique advantages in the process of image processing, especially in the field of visual image processing.

Deep learning was widely used in the field of facial expression recognition. Bolotnikova et al. [1] proposed a real -time facial recognition system that uses blocks to process local binary modes of facial images captured by NAO humanoid robots. In order to improve the recognition results obtained by different color channels of YUV color space, most voting and optimal score fusion methods were used. ParkHi et al. [2] using CNN to learn the task, traversing the complexity of deep network training and facial recognition, and achieved the most advanced results in LFW and YTF facial datasets. Xiaoou Tang et al. [3] proposed two very deep neural network architecture, called Deepid3, for facial recognition. These two architectures were rebuilt and stacked from the initial layer in the VGG network and Googlenet network to make it suitable for facial recognition. The integration of the two architectures proposed, after training, the accuracy rate of 99.53% was achieved in the LFW facial dataset, and the accuracy rate was 96.0% in the FW RANK-1 facial dataset.

Deep learning has proven its effectiveness in the field of facial recognition, but in the application of humanoid robots, the effect was always not ideal, and the accuracy was difficult to meet the actual application requirements. CNN focus on local features, but it ignored the connection between these features. Therefore, this paper designs the fusion model of ResNet and BiGRU and designs the attention mechanism. Model extracted local features and learned shallow information through ResNet, It learned the deep information from forward and backward through BiGRU, The attention mechanism was used to amplify the weights of key features of facial expressions, aiming to improve the performance of the model.

2   Related Work

Facial expressions were caused by the contraction and relaxation of some facial muscles. Therefore, it was best to consider the dynamic factors and time factors in the facial expressions at the same time, although some studies can well extract geometric factors and appearance factors. In one study, [4] manually selected the most expressive features in the image sequence for experiments. This method obtains higher accuracy, however, this is not a reasonable way that verifies the feasibility of this method. Many deep learning methods were used to solve difficult tasks, such as CNN and RNN [5], as well as improved networks [6–8].

CNN has been proven to be an effective method in the field of facial expression recognition. ZHANG et al. [9] uses deep CNN for facial expression recognition based on static images. Ziwei Liu et al. [10] proposed a novel deep learning framework for facial recognition in wild. It has two CNNs, LNET and ANET, which were fine -tuned with attribute labels, but they were different from pre-training. LNET trains the positioning of the facial through a large number of general objects, and ANET was pre-trained by a large number of people's facials for prediction. Mohammad Rasool Izadi et al. [11] use shared CNN architecture and shared learning parameters to predict the facial attributes and identify the facial image of the facial, and then use the features of human facial attributes as auxiliary information to connect the features of the facial to increase the CNN to the person to the person Facial recognition ability. Shiyao Wang et al. [12] share the facial attribute cluster into the group, CNN only shared the features of each group in the stage of later feature extraction. They proposed a simple and effective attribute cluster algorithm, based on observing that certain attributes were more synergwitic than other attributes. Ghayoumi et al. [13] proposed a CNN architecture to give robots the ability to identify emotions. The network consists of three convolutional layers and a complete connection layer, using gesture data and facial expression data as the input of CNN. Although the CNN architecture was only four layers, it has good emotional recognition ability and performs well in the experiment.

RNN has been proposed to process dynamic data in the time sequence. RNN was widely used in context applications, and it has an internal memory to process the input sequence by time. Many studies have shown that RNN was a powerful sequence data model. XU et al. [14] proposed a LSTM-CNN architecture for anti-deception to identify the facial. The model can learn time features by using different attacks [15] facial anti-deception database. Experiments have proved that it can be used well for facial anti-deception. In the literature [16], a multi-model emotional recognition method for human-machine interaction was proposed based on evolutionary calculations. This method was combined with several intelligent algorithms and maximum computing algorithms, with an accuracy rate of 97%. The emotional recognition system in small human robots was practical, and this work can also be adopted in many future humanoid robots interactive applications.

In this paper, we designed a combination model based on ResNet-BiGRU-Attention. The model learns shallow features through CNN and learns deep features through RNN. We have also added attention mechanism to enlarge the key feature weights to classify the expression of the facial.

3   Method

3.1   Convolutional Neural Networks

1) CNN was a feed neural network containing convolutional computing. It was one of the representative algorithms of deep learning. It was successful in the field of computer vision. It consists of five parts, the input layer: the input data, the pixel point of the image and the human facial expression image matrix formed by the RGB channel. Convolution layer: The input person facial expression were featured, and the convolutional calculation was performed through the filter in the image feature matrix to extract the local features. Pooling layer: max pooling extraction and retaining the most important features. Full connection layer: The characteristic space obtained by the front layer (convolution, pooling, etc.) was mapped to the sample marking space. SoftMax: The role of the SoftMax layer was to turn the original output of the neural network into a probability distribution, and the sum of the SoftMax sample component was 1. As shown in Fig. 1 was the basic structure of a convolutional neural network.

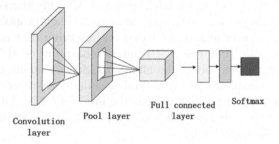

Convolution layer   Pool layer   Full connected layer   Softmax

Fig. 1. Convolutional neural networks.

2) Kaiming He et al. [17] proposed the concept of the residual block. As shown in Fig. 2, after input x, complete the convolution-relu operation, the result is $f(x)$, and add it to the original x, there was $h(x) = f(x) + x$. Compared with the traditional CNN output $H(x) = f(x)$, the residual network is added to the convolution output $F(x)$ to the original x, which is equivalent to calculating a small change to the original x, so that the output obtained in this way. $H(x)$ was the superposition between x and changes. After the gradient transmission, the gradient that was passed to the previous layer was an x gradient. Due to this shortcut, the deep gradient can pass directly and unimpededwhich makes the shallow network layer parameters effective training.

3.2   Bidirectional Gating Recurrent Neural Networks

1) RNN was usually used to process the data sequence of time sequences, and the data needs to be converted to the form of (number of samples, time steps,

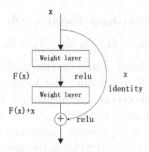

Fig. 2. The concept of residual block.

and number of feature values). During each time step processing process in the RNN network, the features in the sample were multiplied by the corresponding weight, and the deviation parameters were added to the activation function processing. We handle the rectangular feature diagram generated by the human facial expression calculated by convolution, generate a one-dimensional vector, and pass to the RNN part for training.

2) GRU was an enhanced RNN, which was proposed to solve the gradient explosion in long-term memory and back-propagation. In GRU, two gates were used, the reset gate and the update gate, which determines how the new input information was combined with the previous memory, helping to capture short-term dependencies in the time series; the update gate defines the amount of the previous memory saved to the current time step Helps capture long-term dependencies in time series. The design of the two gates helps to learn key features and forget excess expression information, and its internal structure was shown in Fig. 3.

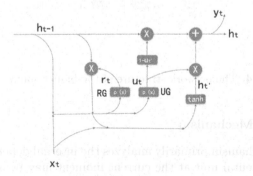

Fig. 3. The internal structure of the GRU unit.

$$r_t = \rho(\omega_{xr}x_t + \omega_{hr}H_{t-1} + b_r) \tag{1}$$

$$u_t = \rho(\omega_{xu}x_t + \omega_{hu}H_{t-1} + b_u) \tag{2}$$

$$h'_t = \tanh(\omega_{xh}x_t + \omega_{hh}(r_t \otimes h_{t-1}) + b_h) \tag{3}$$

$$h_t = (1 - u_t)h'_t + r_t \otimes h_{t-1} \tag{4}$$

where r_t represents the reset gate, u_t the update gate, h'_t represents the candidate hidden state, h_t represents the hidden state, h_{t-1} is the hidden state of time $t-1$. ρ represents the activation function, x_t represents the input of time t, ω_{xr} and ω_{hr}, $\omega_{xu} and \omega_{hu}$, $\omega_{xh} and \omega_{hh}$ mean matrix weights of r_t, u_t, h'_t respectively, $\otimes$ represents the deviation parameter of the point multiplication.b_r, b_u, b_h are the deviation parameter corresponding to r_t, u_t, h'_t respectively. GRU achieves selective forgetting of original hidden information and selective memory of current node information through a reset gate and an update gate. The gate signal interval is $[0, 1]$, the candidate hidden state uses the reset gate to control how much information has been forgotten in the past, and how much new information needs to be accepted from the historical state to update the current state of the gate control. This design addresses the gradient decay problem in recurrent neural networks and better captures the dependence of time steps in time series.

3) 3BiGRU consists of two GRUs that input facial expression features from forward and backward through two input sequences, providing contextual global features to the neural network. Its structure was shown in Fig. 4, where GRU2 represents the forward input and GRU1 represents the reverse input.

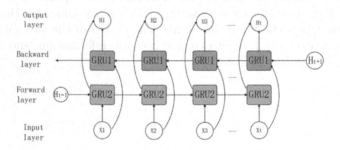

Fig. 4. The network structure of the bidirectional GRU.

3.3   Attention Mechanism

The attention mechanism primarily analyzes the internal dependencies of inputs. The output of a neural unit at the current moment may be affected by feature information that was attached to it or feature information at a distance. Depending on the degree of impact, different weight parameters were assigned to it, so that the model pays attention to the information about the key features. Its structure was shown in Fig. 5.

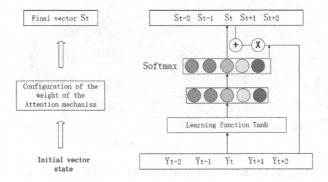

Fig. 5. Structure of attention mechanism.

Generate attention α_t weights, as follows:

$$\alpha_t = \sigma(w_t Y_t + b_t) \tag{5}$$

where σ is the learning function tanh, Y_t is the initial status vector of the characteristic vector of the t feature, w_t is the weight coefficient matrix of the t feature vector, b_t is the deviation of the characteristic vector of the t feature, the change of the weight rate by attention, the softmax function generates probabilities β_t as follows:

$$\beta_t = \frac{\exp(e_t)}{\sum_{i=1}^{t} \exp(e_t)} \tag{6}$$

The generated attention weight is configured to the corresponding hidden state Y_t, so that the attention weight generated by the model comes into play, P is the final output state vector and the S_t weighted average, the weight is a_t, the formula is as follows:

$$P = \sum_{t=1}^{n} \beta_t \cdot Y_t \tag{7}$$

3.4   ResNet-BiGRU-Attention Model

The ResNet-BiGRU-Attention model proposed in this paper was shown in Fig. 6, the facial expression image size was adjusted to 150×150 as the input of CNN, ResNet was choosed in terms of choice in CNN, it extracted local features and BiGRU analysed features. This method was used to overcome the lack of global attention to the CNN and the lack of local attention of BiGRU, combine two points to learn and train the facial expression features from the global and local features, and then enhance the weight of the facial expression features through the attention model, and finally output the results through the softmax layer.

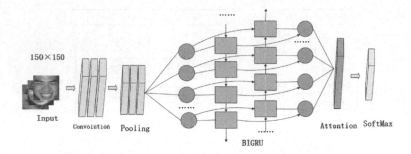

Fig. 6. Model structure of ResNet-BiGRU-Attention.

4   Experiment

This experiment was conducted in the Windows operating system (64-bit), and the GPU was NVIDIA Geforce RTX3050 The CPU was Intel (R) Core (TM) i5-11400(H) with 8 GB of RAM and all the code was used Written in python, built on keras 2.3.1, deep learning platform Tensorflow2.7.0.

4.1   An Introduction to Datasets

The data set used in the experiment named RAF-DB dataset [18]. This database was a large-scale facial expression database. The facial images in the database include different types of facial expression images such as Age, gender, race, posture and light conditions, and processed (such as various filters and special effects), some of its figures were shown in Fig. 7, including 29672 real -world images, including 7 basic emotions, divided for the training set 12271 and 3068 test sets, the two concentrated images were close to the same distribution.

4.2   Experimental Methods

First of all, the training set experimental data was normalized, and then the experimental dataset was increased through the expansion methods. The image enters the convolutional layer in the format of 150 × 150 × 3. In order to extract local information, this paper designed 3 Residual blocks with a convolution filters size of 3 × 3. The activation function was "RELU". The size of the pooling was 2 × 2, and the information of the sample after the pooling was transmitted into the RNN by adjusting the format. In RNN, two BiGRU modules were designed in this paper. The first BiGRU has a total of 256 units, and the second BiGRU has 512 units. The activation function was "Sigmoid". The input feature tensor was 49 × 49, and we transformed it as a one-dimensional vector 1 × 2041. Finally, the amount of tensor trained by RNN was introduced into the Attention model. The model has a large weight distribution of the characteristic information that contribute to the classification task, and the weight of the characteristic information of the small features of the classification task was lightly distributed. This makes the model better complete the classification task.

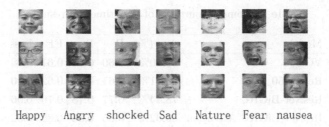

Happy   Angry   shocked   Sad   Nature   Fear   nausea

Fig. 7. Face emoticon data graph.

In this paper, categorical_crossentropy and Adam were used as the loss function and optimizer respectively. The function performed well in the relevant research field. In addition, using Adam has less memory requirements and high algorithm efficiency. In the experiment, when the learning rate was 0.001, the result was the best.

In the experiment, batch_size is 40, the number of neural units of BiGRU is 384, and the activation functions are relu and sigmoid. A total of 50 iterations are performed.

The process of model training is as follows in Fig. 8, some parameters were applied and adjusted in the experiment, as detailed in Table 1.

5   Results and Discussion

In this experiment, 5 experiments were conducted for fairness and exclusion of accidents, and the average of each data was selected as the comparison result of the model, Table 1 was the data of the experimental results.

The results of the comparison of different models on the RAF-DB dataset. Experiments have shown that in experiments with the same dataset, the fusion network ResNet-BiGRU-Attention converges faster and has a higher accuracy

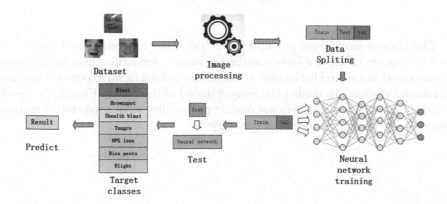

Fig. 8. Workflow diagram.

Table 1. Comparison table of experimental results.

Models	Acc (%)	P	R	F1	Loss
VGG16	65.30%	0.60	0.61	0.61	0.08
ResNet50	62.11%	0.61	0.61	0.62	0.10
ResNet-BiGRU	78.44%	0.77	0.78	0.76	0.06
ResNet-BiGRU-Attention	86.02%	0.85	0.86	0.86	0.02

rate than other networks. It can be seen from the table that the models proposed in this study were better than other network structures in terms of accuracy, especially after the addition of attention mechanisms, the recognition accuracy of the model has been significantly improved.

6   Human Computer Interaction Test

In this paper, the facial expression recognition system was applied to the NAO robot, as shown in Fig. 9, so that it can perform basic facial expression recognition to realize human-machine interaction.

Fig. 9. NAO robot.

The trained model was put into the robot system. Firstly, the camera was used to capture the user's facial expression image. Secondly, these images were preprocessed and stored in the buffer. Then, the trained facial expression recognition model was used to predict the images stored in the buffer. Finally, the result of facial expression and the corresponding probability were predicted. Figure 10 shows the experimental results of the subjects.

happy   sad   angry

Fig. 10. Experimental result of testee.

As can be seen from Fig. 10, the picture on the left was the facial expression result predicted by the model after camera acquisition The picture on the right shows the words and corresponding actions made by the robot. The robot predicts the category of facial expression according to the model, and makes corresponding actions and words to respond to the user. The user was happy, it will respond happily, when the user was sad, it will respond with sympathy, when the user was angry, it will respond with persuasion.

7 Conclusion

Compared with the performance of other neural networks in facial expression data set, the proposed model based on ResNet-BiGRU-Attention in this paper performed better. During the training, its convergence speed was faster, and the training results achieved the goal of improving the recognition accuracy. The model can be used well in facial expression recognition in humanoid robot. In future research, it was necessary to optimize the model structure to adapt to more complex scenes, so as to improve the application scope of the model.

Acknowledgements. This work was supported in part by the National Natural Science Foundation of China under Grants U21A2019, 61873058 and 61933007, the Hainan Province Science and Technology Special Fund under Grant ZDYF2022-SHFZ105, Heilongjiang Natural Science Foundation of China under Grant LH2020F042, the Scientific Research Starting Foundation for Post Doctor from Heilongjiang of China under Grant LBH-Q17134, the Open Fund of the Key Laboratory for Metallurgical Equipment and the Control of Ministry of Education in Wuhan University of Science and Technology under Grants 2018A02 and MECOF 2019B02.

References

1. Bolotnikova, A., Demirel, H., Anbarjafari, G.: Real-time ensemble based face recognition system for NAO humanoids using local binary pattern. Analog Integr. Circ. Sig. Process **92**(3), 467–475 (2017). https://doi.org/10.1007/s10470-017-1006-3
2. Parkhi, O.M., Vedaldi, A., Zisserman, A.: Deep face recognition (2015)
3. Sun, Y., Liang, D., Wang, X., Tang, X.: Deepid3: face recognition with very deep neural networks. arXiv preprint arXiv:1502.00873 (2015)
4. Lopes, A.T., De Aguiar, E., De Souza, A.F., Oliveira-Santos, T.: Facial expression recognition with convolutional neural networks: coping with few data and the training sample order. Pattern Recogn. **61**, 610–628 (2017)

5. Hopfield, J.J.: Neural networks and physical systems with emergent collective computational abilities. Proc. Natl. Acad. Sci. **79**(8), 2554–2558 (1982)
6. Srivastava, N., Hinton, G., Krizhevsky, A., Sutskever, I., Salakhutdinov, R.: Dropout: a simple way to prevent neural networks from overfitting. J. Mach. Learn. Res. **15**(1), 1929–1958 (2014)
7. Ioffe, S., Szegedy, C.: Batch normalization: accelerating deep network training by reducing internal covariate shift. In: International Conference on Machine Learning, pp. 448–456. PMLR, June 2015
8. Glorot, X., Bordes, A., Bengio, Y.: Deep sparse rectifier neural networks. In: Proceedings of the Fourteenth International Conference on Artificial Intelligence and Statistics, pp. 315–323. JMLR Workshop and Conference Proceedings, June 2011
9. Yu, Z., Zhang, C.: Image based static facial expression recognition with multiple deep network learning. In: Proceedings of the 2015 ACM on International Conference on Multimodal Interaction, pp. 435–442, November 2015
10. Liu, Z., Luo, P., Wang, X., Tang, X.: Deep learning face attributes in the wild. In: Proceedings of the IEEE International Conference on Computer Vision, pp. 3730–3738 (2015)
11. Izadi, M.R.: Feature level fusion from facial attributes for face recognition. arXiv preprint arXiv:1909.13126 (2019)
12. Wang, S., Deng, Z., Wang, Z.: Collaborative learning network for face attribute prediction. In: Lai, S.-H., Lepetit, V., Nishino, K., Sato, Y. (eds.) ACCV 2016. LNCS, vol. 10113, pp. 361–374. Springer, Cham (2017). https://doi.org/10.1007/978-3-319-54187-7_24
13. Ghayoumi, M., Bansal, A.K.: Multimodal architecture for emotion in robots using deep learning. In: 2016 Future Technologies Conference (FTC), pp. 901–907. IEEE, December 2016
14. Xu, Z., Li, S., Deng, W.: Learning temporal features using LSTM-CNN architecture for face anti-spoofing. In: 2015 3rd IAPR Asian Conference on Pattern Recognition (ACPR), pp. 141–145. IEEE, November 2015
15. Zhang, Z., Yan, J., Liu, S., Lei, Z., Yi, D., Li, S.Z.: A face antispoofing database with diverse attacks. In: 2012 5th IAPR International Conference on Biometrics (ICB), pp. 26–31. IEEE, March 2012
16. Perez-Gaspar, L.A., Caballero-Morales, S.O., Trujillo-Romero, F.: Multimodal emotion recognition with evolutionary computation for human-robot interaction. Expert Syst. Appl. **66**, 42–61 (2016)
17. He, K., Zhang, X., Ren, S., Sun, J.: Identity mappings in deep residual networks. In: Leibe, B., Matas, J., Sebe, N., Welling, M. (eds.) ECCV 2016. LNCS, vol. 9908, pp. 630–645. Springer, Cham (2016). https://doi.org/10.1007/978-3-319-46493-0_38
18. Li, S., Deng, W., Du, J.: Reliable crowdsourcing and deep locality-preserving learning for expression recognition in the wild. In: Proceedings of the IEEE Conference on Computer Vision and Pattern Recognition, pp. 2852–2861 (2017)

Overtaking Trajectory Planning Based on Model Predictive Control

Zihan Yuan[1] and Jun Xu[1,2(✉)]

[1] School of Mechanical Engineering and Automation, Harbin Institute of Technology,
Shenzhen, China
20S053103@stu.hit.edu.cn
[2] Key Laboratory of System Control and Information Processing, Ministry of Education,
Shanghai, China

Abstract. Autonomous driving technology can greatly increase road safety and reduce accidents, and has become a hot research topic in academia and industry today. However, traditional vehicle motion planning methods often have difficulty in balancing real-time performance with trajectory quality. This paper designs a trajectory planning method based on model predictive control technology, which transforms the motion planning problem into a quadratic planning problem. Compared with previous methods, the proposed method can generate trajectories that meet the requirements of vehicle kinematics and satisfy the requirements of comfort and energy saving while ensuring obstacle avoidance and real-time, and verifies the feasibility of this method in simulation experiments.

Keywords: Model predictive control · Motion planning · Collision avoidance

1 Introduction

With the progress of society and the continuous development of the automotive industry, autonomous driving technology is gaining more and more attention from academia and industry and has become one of the hot spots for research. Autonomous vehicles can greatly increase road safety and reduce the number of human-caused traffic accidents. The national highway traffic safety administration of America (NHTSA) calculates that every 100 million miles driven worldwide results in at least one fatality and more than 50 injuries in traffic accidents, and 94% of the causes of these accidents are human-related [1]. At the same time, autonomous vehicles can increase the capacity of roads and reduce air pollution through the efficient use of fuel.

The general abstraction of the hierarchical scheme for autonomous vehicles can be found in [2, 3]. The trajectory planning problem for overtaking behavior, which is the concern of this paper, belongs to the motion planning level. The main methods at this level include (1) sampling-based path planning methods, represented by RRT [4] and its derivatives, which ensure that feasible solutions are found when they are available in the state space, but the resulting solutions of these methods are often not optimal; (2) Graph search methods, represented by the A* algorithm [5], the performance, computation time and storage cost are related to the denseness of the raster; (3) Optimal control methods, represented by MPC [6, 7], which consider the motion planning problem as a multi-objective optimization problem with constraints, and the solution quality of this method is higher compared to other methods. However, this method is difficult to guarantee real-time performance and often only finds a locally optimal solution and a long solution time if faced with a non-convex optimization problem.

The typical behaviors of autonomous vehicles on the road can be divided into the following categories: following, changing lane, overtaking, merging lane, lane splitting, etc. Among them, overtaking is a relatively complex operation. In contrast to the lane-keeping and lane-changing maneuvers, overtaking is composed of three consecutive actions: changing lane, then driving on an adjacent line and overtaking the overtaken vehicle, and finally changing lane again, during which the overtaking vehicle shifts in time from one lane to the adjacent lane, then lane following, and then back to the same lane once again. In automatic overtaking, control objectives can be achieved by infrastructure-supported methods or in an autonomous manner. The vehicle needs to follow a predefined trajectory, and the trajectory needs to meet several feasibility ground requirements, such as maximum lateral acceleration and maximum steering angle. Some literature has transformed this problem into a sequential quadratic problem (SQP) [8], an approach that is easier to introduce constraints. Some literature is devoted to the use of distributed MPC to solve the highway overtaking and lane changing problems [9, 10]. In literature [11], an overtaking control method based on conflict probability estimation is proposed as a safety index, the method uses model predictive control and integrates the overtaking decision and control into a tracking control problem.

In this paper, we use model predictive control techniques for planning overtaking trajectories. Applying MPC to motion planning faces many problems, firstly, the kinematic model of the vehicle is nonlinear; Secondly, the obstacle avoidance constraint is also non-convex. The literature [12] reduces the self-vehicle to a point mass model and represents the obstacle vehicle as a polyhedron to transform the obstacle avoidance constraint into a convex constraint, but due to poor real-time performance, this method is mostly used in scenarios with slower vehicle speed. In the overtaking scenario, the vehicle speed is faster and there are fewer obstacles around, based on this feature, this paper considers converting the obstacle avoidance constraint into a linear constraint and combining the linearized vehicle kinematic model and the quadratic objective function to formulate the optimization problem into a quadratic programming problem. It should be noted that this method is inaccurate to a certain extent, but considering the specificity of the overtaking situation, the method can accomplish the trajectory planning task very well.

The organization of this paper is as follows. Section 2 introduces the MPC method. Section 3 introduces the kinematic modeling of the vehicle. Section 4 presents the problem modeling of the overtaking problem. Numerical experiments to demonstrate the effectiveness of the proposed method are given in Sect. 5, and conclusions are drawn in Sect. 6.

2 Introduction of Model Predictive Control

Model predictive control is an optimization-based control strategy in which an open-loop optimization problem in a finite time horizon is solved online at each sampling moment based on the current measurement information obtained, and the first element of the resulting control sequence is applied to the controlled object, and the process is repeated at the next sampling moment to refresh the optimization problem with the new measurement values and solve it again.

For a linear time-invariant system:

$$x_{k+1} = Ax_k + Bu_k \tag{1}$$

where $x \in \mathbb{R}^n$ is an n-dimensional state variable, $u \in \mathbb{R}^m$ is an m-dimensional control variable, and the constraint is satisfied that:

$$\forall k \geq 0, x_k \in \chi, u_k \in U$$

The corresponding MPC problem can be written as follows:

$$\min_{u_{k+i|k}} p(x_{k+N|k}) + \sum_{i=0}^{N-1} l(x_{k+i|k}, u_{k+i|k})$$
$$s.t. x_{k+i+1} = Ax_{k+i} + Bu_{k+i}, i = 1, \ldots\ldots, N-1$$
$$x_{k+i|k} \in \chi, u_{k+i|k} \in U, i = 0, \ldots\ldots, N-1$$
$$x_{k|k} = x_k$$

where N is the control time horizon, p is the terminal cost function of the MPC problem, and l is the process cost function of this MPC problem.

In this paper the problem is modeled as a quadratic optimization problem, using a quadratic objective function with linear constraints to model the problem, and this MPC problem can be described as:

$$\min_{u_{k+i|k}} x_{k+N|k}^T P x_{k+N|k} + \sum_{i=0}^{N-1} x_{k+i|k}^T Q x_{k+i|k} + u_{k+i|k}^T R u_{k+i|k}$$
$$s.t. x_{k+i+1} = Ax_{k+i} + Bu_{k+i}, i = 1, \ldots\ldots, N-1$$
$$x_{k+i|k} \in \chi, u_{k+i|k} \in U, i = 0, \ldots\ldots, N-1$$
$$x_{k|k} = x_k$$

The objective function can be changed by adjusting the matrices P, Q, and R.

3 Vehicle Kinematic Model

In the process of modeling vehicle kinematics, the vehicle model is first simplified, and the vehicle model in this paper is based on the bicycle model [13], which has the following assumptions.

(1) The ground is assumed to be flat and in good condition, and the vehicle will not have bumps in the process of driving.

(2) The wheels do not skid and have good contact with the road surface.
(3) The direction of the vehicle is completely controlled by the front wheels.

Taking into account the above assumptions, the vehicle model is simplified to a two-degree-of-freedom bicycle model: two degrees of freedom for the vehicle along the longitudinal motion and the front wheels along the axis perpendicular to the vehicle motion plane. By equating each of the two front wheels and the two rear wheels into a single wheel, a bicycle model with motion in the plane is obtained. The vehicle model is shown in Fig. 1. The subscript f denotes the front wheel, the subscript r denotes the rear wheel, (x_r, y_r) is the center of the rear wheel of the vehicle; l is the distance between the equivalent front wheel center and the equivalent rear wheel center; v_f and v_r are the velocities of the equivalent front wheel center and the equivalent rear wheel center of the vehicle; φ is the turning angle of the vehicle, δ_f is the turning angle of the front wheel; the motion model is illustrated in Fig. 1.

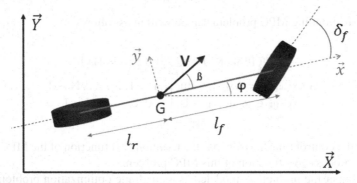

Fig. 1. Two-degree-of-freedom kinematic model of vehicle

The equation of state can be obtained based on the kinematic structure of the vehicle:

$$
\begin{aligned}
\dot{x}_r &= v_r \cos(\varphi) \\
\dot{y}_r &= v_r \sin(\varphi) \\
\dot{\varphi} &= v_r \tan(\delta_f)/(l_r + l_f) \\
\dot{v} &= a
\end{aligned}
\tag{2}
$$

With kinematic model and the initial values of the state of the vehicle, it is possible to calculate the state of the vehicle at the next moment after the control input is given at one moment.

The state quantity X of the vehicle is set to be the current position of the equivalent center of the rear wheels of the vehicle (x_r, y_r), the velocity v_r, and the angle of rotation φ of the body, i.e.

$$
X = \begin{bmatrix} x & y & v & \varphi \end{bmatrix}^T
\tag{3}
$$

For the problem studied in this paper, the kinematic equations of the vehicle are nonlinear equations and the model needs to be linearized in order to guarantee the performance of the planning algorithm. A first-order Taylor expansion is performed for the vehicle kinematic model in the vicinity of the operating point as follows:

$$\dot{X} = f(X_r, U_r) + \frac{\partial f}{\partial X}(X - X_r) + \frac{\partial f}{\partial U}(U - U_r) \tag{4}$$

Subtracting from Eq. (4), then Eq. (3) turns into Eq. (5):

$$\dot{\tilde{X}}(t) = A_c(t)\tilde{X}(t) + B_c(t)\tilde{U}(t) \tag{5}$$

where:

$$A_c(t) = \begin{bmatrix} 0 & 0 & -v_r\sin\varphi_r & \cos\varphi_r \\ 0 & 0 & v_r\cos\varphi_r & \sin\varphi_r \\ 0 & 0 & 0 & \tan\delta_{fr}/l \\ 0 & 0 & 0 & 0 \end{bmatrix}$$

$$B_c(t) = \begin{bmatrix} 0 & 0 \\ 0 & 0 \\ 0 & v_r(\tan^2\delta_{fr} + 1)/l \\ 1 & 0 \end{bmatrix}$$

$$\tilde{X} = X - X_r$$

$$\tilde{U} = U - U_r$$

According to the linear model in continuous time, the linear discrete-time system equation can then obtained:

$$\tilde{X}(k + 1|t) = A_{k,t}\tilde{X}(k|t) + B_{k,t}\tilde{U}(k|t) \tag{6}$$

In Eq. (6), Ak, t = I + TAc(t), Bk, t = Bc(t)dt, and dt is the step size of the MPC. To simplify the calculation, it is assumed that:

$$A_{k,t} = A_t, k = 1, 2, \ldots\ldots, N$$
$$B_{k,t} = B_t, k = 1, 2, \ldots\ldots, N$$

then:

$$\tilde{X}(k + 1|t) = A_t\tilde{X}(k|t) + B_t\tilde{U}(k|t) \tag{7}$$

Equation (7) shows that, given the initial state quantities and the control quantities for each control time horizon, the state quantities can be calculated.

$$\tilde{X}(k|t) = A_t^k\tilde{X}(0|t) + A_t^{k-1}B_t\tilde{U}(0|t) + A_t^{k-2}B_t\tilde{U}(1|t) + \cdots + B_t\tilde{U}(k|t) \tag{8}$$

In this paper, the prediction time horizon and control time horizon are taken to be equal, $N_p = N_c$.

4 Overtaking Problem Algorithm Design

The overtaking problem can be specifically described as a process in which a vehicle overtakes a vehicle leading in its lane through a lane change while returning to its initial lane at the end of the overtaking behavior while avoiding collisions with surrounding vehicles.

The overtaking task can be described as an optimal control problem, the problem is modeled in two main parts, the first part is to determine the objective function of the optimization problem and the second part is to determine the constraints of the optimization problem.

The ego vehicle needs to plan local trajectories based on real-time vehicle state and environment information, which includes the trajectory prediction information of surrounding vehicles, road information, etc. The local trajectory plans the vehicle from the current state to the next state in real time, and the planning process needs to ensure that the constraints (safety constraints, physical constraints) are satisfied. In addition, the local trajectory should minimize the deviation from the overall reference trajectory and minimize other metrics in the planning process.

In this paper, the trajectory planning problem is transformed into a trajectory tracking problem with obstacle avoidance constraints, and the planned trajectory needs to achieve tracking of a predefined reference trajectory under the condition that the obstacle avoidance constraints are satisfied. The reference trajectory is defined as a lane center-line that contains a constant desired speed.

According to the objective function in Sect. 2, the objective function of the optimization problem is then described as follows:

$$J_1 = \sum_{k=N_{p-k}}^{N_p} (X(k|t) - X_{ref})^T Q_1 (X(k|t) - X_{ref}) \tag{9}$$

The first term minimizes the difference between the state volume of the vehicle and the reference trajectory. Such that the state volume is as close as possible to the reference trajectory.

$$J_2 = \sum_{k=1}^{N_c} U(k|t)^T Q_2 U(k|t) \tag{10}$$

The second term minimizes the control volume so that the control volume is not very large, and this part of the objective function is designed for energy conservation considerations.

$$J_3 = \sum_{k=2}^{N_c} (U(k|t) - U(k-1|t))^T Q_3 (U(k|t) - U(k-1|t)) \tag{11}$$

The third term minimizes the amount of variation of the control quantity, for the consideration of comfort.

The constraints of the optimization problem can be described as: firstly, the boundary value constraints.

$$X(0|t) = X_0 \tag{12}$$

In addition, the obstacle avoidance constraint is also considered. Throughout the prediction time horizon, the vehicle cannot collide with other vehicles or the road, and assuming that the vehicle i with which a collision may occur on the road is predicted to be at its future k-th step at moment t as $(x_i(k|t), y_i(k|t))$, the obstacle avoidance constraint can be written as:

$$(X(k|t) - X_i(k|t))^T Q_4 (X(k|t) - X_i(k|t)) < d_{min}^2 \tag{13}$$

This constraint is a nonlinear constraint, and in order to improve the solution performance of MPC algorithm, this paper eventually wants to transform the MPC problem into a quadratic programming problem, thus it is necessary to linearize this constraint here, and choose the initial value of the linearized point position for each trajectory planning, then equation can be transformed into:

$$(X(0|t) - X_i(k|t))^T Q_4 (2X(k|t) - X(0|t) - X_i(k|t)) < d_{min}^2 \tag{14}$$

where:

$$Q_4 = \begin{bmatrix} I_2 & 0 \\ 0 & 0 \end{bmatrix}$$

Considering the constraint between the vehicle and the road edge, assuming that the width of a single lane is w_l, the width of the vehicle is w_c, and the ordinate of the lower boundary of the lane is $y = 0$, then the obstacle avoidance constraint can be written as:

$$2w_l - 0.5w_c < y(k|t) < 0.5w_c \tag{15}$$

Finally, there is a constraint on the size of the control quantity as well as the state quantity, both the state quantity and the control quantity, the size cannot exceed their extreme values. For the vehicle acceleration, the extreme value constraint for the front wheel turning angle can be described as:

$$U_{min} \le U(t) \le U_{max} \tag{16}$$

For the vehicle speed, the extreme value constraint on the turning angle can be described as:

$$X_{min} \le X(t) \le X_{max} \tag{17}$$

In this section, the objective function of overtaking problem is defined as a quadratic function, and all constraints are defined as affine functions. Finally, the overtaking problem is formulated into a quadratic programming problem.

5 Experiments

The simulation environment in this paper is based on the Matlab R2021b, and the actual parameters used for the simulation are as follows:

Table 1. Experiment setup.

Type	Model number
CPU	Intel i7-6700 HQ
Memory	24 GB
GPU	NVIDIA 1060 6 GB
Disk	1 TB HDD
Type	Model number

YALMIP is used for the solution of the optimization problem.

5.1 Scenario

The overtaking scenario used in this paper is shown in Fig. 3. The designed road scenario is a structured two-lane road scenario with each lane being 3.75 m wide.

In the overtaking action, we assume that the following conditions are satisfied: the vehicle being overtaken moves at a constant speed along a straight route. Assume that the ego vehicle must overtake the vehicle in front of it, and that its distance from the car in front is d. The ego vehicle must complete the following three parts of the maneuver: first, the lane change maneuver. Starting from the current position of the self-driving vehicle, it deviates from its original lane, tracks a given reference trajectory for a certain period of time, and switches to another target lane at the end of the first phase. After that, the vehicle drives in a straight line along the lane, tracking a given reference trajectory for a given period of time until it overtakes the overtaken vehicle by a corresponding distance. Finally, after tracking the given reference trajectory, the ego vehicle returns to the lane and reaches the pre-selected position in front of the overtaken vehicle. Specifically, the scene contains an obstacle vehicle, at the initial moment, the ego vehicle and the obstacle vehicle are both in the lane below, the initial coordinates of the obstacle vehicle under the world coordinate system are (55, 1.875), and the obstacle vehicle is in front of the ego vehicle at the position of 50 m. The obstacle vehicle is traveling at a speed of 13 m/s in the lower lane at a constant speed, and all the ego vehicle needs to do is to change lanes to the upper lane first, then accelerate to overtake the obstacle vehicle and finally return to the original lane.

5.2 Simulation Results

It's necessary to generate a reference trajectory based on a known waypoint, which consists of multiple line trajectories stitched together, including: a uniform linear motion in the lane above and a uniform linear motion in the original lane.

The simulation experiments of motion planning for the overtaking problem are carried out in this scenario using linear time-varying MPC. The experimental results are shown in the Figs. 2 and 3.

The subgraph (a)–(d) in Fig. 2 respectively describe the changes of vehicle abscissa, ordinate, steering Angle, and speed with time. The abscissa of the vehicle gradually increases with time, while the ordinate first increases and then decreases with time, finally the vehicle completes the entire overtaking behavior. Figure 3 is an aerial view, in which the red curve is the planned trajectory, and the blue curve is the previous reference trajectory. Our planning method successfully generates a continuous trajectory that meets the requirements of vehicle kinematics. Figures 4 and 5 show the comparison of the motion planning state variables and Aerial view for the linear and nonlinear models under the same conditions, respectively. It can be seen that they are very close to each other, which illustrates that the linear model can be a good substitute for the nonlinear model.

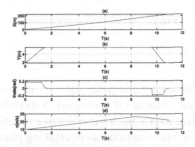

Fig. 2. Motion planning for linear vehicle kinematic model.

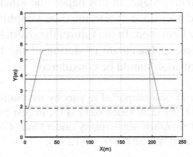

Fig. 3. Aerial view of motion planning.

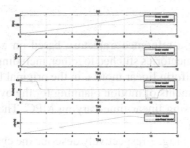

Fig. 4. Motion planning comparison.

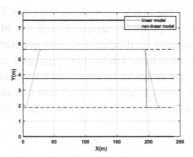

Fig. 5. Aerial view comparison.

6   Conclusion

In this paper, a motion planning method for solving an overtaking task considering dynamic obstacles and static obstacles is presented. It models the overtaking task as a convex optimization problem with a quadratic objective function and linear constraints, and uses the MPC method to plan a reasonable overtaking planning trajectory. From the experiments in Sect. 5, the method is successful, and the method can plan the overtaking trajectory quickly while satisfying the constraints and considering other requirements such as comfort in the planning stage. In this paper, the kinematic model of the vehicle, as well as the obstacle avoidance constraints, are simplified to meet the real-time requirement of the strategy limitation. In the future, the overtaking task should be modeled closer to real situations, and accurate modeling of the traffic environment, road conditions, and other information should be considered.

Acknowledgements. This work was supported in part by the National Natural Science Foundation of China under Grant U1813224, Grant 62173113, in part by the Science and Technology Innovation Committee of Shenzhen Municipality under Grant GXWD20201230155427003-20200821173613001 and Grant JCYJ20200109113412326.

References

1. Santokh, S.: Critical reasons for crashes investigated in the national motor vehicle crash causation survey (2015)

2. González, D., Pérez, J., Milanés, V.: A review of motion planning techniques for automated vehicles. IEEE Trans. Intell. Transp. Syst. **4**(17), 1135–1145 (2016)
3. Paden, B., Cap, M., Yong, S.: A survey of motion planning and control techniques for self-driving urban vehicles. IEEE Trans. Intell. Veh. **1**, 33–55 (2016)
4. Khatib, O.: Real-time obstacle avoidance for manipulators and mobile robots. In: IEEE International Conference on Robotics and Automation, pp. 500–505 (1985)
5. Elbanhawi, M., Simic, M.: Sampling-based robot motion planning: a review. IEEE Access. **2**, 56–77 (2014)
6. Obayashi, M., Uto, K., Takano, G.: Appropriate overtaking motion generating method using predictive control with suitable car dynamics. In: IEEE Conference on Decision and Control, pp. 4992–4997 (2016)
7. Cardoso, V.: A model-predictive motion planner for the IARA autonomous car. In: IEEE International Conference on Robotics and Automation, pp. 225–230 (2017)
8. Qin, J., Badgwell, T.: A survey of industrial model predictive control technology. Control Eng. Pract. **11**(7), 733–764 (2003)
9. Liu, P., Ozguner, U., Zhang, Y.: Distributed MPC for cooperative highway driving and energy-economy validation via microscopic simulations. Transp. Res. Part C **77**, 90–95 (2017)
10. Han, Y., Hegyi, A., Yuan, Y.: Resolving freeway jam waves by discrete first-order modelbased predictive control of variable speed limits. Transp. Res. Part C. **77**, 405–420 (2017)
11. Wang, F., Yang, M., Yang, R.: Conflict-probability estimation-based overtaking for intelligent vehicles. IEEE Trans. Intell. Transp. Syst. **10**(2), 366–370 (2009)
12. Xiaojing, Z., Liniger, A., Borrelli, F.: Optimization-based collision avoidance. IEEE Trans. Control Syst. Technol. **29**(3), 972–983 (2020)
13. Luca, A, Oriolo, G., Samson, C.: Feedback control of a nonholonomic car-like robot. In: Laumond, J.P. (eds) Robot Motion Planning and Control. Lecture Notes in Control and Information Sciences, LNCS, vol. 229, pp. 171–253. Springer, Heidelberg (1998). https://doi.org/10.1007/BFb0036073

H_∞ Switching Adaptive Tracking Control for Manipulator with Average Dwell Time

Hongmei Zhang and Junpeng Shang[✉]

School of Automation, Shenyang Aerospace University, Shenyang 110000, China
zhanghm001@yeah.net, sjp970928@163.com

Abstract. The H_∞ switching adaptive control method with average dwell time is presented in this paper, in order to solve the uncertain problems such as load changes. Due to the change of the load, the parameters of the manipulator change. A switching system is established to simulate the manipulator system whose parameters change. The average dwell time ensures that the switching speed is slow enough that each subsystem can be stabilized, thereby making the entire switching system stable. Simulations show that, under load changes and input disturbances, the manipulator can achieve progressive tracking with the proposed controller.

Keywords: Switching system · Average dwell time · Input disturbance · Manipulator

1 Introduction

As we all know, the manipulator is a complex MIMO nonlinear system. Because of its strong coupling and time-varying characteristics, the trajectory tracking control of the manipulator has always been a difficult task [1–3]. At present, the control methods for manipulators generally include feedforward compensation, adaptive control, sliding mode control, robust control, PID control, neural networks and fuzzy control [4–6]. Reference [7] proposes an adaptive finite-time second-order sliding mode tracking control method for robots, which achieves accurate tracking control, optimized robust performance and parameter tuning; Reference [8] aims at nonlinear robot nonlinearity with input constraints. An adaptive fixed-time fault-tolerant constraint control for trajectory tracking is designed, and the effectiveness and robustness of the method are ensured on simulation. For the unknown upper bound of parameter uncertainty and disturbance, in the literature [9], a robust adaptive tracking controller is proposed, which verifies its global stability with good tracking ability.

For the parameter jump caused by the repeated picking and placing of objects by the manipulator, the concept of switching control is introduced. Reference [10] studies an adaptive switching control strategy based on fuzzy logic system, which introduces non-zero time-varying parameters. The good tracking performance is achieved in the case of unknown robot dynamics. In reference [11] The RBF neural networks are used to approximate the unknown function of the robot, and a robust controller is designed to compensate the neural network approximation error and external disturbance. By switching multiple Lyapunov functions, an adaptive update law and an allowable switching signal are established to ensure the asymptotic Lyapunov stability of the closed-loop system, so that the joint position follows given bounded expected output signal; Reference [12] proposes robust adaptive neural switching control for robots with uncertainty and disturbance, which ensures system tracking stability and error convergence.

In this paper, the unmeasurable error state of the manipulator is studied, and H_∞ adaptive tracking control with average dwell time is designed. Section 2 describes the dynamic model of the manipulator, its basic characteristics, the concept of average dwell time, and the establishment of the switching model. Section 3 presents the design process of the controller and the construction of the high-gain observer. Section 4 verifies the effectiveness of the proposed method through the simulation of a two-degree-of-freedom manipulator. Section 5 is the conclusion.

2 Basic Knowledge Preparation

Consider an N-joint manipulator whose dynamic performance can be described by a second-order nonlinear differential equation:

$$M(q)\ddot{q} + C(q, \dot{q})\dot{q} + G(q) = \tau + \zeta \tag{1}$$

Here, $q, \dot{q}, \ddot{q} \in R^n$ is the displacement vector, velocity vector and acceleration vector of the joint angle respectively. $M(q) \in R^{n \times n}$ is the inertia matrix of the manipulator. $C(q, \dot{q}) \in R^n$ represents the centrifugal force and the Coriolis force. $G(q)$ is the gravity term. $\tau \in R^n$ is the control torque. ζ is the input disturbance. The followings are properties of the manipulator:

Property 1. $M(q) - 2C(q, \dot{q})$ is an obliquely symmetric matrix.

Property 2. The inertia matrix $M(q)$ is a symmetric positive definite matrix, c_1 and c_2 is a positive number, which satisfies the following inequality:

$$m_1 \|x\|^2 \le x^T M(q)x \le m_2 \|x\|^2 \tag{2}$$

Property 3. There is a parameter vector that depends on the parameters of the manipulator, so that $M(q)$, $C(q, \dot{q})$, $G(q)$ satisfy the linear relationship, and the dynamic Eq. (1) can be changed to

$$M(q)\ddot{q} + C(q, \dot{q})\dot{q} + G(q) = W(q, \dot{q}, \ddot{q})\Phi \tag{3}$$

where $W(q, \dot{q}, \ddot{q}) \in R^{n \times m}$ is regression matrix.

2.1 Establishment of Switching Model

Associating each load with a subsystem, we can get the following model of manipulator switching

$$M_\sigma(q)\ddot{q} + C_\sigma(q, \dot{q})\dot{q} + G_\sigma(q) = W(q, \dot{q}, \ddot{q}) = \tau + \zeta \tag{4}$$

where $\sigma(t) : [0, +\infty) \rightarrow \Lambda$ is the switching signal controlled by the load, $\Lambda = \{1, \cdots, N\}$ is a subset of the switching system and the load types, N is the number of loads.

To design a switching controller for system (4) such that the tracking error $e = q - q_d$ is eventually uniformly bounded.

Lemma 1 [13]: For any time point $t_2 > t_1 \geq 0$, let $N_\sigma(t_1, t_2)$ denote the switching times of the switching signal $\sigma(t)$ on (t_1, t_2). If

$$N_\sigma(t_1, t_2) \leq N_0 + (t_2 - t_1)/\varepsilon \tag{5}$$

make $\varepsilon > 0, N_0 > 0$. Then, ε is called the average dwell time (ADT) of the switching signal $\sigma(t)$. The average dwell time of the switching system satisfies $\varepsilon > \frac{\log \mu}{2\lambda_0}$.

The switching system is globally asymptotically stable for each switching signal with an average dwell time (ADT). If every subsystem of the switching system is stable, and the switching speed is slow enough, the switching system (4) is stable.

3 The Controller Design

3.1 High Gain Observer

In the case of unmeasured system state, the following high-gain observer is used to estimate the error E:

$$\dot{\hat{a}}_1 = \hat{a}_2 + \frac{c_1}{b_1}(a_1 - \hat{a}_1); \quad \dot{\hat{a}}_2 = \frac{c_2}{b_2}(a_1 - \hat{a}_1) \tag{6}$$

where, $a_1 = \dot{e}, a_2 = \ddot{e}, \hat{a}_1 = \dot{\hat{e}}, \hat{a}_2 = \ddot{\hat{e}}, b_i, i = 1, 2$ is a small positive number, and $c_i > 0, i = 1, 2$ is chosen so that the roots of $s^2 + b_1 s + b_2 = 0$ have negative real parts. $e = \begin{bmatrix} e_1 & e_2 \end{bmatrix}^T$ is the tracking error of the two joints of the manipulator.

3.2 Switched Adaptive Controller

A switching adaptive controller is designed for system (4) to ensure that progressive tracking can be achieved without disturbance.

For the kinetic Eq. (4), we devise the following control law:

$$\tau = \tau_\sigma = M_0(\ddot{e} + K_v\dot{e} + K_pe) + W(q, \dot{q}, \ddot{q})\hat{\Phi}_\sigma \tag{7}$$

where M_0 is a positive definite matrix, K_p and K_v are the proportional gain matrix and the differential gain matrix respectively, and $\hat{\Phi}_\sigma$ is the estimated value of Φ_i. When the subsystem corresponding to the manipulator is inactive, the estimated parameters will not affect the joint angles of the manipulator. We propose an adaptive law:

$$\begin{cases} \dot{\hat{\Phi}}_i = \Gamma_i W^T M_0^{-1^T} B^T PE \ i = \sigma \\ \dot{\hat{\Phi}}_I = 0 \qquad\qquad i \neq \sigma \end{cases} \tag{8}$$

where $E = \begin{bmatrix} e \ \dot{e} \end{bmatrix}^T$.

Lemma 2 [14]: When $\zeta = 0$, combining (4) and (8), we can get.

$$M_0(\ddot{e} + K_v\dot{e} + K_pe) = W(q, \dot{q}, \ddot{q})(\Phi - \hat{\Phi}_\sigma) = W(q, \dot{q}, \ddot{q})\tilde{\Phi}_\sigma \tag{9}$$

Taking $E = [e; \dot{e}]$, then the system (12) is transformed into a state space model as

$$\dot{E} = \begin{bmatrix} 0_n & I_n \\ -K_p & -K_v \end{bmatrix}E + \begin{bmatrix} 0_n \\ I_n \end{bmatrix}M_0^{-1}W(q, \dot{q}, \ddot{q})\tilde{\Phi}_\sigma = AE + BM_0^{-1}W(q, \dot{q}, \ddot{q})\tilde{\Phi}_\sigma, \tag{10}$$

Choose suitable K_p and K_v, so that A is a Hurwitz matrix. Then, exist $P > 0$ and $Q > 0$ satisfy $A^T P + PA = -Q$. Choose a Lyapunov function

$$V(E, \Psi) = E^T PE + \text{tr}\left(\Psi^T \Gamma^{-1}\Psi\right), \tag{11}$$

where $\Psi^T = \begin{bmatrix} \tilde{\Phi}_1^T, \cdots, \tilde{\Phi}_N^T \end{bmatrix}$, $\Gamma^{-1} = diag\left(\Gamma_1^{-1}, \cdots, \Gamma_N^{-1}\right)$, and $\Gamma_i > 0, i = 1, 2, \cdots, N$.

Take the derivative of (11)

$$\dot{V}(E, \Psi) = -E^T QE + 2\tilde{\Phi}_\sigma^T(W^T (M_0^{-1})^T B^T PE + \Gamma_\sigma^{-1}\dot{\hat{\Phi}}_\sigma) \\ = -E^T QE < 0, \quad \forall E \neq 0, \tag{12}$$

$V(E, \Psi)$ is a non-increasing function on t. Therefore, $V(E(t), \Psi(t)) \leq V(E(0), \Psi(0)), \forall t \geq 0$, it can be seen that $V(E, \Psi)$ is bounded, E and Ψ are also bounded.

Assume that when $t \in R^+$, $q_d(t), \dot{q}_d(t), \ddot{q}_d(t)$ is bounded, E is also bounded, so that $q, \dot{q}, \ddot{q}$ is bounded. At the same time, Properties 1–3 guarantee the boundedness of $W(q, \dot{q}, \ddot{q})$. Therefore, $\dot{E} \in L_\infty$ on Eq. (10). As well as applying Barbalat's lemma, $\lim\limits_{t \to \infty} E(t) = 0$.

Lemma 3 [14]: Given a constant δ, if exists K_p, K_v and P exist, satisfying

$$\begin{bmatrix} Z^T B^T + P^{-1}A^T + AP^{-1} + BZ & B & P^{-1}C^T \\ B^T & -\delta I & 0 \\ CP^{-1} & 0 & -I \end{bmatrix} < 0 \tag{13}$$

where, $Z = KP^{-1}$, and $K = \begin{bmatrix} -K_p & -K_v \end{bmatrix}$. Then, using the controller (7) and the adaptive law (8) to control the system (4) with input disturbance, it can be obtained that under any switching, it still has the H_∞ tracking performance.

As it can be seen from the above, when the system (4) is not disturbed, the trajectory asymptotic tracking can still be maintained. When the disturbance is not zero, we can transform Eq. (10) into

$$\dot{E} = (\overline{A} + BK)E + B\left(M_0^{-1}W(q, \dot{q}, \ddot{q})\tilde{\Phi}_\sigma + d\right) \tag{14}$$

where $\overline{A} = \begin{bmatrix} 0_n & I_n \\ 0_n & 0_n \end{bmatrix}$.

4 Simulation

We verify the feasibility and effectiveness of the proposed controller by simulating a two-degree-of-freedom manipulator. First, considering the zero-interference, the traditional adaptive control is simulated. Then, simulate the controller proposed is applied. Finally, under the input disturbances, the necessity of switching control is illustrated.

The structure of the two degrees of freedom manipulator is shown in Fig. 1, and its dynamic equation is:

$$M(q)\ddot{q} + C(q, \dot{q})\dot{q} = W(q, \dot{q}, \ddot{q}) = \tau + \zeta,$$

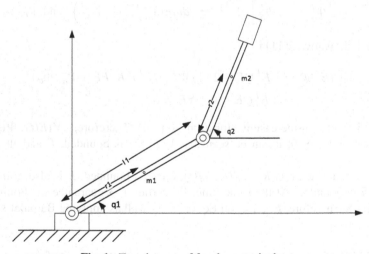

Fig. 1. Two degrees of freedom manipulator

$$M(q) = \begin{bmatrix} J_1 & m_2 r_2 l_1 \cos(q_2 - q_1) \\ m_2 r_2 l_1 \sin(q_2 - q_1) & J_2 \end{bmatrix},$$

$$C(q, \dot{q}) = \begin{bmatrix} 0 & -\dot{q}_2 m_2 r_2 l_1 \sin(q_2 - q_1) \\ \dot{q}_1 m_2 r_2 l_1 \sin(q_2 - q_1) & 0 \end{bmatrix},$$

$$J_1 = \frac{4}{3}m_1r_1^2 + m_2l_1^2, J_2 = \frac{4}{3}m_2r_2^2, J_3 = m_2r_2l_1, \ \Phi = \begin{bmatrix} J_1 & J_2 & J_3 \end{bmatrix}^T,$$

$$W(q, \dot{q}, \ddot{q}) = \begin{bmatrix} \ddot{q}_1 & 0 & \cos(q_2 - q_1)\ddot{q}_2 - \dot{q}_2^2\sin(q_2 - q_1) \\ 0 & \ddot{q}_2 & \cos(q_2 - q_1)\ddot{q}_1 - \dot{q}_1^2\sin(q_2 - q_1) \end{bmatrix}.$$

We simulated the operation of the manipulator with no load and load, and set $\sigma = 2$ to indicate a load and $\sigma = 1$ to indicate no load. The actual parameters of the controller are shown in Table 1. Moreover, when the error state is unpredictable, a high-gain observer is introduced to estimate the errors. Given the desired trajectory of the manipulator $q_d = [0.5\sin t \quad \sin 3t], e_0 = [0.1 \quad 0.2]^T, \dot{e}_0 = [0 \quad 0]^T$. Choose $\lambda_0 = 20$ and $\mu = 450$. According to Lemma 1, if the average dwell time is greater than 0.133, the tracking error e is eventually uniformly bounded.

Table 1. Subsystem parameters.

	m_1	m_2	r_1	r_2	l_1
$\sigma = 1$	1	1	1	1	2
$\sigma = 2$	1	2	1	1.5	2

Simulation 1

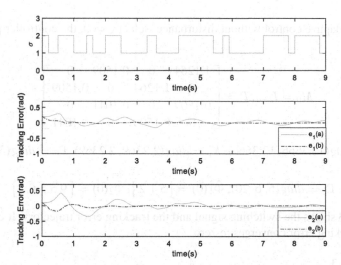

Fig. 2. Comparison of two controllers without interference (a: adaptive control, b: H_∞ switching adaptive control)

Conventional adaptive control without interference is performed. Apply traditional adaptive law [15]. Select the initial value $\hat{\Phi}(0) = [7.3 \quad 3.6 \quad 4]^T, M_0 = 10 \times I_{2\times2}$,

$\Gamma = diag(6, 6, 20)$, and other parameters remain unchanged. As can be seen from Fig. 2, as long as the load is constantly changing, the tracking error will never converge under traditional adaptive control. In contrast, the switch control method in this paper can make the tracking error converge rapidly.

Simulation 2

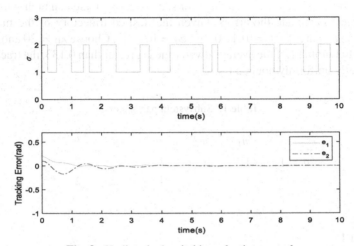

Fig. 3. Undisturbed switching adaptive control

To switch adaptive control without disturbance, select $\zeta = 0$, the controller parameters are

$$M_0 = I_{2\times2}, P = \begin{bmatrix} 1.1264 & 0 & 0.1509 & 0 \\ 0 & 1.1264 & 0 & 0.1509 \\ 0.1509 & 0 & 0.1041 & 0 \\ 0 & 0.1509 & 0 & 0.1041 \end{bmatrix},$$

$K_p = diag(12.3666, 12.3666)$, $K_v = diag(2.2369, 2.2369)$, $\Gamma_1 = diag(3, 3, 20)$

$$\Gamma_2 = diag(6, 6, 20), \hat{\Phi}_1(0) = \begin{bmatrix} 5 & 1 & 2 \end{bmatrix}, \hat{\Phi}_2(0) = \begin{bmatrix} 9 & 5.5 & 6.1 \end{bmatrix}$$

Figure 3 shows the switching signal and the tracking error trajectory. It can be seen that the tracking error converges to zero.

Simulation 3

H_∞ Switching adaptive control is shown in the presence of input disturbances. Choose disturbance $\zeta = 0.5 \sin t$, for a given decay rate $\delta = 0.16$. K_p, K_v and P satisfy inequality (13) in Simulation 1. As it can be seen in Fig. 4, the controller (13) and the adaptive law (14) ensure the tracking characteristic and the tracking error converges at zero.

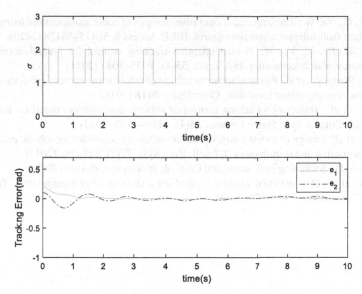

Fig. 4. H_∞ switching adaptive control under interference

5 Conclusion

The adaptive tracking control problem is studied for the manipulator whose parameters change due to the load change. The switching model of the manipulator is established, and an adaptive tracking control of the manipulator with average dwell time is proposed. Finally, the effectiveness is proved in simulations.

References

1. Hayat, R., Buss, M.: Model identification for robot manipulators using regressor-free adaptive control. In: 2016 UKACC 11th International Conference on Control (CONTROL), pp. 1–7. IEEE (2016)
2. Kikuuwe, R.: A sliding-mode-like position controller for admittance control with bounded actuator force. IEEE/ASME Trans. Mechatron. **19**(5), 1489–1500 (2013)
3. Wang, H.: Adaptive control of robot manipulators with uncertain kinematics and dynamics. IEEE Trans. Autom. Control **62**(2), 948–954 (2016)
4. Jie, W., Yudong, Z.B., et al.: Trajectory tracking control using fractional-order terminal sliding mode control with sliding perturbation observer for a 7-DOF robot manipulator. IEEE/ASME Trans. Mechatron. **25**(4), 1886–1893 (2020)
5. Dai, L., Yu, Y.D., et al.: Robust model predictive tracking control for robot manipulators with disturbances. IEEE Trans. Industr. Electron. **68**(5), 4288–4297 (2021)
6. Hu, B., Guan, Z., et al.: Adaptive tracking control of cooperative robot manipulators with markovian switched couplings. IEEE Trans. Ind. Electron. **68**(3), 2427–2436 (2021)
7. Mobayen, S., Mofid, O., Din, S.U., et al.: Finite-time tracking controller design of perturbed robotic manipulator based on adaptive second-order sliding mode control method. IEEE Access **9**, 71159–71169 (2021)

8. Hwang, C., Yu, W.: Tracking and cooperative designs of robot manipulators using adaptive fixed-time fault-tolerant constraint control. IEEE Access **8**, 56415–56428 (2020)
9. Jinzhu, P., Jie, Y., Jie, W.: Robust adaptive tracking control for nonholonomic mobile manipulator with uncertainties. ISA Trans. **53**(4), 1035–1043 (2014)
10. Fan, Y., Wang, W., et al.: Fuzzy adaptive switching control for an uncertain robot manipulators with time-varying output constraint. Complexity **2018** (2018)
11. Lei, Y., et al.: Trajectory switching control of robotic manipulators based on RBF neural networks. Circuits Syst. Signal Process. **33**(4), 1119–1133 (2014)
12. Lei, Y., et al.: Design of robust adaptive neural switching controller for robotic manipulators with uncertainty and disturbances. J. Intell. Rob. Syst. **77**(3), 571–581 (2015)
13. Liberzon, D.: Switching in Systems and Control. Birkhauser, Boston (2003)
14. Xia, W., et al.: H∞ switched adaptive control for a class of robot manipulators. Trans. Inst. Meas. Control **36**(3), 347–353 (2014)
15. Slotine, J.J.E., Li, W.: Applied Nonlinear Control. Englewood Cliffs (1991)

An Inspection Planning Method for Steam Generators with Triangular-Distributed Tubes

Biying Xu, Xuehe Zhang, Yue Ou, Kuan Zhang, Zhenming Xing, Hegao Cai, Jie Zhao, and Jizhuang Fan[⊠]

State Key Laboratory of Robotics and System, Harbin Institute of Technology, Harbin 150001, China
fanjizhuang@hit.edu.cn

Abstract. With the widespread use of nuclear power, steam generators have been widely used, and their periodic inspection is necessary to ensure reliable operation of steam generators. The planning of the steam generator heat transfer tube inspection robot, i.e., the autonomous operation planning of the robot so that it can inspect the heat transfer tube autonomously and without collision with the environment is a difficult research point for nuclear power plant maintenance robots. Based on the triangular distribution of tube plates, an inspection planning method is proposed in this paper, which includes two parts: task planning and path planning. Based on the distribution of the tube plate and the robot motion, the robot inspection methods are classified into three categories and an evaluation index is proposed for selecting the best planning scheme. Based on the planned robot base inspection positions, an improved A* algorithm is proposed in this paper for robot path planning. To verify the reliability of the proposed algorithm, five sets of experiments are conducted in this paper within a steam generator simulation. The experimental results show that the robot can complete the movement and inspection operations on the tube plate according to the planning results, ensuring full coverage inspection for a given heat transfer tube task. Moreover, after comparing the actual running time of the three planning methods, the robot corresponding to the algorithm proposed in this paper has the shortest running time and the highest working efficiency.

Keywords: Inspection planning method · Task planning · Path planning · Steam generator

1 Introduction

Considering the necessary demand for sustainable energy development, the nuclear power industry has entered a period of rapid development as one of the clean energy sources with low carbon emission, cost of power generation, stable and high utilization rate of power generation, and convenient storage and transportation [1]. The fission reaction of nuclear fuel in the pressure vessel generates a large amount of heat energy, which heats up the high-pressure water in the first circuit, and then the main pump in the first circuit sends the heated high-temperature high-pressure water in the pressure vessel

© The Author(s), under exclusive license to Springer Nature Switzerland AG 2022
H. Liu et al. (Eds.): ICIRA 2022, LNAI 13457, pp. 573–584, 2022.
https://doi.org/10.1007/978-3-031-13835-5_52

to the steam generator, which transfers the heat to the second circuit water through the heat transfer tube in the steam generator, causing the second circuit water to boil and generate steam to drive the turbine rotation [2]. Steam is generated to push the turbine to rotate, which drives the generator set to generate electricity. The heat from the first circuit water is transferred to the second circuit water, and then the temperature drops, and then the first circuit main pump enters the pressure vessel again to absorb the heat energy released by nuclear fission, and so on to realize the cycle of nuclear reactor power generation [3].

The special structural design of the steam generator (SG) enables the exchange of heat energy between the first and second circuits, and at the same time confines nuclear radiation in the first circuit, thus ensuring that the equipment in the second circuit is not contaminated by nuclear radiation during normal operation of the unit. Therefore, the working performance of steam generator is the key to realize efficient energy transfer and prevent nuclear radiation contamination of the second circuit equipment [4].

Therefore, regular performance inspection and maintenance of heat transfer tubes are the main means to ensure safe and reliable operation of steam generators and avoid unscheduled shutdown [5]. The tube plates of steam generators are divided into two types: square tube plates and triangular tube plates according to the arrangement of heat transfer tubes. Currently, the main method of eddy current nondestructive testing is to control the robot movement to accurately place the eddy current probe into the specified heat transfer tubes to obtain the testing data, so as to realize the performance inspection of heat transfer tubes [6]. Since the in-service inspection of steam generators is usually a harsh environment with high nuclear radiation and strong corrosion, and requires high positioning accuracy, heavy inspection tasks, and very complex work tasks, special automated equipment must be used to complete [7].

Most of the existing steam generator robots require human intervention, and in the case of complex multi-task heat transfer tube inspection, operators are required to manually assist and select the heat transfer tubes to be inspected in turn. This method of operation is difficult to achieve and requires high operator skills, and improper operation can easily cause collisions between the inspection equipment and the water chamber of the steam generator, with serious consequences, so it is particularly important to plan the robot overhaul operation and make the robot complete the inspection operation independently.

The robot's operation planning is divided into two main parts, firstly, selecting the robot's inspection position according to the inspection task, and secondly, making the robot move from the current position to the target inspection position. Task 1 is a kind of task planning, in our previous research, we planned for a single inspection task, and planned the robot inspection position for a single task according to the robot's workspace, we applied the method to our self-designed robot and conducted a lot of experiments, and the test results showed that the method is simple and effective. However, for multiple inspection tasks, the method can only be traversed one by one, and the operational efficiency is low [8]. Task 2, path planning, has been widely explored by domestic and foreign scholars for path planning of mobile robots. Tomas Lozano-Perez of MIT and Michael A. Wesley of IBM Research proposed the visual graph method in 1979, which uses an optimization algorithm to search for the optimal path from the starting point

S to the target point G. The shortest path from the starting point to the target point is obtained by accumulating and comparing the distances of these lines. Although the optimal path can be found using the visual graph method, the search time is too long [9]. To improve the efficiency of the search, the smarter A* search algorithm was proposed. The A* algorithm adds an estimation function to Dijkstra's algorithm, which is a cost-based heuristic search algorithm that finds the path with the lowest cost from the initial location to the target location [10]. The traditional A* algorithm has its limitations in applying to robots in different fields, and researchers have made many improvements to the A* algorithm according to the actual application areas and requirements. [11] proposed an improved A* algorithm to reduce the processing time, i.e., the value of the heuristic function s is determined only before the collision, instead of at the beginning of the collision, and there is a good decay in the processing time and the algorithm is faster in computation. In [12], A star planning-key fold extraction to remove redundant node inflection points is performed first, and combined with improved dynamic window method for local path planning to solve the problems of many folds, path redundancy, low smoothness and local minimum.

Considering the necessity of heat transfer tube inspection mentioned above and the difficulty of existing operations, this paper proposes an inspection planning method applied to a triangular-sized tube plate to enable a robot to perform multiple heat transfer tube inspection tasks autonomously.

This paper is structured as follows: Sect. 2 introduces the robot and its environment modeling, Sect. 3 introduces the robot's autonomous inspection planning method, Sect. 4 is the robot autonomous inspection planning and motion experiments, and Sect. 5 summarizes the whole paper.

2   System Design and Model Establishing

2.1   System Design

The robot's inspection system is shown in Fig. 1. The operator sends the inspection plan to the robot planner, which plans the robot's base position (i.e., inspection position) and inspection attitude based on multiple inspection tasks, and then plans the robot's motion path based on the robot's current position and sends the planning result to the robot controller so that the robot can complete the inspection operation autonomously.

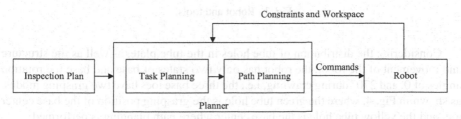

Fig. 1. Robot inspection system.

2.2 Environment and Robot Model

The evaporator tube plate is represented by the grid method, as shown in Fig. 2, with the evaporator tube hole in the center of each grid and the tube plate spacing as the grid center spacing, treating each grid as a node.

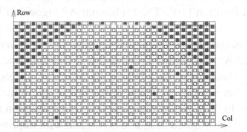

Fig. 2. Triangular-distributed tube plate.

The robot has four degrees of freedom, as shown in Fig. 3(a). The rotation degree of freedom in the middle can ensure the rotation of the foot end when the base is fixed on the pipe plate and the rotation of the base when the foot end is fixed on the pipe plate, and similarly, the movement degree of freedom can ensure the relative movement of the base and the foot end, the elevation degree of freedom can ensure the relative elevation of the base and the foot end, and the tool rotation degree of freedom can make the tool end rotate freely in the range of [−90°, 90°]. In order to improve the inspection °efficiency, the robot carries two tool probes for inspection, as shown in Fig. 3(b).

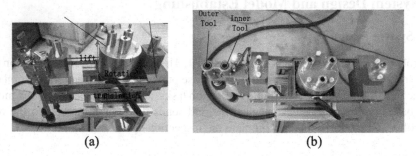

(a)   (b)

Fig. 3. Robot and tools.

Considering the distribution of tube holes in the tube plate, as well as the structure and movement of the robot, the robot has only two states of base and base toe rotation angles of 0, and 270° during crawling, i.e., the three base toes have two grasping modes, as shown in Fig. 4, where the green tube hole is the grasping position of the base center toe, and the yellow tube hole is the base center where path planning is performed.

The robot is an RPR-type robot in planar motion. When two probes are working at the same time, assuming that the tube hole spacing is d, the inner probe tube hole

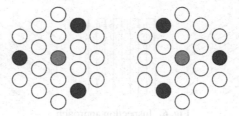

Fig. 4. Robot and tools. (Color figure online)

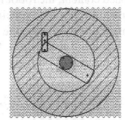

Fig. 5. Tool workspace.

position b1, the outer probe tube hole position b2, and the current base position cb, the base position b satisfies the following conditions.

$$(r_b, c_b) = \{(r, c)|\text{dis}(cb, b)_{min}, \text{dis}(b1, b2) = 2d\} \tag{1}$$

The robot pose is solved as follows, the robot tool workspace is shown in Fig. 5.

$$\begin{cases} \theta_1 = 2d \times \arctan(r_b + \frac{\sqrt{r_{b+}^2 c_b^2}}{c_b}) \\ d_2 = \sqrt{r_{b+}^2 c_b^2} \\ \theta_3 = \arccos(c_{b2} - c_{b1})\text{or } \arcsin(r_{b2} - r_{b1}) \end{cases} \tag{2}$$

3 Method

3.1 Task Planning

Since the outer and inner test tools are separated by two-hole distances and the end of the tool is connected to a cable, in order to ensure that the cable does not interfere, the inspection is efficient, and the robot does not collide with the water chamber, the planning for multiple tasks is based on a single-row task inspection as the planning standard. Considering that the tube plates distributed by the steam generator heat transfer tubes are triangularly distributed tube plates, there are three ways to divide the single-row tasks as follows: left-slanting inspection, inspection by column, and right-slanting inspection, as shown in Fig. 6.

Fig. 6. Inspection approach.

According to the aforementioned content, the robot inspection to a single row as the basic unit, and the tools are separated by two-hole spacing, so we will check the task to 4 as the basic unit of complementary planning, then the inspection form corresponding to the three inspection methods by column as shown in Fig. 7.

Fig. 7. Inspection with groups. (The green thick solid line corresponds to a group of holes as a unit). (Color figure online)

In this paper, we propose the following task planning form. The inspection tasks are first divided into a single row of tasks, and then in units of 4. Based on the workspace calculated in Sect. 2.2, the nearest pedestal location that can check the four inspection tasks from the current position of the pedestal is searched in the workspace of the pedestal until all inspection tasks are planned and a list of pedestals is obtained. The schematic diagram of the search is shown in Fig. 8.

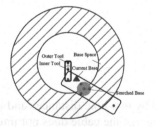

Fig. 8. Inspection with groups.

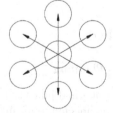

Fig. 9. Six-direction search.

The motion of the robot on the tube plate contains the fixation process and the movement process, that is, when the base is fixed, the foot end moves and rotates, and when the foot end is fixed, the base moves and rotates, and the movement of the robot is completed in this alternating motion. And the fixation process takes a long time, so the planning result should try to make the robot move the shortest distance and the least number of fixation releases. Considering the structure and motion form of the robot, the more the number in the base list, the more positions the base of the robot must be fixed; the farther the planned base is from the current robot position, the more the number of fixation inspections. Therefore, an evaluation index for comparison $Value(i)$, is proposed for selecting the optimal solution from the three inspection methods.

$$Value(i) = w1 \cdot \frac{Num(i)}{\sum_1^3 Num(i)} + w2 \cdot \frac{Length(i)}{\sum_1^3 Length(i)} (i = 1, 2, 3) \qquad (3)$$

For the pedestal results planned by three inspection methods, $Num(i)$ is the number of pedestals planned by the ith inspection method, and $Length(i)$ is the path length obtained by path planning of the ith inspection method. $i = 1$ is left-slanting inspection, $i = 2$ is inspection by column, and $i = 3$ is right-slanting inspection, w1 is the evaluation weight of the number of pedestals, and w2 is the evaluation weight of the path length. The smaller this evaluation value is, the better the planning scheme is. w1 and w2 are determined by experiments.

3.2 Path Planning

Due to the structure of the tube plate positioning robot and the shape of the steam generator tube plate, the robot can only move along the left-slanting direction, column direction, and right-slanting direction of the heat transfer tube pipe during the crawling process, so the search direction is selected as a six-directional search during the path search, as shown in Fig. 9.

The traditional A* algorithm search process is as follows. For the Open table, select the point with the smallest cost among them, find the non-obstructive proximity node n in the search direction of the point, judge its cost f(n), and determine whether it is already in the Open table, if not, directly put the point into the Open table, otherwise, compare the cost of the two arrival methods, and always put the node with the smallest current total cost in the Open table until the smallest node in the Open table is the target point position.

Considering the different walking and rotation times of this tube and plate positioning robot, and the structural design of the robot that allows the tube and plate positioning robot to move a distance larger than one grid at a time, the traditional A* algorithm is improved in two ways: the consideration of the moving direction is added to the cost in the calculation of g (n) and h (n), and the obstacle node is also considered in the search for the proximity node, as described below.

The time spent by the moving action of the pipe plate positioning robot during the crawling process is smaller than the time spent by the rotating action. After the experiment, the cost of moving once directly is selected as Δ, i.e., the cost of moving two adjacent grids in unit of Δ, and the cost of rotating once is 0.8Δ, i.e., the cost of moving one grid after rotation is 1.8Δ. For node n, the valuation function h (n) is taken as the custom distance after adding the rotation variable, and the expression of h (n) is shown as follows.

$$dis(t, n) = \begin{cases} |row_t - row_n| & col_t = col_n \\ |row_t - row_n|/2 & else \end{cases} \qquad (4)$$

$$h(n) = \lceil dis(t, n)/stepmax \rceil \times \Delta + \Delta_r \qquad (5)$$

$$\Delta_r = \begin{cases} 0(col_t = col_n or |row_t - row_n| = |col_t - col_n|) \\ 0.8\Delta \qquad\qquad\qquad\qquad\qquad\qquad (else) \end{cases} \qquad (6)$$

In the process of exploring nodes, three steps are required to determine whether a node is reachable or not. The first step is the accessibility of the base, i.e., whether it satisfies one of the two orientations in Fig. 4. The second step is the reachability of the foot end, i.e., whether the foot end can make the corresponding pipe hole of the foot end a through-hole by moving within the range after the base position is fixed. The third step is to determine whether the robot collides with the water chamber at the current position. A simplified collision model is established for the robot in an enveloping manner, and the two-dimensional sketch of the collision model is shown in Fig. 10, and the robot is collision detected in the depth direction.

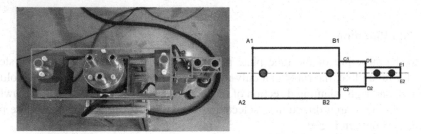

Fig. 10. Robot collision model. (A1…E2 are all detected collision points)

4 Experiment

The tube plate and robot used for the experiment are shown in Fig. 11, where is the base of the robot, is the foot of the robot, and is the corresponding position of the two tools. In this paper, five groups of tasks are selected for the autonomous inspection planning of the robot, and the task-related data corresponding to the tasks in the pipe plate as shown in Fig. 12 (Table 1).

We experimented with the planning results for all three methods, Method 1 for checking by left oblique direction, Method 2 for checking by column direction, and Method 3 for checking by right oblique direction. We recorded the robot running time. The experimental results are shown in Table 2, bolded in black to indicate the method applied by our algorithm planning.

In the first group of experiments, the process of the column-by-column inspection is shown in Fig. 13. The robot follows the planned path, translates and rotates accordingly to reach the inspection position, and then changes its attitude to deliver the two tools to the designated inspection tube holes, where (a)-(g) are the robot's movement process and (h)-(o) are the robot's inspection process.

The number of planning pedestals, planning path length, actual running time and evaluation value of each method were analyzed, and the results are shown in Fig. 14.

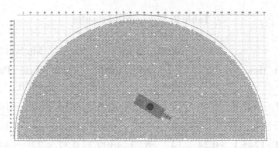

Fig. 11. Environment and robot. (The outer semicircle is the water chamber boundary and the solid round hole is the corresponding position of the heat transfer tube. The large orange rectangle and its solid circles are the foot and its toes, while the small are the tool mechanism and the two tools, and the orange prototype and its solid circle are the base and its toes) (Color figure online)

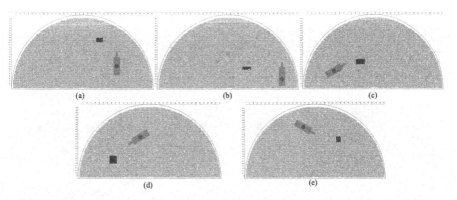

Fig. 12. Experiment tasks. (Black pipe holes are artificially added obstacle pipe holes)

Table 1. Experiment data.

Group	Base Pos	Start Row	Start Col	End Row	End Col	Tube Number
1	47,131	97	106	104	113	36
2	20,155	40	106	45	116	32
3	36,38	50	66	60	76	61
4	84,76	30	38	45	46	72
5	105,73	74	120	85	125	36

From Fig. 14 (a) and (b), it can be seen that the number of pedestals corresponding to each group of experiments is not exactly proportional to the path length, for example, the third group of experiments Method 2 plans the longest path, but the number of pedestals is only higher than the shortest number of pedestals by one. The evaluation value corresponding to each method is calculated and compared with the actual running time of the robot, as shown in Fig. 14 (c), (d). It can be seen that the evaluation value

Table 2. Experiment results.

Group	Method 1				Method 2				Method 3			
	Base Num	Path	time	Value	Base Num	Path	time	Value	Base Num	Path	time	Value
1	4	10.1	542.8	0.45	1	4	**416.5**	**0.15**	3	10.2	441.4	0.40
2	6	21.5	750.23	0.52	2	15.3	656.9	0.28	1	12.2	**602.5**	**0.20**
3	13	26.4	**1245.1**	**0.24**	14	52.3	1309.3	0.37	22	44.2	1560.3	0.39
4	17	34.6	1421.1	0.34	17	23.1	**1400.9**	**0.27**	15	45.1	1440.7	0.39
5	12	41.1	1052.8	0.37	9	38.9	1043.1	0.32	8	40.1	**972.3**	**0.31**

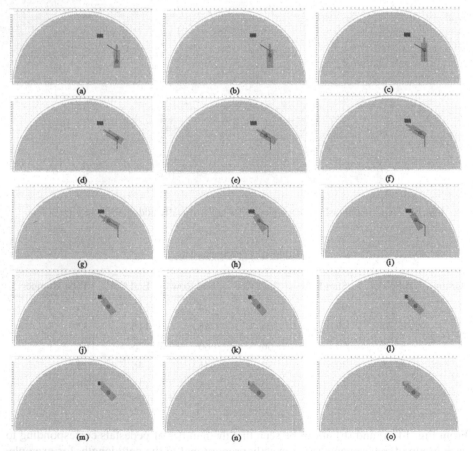

Fig. 13. Robot motion. (The green solid circle in the figure is the planned path, the green hollow circle is the pipe hole to be inspected, and the red hollow circle is the already inspected pipe hole) (Color figure online)

can completely reflect the goodness of the planning scheme, and the results of ranking each group of experiments according to the evaluation value are completely consistent with the running time ranking, i.e., the optimal scheme we choose corresponds to the shortest running time of the robot, the evaluation value evaluation is valid, and all three schemes can ensure that the given Full coverage inspection of heat transfer tubes.

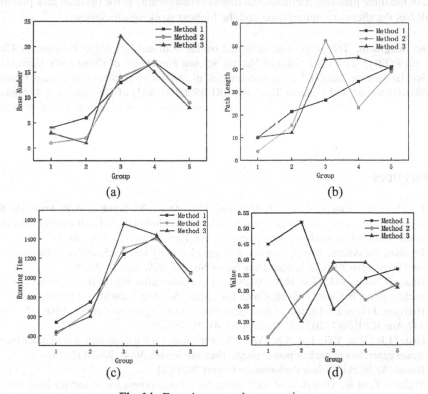

Fig. 14. Experiment results comparison.

5 Conclusion

With the widespread application of nuclear energy, the inspection of heat transfer tubes of steam generators has become a top priority, and it is imperative to perform autonomous inspection planning for robots for multiple inspection tasks so that they can inspect heat transfer tubes autonomously and without colliding with the environment. In this paper, we propose an autonomous inspection planning method based on task planning for robot inspection tasks and path planning for robots based on triangular distribution of tube plates. According to the distribution of the tube plate environment, the inspection methods are divided into three categories, the tasks are subdivided, and an evaluation index of the task planning method is proposed to select the optimal task planning result. Based on the planned base list, path planning is performed based on the current position of the robot, so that the robot moves to the designated inspection position and then inspects the tube holes one by one according to the planned inspection posture. In this paper, five sets of experiments were conducted within the steam generator simulator. The experimental results show that the robot can complete the movement and inspection inspections on the tube plate according to the planning results, ensuring full coverage inspection of the given heat transfer tube task, and after comparing the actual running time of the three planning methods, the robot corresponding to the optimal task planning result has the shortest running time and the highest working efficiency.

Acknowledgment. This work was supported by the National Key R&D Program of China (No. 2019YFB1312101), the National Natural Science Foundation of China (NO. U2013214), the Special funding support for the construction of innovative provinces in Hunan Province (2019GK1010), the Self-Planned Task (NO.SKLRS202001A03) of the State Key Laboratory of Robotics and System (HIT) and Special funding support for the construction of innovative provinces in Hunan Province (2019GK1010).

References

1. Rachkov, V.I., Kalyakin, S.G., Kukharchuk, O.F., Orlov, Y., Sorokin, A.P.: From the first nuclear power plant to fourth-generation nuclear power installations [on the 60th anniversary of the World's First nuclear power plant]. Therm. Eng. **61**(5), 327–336 (2014)
2. International Atomic Energy Agency, Energy, Electricity and Nuclear Power Estimates for the Period up to 2050, Reference Data Series No. 1, IAEA, Vienna (2020)
3. Huan, H., Ding, W.J., Guo, H.B.: Analysis of key issues affecting the development of inland nuclear power in China. J. South China Univ. (Soc. Sci. Edn.). **20**(3), 9–15 (2019)
4. Harrison, J.D., et al.: The use of dose quantities in radiological protection: ICRP publication 147 Ann ICRP 50(1) 2021. J. Radiol. Prot. **41**(2), 410 (2021)
5. Gao, M.H., Han, Y.G., Lei, S.X., Yao, J.Y.: Measures for the operation and maintenance of steam generators in nuclear power plants. Pressure Vessel. **36**(4), 74–78 (2019)
6. Bilbao, S.: World Nuclear Performance Report 2021 [R]
7. Yuchun, T., et al.: Overview of NDT technology development for in-service inspection of pressurized water reactor nuclear power plants. Nondestruct. Test. **31**(12), 959–966 (2009)
8. Xu, B., Li, G., Zhang, K., Cai, H., Zhao, J., Fan, J.: Motion planning of a steam generator mobile tube inspection robot. Nucl. Eng. Technol. **54**, 1374–1383 (2021)
9. Lozano-Perez, T., Wesley, M.: An algorithm for planning collision-free paths among polyhedral obstacles. Commun. ACM **22**(5), 436-450P (1979)
10. Hart, P.E., Nilsson, N.J., Raphael, B.: A Formal basis for the heuristic determination of minimum cost paths. IEEE Trans. Syst. Sci. Cybern. **4**(2), 100–107 (1968)
11. Guruji, A.K., Agarwal, H., Parsediya, D.K.: Time-efficient A* algorithm for robot path planning. Proc. Technol. **23**, 144–149 (2016). ISSN 2212–0173
12. Chen, J., Xu, L., Chen, J., Liu, Q.: Improved A* and dynamic window method for mobile robot path planning. Comput. Integr. Manuf. Syst. 1–17 (2022)

Memory-Based STOMP for Local Path Planning

Wenjie Li[1], Tao Cao[1], Yunfan Wang[2(✉)], and Xian Guo[2]

[1] State Grid Tianjin Electric Power Company, Tianjin, China
[2] Institute of Robotics and Automatic Information System, College of Artificial Intelligence, Nankai University, Tianjin, China
2120210376@mail.nankai.edu.cn, guoxian@nankai.edu.cn

Abstract. Planning and navigation of mobile robots has always been a challenging problem, which has attracted a large number of scholars, especially the research on local path planners. In order to use the past planning experience to guide future path planning, a memory-based stochastic trajectory optimization for motion planning (M-STOMP) is used to solve the local path planning problem. Firstly, the past path planning experience is continuously used to guide the subsequent planning by using memory, which is a method for continuous planning. Then, STOMP algorithm uses Gaussian distribution to generate some smooth paths in the state space, and uses optimized method to update to get a better path. Finally, this method was tested in four different scenarios which validate the proposed method. This paper gave a method for local path planning from a new perspective.

Keywords: Path planning · Mobile robot · Collision avoidance

1 Introduction

Collision avoidance is the primary basic task for mobile robots to work properly. The robot needs to find a collision-free path between a given starting point and an end point so that the robot can reach the end point safely. Path planning techniques emerge to plan a collision-free path. However, today's path-planning techniques are far from making robots as flexible as humans. Robot path planning is divided into global path planning and local path planning like humans. For static scenarios, the global path planner finds a reasonable global path that tells the robot where to go in the future. Following the planned global path, there will always be emergencies, such as some dynamic obstacles such as pedestrians and vehicles. The local path planner can deal with dynamic scenarios based on the sensor data. Local path planning is one of the key technologies for the navigation of mobile robots, which attracts a large number of researchers. This paper focuses on local path planning methods.

This work is supported by State Grid Tianjin electric power company science and technology project (KJ21-1-32).

Many local path planning algorithms have been proposed not only for static but also dynamic obstacles [3,6]. The VFH (Vector field histogram) [2] algorithm uses statistical histogram to represent obstacle occupation of all grids and their influence on the motion direction to obtain the optimal motion direction. This method has similar disadvantages with the artificial potential field method, in addition, the kinematics and dynamics of the robot are not considered. The VFH+ method [13] was proposed to improve the origin VFH with full consideration about the size of the robot, kinematics and dynamics characteristics. However, VFH+ sometimes cannot find the most appropriate direction because of its limited range of perception. VFH* [14] was proposed to address that problem by introducing preplanning.

There is a local planning method for sampling in motion space, which considers the kinematic model and dynamics constraints. The dynamic window approach (DWA) [5] proposed by Fox et al. sample feasible action in action space using the velocity space with dynamic constraints (VSD). VSD gives a feasible velocity space from the current robot velocity. The candidate paths can be obtained by simulating the sampled actions forward. A optimal path is selected by evaluate this candidate paths. Dobrevski et al. proposed a adaptive DWA method [4] which introduces a data-driven method to adjust the parameters of DWA adaptively. The global dynamic path planning fusion algorithm was proposed in [10] combining DWA with jump-A*.

Sampling in state space is more suitable for constrained environment than sampling in action space. A state space sampling strategy was proposed in [7]. Such methods consider uniform sampling in the state space and then obtain control commands by backward solving. Some sampling methods are Bezier curve method, cyclotron curve method and state lattice sampling [9].

In this paper, the stochastic trajectory optimization for motion planning (STOMP) was used to complete local path planning, which is also a state-space sampling method. Using a Gaussian distribution produces a certain number of smooth paths in the state space, which are then optimized appropriately. In particular, this paper uses a memory-based approach that can use past planning experience to guide subsequent path planning.

The remainder of this paper is organized as follows. In Sect. 2, we briefly introduced the STOMP algorithm. In Sect. 3, the memory is introduced to STOMP for local path planning, the matching and correction methods are described in detail, and a basic path tracking method is presented. The memory-based STOMP is tested in four scenarios in Sect. 4. Section 5 concludes this paper.

2   Basic STOMP

STOMP [8] is a optimization method to motion planning problem that can tackle general constraints because no gradient information is required in optimization process. The STOMP involves stochastic trajectory optimization using a certain number of noise trajectories, which turns a planning problem into a optimization problem. STOMP algorithm optimization starts with an initial trajectory Θ that has N intermediate states $\theta_i \in \mathbb{R}^J$, where J is the dimension of every state θ_i. The time between any two adjacent states θ_i and $theta_{i+1}$ is set to ΔT. K noise trajectories will be generated randomly to update current trajectory in each iteration using Gaussian distribution $\mathcal{N}(0, \Sigma)$.

The optimization problem can be described as minimizing the cost function:

$$\min_{\tilde{\theta}} \mathbb{E} \left[\sum_{i=1}^{N} q\left(\tilde{\theta}_i\right) + \frac{1}{2}\tilde{\Theta}^\top R\tilde{\Theta} \right] \tag{1}$$

where $\tilde{\Theta} = [\tilde{\theta}_1, \tilde{\theta}_2, \cdots, \tilde{\theta}_N] \in \mathbb{R}^{J \times N}$ is a noise trajectory, $q\left(\tilde{\theta}_i\right)$ is a state-dependent cost function including obstacle cost, torque cost and constraints cost. $R = A^\top A$ is a semi-position definite matrix, A is a finite differencing matrix.

$$A = \begin{bmatrix} 1 & 0 & 0 & & 0 & 0 & 0 \\ -2 & 1 & 0 & \cdots & 0 & 0 & 0 \\ 1 & -2 & 1 & & 0 & 0 & 0 \\ & \vdots & & \ddots & & \vdots & \\ 0 & 0 & 0 & & 1 & -2 & 1 \\ 0 & 0 & 0 & \cdots & 0 & 1 & -2 \\ 0 & 0 & 0 & & 0 & 0 & 1 \end{bmatrix}$$

The STOMP estimates the gradient of the cost function of Eq. 1 inspired by a work in the areas of path integral reinforcement learning [12] rather than solving its gradient directly in [11]. The stochastic gradient is estimated as follow:

$$\delta\hat{\Theta}_G = \int \exp\left(-\frac{1}{\lambda}S(\Theta)\right)\delta\Theta d(\delta\Theta) \tag{2}$$

where $S(\Theta) = \sum_{i=1}^{N} q(\theta_i)$ is the sum of costs of all intermediate states along the trajectory Θ.

3 STOMP for Local Planning

A memory-based STOMP algorithm is introduced to solve local path planning problem, the algorithm can quickly match a better path from the past empirical memory according to the current local obstacles, and then optimize the path appropriately for several times to obtain a better path. For mobile robot, a state θ can be described by a vector $[x, y, \phi]^\top$, and a trajectory with N intermediate states can be described by $\Theta = [\theta_1, \theta_2, \cdots, \theta_N] \in \mathbb{R}^{3 \times N}$.

3.1 Memory-Based STOMP

Memory. In order to be able to take advantage of past path planning experience and continue to plan better and better, a memory-based STOMP is presented [16]. A memory $\mathcal{M}$ is set up to store past experience like $(e^{past}, \theta_g^{past}, \Theta^{past})$, where e^{past} is a vector to describe the local obstacles perceived by sensors in the past local planning, $\theta_g^{past} = [x_g, y_g, \phi_g]^T$ is the goal state in the past local planning, Θ^{past} is the optimal path obtained in the past local planning under the conditions of e^{past} and θ_g^{past}.

The e^{past} in each triple $(e^{past}, \theta_g^{past}, \Theta^{past})$ is a vector to describe local obstacles. A low-precision 6×6 grid is used to describe obstacles, and this low-precision map can be obtained using low-cost sensors. The advantage of low-precision maps is that they can reduce costs and facilitate fast matching calculations for memory mechanisms. The e^{past} can be obtained by reshaping the 6×6 map into a vector of 36×1.

In the matching process, it is also necessary to match the target, but the mobile robot keeps moving so that the absolute position changes all the time. Therefore, relative position is used in the matching calculation. The θ_g^{past} is a relative state to describe the position of a given local goal θ_{goal}^{local} relative to the current state $\theta^{current}$ of the robot.

$$\theta_g^{past} = \theta_{goal}^{local} - \theta^{current} \tag{3}$$

It doesn't make sense to use absolute position at all because the absolute position of the robot is always changing. The trajectory Θ^{past} stored in memory is also relative to the robot's current position $\theta^{current}$. Here an operation is denoted as

$$\Theta^{current} = \Xi\left(\theta^{current}\right) = [\overbrace{\theta^{current}, \ldots, \theta^{current}}^{N}] \tag{4}$$

$$\Theta^{past} = \Theta^{local} - \Theta^{current} \tag{5}$$

where Θ^{local} is a trajectory in local planning with absolute positions.

Matching. We hope to quickly match past experience in memory to a good path according to the current local obstacle environment and the given local goal. Therefore, the similarity between the current information $(e^{new}, \theta_g^{new})$ and the information in memory must be calculated. Since we consider the similarity between the current local obstacle map and the past obstacle map, mainly the difference in shape and position, rather than the difference in numerical size, we choose cosine similarity as the index of matching calculation. The similarity can be computed as following

$$
\begin{aligned}
s_e &= \frac{e^{new} \cdot e^{past}}{||e^{new}||_2 ||e^{past}||_2} \\
s_g &= \frac{\theta_g^{new} \cdot \theta_g^{past}}{||\theta_g^{new}||_2 ||\theta_g^{past}||_2} \\
s &= s_e \times s_g
\end{aligned}
\tag{6}
$$

where s_e is the similarity between the new obstacle map and the past obstacle map, s_g is the similarity between the new goal and the past goal, s is the comprehensive similarity, considering both obstacles and goal. The path with the greatest similarity will be used as the matched path.

Modification. The matched path is relative path because all states subtracted $\theta^{current}$ so that the start state θ_s of the path is a zero vector. Absolute path can be obtained

$$\Theta = \Theta^{past} + \Xi\left(\theta^{current}\right) = \Theta^{past} + \Theta^{current} \tag{7}$$

The matched path must be corrected because the goal of the matched path is a little different from the given goal θ_g^{new}. After changing the goal of the path to the desired absolute goal $\theta_g^{new} + \theta^{current}$, we also need to modify each intermediate state of the path so that the distance between the intermediate states is evenly distributed. We calculate the corrections for each intermediate state and make corrections to the states in reverse order from state θ_{N-1} to θ_2 except for θ_s and θ_g.

$$\Delta = \frac{\sum_{i=1}^{N-1} \|\theta_{i+1} - \theta_i\|}{N-1}$$
$$\delta\theta_i = \frac{\|\theta_{i+1} - \theta_i\| - \Delta}{\|\theta_{i+1} - \theta_i\|} \left(\theta_{i+1} - \theta_i\right) \tag{8}$$
$$\theta_i = \theta_i + \delta\theta_i$$

where $\|\cdot\|$ is the length of a vector, Δ is average length of the interval between two adjacent states of this path, $\delta\theta_i$ is the correction for ith state along this path. See Algorithm 1 for the pseudocode of matching and correction.

Algorithm 1. Match and modify path

Input: the memory $\mathcal{M}$ storing past $(e^{past}, \theta_g^{past}, \Theta^{past})$; new obstacle environment information e^{new}; new goal configuration θ_g^{new};
Output: a path Θ;
1: **function** MATCHTRAJ($\mathcal{M}, e^{new}, \theta_g^{new}$)
2:     **for** $i = 1, 2, ..., size(\mathcal{M})$ **do**
3:         Compute cosine similarity s_i using Eq. 6
4:     **end for**
5:     $idx = argmax(s)$
6:     $\Theta_m \leftarrow \Theta_{idx}^{past}$
7:     Using Eq. 7 to get absolute path.
8:     **for** $i = N - 1, N - 2, ..., 2$ **do**
9:         Modify state θ_i using Eq. 8
10:     **end for**
11:     **return** Θ_m
12: **end function**

Optimization. The path that has been matched and corrected is used as an candidate initial path, and then optimization is carried out to obtain a better path. another candidate initial path can be get from the global path. Before optimization, compare the two candidate initial paths and choose the better one as the initial path. In order to limit the size of memory and ensure the diversity of memory, it is necessary to decide whether to store experience into memory after optimization. The pseudocode is shown in Algorithm 2.

Algorithm 2. Memory-based STOMP

Input: $\boldsymbol{\theta}_s$, $\boldsymbol{\theta}_g^{new}$, e^{new}, N, $\mathcal{M}$, $Q(\boldsymbol{\Theta}) = \sum_{i=1}^{N} q(\theta_i) + \frac{1}{2}\boldsymbol{\Theta}^\top R\boldsymbol{\Theta}$;
Output: a collision-free path $\boldsymbol{\Theta}$
1: $\boldsymbol{\Theta}_g \leftarrow$ GLOBAL_PATH$(\boldsymbol{\theta}_s, \boldsymbol{\theta}_g^{new}, N)$ —— Get the first N states of the global path
2: $\boldsymbol{\Theta}_m \leftarrow$ MATCHTRAJ$(\mathcal{M}, e^{new}, \boldsymbol{\theta}_g^{new})$ —— Match a path from memory
3: **if** $Q(\boldsymbol{\Theta}_m) < Q(\boldsymbol{\Theta}_g)$ **then** —— Select a better path by comparing
4:     $\boldsymbol{\Theta}_{init} = \boldsymbol{\Theta}_m$
5:     $store$=False
6: **else**
7:     $\boldsymbol{\Theta}_{init} = \boldsymbol{\Theta}_l$
8:     $store$=True
9: **end if**
10: $\boldsymbol{\Theta} \leftarrow$ STOMP$(\boldsymbol{\theta}_s, \boldsymbol{\theta}_g^{new}, \boldsymbol{\Theta}_{init})$ —— To optimize. The pseudo code is in [8]
11: **if** $store$ **then**
12:     $\mathcal{M}.insert((e^{new}, \boldsymbol{\theta}_g^{new}, \boldsymbol{\Theta}))$ —— Store experience in memory
13: **end if**

3.2   Control for Tracking Path

The kinematic model [1] of the differential robot in Fig. 1 is as follows

$$\dot{\xi} = \begin{pmatrix} \dot{x} \\ \dot{y} \\ \dot{\theta} \end{pmatrix} = \begin{pmatrix} \cos\theta & -l_2\cos\theta - l_1\sin\theta \\ \sin\theta & -l_2\sin\theta + l_1\cos\theta \\ 0 & 1 \end{pmatrix} \begin{pmatrix} v \\ w \end{pmatrix} \tag{9}$$

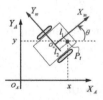

Fig. 1. Robot configuration

Set the position of P_t to $(l_1, 0)$, and control the position of this point.

$$\begin{pmatrix} \dot{x} \\ \dot{y} \end{pmatrix} = \begin{pmatrix} \cos\theta & -l_1\sin\theta \\ \sin\theta & l_1\cos\theta \end{pmatrix} \begin{pmatrix} v \\ w \end{pmatrix} = M \begin{pmatrix} v \\ w \end{pmatrix} \tag{10}$$

with M invertible matrix.

Given a goal position (x_g, y_g), the errors of position can be computed

$$e_x = x - x_g$$
$$e_y = y - y_g$$

(11)

Since the target is constant, the derivative of the error can be obtained

$$\dot{e}_x = \dot{x}$$
$$\dot{e}_y = \dot{y}$$

(12)

We can use a simple proportional controller as follow

$$\begin{pmatrix} v \\ w \end{pmatrix} = -KM^{-1} \begin{pmatrix} e_x \\ e_y \end{pmatrix}$$

(13)

4   Simulation

In order to better evaluate our algorithm, we carried out simulation in several different scenarios [15] including maze, office, room and shopping mall because different scenarios can be used to test the security and flexibility of local planners. We used the Gazebo simulation platform in Ubuntu for simulation because of its increasing popularity among the ROS community and selected the Pioneer 3-DX mobile robot as our differential drive mobile robot.

Simulation in four scenarios is shown in the Fig. 2. The maze and shopping mall in Figs. 2(a) and 2(d) are large-scale scenarios which can evaluate the applicability of local planners. In particular, the maze is the more challenging scenario because it has a narrower passage and the robot needs to make continuous turns to avoid obstacles which can test the robot's flexibility. The room and office scenarios in Figs. 2(c) and 2(b) which have more obstacles can test the obstacle avoidance ability of the algorithm. Each scenario contains a 2-D map and a 3-D Gazebo model. In 2-D map, the green path is given by global path planner, the blue paths are noise paths generated by M-STOMP, the red path is the actual path to track. The paths generated by M-STOMP are shown in Fig. 3 to compare with Bezier curve sampling method. The Bezier curve sampling method samples multiple candidate target points in the state space and constructs Bezier curves which results in a generated path whose target point is not on the global path. In this M-STOMP, a target point is found on the global path, and all generated noise paths will reach the same target point. In this method, a path is selected between the starting point and the target point to "bypass" obstacles. The noise paths generated by this method can cover more state space and plan more kinds of paths.

Three evaluation indexes proposed in [15] were used to compare DWA, Bezier curves and M-STOMP respectively. DWA is a sampling method in control space, Bezier curves is a sampling method in state space. The simulation results are shown in Table 1 and the best results are shown in bold. DWA samples directly in the control space, which has better motion efficiency. Bezier curve sampling method makes use of the smoothness of Bezier curve to sample in the state space, so the velocity smoothness is better. The M-STOMP in this paper has better safety because it covers a larger state space and takes advantage of memory mechanisms.

Table 1. The simulation results of three algorithms

	M-STOMP	Bezier curve	DWA
Safety [%]	**3.81**	4.30	20.20
Motion efficiency [s]	33.11	29.58	**22.04**
Velocity smoothness [m/s^2]	0.126	**0.045**	0.100

In this paper, the local path planning problem of mobile robot is solved from a new perspective. This algorithm uses memory-based methods to make robot planning more and more accurate as the number of planning increases, similar to the continuous learning process of humans. Although this method has no outstanding performance in computing time, the path security planned by this method is much higher. As shown in the Fig. 3(a), the red path has good smoothness and perfect curvature to avoid obstacles as much as possible for better safety.

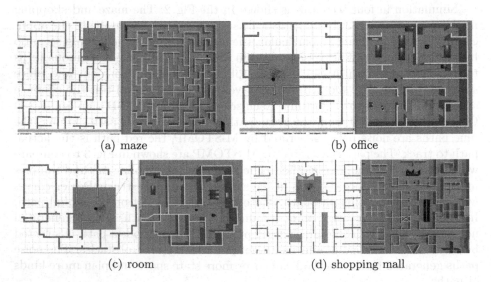

(a) maze

(b) office

(c) room

(d) shopping mall

Fig. 2. Simulation in four scenarios: for each scenario in the subgraph, a 2-D map on left and a Gazebo 3D model on right half are included. The global path is green, the noise path is blue and the actual path tracked is red. (Color figure online)

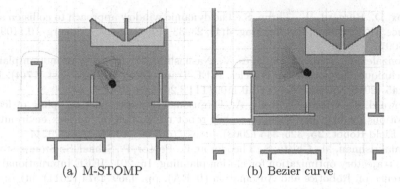

(a) M-STOMP   (b) Bezier curve

Fig. 3. M-STOMP local path planner and Bezier curve local path planner: the green path is global, the blue are paths sampled and the red is the actual path to follow. (Color figure online)

5 Conclusion

The Stochastic trajectory optimization for motion planning (STOMP) was employed on local path planning for mobile robot, and a memory was introduced to utilize past planning experience. The robot can preliminarily match a path from memory based on the current target and local low-precision obstacle map. The multivariate Gaussian distribution can be used to generate smooth noise paths that can bypass obstacles to reach the same target point on the global path. These paths can cover a larger state space and find more diverse local paths than Bezier curve method. In this paper, memory is introduced for continuous planning of the robot, that is, past planning experience can be used to guide subsequent path planning, which is a smart way to make robots more adept and smarter at planning their paths. Finally, our method is validated in four different scenarios.

References

1. Adouane, L.: Orbital obstacle avoidance algorithm for reliable and on-line mobile robot navigation (2009)
2. Borenstein, J., Koren, Y.: The vector field histogram-fast obstacle avoidance for mobile robots. IEEE Trans. Robot. Autom. **7**(3), 278–288 (1991). https://doi.org/10.1109/70.88137
3. Cai, K., Wang, C., Cheng, J., De Silva, C.W., Meng, M.Q.H.: Mobile robot path planning in dynamic environments: a survey. arXiv preprint arXiv:2006.14195 (2020)
4. Dobrevski, M., Skočaj, D.: Adaptive dynamic window approach for local navigation. In: 2020 IEEE/RSJ International Conference on Intelligent Robots and Systems (IROS), pp. 6930–6936 (2020). https://doi.org/10.1109/IROS45743.2020.9340927

5. Fox, D., Burgard, W., Thrun, S.: The dynamic window approach to collision avoidance. IEEE Robot. Autom. Mag. **4**(1), 23–33 (1997). https://doi.org/10.1109/100.580977
6. González, D., Pérez, J., Milanés, V., Nashashibi, F.: A review of motion planning techniques for automated vehicles. IEEE Trans. Intell. Transp. Syst. **17**(4), 1135–1145 (2016). https://doi.org/10.1109/TITS.2015.2498841
7. Howard, T., Green, C., Kelly, A., Ferguson, D.: State space sampling of feasible motions for high performance mobile robot navigation in complex environments. J. Field Robot. **25**, 325–345 (2008). https://doi.org/10.1002/rob.20244
8. Kalakrishnan, M., Chitta, S., Theodorou, E., Pastor, P., Schaal, S.: Stomp: stochastic trajectory optimization for motion planning. In: 2011 IEEE International Conference on Robotics and Automation (ICRA), pp. 4569–4574 (2011). https://doi.org/10.1109/ICRA.2011.5980280
9. Knepper, R.A., Kelly, A.: High performance state lattice planning using heuristic look-up tables. In: 2006 IEEE/RSJ International Conference on Intelligent Robots and Systems, pp. 3375–3380 (2006). https://doi.org/10.1109/IROS.2006.282515
10. Liu, L., et al.: Global dynamic path planning fusion algorithm combining jump-a* algorithm and dynamic window approach. IEEE Access **9**, 19632–19638 (2021). https://doi.org/10.1109/ACCESS.2021.3052865
11. Ratliff, N., Zucker, M., Bagnell, J., Srinivasa, S.: CHOMP: gradient optimization techniques for efficient motion planning, pp. 489–494, June 2009. https://doi.org/10.1109/ROBOT.2009.5152817
12. Theodorou, E., Buchli, J., Schaal, S.: Reinforcement learning of motor skills in high dimensions: a path integral approach. In: 2010 IEEE International Conference on Robotics and Automation (ICRA), pp. 2397–2403 (2010). https://doi.org/10.1109/ROBOT.2010.5509336
13. Ulrich, I., Borenstein, J.: VFH+: reliable obstacle avoidance for fast mobile robots. In: Proceedings of 1998 IEEE International Conference on Robotics and Automation (Cat. No. 98CH36146). vol. 2, pp. 1572–1577 (1998). https://doi.org/10.1109/ROBOT.1998.677362
14. Ulrich, I., Borenstein, J.: VFH/SUP */: local obstacle avoidance with look-ahead verification. In: Proceedings 2000 ICRA. Millennium Conference. IEEE International Conference on Robotics and Automation. Symposia Proceedings (Cat. No. 00CH37065), vol. 3, pp. 2505–2511 (2000). https://doi.org/10.1109/ROBOT.2000.846405
15. Wen, J., et al.: MRPB 1.0: a unified benchmark for the evaluation of mobile robot local planning approaches. In: 2021 IEEE International Conference on Robotics and Automation (ICRA), pp. 8238–8244 (2021). https://doi.org/10.1109/ICRA48506.2021.9561901
16. Yunfan, W., Xian, G.: Memory-based stochastic trajectory optimization for manipulator obstacle avoiding motion planning. In: 2022 7th Asia-Pacific Conference on Intelligent Robot Systems (ACIRS). (Accepted)

Research and Verification of Robot Master-Slave Control Algorithm for Nuclear Power Maintenance Scenarios

Feng Yang[1], Haihua Huang[2], Yanzheng Chen[1], Weiming Li[2], Quanbin Lai[3(✉)], Rui Ma[3], Binxuan Sun[3], and Xingguang Duan[3]

[1] Guangxi Fangchenggang Nuclear Power Co., Ltd., Guangxi 538001, China
[2] China Nuclear Power Technology Research Institute Co., Ltd., Shenzhen 518000, China
[3] Beijing Institute of Technology, Beijing 100081, China
quanbin.lai@bit.edu.cn

Abstract. In this paper, the master-slave control algorithm is investigated and an experimental verification platform is built to validate the master-slave algorithm and the remote maintenance operation flow for the needs of nuclear power remote maintenance scenarios. The paper adopts an incremental master-slave control algorithm based on position-orientation separation method, which overcomes the isomerism and workspace inconsistency problem between the master and slave while ensuring the same motion trend between the master and slave; Secondly, a variety of position mapping scales are designed to meet the needs of nuclear power maintenance operation tasks, taking into account the efficiency and accuracy of the operation. Meanwhile, a safety assurance mechanism is introduced in the master-slave control architecture to eliminate the situation that the slave robot arm moves violently in a short period of time due to operator's misoperation. Finally, the effectiveness of the master-slave control algorithm is verified by simulating a nuclear remote maintenance task on the experimental validation platform.

Keywords: Nuclear robot · Remote maintenance · Master-Slave control

1 Introduction

As a clean energy source that does not produce carbon dioxid, nuclear energy has greater advantages over other clean energy sources such as hydropower, wind power and solar energy, both in terms of technical maturity, economic efficiency and sustainability and future prospects [1]. However, due to the highly damaging nature of nuclear radiation to humans and electrical equipment, the harsh working environment of nuclear power plants poses a series of difficult problems that

This work was supported by the National Key R&D Program of China (Grant No. 2019YFB1310803).

H. Liu et al. (Eds.): ICIRA 2022, LNAI 13457, pp. 595–603, 2022.
https://doi.org/10.1007/978-3-031-13835-5_54

constrain the generation of electricity and reduce the efficiency of power generation. For example, during the operation and maintenance of nuclear power plants, repetitive and time-consuming tasks such as maintenance and replacement of nuclear power facilities need to be carried out in a radioactive environment, limiting the total working time of operators [2]. Given that operators are very restricted in the nuclear environment, robots based on remote control algorithms are used in the nuclear environment to replace operators for nuclear power plant tasks [3].

In terms of nuclear power robotics applications, Joseph S, Kevin R et al. developed a six-legged teleoperated robot in 1990, ROBIN [4], which can move in any direction by means of a six-legged mechanism and carries a robotic arm with a load capacity of 13 kg, giving it a greater advantage in the grasping of discarded objects. In 1999, the JAEA Institute developed the RaBot teleoperated robot in response to a request from the Japanese government [5], but the lack of follow-up attention made the product inadequate and it was not put into use at the Fukushima nuclear power plant, causing huge losses. After the Fukushima nuclear leak in Japan, iRobot urgently produced two teleoperated robots, PackBot [6] and Warrior [7], which were put into the handling of the Fukushima nuclear accident. In terms of master-slave control algorithms, paper [8] presents a teleoperation strategy, using direct angle mapping and CLIK (closed-loop inverse kinematics) methods to implement the manipulation of the slave in position-position mode. In paper [9], Amit Shukla et al. present modeling, simulation, and control of a novel teleoperated mechanism, where two nonisomorphic manipulators are used in one integrated system. Alana Sherman et al. focus on the design and testing of teleoperation controllers which are required to discriminate changes in compliance, addressing the question of which controller architecture performs the best in the high fidelity application of telesurgery in paper [10]. Byeong-Yeon Kim [11] presents a synchronization scheme of bilateral teleoperation systems using composite adaptive controller, solving the position and force tracking problems in free and contact motion.

Current nuclear robots are mostly used in nuclear power plants for emergency and reprocessing tasks, mainly for single tasks such as cleaning and cutting, and are relatively simple to handle. However, in addition to emergency tasks, nuclear power plants also include routine operation and maintenance tasks, such as overhauling damaged pipe connections, bolts and fasteners. In the maintenance tasks, due to the small size of the operated objects and the complex and unpredictable environment, there is a high demand for operational flexibility and precision. The existing post-processing nuclear robots are difficult to meet the needs of operation and maintenance in terms of control flexibility and precision.

This paper investigates the key technology master-slave control algorithm for nuclear power operation and maintenance scenarios, using a mapping algorithm based on position-orientation separation method to improve control flexibility, and designing various mapping scales to improve the accuracy of manipulation. By building an experimental verification system for maintenance tasks, the effectiveness of the nuclear maintenance process and master-slave control algorithm is verified in principle.

2 Experimental Validation System and Workflow

The verification system mainly consists of a 6-DoF collaborative robot, a force feedback master manipulator, a loosening verification end effector and an end effector holder, as shown in Fig. 1-(a). The collaborative robot adopts AUBO-i5 collaborative robot, which has a 5 kg workload and a maximum working radius of 886.5 mm, with a repeatable positioning accuracy of ±0.02 mm. The force feedback master manipulator is Omega.6 from Force Dimension, with six degrees of freedom for Cartesian spatial position and orientation control and force feedback capability in the X, Y, Z translation directions. Loosening verification end effector is similar to a hexagonal socket spanner, as shown in Fig. 1-(b), with a hexagonal profile structure inside the socket for clamping the nut during the loosening/tightening process.

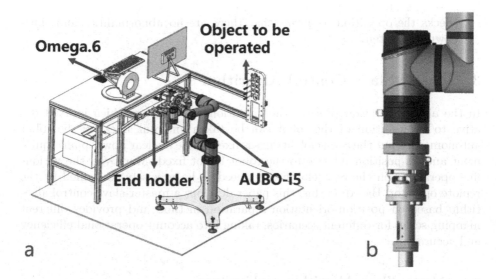

Fig. 1. Verification system components and loosening verification end effector.

2.1 Validation System Workflow

This paper simulates the task of loosening damaged pipe connections (Swagelok fittings) in a nuclear power plant using the maintenance verification system mentioned above. The specific task flow is as follows:

(1) System initialization. Power up the system, perform status self-test on the collaborative robot and master hand, complete the initialization of the position, and enter the working mode.
(2) Autonomously picking the loosening verification end effector. As the position of the end effector holder is fixed in relation to the collaborative robot, in order to improve the efficiency of the operation, the point of the end effector

holder is pre-marked and the collaborative robot moves autonomously to pick and place the loosening verification end effector. In this step, the operator selects the corresponding end effector of the operation in the host computer and then the collaborative robot pick it from the end effector holder.

(3) Loosening of Swagelok fittings based on master-slave control mode. After picking the operating end effector, the collaborative robot enters master-slave control mode, where the operator controls the robot position and orientation via a remote master hand to reach the vicinity of the Swagelok fittings and perform fine operations on the Swagelok fittings, such as alignment, snapping in and Loosening.

(4) Putting back the Loosening end effector. After Loosening the Swagelok fittings in master-slave mode, the operator gives the relevant instructions to the robot to place the damaged Swagelok fittings in a fixed recovery position and to return the operating end effector to the end effector holder.

(5) System shutdown. When all operations have been completed, the operator checks the operation, confirms that there are no abnormalities and shuts down the system.

3   Master-Slave Control Algorithm

In the above operation process, the operation end effector which is fixed relative to the position of the robot can be taken and put back by the robot autonomously, but the Swagelok fittings is fixed in the nuclear power plant equipment and its position relative to the robot is not fixed. Moreover, the various fine operations on the Swagelok fittings need to be precisely controlled by the remote operator. Based on this, this paper develops a master-slave control algorithm based on position-orientation separation method and provides different mapping scales for different scenarios, taking into account operational efficiency and accuracy.

3.1   Master-Slave Algorithm Architecture

As the master hand and slave robot are structurally isomeric, an incremental master-slave control algorithm is required. This algorithm, which is very common in minimally invasive laparoscopic surgery [12], is characterised by allowing a large gap in the workspace between the master hand and slave robot and does not require the master hand and slave robot to be in the same position at all times. The basic principle of the algorithm is to calculate the position increment of the master hand at the current moment relative to the previous moment and superimpose this position increment on the position of the slave robot at the previous moment as the desired position of the robot arm at the current moment. For orientation, as it is not linear, it cannot be superimposed directly like position. If the orientation of the master hand and the slave robot were to be kept consistent all the time in a certain coordinate system (e.g. world coordinate system), this would lead to a sudden movement of the slave robot when the master-slave connection is established to ensure that the orientation of slave robot is consistent with that of master hand. For our workflow, this approach is not suitable. We need to keep the robot stationary after the master hand position has been adjusted and a new master-slave connection has been established. Therefore, this paper adopts a master-slave control algorithm that separates position and orientation: in position, an incremental mapping is made, and in orientation, the motion trend between the two moments is calculated, so that the slave robot maintains the same motion trend as the master hand, instead of absolute following of orientation. If necessary, the orientation can be locked and only the position is mapped. The algorithm architecture is shown in Fig. 2.

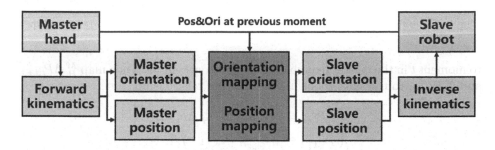

Fig. 2. Master-slave algorithm architecture.

3.2 Incremental Master-Slave Control Algorithm Based on Position-Orientation Separation Method

In this paper, ${}^A_B T_t$ denotes the transformation relationship of coordinate system B with respect to coordinate system A at time t. The coordinate systems are defined as follows: H is the master end effector coordinate system; M is the master base coordinate system; S is the slave robot base coordinate system; I is the slave robot end effector coordinate system. The coordinate transformation relationship is shown in Fig. 3. At moment t, the position ${}^M_H P_t$ and orientation ${}^M_H R_t$ of the master hand can be obtained through the positive kinematics of the master hand, which, after a time period, moves to a new position ${}^M_H P_{t+1}$ and orientation ${}^M_H R_{t+1}$ at moment $t+1$, satisfying the following relation.

$$\begin{cases} {}^M_H \Delta P_{t,t+1} = {}^M_H P_{t+1} - {}^M_H P_t \\ {}^M_H R_{t+1} = {}^M_H R_{t,t+1} * {}^M_H R_t \end{cases} \tag{1}$$

In Eq. 1, ${}^M_H \Delta P_{t,t+1}$ represents the position increment of the end effector coordinate system H at moment $t+1$ with respect to moment t in the master hand base coordinate system M, while ${}^M_H R_{t,t+1}$ is the trend of the orientation transformation of the end effector coordinate system H at moment t+1 with respect

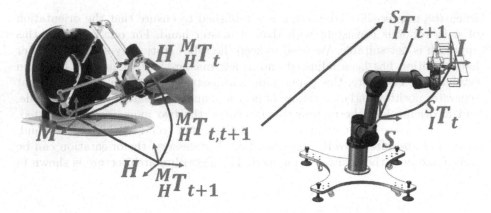

Fig. 3. Definition of coordinate systems and coordinate transformation relationship.

to moment t in the master hand base coordinate system M. Then map $^{M}_{H}\Delta P_{t,t+1}$ and $^{M}_{H}R_{t,t+1}$ to the slave robot in the following relationship.

$$\begin{cases} ^{S}_{I}P_{t+1} = ^{S}_{I}P_{t} + ^{S}_{M}R * ^{M}_{H}\Delta P_{t,t+1} \\ ^{S}_{I}R_{t+1} = ^{S}_{M}R * ^{M}_{H}R_{t,t+1} * ^{S}_{I}R_{t} \end{cases} \tag{2}$$

In Eq. 2, $^{S}_{I}P_{t+1}$, $^{S}_{I}R_{t+1}$ represent the desired position and orientation of the slave robot at $t+1$ moment; $^{S}_{M}R$ represents the transformation relationship between the master hand base coordinate system M and the slave robot base coordinate system S, which can be obtained directly or indirectly by the way the master hand and slave robot are mounted. Therefore, according to the above relationship, the position and orientation $^{S}_{I}T_{t+1}$ (Eq. 3) of the slave robot arm at the moment $t+1$ is obtained.

$$^{S}_{I}T_{t+1} = \begin{bmatrix} ^{S}_{I}R_{t+1} & ^{S}_{I}P_{t+1} \\ 0 & 1 \end{bmatrix} \tag{3}$$

The inverse kinematics is solved to obtain the desired angles of the six joints based on the desired position and orientation of slave robot. This master-slave mapping is then achieved by sending the corresponding salve robot motion control commands. In this algorithm, the master hand can be clutch-switched when it reaches a workspace limit position or an uncomfortable operating position, repositioning the master hand to a comfortable position, thus solving the problem of inconsistent workspace between the master and the slave. Crucially, the method also ensures that there is no sudden movement of the salve robot at any moment after the master-slave connection is established, satisfying the need for Cartesian spatial position and orientation control of the slave robot while ensuring safe handling.

3.3 Security Mechanisms

For both the forward kinematics of the Omega.6 and the inverse kinematics of the AUBO-i5, the device manufacturer has provided encapsulated functions that can be called by the user to achieve the solution. However, it should be noted that up to eight sets of solutions exist for the inverse kinematics of AUBO-i5, which need to be filtered. The set of solutions with the smallest difference to the current joint angle is selected here as the desired joint angle, as shown in Eq. 4, where q represents the joint angle.

$$q_{desired} = \arg\min_{1 \le i \le 8} ||q_i - q_{current}|| \tag{4}$$

At the same time, taking into account the possibility of operator mishandling during operation, resulting in a large position or orientation change of the master hand within a short period of time, a certain safety mechanism needs to be set in order to prevent the slave robot from also following the master hand and experiencing a large and violent movement. This is ensured by setting a maximum difference σ between the desired joint angle and the current joint angle (Eq. 5), i.e. when the difference between the desired joint angle and the current angle exceeds the threshold value σ, the slave robot does not perform this movement. This threshold value is related to the communication frequency of the robot and should be set smaller for robots with high communication frequency and vice versa.

$$||q_{desired} - q_{current}|| \le \sigma \tag{5}$$

3.4 Variable Mapping Scales

As the operating space of the slave robot is much larger than the operating space of the Omega.6, a fixed mapping scale would require repeatedly resetting the master hand to the appropriate position when it has reached its limit position of workspace. On the other hand, when performing fine operations on Swagelok fittings, precise operations such as centering and snapping cannot be achieved due to the large movement of the slave robot. For this reason, three mapping scales of 3:1, 1:1 and 2:1 have been set for the mapping of the positions for the operating conditions, resulting in the following relationships in the position mapping (Eq. 6), where k is the mapping scale set above, $k = \{3, 1, 1/2\}$.

$$^S_I P_{t+1} = {}^S_I P_t + k * {}^S_M R * {}^M_H \Delta P_{t,t+1} \tag{6}$$

4 Experiments and Results

To verify the effectiveness of the master-slave control algorithm, this paper performs the task of unscrewing a damaged Swagelok fittings on an maintenance experimental verification platform. The basic experiment flow is as follows.

(1) The operator controls the slave robot to pick the loosening end effector.
(2) Move the loosening end effector to the vicinity of the Swagelok fittings.
(3) Adjusting the mapping scale to align the loosening end effector with the centre of the Swagelok fittings and slowly snapping it in.
(4) After loosening the Swagelok fittings, withdraw the loosening end effector.
(5) Put the loosening end effector back, waiting for the next command.

The experimental procedure and results are shown in Fig. 4. During this experiment, the entire operation process was fully implemented based on the incremental master-slave control algorithm and variable mapping scales, achieving the task of aligning and snapping in the Swagelok fittings, thus verifying the effectiveness of the algorithm.

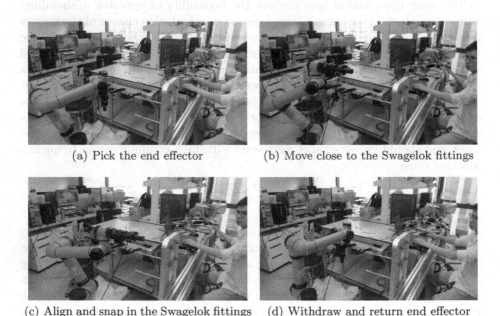

(a) Pick the end effector   (b) Move close to the Swagelok fittings

(c) Align and snap in the Swagelok fittings   (d) Withdraw and return end effector

Fig. 4. Experimental procedure for the maintenance of Swagelok fittings based on the master-slave control algorithm

5   Conclusion

In this paper, the master-slave control algorithm is studied for the nuclear power remote maintenance scenario. The incremental master-slave control algorithm is used to overcome the problem of master-slave isomerism and workspace inconsistency; the position and orientation separation algorithm is used to ensure that the motion trend of the master and the slave is the same and to meet the control needs while ensuring the safety of the control. In the process of master-slave mapping, a safety guarantee mechanism is set to eliminate the violent movement of the slave robot due to operator's misoperation; Finally, on the experimental verification system, the operator maintained the damaged Swagelok fittings by means of master-slave control method, successfully completing the entire operation proces, thus verifying the effectiveness of the algorithm.

References

1. Buongiorno, J., Parsons, J.E., Petti, D.A., Parsons, J.: The future of nuclear energy in a carbon-constrained world (2019)
2. Prăvălie, R., Bandoc, G.: Nuclear energy: between global electricity demand, worldwide decarbonisation imperativeness, and planetary environmental implications. J. Environ. Manag. **209**, 81–92 (2018)
3. Smith, R., Cucco, E., Fairbairn, C.: Robotic development for the nuclear environment: challenges and strategy. Robotics **9**(4), 94 (2020)
4. Dyrd, J.S., DeVries, K.R.: A six-legged telerobot for nuclear applications development. Int. J. Robot. Res. **9**(2), 43–52 (1990)
5. Oka, K., Shibanuma, K.: Development of a radiation-proof robot. Adv. Robot. **16**(6), 493–496 (2002)
6. Sugisaka, M.: Working robots for nuclear power plant desasters. In: 5th IEEE International Conference on Digital Ecosystems and Technologies (IEEE DEST 2011), pp. 358–361. IEEE (2011)
7. Kawatsuma, S., Fukushima, M., Okada, T.: Emergency response by robots to Fukushima-Daiichi accident: summary and lessons learned (2012)
8. Ju, Z., Yang, C., Li, Z., Cheng, L., Ma, H.: Teleoperation of humanoid baxter robot using haptic feedback. In: 2014 International Conference on Multisensor Fusion and Information Integration for Intelligent Systems (MFI), pp. 1–6. IEEE (2014)
9. Shukla, A., Karki, H., Behera, L., Jamshidi, M.M.: Teleoperation by using nonisomorphic mechanisms in the master-slave configuration for speed control. IEEE Syst. J. **12**(2), 1369–1380 (2016)
10. Sherman, A., Çavuşoğlu, M.C., Tendick, F.: Comparison of teleoperator control architectures for palpation task. In: ASME International Mechanical Engineering Congress and Exposition, vol. 26652, pp. 1261–1268. American Society of Mechanical Engineers (2000)
11. Kim, B.Y., Ahn, H.S.: A design of bilateral teleoperation systems using composite adaptive controller. Control. Eng. Pract. **21**(12), 1641–1652 (2013)
12. Ai, Y., Pan, B., Niu, G., Fu, Y., Wang, S.: Master-slave control technology of isomeric surgical robot for minimally invasive surgery. In: 2016 IEEE International Conference on Robotics and Biomimetics (ROBIO), pp. 2134–2139. IEEE

Research on Force Perception of Robot End-Effector Based on Dynamics Model

Zhongshuai Yao, Ming Hu$^{(\boxtimes)}$, Yufeng Guo, Jianguo Wu, and Jing Yang

Faculty of Mechanical Engineering and Automation, Zhejiang Sci-Tech University, Zhejiang, Hangzhou, China
huming@zstu.edu.cn

Abstract. With the wide application of robots in the industrial field, higher requirements are put forward for the use of robots. The force information at the end of the robot is an important execution information of the robot, and the accuracy of its estimation accuracy directly affects the execution precision of the robot. Aiming at this problem, an accurate dynamic model of six-Dofs robot was established, and the torque changes under different working conditions in the process were analyzed. The dynamics simulation model of the robot was built by the co-simulation of MATLAB and Adams software. According to the collected torque information, it will be transformed into the end contact force information. The accuracy of estimating the end force can reach 98.6%.

Keywords: Robot · Dynamic model · Force perception · Accuracy

1 Intorduction

Robots have been widely used in various production fields, and various types of robots have gradually achieved the effects of position tracking and force tracking. The effect of position tracking has reached a very mature technical level in Cartesian space, and there are still some technical restrictions on the coupling of position tracking and force tracking. The dynamic model constructed by Newton Euler equation is often used in the research of machine manpower/position hybrid control. It can achieve both the position control in Cartesian space and the force control requirements. This control research is often used in the application scenario of the interaction force between the end of the manipulator and the external environment.

Robot dynamics clearly expresses the relationship between machine manpower and motion [1], From the perspective of control, the manipulator system belongs to redundant, multivariable and essentially nonlinear automatic control system. It is a complex dynamic coupling problem. It is necessary to realize the functions of high-precision robot motion control, force control and load identification. The dynamic module has become an indispensable part of the research on high-precision motion control. The common dynamic modeling methods include Newton Euler method, Lagrange method and Kane method [2]. The dynamic formulas constructed by different modeling methods are different, but the final dynamic model is the same. Building an accurate dynamic model is

H. Liu et al. (Eds.): ICIRA 2022, LNAI 13457, pp. 604–613, 2022.
https://doi.org/10.1007/978-3-031-13835-5_55

the basis to improve its dynamic characteristics [3], According to the dynamic model, the joint torque information of each joint can be obtained. For spine surgery robots, we should always pay attention to the contact force and deflection force between the end of the manipulator and the human skin and the spine. Obtaining the end contact force can generally be divided into installing a six-dimensional force sensor at the end and calculating the end contact force according to the dynamic model. The installation of six dimensional force sensor will occupy a certain operating space of manipulator [4], This paper will build an accurate dynamic model, and then calculate the end contact force according to the dynamic model. For example, pedicle screw placement has become the main means to treat spinal fractures and degenerative lumbar diseases. Routine surgery depends on vertebral anatomical markers and clinical experience, and the accuracy of screw placement is not high, which is easy to cause damage to important blood vessels and nerves. Therefore, the robot manipulator, which uses computer-aided navigation and provides the precise placement direction of arch root screw, came into being, but the robot assisted nail placement will still have a certain force deviation [5], Therefore, in the process of orthopaedic nail placement, real-time reading of the end contact force and perceived bias force will improve the accuracy of end nail placement.

This paper focuses on the research of force feedback control method based on dynamic model [6–8], Force/position hybrid control of orthopaedic nail placement robot [9, 10]。The dynamic model of the robot is built according to the Newton Euler equation, and the reliability of the dynamic model is verified by the joint simulation of MATLAB and Adams. The joint torque is collected to compare the difference between the ideal model and the actual model. The moment mutation of the robot under different working conditions is studied, and then the moment is transformed into the end contact force according to the numerical value of the moment and the conversion relationship between joint space and Cartesian space, so as to realize the function of predicting the contact force at the end of the manipulator.

2   Robot Dynamics Model

2.1   Introduction to Robot Structure

The mechanical arm adopted in this paper is QJR6–3 six axis series mechanical arm produced by Qianjiang company. The mechanical structure is simple and compact, and can be flexibly installed in production occasions. It has the advantages of high speed, high precision of repeated positioning and wide application range. The structure of the manipulator is shown in Fig. 1 below.

2.2   Dynamic Model

The link of the manipulator can be treated as a rigid body. D'Alembert's principle extends the static equilibrium condition of rigid body to the dynamic problem, considering both the external driving force and the inertial force generated by the acceleration of the object. For any object, the algebraic sum of the external force and the motion resistance (inertial force) in any direction is zero, then D'Alembert's principle comes down to: the

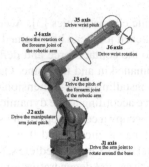

Fig. 1. QJR6–3 six axis series robot

derivatives of linear momentum and angular momentum are equal to the external force and external torque respectively.

Newton Euler uses velocity iteration and force iteration to derive the dynamic equation of the robot connecting rod, including the extrapolation of velocity and angular velocity and the extrapolation of force and torque. That is, push forward from the base, that is, push forward to the end rod, and calculate the angular velocity, angular acceleration and centroid acceleration of each rod step by step, as shown in Fig. 2; Push back from the end joint of the end rod to the first joint, as shown in Fig. 3; Then the torque of each joint is obtained.

The velocity and angular velocity are recursive from inside to outside;

$$
^{i+1}\omega_{i+1} = \begin{cases} ^{i+1}_i R\,^i\omega_i + \dot{\theta}^{i+1}_{i+1} Z_{i+1}\,(\text{Rotating joint } i+1) \\ ^{i+1}_i R\,^i\omega_i \,(\text{Moving joints } i+1) \end{cases} \tag{1}
$$

$$
^{i+1}\dot{\omega}_{i+1} = \begin{cases} ^{i+1}_i R\,^i\dot{\omega}_i + ^{i+1}_i R\,^i\omega_i \times \dot{\theta}^{i+1}_{i+1} Z_{i+1} + \ddot{\theta}^{i+1}_{i+1} Z_{i+1}\,(\text{Rotating joint } i+1) \\ ^{i+1}_i R\,^i\dot{\omega}_i\,(\text{Moving joints } i+1) \end{cases} \tag{2}
$$

$$
^{i+1}\dot{v}_{i+1} = \begin{cases} ^{i+1}_i R\left(^i\dot{\omega}_i \times\,^i P_{i+1} +\,^i \omega_i \times \left(^i\dot{\omega}_i \times\,^i P_{i+1}\right) +\,^i \dot{v}_i\right)(\text{Rotating joint } i+1) \\ ^{i+1}_i R\left(^i\dot{\omega}_i \times\,^i P_{i+1} +\,^i \omega_i \times \left(^i\dot{\omega}_i \times\,^i P_{i+1}\right) +\,^i \dot{v}_i\right) \\ +2\,^{i+1}\omega_{i+1} \times \dot{d}_{i+1}\,^{i+1}z_{i+1} + \ddot{d}_{i+1}\,^{i+1}z_{i+1}\,(\text{Moving joints } i+1) \end{cases} \tag{3}
$$

$$
^{i+1}\dot{v}_{Ci+1} =\,^{i+1}\dot{\omega}_{i+1} \times\,^{i+1} P_{Ci+1} +\,^{i+1}\omega_{i+1} \times \left(^{i+1}\omega_{i+1} \times\,^{i+1} P_{Ci+1}\right) +\,^{i+1}\dot{v}_{i+1}\right) \tag{4}
$$

The centroid moment of the connecting rod can be expressed as;

$$
^{i+1}n_{ci+1} =\,^{ci+1}I_{i+1}\,^{i+1}\dot{w}_{i+1} +\,^{i+1}w_{i+1} \times \left(^{ci+1}I_{i+1}\,^{i+1}w_{i+1}\right) \tag{5}
$$

In the above formula, cRepresents the centroid coordinate system established by the member。$^{ci+1}I_{i+1}$ Represents the centroid inertia tensor of the member, among

$$
^{ci+1}I_{i+1} = \begin{bmatrix} I_{i+1,xx} & -I_{i+1,xy} & -I_{i+1,xz} \\ -I_{i+1,xy} & I_{i+1,yy} & -I_{i+1,yz} \\ -I_{i+1,xz} & -I_{i+1,yz} & I_{i+1,zz} \end{bmatrix}.
$$

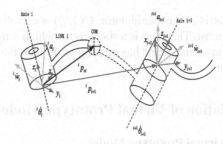

Fig. 2. Velocity and acceleration recurrence diagram

$\dot{\theta}_{i+1}$, $\ddot{\theta}_{i+1}$ Is the angular velocity and angular acceleration of the joint $i + 1$, $_i^{i+1}R$ Represents the rotation matrix from coordinate system i to coordinate system $i + 1$, $^{i+1}P_{Ci+1}$ is Position of $i + 1$ centroid coordinate system under coordinate system $i + 1$, $^iP_{i+1}$ is Position of coordinate system $i + 1$ under coordinate system i.

The forces and moments are recursively derived from the outside to the inside;

$$^if_i = _{i+1}^i R^{i+1}f_{i+1} + ^i F_i \tag{6}$$

$$^in_i = ^i N_i + _{i+1}^i R^{i+1}n_{i+1} + ^i P_{Ci} \times ^i F_i + ^i P_{i+1} \times _{i+1}^i R^{i+1}f_{i+1} \tag{7}$$

$$\tau_i = \begin{cases} n_i^T {}^iZ_i \text{ (Rotating joint)} \\ \overline{f_i^T {}^iZ_i \text{ (Moving joints)}} \end{cases} \tag{8}$$

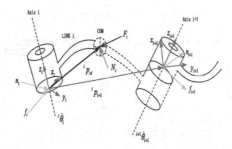

Fig. 3. Recurrence diagram of force and moment

The above recursive formula has two purposes: numerical calculation and derivation of closed form dynamic equations. As long as we know the mass, inertia tensor, centroid position and rotation matrix of each connecting rod, we can solve the joint driving torque and force required by the specified motion through the above equation.

According to the general dynamic expression:

$$\tau_i = M(q)\ddot{q} + C(q, \dot{q}) + G(q) \tag{9}$$

$M(q)$ is the mass matrix of the manipulator, $C(q, \dot{q})$ is coriolis force and centrifugal force, $G(q)$ is a gravity term, This item is a static item, which only depends on the pose of the robot, that is, the joint angle, and has nothing to do with the joint angular velocity and angular acceleration.

3 Dynamic Simulation of Virtual Prototype Model

3.1 Construction of Virtual Prototype Model

The forward and inverse kinematics and dynamics calculation models of the manipulator are built and implemented based on Simulinks in the MATLAB platform. The calculation is completed and the driving torque of each joint is input to observe the spatial position of each joint of the manipulator. It is verified that the tracking position tracking based on dynamics can achieve good results, as shown in Fig. 4 below. In order to better verify the dynamic characteristics of the manipulator, it is necessary to build ADAMS virtual physical model for further dynamic experiments. According to the three-dimensional model of the manipulator, the virtual prototype of the manipulator is constructed according to the link and joint coupling relationship of the manipulator in ADAMS software. The established virtual prototype model is shown in Fig. 5 below.

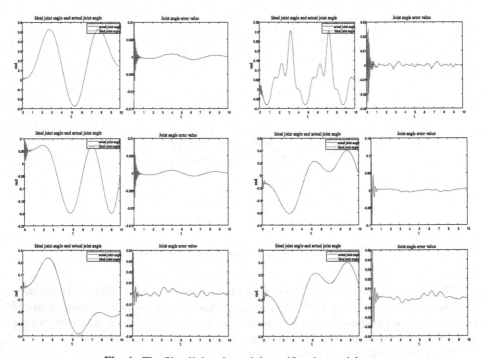

Fig. 4. The Simulink unit module verifies the spatial pose

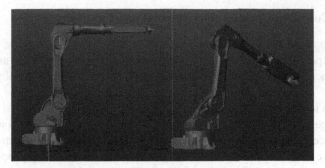

Fig. 5. QJR6–3 Virtual prototype model

3.2 Dynamic Model Validation Simulation

In order to ensure the correctness of the built dynamic model and the feasibility of subsequent experiments, a joint simulation platform was built with Adams and MATLAB. Matlab platform is mainly used to calculate the driving torque of each joint movement and communicate its torque to the virtual prototype built by adamas. It is used to drive the virtual prototype to achieve the preset spatial pose, and collect the calculated torque under the two working platforms for comparison. To further verify the feasibility of applying the dynamic model based on dynamic parameters to spinal screw placement.

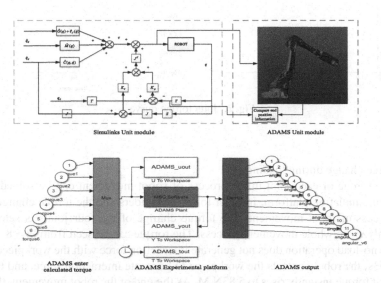

Fig. 6. MATLAB and Adams joint simulation platform and control strategy

3.3 Multi Condition Dynamic Simulation of Movement Process

With the help of the joint simulation platform of MATLAB and Adams, the dynamic simulation experiment of the movement process of robot was carried out, and the torque changes of each joint are obtained respectively, as shown in the Fig. 6 below.

(1) From no load to unloading

The process of the robot movement will go through two stages: No contact with the workpiece, and Contact with the workpiece. The mechanical properties in the two stages are different. The dynamic analysis of the overall loading process is carried out on the above joint simulation platform. The dynamic performance of each joint is shown in Fig. 7 below.

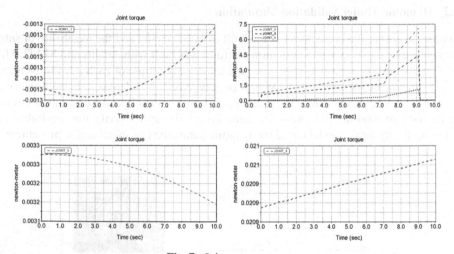

Fig. 7. Joint torque curve

(1) Force change during loading

The torque of each joint in the process of robot movement can be solved by the joint simulation platform, in order to further understand the torque change in the process of robot movement. The torque change of the four joints is selected to analyze the whole movement process. The torque can be seen from Fig. 8. Firstly, the no-load operation does not generate interaction force with the workpiece. After 0.53s, the robot contacts the workpiece to generate interaction force, and the four joint torque instantly rises to 5.83N.M. As the end of the robot movement, the joint torque gradually increases to 16.58N.M, In the next stage, the joint torque climbs to 42.9N.M, reaches the peak moment.

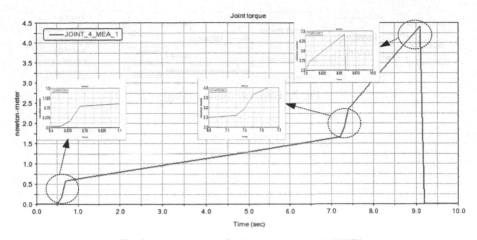

Fig. 0. Joint torque of robot assisted spine surgery

4 End Contact Force Estimation Strategy and Simulation Verification

When the end effector is not in contact with the external environment, the torque required for the joint movement of the manipulator is supplied by the motor, which is expressed as:

$$\tau_i = M(q)\ddot{q} + C(q, \dot{q}) + G(q)$$

Corresponding to the dynamic equation of joint space, the relationship between the operating force and the end acceleration can be expressed as:

$$F = V(q)\ddot{x} + u(q, \dot{q}) + p(q)$$

$V(q)u(q, \dot{q})p(q)$ are inertia matrix, centrifugal force, Coriolis force vector and gravity vector in operation space; F is generalized operating force vector, The relationship between τ_{ext} and joint force vector is:

$$\tau_{ext} = J^T(q)F$$

The contact force signal is transformed into force vector, which is transformed into feedback torque through Jacobian matrix. The final joint torque is obtained by combining the feedback torque with the driving torque driving the manipulator. Then the joint angle position is solved through the inverse dynamic solution, so as to achieve the pose information and contact force information in Cartesian space. The end of the manipulator will execute the preset position information according to the driving torque, reach the estimated force, and the control unit will convert it into feedback torque to continuously adjust the preset position information and generate contact force to achieve the estimated force (Fig. 9).

$$\tau_d = \tau_i + \tau_{ext}$$
$$\tau_d = M(q)\ddot{q} + C(q, \dot{q}) + G(q) + J^T(q)F$$

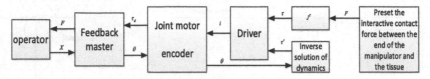

Fig. 9. Force estimation strategy

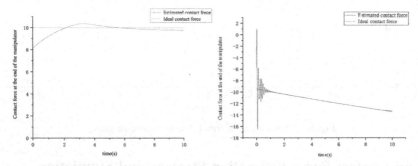

Fig. 10. Comparison of force estimation results with given results

It can be seen from Fig. 10 above that given the ideal end contact force 10N, according to the end estimated force strategy, the estimated force will be stable at 9.86N. There is a force deviation of 0.14N from the ideal contact force. As time goes on, the propulsive force deviation gradually decreases and will eventually stabilize around 10N. Therefore, it can be seen that the above-mentioned predictive force strategy is feasible and effective.

5 Conclusion

1. According to the Newton Euler equation, build an accurate dynamic model, build a matlab platform, drive the joint pose to verify the dynamic model with the joint torque calculated by dynamics, and further establish a joint simulation platform of MATLAB and Adams to verify the joint torque information.
2. According to the dynamic model, the joint simulation is carried out for the multi condition dynamics of the nail placement process, and then the torque information of each joint under each condition is obtained, and the detailed mechanical analysis is carried out for different conditions.
3. The prediction strategy of end contact force and its simulation verification. The prediction strategy of end force is established according to the transformation relationship between joint space dynamic equation and Cartesian space dynamic equation. Through experimental verification, the estimated end contact force can reach 98.6% of the ideal contact force, which can achieve a good force prediction effect.

References

1. Wang, X.L., et al.: kinematics analysis and optimization design of NOVAL 4-DOF parallel mechanism. J. Northeastern Univ. (Nat. Sci.), **39**(04), 532–537 (2018)

2. Leboutet, Q., et al.: Inertial parameter identification in robotics: a survey. Appl. Sci. **11**(9), 4303 (2021)
3. Urrea, C., Pascal, J.: Design, simulation, comparison and evaluation of parameter identification methods for an industrial robot. Comput. Electr. Eng. **67**, 791–806 (2018)
4. Gaz, C., et al.: Dynamic identification of the franka emika panda robot with retrieval of feasible parameters using penalty-based optimization. IEEE Robot. Autom. Lett. **4**(4), 4147–4154 (2019)
5. Yousri, D., et al.: Static and dynamic photovoltaic models' parameters identification using chaotic heterogeneous comprehensive learning particle swarm optimizer variants. Energy Convers. Manag. **182**, 546–563 (2019)
6. Gründel, L., Reiners, C., Lienenlüke, L., Storms, S., Brecher, C., Bitterolf, D.: Frequency-based identification of the inertial parameters of an industrial robot. In: Behrens, B.-A., Brosius, A., Hintze, W., Ihlenfeldt, S., Wulfsberg, J.J. (eds.) Production at the leading edge of technology. LNPE, pp. 429–438. Springer, Heidelberg (2021). https://doi.org/10.1007/978-3-662-62138-7_43
7. Kallu, K.D., et al.: Implementation of a TDMCSPO controller on a 3-dof hydraulic manipulator for position tracking and sensor-less force estimation. IEEE Access **7**, 177035–177047 (2019)
8. Changhong, G., et al.: Hybrid position/force control of 6-dof hydraulic parallel manipulator using force and vision. Indus. Robot Int. J. **43**, 274–283 (2016)
9. Li, Y.J., et al.: Research on a novel parallel spoke piezoelectric 6-DOF heavy force/torque sensor. Mech. Syst. Signal Process. **36**(1), 152–167 (2013)
10. Zeng, F., Xiao, J., Liu, H.: Force/torque sensorless compliant control strategy for assembly tasks using a 6-DOF collaborative robot. IEEE Access **7**, 108795–108805 (2019)

Tactile Robotics

Perceptual Properties of Fingertips Under Electrotactile Stimulation

Ziliang Zhou[1], Yicheng Yang[1], Jia Zeng[1], Xiaoxin Wang[3], Jinbiao Liu[2], and Honghai Liu[3($\boxtimes$)]

[1] The State Key Laboratory of Mechanical System and Vibration, Shanghai Jiao Tong University, Shanghai 200240, China
zzleeeeon@sjtu.edu.cn
[2] The Artificial Intelligence Research Institute, Zhejiang Laboratory, Hangzhou 311100, China
liujinbiao1518@zhejianglab.com
[3] The State Key Laboratory of Robotics and Systems, Harbin Institute of Technology, Shenzhen, China
honghai.liu@icloud.com

Abstract. To sense and represent electrotactile perceptual properties is a crucial milestone in order to achieve intuitive haptics. However, electrotactile perceptual properties are very poorly studied. This study presented an experimental study on the electrotactile perceptual properties of fingertips. A series of experimental paradigms were designed based on self-designed hardware and psychophysical evaluation methods. The detection threshold (DT), pain threshold (PT), just-noticed difference (JND), intensity-quality characteristics and multi-level discrimination ability for pulse amplitude (PA), pulse width (PW) and pulse frequency (PF) have been explored. The experiments verified the individual differences in DT and PT and found that the fingertips were more sensitive to PA and thus more valuable for information encoding. In discrete coding, the recognition accuracy decreases with increasing number of levels, preferably less than 4. The results are expected to provide valuable suggestions for the parameter coding of electrotactile information presentation.

Keywords: Electrotactile · Haptics · Psychophysical evaluation · Information encoding

1 Introduction

Touch is a unique human sensory modality in contrast with other modalities. Tactile receptors in the skin allow humans to perceive pressure, displacement,

Supported by the Shenzhen Science and Technology Program (Grant No. JCYJ202103 24120214040), the Guangdong Science and Technology Research Council (Grant No. 2020B1515120064) and the National Natural Science Foundation of China (Grant No. 61733011 and 62003222).

H. Liu et al. (Eds.): ICIRA 2022, LNAI 13457, pp. 617–627, 2022.
https://doi.org/10.1007/978-3-031-13835-5_56

temperature, pain, etc., which enable humans to manipulate more precisely and sense the environment to avoid injury. According to Heller and Schiff [8], tactile perception is 20 times faster than vision. Geldard et al. [6] highlighted the advantages of tactile sensation and proposed to develop it as a new form of communication.

Tactile information presentation can be achieved in several ways, mainly non-invasive methods that are pneumatically, magnetically, thermally, or piezoelectrically driven [2]. Among them, mechanical stimulation and electrical stimulation have been extensively studied. Compared to mechanical stimulation, electrical stimulation has the advantages of simple structure, low energy consumption and fast response. Electrotactile sensation is the sensation produced by an electric current passing through the skin and activating the tactile receptors [16]. Since there are seven types of mechanoreceptors in human skin [18], the application of different forms of electrical currents to stimulate different receptors can present a variety of tactile sensations. Then, different information can be obtained from different types of tactile sensations. The presentation of electrotactile information can be encoded parametrically or spatially. Electrotactile sensations are usually delivered in the form of electrical pulses, so the parameters that can be used for encoding include pulse amplitude (PA), pulse width (PW) and pulse frequency (PF). Kajimoto [13] and Kaczmarek [10] carried out some early researches into the concept and mechanism of electrotactile displays. Researchers after them have experimented with electrotactile displays on many parts of the human body, including the forehead [12], tongue [9], palms [14], forearms [3], fingertips [19] and so on. The fingertips are more sensitive than other parts of the body, and thus electrical stimulation of the fingertips may have higher spatio-temporal resolution and require smaller amplitudes, which is energy efficient and has the potential for wider applications in electrotactile information presentation.

As a recent review [20] suggested that, despite the advantages of electrotactile stimulation over other methods, there are many challenges that limit the development. The sensations produced by electrical stimulation are influenced by many factors. Besides the electrical parameters themselves, the type and size of the electrodes and the state of the skin (location, hydration) all have influence on the quality of the sensations [11]. On the other hand, due to the weakness of research into the physiological mechanisms of tactile perception, there is no uniform and objective quantitative method for evaluating the intensity and quality of electrotactile perception. Despite much effort by many scholars to overcome the variability of electrotactile sensation, precise control of electrotactile sensation is still very challenging. In terms of electrotactile information presentation, most current research directly adopts linear feedback information using PW [17] and PF [7], however, it is unknown whether the perceives changes in these parameters are linear. Furthermore, the correlations between these parameters and perceptual properties are unclear, and there is a lack of systematic investigation into the differences in human perception of different electrical parameters and the potential for their application in information coding.

The purpose of this paper is to evaluate fingertip electrotactile parameter properties using psychophysical algorithms. The DT, PT, JND, intensity-quality characteristics and multi-level discrimination ability for PA, PW and PF have been explored and the results are expected to provide a theoretical basis for the parameter coding of electrotactile information presentation.

2   Methods

2.1   Subjects and Stimulation System

Due to the individual variation in electrotactile perception, 6 male healthy subjects have been recruited, noted as S1–S6. The same experiment will be conducted on all subjects. It should be noted that all the experimental procedures used in this study were approved by the SJTU School Ethics Committee and the subject has signed the informed consents before the experiments. The electrical stimulation system used was designed in our previous study [21], which was a six-channel constant-current monophasic pulse generator. The psychophysical methods used in this experiment were also integrated into the system. The following is a description of the methods.

2.2   Measurement of DT and PT

Since the intensity of perception is mainly determined by the pulse amplitude (PA) and pulse width (PW) [1], the detection threshold (DT) and pain threshold (PT) of the PA and PW are first measured in order to obtain a reasonable range of electrical parameters. DT is defined as the parameter threshold at which the stimulus can just be perceived, while PT is defined as the parameter threshold at which pain is just beginning to be perceived. DT and PT together determine the operative range of electrical parameters and can reflect the size of the encodable range of parameters.

DT and PT are measured using the staircase method [5]. Subjects manipulate the electrical stimulation hardware for voluntary parameter adjustment while perceiving the stimulus. The stimuli were generated in cycles at a fixed duration (0.5 s) and interval (0.5 s) during the experiment. At the beginning, the parameter value is 0 and the subject increases the parameter at a fixed step (PA: 0.02 mA, PW: 5 us) until the stimulus is just detected or the pain is perceived. Then the value is decreased by the same steps until the sensation or pain disappears and this reversal is taken as DT or PT. This procedure is repeated three times, with a 30 s break at the end of each time, and the final average is taken as the DT or PT test result. To avoid adaptation as much as possible, subjects were asked to quickly adjust the parameters to pain occur when measuring PT. Based on some pre-experimental parameter settings, the PW and PF are set to 150 us and 20 Hz when measuring DT and PT of PA. When measuring the DT and PT of PW, the PA and PF are set to 1 mA and 20 Hz. The dynamic range (DR) is calculated as PT/DT, which reflects the size of the operative setting range of the parameter.

2.3   Measurement of JND

In order to explore the discrimination ability and differences in electrical parameters, just-noticed-difference (JND) was measured for PA, PW and PF under two baselines. JND was defined as the smallest variation that can be discriminated with respect to a parameter baseline, which reflects sensitivity to parameter changes.

JND was measured using the bisection algorithm proposed in our previous study [21], which provides a more efficient measurement method than the traditional [4]. When measuring the JND of PA and PW, the two baselines are (PT − DT) * 0.25 + DT and (PT − DT) * 0.5 + DT respectively. When measuring the JND of PA and PW, the baselines are (PT − DT) * 0.25 + DT and (PT − DT) * 0.5 + DT respectively. For PF, the baselines are 10 Hz and 50 Hz, and are noted as JND-low and JND-high respectively. During the experiments, subjects were asked to continually judge between the baseline and control values and feedback through the software interface. The control value is initially set to half of the baseline and upper values, after which it is continuously updated according to the following:

$$
S_{Control}^{n+1} = \begin{cases} \frac{(S_{Baseline}+S_{Control}^{n})}{2}, A_n > A_T \\[2ex] \frac{(S_{Control}^{n}+S_{Control}^{n-1})}{2}, A_n \leqslant A_T \end{cases} \tag{1}
$$

$$
A_n = \frac{R_n}{N}, S_{Control}^{0} = S_{Upper} \tag{2}
$$

where $S_{Control}^{n}$ is the control value after the nth bisection and $S_{Baseline}$ is the stimuli of the baseline. A_n represents the judgment accuracy of the nth bisection. R_n represents the number of correct judgments in the nth bisection. N represents the total number of judgements made in one bisection. Considering the efficiency and the validity, N is set to 12. A_T is the threshold for judgement accuracy. Considering the incidence of error and randomness, A_T was set to 80%. The experiments ended after 5 bisections and the JND could be measured with an accuracy of $(PT − DT)/2^5$, which is sufficient for the requirements. During the experiments, the baseline and control values were generated in a random order and cycled at a fixed duration (0.5 s) and interval (0.5 s). A response time of 1 s between each cycle was given to the subjects for comparison and manipulation. After each measurement of the baseline there was be one minute for break to avoid fatigue and adaptation. At the end of the experiments, the Weber fraction WF [15], which is defined as JND/baseline, was calculated, enabling comparison of the differences in discrimination ability under different parameters.

2.4   Intensity and Quality Evaluation

Different forms of tactile sensation can be produced by various combinations of parameters. In order to investigate the characteristics, the intensity and quality of perception was evaluated at 10 Hz and 50 Hz with different combinations of PA and PW. Sensitivity indexes (SI) were also calculated to compare the differences in the subjects' perception of intensity.

Intensity and quality evaluation was carried out using a parametric randomized algorithm [21]. Firstly, PA and PW were divided equally into 5 in the range of DT and (PT − DT) * 0.5 + DT, and 25 pairs of parameters were generated by random combination. To avoid pain, the PA and PW are set at parameters much smaller than their PT. The 25 stimuli were delivered in a random order, each with a duration and interval of 0.5 s. After perceiving the stimulus, subjects were first asked to provide feedback on the quality of the perception. Traditionally, the quality of tactile perception was evaluated by feedback from different questionnaires, which may include many kinds of descriptions. This experiment focused on perceptual location and concentration of perceptual quality in order to analyse the possibility of electrotactile spatial coding at the fingertips and therefore a simple questionnaire was designed for a specific evaluation. The questionnaire describes quality in three categories: 1). Local means that the sensation is produced at the point of stimulation and is concentrated; 2). Radiating means that the sensation is produced at the point of stimulation but is scattered and blurred; 3). Referred means that the sensation is not produced at the point of stimulation. The intensity of perception is feedback on a numerical scale from 0 to 10, where 0 means no sensation, while 5 means clear and comfortable stimulation, and 10 means unbearable pain. Subjects were asked to use the mouse to give feedback on the software interface, and each time they finished, the stimuli immediately switched to the next. Various parameter pairs are randomly delivered once without repetition. The experiment was conducted for both 10 Hz and 50 Hz with a 2 min break in between. At the end of the experiment, the sensitivity index (SI) was calculated according to the following formula.

$$SI = \frac{\sum_{i=0}^{N-1} \sum_{j=0}^{N-1} I_{ij}}{N^2} \tag{3}$$

where I_{ij} represents the quantized perception intensity under a certain parameter combination. The value of SI ranges from 0 to 10 and a larger SI represent higher sensitivity.

2.5 Multi-level Discrimination

The measurement of JND reflects the subject's sensitivity to changes of parameters, but cannot directly reflects the ability to discriminate between multiple levels. To explore the potential in the application of information encoding and the differences, multilevel discrimination experiments were conducted. This experiment tested the discrimination accuracy for PA, PW and PF on a level of 3, 4 and 5 respectively.

The PA and PW were divided equally in the range of DT and PT, and the PF was divided in the grading range of 10–100 Hz. The experiments were carried out in the order of PA, PW and PF. Each parameter was divided equally into 3, 4 and 5 and then measured in turn, for a total of 9 trials to be performed.

Each trial began with perceptual training for each level. For training, the stimuli was delivered sequentially from low to high level, each lasting 0.5 s. The experiment was started after 5 turns of training. During the experiment, subjects were asked to judge a randomly generated stimuli and give feedback by clicking the corresponding button on the software interface with the mouse. After each click was completed, the next stimuli was immediately generated and there were 21 continuous judgments in total. At the end of each trial, a two-minute break was taken to avoid fatigue. At the end of the experiment, the accuracy of the judgement was calculated.

2.6   Experimental Procedure

Before the experiment, the subjects were asked to sit in front of a computer with his or her hands outstretched. After briefly cleaning and drying the subjects' hand, electrodes were attached to the palm of left hand and the tip of index finger, respectively, and the right hand was used to operate a mouse or hardware. The electrode at the fingertip is negative and the one at the palm is positive. After a brief introduction to the arrangement and general content of the experiments, DT and PT were measured first, followed by JND, intensity and quality evaluation, and finally a multi-level parameter discrimination experiment. Between each two tests the subjects were free to take a break. The entire duration of the experiment was approximately one and a half hours.

2.7   Statistical Analysis

Visual presentation and significance analysis were carried out for the experimental data. For comparisons of multiple data sets, the normal distribution test was first performed using the shapiro-wilk test (S-W test) and then the homogeneity of variance test using Levene's test. If the data was normally distributed and the variances were homogeneous, a one-way analysis of variance (Welch ANOVA) was used to analyse the variability between the three groups of data, or a T-test was conducted to analyse the variability between two groups of data. If the data does not conform to a normal distribution or the variance is not homogeneous, then non-parametric methods are required. Two groups of data were compared using the Mann-whitney U-test and three with the Kruskai-Wallis H-test. The significance level was set at 0.05. The analysis of the entire data was carried out on the SPSS online platform (SPSSAU) and the data was plotted in MATLAB software (Matlab R2019a).

3   Results

3.1   DT and PT

The results of DT, PT and DR measurements are shown in Table 1. Since PA and PW are not directly comparable, in order to compare the differences between PA and PW on DR, the two groups of data on DR were analysed for differences.

Table 1. Results of DT and PT measurements for PA and PW

Subjects	PA (150 us, 20 Hz)			PW (1 mA, 20 Hz)		
	DT (mA)	PT (mA)	DR = PT/DT	DT (us)	PT (us)	DR = PT/DT
S1	0.28 ± 0.03	3.00 ± 0.26	10.71	0.13 ± 0.01	1.66 ± 0.08	12.77
S2	0.43 ± 0.04	2.62 ± 0.12	6.09	0.16 ± 0.01	0.76 ± 0.08	4.75
S3	0.67 ± 0.06	2.50 ± 0.12	3.73	0.15 ± 0.00	1.05 ± 0.07	7
S4	0.34 ± 0.02	1.97 ± 0.23	5.79	0.15 ± 0.01	1.23 ± 0.06	8.2
S5	0.77 ± 0.03	2.77 ± 0.03	3.6	0.18 ± 0.01	0.37 ± 0.02	2.06
S6	0.63 ± 0.04	3.02 ± 0.83	4.79	0.18 ± 0.01	2.5 ± 0.30	13.89
AVR	0.52 ± 0.19	2.65 ± 0.39	5.79 ± 2.62	0.16 ± 0.02	1.26 ± 0.75	8.11 ± 4.57

A normality test using the S-W test found that the DR for both PA ($p = 0.097$) and PW ($p = 0.758$) were normally distributed. After the variance was tested as being homogeneity ($p = 0.187$) and then the T-test was used to find that the two groups were not significantly different ($p = 0.202$). The data from the tests showed that the DR of the electrical parameters varied considerably between the subjects and that the average DR of the PW, although greater than that of the PA, was not significantly different.

3.2 JND

The results of WF measurements under two baselines are shown in Fig. 1(a). The S-W test indicated that the WF results were largely acceptable as normally distributed ($p = 0.015$) and met the homogeneity of variance requirement ($p = 0.221$). A one-way ANOVA was used which indicated that the WF was significantly different between groups ($p = 0.001$). The results of the between-group t-test showed that PF had a larger WF relative to both PA and PW and was significantly different relative to PA ($p = 0.011$). For both baselines of the same parameter, neither PA nor PW were significantly different, while WF was significantly lower for PA at the higher baseline ($p = 0.034$). The results of the experiments showed that subjects had a higher resolution of PA and were more sensitive to changes at higher baselines. In contrast, subjects were much less able to discriminate between PF changes and remained almost constant across baselines.

3.3 Intensity and Quality

The heat map of the intensity feedback for different pairs of parameters under 10 Hz and 50 Hz is shown in Fig. 2. Both the increase in PW and PA significantly increase the intensity. SI values calculated under the two frequencies are: 3.31 ± 1.08 and 4.66 ± 2.07. As the data was normally and the variances were homogeneous ($p = 0.68$, $p = 0.396$), the T-test was used and showed a significant difference between the SI values ($p = 0.045$). The results show that the perceptual intensity is not only determined by PA and PW. For the same PW and PA parameters, the perceived intensity is greater and more sensitive to high PF.

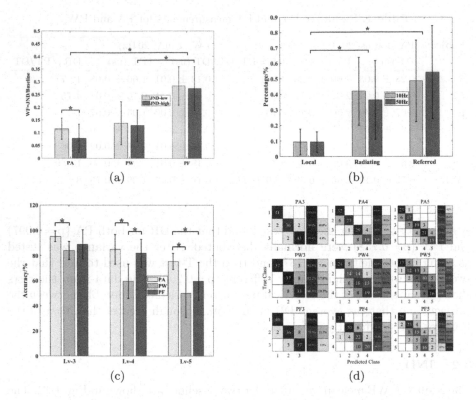

Fig. 1. (a) WF measurement for PA, PW and PF under two baselines. JND-low means the lower baseline calculated by DT and PT (For PF, JND-low is 10 Hz), and JND-high represents the higher baseline (50 Hz for PF). * donates p < 0.05. (b) Perceptual quality at both high and low PF. (c) Discrimination accuracy for PA, PW and PF under 3, 4 and 5 levels. (d) Confusion matrix for the discrimination results.

Figure 1(b) shows the results of the perceptual quality at both high and low PF. The variance in the percentage of all three perceived quality types was relatively large, reflecting the large individual differences in quality feedback among the subjects. Overall, the Local type perception was only about 10%, significantly lower than the radiating and referred type perceptions (10 Hz: p = 0.010, p = 0.031, 50 Hz: p = 0.029, p = 0.026). The difference in perceptual quality between the high and low PF was not significant. The experimental results show that it is difficult to generate specific and focused electrotactile sensations at either high or low frequencies. What the subjects perceived was more of a wide range or shifted sensation.

3.4 Multi-level Discrimination

Figure 1(c) shows the results of the subjects' discrimination accuracy for PA, PW and PF under 3, 4 and 5 levels. It can be intuitively observed that as the

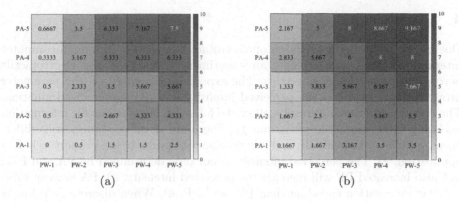

Fig. 2. The heat map of the intensity feedback for different pairs of parameters, (a) PF − 10 Hᴢ. (b) ΓΓ − 50 Iᴌ.

number of levels increases, the subjects' discrimination accuracy decreases in all cases. Independent of the levels, the average accuracy satisfies the following rule: PA > PF > PW. Each group satisfies a normal distribution after normality test, and T-test was used. For the change in accuracy, PA only decreased significantly (p = 0.001) at a level of 5, while accuracy is still greater than 80% at levels 3 and 4. The accuracy of PF decreases significantly (p = 0.03, p = 0.005) as the levels increases, and at level 5 the accuracy is only around 60%. PW has not only a lower accuracy rate relative to PA and PF, but also has a very significant decrease (p = 0.02) at levels greater than 3, which is only about 60%. In terms of differences in parameters, at level 3, all are greater than 80% and PW is slightly lower than PW (p = 0.016) and PF. The difference between PW and PA and PF becomes more significant when the number of levels increases. This experiment illustrates that in terms of multi-level parameter discrimination, subjects were more able to discriminate between PA, followed by PF and PW. PA and PF possess greater potential for electrotactile information encoding compared to PW.

Figure 1(d) shows the confusion matrix for the discrimination results for all subjects. It can be seen that PA, PW and PF all presented a uniform pattern, that is, the level 1 of the parameter had the highest recognition accuracy, and subjects were more likely to be confused when the parameter were increased. For PW, the maximum and minimum values have a higher discrimination accuracy than the medium values, while PF shows a tendency to decrease with increasing parameter values, with an accuracy of only 8.7% for the maximum parameter value at a level number of 5. The whole illustrates that in multi-level parameter discrimination, confusion is more likely to occur between higher parameter values. The accuracy of the perceptual discrimination cannot be guaranteed when the number of levels is more than 3.

4   Conclusion

Due to the promising application of electrotactile sensation in human-computer interaction, this paper presents an experimental study on the electrotactile perceptual properties of fingertips. The experiments focused on the parameter properties and explored the perceived intensity and parameter discrimination. The current experimental results allow the following suggestions for information encoding in electrotactile sensation: 1). There are significant properties differences in different individuals, and it is necessary to evaluate the properties before application. 2). The perceived intensity is not only determined by PA and PW, but also increased PF will increase the perceived intensity. 3). PA is more valuable for information encoding than PW and PF. 4). When discrete encoding is performed, the number of parameter levels should preferably not exceed 4.

References

1. Akhtar, A., Sombeck, J., Boyce, B., Bretl, T.: Controlling sensation intensity for electrotactile stimulation in human-machine interfaces. Sci. Robot. **3**(17), eaap9770 (2018)
2. Asamura, N., Shinohara, T., Tojo, Y., Shinoda, H.: Necessary spatial resolution for realistic tactile feeling display. In: ICRA, pp. 1851–1856. Citeseer (2001)
3. Barros, C.G.C., Bittar, R.S.M., Danilov, Y.: Effects of electrotactile vestibular substitution on rehabilitation of patients with bilateral vestibular loss. Neurosci. Lett. **476**(3), 123–126 (2010)
4. Boring, E.G.: Sensation and perception in the history of experimental psychology (1942)
5. Cornsweet, T.N.: The staircase-method in psychophysics. Am. J. Psychol. **75**(3), 485–491 (1962)
6. Geldard, F.A.: Some neglected possibilities of communication. Science **131**(3413), 1583–1588 (1960)
7. Graczyk, E.L., Schiefer, M.A., Saal, H.P., Delhaye, B.P., Bensmaia, S.J., Tyler, D.J.: The neural basis of perceived intensity in natural and artificial touch. Sci. Transl. Med. **8**(362), 362ra142–362ra142 (2016)
8. Heller, M.A.: The Psychology of Touch. Psychology Press, London (2013)
9. Kaczmarek, K.A.: The tongue display unit (TDU) for electrotactile spatiotemporal pattern presentation. Sci. Iran. **18**(6), 1476–1485 (2011)
10. Kaczmarek, K.A.: The portable neuromodulation stimulator (PoNS) for neurore-habilitation. Sci. Iran. **24**(6), 3171–3180 (2017)
11. Kaczmarek, K.A., Webster, J.G., Bach-y Rita, P., Tompkins, W.J.: Electrotactile and vibrotactile displays for sensory substitution systems. IEEE Trans. Biomed. Eng. **38**(1), 1–16 (1991)
12. Kajimoto, H., Kanno, Y., Tachi, S.: Forehead electro-tactile display for vision substitution. In: Proceedings of EuroHaptics, p. 11 (2006)
13. Kajimoto, H., Kawakami, N., Maeda, T., Tachi, S.: Electro-tactile display with tactile primary color approach. Graduate School of Information and Technology, The University of Tokyo (2004)
14. Kajimoto, H., Suzuki, M., Kanno, Y.: Hamsatouch: tactile vision substitution with smartphone and electro-tactile display. In: CHI 2014 Extended Abstracts on Human Factors in Computing Systems, pp. 1273–1278 (2014)

15. Lawless, H.T., Heymann, H.: Physiological and psychological foundations of sensory function. In: Lawless, H.T., Heymann, H. (eds.) Sensory Evaluation of Food. FSTS, pp. 19–56. Springer, New York (2010). https://doi.org/10.1007/978-1-4419-6488-5_2

16. Pfeiffer, E.A.: Electrical stimulation of sensory nerves with skin electrodes for research, diagnosis, communication and behavioral conditioning: A survey. Med. Biol. Eng. **6**(6), 637–651 (1968)

17. Schiefer, M., Tan, D., Sidek, S.M., Tyler, D.J.: Sensory feedback by peripheral nerve stimulation improves task performance in individuals with upper limb loss using a myoelectric prosthesis. J. Neural Eng. **13**(1), 016001 (2015)

18. Toney, A., Dunne, L., Thomas, B.H., Ashdown, S.P.: A shoulder pad insert vibrotactile display. In: Proceedings of Seventh IEEE International Symposium on Wearable Computers, pp. 35–35. Citeseer (2003)

19. Zhou, Z., Yang, Y., Liu, H.: A braille reading system based on electrotactile display with flexible electrode array. IEEE/CAA J. Autom. Sinica **9**(4), 735–737 (2022)

20. Zhou, Z., Yang, Y., Liu, J., Zeng, J., Wang, X., Liu, H.: Electrotactile perception properties and its applications: a review. IEEE Trans. Haptics 1 (2022). https://doi.org/10.1109/TOH.2022.3170723

21. Zhou, Z., Yang, Y., Zeng, J., Wang, X., Liu, H.: Explore electrotactile parametric properties using an electrical stimulation system. IEEE Sens. J. **22**(7), 7053–7062 (2022)

A Brief Review Focused on Tactile Sensing for Stable Robot Grasping Manipulation

Zhenning Zhou, Zhuangzhuang Zhang, Kaiyi Xie, Xiaoxiao Zhu, and Qixin Cao[✉]

Shanghai Jiao Tong University, Shanghai 200240, China
{zhening_zhou,qxcao}@sjtu.edu.cn

Abstract. In this paper, we briefly investigate recently published literature on robot grasping with tactile information to understand the effect introduced by tactile modality and summarize the current issues of tactile sensing. Moreover, this paper consists of a review of slip detection during grasping, a review of grasp stability assessment to estimate the current contact state and a review of regrasp to select appropriate grasp adjustment action. Finally, we discuss the current limitations and deficiencies that prevent researchers from using tactile sensors, making it challenging to incorporate tactile modalities into robot perception and properly utilize tactile information to achieve effective and stable grasp performances. We consider that the pipeline consisting of grasp outcome prediction and grasp action adjustment based on machine learning is an appropriate scheme to make full use of tactile information and its potential in robot grasping tasks. More studies in this field are expected in the future.

Keywords: Tactile sensing · Grasp stability · Slip detection · Regrasp · Multi-modal perception for grasping

1 Introduction

In recent years, tactile sensing has attracted increasing attention for robotic manipulation, especially robot grasping tasks [1]. Grasping is a fundamental skill requirement for robots to work in an industrial or home-like environment [2–4]. Moreover, a successful grasp could be described as a relationship between an object and a gripper that allows for constraints and conditions of further manipulation [5]. Due to the uncertainties from algorithms, control and grasping process, the planned grasps will hardly be executed without any error. Thus, the stability of the grasp becomes more and more important [6–8]. Recently, stable robotic grasping based on tactile information has been one of the most popular problems researchers have been working on in the field of robotics [9–11], which can not only improve the success rate of grasping tasks, but also effectively serve to subsequent manipulation tasks.

A robust and stable grasp is particularly expected when robots start to work in unstructured environments [12]. Although there exists much work on robotic grasp manipulation with tactile sensing, including analytical methods and machine learning-based methods [13–15], some studies do not focus on stable grasping and belong to exploratory research.

© The Author(s), under exclusive license to Springer Nature Switzerland AG 2022
H. Liu et al. (Eds.): ICIRA 2022, LNAI 13457, pp. 628–639, 2022.
https://doi.org/10.1007/978-3-031-13835-5_57

In this paper, we focus on the research relative to stable grasping with tactile information and summarize the existing research results by combing published literature in this field. To effectively understand the contributions of these literature, this paper is composed of three parts: slip detection, stability assessment and grasp adjustment, which together constitute a complete stable grasping process.

2 Grasp with Slip Detection

The contact state perception between the gripper and object is vital for the control system during grasping manipulation, which helps form a control loop and adjust grasping motion based on the state feedback. While slip, an unstable contact state [16], occurs when the current grasp is performed with improper force or grasp strategy. Therefore, slip detection can assist robots in timely adjusting the grasping force and selecting an appropriate grasp action plan. The sensing of slip plays a vital role in robotic manipulation, and it has long been a challenging problem in the robotic community [17, 18].

2.1 Slip Detection with Tactile Sensor

In the past decades, many approaches have been developed based on tactile sensors to detect slip by physical signals, like vibration, force change, acceleration and relative motion between the gripper and object [19–21], and these all could be concluded as tactile sensing. Some research focused on creating a mechanism to detect slip. A soft skin covered with nibs which produce small vibrations was introduced in [22]. The contact force was observed to detect slip in [23, 24]. For example, authors in [23] detected/corrected slips and regulated grasping forces while manipulating deformable objects with the dynamic center of mass. In [25], they developed center-of-pressure tactile sensors for slip detection. In [26], hidden Markov models were trained to predict slip. In recent years, with the development of deep learning, many learning-based methods with tactile sensors for slip detection have emerged.

How to use biomimetic tactile sensors to extract useful tactile information needed for slip detection was explored in [27]. Different modalities available from the Bio Tac sensor were respectively tested to perform detection of the slip event, and the pressure-based method was proved to have the best performance. A learning-based approach for predicting slip with a Bio Tac sensor was proposed in [28] using high dimensional tactile information. The authors modelled this problem as a self-supervised learning problem. Experimental results showed that multiple unknown objects could be grasped successfully and stably by eliminating the possible slip by using slip prediction in the feedback loop of the controller.

In [29], the authors adopted random forest classifiers to create generalizable slip predictors based on tactile sensing, which could predict slip events and explore the generalization capabilities of supervised learning methods. Zapata-Impata et al. [30] and Meier et al. [31] classified different slip directions based on deep learning. The spatio-temporal tactile features were extracted and learned in [30] using a built ConvLSTM network to detect the direction of a slip of seven categories. Using similar spatio-temporal tactile features, authors in [31] proposed a deep convolutional neural network to classify the contact state and distinguish between rotational and translation slippage by adopting a piezo-resistive sensor array. However, the data collection in these two researches were specifically designed to produce discrete slip directions, which only contain limited slip behaviors.

2.2 Slip Detection with Vision-Based Tactile Sensing

The vision-based tactile sensors/optical tactile sensors could convert signals of the contact deformation into images and thus achieve high spatial resolution, which may help reconstruct the shape of the detected object and obtain rich contact information such as contact position, contact force, et al. [32, 33]. A finger-shaped tactile sensor using an optical waveguide was proposed in [34], which could detect the point where an object contacts the sensor surface and the normal to the surface of the contacted object. In [35], a compact tactile sensor complemented by Ferrier and Brockett successfully reconstructed the coarse 3D shape of the detected object. The similar idea was also adopted in [36–38] to encode edge information and construct contact state information. Moreover, with the tactile signals in the form of images, such as the tactile information from GelSight, the slip events could be detected more directly with appropriate image processing and feature extraction methods.

Authors in [39] presented a novel method of sensing the various load and slip on the contact surface with the GelSight, a vision-based tactile sensor. This method could infer the contact state based on the sequence of images from the GelSight sensor because the displacement field has different variations with the normal load, shear load and in-plane torsional load, respectively, and the displacement magnitude in positive correlation to the load. Results showed that the proposed method was effective in detecting interactions with an object during incipient slip.

A new design of GelSight for robot gripper using a Lambertian membrane and new illumination system was developed in [40], which could help improve geometric accuracy. Researchers performed slip detection with this developed sensor in a grasping experiment. For 37 objects tested in this work, the new sensor can detect both translational and rotational slip during grasping without any prior knowledge of the objects, benefiting the grasp stability.

2.3 Slip Detection Combined Tactile and Visual Information

For robot perception, the tactile and visual modalities can compensate each other. The tactile sensing can obtain the surface texture and contact state information of the object, while the visual sensing can provide information about the size and posture of the object. Therefore, the combination of them is helpful for better robot manipulation tasks, including slip detection during grasping.

In [41], a new framework based on deep neural network (DNN) was proposed for slip detection without any pre-knowledge of the physical parameters of the objects. The training data was acquired by a GelSight tactile sensor and an external camera mounted on the side of the gripper to grasp and lift 94 daily objects with different grasping forces and grasping positions. Using the image sequences obtained from the two sensors when the objects begin to be lifted, the DNN was trained to predict whether a slip occurred or not. Moreover, the proposed model was compared with other methods, including the models with single sources (tactile sensor or camera), and the results indicated that the tactile and visual information are complementary to each other in the slip detection task, especially for those objects with slippery and smooth surfaces. This work is heuristic for subsequent studies on grasp stability assessment, grasping adjustments, grasping strategy selection etc.

3   Grasp Stability Assessment

In the past few years, much research has focused on the stability in the process of grasping, which is critical for robots to estimate the current grasp state and achieve high-quality grasping manipulation [5, 42, 43]. Moreover, the stability analysis can not only help the adjustment of gripper motion during the grasping process, but also predict the grasping outcome before grasping [44]. The tactile information, better describing the contact situation between the gripper and the object, is so popular and pregnant to adopt for the construction of robot grasping quality assessment in recent years [45, 46]. Many studies were conducted based on various methods for evaluating grasp stability during grasping and predicting grasp outcome before grasping.

3.1   Grasp Stability Assessment Based on Analytical Methods

In [47], the intrinsic relations between grasping stability and contact conditions consisting of grasping points and grasping force are detailedly studied, and analytical metrics are established to evaluate the stability of current grasping. Moreover, to perform grasp refinement on three-fingered robotic hands using only tactile and joint position information, the well-justified analytical model was introduced to act as the meaningful reward function for RL algorithms, which is observably improved compared with prior complicated and manually designed optimization objectives in RL. In simulation experiments, the combination of geometric and tactile grasp stability metrics receives the highest average success rates and best performance. This work indicated that the research of grasping stability analysis is very valuable for the optimization of the RL algorithm and the construction of objective function.

3.2   Grasp Stability Assessment Based on Learning

With the rapid development of machine learning, constructing a grasp stability estimator from learning has become a popular field, which has attracted many researchers to explore and optimize stability estimation for grasping [48–50]. Emil et al. [51] proposed an adaptive grasping method to find a stable grasp on novel objects. An SVM classifier was learned based on tactile feedback in [52] to evaluate stability when the object was observed with uncertainty. Authors in [6] adopted the Gaussian Mixture Model to train a grasp stability estimator from successful grasp examples. Moreover, there have been abundant studies on the quality assessment from learning with neural networks recently.

A unified probabilistic framework using Bayesian networks for modelling and stability assessment was presented in [53], which considers both geometric constraint conditions and specific stability demands for task execution. This framework integrated high-level task information by human supervision and low-level robot self-exploration during learning to encode task-relevant requirements. Moreover, the relations of the multi-sensor inputs and tasks were modelled with Bayesian networks in a task-oriented manner. This work not only achieved grasp success prediction of a grasping action, but also helped infer the dependencies between different variables and sensory features relevant for object grasping. In this way, we could select sensory features most relevant for a particular task based on the task constraints, which optimizes the employment of the sensory data and opens a significant and interesting avenue for later studies.

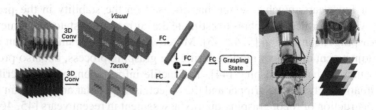

Fig. 1. The diagram of C3D-VTFN model for grasping state assessment.

In [54], in order to quickly determine the force required during grasping, the authors proposed a novel deep neural network (C3D-VTFN) based on the visual and tactile inputs to evaluate the grasping state of various deformable objects, as described in Fig. 1. The features of the modalities were extracted by 3D convolution layers, which provides a new feature extraction scheme for the visual-tactile fusion perception tasks. Moreover, the proposed network was trained and tested on the built GSA Dataset by abundant grasping and lifting experiments with different widths and forces on various deformable objects. Based on this model, some delicate grasp experiments in reality were also implemented. The results demonstrated this model to be effective and accurate enough to assess the grasp state and can be applied to adaptive grasping.

3.3 Grasp Outcome Prediction

For stable grasping and subsequent manipulation tasks, in addition to the assessment of the grasping state during grasping, it is also vital to predict whether a specific grasp will succeed prior to lifting [55, 56]. Bekiroglu et al. [57] assessed grasp quality before manipulating objects. Cockbum et al. [58] proposed an unsupervised feature learning method to train robots from successful and failed grasps, and they could predict whether a grasp attempt will succeed or fail using this knowledge.

In [59], the authors firstly investigated whether touch sensing aids in predicting grasp outcomes compared to pure visual perception. An end-to-end multi-modal sensing framework fusing visual and tactile information was proposed to predict grasp outcome, which requires no characterization of the tactile sensors, nor a model of the robot or object, as shown in Fig. 2. A two-finger gripper equipped with GelSight high-resolution tactile sensors was adopted for grasping trials and data collection. The proposed visuo-tactile deep neural network models were evaluated to directly predict grasp outcomes from either modality individually and from both modalities together. The results showed incorporating tactile reading substantially improves grasping performance.

A novel visual-tactile fusion learning method based on the Self-Attention mechanism (VTFSA) was developed in [60] for a grasp outcome prediction task. To learn effective visual-tactile fusion features, the framework contains a feature extraction module, a VTFSA module and a classification module. The proposed method was compared with traditional methods on two public multimodal grasping datasets, and the experiment results showed that this method could address the problem of different forms of tactile signals and the VTFSA module can further learn some cross-modal position-dependent features, which may be helpful for prediction. In brief, the proposed method had a more comprehensive and robust prediction performance.

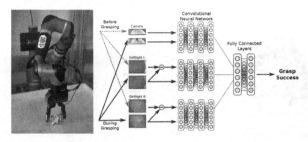

Fig. 2. Diagram of the proposed visual-tactile multi-modal model to predict grasp success

4 Grasp Adjustment and Re-grasp

During manipulation, once a grasp is predicted or evaluated to be unstable with stability assessment methods described in Sect. 2, the grasp adaption adjustment aiming at adjusting hand posture and finger motion is required for an efficient grasping state [6, 61, 62]. Therefore, how to learn regrasp policies and adjust grasp action to acquire complete grasping behaviors attracted the interests of many researchers [63–65].

Chebotar et al. [66] presented a framework based on reinforcement learning (RL) for regrasping behaviors based on tactile data. First, a grasp stability predictor is learned to predict the grasp outcome using spatio-temporal tactile features collected from the early-object-lifting phase. Then, the trained predictor was used to supervise and provide feedback to the RL algorithm that learns the grasp adjustments based on tactile feedback. Abundant experiments on the real robot were conducted. The results indicated that the robot could predict the grasp outcome with high accuracy, and the grasp success rate was greatly improved when allowed to regrasp the object in case of a predicted failure.

This work [67] presented a novel regrasp control policy based on tactile information to plan local grasp adjustments. A tactile-based grasp quality metric consisting of continuous values between 0 and 1 was constructed using a deep convolutional neural network trained on over 2800 grasps. The tactile imprints associated with robot motions relative to the initial grasp were simulated by performing rigid-body transformations of the given tactile measurements. With the newly learned grasp quality network, the newly generated tactile imprints were evaluated, and the best regrasp action could be selected to maximize the grasp quality.

In [68], the authors investigated how to actively and effectively adjust grasp action based on raw visuo-tactile data. To solve this problem, an end-to-end deep, multimodal convolutional network was proposed as action-conditional model to predict the outcome of a candidate grasp adjustment, and then execute a grasp by iteratively selecting the most promising actions. The proposed methods required neither calibration of the tactile sensors nor any analytical modelling of contact forces. To train this model, over 6,000 trials from 65 training objects were collected. The learned model could be adopted to grasp large-scale unseen objects with a high success rate. Moreover, the results demonstrated that the amount of force needed when grasping was easily decreased with this model, while preserving a similar chance of success (Fig. 3).

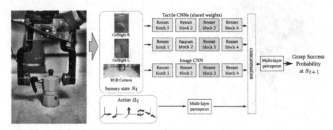

Fig. 3. Action-conditioned visuo-tactile model network architecture in [68]

5 Discussion

According to the survey described above, we have found that there are many studies focusing on grasping with tactile sensing, combined with learned or designed policies to achieve a stable and flexible grasping task, which greatly promotes the rapid development of robot grasping research. However, grasping with tactile perception seems to remain experimental in robotics, which may be attributed to the following reasons:

- **Unhandy to deploy.** Most robot hands/grippers are typically not designed for tactile sensors, so we need to install the tactile sensors in a limited space or design specific mechanisms for installation, which increases the problems of signals, power supply, and circuit wiring.
- **Poor durability and fragile.** The tactile sensors are always fragile because of the direct iteration with objects. Moreover, the properties of tactile sensors may change during long-term use. The inconsistent performance has a significant impact on machine learning, so some tactile sensors often need calibration.
- **Low compatibility with the others.** There are many kinds of tactile sensors, including optics-based, pressure-based and so on. Different data processing and feature extraction methods for these tactile sensors lead to poor compatibility with each other and reduce program reproducibility and reusability.

- **Necessity of tactile sensors.** In most cases, the robotic grasping manipulation could be well implemented without tactile sensors. Therefore, the task scene and target objects are expected to be constrained to help highlight its research significance with tactile sensors.
- **Expensive cost.** Compared to RGB-D cameras, IMUs and other sensors, tactile sensors are relatively expensive. Moreover, some high-performance tactile sensors have not been commercialized, leaving many researchers unable to obtain them.

These limitations and deficiencies prevent researchers from using tactile sensors, which makes it challenging to incorporate tactile modalities into robot grasping tasks and properly use tactile information to achieve stable grasp manipulation.

6 Conclusion

In this paper, we investigate the tactile sensing for robotic grasping manipulation mainly from three aspects, which are slip detection, grasp stability assessment and grasp action adjustment. We find that there are many different types of tactile sensors and methods to extract effective tactile modal information and assist robots in understanding the current contact state when grasping. Through this survey, we discuss the problems of introducing tactile sensors into robotic systems and emphasize the pipeline containing grasp outcome prediction and grasp adjustment based on machine learning because of its feasibility and effectiveness.

References

1. Wettels, N., Santos, V.J., Johansson, R.S., Loeb, G.E.: Biomimetic tactile sensor array. Adv. Robot. **22**(8), 829–849 (2008)
2. Tegin, J., Ekvall, S., Kragic, D., Wikander, J., Iliev, B.: Demonstration-based learning and control for automatic grasping. Intell. Serv. Robot. **2**(1), 23–30 (2009)
3. Goldfeder, C., Allen, P.K., Lackner, C., Pelossof, R.: Grasp planning via decomposition trees. In: Proceedings 2007 IEEE International Conference on Robotics and Automation, Rome, Italy, April 2007, pp. 4679–4684 (2007)
4. Faccio, M., Bottin, M., Rosati, G.: Collaborative and traditional robotic assembly: a comparison model. Int. J. Adv. Manuf. Technol. **102**(5–8), 1355–1372 (2019). https://doi.org/10.1007/s00170-018-03247-z
5. Bekiroglu, Y., Huebner, K., Kragic, D.: Integrating grasp planning with online stability assessment using tactile sensing. In: 2011 IEEE International Conference on Robotics and Automation, Shanghai, China, May 2011, pp. 4750–4755 (2011)
6. Li, M., Bekiroglu, Y., Kragic, D., Billard, A.: Learning of grasp adaptation through experience and tactile sensing. In: 2014 IEEE/RSJ International Conference on Intelligent Robots and Systems, Chicago, IL, USA, September 2014, pp. 3339–3346 (2014)
7. Dang, H., Allen, P.K.: Learning grasp stability. In: 2012 IEEE International Conference on Robotics and Automation, St Paul, MN, USA, May 2012, pp. 2392–2397 (2012)
8. Roa, M.A., Suárez, R.: Grasp quality measures: review and performance. Auton. Robot. **38**(1), 65–88 (2014). https://doi.org/10.1007/s10514-014-9402-3

9. Hyttinen, E., Kragic, D., Detry, R.: Learning the tactile signatures of prototypical object parts for robust part-based grasping of novel objects. In: 2015 IEEE International Conference on Robotics and Automation (ICRA), Seattle, WA, USA, May 2015, pp. 4927–4932 (2015)

10. Dang, H., Weisz, J., Allen, P.K.: Blind grasping: stable robotic grasping using tactile feedback and hand kinematics. In: 2011 IEEE International Conference on Robotics and Automation, Shanghai, China, May 2011, pp. 5917–5922 (2011)

11. Laaksonen, J., Kyrki, V., Kragic, D.: Evaluation of feature representation and machine learning methods in grasp stability learning. In: 2010 10th IEEE-RAS International Conference on Humanoid Robots, Nashville, TN, USA, December 2010, pp. 112–117 (2010)

12. Bierbaum, A., Rambow, M., Asfour, T., Dillmann, R.: Grasp affordances from multi-fingered tactile exploration using dynamic potential fields. In: 2009 9th IEEE-RAS International Conference on Humanoid Robots, Paris, December 2009, pp. 168–174 (2009)

13. Chebotar, Y., Kroemer, O., Peters, J.: Learning robot tactile sensing for object manipulation. In: 2014 IEEE/RSJ International Conference on Intelligent Robots and Systems, Chicago, IL, USA, September 2014, pp. 3368–3375 (2014)

14. van Hoof, H., Hermans, T., Neumann, G., Peters, J.: Learning robot in-hand manipulation with tactile features. In: 2015 IEEE-RAS 15th International Conference on Humanoid Robots (Humanoids), Seoul, South Korea, November 2015, pp. 121–127 (2015)

15. Hellman, R.B., Tekin, C., van der Schaar, M., Santos, V.J.: Functional contour-following via haptic perception and reinforcement learning. IEEE Trans. Haptics 11(1), 61–72 (2018)

16. Hasegawa, T., Honda, K.: Detection and measurement of fingertip slip in multi-fingered precision manipulation with rolling contact. In: Conference Documentation International Conference on Multisensor Fusion and Integration for Intelligent Systems. MFI 2001 (Cat. No.01TH8590), Baden-Baden, Germany, pp. 43–48 (2001)

17. Holweg, E.G.M., Hoeve, H., Jongkind, W., Marconi, L., Melchiorri, C., Bonivento, C.: Slip detection by tactile sensors: algorithms and experimental results. In: Proceedings of IEEE International Conference on Robotics and Automation, Minneapolis, MN, USA, vol. 4, pp. 3234–3239 (1996)

18. Tsujiuchi, N., et al.: Slip detection with distributed-type tactile sensor. In: 2004 IEEE/RSJ International Conference on Intelligent Robots and Systems (IROS) (IEEE Cat. No. 04CH37566), Sendai, Japan, 2004, vol. 1, pp. 331–336 (2004)

19. Howe, R.D., Cutkosky, M.R.: Sensing skin acceleration for slip and texture perception. In: Proceedings, 1989 International Conference on Robotics and Automation, Scottsdale, AZ, USA, 1989, pp. 145–150 (1989)

20. Romano, J.M., Hsiao, K., Niemeyer, G., Chitta, S., Kuchenbecker, K.J.: Human-inspired robotic grasp control with tactile sensing. IEEE Trans. Robot. 27(6), 1067–1079 (2011)

21. Yussof, H.: Sensorization of robotic hand using optical three-axis tactile sensor: evaluation with grasping and twisting motions. J. Comput. Sci. 6(8), 955–962 (2010)

22. Tremblay, M.R., Cutkosky, M.R.: Estimating friction using incipient slip sensing during a manipulation task. In: Proceedings IEEE International Conference on Robotics and Automation, Atlanta, GA, USA, 1993, pp. 429–434 (1993)

23. Kaboli, M., Yao, K., Cheng, G.: Tactile-based manipulation of deformable objects with dynamic center of mass. In: 2016 IEEE-RAS 16th International Conference on Humanoid Robots (Humanoids), Cancun, Mexico, November 2016, pp. 752–757 (2016)

24. Melchiorri, C.: Slip detection and control using tactile and force sensors. IEEE/ASME Trans. Mechatron. 5(3), 235–243 (2000)

25. Gunji, D., et al.: Grasping force control of multi-fingered robot hand based on slip detection using tactile sensor. In: 2008 IEEE International Conference on Robotics and Automation, Pasadena, CA, USA, May 2008, pp. 2605–2610 (2008)

26. Jamali, N., Sammut, C.: Slip prediction using Hidden Markov models: multidimensional sensor data to symbolic temporal pattern learning. In: 2012 IEEE International Conference on Robotics and Automation, St Paul, MN, USA, May 2012, pp. 215–222 (2012)
27. Su, Z., et al.: Force estimation and slip detection/classification for grip control using a biomimetic tactile sensor. In: 2015 IEEE-RAS 15th International Conference on Humanoid Robots (Humanoids), Seoul, South Korea, November 2015, pp. 297–303 (2015)
28. Veiga, F., Peters, J., Hermans, T.: Grip stabilization of novel objects using slip prediction. IEEE Trans. Haptics 11(4), 531–542 (2018)
29. Veiga, F., van Hoof, H., Peters, J., Hermans, T.: Stabilizing novel objects by learning to predict tactile slip. In: 2015 IEEE/RSJ International Conference on Intelligent Robots and Systems (IROS), Hamburg, Germany, September 2015, pp. 5065–5072 (2015)
30. Meier, M., Patzelt, F., Haschke, R., Ritter, H.J.: Tactile convolutional networks for online slip and rotation detection. In: Villa, A.E.P., Masulli, P., Pons Rivero, A.J. (eds.) Artificial Neural Networks and Machine Learning – ICANN 2016. LNCS, vol. 9887, pp. 12–19. Springer, Cham (2016). https://doi.org/10.1007/978-3-319-44781-0_2
31. ZapataImpata, B., Gil, P., Torres, F.: Learning spatio temporal tactile features with a ConvLSTM for the direction of slip detection. Sensors 19(3), 523 (2019)
32. Jiar, Y., Lee, K., Shi, G.: A high resolution and high compliance tactile sensing system for robotic manipulations. In: Proceedings of 1993 IEEE/RSJ International Conference on Intelligent Robots and Systems (IROS 1993), Yokohama, Japan, 1993, vol. 2, pp. 1005–1009 (1993)
33. Ohka, M., Mitsuya, Y., Hattori, K., Higashioka, I.: Data conversion capability of optical tactile sensor featuring an array of pyramidal projections. In: 1996 IEEE/SICE/RSJ International Conference on Multisensor Fusion and Integration for Intelligent Systems (Cat. No. 96TH8242), Washington, DC, USA, 1996, pp. 573–580 (1996)
34. Maekawa, H., Tanie, K., Komoriya, K.: A finger-shaped tactile sensor using an optical waveguide. In: Proceedings of IEEE Systems Man and Cybernetics Conference - SMC, Le Touquet, France, 1993, pp. 403–408 (1993)
35. Ferrier, N.J., Brockett, R.W.: Reconstructing the shape of a deformable membrane from image data. Int. J. Robot. Res. 19(9), 795–816 (2000)
36. Sato, K., Kamiyama, K., Nii, H., Kawakami, N., Tachi, S.: Measurement of force vector field of robotic finger using vision-based haptic sensor. In: 2008 IEEE/RSJ International Conference on Intelligent Robots and Systems, Nice, September 2008, pp. 488–493 (2008)
37. Nagata, K., Ooki, M., Kakikur, M.: Feature detection with an image based compliant tactile sensor. In: Proceedings 1999 IEEE/RSJ International Conference on Intelligent Robots and Systems. Human and Environment Friendly Robots with High Intelligence and Emotional Quotients (Cat. No. 99CH36289), Kyongju, South Korea, 1999, vol. 2, pp. 838–843 (1999)
38. Kamiyama, K., Vlack, K., Mizota, T., Kajimoto, H., Kawakami, K., Tachi, S.: Vision-based sensor for real-time measuring of surface traction fields. IEEE Comput. Grap. Appl. 25(1), 68–75 (2005)
39. Yuan, W., Li, R., Srinivasan, M.A., Adelson, E.H.: Measurement of shear and slip with a GelSight tactile sensor. In: 2015 IEEE International Conference on Robotics and Automation (ICRA), Seattle, WA, USA, May 2015, pp. 304–311 (2015)
40. Dong, S., Yuan, W., Adelson, E.H.: Improved GelSight tactile sensor for measuring geometry and slip. In: 2017 IEEE/RSJ International Conference on Intelligent Robots and Systems (IROS), Vancouver, BC, September 2017, pp. 137–144 (2017)
41. Li, J., Dong, S., Adelson, E.: Slip detection with combined tactile and visual information. In: 2018 IEEE International Conference on Robotics and Automation (ICRA), Brisbane, QLD, May 2018, pp. 7772–7777 (2018)

42. Bekiroglu, Y., Kragic, D., Kyrki, V.: Learning grasp stability based on tactile data and HMMs. In: 19th International Symposium in Robot and Human Interactive Communication, Viareggio, Italy, September 2010, pp. 132–137 (2010)
43. Zapata-Impata, B.S., Gil, P., Torres, F.: Non-Matrix Tactile Sensors: How Can Be Exploited Their Local Connectivity For Predicting Grasp Stability? (2018)
44. Garcia-Garcia, A., Zapata-Impata, B.S., Orts-Escolano, S., Gil, P., Garcia-Rodriguez, J.: TactileGCN: A Graph Convolutional Network for Predicting Grasp Stability with Tactile Sensors (2019)
45. Johansson, R.S., Flanagan, J.R.: Coding and use of tactile signals from the fingertips in object manipulation tasks. Nat. Rev. Neurosci. **10**(5), 345–359 (2009)
46. Gao, Y., Hendricks, L.A., Kuchenbecker, K.J., Darrell, T.: Deep Learning for Tactile Understanding From Visual and Haptic Data (2015)
47. Koenig, A, Liu, Z., Janson, L., Howe, R.: Tactile Grasp Refinement using Deep Reinforcement Learning and Analytic Grasp Stability Metrics. arXiv:2109.11234 [cs, eess], September 2021, Accessed 27 October 2021. http://arxiv.org/abs/2109.11234
48. Miller, A.T., Allen, P.K.: Examples of 3D grasp quality computations. In: Proceedings 1999 IEEE International Conference on Robotics and Automation (Cat. No. 99CH36288C), Detroit, MI, USA, 1999, vol. 2, pp. 1240–1246 (1999)
49. Zheng, Y., Qian, W.-H.: Improving grasp quality evaluation. Robot. Auton. Syst. **57**(6–7), 665–673 (2009)
50. Kwiatkowski, J., Cockburn, D., Duchaine, V.: Grasp stability assessment through the fusion of proprioception and tactile signals using convolutional neural networks. In: 2017 IEEE/RSJ International Conference on Intelligent Robots and Systems (IROS), Vancouver, BC, September 2017, pp. 286–292 (2017)
51. Hyttinen, E., Kragic, D., Detry, R.: Estimating tactile data for adaptive grasping of novel objects. In: 2017 IEEE-RAS 17th International Conference on Humanoid Robotics (Humanoids), Birmingham, November 2017, pp. 643–648 (2017)
52. Dang, H., Allen, P.K.: Stable grasping under pose uncertainty using tactile feedback. Auton. Robot. **36**(4), 309–330 (2013). https://doi.org/10.1007/s10514-013-9355-y
53. Bekiroglu, Y., Song, D., Wang, L., Kragic, D.: A probabilistic framework for task-oriented grasp stability assessment. In: 2013 IEEE International Conference on Robotics and Automation, Karlsruhe, Germany, May 2013, pp. 3040–3047 (2013)
54. Cui, S., Wang, R., Wei, J, Li, F., Wang, S.: Grasp state assessment of deformable objects using visual-tactile fusion perception. In: 2020 IEEE International Conference on Robotics and Automation (ICRA), Paris, France, May 2020, pp. 538–544 (2020)
55. Levine, S., Pastor, P., Krizhevsky, A., Ibarz, J., Quillen, D.: Learning hand-eye coordination for robotic grasping with deep learning and large-scale data collection. Int. J. Robot. Res. **37**(4–5), 421–436 (2018)
56. Yan, G., Schmitz, A., Funabashi, S., Somlor, S, Tomo, T.P., Sugano, S.: A robotic grasping state perception framework with multi-phase tactile information and ensemble learning. IEEE Robot. Autom. Lett., p. 1 (2022)
57. Bekiroglu, Y., Laaksonen, J., Jorgensen, J.A., Kyrki, V., Kragic, D.: Assessing grasp stability based on learning and haptic data. IEEE Trans. Robot. **27**(3), 616–629 (2011)
58. Cockbum, D., Roberge, J.-P., Le, T.-H.-L., Maslyczyk, A., Duchaine, V.: Grasp stability assessment through unsupervised feature learning of tactile images. In: 2017 IEEE International Conference on Robotics and Automation (ICRA), Singapore, Singapore, May 2017, pp. 2238–2244 (2017)
59. R. Calandra et al.: The Feeling of Success: Does Touch Sensing Help Predict Grasp Outcomes?," arXiv:1710.05512 [cs, stat], October 2017, Accessed 08 Mar 2022. http://arxiv.org/abs/1710.05512

60. Cui, S., Wang, R., Wei, J., Hu, J., Wang, S.: Self-attention based visual-tactile fusion learning for predicting grasp outcomes. IEEE Robot. Autom. Lett. **5**(4), 5827–5834 (2020)
61. Steffen, J., Haschke, R., Ritter, H.: Experience-based and tactile-driven dynamic grasp control. In: 2007 IEEE/RSJ International Conference on Intelligent Robots and Systems, San Diego, CA, USA, October 2007, pp. 2938–2943 (2007)
62. Kim, J., Iwamoto, K., Kuffner, J.J., Ota, Y., Pollard, N.S.: Physically-based grasp quality evaluation under uncertainty. In: 2012 IEEE International Conference on Robotics and Automation, St. Paul, MN, USA, May 2012, pp. 3258–3263 (2012)
63. Felip, J., Morales, A.: Robust sensor-based grasp primitive for a three-finger robot hand. In: 2009 IEEE/RSJ International Conference on Intelligent Robots and Systems, St. Louis, MO, USA, pp. 1811–1816, October 2009
64. Chebotar, Y., Hausman, K., Kroemer, O., Sukhatme, G.S., Schaal, S.: Generalizing regrasping with supervised policy learning. In: Kulić, D., Nakamura, Y., Khatib, O., Venture, G. (eds.) 2016 International Symposium on Experimental Robotics. SPAR, vol. 1, pp. 622–632. Springer, Cham (2017). https://doi.org/10.1007/978-3-319-50115-4_54
65. Dang, H., Allen, P.K.: Grasp adjustment on novel objects using tactile experience from similar local geometry. In: 2013 IEEE/RSJ International Conference on Intelligent Robots and Systems, Tokyo, pp. 4007–4012, November 2013
66. Chebotar, Y., Hausman, K., Su, Z., Sukhatme, G.S., Schaal, S.: Self-supervised regrasping using spatio-temporal tactile features and reinforcement learning. In: 2016 IEEE/RSJ International Conference on Intelligent Robots and Systems (IROS), Daejeon, South Korea, pp. 1960–1966, October 2016
67. Hogan, F.R., Bauza, M., Canal, O., Donlon, E., Rodriguez, A.: Tactile regrasp: grasp adjustments via simulated tactile transformations. In: 2018 IEEE/RSJ International Conference on Intelligent Robots and Systems (IROS), Madrid, pp. 2963–2970, October 2018
68. Calandra, R., et al.: More than a feeling: learning to grasp and regrasp using vision and touch. IEEE Robot. Autom. Lett. **3**(4), 3300–3307 (2018)

A Soft Neuromorphic Approach for Contact Spatial Shape Sensing Based on Vision-Based Tactile Sensor

Xiaoxin Wang[1], Yicheng Yang[2], Ziliang Zhou[2], Guiyao Xiang[1], and Honghai Liu[1(✉)]

[1] Harbin Institute of Technology Shenzhen, Shenzhen, China
xiaoxin.wang@stu.hit.edu.cn, honghai.liu@icloud.com
[2] Shanghai Jiao Tong University, Shanghai, China

Abstract. Robots with tactile sensors can distinguish the tactile property of the object, such as the spatial shape, in many robotic applications. The neuromorphic approach offers a new solution for information processing to encode tactile signals. Vision-based tactile sensing has gradually attracted attention in recent years. Although some work has been done on proving the capacity of tactile sensors, the soft neuromorphic method inspired by neuroscience for spatial shape sensing is remarkably rare. This paper presented a soft neuromorphic method for contact spatial shape sensing using a vision-based tactile sensor. The outputs from the sensor were fed into the Izhikevich neuron model to emit the spike trains for emulating the firing behavior of mechanoreceptors. 9 spatial shapes were evaluated with an active touch protocol. The neuromorphic spike trains were decoded for discriminating spatial shapes based on k-nearest neighbors (KNN). Three spike features were used: average firing rate (FR), the coefficient of variation of the interspike interval (ISI CV), and the first spike firing time (FST). The results demonstrated the ability to classify different shapes with an accuracy as high as 93.519%. Furthermore, we found that FST significantly improved spatial shape classification decoding performance. This work was a preliminary study to apply the neuromorphic way to convey the tactile information obtained from the vision-based tactile sensor. It paved the way for using the neuromorphic vision-based tactile sensor in neurorobotic applications.

Keywords: Soft neuromorphic approach · Spatial shape sensing · Vision-based tactile sensing · Spike train · Robotics

1 Introduction

Robots equipped with tactile sensation, just like a human, have more advantages in completing complex tasks. Neuromorphic engineering is an interdisciplinary

Supported by the Shenzhen Science and Technology Program (Grant No. JCYJ202103 24120214040), the Guangdong Science and Technology Research Council (Grant No. 2020B1515120064).

subject that takes inspiration from neuroscience as a new solution for information processing for robots. It intends to mimic neuro-biological architectures present in the nervous system via artificial sensory devices [1]. During the past decade, many neuromorphic designs and hardware development have made significant progress in the industry and academia. For instance, neuromorphic silicon retinas and silicon cochleas have been presented to reproduce the functionality of these in biological system [2]. Besides hardware development, another approach to developing neuromorphic engineering is called soft-approach [3]. It concentrates on using a software algorithm to replicate the spike-based representation of information in a biological neuron system. First, the physical stimuli were transformed into signals via the artificial sensors, and then signals were encoded into spike trains with the artificial neuron model, such as the Izhikevich model [4]. Even though the soft approach to reproducing the spike trains is hard to avoid the disadvantages of the conventional artificial sensors, for instance, highly integrated sensors suffer the readout delay and large power consumption [5], it is a preliminary attempt to establish the artificial sensory system.

In recent years, the soft neuromorphic approach has been developed in several tactile sensation applications, for instance, representation of local curvature in contact [6], and texture discrimination tasks [7]. However, the research about the soft neuromorphic approach applied to tactile surface shape recognition is especially rare. The task of surface shape recognition is a basic and important component for tactile sensing in object recognition [8,9]. For instance, Liu et al. [10] presented a set of low-resolution pressure maps to develop an object shape recognition method. Du et al. [11] proposed the FingerVision sensor with a random color pattern as the tracking target and a dense optical flow algorithm to track the deformation. Yang et al. [12,13] customized an enhanced FingerVision for sensing the spatial surface shape via the surface reconstruction and recognition two-step method. Therefore, this paper intends to fill the gap by adopting a soft neuromorphic method for tactile surface shape recognition.

Another motivation for this paper originates from bionic engineering, for instance, the artificial tactile sensory system. Tactile sensation is essential for robotics and prosthetics [14,15]. As a part of artificial tactile sensors, the vision-based tactile sensor has become a promising solution for tactile sensing over the past decade. Starting in 2009, the Gelsight was developed as a graphics sensor reflecting the deformation of the elastomer via the reflective coating [16, 17]. It was applied in many applications such as robotic manipulation [18] and slippage detection [19]. Lately in 2017, the FingerVision was presented as a new vision-based tactile sensor for tactile sensing through the embedded marker displacements [20] and showed capabilities of object pose estimation and force estimation [21]. Compared the conventional tactile sensors, such as capacitive sensors [22] and piezoresistive sensors [23], the vision-based tactile sensor has the advantages that the structure is simple and the parts are affordable. Besides, the capability of shape recognition has been verified in work [13]. In the human body, the tactile stimuli are detected by the mechanoreceptors in the skin, and the tactile signals will be transformed via the tactile afferent with the spike trains.

However, the outputs of the artificial tactile sensors are usually continuous and not processed directly in artificial neuron systems such as spike neural networks. Therefore, the research of artificial tactile sensors with spike trains combined with a spiking neural network to form the artificial sensory system provides new insight into developing advanced neurorobotics and neuroprostheses. In this paper, the first step of acquiring spike trains was achieved.

For this paper, the main contributions are listed as follows. 1) Spatial shape was encoded with spiking neuron models using the vision-based tactile sensor. 2) The outputs of spike trains were decoded via a KNN classifier to demonstrate surface shape recognition.

The rest of this paper is organized as follows. Section 2 introduced the hardware of the vision-based tactile sensor and the artificial spiking neuron. Section 3 demonstrated the surface shape classification via experiments on different surface shapes and discussed the work. Finally, Sect. 4 concluded the results in this paper.

2   Materials and Methods

2.1   Custom Vision-Based Tactile Sensor

The vision-based tactile sensor was customized as the enhanced *FingerVision*, which was introduced in detail in [13], as depicted in Fig. 1. The elastomer was fabricated based on the silicone gel, had elasticity and determinable hardness, and directly contacted the different spatial surfaces. The position of markers embedded in the elastomer was offset during the contact, indicating the surface topography information. The camera behind the elastomer captured the projection of markers offset in the image plane. A 3D-printed framework connected the elastomer and the camera using the fastening of bolts and nuts.

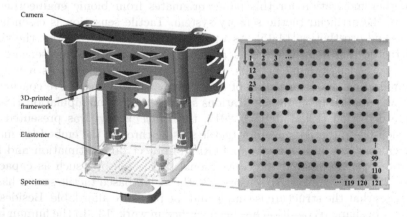

Fig. 1. The vision-based tactile sensor with 11 × 11 markers.

2.2 Experimental Setup and Protocol

The vision-based tactile sensor was fixed on the three-axis motion platform, as shown in Fig. 2. The additional light source ensured the consistency of light intensity. During touch, the sensor contacted the spatial shape perpendicularly via 3 phases: pressing, holding, and release.

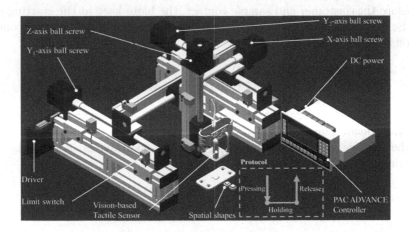

Fig. 2. The experimental setup and protocol.

The 3D-printed spatial shapes were designed as the specimens according to the essential elements of the shape in the first contact with the elastomer: point, line, and surface. Three types with three sizes, a total of 9 shapes, were shown in Fig. 2. The height of the shapes was consistent and set to 4 mm. The type and size were listed in Table 1.

Table 1. The type and size of different shapes

Type		Sphere			Cylinder			Square		
Identifier		Sp1	Sp2	Sp3	Cy1	Cy2	Cy3	Sq1	Sq2	Sq3
Size	Parameter	R			$R \times L$			$L \times L$		
	Value	6	8	10	2×10	4×10	6×10	6×6	10×10	14×14

Starting from the surface of the elastomer, each shape was pressed to the same depth, 1.5 mm. Each shape was contacted 80 times. Finally, there were 720 sets of data.

2.3 Data Acquisition and Noise Filter

The outputs of the vision-based tactile sensor were a series of videos. During the offline data processing, the markers were detected as the blobs in the image plane based on the *Simple Blob Detector* algorithm from *OpenCV* during the offline data processing. The coordinates with X and Y directions of blobs were extracted as the 121×1 vector, expressed as

$$\begin{cases} X(i,t) = \{x(1,t), x(2,t), ..., x(121,t)\} \\ Y(i,t) = \{y(1,t), y(2,t), ..., y(121,t)\} \end{cases} \quad (1)$$

Before the elastomer and sample contact, the blobs keep at the starting position. So we selected the first frame as the original coordinates for each contact. The offset of blobs was expressed as

$$\begin{cases} \Delta x(i,t) = x(i,t) - x(i,0) \\ \Delta y(i,t) = y(i,t) - y(i,0) \end{cases} \quad (2)$$

Considering the overall offset of the elastomer, we selected 4 blobs as the correction point. The average coordinates of the selected blobs were calculated, and the average value was subtracted from the coordinates of all blobs. The equations are

$$\begin{cases} \Delta \bar{x}_c(t) = \frac{\Delta x(1,t) + \Delta x(11,t) + \Delta x(111,t) + \Delta x(121,t)}{4} \\ \Delta \bar{y}_c(t) = \frac{\Delta y(1,t) + \Delta y(11,t) + \Delta y(111,t) + \Delta y(121,t)}{4} \end{cases} \quad (3)$$

$$\begin{cases} \Delta x'(i,t) = \Delta x(i,t) - \Delta \bar{x}_c(t) \\ \Delta y'(i,t) = \Delta y(i,t) - \Delta \bar{y}_c(t) \end{cases} \quad (4)$$

The detection of blobs was affected by the experimental noise, such as the light and the vibration of motion platform, and the stability of algorithm. Therefore, we set the threshold T_{hres} to eliminate insignificant fluctuations. The data was adjusted as

$$\begin{cases} \Delta x''(i,t) = \Delta x'(i,t) - T_{hres} \\ \Delta y''(i,t) = \Delta y'(i,t) - T_{hres} \end{cases} \quad (5)$$

The shifted distance for each blob was calculated based on the Euclidean distance.

$$\begin{aligned} disp(i,t) &= \sqrt{\Delta x''(i,t)^2 + \Delta y''(i,t)^2} \\ D(i,t) &= \{disp(1,t), disp(2,t), ..., disp(121,t)\} \end{aligned} \quad (6)$$

2.4   Neuron Model

The offset for each marker in elastomer was regarded as the sensor outputs with the analog form. The analog outputs were converted into spiking trains via the spiking neuron model. The spiking neuron model replicated the spike-based information of regular spiking behaviors in neurons.

The Izhikevich neuron model [4] was selected as the spiking neuron model for its computational efficiency and biological plausibility. The sensors outputs (S_{output}) were multiplied by a gain (G) and served as input current (I_{input}) to the Izhikevich model. Following the prior studies [23], the inter-spike interval histograms of sensor responses with the gain were computed to strike the optimal value of gain. The optimal value of gain was chosen to reach a balance between the firing rate and sparse responses. Therefore, we selected the gain as 10 in this paper.

The parameters of the Izhikevich model were updated following the two equations:

$$\dot{v} = 0.04v^2 + 5v = 140 - u + I_{input}$$
$$\dot{u} = a(bv - u) \tag{7}$$

where v represents the membrane potential, u represents the membrane recovery variable. $I_{input} = S_{output} \times G$ is the current value, S_{output} represents the sensors outputs and G is the gain.

The model produces a spike when the membrane potential reaches 30 mV, which following the equation with after-spike resetting:

$$\text{if } v > 30 \text{ mV}, \text{then} \begin{cases} v \leftarrow c \\ u \leftarrow u + d \end{cases} \tag{8}$$

Here, a, b, c, and d are the dimensionless variables, which were chosen to imitate regular spiking neuron behaviours [4]. The values used in this paper were: $a = 0.02, b = 0.2, c = -65\,\text{mV}, d = 2$.

2.5 Spike Trains Decoding Method

The identity of the tactile stimuli was decoded from the features of the spike trains produced by the multi-channels during the contact phase of the experimental protocol.

Generally, a bulk of sensory neurons were considered to convey information by average firing rate (FR) [24], which only considers the interval between the first spike time and the last spike time. The average firing rate is directly related to the inverse of the average interspike interval (ISI). The second feature is the ISI coefficient of variation (CV) during the same phase. Another equally important spike feature is first spike latency, which refers to the first spike firing time (FST). The first spike latencies with the timing were found to convey the tactile information of surface shape more reliably [25]. The two features were defined as

$$FR = \frac{t_{spike_n} - t_{spike_0}}{n} \tag{9}$$

$$ISI(n) = t_{spike_n} - t_{spike_{n-1}}$$
$$ISI\ CV = \frac{std(ISI)}{average(ISI)} \tag{10}$$

$$FST = t_{spike_0} \tag{11}$$

In this work, the features above were evaluated to classify the different spatial shape surfaces. In addition, the FST feature was ensured for the stable contact operation based on the controller and the well-performed blob detection method.

The decoding evaluation was performed via the 3-D space of response using a k-nearest neighbors (KNN) algorithm. The KNN classifier with 5-fold cross-validation and Euclidean distance was selected to classify different shapes for it was easy to implement. The feature extraction and the classification were carried out using *MATLAB*.

3 Results and Discussion

3.1 Spiking Encoding of Shapes

The elastomer contacted different shapes, and the embedded markers shifted according to the spatial features of shapes. Each marker was considered a sensing element. The coordinates of markers were extracted along the time, which was associated with three phases, as shown in Fig. 3.

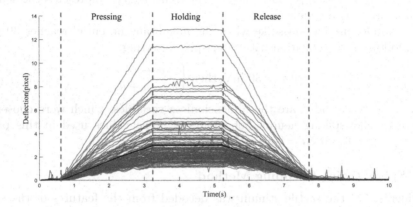

Fig. 3. The deflection of blobs in three phases: pressing, holding, release.

The data containing the changes of markers coordinates was fed into a number of neurons, as introduced in Sect. 2.4. Each sensing element corresponds to a neuron, which generates one spike train. Therefore, 121 × 1 serial spike trains were in the output of 121 neurons. From Fig. 4, we found that the first spiking firing was closely related to the position of the shape contacted with the elastomer. The second column was the deflection of each blob from the original position. Finally, the displacement of shifted blobs was encoded as the spike trains, shown in the time domain as 2D in the third column and 3D in the fourth. Intuitively, the number of spikes for each sensing element depended on the contacted depth.

3.2 Classification of Different Shapes

The KNN classifier was implemented to identify shapes based on FR, FST, and ISI CV features. Then, the 5-fold cross-validation was conducted to find a suitable model for the task.

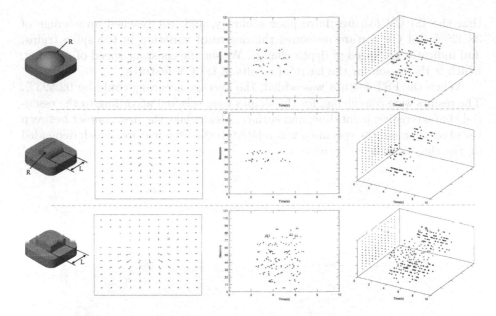

Fig. 4. The outputs with spike trains from the encoding processing.

Considering the noise from external conditions, we set a threshold and observed the influence of different values. The source of the noise included the varying light intensity that interferes with the blob detection accuracy, and the motion platform that usually produces periodic vibration. The smaller threshold value allowed more fluctuations to decrease the accuracy of identified shapes. However, the larger one would lose more useful information on blob deflections. From the results of Fig. 5, we selected the suitable T_{hres} as 4.

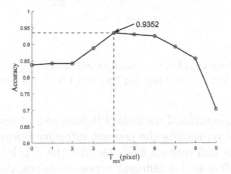

Fig. 5. The influence of the threshold T_{hres} to the classification.

To evaluate the efficiency of different features, we drew the confusion matrix to observe the results of different features added, as depicted in Fig. 6. We found that the ISI CV features have poor accuracy, and just reached an average of 38.426%. ISI CV feature measures the degree of variation in the spike trains, and indicates the speed of depth change. We set the constant speed of pressing, which is the reason for the harmful results of ISI CV features.

When the FST feature was added, the average accuracy could be 92.593%. The results were convincing, for the shapes were selected according to the essential characteristics: point, line, and surface. Meanwhile, the first contact between the elastomer and the specimen was related to the FST feature, which depended on the shape's characteristics.

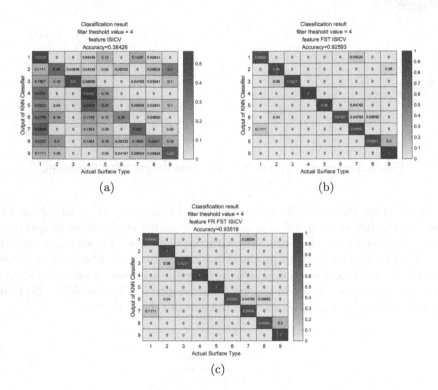

Fig. 6. The confusion matrix of KNN classifier in spatial shapes classification with the $T_{hres} = 4$. (a) feature ISI CV, (b) feature FST ISI CV, (c) feature FR FST ISI CV

The classification combined with the FR feature had an average accuracy of 93.519%. FR feature represents the contact intensity information, which refers to the pressing depth and contact field. Despite the depth being consistent, the size varied on a small scale for different types of shapes. So the FR feature has improved in the classification but is weak.

The proportion of the train set was another essential parameter for the classifier. It indicated the performance of the classification algorithm in the dataset. Therefore, we got the results by a set different proportion of train set, as shown in Fig. 7. We found that the accuracy tended to be stable when the value reached 0.4.

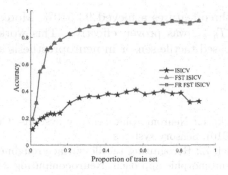

Fig. 7. The classification results of different proportion of train set.

3.3 Discussion

The soft neuromorphic approach was implemented using a vision-based tactile sensor to classify different shapes. The results showed that the Izhikevich neuron model was significant in encoding the data from the outputs of the sensor as spike trains. The input of the neuron model was the Euclidean distance of deflection of blobs. However, it lost the direction information about the shifted blobs, which indicated the characteristics of the contacted surface of the shape.

The KNN algorithm could decode the spike trains based on selected features. The FST and FR feature offered useful information about the shape, but the ISI CV feature seemed to play a small role. The varying speed of pressing and multiple depths maybe improve the above situation.

We just designed three types of shapes with three sizes for the specimens. The essential characteristics of shape about the first contact with the sensor were considered. Then, more characteristics relative to the shape could be deliberated, such as the change rate of height from a point, the orientation of the line edge, and the curvature of a surface.

4   Conclusion

This paper developed a soft neuromorphic method for classifying different shapes based on vision-based tactile sensing. A custom vision-based tactile sensor attached to the three-axis motion platform contacted different shapes following the protocol of three phases: pressing, holding, and release. The specimens were designed based on the essential characteristics of a shape in the first contact with the sensor: point, line, and surface. The blobs from the sensor were detected, the coordinates were extracted, and the deflection data of blobs was fed into the Izhikevich neuron model to reproduce spike trains. Three features were selected from the spike trains: FR, FST, and ISI CV. The KNN classifier decoded the different shapes based on the above features. We found that the FST feature significantly improved the classification of shapes, which was consistent with the results of a physiological experiment. The final average accuracy

650   X. Wang et al.

combined with the three features achieved 93.519%. Moreover, the noise filter
with the threshold, T_{hres}, was proven effective. This work paves the way for
developing a vision-based tactile sensor in neuroprosthesis and neurorobotics.

References

1. Liu, S.C., Delbruck, T.: Neuromorphic sensory systems. Curr. Opin. Neurobiol.
   20(3), 288–295 (2010). Sensory systems
2. Zhengkun, Y., Yilei, Z.: Recognizing tactile surface roughness with a biomimetic
   fingertip: a soft neuromorphic approach. Neurocomputing **244**, 102–111 (2017)
3. Spigler, G., Oddo, C.M., Carrozza, M.C.: Soft-neuromorphic artificial touch for
   applications in neuro-robotics. In: 2012 4th IEEE RAS EMBS International Conference on Biomedical Robotics and Biomechatronics (BioRob), pp. 1913–1918
   (2012)
4. Izhikevich, E.: Simple model of spiking neurons. IEEE Trans. Neural Netw. **14**(6),
   1569–1572 (2003)
5. Oballe-Peinado, S., Hidalgo-López, J.A., Sánchez-Durán, J.A., Castellanos-Ramos,
   J., Vidal-Verdú, F.: Architecture of a tactile sensor suite for artificial hands based
   on FPGAs. In: 2012 4th IEEE RAS EMBS International Conference on Biomedical
   Robotics and Biomechatronics (BioRob), pp. 112–117 (2012)
6. Lee, W.W., Cabibihan, J., Thakor, N.V.: Bio-mimetic strategies for tactile sensing.
   In: SENSORS 2013, pp. 1–4. IEEE (2013)
7. Sankar, S., et al.: Texture discrimination with a soft biomimetic finger using a
   flexible neuromorphic tactile sensor array that provides sensory feedback. Soft
   Robot. **8**(5), 577–587 (2021)
8. Liu, H., Guo, D., Sun, F.: Object recognition using tactile measurements: kernel
   sparse coding methods. IEEE Trans. Instrum. Meas. **65**(3), 656–665 (2016)
9. Xu, Z., Chen, M., Liu, C.: Object tactile character recognition model based on
   attention mechanism LSTM. In: 2020 Chinese Automation Congress (CAC), pp.
   7095–7100 (2020)
10. Liu, H., Greco, J., Song, X., Bimbo, J., Seneviratne, L., Althoefer, K.: Tactile image
    based contact shape recognition using neural network. In: 2012 IEEE International
    Conference on Multisensor Fusion and Integration for Intelligent Systems (MFI),
    pp. 138–143 (2012)
11. Du, Y., Zhang, G., Zhang, Y., Wang, M.Y.: High-resolution 3-dimensional contact
    deformation tracking for FingerVision sensor with dense random color pattern.
    IEEE Robot. Autom. Lett. **6**(2), 2147–2154 (2021)
12. Zhang, Y., Yang, Y., He, K., Zhang, D., Liu, H.: Specific surface recognition using
    custom finger vision. In: 2020 International Symposium on Community-centric
    Systems (CcS), pp. 1–6 (2020)
13. Yang, Y., Wang, X., Zhou, Z., Zeng, J., Liu, H.: An enhanced FingerVision for
    contact spatial surface sensing. IEEE Sens. J. **21**(15), 16492–16502 (2021)
14. Dahiya, R.S., Metta, G., Valle, M., Sandini, G.: Tactile sensing-from humans to
    humanoids. IEEE Trans. Robot. **26**(1), 1–20 (2010)
15. Huang, X., et al.: Neuromorphic vision based contact-level classification in robotic
    grasping applications. Sensors **20**(17), 4724 (2020)
16. Johnson, M.K., Adelson, E.H.: Retrographic sensing for the measurement of surface
    texture and shape. In: 2009 IEEE Conference on Computer Vision and Pattern
    Recognition, pp. 1070–1077 (2009)

17. Jia, X., Li, R., Srinivasan, M.A., Adelson, E.H.: Lump detection with a gelsight sensor. In: 2013 World Haptics Conference (WHC), pp. 175–179 (2013)
18. Li, R., et al.: Localization and manipulation of small parts using gelsight tactile sensing. In: 2014 IEEE/RSJ International Conference on Intelligent Robots and Systems, pp. 3988–3993 (2014)
19. Dong, S., Yuan, W., Adelson, E.H.: Improved gelsight tactile sensor for measuring geometry and slip. In: 2017 IEEE/RSJ International Conference on Intelligent Robots and Systems (IROS), pp. 137–144 (2017)
20. Yamaguchi, A., Atkeson, C.G.: Implementing tactile behaviors using FingerVision. In: 2017 IEEE-RAS 17th International Conference on Humanoid Robotics (Humanoids), pp. 241–248 (2017)
21. Yamaguchi, A., Atkeson, C.G.: Tactile behaviors with the vision-based tactile sensor FingerVision. Int. J. Humanoid Robot. **16**(03), 1940002 (2019)
22. da Rocha, J.G.V., da Rocha, P.F.A., Lanceros-Mendez, S.: Capacitive sensor for three-axis force measurements and its readout electronics IEEE Trans. Instrum. Meas. **58**(8), 2830–2836 (2009)
23. Gupta, A.K., Nakagawa-Silva, A., Lepora, N.F., Thakor, N.V.: Spatio-temporal encoding improves neuromorphic tactile texture classification. IEEE Sens. J. **21**(17), 19038–19046 (2021)
24. Gerstner, W., Kistler, W.M.: Spiking Neuron Models: Single Neurons, Populations, Plasticity. Cambridge University Press, Cambridge (2002)
25. Johansson, R.S., Birznieks, I.: First spikes in ensembles of human tactile afferents code complex spatial fingertip events. Nat. Neurosci. **7**(2), 170–177 (2004)

Contact Information Prediction Based on Multi-force Training for Tactile Sensor Array with Elastomer Cover

Qiang Diao[1,2], Wenrui Chen[1,2(✉)], Yaonan Wang[1,2], Qihui Jiang[1,2], and Zhiyong Li[1,2]

[1] National Engineering Research Center of Robot Visual Perception and Control Technology, Hunan University, Changsha, China
chenwenrui@hnu.edu.cn
[2] School of Robotics, Hunan University, Changsha, China

Abstract. Tactile perception is essential for the grasping and manipulation of the robotic hand. The contact force and position can be detected by the tactile sensor. Tactile sensors with continuous surface cover can achieve higher detection accuracy in some cases than independent sensing units, but the calibration is also more troublesome. In this paper, we propose a contact information prediction method based on multi-force training using a BP neural network. The contact force could be predicted from the output of the sensor units through the mixed training of force and position, where the corresponding calibration data set is generated by collecting multiple forces at each selected point on the surface of the tactile sensor. The feasibility of the proposed calibration algorithm could be verified by comparison experiments.

Keywords: Tactile sensing · Elastomer cover · Neural network · Robotic hand

1 Introduction

With the rapid development of robotics, robotic hands are widely used in aerospace, intelligent manufacturing, industrial production, and home services [1]. Robotic hands can help robots to perform human-like manipulation, and also help disabled people to handle some basic daily tasks [2]. To improve the grasping and manipulation capabilities of robotic hands, robotic hand tactile sensors are used.

Current principles of tactile sensors are mainly based on piezoresistive [3], capacitive [4], piezoelectric [5], magnetic [6], and optical vision [7, 8]. Tactile sensors can provide a wealth of contact information for the robotic hand, including contact force, contact position, and so on. The reliability of the sensor output information prediction is highly dependent on the accuracy of the calibration process [9]. Therefore, a good and accurate tactile sensor calibration method is an important guarantee to maximize the use of the sensor.

Most tactile sensors consist of a sensing array, each unit of which is called a taxel. The contact information can be estimated from the activated taxels [10, 11]. At present, many tactile sensors use independent sensing units to estimate contact information.

H. Liu et al. (Eds.): ICIRA 2022, LNAI 13457, pp. 652–660, 2022.
https://doi.org/10.1007/978-3-031-13835-5_59

Although this can simplify the calibration process, the spatial detection resolution of sensors is reduced due to the limitations of physical integration and wire complexity. Compared with the independent sensor units, the tactile sensor with continuous elastic coverage which is more similar to the shape of human skin and protects the sensor units from environmental damage, is more suitable for grasping and manipulation of the robotic hand. However, elastomer cover also leads to the diffusion effect for contact force, that is, the elastomer layer has a coupling effect on contact information, which greatly increases the difficulty of calibration, makes the calibration cannot be only for a certain unit, and needs to consider the force response of adjacent elements. Therefore, Liu et al. in [12] proposed an inverse solution strategy of contact force. Based on a small number of sensing units, the amplitude and position of unknown loading even between two points can be detected by using the correlation coefficient method on the continuous elastic cover, thus achieving higher spatial resolution. However, this calibration method requires high precision motion equipment and a large amount of comprehensive data acquisitions, which is not conducive to the low-cost manufacturing and widespread use of sensors. Applying a simple and rapid calibration process on a small number of sensor units with elastomer cover is needed to be studied deeply.

Therefore, this paper proposes a calibration method based on the BP neural network for multi-force training, which can simplify the calibration process of tactile sensor with continuous surface to a greater extent and make them easy to test and use.

2 Method

2.1 Contact Analysis

In order to verify the feasibility of the proposed calibration algorithm, a planar tactile sensor model is established. The tactile sensor model is divided into three layers. The lower layer is a rigid base layer that provides rigid support and robotic hand interface. The middle layer is the circuit layer, on which 12 tactile sensor units at the same height are arranged neatly. The upper layer is an elastomer layer, made of rubber material, which simulates human skin and is used to protect the sensing units and facilitate the grasp of the robotic hand. The schematic diagram of the sensor model is shown in Fig. 1.

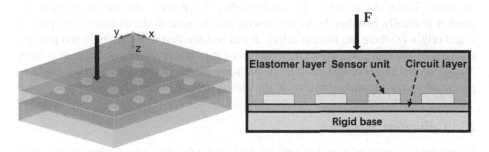

Fig. 1. Sensor model

When the loading force is in contact with the tactile sensor surface, the stress response from sensor units under the area near the loading force will be excited. Since each sensor unit can only sense unidirectional force, we only analyze the normal stress of each sensor unit. Thus, the contact model of the sensor surface can be simplified because of the linear elastic behavior of the rubber material used in the elastomer layer and only point contact case considered. According to contact mechanics [13], in an elastic half-space, under the action of a single normal concentrated point force, the z-axis stress component at a certain point A in the elastomer layer is expressed as:

$$\sigma_z = -\frac{3Fz^3}{2\pi\rho^5} \tag{1}$$

where F represents the normal concentrated force perpendicular to the contact surface, and the distance between the point A and the applied force F is $\rho = \left(r^2 + z^2\right)^{1/2} = \left(x^2 + y^2 + z^2\right)^{1/2}$. The model of concentrated force action is shown in Fig. 2.

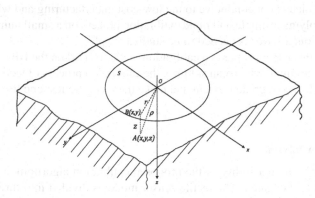

Fig. 2. Schematic diagram of the single concentrated point force loading

According to Formula (1), there is a linear relationship between the z-direction stress at any point A and the magnitude of the normal concentrated force F applied on the cover surface. Since all sensor units are at the same depth, the z coordinates remain the same. Under the action of the single loading force, the z-directional stress at any point A gradually nonlinearly decreases with the increase of the distance from point A to the origin O where the force is acting. It can be seen that the magnitude and position changes of the force will cause the changes of the output signals of the sensor units. Therefore, the position and intensity of the force acted on the cover surface could be predicted by corresponding outputs of the sensor units theoretically.

2.2 Calibration Strategy

Due to the nonlinear relationship between the contact force and the outputs of the sensor units and the uneven rubber cover error caused by the manufacturing process of the tactile sensor, the conventional nonlinear fitting is not applicable. In addition, the calibration algorithm aims to predict more contact information with a simple calibration process and a small number of samples. Therefore, a BP neural network with strong nonlinear mapping ability is selected, which is a multi-layer feed-forward neural network trained according to error backward propagation algorithm, and is one of the most widely used neural network models.

contact forces with random intensities are loaded at several random positions, and the corresponding sensor array outputs are calculated from Formula (1). The purpose of neural network is to map the relationship between loading force information and sensor outputs information, which can be expressed as,

$$\left[F \, x \, y \right]^{T} = f ([\sigma_{z1}, \sigma_{z2}, ... \sigma_{z12}]^{T}) \tag{2}$$

where F is the intensity of loading force on the sensor surface obtained from the standard force sensor and the position corresponding to the loading force is (x, y), which is obtained by the precision biaxial motion stage. $\sigma_{z1}, \sigma_{z2},...\sigma_{z12}$ are treated as the z-directional stresses of 12 sensing units corresponding to F. Since all sensing units adopt the same type of force sensing chips, their outputs can be collected uniformly.

3   Calibration Experiments

3.1   Database Collection

The algorithm comes from the requirement to develop and calibrate the sensor for the two-finger gripper [14] in the laboratory, so its size is used as a reference for the design of the sensor model. The sensor is 30mm long and 18mm wide, and a total of 12 sensor units are placed evenly, as shown in Fig. 1. In order to avoid boundary effect, the detection range is the inner area slightly away from the surrounding area, which can be regarded as an ideal elastic half space, and the detection accuracy is required to be 1.5 mm. The pressure range of the sensor is 0.01–5 N, and the resolution is required to be 0.3 N.

Specifically, data collection can be divided into three steps. Firstly, select several points randomly in the plane area. Here, 200 points are randomly selected in the inner region, which is ranged from 2 to 16 mm in the x direction and 2 to 28 mm in the y direction, with a resolution of 0.1 mm. The largest location accuracy is 0.01 mm representing the position resolution of XY biaxial translation platform. The location distribution of points is shown in Fig. 3. Secondly, each selected point is pressed by a single random force, which represents the randomness of the data, with a resolution of 0.01 N. Thirdly, collect the forces and positions of all points and the corresponding outputs of 12 tactile sensors. In 200 sets of data, the proportions of training set, validation set and test set are set as 70%, 15%, and 15%, respectively. Two controlled experiments are conducted.

3.2   Experimental Results

In the first experiment, two neural networks are used to detect the contact force and contact position, respectively. The inputs of both neural networks are 12 sensor units output signals. The output of the first neural network is one-dimensional contact force F, and the outputs of the second neural network are the contact position (x, y). Experimental results are shown in Fig. 4.

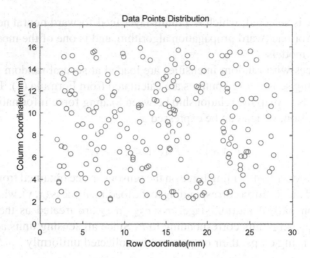

Fig. 3. Location distribution of calibration points

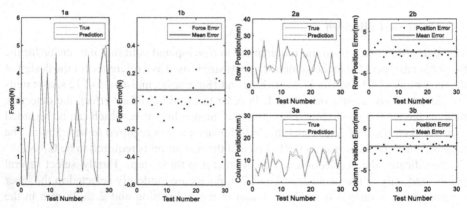

Fig. 4. 1a and 1b are contact force prediction. 2a and 2b are the contact position prediction for *x*. 3a and 3b are the contact position prediction for *y*.

It can be seen from Fig. 4 that the prediction accuracy of contact forces is high with small error, while the prediction error of contact positions is relatively large.

In the second experiment, in order to test the performance of neural network prediction, only a neural network is used for mixed prediction of contact signals. The network input is still the output signals of 12 sensor units, and the network output is the combination of *F*, *x*, and *y*. The experimental results are shown in Fig. 5.

It is observed in Fig. 5 that both force error and position error have good fitting. The detailed prediction error parameters are shown in Table 1.

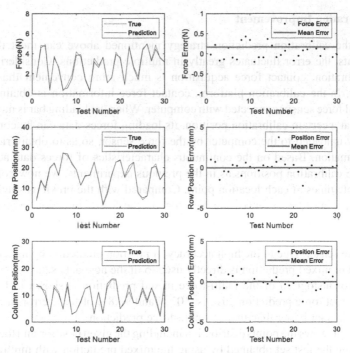

Fig. 5. Mixed prediction of contact force and position

Table 1. Network prediction performance

Neural network	Error (force)	Proportional (force < 0.3 N)	Error (position)	Proportional (distance < 1.5 mm)
Force-only	0.08N	96.67%		
Position-only			1.6036 mm	56.67%
Force and position	0.1662N	80%	0.8669 mm	83.33%

As can be seen from Table 1, the prediction accuracy of single contact force is high, while that of position is low. On the contrary, the position error of the hybrid prediction neural network is much smaller than that of the single prediction neural network, while the force detection error is slightly larger, which can only meet the basic requirements. The reason for this situation may be that the outputs of the sensing units are triggered by contact force and the contact position is also generated by the contact force. Therefore, mixing contact force and contact position during the training process can enhance the prediction of contact information.

3.3 Calibration Improvement

Although the calibration prediction strategy mentioned above can meet the simple requirements, the error fluctuates greatly in multiple predictions. Considering that in actual calibration, contact force acquisition is much more convenient than position acquisition. In the calibration platform, contact force information is obtained by the commercial force sensor connected with computer. When the loading bar is moved along the Z-axis at a certain calibration position, its loading forces data can be continuously and rapidly uploaded to the computer by the force sensor, so as to obtain rich contact force information. Based on the continuous characteristics of forces data acquisition, in the same calibration positions as in the previous experiments, we now collect force data multiple times at each location point. Compared with the previous single random contact force, in order to reduce the data runout, the force collection interval at each position point is set as 0.1 N, with a range of 0.1–5 N, to produce the data set. This process is called as 'multi-force' collection at each point on the elastomer cover surface of the tactile sensor. Due to the high accuracy of position prediction by mixed training, the method of mixed prediction is directly used to fit the new data set.

The error histogram of the multi-force mixed prediction is shown in Fig. 6. The average contact force prediction error is 0.07 N and 95.8% of force errors are less than 0.2 N, which is far better than that of single-force prediction.

In Fig. 7, it shows the points distribution including the given position and the predicted position from the test set obtained by using the mixed prediction with multiple forces. It can be seen that the position errors between the predicted points and the given points are much smaller than that of the prediction of single force. Through calculation, the average error of position predictions is 0.13 mm and 98.9% of position errors are less than 0.5 mm, which can meet our target very well.

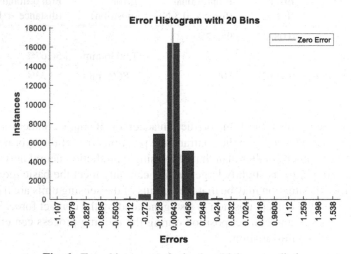

Fig. 6. Error histogram of mixed multi-force prediction

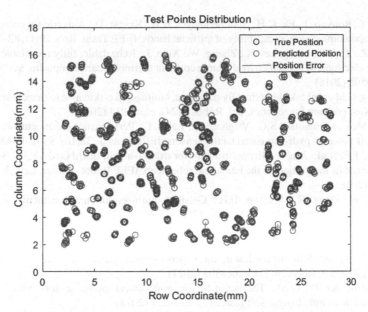

Fig. 7. Point positions distribution of mixed multi-force prediction

4 Conclusion

For the problems of complex data acquisition and calibration processing for the tactile sensor with continuous elastomer cover, this paper proposes a calibration method which can well predict the required contact force information based on multi-force training. Simulation experiments are carried out to compare the results of training methods of single-force and multi-force, respectively, and finally, it was concluded that the hybrid prediction method of multi-force could better map the connection between contact information and tactile array signals. In the future work, we consider how to apply the method to actual tactile sensor calibration quickly and accurately. In addition, there are still some shortcomings. In order to test the performance of the sensor, the number of points selected is still too much, how to choose fewer particular points to predict contact force will be a problem worth studying. In addition, the curved surface tactile sensors are often used in the robotic hand, so how to calibrate the curved tactile sensor also needs to be explored more deeply.

Acknowledgement. This work is supported by the National Key R&D Program under Grant 2018YFB1308604, the Foundation of Science and Technology on Space Intelligent Control Laboratory under Grant 2021-JCJQ-LB-010-12 and the Natural Science Foundation of Hunan Province under Grant 2020JJ5054.

References

1. Billard, A., Kragic, D.: Trends and challenges in robot manipulation. Science **364**(6446), eaat8414 (2019)

2. Feix, T., Romero, J., Ek, C.H., Schmiedmayer, H.B., Kragic, D.: A metric for comparing the anthropomorphic motion capability of artificial hands. IEEE Trans. Rob. **29**(1), 82–93 (2012)
3. Zou, Z., Zhu, C., Li, Y., Lei, X., Zhang, W., Xiao, J.: Rehealable, fully recyclable,and malleable electronic skin enabled by dynamic covalent thermoset nanocomposite. Sci. Adv. **4**(2), eaaq0508 (2018)
4. Boutry, C.M., et al.: A hierarchically patterned, bioinspired e-skin able to detect the direction ofapplied pressure for robotics. Sci. Robot. **3**(24), eaau6914 (2018)
5. Hari, M.A., Karumuthil, S.C., Varghese, S., Rajan, L.: Performance enhancement of flexible and self-powered pvdf-zno based tactile sensors. IEEE Sens. J. **22**(10), 9336–9343 (2022)
6. Tomo, T.P., et al.: A new silicone structure for uskin—a soft, distributed, digital 3-axis skin sensor and its integration on the humanoid robot icub. IEEE Robot. Autom. Lett. **3**(3), 2584–2591 (2018)
7. Yuan, W., Dong, S., Adelson, E.H.: Gelsight: high-resolution robot tactile sensors for estimating geometry and force. Sensors **17**(12), 2762 (2017)
8. Lambeta, M., et al.: Digit: a novel design for a low-cost compact high-resolution tactile sensor with application to in-hand manipulation. IEEE Robot. Autom. Lett. **5**(3), 3838–3845 (2020)
9. Yan, Y., et al.: Soft magneticskin for super-resolution tactile sensing with force self-decoupling. Sci. Robot. **6**(51), eabc8801 (2021)
10. Ward-Cherrier, B., et al.: The tactip family: soft optical tactile sensors with 3D-printed biomimetic morphologies. Soft Rob. **5**(2), 216–227 (2018)
11. Jamali, N., Maggiali, M., Giovannini, F., Metta, G., Natale, L.: A new design ofa fingertip for the iCub hand. In: 2015 IEEE/RSJ International Conference on Intelligent Robots and Systems (IROS), pp. 2705–2710. IEEE (2015)
12. Liu, W., Gu, C., Zeng, R., Yu, P., Fu, X.: A novel inverse solution of contact force based on a sparse tactile sensor array. Sensors **18**(2), 351 (2018)
13. Johnson, K.L., Johnson, K.L.: Contact Mechanics. Cambridge University Press, Cambridge (1987)
14. Chen, W., Xiong, C., Wang, Y.: Analysis and synthesis of underactuated compliant mechanisms based on transmission properties of motion and force. IEEE Trans. Rob. **36**(3), 773–788 (2020)

Hand Rehabilitation Modes Combining Exoskeleton-Assisted Training with Tactile Feedback for Hemiplegia Patients: A Preliminary Study

Bo He, Min Li[✉], and Guoying He

Department of Mechanical Engineering, Xi'an Jiaotong University, Xi'an 710049, China
Min.li@mail.xjtu.edu.cn

Abstract. Within the field of rehabilitation for people with hemiplegia, this paper presents a novel training system for hand function rehabilitation. This training system mainly includes a hand rehabilitation exoskeleton, tactile feedback devices and a virtual reality scene. Tactile feedback devices are designed as electric stimulation slip feedback actuator and pneumatic contact force feedback actuator respectively. The virtual reality scene is a human-computer interaction interface built by Unity 3D. Three rehabilitation training modes including a contact force enhanced rehabilitation mode, a mirror therapy mode and an active rehabilitation mode are proposed to provide different feedback stimulation for patients at different rehabilitation stages to obtain better rehabilitation training effect. Verification experiments were conducted to preliminarily show the feasibility of those modes.

Keywords: Hand function rehabilitation · Virtual reality · Tactile feedback · Mirror therapy

1 Introduction

Stroke has become the second leading cause of death worldwide, heavily affecting a large of people. Over 69% of the patients have hand dysfunction in the early stages of the disease, and 37% still have imprecise control of hand grasping and extension movements after three months [1]. Due to the high plasticity of the central nervous system, stroke patients are able to restore their hand function through rehabilitation training [2]. However, as the hand is one of the most complex organs with its elaborate anatomical structure and corresponding central nerves, hand dysfunction rehabilitation after stroke is complicated. These patients are likely to suffer from hemiplegia, a condition characterized by partial or total loss of motor and/or tactile perception in one hand, resulting in abnormal hand function. They need timely and regular effective hand function rehabilitation training.

Mirror therapy is an effective and feasible method for patients with hemiplegia [3]. The method requires the patient to place the healthy hand in front of a mirror and the affected hand behind the mirror. During rehabilitation training, the healthy hand and

H. Liu et al. (Eds.): ICIRA 2022, LNAI 13457, pp. 661–669, 2022.
https://doi.org/10.1007/978-3-031-13835-5_60

the affected hand do the same rehabilitation movement at the same time. The patient observes the mirror from the healthy hand side. By "tricking" the brain in this way, patients can imitate and relearn the correct movement and promote their brain function remodeling. Advances in robotics and virtual reality (VR) have made mirror therapy more effective. Game scenes adapted to hand movement can be constructed in a virtual environment. The movement of the healthy hand was monitored by external sensors in real time. The virtual motion posture of the affected hand was constructed according to the motion data of the healthy hand. Hand function rehabilitation robots can help hemiplegia patients to effectively replicate the movements of the healthy hand on the affected hand [4, 5]. Using a computer screen as a mirror, the method above can be used to duplicate mirror therapy. Rehabilitation robots combined with VR can lead to better results in mirror therapy for hemiplegia patients [6–8].

There are a number of studies on rehabilitation training in VR environments. Daria et al. employed data gloves and VR technology to develop an immersive VR training system based on Alice in Wonderland [9]. A rich VR environment attracted patients' attention and make them focus on rehabilitation training movements such as grasping and side pinching. However, the system didn't consider bilateral rehabilitation. Patricio et al. proposed a bilateral fine motor rehabilitation system for the recovery of hand mobility based on VR environment [8]. The system could assist the affected limb to carry out fine motor training with the help of hand orthosis. However, the system only provided visual feedback for the patient's hand movement in VR environment, and lacked stimulation for the patient's sensory loop.

In conclusion, the rehabilitation training system combined with VR environment can provide visual feedback of hand posture, which is conducive to fine grasping training. Different training scenarios can be built in the virtual environment to attract patients' attention. However, the existing rehabilitation system rarely integrates tactile and motor feedback in VR environment. What's more, the rehabilitation training mode is single and difficult to adapt to the different stages of hand function rehabilitation training. Therefore, this paper presents hand rehabilitation modes combining exoskeleton-assisted training with tactile and motor feedback for hemiplegia patients in different rehabilitation periods.

2 Method

2.1 Analysis of Hand Characteristics in Different Rehabilitation Stages

Reasonable rehabilitation is essential for hand function rehabilitation. Patients with hand dysfunction are divided into different rehabilitation stages depending on the impairment level of their hand abilities.

In the acute phase of stroke, muscles cannot contract autonomously. Normal activities should be maintained to prevent complications. Under the circumstances, the main training focus is on motor feedback, supplemented by tactile feedback. In the training system designed in this paper, corresponding tactile stimulation was applied according to the robot's movements, with priority restoring the patient's motor abilities.

In the convalescent period of stroke, patients have hypertonic muscle associated with abnormal motor patterns. This stage is three weeks to six months after the onset of stroke. It is necessary to suppress spasm, promote recovery of separation movement, and strengthen active activities of hemiplegic limbs in line with daily living activities. In this stage, mirror therapy combined with VR technology was employed for rehabilitation training.

Six months after the onset of stroke is called the sequelae stage. At this stage, the patient's hand function recovery slowly, accompanied by various sequelae such as poor control of hand movement. The rehabilitation training is mainly tactile stimulation, supplemented by motor stimulation, focusing on the patient's ability to perform fine movements.

2.2 Design of the Rehabilitation Training System

Rehabilitation training system mainly includes a principal computer, a slave computer and other hardware equipment shown in Fig. 1. Figure 2 shows the software structure. The principal computer is a PC, running on Windows 10 system. The virtual environment built by Unity 3D run on PC to provide rehabilitation training scenes and control instructions. A Leap Motion was used to monitor the movement of the healthy hand. A DAM module was adapted to transmit control commands from the principal computer to the pneumatic proportional valve (IVT0030-2BL, SMC, Japan). An Arduino was used to control slip feedback actuator's current strength, frequency, duty cycle and the switch of the electrode array.

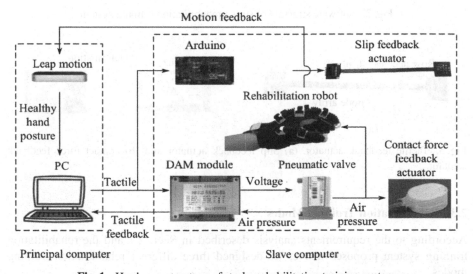

Fig. 1. Hardware structure of stroke rehabilitation training system

A commercially pneumatic hand function rehabilitation exoskeleton was employed to assist the affected hand in rehabilitation training. A flexible printed electrode array was used to reproduce slip (see Fig. 3(a)), consisting of 1 cathode and 13 anodes. Slip sensation is reproduced by controlling the on/off of the anode. The contact force feedback actuator was designed with an air cavity structure. When inflated, the working surface is deformed, creating a contact force on the fingers. The principle is shown in Fig. 3(b) left.

The actuator is manufactured using flexible 3D printing technology shown in Fig. 3(b) right. The working pressures of the contact force feedback actuator and the pneumatic rehabilitation robot were controlled by the pneumatic proportional valve.

As shown in Fig. 2, the principal computer interacts with Leap Motion, Arduino Mega2560 and the pneumatic proportional valve through USB3.0 Micro B, Bluetooth and DAM modules, respectively.

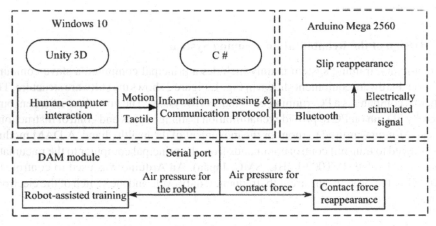

Fig. 2. Software structure of stroke rehabilitation training system

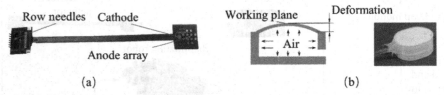

Fig. 3. Tactile feedback actuator. (a) Slip feedback actuator and (b) contact force feedback actuator.

2.3 Rehabilitation Training Modes

According to the requirements analysis described in Sect. 2.1 and the rehabilitation training system proposed above, we designed three different rehabilitation training modes.

Contact Force Enhanced Rehabilitation Mode

In the acute phase of stroke, a contact force enhanced rehabilitation mode was adopted. The rehabilitation training at this stage was mainly based on motor stimulation, supplemented by tactile stimulation. The hand exoskeleton derived the patient's fingers to carry out continuous passive rehabilitation training. The contact force feedback actuators applied force to the fingertips in response to changes in joint angles as the fingers move. In this mode, only contact force feedback was integrated to the exoskeleton in passive rehabilitation training. Therefore, we called it contact force enhanced rehabilitation mode. Figure 4 shows the hand exoskeleton with contact force feedback actuators.

The feedback actuator and the exoskeleton were controlled by both the principal and slave computers. The principal computer sends start and end instructions to the slave computer to ensure that the exoskeleton's motion changes in sync with the contact force feedback.

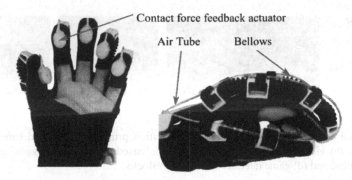

Fig. 4. Pneumatic rehabilitation exoskeleton with contact force feedback actuators.

Mirror Therapy Mode

Mirror therapy was introduced in the convalescent period of stroke. The exoskeleton was worn on the affected hand during training. The movement information of the healthy hand was collected through Leap Motion. The health hand motion information was employed to construct the virtual affected hand in VR environment and control the exoskeleton to make the affected hand exercise. When the virtual affected hand touched the object in VR environment, the contact force feedback actuator and the slip feedback actuator started to work, applying contact and slip stimulation to fingers.

In this mode, the mirror image of the healthy hand model (the virtual affected hand) needed to be presented in VR environment. As shown in Fig. 5(a), a mirror and two cameras were created. One main camera adjusted lens. The other camera, as a mirror camera, maintains a symmetric relationship with the main camera relative to the mirror. The view of the main camera is adjusted by holding down the right mouse button and dragging the mouse. The construction of the affected hand in VR environment is shown in Fig. 5(b).

Active Rehabilitation Mode

In the sequelae stage, patients have certain motor ability, and the goal of rehabilitation training is to improve the fine operation of the hand. So we designed two VR games for rehabilitation training. The rehabilitation exoskeleton was removed in this mode.

One game called Dodging Bullets focuses more on fine motor training, with the tactile feedback only as a reminder. As shown in Fig. 5(c), bullets randomly appeared around the screen and moved in different directions. Patients use Leap Motion to control the movement of the character in the game to avoid bullets. Only after the patient made the correct gesture did the character follow. Tactile stimuli were applied to the patient's fingertips as the game character moved. The longer the character lived in the game, the higher the score.

The other game named Building Blocks focused more on the patient's tactile experience. In this game, patients need to make building blocks appear through correct gesture. Patients need to keep piling up blocks to make them higher. The height of the blocks at a given time determines the patient's score.

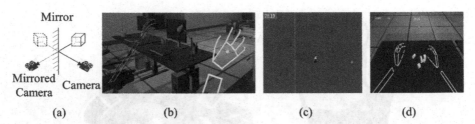

Fig. 5. Virtual environment construction. (a) Realization principle of affected hand in virtual environment; (b) virtual hand model of affected side based on mirror; (c) game interface of Dodging Bullets, and (d) game interface of Building Blocks.

3   Experimental Analysis and Results

Verification experiments were conducted to preliminarily show the feasibility of the system.

3.1   Performance of the Contact Force Feedback Actuator

The contact force feedback actuator played an important role in the rehabilitation training system, so its performance was verified and analyzed first.

The actuator applied force to the fingertip by inflating. In our previous studies, the relation between the pressure of the actuator (P_a/kPa) and the output force (F/N) can be expressed by formula 1.

$$F = 0.02913P_a - 0.2957 \tag{1}$$

The actuator's output force calculated by the pressure was called the feedback force. The force generated by the virtual hand touching the object was called the target force. The output force of the feedback actuator measured by a standard force sensor was called the practical force.

In the experiment, the upper computer sent a command to the DAM module every 0.1 s to control the actuator to raise or lower the pressure of 5 kPa. The pressure of the actuator was controlled to rise from 0 kPa to 350 kPa and then fall back to 0 kPa as an trail. Three trails were repeated. The practical force measured by a standard force sensor and pressures fed back by pneumatic proportional valves were recorded. The feedback force and the target force were calculated and plotted together with the practical force in Fig. 6.

The three almost identical curves indicate that the performance of the contact force feedback actuator can meet the requirements of VR rehabilitation training. This experiment also confirms that the commercial pneumatic hand exoskeleton integrated contact force feedback actuator shown in Fig. 4 can reliably assist patient in rehabilitation training according to the contact force enhanced rehabilitation mode.

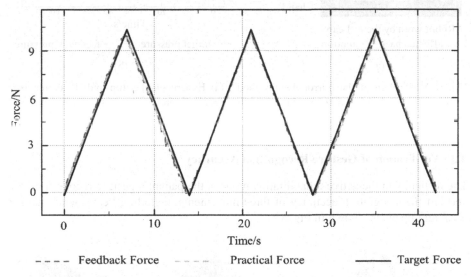

Fig. 6. Performance of the contact force feedback actuator

3.2 Verification of the Mirror Therapy Mode

This experiment verifies the reliability of the hand exoskeleton control. The metacarpophalangeal joint motion angle of the healthy hand was monitored by Leap Motion and used to control the exoskeleton worn by the affected hand. The relationship between the working air pressure of the exoskeleton (P_r/kPa) and the metacarpophalangeal joint motion angle of the healthy hand (θ/°) was as follows:

$$P_r = 5/3\theta \tag{2}$$

A health man was invited to take the test. The subject's left hand was fitted with the exoskeleton to simulate the affected hand. The participant was asked to extend his palm with fingers in a horizontal position at first. He made a slow fist and then extend his fingers as one trial. The experiment was repeated three times.

The control pressure in VR environment was calculated by Formula 2 (target pressure). The actual exoskeleton working pressure was fed back to the principal by the proportional valve (feedback pressure). The target pressure and the feedback pressure were recorded simultaneously. Figure 7(b) shows that when the healthy hand joint moves gently, the target pressure curve basically coincides with the feedback pressure curve. The experiment indicates that the designed hand rehabilitation system can meet the requirements of the mirror therapy mode.

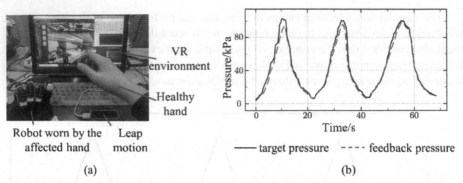

(a)   (b)

Fig. 7. Verification of the mirror therapy mode. (a) Experimental setup and (b) comparison between the exoskeleton robot working pressure (feedback pressure) and the control pressure in VR environment (target pressure).

3.3 Verification of Gesture Recognition Accuracy

The difficulty in the active rehabilitation mode is the patient's gesture recognition. We verified the recognition accuracy of three movements, including heavy wrap, palmar wrap and tip pinch, shown in Fig. 8.

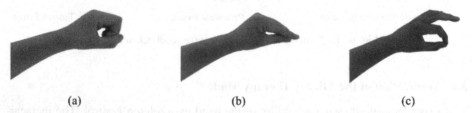

(a)   (b)   (c)

Fig. 8. The hand rehabilitation training movements adopted by the rehabilitation training system. (a) Heavy wrap, (b) palmar wrap and (c) tip pinch.

In the experiment, a participant completed the above three actions in random order as one trail. The experiment was repeated six times. The result shows that all the movements can be identified with 100% accuracy. The experiment also indicated that the participant could complete the rehabilitation training task in the active rehabilitation mode.

4   Conclusion and Future Work

This paper presents a hand function rehabilitation system for hemiplegia patients at different rehabilitation stages. On the basis of a pneumatic rehabilitation exoskeleton, haptic feedback devices and VR scene are added to form the proposed rehabilitation system. In the acute phase of stroke, we proposed a contact force enhancement rehabilitation mode based on the hand exoskeleton and contact force feedback. In the convalescent period of stroke, a mirror therapy mode was introduced combining exoskeleton-assisted hand motion training with VR and tactile feedback. In the sequelae stage, an active rehabilitation mode was applied. Verification experiments were conducted to preliminarily show the feasibility of those modes. The first validation experiment indicates that the contact force feedback actuator has a satisfactory performance. The second experiment verifies that the exoskeleton can follow the motion posture of the healthy hand to assist the rehabilitation training of the affected hand. The last experiment shows that hand gestures can be accurately recognized.

The possible beneficial effects of the rehabilitation training method are as follows. First, the training system combines the exoskeleton with contact force feedback and slip feedback to promote the sensory function recovery of stroke patients. Various feedback stimuli with VR environment promote patients to maintain concentration to improve the effect of rehabilitation training. Second, virtual reality is deployed to reproduce mirror therapy, which is very friendly to the hand function rehabilitation of hemiplegia patients. What's more, three training modes assist patients in receiving appropriate feedback stimulation at different stages of rehabilitation. For example, in the acute phase of stroke, the patient experiences predominantly motor feedback stimulation, supplemented by tactile feedback stimulation.

In future work, more participants should be involved in the validation of the system, especially stroke patients, to verify the possible beneficial effects of the proposed system. More virtual game scenarios also need to be designed to further improve the system.

Acknowledgements. This work was supported by the National Natural Science Foundation of China under Grant (51975451).

References

1. Jia, J.: Hand Function rehabilitation. Publishing House of Electronics Industry, Bei Jing (2019)
2. Li, M., Guanghua, X., Xie, J., et al.: Motor rehabilitation with control based on human intent for stroke survivors. ROBOT **39**(5), 759–768 (2017)
3. Gandhi, D.B., Sterba, A., Khatter, H., et al.: Mirror therapy in stroke rehabilitation: current perspectives. Ther. Clin. Risk Manag. **16**, 75–85 (2020)
4. Hesse, S., Schmidt, H., Werner, C.: Machines to support motor rehabilitation after stroke: 10 Years of experience in Berlin. J. Rehab. Res. Develop. **43**(5), 671–678 (2006)
5. Hesse, S., Schulte-Tigges, G., Konrad, M., et al.: Robot-assisted arm trainer for the passive and active practice of bilateral forearm and wrist movements in hemiparetic subjects. Arch. Phys. Med. Rehab. **84**(6), 915–920 (2003)
6. Yah-Ting, W., Chen, K.-H., Ban, S.-L., et al.: Evaluation of leap motion control for hand rehabilitation in burn patients: an experience in the dust explosion disaster in Formosa Fun Coast. Burns **45**(1), 157–164 (2019)
7. Shin, J.-H., Kim, M.Y., Lee, J.Y., et al.: Effects of virtual reality-based rehabilitation on distal upper extremity function and health-related quality of life: a single-blinded, randomized controlled trial. J. NeuroEng. Rehab. **13**(1), 1:10 (2016)
8. Cartagena, P.D., Naranjo, J.E., Saltos, L.F., et al.: Multifunctional exoskeletal orthosis for hand rehabilitation based on virtual reality. Inf. Commun. Technol. Ecuador **884**, 209–221 (2019)
9. Tsoupikova, D., et al.: Virtual immersion for post-stroke hand rehabilitation therapy. Ann. Biomed. Eng. **43**(2), 467–477 (2014). https://doi.org/10.1007/s10439-014-1218-y

Co-manipulation System with Enhanced Human-Machine Perception

Behavior Tree Based Dynamic Task Planning Method for Robotic Live-Line Maintenance

Feng Jiabo[1] , Shi Lirong[2], Liu Lei[1], and Zhang Weijun[1(✉)]

[1] Shanghai Jiao Tong University, 800 Dongchuan Road, Shanghai, China
zhanweijun@sjtu.edu.cn
[2] Qujing Power Supply Bureau of Yunnan Power Grid Co., Ltd., Yunnan, China

Abstract. The biggest challenge for robotic automation in the field is unexpected events caused by uncertainties in an unstructured environment. In classical task planning, the planning and execution of tasks are separated, which makes it difficult to deal with unexpected events in the execution process. However, robots must be able to handle unexpected events to ensure the smooth execution of tasks in complex dynamic environments. This paper introduces a method for dynamic task planning using behavior trees, which is used for robots to perform live-line maintenance operations on overhead lines in distribution networks. This method realizes the dynamic planning of tasks and the handling of unexpected events by structuring the task behavior tree. Experiments and field operations show that the method can realize complex field operations and have unexpected handling capabilities.

Keywords: Live-line maintenance robot · Behavior tree · Autonomous

1 Introduction

Live line maintenance is the overhaul, maintenance, and testing of electrical equipment without power interruption. Using robots to replace manual for live-line maintenance live electricity can effectively avoid the dangers of high voltage. This task is a field work, and the work environment is complex and diverse. Robots face the challenges of various unexpected events during operation. To solve this problem, we introduce the Behavior Tree method.

Behavior Tree (BT) is a modeling developed for non-player characters in computer games [1, 2]. Researchers apply it to the operation of various types of robots [3–8]. Bagnell [8] use the BT architecture to arrange tasks and drive robots to complete autonomous grasping tasks. Hu Danying [9] proposed a method to achieve semi-automatic surgical tasks using a BT framework for the surgical robot Raven II. In Stuede' research, BTs are used to solve problem of people search by a mobile social robot [10]. Wang used BT for task perception, allocation, and execution [11].

Compared with traditional robot control methods BT has unique advantages. Compared with State Machine, BT has better maintainability, extensibility and reusability. The addition or subtraction of states in a state machine requires redefining state transitions. And BT can easily add or delete nodes or branches. Decision tree and BT have

H. Liu et al. (Eds.): ICIRA 2022, LNAI 13457, pp. 673–685, 2022.
https://doi.org/10.1007/978-3-031-13835-5_61

a similar hierarchical structure, which can be modularized and have good readability. But the nodes of the decision tree have no information flow, making fault handling very difficult. BTs are reactive, that is, the execution of a node returns the result of the execution, giving it the ability to react quickly to changes. In unstructured environments, BTs can make decisions based on changing world states.

Based on the modularity and reactivity advantages of BTs, this paper proposes a dynamic task planning method for live-line maintenance tasks. Firstly, according to the characteristics and requirements of live work task execution, the nodes of the BT are transformed to build the task BT; secondly, a dynamic task planning method based on hierarchical state space is proposed. The dynamic response of the task execution process is realized by using the reactiveness of the BT. Third, based on the task BT, the accident handling methods of the automatic process are proposed, allowing professionals to guide the operation process. Experiments and field operations show that the method can realize the automation of the operation process and has certain fault handling ability.

2   Problem Statement

2.1   Robot System

The live working robot is composed of a lift truck and an operating platform, as shown in Fig. 1. During operation, the insulating arm lifts the platform to the vicinity of the overhead line. The three six-axis robotic arms on the platform will perform the operation.

Operation platform

Insulated boom

Crawler chassis

Fig. 1.   Structure of live-line maintenance working robot

2.2   Live-Line Maintenance

Live-line maintenance involve multiple operations, such as install/uninstall drainage wires drain wires, installing grounding rings, and removing foreign bodies. During the operation, the robot uses special tools to complete the corresponding operation. Taking drainage operation as an example, the operation includes positioning, electrical inspection, wire stripping, and installation of wire clamps, as shown in Fig. 2. The tools used are camera, electroscope, wire stripper, and wire clamp installer.

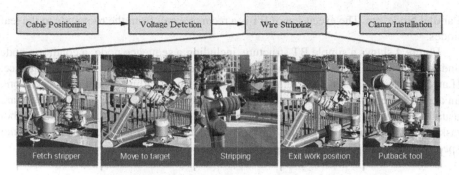

Fig. 2. Schematic diagram of drainage process and wire stripping operation

2.3 Uncertainty in Operations

In the actual operation process, various unexpected situations will occur, making it difficult for the robot to perform tasks according to the set program. As shown in Fig. 3, changes in the external environment, differences in goals, and system reliability all affect the execution of tasks. For example, during operation, the lighting changes and the camera cannot be positioned in direct sunlight. However, the preset program cannot adjust the camera according to the scene situation. When external factors cause the task execution to fail, the preset program cannot eliminate these failures and continue the operation.

Fig. 3. Common problems in the operation of robots. (a. Sunlight: changes in light during operation affect camera shooting; b. Stripping failure: the cutting depth of the tool does not match the thickness of the insulating layer; c. Overload: Twisted hard cable overloads the robot; d. The removed drainage wire is stuck on the stripper)

3 Behaviour Tree for Live-Line Maintenance Task

3.1 Principle of BT

A BT is a tree-like structure consisting of a series of logical nodes and execution nodes. We combine various nodes like building blocks to obtain a Decision-Tree-like structure. Execution nodes (leaf nodes), including condition nodes and action nodes, are the leaves of the BT. Logical nodes are forks in the BT, including Sequence Node, Select Node,

Parallel Node, etc. The execution of BT is a recursive call from the root node to the leaf nodes.

Figure 4 shows a simple BT structure, including a sequence node, a condition node and a action node. The sequential node mechanism executes the child nodes in sequence. If any child node fails, the execution is terminated and a failure is returned. Therefore, an action node will only be executed if the condition node is met.Condition nodes are usually used alone in normal BTs. However, tasks and preconditions are paired, in robot tasks. So in the task BT, we use the graph structure as a module: task node. If not specified, the node in the following refers to task node.

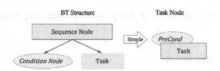

Fig. 4. Sequence node branch and task node

3.2 Execute Tasks with Nodes

In the task BT, we use action nodes to implement basic robot operations, including move PTP, mve Line, etc. And use the logical nodes to combine them into more complex tasks, and finally realize the complex operation process.

Figure 5 shows the BT implementation of the Fetch task. The child nodes < Plan > (planning path), < Move(PTP) >, < Move(line) >, < Grasp(IO) > are action nodes. These nodes are basic action that can be directly executed by the robot. The pre(*) is a precondition for node execution. The parent node is the Select Node. The principle is to execute the nodes sequentially from left to right until one node is successfully executed. This means that only one child node will be executed at a time. Set the precondition of the child node to the execution result of the previous child node, and all child nodes will be executed in turn to realize the grabbing process.

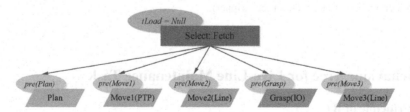

Fig. 5. The BT structure of the Fetch task

The above node is called Branch Node. In the live job, the branch node also includes Enter (enter the work position), Operate (use tools), Exit (exiting the work position), and Putback (put the tool back). These branch nodes can continue to be combined to complete more complex tasks, such as the wire stripping operation shown in Fig. 2. The Wire Stripping node is a Select node with 5 branch nodes as child nodes. Such nodes are called module task nodes. The module task node can control the robot to use a tool to complete the corresponding operation.

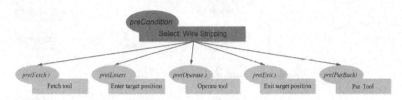

Fig. 6. The BT structure of the wire stripping task

The drainage operation process shown in Fig. 2 includes four module task nodes in total. During the operation, the robotic arm of the robot uses the camera, electroscope, wire stripper, and wire clip installer in sequence to complete the operation. This again involves the control of the three six-axes robots. In our design, the three robot can work independently or collaboratively. For example, when stripping a wire with robot, another may be required to clamp the cable. Therefore we use one parallel node to control the three robotic arms in parallel. The principle of parallel parallel nodes is to execute all child nodes in sequence, regardless of whether the previous child nodes are executed successfully. As shown in Fig. 7, robot i represents the manipulators. Each time the BT is executed, the three manipulators are executed in parallel.

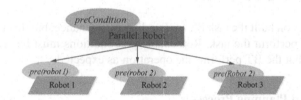

Fig. 7. BT structure for parallel control of multiple manipulators

3.3 Task BT

According to the execution process, task nodes can be combined to form a task BT, as shown in Fig. 8. There are 5 layers of structure in the task BT, namely root layer, robot layer, module layer, branch layer and action layer.

Each robot node contains multiple module tasks as child node. For example, the Robot1 node includes operations such as Stripping wires, Installing wire clips, and Detecting electricity. The observation robot (Robot3 node) can perform task of positioning. Each module task node contains five branch nodes, which constitute the branch layer (most branches in the Fig. 8 are collapsed). The child nodes of the branch task are the action nodes (or leaf nodes), which are the tips of the BT. In the task BT, the module and branch nodes decide the leaf nodes to be executed according to the preconditions, and the robot executes the actions.

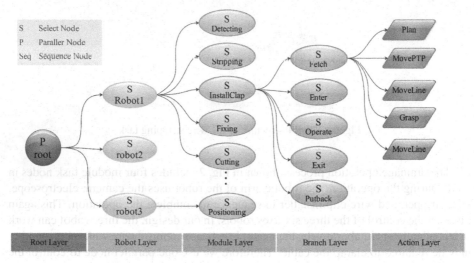

Fig. 8. Task BT structure for live-line maintenance.

4   Task Planning Based on BT

The previous section built the task BT for live-line maintenance, but this was not enough to make the BT perform the task. Reasonable preconditions must be set for each task node to ensure that the BT performs the operation as expected.

4.1   State-Based Planning Processes

As shown in the BT structure shown in Fig. 4, the execution of the task node must satisfy the preconditions. In robotics tasks, a precondition is usually a set of states. These states may be sensor feedback or internal logic flag. The execution of the task will cause these state changes. In Fig. 5, the precondition of < Plan > is to complete the target positioning, and the precondition of < Move1(PTP) > is to complete the path planning.

Definition of Hierarchical State. To describe robotic system state, we define a set of states that describe the effects of task execution on the system. The system state is a triple consisting of the module state, the branch state, and the action state, as in Eq. 1.

$$S = (S_{mod}, S_{sub}, S_{pri}) \tag{1}$$

These three groups of states respectively represent the influence of different levels of task nodes execution on the system state. For example, the module state includes:

positioning or not, wire stripped or note, wire clip installed or not, etc., as in Eq. 2. These states correspond to the results of the robot's execution of the module tasks. The branch state (S_{sub}) is represented by three tool-related variables, namely tLoad (Load the tool or not), tPos (in Opeate position or not), and tOperate (Has the tool been used). The state of action layer(S_{pri}) is the feedback of basic actions.

$$S_{mod} = \{modPositioned, modGripped, modClampInstalled, modDetected\} \quad (2)$$

$$S_{sub} = \{tLoad, tPos, tOperate\} \quad (3)$$

$$S_{pri} = \{pPlan, pPTP, pLine, pIO, pCam\} \quad (4)$$

Each variable in the above formula has three values {*True, Null, False*}. Such as *tLoad = True* means the tool is loaded, and *tLoad = False* means the wrong tool is loaded.

As shown in Fig. 9, the red, green and the blue borders represent tasks that are being executed, completed and to be executed. The text below the task is the state variable affected by the task. For example, the task < Cable Positioning > has been completed, and the system state is *modPositioned = True*.

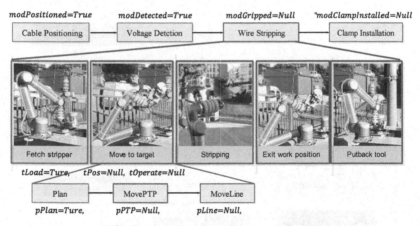

Fig. 9. Operating process and system state

Hierarchical State Planning. When defining states, we intentionally map the state level to the task node type. In this way, the preconditions of task nodes are only related to the state of the corresponding level. This layered nature makes it possible to plan tasks hierarchically, reducing the difficulty of planning and increasing the degree of modularity .

During the drainage operation in Fig. 9, the precondition of performing the wire stripping task is to complete the cable positioning and the electrical inspection operation.

Therefore, the precondition of this task node is shown in Eq. 5.

$$S_{mod} = \{modPositioned = True, modDetected = True,$$
$$modGripped = Null, modClampInstalled = Null \ldots\} \quad (5)$$

Similarly, the preconditions of branch task node and action task node are only related to branch state and action state, as in Eq. 6 and Eq. 7.

$$S_{sub} = \{tLoad = Ture, tPos = Null, tOperate = Null\} \quad (6)$$

$$S_{pri} = \{pPlan = Ture, pPTP = Null, pLine = Null, \ldots\} \quad (7)$$

4.2 State Planning for Stochastic Processes

As mentioned above, there are many uncertainties in the field operation process that prevent the task from being performed as expected. In planning problems, it is manifested as the uncertainty of state transition. That is, the node execution does not necessarily result in the desired state. For example, the obstacle has changed during the robot movement, which causes the $<$ PTP $>$ node to fail. Therefore, when the task is executed, the child nodes in Figs. 5, 6 and 7 are not executed in the order from left to right, but depend on the actual system state. Taking the branch layer task as an example, the nodes to be executed in different states are shown in Fig. 10 (For details about node $<$ DealwithFalse $>$, see Sect. 5.3).

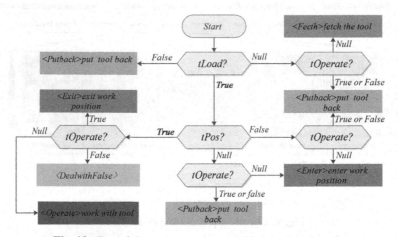

Fig. 10. Branch layer state and executable branch task nodes

The preconditions for branch node execution are shown in Fig. 10. For example, the precondition of $<$ Fetch $>$ is Eq. 8. The execution of the node only depends on the branch state, and has nothing to do with the historical state and other system states. Therefore, this is a planning method for stochastic processes. BT can make decisions in real time based on changes in field conditions.

$$pre(Fetch) = \{tLoad = Null, tOperate = Null\} \quad (8)$$

5 Handling Unexpected Incidents

This part will introduce the handling method of uncertain events in the job process based on task BT. During the task execution, we may encounter various unexpected failures. Depending on the source, problems can basically be divided into three categories.

1. Robot execution failures, such as robotic arm degradation, torque overload, path planning failure, etc. These problems may cause the robot to alarm and interrupt task execution.
2. Process control problems, for example, in the absence of planning solutions, the path planning nodes will continue to re-plan, causing the program to fall into an infinite loop;
3. Tool failure. Since the tool has a physical interaction with the outside world, it is more prone to failure. For example, the wire stripper gets stuck.

For these situations, we design a fault handling method based on the BT.

5.1 Robot Execution Failure

Robot execution failure is a common type of failure. The cause of these failures can be obtained through the system failure code, and there are clear solutions. In the BT framework, we introduce a fault handling node, as shown in Fig. 11. This node is entered when there is an error in the layered state.

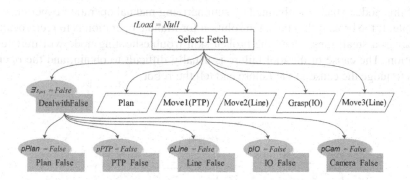

Fig. 11. Troubleshooting node for robot execution failure

Take < *Fetch* > for example. This task is completed by 5 action nodes. These nodes may fail during execution. For example, if there is no planning solution when planning the path, then the action state *pPlan = false*. In the next cycle, because the layer state is false, it will enter the fault processing node. The current layer state *pPlan = fasle*, then it will enter the < *Plan False* > node to process the planning error. According to the type of error returned by the planning task, re-planning, attitude adjustment, etc. are taken.

5.2 Process Control Problems

BT execution is based on state. If the state does not change, the BT may fall into the dilemma of repeatedly executing some nodes. For example, during path planning, if the planning fails, the robot will try to re-plan. If there is no planning solution for the current position, the robot will keep trying to plan a path.

For such problems, a decoration node is added to limit the execution time and the number of failures of nodes, as shown in Fig. 12. The decoration node does not have the function of logical processing. Its function is to record the execution time and the number of failures of the child node, and decide whether to execute the child node.

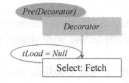

Fig. 12. Decorated nodes in the task BT

5.3 Tool Failure

When a tool faulure occurs, node < Tool False > will be executed according to the branch state, as shown in Fig. 13. There are processing methods for different fault types under this node, which are obtained by summarizing manual operation experience. For example, if the broken skin fails, the solution for manual operation is to reciprocate the stripper in a small range, then the broken skin troubleshooting node will imitate this operation. The cause of the tool failure is usually difficult to obtain, and the operator needs to judge the cause of the failure and tell the robot.

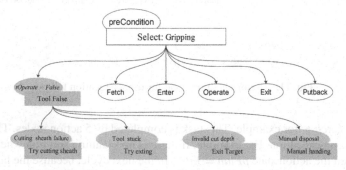

Fig. 13. Tool fault handling based on task BT

6 Experiments and Field Work

In view of the failure problems in the operation process, the ability of the robot to eliminate failures is verified on the experimental platform. During the stripping process, faults are artificially created by dragging the cable, placing the cable incorrectly, and using insufficient cutting depth. According to the decision of the < *Tool False* > node, the robot handles the fault according to the preset strategy. The test results are shown in Table 1.

Table 1. Wire stripping troubleshooting test

Cause of the failure	Number of tests	Number of successes (rate)
Insufficient cutting depth	5	5 (100%)
Failed to cut off sheath	8	6 (75%)
Insufficient clamping	6	6 (83%)
Cut into the metal core	3	2 (67%)
Slack cable	7	7 (100%)
Total	29	26 (89.7%)

In September 2021, we carried out broken drainage in Guandu District, Kunming City, as shown in Fig. 14. Since the power supply area does not need power supply from the distribution network, the power supply equipment and drainage lines need to be removed. The purpose of the drainage operation is to remove the drainage line on the overhead line.

Since this is the first field broken drainage operation of the robot, we encountered a new requirement. In the original plan, the operation of the fire demolition operation only required cutting the drainage line at the line clamp. After arriving at the site, the power grid technicians required to cut the drainage wire both at the overhead line (1st cutting in Fig. 14d) end and the insulated terminal end (2nd cutting in Fig. 14e), and remove the cable safely. We have encountered this kind of problem in the drainage operation and have experience in dealing with it. The stochastic process-oriented task planning method based on BTs allows us to adjust task execution by modifying the task state. When the first disconnection is done (Fig. 14d), we reset the state mod*Positioned* = *Null*. After the state changes, task BT re-decisions based on current state, and will re-execute the < position > (Fig. 14e) and < Cutting > (Fig. 14f) task nodes.

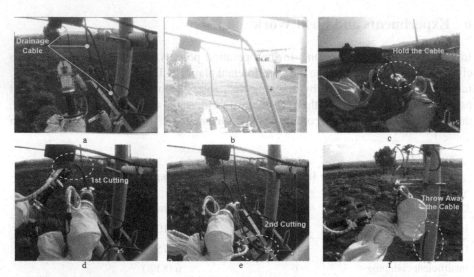

Fig. 14. Field work: broken drainage operation on overhead lines (a. The drainage cable to be removed, b. Locate the cable, c. Hold the cable with the auxiliary arm, d. Break the wire on the side of the overhead line, e. Break the wire on the side of the insulation terminal, f. Throw away drainage wire)

7   Conclusion

This paper introduces a method to realize dynamic task planning of live working robot by using BT. According to the job process, a task BT is constructed to realize the dynamic planning and execution of tasks. Aiming at the uncertainty of task execution, a stochastic process-oriented task planning method is proposed. Aiming at unexpected events, a method of fault handling is designed. Experiments and field operations show that the method can be adapted to complex field operations.

References

1. Colledanchise, M., Ögren, P.: How BTs modularize hybrid control systems and generalize sequential behavior compositions, the subsumption architecture, and decision trees. IEEE Trans. Rob. **33**(2), 372–389 (2017)
2. Mateas, M., Stern, A.: A behavior language for story-based believable agents. IEEE Intell. Syst. **17**(4), 39–47 (2002)
3. Nicolau, M., Perez-Liebana, D., O'Neill, M., Brabazon, A.: Evolutionary BT approaches for navigating platform games. IEEE Trans. Comput. Intell. AI Games **9**(3), 227–238 (2016)
4. Shoulson, A., Garcia, F.M., Jones, M., Mead, R., Badler, N.I.: Parameterizing behavior trees. In: Allbeck, J.M., Faloutsos, P. (eds.) Motion in Games. MIG 2011. LNCS, vol. 7060, pp. 144–155. Springer, Berlin, Heidelberg (2011). https://doi.org/10.1007/978-3-642-25090-3_13
5. Bojic, I., Lipic, T., Kusek, M., Jezic, G.: Extending the jade agent behaviour model with jbehaviourtrees framework. In: O'Shea, J., Nguyen, N.T., Crockett, K., Howlett, R.J., Jain, L.C. (eds.) KES-AMSTA 2011. LNCS (LNAI), vol. 6682, pp. 159–168. Springer, Heidelberg (2011). https://doi.org/10.1007/978-3-642-22000-5_18

6. Ögren, P.: Increasing modularity of UAV control systems using computer game BTs. In: AIAA Guidance, Navigation, and Control Conference, p. 4458. Minneapolis (2012)

7. Marzinotto, A., Colledanchise, M., Smith, C., Ögren, P.: Towards a unied BTs framework for robot control. In: 2014 IEEE International Conference on Robotics and Automation (ICRA), pp. 5420–5427. IEEE (2014)

8. Bagnell, J., Cavalcanti, F., Cui, L., et al.: An integrated system for autonomous robotics manipulation, In: 2012 IEEE/RSJ International Conference on Intelligent Robots and Systems, pp. 2955–2962. IEEE (2012)

9. Gubisch, G., Steinbauer, G., Weiglhofer, M., Wotawa, F.: A Teleo-reactive architecture for fast, reactive and robust control of mobile robots. In: Nguyen, N.T., Borzemski, L., Grzech, A., Ali, M. (eds.) IEA/AIE 2008. LNCS (LNAI), vol. 5027, pp. 541–550. Springer, Heidelberg (2008). https://doi.org/10.1007/978-3-540-69052-8_57

10. Stuede, M., et al.: Behavior-tree-based person search for symbiotic autonomous mobile robot tasks. In: 2021 IEEE International Conference on Robotics and Automation, pp. 2414–2420. IEEE (2021)

11. Wang, T., Shi, D., Yi, W.: Extending behavior trees with market-based task allocation in dynamic environments. In: 2020 4th International Symposium on Computer Science and Intelligent Control. pp. 1–8 (2020)

Design of Multi-unit Passive Exoskeleton for Running

Nianfeng Wang$^{(\boxtimes)}$, Fan Yue, Jiegang Huang, and Xianmin Zhang

Guangdong Provincial Key Laboratory of Precision Equipment
and Manufacturing Technology, School of Mechanical and Automotive Engineering,
South China University of Technology, Guangzhou 510640, China
menfwang@scut.edu.cn

Abstract. The passive exoskeleton used to assist the human gait and reduce the energy consumption of the human body. In this paper, through the mathematical expression of the man-machine mechanical power model and the installation design area, combined with the optimization algorithm, some passive exoskeleton structure designs that can reduce the mechanical power consumption of the whole lower limb of the human body are found. The designed passive exoskeleton enables an average reduction of 4.4% compared to disability metabolism by building experimental prototypes for metabolic experiments.

Keywords: Passive exoskeleton · Running assistance · Optimal design

1 Introduction

Exoskeletons are used to assist or enhance human movement. It is usually used for medical rehabilitation, weight reduction or movement support [1]. Exoskeletons are usually divided into two categories according to the power source. Some are the powered exoskeleton that are assisted by motors or other power components, such as Berkeley [2], HAL [3] or Exosuits [4]. Others are the passive exoskeleton that use elastic elements to store and release energy by analyzing gait characteristics. Compared with the powered exoskeletons, the passive exoskeletons do not need to carry energy storage devices and the power source devices. So they are lighter in weight, relatively simple and reliable in structure. They also have high safety when assisting the human body. However, passive exoskeletons cannot provide power by themselves. All power needs to be stored and released from the movement of the human body. We cannot rely on passive exoskeletons to assist all the joint torques of a certain joint. It is difficult to use methods such as "human in the loop" [5] to adjust training parameters at any time as well. Therefore, general research usually adopts the method of establishing a model. Then they complete the design of passive exoskeletons by analyzing and solving the model with inputting biological signals and ingeniously designing a mechanical structure in a suitable position to assist the human body.

H. Liu et al. (Eds.): ICIRA 2022, LNAI 13457, pp. 686–697, 2022.
https://doi.org/10.1007/978-3-031-13835-5_62

Some human or man-machine models that can be used for passive exoskeleton design usually fall into the following categories [6]. Some are abstract models similar to the inverted pendulum. The exoskeleton is designed by studying the relationship between the position of the center of mass of the human body and the ground reaction force. Some are the Rigid dynamic models. Ren, L, Jones and others of Stanford University established an inverse dynamic 7 link model to explore the influence of backpacks on the human body [7]. Salman Faraji proposed a simpler 3 link model to calculate the walking power of human walking [8]. Others are muscle models, which judge whether the exoskeleton is effective by combining the relevant theories of biomechanics.

Some passive exoskeletons were designed through the above models. In 2006, Professor Sunil K. Agrawal and his team from the University of Delaware designed a gravity-balanced lower extremity exoskeleton [9]. The exoskeleton relies on the link mechanism and the spring to balance the gravity. In 2015, French Yannick Aoustin proposed a 7 link human body model, which was also used on exoskeleton similar to humans [10]. It theoretically proves the feasibility and effectiveness of the passive exoskeleton with locking knee joints. In 2015, Professor Sawicki and his team from north carolina state University designed a passive lower limb exoskeleton [11, 12]. They used the Hill muscle model to build an ankle joint model and obtained the best stiffness of the passive exoskeleton spring by adding a spring to the outside of the ankle model. It can reduce 7.2% of people's metabolic consumption when walking. In 2018, Xiong proposed a four-muscle model based on the hip joint and design the passive exoskeleton [13]. In 2020, Cseke uses opensim as a modeling tool to establish a skeletal muscle model to simulate the ideal auxiliary exoskeleton acting on the gait of the elderly [14]. In 2020, Zhou designed a passive lower extremity exoskeleton with a combination of hip and knee joints for human walking assistance [15]. The exoskeleton has spring mechanisms at two joint positions to generate assist torque.

The design of an exoskeleton first needs to determine the auxiliary joints or areas. The determination of joints usually requires observing the changes of joint torque during the human gait process, so as to find potential joints for assistance. But at the same time, this may miss some of the results of cross-joint assistance or multi-joint assistance. Something is required to find some possible exoskeleton structures from the lower limbs of the entire human body to assist the human gait through simple elastic elements. We establish a multi-rigid body dynamics model to find the passive exoskeleton structure of the entire lower limbs that has the potential of boosting through the goal of the minimum mechanical power for human running. In order to achieve this goal, each part of the model usually needs to be independently calculated. Therefore, the model can quickly calculate the inverse dynamic solution when the passive exoskeleton structure changes. We achieve this goal by rewriting the Newton-Euler iterative equation.

2   Model and Installation Area

The human body is regarded as a 2-dimensional multi-rigid body model. Parameters of human body parts (HAT, left and right thighs, left and right shanks, left and right feet) include length, mass, center of mass position, and inertia matrix. The human body calculates the joint torques through the inverse dynamic method by inputting the posture of body parts. The gravitational acceleration is in the $-z$ direction. The human body travels in the x direction and the angular velocity of joint rotate in the y direction during the movement. Human body parts are regarded as rigid bodies. The position, velocity and acceleration of other points of body part can be calculated by Eq. 1 from the point of which kinematics is known.

$$
\begin{aligned}
{}^{G}p_i &= {}^{G}p_k + {}^{G}_{L}R({}^{L}p_i - {}^{L}p_k) \\
{}^{G}v_i &= {}^{G}v_k + {}^{G}\omega \times {}^{G}_{L}R({}^{L}p_i - {}^{L}p_k) \\
{}^{G}a_i &= {}^{G}a_k + {}^{G}\omega \times ({}^{G}\omega \times {}^{G}_{L}R({}^{L}p_i - {}^{L}p_k)) \\
&\quad + {}^{G}\alpha \times {}^{G}_{L}R({}^{L}p_i - {}^{L}p_k)
\end{aligned}
\tag{1}
$$

${}^{G}p_i$ is the coordinates of a point on the rigid body in the ground coordinate system. ${}^{G}p_i$ is the coordinates of a known point on the rigid body in the ground coordinate system. ${}^{L}p_i$ is the coordinates of a point on the rigid body in the local coordinate system. ${}^{L}p_k$ is the coordinates of a known point on the rigid body in the local coordinate system. ${}^{G}v_i$, ${}^{G}a_i$ are the speed and acceleration of a point. ${}^{G}v_k$, ${}^{G}a_k$ are the speed and acceleration of a known point. ${}^{G}\omega$, ${}^{G}\alpha$ are the angular velocity and angular acceleration of the rigid body. ${}^{G}_{L}R$ is the transformation matrix from the local coordinate system to the ground coordinate system.

The dynamics of a part is determined according to the following formula as:

$$
\begin{aligned}
{}^{G}f_o &= m\,{}^{G}a_{cm} - \sum_{i=1(i\neq o)}^{N} {}^{G}f_i - mg \\
{}^{G}n_o &= {}^{G}_{L}RI({}^{G}_{L}R)^{T}({}^{G}\alpha) + {}^{G}\omega \times {}^{G}_{L}RI({}^{G}_{L}R)^{T}({}^{G}\omega) \\
&\quad - \sum_{i=1}^{N} {}^{G}_{L}R({}^{L}p_i - {}^{L}p_{cm}) \times {}^{G}f_i - \sum_{i=1(i\neq o)}^{N} {}^{G}n_i
\end{aligned}
\tag{2}
$$

${}^{G}f_o$, ${}^{G}n_o$ are the point force and moment. m is the rigid body mass. ${}^{G}a_{cm}$ is the acceleration of the rigid body's center of mass. g is the acceleration of gravity. I is the inertia tensor. ${}^{G}f_i$, ${}^{G}n_i$ are the forces and moments of other points. and ${}^{L}p_{cm}$ is the position of the center of mass in the local coordinate system.

The force and moment that passive exoskeleton produces on the human body is determined by the kinematic results. The formula can be expressed as:

$$
\begin{aligned}
f_{bot,1} = -f_{bot,2} &= \begin{cases} k_{bot}(p_1 - p_2), \|p_1 - p_2\| > L_0 \\ 0, \|p_1 - p_2\| \leq L_0 \end{cases} \\
n_{bot,1} = n_{bot,2} &= 0
\end{aligned}
\tag{3}
$$

f_{bot} is the exoskeleton force. n_{bot} is the exoskeleton moment. p_1, p_2 are the two points where the exoskeleton unit is installed on the human body. k_{bot} is the stiffness coefficient of the passive exoskeleton unit. L_0 is the minimum length of the passive exoskeleton unit enabled.

We hope that every viable part of the human body can be mounted with elastic devices to reduce the mechanical work of the human when running.

Therefore, it is necessary to mathematically express the installation design area of the passive exoskeleton. Rectangular areas are drawn on the front and back sides of each part of the human body for the 2-dimensional body model. One end of the elastic device can be installed at any point in the rectangular area. The value of the design area parameter refers to the length and width of each part of the human body, as shown in Fig. 1.

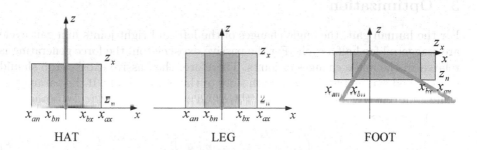

HAT   LEG   FOOT

Fig. 1. Installation design area of the passive exoskeleton

For the exact relative coordinates of the arrangement position, the body parts where one end of the elastic devices are installed need to be first determined. If the seven parts of the human body are numbered, the installation part can be determine by the body part number i. Secondly, two parameters ε_x and ε_z are used to determine the relative coordinates as follows:

$$
x_{inst} = \begin{cases} x_{an}L_i + \varepsilon_x(x_{ax} - x_{bx} + x_{bn} - x_{an})L_i \\ \quad (\varepsilon_x \leq \frac{x_{bn} - x_{an}}{x_{ax} + x_{bn} - x_{bx} - x_{an}}) \\ x_{bx}L_i + \varepsilon_x x_{ax} - \varepsilon_x x_{bx} + (\varepsilon_x - 1)x_{bn} \\ \quad +(1 - \varepsilon_x)x_{an}L_i \\ \quad (\varepsilon_x > \frac{x_{bn} - x_{an}}{x_{ax} + x_{bn} - x_{bx} - x_{an}}) \end{cases}
\tag{4}
$$
$$
z_{inst} = z_n L_i + \varepsilon_z(z_x - z_n)L_i
$$

i and ε_x are merged into a new variable χ in order to reduce the number of variables in the optimization process and maintain the continuity of the variables by Eq. 5.

$$
\chi = \varepsilon_x + i - 1
\tag{5}
$$

The variable χ includes the installation part of the passive exoskeleton and the x relative position in the local coordinate system. χ is reduced to i and ε_x by Eq. 6 when needed.

$$
i = \begin{cases} 1, \chi = 0 \\ \lceil \chi \rceil, \chi > 0 \end{cases}
\tag{6}
$$
$$
\varepsilon_x = \chi - i + 1
$$

Mechanical work of the human body can be calculated as follow:

$$W = \sum_{j=1}^{k} \int_{t_0}^{t_1} |M_j \cdot \omega_j| dt \qquad (7)$$

M_j is the torque of a joint and ω_j is the angular velocity of the joint.

3 Optimization

For the human gait, the angle changes of the left and right joints in a gait cycle are staggered for half a cycle. For the passive exoskeleton, the force generating is related to the angle changes of joints. Therefore, the passive exoskeleton should be designed symmetrically with both sides of the human body. If the parameters i and ε of one side are determined, the i and ε of its symmetrical position can be expressed as

$$\begin{cases} i_{u'} = \phi(i_u) \\ \varepsilon_{u',ori} = \varepsilon_{u,ori}, ori \notin T \\ \varepsilon_{u',ori} = 1 - \varepsilon_{u,ori}, ori \in T \end{cases} \qquad (8)$$

$\phi(i_u)$ is the number of the symmetrical human body unit of i. T is the set of coordinate axis directions perpendicular to the sagittal plane of the human body (Fig. 2).

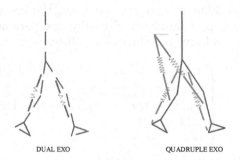

DUAL EXO   QUADRUPLE EXO

Fig. 2. Examples of passive exoskeleton structures

Considering that a single elastic device is used to assist human running, two elastic device placement positions are generated based on symmetry, that is, a dual unit passive exoskeleton. For two elastic devices to assist, four elastic element placements are generated based on symmetry (quadruple unit passive exoskeleton). If the minimum mechanical power of the human running is used as the optimization goal, the optimization problem of the dual unit passive exoskeleton can be expressed as:

$$\begin{aligned} \min \quad & W \\ \text{s.t.} \quad & 0 \leq \chi 1 \leq 7, 0 \leq \chi 2 \leq 7, 0 \leq \varepsilon_{z1} \leq 1, 0 \leq \varepsilon_{z2} \leq 1 \\ & 0 \leq L_0 \leq 1.5, 1000 \leq k_{bot} \leq 5000 \end{aligned} \qquad (9)$$

If it is a quadruple unit passive exoskeleton, the optimization problem can be expressed as:

$$
\begin{aligned}
\min \quad & W \\
\text{s.t.} \quad & 0 \le \chi 1 \le 7, 0 \le \chi 2 \le 7, 0 \le \varepsilon_{z1} \le 1, 0 \le \varepsilon_{z2} \le 1 \\
& 0 \le \chi 3 \le 7, 0 \le \chi 4 \le 7, 0 \le \varepsilon_{z3} \le 1, 0 \le \varepsilon_{z4} \le 1 \\
& 0 \le L_{0,1} \le 1.5, 1000 \le k_{bot,1} \le 5000 \\
& 0 \le L_{0,3} \le 1.5, 1000 \le k_{bot,3} \le 5000
\end{aligned}
\tag{10}
$$

The reasons for the constraints of the above optimization problem are as follows. The maximum value of i is 7 for the 7 part human body model. The value of ε is constrained to be between 0–1 by definition. The value of L_0 is usually determined according to the system structure, but any range will always produce optimization results. The upper limit is set to the farthest value of the theoretical two ends of the human body (usually 1–2 m). The setting of the stiffness k of the elastic device is generally selected according to the actual situation of the engineering problem. If the elastic device is a tension spring, the common stiffness range is between 1000–5000 N/m.

The objective function is discontinuous since χ will produce mutations in different parts of the human body. So the genetic algorithm is used to optimize the problem. Table 1 is the parameters of the design area.

Table 1. Parameters of the design area

Unit	i	$\phi(i)$	x_{an}	x_{bn}	x_{bx}	x_{ax}	z_n	z_x
Foot(L)	1	2	−0.6	−0.4	0.5	0.7	−0.5	0
Foot(R)	2	1	−0.6	−0.4	0.5	0.7	−0.5	0
Shank(L)	3	4	−0.4	−0.3	0.3	0.4	0	1
Shank(R)	4	3	−0.4	−0.3	0.3	0.4	0	1
Thigh(L)	5	6	−0.4	−0.3	0.3	0.4	0	1
Thigh(R)	6	5	−0.4	−0.3	0.3	0.4	0	1
HAT	7	7	−0.4	−0.24	0.24	0.4	0	0.5

Figure 3 shows the optimization result of the dual unit passive exoskeleton. The left picture is the installation position (Red is the optimization result, purple is the optimization process result). The right picture shows the auxiliary force of the exoskeleton during the gait cycle. The final optimization result can reduce the mechanical power of the human body by 24.37% in theory. The parameters of optimization result are shown in Table 2.

Table 2. Parameters of dual passive exoskeleton optimization

$\chi 1$	$\chi 2$	ε_{z1}	ε_{z2}	L_0	k_{bot}
4.5274	5.2880	0.4084	0.3364	0.2097	1427.6

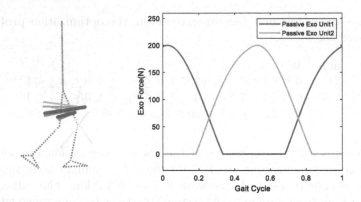

Fig. 3. Results of dual unit passive exoskeleton optimization (Color figure online)

Figure 4 shows the optimization result of the quadruple unit passive exoskeleton. The final optimization result can reduce the mechanical power of the human body by 25.58% in theory. The parameters of optimization result are shown in Table 3.

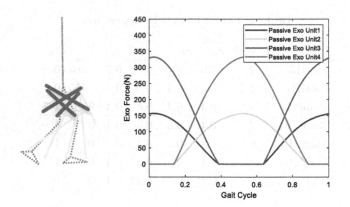

Fig. 4. Results of quadruple unit passive exoskeleton optimization

Table 3. Parameters of quadruple passive exoskeleton optimization

Unit	$\chi 1(\chi 3)$	$\chi 2(\chi 4)$	$\varepsilon_{z1}(\varepsilon_{z3})$	$\varepsilon_{z2}(\varepsilon_{z4})$	$L_{0,i}$	$k_{bot,i}$
1	4.5655	5.1967	0.2243	0.9904	0.3663	2173.0
3	5.1080	4.7656	0.2741	0.8331	0.3199	3622.9

Some structures may interfere during human running if considering the actual design factors, including the following structures: (1) Mount the elastic device from the left leg to the right leg. (2) Mount the elastic device from the front to the back of one human body part. (3) Mount the elastic device from the front side of the knee. Considering that the optimization should eliminate these structures as much as possible, penalty terms can be imposed on the objective function:

$$\begin{aligned}
&W' = W + \lambda_{sy}M_{sy}, i_1 \in Y_i \& i_2 \notin Y_i \\
&W' = W + \lambda_{fb}M_{fb}, (\varepsilon_{x1} - \mu_1)(\varepsilon_{x2} - \mu_2) < 0 \\
&(\mu_i = \frac{x_{bn,i} - x_{an,i}}{x_{ax,i} + x_{bn,i} - x_{bx,i} - x_{an,i}}) \\
&W' = W + \lambda_{kn}M_{kn}
\end{aligned} \tag{11}$$

W' is the objective function. λ_{sy}, λ_{fb} and λ_{kn} are the weighting factors. ms are the penalty items.

Then the optimization problem can be described as

$$\begin{aligned}
\min \quad & W + \lambda_{sy}M_{sy} + \lambda_{fb}M_{fb} + \lambda_{kn}M_{kn} \\
\text{s.t.} \quad & 0 \le \chi 1 \le 7, 0 \le \chi 2 \le 7, 0 \le \varepsilon_{z1} \le 1, 0 \le \varepsilon_{z2} \le 1 \\
& 0 \le \chi 3 \le 7, 0 \le \chi 4 \le 7, 0 \le \varepsilon_{z3} \le 1, 0 \le \varepsilon_{z4} \le 1 \\
& 0 \le L_{0,1} \le 1.5, 1000 \le k_{bot,1} \le 15000 \\
& 0 \le L_{0,3} \le 1.5, 1000 \le k_{bot,3} \le 15000
\end{aligned} \tag{12}$$

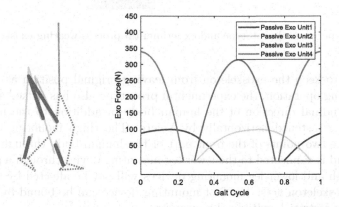

Fig. 5. Results of quadruple unit passive exoskeleton optimization with restriction

We relax the restriction on k so that the optimization can be carried out more efficiently. Figure 5 shows the optimization result of the quadruple part passive exoskeleton with restrictions. The final optimization result can reduce the mechanical power of the human body by 7.9% in theory. The parameters of the optimization result are shown in Table 4. If the spring stiffness is reduced to 5000N/m, the human body mechanical work can be reduced to 4.18%.

Table 4. Parameters of quadruple passive exoskeleton optimization with restriction

Unit	$\chi 1(\chi 3)$	$\chi 2(\chi 4)$	$\varepsilon_{z1}(\varepsilon_{z3})$	$\varepsilon_{z2}(\varepsilon_{z4})$	$L_{0,i}$	$k_{bot,i}$
1	2.3859	0.2265	0.4576	0.5834	0.2166	14228
3	5.4989	6.1505	0.2734	0.4741	0.5189	13741

4 Experiment

In order to verify the effect of the passive exoskeleton design, we built a prototype for experiments (Fig. 6). The elastic devices is realized by tension springs. In order to facilitate the adjustment of the installation position, an aluminum profile frame is designed at the waist. The positions of the spring fixing points can be adjusted along the aluminum profile. The frame can be adjusted up and down by stretching the backpack elastic band. A triangular mounting device is designed at the position of the thigh and shank.

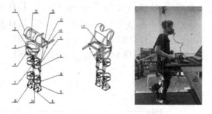

Fig. 6. Experimental prototype and experimental process wearing exoskeleton

In order to keep the exoskeleton from leaving original position as much as possible during operation, the experimental prototype also has a fixed structure in the longitudinal direction of the human body in addition to the mounting position being fastened horizontally by Velcro. The thigh mounting device is fixed with the two points of the front part of the human body through a strap. The lower end is connected to the lower leg mounting device through a strap, so that the thigh and lower leg mounting devices will not be affected by the force when the exoskeleton acts. The foot mounting device can be bound by the sole of the foot to restrict longitudinal movement.

The experiment is divided into eight groups. Each group consists of an experimental group wearing exoskeleton and a control group where the exoskeleton spring cannot work. In the experiment, the experimental group and the control group ran for 5 min each time, and then took another group after a five-minute rest. The running speed is 4 km/h. The actual calculation data only takes the last three minutes of each group to prevent the initial interference, then calculated the average metabolic consumption as the result of the group of experiments. The effectiveness of the passive exoskeleton design is verified by comparing the results of the experimental group and the control group.

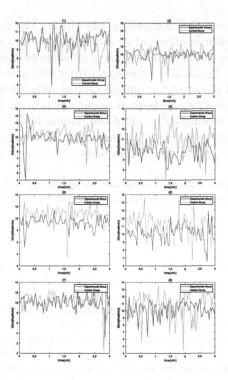

Fig. 7. Metabolic test results of the wearing exoskeleton experiment

Table 5. Average metabolic test results of the wearing exoskeleton experiment

	Group1	Group2	Group3	Group4	Group5	Group6	Group7	Group8	Average
Test group	10.12	9.94	9.79	9.83	9.32	10.16	10.07	10.23	9.93
Control group	9.60	9.93	10.23	10.75	10.55	11.16	10.33	10.74	10.41
Reduce metabolism	−5.44%	−0.12%	4.31%	8.56%	11.67%	8.88%	2.49%	4.82%	4.40%

The results shows in Table 5 and Fig. 7. It can be seen that the metabolism of the first group increased after wearing the exoskeleton. The second group was basically the same. The metabolism of the other six groups decreased to varying degrees after the exoskeleton was used. Overall, after wearing the exoskeleton, the human metabolism is reduced by 4.40% on average compared with the spring not working.

5   Conclusion

In this paper, the overall structure design of the passive exoskeleton of the lower limbs is realized based on the man-machine model. The description of the exoskeleton installation design area is realized. The mechanical work of the human body system is taken as the objective function. Then the passive exoskeleton is optimized through genetic algorithm. The results show that the dual passive exoskeleton is arranged at a specific position of the hip joint and the theory can reduce the mechanical power consumption of the human system in the running state by 24.37%. The quadruple unit passive exoskeleton can make the mechanical power of the human system reduced by 25.58% in theory. The quadruple unit passive exoskeleton under engineering restrictions can theoretically reduce the mechanical work of the human body by 7.9%. The human metabolism is reduced by 4.4% on average through the experiment of wearing the exoskeleton prototype on the human body.

Acknowledgment. The authors would like to gratefully acknowledge the reviewers comments. This work is supported by National Key R&D Program of China (Grant Nos. 2019YFB1310200), National Natural Science Foundation of China (Grant Nos. 520751807) and Science and Technology Program of Guangzhou (Grant Nos. 201904020020).

References

1. Herr, H.: Exoskeletons and orthoses: classification, design challenges and future directions. J. Neuroeng. Rehabil. **6**(1), 1–9 (2009)
2. Kazerooni, H., Steger, R.: The Berkeley lower extremity exoskeleton (2006)
3. Suzuki, K., Mito, G., Kawamoto, H., Hasegawa, Y., Sankai, Y.: Intention-based walking support for paraplegia patients with robot suit HAL. Adv. Robot. **21**(12), 1441–1469 (2007)
4. Panizzolo, F.A., et al.: A biologically-inspired multi-joint soft exosuit that can reduce the energy cost of loaded walking. J. Neuroeng. Rehabil. **13**(1), 1–14 (2016)
5. Ding, Y., Kim, M., Kuindersma, S., Walsh, C.J.: Human-in-the-loop optimization of hip assistance with a soft exosuit during walking. Sci. Robot. **3**(15), eaar5438 (2018)
6. Silva, M., et al.: Current perspectives on the biomechanical modelling of the human lower limb: a systematic review. Arch. Comput. Methods Eng. **28**(2), 601–636 (2021)
7. Ren, L., Jones, R.K., Howard, D.: Dynamic analysis of load carriage biomechanics during level walking. J. Biomech. **38**(4), 853–863 (2005)
8. Faraji, S., Wu, A.R., Ijspeert, A.J.: A simple model of mechanical effects to estimate metabolic cost of human walking. Sci. Rep. **8**(1), 1–12 (2018)
9. Agrawal, S.K., et al.: Assessment of motion of a swing leg and gait rehabilitation with a gravity balancing exoskeleton. IEEE Trans. Neural Syst. Rehabil. Eng. **15**(3), 410–420 (2007)
10. Aoustin, Y.: Walking gait of a biped with a wearable walking assist device. Int. J. Humanoid Rob. **12**(04), 1550018 (2015)
11. Collins, S.H., Wiggin, M.B., Sawicki, G.S.: Reducing the energy cost of human walking using an unpowered exoskeleton. Nature **522**(7555), 212–215 (2015)
12. Sawicki, G.S., Khan, N.S.: A simple model to estimate plantarflexor muscle-tendon mechanics and energetics during walking with elastic ankle exoskeletons. IEEE Trans. Biomed. Eng. **63**(5), 914–923 (2015)
13. Chen, W., Wu, S., Zhou, T., Xiong, C.: On the biological mechanics and energetics of the hip joint muscle-tendon system assisted by passive hip exoskeleton. Bioinspir. Biomim. **14**(1), 016012 (2018)

14. Stollenmaier, K., Rist, I.S., Izzi, F., Haeufle, D.F.: Simulating the response of a neuro-musculoskeletal model to assistive forces: implications for the design of wearables compensating for motor control deficits. In: 2020 8th IEEE RAS/EMBS International Conference for Biomedical Robotics and Biomechatronics (BioRob), pp. 779–784. IEEE (2020)
15. Zhou, L., Chen, W., Chen, W., Bai, S., Zhang, J., Wang, J.: Design of a passive lower limb exoskeleton for walking assistance with gravity compensation. Mech. Mach. Theory 150, 103840 (2020)

Force Tracking Impedance Control Based on Contour Following Algorithm

Nianfeng Wang[1,2](✉), Jianbin Zhou[2], Kaifan Zhong[2], Xianmin Zhang[2], and Wei Chen[3]

[1] Guangdong Artificial Intelligence and Digital Economy Laboratory (Guangzhou), Guangzhou, China
menfwang@scut.edu.cn
[2] Guangdong Key Laboratory of Precision Equipment and Manufacturing Technology, School of Mechanical and Automotive Engineering, South China University of Technology, Guangzhou 510640, People's Republic of China
[3] Shenzhen Polytechnic, Shenzhen, China
chenwei1@szpt.edu.cn

Abstract. The original impedance control is a main force control scheme widely used in robotic force tracking. However, it is difficult to achieve a good force tracking performance in uncertain environment. This paper introduces a modification of the impedance control scheme which has the adaptability to track the desired force in uncertain environment (in terms of the varying location of the environment relative to the manipulators). The relation function of contact force in adjacent control period is derived to estimate the trajectory inclination angle deviation (IAD) of the manipulator. After that, the contour following algorithm which is implemented under a PID controller is proposed. To achieve force tracking impedance control under uncertain environment location, the movement of the manipulator in one control period is determined by estimating the new velocity vector and calculating the impedance correction online, which is based on the position-based impedance control (PBIC). Experiments was presented for testing the performance of IAD estimation and force tracking.

Keywords: Force tracking · Impedance control modification · Contour following · Uncertain environment

1 Introduction

Robot manipulators have evolved and they are often designed to interact with the environments. Typical examples include peg-in-hole operation [1], deburring [2], polishing [3], and dual-robot coordination [4,5]. When the manipulators executing these tasks, interaction force control is a central importance for improving the operation compliance. The constant-force mechanisms can provide a near constant force output without using force sensor and controller [6]. In the previous researches, another promising methods to realize force tracking applications

H. Liu et al. (Eds.): ICIRA 2022, LNAI 13457, pp. 698–709, 2022.
https://doi.org/10.1007/978-3-031-13835-5_63

is provided by indirect force controller (IFC). The popular variations of the IFC is the impedance control introduced by Hogan in [7] and the hybird position and force control introduced by Raibert and Craig in [8], and the impedance control is considered as a practical one to achieve force tracking in a position-controlled manipulators system.

However, the force tracking performance of the original impedance control is not good enough in uncertain environment. To deal with this problem, vast investigations have been made. The variable impedance control is used in [9,10] by varing the target stiffness and damping of the impedance model on-line to regulate the contact force without any knowledge of the environment. Under this category of methods, the impedance parameters is adjusted according to the force feedback. In addition to those efforts, the more direct ways that generate the reference trajectory by estimating the environment stiffness and location is presented in [11,12]. Besides, the another way that compensates the robot dynamic uncertainties by contact force information is proposed in [13]. Further than that, with the development of intelligent learning method, neural network (NN) or fuzzy technique was applied in impedance controller to compensate the uncertainties. In [14,15], an impedance controller combined with NN is developed to track the desired contact force of the end-effector and the desired trajectories of the manipulator. In [16], the adaptive fuzzy NN based impedance control method is proposed to approximate the robot and environment dynamical model.

Fractional Order Impedance Control

In this paper, a modification of the impedance control scheme combined with an contour following algorithm is proposed in order to perform force tracking impedance control despite the presence of environment uncertainties. This method defines the movement of the manipulator in one control period which can be easily implemented in discrete systems. During the analysis, the relation of contact force in adjacent control period is derived and the contour following algorithm is proposed in this paper. Experiments of IAD estimation and force tracking for straight lines and arcs are presented to verify the performance of the method.

2 System Modeling and Control

In this part, the interaction model is discussed and the IAD estimation law based on the interaction force is proposed in Sect. 2.1. To reduce the force tracking error caused by environment location uncertainty, a modification of the impedance control algorithms, which is combined with the IAD estimation law, is proposed for the PBIC system in Sect. 2.2.

2.1 Interaction Model and IAD Estimation

The interaction model when end effector keeps contact with the environment is presented in Fig. 1, where N_i refers to the contact points in current cycle and v refers to the velocity of the end effector. When the end effector reaches the next planned point N'_{i+1}, the distance between N_i and N'_{i+1} is $l = v \cdot T_s$ (T_s is the system control cycle). Denote δ and δ' the normal deformation (penetration depth) caused by the interaction in current and next cycle respectively. From Fig. 1 we can know that if the end effector run close to the environment, the relation of normal deformation will be $\delta' > \delta$, if the end effector run away from the environment, it will be $\delta' < \delta$. $F_n(i)$ and $F'_n(i+1)$ are the normal contact force produced under the action of the deformation. Assume k_e is the environment stiffness, then $F_n(i)$ in current cycle is $F_n(i) = k_e \cdot \delta$, $F'_n(i+1)$ in next cycle is $F'_n(i+1) = k_e \cdot \delta'$.

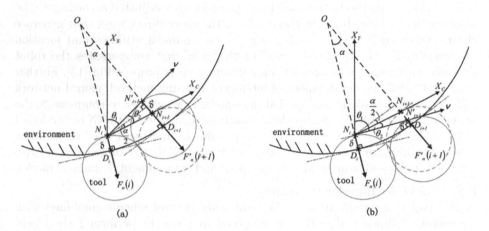

(a)   (b)

Fig. 1. Interaction model of manipulator and the environment. (a) Run close to environment. (b) Run away from environment.

For simplifying calculation, a reference line X_C parallel to the secant of $D_i\widehat{D}_{i+1}$ is used as the tangential direction of the environment. X_S is the X-axis of the sensor frame $O_S - X_S Y_S Z_S$, θ_1 is the inclination angle of the motion velocity in current cycle, and θ_2 is the included angle between v and X_C, i.e. IAD. The purpose of IAD estimation is to make the IAD to zero or minimum.

Generally, contour following refers to a constrained-motion task in which a manipulator must track along an environment surface. A problem in the contour-following control is that the unexpected environment disturbances that degrade the tracking performance. For instance, the pre-planned path is not feasible due to uncertainties in the model used by the path planner. If the velocity direction v of the end effector can be adjusted to be close to the environment direction X_C in each cycle, better contour-following performance may be expected. A general method for estimating the IAD to compensate the uncertainties of the environment is given below.

When the normal deformation between two cycles are different, interaction force deviation in adjacent contact points occurs. Assume N_{i+1} is the ideal planned point that has the same penetration depth as N_i, the difference of normal deformation $\Delta\delta = |\delta - \delta'|$ (as $N_{i+1}N'_{i+1}$ shown in Fig. 1) between two cycle can be expressed as

$$\Delta\delta = \begin{cases} vT_s \cdot \left[sin(\theta_2 - \frac{\alpha}{2}) + cos(\theta_2 - \frac{\alpha}{2}) \cdot tan\frac{\alpha}{2} \right] (\delta' > \delta) \\ vT_s \cdot \left[sin(\theta_2 + \frac{\alpha}{2}) - cos(\theta_2 + \frac{\alpha}{2}) \cdot tan\frac{\alpha}{2} \right] (\delta' < \delta) \end{cases} \tag{1}$$

where α refers to the inclination angles between adjacent contact points (as shown in Fig. 1). According to the analysis in Sect. 2.1, the normal contact force in next cycle $F'_n(i+1)$ can be expressed as

$$F'_n(i+1) = F_n(i) + k \cdot \Delta\delta \tag{2}$$

where k refers to the stiffness of the environment. Simplifying Eq. 1 and substituting it into Eq. 2, yields

$$F'_n(i+1) = \begin{cases} F_n(i) + \\ kvT_s sin\theta_2(cos\frac{\alpha}{2} + sin\frac{\alpha}{2} \cdot tan\frac{\alpha}{2})(\delta' > \delta) \\ \\ F_n(i) - \\ kvT_s sin\theta_2(cos\frac{\alpha}{2} + sin\frac{\alpha}{2} \cdot tan\frac{\alpha}{2})(\delta' < \delta) \end{cases} \tag{3}$$

If $0 < \alpha < \frac{\pi}{2}$ and $0 < \theta_2 < \frac{\pi}{2}$ (the inclination angles between adjacent contact points is far less than $\frac{\pi}{2}$ in practice), the following conclusion can be drawn.

$$\begin{cases} F'_n(i+1) > F_n(i)(\delta' > \delta) \\ F'_n(i+1) < F_n(i)(\delta' < \delta) \end{cases} \tag{4}$$

Equation 4 shows that contact force will increase and decrease when the manipulator run close to and away from the environment respectively. Observing Eq. 3 we can find that both of the cases have similar forms of expression. So the IAD estimation law is proposed as

$$\theta_2(i) = arcsin \left[\frac{F'_n(i+1) - F_n(i)}{kvt_s(cos\frac{\alpha}{2} + sin\frac{\alpha}{2} \cdot tan\frac{\alpha}{2})} \right] \tag{5}$$

The proposed law Eq. 5 indicates the relation between IAD and the interaction force deviation. For convenient applications in the position-based control of industrial robots, the inclinational angle θ_1 in each sampling period can be adjusted by estimating IAD according to the interaction force, having the form as

$$\theta_1(i+1) = \theta_1(i) + arcsin \left[\frac{F'_n(i+1) - F_n(i)}{kvt_s(cos\frac{\alpha}{2} + sin\frac{\alpha}{2} \cdot tan\frac{\alpha}{2})} \right] \tag{6}$$

2.2   Modification of Impedance Control and Force Tracking

A manipulator is modelled by a second order mass-spring-damper system as shown in Fig. 2, and the environment is considered as a simplified spring system.

The system model of impedance control without contact and with contact is presented in Fig. 2, where m, b, and k are respectively the mass, damping, and stiffness of the manipulator, k_e is the stiffness of the environment, x is the position of the manipulator, x'_e is the position of environment without any contact and x_e is the contact position of environment. The typical target impedance

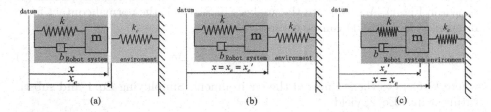

Fig. 2. Impedance control model. (a) without any contact between the end effector and the environment. (b) just at contact $f_e = 0$ and (c) contact with $f_e \neq 0$

is chosen as a linear second order system by Hogan in [7], so that the one-dimensional dynamical relationship between the contact force f_e and the position perturbation $\Delta x = x - x_r$ is given by

$$m_d \ddot{\Delta x} + b_d \dot{\Delta x} + k_d \Delta x = f_d - f_e = -e_f \qquad (7)$$

where x_r refers to the reference position, f_d is the desired contact force and e_f is the contact force error. Suppose

$$\begin{cases} x_1 = \Delta x \\ x_2 = \dot{x}_1 = \dot{\Delta x} \end{cases} \qquad (8)$$

Then the continuous time state equation of Eq. 7 can be expressed as

$$\dot{\boldsymbol{x}} = \begin{bmatrix} \dot{x}_1 \\ \dot{x}_2 \end{bmatrix} = \begin{bmatrix} 0 & 1 \\ -m_d^{-1}k_d & -m_d^{-1}b_d \end{bmatrix} \begin{bmatrix} x_1 \\ x_2 \end{bmatrix} - \begin{bmatrix} 0 \\ m_d^{-1} \end{bmatrix} \cdot e_f \qquad (9)$$

where $\boldsymbol{x}$ is the vector of the state equation.

For convenient applications in the discrete control of industrial robots, Eq. 9 should be implemented in a discrete format. As done in Sect. 2.1, assume that the control system is subject to sampling process with an interval of T_s. The discrete time approximation of Eq. 9 can be written as

$$\boldsymbol{x}(k+1) = \begin{bmatrix} 1 & T_s + 1 \\ 1 - m_d^{-1}k_d T_s & 1 - m_d^{-1}b_d T_s \end{bmatrix} \boldsymbol{x}(k)$$
$$- \begin{bmatrix} 0 \\ m_d^{-1}T_s \end{bmatrix} \cdot e_f(k) \qquad (10)$$

From Eq. 10 we can calculate the impedance correction Δx to modify the reference position x_r by $x_r = x_r + \Delta x$ in each sampling period to achieve force tracking. This process is known as PBIC system, which is established as shown in Fig. 3. Where F_e and F_d refer to the actual and desired contact force respectively, and $E = F_e - F_d$ refers to the force error which is used as the input of the impedance controller. However, the use of only impedance control turns out

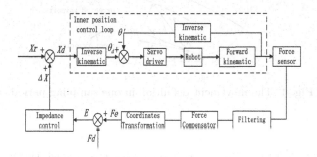

Fig. 3. The position-based impedance control (PBIC) system.

to be inadequate. Simulations and experiments conducted in [9] show that the traditional constant impedance control cannot track the desired force or even the force tracking is non-convergent in uncertain environment. Thus it is necessary to modify the form of the traditional impedance control to achieve the robust force tracking performance. A modification of the impedance control is proposed below to improve the robustness of the original algorithms.

To ensure the operation quality, the proposed online force tracking algorithm needs to satisfy the following two conditions:

- The velocity of the end effector along to the direction of the environment is kept constant.
- The interaction force between end effector and the environment is kept approximately constant.

According to the above two conditions, the movement definition in one sampling period is defined in Fig. 4. Known information includes magnitude and direction of current velocity v. θ_2 is the estimation of IAD which is obtained by Eq. 5, and v' is the velocity after the inclination angle is adjusted. With the IAD estimation and the magnitude $|v'| = |v|$, v' can be obtained as

$$
\begin{cases}
cos\theta_2 = \dfrac{v \cdot v'}{|v||v'|} \\[2mm]
|v'| = \sqrt{a^2 + b^2}
\end{cases}
\tag{11}
$$

where a, b is the coordinate of point C' relative to point P. Therefore, the IAD is estimated in order to obtain v'. vector v' can be regarded as the vector of direction compensation. The vector Δx, which represents the impedance correction

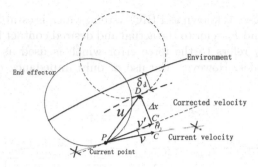

Fig. 4. The movement definition in one sampling period.

calculated by Eq. 10, is vertical to the vector v' to compensate the penetration depth in current period. After calculating vector v' and Δx, the movement u in one period can be obtained as

$$u = \Delta x + v' \qquad (12)$$

The form of proposed modification of the impedance control is given in Eq. 5, Eq. 10, Eq. 11 and Eq. 12. The above analysis shows that the target point D in Fig. 4 can be estimated through the force and position measurements. The whole proposed method includes inclination angle estimation and interaction force tracking and it is, in essence, the motion direction and the penetration depth control of the end effector. According to the method previously described, the total process when manipulator executes an online task involving interaction with the environment is shown in Fig. 5.

3   Experiments and Discussion

To test the proposed IAD estimation and modified impedance control method, a series of experiments are conducted and presented in this section. The test platform consist of self-developed open controller, a GMERI SGR02 industrial manipulator, a SRI M3714B3 6-axis force sensor, a SRI M8128 interface box and the end effector. The hardware architecture of the test platform is presented in Fig. 6. The open controller of manipulator and the force control system are communicated through TCP with the communication cycle $T_s = 28$ ms.

3.1   Force Tracking Quality Testing

The force tracking performance of the proposed control method is tested in the following experiments. Firstly, we conducted the experiment is tested on a planar workpiece which is shown in Fig. 7(a). Then in order to demonstrate the robustness of the proposed method, experiments are conducted on a big circular nozzle (which can be fitted at a dyeing machine) surface and a curved

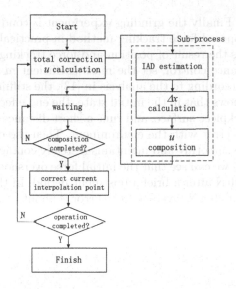

Fig. 5. The process of interaction control.

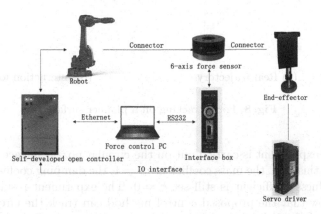

Fig. 6. The hardware architecture of the test platform.

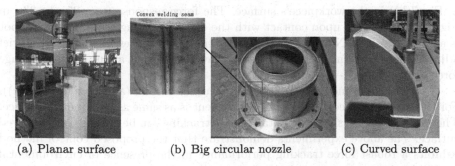

(a) Planar surface   (b) Big circular nozzle   (c) Curved surface

Fig. 7. Workpieces for experiments

surface respectively. Finally the grinding experiment is conducted to tested the feasibility of the proposed force tracking method in practical applications.

Figure 8 shows us the result of position and force tracking on the planar surface. For the impedance control, set the mass coefficient $m = 1$ and damping coefficient $b = 45$. According to the analysis in [13], the stiffness coefficient is set $k = 0$. Figure 8(a) shows that in the initial state, the end effector moves from the free space to the workpiece surface, and runs a short distance along the direction which has a distinct error with the environment. Then the end effector adjusts the inclination angle smoothly and maintains a steady contact with the environment. Form Fig. 8(b) we can see that the initial force overshoot is happening and the force settles to 40 N after a brief adjustment period. In the stable-stage, the average force is about 39.4 N (average force error is about −0.6 N).

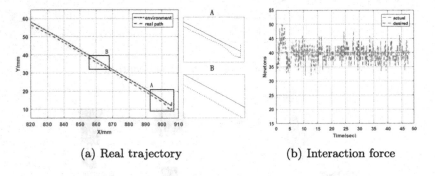

(a) Real trajectory   (b) Interaction force

Fig. 8. Force tracking on a planner surface

Another experiment is carried out on the circular nozzle surface as shown in Fig. 7(b). In this task, the mass coefficient $m = 1$, the damping coefficient $b = 55$, and the stiffness coefficient is still set $k = 0$. The experiment results displayed in Fig. 9 show that the proposed control method can track the circular surface although the initial direction of the path has some error. From $x = 777\,\text{mm}$ to $x = 758\,\text{mm}$, the end effector through the convex welding seam (as shown in Fig. 7(b)) in the workpiece's surface. The force response from 25 s to 33 s in Fig. 9(b) shows that upon contact with the convex welding seam, the overshoot is approximately 10 N and then the interaction force settles to 40 N after a brief adjustment period. In the stable-stage, the average force is about 39.2 N (average force error is about −0.8 N).

A further experiment is conducted on a curved surface (as shown in Fig. 7(c)). For the curved surface, the damping coefficient is as same as the circular surface. The result in Fig. 10 shows that stable force tracking can be obtained on a curved surface. The above experiments demonstrate that the proposed control method exhibits a robust force tracking performance in the presence of environmental uncertainty.

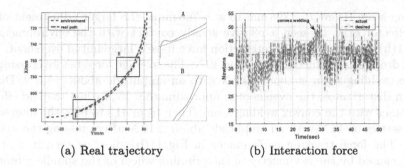

(a) Real trajectory   (b) Interaction force

Fig. 9. Force tracking on a circular surface

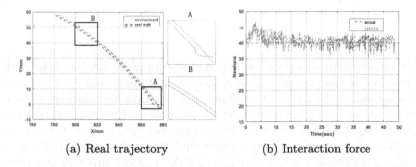

(a) Real trajectory   (b) Interaction force

Fig. 10. Force tracking on a non-circular curved surface

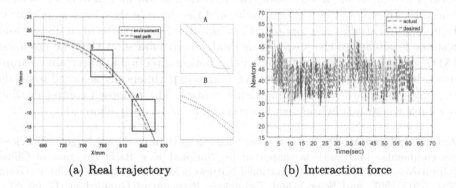

(a) Real trajectory   (b) Interaction force

Fig. 11. Grinding experiment on a circular surface

In order to test the force tracking performance in practical applications, grinding experiment is conducted on the big circular nozzle. A fiber grinding wheel is used as the end effector, the desired force tracking effect can be achieved by setting $m = 1, b = 75$ and $k = 0$. From Fig. 11(a) we can see that the end effector can still track the contour of the workpiece roughly in the presence of the system disturbance in a uncertain environment. After crossing the convex welding seam (from $x = 795$ mm to $x = 765$ mm), the larger adjustment of the end effector exist to keep a relative steady contact with the environment. In Fig. 11(b) we know that the interaction force have a large initial overshoot, then it has dropped and fluctuated around 40 N. The average force before crossing the convex welding seam is about 40.2 N with an amplitude about ± 7.5 N. Due to system disturbance, the overshoot is approximately 15 N when the end effector in contact with the convex welding seam. Then from 41 s to 62 s, the interaction force settles to 40 N with an amplitude about ± 10 N after crossing the welding seam. The force tracking performance in Fig. 11(b) show us even in a strong noise (caused by the asymmetry of the grinding wheel or the spindle vibration) environment, the desired force can be tracked by the manipulator under the control of the proposed method.

4   Conclusion

In this paper, a modification of impedance control is proposed to perform force tracking in the presence of the environmental uncertainties. The proposed method estimates the IAD of the manipulator motion and calculates the total correction in one control period based on the force and position measurements. In order to establish the relation of IAD and the interaction force, the interaction model when the end effector keep contact with the environment is presented. A movement calculation method that includes the motion direction and penetration depth compensation is defined. For convenient applications in the discrete control system of industrial robot, the IAD estimation and movement calculation are implemented by PID controller and the discrete time form respectively. Experimental studies are conducted in a self-developed platform to discuss and test the feasibility of the proposed method. The results show that the proposed IAD estimation can be used to correct the motion direction in uncertain environment. In addition, the desired force tracking is experimentally achieved based on the proposed modification of impedance control. The proposed control method is robust when the environment is uncertain or is abruptly changed.

Acknowledgment. The authors would like to gratefully acknowledge the reviewers comments. This work is supported by National Key R&D Program of China (Grant Nos. 2019YFB1310200), National Natural Science Foundation of China (Grant Nos. 520751807) and Science and Technology Program of Guangzhou (Grant Nos. 201904020020).

References

1. Car, M., Ivanovic, A., Orsag, M., Bogdan, S.: Impedance based force control for aerial robot peg-in-hole insertion tasks. In: 2018 IEEE/RSJ International Conference on Intelligent Robots and Systems (IROS), pp. 6734–6739, October 2018
2. Niknam, S.A., Davoodi, B., Davim, J.P., Songmene, V.: Mechanical deburring and edge-finishing processes for aluminum parts—a review. Int. J. Adv. Manuf. Technol. **95**(1), 1101–1125 (2017). https://doi.org/10.1007/s00170-017-1288-8

3. Ma, Z., Poo, A.N., Ang, M.H., Hong, G.S., See, H.H.: Design and control of an end-effector for industrial finishing applications. Robot. Comput.-Integr. Manuf. **53**, 240–253 (2018)
4. Duan, J.J., Gan, Y.H., Chen, M., Dai, X.Z.: Symmetrical adaptive variable admittance control for position/force tracking of dual-arm cooperative manipulators with unknown trajectory deviations. Robot. Comput.-Integr. Manuf. **57**, 357–369 (2019)
5. Zhao, X., Bo Tao, L., Qian, Y.Y., Ding, H.: Asymmetrical nonlinear impedance control for dual robotic machining of thin-walled workpieces. Robot. Comput.-Integr. Manuf. **63**, 101889 (2020)
6. Wang, P., Qingsong, X.: Design and modeling of constant-force mechanisms: a survey. Mech. Mach. Theory **119**, 1–21 (2018)
7. N. Hogan: Impedance control-an approach to manipulation. I-theory. II-implementation. III-applications. J. Dyn. Syst. Measur. Control **107**(17), 1–24 (1985)
8. Raibert, M.H., Craig, J.J.: Hybrid position/force control of robot manipulators. J. Dyn. Syst. Meas. Control **103**(2), 126–133 (1982)
9. Duan, J., Gan, Y., Chen, M., Dai, X.: Adaptive variable impedance control for dynamic contact force tracking in uncertain environment. Robot. Auton. Syst. **102**, 54–65 (2018)
10. Souzanchi-K, M., Arab, A., Akbarzadeh-T, M.R., Fateh, M.M.: Robust impedance control of uncertain mobile manipulators using time-delay compensation. IEEE Trans. Control Syst. Technol. **26**(6), 1942–1953 (2018)
11. Zhang, X., Khamesee, M.B.: Adaptive force tracking control of a magnetically navigated microrobot in uncertain environment. IEEE/ASME Trans. Mechatron. **22**(4), 1644–1651 (2017)
12. Roveda, L., Iannacci, N., Vicentini, F., Pedrocchi, N., Braghin, F., Tosatti, L.M.: Optimal impedance force-tracking control design with impact formulation for interaction tasks. IEEE Robot. Autom. Lett. **1**(1), 130–136 (2016)
13. Jung, S., Hsia, T.C., Bonitz, R.G.: Force tracking impedance control of robot manipulators under unknown environment. IEEE Trans. Control Syst. Technol. **12**(3), 474–483 (2004)
14. Yang, Z., Peng, J., Liu, Y.: Adaptive neural network force tracking impedance control for uncertain robotic manipulator based on nonlinear velocity observer. Neurocomputing **331**, 263–280 (2019)
15. Yao, B.T., Zhou, Z.D., Wang, L.H., Xu, W.J., Liu, Q., Liu, A.M.: Sensorless and adaptive admittance control of industrial robot in physical human-robot interaction. Robot. Comput.-Integr. Manuf. **51**, 158–168 (2018)
16. Peng, J., Yang, Z., Ma, T.: Position/force tracking impedance control for robotic systems with uncertainties based on adaptive Jacobian and neural network. Complexity (2019)

Guidance Method for UAV to Occupy Attack Position at Close Range

Xu Bingbing[1], Meng Guanglei[1,2(✉)], Wang Yingnan[1], and Zhao Runnan[2]

[1] School of Automation, Shenyang Aerospace University, Shenyang 110136, China
mengguanglei@yeah.net
[2] Liaoning Provincial Key Laboratory of Advanced Flight Control and Simulation Technology,
Shenyang 100136, China

Abstract. Unmanned aerial vehicles (UAVs) have become an important role in modern air combat. Aiming at the requirement that UAVs can autonomously maneuver according to the battlefield information to obtain the advantage of attack position in close-range air combat scenarios, a solution based on the constrained gradient method to solve the optimization guidance index of UAV attack position occupation to control UAV maneuvering is proposed. The UAV kinematic model is used as an algorithm control carrier. According to the actual air combat confrontation situation, it judges whether the distance and angle meet the attack or avoid conditions, and designs corresponding optimization indicators. Based on the input target state information, the constrained gradient method is used to optimize the attack or avoidance indicators. Perform the solution to obtain the guidance instructions, and input the instructions into the corresponding UAV kinematics model to complete the UAV's attack position occupation guidance. According to the engineering application requirements, a typical 1V1 air combat simulation test scenario is established. The simulation results show that the method in this paper can guide the UAV to obtain the advantage of attacking position.

Keywords: Occupy guidance · Optimization Index · Optimal control

1 Introduction

In modern warfare, the influence of air supremacy on the outcome of a war is increasingly important [1–5]. As more drones have exchanged small casualties for big success on the battlefield, major countries in the world have begun to pay attention to the development and application of drones in air combat. In air combat confrontations, the acquisition of attack position advantage is the key to the battle between the two sides. At present, scholars at home and abroad have proposed a variety of UAV maneuver decision-making or attack position occupation guidance methods. One kind of research scheme is based on maneuvering action library and uses artificial intelligence method to realize maneuvering decision in different situations [7–18]. The second method designs the guidance index function respectively for the attack and escape situations, and then uses the optimal control method to solve the guidance parameters, so as to meet the optimality requirements of space occupying guidance in air combat [19–21]. However, due to the curing of maneuver, the guidance trajectory lacks the flexibility to adjust in time with the slight change of the situation, which becomes the key factor affecting the decision fidelity and the optimization of position occupying guidance. The above domestic and foreign research methods provide theoretical reserves for the application of UAV attack position occupation guidance in future air combat.

In this paper, based on the constrained gradient method, the optimal control index is solved to obtain the optimal control quantity of the UAV, and it is converted into data and input into the UAV kinematics model to lead the UAV to complete the attack position occupation process. The simulation results show that the method can quickly reach the attack state or avoid the threat by occupying a reasonable attack position, which has good engineering application value. It also provides a new perspective for solving problems in the field of autonomous maneuvering of UAV air combat.

2   UAV Kinematic Model

2.1   Definition and Transformation Method of Coordinate System

Ground coordinate system is a coordinate system fixed on the earth's surface. The origin is located at an arbitrarily selected fixed point on the ground; The axes Ox_g point east; The axes Oy_g point north; The axes Oz_g are perpendicular to the local horizontal plane and upward along the local perpendicular. Track coordinate system is also called the ballistic fixed coordinate system. The origin is located at the center of mass of the aircraft, and its coordinate axes Ox_k always point to the ground velocity direction of the aircraft. The coordinate axis Oy_k is located in the symmetrical plane, pointing upwards perpendicular to the coordinate axis; The axes Oz_k are pointing to the right perpendicular to the plane.

Track Deviation Angle χ, which is the included Angle between the projection of the speed axis Ox_a on the horizontal plane Ox_gy_g and the coordinate axis Ox_g. It is stipulated that the track is positive when it is deflected to the right. Track Inclination Angle γ, also known as the climb Angle, that is, the included Angle between the velocity axis Ox_a and the horizontal plane Ox_gy_g. Positive when the track inclines upward.

In this paper, the method of converting from ground coordinate system to track coordinate system is used. Firstly, the Angle χ is rotated around the axis z_g, and then the Angle γ is rotated around the axis y_k. At this time, the ground coordinate system and track coordinate system will completely coincide (see Fig. 1).

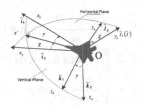

Fig. 1. Conversion diagram from ground coordinate system to track coordinate system

2.2 Kinematics Equation of UAV Center of Mass

Taking the Track Coordinate System as the benchmark and taking the movement direction of the center of mass of the aircraft as the Ox_k axis, the projection of the velocity vector on the three axes is $[V, 0, 0]^T$, and the flight speed is projected to the ground coordinate system:

$$
\begin{bmatrix} V_x \\ V_y \\ V_z \end{bmatrix}_g = L_{gk} \begin{bmatrix} V \\ 0 \\ 0 \end{bmatrix} = L_{kg}^T \begin{bmatrix} V \\ 0 \\ 0 \end{bmatrix} \tag{2}
$$

In formula (1), L_{kg} is the transformation matrix from the ground coordinate system to the velocity coordinate system, and its specific form is:

$$
L_{kg} = \begin{bmatrix} \cos \gamma \cos \chi & \cos \gamma \sin \chi & -\sin \gamma \\ \sin \gamma \sin \mu \cos \chi - \cos \mu \sin \chi & \sin \gamma \sin \mu \sin \chi + \cos \mu \cos \chi & \sin \mu \cos \gamma \\ \sin \gamma \cos \mu \cos \chi + \sin \mu \sin \chi & \sin \gamma \cos \mu \sin \chi - \sin \mu \cos \chi & \cos \mu \cos \gamma \end{bmatrix} \tag{2}
$$

Substituting formula (2) into formula (1), considering that the velocity component of the ground coordinate system is the differential of the corresponding aircraft space coordinate axis, the UAV centroid motion equation can be obtained:

$$
\begin{cases} \dfrac{dx_g}{dt} = V \cos \gamma \cos \chi \\ \dfrac{dy_g}{dt} = V \cos \gamma \sin \chi \\ \dfrac{dz_g}{dt} = V \sin \gamma \end{cases} \tag{3}
$$

2.3 UAV Motion Equation

The UAV motion model not only needs the UAV centroid motion equation to describe the UAV position information in space, but also needs three force equations to describe the UAV forces. The equation of state describing the stress on the UAV is as follows:

$$
\begin{cases} \dot{V} = g\left(\dfrac{\eta P - D}{m} - \sin \gamma\right) \\ \dot{\gamma} = \dfrac{g}{V}(n_z \cos \mu - \cos \gamma) \\ \dot{\chi} = \dfrac{g}{V \cos \gamma} n_z \sin \mu \end{cases} \tag{4}
$$

In formula (4), $\dot{V}$ represents the rate of change of UAV speed, that is the magnitude of acceleration; V is the UAV rate; η is the thrust coefficient, the value is between 0 and 1; P is the maximum thrust that the UAV can achieve, which is the same as the speed direction; D is the resistance, including air resistance, downwash resistance, shock wave resistance, etc.; g is the local gravitational acceleration; $\dot{\gamma}$ is the change rate of the track inclination; γ is the size of the track inclination; n_z is the normal overload, let the longitudinal overload $U_1 = n_z \cos\mu$ and the lateral overload $U_2 = n_z \sin\mu$; μ is the aircraft roll angle; $\dot{\chi}$ is the change rate of the aircraft track declination angle, and χ is the aircraft track declination angle.

Simultaneous formula (3) and formula (4) can obtain the three-degree-of-freedom motion model of UAV. It can be known from the kinematic model of UAV that when the three physical quantities of UAV thrust, normal overload and roll angle are determined, the values of track inclination γ, track declination χ and speed V are given by Numerical integration can obtain the variation law of these three values with time, and then the spatial position coordinates (x, y, z) of the three axes of the UAV can be obtained, and finally the motion trajectory of the UAV can be obtained. Therefore, set the state vector of the UAV is $X = [x, y, z, V, \gamma, \chi]^T$ and the control vector is $u = [P, U_1, U_2]^T$.

3 UAV Attack Positions Occupy the Guide Optimization Indicator Solution

3.1 Design of Optimization Indicators for Attack Positions Occupation Guidance

In the process of air combat, the tail attack is the ideal attack state in the air combat confrontation, and the tail attack is the most unfavorable situation for oneself. According to the air combat situation on the battlefield, our UAV need to reasonably choose to attack the target or avoid the target. When our UAV is at an advantage, we need to reasonably adjust the attack angle and attack distance according to the battlefield conditions to achieve the conditions for rear-end attack. When our UAV is at a disadvantage, we also need to adjust its posture and position to avoid the attack of enemy fighters. Therefore, the optimization index can be divided into the attack optimization index set and the avoidance optimization index set.

Attack Optimization Index
Angle Optimization of Attack Index. When our UAV is in an attack advantage, and the enemy target is within our attack range, but the attack angle does not meet the attack conditions, select the angled attack indicator guides our UAV to occupy a position in an advantageous attack position. The specific form of the angle attack indicator is as follows.

$$J_{\min} = \int_{t_0}^{t_f} (\cos\alpha - \cos\beta)dt \tag{5}$$

$$\cos\beta = \frac{r_{AB} \cdot V_B}{|r_{AB}| \cdot |V_B|} \tag{6}$$

In the above two formulas α is the target entry angle that the UAV expects to fly around; β is the target entry angle; r_{AB} is the displacement vector between the two aircraft; V_B is the enemy target velocity vector; $|V_B|$ The speed of the enemy target. The optimized guidance amount calculated from the angle-optimized attack index makes the entry angle of our UAV satisfy the tail-end attack condition.

Distance Optimization of Attack Index. When our UAV is in an attack advantage, and the enemy's attack angle satisfies the tail attack condition, the distance attack index is 5 adopted so that the attack distance also meets the attack condition. The specific form of the distance attack indicator is as follows.

$$J_{min} = \int_{t_0}^{t_f} |r_{AB}| dt \tag{7}$$

In formula (7), J_{min} represents the established optimized guidance index; $t_0 \sim t_f$ represents the target trajectory prediction extrapolation time; r_{AB} is the displacement vector between our fighter and the enemy target. The optimal guidance amount is calculated from the distance-optimized attack index, so that our UAV maneuver adjustment can reach the condition of the attack distance behind the tail.

Avoid Optimization Index

Angle Optimization of Avoid Index. When the enemy target has an attack advantage and the attack angle meets the attack conditions, in order to reduce the risk of being hit, our UAV needs to be out of the state of being attacked, and the design angle avoidance index is as follows.

$$J_{min} = \int_{t_0}^{t_f} (1 - \cos \beta) dt \tag{8}$$

In formula (8), $t_0 \sim t_f$ represents the target trajectory prediction extrapolation time; β is the target entry angle. By solving the above-mentioned evasion index, the optimized guidance amount is obtained, so that our UAV can increase the entry angle to avoid the enemy's attack.

Distance Optimization of Avoid Index. When the enemy UAV has an attack advantage and the attack distance satisfies the tail attack condition, our UAV needs to quickly move away from the enemy target to destroy the attack distance condition. The distance avoidance indicator is designed as follows.

$$J_{min} = \int_{t_0}^{t_f} (|r_{AB}| - D)^2 dt \tag{9}$$

In formula (9), $|r_{AB}|$ is the displacement between our fighter jets and the enemy fighter jets; D is the expected flying around distance or avoidance distance. The optimal control algorithm is used to solve this index to obtain the corresponding optimal guidance amount, so that our UAV can avoid enemy attacks by increasing the distance between the two aircraft.

3.2 UAV Flight Performance Constraint Operator

In the actual air combat process, compared with manned aircraft, UAV have better aircraft performance and better maneuvering performance, but different UAV have their flight performance constraints, that is, UAV perform maneuvering actions. The maximum thrust that can be achieved, the maximum overload, etc.

In the calculation process of the optimal control constraint gradient method, the constraints such as flight speed and flight overload caused by the performance of the UAV can be ignored, and the calculation is still carried out according to the initial control amount., the obtained control variable is controlled within a reasonable range through the constraint operator, and the control variable within a reasonable range is used as the initial control variable for the next iteration, and the control variable tends to converge after repeated iterations. Set UAV flight performance constraints including UAV speed V, speed change rate ΔV, UAV thrust P, UAV normal overload n_z, and UAV roll angle change rate $\Delta \mu$ and other constraints, the specific settings are as follows.

$$\begin{cases} V_{\min} \leq V \leq V_{\max} \Delta V \leq \Delta V_{\max} \\ 0 \leq P \leq_{\max} n_z \leq n_{z \max}, \Delta \mu \leq \Delta \mu_{\max} \end{cases} \tag{10}$$

In the above formula, the subscripts "max" and "min" represent the upper and lower bounds of the corresponding variables.

3.3 Constrained Gradient Algorithm Based on Optimal Control

The core idea of the constrained gradient method is that for a controlled object in the form of a differential equation, given its initial state, transversal conditions, and critical state conditions that the controlled object can achieve, calculate its performance index within a certain period of time. The optimal control vector for the minima.

Constrained Gradient Algorithm Flow. In the process of solving the optimization index with the constrained gradient method, the input to the algorithm is the state information of our UAV and the enemy UAV, and the state information of the target is predicted by the target trajectory prediction model [6]. At the beginning of each solution cycle, we need to update the UAV's initial guidance, including the UAV's overload and thrust coefficient, and use the updated guidance as the initial control for the next solution, and then according to the UAV's motion model and optimization index set are used to establish the Hamilton function and solve the co-state equation. Runge-Kutta methods are used to solve the numerical solution of the state equation and the co-state equation. The gradient vector is inversely derived from the fitting curve to modify the guidance amount, and iteratively iterates until the guidance amount tends to converge, output the optimal control guidance amount, and input the obtained optimal control guidance amount into the UAV kinematics model to realize the attack positions to occupy guidance optimization of the UAV. The specific flow of the algorithm implementation is shown in the figure (see Fig. 2).

Optimization Index Solution Steps. The designed optimization index is substituted into the optimal control constraint gradient solution algorithm, and the optimization occupancy guidance index of UAV is solved in real time. The solution steps are as follows.

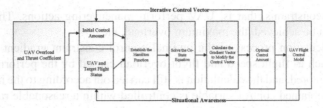

Fig. 2. Optimal control constraint gradient algorithm flow

Step1. Establish the Hamilton function, combine the state equation of UAV and the optimization index established in the air combat situation, and establish the Hamilton function of the optimization index.

$$H = J_{\min} + \lambda_1 V \cos \gamma \cos \chi + \lambda_2 V \cos \gamma \sin \chi + \lambda_3 V \sin \gamma + \lambda_4 \left(\frac{P-D}{m} - g \sin \gamma \right)$$
$$+ \lambda_5 \frac{g}{V} (n_z \cos \mu - \cos \gamma) + \lambda_6 \frac{g}{V \cos \gamma} n_z \sin \mu$$

$$(11)$$

Step2. Integrate the state equation, given an initial control vector $U^k(t) = U^0(t)$ and initial state information $X(t_0)$, through the fourth-order Runge-Kutta methods in the time t_0 to t_f, integrate the state equation forward, and obtain the state vector $X^k(t)$.

Step3. Integrate the state equation, Solve the co-state equation, and obtain the partial derivative of each state variable in the Hamilton function H to obtain the co-state equation corresponding to each state variable.

$$\dot{\lambda}_1 = -\frac{\partial H}{\partial x} \cdot \dot{\lambda}_2 = -\frac{\partial H}{\partial y} \cdot \dot{\lambda}_3 = -\frac{\partial H}{\partial z} \cdots \dot{\lambda}_6 = -\frac{\partial H}{\partial \chi} \qquad (12)$$

Step4. To solve the costate vector, the control vector $U^k(t)$, the terminal value $\lambda(t_f)$ and the state vector $X^k(t)$ obtained from the transversal condition are reversely integrated from the time to be solved t_f to t_0 through the fourth-order Runge-Kutta methods, find the co-state vector $\lambda^k(t)$.

Step5. calculate the gradient vector g^k of the Hamilton function H to the control Solve the gradient vector and vector U.

$$g^k = \left(\frac{\partial H}{\partial U} \right)_k \qquad (13)$$

Step6. To modify the control vector, use the one-dimensional optimization method (0.618) to determine the step size factor τ, and modify the control vector.

$$U^{k+1}(t) = U^k(t) - \tau g^k \qquad (14)$$

Step7. Loop the output control variable, make ε less than a certain minimum value, calculate whether the control vector $U^{k+1}(t)$ satisfies the following output conditions, and output if it satisfies, otherwise return to Step 2, and use the control vector $U^{k+1}(t)$ as the initial control variable for the next settlement, so that analogy.

$$\left| \frac{J(U^{k+1}) - J(U^k)}{J(U^k)} \right| < \varepsilon \tag{15}$$

$$\left\| g^k \right\| < \varepsilon \tag{16}$$

4 Simulation and Analysis

4.1 UAV's Attack Mission Air Combat Simulation Experiment

Angle Optimization Attack Simulation Experiment. To set the initial battlefield situation information, the red and blue sides use the same dynamic model, and the two sides have the same maneuverability. The red-side UAV uses the optimized occupancy positions guidance method proposed in this paper to control the flight, while the blue-side UAV is controlled by a maneuvering library algorithm based on expert experience according to the air combat situation. The initial state information of both parties is shown in Table 1.

Table 1. Initial state information table.

UAV	X(m)	Y(m)	Z(m)	Speed(m/s)	Yaw(°)
Red	10000	−8000	6000	300	0
Blue	10000	2000	6000	300	0

In the initial battlefield situation, the attack distance of the Red UAV meets the attack conditions, but the attack angle does not meet the attack requirements, so the angle attack index is used to calculate the guidance amount. The figure shows the simulation diagram of the 3D trajectory of UAV's 1V1 air combat (see Fig. 3).

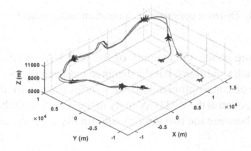

Fig. 3. Angle optimization simulation attack trajectory plot

As shown in figure of the simulation trajectory, at the beginning of the air combat confrontation, the blue UAV performed a jump maneuver to try to reduce the attack advantage of the Red UAV; in the mid-air combat, the blue UAV performed a snake-like maneuver to get rid of the Red UAV pursued; In the late stage of the close air combat, the blue UAV performed maneuvers such as left combat turns and dives to try to get rid of the Red UAV's tail-chasing situation. The simulation results show that under the guidance of the angle optimization control, the Red UAV can adjust the attack angle in time in a highly dynamic air combat environment, follow the maneuvering changes of the blue UAV, and then continue to occupy the rear attack position of the blue UAV, forming a attack positions occupancy advantage, which constitutes favorable offensive conditions.

Distance Optimization Attack Simulation Experiment. Set the initial situation information of the battlefield. The initial state information of the red and blue parties is shown in Table 2.

Table 2. Initial state information table.

UAV	X(m)	Y(m)	Z(m)	Speed(m/s)	Yaw(°)
Red	20000	130000	5000	300	90
Blue	20000	20000	3000	300	−90

On the premise that the attack angle satisfies the attack conditions, the distance optimization attack index is used to calculate the flight control quantity, and guide the Red UAV to quickly move into the distance between the blue UAV and the blue UAV. The simulation diagram of UAV air combat trajectory is shown in figure (see Fig. 4).

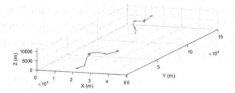

Fig. 4. Distance optimization simulation attack trajectory plot

As shown in figure above, the azimuth of the Red UAV relative to the Blue UAV clearly meets the attack conditions, but the distance between the two is too far to exceed the attack range. The distance optimization attack index is used to calculate and optimize the guidance amount, control the Red UAV to fly in the direction of the blue UAV, quickly shorten the distance between the two aircraft, and finally meet the attack distance index requirements.

4.2 UAV's Avoid Mission Air Combat Simulation Experiment

Angle Optimization Avoid Simulation Experiment. Set the initial battlefield situation information, the dynamic model used by the red and blue parties is the same, and the mobility performance of the two parties is the same. The initial state information of the red and blue parties is shown in Table 3.

Table 3. Initial state information table.

UAV	X(m)	Y(m)	Z(m)	Speed(m/s)	Yaw(°)
Red	10000	0	8000	300	−90
Blue	10000	30000	6000	300	−90

From the initial situation information, it can be seen that the blue plane satisfies the attack angle condition relative to the red UAV, so the angle avoidance index is used to calculate the guidance amount to control the red UAV to avoid the angle. The UAV air combat trajectory simulation diagram is shown in figure (see Fig. 5).

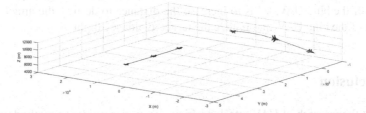

Fig. 5. Angle optimization simulation avoid trajectory plot

As shown in the figure above, in the initial stage of air combat, the red UAV is in front of the blue UAV, and the blue UAV meets the attack angle requirement, but the attack distance condition has not yet been reached. The angle avoidance index is used to calculate the flight control amount, and the red UAV is guided to fly horizontally, so as to destroy the angle attack conditions of the blue UAV, and finally avoid the target attack.

Distance Optimization Avoid Simulation Experiment. In order to carry out the trajectory simulation of the distance avoidance index solution, the initial battlefield situation information is set, and the initial state information of the red and blue parties is shown in Table 4.

From the initial state information, the distance between the blue machine and the red UAV satisfies the attack distance condition, so the distance avoidance index is used to guide the red UAV to quickly open the distance to escape. The UAV 1V1 air combat trajectory simulation diagram is shown in in figure (see Fig. 6).

Table 4. Initial state information table.

UAV	X(m)	Y(m)	Z(m)	Speed(m/s)	Yaw(°)
Red	−5000	−5000	4500	300	0
Blue	5000	5000	4500	300	135

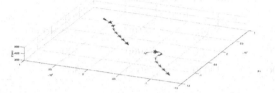

Fig. 6. Distance optimization simulation avoid trajectory plot

As shown in the figure above, the blue-side UAV flies straight toward the red-side UAV. The attack angle does not meet the attack conditions, but the attack distance meets the attack conditions. The distance avoidance index is used to solve and optimize the guidance amount, and the red UAV is controlled to accelerate the flight in the opposite direction of the blue UAV, so as to increase the distance to destroy the attack distance condition of the blue UAV, and realize the target avoidance flight.

5   Conclusion

Aiming at the research of UAV attack position occupation guidance method, this paper proposes an optimal control index solution method based on constrained gradient method to realize UAV autonomous maneuver decision. In 1V1 air combat simulation, our UAV makes reasonable and effective maneuvers according to the situation of enemy UAV immediately, and obtains the attack position advantage.

References

1. Evdokimenkov, V.N., Kozorez, D.A., Rabinskiy, L.N.: Unmanned aerial vehicle evasion manoeuvres from enemy aircraft attack. J. Mech. Behav. Mater. **30**(1), 87–94 (2021)
2. Zhou, H, Zhang, X., Zhang, Z.: Reinforcement learning technology for air combat confrontation of unmanned aerial vehicle. In: International Conference on Computer Graphics, Artificial Intelligence, and Data Processing (ICCAID 2021). SPIE, 12168: 454–459 (2022)
3. Pope, A.P., Ide, J.S., Mićović, D., et al.: Hierarchical reinforcement learning for air-to-air combat. In: 2021 International Conference on Unmanned Aircraft Systems (ICUAS). IEEE, 275–284 (2021)
4. Zhang, Y., Li J., Hu, B., Zhang, J.: An improved PSO algorithm for solving multi-uav cooperative reconnaissance task decision-making problem. In: Proceedings of 2016 IEEE/CSAA International Conference on Aircraft Utility Systems(AUS). 434–437 (2016)

5. Zhao, Y., Wang, X., Kong, W., Shen, L., Jia, S.: Decision making of UAV for Tracking Moving Target via Information Geometry. In: 2016 35th Chinese Control Conference (CCC), pp. 552–558 (2016)
6. Guanglei, M., Mingzhe, Z., Haiyin, P., Huimin, Z.: Threat assessment method of two aircraft formation based on Cooperative tactical identification. Syst. Eng. Electron. Technol. 42(10): 2285–2293 (2020)
7. Virtanen, K., Raivio, T., Hamalainen. R.P.: Modeling pilot's sequential maneuvering decisions by a multistage influence diagram. J. Guidance Control Dyn. 27(4) (2012)
8. Lin, Z., Ming'an, T., Wei, Z., Shengyun, Z.: Sequential maneuvering decisions based on multi-stage influence diagram in air combat. J. Syst. Eng. Electron. 18(3)(2007)
9. Virtanen, K., Karelahti, J., Raivio, T.: Modeling air combat by a moving horizon influence diagram game. J. Guid. Control Dyn. 29(5) (2006)
10. Lin, Z., Ming'an, T., Wei, Z.: Application of impact map countermeasures in multi-aircraft coordinated air combat. J. BUAA, 04):450–453. https://doi.org/10.13700/j.bh.1001-5965 (2007)
11. McGrew, J.S., How, J.P., Williams, B.. Air-combat strategy using approximate dynamic programming. J. Guid. Control. Dyn. 33(5), 1641–1654 (2010)
12. Ma, Y.F., Ma, X.L., Song, X.: A case study on air combat decision using approximated dynamic programming. Math. Probl. Eng. 4 (2004)
13. Li, H.F., Yi, W.F., Cheng, X.M.: Target tracking control algorithm based on approximate dynamic programming. J. Beijing Univ. Aeronaut. Astronaut. 03, 597–605 (2019)
14. Huang, C.Q., Zhao, K.X., Hang, B.J., Wei, Z.L.: Maneuvering decision-making method of UAV based on approximate dynamic programming. J. Electron. Inf. Technol. 40(10), 2447–2452 (2018)
15. Xu, G.D,, Lv, C., Wang, G.H., et al.: Research on UCAV autonomous air combat maneuvering decision-making based on bi-matrix game. Ship Electron. Eng. 37(11), 24–28–39 (2017)
16. Chang, Y., Jiang, C.S., Chen, Z.W.: Decision-making based on fuzzy neural network for air combat of multi-aircraft against multitarget. Electron. Opt. Control 18(04), 13–17 (2011)
17. Gao, Y.Y., Yu, M.J., Han, Q.S., Dong, X.J.: Air combat maneuver decision-making based on improved symbiotic organisms search algorithm. J. Beijing Univ. Aeronaut. Astronaut. 03, 429–436 (2019)
18. Rodin, E.Y., Lirov, Y., Mittnik, S., et al.: Artificial intelligence in air combat games. Comput. Math. Appl. 3(1):261–274 (1987)
19. Imado, F., Kuroda, T.: Family of local solutions in a missile aircraft differential game. J. Guid. Control. Dyn. 34(2), 583–591 (2015)
20. Park, H., Lee, B.Y., Tahk, M.J., et al.: Differential game based air combat maneuver generation using scoring function matrix. Int. J. Aeronaut. Space Sci. 17(2), 204–213 (2016)
21. Huang, C.Q., Dong, K.S., Huang, H.Q., et al.: Autonomous air combat maneuver decision using Bayesian inference and moving horizon optimization. J. Syst. Eng. Electron. 29(01), 86–97 (2018)

The Variation Characteristic of EMG Signal Under Varying Active Torque: A Preliminary Study

Boxuan Zheng, Xiaorong Guan[✉], Zhong Li, Shuaijie Zhao, Zheng Wang, and Hengfei Li

School of Mechanical Engineering, Nanjing University of Science and Technology, Nanjing 210094, China
gxr@njust.edu.cn

Abstract. Surface Electromyography (sEMG) or EMG contains a large amount of information about human kinematics and kinetics, and has been applied in different working environments. Devices like exoskeletons, smart bracelet performs better with information from EMG introduced into the system. For example, some rehabilitation exoskeletons designed for subjects suffered from nerve injuries are controlled under the strategy called "assist-as-needed". In these studies, various methods, especially machine learning, have been used to establish a large number of nonlinear relationships between EMG and kinematics, as well as kinetics. However, some conditions that have not been studied before but occur in the system will lead to errors in the overall response of the control system. In this paper, human muscle tissue is regarded as a device with input and output responses, the relationship between the least squares slope of AEMG (Averaged EMG) and the current change in muscle contraction torque ΔT is studied when the torque generated by muscle contraction is T, the joint angle is θ, and the joint movement angular velocity is ω. The established relationship provides a potential closed-loop EMG control pathway from human to machine for human-machine interaction devices.

Keywords: Electromyogram · Human-machine interface · Muscle biomechatronics response equation

1 Introduction

Surface electromyography (sEMG) or EMG is a technique concerned with the recording and analysis of myoelectric signals and is an essential element in human-robot collaboration systems, as well as human-machine interfaces. It's influenced by physiological variations in the state of muscle fiber membranes [1]. At present, a variety of EMG control equipment has been developed, such as: exoskeleton based on EMG control, EMG control bracelet (the company has been acquired by Google) and so on [2]. Especially exoskeleton, since the appearance of the concept, relative control methods have always been an extremely important part. From the initial control method by increasing the closed loop system sensitivity [3] to EMG based control [2], EEG based control [4] and

© The Author(s), under exclusive license to Springer Nature Switzerland AG 2022
H. Liu et al. (Eds.): ICIRA 2022, LNAI 13457, pp. 722–730, 2022.
https://doi.org/10.1007/978-3-031-13835-5_65

even EMG-EEG based control, in this process, the human-machine cooperation performance or human-machine coupling of the exoskeleton has been greatly improved. But there is still considerable room for the improvement of human-machine collaboration.

In 2003, Kazuo Kiguchi et al. proposed a neuro-fuzzy controller [5]. Then in 2008, they [6] applied the proposed neuro-fuzzy controllers to a 3-DOF upper limb assist device, among which each neuro-fuzzy controller was established based on experiment results in advance. The relationship between EMG and torque generated by human arm changes a lot at different joint positions, so it's established according to joint position. In 2012, the neuro-fuzz controller in the original scheme [7] was improved considering the different joint positions and was applied into a 7-DOF upper limb power-assist exoskeleton. In this scheme, the EMG control part first takes the exoskeleton joint angle and predetermined 16-channel EMG signals as input. Among it, the joint angle determines the selection of the neuro-fuzzy matrix, so that the formula for estimating the joint torque through the EMG signals corresponds to the changes in the joint angle, which leads to the difference in anatomical muscle output properties. This is because that under different motion postures, the joint angle positions are different, and the same muscle has different effects even though with the same activation degree. Finally, use the dynamic formula to calculate the torque required by each joint motor. In the way mentioned above, the human-machine cooperation is implemented.

In 2018, Tatsuya Teramae, etc. proposed an EMG-based optimal control framework for a new type of rehabilitation exoskeleton by AAN (Assist-As-Needed) control strategy based on model prediction control (MPC) method. This framework is established under a linear torque estimation model proposed by Kazuo Kiguchi, etc. in 2012 [8]. In 2019, Zhang Lei, etc. [9] mapped the EMG signals with respect to the joint angles by a nonlinear relationship so as to estimate the movement of upper limb. The control methods mentioned above established the relationship between EMG signal and human muscle torque output or joint angel velocity by means of machine learning, but the influence of power-assist disturbances on EMG signal has not yet been considered for the time being. Related research has attracted a group of researchers. Similar researches are [10, 11].

Jacob A. George et al. [12] tried to solve this problem by means of data-driven. They first set 5 assist levels, 8-channel EMG signals from each leg and the hip joint torque generated by the exoskeleton system were acquired under various assist levels in the experiment. Then relationship between the EMG signals and the torque generated by the human body under different assist levels is established through the KF and CNN convolutional neural networks. Through the analysis of the collected data, researchers came to several qualitative conclusions, including the degree of influence of exoskeleton assist changes on EMG signals and kinetics, as well as several methods of training nonlinear mapping models by machine learning methods.

This paper contains two parts, firstly it solves the problem mentioned above in a brand new approach. In the experiment, the simple movement of elbow flexion and extension is selected, and different torque deficits ΔT (torque that is needed to implement determined movement of human-machine system but not satisfied), angular velocity of the joint rotation ω, joint angle θ when the torque T provided by the human body changes and T are realized through a specially designed experimental device. Then relationship between the least squares slope of the EMG signal smoothed by a time window of 100 ms was explored, the result was called the muscle biomechatronics response equation.

2   Experiment

2.1   Objects

One subject (one male, age: 27) without any known neural or muscular disorders were recruited in this study. No strenuous activity in the past week, no muscle soreness, discomfort and other symptoms.

2.2   Experimental Equipment

In the experiment, the Cometa PicoEMG surface EMG acquisition system (the sampling frequency is 2000 Hz) was used to acquire the original EMG signals of the targeted muscle (raw EMG signals were first filtered using 20–250 Hz butterworth bandpass filter, then remove baseline offsets of the output, as well as the acceleration signal, acting as an action trigger.

In order to simulate the change of external resistance torque, a simulation device is specially designed, as shown in Fig. 1(a). A weight that simulates the change of external resistance torque is connected to a small steel frame by a rope as a load with an acceleration trigger pasted on it as shown in Fig. 1(b).

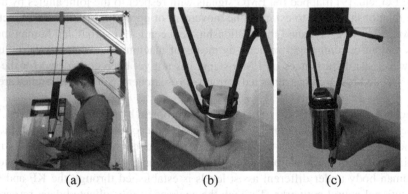

| (a) | (b) | (c) |

Fig. 1. (a) External resistance change simulation device. With the help of it, sudden change of external resistance change could be simulated precisely. (b) The weight of external resistance change simulation device and the acceleration sensor attached to it. (c) The spring used to trigger the weight when external resistance change is 0 N.m.

2.3   Preparation

Firstly, explain the experiment action to the subjects. In particular, the subjects should pay attention to following the beats to move the hand-held weight to a predetermined position during the experiment, rather than paying attention to the force generated by the muscles. This is to make the action in the experiment closer to the typical actions in daily life, such as grasping objects. These routines focus more on the end position rather than muscle contraction as in body building. In this way, the experiments performed are more consistent with that in daily life.

Then place the electrodes. Use a blade to remove the surface body hair, and then use a non-woven fabric dipped in 75% medical alcohol to wipe the skin where the EMG electrodes would be placed to ensure that the dirt affects signal acquisition is removed. Electrodes are supposed to be placed at the peak position of the short head of the biceps in flexion and the triceps.

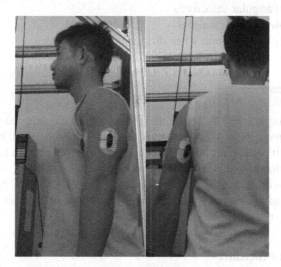

Fig. 2. Electrodes and sticking positions. There are 3 electrodes pasted on the arm.

Since this experiment used a single experimenter as the experimental object, MVC (Maximum Voluntary Contraction) was not performed. A metronome was used in the experiment to make it easy for the experimenter to control the angular velocity of his arm movement. The metronome was set to 200 bpm, see below for a more specific introduction.

2.4   Target Muscle Selection

Throughout the experiment, the elbow flexion-extension freedom was concerned only. Muscles related to elbow flexion-extension include biceps brachii, triceps brachii. Although the triceps brachii is not the main part, it plays an auxiliary role to guarantee stability. See Fig. 2 for electrodes and sticking positions. In fact, only EMG of biceps brachii is analyzed.

2.5 Variable Settings

During the rotation of elbow at a constant angular velocity (the angular velocity is constant, see the introduction in the following section for specific implementation), the parameters that can be controlled are:

1. The size of the torque deficit ΔT
   It is a positive value when the joint torque provided by the muscles related to the elbow joint is increased (simulating a decrease in the external assist torque), and a negative value otherwise.
2. Elbow rotation angular velocity ω
3. Position of power assist change θ
   That is, the angle of the joint when the power assist changes.
4. Human muscle contraction torque T at the moment before the torque changes
   Under different contraction torques T, the muscle biomechatronics response equation may be different.

In this experiment, $\omega = 1.745$ rad/s, and the subjects were required to complete 120° of elbow joint movement in 4 time intervals under the rhythm at 200 bpm. In this way, the angular velocity was controlled to be constant: $\theta = 90°$, at which position the upper arm is vertically downward, the forearm is horizontal; $T = 19.6$ N × moment arm A (holding a 2 kg weight), the assist change is set to 4.9 N × A, 9.8 N × A, 14.7 N × A, 19.6 N × A (add 0.5 kg weight each time). The value of A is set according to the length of forearm of the experimenter.

2.6 Experiment Procedure

According to 4 different levels of torque deficit, the experiment is divided into 5 similar parts, in which the initial load is 19.6N (2 kg), and the torque deficits are 0 N × A, 4.9 N × A, 9.8 N × A, 14.7 N × A and 19.6 N × A. In each group, the same movement is repeated 8 times. In order to reduce the effect of fatigue, there is a 10-min time interval between two groups. In the power-assist-unchanged group, a light spring, as shown in Fig. 1(c), was held by the subject's hand to trigger the weight and the pasted acceleration sensor when $\theta = 90°$. The use of a spring not only ensures the effective triggering of the weights, but also makes sure not to affect the subsequent joint movement when θ is 90°–120° in the same assist group, because the spring can be deformed.

In each group, the subject first faces the external resistance change simulation device, flex the elbow to 90° and the forearm should be level with the ground, then adjust the standing position and the height of weight until the weight just contact the palm. Thirdly, instructed by the metronome, start the movement after the initial beat, and then make sure the elbow has rotated to 30°, 60°, 90° and 120° when the next 4 beats are played. At the moment when contact with the weight, the subject should maintain the original angular velocity as much as possible. Finally, fully relax the arm, reset the position of weights and repeat the whole process 7 times.

3 Data Analysis

3.1 Pre-processing

During the experiment, a total of 40 (5 × 8) sets of motion data were collected. When analyzing, first select an appropriate threshold to judge the trigger point. Subsequently, the data were smoothed using full-wave rectification and averaged over a period of 100 ms [1] (moving average on a sample by sample basis of the past 100 ms).

$$AEMG = \frac{\sum_{i=1}^{N} v_i}{N} \tag{1}$$

N denotes the number of points selected to calculate AEMG of the EMG discrete time series.

8 discrete time series were extracted from the collected data in each group. The trigger point is manually set at 3 s, and each one extracted last 4 s. Finally, we get 40 of them.

3.2 The Differential

The motion of the human body is not as consistent as the motion of mechanism. Identical as the two motion processes are, there will be large or small differences in the preprocessed EMG signals. In the process of the experiment, in order to explore the impact of power-assist change (or torque deficit) on EMG, the experimental data of the power-assist-unchanged group and the power-assist-changed group are both needed. But "how to judge if one of the 8 data is useful for data analysis and which two data are supposed to be put together" turns out to be a problem that needs to be solved in the study of the muscle biomechatronics response equation.

For example, there are 8 data in the power-assist-unchanged group, and the same number as in the power-assist-changed group when T = 4.9 N × A. EMG signals in the first 3 s in these two data sets corresponds to the same action, that is, the subject does a curl at ω = 1.745 rad/s holding a 19.6 N weight. After 3 s, the power-assist changed in power-assist-changed group, but the subjects still maintained the same movement speed. Due to the randomness of EMG signals generated by human movement, we choose to analyze the difference between the EMG signals in the two data groups within 0–3 s, treat the two data with the smallest difference as exactly collected from the same action and analysis them. That's to avoid the influence by arbitrariness of EMG signals. To this end, a degree of difference calculation method is proposed.

Firstly, trend analysis of the EMG signals filtered by 100 ms average filtering is carried out, then a proper threshold is set manually to detect the first obvious higher value of the EMG signals, shown as the green and red solid dot in Fig. 3. Secondly one of the two data sets is used as benchmark to scale the other data set so that the size of contracted discrete time series values between the threshold point and the trigger point is the same. The solid green line representing the scaled part is the same size as the red one, while the dashed green line representing the part before scaling is larger.

Finally, calculate the difference (referenced from the definition of error energy in signal correlation).

$$Diff = \sqrt{\frac{\sum_{i=1}^{N}(a_i - b_i - average)^2}{N}}, i = 1, 2, ..., N \tag{2}$$

$$average = \frac{\sum_{i=1}^{N}(a_i - b_i)}{N} \tag{3}$$

N is the total number of discrete time series values from the threshold point to the trigger point after scaling, a_i and b_i are all discrete time series values from the threshold point to the trigger point in the power-assist-unchanged group and the power-assist-changed group respectively.

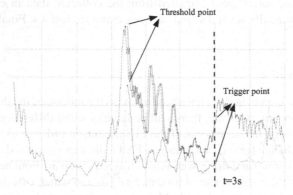

Threshold point

Trigger point

t=3s

Fig. 3. A data set pair with a lower degree of difference. Among them, the yellow part and the magenta part are power-assist-unchanged group and power-assist-changed group ($\Delta T = 9.8$ N × A) respectively, the red part and the green part represent the data after being scaled respectively. The green part is scaled with the red part as the scaling reference, and the green dot is the threshold point of the scaling, so it is with the red dot. (Color figure online)

3.3 Linear Fitting

Currently, no one has been engaged in research in this direction as far as know. After trying several features, it is found that selecting 40 ms AEMG after the trigger point and using the least squares method to perform linear fitting produces a better law. It is worth noting that, in order to simulate a real-time system, all AEMG time windows are within the time range from a period of time ago to the current moment. The specific process is as follows.

Firstly, values of difference of each two data groups collected are calculated in pairs, and the slope K after the least squares fitting of the data pairs with the lowest 3 values is selected, then the average value of them is taken as shown in Table 1.

As depicted in Fig. 4, under four power-assist-change levels, the average values of the slopes are K = −74.3, −26.3, 24.0,147.1 (mv/s), and K is roughly linear with power-assist change. When the power-assist change position of the elbow is 90°, the Human

Table 1. Slope K

Power-assist change level	Weight (kg)	Slope K (mv/s)			Average value (mv/s)
		Data pair 1	Data pair 2	Data pair 3	
1	0.5	−102.3	−20.5	−100.2	−74.3
2	1.0	−64.7	161.4	−175.5	−26.3
3	1.5	−32.6	84.2	20.4	24.0
4	2.0	174.3	102.4	164.6	147.1

muscle contraction torque is 6.468 N·m (19.6 N × A, A = 0.33 m) and the angular velocity is 1.745 rad/s, the EMG signal smoothed by 100ms time window, the functional relationship between the least squares slope and the power-assist change within 40 ms after the assist level changes is roughly as follows:

$$\Delta T = 0.024 \times K \qquad (4)$$

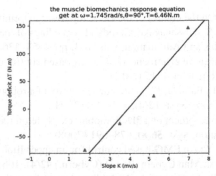

Fig. 4. The muscle biomechatronics response equation get at ω = 1.745 rad/s, θ = 90°, T = 6.46 N.m.

4 Conclusion

This paper preliminarily studies the relationship between the EMG signal feature and the change of muscle torque output under specific joint motion speed, specific muscle torque output and specific joint angle, and the muscle biomechatronics response equation under specific conditions is obtained. The established relationship would be subsequently used to improve the existing control methods of human-machine interaction equipment, to realize "Man-in-loop" better and to achieve a better human-machine interaction/human-machine collaboration performance. Due to the randomness of human motion, final correction torque calculated by this equation may not be completely accurate in value, but it can better improve the compliance in the process of human-computer interaction. Our team will conduct more in-depth research on the application of this equation and more experiments to improve the generalization performance of the equation, which would reveal the muscle biomechatronics response equation of different individuals under different joint motion speeds, different muscle torque outputs as well as different joint angles. In addition, the application of this equation relies on the detection of power-assist changes, so methods to detect sudden changes in muscle output is also worthy of further study. In conclusion, it is foreseeable that this equation would play a role in a wider range of human-machine interaction.

Acknowledgements. This work was supported in part by the China national defense basic scientific research No. JCKY2019209B003.

References

1. Konrad, P.: The ABC of EMG A Practical Introduction to Kinesiological Electromyography. Version 1.4 (2006). Noraxon INC [Электронный ресурс]. http://www.noraxon.com/docs/education/abc-of-emg.pdf
2. Bi, L., Guan, C.: A review on EMG-based motor intention prediction of continuous human upper limb motion for human-robot collaboration. Biomed. Signal Process. Control **51**, 113–127 (2019)
3. Kazerooni, H., et al.: On the control of the Berkeley lower extremity exoskeleton (BLEEX). In: Leal, J., Scheding, S., Dissanayake, G. (eds.) Proceedings of the 2005 IEEE International Conference on Robotics and Automation, vols. 1–4, pp. 4353–4360. IEEE (2005)
4. Meng, J., et al.: Noninvasive electroencephalogram based control of a robotic arm for reach and grasp tasks. Sci. Rep. **6**(1), 1–15 (2016)
5. Kiguchi, K., Tanaka, T., Fukuda, T.: Neuro-fuzzy control of a robotic exoskeleton with EMG signals. IEEE Trans. Fuzzy Syst. **12**(4), 481–490 (2004)
6. Kiguchi, K., et al.: Development of a 3DOF mobile exoskeleton robot for human upper-limb motion assist. Rob. Auton. Syst. **56**(8), 678–691 (2008)
7. Kiguchi, K., Hayashi, Y.: An EMG-based control for an upper-limb power-assist exoskeleton robot. IEEE Trans. Syst. Man Cybern. Part B (Cybern.) **42**(4), 1064–1071 (2012)
8. Teramae, T., Noda, T., Morimoto, J.: EMG-based model predictive control for physical human–robot interaction: application for assist-as-needed control. IEEE Robot. Autom. Lett. **3**(1), 210–217 (2017)
9. Lei, Z.: An upper limb movement estimation from electromyography by using BP neural network. Biomed. Signal Process. Control **49**, 434–439 (2019)
10. Wang, J., Liu, J., Zhang, G., Guo, S.: Periodic event-triggered sliding mode control for lower limb exoskeleton based on human–robot cooperation. ISA Trans. **123**, 87–97 (2022)
11. Qingcong, W., Chen, Y.: Development of an intention-based adaptive neural cooperative control strategy for upper-limb robotic rehabilitation. IEEE Robot. Autom. Lett. **6**(2), 335–342 (2021)
12. George, J.A., et al.: Robust torque predictions from electromyography across multiple levels of active exoskeleton assistance despite non-linear reorganization of locomotor output. Front. Neurorobot. **15** (2021)

A VPRNN Model with Fixed-Time Convergence for Time-Varying Nonlinear Equation

Miaomiao Zhang$^{(\boxtimes)}$ (ID) and Edmond Q. Wu (ID)

Department of Automation, Shanghai Jiao Tong University, Shanghai, China
mmzhang1997@163.com

Abstract. Robots are widely used in various engineering fields, and the solution to their trajectory tracking problem has attracted increasing attention. Such a problem can be typically transformed into a time-varying nonlinear equation (TVNE). For complex and high-precision robot trajectory tracking problems, a fast and low-error tracking solution is necessary. Therefore, a varying-parameter recurrent neural network (VPRNN) model with a modified power-type time-varying parameter is proposed for solving TVNE. An improved sign-bi-power function is selected for the activation function, then the VPRNN model achieves fixed-time convergence. Numerical comparisons with the general fixed-parameter recurrent neural network model are performed, which demonstrates the superiority of our VPRNN model. Besides, the proposed VPRNN model is successfully used to solve the trajectory tracking problem of a three-link robot, which shows its feasibility in practical applications.

Keywords: Varying-parameter recurrent neural network ·
Time-varying nonlinear equation · Fixed-time convergence · Robot
manipulator control

1 Introduction

The trajectory tracking problem of robots is hoping that through settings and optimization, robots can perform certain tasks more accurately, thereby reducing labor costs. Mathematically, the trajectory tracking problem of a robot can be translated into a time-varying nonlinear equation (TVNE). For static nonlinear equations, of course, linear equations can be used as a special case of it, different numerical methods have been devised in the past to solve them [1,6]. However, while these methods can efficiently solve static nonlinear equations, they are no longer suitable for solving TVNE because they do not meet the requirements of continuous real-time computation. Therefore, it is necessary to develop some efficient methods for solving the TVNE.

This work was supported in part by the National Natural Science Foundation of China under Grant 62171274 and Grant U1933125.

With the gradual deepening of research on deep learning, neural networks have been widely used in solving various mathematical problems due to their parallel processing characteristics. Among neural networks, the recurrent neural network (RNN) is a powerful one. For example, Wang et al. used a RNN model to solve the simultaneous linear equation [8]. However, when this RNN model is applied to solve the time-varying problems, the solutions can only approximately converge to the theoretical solution, which means that this model cannot find the true solution to the problem. Based on this, Zhang et al. proposed a special RNN model in [12], which can accurately find theoretical solutions to time-varying problems since the information of the time derivatives of parameters is introduced into this model. Their experiments show that this RNN model can reach exponential convergence, ensuring that the true solution to the time-varying problem can be found. But exponential convergence means waiting infinitely long to get the true solution, which is obviously not practical. Therefore, Li et al. proposed a finite-time convergence RNN model for the time-varying Sylvester equation in [4]. The fact that such a RNN model can achieve finite-time convergence during the solution process is mainly due to the design of the activation function. They propose a new activation function: sign-bi-power (SBP) function. The finite-time convergence of this RNN model means that the convergence time of the model has an upper bound, which is not only related to the parameters in the model but also positively related to the initial value of the error function. This shows that the upper bound of the convergence time may be estimated to be very large [7], which also leads to an inaccurate estimation of the upper bound of the convergence time. Therefore, some researchers have considered RNN models in which the convergence time does not depend on the initial values and only on the model parameters, in fact, this is called fixed-time convergence. Xiao et al. presented a novel RNN model which can achieve fixed-time convergence when solving the time-varying problems in [9]. This study breaks the research ice. A more general form of this novel RNN model was also investigated by Zhang et al. in [11].

Although the RNN models proposed in [9,11] have fixed-time convergence, they still have a shortcoming, that is, the design parameter in the aforementioned RNN model is always set to be a real and positive constant number. Since the design parameters are related to the convergence rate of the model, some scholars have proposed whether the fixed-value parameter can be replaced by a time-varying function and whether it is possible to improve the convergence performance of the model. To this end, Zhang et al. designed a novel varying-parameter RNN (VPRNN) model for solving the time-varying matrix equation in [14], which has a power-type time-varying design parameter. They show that such a VPRNN model can achieve super-exponential convergence when solving the time-varying matrix equation, which is obviously better than the previous fixed-parameter RNN (FPRNN) models. However, in practical applications, the convergence time of the model is the main criterion for measuring its quality, and the convergence time of such a VPRNN model is not given in [14].

Hence, this paper improves the VPRNN model by modifying the power-type time-varying design parameter, and such a VPRNN model achieves fixed-time convergence when solving TVNE. In this way, the robot trajectory tracking problem is also solved, which verifies the applicability and operability of our VPRNN model in practical applications.

2   Problem Formulation

In this paper, our task is to solve the following TVNE:

$$f(x(t), t) = 0, \tag{1}$$

where $x(t) \in \mathbb{R}^n$ is the unknown time-varying vector, t is the time, and $f(\cdot)$ is a nonlinear function. For the sake of research, we always assume that there is at least one theoretical solution $x^*(t)$ exists for the TVNE (1). Next, we will build the VPRNN model that solves TVNE (1).

2.1   Varying-Parameter RNN Model

From the construction theory of the VPRNN model, we can get the following design formula:

$$\dot{e}(t) = -\varphi(t)\Phi(e(t)) \tag{2}$$

where $e(t) \in \mathbb{R}^m$ is the error function and $\dot{e}(t)$ is its derivative with respect to time, $\varphi(t)$ is a time-varying design parameter, and $\Phi(\cdot) : \mathbb{R}^m \to \mathbb{R}^m$ is the activation function.

Then, for solving the TVNE (1), we design the following error function firstly:

$$e(t) = f(x(t), t).$$

In this way, according to the construction idea of the VPRNN model, as long as the error function $e(t)$ converges to zero, the solution of the TVNE (1) can be obtained.

Second, according to the design formula (2), we need to give the time derivative of the error function $e(t)$. Taking the derivative from both sides of the error equation, we have

$$\frac{de(t)}{dt} = \frac{\partial f}{\partial x}\frac{\partial x}{\partial t} + \frac{\partial f}{\partial t}. \tag{3}$$

Finally, as long as the error function $e(t)$ and the equation (3) are substituted into the design formula (2), the VPRNN model can be obtained:

$$\frac{\partial f}{\partial t}\dot{x}(t) = -\varphi(t)\Phi(f(x(t), t)) - \frac{\partial f}{\partial t}. \tag{4}$$

For the setting of the time-varying parameter $\varphi(t)$, Zhang *et al.* proposed the following power-type time-varying design parameter in [14]

$$\nu(t) = t^r + r,$$

where $r > 0$.

In this paper, we modify the above time-varying parameter and propose the following design parameter

$$\varphi(t) = \begin{cases} t^r + \frac{1}{r}, 0 < r \le 1 \\ t^r + r, \quad r > 1. \end{cases}$$

The reason for the above modification is to make the VPRNN model composed of the time-varying parameter $\varphi(t)$ to achieve fixed-time convergence, and the explanation for this will be seen in Sect. 3.

2.2   Fixed-Parameter RNN Model

In general RNN models, the design parameter is generally a fixed value, we call them fixed-parameter RNN models (FPRNNs). In order to highlight the superiority of our VPRNN model (4), here we also give the specific form of the FPRNN model.

First, we give the design formula of the FPRNN model:

$$\dot{e}(t) = -\beta\Phi(e(t)),$$

where β is the fixed-valued design parameter.

Then, similar to the construction process of the VPRNN model, we can get the following FPRNN model

$$\frac{\partial f}{\partial t}\dot{x}(t) = -\beta\Phi(f(x(t), t)) - \frac{\partial f}{\partial t}. \tag{5}$$

Obviously, it can be seen from the specific expressions of the VPRNN model (4) and the FPRNN model (5) that when the time-varying design parameter is set to a constant value, i.e., $\varphi(t) = \beta$, the VPRNN model (4) can reduce into the FPRNN model (5). Moreover, we also can find that the RNN model behaves differently under different activation functions $\Phi(\cdot)$. Regarding the choice of activation function $\Phi(\cdot)$, it is known that any odd function which is monotonically increasing can be used [2,3,5,10]. In this paper, we use the following improved sign-bi-power (ISBP) function [11]:

$$\phi(x) = (k_1|x|^\eta + k_2|x|^\omega)^k \text{sign}(x) + k_3 x, \tag{6}$$

with k, k_1, k_2, and $k_3 > 0$, $0 < k\eta < 1$, and $k\omega > 1$. In particular, the operation $\text{sign}(x)$ is defined as

$$\text{sign}(x) = \begin{cases} 1, & x > 0 \\ 0, & x = 0 \\ -1, & x < 0. \end{cases}$$

3   Fixed-Time Convergence of the VPRNN Model

In this section, the convergence of the VPRNN model (4) is discussed.

Theorem 1. *Given a solvable TVNE* (1), *if the VPRNN model* (4) *is used, then this model can converge in a fixed time*

$$t_{\max} = [\frac{1+r}{k_1(1-k\eta)} + \frac{1+r}{k_2(k\omega-1)}]^{\frac{1}{1+r}}, \tag{7}$$

where the parameters r, k, k_1, k_2, η, *and* ω *satisfy the preceding requirements.*

Proof. When the VPRNN model (4) is used to solve TVNE (1), we have

$$\dot{e}(t) = -\varphi(t)\psi(e(t))$$
$$= -\varphi(t)((k_1|e(t)|^\eta + k_2|e(t)|^\omega)^k \mathrm{sign}(e(t)) + k_3 e(t)).$$

To study the convergence time of the VPRNN model (4), a Lyapunov function $l_i(t) = |e_i(t)| \geq 0$ is set firstly, and then its time derivative satisfies that

$$\dot{l}_i(t) = \dot{e}_i(t)\mathrm{sign}(e_i(t))$$
$$= -\varphi(t)((k_1|e_i(t)|^\eta + k_2|e_i(t)|^\omega)^k + k_3|e_i(t)|) \tag{8}$$
$$= -\varphi(t)((k_1 l_i^\eta(t) + k_2 l_i^\omega(t))^k + k_3 l_i(t)).$$

When $0 < r \leq 1$, the time-varying design parameter is taken as $\varphi(t) = t^r + 1/r$, and thus from (8) we have

$$\dot{l}_i(t) = -(t^r + 1/r)((k_1 l_i^\eta(t) + k_2 l_i^\omega(t))^k + k_3 l_i(t))$$
$$\leq -t^r((k_1 l_i^\eta(t) + k_2 l_i^\omega(t))^k + k_3 l_i(t)). \tag{9}$$

Next, the convergence time of the VPRNN model (4) is given via the following two steps.

First, if the initial error satisfies $|e_i(0)| > 1$, we can find the time t_1 such that the error function satisfies $|e_i(t_1)| = 1$. From the inequalities (9), it follows:

$$\dot{l}_i(t) \leq -t^r k_2 l_i^{k\omega}(t),$$

i.e.,

$$l_i^{-k\omega}(t)\dot{l}_i(t) \leq -k_2 t^r. \tag{10}$$

To solve the differential inequality (10), it can simultaneously integrate from 0 to t_1 on both sides of it

$$\int_0^{t_1} l_i^{-k\omega}(t)\dot{l}_i(t)dt \leq \int_0^{t_1} -k_2 t^r dt,$$

i.e.,

$$\frac{1}{1-k\omega}(1 - l_i^{1-k\omega}(0)) \leq -\frac{k_2}{1+r}t_1^{1+r}.$$

Hence, we have

$$t_1 \leq \left[\frac{(1+r)(1 - l_i^{1-k\omega}(0))}{k_2(k\omega - 1)}\right]^{\frac{1}{1+r}}$$

$$\leq \left[\frac{1+r}{k_2(k\omega - 1)}\right]^{\frac{1}{1+r}},$$

since $0 < 1 - l_i^{1-k\omega}(0) < 1$.

Secondly, find the time t_2 such that the error function satisfies $|e_i(t_2)| = 0$. In this case, the inequalities (9) can be written as

$$l_i^{-k\eta}(t)\dot{l}_i(t) \leq -k_1 t^r. \tag{11}$$

Similarly, integrating from t_1 to t_2 on both sides of the inequality (11), it can be obtained that

$$t_2^{1+r} \leq t_1^{1+r} + \frac{1+r}{k_1(1 - k\eta)},$$

i.e.,

$$t_2 \leq \left(t_1^{1+r} + \frac{1+r}{k_1(1 - k\eta)}\right)^{\frac{1}{1+r}}$$

$$\leq \left[\frac{1+r}{k_1(1 - \eta)} + \frac{1+r}{k_2(k\omega - 1)}\right]^{\frac{1}{1+r}}$$

$$= t_{\max}.$$

So far, the fixed convergence time of the VPRNN model (4) when $r \leq 1$ is now proved.

When $r > 1$, the same method as above can be used to discuss the convergence time of the VPRNN model (4). It can be easily obtained that a clear upper bound of the convergence time of the VPRNN model (4) in this case $r > 1$ is also $t_{\max}$. Due to the limited space, we will not give detailed proof here. The proof is thus completed.

Remark 1. From the proof of Theorem 1, it can be found that only changing the time-varying parameter $\nu(t)$ to $\varphi(t)$, the value of the time-varying parameter of the VPRNN model (4) can always be greater than 1. In this way, the fixed-time convergence of the VPRNN model (4) is established when the parameter r satisfies $0 < r \leq 1$.

4   Numerical Experiments

A numerical example is proposed in this section to compare the convergence performance of the VPRNN model (4) and of the FPRNN model (5) in solving the TVNE (1).

In particular, the fixed-valued design parameter β of the FPRNN model (4) is set to $\beta = 1$ and the time-varying design parameter of the VPRNN model (4) is set to:

(i) $\varphi(t) = t^{1/3} + 3$; and $\nu(t) = t^{1/3} + 1/3$, if $r \le 1$;
(ii) $\varphi(t) = \nu(t) = t^2 + 2$, if $r > 1$.

Additionally, the parameters in ISBP activation function are set to $k = k_1 = k_2 = k_3 = 1$, $\eta = 1/3$, and $\omega = 2$. From Theorem 1, the fixed convergence time $t_{\max}$ of the VPRNN model (4) is thus 2.0868 s $(r = 1/3)$, and1.82 s $(r = 2)$.

For the numerical example, the following TVNE is considered

$$g(x(t), t) = \begin{pmatrix} \ln(x_1(t) - 1/(t+1)) \\ x_1(t)x_2(t) - 0.3\exp(3/(2t+2))\sin(t) \end{pmatrix},$$

where the unknown vector is $x(t) = [x_1(t), x_2(t)]^T \in \mathbb{R}^2$.

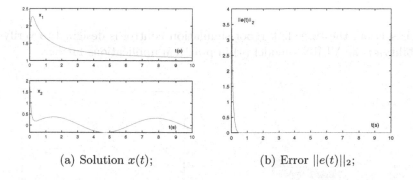

(a) Solution $x(t)$; (b) Error $\|e(t)\|_2$;

Fig. 1. The process of the VPRNN model (4) solving the TVNE, when the time-varying design parameter is set to $\varphi(t) = t^{1/3} + 3$.

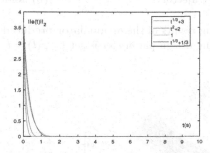

Fig. 2. The convergence of the error $\|e(t)\|_2$ produced by the VPRNN model (4) and FPRNN model (5) when solving the TVNE.

The simulation results are given in Fig. 1 and Fig. 2. As shown in Fig. 1(a), the solution found by the VPRNN model (4) composed of the time-varying design parameter $\varphi(t) = t^{1/3} + 3$ always changes with time, even if the initial state is randomly selected in $[-2, 2]^{2 \times 1}$. Obviously, this satisfies the requirement of a real-time solution. In addition, it can be seen from Fig. 1(b), the norm of the error function $||e(t)||_2$ can converge to zero in about 0.4 s, which is within the fixed convergence time. Similarly, when the time-varying design parameter is set to $\varphi(t) = t^2 + 2$, the results of the VPRNN model (4) are similar, and we will not give details. For comparison, we also solve this TVNE with the VPRNN model composed of the time-varying design parameter $\nu_1(t) = t^{1/3}+1/3$ and the FPRNN model. The convergence of the error norm $||e(t)||_2$ is given in Fig. 2. We can find that although the error norm $||e(t)||_2$ all can converge to zero, the VPRNN model (4) we proposed has a shorter convergence time than others. In general, these results are sufficient to demonstrate the effectiveness and advantages of our proposed VPRNN model (4) for solving TVNE.

5   Robot Manipulator Application

In this section, the three-link robot simulation control is designed to verify the feasibility of the VPRNN model (4) in practical applications further.

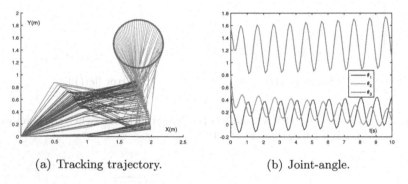

(a) Tracking trajectory.   (b) Joint-angle.

Fig. 3. The trace tracking results of the manipulator produced by the VPRNN model (4), when the time-varying design parameter is set to $\varphi(t) = t^{1/3} + 3$.

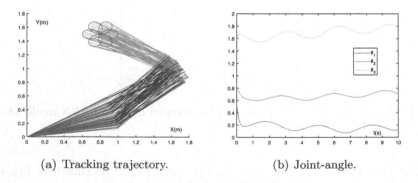

(a) Tracking trajectory.   (b) Joint-angle.

Fig. 4. The trace tracking results of the manipulator produced by the VPRNN model (4), when the time-varying design parameter is set to $\varphi(t) = t^2 + 2$.

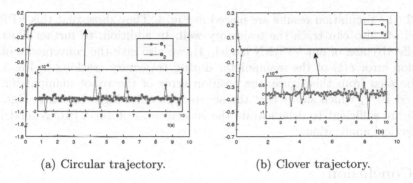

(a) Circular trajectory.   (b) Clover trajectory.

Fig. 5. The convergence of the tracking error produced by the VPRNN model (4) when using the manipulator to trace the circular trajectory and the clover trajectory.

For the trajectory tracking problem of the robot manipulator, the position level kinematics equation of it as follows [13]:

$$r_d(t) = y(\theta(t), t), \tag{12}$$

where $r_d(t)$ is the position vector of the desired path, $\theta(t)$ is the joint-angle vector of the manipulator, and $y(\cdot)$ is the forward kinematics nonlinear mapping of the manipulator.

Generally, the position level kinematics equation (12) of the manipulator is a time-varying linear equation. Thus, the trajectory tracking problem of the manipulator can be solved by the VPRNN model (4). According to the VPRNN model building process, we set the following error function:

$$e(t) = r_d(t) - y(\theta(t), t).$$

Then, the VPRNN model for the trajectory tracking problem of the robot manipulator is:

$$J(\theta(t))\dot{\theta}(t) = \dot{r}_d(t) - \varphi(t)\Phi(r_d(t) - y(\theta(t), t)), \tag{13}$$

where $J(\theta(t)) = \partial y(\theta(t), t)/\partial t$ is a Jacobian matrix, and $\dot{\theta}(t)$ and $\dot{r}_d(t)$ are the time derivative of $\theta(t)$ and $r_d(t)$, respectively.

In this simulation experiment, the three-link robot will track the circular trajectory and the clover trajectory on a two-dimensional plane, and the initial state is set to $[\pi/6; \pi/4; \pi/2]$.

All simulation results are placed in Figs. 3, 4 and 5. By observing Fig. 3(a), it can be concluded that when the time-varying design parameter is selected as $\varphi(t) = t^{1/3} + 3$, the manipulator controlled by the VPRNN model (4) can perfectly complete the trajectory tracking task. Moreover, from Fig. 3(b), the joint angles $\theta(t)$ of the robot manipulator change continuously, which shows that the trajectory planning scheme obtained by the VPRNN model (4) is reasonable and effective. Similarly, when the time-varying design parameter is set to $\varphi(t) =$

$t^2 + 2$, the simulation results are placed in Fig. 4. They show that this VPRNN model (4) also can track the trajectory well. In addition, to further illustrate the effectiveness of our VPRNN model (4), we also give the convergence of the position error $e(t)$ of the manipulator during trajectory tracking in Fig. 5. As can be seen from this figure, the position error of the robot manipulator has reached 10^{-6}, which shows that the accuracy is quite high. In short, Figs. 3, 4 and 5 are sufficient to demonstrate the effectiveness of our VPRNN model (4) in practical applications.

6   Conclusion

This paper presents an efficient varying-parameter recurrent neural network (VPRNN) model for solving the time-varying nonlinear equation (TVNE) via modifying the power-type time-varying design parameter. We proved that this VPRNN model activated by the improved sign-bi-power function possesses the fixed-time convergence when it is used to solve the TVNE. Some numerical experiments are performed to show the superiority of the proposed VPRNN model over the previous VPRNN models and the fixed-parameter RNN model. Furthermore, we applied this VPRNN model to solve the trajectory tracking problem of a three-link robot, showing its applicability in practice.

References

1. Argyros, I.K., Kansal, M., Kanwar, V.: On the local convergence of an eighth-order method for solving nonlinear equations. Ann. West Univ. Timisoara Math. Comput. Sci. **54**(1), 3–16 (2016)
2. Guo, D., Zhang, Y.: Zhang neural network for online solution of time-varying linear matrix inequality aided with an equality conversion. IEEE Trans. Neural Netw. Learn. Syst. **25**(2), 370–382 (2014)
3. Guo, D., Zhang, Y.: ZNN for solving online time-varying linear matrix-vector inequality via equality conversion. Appl. Math. Comput. **259**, 327–338 (2015)
4. Li, S., Chen, S., Liu, B.: Accelerating a recurrent neural network to finite-time convergence for solving time-varying Sylvester equation by using a sign-bi-power activation function. Neural Process Lett. **37**, 198–205 (2013)
5. Li, S., Li, Y.: Nonlinearly activated neural network for solving time-varying complex sylvester equation. IEEE Trans. Cybern. **44**(8), 1397–1407 (2014)
6. Ngoc, P.H.A., Anh, T.T.: Stability of nonlinear Volterra equations and applications. Appl. Math. Comput. **341**(15), 1–14 (2019)
7. Shen, Y., Miao, P., Huang, Y., Shen, Y.: Finite-time stability and its application for solving time-varying Sylvester equation by recurrent neural network. Neural Process Lett. **42**, 763–784 (2015)
8. Wang, J.: Electronic realisation of recurrent neural network for solving simultaneous linear equations. Electron. Lett. **28**(5), 493–495 (2002)
9. Xiao, L., Zhang, Y., Dai, J., Li, J., Li, W.: New noise-tolerant ZNN models with predefined-time convergence for time-variant Sylvester equation solving. IEEE Trans. Syst. Man Cybern. Syst. **51**(6), 3629–3640 (2021)

10. Xiao, L., Zhang, Y.: Different Zhang functions resulting in different ZNN models demonstrated via time-varying linear matrix-vector inequalities solving. Neurocomputing **121**, 140–149 (2013)
11. Zhang, M., Zheng, B.: Accelerating noise-tolerant zeroing neural network with fixed-time convergence to solve the time-varying Sylvester equation. Automatica **135**, 109998 (2022)
12. Zhang, Y., Ge, S.S.: Design and analysis of a general recurrent neural network model for time-varying matrix inversion. IEEE Trans. Neural Networks **16**(6), 1477–1490 (2005)
13. Zhang, Y., Yang, M., Chen, D., Li, W., Yan, X.: Proposing, QP-unification and verification of DLSM based MKE-IIWT scheme for redundant robot manipulators. In: Proceedings. 2017 IEEE 3rd Information Technology and Mechatronics Engineering Conference, pp. 242–248 (2017)
14. Zhang, Z., Zheng, L., Weng, J., Mao, Y., Lu, W., Xiao, L.: A new varying-parameter recurrent neural-network for online solution of time-varying Sylvester equation. IEEE Trans. Cybern. **48**(11), 3135–3148 (2018)

Surface Electromyography-Based Assessment of Muscle Contribution in Squatting Movements

Zheng Wang, Xiaorong Guan(✉), Zhong Li, Boxuan Zheng, Hengfei Li, and Yu Bai

School of Mechanical Engineering, Nanjing University of Science and Technology, Nanjing, China
gxr@njust.edu.cn

Abstract. The surface EMG signal is an electrophysiological signal generated by muscle contraction and collected by placing electrodes on the skin surface, which contains rich information about muscle function and state. The current exoskeleton design also urgently needs to evaluate the muscle contribution to assist joint or part movement, and this result will directly affect the theoretical design of the exoskeleton. From this perspective, in this paper, we measured the surface EMG data during squatting for 10 test subjects, and set up a control group and an test group, with each control group doing 10 continuous squats and each test group doing 10 continuous squats with a hand weight of 10 kg. In this paper, 60 sets of surface EMG data of squatting movements of 10 test subjects were analyzed, and the contribution of 12 different parts of muscles was evaluated based on covariance matrix, and it was obtained that rectus femoris contributed more than 15% of the 12 muscles without weight-bearing, but the contribution of rectus femoris decreased by 50% under weight-bearing condition, and the contribution of medial femoris and biceps femoris increased significantly to more than 15% of the overall.

Keywords: Surface EMG · Muscle contribution · Exoskeleton · Feature extraction · Covariance matrix

1 Introduction

Motor tasks are achieved by activating an appropriate set of muscles [1]. The number of recruited muscles depends on the task constraints of a precise movement [2]. The central nervous system (CNS) plays the main role in the motor control since it activates the precise muscle choosing both the magnitude and the timinimumsg of the activation [3].

The problem of redundant control is involved in the field of human motion control, whether for overall motion description or for local motion description of limbs. Muscle synergy theory suggests that the nervous system reduces the computational burden of redundant motor control by recruiting several muscles to synergize simultaneously in a modular control fashion [1]. The study of muscle contribution to precise movements helps to give significant theoretical support to exoskeletons in the design phase, which can make exoskeletons to power precise muscles and thus make exoskeletons do better in

H. Liu et al. (Eds.): ICIRA 2022, LNAI 13457, pp. 742–752, 2022.
https://doi.org/10.1007/978-3-031-13835-5_67

human-computer interaction. Therefore, muscle system theory is important for the study of exoskeletons in the field of human-computer interaction. The activation of muscle synergies, rather than each muscle individually, represents the most appealing idea to explain how the CNS bypasses the difficulty in controlling a large variety of muscles [4–7]. These modules are commonly named muscle synergies, which are defined as the coherent activation, in space and time, of a group of muscles. The brain generates electrical signals for motor intent, which are transmitted through the spinal cord to the body part to be controlled, stimulating the motor nerves in that part to control the muscle groups to produce movement. Muscles generate surface EMG signals during movement, and different movements correspond to the different surface EMG signals, which establishes a relationship between surface EMG signals and human movement [8].

Muscle synergies can be extracted by factorizing data acquired by surface electromyography (sEMG). Nonnegative matrix factorization [9] is the most widespread algorithm used for factorization, but it was demonstrated that similar results can be obtained by applying other methods, such as principal component analysis(PCA) or independent component analysis and inverse Gaussian [10, 11].

In this paper, the covariance matrix was used to analyze the sEMG data collected during the human squatting movement, so as to obtain the contribution of different muscles during the squatting process. Firstly, a control group and a test group were set up to obtain the different surface EMG data by changing the weight. Then the data were preprocessed and the mean absolute value (MAV), root mean square (RMS), mean power frequency (MPF), and median frequency (MF) were extracted. Finally, the data were analyzed for each of the four different eigenvalues to obtain the muscle contributions during squatting and the eigenvalues that more easily reflect this feature, and to mark the muscles with a greater increase in the muscle contributions after weight-bearing, which provides theoretical support for subsequent exoskeleton design and human-computer interaction analysis of the exoskeleton.

2   Materials and Methods

2.1   Selection of Acquisition Equipment

The test equipment selected in this paper is the wave plus system. The following figure shows the typical wave plus components (Fig. 1).

Wave Plus system is an innovative multi-channel wireless surface electromyographic system with accelerometers. Wave Plus is a system for the data collection of biologic signals; the main system feature is the absence of cables between the transmitters on the patient and the data receiver/recording unit. This allows the acquisition of EMG, accelerometer signal and inertial data while the patient is free to move. This feature is very useful for clinical and scientific applications, for example in pathologic gait analysis or in rehabilitation. Low impassivity and high safety allow to use Wave Plus system for patients who tolerate the adhesive electrodes and conductive gel for SEMG detection through medical electrodes.

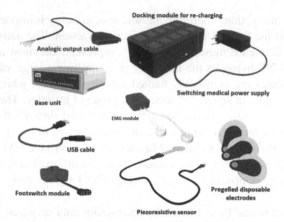

Fig. 1. Typical Wave Plus components

The PicoEMG is composed like minimumsi Wave but without the cable clips. This feature reduces the antenna effect and its symmetrical construction reduces motion artefacts. PicoEMG is applied directly on the muscle and supported by the pre-gelled sensors themselves, without additional stickers (Fig. 2).

Fig. 2. PicoEMG sensor

2.2 Test Process Design

Subjects: The subjects were 10 young males aged 22–26 years, healthy, 165–185 cm in height, 60–80 kg in weight, right hand as their dominimumsant hand and no history of upper limb muscle strain, and with exercise habits. No strenuous exercise was performed within 72 h before the test to avoid the influence of other fatigue factors on the test results. Training on the test movements was conducted before the muscle sEMG collection to ensure the proficiency of the test movements.

Test procedure: Subjects were informed of the test task before the test, and their height, weight, and age were recorded. Because of the influence of temperature on EMG signal generation, the ambient temperature of the test was set to 24 °C. The subjects were warmed up for 10 minimumsimums, and 12 muscles were selected, including two-sided latissimus dorsi, two-sided external abdominous obliques, two-sided tensor muscle of the fascia lata, two-sided rectus femoris, two-sided vastus medialis, and two-sided biceps femoris. The skin near the electrode placement point and the placement point was then depilated and washed with water after depilatory treatment, and the skin was repeatedly wiped with 75% medical alcohol after drying with paper towels. After the electrodes are pasted, it is necessary to confirm the reliability of the paste and determinimumsed whether the measured muscle electrodes are correctly connected to the corresponding channels. When ready, the test is performed according to the prescribed action. The placement of the chip electrode is shown in Figs. 3 and 4 (Table 1).

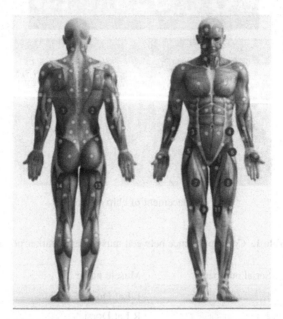

Fig. 3. Selecting precise test muscles in the software

Test group: The experimenter completed the squatting reciprocal process and carried 10 kg of goods in his hands. In the squat and finished standing need to keep straight for one second, each group ten times. When the subject is ready, he/she reports to the test recorder and starts the test after hearing the "start" command from the recorder, while the software starts to record the EMG signal during the test, and then stops recording. After each test, the data was saved and backed up, and the subject could rest for 10 minimums before the next test.

Control group: The experimenter did not hold the goods in his hands during the completion of the squatting reciprocation. In the squat and finished standing need to keep upright for one second, each group 10 times. When the subject was ready, he/she reported to the test recorder and started the test after hearing the "start" command from the recorder, while the software started to record the EMG signal during the test, and then stopped recording. The data were saved and backed up after each trial, and the subjects were allowed to rest for 10 minimums before the next trial, which was conducted three times. Because the experiment required control variables, the same group of subjects

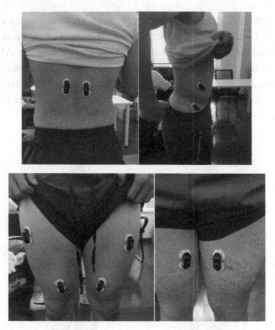

Fig. 4. Placement of chip electrodes

Table 1. Correspondence between muscles and marker points

Serial number	Muscle name
1	L.Lat.Dorsi
2	R.Lat.Dorsi
3	R.Ext.Oblique
4	L.Ext.Oblique
5	R.Tensor Fl.
6	L.Tensor Fl.
7	R.Rectus Fem.
8	L.Rectus Fem.
9	R.Vmo
10	L.Vmo
11	R.Biceps Fem.
12	L.Biceps Fem.

was used for the test and control groups, allowing the subjects to perform the experiment on two different days to reduce errors (Fig. 5).

3 Theory and Calculation

3.1 Data Pre-processing

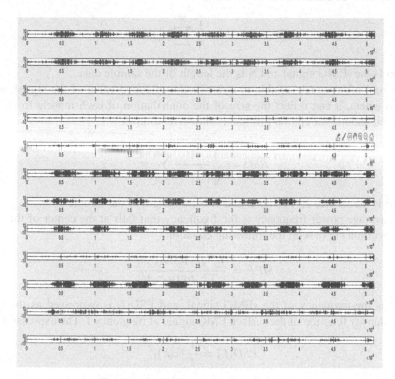

Fig. 5. sEMG signal after pre-processing.

In the acquisition process of surface EMG signals, although there are generally amplification and filtering circuits in the acquisition equipment, which can reduce the interference of noise, to a certain extent, they cannot be completely luminous, and the signals are still mixed with other noise components, such as other electronic devices in the surrounding environment (e.g., cell phones, incandescent lamps, etc.), artifact noise due to the movement of the electrodes relative to the skin due to the activity of the limbs, and noise introduced by the acquisition system noise introduced by electronic devices. These noises can lead to poor quality of the detected surface EMG signals, and if these raw EMG signals are not first denied, it will affect the feature differentiation used to characterize the action patterns and thus reduce the recognition of the action. Since the energy distribution of surface EMG signals is mainly concentrated in 20–500 Hz, the high pass filter and the low pass filter are used to filter the wake noise within 20 Hz and the ambient noise above 500 Hz. Since the surface myoelectric signal is also affected by the 220 V AC voltage, 50 Hz on the sensor, we also need a 50 Hz digital trap to filter out the IEE noise interference.

3.2 Data Post-processing

The amplitude of the acquired sEMG signal varies when different limb movements are performed, and the absolute mean value can describe the average intensity of the EMG signal, which is calculated as shown below.

$$MAV = \frac{1}{N} \sum_{i=1}^{N} |x_i|$$

where xi is the sEMG signal and N is the length of the sample data.

The root mean square is able to describe the effective value of the signal, and to a certain extent, it can reflect the size of the contribution of each muscle to the limb movement, and its calculation formula is shown as follows.

$$RMS = \sqrt{\frac{1}{N-1} \sum_{i=1}^{N} x_i^2}$$

where xi is the surface EMG signal and N is the length of the sample data.

The average power frequency is the frequency that falls at the center of the signal power spectrum curve with the following equation.

$$MPF = \frac{\int_0^\infty f \cdot PSD(f)df}{\int_0^\infty PSD(f)df}$$

where f is the frequency of the sEMG signal, and PSD(f) is expressed as the power spectral density function of the surface EMG signal at frequency f. The expressions are:

$$PSD(f) = \frac{1}{T} |x(k)|^2$$

The median frequency is the frequency at which the signal power spectrum curve is divided into two regions of equal area, which is given by the following equation.

$$MF = \frac{1}{2} \int_0^\infty PSD(f)df$$

The average absolute value, root mean square value, average power frequency and median frequency characteristics of the 12 channels' sEMG signals were calculated using the above eigenvalue equations, respectively.

The four eigenvalues obtained above are subjected to the covariance matrix operation respectively, and let $X(x_1, x_2, x_3 \ldots x_n)^T$ is an n-dimensional random variable, called the matrix $C = (c_{ij})_{n \times n} = \begin{pmatrix} c_{11} & \cdots & c_{1n} \\ \vdots & \ddots & \vdots \\ c_{n1} & \cdots & c_{nn} \end{pmatrix}$ is the covariance matrix of the n-dimensional random variable X, also denoted as D(X). Of which $C_{ij} = cov(x_i x_j)$, $i, j = 1, 2, 3 \ldots n$, is the covariance of the components Xi and Xj of X. Then calculate $p_i = \frac{\sum_{i=1}^{n} |c_{ij}|}{\sum_{i=1}^{n} \sum_{j=1}^{n} |c_{ij}|} \times 100\%$, the percentage of the relationship between each component and the other components is obtained. Pi can be approximated as the contribution of each muscle in the movement.

4   Results and Discussions

With the above data processing method, the 60 sets of 12 channels of data are processed, and the following 4 graphs can be obtained.

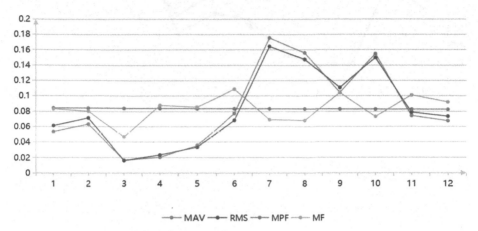

Fig. 6. Muscle contribution rate of control group

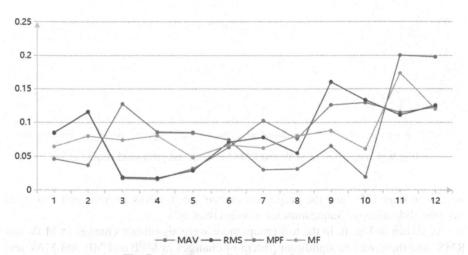

Fig. 7. Muscle contribution rate of test group

As shown in Fig. 6, it can be seen that in the control group, MAV and RMS have obvious curve changes, MPF and MF have no obvious change pattern, and MAV and RMS demonstrate the relationship between the size of the contribution of the corresponding muscles, and the same muscles on the left and right sides are a group, and they are arranged from the largest to the smallest in the order of two-sided rectus femoris, two-sided medial femoris, two-sided biceps femoris, two-sided latissimus dorsi, two-sided latissimus fasciae, two-sided abdominous The proportion of two-sided rectus femoris

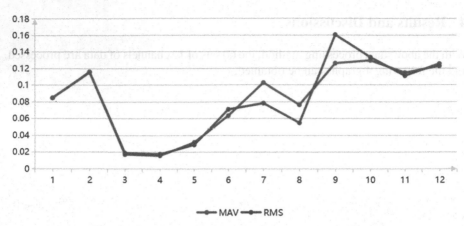

Fig. 8. Muscle contribution rate of test group (MAV,RMS)

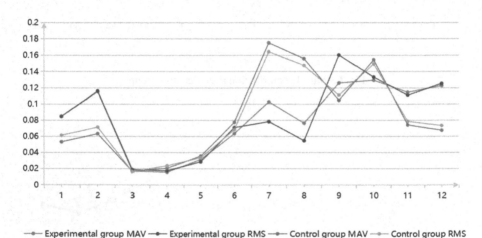

Fig. 9. Comparison of MAV and RMS between test group and control group

was more than 15%, and the proportion of two-sided vastus lateralis and two-sided external abdominous oblique muscles was less than 5%.

As shown in Fig. 6. In the test group, there were significant changes in MAV and RMS, and there was no significant pattern of changes in MPF and MF, and MAV and RMS demonstrated the relationship between the magnitude of contribution of the corresponding muscles, with the same muscles on the left and right sides as a group, arranged from largest to smallest in order of two-sided medial femoral muscles, two-sided biceps femoris, two-sided latissimus dorsi, two-sided rectus femoris, two-sided vastus fasciae tensor, and two-sided external abdominous oblique muscles, of which two-sided medial femoral muscles, two-sided medial femur, two-sided biceps femoris and two-sided latissimus dorsi accounted for more than 10%, and two-sided external abdominous obliques accounted for less than 2% (Figs. 7 and 8).

As shown in Fig. 9, by comparing the MAV and RMS obtained from the test group and the control group, it is found that the bilateral medial femoral muscle decreases by 50%. while the two-sided medial femoral muscles, two-sided biceps femoris, and two-sided latissimus dorsi muscles increased, and the two-sided latissimus dorsi muscles and two-sided external abdominous obliques remained basically unchanged.

The calculation method in this paper has no simulation for verification, and the subsequent research can be continued. The results obtained so far are for theoretical reference only and are subject to subsequent verification.

5 Conclusion

Through the above data processing methods, 60 groups of 12 channels of data were processed, and the results were analyzed to obtain the following conclusions.

(1) In the calculation of muscle contribution using covariance matrix, there is a clear pattern for MAV and RMS, and no clear pattern for MPF and MF, which is not applicable to this method.

(2) During squatting, the two-sided rectus femoris contributed the most and the two-sided external abdominous obliques contributed the least, i.e.. The two-sided rectus femoris was most susceptible to muscle fatigue and the two-sided external abdominous obliques were least susceptible to fatigue during squatting.

(3) During weighted squatting, the contribution of two-sided rectus femoris decreased, while the contribution of two-sided medial femoris, two-sided biceps femoris and two-sided latissimus dorsi increased and was significantly greater than that of non-weighted squatting. This indicates that the two-sided medial femoral muscles, two-sided biceps femoris and two-sided latissimus dorsi are more susceptible to muscle fatigue during weighted squats.

(4) In the subsequent design of the lumbar-assisted exoskeleton, emphasis should be placed on protecting the two-sided medial femoral muscles, two-sided biceps femoris and two-sided latissimus dorsi muscles to prevent injury to the wearer during weighted squats.

References

1. Yang, Y., Peng, Y.X., Zengminimumsg, H., Liu, Y, Wang, X., Jian, W.: Research progress and prospect of muscle synergy theory for redundant control of complex human movement. Sports Sci. **40**(12), 63–72 (2020). https://doi.org/10.16469/j.css.202012006
2. Freund, H.J.: Motor unit and muscle activity in voluntary motor control. Physiol. Rev. **63**(2), 387–436 (1983)
3. Winter, D.A.: Biomechanics and Motor Control of Human Movement, 3rd edn. John Wiley & Sons Inc., Hoboken (2005)
4. Cheung, V.C.K., d'Avella, A., Bizzi, E.: Adjustments of motor pattern for load compensation via modulated activations of muscle synergies during natural behaviors. J. Neurophysiol. **101**(3), 1235–1257 (2009)

5. Bizzi, E.: Motor control revisited: a novel view. Curr. Trends Neurol. **10**, 75–80 (2016)
6. Bizzi, E., Cheung, V.C.K., d'Avella, A., Saltiel, P., Tresch, M.: Combining modules for movement. Brain Res. Rev. **57**(1), 125–133 (2008)
7. Tresch, M.C., Jarc, A.: The case for and against muscle synergies. Curr. Opin. Neurobiol. **19**(6), 601–607 (2009)
8. Chu, J.-U., Moon, I., Mun, M.-S.: A real-time EMG pattern recognition based on linear-nonlinear feature projection for multifunction myoelectric hand. In: 9th International Conference on Rehabilitation Robotics, 2005. ICORR 2005, pp. 295–298 (2005)
9. Lee, D.D., Seung, H.S.: Learning the parts of objects by non-negative matrix factorization. Nature **401**(6755), 788–791 (1999)
10. Santuz, A., Ekizos, A., Janshen, L., Baltzopoulos, V., Arampatzis, A.: On the methodological implications of extracting muscle synergies from human locomotion. Int. J. Neural Syst. **27**(5),1750007 (2017)
11. Tresch, M.C., Cheung, V.C.K., d'Avella, A.: Matrix factorization algorithms for the identification of muscle synergies: evaluation on simulated and test data sets. J. Neurophysiol. **95**(4), 2199–2212 (2006)

Energy Gradient Descent Method for Actuation of a Direct-Drive Spherical Robotic Wrist

Mengke Li, Yaqing Deng, and Kun Bai[(✉)]

Huazhong University of Science and Technology, Wuhan 430074, China
kbai@hust.edu.cn

Abstract. This paper presents an energy gradient descent method for actuating a spherical robotic wrist which is capable of providing three-DOF rotations in one joint. By formulating the relationship between the magnetic energy for driving the spherical rotor and the current inputs supplied to the motor, an energy gradient descent method is proposed by adjusting the supplied current inputs for shaping a minimum magnetic energy point at the desired rotor state. As a result, the rotor will approach to the desired state automatically without the need of any feedback control laws. The solutions to the supplied currents for shaping a desired energy profile can be computed in real-time with a magnetic-flux-based model. The proposed method has been validated with both numerical simulations and experimental tests performed on a cooperative robotic manipulator equipped with a spherical wrist actuator.

Keywords: Robotic joint · Spherical motor · Compliant control

1 Introduction

Actuators with dexterous motions and direct force/torque manipulations are always desired for robotic manipulators. In order to achieve complicated works in multi-dimensional robot task space [1–3], existing robotic manipulators are primarily based on serially/parallel connected motors with coupling mechanisms [2, 4], which results in bulky structures and singularities/backlashes in motion as well as non-backdrivable joints which are undesired for force/compliant manipulations.

In order for dexterous and compliant manipulations, several actuator systems have been developed. Among them are the spherical motors that can achieve multi-DOF rotational motions in one joint [5–8]. The transmission-free configurations of spherical motors allow for singularity-free and backlash-free motions as well as direct torque manipulations for robotic joints. Existing applications of spherical motors include motion stage for manufacturing [9], robotic wrist [10] as well as haptic device [11]. The actuation of spherical motors relies on the interactions between the electro-magnets (EMs) and permanent-magnets (PMs) distributed on the spherical surfaces of the socket-like rotor and ball-like stator. By establishing the relationship between the multi-dimensional magnetic torque applied on the rotor and the current inputs supplied into the EMs at any orientation [9], the desired currents can be computed with the actuation model for a

H. Liu et al. (Eds.): ICIRA 2022, LNAI 13457, pp. 753–764, 2022.
https://doi.org/10.1007/978-3-031-13835-5_68

desired torque that is determined by the control law. In order to achieve precise multi-DOF orientation regulation/tracking and impedance control for compliant manipulations as robotic joints, a variety of feedback control methods have been developed. In [12], a complementary control method that precisely controlling the multi-DOF orientation of spherical motors in presence of external disturbances as well as model uncertainties and inaccuracies are proposed. The proposed controller featured with a two-DOF structure is composed of an H_2 controller for a nominal plant and then complements it with an additional regulator designed in H_∞ sense to assure robustness which can be adjusted online in accordance with the monitored modeling mismatch to improve the conservativeness of traditional robust control. In [10], a back-drivable spherical wrist with smart compliance for rendering human wrist-like capabilities in robotic applications is presented. In order to synthetically impose both motion accuracy and active compliance for dedicated wrist manipulations, a robust hybrid control method is proposed that can switch between motion control (at free motion) and impedance control (at interactions with the environment). Existing torque and impedance manipulations of spherical motors rely on feedback controls that require complicated multi-DOF orientation measurements and computationally demanding control laws which are based on the nonlinear dynamic models of the rotor. It is desired that a highly efficient actuation method is derived that allows intuitive low-level stability and direct stiffness/impedance manipulations. This paper presents an energy gradient descent method which draws minimum magnetic energy at the desired state (and thus a stable state) by adjusting the supplied motor currents so that the rotor automatically approaches the desired state in an asymptotically way without any feedback.

2 Energy Gradient Descent Method for Spherical Motor

Figure 1(a) illustrates a robotic manipulator configured with a direct-drive spherical wrist for performing dexterous motions and compliant interactions. As detailed in Fig. 1(b), the spherical wrist is directly actuated by the electromagnetic interactions between the electromagnets (EMs, housed on the outer surface of the stator) and the permanent magnets (PMs, strategically embedded in the rotor). The rotor is supported concentrically through a low friction spherical rolling bearing which allows continuous three-DOF rotations. When the EMs are applied with currents, a three-dimensional magnetic torque will be applied on the rotor which translates into three-DOF rotations of the rotor. The rotor orientation is defined in terms of Euler angles (roll, pitch, yaw) $\mathbf{q} = [\alpha, \beta, \gamma]^T$. The rotation matrix $\mathbf{R}$ of the rotor can be expressed as (1):

$$\mathbf{R}(\alpha, \beta, \gamma) = \begin{bmatrix} C_\gamma C_\beta & -S_\gamma C_\beta & S_\beta \\ S_\gamma C_\alpha + C_\gamma S_\beta S_\alpha & C_\gamma C_\alpha - S_\gamma S_\beta S_\alpha & -C_\beta S_\alpha \\ S_\gamma S_\alpha - C_\gamma S_\beta C_\alpha & C_\gamma S_\alpha + S_\gamma S_\beta C_\alpha & C_\beta C_\alpha \end{bmatrix} \quad (1)$$

In (1), S and C represent sine and cosine respectively. The dynamic model of the spherical wrist can be derived with Lagrange formulation as (2):

$$\mathbf{M}(\mathbf{q})\dot{\mathbf{q}} + \mathbf{C}(\mathbf{q}, \dot{\mathbf{q}}) + \mathbf{G}(\mathbf{q}) = \tau + \tau_f \quad (2)$$

In (2), $\mathbf{M}(\mathbf{q})$ is the rotor inertia matrix; $\mathbf{C}(\mathbf{q}, \dot{\mathbf{q}})$ is the combined centripetal and Coriolis torque vector; $\mathbf{G}(\mathbf{q})$ is the gravitational torque vector; $\boldsymbol{\tau}$ is the electromagnetic actuating torque applied on the rotor; and $\boldsymbol{\tau}_f$ is the friction torque applied on the rotor. The detailed formulation of the dynamic model can be found in [9].

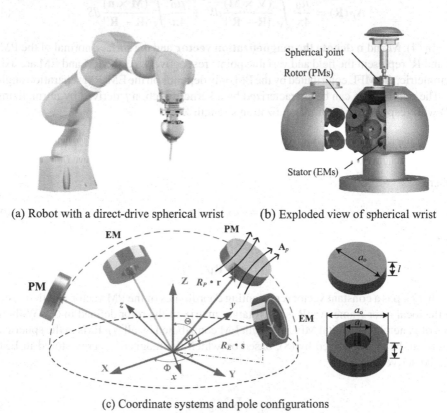

(a) Robot with a direct-drive spherical wrist   (b) Exploded view of spherical wrist

(c) Coordinate systems and pole configurations

Fig. 1. Illustration of robot with a direct-drive spherical wrist.

The pole configurations are presented in Fig. 1(c), where XYZ and xyz represent the stator and rotor coordinates respectively. In Fig. 1(c), $\mathbf{s}$ and $\mathbf{r}$ represent the unit vectors in XYZ frame from the origin to the geometrical centers of the EMs and PMs, respectively; σ is the separation angle between $\mathbf{s}$ and $\mathbf{r}$; R_P, R_E are the radial distance of PMs and EMs, respectively.

For an EM-PM pair, the total magnetic flux linkage (MFL) through the EM can be obtained as follows [13, 14]:

$$\Lambda = \frac{1}{a} \int_V (\mathbf{A}_P \cdot \mathbf{I}) \, dv \qquad (3)$$

In (3), l is the direction vector of the current; a and V denote the wire cross-sectional area and winding volume respectively; and $\mathbf{A}_P$ is the magnetic vector potential of the PM which can be computed using (4)

$$\mathbf{A}_P(\mathbf{R}) = \frac{\mu_0}{4\pi} \int_V \frac{(\nabla \times \mathbf{M})}{|\mathbf{R} - \mathbf{R}'|} dV + \frac{\mu_0}{4\pi} \int_S \frac{(\mathbf{M} \times \mathbf{n})}{|\mathbf{R} - \mathbf{R}'|} dS \qquad (4)$$

In (4), $\mathbf{M}$ and $\mathbf{n}$ **denote the magnetization vector** and the surface normal of the PM; $\mathbf{R}$ and $\mathbf{R}'$ represent the field and variable points respectively. As the PM and EM are axis symmetric, the MFL contributed by the PM only depends on the EM-PM separation angle σ. The relationship can be characterized by a kernel function f derived by normalizing (3) with respect to the PM magnetization strength λ

$$f(\sigma) = \frac{\Lambda}{\lambda} = \frac{1}{a\lambda} \int_V (\mathbf{A}_P \cdot \mathbf{I}) \, dv \qquad (5)$$

where

$$\sigma = cos^{-1}(\mathbf{s} \cdot \mathbf{r}) \qquad (6)$$

and

$$\mathbf{r} = \mathbf{R}\mathbf{p} \qquad (7)$$

In (7), $\mathbf{p}$ is a constant vector representing coordinates of the PM vector $\mathbf{r}$ with respect to the local rotor frame xyz; $\mathbf{R}$ is the rotation matrix of the rotor defined in (1). Without loss of generality, the total MFL in the jth EM contributed by all N_P PMs in the spherical wrist can be characterized by (8), based on which the magnetic energy stored in EM$_j$ can be derived as (9)

$$\Lambda_j = \sum_{i=1}^{N_p} \lambda_i f\left(\sigma_{ij}\right) \qquad (8)$$

$$E_j = u_j \Lambda_j \qquad (9)$$

In (8) and (9), σ_{ij} refers to the separation angle between the jth EM (EM$_j$) and ith PM (PM$_i$); and u_j is current input of EM$_j$. For a spherical wrist consisting of N_E EMs, the total magnetic energy at any rotor orientation $\mathbf{q}$, which transforms into the kinetic energy of the rotor, can be obtained as

$$E(\mathbf{q}) = \sum_{j=1}^{N_E} E_j(\mathbf{q}) \qquad (10)$$

In order that the rotor automatically approaches any desired state $\mathbf{q}_d$, the energy field is shaped by (11) so that it reaches a minimum at $\mathbf{q}_d$:

$$\begin{cases} \nabla E|_{\mathbf{q}=\mathbf{q}_d} = \mathbf{0} \\ \mathbf{H}(E)|_{\mathbf{q}=\mathbf{q}_d} \succ 0 \end{cases} \qquad (11)$$

where $\mathbf{H}(\cdot)$ is the Hessian Matrix of a scalar field [15]. (11) can be derived as (12a, b) with substitution of (8 and 9):

$$\nabla E = \sum_{j=1}^{N_E} \nabla E_j = \sum_{j=1}^{N_E} u_j \frac{\partial \Lambda_j(\mathbf{q})}{\partial \mathbf{q}} \tag{12a}$$

$$\mathbf{H}(E) = \sum_{j=1}^{N_E} u_j \frac{\partial \Lambda_j}{\partial \mathbf{q} \partial \mathbf{q}^{\mathrm{T}}} \tag{12b}$$

Substituting (6–7) into (12a), yields

$$\nabla E = \mathbf{K}(\mathbf{q})\mathbf{u} \tag{13}$$

where

$$\mathbf{u} = \left[u_1, \cdots, u_j, \cdots, u_{N_E} \right]^{\mathrm{T}} \tag{14}$$

and

$$\mathbf{K} = \left[\mathbf{K}_1(\mathbf{q}), \cdots, \mathbf{K}_j(\mathbf{q}), \cdots, \mathbf{K}_{N_E}(\mathbf{q}) \right] \tag{15}$$

$$\mathbf{K}_j(\mathbf{q}) = \sum_{i=1}^{N_P} \left(-\frac{\lambda_i f'(\sigma_{ij})}{\sin \sigma_{ij}} \begin{bmatrix} \mathbf{s}_j^{\mathrm{T}} \mathbf{a} \mathbf{p}_i \\ \mathbf{s}_j^{\mathrm{T}} \mathbf{b} \mathbf{p}_i \\ \mathbf{s}_j^{\mathrm{T}} \mathbf{c} \mathbf{p}_i \end{bmatrix} \right) \tag{16}$$

In (16), $\mathbf{a} = \partial \mathbf{R}/\partial \alpha$, $\mathbf{b} = \partial \mathbf{R}/\partial \beta$, $\mathbf{c} = \partial \mathbf{R}/\partial \gamma$, and $f' = df/d\sigma$.
Similarly, (12b) can be rewritten as (17) with substitution of (6–7) into (12b):

$$\mathbf{H}(E) = \left[\sum_{j=1}^{N_E} \mathbf{N}_{\alpha,j}(\mathbf{q}) u_j \ \sum_{j=1}^{N_E} \mathbf{N}_{\beta,j}(\mathbf{q}) u_j \ \sum_{j=1}^{N_E} \mathbf{N}_{\gamma,j}(\mathbf{q}) u_j \right] \tag{17}$$

where

$$\mathbf{N}_{\alpha,j}(\mathbf{q}) = \sum_{i=1}^{N_P} \frac{\lambda_i}{\sin^3 \sigma_{ij}} \mathbf{I}_{3\times3} \otimes \mathbf{s}_j^{\mathrm{T}} \left[\eta(\sigma_{ij}) \left(\mathbf{s}_j^{\mathrm{T}} \mathbf{a} \mathbf{p}_i \right) \begin{bmatrix} \mathbf{a} \\ \mathbf{b} \\ \mathbf{c} \end{bmatrix} - \zeta(\sigma_{ij}) \begin{bmatrix} \partial \mathbf{a}/\partial \alpha \\ \partial \mathbf{a}/\partial \beta \\ \partial \mathbf{a}/\partial \gamma \end{bmatrix} \right] \mathbf{p}_i$$

$$\mathbf{N}_{\beta,j}(\mathbf{q}) = \sum_{i=1}^{N_P} \frac{\lambda_i}{\sin^3 \sigma_{ij}} \mathbf{I}_{3\times3} \otimes \mathbf{s}_j^{\mathrm{T}} \left[\eta(\sigma_{ij}) \left(\mathbf{s}_j^{\mathrm{T}} \mathbf{b} \mathbf{p}_i \right) \begin{bmatrix} \mathbf{a} \\ \mathbf{b} \\ \mathbf{c} \end{bmatrix} - \zeta(\sigma_{ij}) \begin{bmatrix} \partial \mathbf{b}/\partial \alpha \\ \partial \mathbf{b}/\partial \beta \\ \partial \mathbf{b}/\partial \gamma \end{bmatrix} \right] \mathbf{p}_i$$

$$\mathbf{N}_{\gamma,j}(\mathbf{q}) = \sum_{i=1}^{N_P} \frac{\lambda_i}{\sin^3 \sigma_{ij}} \mathbf{I}_{3\times3} \otimes \mathbf{s}_j^{\mathrm{T}} \left[\eta(\sigma_{ij}) \left(\mathbf{s}_j^{\mathrm{T}} \mathbf{c} \mathbf{p}_i \right) \begin{bmatrix} \mathbf{a} \\ \mathbf{b} \\ \mathbf{c} \end{bmatrix} - \zeta(\sigma_{ij}) \begin{bmatrix} \partial \mathbf{c}/\partial \alpha \\ \partial \mathbf{c}/\partial \beta \\ \partial \mathbf{c}/\partial \gamma \end{bmatrix} \right] \mathbf{p}_i$$

and $\eta(\sigma_{ij}) = f''(\sigma_{ij}) \sin \sigma_{ij} - f'(\sigma_{ij}) \cos \sigma_{ij}$, $\zeta(\sigma_{ij}) = f'(\sigma_{ij}) \sin^2 \sigma_{ij}$.
in (17)(a–c), $\otimes$ donates the Kronecker product [16].

(17) can be rewritten as (18) by transforming $\mathbf{H}(E)$ into vector form:

$$vec[\mathbf{H}(E)] = \mathbf{Nu} \tag{18}$$

where

$$\mathbf{N} = \begin{bmatrix} \mathbf{N}_{\alpha,1}(\mathbf{q}) & \mathbf{N}_{\alpha,j}(\mathbf{q}) & \mathbf{N}_{\alpha,N_E}(\mathbf{q}) \\ \mathbf{N}_{\beta,1}(\mathbf{q}) & , \cdots & \mathbf{N}_{\beta,j}(\mathbf{q}) & , \cdots & \mathbf{N}_{\beta,N_E}(\mathbf{q}) \\ \mathbf{N}_{\gamma,1}(\mathbf{q}) & \mathbf{N}_{\gamma,j}(\mathbf{q}) & \mathbf{N}_{\gamma,N_E}(\mathbf{q}) \end{bmatrix}$$

in (18), $vec[\cdot]$ represents the vector operator of a matrix [16]. (13) and (18) can be augmented as (19)

$$\begin{bmatrix} \nabla E \\ vec[\mathbf{H}(E)] \end{bmatrix} = \begin{bmatrix} \mathbf{K} \\ \mathbf{N} \end{bmatrix} \mathbf{u} \tag{19}$$

Let $\nabla E = 0$ and $\mathbf{H}(E) = \mathbf{L} = diag(\lambda_1, \lambda_2, \lambda_3)$, where $\lambda_1, \lambda_2, \lambda_3 > 0$. As $\mathbf{H}(E)$ is positive definite, (11) is satisfied which allows a minimum magnetic energy point at the desired state. Based on the current-to-torque relationship in (19), for a spherical motor featured with redundant inputs (the number of current inputs is higher than the number of linear equations), an optimal $\mathbf{u}$ can be found in the form of pseudoinverse from (20) to meet the condition (11):

$$\mathbf{u} = \begin{bmatrix} \mathbf{K} \\ \mathbf{N} \end{bmatrix}^T \left(\begin{bmatrix} \mathbf{K} \\ \mathbf{N} \end{bmatrix} \begin{bmatrix} \mathbf{K} \\ \mathbf{N} \end{bmatrix}^T \right)^{-1} \begin{bmatrix} \mathbf{0}_{3 \times 1} \\ vec(\mathbf{L}) \end{bmatrix} \tag{20}$$

3   Results and Discussions

The proposed method has been validated using numerical simulations and experimental tests based on a spherical wrist joint configured on a robotic manipulator as shown in Fig. 2. The parameter values and those defining the EM-PM locations in Fig. 1 are list in Table 1. Note that the rotor gravity of the spherical wrist has been compensated in the tests.

The computation of the multiport model (16) and (17) requires an explicit form of the kernel function f. Following (5), the MFL of an EM-PM pair in the spherical motor (as shown in Fig. 2) was computed with numerical integration using the EM-PM parameters presented in Table 1. A closed-form expression can be obtained as (21) by curve fitting the numerical results

$$f(\sigma) = \sum_{j=0}^{6} \left[a_j \cos(jw\sigma) + b_j \sin(jw\sigma) \right] \tag{21}$$

In (20), $[a_0-a_6] = [28.38, 5.82, -35.95, -4.46, 11.97, 2.64, -0.46] \times 10^{-3}$, $[b_1-b_6] = [-50.23, -6.23, 2.29, 3.99, 3.83, 0.71] \times 10^{-3}$, and $w = 0.031$. f' and f'' in (16) and (17) can be derived explicitly by taking the derivative and the second derivative of (21).

Fig. 2. Robotic manipulator with a spherical wrist joint

Table 1. Spherical motor parameters.

Rotor PMs	$a_o = 20$ mm, $l = 5$ mm, $\mu_0 M_0 = 1.465\ T$			
	PM$_i$ centroid	Index(i)	(Θ, Φ) in xyz	Polarity
	$R_P = 45.5$ mm	1–12	105°	$(i-1) \times 30° + 15°$	$(-1)^i$
		13–24	75°	$(i-3) \times 30° + 15°$	$(-1)^{i-1}$
Stator EMs	$a_o = 20$ mm, $a_i = 8$ mm, $l = 6$ mm, $d = 0.3$ mm, # of turns: 400			
	EM$_j$ centroid	Index(j)	(Θ, Φ) in xyz	
	$R_E = 38.3$ mm	1–8	115°	$(j-1) \times 30°$
		9–16	65°	$(j-9) \times 30°$
		17–24	90°	$(j-17) \times 30°$
Rotor properties	Mass: $m = 0.484$ kg Centroid: $h_z = 6.937$ mm Moment of inertia (kg·mm²): $I_{xx} = 606.43$, $I_{yy} = 605.96$, $I_{zz} = 847.34$			

3.1 Simulation Results

The capability of the proposed energy gradient descent method for point-to-point positioning in an open-loop fashion was investigated. Figure 3 presents the simulated responses for a step response where the wrist orientation changed from initial position $\mathbf{q}_0 = [0, 0, 0]^T$ to a desired state at $\mathbf{q}_d = [15, 10, 0]^T$ by setting $\mathbf{L} = diag\ (0.3, 0.3, 2.5)$ in (20). In the simulation, a friction torque is applied with $\tau_f = -\nu\dot{\mathbf{q}}$, where $\nu = 0.011$ kg·m²/s. It can be seen that the spherical wrist approached to the desired state from the initial state with the shaped energy profile which required no feedback control.

To assist understanding, the resultant magnetic energies with the supplied currents at different rotor orientations are computed and the results are shown in Fig. 4. For visualization, the energy profile was plotted a function of α, β in the figure. It can be seen that the energy profile form a minimum point at the desired state. The simulated trajectory was superimposed on Fig. 4(a), which demonstrate that the spherical motor rotor

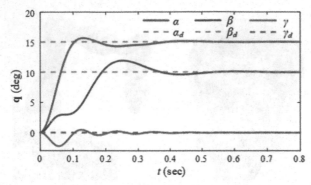

Fig. 3. Tracking step responses with energy gradient descent method ($\mathbf{q}_0 = [0, 0, 0]^T$ and $\mathbf{q}_d = [15, 10, 0]^T$).

asymptotically moved from the starting point to the desired state in the energy profile designed by the gradient descent method. The magnetic torque components at different orientations are also presented in Figs. 4(b–c). According to the virtual displacement [17], the results verified that the magnetic torque pushed the rotor to the desired state with the shaped energy profile.

The capability of the proposed method is also investigated for following a trajectory in an open-loop sense. To compensate the dynamics of the rotor, a torque in the following form has been complemented in a feedforward sense:

$$\tau_0 = \mathbf{M}(\mathbf{q}_d)\ddot{\mathbf{q}}_d + \mathbf{C}(\mathbf{q}_d, \dot{\mathbf{q}}_d) + \mathbf{G}(\mathbf{q}_d)$$

Figures 5(a–c) presents the control responses for the wrist end to track a circle. The desired and simulated orientations are shown in Fig. 5(a) and the errors are plotted in Fig. 5(b). The reference and simulated trajectories of the end-effector are compared in Fig. 5(c). The results show that the proposed control method is capable of precisely tracking a continuous trajectory.

3.2 Experimental Results

The effectiveness of the proposed energy gradient descent method is experimentally demonstrated on the spherical motor configured as a robot wrist as shown in Fig. 2. The step response of the spherical wrist is first tested with the energy descent method and capability of the wrist for rendering a controllable joint stiffness is also investigated.

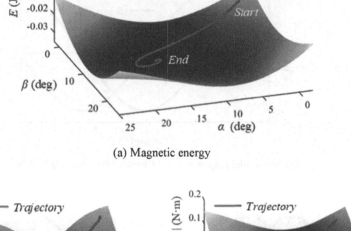

(a) Magnetic energy

(b) Magnetic torque component τ_α (c) Magnetic torque component τ_β

Fig. 4. Mesh of the total potential energy and resultant external torque.

Figure 6 presents the spherical rotor wrist responses of the energy gradient descent control method when the reference changed from $\mathbf{q}_0 = [0, 0, 0]^T$ to $\mathbf{q}_d = [10, 5, 0]^T$ for $\mathbf{L} = diag\,(0.2, 0.2, 1.65)$. The result shows that the energy gradient descent control method has good performance on point-to-point positioning, where the steady-state error can be observed due to model inaccuracies.

As the designed energy field tend to push back the rotor when it deviate from the desired state, the capability of the proposed method for rendering the controllable joint stiffness is experimentally tested. Figure 7(a) presents the experimental setup where the rotor end-effector is manually pushed away from an equilibrium point and the magnetic torque for pushing back the rotor was measured at different wrist orientations. Figures 7(b–c) presents the resistive torque along the α and β directions; for comparison, the resistive torques are tested for different $\mathbf{L}$ values which are shown in Figs. 7(b) and (c) respectively. It can be seen from the experimental results that when the spherical robotic wrist deviated from the desire state due to the interaction with the external environment, a restoring torque was applied on the rotor which is proportional to the magnitude of the deviation depending on the values of $\mathbf{L}$ matrix. It can be shown that the spherical robotic wrist has a controllable stiffness which can be achieved by directly manipulating the $\mathbf{L}$ matrix through the energy gradient descent method.

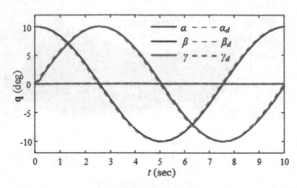

(a) Sinusoidal response $\mathbf{q}_d = [10\sin(0.2\pi t), 10\cos(0.2\pi t), 0]^T$.

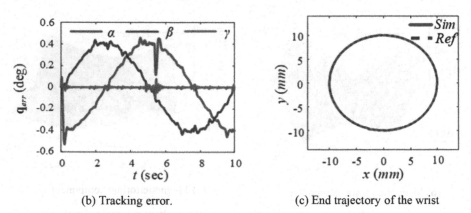

(b) Tracking error.   (c) End trajectory of the wrist

Fig. 5. Trajectory tracking response

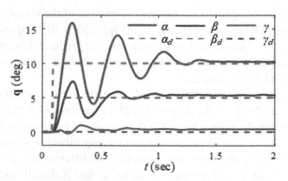

Fig. 6. Point to point response

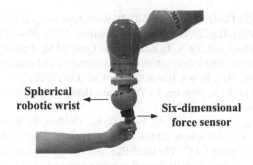

(a) Disturbance experiment

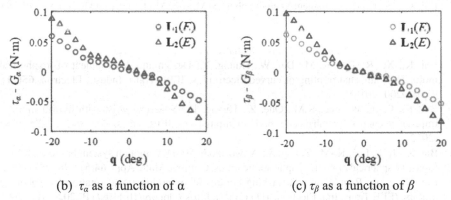

(b) τ_α as a function of α (c) τ_β as a function of β

Fig. 7. Controllable joint stiffness $\mathbf{q}_d = [0, 0, 0]^T$, $\mathbf{L}_1(E) = diag$ (0.065, 0.065, 0.5), $\mathbf{L}_2(E) = diag$ (0.1 0.1, 0.85)

4   Conclusion

This paper presents an energy gradient descent method for actuating three-DOF rotations and regulating three-DOF orientations of a spherical robotic wrist without the need of any feedback control laws. Unlike conventional supplied currents calculation method, the proposed method regulates the spherical robotic wrist to a desire state by shaping a minimum magnetic energy point. In addition, the spherical wrist is capable of delivering a controllable stiffness to compliant to environment with the configured second-order partial derivative of the magnetic energy. The simulation results show that the proposed method provides good step response and tracking performance. The effectiveness of the proposed method for point-to-point positioning and disturbance rejection as well as the controllable stiffness have been experimentally demonstrated on a cooperative robotic manipulator equipped with a spherical wrist actuator.

References

1. Gruijthuijsen, C., Borghesan, G., Reynaerts, D., Poorten, E.V.: A hybrid active/passive wrist approach for increasing virtual fixture stiffness in comanipulated robotic minimally invasive surgery. IEEE Robot. Autom. Lett. **4**(3), 3029–3036 (2019)

2. Hong, M.B., Jo, Y.: Design of a novel 4-DOF wrist-type surgical instrument with enhanced rigidity and dexterity. IEEE/ASME Trans. Mechatron. **19**(2), 500–511 (2014)

3. Wu, G.C.Y., Podolsky, D.J., Looi, T., Kahrs, L.A., Drake, J.M., Forrest, C.R.: A 3 mm wristed instrument for the da vinci robot: setup, characterization, and phantom tests for cleft palate repair. IEEE Trans. Med. Robot. Bionics. **2**(2), 130–139 (2020)

4. Al-Widyan, K., Ma, X.Q., Angeles, J.: The robust design of parallel spherical robots. Mech. Mach. Theory **46**(3), 335–343 (2011)

5. Rossini, L., Mingard, S., Boletis, A., Forzani, E., Onillon, E., Perriard, Y.: Rotor design optimization for a reaction sphere actuator. IEEE Trans. Ind. Appl. **50**(3), 1706–1716 (2014)

6. Fernandes, J.F.P., Branco, P.J.C.: The shell-like spherical induction motor for low-speed traction: electromagnetic design, analysis, and experimental tests. IEEE Trans. Industr. Electron. **63**(7), 4325–4335 (2016)

7. Bai, K., Lee, K.-M.: Permanent Magnet Spherical Motors: Model and Field Based Approaches for Design Sensing and Control. Springer, New York (2018)

8. Bai, K., Lee, K.-M.: Direct field-feedback control of a ball-joint-like permanent-magnet spherical motor. IEEE/ASME Trans. Mechatron. **19**(3), 975–986 (2014)

9. Bai, K., Xu, R., Lee, K.-M., Dai, W., Huang, Y.: Design and development of a spherical motor for conformal printing of curved electronics. IEEE Trans. Industr. Electron. **65**(11), 9190–9200 (2018)

10. Bai, K., Chen, W., Lee, K.M., Que, Z., Huang, R.: Spherical wrist with hybrid motion-impedance control for enhanced robotic manipulations. IEEE Trans. Rob. **38**(2), 1174–1185 (2022)

11. Bai, K., Ji, J., Lee, K.-M., Zhang, S.: A two-mode six-DOF motion system based on a ball-joint-like spherical motor for haptic applications. Comput. Math. Appl. **64**(5), 978–987 (2012)

12. Bai, K., et al.: Regulation and tracking control of omni-directional rotation for spherical motors. IEEE Trans. Ind. Electron. **1**(1) (2022). https://doi.org/10.1109/TIE.2022.3163566

13. Jackson, J.D.: Classical Electrodynamics. Wiley, Hoboken (1998)

14. Cheng, D.K.: Field and Wave Electromagnetics. Pearson, London (2007)

15. Boyd, S., Vandenberghe, L.: Convex Optimization. Cambridge University Press, New York (2004)

16. Magnus, J.R., Neudecker, H.: Matrix Differential Calculus with Applications in Statistics and Econometrics. John Wiley & sons, Chichester (1999)

17. Shabana, A.: Dynamics of Multibody Systems. Cambridge University Press, New York (2020)

Compliant Mechanisms and Robotic Applications

Design and Modeling of a Novel Compliant Ankle Mechanism with Flexible Slider-Crank Limbs

Shujie Tang[2,3], Genliang Chen[1,2(✉)], Wei Yan[3], and Hao Wang[1,3]

[1] State Key Laboratory of Mechanical Systems and Vibration,
Shanghai Jiao Tong University, Shanghai 200240, China
{leungchan,ywgump}@sjtu.edu.cn
[2] Meta Robotics Institute, Shanghai Jiao Tong University,
Shanghai 200240, China
sjtang@sjtu.edu.cn
[3] Shanghai Key Laboratory of Digital Manufacturing for Thin-Walled Structures,
Shanghai Jiao Tong University, Shanghai 200240, China
wanghao@sjtu.edu.cn

Abstract. This paper presents the conceptual design and modeling of a novel compliant ankle mechanism, which has flexible slider-crank limbs. Two elastic beams are utilized as the springy elements to connect the sliders and crank, which provides the ankle joint with passive rotational stiffness when two sliders are driven independently. Both the forward and inverse kinetostatic model are derived to determine the equilibrium configuration and the corresponding actuation variables. Besides, the rotational stiffness of the studied ankle mechanism is modeled based on results from the kinetostatic model. Results of stiffness analysis reveal that the proposed ankle joint is capable of varying its rotational stiffness if the sliders are controlled properly. The kinetostatic and stiffness models developed in this paper lay a foundation for stiffness design and prototype development in the future work.

Keywords: Compliant ankle joint · Kinetostatic modeling · Stiffness

1 Introduction

For decades, humanoid robots designed for various task and environment have been extensively studied. Different capabilities of the existing humanoid robots allow a variety of applications, such as rescue, education, assisting, entertainment, etc. [1]. The humanoid robot ankle, which is not only a weight-bearing but also the shock-absorbing structure [2], plays an important role during locomotion.

In recent years, a variety of novel ankle mechanisms have been developed, most of which use serial- or parallel-arranged structure with rigid linkages. Liang and Wang [2] proposed a 3 degree of freedom (DOF) ankle joint composed of three identical UPS limbs and one UR limb. Kumar et al. [3] developed a novel

© The Author(s), under exclusive license to Springer Nature Switzerland AG 2022
H. Liu et al. (Eds.): ICIRA 2022, LNAI 13457, pp. 767–778, 2022.
https://doi.org/10.1007/978-3-031-13835-5_69

ankle mechanism of 2SPRR+1U type. The rigid-linkage design provides high stiffness and kinematic accuracy, but also leads to heavy and bulky structures at the same time, moreover, the compliance that is important for absorption of shocks is hart to be guaranteed.

Generally, there are two kinds of compliance, namely active compliance and passive compliance. The former one, active compliance, can be realized through force-based feedback control strategies, which has been extensively studied and widely used in human-robot interaction [6,7]. Related application of active compliance in the design of ankle mechanism can also be found, for example, Stoeffler et al. [5] designed a variable stiffness ankle mechanism that combines parallel redundant mechanism and variable impedance actuator. However, too much dependency on the control algorithm and the rigid structure itself will also reduce the reliability. The other kind of compliance, the passive compliance, is realized by passive deformation of the elastic elements. For example, Van Oort et al. [4] presented an ankle actuation mechanism that has four springs arranged in parallel. Since it is an intrinsic property of the mechanism, this kind of compliance is more sensitive and reliable, which is more suitable for ankle mechanism design.

Parallel Continuum Robots (PCRs) [8], which is one of the popular research topics in the current robotics community, achieve its intrinsic compliance through large deformation of the parallel-arranged flexible links. Inspired by the structure of PCRs, a novel ankle mechanism that has two flexible crank-slider limbs is presented in this paper. Elastic beams are used to connect one common crank and two sliders that are driven independently. On one hand, the two-slider-crank limbs provide the ankle joint with passive stiffness which is useful for shock absorption, on the other hand, the parallel structure guarantees sufficient strength and precision.

The paper is organized as follows: Sect. 2 presents the mechanism description for the studied compliant ankle mechanism. Then, the kinestatic models, including forward and inverse kinetostatic model, are derived based on a discretization-based approach in Sect. 3. To analyze the stiffness characteristics of the mechanism, the derivation of stiffness model is given in Sect. 4. Finally, conclusions are drawn in Sect. 5

2   Mechanism Description

Flexible slider-crank mechanism is a kind of compliant mechanism, that use flexible beam to replace the rigid linkage of traditional slider-crank mechanism, as exhibited in Fig. 1. The elastic beam connects the slider and crank fixedly with a pre-specified angle, which results to a pre-deformation of the flexible beam. The slider is actively controlled, which gives rise to the bending deformation of the flexible beam and the passive rotation of the rigid crank. Due the elasticity of the flexible beam, there exists passive rotation stiffness at the revolute joint of the crank. Furthermore, the passive stiffness of the joint varies with the translation of slider, since the magnitude of the flexible beam's bending deformation would change accordingly. The passive elasticity of the revolute joint is an intrinsic property of the compliant slider-crank mechanism, which is exactly what the ankle mechanism design needs. Therefore, as shown in Fig. 2, a compliant ankle mechanism is obtained by assembling two compliant slider-crank mechanism.

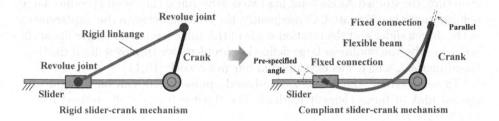

Fig. 1. Compliant slider-crank mechanism

The studied compliant ankle mechanism comprises a rigid frame and two flexible limbs, and each of the flexible limb is a compliant slider-crank mechanism. The flexible beams used in the limbs are made of spring steel stripes with uniform rectangular cross section. The two cranks are fixed together to form a common one, and the two sliders are driven independently. Due to the inherent elasticity, the flexible beam would bend in the working plane when the ankle joint is rotated, which provides passive stiffness to the ankle joint. Besides, the ankle joint is capable of varying its rotational stiffness by adjusting the displacement of the two sliders. Moreover, by leveraging the redundancy in actuation, active stiffness control can be achieved based on the kinetostatic and stiffness model. Figure 2 displays the conceptual design scheme, and the prototype will be developed in future works.

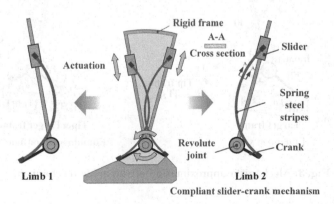

Fig. 2. Compliant ankle mechanism with two-slider-crank limbs.

3 Kinetostatic Modeling

This section introduces the kinetostatic modeling of the proposed compliant ankle mechanism. As exhibited in Sect. 2, in addition to the rigid supporting structure, the studied Ankle Joint has two flexible limbs that would produce large deformation when actuated. Consequently, the relation between the displacement of the driven slider and the rotation angle of the ankle joint is no longer linear. In order to solve the nonlinear large deflection problem, we employ a discretization-based method, which was developed in our prior work [10, 11].

To some extent, the discretization-based approach [10] can be thought as a special kink of finite element method. The flexible beam is discretized into n small segments, and each segment is approximated by a 6 degrees of freedom (DOF) serial manipulator, which is based on the principal decomposition of the structure compliance matrix [9].

It is worth noting that, for spring steel stripe used in the studied mechanism, its compression/elongation deformation is negligible compared to bending and torsional ones, furthermore, in planar case, only one bending effect needs considering. Hence, only one revolute joint is taken into account in the approximated mechanism. As a result, the flexible beam can be approximated by a serial hyper-redundant mechanism with passive but elastic joints, as illustrated in Fig. 3.

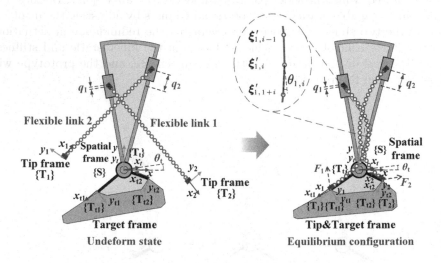

Fig. 3. Mechanism approximation of the ankle mechanism.

3.1 Forward Kinetostatic Model

In forward problem of kinetostatic modeling, the inputs are the displacements of two driven sliders, namely q_1, q_2, and the rotation angle of the ankle joint, namely θ_t, should be identified accordingly. In order to determine the final equilibrium state of the ankle mechanism, both the geometric constraint at the tip and the force equilibrium in joint space should be taken into account.

It is worth noting that the passive stiffness of the ankle joint is zero if no flexible link is connected to it, which means no reacted moment could be generated at the joint to resist external torque. Thus, the moment generated by two flexible links should be balanced at the joint. As a result, the system forward kinetostatic model of the compliant ankle joint can be represented by a set of nonlinear equations as

$$
C_{fwd}(\boldsymbol{\theta_1}, \boldsymbol{\theta_2}, \theta_t, \boldsymbol{F}_1, \boldsymbol{F}_2) =
\begin{bmatrix}
\left(\ln(\mathbf{g}_{st1}\mathbf{g}_{t1}^{-1})\right)^{\vee} \\
\left(\ln(\mathbf{g}_{st2}\mathbf{g}_{t2}^{-1})\right)^{\vee} \\
\mathbf{K}_1\boldsymbol{\theta}_1 - \mathbf{J}_1^T\boldsymbol{F}_1 \\
\mathbf{K}_2\boldsymbol{\theta}_2 - \mathbf{J}_2^T\boldsymbol{F}_2 \\
\boldsymbol{\xi}_t(-\boldsymbol{F}_1 - \boldsymbol{F}_2)
\end{bmatrix}
=
\begin{bmatrix}
\boldsymbol{y}_1 \\
\boldsymbol{y}_2 \\
\boldsymbol{\tau}_1 \\
\boldsymbol{\tau}_2 \\
\tau_0
\end{bmatrix}
=
\begin{bmatrix}
\boldsymbol{y} \\
\boldsymbol{\tau}
\end{bmatrix}
\tag{1}
$$

where $\boldsymbol{\theta}_1 = [\theta_{1,1}, \theta_{1,2}, ..., \theta_{1,N1}]^T \in \mathbb{R}^{N1 \times 1}, \boldsymbol{\theta}_2 = [\theta_{2,1}, \theta_{2,2}, ..., \theta_{2,N1}]^T \in \mathbb{R}^{N2 \times 1}$ are the joint displacement vectors of the flexible links in the left and right side, θ_t relates to the rotation angle of the ankle joint, and $\boldsymbol{F}_1, \boldsymbol{F}_2$ represent the external wrench at the connection points between the elastic beam and the crank, as shown in Fig. 3. $\mathbf{g}_{st1}, \mathbf{g}_{st2} \in SE(3)$ denote the pose of tip frame $\{T_1\}, \{T_2\}$ with respect to the spatial frame $\{S\}$, and $\mathbf{g}_{t1}, \mathbf{g}_{t2 \in SE(3)}$ are the pose of target frame $\{T_{t1}\}, \{T_{t2}\}$ with respect to the spatial one. $\boldsymbol{\xi}_t$ is the joint twist of the ankle joint.

$\left(\ln(\mathbf{g}_{st1}\mathbf{g}_{t1}^{-1})\right)^{\vee}, \left(\ln(\mathbf{g}_{st2}\mathbf{g}_{t2}^{-1})\right)^{\vee} \in \mathbb{R}^{6 \times 1}$ relate to the pose deviation of the current pose of tip frame from its target one. The vector $\boldsymbol{\tau}_1 \in \mathbb{R}^{N1 \times 1}, \boldsymbol{\tau}_2 \in \mathbb{R}^{N2 \times 1}$ represent the resultant moment in the joint space of the approximated mechanism, and $\tau_1 \in \mathbb{R}^{1 \times 1}$ represents the resultant moment at the ankle's revolute joint. $\mathbf{K}_1 = \mathrm{diag}(k_{1,1}, \cdots, k_{1,N_1}) \in \mathbb{R}^{N_1 \times N_1}, \mathbf{K}_2 = \mathrm{diag}(k_{2,1}, \cdots, k_{2,N_2}) \in \mathbb{R}^{N_2 \times N_2}$ denote the inherent stiffness of the elastic joints in the approximate hyper-redundant mechanism. The Jacobian matrix $\mathbf{J}_1, \mathbf{J}_2$ can be derived by differentiating the tip pose as

$$
\begin{cases}
\left(\dot{\mathbf{g}}_{st1}\mathbf{g}_{st1}^{-1}\right)^{\vee} = \mathbf{J}_1\dot{\boldsymbol{\theta}}_1 \Rightarrow \mathbf{J}_1 = [\boldsymbol{\xi}'_{1,1}, \boldsymbol{\xi}'_{1,2}, \cdots, \boldsymbol{\xi}'_{1,N_1}] \in \mathbb{R}^{6 \times N_1} \\
\left(\dot{\mathbf{g}}_{st2}\mathbf{g}_{st2}^{-1}\right)^{\vee} = \mathbf{J}_2\dot{\boldsymbol{\theta}}_2 \Rightarrow \mathbf{J}_2 = [\boldsymbol{\xi}'_{2,1}, \boldsymbol{\xi}'_{2,2}, \cdots, \boldsymbol{\xi}'_{2,N_2}] \in \mathbb{R}^{6 \times N_2}
\end{cases}
\tag{2}
$$

where $\boldsymbol{\xi}'_{1,i} = \mathrm{Ad}(\exp(\hat{\boldsymbol{\xi}}_{1,1}\theta_{1,1})\exp(\hat{\boldsymbol{\xi}}_{1,2}\theta_{1,2}) \cdots \exp(\hat{\boldsymbol{\xi}}_{1,i-1}\theta_{1,i-1}))\boldsymbol{\xi}_{1,i} \in se(3)$ is the 6×1 form joint twist, in current configuration, which is derived through the adjoint operator [12] $\mathrm{Ad}(\cdot)$ associated with elements in $SE(3)$, and $\boldsymbol{\xi}'_{2,i}$ can be derived in the same way. Here $\hat{\boldsymbol{\xi}}_{1,i}, \hat{\boldsymbol{\xi}}_{2,i} \in se(3)$ refer to the joint twist in undeformed state, which are represented in 4×4 standard form.

The total number of unknowns in the nonlinear algebraic equations is $N_1 + N_2 + 7$, which equals to the number of equation, therefore, the forward problem is deterministic. Newton-Raphson method is used here to solve these equations efficiently.

The upper four equations in Eq. 1 denote the geometric constraint and static equilibrium condition for the left and right flexible link. The last equation describes the coupling condition of two flexible links, representing the sum of moment projection at the joint of two reactive force induced by flexible links, which should equal to zeros when equilibrium state is reached. Then, the gradient matrix can be derived as

$$\nabla_{fwd} = \begin{bmatrix} \frac{\partial y}{\partial \theta} & \frac{\partial y}{\partial \theta_t} & \frac{\partial y}{\partial F} \\ \frac{\partial \tau}{\partial \theta} & \frac{\partial \tau}{\partial \theta_t} & \frac{\partial \tau}{\partial F} \end{bmatrix} \tag{3}$$

where the derivatives of pose deviation with respect to joint displacement vector $\theta = [\theta_1^T, \theta_2^T]^T \in \mathbb{R}^{(N1+N2)\times 1}$, and the ankle rotation angle θ_t can be obtained as

$$\frac{\partial y}{\partial \theta} = \begin{bmatrix} \frac{\partial y_1}{\partial \theta_1} & \frac{\partial y_1}{\partial \theta_2} \\ \frac{\partial y_2}{\partial \theta_1} & \frac{\partial y_2}{\partial \theta_2} \end{bmatrix} = \begin{bmatrix} J_1 & 0 \\ 0 & J_2 \end{bmatrix}, \quad \frac{\partial y}{\partial \theta_t} = \begin{bmatrix} \frac{\partial y_1}{\partial \theta_t} \\ \frac{\partial y_2}{\partial \theta_t} \end{bmatrix} = \begin{bmatrix} -\mathrm{Ad}(g_{st1}g_{t1}^{-1})\xi_t \\ -\mathrm{Ad}(g_{st2}g_{t2}^{-1})\xi_t \end{bmatrix} \tag{4}$$

The pose deviation is independent of external wrenches, so the corresponding item in gradient matrix is $\partial y/\partial F = 0$. The system overall stiffness matrix is represented by a block diagonal matrix as

$$\frac{\partial \tau}{\partial \theta} = \begin{bmatrix} \frac{\partial \tau_1}{\partial \theta_1} & \frac{\partial \tau_1}{\partial \theta_2} \\ \frac{\partial \tau_2}{\partial \theta_1} & \frac{\partial \tau_2}{\partial \theta_2} \\ \frac{\partial \tau_0}{\partial \theta_1} & \frac{\partial \tau_0}{\partial \theta_2} \end{bmatrix} = \begin{bmatrix} K_1 - K_{J1} & 0 \\ 0 & K_2 - K_{J2} \end{bmatrix} \tag{5}$$

where $K_{J1} = \partial J_1^T F_1/\partial \theta_1, K_{J2} = \partial J_2^T F_2/\partial \theta_2$ represent the configuration-dependent item of the overall stiffness matrix (please refer to [10] for details). The joint moment is independent of ankle rotation angle θ_t, hence $\partial \tau/\partial \theta_t = 0$. Likewise, the derivative of joint moment with respect to external wrench $F = [F_1^T, F_2^T]^T$ can be expressed by Jacobian matrix of two flexible links and joint twist of the ankle joint as

$$\frac{\partial \tau}{\partial F} = \begin{bmatrix} \frac{\partial \tau_1}{\partial F_1} & \frac{\partial \tau_1}{\partial F_2} \\ \frac{\partial \tau_2}{\partial F_1} & \frac{\partial \tau_2}{\partial F_2} \\ \frac{\partial \tau_0}{\partial F_1} & \frac{\partial \tau_0}{\partial F_2} \end{bmatrix} = \begin{bmatrix} -J_1^T & 0 \\ 0 & -J_2^T \\ -\xi_t & -\xi_t \end{bmatrix} \tag{6}$$

All those items in gradient matrix can be derived analytically, therefore, the rotation angle of ankle joint, together with equilibrium configuration of the flexible links and corresponding external wrench, can be specified iteratively, using the following update theme.

$$\begin{bmatrix} \delta\theta \\ \delta\theta_t \\ \delta F \end{bmatrix} = -\nabla_{fwd} C_{fwd} \Rightarrow \begin{cases} \theta^{j+1} = \theta^j + \delta\theta \\ \theta_t^{j+1} = \theta_t^j + \delta\theta_t \\ F^{j+1} = F^j + \delta F \end{cases} \tag{7}$$

The actuation variables $q_1, q_2 \in [-10\,\text{mm}, 10\,\text{mm}]$ are discretized evenly with the increment of 0.5 mm, the corresponding rotation angle is calculated using the forward kinetostatic model developed in this section, as shown in Fig. 4.

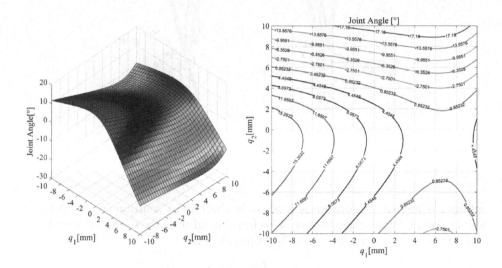

Fig. 4. Solutions of forward problems.

3.2 Inverse Kinetostatic Model

The inverse problem of kinetostatic modeling can be stated as to specify the corresponding displacement of two sliders, namely q_1, q_2, given the target rotation angle θ_t of ankle joint. For the inverse problem, the geometric constraints and equilibrium condition are identical with that of the forward problem, so the system inverse kinetostatic model is formulated as the same nonlinear algebraic equations as in Eq. 1

$$C_{inv}(\boldsymbol{\theta_1}, \boldsymbol{\theta_2}, \boldsymbol{F_1}, \boldsymbol{F_2}, q_1, q_2) = \begin{bmatrix} \left(\ln(\boldsymbol{g}_{st1}\boldsymbol{g}_{t1}^{-1})\right)^{\vee} \\ \left(\ln(\boldsymbol{g}_{st2}\boldsymbol{g}_{t2}^{-1})\right)^{\vee} \\ \mathbf{K}_1\boldsymbol{\theta_1} - \mathbf{J}_1^T\boldsymbol{F_1} \\ \mathbf{K}_2\boldsymbol{\theta_2} - \mathbf{J}_2^T\boldsymbol{F_2} \\ \boldsymbol{\xi}_t(-\boldsymbol{F_1} - \boldsymbol{F_2}) \end{bmatrix} = \begin{bmatrix} \boldsymbol{y_1} \\ \boldsymbol{y_2} \\ \boldsymbol{\tau_1} \\ \boldsymbol{\tau_2} \\ \boldsymbol{\tau_0} \end{bmatrix} = \begin{bmatrix} \boldsymbol{y} \\ \boldsymbol{\tau} \end{bmatrix} \qquad (8)$$

The only difference between the inverse and forward kinetostaic model is that the known variables q_1, q_2 in forward model are converted to unknown ones, and the unknown variable θ_t in forward model is converted to known one. Hence, the numbers of nonlinear algebraic equations is $N_1 + N_2 + 7$, while the number of corresponding unknowns is $N_1 + N_2 + 8$, which means the number of solution is

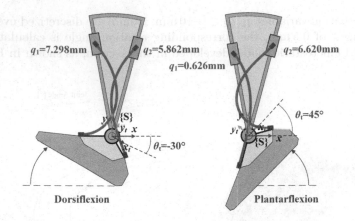

Fig. 5. Solutions of inverse problems.

infinite. If iterative algorithm is used, only the closest solution to initial guess will be found. Extra constraints can be introduced to make the solution unique. The gradient of the inverse model is represented as

$$\boldsymbol{\nabla}_{inv} = \begin{bmatrix} \frac{\partial y}{\partial \theta} & \frac{\partial y}{\partial F} & \frac{\partial y}{\partial q} \\ \frac{\partial \tau}{\partial \theta} & \frac{\partial \tau}{\partial F} & \frac{\partial \tau}{\partial q} \end{bmatrix} \tag{9}$$

where the displacement vector of flexible links is $\boldsymbol{\theta} = [\boldsymbol{\theta}_1^T, \boldsymbol{\theta}_2^T]^T$, and the actuation variable is denoted as $\boldsymbol{q} = [q_1, q_2]^T \in \mathbb{R}^{2 \times 1}$. The left four items in gradient matrix Eq. 9, namely $\partial y/\partial \theta, \partial y/\partial F, \partial \tau/\partial \theta, \partial \tau/\partial F$, have been derived in Eq. 4–6. The derivative of pose deviation with respect to actuation variable can be represented as

$$\frac{\partial y}{\partial q} = \begin{bmatrix} \frac{\partial y_1}{\partial q_1} & \frac{\partial y_1}{\partial q_2} \\ \frac{\partial y_2}{\partial q_1} & \frac{\partial y_2}{\partial q_2} \end{bmatrix} = \begin{bmatrix} \mathbf{J}_{q1} & \mathbf{0} \\ \mathbf{0} & \mathbf{J}_{q2} \end{bmatrix} \tag{10}$$

where $\mathbf{J}_{q1}, \mathbf{J}_{q2} \in \mathbb{R}^{6 \times 1}$ are the Jacobian matrix of flexible links associated with actuation variables (refer [10] for details). this two matrices can be derived according to differential of Lie group $SE(3)$ as

$$\mathbf{J}_{q1} = \frac{(\partial \mathbf{g}_{st1} \mathbf{g}_{st1}^{-1})^\vee}{\partial q_1}, \quad \mathbf{J}_{q2} = \frac{(\partial \mathbf{g}_{st2} \mathbf{g}_{st2}^{-1})^\vee}{\partial q_2} \tag{11}$$

The last item $\partial \tau/\partial q$ in gradient matrix can be obtained as

$$\frac{\partial \tau}{\partial F} = \begin{bmatrix} \frac{\partial \tau_1}{\partial q_1} & \frac{\partial \tau_1}{\partial q_2} \\ \frac{\partial \tau_2}{\partial q_1} & \frac{\partial \tau_2}{\partial q_2} \\ \frac{\partial \tau_0}{\partial q_1} & \frac{\partial \tau_0}{\partial q_2} \end{bmatrix} = \begin{bmatrix} -\mathbf{J}_{1q1}^T \mathbf{F}_1 & \mathbf{0} \\ \mathbf{0} & -\mathbf{J}_{2q2}^T \mathbf{F}_2 \\ \mathbf{0} & \mathbf{0} \end{bmatrix} \tag{12}$$

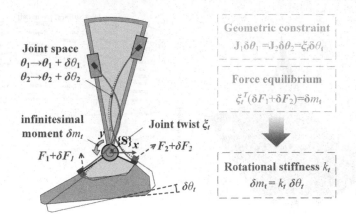

Fig. 6. Stiffness model derivation.

where $\mathbf{J}_{1q1}, \mathbf{J}_{2q2}$ denote the derivatives of Jacobian matrix $\mathbf{J}_1, \mathbf{J}_2$ with respect to actuation variables q_1, q_2, which can be represented as

$$\mathbf{J}_{1q1} = \left[\frac{\partial \boldsymbol{\xi}'_{1,1}}{\partial q_1}, \cdots, \frac{\partial \boldsymbol{\xi}'_{1,N_1}}{\partial q_1}\right], \quad \mathbf{J}_{2q2} = \left[\frac{\partial \boldsymbol{\xi}'_{2,1}}{\partial q_2}, \cdots, \frac{\partial \boldsymbol{\xi}'_{2,N_2}}{\partial q_2}\right] \quad (13)$$

Analogously, the actuation variables, along with equilibrium configuration of the flexible links and corresponding external wrench, can be specified iteratively using gradient-based searching algorithm, following the update theme

$$\begin{bmatrix} \delta\boldsymbol{\theta} \\ \delta\boldsymbol{F} \\ \delta\boldsymbol{q} \end{bmatrix} = -\boldsymbol{\nabla}_{inv}\,\boldsymbol{C}_{inv} \Rightarrow \begin{cases} \boldsymbol{\theta}^{j+1} = \boldsymbol{\theta}^j + \delta\boldsymbol{\theta} \\ \boldsymbol{F}^{j+1} = \boldsymbol{\theta}^j_F + \delta\boldsymbol{F} \\ \boldsymbol{q}^{j+1} = \boldsymbol{q}^j + \delta\boldsymbol{q} \end{cases} \quad (14)$$

Figure 5 displays two solutions of the inverse problem using the inverse kineto-static model developed in this section.

4 Stiffness Modeling

The studied compliant ankle joint in this paper achieves passive elasticity through its springy element in the flexible links. As illustrated in Fig. 2, when the ankle rotates around the joint, the elastic beam would bend accordingly, which produce passive rotational stiffness at the joint. Due to the nonlinear large defor-mation of the elastic beam, the rotational stiffness varies non-linearly with the rotation angle, which is hard to determine. In this section, the rotational stiffness model of the studied ankle joint is derived, based on results from kinetostatic model.

Let δm_t be an infinitesimal external moment exerted at the joint, as shown in Fig. 6, then, due to the external moment, the static equilibrium condition of

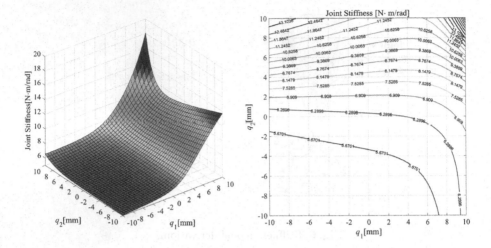

Fig. 7. Joint stiffness of the studied ankle mechanism.

the approximated hyper-redundant mechanism, as formulated in Eq. 1 and 8, could be updated as

$$\begin{cases} \boldsymbol{\tau}_1 = \mathbf{K}_1(\boldsymbol{\theta}_1 + \delta\boldsymbol{\theta}_1) - \mathbf{J}_1^T(\boldsymbol{F}_1 + \delta\boldsymbol{F}_1) = \boldsymbol{0} \\ \boldsymbol{\tau}_2 = \mathbf{K}_2(\boldsymbol{\theta}_2 + \delta\boldsymbol{\theta}_2) - \mathbf{J}_2^T(\boldsymbol{F}_2 + \delta\boldsymbol{F}_2) = \boldsymbol{0} \end{cases} \tag{15}$$

where $\delta\boldsymbol{\theta}_1, \delta\boldsymbol{\theta}_2$ are the infinitesimal displacement induced by external moment at the joint, and $\delta\boldsymbol{F}_1, \delta\boldsymbol{F}_2$ denote the additional force component caused by δm_t. Considering the original equilibrium condition as

$$\begin{cases} \mathbf{K}_1\boldsymbol{\theta}_1 - \mathbf{J}_1^T\boldsymbol{F}_1 = \boldsymbol{0} \\ \mathbf{K}_2\boldsymbol{\theta}_2 - \mathbf{J}_2^T\boldsymbol{F}_2 = \boldsymbol{0} \end{cases} \tag{16}$$

Substituting Eq. 16 into Eq. 15, the infinitesimal displacement can be represented as

$$\begin{cases} \delta\boldsymbol{\theta}_1 = \mathbf{C}_1\mathbf{J}_1^T\delta\boldsymbol{F}_1 \\ \delta\boldsymbol{\theta}_2 = \mathbf{C}_2\mathbf{J}_2^T\delta\boldsymbol{F}_2 \end{cases} \tag{17}$$

where $\mathbf{C}_1 = \mathbf{K}_1^{-1}, \mathbf{C}_2 = \mathbf{K}_2^{-1}$ refer to the compliance of the approximated joints in the flexible links. Note that the geometric constraints of each flexible link still exist, namely Eq. 18, which means the small changes in two joint space would cause the same tiny rotation at the tip.

$$\mathbf{J}_1\delta\boldsymbol{\theta}_1 = \mathbf{J}_2\delta\boldsymbol{\theta}_2 = \boldsymbol{\xi}_t\delta\theta_t \tag{18}$$

Premultiplying Eq. 17 by $\mathbf{J}_1$ and $\mathbf{J}_2$ gives

$$\begin{cases} \mathbf{J}_1\delta\boldsymbol{\theta}_1 = \mathbf{J}_1\mathbf{C}_1\mathbf{J}_1^T\delta\boldsymbol{F}_1 = \boldsymbol{\xi}_t\delta\theta_t \\ \mathbf{J}_2\delta\boldsymbol{\theta}_2 = \mathbf{J}_2\mathbf{C}_2\mathbf{J}_2^T\delta\boldsymbol{F}_2 = \boldsymbol{\xi}_t\delta\theta_t \end{cases} \tag{19}$$

where $\mathbf{J}_1\mathbf{C}_1\mathbf{J}_1^T = \mathbf{C}_{1t}, \mathbf{J}_2\mathbf{C}_2\mathbf{J}_2^T = \mathbf{C}_{2t} \in \mathbb{R}^{6\times 6}$ represent the two flexible links' compliance at the ankle joint. Further, taking account of moment equilibrium condition at the joint, which can be expressed as

$$\boldsymbol{\xi}_t^T(\delta\boldsymbol{F}_1 + \delta\boldsymbol{F}_2) = \delta m_t \tag{20}$$

where $\delta\boldsymbol{F}_1, \delta\boldsymbol{F}_2$ can be derived as Eq. 21, according to Eq. 19.

$$\begin{cases} \delta\boldsymbol{F}_1 = \mathbf{C}_{1t}^{-1}\boldsymbol{\xi}_t\delta\theta_t \\ \delta\boldsymbol{F}_2 = \mathbf{C}_{2t}^{-1}\boldsymbol{\xi}_t\delta\theta_t \end{cases} \tag{21}$$

Here $\mathbf{C}_{1t}^{-1} = \mathbf{K}_{1t}, \mathbf{C}_{2t}^{-1} = \mathbf{K}_{2t} \in \mathbb{R}^{6\times 6}$ represent the tip stiffness of two flexible links at the ankle joint. By substituting Eq. 21 into Eq. 20, the relation between the infinitesimal moment δm_t and the corresponding tiny rotation $\delta\theta_t$ can be obtained as

$$\boldsymbol{\xi}_t^T(\mathbf{K}_{1t} + \mathbf{K}_{2t})\boldsymbol{\xi}_t\delta\theta_t = \delta m_t \tag{22}$$

where $\mathbf{K}_t = \mathbf{K}_{1t} + \mathbf{K}_{2t} \in \mathbb{R}^{6\times 6}$ is the stiffness matrix of the two flexible links at the ankle joint, and $\boldsymbol{\xi}_t^T\mathbf{K}_t\boldsymbol{\xi}_t \in \mathbb{R}^{1\times 1}$ represents the rotation component, namely the rotational stiffness.

According to the stiffness model derived in this section, the rotational stiffness of the ankle mechanism is evaluated, as displayed in Fig. 7.

5   Conclusion

In this paper, a novel ankle mechanism which has two compliant limbs is proposed. Each of the compliant limbs can be regarded as a slider-crank mechanism that use elastic beam to fixedly connect the crank and driven slider. The proposed ankle mechanism incorporates the strength and accuracy of parallel mechanism and the intrinsic compliant property of elastic beam, which is beneficial to shock-absorption during ambulation. Forward and inverse kinetostatic models are derived using a disretization-based method. The rotational stiffness of the ankle joint is also analyzed. Based on the kinetostatic and stiffness model derived in this paper, a prototype will be developed in the next step, and future work will focus on parameters optimization and stiffness design.

Acknowledgement. This research work was supported in part by the National Key R&D program of China under the Grant 2019YFA0709001, and the National Natural Science Foundation of China under the Grant 52022056 and 51875334.

References

1. Saeedvand, S., Jafari, M., Aghdasi, H.S., Baltes, J.: A comprehensive survey on humanoid robot development. Knowl. Eng. Rev. 34 (2019)
2. Liang, Q., Wang, Y.: Flexible ankle based on PKM with force/torque sensor for humanoid robot (2011)

3. Kumar, S., Nayak, A., Peters, H., Schulz, C., Müller, A., Kirchner, F.: Kinematic analysis of a novel parallel 2SPRR+1U ankle mechanism in humanoid robot. In: Lenarcic, J., Parenti-Castelli, V. (eds.) ARK 2018. SPAR, vol. 8, pp. 431–439. Springer, Cham (2019). https://doi.org/10.1007/978-3-319-93188-3_49

4. van Oort, G., Reinink, R., Stramigioli, S.: New ankle actuation mechanism for a humanoid robot. IFAC Proc. Vol. 44(1), 8082–8088 (2011)

5. Stoeffler, C., Kumar, S., Peters, H., Brüls, O., Müller, A., Kirchner, F.: Conceptual design of a variable stiffness mechanism in a humanoid ankle using parallel redundant actuation. In: 2018 IEEE-RAS 18th International Conference on Humanoid Robots (Humanoids), pp. 462–468. IEEE (2018)

6. Zeng, G., Hemami, A.: An overview of robot force control. Robotica 15(5), 473–482 (1997)

7. Hogan, N., Buerger, S.: Robotics and automation handbook, chapitre impedance and interaction control, pages 19.1–19.24, vol. 10, p. 47. CRC Press, New York (2004)

8. Bryson, C.E., Rucker, D.C.: Toward parallel continuum manipulators. In: 2014 IEEE International Conference on Robotics and Automation (ICRA), pp. 778–785. IEEE (2014)

9. Chen, G., Wang, H., Lin, Z., et al.: The principal axes decomposition of spatial stiffness matrices. IEEE Trans. Rob. 31(1), 191–207 (2015)

10. Chen, G., Zhang, Z., Wang, H.: A general approach to the large deflection problems of spatial flexible rods using principal axes decomposition of compliance matrices. ASME J. Mech. Robot. 10(3), 031012 (2018)

11. Chen, G., Kang, Y., Liang, Z., Zhang, Z., Wang, H.: Kinetostatics modeling and analysis of parallel continuum manipulators. Mech. Mach. Theory 163, 104380 (2021)

12. Selig, J.M.: Geometric Fundamentals of Robotics, vol. 128. Springer, New York (2005). https://doi.org/10.1007/b138859

Adaptive Compliance Control of Flexible Link Manipulator in Unknown Environment

Cianyi Yannick[1], Xiaocong Zhu[1(✉)], and Jian Cao[2]

[1] State Key Laboratory of Fluid Power and Mechatronic Systems,
Zhejiang University, Hangzhou 310027, China
zhuxiaoc@zju.edu.cn
[2] School of Mechanical Engineering, Hefei University of Technology,
Hefei 230009, China

Abstract. The present work proposes an Adaptive Compliant Control scheme based on a closed-form output-redefined and perturbed dynamic model of a Single-link Flexible Manipulator (SLFM) in Unknown Environment. The control scheme is composed of inner and outer controllers. The inner control is designed based on Two-Time Scale Adaptive Robust Control (TTARC) to ensure fast and precise motion control, while the outer control is based on the impedance dynamics aiming to offer a desired compliant behavior in constrained motion. External force is estimated based on the extended Kalman Filter (EKF). The stability of the closed-loop system is verified through Lyapunov theory. The effectiveness of the overall control scheme is verified through simulation.

Keywords: Collaborative robots · Flexible-link manipulators · Compliance control · Two-time scale · Force observers

1 Introduction

Collaborative robots could meet the human's demand further by extending their application fields since traditional robots have limitations on handling complex products, being suitable for unstructured environments, and guaranteeing human safety. The expansion of collaborative robots could allow industrial robotics to be more attractive, with an estimation of 4 millions in 2022 [4]. Collaborative robots are characterized by their safety and flexibility, while still facing problems to be solved, such as accurate dynamic modeling and precise motion control. Most of collaborative robots designed in literature are usually equipped with rigid links, which cause hard collision problem during interactive operation with

This work was supported by the National Natural Science Foundation of China (Nos 51675471 and 51375432) and Science Fund for Creative Research Groups of National Natural Science Foundation of China (No. 51821093), and also supported by the Fundamental Research Funds for the Central Universities (2019QNA4002).

H. Liu et al. (Eds.): ICIRA 2022, LNAI 13457, pp. 779–790, 2022.
https://doi.org/10.1007/978-3-031-13835-5_70

humans [2]. Considering the core issue of safety and compliance, manipulators with flexible joints are recently presented [6]. Besides, if the manipulator link has flexible structure or is operating at high speed, the manipulator will exhibit flexible characteristics rather than rigid behavior. Therefore, the high performance control of flexible link manipulator (FLM) needs to be further developed for wide application of collaborative robots by handling the following well-known addressed problems: (i) link vibration, (ii) system nonlinearity, (iii) inevitable uncertainties, and (iv) instability in the internal dynamics.

Besides passive [10] and active compliant controls [16], Impedance control has been verified as best alternative way to achieve compliance behavior of the robot through regulation of its inertia, stiffness, and damping [13]. Because of modeling uncertainties, both unknown disturbances and environments, robust [5], adaptive [8,11], and learning technique [14] controls have been investigated and used to enforce the basic impedance control of robot manipulators. Most of the above different impedance control techniques are widely implemented on rigid, parallel rigid, and flexible joint robots. However, research on the implementation of compliant control on Cobots with flexible link are limited to adaptive impedance [1], dynamic hybrid position/force [9], backstepping approach [7] controls, and composite impedance control based singular perturbation (SP) theory [3]. Unfortunately, most of control designs are based on complex dynamics equations with hard task either to measure the vibration states or to retrieve them through accurate sensors.

The current research aims firstly to develop an explicit dynamics model for a SLFM system with high order vibration modes based on the combined Assumed Modal and Lagrange formulation methods. Then, a redefined closed-form dynamic model with both parametric and nonlinear uncertainties under necessary conditions for stability of the internal dynamics is proposed. Secondly, the control scheme comprises an inner control designed based on singular-perturbed and two-time scale sub-system dynamics. The outer control is designed based on impedance dynamics to enable the robot with compliance characteristic for the safety of both robot and unknown environment, during constrained motion. The unknown environment parameters includes contact force, stiffness and equilibrium position. The contact force is estimated by a designed force observer based on the extended Kalman filter (EKF) algorithm.

2   Dynamic of FLM

The SLFM in Fig. 1 consists of thin flexible link regarded as an Euler-Bernoulli beam of length l and a deflection w derived from the assumed modal method.

$$w(x,t) = \sum_{i=0}^{\infty} \phi_i(x)q_i(t) \tag{1}$$

where $\phi_i(x)$ and $q_i(t)$ are respectively link i-th mode shape function and its associated time generalized coordinate. The link, at one end (i.e., the hub), is driven

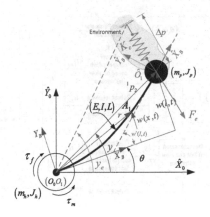

Fig. 1. Schematics of a rotary SLFM

by a rotary actuator and the other end attached to a payload attached while interacting unknown environment. In addition, the following assumptions are considered: (i) the link material property follows Hook's law; (ii) the link deflection is small; (iii) no longitudinal stiffness and length's variation are considered in the link; (iv) the environments is compliant and described by a massless spring.

By only selecting the first vibration mode while considering higher-order vibration modes as system uncertainties, the FLM dynamic model with uncertainties is given by [17]

$$\begin{cases} a_0\ddot{\theta} + a_1\ddot{q}_1 + (\kappa_2 + b_v)\dot{\theta} + A_f \tanh(\lambda_v\dot{\theta}) + \Delta_n = \kappa_1 u - \tau_{\theta,e} \\ a_1\ddot{\theta} + \ddot{q}_1 + 2\xi_1\omega_1\dot{q}_1 + \omega_1^2 q_1 = -\tau_{q,e} \end{cases} \quad (2)$$

where $a_0 = J_h + ml^2 + \rho A_b l^3/3$, $a_i = \rho A_b \int_0^l x\phi_i dx + ml\phi_{ie}$, $\Delta_n = \sum_{i=1}^{\infty}(a_i\ddot{q}_i) - a_1\ddot{q}_1$, $i = 1, 2, ..., n$. $\tau_{\theta,e} = J_\theta^T(\theta, q)f_e$ and $\tau_{q,e} = J_q^T(\theta, q)f_e$ are joint and flexible body frame joint torques, respectively, due to contact force. κ_1 and κ_2 are dc-motor parameters, A_f and b_v are the unknown coefficient of Column and viscous friction torques, respectively, and λ_v is a large positive coefficient.

According to the above assumptions and to the link deflection (1), the total tip-point angle of the link is given by $y_t(l,t) = \theta + \alpha(t)$ where $\alpha(t) = \arctan\left(\sum_{i=0}^{\infty}\bar{\phi}_{ie}q_i(t)\right)$, with $\bar{\phi}_{ie} = \phi_{ie}/l$, and $\phi_{ie} = \phi(l)$, in which the vibration mode of link can be expressed as

$$q_1 = \bar{\phi}_{1e}^{-1}\alpha + \bar{\phi}_{1e}^{-1}\Delta_q \quad (3)$$

where Δ_q is the approximation error of tip-end deflection of link, which is given by $\Delta_q = q_1\bar{\phi}_{1e} - \arctan\left(\sum_{i=1}^{\infty}\bar{\phi}_{ie}q_i\right)$. Substituting (3) into (2) and expressing the results in term of system parameters gives

$$\begin{cases} \ddot{\theta} = \zeta_1 u + \zeta_2\alpha + \zeta_3\dot{\theta} + \zeta_4\dot{\alpha} + \zeta_9\tanh(\lambda_v\dot{\theta}) + \zeta_{11}f_e + \zeta_{13} \\ \ddot{\alpha} = \zeta_5 u + \zeta_6\alpha + \zeta_7\dot{\theta} + \zeta_8\dot{\alpha} + \zeta_{10}\tanh(\lambda_v\dot{\theta}) + \zeta_{12}f_e + \zeta_{14} \end{cases} \quad (4)$$

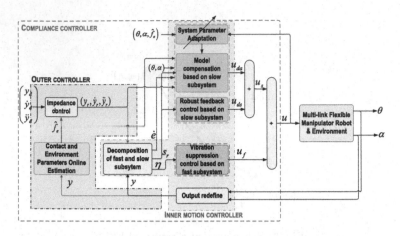

Fig. 2. Compliance control scheme of SLFM

where $\zeta_1 = \frac{\kappa_1}{a_0-a_1^2}$, $\zeta_2 = \frac{a_1\omega_1^2\bar{\phi}_{1e}^{-1}}{a_0-a_1^2}$, $\zeta_3 = -\frac{\kappa_2+b_v}{a_0-a_1^2}$, $\zeta_4 = \frac{2a_1\xi_1\omega_1\bar{\phi}_{1e}^{-1}}{a_0-a_1^2}$, $\zeta_5 = -\frac{a_1\kappa_1\bar{\phi}_{1e}}{a_0-a_1^2}$, $\zeta_6 = -\frac{a_0\omega_1^2}{a_0-a_1^2}$, $\zeta_7 = \frac{a_1\bar{\phi}_{1e}}{a_0-a_1^2}(\kappa_2+b_v)$, $\zeta_8 = -\frac{2a_0\xi_1\omega_1}{a_0-a_1^2}$, $\zeta_9 = -\frac{1}{a_0-a_1^2}A_f$, $\zeta_{10} = \frac{a_1\bar{\phi}_{1e}}{a_0-a_1^2}A_f$, $\zeta_{11} = \frac{a_1J_\theta^T-J_\theta^T}{a_0-a_1^2}$, $\zeta_{12} = \frac{(a_1J_\theta^T-a_0J_q^T)\bar{\phi}_{1e}}{a_0-a_1^2}$, $\zeta_{13} = \frac{a_1}{a_0-a_1^2}\Delta_1 - \frac{1}{a_0-a_1^2}\Delta_2$, $\zeta_{14} = -\frac{a_0\bar{\phi}_{1e}}{a_0-a_1^2}\Delta_1 + \frac{a_1\bar{\phi}_{1e}}{a_0-a_1^2}\Delta_2$. and $\Delta_1 = \bar{\phi}_{1e}^{-1}[\ddot{\Delta}_q + 2\xi_1\nu_1\dot{\Delta}_q + \nu_1^2\Delta_q]$, $\Delta_2 = \bar{\phi}_{1e}^{-1}a_1\ddot{\Delta}_q + \Delta_n$. ζ_{13} and ζ_{14} are regarded as the nonlinear uncertainty of FLM, including modeling error from neglected high-order vibration modes, unmodeled complex friction torque, approximation error of tip deflection and unknown disturbances, etc.

3 Control Design

The proposed compliance control strategy comprises two main controllers: an Impedance Dynamics-based Control and the Two-Time Scale Adaptive Robust Control (TTARC) as outer and inner controllers Fig. 2. The feedback for both controllers is realized by an output redefined function. During constrained motion, a force observer estimates the parameters of the environments. In the following, each control part is designed, as well as the stability of the closed-loop system is verified.

3.1 Output Redefined Model

Consider a new output redefine function $y_\Gamma \triangleq \theta + \Gamma\alpha$. Taking use of (4), the second derivative of y_Γ helps to obtain a refined dynamics model.

$$\begin{cases} \ddot{y}_\Gamma = \phi_r^T\vartheta_r + \Delta(t) \\ \ddot{\alpha} = \phi_f^T\vartheta_f + \Delta_\alpha \end{cases} \tag{5}$$

where $\vartheta_r = [\zeta_1+\Gamma\zeta_5, \zeta_2+\Gamma\zeta_6, \zeta_3+\Gamma\zeta_7, \zeta_4+\Gamma\zeta_8, \zeta_9+\Gamma\zeta_{10}, \zeta_{11}+\Gamma\zeta_{12}, d_n]^T$ is the vector parameters, $\phi_r = [u, \alpha, \dot{\theta}, \dot{\alpha}, \tanh(\lambda_v\dot{\theta}), f_e, 1]^T$ its corresponding regressor.

$\vartheta_f = [\zeta_5, \zeta_6, \zeta_7, \zeta_8, \zeta_{10}, \zeta_{12}, \Delta_a]^T$ and $\phi_f = \phi_f$ are the vector parameters of the flexible dynamics and its corresponding regressor, respectively. $\Gamma > 0$ and $\Gamma \in [0, \Gamma^*]$. Γ^* is a critical value above which the internal dynamics becomes unstable

3.2 Two-Time Scale Adaptive Robust Control Design

The dynamics (5) naturally have a higher frequency in the dynamics associated with the vibration of flexible link than in the one associated with the movement of rigid joint, especially during the motion and/or in the case of high stiffness system. Therefore, (5) can be divided into two subsystems, slow and fast, and the control design can be reduced to slow and fast slow and fast controllers.

Slow Dynamics: actual tip-trajectory y_Γ tracks a reference tip-trajectory given by y_r with a tracking error $e_r \triangleq y_\Gamma - y_d$. Consider a sliding mode function s_r such that $s_r \to 0$ occurs when $e_r \to 0$ as $t \to \infty$:

$$s_r = \dot{e}_r + k_1 e_r = \dot{y}_\Gamma - x_{2eq} \tag{6}$$

with $x_{2eq} \triangleq \dot{y}_d - k_1 e_r$, k_1 a positive value. According to (5) and (6) the time derivative of s_r gives the error dynamic equation.

$$\dot{s}_r = \ddot{y}_\Gamma - \dot{x}_{2eq} = K_u u + \phi_{ra}^T \hat{\vartheta}_{ra} - \dot{x}_{2eq} - \phi_r^T \tilde{\vartheta}_r + \tilde{d}(t) \tag{7}$$

where $K_u = \hat{\zeta}_1 + \Gamma\hat{\zeta}_5$, $\phi_{ra} = [\alpha, \dot{\theta}, \dot{\alpha}, \tanh(\lambda_v \dot{\theta}), f_e, I]^T$ is the regressor vector, and $\tilde{\vartheta}_r = \hat{\vartheta}_r - \vartheta_r$ is the system parameter estimation error, and $\hat{\vartheta}_{ra} = [\hat{\zeta}_2 + \Gamma\hat{\zeta}_6, \hat{\zeta}_3 + \Gamma\hat{\zeta}_7, \hat{\zeta}_4 + \Gamma\hat{\zeta}_8, \hat{\zeta}_9 + \Gamma\hat{\zeta}_{10}, \hat{\zeta}_{11} + \Gamma\hat{\zeta}_{12}, d_n]^T$ and $\tilde{d}_t(t)$ are respectively the estimated parameter vector and nonlinear uncertainty term, which are both assumed to be bounded and satisfy the following inequalities.

$$\Omega_{\vartheta_r} \triangleq \{\vartheta_{r,i,\min} \leq \vartheta_{r,i} \leq \vartheta_{r,i,\max}\}, \text{ and } \Omega_\Delta \triangleq |\tilde{d}_t(t)| \leq \varrho_0 \tag{8}$$

where $\vartheta_{r,i,\min}$ and $\vartheta_{r,i,\max}$ are known lower and upper bound vectors of ϑ_r, and ϱ_0 is a known constant value. $\hat{\vartheta}_r$ can be estimated through the parameter adaptation law

$$\dot{\hat{\vartheta}}_r = \text{Proj}_{\hat{\vartheta}_r}(\Gamma_r \phi_r s_r) \tag{9}$$

where Γ_r is chosen as a symmetric positive definite adaptation rate matrix, and $\text{Proj}_\bullet$ is the projection mapping defined as

$$\text{Proj}_{\hat{\vartheta}_r}(\bullet) = \begin{cases} 0 & \text{if } \hat{\vartheta}_{r,i} = \hat{\vartheta}_{r,i,\max} \text{ and } \bullet > 0 \\ 0 & \text{if } \hat{\vartheta}_{r,i} = \hat{\vartheta}_{r,i,\min} \text{ and } \bullet < 0 \\ \bullet & \text{otherwise} \end{cases} \tag{10}$$

such that the following property is satisfied:

$$\begin{aligned} &(i) \quad \hat{\vartheta}_r \in \Omega_{\vartheta_r} \triangleq \{\hat{\vartheta}_r : \vartheta_{r,\min} \leq \hat{\vartheta}_r \leq \vartheta_{r,\max}\}, \quad \forall t \\ &(ii) \quad \tilde{\vartheta}_r^T \left[\Gamma_r^{-1}\text{Proj}_{\hat{\vartheta}}(\Gamma_r \phi_r s_r) - \phi_r s_r\right] \leq 0, \quad \forall t \end{aligned} \tag{11}$$

Let the control input be synthesized as follows

$$u = u_{slow} + u_{fast} = u_{da} + u_{ds} + u_{fast} \tag{12}$$

where u_{da} is the model compensation control law including the contact force model compensation law given by $u_{da} = K_u^{-1}(-\phi_{ra}^T \hat{\vartheta}_{ra} + \dot{x}_{2eq})$, the robust control law $u_{ds} = K_u^{-1} u_s$, and the fast controller law $u_{fast} = K_u^{-1} u_f$, with u_s and u_f the control laws to be synthesized later.

The substitution of (12) into (7) leads to following output tracking error dynamics considered as closed-form slow subsystem dynamics:

$$\dot{s}_r = -\phi_r^T \tilde{\vartheta}_r + \tilde{d}(t) + u_s + u_f \tag{13}$$

Fast Dynamics: Consider a new variable η such that $\eta = \alpha/\mu^2$ and by taking (12) into second equation in (5) gives

$$\mu^2 \ddot{\eta} = \hat{\zeta}_5 K_u^{-1}(-\phi_{rb}^T \hat{\vartheta}_{rb} + \dot{x}_{2eq} + u_s + u_f) + [\hat{\zeta}_6 - \hat{\zeta}_5 K_u^{-1}(\hat{\zeta}_2 + \Gamma \hat{\zeta}_6)]\alpha \tag{14}$$
$$+ \phi_{fb}^T \hat{\vartheta}_{fb} - \phi_f^T \tilde{\vartheta}_f$$

where μ is the singular perturbation parameter, $\phi_{rb} = [\dot{\theta}, \dot{\alpha}, \tanh(\lambda_v \dot{\theta}), f_e, 1]^T$, $\vartheta_{fb} = [\zeta_7, \zeta_8, \zeta_{10}, \zeta_{12}, \Delta_\alpha]^T$, $\vartheta_{rb} = [\zeta_3 + \Gamma\zeta_7, \zeta_4 + \Gamma\zeta_8, \zeta_9 + \Gamma\zeta_{10}, \zeta_{11} + \Gamma\zeta_{12}, d_n]^T$, $\phi_{fb} = \phi_{rb}$, $\phi_f = \phi_r$, and $\vartheta_f = [\zeta_5, \zeta_6, \zeta_7, \zeta_8, \zeta_{10}, \zeta_{12}, \Delta_\alpha]^T$.

By definition of the following new variables $K_{cl} = \min\{\hat{\zeta}_6 - \hat{\zeta}_5 K_u^{-1}(\hat{\zeta}_2 + \Gamma\hat{\zeta}_6)\}$, $\mu^2 = |K_{cl}|^{-1}$, and $K_{clf} = \mu^2 K_{cl}$, (14) shortly becomes

$$\mu^2 \ddot{\eta} = K_{clf}\eta + \bar{N}_1(\dot{\theta}, f_e) + \Delta_N(t) + N_2 u_s + N_2 u_f \tag{15}$$

where $N_1(\dot{\theta}, f_e) = \hat{\zeta}_5 K_u^{-1}(-\phi_{rb}^T \hat{\vartheta}_{rb} + \dot{x}_{2eq}) + \phi_{fb}^T \hat{\vartheta}_{fb} - \phi_f^T \tilde{\vartheta}_f = \bar{N}_1(\dot{\theta}, f_e) + \Delta_N(t)$, with $\bar{N}_1(\dot{\theta}, f_e)$ and $\Delta_N(t)$ being slow and fast time-variant parts of $N_1(\dot{\theta}, f_e)$ respectively.

Moreover, by letting $\mu = 0$ into (15), the invariant manifold

$$\eta_s = -K_{clf}^{-1}[\bar{N}_{1s}(\dot{\theta}, f_e) + N_2 u_s] \tag{16}$$

is designed so that for canceling out effect of force contact in the fast time-varying part of $N_1(\dot{\theta}, f_e)$, the following new variables $\eta_1 \triangleq \eta - \eta_s$ and $\eta_2 \triangleq \mu^{-1}\dot{\alpha}$ can be defined as fast subsystem state variables associated to the following fast subsystem dynamics

$$\mu\dot{\eta}_2 = K_{clf}\eta_1 + N_2 u_f + \Delta_N(t) \tag{17}$$

By introducing a new time-scale variable $\varsigma = t/\mu$, (17) can be expressed in closed-form as

$$d\bar{\eta}/d\varsigma = A_f \bar{\eta} + B_f u_f + \Delta_f \tag{18}$$

where $\bar{\eta} = [\eta_1, \eta_2]^T$, $A_f = \begin{bmatrix} 0 & 1 \\ K_{clf} & 0 \end{bmatrix}$, $B_f = [0, N_2]^T$, and $\Delta_f = [0, \Delta_N(t)]^T$.

Control Design for Slow Subsystem: In completion of the control law (12), the robust control law of slow subsystem u_s is designed as

$$u_s = -k_r \ s_r - S(hsgn(s_r)) \qquad (19)$$

where k_r is the feedback gain to be designed during the closed-loop analysis. The nonlinear term $S(hsgn(s_r))$ is defined such that the following properties are satisfied:

$$
\begin{aligned}
(i) & \quad -s_r \ S(hsgn(s_r)) \leq 0 \\
(ii) & \quad s_r[-S(hsgn(s_r)) - (\phi_r^T \tilde{\vartheta} - \tilde{d}_t)] \leq \epsilon(t)
\end{aligned}
\qquad (20)
$$

where $\epsilon(t)$ is a bounded time-varying scalar, i.e. $0 < \epsilon(t) \leq \epsilon_M$, with $\epsilon_M > 0$.

Control Design for Fast Subsystem: The control law u_f aims to suppress effectively the vibration within the link and especially at the tip link. u_f is synthesized as a state feedback control based on fast subsystem [15]

$$u_f = -\mu_f K_f \bar{\eta} \qquad (21)$$

where $K_f = [K_{f_1} \ K_{f_2}]$ is the feedback gain to be synthesized by solving the closed-loop characteristic equation.

$$s^2 + (N_2 K_2) \ s + (N_2 K_1 - K_{clf}) = s^2 - 2p_{f_d}s + p_{f_d}^2 \qquad (22)$$

where p_{f_d} is the desired pole. By identification, the feedback gains are given by $K_{f_1} = \frac{p_{f_d}^2 + K_{clf}}{N_2}$ and $K_{f_2} = \frac{-2p_{f_d}}{N_2}$ and computed after free placement of p_{f_d}.

3.3   Stability of the Controller

Lyapunov Stability of the Closed-Loop Slow Subsystem: The Lyapunov candidate for closed-loop slow subsystem and its time derivative are given in (23)

$$
\begin{cases}
V_1 = \dfrac{1}{2}s_r^2, \text{ with } V_1 \geq 0 \ \forall \ s_r \neq 0 \\
\dot{V}_1 = s_r \ \dot{s}_r \leq -k_r \ s_r^2 + \epsilon_M + l_\psi
\end{cases}
\qquad (23)
$$

where ϵ_M is defined in (20) and $l_\psi = ||s_r \ u_f||$. The passivity condition of the closed-loop slow subsystem relies in proper design of ϵ_M and l_ψ. Expressing (23) in term of V_1 as in (24)

$$\dot{V}_1 + 2k_r V_1 \leq (\epsilon_M + l_\psi) \qquad (24)$$

and multiplying both side of (24) by $e^{-2k_r \ t}$, and by finally integrating over time leads to

$$V_1(t) = e^{-2k_r \ t}V_1(0) + \frac{\epsilon_M + l_\psi}{2k_r} \left(1 - e^{-2k_r \ t}\right) \qquad (25)$$

For fast convergence in the transient part of (25), k_r is desirable as large as possible. The comparison Lemma [12] helps to write

$$|s_r(t)|^2 \le e^{-2k_r t}|s_r(0)|^2 + \frac{\epsilon_M + l_\psi}{2k_r}\left(1 - e^{-2k_r t}\right) \qquad (26)$$

so one can easily shows that $s_r(\infty) \to 0$ for large k_1 and k_r, and very small ϵ_M and l_ψ. Small l_ψ also implies playing with μ_f in (21).

In case of $\Delta(x,t) \ne 0$, the asymptotic output tracking error can be achieved by choosing a new Lyapunov candidate

$$V_2 = V_1 + \frac{1}{2}\tilde{\vartheta}_r^T \Gamma_r^{-1}\tilde{\vartheta}_r \qquad (27)$$

where $V_2 \ge 0$ for $s_r = 0$, and $\tilde{\vartheta}_r = 0$, and $V_2 > 0$ $\forall$ $s_r \ne 0$, $\tilde{\vartheta}_r \ne 0$, since $\Gamma_r \ge 0$ and $V_1 \ge 0$. The time derivative of (27) gives

$$\dot{V}_2 = \dot{V}_1 + \frac{\partial V_a}{\partial \tilde{\vartheta}}\dot{\tilde{\vartheta}}_r \le -k_r\, s_r^2 + l_\psi \qquad (28)$$

where $\dot{\tilde{\vartheta}}_r = \dot{\hat{\vartheta}}_r$, since ϑ_r is constant vector. Therefore, the passivity condition relies in proper design of l_ψ. If $l_\psi \to 0$ $\forall$ s_r, then $\dot{V}_2 \le 0$. In addition, according to Barbalat's lemma [12], $\dot{V}_2 \to 0$ while $t \to \infty$ because (i) V_2 is lower bounded (27), (ii) $\dot{V}_2 \le 0$, and (iii) $\dot{V}_2$ is uniformly continuous in time. Therefore, one can concludes that s_r is asymptotically stable, which according to (6), implies that $e_r = \exp(-k_1 t)$, hence $e_r(\infty) = 0$ since $k_1 > 0$.

Stability of the Closed-Loop Fast Subsystem: The closed-loop internal dynamic is obtained by substitution of fast control input (21) and fast state variables $\bar{\eta}$ into internal dynamic (15):

$$\ddot{\alpha} + 2\xi_f\omega_f\dot{\alpha} + \omega_f^2\alpha = \mu^2\omega_f^2\eta_s + \Delta_N \qquad (29)$$

where $\omega_f^2 = \frac{1}{\mu}(\mu_f N_2 K_{f_1} - \bar{K}_{clf})^{1/2}$ and $\xi_f = \frac{\mu_f N_2 K_{f_2}}{2\mu\omega_f}$, respectively frequency and damping ratio of the fast closed-loop internal dynamics, all depending on Γ, desired poles p_{f_d}, and system parameters ζ_i. Because of stability analysis, let define new variables $\sigma = [\alpha^T, \dot{\alpha}^T]^T$ such that (29) can be written as

$$\dot{\sigma} = A_\sigma\sigma + d(t) \qquad (30)$$

where $A_\sigma = \begin{bmatrix} 0 & 1 \\ -\omega_f^2 & -2\xi_f\omega_f \end{bmatrix}$, $d(t) = [0,\ N_3]^T$, $N_3 = K_a\eta_s + \Delta_s(t)$, and the gain $K_a = \mu_f N_2 K_{f_1}$.

The stability of inner closed-loop dynamics (29) requires the real part of the pole P_d of (30) to be negative while keeping small disturbance $d(t)$. The selection of stability region is then a trade off between small $\mathbb{R}_e(A_\sigma)$, small K_a, and small $1/K_u$ as shown in Fig. 3 under varying Γ and P_{d_f}. It can be seen that the smaller is the desired fast dynamics pole P_{d_f}, the more the pole P_d is close to zero, the more the dynamics (30) is unstable, and the larger is $1/K_u$, even though K_a is getting smaller. Thus, $\Gamma \in [0.3, 0.7]$ is suitable range for internal dynamics stability and further good control performance.

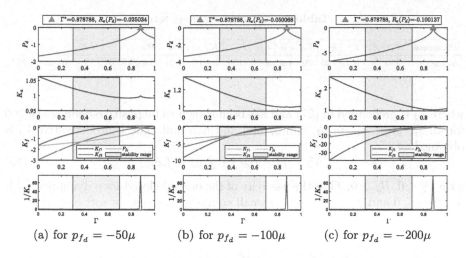

(a) for $p_{f_d} = -50\mu$ (b) for $p_{f_d} = -100\mu$ (c) for $p_{f_d} = -200\mu$

Fig. 3. Selection of output redefine parameter Γ

3.4   Impedance Control Design

In order to prescribe a robot dynamic behavior during constrained motion, the impedance dynamics is given by

$$M_d(\ddot{y}_r - \ddot{y}_d) + B_d(\dot{y}_r - \dot{y}_d) + K_d(y_r - y_d) = f_e \qquad (31)$$

where $M_d > 0$, $B_d > 0$, and $K_d > 0$ are respectively desired impedance inertia, damping and stiffness. y_r and y_d are reference and desired tip-trajectories in joint-space. f_e is the contact force between the robot end-effector and the unknown compliant environment given by

$$f_e = K_e(y - y_e)l \qquad (32)$$

where K_e is environment stiffness, y is the actual position of the robot end-effector, and l is the length of robot link. K_e, y_e and f_e are the environment parameters considered to be unknown.

Stability Analysis of the Outer Closed-Loop Dynamics: the outer closed-loop dynamics is a combination of the impedance dynamics (31), the interaction force (32), and the inner closed-loop dynamics (13)

$$\begin{cases} M_d(\ddot{y}_r - \ddot{y}_d) + B_d(\dot{y}_r - \dot{y}_d) + K_d(y_r - y_d) = K_e(y - y_e)l \\ \dot{s}_r = -\phi_r^T \tilde{\vartheta}_r + \tilde{d}(t) + u_s + u_f \end{cases} \qquad (33)$$

Another Lyapunov candidate is chosen as

$$V_3 = V_2 + \frac{1}{2}M_d(\dot{y}_d - \dot{y}_r)^2 + \frac{1}{2}K_d(y_d - y_r)^2 + \frac{1}{2}K_e(y - y_e)^2 \qquad (34)$$

Table 1. Control parameters setup

Parameter	$\Gamma_r(8,8)$	Γ	k_1	k_r	ϵ_M	h_M	P_d	K_d	M_d	B_d	K_e	y_e
Value	250	0.7	120	70	1.0	5	-120	2 - 10	0.01	$0.8\sqrt{4M_dK_d}$	2 - 10	$15° - 25°$

where V_2 is predefined in (27) and has been shown to be positive-definite. $V_3 \geq 0$ for all s_r, y, y_d, y_r, $\dot{y}$, $\dot{y}_d$, and $\dot{y}_r$ null and non-null. The time derivative $\dot{V}_3$ is obtained as

$$\dot{V}_3 = \dot{V}_2 - B_d e_d^2 + f_e \dot{y}_d + f_e \dot{e}_r \tag{35}$$

with $\dot{V}_2 \leq 0$, $B_d > 0$. Thus the passivity of the outwer closed-loop dynamics holds for $f_e \dot{y}_d \leq 0$ and $f_e \dot{e}_r \leq 0$, i.e. (i) small contact force (use of soft environments - small K_e); (ii) accurate inner motion control ($e_r \approx 0$); and (iii) the use of a passive or compliant environment.

Environment Parameters Estimation: The contact force f_e is estimated using force observer based on EKF algorithm (36)

$$\begin{cases} \hat{v}_k^- = \hat{v}_k^- + T_s \, f(\hat{v}_{k-1}, u_{s,k}) \\ \hat{P}_k^- = \hat{F}_{k-1}\hat{P}_{k-1}\hat{F}_{k-1}^T + \hat{H}_{k-1}\tilde{N}_{k-1}\hat{H}_{k-1}^T \\ K_k = \hat{P}_k^- C_{v,k}^T (C_{v,k}\hat{P}_k^- C_{v,k}^T + \tilde{W}_k)^{-1} \end{cases} \quad \begin{cases} \hat{v}_k^+ = \hat{v}_k^- + K_k \left(\tilde{y}_k - C_{v,k}\hat{v}_k^-\right) \\ \hat{P}_k = (I - K_k C_{v,k}) \hat{P}_k^- \\ f_{e_k} = \hat{v}_k^+ (\text{end}) \end{cases}$$

$$\tag{36}$$

where $v \triangleq [\dot{\theta}, \theta, \dot{\alpha}, \alpha, f_e]^T$, f is the state transition function based on the dynamics equation (4), $(\hat{v}_k^-, \hat{P}_k^-)$ and $(\hat{v}_k, \hat{P}_k)$ are the predicted and estimated states and their associated covariance, respectively. K_k is the Kalman filter gain to correct the prediction on time step k.

Finally, by defining a threshold value for the contact force f_e^*, such that at instance $|\hat{f}_e| > f_e^*$ the contact can be detected. Thus, the actual position y at that instance is considered as the estimated rest position of the environment $\hat{y}_e$. The environment stiffness can be computed based on the Eq. (32).

4   Simulation Results

The effectiveness of the proposed controller is verified on a SFLM with model parameters given in [17], tracking from its tip, a desired square wave trajectory given by $y_d = [0 - 40]°$, with $\dot{y}_{d,max} = 80°/s$ and $\ddot{y}_{d,max} = 240°/s^2$. Table 1 shows control parameters set for good control performance such as accurate inner motion control, robustness, and fast response.

For given a compliant soft environment of $K_e = 2\,\text{N/m}$, located at $y_e = 25°$ and $y_e = 15°$, for a period of 1.35 s, from 5.5 to 7.4 s and from 9.415 to 11.4 s respectively, Fig. 4 shows effect of stiff robot by setting up the desired impedance stiffness to $K_d = 5\,\text{N/m}$. The robot's end-effector is able to penetrate within the environment, and damages the environment with low contact force $\hat{f}_{e,ss} \approx 0.189\,\text{N}$. Therefore, for safety of soft environment, a small value of

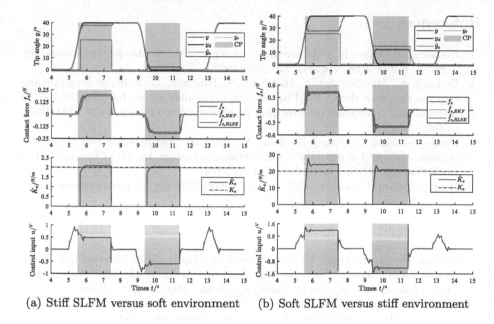

(a) Stiff SLFM versus soft environment   (b) Soft SLFM versus stiff environment

Fig. 4. Numerical simulation results of Compliant control of SLFM

K_d is suitable to maintain the robot end-effector at the equilibrium position of environment. Moreover, for given stiff compliant environment of $K_e = 20\,\mathrm{N/m}$, setting small $K_d = 2\,\mathrm{N/m}$ (soft robot), prevents robot end-effector to penetrate the environment and keep itself safe from hard collision. In addition, for high environment stiffness the contact force becomes larger $\hat{f}_{e,ss} \approx 0.5\,\mathrm{N}$ and the transient response could suffer from large overshoot.

5 Conclusion

In this paper, an adaptive compliance control of a SLFM in unknown environment has been proposed in term of inner and outer controllers. The inner controller has been designed firstly based on an output-redefined and singular-perturbed slow dynamics for precise tip-trajectory tracking and secondly based on two-time scales fast dynamics to suppress tip-link vibrations. Lyapunov theory has been used to point out necessary passivity conditions for both closed-loop inner and outer dynamics. The unknown environment parameters have been estimated through two force observer based on EKF algorithm and compare with RLSE method. System parameters have been updated through online adaptation law. The effectiveness of the proposed controller has been verified through numerical simulation.

References

1. Colbaugh, R., Glass, K.: Adaptive task-space control of flexible-joint manipulators. J. Intell. Robot. Syst. **20**(2–4), 225–249 (1997)
2. De Luca, A., Albu-Schaffer, A., Haddadin, S., Hirzinger, G.: Collision detection and safe reaction with the DLR-III lightweight manipulator arm. In: 2006 IEEE/RSJ International Conference on Intelligent Robots and Systems, pp. 1623–1630. IEEE (2006)
3. Deng, D., Sun, T., Guo, Z., Pan, Y.: Singular perturbation-based variable impedance control of robots with series elastic actuators. In: 2019 Chinese Control Conference (CCC), pp. 4397–4402. IEEE (2019)
4. Heer, C.: World robotics 2021 reports. https://ifr.org/ifr-press-releases/news/robot-sales-rise-again. Accessed 6 June 2022
5. Izadbakhsh, A., Khorashadizadeh, S.: Robust impedance control of robot manipulators using differential equations as universal approximator. Int. J. Control **91**(10), 2170–2186 (2018)
6. Jianbin, H., Zhi, L., Hong, L.: Development of adaptive force-following impedance control for interactive robot. In: Tan, Y., Shi, Y., Tang, Q. (eds.) Advances in Swarm Intelligence, pp. 15–24. Springer, Cham (2018). https://doi.org/10.1007/978-3-319-93818-9_2
7. Jiang, Z.H., Irie, T.: A new impedance control method using backstepping approach for flexible joint robot manipulators. Int. J. Mech. Eng. Robot. Res. **9**(6), 1–11 (2020)
8. Li, P., Ge, S.S., Wang, C.: Impedance control for human-robot interaction with an adaptive fuzzy approach. In: 2017 29th Chinese Control and Decision Conference (CCDC), pp. 5889–5894. IEEE (2017)
9. Matsuno, F., Yamamoto, K.: Dynamic hybrid position/force control of a two degree-of-freedom flexible manipulator. J. Robot. Syst. **11**(5), 355–366 (1994)
10. Park, D.I., et al.: Automatic assembly method with the passive compliant device. In: 2017 11th Asian Control Conference (ASCC), pp. 347–348. IEEE (2017)
11. Sharifi, M., Behzadipour, S., Vossoughi, G.: Nonlinear model reference adaptive impedance control for human-robot interactions. Control Eng. Pract. **32**, 9–27 (2014)
12. Slotine, J.J.E., et al.: Applied Nonlinear Control, vol. 199. Prentice Hall Englewood Cliffs, NJ (1991)
13. Song, P., Yu, Y., Zhang, X.: A tutorial survey and comparison of impedance control on robotic manipulation. Robotica **37**(5), 801–836 (2019)
14. Sun, T., Cheng, L., Peng, L., Hou, Z., Pan, Y.: Learning impedance control of robots with enhanced transient and steady-state control performances. Sci. China Inf. Sci. **63**(9), 1–13 (2020). https://doi.org/10.1007/s11432-019-2639-6
15. Vossoughi, G., Karimzadeh, A.: Impedance control of a two degree-of-freedom planar flexible link manipulator using singular perturbation theory. Robotica **24**(2), 221 (2006)
16. Zeng, F., Xiao, J., Liu, H.: Force/torque sensorless compliant control strategy for assembly tasks using a 6-DOF collaborative robot. IEEE Access **7**, 108795–108805 (2019)
17. Zhu, X., Yannick, C., Cao, J.: Inverse dynamics-based control with parameter adaptation for tip-tracking of flexible link robot. In: 2021 WRC Symposium on Advanced Robotics and Automation (WRC SARA), pp. 174–180. IEEE (2021)

A Novel Discrete Variable Stiffness Gripper Based on the Fin Ray Effect

Jiaming Fu[1], Han Lin[1], I. V. S. Prathyush[2], Xiaotong Huang[1], Lianxi Zheng[3], and Dongming Gan[1(✉)]

[1] Purdue University, West Lafayette, IN 47907, USA
dgan@purdue.edu
[2] Birla Institute of Technology and Science, Pilani 333031, India
[3] Khalifa University, Abu Dhabi 127788, UAE

Abstract. Variable stiffness grippers can adapt to objects with different shapes and gripping forces. This paper presents a novel variable stiffness gripper (VSG) based on the Fin Ray effect that can adjust stiffness discretely. The main structure of the gripper includes the compliant frame, rotatable ribs, and the position limit components attached to the compliant frame. The stiffness of the gripper can be adjusted by rotating the specific ribs in the frame. There are four configurations for the gripper that were developed in this research: a) all ribs OFF (Flex) mode; b) upper ribs ON and lower ribs OFF (Hold) mode; c) upper ribs OFF and lower ribs ON (Pinch) mode; d) all ribs ON (Clamp) mode. Different configurations can provide various stiffness for the gripper's finger to adapt the objects with different shapes and weights. To optimize the design, the stiffness analysis under various configurations and force conditions was implemented by finite element analysis (FEA). The 3-D printed prototypes were constructed to verify the feature and performance of the design concept of the VSG compared with the FEA results. The design of the VSG provides a novel idea for industrial robots and collaborative robots on adaptive grasping.

Keywords: Variable stiffness gripper · Fin Ray effect · Discrete stiffness change · Robotic grasping · Adaptive grasping

1 Introduction

Compared with traditional rigid manipulators, adaptive grippers are able to fulfill variable tasks in an unstructured environment. Most traditional rigid grippers are not compliant enough to grip deformable or delicate objects. Therefore, the expansion of soft and adaptive grippers would provide better solutions for the robotics field. Adaptive grippers are widely-used, both for industrial robots and collaborative robots [1].

Many solutions of adaptive grippers have been developed [2, 3] such as pneumatic 3D printed soft grippers [4], tendon-driven adaptive grippers [5–7], structural transformation based compliant variable stiffness grippers [8], Fin Ray grippers [9], etc. There are also a bunch of studies on the materials of grippers, for example, composites materials [10],

H. Liu et al. (Eds.): ICIRA 2022, LNAI 13457, pp. 791–802, 2022.
https://doi.org/10.1007/978-3-031-13835-5_71

dielectric elastomer [11], memory alloy [12], and low-melting-point alloy [13]. Lots of innovative grippers with variable stiffness have also been proposed recently, they can adjust the stiffness by air-operated [14], magnetic [15], and rotating built-in elements [16, 17]. Additionally, there have been several excellent research publications on the characteristics, shape, structure, and parameters of Fin Ray [18–22].

Based on those ideas, this work will also introduce a novel variable stiffness gripper based on the Fin Ray effect that can adjust stiffness discretely. The main structure of the gripper includes the compliant frame, rotatable ribs, and the position limit components attached to the compliant frame. The stiffness of the gripper can be adjusted by rotating the specific ribs in the frame. This paper will focus on the mechanical design and performance of the VSG instead of building a mathematical model for fin ray structure which has been done by [23, 24].

The VSG can take into account both accuracy and speed, and it can grasp objects with a variety of hardness and shapes. For most soft grippers, it is difficult to ensure accuracy because of the low stiffness. In addition, the response speed of the VSG is very fast, as long as the motor drives the pulley to rotate, the stiffness can be changed rapidly in offline mode. Also, the VSG is low energy consumption. The servo motor only consumes power when the stiffness needs to be changed, but not when it is on standby. Third, the VSG has a simple structure and is easy to assemble. Its manufacturing cost is also low, and it is easy to replace if damaged.

The paper is structured as follows. Section 2 introduces the mechanical design of the VSG, and the concept implemented for adjusting the stiffness. Section 3 compares FEA and experiment data. Section 4 discusses the result and shows demos while Sect. 5 summarizes the work.

2 Concept of the Design

As shown in Fig. 1, the VSG is composed of two units: the driving mechanism and the grasping mechanism. The driving mechanism is used to realize the opening and tightening of the manipulator. The crank gear, rocker, and connecting rod constitute a parallelogram mechanism. The gear drive makes the two parallelogram mechanisms move synchronously. The motor transmits the rotation to the upper gear crank, which drives the movement of the two fingers. This is a common manipulator mechanism. The advantages of these mechanisms are simple and compact, which can achieve fast and precise control.

The overall structure of the grasping mechanism adopts the Fin Ray effect. The structure of the Fin Ray is a V-shaped frame with two bones on the sides and several ribs connected in between. For the VSG, the frame is designed as compliant, and the four ribs that support the frame have convertible angles, to realize discrete stiffness adjustment. The specific method is to connect two thin rods between the tip of the frame and the base to hold the ribs. The rod may increase the stiffness of the fingers, but it is designed to be as thin as possible and made of a compliant material to avoid interference with the overall stiffness as much as possible. Two belt pulleys are fixed on each rod, which is respectively connected with the upper two ribs and the lower two ribs through shafts. The pulley is connected to the servo motor through a belt. Each finger has 2 servo motors.

One motor controls the angular position of the lower two ribs, and the other controls the upper two ribs. In order to prevent the ribs from sliding and tilting to undesired angles, the ribs can be slidingly fitted into the grooves on the frame; this design is to prevent the ribs from sliding into other angles and causing unnecessary deflection in different rigid areas. When the servo motor is in the locked position, the ribs will be locked accordingly, and the locked movement will be transmitted to the pulley and ribs through the belt. Two fingers are defined as a synchronized configuration.

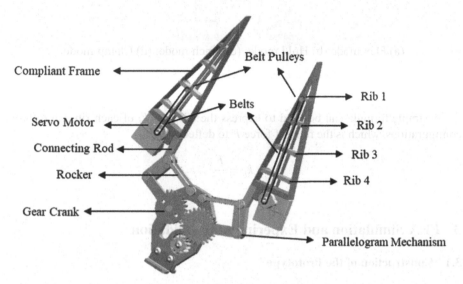

Fig. 1. 3-D model of the VSG.

Therefore, this mechanism has four configurations to achieve four stiffness levels to suit the objects with various hardness and dimension, as shown in Fig. 2. When all the ribs are out of contact with the frame, the system is in all ribs OFF status, also called Flex mode. This mode is suitable for grabbing larger soft objects or fragile objects. At this time, the priority of protecting items is higher than precision and speed. When the upper two ribs stay in contact with the frame and the lower two ribs leave the frame, the system is in upper ribs ON and lower ribs OFF status, also called Hold mode. This mode is suitable for grabbing heavy soft objects or fragile objects. The two fingers will wrap the object gently. When the upper two ribs leave the frame and the lower two ribs stay in contact with the frame, the system is in upper ribs OFF and lower ribs ON status, also called Pinch mode. This mode is suitable for grabbing light and small soft objects or fragile objects while ensuring high accuracy; when all ribs are in contact with the frame, the system is in all ribs on status, also called Clamp mode. This mode is suitable for grabbing hard objects with a variety of sizes, while the system is at high-speed operation to ensure maximum precision.

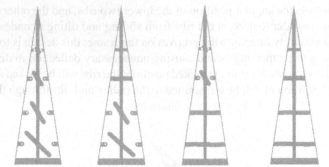

(a) Flex mode;(b) Hold mode; (c) Pinch mode; (d) Clamp mode.

Fig. 2. Four configurations of the VSG.

A simple formula can be used to express the stiffness k_i of each rib i in different configurations, which is the ratio of force F to deflection δ_i:

$$k_i = \frac{F}{\delta_i} \tag{1}$$

3   FEA Simulation and Experimental Validation

3.1   Construction of the Prototype

According to the concept of design in Sect. 2, a prototype was constructed based on 3D printing. PLA was selected as the main material due to its high toughness and high strength characteristics. TPU 95A was not adopted in this case because the stiffness in Flex mode was too low to hold the object. When building the prototype, the design of the VSG was simplified, so pulleys and motors were not be installed. Therefore, pins are added between the two ends of the ribs and the compliant frame to prevent the ribs from being separated from the frame due to excessive force. This was to contrive the situation equivalent to the servo motor and the toothed pulley locking the ribs. This would allow ribs to rotate to a certain angle while force is being exerted and not to be separated from the frame. In 3D printing, the infill of the prototype was set to 40%, and the layer height was set to 0.1 mm.

3.2   Determination of Material Properties

The material properties of the same material under different printing configurations are different. The supplier did not provide the material properties of PLA at 40% infill, including density, Young's modulus, and Poisson's ratio. Measures were taken to obtain Young's modulus of our test specimen. According to the definition of Young's modulus, the longitudinal stress was divided by the strain, but the result was too small. A possible reason is that the 3-D printed parts are anisotropic, because of the different patterns and infills when printing. Therefore, the deflection formula of the cantilever beam is used because it is the closest to the testing scenario:

$$\delta = \frac{FL^3}{3EI} \tag{2}$$

where L is the length of the beam; F is the force applied on one end of the beam; I is the moment of inertia of the beam; δ is the maximum deflection of the beam. The F and δ can be measured then substitute them to the equation to calculate E that is 3694 MPa. To make the results as accurate as possible, a cantilever beam with a size similar to one side frame and the same printing configuration was used, which is 200 × 1 × 2.4 mm. Moreover, we measured the density of PLA at 40% infill, and 0.1 mm layer height is 1.16 g/cm^3. In addition, Poisson's ratio has also been determined according to the negative of the ratio of transverse strain to axial strain, which is 0.39.

3.3 FEA Simulation

In order to evaluate the accuracy of our experiments on the prototype we created, FEA was used to implement static analysis of various force situations in ANSYS. A new PLA material was added to the engineering database, based on the parameters measured in Sect. 3.2. The simulation is to obtain 16 sets of deformation results for the four ribs under four configurations with a force ranging from 0 to 10N. As shown in Fig. 3, the animation ratio is 1:1. The parameters of the 3-D model used in the simulation are consistent with the prototype used in the experiment. The smallest deformation is in Clamp mode, when the probe exerts 10 N force on Rib 4, the deflection of Rib 4 is 0.29 mm. The largest deformation is in Flex mode, when the probe exerts 10 N force on Rib 3, the deflection of Rib 3 is 8.02 mm.

3.4 Experimental Validation

To verify the accuracy of the FEA simulation, experiments on the VSG were implemented. As shown in Fig. 4, a simplified 3-D printed VSG was fixed on a bench vise, and the bench vise was fixed on the leg of the experimental table. The Mark-10 M5-100 force gauge is installed on the ESM303 test stand and is used to measure the force applied on the ribs. The test stand has a travel display function, which can detect the deformation of the contact point. A flat tip shape probe was chosen because it would be best to simulate the actual force exertion onto the VSG when grasping an object. Then the probe was placed on the frame and the ribs were aligned. Next, we zeroed force and displacement and set the force threshold to 10N. The probe would then automatically press down until it reaches the threshold. These settings were the same as they were in ANAYS. To reduce the error, the experiment was repeated three times for 16 cases, and the results were averaged afterward.

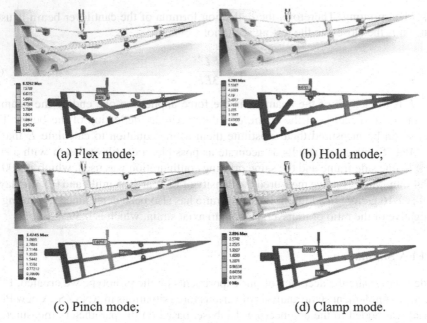

(a) Flex mode;   (b) Hold mode;

(c) Pinch mode;   (d) Clamp mode.

Fig. 3. The comparation between FEA simulation and experiment under different configurations on Rib 3.

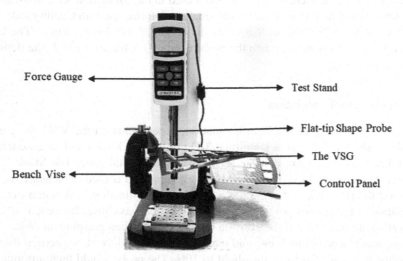

Fig. 4. Experimental setup.

Table 1. Main specifications of the VSG

Parameters	Values	Units
Hight of the VSG	200	mm
Width of the VSG	60	mm
Thickness of the VSG	2.4	mm
The thickness of the compliant frame	1	mm
Weight of a VSG prototype	38	g
Peak load	40	N
Range of stiffness variation on Rib 4	4.13–33.33	N/m

4 Results

According to the FEA and experimental data, the comparison plots of different ribs under the same configuration were obtained, as shown in Fig. 5. Figure 5(a) shows the relationship between force and deflection of the four ribs in Flex mode. It could be seen that the deflection of all the ribs has reached the maximum level. Figure 5(b) presents the relationship between force and deflection of the four ribs in Hold mode. We can see the deflections of Ribs 1–3 are relatively large. Figure 5(c) shows the relationship between force and deflection of the four ribs in Pinch mode. The deflections of Rib 1–2 are relatively large here. Figure 5(d) shows the relationship between the force and deflection of the four ribs in Clamp mode. The deflections of all ribs are relatively small, especially Rib 4. In Hold mode and Pinch mode, the error of Rib 1 between the experimental values and FEA is relatively large, reaching 21%. One possible reason is the anisotropy caused by the different filling patterns of the 3-D printed parts, which can be accepted. The errors of other data are within 10%, This further proves the VSG design is feasible.

According to the FEA and experimental data, the comparison diagrams of the same stressed ribs under different configurations were obtained, as shown in Fig. 6. Figure 6(a) shows the relationship between force and deflection of Rib 1 in four configurations. Its stiffness variation range is very small, only 1.4 times the original stiffness. Figure 6(b) presents the relationship between force and deflection of Rib 2 in four configurations. Its stiffness variation range is also quite small, only 1.5 times. Figure 6(c) illustrates the relationship between force and deflection of Rib 3 in four configurations, and its stiffness variation range is moderate, which is 3 times. Rib 3 is the most commonly used position for grabbing objects in reality. Figure 6(d) shows the relationship between force and deflection of Rib 4 in four configurations. Its stiffness varies in a large range up to 8 times its original stiffness, but the deflection itself is not large enough.

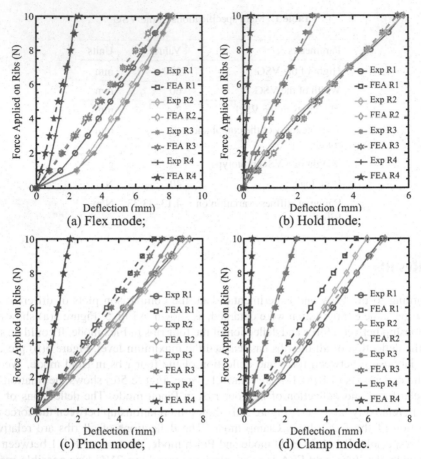

Fig. 5. Comparison between FEA simulation and experiment with different ribs under same configurations.

Figure 7 shows the comparison of maximum and minimum stiffness when the probe exerts a force on Rib 4 in FEA. Regardless of the position of the ribs and considering the global stiffness, the maximum stiffness of the VSG in Clamp mode is 11 times that in Flex mode.

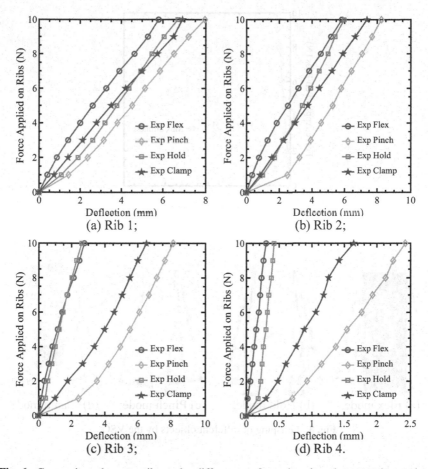

Fig. 6. Comparison the same ribs under different configurations based on experiment data.

The VSG can grab various objects in four configurations. Figure 8(a) shows the situation of the VSG grabbing a large piece of foam in Flex mode. In this case, the force required for this task is very small. Figure 8(b) illustrates the case of the VSG holding the paper cup in Hold mode where the deformation of the paper cup is inconspicuous. Figure 8(c) presents the situation of the VSG pinching the egg in Pinch mode, where the deformation of the frame is not large, and the egg is not crushed. Figure 8(d) shows the case where the VSG clamps the solid box in Clamp mode. It can be seen from the picture that the deformation of the frame is not obvious, and the box does not slip off. The demonstration of these demos proves that the design of the VSG is feasible.

800   J. Fu et al.

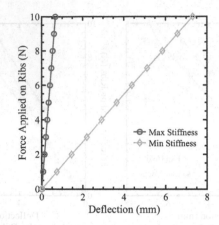

Fig. 7. FEA simulation under configurations of minimum and maximum stiffness.

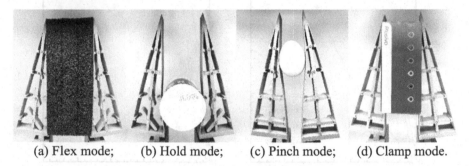

(a) Flex mode;   (b) Hold mode;   (c) Pinch mode;   (d) Clamp mode.

Fig. 8. Grasping of different objects by the VSG.

5   Conclusions

This paper proposes an innovative design concept of a variable stiffness gripper (VSG) based on the Fin Ray effect that can adjust its stiffness discretely for industrial robots and collaborative robots on adaptive grasping. The basic principle of this concept was to change the stiffness of a gripper of a fin ray design by allowing the ribs to rotate to allow such features to be realized. The ribs were divided into two sets of groups and there are four modes for our gripper design: the clamp, hold, pinch and flex modes. We measured the material properties of PLA in a specific configuration and imported it into FEA to simulate the deformation of the four ribs in different configurations. Also, a prototype was built, and our experimental results are in good agreement with the FEA. A grasp test was conducted to identify its ability to adapt objects with different sizes and hardness for better observation. The experiment was set to exert a 10 N force onto the gripper under 16 situations and the results matched our expectation of the FEA. Most of the results fell within a 10% range of difference from the FEA results, and it proves to achieve a maximum of 8 times change in stiffness compared to its original characteristics. Theoretically, the ribs would be operated by two servo motors through a belt and pulley system to change their positions. We contrived this feature in our prototype and there would be further studies underway to improve its performance.

Acknowledgment. This work is partially supported by the Purdue-Khalifa University collaboration project, under award No. CIRA-2020-024 and the National Science Foundation (NSF) grant under FRR-2131711.

References

1. Muthusamy, R., Huang, X., Zweiri, Y., Seneviratne, L., Gan, D., Muthusamy, R.: Neuromorphic event-based slip detection and suppression in robotic grasping and manipulation. IEEE Access **8**, 153364–153384 (2020)
2. Huang, X., et al.: Neuromorphic vision based contact-level classification in robotic grasping applications. Sensors **20**, 4724. 20, 4724 (2020)
3. Wei, Y., et al.: A novel, variable stiffness robotic gripper based on integrated soft actuating and particle jamming. Soft Robot. **3**, 134–143 (2016)
4. Zhang, P., Chen, W., Tang, B.: Design and feasibility tests of a lightweight soft gripper for compliant and flexible envelope grasping (2021). https://home.liebertpub.com/soro
5. Al Abeach, L.A.T., Nefti-Meziani, S., Davis, S.: Design of a variable stiffness soft dexterous gripper. Soft Robot. **4**, 274–284 (2017)
6. Hussain, I., et al.: Compliant gripper design, prototyping, and modeling using screw theory formulation: Int. J. Robot. Res. **40**, 55–71 (2020). https://doi.org/10.1177/0278364920947818
7. Chen, R., et al.: Bio-inspired shape-adaptive soft robotic grippers augmented with electroadhesion functionality. Soft Robot. **6**, 701–712 (2019). https://home.liebertpub.com/soro
8. Hussain, I., et al.: Modeling and prototyping of an underactuated gripper exploiting joint compliance and modularity. IEEE Robot. Autom. Lett. **3**, 2854–2861 (2018)
9. Hussain, I., et al.: Design and prototype of supernumerary robotic finger (SRF) inspired by fin ray® effect for patients suffering from sensorimotor hand impairment. RoboSoft 2019—2019 .In: EEE International Conference on Soft Robot, pp. 398–403 (2019)
10. Hussain, I., et al.: Design and prototyping soft–rigid tendon-driven modular grippers using interpenetrating phase composites materials: Int. J. Robot. Res. **39**, 1635–1646 (2020). https://doi.org/10.1177/0278364920907697.
11. Yang, Y., Chen, Y., Li, Y., Wang, Z., Li, Y.: Novel variable-stiffness robotic fingers with built-in position feedback. Soft Robot. **4**, 338–352 (2017)
12. Wang, W., Ahn, S.H.: Shape memory alloy-based soft gripper with variable stiffness for compliant and effective grasping. Soft Robot. **4**, 379–389 (2017). https://home.liebertpub.com/soro
13. Hao, Y., et al.: A variable stiffness soft robotic gripper with low-melting-point alloy. In: Chinese Control Conference CCC, pp. 6781–6786 (2017)
14. Arachchige, D.D.K., Chen, Y., Walker, I.D., Godage, I.S.: A novel variable stiffness soft robotic gripper. In: International Conference on Automation Science and Engineering, 2021-August, pp. 2222–2227 (2020)
15. Memar, A.H., Mastronarde, N., Esfahani, E.T.: Design of a novel variable stiffness gripper using permanent magnets. In: Proceedings of International Conference on Robotics and Automation, pp. 2818–2823 (2017)
16. Li, X., Chen, W., Lin, W., Low, K.H.: A variable stiffness robotic gripper based on structure-controlled principle. IEEE Trans. Autom. Sci. Eng. **15**, 1104–1113 (2018)

17. Chandrasekaran, K., Somayaji, A., Thondiyath, A.: A novel design for a compliant mechanism based variable stiffness grasper through structure modulation. J. Med. Devices Trans. ASME **15**, (2021)
18. Yang, Y., Jin, K., Zhu, H., Song, G., Lu, H., Kang, L.: A 3D-printed fin ray effect inspired soft robotic gripper with force feedback. Micromachines **12**, 1141. 12, 1141 (2021)
19. Basson, C.I., Bright, G.: Geometric conformity study of a fin ray gripper utilizing active haptic control. In: International Conference on Control, Automation ICCA. 2019-July, pp. 713–718 (2019)
20. Elgeneidy, K., Lightbody, P., Pearson, S., Neumann, G.: Characterising 3D-printed soft fin ray robotic fingers with layer jamming capability for delicate grasping. RoboSoft 2019 2019. In: IEEE 4th International Conference on Soft Robotics, pp. 143–148 (2019)
21. Elgeneidy, K., Fansa, A., Hussain, I., Goher, K.: Structural optimization of adaptive soft fin ray fingers with variable stiffening capability. In: 2020 3rd IEEE International Conference on Soft Robotics (RoboSoft), pp. 779–784 (2020)
22. Ali, M.H., Zhanabayev, A., Khamzhin, S., Mussin, K.: Biologically inspired gripper based on the fin ray effect. In: 2019 5th International Conference on Control, Automation and Robotics, ICCAR 2019, pp. 865–869 (2019)
23. Armanini, C., Hussain, I., Iqbal, M.Z., Gan, D., Prattichizzo, D., Renda, F.: discrete cosserat approach for closed-chain soft robots: application to the fin-ray finger. IEEE Trans. Robot. **37**, 2083–2098 (2021)
24. Anwar, M., Khawli, T. Al, Hussain, I., Gan, D., Renda, F.: Modeling and prototyping of a soft closed-chain modular gripper. Ind. Rob. **46**, 135–145 (2019)

Author Index

Ai, Qingsong 150

Bai, Kun 753
Bai, Yu 742
Bai, Yu-Long 71
Balandiz, Kemal 174
Bi, Yuanzhen 453
Bian, Sai Yinguan 497
Bingbing, Xu 710

Cai, Hegao 573
Cao, Guang-Zhong 90, 205
Cao, Jian 779
Cao, Jingwei 453
Cao, Qixin 628
Cao, Tao 585
Chang, Jiachen 162
Chen, Fayin 59
Chen, Genliang 767
Chen, Hanwei 3
Chen, Jiang-Cheng 90
Chen, Miao 197
Chen, Wei 698
Chen, Wenrui 652
Chen, Yanzheng 595
Cheng, Hao 409
Cui, Tong 229
Cui, Yuanzhe 345

Dai, Dongyan 532
Deng, Yaqing 753
Diao, Qiang 652
Ding, Han 485
Ding, Zilin 477
Dou, Jiansong 311
Du, Fuxin 409, 440
Duan, Xingguang 595
Duan, Ye 497

Fan, Jizhuang 573
Fang, Lingshen 189
Fei, Jian 357
Fei, Shihan 197
Feng, Kaixiang 113

Feng, Lijuan 367
Feng, Shuo 520
Fu, Hongrui 440
Fu, Jiaming 791
Fu, Xin 311
Fu, Zeyu 357
Fu, Zhuang 357

Gan, Dongming 791
Gao, Changqing 255
Gao, Gunyao 453
Gao, Tian-Hao 71
Gong, Wenzhi 279
Gu, Jian 127, 138
Guan, Bo 396
Guan, Xiaorong 722, 742
Guanglei, Meng 710
Guo, Chuangqiang 420
Guo, Xian 585
Guo, Yufeng 604
Guo, Zhao 49

Han, Bing 216
Han, Yali 162
Hao, Yongping 466
He, Bo 661
He, Guoying 661
He, Tianbao 420
He, Tianyu 138
Hong, Lin 289, 299
Hou, Licheng 388
Hou, Nan 520
Hou, Yixuan 541
Hu, Ming 604
Hu, Yi-Qian 71
Huang, Haihua 595
Huang, Hailin 255
Huang, Jiegang 686
Huang, Ruining 240
Huang, Xiaotong 791

Jiabo, Feng 673
Jian, Zhen 520
Jiang, Li 420

Jiang, Qihui   652
Jiao, Yafei   509
Jin, Zhuangzhuang   162

Lai, Quanbin   595
Lei, Liu   673
Li, Bing   255
Li, Dehao   268
Li, Hanyang   520
Li, Hengfei   722, 742
Li, Jiangbo   197
Li, Jianmin   396, 430
Li, Ling-Long   90
Li, Mengke   753
Li, Min   661
Li, Tianliang   59
Li, Weiming   595
Li, Wenjie   585
Li, Wenna   197
Li, Xuegui   520
Li, Xuerong   532
Li, Yuchong   279
Li, Zheng   13
Li, Zhiyong   652
Li, Zhong   722, 742
Li, Zihao   430
Lin, Han   791
Ling, Zi-Qin   90
Lirong, Shi   673
Liu, Fengyi   335
Liu, Hansong   420
Liu, Honghai   3, 79, 617, 640
Liu, Jinbiao   617
Liu, Juan   24
Liu, Keping   138
Liu, Pengfei   541
Liu, Quan   37, 150
Liu, Shunyu   162
Liu, Siyu   49
Liu, Wanting   541
Liu, Xiaomeng   268
Liu, Xingchi   396
Liu, Yaojie   24
Liu, Yifan   3, 79
Liu, Yongbai   127
Lu, Linjun   49
Lu, Rong-Rong   71
Lu, Yang   541
Luo, Qiang   150

Ma, Rui   595
Ma, Zhikang   396
Meng, Jianjun   3
Meng, Wei   37, 150
Mu, Tian   453

Ni, Wei-Dian   205
Ning, Chuanxin   103

Ou, Yue   573

Pan, Lizhi   430
Pang, Wen   323
Peng, Nian   37
Prathyush, I. V. S.   791

Qi, Peng   409

Ren, Lei   174
Runnan, Zhao   710

Shang, Junpeng   564
Shao, Weiping   466
Shen, Yichao   345
Shi, Chunjing   466
Shi, Xiang Qian   13
Song, Jinbo   509
Song, Rui   440
Su, Yifei   59
Sui, Chenxin   357
Sun, Binxuan   595
Sun, Wenbin   150
Sun, Yanxu   311
Sun, Zhigang   279
Sun, Zhongbo   127, 138

Tam, Sikyuen   388
Tan, Dong-Po   90
Tan, Min   367
Tang, Qirong   345
Tang, Shujie   767
Tao, Bo   388
Tian, Qiyan   268
Tong, Kai Yu   13
Tu, Mingyang   197

Wang, Baitong   477
Wang, Hao   767
Wang, Honghui   409
Wang, Kai   466
Wang, Linling   323

Wang, Nianfeng   686, 698
Wang, Ran   229
Wang, Xianfeng   477
Wang, Xiaohui   268
Wang, Xiaoxin   617, 640
Wang, Xin   289, 299
Wang, Yaonan   652
Wang, Yaxing   268
Wang, Yunfan   585
Wang, Zheng   722, 742
Wang, Zhuo   279
Wei, Guowu   174
Wei, Hangxing   409
Wei, Yufei   197
Weijun, Zhang   673
Wen duo, Jia   378
Wen, Pengyu   532
Wu, Edmond Q.   731
Wu, Jianguo   604
Wu, Xiaoxiao   541
Wu, Xinggang   229

Xia, Zeyang   367
Xiang, Guiyao   640
Xiao, Li   279
Xiao, Xiaohui   49
Xiao, Zhen-Long   289
Xie, Kaiyi   628
Xie, Shengquan   37
Xing, Zhenming   573
Xiong, Jing   367
Xu, Biying   573
Xu, Changxian   127, 138
Xu, Chao   509
Xu, Hang   299
Xu, Jie   189
Xu, Jun   553
Xu, Pengjie   345
Xu, Xiaohu   485

Yan, Sijie   485
Yan, Wei   767
Yang, Fan   509
Yang, Feng   595
Yang, Hongyu   79
Yang, Jing   604
Yang, Xingchen   3, 79
Yang, Xuejiao   268
Yang, Yicheng   617, 640
Yang, Zeyuan   485

Yannick, Cianyi   779
Yao, Jianfeng   357
Yao, Zhongshuai   604
Ye, Songtao   485
Yin, Zongtian   3, 79
Yingnan, Wang   710
Yu, Dai   378
Yu, Dianyong   497
Yuan, Ye   90
Yuan, Zihan   553
Yue, Chengtao   335
Yue, Fan   686

Zeng, Han   440
Zeng, Jia   617
Zeng, Pengfei   466
Zeng, Tian   279
Zhang, Daohui   311
Zhang, Gang   409, 440
Zhang, Hongmei   564
Zhang, Jialiang   24
Zhang, Jinnan   532
Zhang, Kuan   573
Zhang, Miaomiao   731
Zhang, Ning   3
Zhang, Qifeng   268
Zhang, Qingxin   229
Zhang, Shuai   520
Zhang, Ting   103, 113
Zhang, Xianmin   686, 698
Zhang, Xinmeng   541
Zhang, Xuehe   573
Zhang, Yang   255
Zhang, Yue-Peng   90
Zhang, Zhuangzhuang   628
Zhao, Jianchang   396
Zhao, Jie   573
Zhao, Liming   127, 138
Zhao, Ming   289, 299
Zhao, Shuaijie   722
Zhao, Tong   477
Zhao, Xingang   311
Zhao, Xingwei   388
Zheng, Boxuan   722, 742
Zheng, Jiajun   189
Zheng, Lianxi   791
Zhong, Kaifan   698
Zhou, Chang Qiu   13
Zhou, Jianbin   698

Zhou, Lei 162
Zhou, Xuewei 240
Zhou, Zhenning 628
Zhou, Zhiyong 49
Zhou, Ziliang 617, 640
Zhu, Daqi 323
Zhu, Wei 345
Zhu, Xiaocong 779

Zhu, Xiaoxiao 628
Zhu, Yu 216
Zhuang, Jie 71
Zi feng, Jiang 378
Zi, Qianlong 520
Zou, Yuanyuan 189
Zou, Yuelin 396
Zuo, Weilong 453

Printed in the United States
by Baker & Taylor Publisher Services